logy

BUSINESS & COMPANY RESOURCE CENTER

Business & Company Resource Center puts a complete business library at your students' fingertips. BCRC is a premier online business research tool that allows you to seamlessly search thousands of periodicals, journals, references, financial information, industry reports, company histories, and much more.

INFOTRAC®

InfoTrac® College Edition (ICE), packaged free with every new text, is a fully searchable online database that gives instructors and students 24-hour access to full-text articles from a variety of well-known periodicals and scholarly journals.

MARKETINGNOW!

New! MarketingNow for *Contemporary Marketing, 12e,* is an online assessment-driven and student-centered tutorial that provides students with a personalized learning plan. Based on a diagnostic Pre-Test, a customized learning path is generated for each student's personalized study needs, helping them to visualize, organize, practice, and master the material from the text. Media resources enhance problem-solving skills and improve conceptual understanding. An access code to MarketingNow for *Contemporary Marketing, 12e,* can be bundled with new textbooks at a nominal additional cost.

contemporary marketing

Louis E. Boone
University of South Alabama

David L. Kurtz
University of Arkansas

12th edition

Australia · Canada · Mexico · Singapore · Spain · United Kingdom · United States

To the more than two million students around the globe who began their marketing studies using **Contemporary Marketing** *in their classes*

and

To the Text and Academic Authors Association, which awarded **Contemporary Marketing** *the William Holmes McGuffey Award for Excellence and Longevity, the first basic marketing text to receive this prestigious award.*

Contemporary Marketing, 12/e

Louis E. Boone & David L. Kurtz

VP/Editorial Director:
Jack W. Calhoun

VP/Editor-in-Chief:
Dave Shaut

Publisher:
Melissa Acuña

Executive Editor:
Neil Marquardt

Developmental Editor:
Rebecca von Gillern

Marketing Manager:
Nicole Moore

Senior Promotions Manager:
Terron Sanders

Production Editor:
Margaret M. Bril

Technology Project Editor:
Kristen Meere

Media Editor:
Karen Schaffer

Manufacturing Coordinator:
Diane Lohman

Production House:
Lachina Publishing Services

Printer:
R. R. Donnelley
Willard, Ohio

Art Director:
Michelle Kunkler

Cover and Internal Designer:
Liz Harasymczuk Design

Cover Images:
© Getty Images and © Corbis

Photography Manager:
John Hill

Photo Researchers:
Darren Wright and Annette Coolidge

Printed in the United States of America
1 2 3 4 5 07 06 05 04

ISBN: 0-324-23673-5—Student Edition (Pkg)
0-324-23674-3—Student Edition (Text Only)
0-324-31713-1—Instructor's Edition (Pkg)
0-324-31712-3—Instructor's Edition (Text Only)
Library of Congress Control Number: 2004111568

For more information contact South-Western,
5191 Natorp Boulevard,
Mason, Ohio 45040.
Or you can visit our Internet site at:
http://www.swlearning.com.

preface

Dear Fellow Principles of Marketing Instructor:

The story of **Contemporary Marketing** is a history of innovations in marketing education. We have always strived to keep our book the most current in its field; and this new edition is no exception. It contains all the latest aspects of marketing, from one-to-one marketing and RFID (radio frequency identification) to viral marketing and offshoring.

One of our most successful innovations has involved presenting a unique theme with each new edition. For the 12th edition, we have selected event marketing as our theme—more specifically, sports marketing. Marketing conversations and written communications increasingly use sports metaphors to make business points:

- "Apple hit a home run with the iPod."
- "Airbus is certainly going for the gold in its competitive battles with Boeing."
- "That may have been the best product presentation I ever heard. Melissa was really in the zone."

The continuing case for the new edition is Major League Soccer (MLS). As in past editions, both written and video cases are included. We continue to demonstrate the applicability of marketing concepts by focusing on different sports as chapter-opening features. They include such diverse topics as:

- "Marketing Creates a Winner: The New NASCAR"
- "ESPN's Marketing Strategy Goes to Extremes"
- "The Unplayable Lie" (women's golf)
- "Sports Memorabilia Goes Online"

In addition, we have a brand new feature at the end of each part, entitled "Marketer's Minute." Recognizing the similarities of marketing responsibilities of executives of both traditional consumer and business products and those of sports organizations, we decided to interview top marketing executives from major sports organizations, people such as;

- Eric Stisser, Director of Corporate Sales and Marketing for the St. Louis Rams;
- Michael McCullough, Executive Vice President and Chief Marketing Officer for the NBA's Miami Heat; and
- Suzy Christopher, Senior Director of Marketing for MLS's Columbus Crew.

And to assist you with examples and illustrations for your classroom lectures, we have created **The One Thousand Best Things Ever Said About Sports, Management, and Marketing.** This extensive collection of humorous—and relevant—materials relating business, management, and marketing to the world of sports is organized to match coverage in **Contemporary Marketing.** This special supplement is available at no cost to instructors who use the text in their classes.

After reviewing the final chapters of **Contemporary Marketing, 12e**, we're convinced that it's a game-winning touchdown. We hope you agree.

Welcome to the clubhouse!

Gene Boone

Louis E. Boone

Dave Kurtz

David L. Kurtz

SCORE!

Contemporary Marketing, 12e, has the hottest game on the market!

Contemporary Marketing, 12e, covers all the hot issues and latest developments, immersing students in the excitement of the dynamic marketing arena:

OPENING VIGNETTES

NEW! Sports-related opening vignettes reflect the exciting new theme of the 12th edition and set the stage for each chapter as they turn the spotlight on how real-life companies rise to the marketing challenge.

REAL-WORLD ETHICS

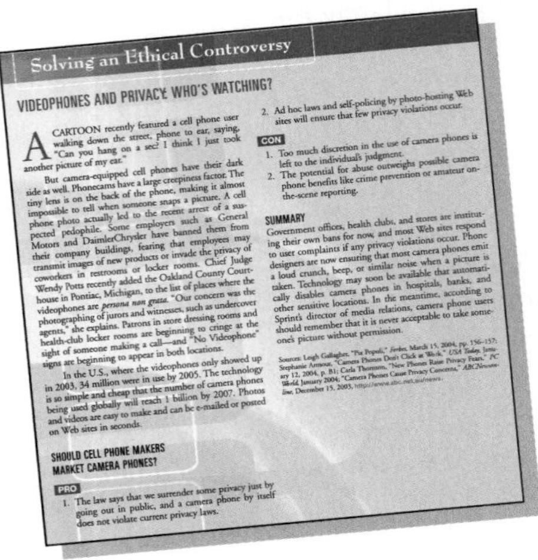

Solving an Ethical Controversy

VIDEOPHONES AND PRIVACY: WHO'S WATCHING?

A CARTOON recently featured a cell phone user walking down the street, phone to ear, saying, "Can you hang on a sec? I think I just took another picture of my ear."

But camera-equipped cell phones have their dark side as well. Phonecams have a large creepiness factor. The tiny lens is on the back of the phone, making it almost impossible to tell when someone snaps a picture. A cell phone photo actually led to the recent arrest of a suspected pedophile. Some employers such as General Motors and DaimlerChrysler have banned them from their company buildings, fearing that employees may transmit images of new products or invade the privacy of coworkers in restrooms or locker rooms. Chief Judge Wendy Potts recently added the Oakland County Courthouse in Pontiac, Michigan, to the list of places where the videophones are *persona non grata.* "Our concern was the photographing of jurors and witnesses, such as undercover agents," she explains. Patrons in store dressing rooms and health-club locker rooms are beginning to cringe at the sight of someone making a call—and "No Videophone" signs are beginning to appear in both locations.

In the U.S., where the videophones only showed up in 2003, 34 million were in use by 2005. The technology is so simple and cheap that the number of camera phones being used globally will reach 1 billion by 2007. Photos and videos are easy to make and can be e-mailed or posted on Web sites in seconds.

SHOULD CELL PHONE MAKERS MARKET CAMERA PHONES?

PRO

1. The law says that we surrender some privacy just by going out in public, and a camera phone by itself does not violate current privacy laws.
2. Ad hoc laws and self-policing by photo-hosting Web sites will ensure that few privacy violations occur.

CON

1. Too much discretion in the use of camera phones is left to the individual's judgment.
2. The potential for abuse outweighs possible camera phone benefits like crime prevention or amateur on-the-scene reporting.

SUMMARY

Government offices, health clubs, and stores are instituting their own bans for now, and most Web sites respond to user complaints if any privacy violations occur. Phone designers are now ensuring that most camera phones emit a loud crunch, beep, or similar noise when a picture is taken. Technology may soon be available that automatically disables camera phones in hospitals, banks, and other sensitive locations. In the meantime, according to Sprint's director of media relations, camera phone users should remember that it is never acceptable to take someone's picture without permission.

Sources: Leigh Gallagher, "Pix Populi," *Forbes,* March 15, 2004, pp. 156–157; Stephanie Armour, "Camera Phones Don't Click at Work," *USA Today,* January 12, 2004, p. B1; Carla Thornton, "New Phones Raise Privacy Fears," *PC World,* January 2004; "Camera Phones Cause Privacy Concerns," *ABCNewsonline,* December 15, 2003, http://www.abc.net.au/news.

ALL NEW! Solving an Ethical Controversy features integrated in each chapter spark lively class discussions as they list the pros and cons to real-world ethics quandaries, such as "Will the Ad-Zapper Mean the Death of TV Commercials?" "Videophones and Privacy: Who's Watching?" and much more.

END-OF-CHAPTER ETHICS EXERCISES

NEW! end-of-chapter **Ethics Exercises** give students additional hands-on experience grappling with ethical decisions.

NEW! ETIQUETTE TIPS

NEW! Etiquette Tips for the Marketing Professional in each chapter equip students with a winning playbook for business and social settings. Topics include "Make Your Next Business Dinner a Marketing Success," "Body Art: Beauty Is in the Eye of the Beholder," "E-Mail and Fax Etiquette," and many more.

NEW! MARKETER'S MINUTE

NEW! Marketer's Minute end-of-part interviews get one-on-one with high-profile marketing professionals, who share how their education and background have contributed to their career achievements as well as the success of their organizations.

part 3

marketer's minute

Talking about Marketing Careers with Michael McCullough, Executive Vice President and Chief Marketing Officer of the Miami Heat

Boone & Kurtz: Tell us a little about your background and how your sports marketing career began.

I was a college basketball player for Utah State University on a basketball scholarship. I majored in political science with a business minor, and, after college, I spent four years working in retail management and buying. I worked at a department store, going through the long training program. I was still playing pretty competitive ball on a part-time basis. That's how I met an executive for the NBA's Sacramento Kings, who said he might have a position in promotions/marketing/sales. With the Kings, I did a little bit of everything. I must have been doing a good job, though, because within a few months I was promoted to director of broadcasting. From there I went on to work for the NBA league office as a broadcasting coordinator. At that time the NBA had only 27 teams, and I worked with each of the teams on their local broadcasts and also with NBC and TNT on the nationally televised games.

Later on, I was contacted by the new owners of the Kings to come back as vice president of marketing and broadcasting, which I did for some time. I was in charge of sponsorships, marketing, and promotion—everything but finance and trading players. Then a headhunter contacted me about a position with the Miami Heat, which ultimately resulted in the position I currently hold. My current position is fairly similar to my previous job in Sacramento, but now I'm not responsible for ticket sales. My work deals with all the aspects of the game experience that touch the public. We're the front line between the Heat and the public: the public face of the franchise.

The best thing about sports is that people are passionate, whether it's good or bad. You can always strike up a conversation. As a marketer you get to find out what people think of your product. You can really gauge the public pulse just by wearing a Miami Heat T-shirt. Other fields just don't have that.

MICHAEL MCCULLOUGH, EXECUTIVE VICE PRESIDENT AND CHIEF MARKETING OFFICER OF THE MIAMI HEAT

Boone & Kurtz: Describe a typical day in the life of the Heat's chief marketing officer.

There's really no such thing as a typical day. No two days are the same because of all the different areas I am in charge of. I have a lot of phone calls each day, and then there are meetings, both scheduled and impromptu. We are always brainstorming or finalizing or changing a project. Today I reviewed a movie trailer with our ad agency, and then dealt with some employee issues. Then we went over some graphics for a mailing to season-ticket holders and began work on the season-ticket renewal program. The season hasn't even started yet, and we are already working on the following year. My days really vary; tomorrow will be different from today, but that's the good part about this job.

Boone & Kurtz: The Heat's big news of late is the "man in black," Shaquille O'Neal. How does the addition of this high-profile celebrity and outstanding athlete affect this year's marketing plans?

Our marketing plan "before Shaq" was a sales-driven model. We concentrated mostly on ticket sales. But the first rumors about Shaq made the phones really start ringing, and once it was official the phones exploded. Ticket sales have been phenomenal; we've sold more season tickets than ever before. Because of this sellout situation our focus has changed from sales to renewal, retention, and service. We've been able to redirect sales and advertising and beef up communications with season-ticket holders, especially first-time season-ticket holders. We want to treat everyone as a brand-new ticket holder and ensure that they are always reminded of the value of holding those tickets. Now our ads are more about the brand and selling merchandise, the Web site, and enhancing the experience.

Shaq is his own entity, and having him as a presence on the team adds another layer to the checks and balances we go through with ads, graphics, etc. We have to communicate with Shaq's people; when you have someone of that caliber, there are extra steps you have to go through.

Boone & Kurtz: Miami is one of the most bilingual cities in the United States. How do the Heat's marketing strategies address this duality?

The Hispanic community is a big part of what we do here. We're really focused on reaching them and ingratiating ourselves with them, letting these folks know they are important to us before expecting them to commit money to our product. Before we ran any advertising directed to the Hispanic community, we had players participate in philanthropic efforts in that community so they could see how involved the team is. Most things we do, we do in both English and Spanish. We have Spanish-language radio broadcasts and are cur-

PHOTO: COURTESY OF MICHAEL MCCULLOUGH

346

NEW! MARKETING CONCEPT CHECKS

NEW! Marketing Concept Checks are brief two- or three-question checkpoints following coverage of major topics to ensure students understand core concepts before moving on to the next major topic.

1. What is utility?
2. Define the term *marketing.*
3. Why is the U.S. an attractive market for foreign competitors?

Technically superior, *Contemporary Marketing,* 12e, remains unrivaled!

The new 12th edition of *Contemporary Marketing* hits a grand slam with the most technologically advanced package available. *Contemporary Marketing* takes advantage of the latest technology to bring more innovation, flexibility, and excitement to your classroom.

CONTINUING VIDEO CASE

ALL NEW! The End-of-Part Continuing Video Case highlights **Major League Soccer** — providing a topic marketing students will cheer about. Available on DVD, this special seven-segment video case and accompanying written cases emphasize strategy, enabling students to follow one company case throughout the various marketing functions.

END-OF-CHAPTER VIDEO PACKAGE

ALL NEW! The End-of-Chapter Video Package includes 19 completely new videos to accompany the cases at the end of each chapter, enabling students to see how real companies — like Doc Martens, Wrigley, and Monster.com — deal with various marketing scenarios.

XTRA!

Xtra! Online brings marketing concepts to life. It includes digitized videos for the Major League Soccer Continuing Case and End-of-Chapter Videos, Student PowerPoint presentation slides, a Marketing Plan with related exercises, and Xtra! Quizzing to reinforce concepts throughout the text to help students prepare for future exams.

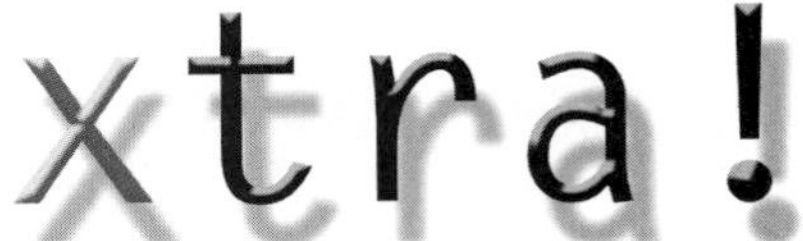

MARKETINGNOW!

New! MarketingNow for *Contemporary Marketing, 12e,* is an online assessment-driven and student-centered tutorial that provides students with a personalized learning plan. Based on a diagnostic Pre-Test, a customized learning path is generated for each student's personalized study needs, helping them to visualize, organize, practice, and master the material from the text. Media resources enhance problem-solving skills and improve conceptual understanding. An access code to MarketingNow for *Contemporary Marketing, 12e,* can be bundled with new textbooks at a nominal additional cost.

AUDIO CHAPTER REVIEWS

Audio Chapter Reviews on CD-ROM are packaged free with every new copy of *Contemporary Marketing, 12e,* allowing students to study in an all-new way. Students can listen to these reviews of chapter summaries and objectives while exercising, driving to class, or walking around campus.

THE WALL STREET JOURNAL

The Wall Street Journal delivers the latest marketing news to students' doorsteps or computer desktops. Available as an optional package with the text, students receive a 15-week subscription to both *The Wall Street Journal* print and online versions for a nominal additional cost.

INFOTRAC®

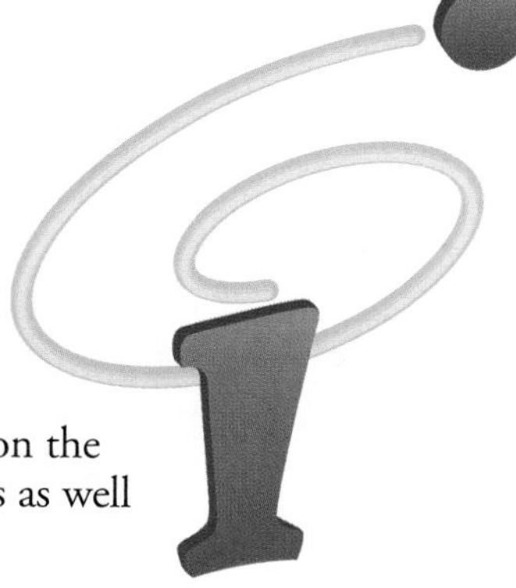

InfoTrac® College Edition (ICE), packaged free with every new text, is a fully searchable online database that gives instructors and students 24-hour access to full-text articles from a variety of well-known periodicals and scholarly journals.

InfoTrac Exercises, located in every chapter of the text as well as on the book's Web site, provide additional learning experiences for students as well as offer guidance on conducting online research.

WEBTUTOR™ ADVANTAGE

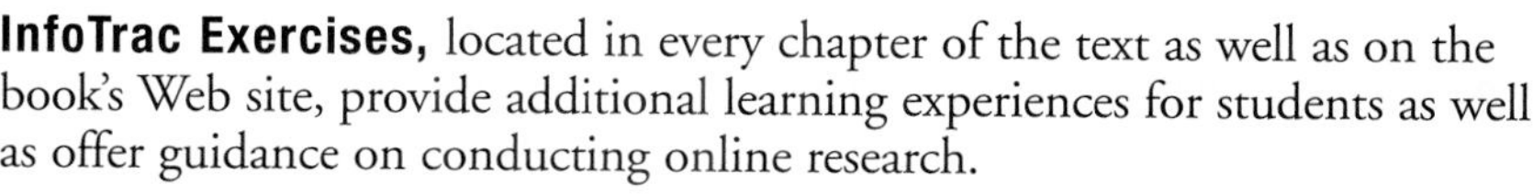

WebTutor™ Advantage for WebCT™/Blackboard® easily and effectively takes your course online, offering in-depth content, digitized end-of-chapter case videos, instructor customization, flashcards, quizzing, discussion questions, tutorials, e-mail, and more.

When it comes to instructor resources, Boone & Kurtz *Contemporary Marketing*, *12e*, has no competition.

Behind every effective leader is a solid support system. In Boone & Kurtz tradition, *Contemporary Marketing, 12e,* equips instructors with the most thorough teaching tools available—bringing innovation to their fingertips.

INSTRUCTOR'S MANUAL & MEDIA GUIDE

The Instructor's Manual and Media Guide provides an excellent resource for instructors at every stage of the game—from its play-by-play guidelines for first-year instructors to its fresh ideas for veteran marketing professors. Each chapter of the IM begins with a transition guide for the 12th edition, followed by a complete set of teaching tools including Annotated Chapter Objectives and detailed Lecture Outlines. Brand new for this edition of the IM are complete guidelines for how to best incorporate the PowerPoint Presentation slides into your lectures. In addition, the Instructor's Manual includes complete solutions to all the end-of-chapter questions, teamwork projects, 'netWork assignments, cases, and video cases. At the end of the IM is a media guide that includes information for the media elements of the text, including all 19 new chapter video cases and the seven brand new Major League Soccer Continuing Case Videos. Each Video Case Guide includes learning goals, chapter concepts spotlighted in the video, video case synopsis, as well as video case questions and answers.

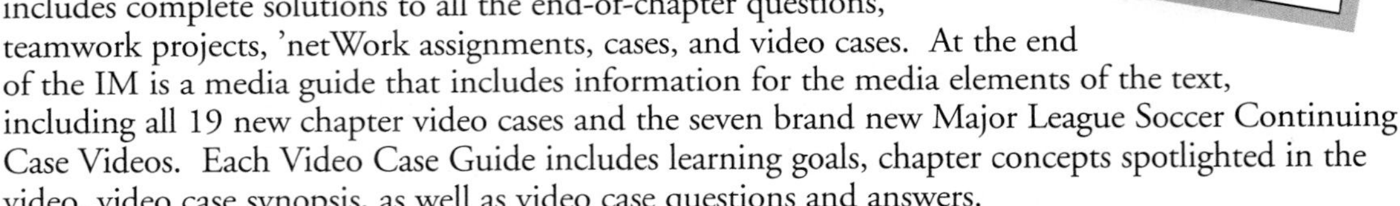

POWERPOINT® PRESENTATION SLIDES

PowerPoint® Presentation Slides provides a complete teaching experience for instructors and a memorable learning experience for students. Instructors have their choice of either a basic presentation that contains approximately 25–30 slides per chapter or an expanded presentation that contains 40–60 slides per chapter. Both presentations contain chapter objectives, the main chapter objectives outlined and explained, figures from the text to enhance student learning, and embedded Web links. The expanded presentation contains a wider scope of embedded Web links and also contains embedded video links. Each chapter ends with a clearly presented summary of the chapter's objectives and key concepts.

COLLABORATIVE LEARNING HANDBOOK

NEW! Collaborative Learning Handbook includes additional interactive exercises specific to each chapter for instructors to assign as group activities or individual exercises. Averaging three per chapter, these 5- to 20-minute exercises range from quick team projects to questions that spark in-class debates. Teaching tips offer insight on how to effectively implement the exercises in class to create a more dynamic and engaging environment for students and instructors.

VIDEO PACKAGE ON DVD

ALL NEW! Video Package available on DVD. *Contemporary Marketing* shoots and scores big with the new video segments, drawing applause from instructors and students alike. The **End-of-Part Continuing Video Case** highlights **Major League Soccer**, giving students a familiar topic to kick around. This special seven-segment video and accompanying written cases enable students to build on their knowledge as they follow one organization through the various marketing functions. In addition, a new **End-of-Chapter Video Package** includes 19 completely new videos to accompany in-text cases that illustrate how real companies such as Green Mountain Coffee, Teenage Research Unlimited, and Jiffy Lube deal with various marketing scenarios.

SUPPORT WEB SITE

Contemporary Marketing, 12e, Support Web site (**http://boone.swlearning.com**) provides an array of useful resources for both students and instructor, and includes:

- ExamView Computerized Testing Software
- Instructor's Resource Center including: Resource Integration Guide, Instructor's Manual and Media Guide, and Test Bank
- Interactive Study Center for students including: Quizzes, Internet Exercises, Flashcards, Personal Development information, and a Newsroom
- Access to WebTutor™ Advantage on Blackboard® and WebCT™
- Access to MarketingNow

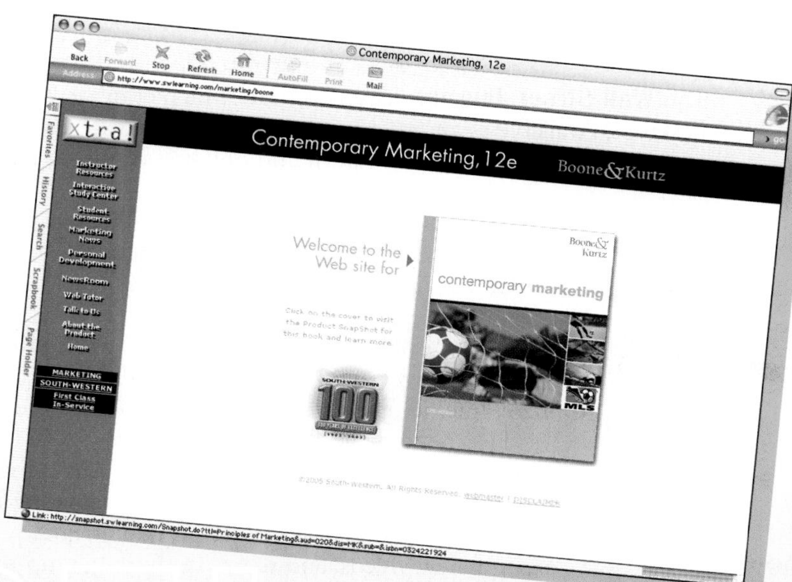

SCORE! with the best the game has to offer

State-of-the-art equipment readies *Contemporary Marketing*, *12e*, students for big league play.

Athletes need the very best equipment to thrive at their game. Boone & Kurtz *Contemporary Marketing, 12e,* delivers the best. These innovative supplements immerse students in the game, giving them hands-on experience with real-world marketing issues and a firsthand view of the excitement in the powerfully charged marketing arena.

STUDENT SUPPLEMENTS

Study Guide contains the following features for each chapter in the text:

- A Chapter Overview that briefly discusses the chapter objectives
- A Complete Chapter Outline
- A Self Quiz
- Set of Critical Thinking Questions

Each chapter ends with a Surfing the Net section in which students are provided with online resources related to the chapter concepts.

xtra!

Xtra! Online brings marketing concepts to life. It includes digitized videos for the Major League Soccer Continuing Case and End-of-Chapter Videos, Student PowerPoint presentation slides, a Marketing Plan with related exercises, and Xtra! Quizzing to reinforce concepts throughout the text to help students prepare for future exams.

Audio Chapter Reviews on CD-ROM are packaged free with every new copy of *Contemporary Marketing, 12e,* allowing students to study in an all-new way. Students can listen to these reviews of chapter summaries and objectives while exercising, driving to class, or walking around campus.

The Wall Street Journal delivers the latest marketing news to student's doorsteps or computer desktops. Available as an optional package with the text, students receive a 15-week subscription to both *The Wall Street Journal* print and online versions for a nominal additional cost.

InfoTrac® College Edition (ICE), packaged free with every new text, is a fully searchable online database that gives instructors and students 24-hour access to full-text articles from a variety of well-known periodicals and scholarly journals.

***Contemporary Marketing, 12e,* Support Web site** (**http://boone.swlearning.com**) offers additional learning resources for students, such as Interactive Study Center including: Quizzes, Internet Exercises, Flashcards, Personal Development information, and a Newsroom.

Boone & Kurtz *Contemporary Marketing, 12e,* brings the principles of marketing course to a whole new level of play. Combining signature Boone & Kurtz pedagogy, innovative new features (like the sports theme, audio reviews, etiquette and ethics emphasis), exciting new videos, and the most thorough, up-to-the-minute coverage available, *Contemporary Marketing, 12e,* is hands down the best the game has to offer!

preface

It's as current as today's headlines. A hallmark of any Boone & Kurtz text is its focus on how marketing concepts apply to today's business issues. And instructors who have used earlier editions of this text in their classes already know that when students ask questions like:

- "How big a threat to our privacy—and our bank account—is identity theft?";
- "What is one-to-one marketing? Will VOIP Internet phones mean the death of the Bell System and landline-based telephones?";
- "If Congress can protect us from telemarketers, why won't they take on the SPAM problem?";
- and "How can marketers turn cell phones and Internet Weblogs *(blogs)* into promotional tools?"

the questions will be discussed—and answered correctly—in *Contemporary Marketing 12e.* After all, the book's position as the benchmark in measuring overall quality has been recognized by fellow U.S. and Canadian authors who voted it the first marketing text to receive the prestigious McGuffey Award for Excellence and Longevity.

But *Contemporary Marketing 12e* goes far beyond ensuring overall accuracy and quality. Instructors have come to expect additional qualities from a Boone & Kurtz text: complete, easy-to-understand coverage of all relevant topics in a lively, engaging writing style that makes students forget that they are reading a college-level textbook. And when students ask:

- "Why is it impossible for a principles of marketing text to cover the subject in less than 660 pages and under 20 chapters?"
- and "Are there any marketing textbooks out there that include high-quality coverage of the importance of business ethics?"

you can simply point to the text in hand. After all, from the very first edition, *Contemporary Marketing* has been a book of firsts. No introductory marketing text in print has been used by as many students—either in the U.S. or abroad. And the best continues to get better.

Briefly Speaking

First, we will be best, and then we will be first.

Grant Tinker (b. 1926)
American television executive

KEY FEATURES OF THE NEW 12TH EDITION

The new edition of *Contemporary Marketing* is packed full of innovations. Here are some of the exciting new features of the 12th edition.

MAJOR EXPANSION OF TEXT COVERAGE OF MARKETING ETHICS

In the wake of the recent crises in business ethics, business programs in colleges and universities are examining their curricula and evaluating the extent and quality of their coverage of ethical issues. A number of universities, including Rutgers University and Ohio State University, are either adding new courses or expanding existing elective courses in ethics. Still others advocate the integration of ethics throughout the courses that comprise their business core curriculum. Many of the latter are currently engaged in extensive review of course contents to determine the adequacy of current coverage.

The new 12th edition of *Contemporary Marketing* provides instructors and students with a thorough treatment of ethical issues affecting marketing, both from a macro perspective and in relation to specific aspects of marketing. The value of marketing ethics is introduced in Chapter 1 and then followed with a detailed analysis in Chapter 3, which focuses specifically on ethical and social responsibility issues. Topics discussed in this chapter include ethical problems in marketing research, product decisions, pricing, distribution, and promotional strategy.

Chapter 4 analyzes the ethical issues surrounding online marketing and the Internet. Topics examined here include copyright issues, and there is a lengthy discussion of privacy issues and the potential misuse of customer information by e-commerce firms. The importance of acting in an ethical manner as a key to developing effective marketing relationships is discussed in Chapter 10. A separate section in Chapter 16 examines advertising ethics and ethical issues in public relations. Ethical issues in personal selling and sales promotion are examined in a separate section in Chapter 17.

Every chapter includes a special experiential feature called *Solving an Ethical Controversy.* This feature is designed to facilitate class debates of current ethical issues. Each begins with a brief background and is followed by a series of pro and con points designed to elicit class discussion of the issues. Examples of these features in the 12th edition include:

- "Identity Theft: Is Privacy Also Stolen?"
- "Will the Ad-Zapper Mean the Death of TV Commercials?"
- "Fighting Internet Piracy: Are All Means Fair?"
- "Must Americans Always Pay More for Prescription Drugs?"
- "MTV's Super Bowl Disaster: Who is Responsible?"
- "Ticketmaster: Who Pays the Price?"
- "Captive Advertising"
- "Videophones and Privacy: Who's Watching?"

Contemporary Marketing's extensive coverage of business ethics is further enhanced by 19 end-of-chapter *Ethics Exercises,* short case scenarios that can be used as homework assignments or as a basis for classroom discussion.

A SHORTER TEXT

A common complaint among both instructors and students is that principles of marketing texts are much too long to be covered in a single term. At the same time, they quickly state that they do not want a watered-down version of a text in the form of an "essentials" edition.

During the past two editions, the authors have worked diligently to create a "right-sized" text of 19 chapters and 660 pages that offers the rigor and comprehensiveness instructors expect but still is short enough to cover. In the new 12th edition, we have accomplished this objective. We think you—and your students—will agree.

A NEW, MORE STRATEGIC FOCUS

In response to numerous instructors who made complaints about the overly descriptive nature of the typical principles of marketing text, the new 12th edition of *Contemporary Marketing* has made significant changes. First, the marketing planning chapter has been relocated so that it can be assigned much earlier in the term, helping to equip students with a solid foundation of strategic thinking.

"Creating an Effective Marketing Plan"—previously an end-of-book appendix—has been completely rewritten to provide more detailed, real-life planning material and immediately follows the discussion of strategic marketing planning in Chapter 2. It also includes an extensive planning case that illustrates the strategic marketing planning concepts discussed in the chapter.

Each chapter closes with a special section assessing strategic implications of chapter concepts on marketing, and an end-of-book appendix, "Financial Analysis in Marketing," provides additional strategic and analytic tools for the reader.

REVISED—AND EXPANDED—MARKETING CAREER COVERAGE

The new 12th edition has responded to the career interests of today's students by featuring a completely rewritten "Planning a Career in Marketing" and moving it to the beginning of the textbook.

This special Prologue to the text offers practical insights to help students prepare for a successful business career. In response to students' interest in relating their own backgrounds and interests to successful marketers, we have included special interviews at the end of each part. The book's sports theme is also reinforced by career profiles. The importance of marketing in every organization is obvious in these profiles of top marketing executives in sports organization. We recently conducted these interviews to provide the reader with an "up close and personal" examination of these marketers' backgrounds, their job descriptions, and how they contribute to overall organizational success. Examples include Jennifer Gardner, director of sales for MLB's Cincinnati Reds; Suzy Christopher, senior director of marketing for Major League Soccer's Columbus Crew; and Michael McCullough, executive vice president and chief marketing officer for the NBA's Miami Heat.

TWO CASES FOR EVERY CHAPTER

Many reviewers of the previous edition requested alternative cases to provide more flexibility for different assignments from one academic term to the next. The new 12th edition now includes two case assignments for every chapter, providing the instructor with flexibility to adjust to time constraints and multiple sections or to use different case assignments for different terms. One case in every chapter is accompanied by a professionally created video that brings to life the written case materials.

19 ALL NEW! VIDEOS

Professionally written and produced, the new video case package provides intriguing, relevant, and current real-world insight into the modern marketplace. Tied directly to chapter concepts, the videos highlight how real-world organizations struggle with the challenges of the 21st century marketplace. Each video is supported by a written case with applications questions. They include:

- Video Case 1.2: Toyota's Hybrid Is Hip with Customers
- Video Case 2.2: Hewlett-Packard's Strategic Plans Shine in B2B Markets
- Video Case 3.2: Green Mountain Coffee Roasters
- Video Case 4.2: Job-Hunting in the Digital Age: Monster.com
- Video Case 5.2: Vida Wellness Spa Wishes You Well
- Video Case 6.2: Technomic Helps Businesses Serve Good Food
- Video Case 7.2: Doc Martens Makes Strides around the World
- Video Case 8.2: Teenage Research Unlimited Has the True Story on Teens
- Video Case 9.2: Orange Glo Cleans Up the Marketplace
- Video Case 10.2: International Flavors & Fragrances Makes Marketing Personal
- Video Case 11.2: Curves: A New Angle on Fitness
- Video Case 12.2: Everything Is Beautiful at L'Oréal
- Video Case 13.2: 1-800-Flowers.com: Great Gifts by Phone or Online
- Video Case 14.2: Westfield Group Creates a Shopper's Paradise
- Video Case 15.2: Jimmy John's Sandwich Shops Give Customers Something to Chew On
- Video Case 16.2: Ride the White Wave with Silk Soymilk
- Video Case 17.2: Chicago Show, Inc. Puts on a Show
- Video Case 18.2: Wrigley's Gives Everyone Something to Chew On
- Video Case 19.2: Jiffy Lube: The Well-Oiled Machine

MAJOR LEAGUE SOCCER: AN EXCITING NEW CONTINUING VIDEO CASE

Each part of the new 12th edition is linked with a continuing case that focuses on event marketing and features one of the major recent marketing challenges in sports: how to transform the world's most popular sport into a marketing success in the U.S. Although soccer has gathered widespread acceptance by both parents and school-age boys and girls, this global sport with its rabid international following has never made it into the high-appeal, high-attendance, and highly watched rankings enjoyed in the U.S. by football, baseball, and basketball. The huge growth of youth soccer and the rapid expansion of Major League Soccer to cities across the U.S. have prompted sports marketing specialists to begin to apply 21st century marketing concepts and strategies in an effort to convert soccer into a major American sport.

This special seven-segment video was created and filmed to support the written cases that appear at the end of each part. This continuing case video is in addition to the 19 videos available with the newly written video cases at the end of each chapter.

ETIQUETTE TIPS FOR MARKETING PROFESSIONALS

Across the nation, business programs are finding ways to help their students succeed—both in business settings and in social encounters with customers, peers, and senior members of the organization. Some offer elective courses. Others sponsor special dinners for soon-to-be-graduated students in which the student engages in conversation with wine stewards (on wine selection and how to tell if a bottle of wine is acceptable); maitre d's (on the roles they play); waiters (on which fork and spoon are used for what); and other guests (who discuss business interactions and appropriate conversation topics). Still other schools, recognizing the popularity of golf among executives, offer golf matches attended by students, instructors, and businesspeople who offer advice.

Today's marketing students need to know how to handle themselves in a variety of business and social settings. In the new 12th edition, every text chapter contributes to the student's etiquette database by covering topics such as:

- How to dress for the job interview
- How to remember names
- Communicating through body language
- Making your next business dinner a marketing success
- How to be a good listener
- Body art: Beauty is in the eye of the beholder
- Dos and don'ts of business invitations

As noted above, your authors have always strived to keep *Contemporary Marketing* truly "contemporary." We want our student readers to have the most current marketing information available. So look at what else is new in the 12th edition.

PEDAGOGICAL CHANGES

The authors conducted a thorough review of *Contemporary Marketing*'s pedagogy. The new 12th edition has numerous user-friendly features.

Greatly Expanded—and More Diverse—End-of-Chapter Materials

Probably our biggest pedagogical change is in the end-of-chapter materials. Here is the new organizational format for the chapter review, student assignments, and other class projects:

1. *Review of Chapter Objectives.* In addition to a review of each chapter learning objective, a series of review questions—which accounted for most of the chapter questions in previous editions—is now included as part of the chapter review rather than as homework assignments.
2. *Marketing Terms You Need to Know.* Page numbers are included.
3. *Other Important Marketing Terms.* Page numbers are included.

4. *Projects and Teamwork Exercises.* This section includes discussion questions.
5. *Applying Chapter Concepts.* Multiple assignments get students actively involved with the chapter's content.
6. *Ethics Exercise.* Offers an in-depth description of actual ethical issues facing a real company with two or more in-depth questions that can be used as a written class assignment or as focal points for in-class discussions.
7. *'netWork Exercises.* Three new content-related Internet exercises are included for each chapter.
8. *InfoTrac Citations and Exercises.* The InfoTrac database gives students direct access to the real world of marketing through academic journals, newspapers, and an assortment of government publications. A subscription to InfoTrac is provided with each new book purchase. The InfoTrac component of the end-of-chapter materials involves assignments linked to the database.
9. Two *cases* appear at the end of every chapter.
10. A *Marketer's Minute* career interview appears at the end of each part, along with a segment of the *Major League Soccer Continuing Video Case*

Marketing Concept Checks

Two or three review-type questions are inserted following every major head in each chapter. This feature lets students assess their progress as they complete each reading assignment.

CONTENT CHANGES

When publisher Merriam-Webster updated its *Collegiate Dictionary* recently, a major task of its editors was to decide which new terms had become prominent enough to merit a place in the new edition. Among the terms making the cut were *MP3, digital subscriber line (DSL),* and *information technology* (also better known by its acronym *IT*).

Ensuring that students introduced to marketing by studying *Contemporary Marketing* are exposed to the most current marketing terms is one of the many responsibilities we assumed as we developed the new edition. And a number of new concepts were added, including the following:

viral marketing	sustainable competitive advantage
grass roots marketing	Wi-Fi
blog (or Weblog)	radio frequency identification (RFID)
one-to-one marketing	virtual relationship
bots (shopbots)	offshoring
virtual sales team	

In addition to new terminology, the 12th edition of *Contemporary Marketing* is filled with new concepts. It is clearly the most up-to-date book in the field. Consider just a few of the new materials introduced in this edition:

- Radio frequency identification (RFID) is an important technological innovation and is expected to replace bar codes and offer new marketing efficiencies. RFID uses tiny computer chips to track inventory and monitor the supply chain.
- Offshoring—the movement of domestic jobs outside the U.S.—has attracted significant attention as nations struggle to create additional higher-paying jobs for their domestic workforces.
- Chapter 2 on strategic planning now covers both first and second mover advantages. In addition, discussion of Porter's Five Forces model has been added to the chapter. A special appendix, "Creating an Effective Marketing Plan," now follows this chapter and features a detailed analysis of the elements of an actual marketing plan.
- One-to-one marketing—discussed in detail in Chapter 10, the relationship marketing chapter—carries segmentation to the ultimate: targeting individuals. Chapter 10 has also been

strengthened with new sections on comarketing and cobranding, topics that formerly appeared in the product section.

- Chapter 4, the e-commerce chapter, now includes new concepts such as viral marketing, VOIP (voice over Internet protocol), and promotional applications of blogs and cell phones.
- The new 12th edition also offers expanded coverage of data mining, interpretive research, business units, and business and competitive intelligence.
- A new section on major advertising appeals has been added to Chapter 16, the advertising and public relations chapter.

ORGANIZATIONAL CHANGES

Here are some of the organizational changes that users of the previous edition will recognize:

1. Chapters have been rearranged in Parts 1, 2, and 3. Our plan was to cover the broader, more general topics first, then move to more specific, "how to" chapters on topics like marketing research and segmentation strategies.
2. Unlike competitive texts that fail to cover electronic marketing until the end of the text or—worse yet—shift the entire chapter from the text to a separate Web site, the *Contemporary Marketing 12e* e-commerce chapter has been renamed and moved up as one of the macro concepts covered in Part 1.
3. Adopter comments persuaded us to return to our earlier format of putting the pricing section last.

ADDITIONAL FEATURES OF THE NEW 12TH EDITION

Contemporary Marketing 12e is packed full of innovations. Here are some other exciting new features:

- **NEW!** The rapid growth of the Hispanic-American market segment and its current ranking as the largest ethnic segment in the U.S. is discussed in detail in the market segmentation chapter. The other major ethnic segments—including the African-American and Asian-American segments—are also examined in this and other chapters.
- **EXPANDED!** Category management, a major organizational development among firms with extensive product lines, is discussed in detail in Chapter 12.
- **NEW!** All 19 chapter-opening marketing vignettes and *Solving an Ethical Controversy* boxes are new. Examples of each have been mentioned in the introductory letter to your marketing instructor or earlier in the Preface. In addition, every *Marketing Hit* and *Marketing Miss* feature in the new edition is new.

UNPARALLELED RESOURCE PACKAGE

Like the 11 editions before it, *Contemporary Marketing 12e* is filled with innovations. The result: the most powerful marketing package available.

Boone & Kurtz lead the market with precedent-setting learning materials, as well as continuing to improve on signature package features—equipping students and instructors with the most comprehensive collection of learning tools, teaching materials, and innovative resources available. As expected, the new 12th edition delivers the most extensive, technologically advanced, user-friendly package on the market.

FOR THE PROFESSOR

NEW! The One Thousand Best Things Ever Said about Sports, Management, and Marketing

Gene Boone, a well-known editor of books of quotations, teamed up with Dave Kurtz to develop one of the largest collections of marketing-related sports quotations ever. A copy of the book is provided free to instructors using *Contemporary Marketing 12e* in their classes by requesting one from your Thomson sales representative.

To assist you in adding insightful, relevant, and humorous materials to your classes, the authors have prepared this supplement packed with insights on the relationships between management, marketing, and the tasks facing every marketer. From relationship marketing and buyer behavior to pricing decisions and product planning, the materials included in this book emphasize—in frequently humorous ways—that *marketing* is a universal function and its successful application is equally essential to any organization. Whether your "product" is consumer or business goods or services—or as diverse as *places* (tourism, attracting new industry or new residents to an area); *events* (sports, entertainment, cultural); *causes* (charitable undertakings); *people* (politicians, celebrities); *not-for-profit organizations* (The Susan G. Komen Breast Cancer Foundation, The ALS [Lou Gehrig's Disease] Association)—successful application of marketing concepts is equally important in achieving success in the marketplace.

NEW! MarketingNOW

This brand-new online assessment-driven and student-centered tutorial provides students with a personalized learning plan. Based on a diagnostic Pre-Test, a customized learning path is generated for each student that targets his or her study needs and helps to visualize, organize, practice, and master the material in the text. Media resources enhance problem-solving skills and improve conceptual understanding. An access code to MarketingNow can be bundled with any new *Contemporary Marketing, 12e* textbook.

Test Bank and Examview Testing Software

Providing over 4,000 total questions, the test bank fills every need you have in testing your students on the chapter contents. Each chapter of the test bank is organized following the chapter objectives, and every question is categorized by type of question (including Knowledge, Application, and Analysis), question format (multiple choice, true/false, and essay), difficulty level, and text page reference. Every chapter of the test bank also includes a matrix that lists all of the questions in the chapter by type so you can easily create a comprehensive test—or a test on one or two specific objectives. The Examview testing software is a Windows-based software program that is both easy to use and attractive. You won't believe that testing software has come this far!

Instructor's Manual and Media Guide

Each chapter of the IM begins with an introduction to the chapter and a concise guide to changes in the new 12th edition. After this easy transition guide, instructors will find a complete set of teaching tools including the following:

- *Annotated chapter objectives.* A quick summary of each objective for the instructor that also shows how it relates to the rest of the chapter materials.
- *Detailed lecture outline.* Includes suggestions for use of other appropriate support materials for each lecture. These support materials include additional examples, articles, activities, and discussion suggestions.
- *Guide for using PowerPoint Presentation slides.* Included as part of the lecture outline, this guide describes in detail where to make the best use of the PowerPoint Presentation slides and where in your lecture they would fit most appropriately.

In addition, the IM includes complete solutions to all the end-of-chapter questions, teamwork projects, 'netWork assignments, cases, and video cases, as well as suggestions for where the instructor may be able to find good guest speakers for each chapter.

At the end of each chapter, there is a media portion of the IM that includes information for that chapter's media elements, including the 19 video cases and the seven Major League Soccer continuing video case segments. Each video case guide includes learning goals, chapter concepts spotlighted in the video, video case synopsis, and video case questions and suggested answers.

Transparency Acetates with Teaching Notes

Over 250 full-color transparency acetates are available to support each chapter and related PowerPoint Presentation in *Contemporary Marketing 12e.* The transparencies consist of important figures and ads from the text as well as special content acetates outlined specifically for *Contemporary Marketing 12e.* Included with the transparency acetates is a complete set of teaching notes describing how best to use them in a classroom lecture or discussion.

PowerPoint Presentation Software

The *Contemporary Marketing 12e* PowerPoint Presentation software is clearly one of the best you'll find. It provides a complete teaching experience for instructors and a memorable learning experience for students. For your convenience, there are two presentations for this text. The Basic presentation includes 25 to 40 slides per chapter, containing chapter objectives, the main concepts discussed as part of each chapter objective, numerous figures from the text that enhance student learning, and embedded Web links. There is also an Expanded presentation that contains 40 to 60 slides per chapter as well as more Web links and video links that give students a strong, complete visual presentation of the chapters' main concepts. Each chapter ends with a clearly presented summation of the chapter objectives and key concepts from the chapter.

Instructor's Resource CD-ROM

It's so easy to organize your support materials when they're all in one place! New with the 12th edition of *Contemporary Marketing* is an Instructor's Resource CD-ROM that contains all of the key instructor supplements: instructor's manual and media guide, test bank, Examview testing software, and PowerPoint Presentation software with embedded videos.

WebTutor Advantage on Blackboard and/or WebCT

WebTutor Advantage puts you ahead of the game in providing online teaching and learning for your students. It contains all of the interactive study guide components that you could ever want and three valuable technology-oriented additions you never thought you'd get!

Included in our WebTutor Advantage offerings for *Contemporary Marketing 12e* are the following:

- Chapter objectives
- Chapter flashcards
- Chapter quizzing
- E-lectures for each chapter
- Video cases digitized with exercises
- Threaded discussion questions for online discussions
- Links to the text Web site: http://boone.swlearning.com

Video Cases

Would this be *Contemporary Marketing 12e* without a brand-new custom video package containing a video case for every chapter in the text? Of course not! And these videos will exceed your every expectation. Each of the 19 videos was professionally produced within a few months of the book's publication and is tied directly to the key concepts in each chapter. Each video is new and highlights marketers as small as marketing research specialist Teenage Research Unlimited and as large as online job search Web site Monster.com. Each gives students a glimpse into how marketers actually work, strategize, and meet challenges in the real world. The video-creation process begins with written cases prepared by the authors and contained in the text. Each is a significant improvement over corporate public relations–type cases used by competing texts.

Video synopses and guides as well as answers to the case questions can be found in the instructor's manual and media guide.

Major League Soccer (MLS) Continuing Video Case

This brand-new feature has been created for the new 12th edition. The written and video case elements are divided into seven sections and appear at the end of each part in *Contemporary Marketing.* The continuing case relates the parts of the text to an exciting, fast-paced example of event marketing: the story of how Major League Soccer and each of its teams are applying marketing concepts to build the world's most popular sport into a prominent position among other professional sports in the U.S.

The written case segments include learning concepts and discussion questions. Video synopses and guides as well as answers to the case questions can be found in the instructor's manual and media guide.

FOR THE STUDENT

Study Guide

Completely updated for the 12th edition, the study guide contains the following features for each chapter in the text:

- Chapter overview that briefly discusses the chapter objectives
- Complete chapter outline
- Self quiz
- Set of critical thinking questions

Each chapter ends with a *Surfing the Net* section in which students are provided with online resources related to the chapter concepts.

Audio Chapter Reviews on CD-ROM

Every *Contemporary Marketing 12e* chapter now comes with an audio review! These audio reviews are provided on CD-ROM for student use. Listen to them while you're exercising, or listen to them while you're walking around campus. Listen to them on the way to class as a preview of what you'll be learning that day! Just listen to them, because they'll supply you with a concise summary of the chapter objectives and the major concepts in a chapter. Step to the head of the class, because they'll get you prepared in a completely new way!

Xtra! Online

Xtra! Online brings marketing concepts to life! It includes digitized videos for the Major League Soccer continuing video case and end-of-chapter videos, student PowerPoint slides, a marketing plan with related exercises, and Xtra! quizzing to reinforce the text's concepts to help you prepare for exams. Xtra! access is available as an optional package with new textbooks. Ask your professor about this exciting study option.

TECHNOLOGY PRODUCTS FOR BOTH INSTRUCTORS AND STUDENTS

Boone & Kurtz Web Site

The Boone & Kurtz Web site contains a complete array of supplementary materials for both instructors and students. Instructors will find many ways of enhancing their courses using the Instructor's Resources section, where they will find the major text supplements in electronic format for viewing or downloading. Students will find a Web site designed specifically for *Contemporary Marketing 12e* that includes both a Student Resources section and an Interactive Study Center. The Student Resources section consists of information about study aids that can help students ace their course. The Interactive Study Center, a dynamic online learning center, consists of interactive quizzes, career information, and more in-depth work including:

- *Internet resources.* These resources direct you to extensive support for marketing topics discussed in the text. Here you'll find articles, exercises, company data, and company profiles, as well as a special feature on *time management.* This feature includes advice and guidelines on effectively managing work and leisure time as a student.
- *Internet applications.* These online marketing exercises use some of the links from the 12th edition and test students on chapter concepts.

ACKNOWLEDGMENTS

Through the first 12 editions of *Contemporary Marketing,* your authors have benefited immensely from the comments and suggestions of more than 1,000 reviewers and colleagues. This input has come via focus groups, publisher reviews, contributions to supplementary text materials, e-mailed suggestions, conference networking, classroom visits, and coffee shop chats. Regardless of the format, all these ideas have helped shape *Contemporary Marketing* into a text that serves as the benchmark for other texts . . . one that has been used by over 2 million students.

Contributors to the current edition include:

Keith Absher
University of North Alabama

Alicia T. Aldridge
Appalachian State University

Amardeep Assar
City University of New York

Tom F. Badgett
Angelo State University

Joe K. Ballenger
Stephen F. Austin State University

Michael Bernacchi
University of Detroit Mercy

David Blanchette
Rhode Island College

Barbara Brown
San Jose State University

Reginald E. Brown
Louisiana Tech University

Marvin Burnett
St. Louis Community College—Florissant

Scott Burton
University of Arkansas

Howard Cox
Fitchberg State University

James Coyle
Baruch College

Elizabeth Creyer
University of Arkansas

Geoff Crosslin
Kalamazoo Valley Community College

William Demkey
Bakersfield College

Michael Drafke
College of DuPage

Joanne Eckstein
Macomb Community College

John Frankel
San Juan College

Robert Georgen
Trident Technical College

Robert Googins
Shasta College

Arlene Green
Indian River Community College

Joel Haynes
State University of West Georgia

Mabre Holder
Roane State Community College

Andrew W. Honeycutt
Clark Atlanta University

Dr. H. Houston
California State University—Los Angeles

John Howe
Santa Ana College

Tom Jensen
University of Arkansas

Marcella Kelly
Santa Monica College

Stephen C. King
Keene State College

Kathleen Krentler
San Diego State University

Laddie Logan
Arkansas State University

Kent Lundin
College of the Sequoias

Patricia Macro
Madison Area Tech College

Frank Markley
Arapahoe Community College

Tom Marshall
Owens Community College

Dennis C. Mathern
The University of Findlay

Lee McGinnis
University of Nebraska

Michael McGinnis
Pennsylvania State University

Norma Mendoza
University of Arkansas

Mohan Menon
University of South Alabama

Anthony Miyazaki
University of Miami

Jerry W. Moorman
Mesa State College

Linda Morable
Richland College

Diane Moretz
Ashland University

Eugene Moynihan
Rockland Community College

Margaret Myers
Northern Kentucky University
Thomas S. O'Connor
University of New Orleans
Nita Paden
Northern Arizona University
George Palz
Erie Community College—North
George Prough
University of Akron
Warren Purdy
University of Southern Maine
Salim Qureshi
Bloomsburg University
Thomas Read
Sierra College
Joel Reedy
University of South Florida
Dominic Rella
Polk Community College
Ken Ridgedell
Southeastern Louisiana University
Fernando Rodriguez
Florida Community College
Lillian Roy
McHenry County College
Arthur Saltzman
California State—San Bernardino
Elise T. Sautter
New Mexico State University
Jonathan E. Schroeder
University of Rhode Island
Farouk Shaaban
Governors State University
John Sondey
South Dakota State University
James Spiers
Arizona State University
David Starr
Shoreline Community College
Bob Stassen
University of Arkansas
Sue Taylor
Belleville Area College
Lars Thording
Arizona State University—West Campus
Rajiv Vaidyanathan
University of Minnesota
Sal Veas
Santa Monica College
Charles Vitaska
Metro State College of Denver
Cortez Walker
Baltimore City Community College
Roger Waller
San Joaquin Delta College
Mary M. Weber
Emporia State University
Vicki L. West
Southwest Texas State University
Elizabeth White
Orange County Community College
David Wiley
Anne Arundel Community College
William Wilkinson
Governors State University
James Williams
Richard Stockton College of New Jersey
Mary Wolfindarger
California State University—Long Beach
Joyce Wood
North Virginia Community College

Earlier contributors include:

Keith Absher
Kerri L. Acheson
Zafar U. Ahmed
M. Wayne Alexander
Bruce Allen
Linda Anglin
Allen Appell
Paul Arsenault
Dub Ashton
Amardeep Assar
Tom F. Badgett
Joe K. Ballenger
Wayne Bascom
Richard D. Becherer
Tom Becker
Richard F. Beltramini
Robert Bielski
Carol C. Bienstock
Roger D. Blackwell
Jocelyn C. Bojack
Michele D. Bunn
James Camerius
Les Carlson
John Carmichael
Jacob Chacko
Robert Collins
Elizabeth Cooper-Martin
Deborah L. Cowles
Howard B. Cox
John E. Crawford
Michael R. Czinkota
Kathy Daruty
Grant Davis
Gilberto de los Santos
Carol W. DeMoranville
Fran DePaul
Gordon Di Paolo
John G. Doering
Jeffrey T. Doutt
Sid Dudley
John W. Earnest
Philip E. Egdorf
Michael Elliot
Amy Enders
Bob Farris
Lori Feldman
Sandra M. Ferriter
Dale Fodness
Gary T. Ford
Michael Fowler
Edward Friese
Sam Fullerton
Ralph M. Gaedeke
G. P. Gallo
Nimish Gandhi
Sheryl A. Gatto
Robert Georgen
Don Gibson
David W. Glascoff
James Gould
Donald Granbois
John Grant
Paul E. Green
William Green
Blaine Greenfield
Matthew Gross
Robert F. Gwinner
Raymond M. Haas
John H. Hallaq
Cary Hawthorn
E. Paul Hayes
Hoyt Hayes
Betty Jean Hebel
Debbora Heflin-Bullock
John (Jack) J. Heinsius
Sanford B. Helman
Nathan Himelstein
Robert D. Hisrich
Ray S. House
George Housewright
Donald Howard
Michael D. Hutt
Gregory P. Iwaniuk
Don L. James
James Jeck
Candida Johnson
David Johnson
Eugene M. Johnson
James C. Johnson
Harold H. Kassarjian
Bernard Katz
Stephen K. Keiser
Michelle Keller
J. Steven Kelly
James H. Kennedy
Charles Keuthan

Maryon King
Randall S. Kingsbury
Donald L. Knight
Linda S. Koffel
Philip Kotler
Terrence Kroeten
Russell Laczniak
Martha Laham
L. Keith Larimore
Edwin Laube
Ken Lawrence
Francis J. Leary, Jr.
Mary Lou Lockerby
James Lollar
Paul Londrigan
David L. Loudon
Dorothy Maass
James C. Makens
Lou Mansfield
Warren Martin
James McCormick
Carl McDaniel
Michael McGinnis
James McHugh
Faye McIntyre
H. Lee Meadow
Mohan Menon
William E. (Gene) Merkle
John D. Milewicz
Robert D. Miller
Laura M. Milner
Banwari Mittal
Harry J. Moak
J. Dale Molander
John F. Monoky
James R. Moore
Thomas M. Moran
Susan Logan Nelson
Colin F. Neuhaus
Robert T. Newcomb
Jacqueline Z. Nicholson
Tom O'Connor
Robert O'Keefe
Sukgoo Pak
Eric Panitz
Dennis D. Pappas
Constantine Petrides
Barbara Piasta
Dennis D. Pitta
Barbara Pletcher
Carolyn E. Predmore
Arthur E. Prell
Bill Quain
Rosemary Ramsey
Thomas C. Reading
Gary Edward Reiman
Glen Riecken
Arnold M. Rieger
C. Richard Roberts
Patrick J. Robinson
William C. Rodgers
William H. Ronald
Bert Rosenbloom
Barbara Rosenthal
Carol Rowery
Ronald S. Rubin
Don Ryktarsyk
Rafael Santos
Duane Schecter
Dennis W. Schneider
Larry J. Schuetz
Bruce Seaton
Howard Seigelman
Jack Seitz
Steven L. Shapiro
F. Kelly Shuptrine
Ricardo Singson
Norman Smothers
Carol S. Soroos
James Spiers
Miriam B. Stamps
William Staples
David Steenstra
Bruce Stern
Robert Stevens
Kermit Swanson
G. Knude Swenson
Cathy Owens Swift
Clint B. Tankersley
Ruth Taylor
Donald L. Temple
Vern Terpstra
Ann Marie Thompson
Howard A. Thompson
John E. Timmerman
Frank Titlow
Rex Toh
Dennis H. Tootelian
Fred Trawick
Richard Lee Utecht
Rajiv Vaidyanathan
Toni Valdez
Peter Vanderhagen
Dinoo T. Vanier
Gayle D. Wasson
Donald Weinrauch
Fred Weinthal
Susan B. Wessels
John J. Whithey
Debbora Whitson
Robert J. Williams
Nicholas C. Williamson
Cecilia Wittmayer
Van R. Wood
Julian Yudelson
Robert J. Zimmer

Finally, this new edition would never have become a reality without our highly competent editorial, production, marketing, and video teams at South-Western/Thomson Learning. Sincere thanks go to Jack W. Calhoun, vice president and editorial director; Dave Shaut, vice president and editor-in-chief; Melissa Acuña, publisher; Neil Marquardt, executive editor; Rebecca von Gillern, developmental editor; Marge Bril, production editor; Vicky True and Kristen Meere, video and technology experts; Nicole Moore, marketing manager; and Heather Churchman, editorial assistant. Thanks also to Ronn Jost of Lachina Publishing Services.

We are grateful for the many suggestions and contributions of dozens of people who teach the introductory marketing course on a regular basis and are in the best position to comment on what works best—and what doesn't work at all. Every recommendation made a difference in the creation of the new edition.

We would also like to express our appreciation to our research and editorial assistants, Karen Hill and Mikhelle Taylor. Their untiring efforts on our behalf are most appreciated.

In addition, we applaud the contributions of the high-quality instructors who participated in making the *Contemporary Marketing* supplements an outstanding and innovative teaching and learning package:

Geoff Crosslin
Kalamazoo Valley Community College

Doug Hearth
University of Arkansas

Marcella Kelly
Santa Monica College

Thomas S. O'Connor
University of New Orleans

Fernando Rodriguez
Florida Community College

Sal Veas
Santa Monica College

Louis E. Boone & David L. Kurtz

about the authors

Gene Boone was born about the time World War II began and had a relatively quiet childhood until 1956, when he received a 45 rpm RCA Victor recording of "Heartbreak Hotel" by Elvis Presley. Within a year he had discovered Buddy Holly, Little Richard, and Chuck Berry—and he wanted more. So he decided to combine high school with a two-year gig as a part-time DJ at a local radio station. Playlists didn't exist in those days, and as long as irate listeners didn't call in and demand that the station manager fire you, you could play anything you liked. A diverse group of fellow DJs introduced him to artists who were quickly added to his growing list of favorites: blues greats John Lee Hooker and B. B. King; the haunting, poetry-like songs of Simon & Garfunkel; the unique vocal blending of the Everly Brothers, whose work impacted the groups who led the British Invasion of the 1960s; and the riveting, soulful music by the son of an Arkansas cotton farmer—a man named Johnny Cash.

But few people spend a lifetime career spinning tunes at a small-time radio station, and, following graduation, he started looking for something fun that paid a bit more. College professor sounded like a cool occupation that would keep him indoors and, perhaps, help him meet women (assuming they considered tweed jackets attractive). Nobody told him until it was too late that it was going to take another eight years in college to achieve his ambition—eight more years!—but he struggled through it. He's happy he did because he was able to affect (at least a little) the lives of thousands of his young, middle-age, and older students in a half-dozen universities throughout the United States, as well as in Australia, England, and Greece. These gigs proved to be almost as much fun as the first.

But his love of music, which had never died, was rekindled during an evening section of a Principles of Marketing class several decades ago at the University of Southern Mississippi in which one of his students—sitting on the back row—would soon make music that linked him forever to tequila-flavored drinks and talking tropical birds. Short in stature and soft-spoken, Jimmy Buffett hardly looked the part of a pop music star, but over the decades he consistently demonstrated just how much he had learned about marketing in that fall semester course.

During his high-school days, no one in Salisbury, Maryland, would have mistaken **Dave Kurtz** for a scholar. In fact, he was a mediocre student, so bad that his father steered him toward higher education by finding him a succession of back-breaking summer jobs. Thankfully, most of them have been erased from his memory, but a few linger, including picking peaches, loading watermelons on trucks headed for market, and working as a pipe fitter's helper. Unfortunately, these jobs had zero impact on his academic standing. Worse yet for Dave's ego, he was no better than average as a high-school athlete in football and track.

But four years at Davis & Elkins College in Elkins, West Virginia, turned him around. Excellent teachers helped get Dave on a sound academic footing. His grade point average soared—enough to get him accepted by the graduate business school at the University of Arkansas, where he met Gene Boone. After graduate school, the two became career co-authors, with over 50 books between them. Gene and Dave also got involved in several entrepreneurial ventures.

Today, Dave Kurtz is back teaching at the University of Arkansas after duty tours in Ypsilanti, Michigan; Seattle; and Melbourne, Australia. He is the proud grandfather of five "perfect" kids and a sportsman with a golfing handicap too high to mention. Dave, his wife, Diane, and two demanding Yorkies live in Rogers, Arkansas, where he holds a university professorship at the Sam M. Walton College of Business in nearby Fayetteville.

contents in brief

Preface xi

PART 1 **DESIGNING CUSTOMER-ORIENTED MARKETING STRATEGIES 1**
Chapter 1 Marketing: Creating Satisfaction through Customer Relationships 2
Chapter 2 Strategic Planning and the Marketing Process 38
Appendix Creating an Effective Marketing Plan 62
Chapter 3 The Marketing Environment, Ethics, and Social Responsibility 76
Chapter 4 E-Commerce: Marketing in the Digital Age 114

PART 2 **UNDERSTANDING BUYERS AND MARKETS 155**
Chapter 5 Consumer Behavior 156
Chapter 6 Business-to-Business (B2B) Marketing 186
Chapter 7 Serving Global Markets 218

PART 3 **TARGET MARKET SELECTION 255**
Chapter 8 Marketing Research, Decision Support Systems, and Sales Forecasting 256
Chapter 9 Market Segmentation, Targeting, and Positioning 286
Chapter 10 Relationship Marketing, Customer Relationship Management (CRM), and One-to-One Marketing 316

PART 4 **PRODUCT DECISIONS 349**
Chapter 11 Product and Service Strategies 350
Chapter 12 Category and Brand Management, Product Identification, and New-Product Development 380

PART 5 **DISTRIBUTION DECISIONS 413**
Chapter 13 Marketing Channels and Supply Chain Management 414
Chapter 14 Direct Marketing and Marketing Resellers: Retailers and Wholesalers 446

PART 6 **PROMOTIONAL DECISIONS 479**
Chapter 15 Integrated Marketing Communications 480
Chapter 16 Advertising and Public Relations 518
Chapter 17 Personal Selling and Sales Promotion 552

PART 7 **PRICING DECISIONS 595**
Chapter 18 Price Concepts and Approaches 596
Chapter 19 Pricing Strategies 626

Appendix A-1

Video Cases VC-1

Notes N-1

Glossary G-1

Indexes I-1

contents

Preface xi

part 1

DESIGNING CUSTOMER-ORIENTED MARKETING STRATEGIES 1

chapter 1

MARKETING: CREATING SATISFACTION THROUGH CUSTOMER RELATIONSHIPS 2

Opening Vignette
Marketing Creates a Winner: The New NASCAR 2

Marketing Miss
How Segway Swerved Away from Success 12

Solving an Ethical Controversy
Identity Theft: Is Privacy Also Stolen? 14

Etiquette Tips for Marketing Professionals
How to Remember Names 28

What Is Marketing? 6
A Definition of Marketing 7 | Today's Global Marketplace 8

Four Eras in the History of Marketing 9
The Production Era 9 | The Sales Era 10 | The Marketing Era 10
Emergence of the Marketing Concept 11 | The Relationship Era 11
Converting Needs to Wants 12

Avoiding Marketing Myopia 13

Extending the Traditional Boundaries of Marketing 15
Marketing in Not-for-Profit Organizations 15 | Characteristics of Not-for-Profit Marketing 16

Nontraditional Marketing 17
Person Marketing 17 | Place Marketing 18 | Cause Marketing 19
Event Marketing 20 | Organization Marketing 20

Creativity and Critical Thinking 21

The Technology Revolution in Marketing 22
Interactive Marketing 23 | The Internet 23 | Broadband 24 | Wireless 25
Interactive Television Service 25 | How Marketers Use the Web 25

From Transaction-Based Marketing to Relationship Marketing 26
One-to-One Marketing 27 | Developing Partnerships and Strategic Alliances 29

Costs and Functions of Marketing 30

Ethics and Social Responsibility: Doing Well by Doing Good 31

Strategic Implications of Marketing in the 21st Century 32
Review of Chapter Objectives 33 | Marketing Terms You Need to Know 34
Other Important Marketing Terms 34 | Projects and Teamwork Exercises 35
Applying Chapter Concepts 35 | Ethics Exercise 36 | 'netWork Exercises 36
InfoTrac Citations and Exercises 36

Case 1.1 How the Rolling Stones Keep Rolling 37

Video Case 1.2 Toyota's Hybrid Is Hip with Customers 37

chapter 2

STRATEGIC PLANNING AND THE MARKETING PROCESS 38

Marketing Planning: The Basis for Strategy and Tactics 40
Strategic Planning versus Tactical Planning 41 | Planning at Different Organizational Levels 41

Steps in the Marketing Planning Process 42
Defining the Organization's Mission and Objectives 42
Assessing Organizational Resources and Evaluating Environmental Risks and Opportunities 44
Formulating, Implementing, and Monitoring a Marketing Strategy 44

Successful Strategies: Tools and Techniques 44
Porter's Five Forces Model 44 | First Mover and Second Mover Strategies 46
SWOT Analysis 46 | The Strategic Window 48

Elements of a Marketing Strategy 48
The Target Market 48 | Marketing Mix Variables 49 | The Marketing Environment 51

Methods for Marketing Planning 54
Business Portfolio Analysis 54 | The BCG Matrix 55

Strategic Implications of Marketing in the 21st Century 56
Review of Chapter Objectives 56 | Marketing Terms You Need to Know 57
Other Important Marketing Terms 58 | Projects and Teamwork Exercises 58
Applying Chapter Concepts 58 | Ethics Exercise 59 | 'netWork Exercises 59
InfoTrac Citations and Exercises 59

Case 2.1 Starbucks' Strategy: It's a Small World After All 60

Video Case 2.2 Hewlett-Packard's Strategic Plans Shine in B2B Markets 61

Opening Vignette
ESPN's Strategy Goes to Extremes 38

Marketing Miss
Target's New Tactic: Stocking Its Shelves with Food 46

Solving an Ethical Controversy
Oracle and PeopleSoft: Competition or Antitrust? 53

Etiquette Tips for Marketing Professionals
How to Network 54

appendix

CREATING AN EFFECTIVE MARKETING PLAN 62

Components of a Business Plan 62

Creating a Marketing Plan 63
Formulating an Overall Marketing Strategy 63
The Executive Summary, Competitive Analysis, and Mission Statement 65
Description of the Company 66 | Statement of Goals and Core Competencies 66
Outline of the Marketing Environment (Situation Analysis) 66
The Target Market and Marketing Mix 67 | Budget, Schedule, and Monitoring 67

Sample Marketing Plan 68
Five-Year Marketing Plan Blue Sky Clothing, Inc. 69

chapter 3

THE MARKETING ENVIRONMENT, ETHICS, AND SOCIAL RESPONSIBILITY 76

Environmental Scanning and Environmental Management 79

Opening Vignette
The Unplayable Lie 76

Marketing Hit
Curves: Walk in, Exercise, Walk Out 83

Etiquette Tips for Marketing Professionals
Smoking Etiquette 104

Solving an Ethical Controversy
Videophones and Privacy: Who's Watching? 105

The Competitive Environment 80
Types of Competition 80 | Developing a Competitive Strategy 82
Time-Based Competition 82

The Political-Legal Environment 84
Government Regulation 84 | Government Regulatory Agencies 85
Other Regulatory Forces 87 | Controlling the Political-Legal Envionment 88

The Economic Environment 89
Stages in the Business Cycle 89 | Inflation and Deflation 91 | Unemployment 91
Income 92 | Resource Availability 92 | The International Economic Environment 92

The Technological Environment 93
Applying Technology 94

The Social-Cultural Environment 95
Consumerism 96

Ethical Issues in Marketing 97
Ethical Problems in Marketing Research 99 | Ethical Problems in Product Strategy 100
Ethical Problems in Distribution Strategy 101
Ethical Problems in Promotional Strategy 101 | Ethical Problems in Pricing 102

Social Responsibility in Marketing 102
Marketing's Responsibilities 103 | Marketing and Ecology 106

Strategic Implications of Marketing in the 21st Century 107
Review of Chapter Objectives 108 | Marketing Terms You Need to Know 110
Other Important Marketing Terms 110 | Projects and Teamwork Exercises 110
Applying Chapter Concepts 111 | Ethics Exercise 111 | 'netWork Exercises 111
InfoTrac Citations and Exercises 112

Case 3.1 Is Detroit Losing the Race to Hybrids? 113

Video Case 3.2 Green Mountain Coffee Roasters 113

chapter 4
E-COMMERCE: MARKETING IN THE DIGITAL AGE 114

Opening Vignette
Sports Memorabilia Go Online 114

Etiquette Tips for Marketing Professionals
E-Mail and Fax Etiquette 122

Marketing Miss
Why Are Online Exchanges Dying? 128

Solving an Ethical Controversy
Fighting Internet Piracy: Are All Means Fair? 137

What Is E-Commerce? 117

Interactivity and E-Commerce 119
The Internet 119 | The World Wide Web 120 | Four Web Functions 121

Accessing the Internet 124

E-Commerce and the Economy 126
Business-to-Business Online Marketing 126 | Online Consumer Marketing 129
Benefits of Online Consumer Marketing 132
Online Marketing Is International Marketing 134 | Security and Privacy Issues 135

Who Are the Online Buyers and Sellers? 136
Online Buyers 136 | Online Sellers 138

Interactive Marketing Channels 138
Company Web Sites 139 | Advertising on Other Web Sites 140
Online Communities 140 | Other Interactive Marketing Links 141

Creating an Effective Web Presence 143
Building an Effective Web Site 143 | Managing a Web Site 143
Measuring the Effectiveness of Online Marketing 144

Strategic Implications of Marketing in the 21st Century 145
Review of Chapter Objectives 146 | Marketing Terms You Need to Know 147
Other Important Marketing Terms 147 | Projects and Teamwork Exercises 148
Applying Chapter Concepts 148 | Ethics Exercise 149 | 'netWork Exercises 149
InfoTrac Citations and Exercises 149

Case 4.1 Match.com: The Love Algorithm 150

Video Case 4.2 Job-Hunting in the Digital Age: Monster.com 151

Marketer's Minute: Talking about Marketing Careers with Eric Stisser, Director of Corporate Sales and Marketing for the St. Louis Rams 152

Major League Soccer Continuing Video Case: The Meeting Place for U.S. Soccer Fans 154

part 2
UNDERSTANDING BUYERS AND MARKETS 155

chapter 5
CONSUMER BEHAVIOR 156

Interpersonal Determinants of Consumer Behavior 158
Cultural Influences 159 | Social Influences 163 | Family Influences 164

Personal Determinants of Consumer Behavior 166
Needs and Motives 167 | Perceptions 169 | Attitudes 171 | Learning 173
Self-Concept Theory 174

The Consumer Decision Process 175
Problem or Opportunity Recognition 176 | Search 177 | Evaluation of Alternatives 177
Purchase Decision and Purchase Act 178 | Postpurchase Evaluation 178
Classifying Consumer Problem-Solving Processes 179

Strategic Implications of Marketing in the 21st Century 180
Review of Chapter Objectives 180 | Marketing Terms You Need to Know 181
Other Important Marketing Terms 182 | Projects and Teamwork Exercises 182
Applying Chapter Concepts 182 | Ethics Exercise 183 | 'netWork Exercises 183
InfoTrac Citations and Exercises 183

Case 5.1 Cabela's: Marketing to the Consumer Who Hates to Shop 184

Video Case 5.2 Vida Wellness Spa Wishes You Well 185

Opening Vignette
Catering to the Long-Distance Fan 156

Marketing Hit
Bread Makers Responding to a Double-Wide Nation 168

Solving an Ethical Controversy
Assuring Consumers the Beef Supply Is Safe 172

Etiquette Tips for Marketing Professionals
Communicating through Body Language 175

Opening Vignette
Rawlings and Major League Baseball: They Fit Like Ball in Glove 186

Etiquette Tips for Marketing Professionals
Make Your Next Business Dinner a Marketing Success 196

Marketing Hit
The New Saab Is No Sob Story 197

Solving an Ethical Controversy
Who Gets the Contracts to Rebuild Iraq? 210

chapter 6
BUSINESS-TO-BUSINESS (B2B) MARKETING 186

Nature of the Business Market 188
Components of the Business Market 190 | B2B Markets: The Internet Connection 191
Differences in Foreign Business Markets 191

Segmenting B2B Markets 192
Segmentation by Demographic Characteristics 192 | Segmentation by Customer Type 192
Segmentation by End-Use Application 193 | Segmentation by Purchase Categories 193

Characteristics of the B2B Market 194
Geographic Market Concentration 194 | Sizes and Numbers of Buyers 194
The Purchase Decision Process 195 | Buyer–Seller Relationships 195
Evaluating International Business Markets 196

Business Market Demand 197
Derived Demand 197 | Volatile Demand 198 | Joint Demand 198
Inelastic Demand 198 | Inventory Adjustments 199

The Make, Buy, or Lease Decision 199
The Rise of Outsourcing and Offshoring 200
Problems with Outsourcing and Offshoring 201

The Business Buying Process 202
Influences on Purchase Decisions 202 | Model of the Organizational Buying Process 204
Classifying Business Buying Situations 206 | Analysis Tools 207

The Buying Center Concept 207
Buying Center Roles 207 | International Buying Centers 208 | Team Selling 209

Developing Effective Business-to-Business Marketing Strategies 209
Challenges of Government Markets 209 | Challenges of Institutional Markets 211
Challenges of International Markets 212

Strategic Implications of Marketing in the 21st Century 213
Review of Chapter Objectives 213 | Marketing Terms You Need to Know 215
Other Important Marketing Terms 215 | Projects and Teamwork Exercises 215
Applying Chapter Concepts 216 | Ethics Exercise 216 | 'netWork Exercises 216
InfoTrac Citations and Exercises 216

Case 6.1 Siebel and Sun Microsystems Keep Their Customers Satisfied 217

Video Case 6.2 Technomic Helps Businesses Serve Good Food 217

Opening Vignette
Manchester United Tries to Score with Soccer in America 218

Marketing Hit
Made—and Branded—in China 226

Etiquette Tips for Marketing Professionals
When in Rome . . . 229

Solving an Ethical Controversy
Must Americans Always Pay More for Prescription Drugs? 232

chapter 7
SERVING GLOBAL MARKETS 218

The Importance of Global Marketing 221
Service and Retail Exports 222 | Benefits of Going Global 223

The International Marketplace 224
Market Size 224 | Buyer Behavior 226

The International Marketing Environment 227
International Economic Environment 227 | International Social-Cultural Environment 228
International Technological Environment 230 | International Political-Legal Environment 230
Trade Barriers 233 | Dumping 234

Multinational Economic Integration 235
GATT and the World Trade Organization 236 | The NAFTA Accord 237
The Free Trade Area of the Americas 237 | The European Union 237

Going Global 238

First Steps in Deciding to Market Globally 239
Strategies for Entering International Markets 239 | Contractual Agreements 240
International Direct Investment 242

From Multinational Corporation to Global Marketer 242

Developing an International Marketing Strategy 243
International Product and Promotional Strategies 244 | International Distribution Strategy 245
Pricing Strategy 245 | Countertrade 246

The U.S. as a Target for International Marketers 246

Strategic Implications of Marketing in the 21st Century 247
Review of Chapter Objectives 247 | Marketing Terms You Need to Know 248
Other Important Marketing Terms 249 | Projects and Teamwork Exercises 249
Applying Chapter Concepts 249 | Ethics Exercise 250 | 'netWork Exercises 250
InfoTrac Citations and Exercises 250

Case 7.1 MTV Updates Its Global Strategy 251

Video Case 7.2 Doc Martens Makes Strides around the World 251

Marketer's Minute: Talking about Marketing Careers with Roger Curtis, Vice President of Marketing and Sales for California Speedway 252

Major League Soccer Continuing Video Case: Can MLS Speak the International Language? 254

part 3

TARGET MARKET SELECTION 255

chapter 8

MARKETING RESEARCH, DECISION SUPPORT SYSTEMS, AND SALES FORECASTING 256

The Marketing Research Function 258
Development of the Marketing Research Function 258
Who Conducts Marketing Research? 259 | Customer Satisfaction Measurement Programs 260

Opening Vignette
Charlotte NBA Team Hunts a New Identity 256

Solving an Ethical Controversy
Did Test Results Go Better with Coke? 263

Etiquette Tips for Marketing Professionals
How to Be a Good Listener 269

Marketing Hit
Ben & Jerry's Seeks Intelligence in Ice Cream 276

The Marketing Research Process 260
Define the Problem 260 | Conduct Exploratory Research 261
Formulate a Hypothesis 262 | Create a Research Design 262 | Collect Data 262
Interpret and Present Research Information 264

Marketing Research Methods 264
Secondary Data Collection 264 | Sampling Techniques 266
Primary Research Methods 267 | Conducting International Marketing Research 273

Interpretative Research 274

Computer Technology in Marketing Research 275
Marketing Information Systems (MISs) 275
Marketing Decision Support Systems (MDSSs) 275 | Data Mining 275
Business Intelligence 276 | Competitive Intelligence 277

Sales Forecasting 277
Qualitative Forecasting Techniques 277 | Quantitative Forecasting Techniques 279

Strategic Implications of Marketing in the 21st Century 279
Review of Chapter Objectives 280 | Marketing Terms You Need to Know 282
Other Important Marketing Terms 282 | Projects and Teamwork Exercises 282
Applying Chapter Concepts 283 | Ethics Exercise 284 | 'netWork Exercises 284
InfoTrac Citations and Exercises 284

Case 8.1 Marketing Research Goes to the Movies 285

Video Case 8.2 Teenage Research Unlimited Has the True Story on Teens 285

chapter 9
MARKET SEGMENTATION, TARGETING, AND POSITIONING 286

Types of Markets 288

The Role of Market Segmentation 289
Criteria for Effective Segmentation 289

Segmenting Consumer Markets 290

Geographic Segmentation 291
Using Geographic Segmentation 292 | Geographic Information Systems (GISs) 293

Demographic Segmentation 293
Segmenting by Gender 293 | Segmenting by Age 294 | Segmenting by Ethnic Group 296
Segmenting by Family Life Cycle Stages 298 | Segmenting by Household Type 300
Segmenting by Income and Expenditure Patterns 300
Demographic Segmentation Abroad 301

Psychographic Segmentation 301
What Is Psychographic Segmentation? 302 | VALS2 302
Psychographic Segmentation of Global Markets 303 | Using Psychographic Segmentation 304

Opening Vignette
Arte Moreno: An Angel to Major League Baseball 286

Solving an Ethical Controversy
What Kind of Information Should Marketers Collect? 299

Etiquette Tips for Marketing Professionals
Body Art: Beauty Is in the Eye of the Beholder 303

Marketing Miss
Who Buys the Pants in the Family? 310

Product-Related Segmentation 305

Segmenting by Benefits Sought 305 | Segmenting by Usage Rates 305
Segmenting by Brand Loyalty 305 | Using Multiple Segmentation Bases 305

The Market Segmentation Process 306

Develop a Relevant Profile for Each Segment 306 | Forecast Market Potential 306
Forecast Probable Market Share 306 | Select Specific Market Segments 307

Strategies for Reaching Target Markets 307

Undifferentiated Marketing 307 | Differentiated Marketing 307
Concentrated Marketing 308 | Micromarketing 308
Selecting and Executing a Strategy 308

Strategic Implications of Marketing in the 21st Century 311

Review of Chapter Objectives 311 | Marketing Terms You Need to Know 312
Other Important Marketing Terms 312 | Projects and Teamwork Exercises 313
Applying Chapter Concepts 313 | Ethics Exercise 313 | 'netWork Exercises 314
InfoTrac Citations and Exercises 314

Case 9.1 Scion: Toyota's Next Generation 315

Video Case 9.2 Orange Glo Cleans Up the Marketplace 315

chapter 10

RELATIONSHIP MARKETING, CUSTOMER RELATIONSHIP MANAGEMENT (CRM), AND ONE-TO-ONE MARKETING 316

The Shift from Transaction-Based Marketing to Relationship Marketing 318

Elements of Relationship Marketing 320 | Internal Marketing 320

The Relationship Marketing Continuum 321

First Level: Focus on Price 322 | Second Level: Social Interactions 322
Third Level: Interdependent Partnership 322

Enhancing Customer Satisfaction 324

Understanding Customer Needs 324
Obtaining Customer Feedback and Ensuring Customer Satisfaction 324

Building Buyer–Seller Relationships 325

How Marketers Keep Customers 325 | Database Marketing 327
One-to-One Marketing 328

Customer Relationship Management 329

Benefits of CRM 329 | Problems with CRM 330 | Managing Virtual Relationships 331
Retrieving Lost Customers 331

Buyer–Seller Relationships in Business-to-Business Markets 332

Choosing Business Partners 333 | Types of Partnerships 333
Cobranding and Comarketing 333

Improving Buyer–Seller Relationships in Business-to-Business Markets 335

National Account Selling 335 | Business-to-Business Databases 335

Opening Vignette
The Women's National Basketball Association (WNBA) Rebounds 316

Solving an Ethical Controversy
When Is a Close Relationship Too Close? 323

Marketing Hit
Carmakers Pitch to the Gay Community 334

Etiquette Tips for Marketing Professionals
It's the Thought That Counts: Dealing with Gifts and Greetings 336

Electronic Data Interchange 335 | Vendor-Managed Inventory 336
Managing the Supply Chain 337 | Business-to-Business Alliances 337

Evaluating Customer Relationship Programs 339

Strategic Implications of Marketing in the 21st Century 340

Review of Chapter Objectives 340 | Marketing Terms You Need to Know 342
Other Important Marketing Terms 342 | Projects and Teamwork Exercises 342
Applying Chapter Concepts 343 | Ethics Exercise 343 | 'netWork Exercises 344
InfoTrac Citations and Exercises 344

Case 10.1 Hilton Is OnQ with Customers 345

Video Case 10.2 International Flavors & Fragrances Makes Marketing Personal 345

Marketer's Minute: Talking about Marketing Careers with Michael McCullough, Executive Vice President and Chief Marketing Officer of the Miami Heat 346

Major League Soccer Continuing Video Case: Does MLS Need a Superhero? 348

part 4

PRODUCT DECISIONS 349

chapter 11

PRODUCT AND SERVICE STRATEGIES 350

Opening Vignette
The New Angle on Fishing 350

Etiquette Tips for Marketing Professionals
Telephone Manners: Hello, Goodbye, and in Between 365

Solving an Ethical Controversy
MTV's Super Bowl Disaster: Who Is Responsible? 367

Marketing Hit
Birkenstocks: They're Not Just for Hippies Anymore 370

What Is a Product? 352

What Are Goods and Services? 352

Importance of the Service Sector 354

Classifying Goods and Services for Consumer and Business Markets 355

Types of Consumer Products 355 | Classifying Consumer Services 358
Applying the Consumer Products Classification System 359
Types of Business Products 360

Quality as a Product Strategy 364

Worldwide Quality Programs 364 | Benchmarking 364 | Quality of Services 365

Development of Product Lines 366

Desire to Grow 367 | Enhancing the Company's Position in the Market 368
Optimal Use of Company Resources 368

The Product Mix 368

Product Mix Width 368 | Product Mix Length 369 | Product Mix Depth 369
Product Mix Decisions 369

The Product Life Cycle 370

Introductory Stage 371 | Growth Stage 372 | Maturity Stage 372 | Decline Stage 373

Extending the Product Life Cycle 373

Increasing Frequency of Use 373 | Increasing the Number of Users 374
Finding New Uses 374 | Changing Package Sizes, Labels, or Product Quality 374

Product Deletion Decisions 375

Strategic Implications of Marketing in the 21st Century 375

Review of Chapter Objectives 375 | Marketing Terms You Need to Know 377
Other Important Marketing Terms 377 | Projects and Teamwork Exercises 377
Applying Chapter Concepts 377 | Ethics Exercise 378 | 'netWork Exercises 378
InfoTrac Citations and Exercises 378

Case 11.1 Kevlar: A Product in Search of a Need 379

Video Case 11.2 Curves: A New Angle on Fitness 379

chapter 12

CATEGORY AND BRAND MANAGEMENT, PRODUCT IDENTIFICATION, AND NEW-PRODUCT DEVELOPMENT 380

Managing Brands for Competitive Advantage 382

Brand Loyalty 382 | Types of Brands 384 | Brand Equity 387
The Role of Category and Brand Management 388

Product Identification 388

Brand Names and Brand Marks 388 | Trademarks 391 | Developing Global Brand Names and Trademarks 392 | Packaging 393 | Brand Extensions 395
Brand Licensing 396

New-Product Planning 396

Product Development Strategies 396 | The Consumer Adoption Process 398
Adopter Categories 398 | Identifying Early Adopters 399
Organizing for New-Product Development 400

The New-Product Development Process 401

Idea Generation 402 | Screening 402 | Business Analysis 402 | Development 403
Test Marketing 403 | Commercialization 403

Product Safety and Liability 403

Strategic Implications of Marketing in the 21st Century 404

Review of Chapter Objectives 405 | Marketing Terms You Need to Know 406
Other Important Marketing Terms 406 | Projects and Teamwork Exercises 406
Applying Chapter Concepts 407 | Ethics Exercise 407 | 'netWork Exercises 408
InfoTrac Citations and Exercises 408

Case 12.1 What Will Become of the Box? 409

Video Case 12.2 Everything Is Beautiful at L'Oréal 409

Marketer's Minute: Talking about Marketing Careers with David Abrutyn, Senior Vice President of IMG Consulting 410

Major League Soccer Continuing Video Case: MLS Finds Fertile New Ground 412

Opening Vignette
Teaming Up to Market Merchandise Featuring College Logos 380

Solving an Ethical Controversy
Counterfeiters: Is It Worth the Fight to Stop Them? 384

Etiquette Tips for Marketing Professionals
How to Run a Business Meeting 389

Marketing Miss
SPAM versus Spam: Who Will Win? 390

part 5

DISTRIBUTION DECISIONS 413

chapter 13

MARKETING CHANNELS AND SUPPLY CHAIN MANAGEMENT 414

Opening Vignette
Swoosh! Nike's Bid for Channel Dominance 414

Solving an Ethical Controversy
Ticketmaster: Who Pays the Price? 425

Etiquette Tips for Marketing Professionals
Developing Relationships with Supply Chain Contacts in China 430

Marketing Hit
IBM Overhauls Its Supply Chain 431

The Role of Marketing Channels in Marketing Strategy 416

Types of Marketing Channels 417
Direct Selling 419 | Channels Using Marketing Intermediaries 419
Dual Distribution 420 | Reverse Channels 420

Channel Strategy Decisions 421
Selection of a Marketing Channel 421 | Determining Distribution Intensity 422
Who Should Perform Channel Functions? 424

Channel Management and Leadership 426
Channel Conflict 426 | Achieving Channel Cooperation 427

Vertical Marketing Systems 427
Corporate and Administered Systems 428 | Contractual Systems 428

Logistics and Supply Chain Management 429
Radio Frequency Identification (RFID) 431 | Enterprise Resource Planning 432
Logistical Cost Control 432

Physical Distribution 433
The Problem of Suboptimization 433 | Customer-Service Standards 434
Transportation 434 | Warehousing 438 | Inventory Control Systems 439
Order Processing 439 | Protective Packaging and Materials Handling 440

Strategic Implications of Marketing in the 21st Century 440
Review of Chapter Objectives 441 | Marketing Terms You Need to Know 442
Other Important Marketing Terms 442 | Projects and Teamwork Exercises 443
Applying Chapter Concepts 443 | Ethics Exercise 443 | 'netWork Exercises 444
InfoTrac Citations and Exercises 444

Case 13.1 BAX to the Future: How a Logistics Firm Has Survived and Grown 445

Video Case 13.2 1-800-Flowers.com: Great Gifts by Phone or Online 445

chapter 14

DIRECT MARKETING AND MARKETING RESELLERS: RETAILERS AND WHOLESALERS 446

Opening Vignette
REI: The Retailer with 2 Million Owners 446

Marketing Hit
Netflix: Movies by Mail 451

Etiquette Tips for Marketing Professionals
Dos and Don'ts of Business Invitations 455

Solving an Ethical Controversy
Ask Your Doctor—or Not? 457

Retailing 448
Evolution of Retailing 448

Retailing Strategy 449

Selecting a Target Market 449 | Merchandising Strategy 450
Customer-Service Strategy 451 | Pricing Strategy 452 | Location/Distribution Strategy 453
Promotional Strategy 454 | Store Atmospherics 456

Types of Retailers 457

Classification of Retailers by Form of Ownership 458 | Classification by Shopping Effort 458
Classification by Services Provided 458 | Classification by Product Lines 459
Classification of Retail Transactions by Location 461
Retail Convergence and Scrambled Merchandising 461

Wholesaling Intermediaries 462

Functions of Wholesaling Intermediaries 462 | Types of Wholesaling Intermediaries 463
Retailer-Owned Cooperatives and Buying Offices 467

Direct Marketing and Other Nonstore Retailing 467

Direct Mail 467 | Direct Selling 468 | Direct-Response Retailing 468
Telemarketing 469 | Internet Retailing 469 | Automatic Merchandising 469

Strategic Implications of Marketing in the 21st Century 469

Review of Chapter Objectives 470 | Marketing Terms You Need to Know 471
Other Important Marketing Terms 472 | Projects and Teamwork Exercises 472
Applying Chapter Concepts 473 | Ethics Exercise 473 | 'netWork Exercises 474
InfoTrac Citations and Exercises 474

Case 14.1 Costco Challenges Mighty Wal-Mart 475

Video Case 14.2 Westfield Group Creates a Shopper's Paradise 475

Marketer's Minute: Talking about Marketing Careers with Jennifer Gardner, Director of Sales for the Cincinnati Reds 476

Major League Soccer Continuing Video Case: MLS Delivers the Goods 478

part 6

PROMOTIONAL DECISIONS 479

chapter 15

INTEGRATED MARKETING COMMUNICATIONS 480

Integrated Marketing Communications 483

Importance of Teamwork 485 | Role of Databases in Effective IMC Programs 486

The Communication Process 486

Objectives of Promotion 490

Provide Information 490 | Increase Demand 491 | Differentiate the Product 491
Accentuate the Product's Value 492 | Stabilize Sales 492

Elements of the Promotional Mix 492

Personal Selling 493 | Nonpersonal Selling 493

Opening Vignette
Tour de Lance 480

Etiquette Tips for Marketing Professionals
How to Write an Effective Letter 488

Marketing Miss
How the Gap Lost Its Groove 489

Solving an Ethical Controversy
Captive Advertising 494

Sponsorships 497
Sponsorship Spending 498 | Growth of Sponsorships 499
How Sponsorship Differs from Advertising 499 | Assessing Sponsorship Results 500

Direct Marketing 500
Direct Marketing Communications Channels 501 | Direct Mail 501 | Catalogs 502
Telemarketing 502 | Direct Marketing via Broadcast Channels 503
Electronic Direct Marketing Channels 503 | Other Direct Marketing Channels 504

Developing an Optimal Promotional Mix 504
Nature of the Market 504 | Nature of the Product 505
Stage in the Product Life Cycle 505 | Price 506 | Funds Available for Promotion 506

Pulling and Pushing Promotional Strategies 507

Budgeting for Promotional Strategy 508

Measuring the Effectiveness of Promotion 510
Measuring Online Promotions 510

The Value of Marketing Communications 511
Social Importance 511 | Business Importance 512 | Economic Importance 512

Strategic Implications of Marketing in the 21st Century 513
Review of Chapter Objectives 513 | Marketing Terms You Need to Know 514
Other Important Marketing Terms 515 | Projects and Teamwork Exercises 515
Applying Chapter Concepts 515 | Ethics Exercise 516 | 'netWork Exercises 516
InfoTrac Citations and Exercises 516

Case 15.1 IMC Strategy Launches New $20 Bill 517

Video Case 15.2 Jimmy John's Sandwich Shops Give Customers Something to Chew On 517

chapter 16

ADVERTISING AND PUBLIC RELATIONS 518

Opening Vignette
The Dark Side of Celebrity Endorsements 518

Marketing Hit
Cell Phone Messages Ring True 525

Solving an Ethical Controversy
Will the Ad-Zapper Mean the Death of TV Commercials? 532

Etiquette Tips for Marketing Professionals
Voice-Mail Etiquette 538

Advertising 520
Types of Advertising 521 | Objectives of Advertising 521

Advertising Strategies 522
Comparative Advertising 522 | Celebrity Testimonials 523 | Retail Advertising 524
Interactive Advertising 525

Creating an Advertisement 526
Translating Advertising Objectives into Advertising Plans 526

Advertising Messages 527
Advertising Appeals 527 | Developing and Preparing Ads 528
Creating Interactive Ads 528

Media Selection 530
Television 530 | Radio 531 | Newspapers 533 | Magazines 533 | Direct Mail 534
Outdoor Advertising 534 | Interactive Media 535 | Other Advertising Media 535

Media Scheduling 536

Organization of the Advertising Function 537
Advertising Agencies 537

Public Relations 538
Marketing and Nonmarketing Public Relations 539 | Publicity 540

Cross Promotion 540

Measuring Promotional Effectiveness 541
Measuring Advertising Effectiveness 541 | Measuring Public Relations Effectiveness 543
Evaluating Interactive Media 543

Ethics in Nonpersonal Selling 544
Advertising Ethics 544 | Ethics in Public Relations 545

Strategic Implications of Marketing in the 21st Century 545
Review of Chapter Objectives 545 | Marketing Terms You Need to Know 547
Other Important Marketing Terms 547 | Projects and Teamwork Exercises 548
Applying Chapter Concepts 548 | Ethics Exercise 549 | 'netWork Exercises 549
InfoTrac Citations and Exercises 550

Case 16.1 Will Technology Kill the Advertising Star? 551

Video Case 16.2 Ride the White Wave with Silk Soymilk 551

chapter 17
PERSONAL SELLING AND SALES PROMOTION 552

The Evolution of Personal Selling 554

The Four Sales Channels 556
Over-the-Counter Selling 556 | Field Selling 557 | Telemarketing 558
Inside Selling 560 | Integrating the Various Selling Channels 560

Trends in Personal Selling 561
Relationship Selling 561 | Consultative Selling 562 | Team Selling 563
Sales Force Automation 564

Sales Tasks 565
Order Processing 566 | Creative Selling 566 | Missionary Selling 566

The Sales Process 567
Prospecting and Qualifying 567 | Approach 568 | Presentation 569
Demonstration 569 | Handling Objections 569 | Closing 570 | Follow-Up 571

Managing the Sales Effort 571
Recruitment and Selection 572 | Training 573 | Organization 573 | Supervision 574
Motivation 575 | Compensation 576 | Evaluation and Control 576

Ethical Issues in Sales 578

Sales Promotion 579
Consumer-Oriented Sales Promotions 580 | Trade-Oriented Promotions 583

Opening Vignette
The Williams Sisters: Selling Talent and Tennis 552

Solving an Ethical Controversy
Who's Calling? 559

Etiquette Tips for Marketing Professionals
Get in the Swing with Good Golf Manners 562

Marketing Hit
Salesforce.com Leases Software for Less 564

Strategic Implications of Marketing in the 21st Century 585

Review of Chapter Objectives 585 | Marketing Terms You Need to Know 587
Other Important Marketing Terms 587 | Projects and Teamwork Exercises 588
Applying Chapter Concepts 589 | Ethics Exercise 589 | 'netWork Exercises 589
InfoTrac Citations and Exercises 590

Case 17.1 The Independent Sales Force 591

Video Case 17.2 Chicago Show, Inc. Puts on a Show 591

Marketer's Minute: Talking about Marketing Careers with Suzy Christopher, Senior Director of Marketing for the Columbus Crew 592

Major League Soccer Continuing Video Case: MLS Promotes Soccer, and Reading, and Jobs 594

part 7 PRICING DECISIONS 595

chapter 18 PRICE CONCEPTS AND APPROACHES 596

Opening Vignette
Outfitting a Cheerleading Squad: How Marketers Turn Team Spirit into Booming Sales 596

Etiquette Tips for Marketing Professionals
Learning the Rules about Tipping 607

Solving an Ethical Controversy
Why Do Prescription Drugs Cost So Much? 609

Marketing Miss
Oh, Those Fees and Hidden Charges 612

Pricing and the Law 598

Robinson-Patman Act 599 | Unfair-Trade Laws 600 | Fair-Trade Laws 600

Pricing Objectives and the Marketing Mix 601

Profitability Objectives 602 | Volume Objectives 602 | Prestige Objectives 605

Pricing Objectives of Not-for-Profit Organizations 605

Methods for Determining Prices 606

Price Determination in Economic Theory 608

Cost and Revenue Curves 608 | The Concept of Elasticity in Pricing Strategy 609
Practical Problems of Price Theory 613

Price Determination in Practice 613

Alternative Pricing Procedures 614 | Breakeven Analysis 614

Toward Realistic Pricing 616

The Modified Breakeven Concept 616 | Yield Management 618

Global Issues in Price Determination 619

Strategic Implications of Marketing in the 21st Century 620

Review of Chapter Objectives 621 | Marketing Terms You Need to Know 622
Other Important Marketing Terms 622 | Projects and Teamwork Exercises 623
Applying Chapter Concepts 623 | Ethics Exercise 624 | 'netWork Exercises 624
InfoTrac Citations and Exercises 624

Case 18.1 Universal Slashes Prices of CDs by 30 Percent 625

Video Case 18.2 Wrigley's Gives Everyone Something to Chew On 625

chapter 19

PRICING STRATEGIES 626

Pricing Strategies 628
Skimming Pricing Strategy 629 | Penetration Pricing Strategy 631
Competitive Pricing Strategy 632

Price Quotations 634
Reductions from List Price 634 | Geographic Considerations 637

Pricing Policies 639
Psychological Pricing 640 | Price Flexibility 640 | Product-Line Pricing 641
Promotional Pricing 641 | Price-Quality Relationships 642

Competitive Bidding and Negotiated Prices 643
Negotiating Prices Online 644

The Transfer Pricing Dilemma 645

Global Considerations and Online Pricing 646
Traditional Global Pricing Strategies 646 | Characteristics of Online Pricing 646
Bundle Pricing 647

Strategic Implications of Marketing in the 21st Century 648
Review of Chapter Objectives 649 | Marketing Terms You Need to Know 650
Other Important Marketing Terms 650 | Projects and Teamwork Exercises 651
Applying Chapter Concepts 651 | Ethics Exercise 652 | 'netWork Exercises 652
InfoTrac Citations and Exercises 652

Case 19.1 Solving the Pricing Puzzle 653

Video Case 19.2 Jiffy Lube: The Well-Oiled Machine 653

Marketer's Minute: Talking about Marketing Careers with Pat Gavin, Director of the Professional Golf Management (PGM) Program at New Mexico State University 654

Major League Soccer Continuing Video Case: Major League Soccer: The Price of Admission 656

Appendix A-1

Video Cases VC-1

Notes N-1

Glossary G-1

Indexes I-1

Opening Vignette
How Hockey Teams Set Ticket Prices 626

Marketing Miss
Milk Is in Demand 629

Solving an Ethical Controversy
When Is a Rebate Not a Rebate? 638

Etiquette Tips for Marketing Professionals
How to Ask for a Price Break 644

Planning a Career in Marketing

STUDY OF MARKETING EXPANDS INTO OTHER ACADEMIC PROGRAMS

As you meet more and more of your marketing classmates during the months ahead, you are likely to be amazed at the diversity of interests—to say nothing of career interests—of your fellow students. Many of them will be taking this course as a requirement for one of the different majors in your school's business program. But you are also likely to find more academic diversity than ever before. They come from majors ranging from the fine arts and interior design to leisure services, hospitality management, and sport marketing and management. But each of them is as interested as you to learn about marketing and how to apply it to his or her chosen field of interest.

Today, marketing is recognized a an invaluable tool in all kinds of industries, not just in the traditional areas involving consumer products like fashion accessories, autos, and flat-screen TVs. Now marketing concepts and strategies are put to use more and more frequently in marketing:

- *people* (such as celebrities and political candidates)
- *organizations* (such as nonprofits and even hospitals and medical practices)
- *places* (such as cities vying to host conventions and sports tournaments, attract new businesses, and entice tourists and permanent residents to visit)
- *causes* (such as environmental protection and gay rights)
- *events* (such as concerts, rallies, and sporting events)

© ARIEL SKELLEY/CORBIS

The growing popularity of marketing courses in sports management programs is a good example. These programs were formerly found almost exclusively in hospitality, tourism, leisure services, and separate sport management programs. They have recently expanded to a growing number of business school marketing programs in acknowledgment of student interest in applying business and marketing knowledge to a career in sports—and in recognition of the need to identify target markets and design marketing mixes to satisfy customers (fans) in a successful sports career.

Collegiate programs in sports management combine academic and practical training in professional sports, sport marketing and promotion, facility and event management, management of amateur sports, manufacturing and sale of sporting goods, sports club management, sports media and communication, and athletic representation. These programs also include extensive coursework in science, the humanities, math and technology, accounting, communication, and computer applications.

Individualized programs are available for many sports. Golf management programs operate in cooperation with the PGA—the not-for-profit organization comprised of more than 28,000 men and women golfing professionals that promotes the game of golf while continuing to enhance the standards of the profession. These programs are currently being offered by 16 colleges and universities, including Penn State, Mississippi State, New Mexico State, Florida State, and Ferris State (Michigan). Curricula typically include internships and on-the-job experiences at country clubs, resorts, or other golf facilities. The full program of study includes workshops, seminars, and specialized courses ranging from Merchandising and Tournament Operations to Food and Beverage Operations and Business Writing. And of course, the marketing concepts you'll learn in this course are among the first things sport marketing majors learn about when they study the business of sports.[1]

Overview

Congratulations on your decision to take this course. After all, marketing is a pervasive element in our lives. In one form or another, it reaches every person. As you begin this course, you should be aware of three important facts about marketing.

The person who knows *how* will always have a job. The person who knows *why* will always be his boss.

Diane Ravitch (b. 1938)
American educator

MARKETING COSTS ARE A BIG COMPONENT OF YOUR TOTAL BUDGET

Approximately 50 percent of the total costs of products you buy are marketing costs. In short, half of the $20 you pay for that chart-topping CD goes, not for the plastic disc, protective sleeve, paper jacket, or the physical act of burning the tracks onto the disk, but for marketing costs. The same is true of the price of a new flat-screen monitor for your desktop, your DVD player, and the $26,000 Toyota Prius you want so badly.

But costs alone do not indicate the value of marketing. The high living standard that you, your family, and your friends enjoy is in large part a function of our nation's efficient marketing systems. When considered in this perspective, the costs of marketing seem more reasonable. For example, effective marketing can expand overall sales, thereby spreading fixed production costs over more units of output and reducing total output costs.

If I had my life to live over again, I would be a trader of goods rather than a student of science. I think barter is a noble thing.

Albert Einstein (1879–1955)
American physicist

MARKETING PROVIDES AN OPPORTUNITY TO CONTRIBUTE TO SOCIETY AS WELL AS TO AN INDIVIDUAL COMPANY

Marketing decisions affect everyone's welfare. How much quality should be built into a product? Will people buy a safer product if it costs twice as much as the current version? Should every community adopt recycling programs? Because ethics and social responsibilities are critical factors for marketers in a business environment tarnished by both ethical and legal failings of a number of well-known companies and their leaders, it is essential that marketers strive to exceed customer and government expectations of ethical behavior. Reading the "Solving an Ethical Controversy" feature included in every chapter will increase your awareness of the role of high ethical standards in every dimension of marketing and allow you to examine the not always black-and-white ethical issues such as prescription

Becoming a successful executive often starts with a degree in marketing or business. However, it is also common for high achievers who wish to acquire the knowledge and credentials associated with an advanced degree to pursue additional studies on a part-time basis while holding down a full-time job. As this promotional message from the J. Mack Robinson College of Business at Georgia State University proclaims, the GSU program has the flexibility to match the needs of individual students.

drug pricing, online privacy, advertising to children, and invasive practices such as spam, pop-up ads, and telemarketing.

Not only does marketing influence numerous facets of our daily lives, but decisions regarding marketing activities also affect everyone's welfare. Opportunities to advance to more responsible decision-making positions come sooner in marketing than in most occupations. This combination of challenges and opportunities has made marketing one of the most popular fields of academic study.

A recent survey by executive recruiter Korn/Ferry International revealed that the best route to the top of the corporate ladder begins in a company's marketing team. The growing global economy demands proven market leaders in winning the fight to increase a firm's worldwide market shares—part of the reason why three of every eight CEOs have marketing backgrounds. Finance, which had long dominated as the top career path for senior executives, fell to third place, and executives who had completed international assignments—many of the assignments being marketing related—came in second.

YOU MAY CHOOSE A CAREER IN MARKETING

When asked about their conception of an ideal entry-level job following graduation, most students mention salary and opportunity for professional growth and advancement. While compensation is almost always an issue, the 21st century job seeker also wants to feel recognized for his or her achievements, be assigned new responsibilities, and work in continuous-learning environments. Many will also include as an important issue working for a family-friendly organization that offers a high quality of life.

Of the many career paths chosen by business graduates, marketing is the single largest employment category in the U.S. labor force, and job growth in the field is expected to accelerate. The U.S. Bureau of Labor Statistics estimates that the number of jobs in marketing, advertising, and public relations management will grow much faster than the average for all occupations. Every successful organization—profit-seeking or not-for-profit—recognizes the necessity of effective marketing in accomplishing its goal of providing customer satisfaction by hiring highly motivated, professionally educated marketing specialists to design and implement these customer-driven programs.

Marketing-related occupations account for 25 to 30 percent of jobs in the typical highly industrialized nation. History has shown that the demand for effective marketers is not affected by cyclical economic fluctuations.

YOUR QUEST FOR A SUCCESSFUL, REWARDING CAREER

Selecting a career may be the most important decision you will ever make. That's why *Contemporary Marketing* begins by discussing the best way to approach career decisions and how to prepare for an *entry-level position*—your first permanent employment after leaving school. We then look at a range of marketing careers and discuss employment opportunities in fields related to each major part of the text.

Until recently, entry-level positions had been more difficult to find. As the economy suffered after September 11, 2001, so did the job market. Today, economic conditions are improving, and job prospects are brighter for most students. According to a National Association of Colleges and Employers survey, the class of 2004 could expect to find about 11 percent more job openings than the preceding class, and sales and marketing jobs are expected to rebound in many industries as the economy recovery continues.[2] Still, you need to do everything you can to enhance your career opportunities. You've already taken an important first step by enrolling in a class using this textbook. You will need to continue to be creative in your job search. But as you know, creativity has never been in short supply on the nation's campuses.

During the next few months, you will be introduced to all the key functional areas of marketing. As you learn about marketing concepts, you will also be able to identify areas of employment that you may wish to pursue.

Education will improve your prospects of finding and keeping the right job. In a recent year, the average full-time employee 18 or older with a high school diploma earned just under $23,000. By contrast, the average employee with a bachelor's degree earned $40,000-plus annually—one and three-fourths more than the pay of the high school grad. Better educated graduates also found jobs more quickly than others.[3] Applying yourself in class, expanding your experiences through career-directed volunteer efforts, part-time and summer jobs, and high-quality internships—and selecting the right major—will put you well on your way to improving these salary statistics when you launch your career.

In addition to taking classes, try to gain related experience either through a job and/or by participating in campus organizations. Internships, carefully selected summer and part-time jobs, and volunteer activities on campus and in your community can also give you invaluable hands-on experience while you pursue your education. During the recent tight job markets when youth unemployment soared to 12 percent, work experience often set people apart from other job seekers in the eyes of recruiters.[4] Work-related experience—including internships—is often invaluable for traditional students who entered college immediately following graduation from high school and who possess little or no work experience.

This career-focused Prologue provides you with a brief look at the trends and opportunities available for future marketers in an increasingly diversified professional field. It describes essential elements of an effective résumé and discusses the latest trends in electronic job searches. Finally, it provides a listing of primary marketing information sources that contain answers to many of the questions typically asked by applicants. This information will provide valuable career-planning assistance in this and other future courses, whether your career plans involve marketing or you decide to major in another field.

Many of the marketing positions you read about throughout the text are described here. Specifically, the job summaries describe the job and the responsibilities and duties that are typically required as well as the usual career path for each of these marketing-related positions.

Marketing your skills to a prospective employer is much the same as marketing a product to a consumer. Increasingly, job seekers are selling their skills online, bypassing intermediaries such as employment agencies, and leveling the playing field between applicant and potential employer. The greatest challenge for online job seekers is learning how to market themselves.

Despite the vast databases and fancy tools of the giant career sites such as Monster.com and CareerBuilder (http://www.careerbuilder.com), which may receive hundreds of thousands of visits each day, savvy job seekers often find their time better spent zeroing in on niche boards offering more focused listings.[5] For example, sales applicants can check out Salesgiant.com.

In many instances, students desiring interviews with specific employers or in certain geographic locations will go directly to the employer's or region's Web site to learn of available positions. Most

An ideal job is one that makes you want to go to work every morning. It's working at something you enjoy and for which you get rewarded handsomely for performing at a superior level that provides satisfaction.

Some jobs—or even internships for students working in those jobs—are so enticing that they become the subject of contests, pitting applicants against each other. ESPN SportsCenter created a contest in which finalists would vie for their dream job as a news anchor.

COURTESY OF MONSTER WORLDWIDE, INC.

Monster.com is one of the 3,000-plus online career sites available for use by online job seekers. Graduates may find niche sites just as useful as larger ones like Monster.

employers include an employment site as part of their home page. Some offer virtual tours of what it is like to work for the firm. For example, the Enterprise Rent-a-Car Web site features profiles of young assistant managers as they perform daily work activities.

After spending $1.8 million in a single year to hire between 12,000 and 14,000 people, Lockheed Martin decided to make better use of its corporate Web site in recruiting job candidates. The defense contractor hired the same number of new employees the following year, but its cost-cutting approach made it possible to fill its vacancies and spend only $750,000 on commercial job boards.[6]

Your online job search can focus on positions in a specialized field or location, or these positions can be posted on metasites like Monster.com with few if any particular limitations on company or location. In either case, the key to getting the job you want is letting the market know who you are and what you can do. While few college graduates are hired directly based on their response to an online listing, this approach is often an important first step in zeroing in on specific employers of interest and then soliciting interviews that may lead to job offers.

As you begin your career, you will apply many of the principles and concepts discussed in the text, including how to do the following: target a market, capitalize on brand equity, position a product, and use marketing research techniques. Even in jobs that seem remote from the marketing discipline, this knowledge will help you stay focused on the most important aspect of business: the consumer.[7]

STANDING OUT FROM THE CROWD OF JOB SEEKERS

True terror is to wake up one morning and discover that your high school class is running the country.

Kurt Vonnegut Jr. (b. 1922)
American author

In a tight job market, employers can afford to be choosy in deciding which applicants will make the cut, be interviewed, and possibly, be offered a position. And often the applicant's accumulated job and leadership experiences will be key decision criteria in determining whether he or she is given serious consideration as a potential employee.

Students often choose to continue their studies following graduation and pursue an MBA degree or enter a master's program specially suited to their career goals. For example, students interested in a marketing research career may decide to study for a specialized master's degree in this field offered by a growing number of universities. A student who wishes to extend formal education in a specialized degree program should seek advice on specific programs from instructors who teach in that area. For example, a marketing research professor is likely to have information on master's programs in that field at different universities.

Other activities that enhance your personal worth are internships and volunteering. Internships have been described as a critical link in bridging the theory–practice educational gap. They help to carry students between the academic present and the professional future. They provide students with an opportunity for learning how classroom theory is applied in real-world business environments.

An internship is a partnership between the student, the academic institution, and the agency or internship site. All these parties assume definite responsibilities, perform specific functions, and achieve benefits as a result of their involvement. In addition, internships can serve as critical networking and job-hunting tools. In some instances, internships are precursors of specific employment opportunities, allowing students to demonstrate technical proficiency while providing cost-effective employee training for the company or not-for-profit organization.[8] Students interested in blending marketing with a career in sports find internships are almost essential in landing entry-level positions. Nearly 90 percent of sports organizations offer internships in a broad variety of areas and departments.[9]

Excellent sources of information about the nation's outstanding internships can be found at your local bookstore. One particularly useful publication by Mark Oldman and Samer Hamadeh is *America's Top 100 Internships*, published annually by Villard Books in New York.

Résumé Blunders

The following list of errors appeared in job résumés, applications, and cover letters received by Robert Half, the late founder of Accountemps:

- "I have worked in a fairy wide range of industries."
- "Great eye for derail."
- "I have incredibly entertaining hair."
- "I am accustomed to being in the hot seat."
- "EDUCATION: Some."

YOUR RÉSUMÉ

Writing a résumé is a task that almost every job seeker dislikes—and one that is often postponed until the last minute. "After all," the thinking usually goes, "I won't be involved in interviewing for another year." However, this task is made less daunting with the help of your faculty adviser or career counselor, a growing number of books and articles on résumé writing, and numerous computer software packages that require little more than filling in the blanks.[10]

A résumé is probably the most important document that a job seeker can provide to a potential employer because it frequently is the only written record of credentials available with which an evaluation and the selection of a job candidate can be made. It is a concise summary of academic, professional, and personal accomplishments that makes focused statements about the job applicant.

Three basic formats are used in preparing a résumé. A *chronological résumé* arranges information in reverse chronological order, emphasizing job titles and organizations and describing responsibilities held and duties performed. This format highlights continuity and career growth. A *functional résumé* accents accomplishments and strengths, placing less emphasis on job titles and work history, and often omits job descriptions. A functional résumé prepared by a recent graduate is shown in Figure 1. Some applicants use a *combined résumé* format, which emphasizes skills first, followed by employment history. This format highlights a candidate's potential and suits students who often have little experience directly related to their desired positions.

Most résumés include full names as well as mail and e-mail addresses. If the username of your e-mail address is "MachoDude" or "SnowboardDoll," replace it with one related to your real name or location to convince employers to take you seriously.

A statement of career objectives typically follows. Academic information is provided next, followed by experience and work history. Applicants with limited work histories and no internship experiences typically focus on relevant personal activities and interests. Any and all professional and extracurricular activities, as well as academic, work, and internship experiences, should be included on your résumé. Most résumés close with lists of references.

Whether yours is a traditional résumé on paper or posted on an Internet résumé listing, the important point to remember in creating an effective résumé is to present the most relevant information in a clear, concise manner that emphasizes your best attributes.

COVER LETTER

An employer is typically first introduced to a job applicant through a cover letter. Like gift wrapping on a present, a cover letter should attract attention and interest about what is inside and should be addressed to a specific person. The cover letter must provide specifically targeted information, state the particular position you are applying for, where you learned about the position, and why you are interested in it. It should also describe attributes of your personality, such as dependability, responsibility, energy level, and technical skills, without sounding overly boastful or arrogant.[11]

Next, your cover letter should specifically state when you will follow up with a phone call or letter. Your cover letter then should close with an expression of appreciation for being considered for the position. Make certain that your cover letter is neat and grammatically correct, since employers often use it to evaluate written communication skills. Finally, sign the letter in blue or black ink.

Mark your calendar and follow up your cover letter and résumé when you stated you would. If you indicated that you would call, then use this opportunity to ask any additional questions and set a possible date for an interview.

A résumé is a balance sheet without any liabilities.

Robert Half (1918–2001)

American personnel agency executive

figure 1
Functional Résumé

Jorge Paz
Two Seaside Drive, Apt. 3A
Los Angeles, CA 90026
215-555-7092
JPAZ@hotmail.com

Objective
Joining a growth-oriented company that values highly productive employees. Seeking an opportunity that leads to senior merchandising position.

Professional Experience
Administration
Management responsibilities in a major retail buying office included coordinating vendor relation efforts. Supervised assistant buyers.

Category Management
Experience in buying home improvement and sport, recreation, and fitness categories.

Planning
Leader of a team charged with reviewing the company's annual vendor evaluation program.

Problem Solving
Successfully developed a program to improve margins in the tennis, golf, and fishing product categories.

Work Experience
Senior Buyer
Southern California Department Stores 2005–Present

Merchandiser
Pacific Discount Stores, a division of Southern California Department Stores 2003–2005

Education
Bachelor of Science degree in business
Double major in marketing and retailing
California State University–San Bernardino 2001–2005

Computer Skills
Proficient with IBM-compatible computers and related software, including spreadsheets, graphics, desktop publishing, and word processing.
Packages: Excel, Lotus 1-2-3, Harvard Graphics, PowerPoint, Microsoft Word

Familiar with Adobe PageMaker and the Macintosh.

Language Skills
Fluent in speaking and writing Spanish.

LETTERS OF RECOMMENDATION

Letters of recommendation serve as testimonials to your performance in academic and work settings. The best references provide information relevant to the desired industry or marketing specialty as well as opinions of your skills, abilities, and character. References may be obtained from former or current employers, supervisors from volunteer experiences, professors, and others who can attest to your academic and professional competencies.

An effective letter of recommendation typically contains the following elements:

1. Statement of the length and nature of the relationship between the writer and the job candidate
2. Description of the candidate's academic and career growth potential
3. Review of important achievements
4. Evaluation of personal characteristics (what kind of colleague the candidate will make)
5. Summary of the candidate's outstanding strengths and abilities

Because letters of recommendation take time and effort, it helps to provide a résumé and any other information relevant to the recommendation, along with a stamped, addressed (typed) envelope. When requesting letters of recommendation, you should allow ample time for your references to compose them—as long as a month is not unusual.

In addition to including a cover letter, résumé, and letters of recommendation, candidates should include photocopies of transcripts, writing samples, or other examples of work completed. For example, if you are applying for a position in public relations, advertising, or sports marketing, you may want to include examples of professional writing, graphics, and audio/visual tapes and DVDs to support written evidence of your credentials. Research and service projects that resulted in published or unpublished articles may also enhance your portfolio.

Briefly Speaking

Put it to them briefly so they will read it; clearly, so they will appreciate it; picturesquely, so they will remember it—and, above all, accurately, so they will be guided by its light.

Joseph Pulitzer
(1847–1911)
American journalist

DEALING WITH AUTOMATED SYSTEMS

Employers are quickly moving to automated (paperless) résumé processing and applicant-tracking systems. As a result, if you prepare a technology-compatible résumé and cover letter, you'll enjoy an edge over applicants whose résumés and cover letters can't be added to the firm's database. Also, remember that résumés are often transmitted electronically. Figure 2 contains a number of tips for creating an effective, technology-compatible résumé.

Employers who review electronic résumés and those posted on some of the 3,000 Web sites currently carrying job postings frequently save time by using computers to search for keywords in job titles, job descriptions, or résumés to narrow the search. In fact, *manager* is the No. 1 word for which companies search. Regardless of the position you seek, the key to an effective electronic résumé is to use exact words and phrases, emphasizing nouns rather than the action verbs you are likely to use in a printed résumé. For example, a company looking for a marketing account manager with experience in Lotus 1-2-3, Microsoft Word, and Microsoft Excel programs is likely to conduct computer searches for only those résumés that include the job title and the three software programs.

figure 2

Tips for Preparing an Electronic Résumé

Tips for Preparing an Electronic Résumé

- Use a plain font. Use a standard serif typeface, such as Courier, Times, Arial, Univers, or Futura. Simplicity is key.
- Use 11- to 14-point type sizes.
- Keep your line length to no more than 65 characters (letters, spaces, and punctuation).
- Do not use graphics, bullets, lines, bold, italics, underlines, or shading.
- Use capital letters for your headings.
- Justify your text to the left.
- Use vertical and horizontal lines sparingly. Lines may blur your type.
- Omit parentheses and brackets, even around telephone numbers. These can blur and leave the number unreadable.
- Use white paper and black type.
- Use a laser-quality printer.
- Print on one side of the paper only.
- Don't compress space between letters. Use a second page rather than pack everything into one page and have it scan unclearly.
- Do not staple pages of a résumé together.
- Use industry buzzwords. Keyword searches often look for industry jargon.
- Place your name as the first text on the résumé. Do not put anything else on that line.
- Fax résumés on the *fine mode* setting. It is much easier to read than the *standard mode* setting.
- Do not fold your résumé. A crease makes scanning—and retrieving—difficult.
- If you are sending your résumé in the body of an e-mail transmission, do not distinguish between pages, as the full e-mail will download into the database as one sheet.
- Don't send a résumé as an e-mail attachment unless you are specifically instructed to do so. Many employers discard unsolicited attachments.

Source: Mary Dixon Werdler, "Translate Your Résumé for Electronic Eyes," http://www.jobweb.com, accessed February 1, 2002. © National Association of Colleges and Employers. Used by permission.

LEARNING MORE ABOUT JOB OPPORTUNITIES

You should carefully study the various employment opportunities you have identified. Obviously, you will like some more than others, but you should examine a number of factors when assessing each job possibility:

1. Actual job responsibilities
2. Industry characteristics
3. Nature of the company
4. Geographic location
5. Salary and opportunities for advancement
6. How the job is likely to contribute to your long-range career opportunities

Too many job applicants consider only the most striking features of a job, perhaps its location or the salary offered. However, a comprehensive review of job openings should provide a balanced perspective of the overall employment opportunity, including both long-run and short-run factors.

JOB INTERVIEWS

The first objective of your job search is obtaining an interview with a prospective employer. This interview demands considerable planning and preparation on your part. You want to enter the interview equipped with a good understanding of the company, its industry, and its competitors. The executive director of the National Association of Colleges and Employers says, "Each year, employers cite researching the organization as the single most important piece of advice they can offer candidates."[12]

Prepare yourself by researching the following basic information about the firm:

- When was the company founded?
- What is its current position in the industry?
- What is its financial status?
- In which markets does it compete?
- How is the firm organized?
- Who are its competitors?
- How many people does it employ?
- Where are its production facilities and offices located?
- Does it have a written code of ethics? How is it administered?

The future belongs to those who believe in the beauty of their dreams.

Eleanor Roosevelt (1884–1962)

first lady of the United States (1933–1945)

This information is useful in several ways. First, knowing so much about the firm should give you a feeling of confidence during the interview. Second, it can help you avoid making an unwise employment decision. Third, it may help you to impress an interviewer, who may try to determine how much you know about the company as a means of evaluating your interest level. A job applicant who fails to make an effort to obtain such information often risks elimination from further consideration.

But where do you find this company information? First, your school's career center is likely to have detailed information on prospective employers. Your marketing and business professors may also provide tips. In addition, the college's or university's reference librarian can direct you to sources to use in investigating a firm. Also, you can write directly to the company. Companies typically maintain informative Web sites; others publish career brochures. Finally, ask friends and relatives for input. Either they or people they know may have had experience with the company.

Interviewers usually cite poor communication as the main reason for an unsuccessful job interview. The job seeker either is inadequately prepared for the interview or lacks confidence. Remember that the interviewer will certainly make a determination of whether you can communicate directly based on the question-and-answer sequence that comprises this meeting. You should be specific in answering and asking questions, and you should clearly and positively express your concerns. The questions that interviewers ask most often include the following:

- "Why do you want this job?"
- "Where do you see yourself 10 years from now?"
- "What are your strengths?"
- "What are your weaknesses?"
- "Why should I hire you?"

It is important to know the name of the person (or persons) who will conduct the interview, what the interviewer's regular job responsibilities are, and who will make the final hiring decisions. In many cases, the people who conduct initial job interviews work in the human resources unit of their company. These interviewers typically make recommendations to line managers about which applicants appear most suitable for the vacancy. Line managers who head the units in which the applicant would be employed will get involved later in the hiring process. Some hiring decisions result from joint interviews conducted by both human resources personnel and the immediate supervisor of the prospective employee. Most often, however, immediate supervisors make the decision alone or in combination with input from senior employees in the department who will be colleagues of the new hire. Rarely does the human resources department have sole hiring authority for professional marketing positions.

One of the things you will discover by researching a firm prior to your interview is how well its employees reflect the diversity of the marketplace.

Remember that preparing for an interview doesn't end here. You need to dress for the occasion, as the "Etiquette Tips for Marketing Professionals" feature explains.

In a typical format, the interviewer talks little during the interview. This approach, referred to as an *open-ended interview,* forces you to talk about yourself and your career goals. If you appear unorganized, the interviewer may eliminate you on that basis alone. When faced with this type of interview, be sure to express your thoughts clearly and keep the conversation on target. Talk for about 10 minutes and then ask some specific questions of the interviewers. Come prepared with questions to ask. Listen carefully to the responses. Remember that if you prepare for a job interview, it will become a mutual exchange of information.

A successful first interview will probably result in an invitation to return for another interview. In some cases, this invitation will include a request to take a battery of tests. Most students do very well on these tests because they have had plenty of practice in the classroom!

ETIQUETTE TIPS

FOR MARKETING PROFESSIONALS

How to Dress for Your Job Interview

LANDING a job interview is a big step on the road to starting your career. Making the most of the opportunity to create a good impression—and to learn something about the company you might work for—begins with presenting yourself well. This means being prepared; projecting confidence, eagerness, and dependability; and looking the part. Here are some tips for dressing for the interview. Unless you are applying for a very unusual job, in which case you can actually call ahead and find out what attire is appropriate, these suggestions will serve you well.

1. Dress conservatively. A dark two-piece suit in a current style is best for men and women, with a conservative long-sleeved shirt or blouse. Men should choose a conservatively patterned tie. Keep conventional jewelry and makeup to an unnoticeable minimum.
2. Make sure your clothes are clean and well-pressed and that there are no runs in stockings or holes in socks.
3. Wear clean, well-polished shoes.
4. Make sure your nails are clean and short. If you wear polish, use a conservative color.
5. Use a minimum of cologne or perfume.
6. Keep your pockets free of noisy coins and keys or bulging items like phones or pagers.
7. Leave nose rings, eyebrow rings, and other unusual body ornaments at home.
8. Keep your hair neat, groomed, and short (for men) or off your face (for women). Men should be clean-shaven.
9. Carry a portfolio or briefcase (women might carry one instead of a purse to avoid clutter).

Looking professional is the first step to conducting a successful interview—and landing a job. So think first what the interviewer would like to see in a job candidate and dress accordingly. Then both you and the interviewer will be more at ease.

Sources: "Dress for Interview Success," http://www.collegegrad.com/jobsearch/, accessed June 30, 2004; Randall S. Hansen, "When Job-Hunting: Dress for Success," *Quintessential Careers*, http://www.quintcareers.com, accessed June 30, 2004; Joann S. Lublin, "Dated Suit, Dirty Nails Can Tip the Balance If You're Job Hunting," *The Wall Street Journal*, June 1, 2004, p. B1.

It is not uncommon for applicants to receive an attractive job offer only after being rejected one or more times previously. Students at an Arizona university once pooled their rejection letters from would-be employers, reviewed them, and then voted on the company that had written the worst rejection letter. Here are excerpts from the five finalists:

- "After most careful consideration of your qualifications and background, we are unable to identify anything you can do for us . . . "
- "We're certain you could be more useful someplace else . . . "
- " . . . but we're sure you will find something you can do."
- "My conscience doesn't allow me to encourage you . . . "
- "Unfortunately, we have to be selective . . . "[13]

EMPLOYMENT DECISIONS

Employers still considering you to be a viable job candidate now know a lot about you. You should also know a lot about the company. The primary purpose of further interviews is to determine whether you can work effectively within the organization.

If you continue to create a positive impression during subsequent interviews, you may be offered a position with the firm. Again, your decision to accept the offer should depend on how well the opportunity matches your career objectives. Make the best entry-level job decision you can and learn from it. Learn your job responsibilities as quickly and thoroughly as possible; then start looking for ways to improve your performance and that of your employer.

table 1 *Text Chapters Describing Responsibilities of Different Marketing Positions*

MARKETING POSITION	CONTEMPORARY MARKETING CHAPTER(S) MOST DIRECTLY RELATED TO THE MARKETING POSITION
Marketing, Advertising, Product, and Public Relations Managers	Chapters 1–2 (marketing)
	Chapters 11–12 (product)
	Chapters 15–16 (advertising and public relations)
Sales Representatives and Sales Managers	Chapter 17
Advertising Specialists	Chapters 15–16
Public Relations Specialists	Chapters 15–16
Purchasing Agents and Managers	Chapter 6
Retail and Wholesale Buyers and Merchandise Managers	Chapter 14
Marketing Research Analysts	Chapter 8
Logistics: Material Receiving, Scheduling, Dispatching, and Distributing Occupations	Chapter 13

MARKETING POSITIONS

The basic objective of any firm is to market its goods or services. Marketing responsibilities vary among organizations and industries. In a small firm, the owner or president may assume many of the company's marketing responsibilities. A large firm needs a staff of experienced sales, marketing, and advertising managers to coordinate these activities. Table 1 identifies the text chapters directly related to the responsibilities of each position. Note also that specific titles of different marketing positions may vary among firms. For example, the person holding the top marketing position in a company may have such titles as vice president of sales and marketing, director of marketing, or senior marketing manager. Job descriptions and typical career paths of eight major marketing positions are included in Table 2.

table 2 *Job Descriptions and Career Paths for Eight Major Marketing Positions*

MARKETING, ADVERTISING, PRODUCT, AND PUBLIC RELATIONS MANAGERS

Marketing management spans a range of positions, including vice president of marketing, marketing manager, sales manager, product manager, advertising manager, promotion manager, and public relations manager. The vice president directs the firm's overall marketing policy, and all other marketers report through channels to this person. Sales managers direct the efforts of sales professionals by assigning territories, establishing goals, developing training programs, and supervising local sales managers and their personnel. Advertising managers oversee account services, creative services, and media services departments. Promotion managers direct promotional programs that combine advertising with purchase incentives designed to increase the sales of the firm's goods or services. Public relations managers are responsible for communicating with the firm's various publics, conducting publicity programs, and supervising the specialists who implement these programs.

Job Description

As with senior management positions in production, finance, and other areas, top marketing management positions often involve long hours and extensive travel. Work under pressure is also common. For sales managers, job transfers between headquarters and regional offices may disrupt one's personal life. Approximately 460,000 marketing, advertising, product, and public relations managers are currently employed in the U.S. The Bureau of Labor Statistics estimates for the first decade of this century show strong growth of 168,000 new positions in these categories, the seventh-largest growth category.[a]

table 2 *continued*

Career Path

A degree in business administration, preferably with a concentration in marketing, is usually required for these positions. In highly technical industries, such as computers, chemicals, and electronics, employers typically prefer bachelor's degrees in science or engineering combined with master's degrees in business administration. Liberal arts students can also find many opportunities, especially if they have business minors. Most managers are promoted from positions such as sales representatives, product or brand specialists, and advertising specialists within their organizations. Skills or traits that are most desirable for these jobs include high motivation levels, maturity, creativity, resistance to stress, flexibility, and the ability to communicate persuasively.

SALES REPRESENTATIVES AND SALES MANAGERS

Millions of items are bought and sold every day. The people in the firm who carry out this activity may have a variety of titles—sales representative, account manager, manufacturer's representative, sales engineer, sales agent, retail salesperson, wholesale sales representative, and service sales representative. Sales managers are typically selected from people in the current sales force who have demonstrated that they possess the managerial skills needed to lead teams of sales representatives. In addition, many organizations require that all marketing professionals spend some time in the field to experience the market firsthand and to understand the challenges faced by front-line personnel.

The best way to get what you want is to help other people get what they want.

Zig Ziglar (b. 1927)

American motivational speaker

Job Description

Salespeople are usually responsible for developing prospective client lists, meeting with current and prospective customers to discuss the firm's products, and then following up to answer questions and supply additional information. By knowing the business needs of each customer, the sales representative can identify products that best satisfy these needs. Following a customer purchase, they are likely to revisit their customers to ensure that the products are meeting the customers' needs and to explore further business opportunities or referrals provided by satisfied buyers. Some sales of technical products involve lengthy interactions. In these cases, a salesperson may work with several clients simultaneously over a large geographic area. Those responsible for large territories may spend most of their workdays on the phone, receiving and sending e-mail messages, or on the sales floor. Recent compensation data revealed that top-level professional salespeople received total annual pay of $140,000 on average, a 9 percent increase over the previous year—even in the midst of a recession.[b]

Work as a sales representative or sales manager can be rewarding for those who enjoy interacting with people, those invigorated by competition, and those who feel energized by the challenge of expanding sales in their territories. Successful sales professionals—both individual sales reps and sales managers—should be goal-oriented, persuasive, self-motivated, and independent. In addition, patience and perseverance are important qualities.

Career Path

The background needed for a sales position varies according to the product line and market. Most professional sales jobs require a college degree, and many companies run their own formal training programs that can last up to two years for sales representatives in technical industries. This training may take place in a classroom, in the field with a mentor, or most often using a combination of both methods. Sales managers are usually promoted from the field; they are likely to include successful sales representatives who exhibit managerial skills and promise. Sales management positions begin at a local or district level, then advance to positions of increased authority and responsibility such as area, regional, national, and international sales manager.

ADVERTISING SPECIALISTS

Most companies, especially firms serving consumer markets, maintain small groups of advertising specialists who serve as liaisons between the marketer and its outside advertising agencies. The leader of this liaison function is sometimes called a *marketing communications manager.* Positions in an advertising agency include specialists in account services, creative services, and media services. Account services functions are performed by account executives, who work directly with clients. An agency's creative services department develops the themes and presentations of the advertisements. This department is supervised by a creative director, who oversees the copy chief, art director, and their staff members. The media services department is managed by a media director, who oversees the planning group that selects media outlets for ads.

Job Description

Advertising can be one of the most glamorous and creative fields in marketing. Because the field combines the best of both worlds—that is, the tangible and scientific aspects of marketing along with creative artistry—advertising attracts people with a broad array of abilities.

table 2 *continued*

Career Path

Most new hires begin as assistants or associates for the position they hope to acquire, such as copywriter, art director, and media buyer. Often, a newly hired employee must receive two to four promotions before becoming manager of these functions. College degrees in liberal arts, graphic arts, communications, psychology, or sociology, in addition to marketing training, are preferred for entry-level positions in advertising.

PUBLIC RELATIONS SPECIALISTS

Specialists in public relations strive to build and maintain positive relationships with various publics. They may assist management in drafting speeches, arranging interviews, overseeing company archives, responding to information requests, and handling special events, such as sponsorships and trade shows, that generate promotional benefits for the firm.

Job Description

While public relations specialists normally work a standard 40-hour week, they will occasionally rearrange their normal schedules to meet deadlines or prepare for major events. Occasionally, they are required to be on the job or on call around the clock to respond to an emergency or crisis. About 110,000 public relations specialists are currently employed in the U.S., two-thirds of them in service industries. Public relations positions tend to be concentrated in large cities near major press services and communications facilities. However, this centralization is changing with the increased popularity of new communications technologies, such as satellite uplinks, wireless technologies, and the Internet, which allow more freedom of movement. Most public relations consulting firms are concentrated in New York, Los Angeles, Chicago, and Washington, D.C.

Essential characteristics for a public relations specialist include creativity, initiative, good judgment, and the ability to express thoughts clearly and simply—both verbally and in writing. An outgoing personality, self-confidence, and enthusiasm are also recommended traits.

COURTESY OF MAY DEPARTMENT STORES COMPANY

Thousands of retailers such as May Department Stores—parent of such widely known and highly regarded retailers as Famous-Barr, Filene's, Foley's, Hecht's, Kaufmann's, Marshall Field's, Lord & Taylor, and Robinson May—employ hundreds of thousands of college graduates who decide on a career in retailing.

Career Path

A college degree combined with public relations experience, usually gained through one or more internships, is considered excellent preparation for public relations. Many entry-level public relations specialists hold degrees with majors in advertising, marketing, public relations, or communications. New employees in larger organizations are likely to participate in formal training programs; those who begin their careers at smaller firms typically work under the guidance of experienced staff members. Entry-level positions carry such titles as research assistant or account assistant. A potential career path includes a promotion to account executive, account supervisor, vice president, and eventually senior vice president.

PURCHASING AGENTS AND MANAGERS

In the 21st century business world, the two key marketing functions of buying and selling are performed by trained specialists. Just as every organization is involved in selling its output to meet the needs of customers, so too must all companies make purchases of goods and services required to operate their businesses and turn out items for sale.

Modern technology has transformed the role of the purchasing agent. The transfer of routine tasks to computers now allows contract specialists, or procurement officers, to focus on products, suppliers, and contract negotiations. The primary function of this position is to purchase the goods, materials, component parts, supplies, and services required by the organization. These agents ensure that suppliers deliver quality and quantity levels that match the firm's needs; they also secure these inputs at reasonable prices and make them available when needed.

Purchasing agents must develop good working relationships both with colleagues in their own organizations and with suppliers. As the popularity of outsourcing has increased, the selection and management of suppliers have become critical functions of the purchasing department. In the government sector, this role is dominated by strict laws, statutes, and regulations that change frequently.

table 2 *continued*

Job Description

Purchasing agents can expect a standard work week with some travel to suppliers' sites, seminars, and trade shows. Over 600,000 people are employed in purchasing positions in the U.S., most of them in manufacturing and government.

Career Path

Organizations prefer college-educated candidates for entry-level jobs in purchasing. Strong analytical and communication skills are required for any purchasing position. New hires often begin their careers by enrolling in extensive company training programs in which they learn procedures and operations. Training may include assignments dealing with production planning. Professional certification is becoming an essential criterion for advancement in both the private and the public sectors. A variety of associations serving the different categories of purchasing confer certifications on agents, including Certified Purchasing Manager, Professional Public Buyer, Certified Public Purchasing Officer, Certified Associate Contract Manager, and Certified Professional Contract Manager.

RETAIL AND WHOLESALE BUYERS AND MERCHANDISE MANAGERS

Buyers working for retailers and wholesale businesses purchase goods for resale. Their goal is to find the best possible merchandise at the lowest prices. They also influence the distribution and marketing of this merchandise. Successful buyers must understand what appeals to consumers and what their establishments can sell. Product bar codes and point-of-purchase terminals allow organizations to accurately track goods that are selling and those that are not; buyers frequently analyze this data to improve their understanding of consumer demand. Buyers also check competitors' prices and sales activities and watch general economic conditions to anticipate consumer buying patterns.

Anyone who keeps learning stays young.

Henry Ford (1863–1947)

American automobile manufacturer

Job Description

Approximately 260,000 people are currently employed in the U.S. as retail and wholesale buyers and merchandise managers. These jobs often require substantial travel, as many orders are placed on buying trips to shows and exhibitions. Effective planning and decision-making skills are strong assets in this career. In addition, the job involves anticipating consumer preferences and ensuring that the firm keeps needed goods in stock. Consequently, the people filling these positions must possess such qualities as resourcefulness, good judgment, and self-confidence.

Career Path

Most retail and wholesale buyers begin their careers as assistant buyers or trainees. Larger retailers seek college-educated candidates, and extensive training includes job experience in a variety of positions. Advancement often comes when buyers move to departments or new locations with larger volumes—or become merchandise managers to coordinate or oversee the work of several buyers.

MARKETING RESEARCH ANALYSTS

These marketing specialists provide information that assists marketers in identifying and defining opportunities. They generate, refine, and evaluate marketing actions and monitor marketing performance. Marketing research analysts devise methods and procedures for obtaining needed, decision-oriented data. Once they compile data, analysts evaluate it and then make recommendations to management.

Job Description

Firms that specialize in marketing research and management consulting employ the majority of the nation's marketing research analysts. These positions are often concentrated in larger cities, such as New York, Los Angeles, and Chicago. Those who pursue careers in marketing research must be capable of working accurately with detail, display patience and persistence, work effectively both independently and with others, and operate objectively and systematically. Significant computer and analytical skills are essential for success in this field.

Career Path

A bachelor's degree with an emphasis in marketing provides sufficient qualifications for many entry-level jobs in marketing research. Because of the importance of quantitative skills and the need for competence in using analytical software packages, this education should include courses in calculus, linear algebra, statistics, sampling theory and survey design, computer science, and information systems. Students should try to gain experience in conducting interviews or surveys while still in college. A master's degree in business administration or a related discipline is advised for improving advancement opportunities.

table 2 *continued*

LOGISTICS: MATERIAL RECEIVING, SCHEDULING, DISPATCHING, AND DISTRIBUTING OCCUPATIONS

Logistics offers a myriad of career positions. Job titles under this broad heading include material receiving, scheduling, dispatching, materials management executive, distribution operations coordinator, distribution center manager, and transportation manager. The logistics function includes responsibilities for production and inventory planning and control, distribution, and transportation.

Job Description

Approximately 3.8 million people are currently employed in logistics positions in the U.S., including material receiving, scheduling, dispatching, and distribution. These positions demand good communication skills and the ability to work effectively under pressure.

Career Path

Computer skills are highly valued in these jobs. Employers look for candidates with degrees in logistics and transportation. However, graduates in marketing and other business disciplines may succeed in this field.

[a] Paul Kaihla, "How to Land Your Dream Job," Business 2.0, November 2004, pp. 103–114; Deborah L. Vance, "Demand for Managers Grows," *Marketing News,* October 15, 2004, pp. 11–13.

[b] Meghan A.T.B. Reese, "Advice for Landing That First Job," *USA Today,* September 1, 2004, p. D8.

ADDITIONAL INFORMATION SOURCES

A wealth of helpful career information is continually updated for you at the Boone and Kurtz Web site: **http://boone.swlearning.com**. You'll find a complete "Marketing Careers" section located under the heading "Marketing Topics" on the left-hand navigation bar. Here you'll learn more about marketing careers and be able to locate currently posted job opportunities. The site provides a vast number of career resources such as links to job sites, career guidance sites, U.S. newspaper job ads, and company information. It also provides ways for researching cities of special interest to you.

Marketer's Minute: Talking about Marketing Careers, a new feature at the end of each of the seven parts of *Contemporary Marketing, 12e,* consists of an interview with a top marketing executive in a major sports organization. In reading the sports marketing executive's description of his or her background, how the position was filled, and the other members of the marketing department, you will be able to compare the similarities—and differences—between this industry and more traditional businesses. Most persons interviewed also discuss how to stand out in applying for internships.

The "Personal Development" section of the Web site contains career guidance tips, including interviewing techniques and résumé writing advice. The site is updated regularly.

part 1

DESIGNING CUSTOMER-ORIENTED MARKETING STRATEGIES

chapter 1	Marketing: Creating Satisfaction through Customer Relationships
chapter 2	Strategic Planning and the Marketing Process
	Appendix: Creating an Effective Marketing Plan
chapter 3	The Marketing Environment, Ethics, and Social Responsibility
chapter 4	E-Commerce: Marketing in the Digital Age

PHOTO: COURTESY OF WIREIMAGES.COM

chapter 1

Marketing: Creating Satisfaction through Customer Relationships

chapter objectives

1. Explain how marketing creates utility through the exchange process.
2. Contrast marketing activities during the four eras in the history of marketing.
3. Explain the importance of avoiding marketing myopia.
4. Describe the characteristics of not-for-profit marketing.
5. Identify and briefly explain each of the five types of nontraditional marketing.
6. Outline the changes in the marketing environment due to technology.
7. Explain the shift from transaction-based marketing to relationship marketing.
8. Identify the universal functions of marketing.
9. Demonstrate the relationship between ethical business practices and marketplace success.

MARKETING CREATES A WINNER: THE NEW NASCAR

NASCAR used to drive the fringes of spectator sports. Until a few years ago, a few thousand diehards stuck plugs in their ears and went out to racetracks in the southeastern U.S. to watch obsessed drivers roar around a big oval. But all of that has changed. Yes, the earplugs are still necessary. And the drivers are still considered daredevils. But now, fans can find racetracks just about anywhere in the country, from the Northeast to the Midwest to the Southwest and beyond. After announcing its intention to build a track in Washington State, NASCAR's only remaining geographic void is New York—and Brian and Lesa France are working diligently to fill it. NASCAR is currently the No. 2 U.S. spectator sport, after professional football. What makes the sport so attractive to so many people? How did this phenomenon spread from the back roads of the Deep South to the golden streets of a place like Las Vegas?

In 1948, "Big Bill" France founded the National Association for Stock Car Auto Racing in Daytona Beach, Florida. His goal as a marketer was to organize and promote a sport that was pretty much the domain of former bootleggers who were looking for

CAMERAS IN ACTION STOCK PHOTOGRAPHY, INC.

something crazy to do. By 1972, when Bill Sr. handed the NASCAR wheel over to his son, Bill Jr., the sport was well established in its southern niche, with followers who were predictable in their conservative political views and love of country music. Under Bill France Jr. and his children Brian and Lesa, NASCAR grew into a multibillion-dollar business with nearly 100 million fans across the country and television contracts with Fox, NBC, and TNT worth $2.8 billion. TV ratings for Fox's Nextel Cup Series nearly double baseball's regular-season average. Thirteen million fans bought tickets to the 2,000-plus races in NASCAR's various divisions last year, with attendance at the big events averaging 186,000—at an average ticket price of $75. And nascar.com is one of the five most heavily trafficked sports Web sites. The image of NASCAR has changed: Whereas it was once the playground of outlaws, it is now a theme park for families.

Exposure on network television—as opposed to small cable channels—has helped NASCAR reach a broader market. "The TV distribution growth from 80 million to 105 million homes has had a dramatic effect," explains George Pyne, chief operating officer of the organization. "Our fans are higher income, better educated and younger than they were five to seven years ago." There has also been a change in NASCAR sponsors. When federal regulations banned tobacco advertising, NASCAR replaced the Winston brand with Nextel Communications. Nextel paid $750 million over 10 years—one of the biggest sponsorship deals ever—to put its name on the Nextel Cup Series. Domino's Pizza has centered all of its sports marketing on NASCAR, with ads featuring driver Michael Waltrip and pizza boxes displaying the NASCAR logo. Domino's marketers believe they will reach more consumers—particularly women—this way than they would if they focused on football. "Unlike the NFL, NASCAR viewership is 50-50 men and women," says Tim McIntyre of Domino's. "The viewership is large, and it's growing, and it's young."

In addition, food giant Kraft recently ran a national NASCAR sweepstakes aimed at moms; winners received prizes such as a customized Mustang and meetings with famous drivers. Even financial institutions have gotten into the act. Several years ago, international bank HSBC hosted a group of Ford employees at the Michigan 500, including a tent for corporate entertaining, a tour of the infield, and special seats. While NASCAR tries to reach the moms of America, they still haven't forgotten a coveted demographic group labeled the *NASCAR dads*—those politically, socially conservative workers who consider themselves patriots and family men. President George W. Bush reached out to this group when he flew to Daytona Beach, donned a racing jacket, and said "Gentlemen, start your engines" to the drivers in front of network TV cameras and the 180,000 fans who attended the 2004 Daytona 500.

Although corporations spend more than $1 billion a year for NASCAR sponsorships and promotions, this number pales in comparison with the $2 million-plus annual sales of NASCAR-licensed merchandise. Marketing NASCAR merchandise to fans has been a booming business in recent years. Reaching way past T-shirts and caps, companies like Sports Image and Action Performance have had huge success with everything from licensed die-cast replicas of famous racecars to sunglasses engraved with drivers' signatures. To attract younger fans, NASCAR signed a six-year exclusive video game deal with Electronic Arts. In turn, EA and Nextel have discussed adding a NASCAR video game on the title sponsor's phones.

NASCAR has hit some speed bumps on its journey. One is the organization's willingness to allow its teams to advertise beer and pills for male enhancement, while at the same time banning advertisements for hard liquor. Another is the issue of safety. When legendary NASCAR driver Dale Earnhardt Sr. was killed at Daytona, the sport suffered a severe blow—and endured much closer scrutiny of safety practices. Improvements have been made in the cars and on the tracks. For example, barriers called "soft walls" have been installed at most NASCAR racetracks to absorb the impact of a crash and reduce the chance of serious injury. Three years after the death of his father, Dale Earnhardt Jr. won the Daytona 500 on a safer track. Then there's the issue of meeting demand. To do so, NASCAR has moved the location of several of its premier races. For 50 years, the Labor Day weekend races were held in Darlington, South Carolina; now they will be run at a newer, larger track in California.

All of NASCAR's marketing efforts strive to reach an important goal: developing a strong, long-lasting relationship with consumers. This effort means enhancing its image to attract more people, finding new avenues for promoting races and merchandise, and determining the best ways to serve a whole new crop of fans. On all of these tracks, NASCAR seems to be cruising in the fast lane.[1]

Chapter Overview

- "That's my favorite restaurant."
- "I always buy my clothes at this store."
- "I only drive one kind of car."
- "They have the best customer service."

THESE words are music to a marketer's ears, much like the roar of NASCAR fans as they cheer their favorite cars and drivers. Customer loyalty is the watchword of 21st century marketing. But today, individual consumers and business purchasers have so many goods and services from which to choose—and so many different ways to purchase them—that marketers must continually seek out new and better ways to attract and keep customers, as the high-tech industry has learned, sometimes the hard way. Just a few years ago, some providers of information technology services such as data storage and communications paid little attention to the individual needs of their customers; today, their focus is squarely on their customers. "Things have fundamentally changed—for the better," notes John W. Cummings of Merrill Lynch & Co. Experts agree that creating loyal business customers is vital because corporate customers control nearly 80 percent of the $1 trillion spent on information technology every year.[2] Other companies, such as Dell, were built with a focus on the individual customer right from the start. As company founder and CEO Michael Dell recalls, "From the start, our entire business—from design to manufacturing to sales—was oriented around listening to the customer, responding to the customer, and delivering what the customer wanted." The nation's largest PC marketer also identifies the characteristics of its best customers and actively seeks to find more of the same.[3]

Briefly Speaking

If you've never been to a Daytona 500, it's hard for me to describe what it's like to be down here with the drivers and to see the huge crowd and to feel the excitement for one of America's great sporting spectacles. This is more than an event; it's a way for life for a lot of people, and you can feel excitement when you're here.

George W. Bush (b. 1946)
43rd president of the United States

Throughout the marketplace, advances in communications technology allow information to be exchanged between buyers and sellers faster, cheaper, and through more media channels than ever before, including broadcast media, print, telecommunications, online computer services, and the Internet. Companies can now offer consumers more product choices and more places to buy. Today's savvy shoppers can visit a brick-and-mortar shopping mall, hire a personal shopper, order from catalogs, watch television home shopping channels, and browse through a tremendous variety of online sites.

The technology revolution continues to change the rules of marketing during this first decade of the 21st century and will continue to do so in years beyond. The combined power of telecommunications and computer technology creates inexpensive, global networks that transfer voice messages, text, graphics, and data within seconds. These sophisticated technologies create new types of products, and they also demand new approaches to marketing existing products. Communications technology contributes as well to the globalization of today's marketplace, where businesses manufacture, buy, and sell across national borders. You can place an eBay bid on a potential bargain or eat a Big Mac or drink Coca-Cola almost anywhere in the world; your DVD or CD player was probably manufactured in China or South Korea. Both Mercedes-Benz and Hyundai sport utility vehicles are assembled in Alabama, while many Volkswagens are imported from Mexico. The customer service call center for the company you are dealing with may be located in India. Finished products and components routinely cross international borders, but successful global marketing also requires knowledge to tailor products to regional tastes. An Asian food store in Austin, Texas, may also sell popular Hispanic foods such as tortillas to satisfy local tastes of shoppers who enjoy both.

Rapidly changing business landscapes create new challenges for companies, whether they are giant multinational firms or small boutiques, profit- oriented or not-for-profit. Organizations must react quickly to shifts in consumer tastes, competitive offerings, and other market dynamics. Fortunately, information technologies give organizations fast, new ways to interact and develop long-term relationships with their customers and suppliers. In fact, such links have become a core element of marketing today.

However, even with today's innovations, companies don't necessarily have to rely solely on investments in high-tech messages to attract and create loyal customers. A recent survey revealed that sandwich shops Panera Bread and Subway scored the highest level of loyalty among similar restaurants, with 12 percent of consumers pledging loyalty to their brand. Loyalty scores for fast-food giants McDonald's and Burger King were much lower, at 6 percent and 4 percent, respectively. Yet Panera and Subway spend far less on advertising and other high-tech methods of communication to reach consumers.[4]

Every company must serve customer needs—create customer satisfaction—to succeed. Two customer satisfaction researchers described its value this way: "Customer satisfaction has come to represent an important cornerstone for customer-oriented business practices across a multitude of companies operating in diverse industries."[5] Marketing strategies provide the tools by which businesspeople identify and analyze customers' needs and then inform these customers about how the company can meet those needs. Tomorrow's market leaders will be companies that can effectively harness the vast amounts of customer feedback and respond with solutions to their needs.

This new edition of *Contemporary Marketing* focuses on the strategies that allow companies to succeed in today's interactive marketplace. This chapter sets the stage for the entire text, examining the importance of creating satisfaction through customer relationships. Initial sections describe the historical development of marketing and its contributions to society. Later sections introduce the technology revolution, the universal functions of marketing, and the relationship between ethical business practices and marketplace success. Throughout the chapter—and the entire book—there will be discussions of customer loyalty and the lifetime value of a customer. ◆◆◆

Briefly Speaking

A sign at Dell headquarters reads "Think Customer." A full 90 percent of employees deal directly with customers. What are the universal attributes of the Dell brand? Customer advocacy.

Mike George
chief marketing officer, Dell, Inc.

table 1.1 *Four Types of Utility*

TYPE	DESCRIPTION	EXAMPLES	ORGANIZATIONAL FUNCTION RESPONSIBLE
Form	Conversion of raw materials and components into finished goods and services	J. P. Morgan Chase checking account; Lincoln Navigator; Ramen Noodles (nutrition for students who are hungry, broke, and can't—or won't—cook)	Production*
Time	Availability of goods and services when consumers want them	Digital photographs; LensCrafters eyeglass guarantee; UPS Next Day Air	Marketing
Place	Availablility of goods and services at convenient locations	Soft-drink machines outside gas stations; on-site day care; banks in grocery stores	Marketing
Ownership (possession)	Ability to transfer title to goods or services from marketer to buyer	Retail sales (in exchange for currency or credit-card payment)	Marketing

*Marketing provides inputs related to consumer preferences, but the actual creation of form utility is the responsibility of the production function.

1 **Explain how marketing creates utility through the exchange process.**

WHAT IS MARKETING?

Production and marketing of goods and services—whether it's a new crop of organically grown vegetables or digital cable service—are the essence of economic life in any society. All organizations perform these two basic functions to satisfy their commitments to society, their customers, and their owners. They create a benefit that economists call **utility**—the want-satisfying power of a good or service. Table 1.1 describes the four basic kinds of utility: form, time, place, and ownership.

utility Want-satisfying power of a good or service.

Form utility is created when the firm converts raw materials and component inputs into finished goods and services. By combining glass, plastic, metals, circuit boards, and other components, Canon makes a digital camera and Pioneer produces a plasma television. With fabric and leather, Prada manufactures its high-fashion line of handbags. Reality television shows like *The Apprentice* and *Survivor* start with contestants, a host, producers, technical crew and equipment, and a filming location. Although the marketing function focuses on influencing consumer and audience preferences, the organization's production function is responsible for the actual creation of form utility.

figure 1.1
DHL: Supplying Customers with Time and Place Utility

COURTESY OF DHL

Marketing creates time, place, and ownership utilities. Time and place utility occur when consumers find goods and services available when and where they want to purchase them. Overnight courier service DHL emphasizes a combination of time and place utility, as illustrated in Figure 1.1. Vending machines and convenience stores focus on providing place utility for people buying newspapers, snacks, and soft drinks. The transfer of title to goods or services at the time of purchase creates ownership utility.

All organizations must create utility to survive. Designing and marketing want-satisfying goods, services, and ideas are the foundation for the creation of utility. Organizations recently have begun to elevate the function of marketing in their hierarchies; top marketing executives may be promoted to senior vice presidential positions. But where does the process start? In the toy industry, manufacturers try to come up with items that children will want to play with—creating utility. But that's not as simple as it sounds. At the Toy Fair held each February in New York, retailers pore through the different booths of manufacturers and suppliers, looking for the next Bratz dolls or Lego building blocks—trends that turn into classics and generate millions in revenues over the years.

For several years, companies such as Sirius Satellite Radio and XM Satellite Radio Holdings have tried to create utility for consumers with satellite radio service. Statistics show that they are succeeding: In 2002, XM claimed 360,000 subscribers; by 2004, the company had attracted more than one million. Marketers from both companies are hoping to attract even more customers from the 100 million households, and 200 million autos, as well as trucks, boats, RVs, trains, jets, and office buildings that exist in the U.S. today. To do so, these marketers must persuade consumers that satellite radio service can create utility for them.[6]

But how does an organization create a customer? A three-step approach is involved: identifying needs in the marketplace, finding out which needs the organization can profitably serve, and developing an offering to convert potential buyers into customers. Marketing specialists are responsible for most of the activities necessary to create the customers the organization wants. These activities include:

- identifying customer needs
- designing goods and services that meet those needs
- communicating information about those goods and services to prospective buyers
- making the goods or services available at times and places that meet customers' needs
- pricing goods and services to reflect costs, competition, and customers' ability to buy
- providing the necessary service and follow-up to ensure customer satisfaction after the purchase[7]

COURTESY OF LVCVA

Marketers for the city of Las Vegas determined that businesses were looking for new locations for meetings—and focused on the same attractions that draw millions of tourists there to satisfy the expectations of business customers and build relationships.

A DEFINITION OF MARKETING

The word *marketing* encompasses such a broad scope of activities and ideas that settling on one definition is often difficult. Ask three people to define marketing, and three different definitions are likely to follow. Continuous exposure to advertising and personal selling leads most respondents to link marketing with selling or to think that marketing activities start after goods and services have been produced. But marketing also involves analyzing customer needs, securing information needed to design and produce goods or services that match buyer expectations, satisfying customer preferences, and creating and maintaining relationships with customers and suppliers. It applies not only to profit-oriented firms but also to thousands of not-for-profit organizations that offer goods and services.

Today's definition takes all these factors into account. **Marketing** is the process of planning and executing the conception, pricing, promotion, and distribution of ideas, goods, services, organizations, and events to create and maintain relationships that will satisfy individual and organizational objectives.

marketing Process of planning and executing the conception, pricing, promotion, and distribution of ideas, goods, services, organizations, and events to create and maintain relationships that will satisfy individual and organizational objectives.

The expanded concept of marketing activities permeates all organizational functions. It assumes that the marketing effort will proceed in accordance with ethical practices and that it will effectively serve the interests of both society and the organization. The concept also identifies the marketing variables—product, price, promotion, and distribution—that combine to provide customer satisfaction. In addition, it assumes that the organization begins by identifying and analyzing the consumer segments that it will later satisfy through its production and marketing activities. In other words, the customer, client, or public determines the marketing program. The concept's emphasis on creating and maintaining relationships is consistent with the focus in business on long-term, mutually satisfying sales, purchases, and other interactions with customers and suppliers. Finally, it recognizes that marketing concepts and techniques apply to not-for-profit organizations as well as to profit-oriented businesses.

TODAY'S GLOBAL MARKETPLACE

Several factors have forced marketers—and entire nations—to extend their economic views to events outside their own national borders. First, international agreements are being negotiated in attempts to expand trade among nations. Second, the growth of electronic commerce and related computer technologies is bringing previously isolated countries into the marketplace for buyers and sellers around the globe. Third, the interdependence of the world's economies is a reality because no nation produces all of the raw materials and finished goods its citizens need or consumes all of its output without exporting some to other countries. Evidence of this interdependence is illustrated by the introduction of the euro as a common currency to facilitate trade among the nations of the European Union and the creation of trade agreements such as the North American Free Trade Agreement (NAFTA) and World Trade Organization (WTO).

A recession in Europe affects business strategies in North America and the Pacific Rim. An economic downturn in the U.S. affects the stock market in Japan. The recent discovery of a single Canada-bred mad cow in Washington State prompted 16 nations—accounting for 90 percent of U.S. beef exports—to briefly bar U.S beef from crossing their borders. Marketers such as Optibrand Ltd. of Fort Collins, Colorado, responded to the need to track cattle from birth to butcher with radio frequency identification (RFID) tags and retinal scans—since the pattern of veins in each cow's retina is unique.[8]

To remain competitive, companies must continually search for the most efficient manufacturing sites and most lucrative markets for their products. U.S. marketers now find tremendous opportunities serving customers not only in traditional industrialized nations but also in Latin America and emerging economies in Eastern Europe, the Middle East, Asia, and Africa, where rising standards of living create increased customer demand for the latest goods and services. Expanding operations beyond the U.S. market gives domestic companies access to 6 billion international customers. In addition, companies based in these emerging economies are beginning to compete as well. Since its acceptance into the World Trade Organization earlier this century, China's exports have risen more than 18 percent. However, companies founded in emerging economies generally lag behind as world competitors. Legend Group Ltd. is China's largest PC manufacturer, but it commands less than 2 percent of the total world market for PCs, compared with Dell (17 percent), Hewlett-Packard (16 percent), and IBM (5.3 percent). This is despite the fact that China is the most populous nation on earth—and potentially, the largest marketplace. Instead, Legend marketers have decided to achieve their short-term growth objectives by setting their sights on more affluent U.S. consumers.[9]

Service firms also play a major role in today's global marketplace. Although the New York Stock Exchange is based in New York City, investors trade more than $50 billion worldwide every day over the exchange. The U.S. Postal Service and private carriers like FedEx, UPS, and DHL deliver packages and documents around the world within a matter of hours. Air travel is another significant component of international marketing, where domestic carriers compete directly with international carriers. Singapore Airlines, illustrated in Figure 1.2, serves more than 60 major cities across the globe.

The U.S. is also an attractive market for foreign competitors because of its size and the high standard of living that American consumers enjoy, which explains why China's Legend Group Ltd. would like to reach more U.S. consumers. Companies such as Nissan, Sony, and Sun Life of Canada operate production, distribution, service, and retail facilities in the U.S. Foreign ownership of U.S. companies has increased as well. Pillsbury and MCA are two well-known firms with foreign parents. Even American-dominated industries like computer software must contend with foreign competition. Although U.S. firms still hold about 75 percent of the market, European companies are quickly gaining market share. They currently supply about 18 percent of the $100 billion worldwide market for packaged software.[10]

In many cases, global marketing strategies are almost identical to those used in domestic markets. However, more and more companies are customizing their marketing efforts to reach foreign markets, making significant changes to adapt to unique tastes or different cultural and legal requirements abroad. It is often difficult to standardize a brand name on a global basis. The Japanese, for example, like the names of flowers or girls for their automobiles, names such as Bluebird, Bluebonnet, Violet, and Gloria. Americans, on the other hand, prefer rugged outdoorsy names like Mountaineer, Expedition, Pathfinder, and Highlander.

1. What is utility?
2. Define the term *marketing.*
3. Why is the U.S. an attractive market for foreign competitors?

COURTESY OF SINGAPORE AIRLINES

figure 1.2

Marketing of Services: A Major Component of the Global Marketplace

FOUR ERAS IN THE HISTORY OF MARKETING

(2) Contrast marketing activities during the four eras in the history of marketing.

The essence of marketing is the **exchange process,** in which two or more parties give something of value to each other to satisfy perceived needs. In many exchanges, people trade money for tangible goods like DVDs, clothes, a notebook computer, or groceries. In other exchanges, they use money to pay for intangible services like dental care, haircuts, or concerts. In many exchanges, people trade for a combination of both tangible goods and intangible services, as in a restaurant where both the food and the service are part of the exchange. In still others, people may donate funds or time for a cause, such as a Red Cross blood drive, a new theater for a school, or a campaign to clean up polluted waterways.

exchange process Activity in which two or more parties give something of value to each other to satisfy perceived needs.

Although marketing has always been a part of business, its importance has varied greatly. Figure 1.3 identifies four eras in the history of marketing: (1) the production era, (2) the sales era, (3) the marketing era, and (4) the relationship era.

THE PRODUCTION ERA

Prior to 1925, most firms—even those operating in highly developed economies in western Europe and North America—focused narrowly on production. Manufacturers stressed production of quality products and then looked for people to purchase them. The prevailing attitude of this era held that a good product (one with high physical quality) would sell itself. This **production orientation** dominated business philosophy for decades; in fact, business success was often defined solely in terms of production victories.

The production era did not reach its peak until the early part of the 20th century. Henry Ford's mass-production line exemplifies this orientation. Ford's slogan, "They [customers] can have any color they want, as long as it's black," reflected the prevalent attitude toward marketing. Production shortages and intense consumer demand ruled the day. It is easy to understand how production activities took precedence.

However, building a new product is no guarantee of success, and marketing history is cluttered with the bones of miserable product failures despite major innovations. In fact, more than 80 percent of new products fail. Inventing an outstanding new product is not enough. That product must also solve a perceived marketplace need. Otherwise, even the best engineered, highest quality product will fail. Even Henry Ford's horseless carriage took a while to catch on. People were afraid of motor vehicles, which spat out exhaust, stirred up dust on dirt roads, got stuck in mud, and tied up horse traffic. Besides, at the wild speed of seven miles per hour, they caused all kinds of accidents and disruption. It

figure 1.3
Four Eras of Marketing History

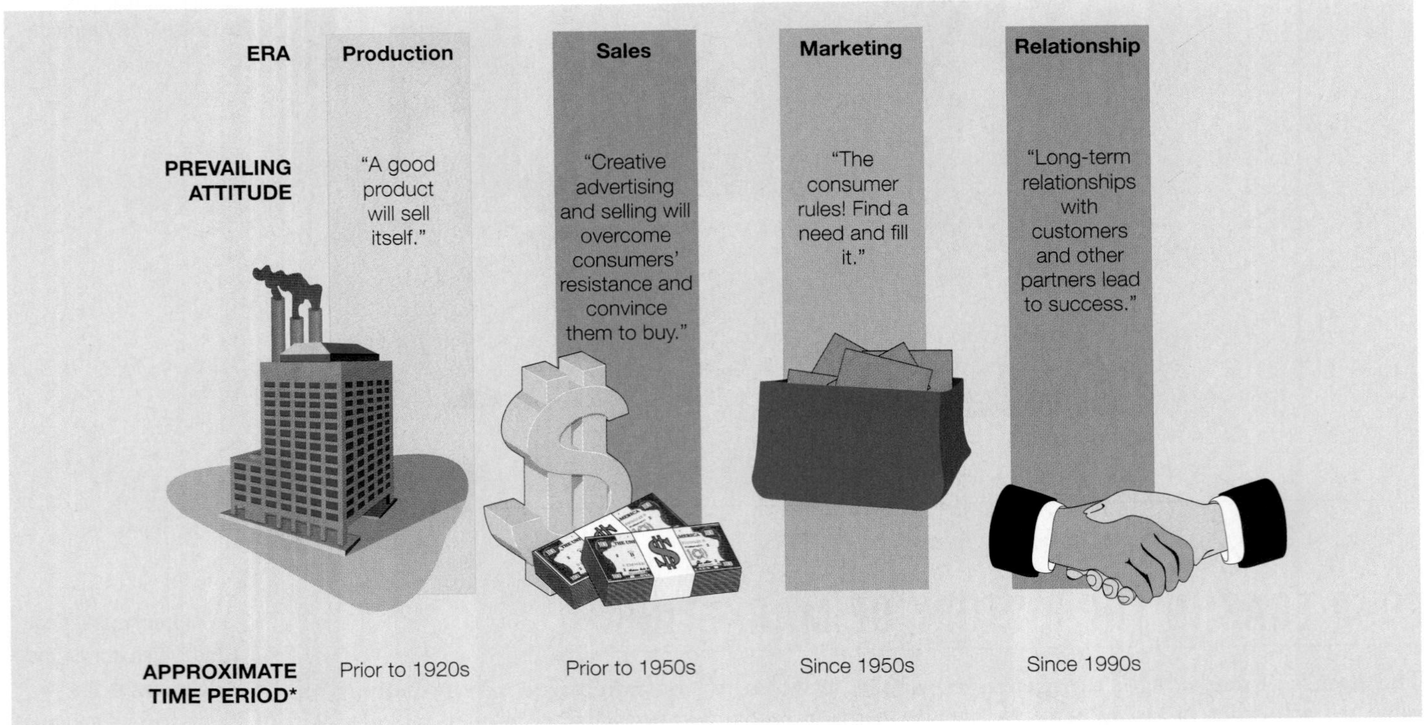

*In the United States and other highly industrialized economies.

took savvy marketing by some early salespeople—and eventually a widespread perceived need—to change people's minds about the product.[11] Today, most of us could not imagine life without a car and have refined that need to preferences for certain types of vehicles, ranging from SUVs to sports cars.

THE SALES ERA

As production techniques in the U.S. and Europe became more sophisticated, output grew from the 1920s into the early 1950s. As a result, manufacturers began to increase their emphasis on effective sales forces to find customers for their output. In this era, firms attempted to match their output to the potential number of customers who would want it. Companies with a **sales orientation** assume that customers will resist purchasing goods and services not deemed essential and that the task of personal selling and advertising is to convince them to buy.

Although marketing departments began to emerge from the shadows of production, finance, and engineering during the sales era, they tended to remain in subordinate positions. Many chief marketing executives held the title of sales manager. But selling is only one component of marketing. As marketing professor Theodore Levitt once pointed out, "Marketing is as different from selling as chemistry is from alchemy, astronomy from astrology, chess from checkers."

THE MARKETING ERA

Personal incomes and consumer demand for goods and services dropped rapidly during the Great Depression of the 1930s, thrusting marketing into a more important role. Organizational survival dictated that managers pay close attention to the markets for their goods and services. This trend ended with the outbreak of World War II, when rationing and shortages of consumer goods became commonplace. The war years, however, created only a pause in an emerging trend in business: a shift in the focus from products and sales to satisfying customer needs.

EMERGENCE OF THE MARKETING CONCEPT

The marketing concept, a crucial change in management philosophy, can be explained best by the shift from a **seller's market**—one in which there were more buyers for fewer goods and services—to a **buyer's market**—one in which there were more goods and services than people willing to buy them. When World War II ended, factories stopped manufacturing tanks and ships and started turning out consumer products again, an activity that had, for all practical purposes, stopped in early 1942.

seller's market Market in which there are more buyers for fewer goods and services.

buyer's market Market in which there are more goods and services than people willing to buy them.

The advent of a strong buyer's market created the need for **consumer orientation** by businesses. Companies had to market goods and services, not just produce and sell them. This realization has been identified as the emergence of the marketing concept. The recognition of this concept and its dominant role in business dates from 1952, when General Electric heralded a new management philosophy:

> [The concept] introduces the [marketer] at the beginning rather than at the end of the production cycle and integrates marketing into each phase of the business. Thus, marketing, through its studies and research, will establish for the engineer, the designer, and manufacturing [person], what the customer wants in a given product, what price he [or she] is willing to pay, and where and when it will be wanted. Marketing will have authority in product planning, production scheduling, and inventory control, as well as in sales, distribution, and servicing of the product.[12]

consumer orientation Business philosophy incorporating the marketing concept that emphasizes first determining unmet consumer needs and then designing a system for satisfying them.

Marketing would no longer be regarded as a supplemental activity performed after completion of the production process. Instead, the marketer would play a leading role in product planning. Marketing and selling would no longer be synonymous terms.

Today's fully developed **marketing concept** is a *companywide consumer orientation* with the objective of achieving long-run success. All facets—and all levels, from top to bottom—of the organization must contribute first to assessing and then to satisfying customer wants and needs. From marketing manager to accountant to product designer, every employee plays a role in reaching potential customers. Even during tough economic times, when companies tend to emphasize cutting costs and boosting revenues, the marketing concept focuses on the objective of achieving long-run success instead of short-term profits.[13] Since the firm's continuity is an assumed component of the marketing concept, companywide consumer orientation will lead to greater long-run profits than managerial philosophies geared toward reaching short-run goals. Consider hugely successful Starbucks. Through its consumer orientation, the company has created an extremely loyal customer base; the average Starbucks customer visits a Starbucks store 18 times a month. Starbucks' welcoming atmosphere, with comfortable seating areas, encourages customers to sit and stay a while—read, chat with friends, and order another coffee. Recently, Starbucks began offering Wi-Fi Internet connections at 2,000 stores—yet another reason to linger and drink coffee. All of these marketing actions translate to what Starbucks marketers and CEO Howard Schultz call "enthusiastically satisfied customers."[14]

marketing concept Companywide consumer orientation with the objective of achieving long-run success.

A strong market orientation—the extent to which a company adopts the marketing concept—generally improves market success and overall performance. It also has a positive effect on new-product development and the introduction of innovative products. Companies that implement market-driven strategies are better able to understand their customers' experiences, buying habits, and needs. These companies can, therefore, design products with advantages and levels of quality compatible with customer requirements. Customers more quickly accept the new products. When Starbucks teamed up with Bank One to offer consumers a Starbucks credit card that also functions as a rechargeable store gift card, loyal customers eagerly adopted the idea.

THE RELATIONSHIP ERA

The fourth era in the history of marketing emerged during the final decade of the 20th century and continues to grow in importance today. Organizations now build on the marketing era's customer orientation by focusing on establishing and maintaining relationships with both customers and suppliers. Naturally, Starbucks continuously establishes and enhances its relationships with new and existing customers. **Relationship marketing** involves long-term, value-added relationships developed over time with customers and suppliers. Strategic alliances and partnerships among manufacturers, retailers, and suppliers often benefit everyone. Ryder System—owner of those yellow rental trucks—has made alliances with such firms as Delphi Automotive, America's largest auto parts supplier, and Toyota Tsusho America, which supplies iron, steel, and textiles to automotive companies. Ryder and Toyota

relationship marketing Development and maintenance of long-term, cost-effective relationships with individual customers, suppliers, employees, and other partners for mutual benefit.

formed a joint venture called TTR Logistics, in which Toyota Tsusho provides the materials and Ryder manages the flow and warehousing of these and other materials such as plastics and wires. Ryder expects the alliance to generate hundreds of millions of dollars in upcoming years. Participants in collaborative relationships generate an estimated 25 percent more sales than independent firms. Teaming up with potential buyers of their products also reduces the risks of new products that might be introduced without advance notice. The concept of relationship marketing, which is the current state of customer-driven marketing, is discussed in detail later in this chapter and in Chapter 10.

CONVERTING NEEDS TO WANTS

Every consumer must acquire goods and services on a continuing basis to fill certain needs. Everyone must satisfy the fundamental needs for food, clothing, shelter, and transportation by purchasing things or, in some instances, temporarily using rented property and hired or leased transportation. By focusing on the benefits resulting from these goods and services, effective marketing converts needs to wants. A need for clothing may be translated into a desire (or want) for designer clothes. The need for a vacation may become the desire to take a Caribbean cruise or visit the Australian outback. But if the need for transportation isn't converted to a desire for a Dodge Durango or a Toyota Prius, there may be extra vehicles sitting unsold on a dealer's lot. Renowned inventor Dean Kamen is now facing this problem with his innovative Segway human transporter, as described in the "Marketing Miss" box.

As easier-to-use software has enabled millions of nontechnical consumers to operate personal computers, and as falling retail prices make these computers affordable to most households, PCs have become fixtures in many schools, offices, and homes. Thousands of tiny and large PC makers have pushed prices below $1,000, and this once-prestigious possession has been reduced to a commodity. Now that computers are viewed as a household need, other needs have arisen, such as protection from identity or information theft through the Internet. Companies such as Symantec, as shown in Figure 1.4, seek to fulfill the need for privacy protection with products such as its Norton antivirus, firewall, and spam-filtering programs.

Marketing-oriented companies addressing privacy issues that can result in identity or information theft focus on providing solutions to these problems, as discussed in the "Solving an Ethical Controversy" feature. They stress product benefits, rather than features, to show the added value that customers will receive from their product offerings.

1. What is the exchange process?
2. What is the major distinction between the sales era and the marketing era?
3. Define *relationship marketing.*

marketing miss How Segway Swerved Away from Success

Background. No one would question Dean Kamen's genius. The New Hampshire–based inventor has come up with brilliant ways to improve people's lives, including a wheelchair that climbs stairs. But when he introduced the Segway Human Transporter to great fanfare, the vehicle dubbed a "scooter" seemed to roll quickly into obscurity.

The Marketing Problem. The Segway is a two-wheeled, self-balancing, electric-powered vehicle designed for individual use around town and inside large buildings—like airport terminals and warehouses. It is easy to use and can travel 10 to 15 miles at 12 miles an hour on a single battery charge. Kamen envisioned a nationwide revolution in personal transportation—commuters, shoppers, tourists, mail carriers, police officers, and others could use this energy-efficient mode of travel. But Segway hit a few roadblocks. First, many states and towns have laws barring the use of motorized vehicles on sidewalks. Second, the new vehicles were virtually unavailable to consumers for the first year, and when they came on the market through Amazon.com, they were expensive—around $5,000. But with no local dealers, would-be purchasers had no place to try them out prior to a purchase and no method of leasing one for a few days or weeks before spending that much money. Third, everyone insisted on calling them "scooters," implying that Segways were a toy. The vehicle didn't seem to have a place in the market: It was slower and—lacking a seat for a passenger or trunk space for

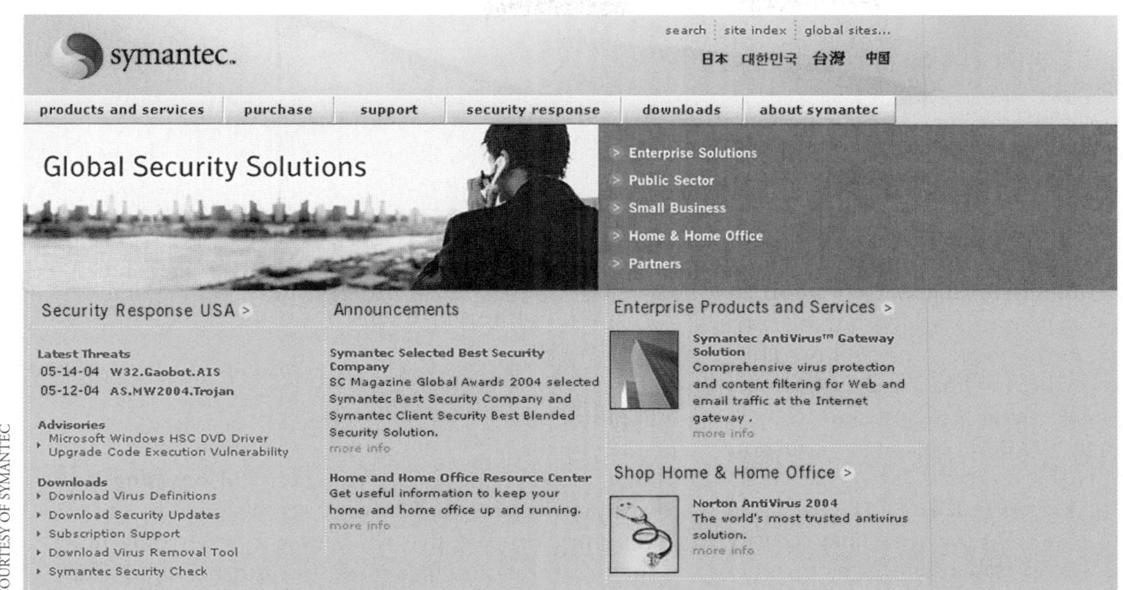

COURTESY OF SYMANTEC

figure 1.4
Fulfilling the Need for Privacy Protection

AVOIDING MARKETING MYOPIA

③ Explain the importance of avoiding marketing myopia.

The emergence of the marketing concept has not been devoid of setbacks. One troublesome problem led marketing scholar Theodore Levitt to coin the term **marketing myopia.** According to Levitt, marketing myopia is management's failure to recognize the scope of its business. Product-oriented rather than customer-oriented management endangers future growth. Levitt cites many service industries—such as dry cleaning and electric utilities—as examples of marketing myopia.

marketing myopia Management's failure to recognize the scope of its business.

Table 1.2 illustrates how firms in a number of industries have overcome myopic thinking by developing broader marketing-oriented business ideas that focus on consumer need satisfaction.

To avoid marketing myopia, companies must broadly define organizational goals oriented toward consumer needs. This approach can help a company stand out from others in highly competitive environments, whether the company is large or small. Charles Revson, founder and president of cosmetics

groceries or other purchases—less practical than a car, but cost far more than a bicycle.

The Outcome. Several cities purchased Segways for their mail carriers and police officers to try, the U.S. military commissioned some for use in a variety of settings, and Chicago's O'Hare Airport bought several for their security staff. A few companies with large warehouses also acquired Segways for their employees to use on the job. Many European cities permit Segways to be used on sidewalks, and local entrepreneurs have begun renting Segways for short-term transportation. Time-pressed tourists attempting to see the sites in major cities have been opting for the more novel Segways rather than renting bikes or scooters, even though their choice immediately labels them as Americans—regardless of what their passport says. With persistent lobbying, at least a dozen states have loosened their sidewalk transportation laws to include the Segway. Justin Timberlake was photographed riding one to the MTV Movie Awards, and former President George Bush got one from his children for Father's Day. You may even witness the occasional Segway cruising down the sidewalk, through the parking lot, and into your local shopping mall, its rider undoubtedly beaming.

Lessons Learned. Segway may prove to be the great invention that Dean Kamen believes it to be, but it needs a market. For now, the vehicle is a novelty—not unlike the horseless carriage of a century ago.

Sources: David Armstrong, "The Segway: Bright Idea, Wobbly Business," *The Wall Street Journal,* February 12, 2004, p. B1; Mike Schneider, "Disney: Visitors May Not Use Segways in Parks," *Mobile Register,* February 8, 2004, p. B4; Kevin Maney, "President's Tumble Off a Segway Seems a Tiny Bit Suspicious," *USA Today,* June 18, 2003, p. B3; George Anders, "Machine Dreams," *The Wall Street Journal,* June 17, 2003, p. D5; Patrick McMahon, "Some Pedestrians Fear SUV of the Sidewalks," *USA Today,* June 17, 2003, p. 1; Lorraine Woellert, "Smoothing the Way for Segway," *BusinessWeek,* April 15, 2003, p. 10.

Solving an Ethical Controversy

IDENTITY THEFT: IS PRIVACY ALSO STOLEN?

MOST of us who own or use computers and use them to shop online, surf the Web for information, or even e-mail our friends harbor at least a tiny fear that somehow our personal information will be stolen without our knowing it. That fear is justified, according to the Federal Trade Commission (FTC), which received more than 500,000 consumer complaints of fraud last year. Identity thieves cost U.S. consumers $5 billion and businesses $33 billion each year, according to the FTC. The problem is now so prevalent that security measures have become a marketable service. Companies such as financial services giant Citigroup have begun to offer free protection against identity theft to its credit-card holders. Everyone agrees that computer technology has revolutionized the way we live our lives and conduct our business. But has it also compromised our right to privacy?

HAS COMPUTER TECHNOLOGY CREATED THE MEANS FOR INVADING OUR PRIVACY AND MADE US MORE VULNERABLE TO CRIME?

PRO

1. Identity theft is one of the easiest crimes to commit—and one of the hardest to catch. Despite billions of dollars lost to identity theft, only about 700 thieves are caught each year. The FBI has labeled identity theft the fastest growing crime in the U.S.
2. The Internet provides a gateway to thousands of databases, credit reports, Social Security numbers, and similar information needed for identity theft. Experts predict that the number of these identity thefts will soar in the next few years.

CON

1. Consumers have many ways to protect themselves from identity theft, including services like the one offered by Citigroup. Visa offers a toll-free hotline through Call for Action and posts fraud-prevention tips on the Web (http://www.callforaction.org).
2. Nearly 50 percent of identity thefts still occur through low-tech means such as digging through trash or peeking over someone's shoulder at the ATM machine. Consumers can go a long way toward protecting themselves by investing in a paper shredder.

SUMMARY

Although the FTC receives, on average, more than 500,000 complaints every year of fraud resulting from identity theft, a national survey commissioned by the federal agency revealed that the problem is not only much greater than that number shows but is rising at an alarming rate. Based on the survey results, the FTC estimates that 10 million U.S. consumers were victimized last year—and only one person in nine was even aware that his or her personal information had been taken until alerted by a crime such as fraudulent charges on an existing credit account or use of the person's identity to open a new account, take out a loan, rent an apartment, or commit a crime. "This report serves as a reality check by confirming that millions of consumers are falling victim to identity theft," says Beth Givens, director of the Privacy Rights Clearinghouse, a not-for-profit consumer information and advocacy organization. Businesses including health insurers, some credit-card companies, and online retailers are trying to respond to their customers' concerns. But consumer advocates say that financial institutions, in particular, need to do more. "If they had to pay for the collateral damage of identity theft, they'd change their practices immediately," says Givens. Others advise consumers to take more control of their own destiny. Brian Keefer, a spokesperson for the industry trade group Your Credit Card Companies, suggests that consumers store their credit cards in a safe place; shred their financial statements; avoid maintaining files containing personal financial statements, tax information, and credit card and bank account numbers on their computer hard drives; and shop only on secure Web sites.

Sources: Andrea Chipman, "Stealing You," *The Wall Street Journal*, April 26, 2004, p. R8; Sara Schaefer Munoz, "Identity Thieves Troll the Internet," *The Wall Street Journal*, April 13, 2004, p. D2; Patrick di Justo, "Public Enemy No. 1: Identity Theft," *Wired*, February 2004, p. 44; Christine Dugas, "Federal Survey: Identity Theft Hits 1 in 4 U.S. Households," *USA Today*, September 4, 2003, p. 10B.

table 1.2 ***Avoiding Marketing Myopia by Focusing on Benefits***

COMPANY	MYOPIC DESCRIPTION	MARKETING-ORIENTED DESCRIPTION
Cingular	"We are a telephone company."	"We are a communications company."
JetBlue Airways	"We are in the airline business."	"We are in the transportation business."
Morgan Stanley	"We are in the stock brokerage business."	"We are in the financial services business."
Sony	"We are in the video game business."	"We are in the entertainment business."

giant Revlon, understood the need for a broader focus on benefits rather than on products. As Revson described it, "In our factory we make perfume; in our advertising we sell hope."

Retailer Anthropologie doesn't just sell clothes—it offers an entire lifestyle to its customers. Consumers who enter an Anthropologie store are greeted by soothing French music and flickering aromatic candles. When they wander into the "Washroom" section of the store, they find luxurious soaps, lotions, and even an exotic medicine cabinet for sale. As they stroll into the "Boudoir" section, they come across soft, crisp sheets, puffy duvet covers and pillows, and of course, a wrought-iron bed available for purchase. In each section of the store, like little boutiques, customers find books, clothing, jewelry, furniture, and home goods that all work in the exotic Anthropologie style. Anthropologie marketers want their customers to feel as though their shopping experience is a treasure hunt.[15]

1. What is marketing myopia?
2. Give an example of how a firm can avoid marketing myopia.

EXTENDING THE TRADITIONAL BOUNDARIES OF MARKETING

Today's organizations—both profit-oriented and not-for-profit—recognize universal needs for marketing and its importance to their success. During a television commercial break, viewers might be exposed to an advertisement for a Nissan Altima, an appeal to help feed children in foreign countries, a message by a political candidate, and a commercial for McDonald's—all in the space of about two minutes. Two of these ads are paid for by firms attempting to achieve profitability and other objectives. The appeal for funds to feed children and the political ad are examples of communications by not-for-profit organizations and individuals.

MARKETING IN NOT-FOR-PROFIT ORGANIZATIONS

Nearly 10 percent of the U.S. workforce works or volunteers in one or more of the 1.6 million not-for-profit organizations across the country. In total, these organizations generate revenues of more than $620 billion each year through contributions and from fund-raising activities.[16] That makes not-for-profit organizations big business.

Not-for-profit organizations operate in both public and private sectors. Federal, state, and local government units and agencies derive revenues from tax collection to pursue service objectives that are not keyed to profitability targets. The Department of Homeland Security is charged with protecting the U.S. from terrorist aggression; an individual state's department of natural resources regulates conservation and environmental programs; a school department is responsible for overseeing educational and curriculum standards for its public school district.

The private sector has an even greater array of not-for-profit organizations, including art museums, the U.S. Ski Team, labor unions, hospitals, private schools, and the Make-a-Wish Foundation® of America. Some, like a successful college football team, may generate enough revenues to pay for other athletic activities at the school, but the team's primary function is to win football games.

NATIONAL PSA PROVIDED BY THE MAKE-A-WISH FOUNDATION® OF AMERICA

The Make-a-Wish Foundation grants wishes to hundreds of terminally ill children each year. To accomplish this huge task, the organization forms alliances with such companies as Disney, American Airlines, the National Football League, and Discover.

In some not-for-profit organizations, adopting the marketing concept can mean forming a partnership with a for-profit company to promote the not-for-profit's message or image. Home Depot has partnered with the National Wildlife Federation to offer environmentally friendly products. These items are marked with National Wildlife Federation stickers and sold in Home Depot retail outlets. Lowe's has a similar partnership with the National Geographic Society, in which the home improvement chain designates shelf space for National Geographic birdhouses and feeders.[17]

Generally, the alliances formed between not-for-profit organizations and commercial firms benefit both. The reality of operating with multimillion-dollar budgets requires not-for-profit organizations to maintain a focused business approach. Consider some current examples:

- McDonald's Ronald McDonald House Charities work with several local and national not-for-profit organizations to help critically ill children and their families through difficult times.
- The fight against breast cancer has generated donations from many organizations, including the U.S. Postal Service, Avon, JCPenney, and Ford Motor Co., among others.
- Tyson Foods donates products to food banks and sponsors a Share Our Strength nutrition program.

The diversity of not-for-profit organizations suggests the presence of numerous organizational objectives other than profitability. In addition to their organizational goals, not-for-profit organizations differ from profit-seeking firms in several other ways.

4 Describe the characteristics of not-for-profit marketing.

CHARACTERISTICS OF NOT-FOR-PROFIT MARKETING

The most obvious distinction between not-for-profit organizations and for-profit—commercial—firms is the financial **bottom line,** business jargon that refers to the overall profitability of an organization. For-profit organizations measure profitability in terms of sales and revenues, and their goal is to generate revenues above and beyond their costs to make money for all stakeholders involved, including employees, shareholders, and the organization itself. Not-for-profit organizations hope to generate as much revenue as possible to support their causes, whether it is feeding children, preserving wilderness, or helping single mothers find work. Historically, not-for-profits have had less exact goals and marketing objectives than for-profit firms, but in recent years, many of these groups have recognized that to succeed, they must develop more cost-effective ways to provide services, and they must compete with other organizations for donors' dollars. Marketing can help them accomplish these tasks.

There are other distinctions between the two types of organizations as well, each of which influences marketing activities. Like profit-seeking firms, not-for-profit organizations may market tangible goods and/or intangible services. The Art Institute of Chicago offers items in its gift shop and through direct-mail catalogs (tangible goods) as well as special exhibits and educational classes (intangible services). But profit-seeking businesses tend to focus their marketing on just one public—their customers. Not-for-profit organizations, however, must often market to multiple publics, which complicates decision making about the correct markets to target. Many deal with at least two major publics—their clients and their sponsors—and often many other publics as well. Political candidates, for example, target both voters and campaign contributors. A college or university targets prospective students as clients of its marketing program, but it also markets to current students, parents of students, alumni, faculty, staff, local businesses, and local government agencies.

A customer or service user of a not-for-profit organization may wield less control over the organization's destiny than would be true for customers of a profit-seeking firm. The children who are fed and sheltered by Save the Children, Childreach, and similar organizations have less influence on the organization's direction than do affluent American children who buy CDs at the local mall. Not-for-profit organizations also often possess some degree of monopoly power in a given geographic area. An individual contributor might object to United Way's inclusion of a particular local agency, but that agency will still receive a portion of that donor's contribution.

In another potential problem, a resource contributor—whether it is a cash donor, a volunteer, or someone who provides office space—may try to interfere with the marketing program in order to promote the message that he or she feels is relevant. Or a donor might restrict a contribution in certain ways that make it difficult for the organization to use. During a capital campaign to raise funds for a new science center, a university alumnus might make a restricted gift to the university theater instead.

1. Give an example of a private sector not-for-profit organization and a public sector not-for-profit organization.
2. Why do for-profit and not-for-profit organizations sometimes form alliances?
3. What is the most obvious distinction between a not-for-profit organization and a commercial organization?

NONTRADITIONAL MARKETING

(5) Identify and briefly explain each of the five types of nontraditional marketing.

As marketing evolved into an organizationwide activity, its application has broadened far beyond its traditional boundaries of for-profit organizations engaged in the creation and distribution of tangible goods and intangible services. In many cases, broader appeals focus on causes, events, individuals, organizations, and places in the not-for-profit sector. In other instances, they encompass diverse groups of profit-seeking individuals, activities, and organizations. Table 1.3 lists and describes five major categories of nontraditional marketing: person marketing, place marketing, cause marketing, event marketing, and organization marketing. These categories can overlap—promotion for an organization may also encompass a cause; a promotional campaign may focus on both an event and a place.

person marketing Marketing efforts designed to cultivate the attention, interest, and preference of a target market toward a person (typically a political candidate or celebrity).

PERSON MARKETING

One category of nontraditional marketing, **person marketing,** refers to efforts designed to cultivate the attention, interest, and preferences of a target market toward a celebrity or authority figure. Celebrities can be real people: former Olympic skier Picabo Street promotes Chapstick; boxing great

table 1.3 ***Categories of Nontraditional Marketing***

TYPE	BRIEF DESCRIPTION	EXAMPLES
Person marketing	Marketing efforts designed to cultivate the attention and preference of a target market toward a person	Celebrity Beyoncé Knowles Athlete LeBron James Political candidate Arnold Schwarzenegger
Place marketing	Marketing efforts designed to attract visitors to a particular area; improve consumer images of a city, state, or nation; and/or attract new business	Hawaii: The Islands of Aloha California: Find Yourself Here Tennessee: Sounds Good to Me
Cause marketing	Identification and marketing of a social issue, cause, or idea to selected target markets	"Reading Is Fundamental." "Friends don't let friends drive drunk." "Be a mentor."
Event marketing	Marketing of sporting, cultural, and charitable activities to selected target markets	NASCAR Pepsi 400 Susan G. Komen Race for the Cure
Organization marketing	Marketing efforts of mutual-benefit organizations, service organizations, and government organizations that seek to influence others to accept their goals, receive their services, or contribute to them in some way	United Way brings out the best in all of us. American Red Cross: Together, we can save a life. Sierra Club: Explore, enjoy, and protect the planet.

figure 1.5

Person Marketing: Alex Rodriguez

© MARY ALTAFFER/AP

George Foreman can be seen in Meineke muffler ads as well as commercials for his indoor barbecue grill; actor James Earl Jones extols the benefits of Verizon phone service; Donald Trump promotes his hit television series, *The Apprentice.* Celebrities can be fictional characters, such as Spongebob Squarepants, who has appeared on boxes of Kraft Macaroni & Cheese. Or they can be widely recognized authority figures. Campaigns for political candidates and the marketing of celebrities are examples of person marketing. In political marketing, candidates target two markets: They attempt to gain the recognition and preference of voters and the financial support of donors.

Briefly Speaking

I don't get my kicks from flirting with death. I flirt with life. It's not that I enjoy the risks, the dangers, and the challenge of the race. I enjoy the life it gives me. When I finish a race, the sky looks bluer, the grass looks greener, and the air feels fresher. It's so much better to be alive.

Jackie Stewart (b. 1939)

Scottish-born auto racer

The big winners among celebrity endorsers are professional athletes. Basketball legend Michael Jordan earns as much as $40 million each year endorsing products such as Oakley sunglasses and Hanes underwear; golfer Tiger Woods lends his celebrity to products ranging from Nike to Accenture business solutions. But no athlete is in more demand today than shortstop Alex Rodriguez of the New York Yankees. For years, the game's best player—and with a long-term contract totaling $252 million, the game's highest paid player—A-Rod spent most of his career with the Seattle Mariners and the Texas Rangers before moving to the Big Apple in 2004. As shown in Figure 1.5, Nike, which has a 10-year endorsement deal with Rodriguez, is certain to reap the benefit of the superstar's change into Yankee pinstripes. Shortly after his signing, the club itself recorded a greeting from A-Rod on its phone lines. Marketers are excited about the player's endorsement prospects. As one sports memorabilia newsletter puts it, "Once you become a Yankee, things go wild. The Yankee brand is the No. 1 sports brand in the world."[18]

With five Grammy awards stowed recently on her shelves, Beyoncé Knowles is another star whose endorsement potential is rising. PepsiCo features Beyoncé prominently in its ads and sponsored a summer concert series on the WB television network.

PLACE MARKETING

place marketing Marketing efforts to attract people and organizations to a particular geographic area.

Another category of nontraditional marketing is **place marketing,** which attempts to attract customers to particular areas. Cities, states, regions, and countries publicize their tourist attractions to lure vacation travelers. They also promote themselves as good locations for businesses. Place marketing has become more important in the world economy, where localities compete for economic advantage, increased employment, trade, and investment. Organizations as varied as the San Diego Zoo, the Alamo in San Antonio, state bureaus of tourism and conventions, and the Seattle Port Authority apply place marketing techniques to attract visitors, residents, and new businesses to their areas. Their strategies include promoting positive images such as friendly residents and beautiful scenery; marketing special attractions such as the Empire State Building or the Eiffel Tower; and focusing on quality of life, such as education, low crime rate, clean air and water, culture and recreation, convenient shopping, and good public transportation.

New York City has gone so far as to hire its first chief marketing officer, Joe Perello, to promote the city to tourists and businesses. Selling the city hasn't been difficult—he's already had offers to rename the city's seat of government Circuit City Hall and to stamp a bottle of vodka with the NYC label. He's refused both of those offers and many others. New York attracts 35 million visitors a year, and many companies unofficially market their products with a New York flavor—like Chock Full o' Nuts coffee, which sells a New York Roast blend. But Perello has a larger vision. He wants to increase the number of tourists to at least 40 million per year and stimulate the growth of additional jobs and new businesses. He wants the city to earn as much as $50 million a year in sponsorship revenues. His first major marketing alliance was a deal with Snapple Beverage Group, which he hopes will yield $20 million a year for the city. As part of the contract, Snapple will spend $12 million a year promoting New York around the country. Why is this important? "New York doesn't have an awareness issue," explains Perello. "The question is how relevant we are to people in Kansas City." He hopes to develop other such relationships. "The revenue potential is great," he says, "but I won't consider this a success unless we get great brands talking about the city in a way they have never talked about us and in places where it needs to be talked about, like Sydney, Australia. . . . We need companies to tell that story."[19]

CAUSE MARKETING

A third category of nontraditional marketing, **cause marketing,** refers to the identification and marketing of a social issue, cause, or idea to selected target markets. Cause marketing covers a wide range of issues, including literacy, physical fitness, gun control, family planning, prison reform, control of

cause marketing Identification and marketing of a social issue, cause, or idea to selected target markets.

figure 1.6

Place Marketing and Cause Marketing

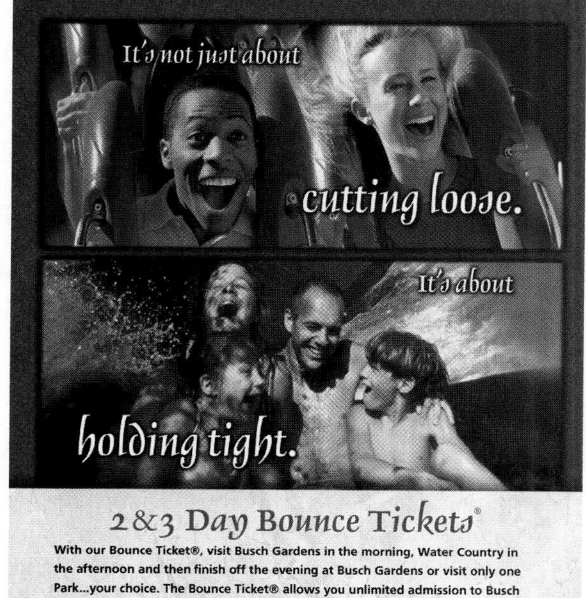

BUSCH GARDENS WILLIAMSBURG

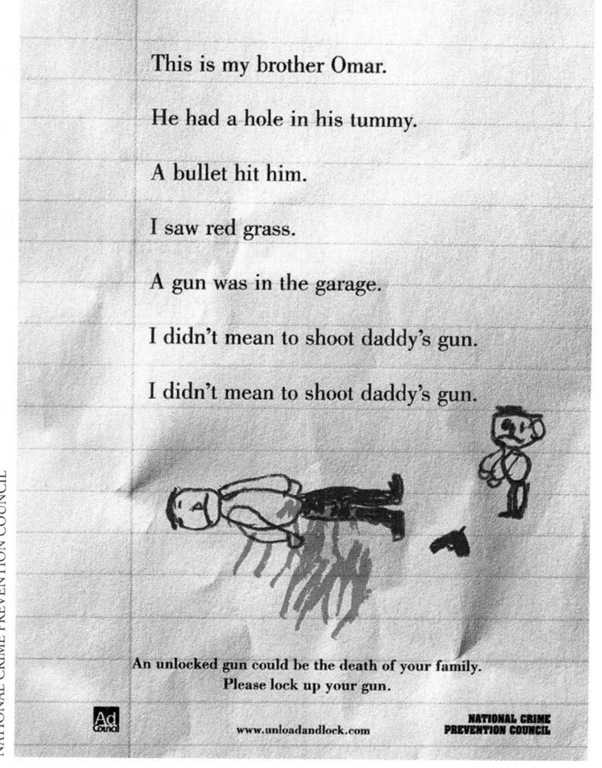

NATIONAL CRIME PREVENTION COUNCIL

overeating, environmental protection, elimination of birth defects, child-abuse prevention, and punishment of convicted drunk drivers.

An increasingly common marketing practice is for profit-seeking firms to link their products to social causes. Companies now spend a whopping $1 billion per year on cause marketing, a practice that essentially began only 20 years ago with an American Express program that linked the use of its card to the renovation of the Statue of Liberty. Mars Inc.'s M&Ms division donates 50 cents to the Special Olympics for each specially marked candy wrapper mailed back to the company by consumers. Crest's Healthy Smiles 2010 campaign supports the Boys and Girls Clubs of America. Avon has long been recognized for its commitment to fighting breast cancer; in one decade, the company raised $250 million for the cause while also creating greater awareness of Avon products. Recently, the nonprofit organization Cause Marketing Forum began issuing the Cause Marketing Halo Awards to organizations for "leadership and outstanding achievements in the field of cause marketing."

Surveys show strong support for cause-related marketing by both consumers and company employees. In one recent survey, 92 percent of consumers have a more positive image of companies that support important social causes, and four of five respondents said that they would change brands to support a cause if the price and quality of the two brands remained equal. "Consumers look for relationships with brands, not just transactions," notes a cause marketing expert.[20] Cause marketing can help build these relationships.

Figure 1.6 illustrates two types of nontraditional marketing. The place marketing ad on the left reminds vacationers that more than a trip back in time awaits them if they choose a holiday to Colonial Williamsburg. Jaw-dropping adventures can be had at the Busch Gardens amusement park nearby. The memorable message on the right makes a powerful statement about the need for trigger locks and/or other secure devices to keep guns away from children.

EVENT MARKETING

event marketing Marketing of sporting, cultural, and charitable activities to selected target markets.

Event marketing refers to the marketing of sporting, cultural, and charitable activities to selected target markets. It also includes the sponsorship of such events by firms seeking to increase public awareness and bolster their images by linking themselves and their products to the events. Sports sponsorships have gained effectiveness in increasing brand recognition, enhancing image, boosting purchase volume, and increasing popularity with sports fans in demographic segments corresponding to sponsor business goals.

Some people might say that the premier sporting event is baseball's World Series. Others might argue that it's the Super Bowl, which many consumers claim they watch only to see the debut of innovative new commercials. Those commercials are expensive and can run as much as $2.3 million for 30 seconds of airtime. And the NFL begins promoting the game—and its potential star athletes—weeks ahead of time. Advertisers in publications such as *Sports Illustrated* gear their ads toward football. But there is a special place in everyone's heart for the Olympics, both summer and winter. Countries the world over compete for the privilege of hosting the games. Television networks bid for the right to cover them. Marketers pour millions into special campaigns tied to the events. Home Depot and UPS, which proudly count a number of athletes among their own employees, create advertisements featuring U.S. Olympians.

ORGANIZATION MARKETING

organization marketing Marketing by mutual-benefit organizations, service organizations, and government organizations intended to influence others to accept their goals, receive their services, or contribute to them in some way.

The category of nontraditional marketing called **organization marketing** involves attempts to influence others to accept the goals of, receive the services of, or contribute in some way to an organization. Organization marketing includes mutual-benefit organizations (conservation groups, labor unions, and political parties), service and cultural organizations (colleges and universities, hospitals, and museums), and government organizations (military services, police and fire departments, and the U.S. Postal Service).

Marketers for the U.S. Department of Defense took an unconventional approach recently, aiming their marketing message at people in a position to influence potential military recruits such as parents, teachers, and religious leaders. "Based on market research, we targeted adult influencers like parents, and especially, reticent mothers," stated an Air Force major who works for the DOD's Joint

Advertising Market Research and Studies Program. "We're looking at adults who have aspirations, hopes, dreams, and ambitions for their children." This approach was a departure from the usual ads featuring strong young adults scaling mountains or parachuting from helicopters. Instead, the approach focused on the military as a "bright future" for recruits.[21]

Organization marketers don't just make appeals for money, labor, or other resources. They must also reassure donors that their contributions are being handled correctly and ethically. The American Red Cross suffered short-term damage to its image when its allocation of funds was questioned following the 9/11 terrorist attacks. The Red Cross created its "Together We Prepare" campaign to respond to new interests, actions, fears, and questions of a post 9/11 America. The ads in this campaign, like the "Give Blood" advertisement in Figure 1.7, demonstrated various empowering ways individuals can prepare themselves and their families to save lives with the help of the Red Cross. By inviting participation, these ads inspired people to see themselves as part of the Red Cross and fostered renewed trust in the organization. During its first year of rotation, the "Together We Prepare" campaign generated $32 million in estimated media placement value.

1. Identify the five major categories of nontraditional marketing.
2. Which category of celebrity endorsers generally earns the most money?
3. How is cause marketing beneficial to organizations that engage in it?

figure 1.7

Organization Marketing by the American Red Cross

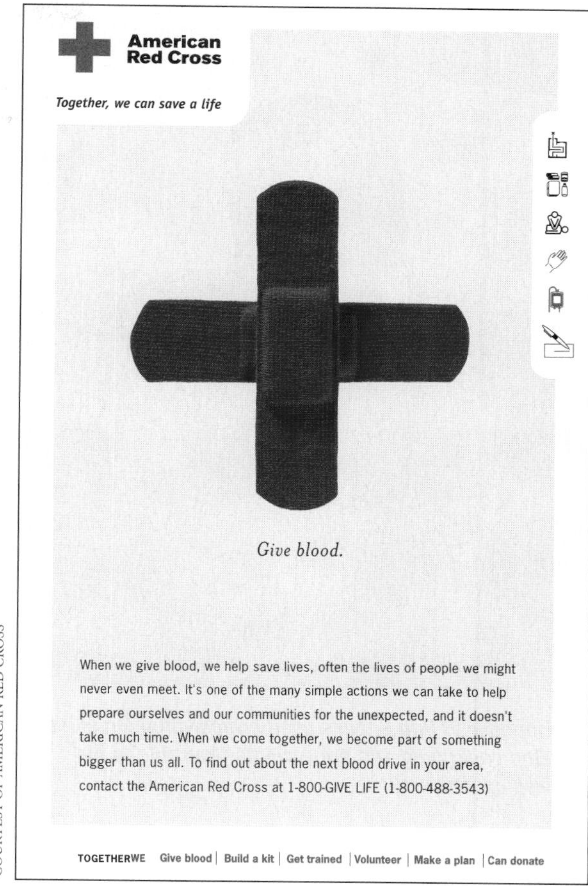

COURTESY OF AMERICAN RED CROSS

CREATIVITY AND CRITICAL THINKING

The challenges presented by today's complex and technologically sophisticated marketing environment require creativity and critical-thinking skills from marketing professionals. **Creativity** is a human activity that produces original ideas or knowledge, frequently by testing combinations of ideas or data to produce unique results. It is an extremely valuable skill for marketers. Creativity helps them develop novel solutions to perceived marketing problems. It has been a part of the human endeavor since the beginning of time. Leonardo da Vinci conceived his idea for a helicopter after watching leaves twirl in the wind. Swiss engineer George de Mestral, noticing that burrs stuck to his wool socks because of their tiny hooks, invented Velcro. Many people think that creativity is the domain of only the young. But famed architect I. M. Pei designed the Rock and Roll Hall of Fame in Cleveland when he was 78 years old.

Critical thinking refers to the process of determining the authenticity, accuracy, and worth of information, knowledge, claims, and arguments. Critical thinkers do not take information at face value and simply assume that it is accurate; they analyze the data themselves and develop their own opinions and conclusions. Critical thinking requires discipline and sometimes a cooling-off period after the creative fire of a new idea. In many instances, it requires analyzing what went wrong with an idea or a process and figuring out how to make it right. James Lindsay, founder of Rap Snacks, Inc., had an idea for a new type of snack food. He knew the multibillion-dollar industry was extremely competitive, but if he succeeded, he could have a share of a very rich pie. But he didn't jump in with both feet until he did his homework—critical thinking. "I've always been curious about the snack industry," says Lindsay, a former sales rep for Warner-Lambert. "If there were inconsistencies in the product, I'd call the

GETTY IMAGES NORTH AMERICA

The founder of Rap Snacks used critical-thinking skills to develop packaging and price points favorable to his desired consumers.

company and find out why." Lindsay also understands his market—inner-city kids who are fans of rap music. So, when his company came out with popcorn, chips, and cheese curls, he packaged the snacks in bags featuring cartoon pictures of famous rap artists like Lil'Romeo, Master P, and Nelly. Every bag also contains album release dates and positive messages for kids. Naturally, Lindsay charges a fee to the music labels for this advertising, which reaches up to 3 million kids per week. Here's the best part: Each bag of Rap Snacks only costs 25 cents, as opposed to the 50- or 75-cent price tag on other snack bags. But Lindsay has reasons for this pricing, too. "In the inner city, every kid has a quarter, but not every kid has a dollar. It's a cheaper way to develop brand loyalty; I'm able to grow with the customer base."[22] Lindsay has used both creativity and critical-thinking skills as a marketer to develop a product and build relationships with consumers and music-industry professionals.

MARKETING Concept Check

1. Define *creativity.*
2. Explain the concept of critical thinking.
3. Why are both of these attributes important for marketers?

THE TECHNOLOGY REVOLUTION IN MARKETING

As we move through the opening decade of the 21st century, we also enter a new era in communication, considered by some as unique as the 15th century invention of the printing press or the first radio and television broadcasts early in the 20th century. **Technology** is the business application of knowledge based on scientific discoveries, inventions, and innovations. Interactive multimedia technologies ranging from computer networks to Internet services to wireless devices have revolutionized the way people store, distribute, retrieve, and present information. These technologies link employees, suppliers, and customers throughout the world.

Technological advances continuously revolutionize marketing. Now that more than half of all U.S. homes and apartments contain at least one personal computer, online services and the Internet offer a new medium over which companies can market products and offer customer service. Marketing and sales departments can quickly access vast databases with information about customers and their buying patterns. Even the U.S. military uses database marketing to contact potential recruits. Several firms, including Merkle Direct Marketing, Inc., and CC3, create databases that identify qualified potential recruits based on age, education, and career interests that they then provide to military recruiters. The databases are so specific that they even indicate a person's preferred medium of contact. "Someone may be highly responsive to interactive marketing or e-mail marketing, but not responsive at all to telemarketing," explains an advertising account executive with the U.S. Air Force.[23]

Briefly Speaking

The question is not what you look at but what you see.

Henry David Thoreau (1817–1862)
American philosopher

6 Outline the changes in the marketing environment due to technology.

Marketers can develop targeted marketing campaigns and zoned advertising programs for consumers located within a certain distance from a store and even within specific city blocks. Newly developed technology makes it possible for marketers to target an individual consumer standing in a supermarket checkout line or walking down a busy city street. Woody Norris's invention—called Hypersonic Sound emitter, or HSS—may be a marketer's dream. With technology that "shoots tightly focused waves of ultrasound," HSS can transmit an audible message to a single person who may be standing 200 feet away from the transmitter. No one standing on either side of the person will hear the message, and if the person steps to the side of the target, the sound disappears. Think of the implications in a supermarket. As you walk down a single aisle, you might receive one message as you pass the popcorn, another as you pass the breakfast cereal, still another as you pass the crackers. And there are no loudspeakers. Already, marketers are flocking to Norris's company, American Technology Corp., to sign up for the new technology. Wal-Mart and McDonald's are testing it, along with Disney. Several undisclosed supermarket chains are eager to nab the product as well. DaimlerChrysler is considering installing the technology so that drivers and passengers can listen to two different music systems without interfering with each other. HSS may be able to provide the ultimate in relationship building with a large market.[24]

Technology can also create convenience—time and place utility—while enhancing customer satisfaction and building customer loyalty. ExxonMobil's Speedpass is a perfect example. At ExxonMobil self-service pumps, customers merely wave their electronic pass—attached to their car keys—across an electric eye to process payment for fuel. This way, fill-ups are quick and easy—and they take place at ExxonMobil stations. But ExxonMobil has taken the technology one step further. In an alliance with McDonald's, in selected locations Speedpass holders may now breeze through a McDonald's drive-up service window, paying for their burger and fries with the wave of a wand.[25]

INTERACTIVE MARKETING

Interactive media technologies combine computers and telecommunications resources to create software that users can direct themselves. They allow people to digitize reports and drawings and transmit them, quickly and inexpensively, over phone lines, coaxial cables, or fiber-optic cables. People can subscribe to personalized news services that deliver article summaries on specified topics directly to their fax machines or computers. They can telecommunicate via e-mail, voice mail, fax, videoconferencing, and computer networks; pay bills using online banking services; and use online resources to get information about everything from theater events to a local car dealer's special sale. With even more recent technology, people can make phone calls via the Internet using Voice over Internet Protocol (VoIP). Ten percent of all calls are now transmitted via VoIP because it is cheaper than conventional phone lines—presenting a potentially important interactive medium for marketers.[26]

Many companies use interactivity in their marketing programs. **Interactive marketing** refers to buyer–seller communications in which the customer controls the amount and type of information received from a marketer. This technique provides immediate access to key product information when the consumer wants it. Interactive techniques have been used for more than a decade; point-of-sale brochures and coupon dispensers are a simple form of interactive advertising. Want to try a new restaurant? Check its Web site for a coupon offering a free appetizer. Interactive marketing also includes two-way electronic communication using a variety of media such as the Internet, CD-ROMs, and virtual reality kiosks.

interactive marketing Buyer–seller communications in which the customer controls the amount and type of information received from a marketer through such channels as the Internet, CD-ROMs, interactive toll-free telephone numbers, and virtual reality kiosks.

Interactive marketing allows marketers and consumers to customize their communication. Customers may come to companies for information, creating opportunities for one-to-one marketing. Interactive marketing can also allow larger exchanges, in which consumers can communicate with one another using e-mail or electronic bulletin boards. These electronic conversations establish innovative relationships between users and the technology, providing customized information based on users' interests and levels of understanding. Interactive technologies support almost limitless exchanges of information. They can help create customer satisfaction and boost customer loyalty. Delta Airlines uses interactivity in several ways to improve customer service and satisfaction. First, travelers can purchase their tickets online. Second, customers can obtain their boarding passes, decide at the last minute to change seats, or check their baggage by using one of the self-service kiosks installed at the airport terminal. Third, they can pick up a Delta Direct phone at the airport to make any flight changes.[27]

Interactive promotions put the customer in control. Consumers can easily get tips on product usage and answers to customer service questions. They can also tell the company what they like or dislike about a product, and they can just as easily click the exit button and move on to another area. As interactive promotions grow in number and popularity, the challenge will be attracting and holding consumer attention.

A series of technological innovations have made major contributions to the ability of consumers to become the major drivers of interactive marketing by controlling the amount and type of information they receive. These innovations—the Internet, broadband technology, wireless communications, and interactive television service—are discussed next.

THE INTERNET

Most of today's discussion of interactive marketing centers on the Internet. The **Internet** (or **Net**) is an all-purpose global network composed of some 50,000 different networks around the world that,

Internet (or **Net**) Worldwide network of interconnected computers that lets anyone with access to a personal computer send and receive images and data anywhere.

within limits, lets anyone with access to a personal computer send and receive images and text anywhere.

The Internet provides an efficient way to find and share information, but until the last decade, most people outside universities and government agencies found it difficult to use and learn. This changed in 1993 with the advent of browser technology that provides point-and-click access to the **World Wide Web (WWW** or **Web)**. The Web is an interlinked collection of graphically rich information sources within the larger Internet. Web sites provide hypermedia resources, a system allowing storage of and access to text, graphics, audio, and video in so-called pages linked to each other in a way that integrates these different media elements. When a user clicks a highlighted word or picture (icon), the browser converts the click to computer commands and brings the requested new information—text, photograph, chart, song, or movie clip—to the user's computer.

World Wide Web (WWW or Web) Collection of resources on the Internet that offers easy access to text, graphics, sound, and other multimedia resources.

Compared with traditional media, the hypermedia resources of the Web offer a number of advantages. Data moves in seconds, without the user noticing that several computers in different locations combine to fulfill a request. Interactive control allows users quick access to other information resources through related pages, either at the same or other sites, and easy navigation through documents. Because it is dynamic, Web site sponsors can easily keep information current. Finally, multimedia capacities increase the attractiveness of these documents.

BROADBAND

broadband technology Extremely high-speed, always-on Internet connection.

Broadband technology—an always-on Internet connection that runs at a speed of 200 kilobytes per second or higher—can deliver large amounts of data at once, making online marketing even faster and easier than it was a few years ago. Consumers can access Web pages and sites can process credit-card purchases much more quickly via broadband. The number of households with broadband connections is increasing rapidly because of this increased speed. Nearly 50 percent of all online U.S. households use a broadband Internet connection, even though subscription costs are about double that of traditional dial-up connections.

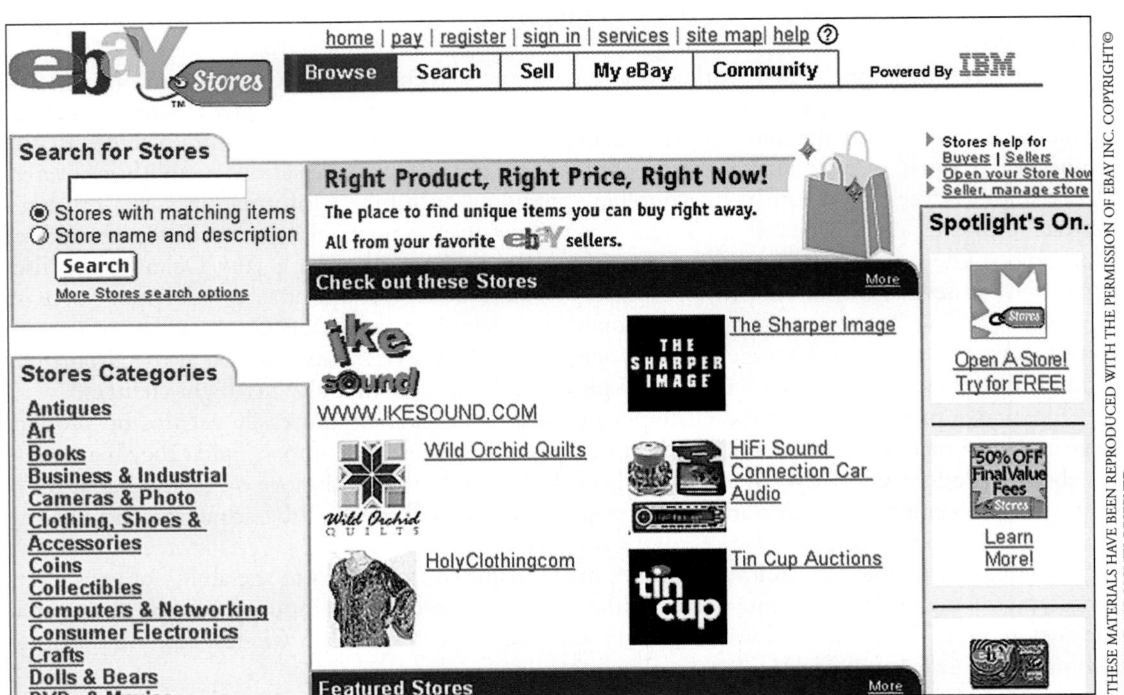

eBay sponsors eBay Stores, a hypermedia used on the Web. This dynamic technology offers quick access to many products in a format with which users are familiar.

The U.S. is certainly not the only market that has embraced broadband. Even emerging economies like South Korea have discovered its benefits. About 11 million South Korean households—70 percent of the nation's citizens—have a broadband connection. NCSoft, a Korean tech firm, is now the largest broadband gaming network, serving 3.2 million subscribers who pay $25 a month. Korea's two top sellers of broadband access, Hanaro and Korea Telecom, are competing frantically to build the world's most advanced wireless Internet infrastructure. If it succeeds, customers could use the same e-mail and network identity no matter where they are—through landlines or over the air.[28]

WIRELESS

More and more consumers now have **wireless** Internet connections for their laptop and handheld computers, which is both a challenge and an opportunity for marketers. In 2003, the number of U.S. consumers with these connections increased 100 percent. Although wireless advertising is still in its infancy, industry watchers predict that wireless ad revenues will soon reach $700 million.[29] This high-tech form of advertising has been slower to catch on with marketers because of the relatively high cost. But wireless ads offer tremendous potential to target certain audiences. And since these ads appear by themselves on a handheld user's screen, they command more attention than a traditional banner ad would. But so far, wireless carriers have limited the amount of wireless advertising they will accept because they do not want to alienate their own customers by bombarding them with advertising messages.

INTERACTIVE TELEVISION SERVICE

Interactive television (iTV) service is another new technology for marketers and consumers alike to embrace. Interactive television service is a package that includes a return path for viewers to interact with programs or commercials by clicking their remote controls. The 18 million U.S. TV viewers who have iTV can request additional information about products or actually purchase them without having to dial their phones. Companies such as Ford have already incorporated iTV into their marketing programs.[30]

HOW MARKETERS USE THE WEB

The Web offers marketers a powerful yet affordable way to reach customers across town or overseas, at almost any time, with interactive messages. The online techniques that companies use to market their businesses fall into four broad categories: virtual storefronts, interactive brochures, online newsletters, and customer service tools.

- The virtual storefront allows customers to view and order merchandise. Amazon.com and eBay are two of the largest such sites. Web stores can be stand-alone operations or grouped in cybermalls with links to 30 to 100 participating retailers. The Internet service provider Yahoo! operates such a mall.

  After the initial rush to establish a virtual storefront, many retailers backed off because they have discovered that their customers are either not interested in shopping for their products online or their product offerings just don't lend themselves to online shopping. Some companies instead set up Web sites that act as information clearinghouses, providing in-depth product information.

- Interactive brochures that provide company and product information are popular Internet marketing applications. These range from simple one-page electronic flyers to multimedia presentations.

- Online newsletters provide current news, industry information, and contacts and links for internal and external customers. *Web Commerce Today*, a monthly online newsletter, helps merchants plan, design, manage, and promote retail or business-to-business Web stores.

- The Web is also a customer service tool. Consumers can order catalogs, get product information, place orders online, and send questions to company representatives.

The Web is probably the most significant innovation affecting marketing and business in the past 50 years. Properly used, it should prove an indispensable tool in promoting connections, building associations, delivering information, and creating online communities. However, to date, few companies have made money on the Internet—and many have lost a bundle. Major beneficiaries have been firms marketing Net-related goods or services—for example, computer networking equipment; software such as access, browser, Web page authoring, and e-mail programs; consultants and Web page creators; Internet access and online service providers like America Online and Earthlink; and companies offering sites where businesses can advertise.

Business-to-business e-commerce has far outweighed e-commerce involving consumers and accounts for 93 percent of all Internet commerce. However, retail sales over the Internet already amount to more than $34 billion a year.[31] As the Web evolves, marketers need to explore its capabilities and learn the best ways to use it effectively in combination with other distribution channels and communications media. Among the questions marketers need to ask are the following:

- What types of goods and services can be successfully marketed on the Web?
- What characteristics make a successful Web site?
- Does the Internet offer a secure way to process customer orders?
- How will Internet sales affect traditional store-based and nonstore retailing and distribution?
- What is the best use of this technology in a specific firm's marketing strategy: promotion, image building, or sales?

The importance of the Internet is reflected throughout this text, and as forthcoming chapters discuss specific marketing topics, we will revisit the Internet and its related technologies to look for answers to the preceding questions.

1. What is interactive marketing?
2. Why are broadband and wireless technologies important to marketers?
3. Identify the four online techniques companies use to market their businesses.

7 Explain the shift from transaction-based marketing to relationship marketing.

FROM TRANSACTION-BASED MARKETING TO RELATIONSHIP MARKETING

lifetime value of a customer Revenues and intangible benefits that a customer brings to an organization over an average lifetime, minus the investment the firm has made to attract and keep the customer.

As marketing progresses through the 21st century, a significant change is taking place in the way companies interact with customers. The traditional view of marketing as a simple exchange process, or **transaction-based marketing,** is being replaced by a different, longer term approach that emphasizes building relationships one customer at a time. Traditional marketing strategies focused on attracting customers and closing deals. Today's marketers realize that, although it's important to attract new customers, it's even more important to establish and maintain a relationship with them so they become loyal repeat customers. These efforts must expand to include suppliers and employees as well. Over the long term, this relationship may be translated to the **lifetime value of a customer**—the revenues and intangible benefits that a customer brings to an organization over an average lifetime, minus the investment the firm has made to attract and keep the customer.

Sirius Satellite Radio marketers estimate the cost of acquiring a single customer at more than $500. At current monthly subscription rates, it takes them almost five years to recoup this investment. Consequently, they must continue to provide a service valuable enough to retain these subscribers for years.

The best way to get what you want is to help other people get what they want.

Zig Ziglar (b. 1926)
American motivational speaker

As defined earlier in this chapter, relationship marketing refers to the development, growth, and maintenance of long-term, cost-effective exchange relationships with individual customers, suppliers, employees, and other partners for mutual benefit. It broadens the scope of external marketing relationships to include suppliers, customers, and referral sources. In relationship marketing, the term *customer* takes on a new meaning. Employees serve customers within an organization as well as outside it; individual employees and their departments are customers of and suppliers to one another. They must apply the same high standards of customer satisfaction to intradepartmental relationships as they do to external customer relationships. Relationship marketing recognizes the critical importance of internal marketing to the success of external marketing plans. Programs that improve customer service inside a company also raise productivity and staff morale, resulting in better customer relationships outside the firm.

Relationship marketing gives a company new opportunities to gain a competitive edge by moving customers up a loyalty hierarchy from new customers to regular purchasers, then to loyal supporters of the firm and its goods and services, and finally to advocates who not only buy its products but recommend them to others, as shown in Figure 1.8. Relationship building begins early in marketing, starting with high-quality products and continuing with excellent customer service during and after purchase. It also includes programs that encourage repeat purchases and foster customer loyalty. Marketers may try to rebuild damaged relationships or rejuvenate unprofitable customers with these practices as well. Sometimes modifying a product or tailoring customer service to meet the needs of these customers can go a long way toward rebuilding a relationship.

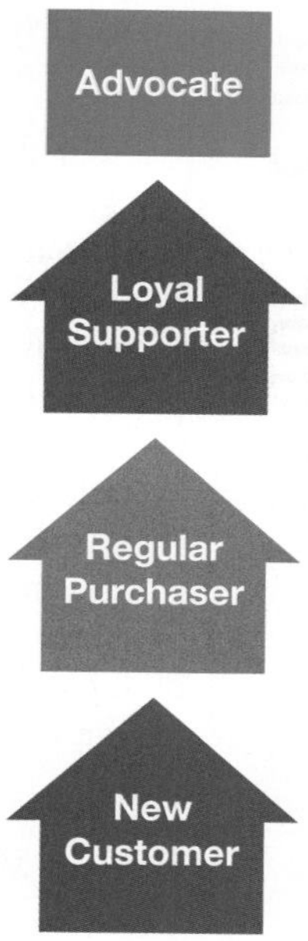

By converting indifferent customers into loyal ones, companies generate repeat sales. As pointed out earlier, the cost of maintaining existing customers is far below the cost of finding new ones, and these loyal customers are profitable ones. Programs to encourage customer loyalty are not new. Frequent purchaser rewards for everything from clothing to groceries are popular examples. Firms in the service industries are among the leaders in building such relationships. Visa teams up with Holiday Inn resorts and hotels during peak vacation months. Holiday Inn advertisements target families, offering a "kids eat free, stay free" program. In addition, travelers who use their Visa cards to stay at one of over 1,000 participating hotels receive a Kids' Activity Book with valuable coupons. Customers who use their Holiday Inn Visa for any purchase receive points for upgrades and free nights at Holiday Inns.[32]

Effective relationship marketing often relies heavily on information technologies such as computer databases that record customers' tastes, price preferences, and lifestyles. This technology helps companies become one-to-one marketers who gather customer-specific information and provide individually customized goods and services. The firms target their marketing programs to appropriate groups rather than relying on mass-marketing campaigns. Companies who study customer preferences and react accordingly gain distinct competitive advantages.

But relationship marketing does not rest entirely on information technology; it also incorporates good manners, or etiquette, such as learning customers' and suppliers' names. The "Etiquette Tips for Marketing Professionals" feature provides a few hints on developing this valuable skill.

figure 1.8

Converting New Customers to Advocates

Advocate

Loyal Supporter

Regular Purchaser

New Customer

one-to-one marketing Customized marketing program designed to build long-term relationships with individual customers.

ONE-TO-ONE MARKETING

To achieve a high level of loyalty, many companies now engage in **one-to-one marketing,** which is exactly what it sounds like: a marketing program customized to build long-term relationships with individual customers. This approach involves identifying a firm's best customers and increasing their loyalty. Many of the tools discussed earlier, such as databases and frequent-purchase programs, support a one-to-one marketing approach. In addition, marketers have found all kinds of new ways to target marketing messages to individual consumers and businesses. Keep in mind that while technology is useful, it is not necessary for every one-to-one marketing communication. At T.G.I. Friday's restaurants, staffers distribute crayons and color-in menus to every child who walks in the door. Younger children also receive balloons when they are ready to leave the restaurant.

The Hypersonic Sound emitter—described earlier in this chapter—which delivers messages to tightly defined areas in a supermarket or outside a store window, is a high-tech method of one-to-one marketing. When the pizza-and-pasta chain Sbarro was searching for a way to reach teens, one of the company's top marketers found LidRock—a firm that sells mini music CDs attached to the inside of a plastic soft-drink lid, as shown in Figure 1.9. Sbarro immediately ordered 500,000 of the lids, estimating that it would take about three months to sell out

figure 1.9

One-to-One Marketing: Sip and Spin with Personalized Entertainment

JEFFREY SALTER/REDUX PICTURES

ETIQUETTE TIPS

FOR MARKETING PROFESSIONALS

How to Remember Names

IT'S a nightmare: You are introduced to someone, and a second later, you have forgotten his or her name. Frantically, you wrack your brain for a shred of memory—but the most you can come up with is that it sounded like the name of your pet goldfish or that the person reminds you of your old girlfriend or boyfriend. Remembering names *is* important in your personal life and your business life—and it is true that the marketer who can remember a name after hearing it only once is considerably ahead of the game. But if you are having trouble with this particular skill, don't despair. Here are some techniques that the experts use to make them seem savvy whenever they are introduced to a new customer.

1. When you are introduced to someone, look at the person's face. This will give you a strong visual image of the individual, with the added bonus that he or she knows you are paying attention. Does he have red hair? Does she wear glasses? Try to zero in on one or two features that are easy to recall.
2. Listen to the person's name. If you do not hear it clearly, ask the person to repeat it. Then repeat it yourself in a friendly voice. You can shake the person's hand and say, "Hello Jenna, I'm so glad to meet you." If possible, use the person's name once or twice during the conversation, including when you say goodbye.
3. Create an association between the person's name and an image that is easy to recall. If it helps, make your mental picture exaggerated and colorful.
4. If the person is with a group, try to remember who else was there; it will help you fill in the missing blank later.
5. The next time you encounter the person, if you have forgotten the name despite all these efforts, don't just run the other way. Instead, reintroduce yourself. Say, "Hello, I'm Demetrice Jones, how are you?" This gracious move allows the person to save face if he or she has forgotten *your* name—and should prompt a reciprocal reintroduction.

Sources: "How to Remember Names," *The Leader's Institute,* http://www.high-impact-leaders.com, accessed January 23, 2004; "How to Remember Names," *Learn That,* http://www.learnthat.com, accessed January 23, 2004.

the supply throughout Sbarro's 700 stores. Every teen who ordered a soft drink would get one. But Sbarro blew through the initial order in just seven weeks and raised its drink revenues 30 percent in the process. So they ordered 2 million more, with a mix of music from Britney Spears, Bubba Sparxxx, and Black Eyed Peas. "We're hitting our target audience, [and] getting the association with technology and music," said marketing executive Anthony Missano. "It's exciting!"[33]

Some marketers have figured out how to target TV commercials to individual neighborhoods and, ultimately, households. Visible World is an ad-targeting technology firm that segments cable television viewers by their buying patterns. Using its own software, Visible World can help advertising agencies prepare thousands of versions of a single commercial that can be altered or updated almost instantaneously on request. Based on database information about interests, past purchases, number of people in a household, and the like, Visible World's technology can modify a commercial to suit a specific need. "It's taking mass medium and turning it into a personal medium," says one advertising executive.[34]

Another way to practice one-to-one marketing is to customize products themselves. This idea isn't new, but it has been taken to new heights by dedicated marketers. At Reflect.com, shoppers can customize cosmetics and skincare formulas to suit their own needs. Customers start with an online questionnaire that includes questions about skin tone, hair texture, fragrance preferences, and the like. Once the questions are answered, a team of technicians in the company's San Francisco laboratory blends specific active ingredients with certain base formulas to create the customized products. Then they inject a preferred fragrance if the customer wants one. Finally, the customer can create an individual brand name for his or her own products. "You're the ultimate brand," says Reflect.com's CEO Richard Gerstein. Shoppers who visit the Lands' End Web site can type in their measurements, answer several questions, and receive a pair of custom-fit jeans three weeks later. One year after the service was launched, nearly half of the jeans that Lands' End sold online were custom fit.[35]

Some marketers don't even need to rely on high technology to create custom products. Maxine Clark, founder of Build-a-Bear Workshop, created a company based on the simple idea that preteen and teenage girls would want to choose, stuff, and dress their own teddy bears. Build-a-Bear Workshop now has franchised booths at shopping malls and other retail locations around the country, and the company offers birthday parties as well. What is the company's ultimate goal? "To create memories," says Maxine Clark.[36]

Customer service is an important feature of successful one-to-one marketing. Perhaps nowhere is superior customer service more vital than in the restaurant business. At their world-famous Inn at Little Washington in Virginia, chef-owners Patrick O'Connell and Reinhardt Lynch stop at nothing to serve their customers the best of everything. When a party arrives at the restaurant, the head waiter quietly rates the mood of his new guests on a scale of 1 to 10. Then the entire staff goes to work to ensure that at the end of the evening, their guests are in the best spirits possible. "No one should leave here below a 9," remarks O'Connell. Restaurant staffers will do just about anything—offer complimentary champagne, extra dessert, a tableside visit by one of the owners, even a tour of the kitchen—to make their guests feel comfortable and happy. "Consciousness to the extreme is great customer service," says O'Connell. Although the inn's five-course dinners—which may include grilled black figs, medallions of veal tenderloin with mushrooms, and a fat slice of chocolate cake with roasted banana ice cream—have gained it a culinary reputation, it's the service that creates the entire dining experience. O'Connell and Lynch focus on hiring employees with positive attitudes, even if they don't have a long history of restaurant experience. "In the hospitality business a desire to please is the key criterion to success," explains O'Connell. "We [have] found that over time, nice people can be taught almost anything."[37]

DEVELOPING PARTNERSHIPS AND STRATEGIC ALLIANCES

But relationship marketing does not apply just to individual consumers and employees. It also affects a wide range of other markets, including business-to-business relationships with the firm's suppliers and distributors as well as other types of corporate partnerships. In the past, companies have often viewed their suppliers as adversaries against whom they must fiercely negotiate prices, playing one off against the other. But this attitude has changed radically, as both marketers and their suppliers discover the benefits of collaborative relationships.

The formation of **strategic alliances**—partnerships that create competitive advantages—is also on the rise. These take many forms, from product-development partnerships that involve shared costs for research and development and marketing to vertical alliances in which one company provides a product or component to another firm, which then distributes or sells it under its own brand. Recently, PepsiCo formed a strategic alliance with Apple's iTunes store, offering free, legal music downloads to consumers who purchased bottles of Pepsi drinks. The two companies launched the program with a television commercial first aired during the Super Bowl. Build-a-Bear Workshop, described earlier, and Limited Too, a retailer of clothing and accessories for preteen and teenage girls, formed an alliance to promote each other's merchandise. Not only do they serve the same market, but the two stores are often located in the same shopping mall.[38]

strategic alliance
Partnerships in which two or more companies combine resources and capital to create competitive advantages in a new market.

Not-for-profit organizations often make use of strategic alliances to raise awareness and funds for their causes. Stride Rite and Save the Children have teamed up in a combined effort to increase shoe sales and raise money for needy children. Figure 1.10 illustrates how Share Our Strength joined forces with companies like American Express and Jenn-Air® to host culinary benefits across North America called Taste of the Nation, whose goal is to raise funds to fight hunger and promote awareness of the sponsoring companies.

MARKETING Concept Check

1. How does relationship marketing give companies a competitive edge?
2. Define *one-to-one marketing.*
3. What is a strategic alliance?

figure 1.10

Strategic Alliance between a Not-for-Profit Organization and For-Profit Firms

COURTESY OF SHARE OUR STRENGTH

8 Identify the universal functions of marketing.

COSTS AND FUNCTIONS OF MARKETING

Firms must spend money to create time, place, and ownership utilities. Numerous attempts have been made to measure marketing costs in relation to overall product costs, and most estimates have ranged between 40 and 60 percent of total costs. On average, one-half of the costs involved in a product, such as a Subway sandwich, an ounce of Safari perfume, or a trip to Australia, can be traced directly to marketing. These costs are not associated with fabrics, raw materials and other ingredients, baking, sewing, or any of the other production functions necessary for creating form utility. What, then, does the consumer receive in return for this 50 percent marketing cost? What functions does marketing perform?

As Figure 1.11 reveals, marketing is responsible for the performance of eight universal functions: buying, selling, transporting, storing, standardizing and grading, financing, risk taking, and securing marketing information. Some functions are performed by manufacturers, others by retailers, and still others by marketing intermediaries called **wholesalers.**

Buying and selling, the first two functions shown in Figure 1.11, represent **exchange functions.** Buying is important to marketing on several levels. Marketers must determine how and why consumers buy certain goods and services. To be successful, they must try to understand consumer behavior. In addition, retailers and other intermediaries must seek out products that will appeal to their customers. Since they generate time, place, and ownership utilities through these purchases, marketers must anticipate consumer preferences for purchases to be made several months later. Selling is the second half of the exchange process. It involves advertising, personal selling, and sales promotion in an attempt to match the firm's goods and services to consumer needs.

Transporting and storing are **physical distribution functions.** Transporting involves the physical movement of goods from the seller to the purchaser. Storing involves warehousing goods until they are needed for sale. Manufacturers, wholesalers, and retailers all typically perform these functions.

The final four marketing functions—standardizing and grading, financing, risk taking, and securing marketing information—are often called **facilitating functions** because they assist the marketer in performing the exchange and physical distribution functions. Quality and quantity control standards and grades, frequently set by federal or state governments, reduce the need for purchasers to inspect each item. Specific tire sizes, for example, permit buyers to request needed sizes and to expect uniform sizes.

Financing is another marketing function because buyers often need access to funds to finance inventories prior to sales. Manufacturers often provide financing for their wholesale and retail cus-

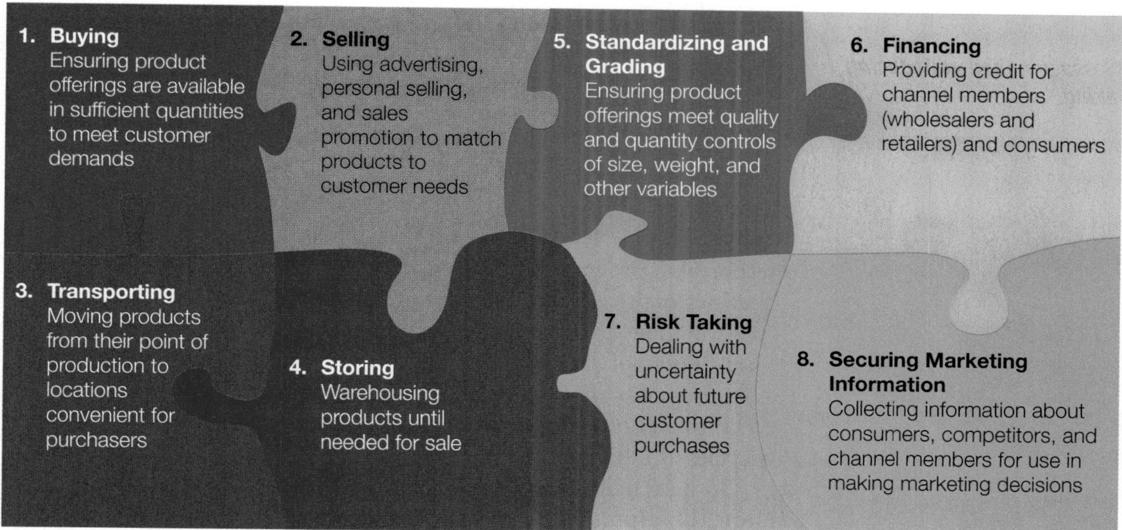

figure 1.11
Eight Universal Marketing Functions

tomers. Some types of wholesalers perform similar functions for their retail customers. Finally, retailers frequently permit their customers to buy on credit.

The seventh function, risk taking, is part of most ventures. Manufacturers create goods and services based on research and their belief that consumers need them. Wholesalers and retailers acquire inventory based on similar expectations of future consumer demand. Entrepreneurial risk takers accommodate these uncertainties about future consumer behavior when they market goods and services.

The final marketing function involves securing marketing information. Marketers gather information to meet the need for decision-oriented input about customers: who they are, what they buy, where they buy, and how they buy. By collecting and analyzing marketing information, marketers also try to understand why consumers purchase some goods and services and reject others.

1. Which two marketing functions represent exchange functions?
2. Which two functions represent physical distribution functions?
3. Which four functions are facilitating functions?

ETHICS AND SOCIAL RESPONSIBILITY: DOING WELL BY DOING GOOD

(9) Demonstrate the relationship between ethical business practices and marketplace success.

Ethics are moral standards of behavior expected by a society. Most companies do their best to abide by an ethical code of conduct, but sometimes organizations and their leaders fall short. Several years ago, the Texas-based energy giant Enron collapsed, taking with it the retirement savings of its employees and investors. Enron's accounting firm, Arthur Andersen, was accused of shredding documents related to the fall of the company. In another scandal, executives from Tyco were accused of using millions of company dollars for their personal benefit. And chemical manufacturer Monsanto was convicted not only of polluting water sources and soil in a rural Alabama area for decades but of ignoring evidence its own scientists had gathered indicating the extent and severity of the pollution.

Despite these and other alleged breaches of ethical standards, most businesspeople do follow ethical practices. Over half of all major corporations now offer ethics training to employees, and most corporate mission statements include pledges to protect the environment, contribute to communities, and improve workers' lives. This book encourages you to follow the highest ethical standards throughout your business and marketing career. Because ethics and social responsibility are so important to marketers, each chapter in this book contains a critical-thinking feature entitled "Solving an Ethical Controversy."

figure 1.12

Anheuser-Busch: Persuasive Message Aimed at Reducing the Incidence of Underage Drinking

ANHEUSER-BUSCH, INC.

Social responsibility involves marketing philosophies, policies, procedures, and actions whose primary objective is the enhancement of society. Many firms—both large and small—include social responsibility programs as part of their overall mission. These programs often produce such benefits as improved customer relationships, increased employee loyalty, marketplace success, and improved financial performance. Timberland Co., manufacturer of boots, outdoor clothing, and accessories, is well known for its high ethical standards and socially responsible programs. The company donates large sums of money to charities each year, and its employees are given paid time off to volunteer for their favorite organizations—from the animal shelter to the local preschool. The company also welcomes ideas for socially responsible programs from its employees. During one recent holiday season, an employee introduced the Trikes for Tots drive, which collected new tricycles and bicycles for needy children.[39]

To help reduce underage drinking, Anheuser-Busch created Operation ID, a program that helps retailers spot fake IDs and verify real ones. Figure 1.12 demonstrates the difficulty of identifying underage drinkers on the basis of appearance and how Anheuser-Busch is taking socially responsible actions aimed at making a difference.

Recent recipients of the annual Excellence in Corporate Philanthropy awards were pharmaceutical giant Pfizer and toy company Hasbro. Hasbro donated thousands of toys to children in war-torn Afghanistan and to equip playrooms in hundreds of hospitals and orphanages. In addition, the company has constructed 100 playgrounds in the U.S. with rubber surfaces that let children in wheelchairs play with friends and siblings. Pfizer's focus has been on getting HIV/AIDS drugs and other medications into the hands of the poor. Over the next five years, it will provide 135 million doses of antibiotic Zithromax to fight trachoma, the world's leading cause of preventable blindness.[40]

1. Define *ethics.*
2. What is social responsibility?
3. Why are these two concepts important to marketers?

Strategic Implications of Marketing in the 21st Century

UNPRECEDENTED opportunities have emerged out of electronic commerce and computer technologies in business today. These advances and innovations have allowed organizations to reach new markets, reduce selling and marketing costs, and enhance their relationships with customers and suppliers. Thanks to the Internet, commerce has grown into a global market.

As a new universe for consumers and organizations is created, marketers must learn to be creative and think critically about their environment. Profit-seeking and not-for-profit organizations must broaden the scope of their activities to prevent myopic results in their enterprises.

Marketers must constantly look for ways to create loyal customers and build long-term relationships with those customers, often on a one-to-one basis. They must be able to anticipate customer needs and satisfy them with innovative goods and services. They must be able to do this faster and better than the competition. And they must conduct their business according to the highest ethical standards.

REVIEW OF CHAPTER OBJECTIVES

1 Explain how marketing creates utility through the exchange process.

Utility is the want-satisfying power of a good or service. Four basic kinds of utility exist: form, time, place, and ownership. Form utility is created when a firm converts raw materials and component inputs into finished goods and services. Marketing creates time, place, and ownership utilities.

1.1. How does a good or service satisfy customers' wants or needs?
1.2. Describe time, place, and ownership utilities.

2 Contrast marketing activities during the four eras in the history of marketing.

During the production era, businesspeople believed that quality products would sell themselves. The sales era emphasized convincing people to buy. The marketing concept emerged during the marketing era, in which there was a companywide focus on consumer orientation with the objective of achieving long-term success. The relationship era focuses on establishing and maintaining relationships with customers and suppliers. Relationship marketing involves long-term, value-added relationships.

2.1. How is the marketing era different from the production and sales eras?
2.2. What are some of the relationships involved in relationship marketing?

3 Explain the importance of avoiding marketing myopia.

Marketing myopia is management's failure to recognize a company's scope of business. To avoid it, companies must broadly define their goals so they focus on fulfilling consumer needs.

3.1. How can companies avoid marketing myopia?

4 Describe the characteristics of not-for-profit marketing.

Not-for-profit organizations operate in both public and private sectors. The biggest distinction between not-for-profits and commercial firms is the bottom line—whether the firm is judged by its profitability levels. Not-for-profit organizations may market to multiple publics. A customer or service user of a not-for-profit organization may have less control over the organization's destiny than do customers of a profit-seeking firm. In addition, resource contributors to not-for-profits may try to exert influence over the organization's activities. Not-for-profits often lack a clear organizational structure but are conservative about spending.

4.1. Identify differences between for-profit firms and not-for-profit organizations.

5 Identify and briefly explain each of the five types of nontraditional marketing.

Person marketing focuses on efforts to cultivate the attention, interest, and preferences of a target market toward a celebrity or authority. Place marketing attempts to attract visitors, potential residents, and businesses to a particular destination. Cause marketing identifies and markets a social issue, cause, or idea. Event marketing promotes sporting, cultural, charitable, or political activities. Organization marketing attempts to influence others to accept the organization's goals or services and contribute to it in some way.

5.1. How might cause and event marketing combine in a single marketing effort?
5.2. How are person and place marketing similar?

6 Outline the changes in the marketing environment due to technology.

Technology now constitutes one of the major elements of the marketing environment. Interactive marketing, the Internet, broadband, wireless, and iTV are all technological advances that can be used by marketers. These new technologies have spawned new industries and products, created new advertising opportunities, redefined competition, significantly impacted marketing mix decisions, and resulted in increased government supervision.

6.1. How has interactive marketing changed the marketing environment?
6.2. Identify four ways that marketers use the Web.

⑦ Explain the shift from transaction-based marketing to relationship marketing.

Relationship marketing represents a dramatic change in the way companies interact with customers. The focus on relationships gives a firm new opportunities to gain a competitive edge by moving customers up a loyalty hierarchy from new customers to regular purchasers and then to loyal supporters and advocates. Over the long term, this relationship may be translated to the lifetime value of a customer. Effective relationship marketing often relies on information technologies, one-to-one marketing, and strategic partnerships and alliances.

7.1. How is customer loyalty an important part of relationship marketing?
7.2. How does one-to-one marketing help build relationships?

⑧ Identify the universal functions of marketing.

Marketing is responsible for eight universal functions, divided into three categories: (1) exchange functions (buying and selling); (2) physical distribution (transporting and storing); and (3) facilitating functions (standardization and grading, financing, risk taking, and securing market information).

8.1 Identify the two halves of the exchange function.
8.2. Who typically performs the physical distribution functions?
8.3. Why are the final four functions referred to as facilitating functions?

⑨ Demonstrate the relationship between ethical business practices and marketplace success.

Ethics are moral standards of behavior expected by a society. Companies that promote ethical behavior and social responsibility usually produce increased employee loyalty and a better public image. This image often pays off in customer growth, since many buyers want to associate themselves with—and be customers of—such firms.

9.1. What are the benefits of ethical and socially responsible behavior on the part of organizations?

MARKETING TERMS YOU NEED TO KNOW

utility 6
marketing 7
exchange process 9
seller's market 11
buyer's market 11
consumer orientation 11
marketing concept 11
relationship marketing 11
marketing myopia 13
person marketing 17
place marketing 18
cause marketing 19
event marketing 20
organization marketing 20
interactive marketing 23
Internet (or Net) 23
World Wide Web (WWW or Web) 24
broadband technology 24
lifetime value of a customer 26
one-to-one marketing 27
strategic alliance 29

OTHER IMPORTANT MARKETING TERMS

production orientation 9
sales orientation 10
bottom line 16
creativity 21
critical thinking 21
technology 22
wireless technology 25
interactive television (iTV) 25
transaction-based marketing 26
wholesalers 30
exchange function 30
physical distribution function 30
facilitating function 30
ethics 31
social responsibility 32

PROJECTS AND TEAMWORK EXERCISES

1. Consider each of the following firms and describe how the firm's goods and/or services can create different types of utility. You can do this alone or in a team.
   a. weekend mountain bike rental outlet
   b. in-store kiosk for viewing and printing disc camera photos
   c. Disney World
   d. eBay
   e. outlet mall
2. With a classmate, choose a U.S.-based company whose products you think will do well in certain markets overseas. The company can be anything from a music group to a clothing retailer—anything that interests you. Then write a plan for how you would target and communicate with overseas markets.
3. Research a company that has been around for decades, such as Ford Motor Co., Kraft Foods, or AT&T, and write a brief description of what the firm's marketing focus would have been during each of these eras: production (if applicable), sales, marketing, and relationship. (Teams can also work together by having a different person write the description of each era.)
4. Choose a company that interests you from the following list, or select one of your own choosing. Research the company in the library or on the Internet to learn what seems to be the scope of its business. Write a brief description of the company's scope of business as it is now—and what it could be in five years, as you imagine it.
   a. General Mills
   b. Bank of America
   c. Marriott Hotels
   d. IBM
   e. Talbot's
5. Which type of nontraditional marketing does each of the following illustrate?
   a. President Bush's efforts to attract enough voters to win reelection as president
   b. a two-page magazine ad with a photograph of the beach at Cancún, Mexico
   c. a poster informing music lovers of an upcoming Kid Rock concert
   d. a recruitment ad for the National Guard
   e. a radio ad advising teenagers not to drink
6. Choose a not-for-profit organization, such as the U.S. Forest Service, Make-a-Wish Foundation, World Health Organization, or the World Wildlife Fund, and design a cause or organization advertisement communicating the organization's marketing message. Be sure to specify the audience to which the message will be directed.
7. Choose a product that you would really like to own but don't yet—a certain car, music system, line of clothing, or sports equipment. Write a plan describing how marketers could use interactive marketing to reach you and other consumers like you.
8. Based on your work in Exercise 7, describe how the different technologies could establish and build a relationship with you and other consumers like you.
9. Team up with one or more classmates to form a strategic alliance. Each group represents an organization—one to be for-profit and the other to be not-for-profit. Identify what business your organization is in, and formulate a plan for an advertisement, event, or some other promotion that would benefit both organizations.
10. Divide into two groups to discuss the ethical or socially responsible conduct of an organization that interests you: Tyco, Wal-Mart, Timberland, U.S. Air, or the Department of Homeland Security. Research the organization on the Internet to come up with information to use in your debate.

APPLYING CHAPTER CONCEPTS

1. How are customer satisfaction and customer loyalty important aspects of today's expanded concept of marketing activities?
2. Describe several factors that have forced countries to extend their economic views to events outside their own national borders. Why are U.S.-based firms actively seeking markets overseas? Why is the U.S. an attractive market for foreign competitors?
3. What is the difference between creativity and critical thinking? What role does each play in an organization's overall marketing strategy?
4. As a marketer, how might you use one-to-one marketing to increase the market for one of the following?
   a. a chain of Mexican restaurants
   b. a line of swimsuits
   c. a new action-thriller movie

ETHICS EXERCISE

While you are being interviewed for a job as a marketer for a large company that manufactures boxed, prepared meals—such as macaroni and cheese or chicken with biscuits—the interviewer steps outside the office. From where you are sitting, you can see a stack of papers on the interviewer's desk that contains advertisements by a competitor who makes similar products. You have an interview scheduled with the competitor for the following week.

1. Would you take a quick look at the ads—and any accompanying marketing notes—while the interviewer is out of the office? Why or why not?
2. In your next interview, would you tell the competitor that you saw the ads? Why or why not?
3. When the interviewer returns, would you mention the ads and offer your own commentary on them? Why or why not?

'netWork EXERCISES

1. **Event marketing.** Visit the Web site for a sporting event, such as the NCAA basketball tournament, the Super Bowl, Olympic Games, or the World Cup. Write a brief report in which you identify the sporting event, the effectiveness of the information presented, and your assessment of the fit between the marketer and the event being promoted.
2. **Not-for-profit marketing.** Virtually all not-for-profit organizations have Web sites. Two examples are the Lance Armstrong Foundation (**http://www.laf.org**) and the National Multiple Sclerosis Society (**http://www.nmss.org**). Visit the Web sites of at least two not-for-profit organizations. Compare and contrast how each uses the Web to support its mission and the role played by marketing. Which site did you find to be the most effective? Defend your answer.
3. **Relationship marketing.** Visit the Web site for a large hotel chain, such as Marriott (**http://www.marriott.com**). Prepare a report listing how the hotel chain has applied some of the principles of relationship marketing discussed in the chapter. Be sure to briefly explain why relationship marketing is so important for a firm like Marriott.

Note: Internet Web addresses change frequently. If you don't find the exact sites listed, you may need to access the organization's or company's home page and search from there or use a search engine such as Google.

INFOTRAC CITATIONS AND EXERCISES

Record: CJ117154646
MTV's Rock the Vote reaches out to young voters via cell phones. *Lori Aratani.* ***Knight Ridder/Tribune News Service,*** May 25, 2004 pK6316

Abstract: The wireless revolution is changing the way an entire generation lives. From digital cameras that send photos instantly over the Internet to cell phones that double as shopping kiosks and minicomputers, wireless appliances help people perform countless daily tasks while granting unlimited mobility. Cell phones, in particular, have been received enthusiastically by the younger generation, becoming for them a status symbol, communications tool, and constant companion. Today's youth use cell phones to chat with friends, make schedules, and send text messages. They are even finding ways to vote using cell phones. MTV's Rock the Vote, a nonpartisan youth voting group that prides itself on being cutting edge, is using wireless technology to boost election turnout among young voters.

1. Using your text, define *utility.* How does the concept of utility relate to the production and marketing of cell phones?
2. Why is it important for marketers to consider the needs of consumers when they plan, design, and manufacture new cell phone models?
3. How is MTV's Rock the Vote utilizing cell phones to increase voter turnout among young people, and why should marketers of wireless goods be paying attention to such innovative uses of their products?

CASE 1.1 How the Rolling Stones Keep Rolling

The Rolling Stones have been singing about relationships for 40 years. And that's the point: not whether you like the British rock group's songs and not whether you think Mick Jagger is too old to be doing what he keeps doing. However, Jagger has been knighted by the queen of England, which is unusual for any CEO. The Rolling Stones are a highly successful company because they have built relationships over the years with thousands of fans who listen to their music and buy tickets to their concerts; with concert promoters and music industry professionals; and with various business partners. Mick Jagger is an excellent marketer. After all, few bands last for four years, and Mick, Keith, and the rest of the band have been at it for more than four decades! In fact, the Stones have made four of the top fifteen most successful North American rock tours of all time—including the No. 1 tour called Voodoo Lounge in 1994, which grossed $121.2 million. Since 1989, the band has generated more than $1.5 billion in gross revenues.

Forming collaborative relationships with other businesses has been an important part of the Stones' marketing strategy. The group has sponsorship deals with companies such as Anheuser-Busch, Microsoft, Sprint, and E*Trade. Then there are the merchandisers, promoters, venue owners, and others who have business relationships with the band.

But most important of all are the fans—consumers who have been buying the group's records, tapes, CDs, and concert tickets for decades. By now, the group has developed hundreds of thousands of fans, mostly baby boomers—yet each Rolling Stones song is like a one-to-one marketing message to a fan. An entire generation grew up, graduated from school, began careers, and has lived their adult lives to tunes like "Jumping Jack Flash," "Shattered," "Under My Thumb," and "Stealing My Heart." Marketing can't get any more personal than that.

Technology has helped the Stones' empire grow over the years, yet the band is one of the last big-name rock 'n' roll acts to go online. That's because much of the group's music was recorded more than 30 years ago, before music was being distributed via the Internet. But Jagger has been a fan of the Internet as an entertainment and communications medium for a number of years. He financed a firm called Jagged Internetworks, a video streaming service. Making the Stones' music available online is a marketing maneuver that should reach both old fans and new ones. In addition to the various promotion and financial managers, the Rolling Stones actually have their own information technology (IT) specialist, Todd Griffith. Griffith is in charge of the band's Web site, **http://www.rollingstones.com**, which handles everything from e-mail for individual band members to computer-aided design drawings of concert venues that are used by the technical crew. About a year ago, Griffith even figured out how to reduce the number of plugs and cables required at a concert venue by making use of wireless networks—no small feat.

The Rolling Stones have proven that they are more than just a rock band. "The thing that we all had to learn is what to do when the passion starts to generate money," explains guitarist Keith Richards. "You don't just start to play your guitar thinking you're going to be running an organization that will maybe generate millions." But generate millions they have. When asked how long they plan to go on playing, Richards answers definitively: "Forever."

Questions for Critical Thinking

1. How important is customer loyalty to the success of the Rolling Stones? Explain your answer.
2. In what ways can you see technology helping or hurting the group's marketing efforts over the next few years?
3. Has the group avoided marketing myopia? Why or why not? How can it do so in the future?

Sources: Company Web site, **http://www.rollingstones.com**, accessed January 4, 2005; Chris Gaither, "Stones to Open Vaults to Net Downloads," *The Boston Globe,* August 18, 2003, **http://www.boston.com**; Ryan Naraine, "Real Gets Rolling Stones; Best Buy Deal," *Internetnews.com,* August 18, 2003, **http://www.internetnews.com**; Rebecca Reid, "Rolling Stones Marry Hi-Fi and Wi-Fi for Concert Shows," *ComputerWorld,* July 30, 2003, **http://www.computerworld.com**; Boby Kurian, "UB to Sponsor Rolling Stones' Indian Summer," *The Hindu Business Line,* February 17, 2003, **http://www.blonnet.com**; Andy Serwer, "Inside the Rolling Stones Inc.," *Fortune,* September 30, 2002, pp. 58–72.

VIDEO CASE 1.2 Toyota's Hybrid Is Hip with Customers

The written case on Toyota appears on page VC-2. The recently filmed Toyota video is designed to expand and highlight the concepts in this chapter and the concepts and questions covered in the written video case.

chapter 2

Strategic Planning and the Marketing Process

chapter objectives

1. Distinguish between strategic planning and tactical planning.
2. Explain how marketing plans differ at various levels in an organization.
3. Identify the steps in the marketing planning process.
4. Describe successful planning tools and techniques, including Porter's Five Forces model, first and second mover strategies, SWOT analysis, and the strategic window.
5. Identify the basic elements of a marketing strategy.
6. Describe the environmental characteristics that influence strategic decisions.
7. Describe the methods for marketing planning, including business portfolio analysis and the BCG matrix.

ESPN'S STRATEGY GOES TO EXTREMES

Every successful sports team plans its winning strategy. A football coach might decide that the best way for the team to win this week's game is to play a passing game. A basketball coach might call for a certain type of defense. A swim coach will probably position the strongest swimmer at the anchor position on a relay squad. When game time arrives, each athlete uses his or her own tactics to get the job done. Keeping this in mind, suppose you ran a cable television network devoted entirely to sports. You need to air all sports, all the time. Naturally, you'd have competitors—major networks that had purchased the rights to televise sports events such as the Super Bowl, the Olympics, the NCAA basketball tournament, the National Football League (NFL), or Major League Baseball (MLB). You have to stand out, to come up with something special to attract viewers—young consumers, if possible—and advertisers. If you were ESPN, here's what your strategy would be: You'd invent a major sports event.

ESPN was launched in Connecticut in 1979 with a slow-pitch softball game between the Kentucky Bourbons and Milwaukee Schlitz (sponsored by Budweiser). Few television industry experts thought the

little cable station would succeed. Today, ESPN Inc., which is owned by Disney and partially by Hearst, operates seven domestic cable networks, including its flagship ESPN station, and has more than 88 million households as subscribers. It does telecast traditional sports, including NFL, MLB, and National Basketball Association (NBA) games. But it also does something unique: It telecasts the annual "X Games." Creating and then televising a series of nontraditional sports competitions similar to the Olympic Games have proved to be a lucrative strategy for the network, which pays a reported $600 million each year for football games, $400 million for basketball games, and about $135 million for baseball. But ESPN doesn't pay a dime for the X Games because it owns the telecast rights to the games it created.

A decade ago, ESPN programmer Ron Semiao noticed that sports like skateboarding were appearing in TV ads—but there was no real media coverage of any organized events, which themselves were few and far between. So Semiao proposed that ESPN host an Olympics-style event—and telecast it. While a handful of executives were skeptical, ESPN decided to give it a try. The first Extreme Games, as they were then called, were held in Providence and Newport, Rhode Island, in 1995. Competitors launched themselves through such fringe activities as kite-skiing, bungee jumping, and, of course, skateboarding. Mountain Dew was one of the original sponsors, hoping to reach the 33 million teenage consumers in the U.S. who wield an impressive $175 billion in buying power. Two years after the first "summer" games took place, ESPN added the "winter" games. Today, the winter athletes compete on everything from snowboards to snowmobiles, motorbikes, and even skis.

After 1995, the Extreme Games became the X Games, and a few of the weirder sports were dropped. Super Modified Shovel Racing never gained wide appeal, perhaps because racers had to plummet down a snow slope at speeds of up to 70 mph—while sitting on a shovel. Kite skiing (a combination of parasailing and water-skiing) was dropped after one contestant was blown off course along the seacoast of Rhode Island and had to catch a cab back to the event. Bungee jumping was eventually determined not to be a "real" sport. And street luge, while exciting, was nearly impossible to practice on a regular basis.

All the while, ESPN has been enjoying the success of the X Games. One recent summer, more than 50 million viewers tuned in to at least part of the Summer X Games, and about 37 million watched the Winter X Games. That's good news for both ESPN and its advertisers. Mountain Dew continues as a major sponsor, and other firms like electronics giant Sony have signed on in an effort to reach young consumers. As the X Games and action sports grow, the event's prize purse also grows, and action sports athletes also gain more visibility worldwide and have more opportunities for sponsorship deals. In the next few years, ESPN marketers will be learning how to strategize with action sports athletes just as if they were a real team.[1]

Chapter Overview

- More and more women are buying trucks. Should we add features to our trucks that are designed specifically for our female customers?
- We have fewer customers eating at our restaurant on weekends. Should we revamp our menu? Lower our prices? Use special promotions? Update the dining room décor?
- Recent marketing research shows we are not reaching our customer target—consumers in their early to mid-20s. Should we consider another advertising agency?

MARKETERS face strategic questions every day—it's part of the job. The marketplace changes continually in response to changes in consumer tastes and expectations, technological developments, competitors' actions, economic trends, and political and legal events, as well as product innovations and pressures from channel members. Although the causes of these changes often lie outside a marketer's control, effective planning can anticipate many of the changes. ESPN created an effective plan to deal with changes in the sports viewing marketplace—and came up with a hit.

If a man watches three football games in a row, he should be declared legally dead.

Erma Bombeck
(1927–1996)
American writer and humorist

This chapter provides an important foundation for analyzing all aspects of marketing by demonstrating the importance of gathering reliable information to create an effective plan. These activities provide a structure for a firm to use its unique strengths. Marketing planning identifies the markets a company can best serve as well as the most appropriate mix of approaches to satisfy the customers in those markets. While this chapter focuses on planning, we will examine in greater detail the task of marketing research and decision making in Chapter 8.

MARKETING PLANNING: THE BASIS FOR STRATEGY AND TACTICS

planning Process of anticipating future events and conditions and of determining the best way to achieve organizational goals.

Plans are nothing; planning is everything.

Dwight D. Eisenhower
(1890–1969)
34th president of the United States

Everyone plans. We plan which courses we want to take, which movie we want to see, and which outfit to wear to a party. We plan where we want to live and what career we want to pursue. Marketers engage in planning as well. **Planning** is the process of anticipating future events and conditions and of determining the best way to achieve organizational objectives. Of course, before marketing planning can even begin, an organization must define its objectives. Planning is a continuous process that includes identifying objectives and then determining the actions through which a firm can attain those objectives. The planning process creates a blueprint for marketers, executives, production staff, and everyone else in the organization to follow for achieving organizational objectives. It also defines checkpoints so that people within the organization can compare actual performance with expectations to indicate whether current activities are moving the organization toward its objectives.

Planning is important both for large and small companies. Because of the millions of dollars required to bring a new automobile to market, auto manufacturers engage in all kinds of planning activities. Chrysler recently spent $400 million updating its Town & Country minivan, including the addition of its new "Stow and Go" technology, which makes it even easier for consumers to change the seating arrangement in the van—using collapsible rear seats that fold away smoothly in the floor—and by offering a tailgate seating option. As part of the planning process, auto companies also build "concept" cars—vehicles not yet ready for the marketplace—that they display and demonstrate at shows like the annual International Auto Show. If enough consumers express interest in the car—for instance, by voting online—the car will be built for the marketplace. Mazda recently introduced a concept minivan called the Flexa, in which adventurous travelers can hang their mountain bikes from the ceiling inside the vehicle.[2]

At the other end of the size spectrum, Jennifer Melton and Brennan Johnson started their business, called Cloud Star Corp., with a simple plan. Jennifer began making her German shepherd's food at home when she realized her pet had severe allergies to commercial dog foods. Recognizing that other dogs had similar diet problems, Melton and Johnson developed their own line of bake-at-home dog treats that were free of many of the ingredients often found in commercial foods. Within a few years, they added dog shampoos and conditioners to their product line. They based much of their planning on feedback from customers. "Most of our growth and our decisions for which area we wanted to go into have been from listening to our customers and what they want from us," explains Melton.[3]

Briefly Speaking

Someone's sitting in the shade today because someone planted a tree a long time ago.

Warren E. Buffett (b. 1930)
American investor

Marketing planning—implementing planning activities devoted to achieving marketing objectives—establishes the basis for any marketing strategy. Product lines, pricing decisions, selection of appropriate distribution channels, and decisions relating to promotional campaigns all depend on plans formulated within the marketing organization.

marketing planning Implementing planning activities devoted to achieving marketing objectives.

An important trend in marketing planning centers on relationship marketing, which is a firm's effort toward developing long-term, cost-effective links with individual customers and suppliers for mutual benefit. Good relationships with customers can arm a firm with vital strategic weapons. Many companies now include relationship-building goals and strategies in their plans. Relationship marketers frequently maintain databases to track customer preferences. These marketers may also manipulate product spreadsheets to answer what-if questions related to prices and marketing performance. In the business-to-business marketplace, firms such as Canadian communications giant Nortel Networks offer technology designed to help other companies plan and execute strategies they will use to achieve product objectives. In doing so, Nortel Networks develops relationships with its customers, as illustrated in Figure 2.1.

STRATEGIC PLANNING VERSUS TACTICAL PLANNING

① **Distinguish between strategic planning and tactical planning.**

Planning is often classified on the basis of its scope or breadth. Some extremely broad plans focus on long-range organizational objectives that will significantly affect the firm for a period of five or more years. Other more targeted plans cover the objectives of individual business units over shorter periods of time.

Strategic planning can be defined as the process of determining an organization's primary objectives and then adopting courses of action that will eventually achieve these objectives. This process includes, of course, allocation of necessary resources. The word *strategy* dates back to a Greek term meaning "the general's art." Strategic planning has a critical impact on a firm's destiny because it provides long-term direction for its decision makers.

strategic planning Process of determining an organization's primary objectives and adopting courses of action that will achieve these objectives.

Strategic planning is complemented by **tactical planning,** which guides the implementation of activities specified in the strategic plan. Unlike strategic plans, tactical plans typically address shorter term actions that focus on current and near-future activities that a firm must complete to implement its larger strategies. In its strategy to gain ground in the diaper wars, Procter & Gamble once employed two tried-and-true tactics against competitor Kimberly-Clark: P&G convinced retailers to cut prices on packages of Pampers *and* launched a campaign showing that Pampers packages contained more diapers than packages of Kimberly-Clark's Huggies. Meanwhile, Kimberly-Clark had essentially instituted a price hike for Huggies by cutting the number of diapers in its packages. P&G's tactic worked. The firm's market share rose, while Kimberly-Clark's dropped. This also illustrates how mistakes in strategic decisions and in tactical planning can be costly.[4]

tactical planning Planning that guides the implementation of activities specified in the strategic plan.

PLANNING AT DIFFERENT ORGANIZATIONAL LEVELS

② **Explain how marketing plans differ at various levels in an organization.**

Planning is a major responsibility for every manager, so managers at all organizational levels devote portions of their workdays to planning. However, the amount of time spent on planning activities and the types of planning typically vary.

figure 2.1

Nortel Networks: Helping Other Companies Plan Their Computer Networks

Top management—the board of directors, chief executive officers (CEOs), chief operating officers (COOs), and functional vice presidents, such as chief marketing officers—spend greater proportions of their time engaged in planning than do middle-level and supervisory-level managers. Also, top managers usually focus their planning activities on long-range strategic issues. In contrast, middle-level managers—such as advertising executives, regional sales managers, and marketing research directors—tend to focus on operational planning, which includes creating and implementing tactical plans for their own units. Supervisors often engage in developing specific programs to meet goals in their areas of responsibility. Table 2.1 summarizes the types of planning undertaken at various organizational levels.

To be most effective, the planning process includes input from a wide range of sources: employees, suppliers, and customers. Some marketing experts advocate developing a network of "influencers"—people who have influence over other people's opinions through authority, visibility, or expertise—to provide input and spread the word about company plans and products.[5] But valuable input can come from almost anywhere. General Electric CEO Jeffrey Immelt believes that his $132 billion company can use some of its own proven best practices to enhance customer and supplier relationships and improve processes. One of the most fundamental of those practices is sharing information. Managers and suppliers share information on productivity innovations; GE offers free information exchange about global markets such as India and China; and customers can access some market information and research data.[6]

1. Define *planning.*
2. Give an example of strategic planning and tactical planning.

STEPS IN THE MARKETING PLANNING PROCESS

③ **Identify the steps in the marketing planning process.**

The marketing planning process begins at the corporate level with the definition of a firm's mission. It then determines its objectives, assesses its resources, and evaluates environmental risks and opportunities. Guided by this information, marketers within each business unit then formulate a marketing strategy, implement the strategy through operating plans, and gather feedback to monitor and adapt strategies when necessary. Figure 2.2 shows the basic steps in the process.

DEFINING THE ORGANIZATION'S MISSION AND OBJECTIVES

mission Essential purpose that differentiates one company from others.

The planning process begins with activities to define the firm's **mission,** the essential purpose that differentiates the company from others. The mission statement specifies the organization's overall goals and operational scope and provides general guidelines for future management actions. Adjustments in this statement reflect changing business environments and management philosophies.

Although business writer Peter Drucker cautions that an effective mission statement should be brief enough "to fit on a T-shirt," companies typically define themselves with slightly longer statements. A statement may be lengthy and formal or brief and informal. Here are several examples:

Bass Pro Shops: "To be the leading merchant of outdoor recreational products, inspiring people to love, enjoy, and conserve the great outdoors."[7]

Ritz-Carlton Hotels: "To be regarded as the quality and market leader of the hotel industry worldwide. We are responsible for creating exceptional, profitable results with the investments entrusted to us by efficiently satisfying customers."[8]

table 2.1 *Planning at Different Managerial Levels*

MANAGEMENT LEVEL	TYPES OF PLANNING EMPHASIZED AT THIS LEVEL	EXAMPLES
Top Management		
Board of directors	Strategic planning	Organization-wide objectives; fundamental strategies; long-term plans; total budget
Chief executive officer (CEO)		
Chief operating officer (COO)		
Divisional vice presidents		
Middle Management		
General sales manager	Tactical planning	Quarterly and semiannual plans; divisional budgets; divisional policies and procedures
Business unit manager		
Director of marketing research		
Supervisory Management		
Zone sales manager	Operational planning	Daily and weekly plans; unit budgets; departmental rules and procedures
Supervisor—telemarketing office		

Briefly Speaking

We're in the second inning of a nine-inning game. We are just beginning to tap into all sorts of new markets, customers, and products.

Howard Schultz (b. 1953)
CEO, Starbucks Corp.

National Collegiate Athletic Association (NCAA): "The NCAA strives to maintain intercollegiate athletics as an integral part of the educational program and the athlete as an integral part of the student body."[9]

Kellogg's: "We build great brands and make the world a little happier by bringing our best to you."[10]

An organization lays out its basic **objectives,** or goals, in its complete mission statement. These objectives in turn guide development of supporting marketing objectives and plans. Soundly conceived objectives should state specific intentions such as the following:

- Generate a 10 percent profit over the next 12 months.
- Attain a 20 percent share of the market by 2010.
- Add 50 new stores within the next year.
- Develop 12 new products in 24 months.

Briefly Speaking

One minor invention every ten days, a major invention every six months.

Thomas A. Edison (1847–1931)
Inventor of the phonograph, incandescent lightbulb, and more

figure 2.2
The Marketing Planning Process

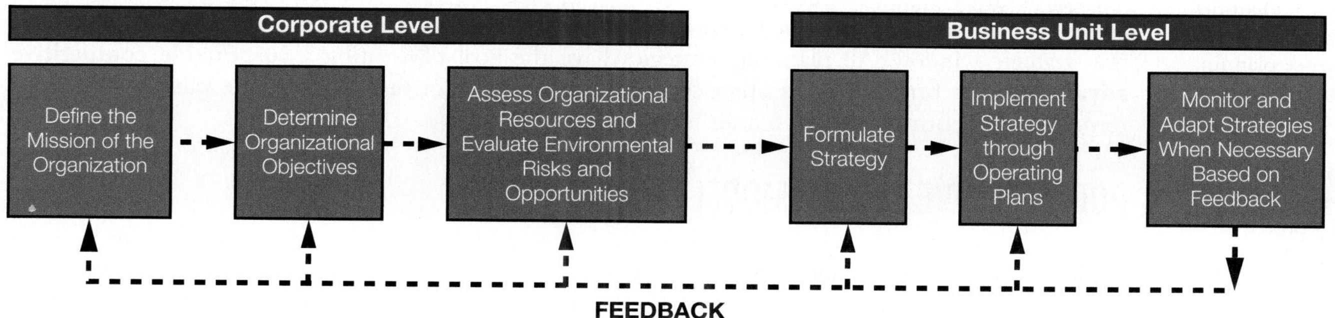

ASSESSING ORGANIZATIONAL RESOURCES AND EVALUATING ENVIRONMENTAL RISKS AND OPPORTUNITIES

The third step of the marketing planning process involves an assessment of an organization's strengths, weaknesses, and available opportunities. Organizational resources include the capabilities of the firm's production, marketing, finance, technology, and employees. An organization's planners pinpoint its strengths and weaknesses. Strengths help them to set objectives, develop plans for meeting those objectives, and take advantage of marketing opportunities.

Chapter 3 will discuss environmental factors that affect marketing opportunities. Environmental effects can emerge both from within the organization and from the external environment. For example, the technological advances provided by the Internet have transformed the way people communicate and do business around the world. In fact, the Internet itself has created entirely new categories of business.

marketing strategy Overall, companywide program for selecting a particular target market and then satisfying consumers in that market through the marketing mix.

FORMULATING, IMPLEMENTING, AND MONITORING A MARKETING STRATEGY

Once a firm's marketers figure out their company's best opportunities, they can develop a marketing plan designed to meet the overall objectives. A good marketing plan revolves around an efficient, flexible, and adaptable marketing strategy.

A **marketing strategy** is an overall, companywide program for selecting a particular target market and then satisfying consumers in that market through a careful blending of the elements of the marketing mix—product, distribution, promotion, and price—each of which is a subset of the overall marketing strategy.

1. Distinguish between an organization's mission and its objectives.
2. What is the importance of the final step in the marketing planning process?

In the two final steps of the planning process, marketers put the marketing strategy into action; then they monitor performance to ensure that objectives are being achieved. Sometimes strategies need to be modified if the product's or company's actual performance is not in line with expected results. When McDonald's introduced its Supersize portions, the firm's marketers certainly thought they had a hit. Offering consumers more of something they already enjoyed looked like the perfect opportunity to increase sales. Today, consumer tastes have changed—instead of asking for a larger serving of fries, they are requesting salads and yogurt. A documentary called *Super Size Me*, which criticized the supersize portioning, and a few attempted lawsuits against the company claiming health risks associated with eating Big Macs and Chicken McNuggets pointed out weaknesses in the firm's menu. So in a new era of concern about overeating, obesity, and minimizing carbohydrate intake, McDonald's began to phase out the Supersize program and phase in its new "Eat Smart, Be Active" marketing program. McDonald's fans will still find their favorites on the new menu—in traditional small, medium, and large sizes. But they'll also be able to buy fruit, yogurt, and salads.[11]

4 **Describe successful planning tools and techniques, including Porter's Five Forces model, first and second mover strategies, SWOT analysis, and the strategic window.**

Porter's Five Forces Model developed by strategy expert Michael Porter, which identifies five competitive forces that influence planning strategies: the threat of new entrants, the threat of substitute products, rivalry among competitors, the bargaining power of buyers, and the bargaining power of suppliers.

SUCCESSFUL STRATEGIES: TOOLS AND TECHNIQUES

We can identify a number of successful marketing planning tools and techniques. This section discusses four of them: Porter's Five Forces model, first and second mover strategies, SWOT analysis, and the strategic window. All planning strategies have the goal of creating a **sustainable competitive advantage** for a firm, in which other companies simply cannot provide the same value to their customers that the firm does—no matter how hard they try.

PORTER'S FIVE FORCES MODEL

A number of years ago, the renowned business strategist and one of the world's best-known business academics Michael E. Porter identified five competitive forces that influence planning strategies in a model called **Porter's Five Forces.** Recently, Porter updated his model to include the impact of the

figure 2.3

Porter's Five Forces Model

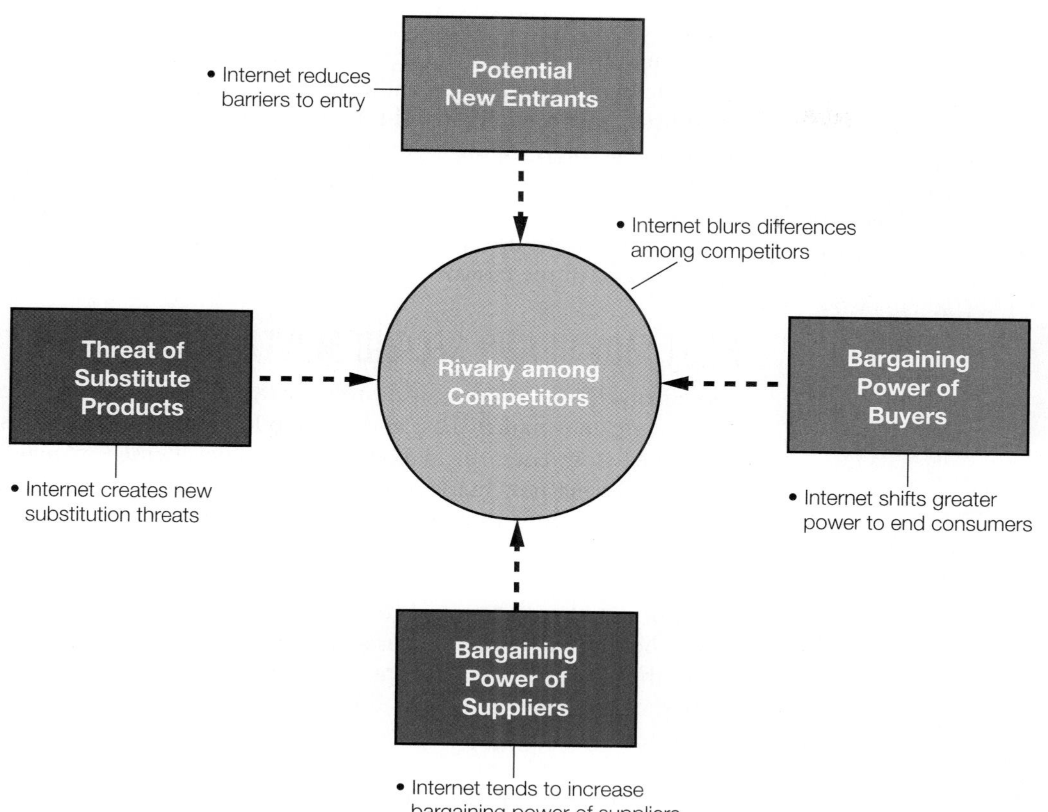

Source: Adapted with permission of The Free Press, a division of Simon & Schuster Adult Publishing Group. From *Competitive Strategy: Techniques for Analyzing Industries and Competitors* by Michael E. Porter. Copyright © 1980, 1998 by The Free Press. All rights reserved.

Internet on the strategies that businesses use. As illustrated by Figure 2.3, the five forces are potential new entrants; bargaining power of buyers; bargaining power of suppliers; threat of substitute products; and rivalry among competitors.

Potential new entrants are sometimes blocked by the cost or difficulty of entering a market. It is a lot more costly and complicated to begin building aircraft than it is to start up an Internet résumé service. In fact, the Internet has reduced the barriers to market entry in many industries.

If customers have considerable bargaining power, they can greatly influence a firm's strategy. The Internet can increase a customer's buying power by providing information that might not otherwise be easily accessible such as supplier alternatives and price comparisons. Currently, a heated debate is taking place over whether U.S. consumers should be able to buy prescription drugs from pharmacies in Canada, where prices are significantly lower.[12] Previously, U.S. consumers purchased all their prescription drugs in this country, where drug manufacturers controlled prices. Now consumers are accessing Canadian online sites, such as CanadaMeds.com and RxNorth.com, or simply driving across the border into Canada—while enforcement agencies look the other way for the time being. This has become a particularly hot issue among seniors and those who live in states that border Canada.

The number of available suppliers to a manufacturer or retailer affects their bargaining power. If a seafood restaurant in the Midwest has only one supplier of Maine lobsters, that supplier has significant bargaining power. But seafood restaurants located along the coast of Maine have many lobster suppliers available, which gives their suppliers less bargaining power.

If customers have the opportunity to replace a company's products with the goods or services from a competing firm or industry, the company's marketers may have to take steps to find a new market, change prices, or compete in other ways to maintain an advantage. When consumers began to be concerned about the amount of sugar in their diets, the sugar industry suffered from the introduction of substitutes like Equal and Splenda. And when news reports questioned the safety of sugar substitutes,

figure 2.4

Equal Sweetener: Fighting the Threat of Substitute Products

Equal countered with promotional messages like the one in Figure 2.4, citing the support of several large health organizations.

The four previous forces influence the rivalry among competitors. In addition, issues like cost and the differentiation or lack of differentiation of products—along with the Internet—influence the strategies that companies use to stand out from their competitors. With the increased availability of information, which tends to level the playing field, rivalry heats up among competitors, who try to differentiate themselves from the crowd.

FIRST MOVER AND SECOND MOVER STRATEGIES

Some firms like to adopt a **first mover strategy**—attempting to capture the greatest market share and develop long-term relationships by being the first to enter the market with a product. Being first may also refer to entering new markets with existing products or creating significant innovations that effectively turn an old product into a new one. Naturally, this strategy has its risks—companies that follow can learn from mistakes by first movers. The online auction site eBay was a first mover that has proved to be enormously successful. Not only was it the first such site, but it is still the most profitable e-commerce site in the world.[13] Amazon.com, which made its name as the world's leading online seller of heavily discounted books, recently expanded into a new retailing category: jewelry. The firm's Web site now offers everything from a $45 freshwater-cultured pearl bracelet to a $93,000 diamond-bedecked platinum radiant-cut necklace.[14] On the other hand, Apple—which has successfully adopted the first mover strategy in many instances—failed terribly with its Newton handheld computer. Firms such as Microsoft thrive on a **second mover strategy**, observing closely the innovations of first movers and then improving on them to gain advantage in the marketplace.

first mover strategy Theory advocating that the company that is first to offer a product in a marketplace will be the long-term market winner.

SWOT ANALYSIS

An important strategic planning tool, **SWOT analysis**, helps planners compare internal organizational strengths and weaknesses with external opportunities and threats. (SWOT is an acronym for **s**trengths, **w**eaknesses, **o**pportunities, and **t**hreats.) This form of analysis provides managers with a critical view of the organization's internal and external environments and helps them evaluate the firm's fulfillment of its basic mission.

marketing miss — Target's New Tactic: Stocking Its Shelves with Food

Background. You've heard of Wal-Mart Supercenter stores—they sell everything from auto parts to groceries. As part of its overall strategy to grow and to compete with Wal-Mart, Target recently started opening its own SuperTarget stores, adding groceries to its retail offerings.

The Marketing Problem. Target has already achieved success with the goods it offers consumers, particularly in fashion. The firm has managed to be a hit by filling its clothing racks and houseware shelves with cool names such as Mossimo, Isaac Mizrahi, and Michael Graves—at affordable prices. But how can a company compete if it doesn't expand? So Target created SuperTargets that contain grocery sections, complete with free samples of roast beef and exotic cheeses, along with fresh-daily sushi and gourmet bread.

The Outcome. Some say Target's grocery sections haven't lived up to expectations, largely because consumers prefer to buy food at their own supermarkets. Supermarket chains—and Wal-Mart—are

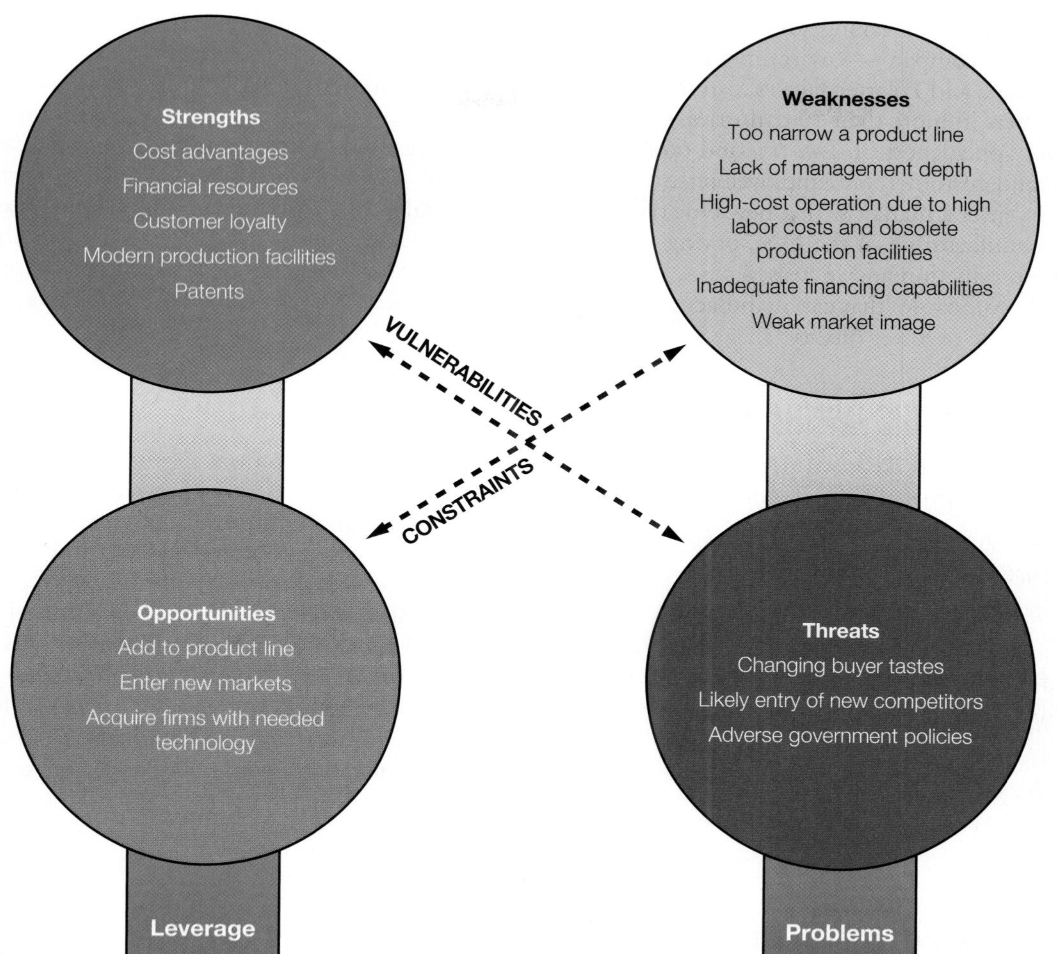

figure 2.5
SWOT Analysis

second mover strategy Theory that advocates observing closely the innovations of first movers and then introducing new products that improve on the original offering to gain advantage in the marketplace.

SWOT analysis Analysis that helps planners compare internal organizational strengths and weaknesses with external opportunities and threats.

A company's strengths reflect its **core competencies**—what it does well. Core competencies are capabilities that customers value and competitors find difficult to duplicate. However, if a company drifts too far from the things it does well, it can stumble, as described in the "Marketing Miss" feature.

As Figure 2.5 shows, matching an internal strength with an external opportunity produces a situation known as *leverage*. Marketers face a problem when environmental threats attack their organization's weaknesses. Planners anticipate constraints when internal weaknesses or limitations prevent their

able to offer better prices, greater selection, and usually a shorter drive to the store. SuperTargets are spread out geographically—there just aren't enough of them—and many are located in congested urban areas where parking is scarce and expenses are high. Although Target claims that its superstores are raking in sales 50 to 100 percent higher than its standard stores, those figures still aren't high enough to compete with Wal-Mart or the supermarket chains.

Lessons Learned. Although a growth strategy is good for a company, not every tactic is successful. Target's core customers are young women with small children who want high fashion, housewares, and other items at low prices. They don't necessarily care about gourmet food, but they want to buy their groceries at the best prices as well. And they need convenience; they don't have the time to drive great distances to do their grocery shopping. So it appears that Target has missed the bulls' eye with this tactic. It may be time to load the quiver with another batch of arrows—and another plan.

Sources: David Ghitelman, "Target Injects Fashion into Food Retailing," *Supermarket News,* December 1, 2003, http://infotrac-college.thomsonlearning.com; "Hallmark of Target's Success," *MMR,* August 25, 2003, http://infotrac-college.thomsonlearning.com; Robert Berner et al., "Has Target's Food Foray Missed the Mark?" *BusinessWeek,* November 25, 2002, p. 76.

organization from taking advantage of opportunities. These internal weaknesses can create vulnerabilities for a company—environmental threats to its organizational strength. Malden Mills, maker of Polarfleece and Polartec fabrics, can identify several strengths: 200 percent growth in the past decade; customers in more than 50 countries; U.S. factory operations; high visibility, with personal profiles in *People,* appearances on *Dateline* and *60 Minutes,* and products listed in the Lands' End and REI catalogs; and customer and employee retention above 95 percent. Opportunities have included being the first to enter a market with a new type of high-performance fabric. Its weaknesses have included keeping manufacturing in the U.S., paying workers higher wages, and a devastating factory fire that shut down production and increased costs. A major threat has appeared in the form of increased competition by companies that can manufacture products at a lower cost, although competitors' products may prove to be of lower quality.[15]

strategic window Limited periods during which the key requirements of a market and the particular competencies of a firm best fit together.

THE STRATEGIC WINDOW

The success of products is also influenced by conditions in the market. Professor Derek Abell has suggested the term **strategic window** to define the limited periods during which the key requirements of a market and the particular competencies of a firm best fit together.[16] The view through a strategic window shows planners a way to relate potential opportunities to company capabilities. Such a view requires a thorough analysis of (1) current and projected external environmental conditions, (2) current and projected internal company capabilities, and (3) how, whether, and when the firm can feasibly reconcile environmental conditions and company capabilities by implementing one or more marketing strategies.

1. **Briefly explain each of Porter's Five Forces.**
2. **What are the benefits and drawbacks of a first mover strategy?**
3. **What are the four components of the SWOT analysis? What is a strategic window?**

(5) **Identify the basic elements of a marketing strategy.**

ELEMENTS OF A MARKETING STRATEGY

Success for a product in the marketplace—whether it is a tangible good, a service, a cause, a person, a place, or an organization—depends on an effective marketing strategy. It's one thing to develop a great product, but if customers don't get the message about it, the product will die. An effective marketing strategy reaches the right buyers at the right time, convinces them to try the product, and develops a strong relationship with them over time. The basic elements of a marketing strategy consist of (1) the target market and (2) the marketing mix variables of product, distribution, promotion, and price that combine to satisfy the needs of the target market. The outer circle in Figure 2.6 lists environmental characteristics that provide the framework within which marketing strategies are planned.

figure 2.6

Elements of a Marketing Strategy and Its Environmental Framework

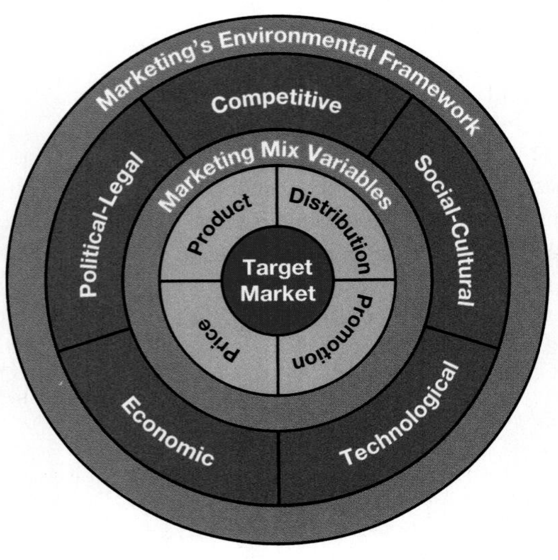

THE TARGET MARKET

A customer-driven organization begins its overall strategy with a detailed description of its **target market:** the group of people toward whom the firm decides to direct its marketing efforts and ultimately its merchandise. Kohl's department stores serve a target market consisting of consumers purchasing for themselves and their families. Other companies, such as Boeing, market most of their products to business buyers like American Airlines and government purchasers. Still other firms provide goods and services to retail and wholesale buyers. In every instance, however, marketers pinpoint their target markets as accurately as possible. Although the concept of dividing markets into specific segments is discussed in more detail in Chapter 9, it's important to understand the idea of targeting a market from the outset. Consider the following examples:

- Just My Size targets plus-size women (who account for more than half of U.S. women) by designing casual wear, lingerie, hosiery, and jeans in sizes 16 and up.

- Solutionz, founded and run by college business student Kirk Fernandez, targets businesses, schools, and government agencies that need conferencing solutions, which his company offers. He got the idea for his business after attending some videoconferencing trade shows and realizing that there was no market leader providing these technologies to organizations.[17]

Diversity plays an ever-increasing role in targeting markets. According to the U.S. Census Bureau, the rapidly growing Hispanic population in the U.S. has now surpassed African Americans. The census reports about 40 million Hispanics in America, an increase of 58 percent over the last decade. With this phenomenal growth, marketers would be wise to pay attention to these and other markets—including women, seniors, and children of baby boomers—as they develop goods and services to offer consumers. Wal-Mart has been targeting the Hispanic market both in the U.S. and just across the border in Mexico, where it owns 607 retail stores.[18]

Timberland, which manufactures boots and outdoor clothing, has been spending more time and effort developing and marketing its products to women instead of focusing mostly on men. For the past few years, a team of six women has reworked the Timberland product line to appeal more to women. New styles include a series of soft leather driving moccasins called the Chauffeur and a grouping of traditional loafers called The New Hampshire Collection (where its headquarters are). "We took the notion of Timberland and the inspiration of outdoors, but made the product more stylish and feminine," explains Meredith Collura Applegate, marketing manager for women's casual footwear at Timberland.[19]

Stouffer's Lean Cuisine targets health- and weight-conscious consumers. This ad, and the new packaging, also takes advantage of an opportunity in the marketplace—the trend toward limiting carbohydrates in the daily diet.

America is not like a blanket—one piece of unbroken cloth, the same color, the same texture, the same size. America is more like a quilt—many pieces, many colors, many sizes, all woven and held together by a common thread.

Rev. Jesse Jackson
(b. 1941)
American civil rights leader

MARKETING MIX VARIABLES

After marketers select a target market, they direct their company's activities toward profitably satisfying that segment. Although they must manipulate thousands of variables to reach this goal, marketing decision making can be divided into four strategies: product, distribution, promotion, and pricing strategies. The total package forms the **marketing mix**—the blending of the four strategic elements to fit the needs and preferences of a specific target market. While the fourfold classification is useful to study and analyze, remember that the marketing mix can—and should—be an ever-changing combination of variables to achieve success.

Figure 2.6 illustrates the focus of the marketing mix variables on the central choice of the target market. In addition, decisions about product, distribution, promotion, and price are affected by the environmental factors in the outer circle of the figure. The environmental variables may play a major role in the success of a marketing program, and marketers must consider their probable effects.

marketing mix Blending of the four strategy elements—product, distribution, promotion, and pricing—to fit the needs and preferences of a specific target market.

Product Strategy

In marketing, the word *product* means more than a good, service, or idea. Product is a broad concept that also encompasses the satisfaction of all consumer needs in relation to a good, service, or idea. So

product strategy Decisions about what goods or services a firm will offer its customers; also includes decisions about customer service, packaging, brand names, and the like.

product strategy involves more than just deciding what goods or services the firm should offer to a group of consumers. It also includes decisions about customer service, package design, brand names, trademarks, patents, warranties, the life cycle of a product, positioning the product in the marketplace, and new-product development. The promotional message for Quaker Toastables in Figure 2.7 illustrates some of these elements. Quaker is a well-known, trademarked brand, and the packaging includes a photograph of a warm pastry filled with tasty fruit. Toastables are aimed at two market segments: busy parents who may not have time to cook a full breakfast, but who want their kids to eat something healthy before they leave for school, and kids who might otherwise skip breakfast or ask for a doughnut instead. The ad emphasizes Quaker's ability to provide high-quality, wholesome food fast in a "win-win" situation where everyone is satisfied.

The growing number of female business travelers has prompted the travel industry to modify its offerings by adding a number of services designed to increase satisfaction among women hotel guests. Based on suggestions by Wyndham Hotels & Resorts' Advisory Board of Women Business Travelers, the chain added a number of features in its product strategy:

- amenities such as loofah mitts and skirt hangers in hotel rooms
- networking tables set aside in hotel restaurants for solo travelers who prefer to eat with others
- a warning call five minutes before room-service delivery to alert guests before a meal is delivered
- jogging partners and, upon return from a run, chilled bottled water, fresh fruit, and plush towels.

This strategy lets Wyndham offer improved customer satisfaction for this growing market. As recently as 1970, women accounted for only 1 percent of all business travelers; today, the number has grown to 50 percent.[20]

distribution strategy Planning that ensures that consumers find their products in the proper quantities at the right times and places.

figure 2.7

Quaker: Using the Product and Promotional Strategies to Appeal to the Toastables Market

Distribution Strategy

Marketers develop **distribution strategies** to ensure that consumers find their products in the proper quantities at the right times and places. Distribution decisions involve modes of transportation, warehousing, inventory control, order processing, and selection of marketing channels. Marketing channels are made up of institutions such as retailers and wholesalers—intermediaries that may be involved in a product's movement from producer to final consumer.

Technology is opening new channels of distribution in many industries. Computer software, a product made of digital data files, is ideally suited to electronic distribution. But all kinds of other products are now bought and sold over the Internet as well. By affecting everything from warehousing to order processing, technology has made the success of Amazon.com and eBay possible. Although these firms operate differently, both rely on technology for various distribution tasks.[21]

Distribution is the perfect place for many companies to form alliances. Sony's music division formed an agreement with Universal Music Group to form Duet, an online music service that will make thousands of songs available to consumers legally over the Internet. Wal-Mart, discussed in more detail in Chapter 13, has been working with its suppliers to implement a new tracking and identification system called *radio frequency identification* (*RFID*), small computer chips which it places on pallets to track and identify products as they move from one location to another. The system reduces labor costs, helps prevent losses caused by out-of-stock items, and helps reduce the number of products lost to theft. But Wal-Mart's suppliers may have to spend as much as $13 million to $23 million to install the system and may not see results for a while.[22]

Promotional Strategy

Promotion is the communications link between sellers and buyers. Organizations use varied ways to send messages about their goods, services, and ideas. They may communicate messages directly through salespeople or indirectly through advertisements and promotions. Figure 2.8 shows a new promotion for a product that has been around since people first walked on earth: milk. The promotion links two ideas in a single marketing message: milk and losing weight. Tea is another ancient product that has been receiving renewed attention from marketers. Restaurants and shops are now promoting high-quality, specialty teas such as rooibos and white tea. Each tea has its own flavor and properties—one type of oolong supposedly suppresses the appetite, while rooibos contains a large concentration of cancer-fighting antioxidants. Establishments like Elaine's Tea Shoppe in Ohio attract customers by advertising custom blends such as UnWrinkle Me, a mixture of white teas that is supposed to improve the drinker's skin tone.[23]

In developing a promotional strategy, marketers blend the various elements of promotion to communicate most effectively with their target market. Many companies use an approach called **integrated marketing communications (IMC)** to coordinate all promotional activities so that the consumer receives a unified and consistent message. Consumers might receive newsletters, e-mail updates, discount coupons, catalogs, invitations to company-sponsored events, and any number of other types of marketing communications about a product. Toyota dealers mail maintenance and service reminders to their customers. Shaw's supermarkets places discount coupons in local newspapers. A political candidate may send volunteer workers through a neighborhood to invite voters to a special reception.

figure 2.8

Promoting the Healthful Benefits of Milk

Pricing Strategy

Pricing strategy deals with the methods of setting profitable and justifiable prices. It is closely regulated and subject to considerable public scrutiny. One of the many factors that influence a marketer's pricing strategy is competition. The computer industry has become all too familiar with price cuts by both current competitors and new market entrants. After years of steady growth, the market has become saturated with low-cost computers, driving down profit margins even farther. There's plenty of competition in the air travel and automobile manufacturing industries as well. Hyundai introduced the first 10-year, 100,000-mile warranty in the auto industry and routinely undersells both U.S. and Japanese-made vehicles. The Hyundai Santa Fe is priced around $18,000—about $5,000 to $10,000 less than SUVs made by Japanese and U.S. firms.[24] In the cell phone industry, competition is fierce. To attract customers, Sprint recently announced that users could tap into their lower cost evening minutes two hours earlier than had been previously allowed. Sprint customers who have plans starting at $35 can tap into their evening minutes for an extra $5 per month.[25]

A good pricing strategy should create value for customers, building and strengthening their relationship with a firm and its products. The promotional message in Figure 2.9 encourages consumers to imagine a watch stylish enough for a teen but durable enough for sports and then offers it to them for less than they expect. Customers get the product they need at a better-than-expected price, creating value.

promotion
Communications link between buyers and sellers. Function of informing, persuading, and influencing a consumer's purchase decision.

pricing strategy
Methods of setting profitable and justifiable prices.

THE MARKETING ENVIRONMENT

6 Describe the environmental characteristics that influence strategic decisions.

Marketers do not make decisions about target markets and marketing mix variables in a vacuum. They must take into account the dynamic nature of the five dimensions of the marketing environment shown back in Figure 2.6: competitive, political-legal, economic, technological, and social-cultural factors.

Concerns about the natural environment have led to new regulations concerning air and water pollution. Automobile engineers, for instance, have turned public concerns and legal issues into

figure 2.9

Timex: Offering Customers Style and Durability—at a Lower Price

opportunities by developing hybrid cars. These new models are fueled by dual energy: a gasoline engine and an electric motor. Toyota was the first to enter the market with its Prius, which depends on both an electric motor and a backup gasoline engine. Another product, the recently designed Electron Stream Carbon Dioxide Reduction system, zaps molecules of air pollution. This system could be marketed to coal-burning plants both in the U.S. and China.[26] Note that the marketing environment is fertile ground for innovators and entrepreneurs.

Businesses are increasingly looking to foreign shores for new growth markets. General Mills has been manufacturing everything from cereal to snack foods for decades—but largely for domestic markets. When the company wanted to expand overseas, instead of starting from scratch, it decided to partner with Nestlé in a venture called Cereal Partners Worldwide. General Mills was the cereal expert, and Nestlé already had a presence in Europe. So far, the strategy has been successful. Since its formation, CPW has expanded its operations into 75 different markets and captured 21 percent of the international cold cereal business.[27]

Technology has changed the marketing environment as well, partly with the advent of the Internet. Throughout this text, you will encounter examples of the ways the Internet and other technological developments are continuously altering how firms do business. And as technology forces these changes, other aspects of the environment must respond. Naturally, there are legal disputes over who owns which innovations. Amazon.com recently won a court battle barring its rival Barnes & Noble.com from using Amazon's patented "one-click" checkout system, which allows shoppers to place their orders with a single click of the mouse instead of rekeying billing information when they are ready to complete a sale. Interestingly, technology moves much more quickly than patenting procedures, which can leave some businesses behind. Amazon founder and chief executive Jeff Bezos has suggested that software and Internet patents should have a shorter life span than other patents—perhaps because of the rapid changes in technology—and that they should be open to public comment before being issued.

Competition is never far from the marketer's mind. In fact, some experts have coined the phrase **rule of three,** meaning that in any industry, the three strongest, most efficient companies dominate between 70 and 90 percent of the market. Here are a few examples—all of which are household names:

- *Fast-food restaurants:* McDonald's, Burger King, Wendy's
- *Cereal manufacturers:* General Mills, Kellogg's, Post
- *Running shoes:* Nike, Adidas, Reebok
- *Airlines:* American, United, Delta
- *Pharmaceuticals:* Merck, Pfizer, Bristol-Myers Squibb[28]

While it may seem like an uphill battle for the remaining hundreds of companies in any given industry, each of these firms can find a strategy for gaining competitive ground. In addition, the federal government keeps a close eye on companies that appear to be swallowing up the competition, as described in the "Solving an Ethical Controversy" feature.

In the highly competitive airline industry, discounters such as JetBlue and Southwest have managed to thrive when some of the larger airlines like USAirways have been pushed into bankruptcy. JetBlue appeals to value-oriented consumers—and delivers by offering services that the larger airlines have reduced or cut out altogether. JetBlue promises a friendly crew, large overhead bins for carry-on luggage, leather seating, and live satellite TV at every seat. Recently, JetBlue was rated by one survey as the No. 1 airline in the U.S. It's about "bringing humanity back to air travel," says CEO David G. Neeleman.[29]

If you are not No. 1 or No. 2 . . . fix it, sell it, or close it.

John F. Welch, Jr. (b. 1935)

retired chairman and CEO, General Electric

Solving an Ethical Controversy

ORACLE AND PEOPLESOFT: COMPETITION OR ANTITRUST?

COMPANIES are always jockeying for power in the marketplace. They employ any number of strategies to become the best, the biggest, the most popular. But sometimes their intentions are questioned by others, including the federal government, particularly when strategies include mergers and acquisitions. Recently, software giant Oracle made a $9.4 billion takeover bid for PeopleSoft. Both firms offer enterprise resource planning (ERP) software, which helps marketers and other managers operate efficiently and create strategic plans for their companies. PeopleSoft did not want to be acquired; Oracle kept pressing shareholders. The federal government took notice of the potential deal, viewing Oracle's move as anticompetitive—a move to take over a competitor to avoid increased competition. Oracle and its supporters argued that the move was necessary for the company to survive.

COULD THE PROPOSED TAKEOVER OF PEOPLESOFT BY ORACLE BE CONSIDERED AN ANTICOMPETITIVE STRATEGY?

PRO

1. According to some experts, the takeover would eliminate competition between the largest suppliers of ERP and financial management software. Only the newly formed company and another giant—SAP—would remain.
2. Customers in the software market want more choice. According to some sources, PeopleSoft customers have been afraid they would lose their choice of products.

CON

1. Software purchases are driven by customers' assessments of the best in the marketplace. Microsoft has a near monopoly in the personal computing market, but it still continues to improve its products.
2. Oracle needs the PeopleSoft acquisition to remain competitive. "Without PeopleSoft, Oracle will be marginalized," argues George Brown, president of Database Solutions.

SUMMARY

Although the takeover bid was unwanted, PeopleSoft has enjoyed a new twist in the story: Publicity about Oracle's move and the federal government's response has thrown PeopleSoft into the limelight, particularly in Europe. "One of the big things is a lot of companies, especially [in Europe], had never heard of us before," says PeopleSoft's chief technology officer Rick Bergquist. "Now, anyone who reads a newspaper has heard of us . . . Now, people see us as the developer of this hot technology that's more flexible [than the competition's], and Oracle wants this. It's given more people a chance to see our wares." PeopleSoft may be the winner after all, provided the antitrust case scheduled for trial in San Francisco federal court ultimately rules in its favor.

Sources: Stacey Cowley, "PeopleSoft CEO Blames Oracle for Poor Sales," *ComputerWeekly.com,* April 23, 2004, http://www.computerweekly.com; David Kirkpatrick, *Fortune,* March 22, 2004, http://www.fortune.com; Dennis Callaghan, "PeopleSoft CTO: Oracle Bid Put PeopleSoft on the Map," *eWeek,* March 18, 2004, http://news.yahoo.com; Jennifer Brown, "Antitrust Suit Marks Final Chapter," *Computing Canada,* March 12, 2004, pp. 1, 6; Barbara Darrow, "Feds Set Out to Sink Oracle's PeopleSoft Bid," *CRN,* March 1, 2004, p. 12.

The social-cultural environment includes a variety of factors, including cultural diversity. As a marketer, you will learn how to meet and talk with many different kinds of people from varying backgrounds. Whether you are naturally outgoing or shy, you can use some of the hints offered in the "Etiquette Tips for Marketing Professionals" feature to smooth the way through these interactions.

The marketing environment provides a framework for all marketing activity. Marketers consider environmental dimensions when they develop strategies for segmenting and targeting markets and when they study consumer and organizational buying behavior.

1. **What are the two components of every marketing strategy?**
2. **Identify the four strategic elements of the marketing mix.**
3. **What are the five dimensions of the marketing environment?**

ETIQUETTE TIPS — FOR MARKETING PROFESSIONALS

How to Network

IT'S tough to be smooth when you are nervous or uncertain in a situation, particularly if it's a business gathering where you hardly know anyone. You're afraid you will be tongue-tied or, worse, say the wrong thing. But as part of your strategy as a marketer, you want to show yourself at your very best. Suppose you find yourself at a dinner meeting, a conference, a reception, or a trade show. Before you get cold feet, take in a few of the following tips from the experts on how to socialize with customers, colleagues, and even competitors with ease. You, too, can network successfully in a crowd.

1. Before the event, try to learn as much as you can about the people who will be attending, particularly those you plan to meet.
2. Try not to carry a lot of excess baggage, such as a large purse or an overstuffed briefcase. That way, you are free to shake hands or to accept any informational material offered to you by a customer or potential employer.
3. Be aware of your body language. Stand up straight and don't fold your arms across your chest. If you appear more confident, you'll begin to feel that way, too.
4. Dress appropriately for the event—business attire for daytime meetings, perhaps a bit more relaxed for evening (but don't show up in party or clubbing clothes). Pay attention to good grooming.
5. Don't interrupt a conversation in progress. Instead, introduce yourself to someone who appears to be alone. Who knows? The person may turn out to be an important contact. Or ask a colleague who knows the person to introduce you. Wait for an appropriate moment to approach anyone else whom you feel you must meet.
6. Offer your handshake as you meet someone, even if you already know the person. Be sure to introduce yourself—or reintroduce yourself. Say why you are attending the event, and ask the person how he or she is enjoying the event. Listen to what the other person is saying; you are gathering information and developing a relationship.
7. When a conversation reaches its conclusion, be sure to thank the person for speaking with you, using his or her name. Tell him or her that you enjoyed the conversation. If appropriate, you may exchange business cards or other contact information.

Sources: "How to Work a Room," *Fox Business Insider*, http://www.sbm.temple.edu, accessed March 9, 2004; "Networking 101," *Massachusetts Institute of Technology*, http://web.mit.edu/career/www/workshops/networking/etiquette.htm, accessed March 9, 2004; "Networking Etiquette & Tactics," *Virtual Technocrats*, December 4, 2001, www.virtualtechnocrats.com, accessed March 9, 2004; Lydia Ramsey, "Etiquette Tip: Appearances Aren't Deceiving in Business," *Savannah Morning News*, October 13, 2001, http://www.savannahnow.com, accessed March 9, 2004.

(7) Describe the methods for marketing planning, including business portfolio analysis and the BCG matrix.

METHODS FOR MARKETING PLANNING

As growing numbers of companies have discovered the benefits of effective marketing planning, they have developed planning methods to assist in this important function. This section discusses two useful methods: the strategic business unit concept and the market share/market growth matrix.

BUSINESS PORTFOLIO ANALYSIS

Although a small company may offer only a few items to its customers, a larger organization frequently offers and markets many products to widely diverse markets. Bank of America offers a wide range of financial products to businesses and consumers; Kraft Foods stocks supermarket shelves with everything from macaroni and cheese to mayonnaise. Top managers at these larger firms need a method for spotting product lines that deserve more investment as well as lines that aren't living up to expectations. So they conduct a **portfolio analysis,** in which they evaluate their company's products and divisions, to determine which are strongest and which are weakest. Much like securities analysts review their portfolios of stocks and bonds, deciding which to retain and which to discard, marketing planners must perform the same assessment of their products, the regions in which they operate, and other marketing mix variables. This is where the concept of an SBU comes in.

Strategic business units (SBUs) are key business units within diversified firms. Each SBU has its own managers, resources, objectives, and competitors. A division, product line, or single product may define the boundaries of an SBU. Each SBU pursues its own distinct mission, and each develops its own plans independently of other units in the organization.

strategic business units (SBUs) Key business units within diversified firms.

Strategic business units, also called **categories,** focus the attention of company managers so that they can respond effectively to changing consumer demand within limited markets. Companies may have to redefine their SBUs as market conditions dictate. You might not think that a company devoted to building robots would have many SBUs. But iBot was launched more than a decade ago by two members of MIT's Artificial Intelligence Lab (Colin Angle and Helen Greiner) and its director, Rodney Brooks. Over the next decade, they hired engineers and built everything from industrial floor waxers to toy balls that "whimpered" when they were rolled into dark corners. Each project was so specific that it became a business unit. Over the years, the business units grew to 12, dwindled, and then grew again. Structuring the company this way was part of the founders' strategic plan to spread the risk. "We had our fingers in all these pies because we had no killer pie," explains CEO Colin Angle. "And we didn't know how to decide what a killer pie was other than to let Darwin do it. Focusing this company too early would have killed it." Eventually, they did come up with a "killer pie"—Roomba, the robotic vacuum, which recently appeared on the best-product lists of *Time, BusinessWeek,* and *USA Today.*[30]

THE BCG MATRIX

To evaluate each of their organization's strategic business units, marketers need some type of portfolio performance framework. A widely used framework was developed by the Boston Consulting Group. This **market share/market growth matrix** places SBUs in a four-quadrant chart that plots market share—the percentage of a market that a firm controls—against market growth potential. The position of an SBU along the horizontal axis indicates its market share relative to those of competitors in the industry. Its position along the vertical axis indicates the annual growth rate of the market. After plotting all of a firm's business units, planners divide them according to the matrix's four quadrants. Figure 2.10 illustrates this matrix by labeling the four quadrants cash cows, stars, dogs, and question marks. Firms in each quadrant require a unique marketing strategy.

Stars represent units with high market shares in high-growth markets. These products or businesses are high-growth market leaders. Although they generate considerable income, they need inflows of even more cash to finance further growth. Apple's popular iPod is the No. 1 selling portable digital music player in the world, but because of rapidly changing technology, Apple will have to continue to invest in ways to update and upgrade the player.[31]

Cash cows command high market shares in low-growth markets. Marketers for such an SBU want to maintain this status for as long as possible. The business produces strong cash flows, but instead of investing heavily in the unit's own promotions and production capacity, the firm can use this cash to finance the growth of other SBUs with higher growth potentials.

Question marks achieve low market shares in high-growth markets. Marketers must decide whether to continue supporting these products or businesses since question marks typically require considerably more cash than they generate. If a question mark cannot become a star, the firm should pull out of the market and target other markets with greater potential. So far, Apple's online iTunes Music Store hasn't turned a profit, but it is an important factor in the success of iPod, selling millions of songs to music buffs. In addition, Apple has signed a deal with Hewlett-Packard (HP) to sell iPods and load iTunes into millions of PCs manufactured by HP. So iTunes could transform itself from a question mark to a star.[32]

figure 2.10

BCG Market Share/Market Growth Matrix

Industry Growth Rate \ Relative Market Share	High	Low
High	**Stars** Generate considerable income **Strategy:** Invest more funds for future growth	**Question Marks** Have potential to become stars or cash cows **Strategy:** Either invest more funds for growth or consider disinvesting
Low	**Cash Cows** Generate strong cash flow **Strategy:** Milk profits to finance growth of stars and question marks	**Dogs** Generate little profits **Strategy:** Consider withdrawing

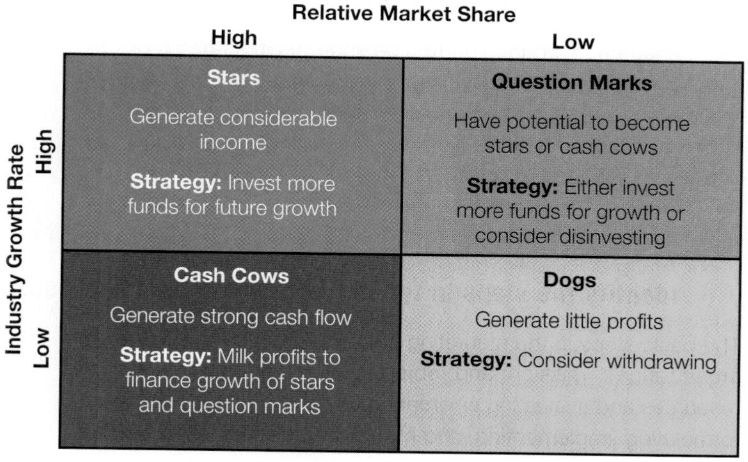

1. What are SBUs?
2. Identify the four quadrants in the BCG matrix.

Dogs manage only low market shares in low-growth markets. SBUs in this category promise poor future prospects, and marketers should withdraw from these businesses or product lines as quickly as possible. In some cases, these products can be sold to other firms, where they are a better fit.

Strategic Implications of Marketing in the 21st Century

NEVER before has planning been as important to marketers as the 21st century speeds ahead with technological advances. Marketers need to plan carefully, accurately, and quickly if their companies are to gain a competitive advantage in today's global marketplace. They need to define their organization's mission and understand the different methods for formulating a successful marketing strategy. They must consider a changing, diverse population and the boundaryless business environment created by the Internet. They must be able to evaluate when it's best to be first to get into a market and when it's best to wait. They need to recognize when they've got a star and when they've got a dog; when to hang on and when to let go. As daunting as this seems, planning can reduce the risk and worry of bringing new goods and services to the marketplace. ◆◆◆

REVIEW OF CHAPTER OBJECTIVES

① Distinguish between strategic planning and tactical planning.

Strategic planning is the process of identifying an organization's primary objectives and adopting courses of action toward these objectives. Tactical planning guides the implementation of the activities specified in the strategic plan.

1.1. State whether each of the following illustrates strategic or tactical planning:
   a. Wal-Mart decides to enter the Japanese market.
   b. A local bakery decides to add coffee to its list of offerings.

② Explain how marketing plans differ at various levels in an organization.

Top management spends more time engaged in strategic planning than do middle- and supervisory-level managers, who tend to focus on narrower, tactical plans for their units. Supervisory managers are more likely to engage in developing specific plans designed to meet the goals assigned to them.

2.1. Summarize in one or two sentences a strategic plan that a top manager in a business unit might be involved with.
2.2. State in a sentence or two a related tactical plan that a middle-level manager might focus on.

③ Identify the steps in the marketing planning process.

The basic steps in the marketing planning process are defining the organization's mission and objectives, assessing organizational resources and evaluating environmental risk and opportunities, and formulating, implementing, and monitoring the marketing strategy.

3.1. What is the difference between a firm's mission and its objectives?
3.2. Define *marketing strategy.*

(4) Describe successful planning tools and techniques, including Porter's Five Forces model, first and second mover strategies, SWOT analysis, and the strategic window.

Porter's Five Forces are identified as the five competitive factors that influence planning strategies: potential new entrants; bargaining power of buyers; bargaining power of suppliers; threat of substitute products; and rivalry among competitors. With a first mover strategy, a firm attempts to capture the greatest market share by being first to enter the market; with a second mover strategy, a firm observes the innovations of first movers and then improves on them to gain advantage. SWOT analysis (strengths, weaknesses, opportunities, and threats) helps planners compare internal organizational strengths and weaknesses with external opportunities and threats. The strategic window identifies the limited periods during which the key requirements of a market and the competencies of a firm best fit together.

4.1. Over which of Porter's Five Forces do consumers have the greatest influence?
4.2. Cite examples of firms that have succeeded with first and second mover strategies.
4.3. When using the strategic window, what three factors must marketers analyze?

(5) Identify the basic elements of a marketing strategy.

Development of a marketing strategy is a two-step process: (1) selecting a target market and (2) designing an effective marketing mix to satisfy the chosen target. The target market is the group of people toward whom a company decides to direct its marketing efforts. The marketing mix blends four strategy elements to fit the needs and preferences of a specific target market. These elements are product strategy, distribution strategy, promotional strategy, and pricing strategy.

5.1. Why is identifying a target market so important to a company?
5.2. Give an example of each of the four strategies in the marketing mix.

(6) Describe the environmental characteristics that influence strategic decisions.

The five dimensions of the marketing environment are competitive, political-legal, economic, technological, and social-cultural. Marketers must be aware of growing cultural diversity in the global marketplace.

6.1. Identify a major way in which technology has changed the marketing environment in the last five years.
6.2. Why is it important for marketers to be aware of the social-cultural environment in which they plan to do business?

(7) Describe the methods for marketing planning, including business portfolio analysis and the BCG matrix.

The business portfolio analysis evaluates a company's products and divisions, including strategic business units (SBUs). The SBU focuses the attention of company managers so they can respond effectively to changing consumer demand within certain markets. The BCG matrix places SBUs in a four-quadrant chart that plots market share against market growth potential. The four quadrants are cash cows, stars, dogs, and question marks.

7.1. What is another name for SBUs?
7.2. Describe the characteristics of each of the four quadrants in the BCG matrix.

MARKETING TERMS YOU NEED TO KNOW

planning 40
marketing planning 41
strategic planning 41
tactical planning 41
mission 42
marketing strategy 44
Porter's Five Forces 44
first mover strategy 46
second mover strategy 46
SWOT analysis 46
strategic window 48
marketing mix 49
product strategy 50
distribution strategy 50
promotion 51
pricing strategy 51
strategic business units (SBUs) 55

OTHER IMPORTANT MARKETING TERMS

objectives 43
sustainable competitive advantage 44
core competencies 47
target market 48
integrated marketing communications (IMC) 51
rule of three 52
portfolio analysis 54
category 55
market share/market growth matrix 55

PROJECTS AND TEAMWORK EXERCISES

1. Choose a company whose goods and services are familiar to you. With at least one other classmate, formulate a mission statement for that company.
2. Once you have formulated the mission statement for your firm, identify at least five objectives.
3. Create a SWOT analysis for yourself, listing your own personal strengths, weaknesses, opportunities, and threats.
4. While Kmart filed for bankruptcy a couple of years ago, Kohl's has been expanding into new regions. Research more information about Kohl's. Then prepare a presentation explaining why this is a good strategic window in which to expand.
5. Use your library resources or an Internet search engine to collect information on one of the following companies (or select one of your own). Identify the firm's target market(s). Note that a large company might have more than one target market. Write a brief proposal for a marketing strategy to reach that market. Suggested firms:
   a. MasterCard
   b. Costco
   c. Volkswagen
   d. Old Navy
   e. Staples
6. With a classmate, choose a company whose products you have purchased in the past. Create two ads for one of the company's products (or product lines). One ad should focus on the product itself—its features, packaging, or brand name. The second ad should focus on pricing. Present your ads to the class for discussion. Which ad is more effective for the product and why?
7. On your own or with a classmate, research a firm that has been around for a long time, such as Ford Motor, General Electric, or DuPont. Use your research to determine the ways that technology has changed the marketing environment for your firm. Present your findings in class.
8. Suppose you are a marketer for a large U.S. toy manufacturer. Top executives at the company have determined that growth overseas is an essential objective. Write a memo to your manager explaining how you think the social-cultural environment may affect your firm's marketing strategy overseas.
9. Team up with one or more classmates to research companies on the Web, looking for firms that have created successful SBUs like L.L. Bean's outdoor and fitness department, which is aimed at women. Then create an advertisement for one of those SBUs.
10. Go back to the firm you selected in Question 5 (or choose a different firm). Further research the company's products so you can create a hypothetical BCG matrix for some of the company's products. Which products are the stars? Which are the cash cows and question marks? Are there any dogs?

APPLYING CHAPTER CONCEPTS

1. Why is it important from a marketing standpoint for an organization to define its goals and objectives?
2. What are the potential benefits and drawbacks if a firm strays from its core competencies?
3. Describe a consumer product that you think is particularly vulnerable to substitution. If you were a marketer for that product, what steps might you take to defend your product's position?
4. Suppose you were a marketer for a luxury skincare line. What factors in the marketing environment might affect your marketing strategy and why?
5. Suppose you were a marketer for a small firm trying to enter one of the dominant industries illustrating the rule of three. Which marketing strategy might you select and why?

ETHICS EXERCISE

Suppose you work for a company that makes surfboards. As part of the marketing team, you have assisted in creating a SWOT analysis for the company and have discovered some good and not-so-good things about your employer. Strengths include customer loyalty, a patented design, and competitive prices. The company has been based on the West Coast, but the owner sees an opportunity to enter the market on the East Coast. But you are concerned about the firm's weaknesses—the product line is narrow, you suspect the company doesn't have the financial resources to expand right now, and the owner keeps a tight rein on everything.

1. Should you speak to your manager about your concerns or keep quiet? Why?
2. Would you look for a job at another firm or remain loyal to the one you work for? Why?

'netWork EXERCISES

1. **Porter's Five Forces Industry Analysis**. Porter's Five Forces industry analysis was briefly described in the chapter. You can learn more about Porter's Five Forces by visiting the Web site listed below. Review the material presented and, working with a partner, apply Porter's Five Forces to a specific industry, such as the airline or grocery retailing industries.

   http://www.quickmba.com/strategy/porter.shtml
2. **Strategic planning versus tactical planning.** During the past couple of years, Eastman Kodak has made a number of major changes to its business practices. One of these has been to exit some of its traditional markets, such as film cameras, while expanding into others, such as digital imaging. Visit the Kodak Web site (**http://www.kodak.com**) as well as several online business news services (such as Yahoo! finance, **http://finance.yahoo.com**). Prepare a report summarizing the recent changes at Kodak. Were these changes the result of strategic or tactical planning? Using Kodak as an example, briefly explain how tactical planning supports strategic planning.
3. **Marketing planning methods**. One of the marketing planning methods discussed in the chapter is the market share/market growth matrix (Figure 2.10). Choose a company that operates in several well-defined markets (such as General Electric, Johnson & Johnson, or 3M). Visit the company's Web site and make a list of each of the firm's major divisions. Next, try to classify each division in terms of market attractiveness and business strengths. Which units did you classify as "stars"? Be prepared to defend your conclusions.

   http://www.ge.com
   http://www.johnsonandjohnson.com
   http://www.3m.com

Note: Internet Web addresses change frequently. If you don't find the exact sites listed, you may need to access the organization's or company's home page and search from there or use a search engine such as Google.

INFOTRAC CITATIONS AND EXERCISES

- **Record:** A112820957
  The Real Satellite Radio Boom Begins.
  Jimmy Schaeffler.
  Satellite News, Feb 2, 2004 v27 i5 p0

Abstract: Having thwarted near financial death less than two years ago, satellite radio is now being embraced by consumers and automakers like never before. The demand for satellite radio streams offering hundreds of channels is rising. XM Satellite Radio is pushing toward two million subscribers, while competitor Sirius hopes to reach one million over the next year. The new technology is attracting high-profile partnerships at an amazing rate. General Motors is installing XM Satellite Radio for new-model vehicles, and Chrysler has provided an equivalent endorsement of Sirius. Satellite radio content is also reaching new heights. A recent seven-year deal between Sirius and the National Football League enables subscribers to hear any football game telecast from anywhere in the country. What cable did for television in the 1980s and '90s, satellite is doing for radio today: improving it and providing audiences with options never before available in the history of the medium.

1. What is *strategic planning,* and how does it play an important role in the success of satellite radio firms XM and Sirius?
2. Based on the information given in the article, what seems to be driving the growth of satellite radio?
3. What is *SWOT analysis,* and how can it steer satellite radio marketers toward business success? What opportunities and threats exist for satellite radio, according to the article?

CASE 2.1 Starbucks' Strategy: It's a Small World After All

If your strategy is growth, you might as well go for the whole cuppa joe. That's what Starbucks is doing—expanding into international markets as if it were the most natural thing to do. To some experts, it *is* the best plan for a company that has been called by Wall Street analysts "the last great growth story." Others are a bit more skeptical. Why, for instance, would an American coffee maker try to pitch its brew against world-famous French dark espresso? "American coffee, it's only water. We call it *jus des chausettes*," sniffs Bertrand Abadie, a documentary filmmaker. (In case you don't speak fluent French, he called your favorite Starbucks flavor "sock juice.") Then there's China—a nation of about 1 billion tea drinkers. How does Starbucks intend to convert a nation whose favorite drink for the past 4,500 years has been tea? Other countries are in the picture as well, such as Japan and Spain. "We're taking the long view that opportunities are so large and that these are the early days," explains Starbucks CEO Howard Schultz.

Starbucks has a plan. Currently, the company has about 6,500 stores worldwide, with about one-fourth of those located in 29 countries outside the U.S. and Canada. According to Schultz, in the next few years, the Seattle-based firm intends to increase that number to 25,000 stores around the world, with 15,000 outside North America. "We're building a brand, not a fad," he explains. The Starbucks brand includes everything from its special flavors to its logo—a mermaid on a green background—which is already one of the most famous product images in the U.S.

Part of the company's strategy is to target younger consumers around the world. Austria's 20-something coffee drinkers already view Starbucks as something new and tasty. "The coffeehouses in Vienna are nice, but they are old. Starbucks is hip," says one newspaper editor. In Spain, the new Starbucks stores are teeming with teens, young adults, and tourists. "We're not going to capture everybody, but I see a younger generation of Spaniards and people of all sorts," observes CEO Schultz. The company is also selling a little bit of luxury in many of these countries, where the average income is lower than in the U.S. A medium-size latté sells for 20 yuan, or about $2.65 in Shanghai, China—a luxury for a household whose monthly income might be around $143. But Chinese consumers view it as an affordable treat.

Scouting the right locations for international shops is also part of Starbucks' planning. In China, local marketers literally stand outside potential locations with handheld clickers, tallying every possible customer who walks by. Young, fashionable couples get enthusiastic clicks. These consumers represent the emerging middle class in China—people with a bit of extra cash to spend and a desire for consumer goods. Starbucks analyzes pedestrian traffic through a location and researches where the newer, trendy areas will be in the next few years. Then marketers figure out where consumers live, work, and play. Finally, they put together a plan for a new store.

Strategic alliances may be a vital factor in Starbucks' ultimate success around the world. In Japan, the firm has partnered with a local handbag manufacturer, Sazaby Inc. In Spain, Starbucks has joined forces with Grupo Vips, the second-largest family-owned restaurant operator in the country. And in France, Starbucks executives have talked with several companies, although Schultz denies he is looking for an outright partner. "Many of those conversations were not so much about partnering but learning about doing business in France and sharing information about their experience," he insists.

Growth is not easy or simple, and Starbucks will have to persevere in an uncertain marketing environment around the world. Some experts accuse Starbucks and other companies of trying to "sell American culture" to international consumers and predict that the novelty will wear off soon. The company has been caught in political turmoil as well. Consumers boycotted a Starbucks store in Lebanon in protest against the U.S.–Iraq war, and Starbucks was forced to close its stores in Tel Aviv because of the violent conflict between Israelis and Palestinians. Then there are the skeptics in France. "The first café was founded in Paris over 300 years ago," claims one French scholar. "Starbucks is not going to compete with the French café. The café isn't just somewhere to drink coffee, it's a place where people go for social contact. In a big place with hundreds of customers, that's difficult."

But Schultz remains optimistic. "Perhaps we can be a great example of something that is American, that is very respectful of the French culture, and we want to bridge that gap." Perhaps Starbucks can get the whole world to sit down and drink a cup of American coffee.

Questions for Critical Thinking

1. Create a brief SWOT analysis of Starbucks focusing on its plans for international growth. Do you think this strategy is a good one for the company? Why or why not?
2. Identify the dimensions of the marketing environment that are mostly likely to affect Starbucks' strategy for global growth and explain why.

Sources: Andy Serwer, "Hot Starbucks to Go," *Fortune,* January 26, 2004, pp. 61–74; Noelle Knox, "Paris Starbucks Hopes to Prove U.S. Coffee Isn't Sock Juice," *USA Today,* January 16, 2004, p. B3; Laurent Rebours, "Starbucks Opens First French Shop to American Joe," *USA Today,* January 15, 2004, http://www.usatoday.com; Geoffrey A. Fowler, "Starbucks' Road to China," *The Wall Street Journal,* July 14, 2003, pp. B1, B3; Jason Singer and Martin Fackler, "In Japan, Adding Beer, Wine to Latté List," *The Wall Street Journal,* July 14, 2003, pp. B1, B3; Amy Wu, "Starbucks' World Won't Be Built in a Day," *Forbes.com,* June 27, 2003, http://www.forbes.com; Gavin Edwards, "The Logo," *Rolling Stone,* May 15, 2003, p. 110; Helen Jung, "Lattés for All: Starbucks Plans Global Expansion," *The News Tribune,* April 20, 2003, http://www.globalexchange.org.

VIDEO CASE 2.2 Hewlett-Packard's Strategic Plans Shine in B2B Markets

The written case on Hewlett-Packard appears on page VC-3. The recently filmed Hewlett-Packard video is designed to expand and highlight the concepts in this chapter and the concepts and questions covered in the written video case.

Creating an Effective Marketing Plan

Overview

"What are our mission and goals?"
"Who are our customers?"
"What types of products do we offer?"
"How can we provide superior customer service?"

THESE are some of the questions addressed by a **marketing plan**—a detailed description of the resources and actions needed to achieve stated marketing objectives. Chapter 2 discussed **strategic planning**—the process of anticipating events and conditions in the marketplace and determining the best way for a firm to achieve its organizational objectives. Marketing planning encompasses all the activities devoted to achieving marketing objectives, establishing a basis for designing a marketing strategy. This appendix deals in depth with the formal marketing plan, which is part of an organization's overall business plan. At the end of this appendix, you'll see what an actual marketing plan looks like. Each plan component for a hypothetical firm called Blue Sky Clothing is presented. ◆◆◆

Briefly Speaking

What do you want to achieve or avoid? The answers to this question are objectives. How will you go about achieving your desired results? The answer to this you can call strategy.

William E. Rothschild
American strategic planning consultant and author

marketing plan Detailed description of the resources and actions needed to achieve stated marketing objectives.

strategic planning Process of anticipating events and market conditions and deciding how a firm can best achieve its organizational objectives.

business plan Formal document that outlines a company's objectives, how they will be met, how the business will achieve financing, and how much money the firm expects to earn.

COMPONENTS OF A BUSINESS PLAN

A company's **business plan** is one of its most important documents. The business plan puts in writing all of the company's objectives, how they will be achieved, how the business will secure necessary financing, and how much money the company expects to earn over a specified time period. Although business plans vary in length and format, most contain at least some form of the following components:

- An *executive summary* briefly answers the who, what, when, where, how, and why questions for the plan. Although the summary appears early in the plan, it is typically written last, after the firm's executives have worked out the details of all the other sections.
- A *competitive analysis* section focuses on the environment in which the marketing plan is to be implemented. Although this section is more closely associated with the comprehensive business plan, factors specifically influencing marketing are likely to be included here.
- The *mission statement* summarizes the organization's purpose, vision, and overall goals. This statement provides the foundation upon which further planning is based.

- The overall business plan includes a series of *component* plans that present goals and strategies for each functional area of the enterprise. They typically include the following:

  The *marketing plan,* which describes strategies for informing potential customers about the goods and services offered by the firm as well as strategies for developing long-term relationships. At the end of this appendix, a sample marketing plan for Blue Sky Clothing is presented.

  The *financing plan,* which presents a realistic approach for securing needed funds and managing debt and cash flows.

  The *production plan,* which describes how the organization will go about developing its products in the most efficient, cost-effective manner possible.

  The *facilities plan,* which describes the physical environment and equipment required to implement the production plan.

  The *human resources plan,* which estimates the firm's employment needs and the skills necessary to achieve organizational goals, including a comparison of current employees with the needs of the firm, and which establishes processes for securing adequately trained personnel should a gap exist between current employee skills and future needs.

This basic format encompasses the planning process used by nearly every successful organization. Whether a company operates in the manufacturing, wholesaling, retailing, or service sector (or a combination), the components described here are likely to appear in its overall business plan. Regardless of the size or longevity of a company, a business plan is an essential tool for a firm's owners because it helps them focus on the key elements of their business. Even small firms that are just starting out need a business plan to obtain financing. Figure 1 shows the outline of a business plan for Blue Sky Clothing.

Briefly Speaking

Make no little plans; they have no magic to stir men's blood and probably themselves will not be realized. Make big plans; aim high in hope and work, remembering that a noble, logical diagram once recorded will not die.

Daniel H. Burnham (1846–1912)

American architect and city planner

CREATING A MARKETING PLAN

Keep in mind that a marketing plan should be created in conjunction with the other elements of a firm's business plan. In addition, a marketing plan often draws from the business plan, restating the executive summary, competitive analysis, and mission statement to give its readers an overall view of the firm. The marketing plan is needed for a variety of reasons:

- To obtain financing because banks and most private investors require a detailed business plan—including a marketing plan component—before they will even consider a loan application or a venture capital investment.
- To provide direction for the firm's overall business and marketing strategies.
- To support the development of long-term and short-term organizational objectives.
- To guide employees in achieving these objectives.
- To serve as a standard against which the firm's progress can be measured and evaluated.

In addition, the marketing plan is where a firm puts into writing its commitment to its customers and to building long-lasting relationships. After creating and implementing the plan, marketers must reevaluate it periodically to gauge its success in moving the organization toward its goals. If changes are needed, they should be made as soon as possible.

FORMULATING AN OVERALL MARKETING STRATEGY

Before creating a marketing plan, a firm's marketers formulate an overall marketing strategy. A firm may use a number of tools in marketing planning, including business portfolio analysis and the BCG matrix. Its executives may conduct a SWOT analysis, take advantage of a strategic window, study Porter's Five Forces model as it relates to their business, or consider adopting a first- or second-mover strategy, all of which are described in Chapter 2.

figure 1

Outline of a Business Plan

The Blue Sky Clothing Business Plan

I. Executive Summary
- Who, What, When, Where, How, and Why

II. Table of Contents

III. Introduction
- Mission Statement
- Concept and Company
- Management Team
- Product

IV. Marketing Strategy
- Demographics
- Trends
- Market Penetration
- Potential Sales Revenue

V. Financing the Business
- Cash Flow Analysis
- Pro Forma Balance Sheet
- Income Statement

VI. Facilities Plan
- Physical Environment
- Equipment

VII. Human Resource Plan
- Employment Needs and Skills
- Current Employees

VIII. Resumés of Principals

spreadsheet analysis Grid that organizes information in a standardized, easily understood format.

In addition to the planning strategies discussed in Chapter 2, marketers are likely to use **spreadsheet analysis,** which lays out a grid of columns and rows that organize numerical information in a standardized, easily understood format. Spreadsheet analysis helps planners answer various "what if" questions related to the firm's financing and operations. The most popular electronic spreadsheet is Microsoft Excel. A spreadsheet analysis helps planners anticipate marketing performance given specified sets of circumstances. For example, a spreadsheet might project the outcomes of different pricing decisions for a new product, as shown in Figure 2.

Once general planning strategies are determined, marketers begin to flesh out the details of the marketing strategy. The elements of a marketing strategy include identifying the target market, studying the marketing environment, and creating a marketing mix.

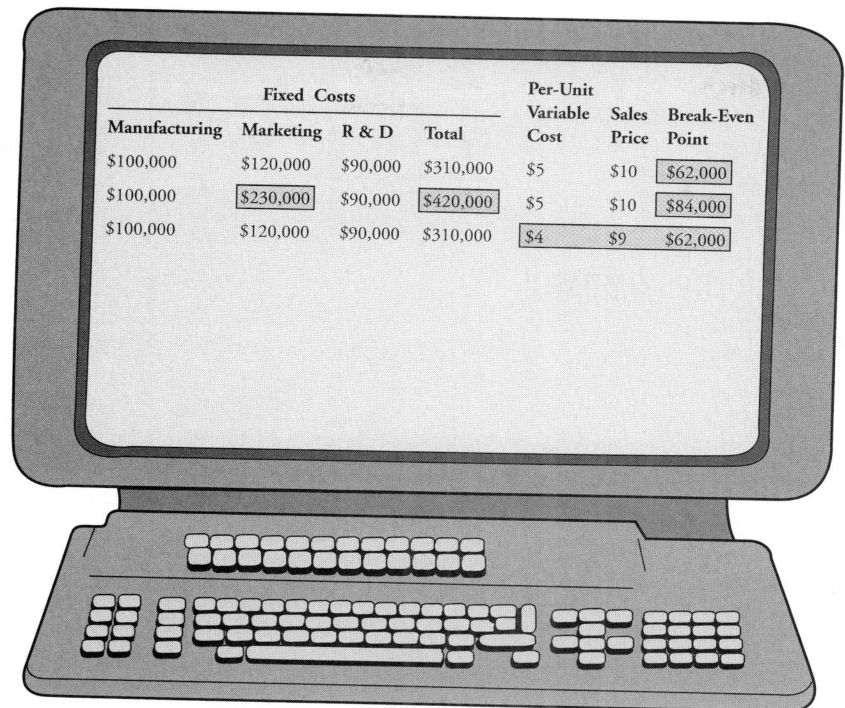

Fixed Costs				Per-Unit Variable Cost	Sales Price	Break-Even Point
Manufacturing	Marketing	R & D	Total			
$100,000	$120,000	$90,000	$310,000	$5	$10	$62,000
$100,000	$230,000	$90,000	$420,000	$5	$10	$84,000
$100,000	$120,000	$90,000	$310,000	$4	$9	$62,000

figure 2
How Spreadsheet Analysis Works

When marketers have identified the target market, they can develop the optimal marketing mix to reach their potential customers:

- *Product strategy.* Which goods and services should the company offer to meet its customers' needs?
- *Distribution strategy.* Through which channel(s) and physical facilities will the firm distribute its products?
- *Promotional strategy.* What mix of advertising, sales promotion, and personal selling activities will the firm use to reach its customers initially and then develop long-term relationships?
- *Pricing strategy.* At what level should the company set its prices?

THE EXECUTIVE SUMMARY, COMPETITIVE ANALYSIS, AND MISSION STATEMENT

Because these three elements of the business plan often reappear in the marketing plan, it is useful to describe them here. Recall that the executive summary answers the who, what, when, where, how, and why questions for the business. The executive summary for the National Collegiate Athletic Association (NCAA) would include reference to its current strategic planning process, which involves "crafting a comprehensive strategic direction based on the balance between the timeless principles of the association and what the association seeks to become within 10 to 30 years."[1] It would go on to answer questions such as who is involved (key people and organizations), what length of time the plan represents, and how the goals will be met.

The competitive analysis focuses on the environment in which the marketing plan is to be implemented. The competitive analysis for warehouse club Costco would likely focus on its efforts to maintain its advantage over Wal-Mart's Sam's Club and BJ's. The analysis might outline Costco's efforts to increase market share over Wal-Mart and BJ's through its strategy of offering high-end luxury goods at rock-bottom prices. Consumers can buy peanuts and toilet paper in bulk at Costco, just as they can at Sam's Club and BJ's—but they can also pick up a Coach handbag, a Lalique crystal vase, or a bottle of Dom Perignon champagne.[2]

Briefly Speaking

Marketing is merely a civilized form of warfare in which most battles are won with words, ideas, and disciplined thinking.

Albert W. Emery (b. 1923)
American advertising agency executive

The mission statement puts into words an organization's overall purpose and reason for being. Ling Chai, a graduate of Beijing University and Princeton, founded Jenzabar, Inc., a small, Massachusetts-based firm that provides Web-based educational software and services to colleges. She describes the mission of her company this way: "Every day, we're supporting millions of students, faculty and administrators on campuses to connect and improve their productivity, learning experiences, and communication with each other." Less than a decade since its inception, Jenzabar's products are used in one of every five universities in the U.S.[3]

DESCRIPTION OF THE COMPANY

Near the beginning of the marketing plan—typically following the executive summary and before the mission statement—a description of the company is included. The company description may include a brief history or background of the firm, the types of products it offers or plans to introduce, recent successes or achievements—in short, it consists of a few paragraphs containing the kind of information often found on the home page of a company's Web site.

STATEMENT OF GOALS AND CORE COMPETENCIES

The plan then includes a statement of the firm's goals and its core competencies—those things it does extremely well or better than anyone else. The goals should be specific and measurable and may be divided into financial and nonfinancial aims. A financial goal might be to add 75 new franchises in the next 12 months or to reach $10 million in revenues. A nonfinancial goal might be to enter the European market or to add a new product line every other year. Texas-based Handango, a wireless software provider for PDAs and cell phones, has experienced growth of 30 percent each quarter for the past three years and now serves 6 million customers. One of its financial goals is to continue that growth; a nonfinancial goal is to increase its customer base to 8 million.[4]

Core competencies are what make a firm stand out from everyone else in the marketplace. Costco, described earlier, started out just like other warehouse clubs, until its marketers realized that the customers they were attracting had more money to spend than they had initially thought—so the company began stocking the shelves with a variety of luxury items in addition to the staples offered by other warehouse clubs. Now one of its core competencies is its ability to offer high-end goods at prices significantly lower than traditional retail outlets. A Costco store actually sold a $106,000 diamond ring recently—but that was considered a bargain compared with the regular retail price. One of its financial goals is to beat the competition in sales on two fronts—against other discounters like Wal-Mart and BJ's and against luxury department stores like Saks Fifth Avenue. A nonfinancial goal is to be perceived as a quality retailer without the high price.[5]

Small businesses often begin with a single core competency and build their business and reputation on it. It is important for a new firm to identify its core competency in the marketing plan so that investors or banks understand why they should lend the firm money to get started or to grow to the next stage. When Todd Graves and Greg Silvey tried to raise funds to open a Louisiana-based chicken-finger restaurant, a few private investors decided to lend them money based on their ability to articulate how strongly they believed in the core competency: the taste and quality of their chicken offerings and the expected growth of this form of fried and baked chicken business. The duo raised enough to open their first Raising Cane restaurant. A decade later, they own 14 more, all located in Louisiana. Their goal is to grow Raising Cane into an international franchise—with each outlet serving great chicken fingers.[6]

OUTLINE OF THE MARKETING ENVIRONMENT (SITUATION ANALYSIS)

Every successful marketing plan takes into consideration the marketing environment—the competitive, economic, political-legal, technological, and social-cultural factors that affect the way a firm formulates and implements its marketing strategy. Marketing plans may address these issues in different ways, but the goal is to present information that describes the company's position or situation within the marketing environment. In-N-Out burger restaurants, based in California, have been around since 1948. Only in the last decade has the company begun to grow, adding about 10 new restaurants per year throughout California, with a few scattered outlets across Nevada and Arizona. All of the restaurants are company owned; there are no franchises. The menu is simple—burgers, fries, soft drinks, and ice cream shakes. Cofounder Esther Snyder, who is now in her early 80s, is still the CEO. In-N-Out has a loyal following that now spans generations.[7] So a marketing plan for In-N-Out would include an evaluation of competing chains such as Burger King and McDonald's; any technological advances that would affect such factors as food preparation; social-cultural issues such as diet preferences of customers and the trend toward wraps and other low-carbohydrate offerings; political-legal issues such as food regulations; and economic issues affecting a pricing strategy.

One such method for outlining the marketing environment in the marketing plan is to include a SWOT analysis, described in Chapter 2. SWOT analysis identifies the firm's strengths, weaknesses, opportunities, and threats within the marketing environment. A SWOT analysis for In-N-Out would identify such strengths as the company's base of long-term customers and its enviable ability to create an advantage that competitors cannot copy, according to industry researcher Paul Westra.[8] Weaknesses might include its limited menu and small number of stores. A major opportunity lies in the fact that In-N-Out has so few stores—and can expand almost anywhere without cannibalizing its own business. Threats include competition from much larger chains. A SWOT analysis can be presented in chart format so it is easy to read as part of the marketing plan. The sample marketing plan in this appendix includes a SWOT analysis for Blue Sky Clothing.

THE TARGET MARKET AND MARKETING MIX

The marketing plan identifies the target market for the firm's products. Premier Cru, a small company that produces music records—not CDs—decided to target radio stations as its initial market. Why? Because many radio disc jockeys prefer the sound that comes from a vinyl record.[9] The target market for Under Armour Performance Apparel is athletes—just about any kind of athlete. Under Armour manufactures T-shirts out of fabric that carries moisture away from the skin. Athletes wear these garments under their uniforms or outerwear to help keep them dry and comfortable during a workout or a game. Within 10 years, Under Armour has secured contracts with the National Hockey League and Major League Baseball, as well as other sports leagues, and its products are available in 4,500 retail outlets nationwide.[10]

The marketing plan also discusses the marketing mix that the firm has selected for its products. When Nokia launched its N-Gage, a handset that plays games, the company used a marketing mix that included product, distribution, promotion, and pricing strategies. By expanding its well-known communications product line to include a new handheld game device, Nokia has set its new product in direct competition with game machines made by Nintendo and Sony. Distribution of N-Gage has proved to be tricky: Nokia has had to finesse agreements with retail outlets that sell games—not just phones—without alienating its core customers in the mobile network industry. Nokia plans to spend an estimated $100 million promoting the new handset. N-Gage has a retail price of $300—higher than competing devices but packed with more features, such as a phone, text messaging, FM radio, and digital-music player.

Perhaps surprisingly, Nokia hasn't just aimed N-Gage at teenagers and twentysomethings who are experts at game playing. Nokia marketers have also targeted other groups of consumers, including socialites and business executives. And as part of its overall marketing strategy, the Finnish telecommunications giant recently divided its organization into four major business units: mobile networks, general mobile phones, wireless entertainment devices, and mobile business products. "Strategically, Nokia is doing the right thing in trying to expand its addressable markets," notes securities analyst Tim Luke of Lehman Brothers.[11] All of these strategies would be included in Nokia's marketing plan for N-Gage.

BUDGET, SCHEDULE, AND MONITORING

Every marketing plan requires a budget, a time schedule for implementation, and a system for monitoring the plan's success or failure. Typically, a budget includes a breakdown of the costs incurred as the marketing program is implemented, offset by projected sales, profits, and losses over the time period of the program.

You have to be fast on your feet and adaptive or else a strategy is useless.

Lou Gerstner (b. 1942)

former chairman, IBM Corp.

Most long-range marketing plans encompass a two- to five-year period, although companies that do business in industries such as auto manufacturing, pharmaceuticals, or lumber may extend their marketing plans further into the future because it typically takes longer to develop these products. However, marketers in most industries will have difficulty making estimates and predictions beyond five years because of the many uncertainties in the marketplace. Firms also may opt to develop short-term plans to cover marketing activities for a single year.

The marketing plan, whether it is long-term or short-term, predicts how long it will take to achieve the goals set out by the plan. A goal may be opening a certain number of new stores, market share growth, or achieving an expansion of the product line. Finally, the marketing program is monitored and evaluated for its performance. Monthly, quarterly, and annual sales targets are usually tracked; the efficiency with which certain tasks are completed is determined; customer satisfaction is measured and so forth. All of these factors contribute to the overall review of the program.

At some point, a firm may opt to implement an *exit strategy*, a contingency plan for the firm leaving the market. A common way for a large company to do this is to sell off a business unit. A number of these strategies have been implemented recently. After attempting for several years to achieve a distinctive competence in its competition with Dell by establishing a number of cow-spot-bedecked retail stores, Gateway recently called the experiment a costly failure and closed the outlets. Facing growing competition in the handheld PDA computer market from increasingly sophisticated smart phones, Sony Electronics recently announced that it has no plans to release new versions of its five Clie models sold in the U.S.[12]

Another example of the implementation of an exit strategy came from jeans icon Levi Strauss, which reported that it was exploring the possibility of selling its Dockers division to help pay down a heavy debt load. The sale of Dockers, which generates $1.4 billion in annual revenues, would help Levi's exit the men's casual clothing market and concentrate instead on its core market of jeans.[13] Smaller firms may exit by merging with other companies. Snapple, which started out as a small beverage company, was eventually sold to Cadbury.

SAMPLE MARKETING PLAN

The following pages contain an annotated sample marketing plan for Blue Sky Clothing. At some point in your career, you will likely be involved in writing—or at least contributing to—a marketing plan. And you'll certainly read many marketing plans throughout your business career. Keep in mind that the plan for Blue Sky is a single example; no one format is used by all companies. Also, the Blue Sky plan has been somewhat condensed to make it easier to annotate and illustrate the most vital features. The important point to remember is that the marketing plan is a document designed to present concise, cohesive information about a company's marketing objectives to managers, lending institutions, and others who are involved in creating and carrying out the firm's overall business strategy.

FIVE-YEAR MARKETING PLAN
BLUE SKY CLOTHING, INC.

TABLE OF CONTENTS

EXECUTIVE SUMMARY

This five-year marketing plan for Blue Sky Clothing has been created by its two founders to secure additional funding for growth and to inform employees of the company's current status and direction. Although Blue Sky was launched only three years ago, the firm has experienced greater-than-anticipated demand for its products, and research has shown that the target market of sports-minded consumers and sports retailers would like to buy more casual clothing than Blue Sky currently offers. They are also interested in extending their product line as well as adding new product lines. In addition, Blue Sky plans to explore opportunities for online sales. The marketing environment has been very receptive to the firm's high-quality goods—casual clothing in trendy colors with logos and slogans that reflect the interests of outdoor enthusiasts around the country. Over the next five years, Blue Sky can increase its distribution, offer new products, and win new customers.

The executive summary outlines the who, what, where, when, how, and why of the marketing plan. Blue Sky is only three years old and is successful enough that it now needs a formal marketing plan to obtain additional financing from a bank or private investors for expansion and the launch of new products.

COMPANY DESCRIPTION

Blue Sky Clothing was founded three years ago by entrepreneurs Lucy Neuman and Nick Russell. Neuman has an undergraduate degree in marketing and worked for several years in the retail clothing industry. Russell operated an adventure business called Go West!, which arranges group trips to locations in Wyoming, Montana, and Idaho, before selling the enterprise to a partner. Neuman and Russell, who have been friends since college, decided to develop and market a line of clothing with a unique—yet universal—appeal to outdoor enthusiasts.

The company description summarizes the history of Blue Sky—how it was founded and by whom, what its products are, and why they are unique. It begins to "sell" the reader on the growth possibilities for Blue Sky.

Blue Sky Clothing reflects Neuman's and Russell's passion for the outdoors. The company's original cotton T-shirts, baseball caps, and fleece jackets and vests bear logos of different sports—such as kayaking, mountain climbing, bicycling, skating, surfing, and horseback riding. But every item shows off the company's slogan: "Go Play Outside." Blue Sky sells clothing for both men and women, in the hottest colors with the coolest names—such as sunrise pink, sunset red, twilight purple, desert rose, cactus green, ocean blue, mountaintop white, and river rock gray.

Blue Sky attire is currently carried by small retail stores that specialize in outdoor clothing and gear. Most of these stores are concentrated in northern New England, California, the Northwest, and a few states in the South. The high quality, trendy colors, and unique message of the clothing have gained Blue Sky a following among consumers between the ages of 25 and 45. Sales have tripled in the last year alone, and Blue Sky is currently working to expand its manufacturing capabilities.

Blue Sky is also committed to giving back to the community by contributing to local conservation programs. Ultimately, the company would like to develop and fund its own environmental programs. This plan will outline how Blue Sky intends to introduce new products, expand its distribution, enter new markets, and give back to the community.

It is important to state a firm's mission and goals, including financial and nonfinancial goals. Blue Sky's goals include growth and profits for the company as well as the ability to contribute to society through conservation programs.

Blue Sky's Mission and Goals

Blue Sky's mission is to be the leading producer and marketer of personalized, casual clothing for consumers who love the outdoors. Blue Sky wants to inspire people to get outdoors more often and enjoy family and friends while doing so. In addition, Blue Sky strives to design programs for preserving the natural environment.

During the next five years, Blue Sky seeks to achieve the following financial and nonfinancial goals:

- *Financial goals*

1. Obtain financing to expand manufacturing capabilities, increase distribution, and introduce two new product lines.
2. Increase revenues by at least 50 percent each year.
3. Donate at least $25,000 a year to conservation organizations.

- *Nonfinancial goals*

4. Introduce two new product lines—customized logo clothing and lightweight luggage.
5. Enter new geographic markets, including southwestern and Mid-Atlantic states.
6. Develop a successful Internet site, while maintaining strong relationships with retailers.
7. Develop its own conservation program aimed at helping communities raise money to purchase open space.

This section reminds employees as well as those outside the company (such as potential lenders) exactly what Blue Sky does so well and how it plans to achieve a sustainable competitive advantage over rivals. Note that here and throughout the plan, Blue Sky focuses on relationships.

Core Competencies

Blue Sky seeks to use its core competencies to achieve a sustainable competitive advantage, in which competitors cannot provide the same value to consumers that Blue Sky does. Already, Blue Sky has developed core competencies in (1) offering a high-quality, branded product whose image is recognizable among consumers; (2) creating a sense of community among consumers who purchase the products; and (3) developing a reputation among retailers as a reliable manufacturer, delivering the requested number of products on schedule. The firm intends to build on these competencies through marketing efforts that increase the number of products offered as well as distribution outlets.

By forming strong relationships with consumers, retailers, and suppliers of fabric and other goods and services, Blue Sky believes it can create a sustainable competitive advantage over its rivals. No other clothing company can say to its customers with as much conviction "Go Play Outside"!

The situation analysis provides an outline of the marketing environment. A SWOT analysis helps marketers and others identify clearly a firm's strengths, weaknesses, opportunities, and threats. Again, relationships are a focus. Blue Sky has also conducted research on the outdoor clothing market, competitors, and consumers to determine how best to attract and keep customers.

Situation Analysis

The marketing environment for Blue Sky represents overwhelming opportunities. It also contains some challenges that the firm believes it can meet successfully. Table A illustrates a SWOT analysis of the company conducted by marketers to highlight Blue Sky's strengths, weaknesses, opportunities, and threats.

The SWOT analysis presents a thumbnail sketch of the company's position in the marketplace. In just three years, Blue Sky has built some impressive strengths while looking forward to new opportunities. Its dedicated founders, the growing number of brand-loyal customers, and sound financial management place the company in a good position to grow. However, as Blue Sky considers expansion of its product line and entrance into new markets, the firm will have to guard against marketing myopia (the failure to recognize the scope of its business) and quality slippages. As the company finalizes plans for new products and expanded Internet sales, its management will also have to guard against competitors who attempt to

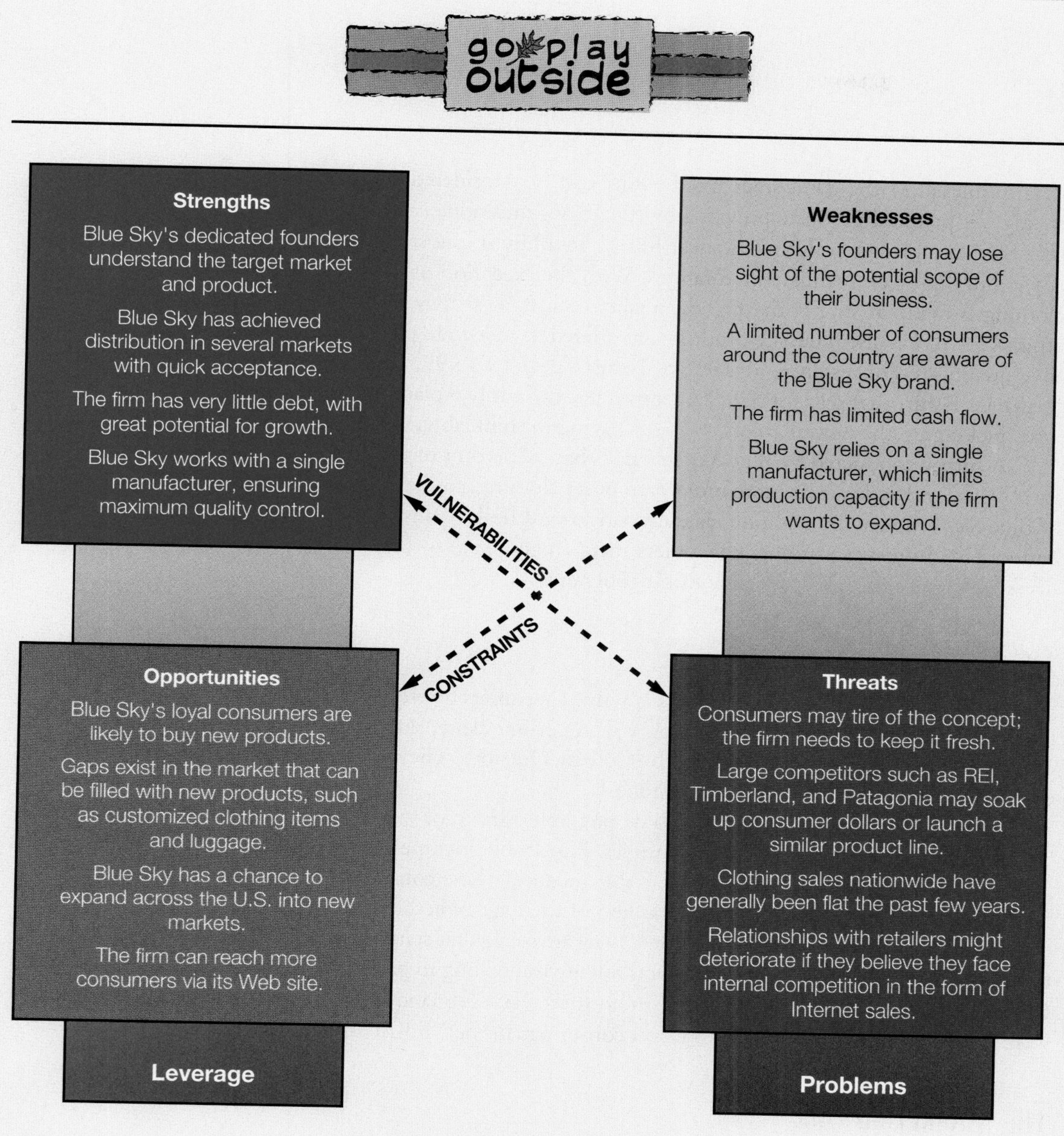

table A

SWOT Analysis for Blue Sky Clothing, Inc.

duplicate the products. However, building strong relationships with consumers, retailers, and suppliers should help thwart competitors.

Competitors in the Outdoor Clothing Market

The outdoor retail sales industry sells about $5 billion worth of goods annually, ranging from clothing to equipment. The outdoor apparel market has many entries. L.L. Bean, REI, Timberland, Bass Pro Shops, Cabello's, and Patagonia are among the most recognizable companies that offer these products. Smaller competitors such as Title IX, which offers athletic clothing for women, and Ragged Mountain, which sells fleece clothing for skiers and hikers, also grab some of the market. The outlook for the industry in general—and Blue Sky in particular—is positive for several reasons. First, consumers are participating in and investing in recreational activities that are near their homes. Second, consumers are looking for ways to enjoy their leisure time with friends and family without overspending. Third, consumers are gaining more confidence in the economy and are willing and able to spend more.

While all of the companies listed earlier can be considered competitors, none offers the kind of trendy, yet practical products provided by Blue Sky—and none carries the customized logos and slogans that Blue Sky plans to offer in the near future. In addition, most of these competitors sell performance apparel in high-tech manufactured fabrics. With the exception of the fleece vests and jackets, Blue Sky's clothing is made of strictly the highest quality cotton, so it may be worn both on the hiking trail and around town. Finally, Blue Sky products are offered at moderate prices, making them affordable in multiple quantities. For instance, a Blue Sky T-shirt sells for $15.99, compared with a competing high-performance T-shirt that sells for $29.99. Consumers can easily replace a set of shirts from one season to the next, picking up the newest colors, without having to think about the purchase.

A survey conducted by Blue Sky revealed that 67 percent of responding consumers prefer to replace their casual and active wear more often than other clothing, so they are attracted by the moderate pricing of Blue Sky products. In addition, as the trend toward health-conscious activities and concerns about the natural environment continue, consumers increasingly relate to the Blue Sky philosophy as well as the firm's contributions to socially responsible programs.

Blue Sky has identified its customers as active people between the ages of 25 and 45. However, that doesn't mean someone who is 62 and prefers to read about the outdoors isn't a potential customer as well. By pinpointing where existing customers live, Blue Sky can make plans for growth into new outlets.

The Target Market

The target market for Blue Sky products is active consumers between the ages of 25 and 45—people who like to hike, rock climb, bicycle, surf, figure skate, in-line skate, ride horses, snowboard or ski, kayak, and other such activities. In short, they like to "Go Play Outside." They might not be experts at the sports they engage in, but they enjoy themselves outdoors.

These active consumers represent a demographic group of well-educated and successful individuals; they are single or married and raising families. Household incomes generally range between $60,000 and $120,000 annually. Despite their comfortable incomes, these consumers are price conscious and consistently seek value in their purchases. Regardless of their age (whether they fall at the upper or lower end of the target range), they lead active lifestyles. They are somewhat status oriented but not overly so. They like to be associated with high-quality products but are not willing to pay a premium price for a certain brand. Current Blue Sky customers tend to live in northern New England, the South, California, and the Northwest. However, one future goal is to target consumers in the Mid-Atlantic states and Southwest as well.

The strongest part of the marketing mix for Blue Sky involves sales promotions, public relations, and nontraditional marketing strategies such as attending outdoor events and organizing activities like day hikes and bike rides.

The Marketing Mix

The following discussion outlines some of the details of the proposed marketing mix for Blue Sky products.

PRODUCT STRATEGY. Blue Sky currently offers a line of high-quality outdoor apparel items including cotton T-shirts, baseball caps, and fleece vests and jackets. All bear the company logo and slogan, "Go Play Outside." The firm has researched the most popular colors for its items and given them names that consumers enjoy—sunset red, sunrise pink, cactus green, desert rose, and river rock gray, among others. Over the next five years, Blue Sky plans to expand the product line to include customized clothing items. Customers may select a logo that represents their sport—say, rock climbing. Then they can add a slogan to match the logo, such as "Get Over It." A baseball cap with a bicyclist might bear the slogan, "Take a Spin." At the beginning, there would be ten new logos and five new slogans; more would be added later. Eventually, some slogans and logos would be retired, and new ones introduced. This strategy will keep the concept fresh and prevent it from becoming diluted with too many variations.

The second way in which Blue Sky plans to expand its product line is to offer items of lightweight luggage—two sizes of duffel bags, two sizes of tote bags, and a daypack. These items would also come in trendy and basic colors, with a choice of logos and slogans. In addition, every product would bear the Blue Sky logo.

DISTRIBUTION STRATEGY. Currently, Blue Sky is marketed through regional and local specialty shops scattered along the California coast, into the Northwest, across the South, and in northern New England. So far, Blue Sky has not been distributed through national sporting goods and apparel chains. Climate and season tend to dictate the sales at specialty shops, which sell more T-shirts and baseball caps during warm weather and more fleece vests and jackets during colder months. Blue Sky obtains much of its information about overall industry trends in different geographic areas and at different types of retail outlets from its trade organization, Outdoor Industry Association.

Over the next three years, Blue Sky seeks to expand distribution to retail specialty shops throughout the nation, focusing next on the Southwest and Mid-Atlantic regions. The firm has not yet determined whether it would be beneficial to sell through a major national chain such as REI or Bass Pro Shops, as these outlets could be considered competitors.

In addition, Blue Sky plans to expand online sales by offering the customized product line via Internet only, thus distinguishing between Internet offerings and specialty shop offerings. Eventually, we may be able to place Internet kiosks at some of the more profitable store outlets so consumers could order customized products from the stores. Regardless of its expansion plans, Blue Sky fully intends to monitor and maintain strong relationships with distribution channel members.

PROMOTIONAL STRATEGY. Blue Sky communicates with consumers and retailers about its products in a variety of ways. Information about Blue Sky—the company as well as its products—is available via the Internet, direct mailings, and in person. The firm's promotional efforts also seek to differentiate its products from those of its competitors.

The company relies on personal contact with retailers to establish the products in their stores. This contact, whether in-person or by phone, helps convey the Blue Sky message, demonstrate the products' unique qualities, and build relationships. Blue Sky sales representatives visit each store two or three times a year and offer in-store training on the features of the products for new retailers or for those who want a refresher. As distribution expands, Blue Sky will adjust to meet greater demand by increasing sales staff to make sure its stores are visited more frequently.

Sales promotions and public relations currently make up the bulk of Blue Sky's promotional strategy. Blue Sky staff works with retailers to offer short-term sales promotions tied to events and contests. In addition, Nick Russell is currently working with several trip outfitters to offer Blue Sky items on a promotional basis. Because Blue Sky also engages in cause marketing through its contribution to environmental programs, good public relations have followed.

Nontraditional marketing methods that require little cash and a lot of creativity also lend themselves perfectly to Blue Sky. Because Blue Sky is a small, flexible organization, the firm can easily implement ideas such as distributing free water, stickers, and discount coupons at outdoor sporting events. During the next year, the company plans to engage in the following marketing efforts:

- Create a Blue Sky Tour, in which several employees take turns driving around the country to campgrounds to distribute promotional items such as Blue Sky stickers and discount coupons.
- Attend canoe and kayak races, bicycling events, and rock climbing competitions with our Blue Sky truck to distribute free water, stickers, and discount coupons for Blue Sky shirts or hats.
- Organize Blue Sky hikes departing from participating retailers.
- Hold a Blue Sky design contest, selecting a winning slogan and logo to be added to the customized line.

PRICING STRATEGY. As discussed earlier in this plan, Blue Sky products are priced with the competition in mind. The firm is not concerned with setting high prices to signal luxury or prestige, nor is it attempting

go play outside

An actual plan will include more specific financial details, which will be folded in to the overall business plan. For more information, see the "Financial Analysis in Marketing" appendix on page A-1 of this book. In addition, Blue Sky states that at this stage, it does not have plans to exit the market by merging with another firm or making a public stock offering.

to achieve the goals of offsetting low prices by selling high quantities of products. Instead, value pricing is practiced so that customers feel comfortable purchasing new clothing to replace the old, even if it is just because they like the new colors. The pricing strategy also makes Blue Sky products good gifts—for birthdays, graduations, or "just because." The customized clothing will sell for $2 to $4 more than the regular Blue Sky logo clothing. The luggage will be priced competitively, offering a good value against its competition.

Budget, Schedule, and Monitoring

Though its history is short, Blue Sky has enjoyed a steady increase in sales since its introduction three years ago. Figure A shows these three years, plus projected sales for the next three years, including the introduction of the two new product lines. Additional financial data are included in the overall business plan for the company.

figure A

Annual Sales for Blue Sky Clothing: 2004–2009

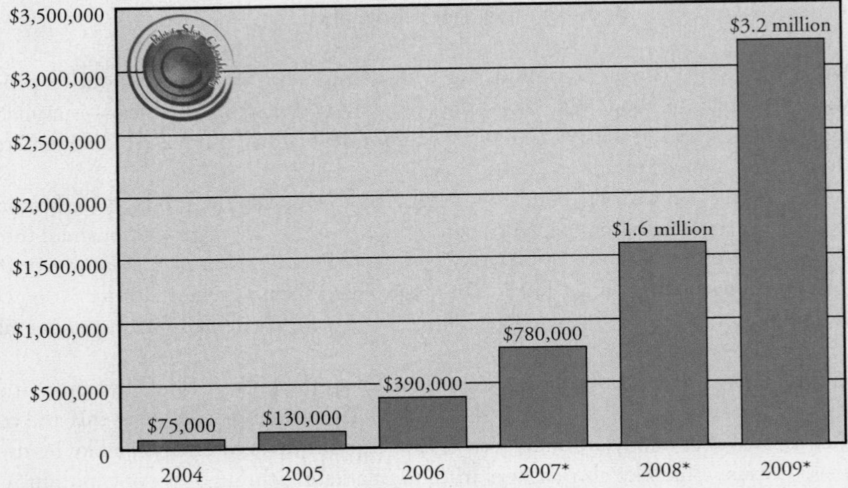

The timeline for expansion of outlets and introduction of the two new product lines is shown in Figure B. The implementation of each of these tasks will be monitored closely and evaluated for its performance.

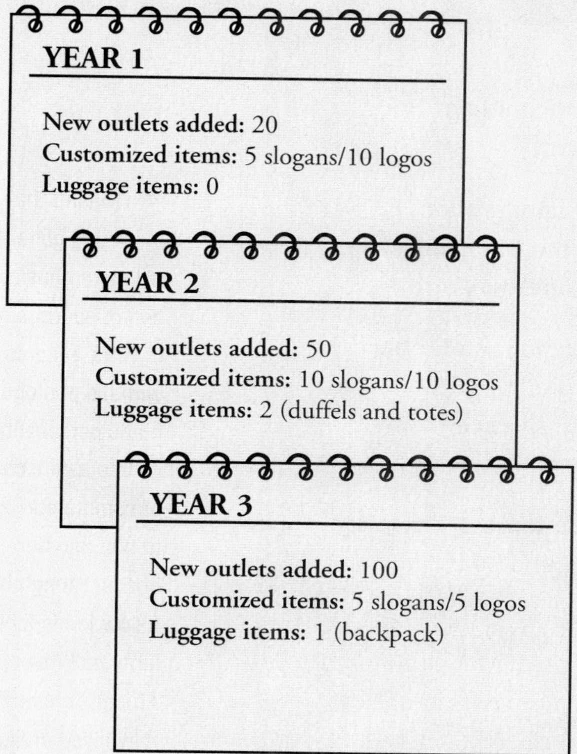

figure B
Timeline for First Three Years of Marketing Plan

Blue Sky anticipates continuing operations into the foreseeable future, with no plans to exit this market. Instead, as discussed throughout this plan, the firm plans to increase its presence in the market. At present, there are no plans to merge with another company or to make a public stock offering.

chapter 3

The Marketing Environment, Ethics, and Social Responsibility

chapter objectives

1. Identify the five components of the marketing environment.
2. Explain the types of competition marketers face and the steps necessary for developing a competitive strategy.
3. Describe how government and other groups regulate marketing activities and how marketers can influence the political-legal environment.
4. Outline the economic factors that affect marketing decisions and consumer buying power.
5. Discuss the impact of the technological environment on a firm's marketing activities.
6. Explain how the social-cultural environment influences marketing.
7. Describe the role of marketing in society and identify the two major social issues in marketing.
8. Identify the four levels of the social responsibility pyramid.

THE UNPLAYABLE LIE

It wasn't that long ago that an amazing young golfer named Tiger Woods sparked the enthusiasm of a whole new generation of sports fans with a spectacular series of world records and championships, along with his photogenic good looks and charismatic personality. Woods, as smart off the course as on, chose carefully from the array of commercial opportunities that opened up to him and burnished his squeaky-clean image. Young players everywhere strove to follow in his footsteps. A recent sports-popularity poll revealed that three times as many African-American fans—13.4 percent—said they loved or liked the PGA Tour now compared with a decade earlier, doubtlessly because of Woods. A new youth-oriented era seemed about to dawn for a sport that had traditionally attracted mostly older players.

Real-estate developers began looking for sites for new golf courses. Equipment and apparel companies made plans to market new product lines to young golfers. Broadcasters anticipated a spike in ad revenues from the wider audiences that televised golf events would attract, and both golfers and tournament organizers began to hope for generous new sponsors. Golf clubs raised their fees with little resistance. The Professional

COURTESY OF SPORTS ILLUSTRATED/ROBERT BECK

Golf Association (PGA) saw an expanding future for its members and their fans.

But within a few years, the boom seemed over before it had really begun. A National Golf Foundation/McKinsey & Co. study reported that golf was losing about 3 million players a year, just as many as it managed to attract over the previous decade. The number of rounds of golf played in the U.S. also dropped steadily. Openings of new golf courses fell sharply after an unbroken climb through the 1990s, and existing courses began to suffer financial difficulties—and occasionally, even foreclosure or sale. Some of these facilities had just undergone millions of dollars of refurbishment and improvements in anticipation of business that never materialized. Apparel and equipment manufacturers began filing for Chapter 11 bankruptcy, including Top-Flite Golf, once known as Spalding and a one-time leader in the production of golf balls.

In addition, an even more public problem had arisen within the sport. Discrimination against women, ranging from petty rules limiting their tee times to complete bans prohibiting women from playing at certain clubs, had long gone unchallenged. Traditional country-club memberships dealt with divorce by expelling the former wife. As Millie Rech, who was banished from her country club when she was divorced, put it, "Rosa Parks was told to go to the back of the bus. I was thrown off the bus."

Matters came to a head during the prestigious Masters Tournament, held at the Augusta (Georgia) National Golf Club, which specifically bars women from membership. Despite public pressure and the nondiscriminatory stance of the PGA and the PGA Tour, the club refused to change its position. Says one top golf executive, "There is no way to explain away the fact that being a member of this club is extraordinary to your professional life, and the fact that women as a category do not have that right—can't get that right—well, that is wrong."

Sports marketers banking on golf are worried about the boom that never came. What went wrong?

The falling stock market—accompanied by the bursting of the dot-com stock price bubble and ethical scandals at Arthur Andersen, Adelphia Communications, Enron, Global Crossing, ImClone, Tyco, and WorldCom—worried many of the game's staunchest players: the retired and the wealthy. Overexpansion of facilities led to overcapacity. Corporate travel and expense budgets were cut in the wake of 9/11, leading to fewer perks like free country-club memberships, golf outings, and business meetings held at swank golf properties. Terry McAndrew of Golfbiz.net also sees another factor: the effect of a new work ethic in an era of rising unemployment. "In today's economy, people are genuinely worried about keeping their jobs and far less likely to slip out of the office early to sneak in a round of golf," he says. Even the willingness of today's parents and grandparents to devote weekends to watching the kids play soccer or baseball instead of pursuing hobbies of their own takes them away from the golf course and its time-consuming ritual. Some observers also believe that golf's slow pace is a poor fit with the harried lives most working couples and families lead today. And despite Tiger Woods's fame, few African-American or Hispanic communities have embraced the sport because of a lack of facilities and the high cost of the game.

It's hard to say for sure how much discrimination against women has hurt the sport. In her book *The Unplayable Lie: The Untold Story of Women and Discrimination in American Golf,* reporter Marcia Chambers describes exclusive golf clubs as "the last caste system in America and a cultural backwater guided by rules and bylaws created at a time when women didn't have the right to vote." Near-perfect play by such women as Annika Sorenstam and Michelle Wie has put women back in the spotlight of professional golf, but are female executives seeing them as role models drawing them back to the game?

So far, golf clubs are responding to the drop in attendance and membership by cutting their fees, but unless golfers materialize in record numbers, marketers may experience only declines in revenue. A lot has changed on the green in just a few short years. Golf is still a great game, but is it a good investment?[1]

Chapter Overview

CHANGE is a fact of life for all people, including marketers. Introducing change to one of the world's oldest organized sports isn't easy, and introducing change that is socially responsible can be even harder.

Although some change may be the result of crises, more often it is gradual. For example, not a video rental outlet could be found in America in 1975, but by 2005, over 21,000 were open for business—with more shelf space devoted to DVDs than to videotapes. During the same period, computer retail outlets exploded in number, increasing 12-fold. Cell phones replaced car phones—and transformed from plain gray into a rainbow of colors and styles while often including video capabilities. Beauty salons reinvented themselves as day spas. The harried lifestyles of today's Americans led consumers to outsource their domestic drudgery, contributing to growth in industries ranging from restaurants to cleaning and lawn-care services.

In addition to planning for change, marketers must set goals to meet the concerns of customers, employees, shareholders, and members of the general public. Industry competition, legal constraints, the impact of technology on product designs, and social concerns are some of the many important factors that shape the business environment. All potentially have impact on a firm's goods and services. Although external forces frequently are outside the marketing manager's control, decision makers must still consider those influences together with the variables of the marketing mix in developing—and occasionally modifying—marketing plans and strategies that take these environmental factors into consideration.

This chapter begins by describing five forces in marketing's external environment—competitive, political-legal, economic, technological, and social-cultural. Figure 3.1 identifies them as the foundation for making decisions that involve the four marketing mix elements and the target market. These forces provide the frame of reference within which all marketing decisions are made. The second focus of this chapter is marketing ethics and social responsibility. This section describes the nature of marketers' responsibilities both to business and to society at large.

Thou shalt not use profanity.

Thou shalt not covet thy neighbor's putter.

Thou shalt not steal thy neighbor's ball.

Thou shalt not bear false witness in the final tally.

Ground rules for a Grand Rapids, Michigan, ministers' golf tournament

ENVIRONMENTAL SCANNING AND ENVIRONMENTAL MANAGEMENT

figure 3.1

Elements of the Marketing Mix within an Environmental Framework

Marketers must carefully and continually monitor crucial trends and developments in the business environment. **Environmental scanning** is the process of collecting information about the external marketing environment to identify and interpret potential trends. The goal is to analyze the information and decide whether these trends represent significant opportunities or pose major threats to the company. The firm is then able to determine the best response to a particular environmental change.

After the first case of mad cow disease in the U.S. was confirmed in late December 2003, some consumers were fearful of eating beef from commercial farms because of concerns about the type of feed used, the production process, and their possible connection with the rare—but deadly—disease. Purveyors of so-called natural or organic beef moved into action, shifting to more aggressive marketing tactics to demonstrate to consumers that their meat was free of disease. Producers were quick to point out that their "natural" beef, produced without artificial growth hormones or most antibiotics, was obtained from cows fed vegetarian diets and was monitored throughout the production process, making it safe to eat. Conventional beef producers were skeptical that organic beef, often from small family farms and priced considerably higher than their own products, would see a permanent gain in its tiny share of the U.S. beef market. But organic farming currently ranks as one of the fastest growing segments of U.S. agriculture. "We think there are consumers who want to know where the food they eat comes from, how it was produced," says Ernie Reeves of Blue Ridge Premium Beef.[2]

environmental scanning Process of collecting information about the external marketing environment to identify and interpret potential trends.

environmental management Attainment of organizational objectives by predicting and influencing the competitive, political-legal, economic, technological, and social-cultural environments.

① **Identify the five components of the marketing environment.**

Environmental scanning is a vital component of effective **environmental management.** Environmental management involves marketers' efforts to achieve organizational objectives by predicting and influencing the competitive, political-legal, economic, technological, and social-cultural environments. In the political-legal environment, managers who are seeking modifications of regulations, laws, or tariff restrictions may lobby legislators or contribute to the campaigns of sympathetic politicians. In an about-face, global tobacco giant Altria, which recently changed its corporate name from Philip Morris, is gathering support among tobacco growers to lobby in favor of a bill to bring the tobacco industry under the regulatory power of the Food and Drug Administration. Company management now favors the move because of the need to create uniform manufacturing and marketing standards that would apply for all tobacco companies.[3]

For many domestic and international competitors, competing with established industry leaders frequently involves **strategic alliances**—partnerships with other firms in which the partners combine resources and capital to create competitive advantages in a new market. Strategic alliances are especially common in international marketing, where partnerships with local firms provide regional expertise for a company expanding its operations abroad. Members of such alliances share risks and profits. Alliances are essential in countries such as China and Mexico, where local laws require foreign firms doing business there to work with local companies.

Through successful research and development efforts, firms may influence changes in their own technological environments. A research breakthrough may lead to reduced production costs or a technologically superior new product.

While changes in the marketing environment may be beyond the control of individual marketers, managers continually seek to predict their impact on marketing decisions and to modify operations to meet changing market needs. Even modest environmental shifts can alter the results of those decisions.

MARKETING Concept Check

1. How does environmental scanning benefit marketers?
2. Does environmental scanning benefit consumers? Why or how?
3. What can managers do to exercise environmental management over the social-cultural environment?

THE COMPETITIVE ENVIRONMENT

As organizations vie to satisfy customers, the interactive exchange creates the **competitive environment.** Marketing decisions by each individual firm influence consumer responses in the marketplace. They also affect the marketing strategies of competitors. As a consequence, decision makers must continually monitor competitors' marketing activities—their products, channels, prices, and promotional efforts.

competitive environment Interactive process that occurs in the marketplace among marketers of directly competitive products, marketers of products that can be substituted for one another, and marketers competing for the consumer's purchasing power.

Few organizations enjoy **monopoly** positions as the sole supplier of a good or service in the marketplace. Utilities, such as natural gas, electricity, water, and cable TV service, have traditionally accepted considerable regulation from local authorities who controlled such marketing-related factors as rates, service levels, and geographic coverage. In exchange, the utilities gained exclusive rights to serve a particular group of consumers. The **deregulation movement** of the past three decades has ended total monopoly protection for most utilities. Today's shoppers can choose from alternative cable TV and Internet providers, cell phone and long-distance telephone carriers, and even gas and electric utilities. The constant stream of solicitations from long-distance telephone companies provides almost daily evidence of increased competition in this formerly monopolized industry.

Some marketers, such as pharmaceutical giants Merck and Pfizer, are able to achieve temporary monopolies from patents on drugs they invest millions to develop. When the Food and Drug Administration approves a new antiarthritis drug, improved blood pressure medicine, or even a pill to stimulate hair growth, the manufacturers are typically granted exclusive rights to produce and market the product during the life of the patent. By being first to market and then holding on to their leadership positions as similar, copycat drugs come on the market, many firms have been able to achieve virtual monopolies. Every single one of the millions of baseballs used in the major leagues is made by Rawlings Sporting Goods.[4]

Through industry megamergers, often on a global scale, some companies seek to dominate markets without ceding the controls that regulated monopolies forfeit. As a result of mergers, the auto, tobacco, accounting, and telecommunications industries are all dominated by three or four giants. Rather than seeking sole dominance of a market, corporations increasingly prefer to share the pie with just a few rivals. Referred to by economists as an **oligopoly,** this structure of a limited number of sellers in an industry where high start-up costs form barriers to keep out new competitors deters newcomers from breaking into markets, while ensuring that corporations remain innovative. In one of the numerous ongoing antitrust actions being pursued against Microsoft, RealNetworks Inc., creator of the media player RealPlayer, alleges that Microsoft "used its monopoly power to restrict how PC-makers install competing media players" and seeks $1 billion or more in damages.[5]

COURTESY OF ALABAMA POWER

Alabama Power, a subsidiary of The Southern Co., promotes its ability to consistently offer its customers rates lower than the national average and avoid the sharp rise in price that occurred during the past 10 years for goods and services ranging from groceries to health care and tuition.

TYPES OF COMPETITION

Marketers face three types of competition. The most *direct* form occurs among marketers of similar products, as when a Shell station opens across the street from BP or Marathon. The rapidly growing cell phone market provides consumers with such alternative suppliers as Verizon, Cingular, and T-Mobile. One of every seven U.S. consumers currently use a cell phone as their primary means of making calls. By not using landlines, these mobile users can save up to $10 a month plus taxes charged for local phone service.[6]

Telecommunications giant Motorola, battered by Finland's Nokia when the market for cell phones exploded, recently fought back with the release of a new line of sleek and stylish phones that serve as fashion accessories as well as communications devices. Motorola hopes that its aggressive design offensive, coupled with the launch of its new 3G handsets—an innovative technology that offers instant access to the Internet—will win back lost market share. In the race for teen dollars, chain store Hot Topic is beating out youth retailers like Gap and American Eagle. Offering funky fashions and oddball gifts—like the glow-in-the-dark tongue ring—the store caters to tastes of almost a fifth of high school students who consider themselves "alternative." Located in easy-to-access suburban malls, Hot Topic keeps in touch with customers' fashion choices, inviting comments and suggestions. Buyers also check out cutting-edge trends at rock concerts and rave parties and by watching at least an hour of MTV each day.[7]

2 Explain the types of competition marketers face and the steps necessary for developing a competitive strategy.

A second type of competition is *indirect* and involves products that are easily substituted. In the business document delivery industry, overnight express mail and messenger services compete with e-mail and voice mail. In the fast-food industry, pizza competes with chicken, hamburgers, and tacos. In transportation, the Greyhound bus line competes with auto rental services, airlines, and train services. Unable to compete directly with substitute transportation services, Amtrak decided to team up with its cruise ship and airline competitors by offering custom-designed vacation packages. Now Amtrak can make travel arrangements to get vacationers where they want to go by air, land, and sea.

Six Flags and Universal Studios amusement parks—the traditional hot spots for family vacations—now compete with outdoor adventure trips. One of every two U.S. adults will decide not to make this year's vacation a tranquil week at the beach or a trip to Disney World. Instead, they'll choose to do something more adventurous—thrill-filled experiences such as skydiving, whitewater rafting, participating in an archeological dig, or climbing Mount Rainier.

A change such as a price increase or an improvement in a product's attributes can also affect demand for substitute products. A major drop in the cost of solar energy would not only increase the demand for solar power but also adversely affect the demand for such energy sources as heating oil, electricity, and natural gas. Oil industry giant British Petroleum (BP) has recently made a competitive move into the solar energy market to broaden its base into renewable energy sources.

Even a "green" product like solar panels is not controversy-free, however. The typical issue involves aesthetics: Neighbors think the rooftop solar-power devices are ugly. These devices took off in popularity during the 1990s, when their costs dropped sharply—thanks to new technology as well as state and federal tax incentives for using them. But their installation has resulted in dozens of lawsuits by homeowners' associations in Sunbelt cities from Florida to California.[8]

One substitute, the Internet access known as wireless fidelity, or Wi-Fi, is experiencing a rocky start-up. While industry observers project that every laptop and handheld computer will soon be able to receive Wi-Fi, it's difficult to predict how many people will want to use it. Many companies, large and small, are carving out local Wi-Fi markets for themselves by setting up radio-linked local area networks to create the "hot spots" where fee-paying users log on. But some of the earliest firms to venture in the market have foundered or even folded, and technical problems plague those who are sticking it out. The wireless connection carries only about 300 feet and is highly vulnerable to hackers. Customer sign-ups have been slow so far, and "it doesn't really look like there are many carriers that are going to be making money," according to one market analyst. In addition, for-fee Wi-Fi must compete with free services offered by McDonald's, Starbucks, and some local governments.[9]

COURTESY OF BP

BP, a major force in the petroleum industry, has invested over $200 million in the firm's goal to make solar power a $1 billion component of its overall energy business by 2007.

The final type of competition occurs among all organizations that compete for consumers' purchases. Traditional economic analysis views competition as a battle among companies in the same industry (direct competition) or among substitutable goods and services (indirect competition). Marketers, however, are aware that all firms compete for a limited amount of discretionary buying power. Competition in this sense means that a Subaru WRX or a wide-screen plasma TV competes with a Colorado ski vacation. For the buyer's entertainment dollar, a Korn compact disc competes with two tickets to a San Antonio Spurs' game.

Because the competitive environment often determines the success or failure of a product, marketers must continually assess competitors' marketing strategies. New-product offerings with technological advances like phonecams, price reductions, special promotions, service requirements, or other competitive variations must be monitored. Then marketers must decide whether to adjust one or more marketing mix components to compete with the new market entry.

DEVELOPING A COMPETITIVE STRATEGY

Marketers at every successful firm must develop an effective strategy for dealing with the competitive environment. One company may compete in a broad range of markets in many areas of the world. Another may specialize in particular market segments, such as those determined by customers' geographic location, age, or income characteristics. Determining a **competitive strategy** involves answering the following three questions:

1. Should we compete?
2. If so, in what markets should we compete?
3. How should we compete?

The answer to the first question depends on the firm's resources, objectives, and expected profit potential. A firm may decide not to pursue or continue operating a potentially successful venture that does not mesh with its resources, objectives, or profit expectations. Semiconductor manufacturer Texas Instruments shed its defense electronics business unit, which makes missile sensors and radar and night-vision systems, to an aircraft company where this unit was a better fit. In a recent move to spin off Medco, its profitable pharmacy-benefits-management subsidiary, pharmaceutical giant Merck cited its decision to concentrate on its core business—the development of breakthrough medicines.[10]

Answering the second question—In what markets should we compete?—requires marketers to acknowledge their firm's limited resources (sales personnel, advertising budgets, product development capability, and the like). They must accept responsibility for allocating these resources to the areas of greatest opportunity.

Some companies gain access to markets or new technologies through acquisitions and mergers. The merger of Cingular Wireless and AT&T Wireless not only created the largest cellular company in the U.S. but also allowed the new company to upgrade its cellular phone technology, expand its territory coverage for users, and provide better clarity for calls—all while reducing overhead costs.[11]

Answering the third question—How should we compete?—requires marketers to make product, distribution, promotion, and pricing decisions that give the firm a competitive advantage in the marketplace. Firms can compete on a variety of bases, including product quality, price, and customer service. For example, retailer Neiman Marcus has gained a competitive advantage by providing superior customer service, while retailer Target competes by providing quality goods at low prices. As Figure 3.2 shows, the urban chic clothing company Urban Outfitters has an extensive Web site. Urban Outfitters competes in the teen clothing market by offering shoppers the ability to purchase their clothing in the online catalog, register for a "Wish List," or buy gift cards for friends or family. But specialized marketing support staff at the firm's headquarters also support the retail sales of its signature stores by directing online shoppers to the nearest Urban Outfitter retailer in their area of the country. Another company, Curves, learned how to compete in the crowded health-club market by offering no-nonsense streamlined fitness centers to meet its customers' needs—and at highly competitive prices (see the "Marketing Hit" box).

TIME-BASED COMPETITION

time-based competition Strategy of developing and distributing goods and services more quickly than competitors.

With increased international competition and rapid changes in technology, a steadily growing number of firms are using time as a strategic competitive weapon. **Time-based competition** is the strategy of developing and distributing goods and services more quickly than competitors. Although a video option on cell phones came late to the U.S. market, the new feature was a big hit, attracting new cus-

COURTESY OF URBAN OUTFITTERS

figure 3.2

The Internet: Important Sales Component of Urban Outfitters' Competitive Strategy

tomers at Verizon Wireless, T-Mobile, and other cell phone competitors. By 2005, most competitors had added this option, and 34 million Americans owned a videophone.[12] The flexibility and responsiveness of time-based competitors enable them to improve product quality, reduce costs, and expand product offerings to satisfy new market segments and enhance customer satisfaction.

In rapidly changing markets like consumer electronics and the computer industry, time-based competition is critical. Consumer demands for speed push developers to work on several generations of their technology simultaneously. In the mid-1990s, high-speed 3-D graphics capability came at a cost exceeding $300,000 and was reserved for high-tech applications such as medical imaging or flight simulations. Today, far more sophisticated graphics programs are available on Sony's PlayStation 2 or Microsoft's Xbox for less than $200. Less than five years ago, a new PC typically came with 20 gigabytes

marketing hit — Curves: Walk in, Exercise, Walk Out

Background. Americans are now the fattest people on the planet, and even fast-food restaurants are beginning to look for ways to jump on the health bandwagon. There have always been gyms. But expensive spa-like facilities are beyond the reach of many, and complicated and demanding exercise routines have a low customer retention rate.

The Challenge. Gary and Diane Heavin, founders of Curves International, wanted to reach a specific market segment—busy women who want to exercise—and offer them an exercise program they could stick to that would promise them weight loss, muscle toning, increased energy, and just plain fun.

The Strategy. Curves, which only began to advertise a couple of years ago, offers a single and inexpensive service—a structured 30-minute workout to music on 8 to 10 exercise machines that provide stretching, aerobics, and strength training. Store hours are short and facilities are small; there are no showers, frills, masseuses, or refreshment bars. A recorded voice guides customers' progress through the workout, and when they're finished, they leave.

The Outcome. The 10-year-old firm, which is privately owned, is the largest fitness franchise and the fastest growing franchise in the world, accounting for one of every four U.S. gyms and taking in about $750 million a year from its 2 million members. New locations are opening at the rate of about 200 per month, and franchise fees are attractively low. By keeping its retail spaces small and by refusing to permit a new franchise to intrude on the market of existing franchises, the Heavins make it possible for their owners to focus on service rather than membership recruitment. And service is what keeps members at its 7,000 worldwide locations coming back.

Sources: Company Web site, http://www.curvesinternational.com, accessed October 11, 2004; Heather Won Tesoriero, "A Slim Gym's Fat Success," *Time*, May 5, 2003; Jill Lerner, "Fitness Chain Curves Makes Boston Push," *Boston Business Journal*, August 29, 2003, http://www.bizjournals.com/boston/; Brian White, "Curves Growing Franchise Network," *Philadelphia Business Journal*, August 1, 2003, http://www.bizjournals.com/philadelphia/.

1. Distinguish between direct and indirect competition and give two examples.
2. What is time-based competition?

of storage; soon a single drive will have a terabyte—or 1,000 gigabytes. That's enough space to hold about 400 movies. The speed at which changes occur in the Internet arena is so great that marketers count time in "Internet years," actually time periods of only several weeks or months.

THE POLITICAL-LEGAL ENVIRONMENT

political-legal environment Component of the marketing environment consisting of laws and interpretations of laws that require firms to operate under competitive conditions and to protect consumer rights.

Before you play the game, learn the rules! It is a bad idea to start playing a new game without first understanding the rules, yet some businesspeople exhibit a lack of knowledge about marketing's **political-legal environment**—the laws and their interpretations that require firms to operate under certain competitive conditions and to protect consumer rights. Ignorance of laws, ordinances, and regulations or noncompliance with them can result in fines, negative publicity, and expensive civil damage suits.

The existing U.S. legal framework was constructed on a piecemeal basis, often in response to issues that were important at the time individual laws were enacted. Businesspeople need considerable diligence to understand its relationship to their marketing decisions. Numerous laws and regulations affect those decisions, many of them vaguely stated and inconsistently enforced by a multitude of different authorities.

Regulations enacted at the federal, state, and local levels affect marketing practices, as do the actions of independent regulatory agencies. These requirements and prohibitions touch on all aspects of marketing decision making: designing, labeling, packaging, distributing, advertising, and promoting goods and services. To cope with the vast, complex, and changing political-legal environment, many large firms maintain in-house legal departments; small firms often seek professional advice from outside attorneys. All marketers, however, should be aware of the major regulations that affect their activities.

(3) Describe how government and other groups regulate marketing activities and how marketers can influence the political-legal environment.

GOVERNMENT REGULATION

The history of U.S. government regulation can be divided into four phases. The first phase was the *antimonopoly period* of the late 19th and early 20th centuries. During this era, major laws such as the Sherman Antitrust Act, Clayton Act, and Federal Trade Commission Act were passed to maintain a competitive environment by reducing the trend toward increasing concentration of industry power in the hands of a small number of competitors. Laws enacted more than 100 years ago still affect business in the 21st century.

The recent Microsoft case is a good example of antitrust legislation at work. The U.S. Department of Justice found the software powerhouse guilty of predatory practices designed to crush competition. By bundling its own Internet Explorer browser with its Windows operating system (which runs 90 percent of the world's personal computers), Microsoft grabbed the majority of the market from rival Netscape. It also bullied firms as large as America Online to drop Netscape Navigator in favor of its browser. Microsoft's supporters countered that consumers have clearly benefited from the integrated features in Windows and that its bundling decisions were simply efforts to offer customer satisfaction through added value. Recently, the European Union charged that Microsoft was up to its old tricks by bundling its Media Player multimedia software into its operating system to beat rival RealNetworks. While the investigation was under way, Microsoft's market share surpassed RealNetworks's. Microsoft is also eyeing the search engine market to take on industry leader Google by offering similar features on its desktop.[13]

The second phase, aimed at *protecting competitors*, emerged during the Depression era of the 1930s, when independent merchants felt the need for legal protection against competition from larger chain stores. Among the federal legislation enacted was the Robinson-Patman Act. The third regulatory phase focused on *consumer protection.* Although the objective of consumer protection underlies most laws—with good examples including the Sherman Act, FTC Act, and Federal Food and Drug Act—many of the major consumer-oriented laws have been enacted during the past 40 years. The fourth phase, *industry deregulation*, began in the late 1970s and continues to the present. During this phase, government has sought to increase competition in such industries as telecommunications, utilities, transportation, and financial services by discontinuing many regulations and permitting firms to expand their service offerings to new markets.

The newest regulatory frontier is *cyberspace*. Federal and state regulators are investigating ways to police the Internet and online services. For example, the FTC has devoted a Web site to publicizing *e-fraud,* schemes such as metatags that falsely lure browsers to sites they have not requested or to start-your-own-business scams. Another popular con is to send consumers a check, apparently with no strings attached. When the check is cashed, the consumer has signed up for a long-term Internet access agreement, usually with an unreliable and overpriced operator. Although the federal government has been slow to regulate *spam*—junk e-mail—many states have enacted legislation and many more have introduced bills to protect consumers and punish offenders. Yet the effectiveness of state campaigns is limited. The Internet is, after all, global, not local.[14]

Privacy and child protection issues are another important—but difficult—enforcement challenge. With the passage of the Children's Online Privacy Protection Act, Congress took the first step in regulating what children are exposed to on the Internet. The primary focus is a set of rules regarding how and when marketers need to get parental permission before obtaining marketing research information from children over the Web.

The government's new *Do Not Call Registry,* a list to which consumers can add their names to avoid telemarketing calls, survived legal challenges and recently went into effect with millions of names and numbers already on the list (10 million people signed up within the first four days). Twelve states maintain similar lists of their own.[15]

Table 3.1 lists and briefly describes the major federal laws affecting marketing. Legislation covering specific marketing practices, such as product development, packaging, labeling, product warranties, and franchise agreements, is discussed in later chapters.

Marketers must also monitor state and local laws that affect their industries. Many states, for instance, allow hard liquor to be sold only in liquor stores; such laws limit the distribution of low-alcohol cocktails made with rum, vodka, whiskey, and bourbon. California's stringent regulations for automobile emissions require special pollution control equipment on cars sold in the state.

Consumers want more control over their telephones. Today we give it to them.

Michael K. Powell (b. 1963)

chairman, Federal Communications Commission (announcing the implementation of national Do Not Call Registry)

GOVERNMENT REGULATORY AGENCIES

Federal, state, and local governments have established regulatory agencies to enforce laws. At the federal level, the Federal Trade Commission (FTC) wields the broadest powers of any agency to influence marketing activities. It has the authority to enforce laws regulating unfair business practices and can take action to stop false and deceptive advertising. The Federal Communications Commission regulates communication by wire, radio, and television. Other federal regulatory agencies include the Consumer Product Safety Commission, the Federal Power Commission, the Environmental Protection Agency, and the Food and Drug Administration (FDA). To protect the public, the FDA recently banned the dietary supplement ephedra, which was linked to 155 deaths.[16]

The FTC uses several procedures to enforce laws. It may issue a consent order through which a business accused of violations can agree to voluntary compliance without admitting guilt. If a business refuses to comply with an FTC request, the agency can issue a cease-and-desist order, which gives a final demand to stop an illegal practice. Firms often challenge cease-and-desist orders in court. The FTC can require advertisers to provide additional information about products in their advertisements, and it can force firms using deceptive advertising to correct earlier claims with new promotional messages. In some cases, the FTC can require a firm to give refunds to consumers misled by deceptive advertising.

The FTC and U.S. Department of Justice can stop mergers if they believe the proposed acquisition will reduce competition by making it harder for new companies to enter the field. In recent years, these agencies have taken a harder line on proposed mergers, especially in the computer, telecommunications, financial services, and health-care sectors.

Removing regulations also changes the competitive picture considerably. Following deregulation of the telecommunications and utilities industries, suppliers no longer have exclusive rights to operate within a territory. Natural gas utilities traditionally competed with electric companies to supply homeowners and businesses with energy needs. Because of deregulation, they now also compete with other gas companies. Customers of KN Energy in southeastern Wyoming can choose from among 12 competing gas companies, some of which deliver gas through out-of-state pipelines. Deregulation also allows new opportunities for start-up companies.

table 3.1 ***Major Federal Laws Affecting Marketing***

DATE	LAW	DESCRIPTION
A. Laws Maintaining a Competitive Environment		
1890	Sherman Antitrust Act	Prohibits restraint of trade and monopolization; identifies a competitive marketing system as national policy goal.
1914	Clayton Act	Strengthens the Sherman Act by restricting such practices as price discrimination, exclusive dealing, tying contracts, and interlocking boards of directors where the effect "may be to substantially lessen competition or tend to create a monopoly"; amended by the Celler Kefauver Antimerger Act to prohibit major asset purchases that would decrease competition in an industry.
1914	Federal Trade Commission Act (FTC)	Prohibits unfair methods of competition; establishes the Federal Trade Commission, an administrative agency that investigates business practices and enforces the FTC Act.
1938	Wheeler-Lea Act	Amends the FTC Act to outlaw additional unfair practices; gives the FTC jurisdiction over false and misleading advertising.
1998	Digital Millennium Copyright Act	Protects intellectual property rights by prohibiting copying or downloading of digital files.
2001	Air Transportation Safety and System Stabilization Act	Enacted in response to terrorist attacks that weakened the airline industry; granted airlines $5 million in cash and $10 million in loan guarantees to keep them in business.
B. Laws Regulating Competition		
1936	Robinson-Patman Act	Prohibits price discrimination in sales to wholesalers, retailers, or other producers; prohibits selling at unreasonably low prices to eliminate competition.
1993	North American Free Trade Agreement (NAFTA)	International trade agreement between Canada, Mexico, and the United States designed to facilitate trade by removing tariffs and other trade barriers among the three nations.
C. Laws Protecting Consumers		
1906	Federal Food and Drug Act	Prohibits adulteration and misbranding of food and drugs involved in interstate commerce; strengthened by the Food, Drug, and Cosmetic Act (1938) and the Kefauver-Harris Drug Amendment (1962).
1970	National Environmental Policy Act	Establishes the Environmental Protection Agency to deal with various types of pollution and organizations that create pollution.
1971	Public Health Cigarette Smoking Act	Prohibits tobacco advertising on radio and television.
1972	Consumer Product Safety Act	Created the Consumer Product Safety Commission, which has authority to specify safety standards for most products.
1998	Children's Online Privacy Protection Act	Empowers FTC to set rules regarding how and when marketers must obtain parental permission before asking children marketing research questions.
2000	Cybersquatting Law	Bans the based-faith purchase of domain names that are identical or confusingly similar to existing registered trademarks.
2001	Electronic Signature Act	Gives electronic signatures the same legal weight as handwritten signatures.
2001	Aviation Security Act	Requires airlines to take extra security measures to protect passengers, including the installation of reinforced cockpit doors, improved baggage screening, and increased security training for airport personnel.
D. Laws Deregulating Specific Industries		
1978	Airline Deregulation Act	Grants considerable freedom to commercial airlines in setting fares and choosing new routes.
1980	Motor Carrier Act and Staggers Rail Act	Significantly deregulates trucking and railroad industries by permitting them to negotiate rates and services.
1996	Telecommunications Act	Significantly deregulates the telecommunications industry by removing barriers to competition in local and long-distance phone and cable and television markets.
2003	Amendments to the Telemarketing Sales Rule	Created a national Do Not Call Registry, which prohibits telemarketing calls to registered telephone numbers; restricted the number and duration of telemarketing calls generating dead air space with use of automatic dialers; cracked down on unauthorized billing; and required telemarketers to transmit their caller ID information. Telemarketers must check the Do Not Call list quarterly, and violators could be fined as much as $11,000 per occurrence. Excluded from the registry's restrictions are charities, opinion pollsters, and political candidates.

The Federal Trade Commission (FTC) is the government's watchdog for marketing activities. It polices business practices from unwanted telemarketing calls to deceptive advertising.

The latest round of deregulation brought the passage of the Telecommunications Act of 1996 and its 2003 amendment, the so-called Do Not Call law for telemarketers. The Telecommunications Act removed barriers between local and long-distance phone companies and cable companies. It allowed the so-called Baby Bells—the seven regional Bell operating companies—to offer long-distance service; at the same time, long-distance companies—such as AT&T, MCI, and Sprint, which control over 90 percent of this market—were able to offer local service. Satellite television providers such as DISH and DirectTV and cable companies like Comcast and Time Warner Cable can offer phone service, and phone companies can get into the cable business. The change promises huge rewards for competitive winners. Capturing 20 percent of the local calling market, for example, is worth $15 billion to $20 billion per year to AT&T. Consumers can shop around for the best deals and packages as more companies compete for their business by bundling services at reduced prices.

However, deregulation is not without its critics. Although the previous decade witnessed a flurry of moves by state authorities to deregulate utilities, California's near disaster from its recent deregulatory moves prompted dozens of states to postpone further consideration of deregulations. Following allegations of financial malpractice at Houston's Enron Corp.—once the poster child of deregulation—the courts recently decided to split the bankrupt company apart and sell it off in pieces. Skyrocketing prices from gas shortages led the Georgia legislature to try to reform the state's deregulated gas market. One bill would re-regulate prices under state rules; another would create a state-regulated supplier to which consumers could switch from privately owned, unregulated gas companies.[17]

OTHER REGULATORY FORCES

Public and private consumer interest groups and self-regulatory organizations are also part of the legal environment. Consumer interest organizations have mushroomed in the past 25 years, and today, hundreds of groups operate at national, state, and local levels. The National Coalition against Misuse of Pesticides seeks to protect the environment. People for the Ethical Treatment of Animals (PETA)

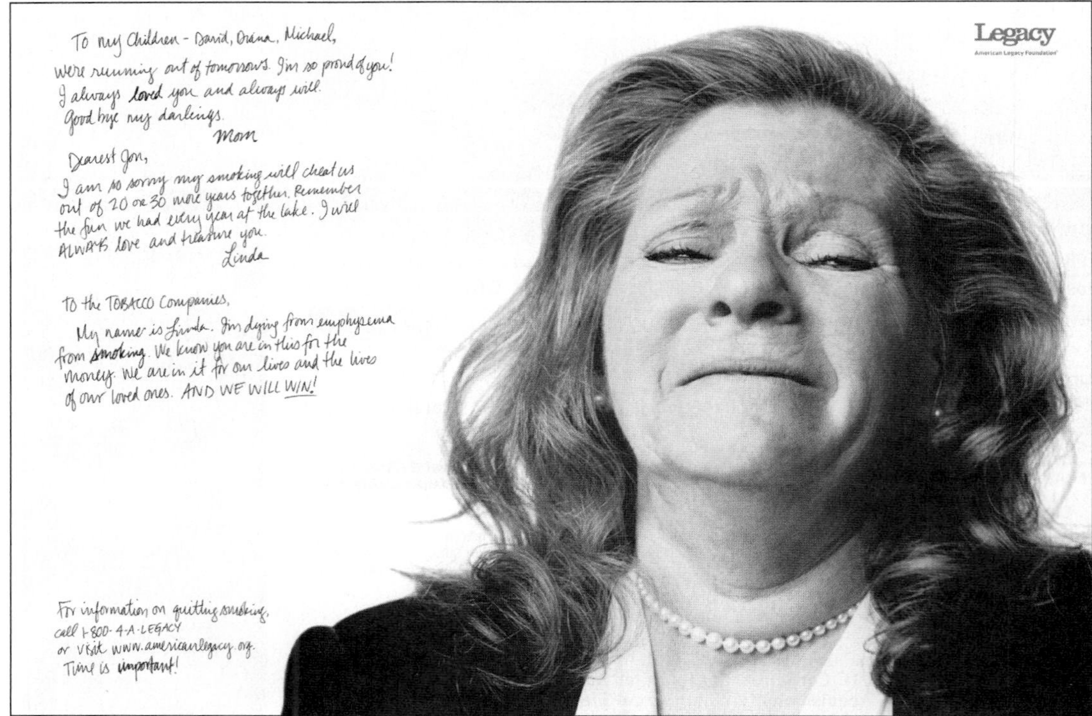

Through funding provided by the tobacco settlement suit, the American Legacy Foundation works to build a future where people will not suffer from smoking-related diseases such as emphysema.

opposes the use of animals for product testing. Other groups attempt to advance the rights of minorities, elderly Americans, and other special-interest causes. The power of these groups has also grown. Pressure from antialcohol groups has resulted in proposed legislation requiring health warnings on all alcohol ads and stricter regulations of alcoholic beverage advertising.

Self-regulatory groups represent industries' attempts to set guidelines for responsible business conduct. The Council of Better Business Bureaus is a national organization devoted to consumer service and business self-regulation. The Council's National Advertising Division (NAD) is designed to promote truth and accuracy in advertising. It reviews and advocates voluntary resolution of advertising-related complaints between consumers and businesses. If NAD fails to resolve a complaint, an appeal can be made to the National Advertising Review Board, which is composed of advertisers, ad agency representatives, and public members. In addition, many individual trade associations set business guidelines and codes of conduct and encourage members' voluntary compliance.

In an effort to protect consumer privacy and curb unwanted mail or phone solicitations, the Direct Marketing Association (DMA) recently approved new rules requiring customers to be notified if information about them—including their name and address—was being shared with other marketers. Companies must also tell consumers that they have the option not to have their information shared. The new rules apply to nearly 4,500 DMA member firms and include 2,600 Internet companies, catalogs, banks, financial institutions, publishers, not-for-profits, and book and music clubs.

As mentioned earlier, regulating the online world poses a challenge. Favoring self-regulation as the best starting point, the FTC sponsored a privacy initiative for consumers, advertisers, online companies, and others as a way to develop voluntary industry privacy guidelines. The Interactive Services Association is also working on its own privacy standards.

CONTROLLING THE POLITICAL-LEGAL ENVIRONMENT

Most marketers comply with laws and regulations because noncompliance can scar a firm's reputation and hurt profits. Yet most also fight regulations they consider unjust. The regional Bell operating companies filed lawsuits to protect their turf against competition from long-distance carriers and cable companies, while GTE claimed the deregulation of local phone service was unconstitutional. Other companies have jumped in to take advantage of new opportunities. Furst Group, a long-distance phone company with no lines or equipment, buys blocks of long-distance time from major carriers at greatly reduced rates and resells them by the minute at a discount. Now the regional Bells and long-distance carriers are competing aggressively to keep their customers. They are also working with **switchless resellers** like Furst to retain small-business customers that they would otherwise lose.

Consumer groups and political action committees within industries may try to influence the outcome of proposed legislation or change existing laws by engaging in political lobbying or boycotts. Lobbying groups frequently enlist the support of customers, employees, and suppliers to assist their efforts.

1. What is the purpose of antitrust legislation?
2. Which federal agency wields the broadest regulatory powers for influencing marketing activities?
3. Name a self-regulatory group and describe its mission.

THE ECONOMIC ENVIRONMENT

(4) Outline the economic factors that affect marketing decisions and consumer buying power.

The overall health of the economy influences how much consumers spend and what they buy. This relationship also works the other way. Consumer buying plays an important role in the economy's health; in fact, consumer outlays perennially make up some two-thirds of overall economic activity. Since all marketing activity is directed toward satisfying consumer wants and needs, marketers must understand how economic conditions influence consumer purchasing behavior.

Marketing's **economic environment** consists of forces that influence consumer buying power and marketing strategies. They include the stage of the business cycle, inflation and deflation, unemployment, income, and resource availability.

economic environment Factors that influence consumer buying power and marketing strategies, including stage of the business cycle, inflation, unemployment, income, and resource availability.

STAGES IN THE BUSINESS CYCLE

Historically, the economy has tended to follow a cyclical pattern consisting of four stages: prosperity, recession, depression, and recovery. No depressions have occurred in the U.S. since the 1930s, and many economists argue that society is capable of preventing future depressions through intelligent use of various economic policies. Good decision making by government agencies, industry groups, and major businesses should ensure that a recession would give way to a period of recovery rather than sinking further into depression.

Consumer buying differs in each stage of the **business cycle,** and marketers must adjust their strategies accordingly. In times of prosperity, consumer spending maintains a brisk pace, and buyers are willing to spend more for premium versions of well-known brands. Marketers respond by expanding product lines, increasing promotional efforts and expanding distribution to raise market share, and raising prices to widen profit margins. As the economy began to recover from the recession of the early years of the 21st century, consumer spending grew at a brisk pace. Some observers referred to these actions as an example of the so-called *wealth effect.* As millions of retirement accounts recovered from the huge sell-off of 2001, consumers looked at their monthly 401(k) retirement accounts, saw them returning in value to their prerecession levels, and *felt* richer and more confident about the future. So they began to reward themselves with expensive purchases they had wanted for years. Figure 3.3 illustrates how marketers appeal to shoppers' desires to indulge themselves with luxury items in response to the wealth effect—such as a Bermudan vacation.

During the recent recession, consumers shifted their buying patterns to emphasize more basic, functional products that carried lower price tags. They limited travel, restaurant meals, entertainment, and convenience purchases like expensive vacations, preferring to spend money on video rentals and home cooking. In recessionary periods, sales of lower priced brands of grocery and household-goods products and private-label goods rise. To compete, marketers consider lowering prices, eliminating marginal products, improving customer service, and increasing promotional outlays to stimulate demand. They may also launch value-priced products likely to appeal to cost-conscious buyers.

figure 3.3
The Wealth Effect: Spending for Luxury Products Increases during Recovery and Prosperity Stages

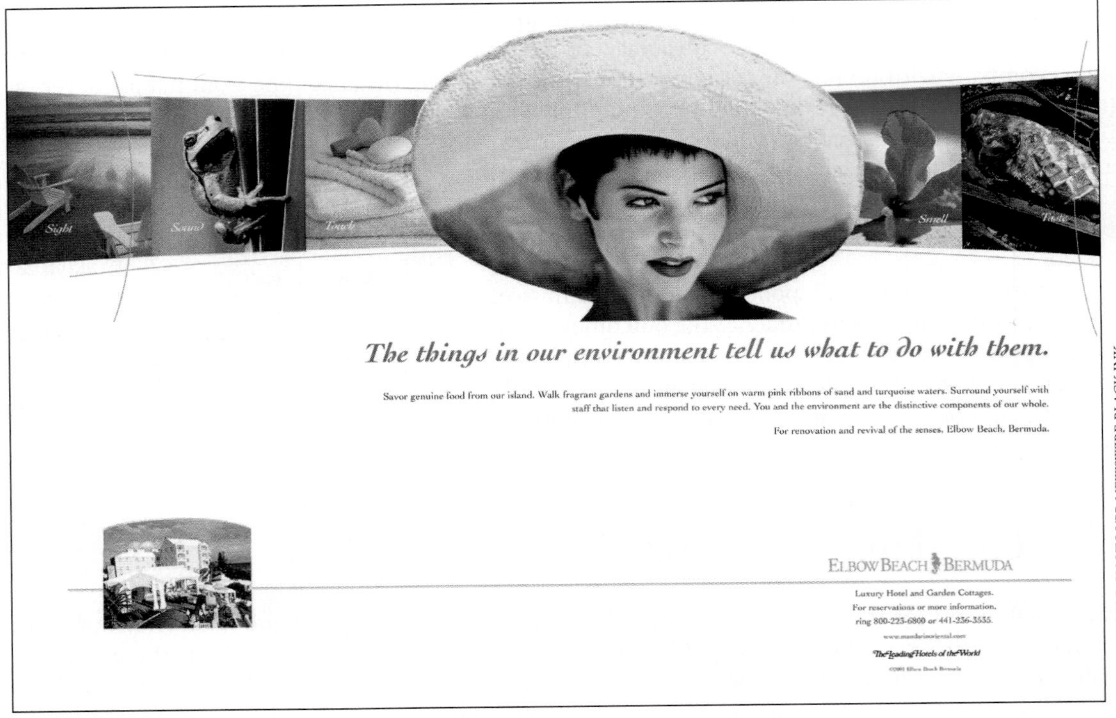

AP/WIDE WORLD PHOTOS/PR NEWSWIRE BLACK INK

Consumer spending sinks to its lowest level during a depression. The last true depression in the U.S. occurred during the 1930s. Although a severe depression could occur again, most experts see it as a slim possibility. Through its monetary and fiscal policies, the federal government attempts to control extreme fluctuations in the business cycle that lead to depression.

In the recovery stage, the economy emerges from recession and consumer purchasing power increases. But while consumers have money to spend, caution often restrains their willingness to buy. During the recovery of an earlier recession a decade ago, for instance, U.S. consumers paid down their car loans and bank loans and borrowed less on their credit cards. With lower principal and interest payments, they actually had higher levels of disposable income to spend. But they continued to spend cautiously. Usually, as a recovery strengthens, consumers become more indulgent, buying more convenience products and higher priced goods and services.

The most recent economic slowdown began in 2001, as growth stalled, unemployment levels rose, and the stock market nosedived. In attempts to cut costs and hold on to profits, corporations made massive layoffs. Telecommunications company Motorola shed a third of its worldwide workforce. Consumer debt rose faster than income, delinquent credit-card payments reached new highs, and personal bankruptcy filings increased fivefold over the previous year.[18] By 2003, following federal interest rate cuts and tax cuts aimed at stimulating the economy, the worst was over. Productivity continued at high levels, low interest rates encouraged consumers to refinance or purchase new homes, the stock market made a significant recovery, and unemployment rates declined. A number of concerns continued: international uncertainties with more than 100,000 U.S. troops stationed in Iraq and Afghanistan; a hint of inflation resulting from a combination of record gasoline prices, the largest federal budget deficit in history, and mortgage interest rate hikes; and concerns about job growth as businesses continue to outsource jobs to foreign countries.

WENDY'S INTERNATIONAL, INC.

Consumers respond to recession by trimming expenses. Restaurants that offer value-priced meals often do better during economic downturns.

Recovery remains a difficult stage for businesses just climbing out of a recession since it requires them to earn profits while trying to gauge uncertain consumer demand. Many cope by holding down costs. Some trim payrolls and close branch offices. Others cut back on business travel budgets. DaimlerChrysler pared spending on airline tickets by two-thirds during a single year. Teleconferencing and videoconferencing took the place of nonessential travel. Some industries struggle more than others during recovery periods. Among the hardest hit after the recent recession were the airline and lodging industries and the nation's major theme parks. Not only were consumers reluctant to fly following the terrorist attacks of September 11, but many of them viewed such services as travel and entertainment as unnecessary luxuries.

Despite the recent slowdown, economic growth is expected to continue at an annual rate of 3 percent for the remainder of this decade. Inflation should remain relatively low, and the standard of living will rise. During the first decade of this century, established industries such as finance, media, wholesale, and retail will change dramatically, and new industries will be created at an astounding pace.

Business cycles, like other aspects of the economy, are complex phenomena that seem to defy the control of both government officials and marketers. Success depends on flexible plans that can be adjusted to satisfy consumer demands during the various business cycle stages.

INFLATION AND DEFLATION

A major constraint on consumer spending, which can occur during any stage of the business cycle, is **inflation**—rising prices caused by some combination of excess demand and increases in the costs of raw materials, component parts, human resources, or other factors of production. Inflation devalues money by reducing the products it can buy through persistent price increases. These rising prices increase marketers' costs, such as expenditures for wages and raw materials, and the resulting higher prices may therefore negatively affect sales. U.S. inflation hit a heart-stopping high in 1979 of 13.3 percent.

If inflation is so bad, is its opposite, *deflation*, better? At first, it might seem so. Falling prices mean that products are more affordable. But deflation can be a long and damaging downward spiral, causing a freefall in business profits, lower returns on most investments, and widespread job layoffs. The last time that the U.S. experienced significant deflation was in the Great Depression of the 1930s. During the recent recession, economists worried about deflation, as interest rates declined and some product prices declined. Still, other than the cost of energy and food prices, which can fluctuate wildly, inflation is rising at about a 1 percent rate annually, in part due to rising energy and health-care costs and services—a sector that makes up 60 percent of the consumer price index. Productivity gains have also helped keep U.S. prices in neutral, with neither inflation nor deflation a significant threat.

UNEMPLOYMENT

Unemployment is defined as the proportion of people in the economy who do not have jobs and are actively looking for work. Unemployment rises during recessions and declines in the recovery and prosperity stages of the business cycle. Like inflation, unemployment affects marketing by modifying consumer behavior. Unless unemployment insurance, personal savings, and union benefits effectively offset lost earnings, unemployed people have relatively little income to spend. Even if these protections completely compensate people for lost earnings, their purchase behavior is still likely to change. Instead of committing limited funds to new purchases, they may choose to build their savings.

The relationship between unemployment and stages in the business cycle was illustrated in the past dozen years. After peaking near 8 percent during the recession of 1992, unemployment declined steadily in the midst of the extended period of prosperity from the mid-1990s to the early years of this century, reaching a low of 3.9 percent in 2001. It crept back up to the 6 percent mark when the nation experienced a double blow of an economic downturn combined with the terrorist attacks.[19] Since that time, unemployment has declined in the wake of an improved economy, though recent rates of job creation have been below expectations and thousands of job seekers have dropped out of the job market.[20]

Internet job boards are cutting into the job-search market once controlled by matchmaking personnel agencies and newspaper advertising. The Web now accounts for about 15 percent of employment advertising, up from only 2 percent just a few years ago. Thousands of large and medium-sized employers include an "Available Positions" section on their Web sites. Online recruiters like

HotJobs.com and Monster.com are both popular with job seekers and growing rapidly. HotJobs.com, one of the big success stories in online recruiting, is a regular advertiser on annual Super Bowl telecasts. It maintains a database of almost 10 million registered job seekers—and has in excess of 70,000 job listings.[21]

INCOME

Income is another important determinant of marketing's economic environment because it influences consumer buying power. By studying income statistics and trends, marketers can estimate market potential and develop plans for targeting specific market segments. For example, U.S. household incomes have grown in recent years. Coupled with a low rate of inflation, this increase has boosted purchasing power for millions of consumers. A rise in income represents a potential for increasing overall sales. However, marketers are most interested in **discretionary income,** the amount of money people have to spend after buying necessities such as food, clothing, and housing.

Changes in average earnings powerfully affect discretionary income. Historically, periods of major innovation have been accompanied by dramatic increases in living standards and rising incomes. During the first half of the 20th century—a period of unprecedented innovations in transportation from the railroads to supersonic jets—real per-capita incomes tripled and even quadrupled, fueled by rising productivity. The 21st century could see similar income gains with the growth of electronic technologies. Some predictions indicate a 9 percent rise in real wages, a more than 50 percent rise in corporate earnings, and interest rates below 4 percent. These rapidly climbing income rates could lead to a 25 percent growth in the overall economy.

RESOURCE AVAILABILITY

Resources are not unlimited. Shortages—temporary or permanent—can result from several causes, including lack of raw materials, component parts, energy, or labor. A continuing concern of both business executives and government officials is the nation's dependence on imported oil and the risk that these imports might be curtailed by exporting countries attempting to influence U.S. foreign policy. Also, brisk demand on a global scale may bring in orders that exceed available petroleum and natural gas stockpiles, overwhelm manufacturing capacity, or outpace the response time required to gear up a production line. During the past two years, gasoline purchasers have experienced declines in discretionary income as gas prices moved above the $2-per-gallon range. Regardless of the cause, shortages require marketers to reorient their thinking.

demarketing Process of reducing consumer demand for a good or service to a level that the firm can supply.

One reaction is **demarketing,** the process of reducing consumer demand for a product to a level that the firm can reasonably supply. Oil companies publicize tips on how to cut gasoline consumption, and utility companies encourage homeowners to install more insulation to reduce heating costs. Many cities discourage central business-district traffic by raising parking fees and violation penalties and promoting mass transit and carpooling.

A shortage presents marketers with a unique set of challenges. They may have to allocate limited supplies, a sharply different activity from marketing's traditional objective of expanding sales volume. Shortages may require marketers to decide whether to spread limited supplies over all customers or limit purchases by some customers so that the firm can completely satisfy others.

Marketers today have also devised ways to deal with increased demand for fixed amounts of resources. Reynolds Metal Co. addresses the dwindling supply of aluminum through its recycling programs, including cash-paying vending machines. Such "reverse" vending machines allow people to insert empty cans into the machines and receive money, stamps, and/or discount coupons for merchandise or services.

THE INTERNATIONAL ECONOMIC ENVIRONMENT

In today's global economy, marketers must also monitor the economic environment of other nations. Just as in the U.S., a recession in Europe or Japan changes buying habits. Changes in foreign currency rates compared with the U.S. dollar also affect marketing decisions. Problems in Asian economies hurt companies such as BP, whose foreign sales fell nearly 20 percent in just two years. Even beverage giant Coca-Cola Co. is not immune. With 75 percent of its operating profit generated overseas, currency fluctuations risk damaging overall performance. Rival PepsiCo gets only a fifth of its earnings from international sales.[22]

For the most part, however, U.S. companies have posted higher revenue gains in overseas operations. Technology companies are the biggest beneficiaries. Combined, Lucent Technologies, Dell, and Seagate Technology account for well over $12 billion in annual sales from outside the U.S.

In China, where the market for cell phones shows growth at the phenomenal rate of 50 percent while demand in Europe slows down, technology companies foresee a similarly explosive market for wireless Internet access. In fact, overall exports to China have recently risen dramatically, increasing faster than exports to the U.S., and the Chinese economy may soon become the world's second most important engine of growth.[23]

1. **What are the stages of the business cycle?**
2. **What is inflation and how does it affect consumer buying decisions?**
3. **How does the international economic environment affect U.S. marketers?**

THE TECHNOLOGICAL ENVIRONMENT

5 **Discuss the impact of the technological environment on a firm's marketing activities.**

technological environment Applications to marketing of knowledge based on discoveries in science, inventions, and innovations.

The **technological environment** represents the application to marketing of knowledge in science, inventions, and innovations. Technology leads to new goods and services for consumers; it also improves existing products, offers better customer service, and often reduces prices through new, cost-efficient production and distribution methods. Technology can quickly make products obsolete—e-mail, for example, quickly eroded both letter writing and the market for fax machines—but it can just as quickly open new marketing opportunities.

As we discussed in Chapter 1, technology is revolutionizing the marketing environment, transforming the way companies promote and distribute goods. Technological innovations create not only new products and services but also entirely new industries. Among the new businesses developing as a result of the Internet are Web-page designers, new types of software firms, interactive advertising agencies, and companies such as VeriSign that allow customers to make secure financial transactions over the Web. Industrial and medical use of lasers, superconductor transmission of electricity, wireless communications products, seeds and plants enhanced by biotechnology, and genetically engineered proteins that fight disease are a few more examples of technological advances.

ConocoPhillips has revamped its manufacturing operations with new software applications. A new planning and optimization program, designed to help refinery operations comply with stiff federal environmental regulations that took effect in 2004, also cut supply chain and manufacturing costs.[24]

Technology can sometimes address social concerns. In response to pressure from the World Trade Organization and the U.S. government, Japanese automakers were first to use technology to develop more fuel-efficient vehicles and reduce dangerous emissions with offerings like the Toyota Prius and a hybrid version of the Honda Civic. The Japanese are already rolling out their second generation of "hybrid vehicles" that combine a conventional gasoline engine with a battery-powered electric motor, and Ford Motor Co.'s hybrid Escape sport-utility vehicle (SUV) promises up to 40 mpg in the city.[25] Figure 3.4 shows the Prius, Toyota's successful hybrid vehicle capable of achieving up to 52 miles per gallon in highway driving. Although 47,000 units were built in 2004, buyers had to wait as long as six months to buy one. Case 3.1 at the end of the chapter describes some of the strategies U.S. automakers have chosen to cope with technology change.

Industry, government, colleges and universities, and other not-for-profit institutions all play roles in the development of new technology—but improvements often come at a price. A recent study found, for instance, that the cost of saving one life by insulating airplane cabins to protect against fire would be $300,000, while strengthening side doors on automobiles would cost $1.1 million per life saved. Flame-retardant children's sleepwear would save lives at a cost of $2.2 million each for implementing safety regulations.[26]

Research and development efforts by private industry represent a major source of technological innovation. Pfizer, a U.S.-based global pharmaceutical company, discovers, develops, manufactures, and markets innovative medicines, spending billions each year on research. Among its most publicized

figure 3.4

The Toyota Prius: One of the First Hybrid Automobiles Available to U.S. Auto Buyers

JOHN HILLERY/REUTERS/LANDOV

breakthroughs are the cholesterol-lowering drug Lipitor, which ranks as the biggest selling prescription drug in the U.S.; Viagra, a revolutionary treatment for erectile dysfunction; and Trovan, one of the most prescribed antibiotics in the U.S. Pfizer Animal Health develops animal vaccines, feed additives, and the first arthritis medication in the U.S. specifically for dogs. To maximize the strength of its product lines, Pfizer invests nearly $3 billion in research and development annually. Its U.S. sales force, which doubled in number in just three years, has ranked No. 1 in overall quality for the last four years.

Another major source of technology is the federal government, including the military. Air bags originated from Air Force ejection seats, digital computers were first designed to calculate artillery trajectories, and the microwave oven is a derivative of military radar systems.

Although the U.S. has long been the world leader in research, competition from rivals in Europe, Japan, and other Asian countries is intense. While U.S. companies spearheaded the technologies behind personal computers, networking systems, and the Internet, Japanese firms capitalized on their ability to transfer those technologies into commercial products. For instance, Sony and JVC commercialized videocassette recorders—an American technology—into one of the most successful new products of the past two decades. Chinese companies, which traditionally operated as subcontractors for U.S. firms, are working to build their own international brands—much like current Japanese competitors did 30 years ago.[27]

APPLYING TECHNOLOGY

The technological environment must be closely monitored for a number of reasons. For one, creative applications of new technologies not only give a firm a definite competitive edge but can also benefit society. As shown in Figure 3.5, Scottsdale, Arizona-based First Solar developed solar-energy-powered refrigerators—powered by rooftop solar panels—to help Native American Navajo in remote areas maintain their food supplies without making long trips every other day for block ice. The Navajo were far away from any power grids and could not tap typical electricity sources. So, First Solar developed the refrigerators to tap the power of the sun, which is plentiful in Arizona.[28]

Marketers who monitor new technology and successfully apply it may also enhance customer service. Breakthroughs in electronic communications have brought consumers the convenience of in-home shopping and 24-hour banking at automated teller machines and via the Internet. Some restaurants provide faster service by equipping serving staff with palmtop computers that transmit patrons' orders to the kitchen staff.

Vonage, a start-up communications company in New Jersey, offers customers low-priced phone service and an extraordinary array of sophisticated service extras thanks to its use of the Internet to route local and long-distance calls. Vonage calls its product Digital Voice service; the generic name of the new technology is *VoIP*, or Voice over Internet Protocol, and it's expected to revolutionize the phone industry by using a high-speed Internet connection instead of a conventional phone line. Despite some concerns about the reliability of the service, which requires customers to have high-speed or broadband Internet connections and which does not work during a power outage, AT&T, Qwest, and Verizon are preparing to adopt the new technology, as are cable and Internet providers like Cablevision, Comcast, and Time Warner Cable.[29] No one knows for sure how many customers will adopt the VoIP technology, and there is no guarantee of success for the firms that rush to provide it. Subsequent chapters discuss in more detail how companies apply technologies—such as databases, electronic data interchange, and interactive promotional techniques—to create a competitive advantage.

figure 3.5

How Technology Advances Meet Consumer Needs

JACQUELINE BOHNERT PHOTOGRAPHY

MARKETING Concept Check

1. What are some of the consumer benefits of technology?
2. Are there any drawbacks to applications of new technology?

THE SOCIAL-CULTURAL ENVIRONMENT

(6) **Explain how the social-cultural environment influences marketing.**

As a nation, the U.S. is becoming older, more affluent, and more culturally diverse. The birthrate is falling, and subculture populations are rising. People express concerns about the environment, buying ecologically friendly products that reduce pollution. They value the time at home with family and friends, watching videos and eating microwavable snacks. These aspects of consumer lifestyles help shape marketing's **social-cultural environment**—the relationship between marketing and society and its culture.

social-cultural environment Component of the marketing environment consisting of the relationship between the marketer and society and its culture.

To remain competitive, marketers must be sensitive to society's demographic shifts and changing values. These variables affect consumers' reactions to different products and marketing practices. College students—a core market for new releases on compact disc or DVD—have found new ways to get hold of popular music and movies. Napster, the song-swapping service that allowed friends to trade pirated music over the Web, has been silenced by litigation. After its suit against Morpheus was thrown out of court in 2003, the Recording Industry Association of America (RIAA) responded to music file sharing on the Internet by filing lawsuits for copyright infringement against over 250 music fans of all ages, some as young as 12. The first result of the suits was a public relations flap in which even pop recording artists took sides, but the RIAA is pursuing its case, while offering to accept cash settlements from the defendants and setting up an amnesty program. "We knew that the press would find poster children as a result of this program," says RIAA president Cary Sherman. "But you have to choose between your wish to be loved and your wish to survive. The purpose is to get the message out."[30]

Another social-cultural consideration is the increasing importance of cultural diversity. The U.S. is a mixed society composed of various submarkets, each with its unique values, cultural characteristics, consumer preferences, and purchasing behaviors. Advertising firm Dieste Harmel specializes in

No es lo mismo
sin Verizon Wireless.

COURTESY OF VERIZON WIRELESS

Verizon Wireless, competing for the No. 1 position in the U.S. cell phone market and being challenged by Cingular's purchase of AT&T Wireless, sees the Hispanic market as a major source of growth and its line of videophones as a major product attraction. The rapidly growing U.S. Hispanic market is an even larger ethnic segment than African-American consumers, previously the nation's largest ethnic segment.

targeting the Hispanic market. When research showed that Hispanic consumers ate only half as many salty snacks as non-Hispanic consumers, Dieste went to work. The resulting campaign featured two Latin music stars and created a fun, party atmosphere around the client's product, Doritos. Sales shot up by 25 percent. Even better, a campaign tie-in showcased Pepsi, whose sales in Hispanic markets tripled.[31]

The social-cultural context often exerts a more pronounced influence on marketing decision making in the international sphere than in the domestic arena. Learning about cultural and societal differences among countries is paramount to a firm's success abroad. Marketing strategies that work in the U.S. often fail when directly applied in other countries, and vice versa. In many cases, marketers must redesign packages and modify products and advertising messages to suit the tastes and preferences of different cultures. Chapter 7 explores the social-cultural aspects of international marketing.

CONSUMERISM

Changing societal values have led to **consumerism,** defined as a social force within the environment that aids and protects the buyer by exerting legal, moral, and economic pressures on business. Today, everyone—marketers, industry, government, and the public—is acutely aware of the impact of consumerism on the nation's economy and general well-being.

In recent years, marketers have witnessed increasing consumer activism. No organization or industry is immune. Marketers of canned tuna have been criticized for promoting sales of tuna caught by nets that also trap and kill dolphins. Private airport security firms have been replaced by federal employees in response to heightened concerns over the threat of terrorist attacks. Protesters oppose moves to allow oil drilling in the Alaska wildlife refuge. Boycotts, another means through which consumers make their objections known, have increased in recent years to include companies from almost every industry: Nike, McDonald's, Disney, Monsanto, and British Airways have all been targeted in recent years. Just the threat of a boycott can sometimes bring results.

You are not anonymous. We're going to begin to take names.

Cary Sherman

president, Recording Industry Association of America (to millions of Web users who download copyrighted music)

consumerism Social force within the environment designed to aid and protect the consumer by exerting legal, moral, and economic pressures on business and government.

But firms do not always give in to consumer demands. The economic system cannot work if excessive demands prevent firms from achieving reasonable profit objectives. This choice between pleasing all consumers and remaining viable defines one of the most difficult dilemmas facing business. Given these constraints, what should buyers have the right to expect from the competitive marketing system?

The most frequently quoted answer came from a speech made by President John F. Kennedy more than four decades ago. Although this list does not amount to a definitive statement, it offers good rules of thumb that explain basic **consumer rights:**

1. *The right to choose freely.* Consumers should be able to choose from among a range of goods and services.
2. *The right to be informed.* Consumers should be provided with enough education and product information to enable them to be responsible buyers.
3. *The right to be heard.* Consumers should be able to express their legitimate displeasure to appropriate parties—that is, sellers, consumer assistance groups, and city or state consumer affairs offices.
4. *The right to be safe.* Consumers should be assured that the goods and services they purchase are not injurious with normal use. Goods and services should be designed in such a way that the average consumer can use them safely.

These rights have formed the conceptual framework of much of the legislation enacted during the first 40 years of the consumer rights movement. However, the question of how best to guarantee them remains unanswered. Sometimes state or federal authorities step in. California's "lemon law" gives car dealers only three chances to repair a defective auto. Following the terrorist attacks of September 11, airlines were immediately required to install titanium cockpit doors. Food labeling regulations force disclosure of such details as expiration date, ingredients, and nutritional values on packaged foods.

consumer rights In their most basic form, these rights include a person's right to choose goods and services freely, to be informed about these products and services, to be heard, and to be safe. These four basic rights form the conceptual framework for a more thorough and legislative explanation of consumer rights that has developed and changed since 1962 when President Kennedy outlined consumer rights.

For years, studies have shown that automobiles are safer, better designed, and more sturdily built than ever before. But why does the number of recalls continue to grow? One in twelve cars was recalled last year—some 19.5 million vehicles in all and roughly three percentage points higher than a decade ago. Automakers are required to notify customers when they determine a vehicle is defective or doesn't comply with federal safety regulations. The recent increases in auto recalls have been fueled by tougher safety laws passed in response to a series of rollover deaths in Ford Explorers using Firestone tires. Another major contributor is advanced computer systems that now allow dealers to spot problems sooner. Consequently, the vast majority of recalls—three of four last year—are voluntary. At the top of the "Most Recalled Vehicles" list is the 1997 Ford F-150, which has been recalled 13 times. Just behind the popular truck are the 2000 BMW X5 (12 recalls) and the 2000 Ford Focus (11 recalls).[32]

Consumers will soon have more providers to choose from in selecting their type of phone service, whether traditional land line or wireless, without having to give up their familiar phone numbers in the process. New regulations allow customers who switch from corded phones to cell phones to keep their phone numbers as long as the wireless company serves the same area. A smaller percentage of customers who switch in the other direction can keep their phone numbers. Chris Murray, legislative counsel for *Consumer Reports* magazine, expects the change to improve service and lower prices. "Wireless is the only near-term hope for real consumer choice," he says.[33]

1. What is consumerism?
2. What can marketers do to protect the consumer's right to be heard?
3. How does protecting consumers' rights benefit marketers?

The social-cultural environment for marketing decisions at home and abroad is expanding in scope and importance. Today, no marketer can initiate a strategic decision without considering the society's norms, values, culture, and demographics. Understanding how these variables affect decisions is so important that some firms have created a new position—typically, manager of public policy research—to study the changing societal environment's future impact on their organizations.

ETHICAL ISSUES IN MARKETING

(7) Describe the role of marketing in society and identify the two major social issues in marketing.

The five environments described so far in this chapter do not completely capture the role that marketing plays in society and the consequent effects and responsibilities of marketing activities. Because marketing is closely connected with various public issues, it invites constant scrutiny by the public. Moreover, since marketing acts as an interface between an organization and the society in which it operates, marketers often carry much of the responsibility for dealing with social issues that affect their firms.

Marketing operates in an environment external to the firm. It reacts to that environment and in turn is acted upon by environmental influences. Relationships with customers, employees, the government, vendors, and society as a whole form the basis of the social issues that

Nutrition labeling helps protect consumer rights. The United States Potato Board promotes the health benefits of America's favorite vegetable.

When the SEC and the Justice Department get their act together and start sending some CFOs and CEOs to jail, you'll see a real wake-up call.

Philip B. Livingston

president, Financial Executives International

confront contemporary marketers. While these concerns often grow out of the exchange process, they produce effects coincidental to the primary sales and distribution functions of marketing. Marketing's relationship to its external environment has a significant effect on the firm's eventual success. It must continually find new ways to deal with the social issues facing the competitive system.

The diverse social issues that marketers face can be divided into two major categories: marketing ethics and social responsibility. While the overlap and classification problems are obvious, this simple framework provides a foundation for systematically studying these issues.

In a number of instances, ethical abuses result in so much harm—to customers, employees, investors, and the general public—that governments enact laws to punish them. The wave of corporate fraud and conflicts of interest on Wall Street and in Big Business during the past decade is still being addressed in the form of court trials and guilty pleas by wrongdoers. Following guilty pleas by such high-profile executives as Sam Waksal, founder and CEO of ImClone Systems, Scott D. Sullivan of WorldCom, and Andrew S. Fastow of Enron, state and federal trials began. Domestic diva Martha Stewart was convicted in a high-profile trial that wrapped up a few weeks after the conviction of Adelphia Communications Corp. founder John Rigas and his son. In 2005, trials began for WorldCom founder and CEO Bernard J. Ebbers, Tyco International's Mark Schwartz and L. Dennis Kozlowski, Enron founder Ken Lay and CEO Jeffrey K. Skilling, and HealthSouth Corp.'s Richard M. Scrushy.[34]

marketing ethics Marketers' standards of conduct and moral values.

Environmental influences have directed increased attention toward **marketing ethics,** defined as the marketer's standards of conduct and moral values. Ethics concern matters of right and wrong: the responsibility of individuals and firms to do what is morally right. As Figure 3.6 shows, each element of the marketing mix raises its own set of ethical questions. Before any improvements to the marketing system can be made, each of them must be evaluated.

Increased recognition of the importance of marketing ethics is evident from the more than 600 full-time corporate ethics officers in firms ranging from Dun & Bradstreet, Dow Corning, and Texas Instruments to even the Internal Revenue Service. The Federal Sentencing Guidelines for Organizations provides a framework for evaluating misconduct in business activities, such as fraud or price fixing. The sentencing guidelines act as an incentive for corporations to implement effective ethics compliance programs—if they are hauled into court, the existence of such a program can help reduce fines or sentences. A step-by-step framework for building an effective program is shown in Figure 3.7.

In a recent judgment against Wal-Mart, a federal jury found that the world's largest retailer forced employees at 18 Oregon stores to work unpaid overtime, a practice that the company maintains is against its policies. Compensation to the employees is still being determined. In the meantime, the world's largest retailer faces some three dozen similar lawsuits nationwide, so ethical violations such as these, if found to be true, could become costly not only in monetary terms but in harm to the firm's reputation.[35]

Ensuring ethical practices means promising customers and business partners not to sacrifice quality and fairness for profit. In exchange, organizations hope for increased customer loyalty toward their

figure 3.6
Ethical Questions in Marketing

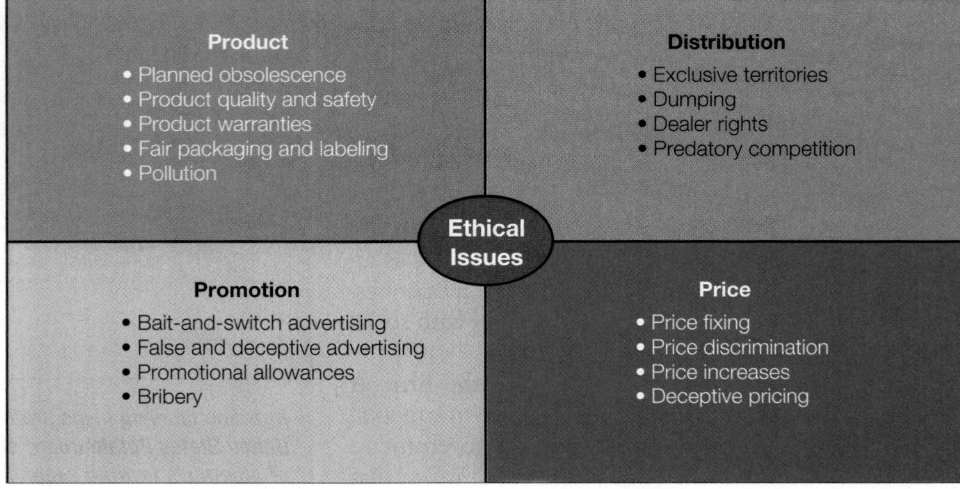

brands. Yet issues involving marketing ethics are not always clear-cut. The issue of cigarette advertising, for example, has divided the ranks of advertising executives. Is it right for advertisers to promote a product that, while legal, has known health hazards?

For years, charges of unethical conduct have plagued the tobacco industry. In the largest civil settlement in U.S. history, tobacco manufacturers agreed to pay $206 billion to 46 states. Four other states—Florida, Minnesota, Mississippi, and Texas—had separate settlements totaling another $40 billion. The settlement frees tobacco companies from state claims for the cost of treating sick smokers. For their part, cigarette makers can no longer advertise on billboards or use cartoon characters in ads, nor can they sell nontobacco merchandise containing tobacco brands or logos. A University of Michigan study credits the lawsuits and the resulting advertising restrictions—especially the elimination of the teen-oriented Joe Camel campaign—with reducing teen smoking by up to 9 percent in a single year. Aggressive state-run antismoking campaigns, paid for out of the tobacco settlements, were another key factor. However, researchers reported a fourfold rise in smoking among college students over a recent five-year period. Consumer groups are also pointing their fingers at cigarette marketers, though some class-action lawsuits against tobacco companies have recently been thrown out of court because they "involve too many individual issues to be tried as class actions." Says one analyst, "Tobacco is still a highly profitable business and companies are going to remain competitive with each other. You may not be able to put up a 50-foot sign on the street, but you can still send it in the mail to smokers. I would expect to see more emphasis on direct-to-consumer marketing."[36]

People develop standards of ethical behavior based on their own systems of values, which help them deal with ethical questions in their personal lives. However, the workplace may generate serious conflicts when individuals discover that their ethical beliefs are not necessarily in line with those of their employer. For example, employees may think that shopping online during a lunch break using a work computer is fine, but the company may decide otherwise. The quiz in Figure 3.8 highlights other everyday ethical dilemmas.

figure 3.7

Ten Steps for Corporations to Improve Standards of Business Ethics

1. Appoint a senior-level ethics compliance officer.
2. Set up an ethics code capable of detecting and preventing misconduct.
3. Distribute a written code of ethics to employees, subsidiaries, and associated companies and require all business partners to abide by it.
4. Conduct regular ethics training programs to communicate standards and procedures.
5. Establish systems to monitor misconduct and report grievances.
6. Establish consistent punishment guidelines to enforce standards and codes.
7. Encourage an open-door policy, allowing employees to report cases of misconduct without fear of retaliation.
8. Prohibit employees with a track record of misconduct from holding positions with substantial discretionary authority.
9. Promote ethically aware and responsible managers.
10. Continually monitor effectiveness of all ethics-related programs.

Source: Adapted from O. C. Ferrell, John Fraedrich, and Linda Ferrell, *Business Ethics: Ethical Decision Making and Cases*, Sixth Edition, pp. 61–62 and 172–173. Copyright © 2005 by Houghton Mifflin Company. Reprinted with permission.

How can these conflicts be resolved? In addition to individual and organizational ethics, individuals may be influenced by a third basis of ethical authority—a professional code of ethics that transcends both organizational and individual value systems. A professional peer association can exercise collective oversight to limit a marketer's individual behavior.

Any code of ethics must anticipate the variety of problems that marketers are likely to encounter. Promotional matters tend to receive the greatest attention, but ethical considerations also influence marketing research, product strategy, distribution strategy, and pricing.

ETHICAL PROBLEMS IN MARKETING RESEARCH

Invasion of personal privacy has become a critical issue in marketing research. The proliferation of databases, the selling of address lists, and the ease with which consumer information can be gathered through Internet technology have all increased public concern. The issue of privacy will be explored in greater detail in Chapter 4. From an ethical standpoint, a marketing research practice that is particularly problematic is the promise of cash rewards or free offers in return for marketing information that can then be sold to direct marketers. Consumers commonly disclose their demographic information in return for an e-mail newsletter or a favorite magazine.

Privacy issues have grown as rapidly as companies on the Web—and consumers are fighting back. Following a recent investigation by the Federal Trade Commission (FTC) into its consumer research practices, online advertiser DoubleClick.com paid out $1.8 million to settle federal and state class-action

There's no incompatibility between doing the right thing and making money.

William Clay Ford Jr.
(b. 1958)
CEO, Ford Motor Co.

figure 3.8

Test Your Workplace Ethics

Workplace Ethics Quiz

The spread of technology into the workplace has raised a variety of new ethical questions, and many old ones still linger. Compare your answers with those of other Americans surveyed on page 112.

Office Technology

1. Is it wrong to use company e-mail for personal reasons?
   ❑Yes ❑No
2. Is it wrong to use office equipment to help your children or spouse do schoolwork?
   ❑Yes ❑No
3. Is it wrong to play computer games on office equipment during the workday?
   ❑Yes ❑No
4. Is it wrong to use office equipment to do Internet shopping?
   ❑Yes ❑No
5. Is it unethical to blame an error you made on a technological glitch?
   ❑Yes ❑No
6. Is it unethical to visit pornographic Web sites using office equipment?
   ❑Yes ❑No

Gifts and Entertainment

7. What's the value at which a gift from a supplier or client becomes troubling?
   ❑$25 ❑$50 ❑$100
8. Is a $50 gift to a boss unacceptable?
   ❑Yes ❑No
9. Is a $50 gift from the boss unacceptable?
   ❑Yes ❑No
10. Of gifts from suppliers: Is it OK to take a $200 pair of football tickets?
    ❑Yes ❑No
11. Is it OK to take a $120 pair of theater tickets?
    ❑Yes ❑No
12. Is it OK to take a $100 holiday food basket?
    ❑Yes ❑No
13. Is it OK to take a $25 gift certificate?
    ❑Yes ❑No
14. Can you accept a $75 prize won at a raffle at a supplier's conference?
    ❑Yes ❑No

Truth and Lies

15. Due to on-the-job pressure, have you ever abused or lied about sick days?
    ❑Yes ❑No
16. Due to on-the-job pressure, have you ever taken credit for someone else's work or idea?
    ❑Yes ❑No

SOURCE: Ethics Officer Association, Belmont, Massachusetts; Leadership Group, Wilmette, Illinois; surveys sampled a cross section of workers at large companies and nationwide; used with permission from Ethics Officer Association.

suits. In addition, DoubleClick sent out more than 300 million consumer-privacy banner ads, inviting consumers to learn more about protecting their privacy online.[37]

Several agencies, including the FTC, offer assistance to Internet consumers. For information on how to stop junk mail and telemarketing calls, a good place to start is at **http://www.ftc.gov/privacy**. The Direct Marketing Association also provides services, such as the Mail, Telephone, and E-Mail Preference Services, to help consumers get their names removed from marketers' targeted lists. Registration on the U.S. government's Do Not Call list for shielding your phone number is available at (888) 382-1222 and **http://www.donotcall.gov**. UnlistMe.com and Junkbusters are free Web services that also help consumers remove their names from direct mail and telemarketing lists.

Radio-frequency identification (RFID) is an old technology being put to new uses. In dozens of applications, RFID readers already use radio waves to scan chips attached to everything from cars passing through tollbooths to museum masterpieces, pets, and livestock, tracking their locations and movement. Some consumer advocates are already alarmed at the possibility that RFID readers can collect and correlate information about purchases without the buyer's even being aware. Safeguards are in the works. "Privacy mavens are going to wring their hands over this, and I'm sympathetic," says futurist Paul Saffo, "but RFID is too good to stop."[38]

ETHICAL PROBLEMS IN PRODUCT STRATEGY

Product quality, planned obsolescence, brand similarity, and packaging questions are of critical importance to the success of a brand. Not surprisingly, competitive pressures have forced some marketers into packaging practices that may be considered misleading, deceptive, or unethical. Larger packages help gain shelf space and consumer exposure in the supermarket. Oddly sized packaging makes price comparisons difficult. Bottles with concave bottoms give the impression that they contain more liquid than they actually do. Are these practices justified in the name of competition or can they be considered deceptive? Growing regulatory mandates appear to be narrowing the range of discretion in this area.

When serving sizes of kid-friendly meals became intertwined with growing concerns about a startling increase in obesity among children, fast-food restaurants—led by industry giant McDonald's—decided to modify their product strategies and slim down their menus. During 2003, McDonald's added entrée salads and moved to provide more fruit, vegetable, and yogurt options with its Happy Meals. Although company officials denied that their decision was influenced by a highly publicized documentary *Super Size Me,* in which the filmmaker eats nothing but McDonald's food for a month and gains 25 pounds, supersizing was clearly out of step with societal concerns. By 2005, McDonald's had eliminated the supersizing option for fries and drinks in all of its 13,000-plus U.S. outlets. The old 7-ounce Supersize fries contained 610 calories. Today, the biggest size weighs an ounce less and contains 540 calories.

Nobody is forced to eat at McDonald's.

Robert W. Sweet

U.S. federal judge (dismissing a class-action lawsuit seeking damages from McDonald's for causing obesity)

About 20 states currently restrict students' access to junk food until after lunch, and another two dozen are considering total bans or limits on vending machine products. The Texas Agriculture Department responded to reports that 38 percent of Texas fourth-graders are overweight by banning deep fat frying and whole milk in public schools.[39]

Timber manufacturer Boise Cascade recently agreed to stop buying wood products from endangered forests around the world and to halt timber cutting from virgin forests in the U.S. as well. The firm also plans to pressure suppliers to follow its example by tracking the origins of paper and wood products it receives. "I think they know their consumer brand won't survive if it's attached to old-forest destruction," says Jennifer Krill, organizer for the Rainforest Action Network, which called for boycotts of Boise in an effort to win a policy change. Boise may in fact have lost some customers before adopting its new stance, including copy company Kinko's Inc., which already avoids using paper products from endangered forests.[40]

ETHICAL PROBLEMS IN DISTRIBUTION STRATEGY

Two ethical issues influence a firm's decisions regarding channel strategy:

1. What is the appropriate degree of control over the channel?
2. Should a company distribute its products in marginally profitable outlets that have no alternative source of supply?

The question of channel control typically arises in relationships between manufacturers and franchise dealers. For example, should an automobile dealership, a gas station, or a fast-food outlet be coerced to purchase parts, materials, and supplementary services from the parent organization?

The second question concerns marketers' responsibility to serve unsatisfied market segments even if the profit potential is slight. Should marketers serve retail stores in low-income areas, serve users of limited amounts of the firm's product, or serve a declining rural market? These problems are difficult to resolve because they often involve individuals rather than broad segments of the general public. An important first step is to ensure that the firm consistently enforces its channel policies.

ETHICAL PROBLEMS IN PROMOTIONAL STRATEGY

Promotion is the component of the marketing mix that gives rise to the majority of ethical questions. Personal selling has always been a target of criticism. Early traders, pack peddlers, drummers, and today's used-car salespeople have all been accused of marketing malpractices that range from exaggerating product merits to outright deceit. Gifts and bribes are common ethical abuses.

The means through which marketers target specific demographic groups sometimes falls short of ethical standards. Prescription drug manufacturers routinely market their products to the doctors who recommend them to patients. But Biovail Corp., a large Canadian drug company, has been accused of paying $1,000 each to thousands of U.S. doctors who prescribe its Cardizem LA, a heart medication. Concerned that such payments might influence doctors' judgment, the government has been issuing guidelines for compliance with federal fraud and abuse laws, which ban such compensation when its primary purpose is to encourage sales. Biovail claims it is in compliance with all regulations.[41]

The pharmaceutical industry has frequently attracted attention for its questionable advertising practices. Increasingly, television advertising directed at consumers suggests that viewers take a proactive role in family health care by requesting that their doctors prescribe the medications they see advertised. Opponents allege that such advertising puts undue pressure on physicians to prescribe costly branded drugs rather than nondrug remedies or over-the-counter alternatives. Not only may consumer-driven prescriptions lead to unnecessary or even harmful drug use, but they also ratchet up the cost of insurance coverage. The pharmaceutical industry argues that direct-to-consumer advertising educates patients while leaving physicians in control of treatment.[42]

In yet another promotional controversy, KFC Corp. recently depicted its Kentucky Fried Chicken meals as a health food, creating a series of ads in which customers claimed the food was low in calories and helped them lose weight. KFC had to pull the campaign in the uproar that followed.

ETHICAL PROBLEMS IN PRICING

Pricing is probably the most regulated aspect of a firm's marketing strategy. As a result, most unethical price behavior is also illegal. Schering-Plough Corp., for example, is under investigation for offering pharmaceuticals at no cost or at extremely deep discounts to managed-care plans that include Schering-Plough drugs on HMO lists of drugs for which companies are reimbursed.[43] Some aspects of pricing, however, are still open to ethics abuses. For example, should some customers pay more for merchandise if distribution costs are higher in their areas? Do marketers have an obligation to warn vendors and customers of impending price, discount, or return policy changes?

Overstock.com, a $240-million e-tailer carrying about 12,000 items, promotes itself as the place to shop with savings up to 80 percent below list price. That alone is a compelling argument for visiting its Web site, assuming the list prices quoted are accurate. But a recent *BusinessWeek* check found almost 100 instances where the list prices were misstated. Although the prices were more reliable for watches and books, consumer electronics list prices were most likely to be incorrect. Some mistakes were significant. Toshiba's Model 36AF43 carried a $1,699 list price on the Overstock.com site; the actual manufacturer's list was $999.37. Although the overly high list price doesn't affect the seller's return on each unit sold, it does cause purchasers to believe that they are receiving a higher price discount on the item. Company representatives blame the problem on manufacturers who change the list prices for their products.[44]

All these concerns must be dealt with in developing a professional ethic for pricing products. The ethical issues involved in pricing for today's highly competitive and increasingly computerized markets are discussed in greater detail in Chapters 18 and 19.

1. What is the relationship between ethical practices and profit?
2. What are some of the privacy issues inherent in marketing research?
3. How does pricing become an ethical issue?

SOCIAL RESPONSIBILITY IN MARKETING

social responsibility Marketing philosophies, policies, procedures, and actions that have the enhancement of society's welfare as a primary objective.

As several of the examples in this chapter demonstrate, companies can benefit from their contributions to society and at the same time minimize the negative impact they have on the natural and social environments. **Social responsibility** demands that marketers accept an obligation to give equal weight to profits, consumer satisfaction, and social well-being in evaluating their firm's performance. They must recognize the importance of relatively qualitative consumer and social benefits as well as the quantitative measures of sales, revenue, and profits by which firms have traditionally measured marketing performance.

Social responsibility allows for easier measurement than marketing ethics. Government legislation can mandate socially responsible actions. Consumer activism can also promote social responsibility by business. Actions alone determine social responsibility, and a firm can behave responsibly, even under coercion. Government requirements may force firms to take socially responsible actions in matters of environmental policy, deceptive product claims, and other areas. Also, consumers, through their power to repeat or withhold purchases, may force marketers to provide honest and relevant information and fair prices. Ethically responsible behavior, on the other hand, requires more than appropriate actions; ethical intentions must also motivate those actions. The four dimensions of social responsibility—eco-

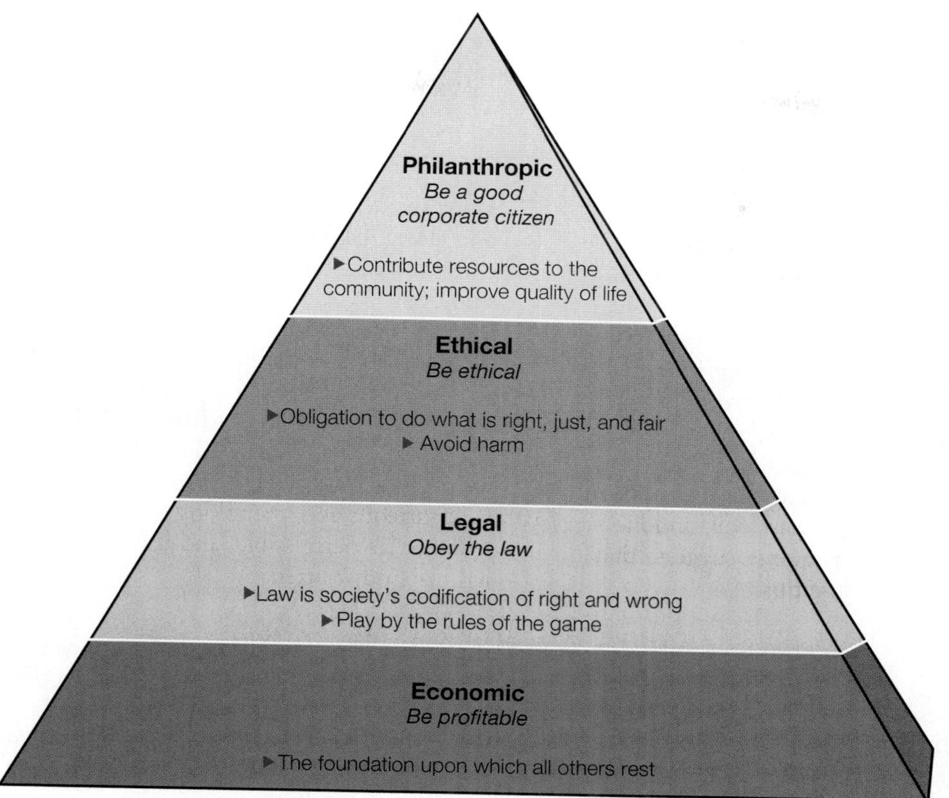

figure 3.9

The Four-Step Pyramid of Corporate Social Responsibility

Source: Archie B. Carroll, "The Pyramid of Corporate Social Responsibility: Toward the Moral Management of Organizational Stakeholders," *Business Horizons* 34, July–August, 1991. Used with permission.

nomic, legal, ethical, and philanthropic—are shown in Figure 3.9. The first two dimensions have long been recognized, but ethical obligations and the need for marketers to be good corporate citizens have increased in importance in recent years.

The locus for socially responsible decisions in organizations has always been an important issue. But who should accept specific accountability for the social effects of marketing decisions? Responses range from the district sales manager to the marketing vice president, the firm's CEO, and even the board of directors. Probably the most valid assessment holds that all marketers, regardless of their stations in the organization, remain accountable for the social aspects of their decisions.

The "Etiquette Tips for Marketing Professionals" box discusses the issue of smoking's effect on everyone in the workplace as well as others who interact with the smoker. The issue of secondhand smoke and the varying degrees of discomfort felt by nonsmokers who come into close contact with smokers should be recognized by the smokers, and appropriate steps should be taken to deal with it in a way that satisfies all affected parties.

MARKETING'S RESPONSIBILITIES

The concept of business's social responsibility traditionally has concerned managers' relationships with customers, employees, and stockholders. In general, managers traditionally have felt responsible for providing quality products at reasonable prices for customers, adequate wages and decent working environments for employees, and acceptable profits for stockholders. Only occasionally did the concept extend to relations with the government and rarely with the general public.

Today, corporate responsibility has expanded to cover the entire societal framework. A decision to temporarily delay the installation of a pollution-control device may satisfy the traditional sense of responsibility. Customers would continue to receive an uninterrupted supply of the plant's products, employees would not face layoffs, and stockholders would still receive reasonable returns on their investments. Contemporary business ethics, however, would not accept this choice as socially responsible.

ETIQUETTE TIPS — FOR MARKETING PROFESSIONALS

Smoking Etiquette

INDIVIDUALS need to be aware of their own social responsibilities. With the increased focus on the unhealthy aspects of smoking, it should be no surprise that in many circles the cigarette habit has come to be seen as rude behavior, imposing second-hand smoke and litter on an increasingly intolerant and vocal population. You probably work, or will work, in a no-smoking environment, and you may live in a city where smoking in hotels, restaurants, clubs, and entertainment centers is all but prohibited. While challenges to such restrictions will undoubtedly continue, good business etiquette suggests that you consider a few commonsense tips.

IF YOU SMOKE

1. When in a business setting, look around for ashtrays. If there are none, take the hint and don't ask whether you may smoke, even if smoking is not expressly forbidden.
2. In an informal setting or in someone's home, offer to step outside before lighting up.
3. Avoid smoking when conducting business internationally, even if the other party smokes.
4. Always be sensitive to the needs and desires of nonsmokers and sit in the nonsmoking section unless everyone in your group agrees otherwise. Never ask a nonsmoker to sit in the smoking section.
5. Even in the smoking section, avoid smoking during meals; wait until dessert is over.
6. Remember that many people have allergies that are exacerbated by exposure to smoke.
7. Don't smoke in cars, whether your own or someone else's. Ask the rental car agent if the company has cars designated as smoking (or nonsmoking).
8. If a nonsmoker asks you not to smoke, accept the decision with grace.
9. If a nonsmoker agrees that you may smoke, keep your cigarette as far away from the other person as you can, don't flick ashes, and don't exhale in anyone's face.
10. Be courteous about smoking outdoors. First ask whether it's permissible, and if you're allowed to light up, don't litter.

IF YOU DON'T SMOKE

1. Don't ask smokers why they smoke. They know it's unhealthy.
2. Don't fake coughing and hacking when in the presence of smokers.
3. Remember that smokers are allowed to smoke in designated areas. You may wish to avoid these areas.
4. Be firm but polite if you would like someone to put out his or her cigarette.

Sources: Lewena Bayer and Karen Mallett, "You Light Up My Life . . . or Not," *Lifewise*, http://lifewise.canoe.ca, accessed January 27, 2004; "Interview with Judith Martin," *American Enterprise*, June 2003, http://www.findarticles.com; Steven Ruszczycky, "A Guide to Smoking Etiquette," *Daily Nexus Online*, April 13, 2001, http://www.dailynexus.com.

Similarly, a firm that markets foods with low nutritional value may satisfy the traditional concept of responsibility, but such behavior is questionable in contemporary perspective. This is not to say that all firms should distribute only foods of high nutritional value; it means merely that the previous framework for evaluation is no longer considered comprehensive in terms of either scope or time. Access to phonecams appears to be a means by which marketers can provide services previously unavailable to users of wireless telephones, but their use can result in invasions of personal privacy. See the "Solving an Ethical Controversy" box for a look at the pros and cons of marketing camera phones.

Contemporary marketing decisions must consider the entire societal framework, not only in the U.S. but throughout the world. Recently, apparel manufacturers and retailers have come under fire for buying from foreign suppliers who force employees to work in dangerous conditions, pay less than a living wage, or violate child-labor laws. Giant pharmaceutical companies, for example, that refuse to allow the development of low-cost versions of their patented drugs to combat epidemics like AIDS,

Solving an Ethical Controversy

VIDEOPHONES AND PRIVACY: WHO'S WATCHING?

A CARTOON recently featured a cell phone user walking down the street, phone to ear, saying, "Can you hang on a sec? I think I just took another picture of my ear."

But camera-equipped cell phones have their dark side as well. Phonecams have a large creepiness factor. The tiny lens is on the back of the phone, making it almost impossible to tell when someone snaps a picture. A cell phone photo actually led to the recent arrest of a suspected pedophile. Some employers such as General Motors and DaimlerChrysler have banned them from their company buildings, fearing that employees may transmit images of new products or invade the privacy of coworkers in restrooms or locker rooms. Chief Judge Wendy Potts recently added the Oakland County Courthouse in Pontiac, Michigan, to the list of places where the videophones are *persona non grata.* "Our concern was the photographing of jurors and witnesses, such as undercover agents," she explains. Patrons in store dressing rooms and health-club locker rooms are beginning to cringe at the sight of someone making a call—and "No Videophone" signs are beginning to appear in both locations.

In the U.S., where the videophones only showed up in 2003, 34 million were in use by 2005. The technology is so simple and cheap that the number of camera phones being used globally will reach 1 billion by 2007. Photos and videos are easy to make and can be e-mailed or posted on Web sites in seconds.

SHOULD CELL PHONE MAKERS MARKET CAMERA PHONES?

PRO

1. The law says that we surrender some privacy just by going out in public, and a camera phone by itself does not violate current privacy laws.
2. Ad hoc laws and self-policing by photo-hosting Web sites will ensure that few privacy violations occur.

CON

1. Too much discretion in the use of camera phones is left to the individual's judgment.
2. The potential for abuse outweighs possible camera phone benefits like crime prevention or amateur on-the-scene reporting.

SUMMARY

Government offices, health clubs, and stores are instituting their own bans for now, and most Web sites respond to user complaints if any privacy violations occur. Phone designers are now ensuring that most camera phones emit a loud crunch, beep, or similar noise when a picture is taken. Technology may soon be available that automatically disables camera phones in hospitals, banks, and other sensitive locations. In the meantime, according to Sprint's director of media relations, camera phone users should remember that it is never acceptable to take someone's picture without permission.

Sources: Leigh Gallagher, "Pix Populi," *Forbes,* March 15, 2004, pp. 156–157; Stephanie Armour, "Camera Phones Don't Click at Work," *USA Today,* January 12, 2004, p. B1; Carla Thornton, "New Phones Raise Privacy Fears," *PC World,* January 2004; "Camera Phones Cause Privacy Concerns," *ABCNewsonline,* December 15, 2003, http://www.abc.net.au/news.

malaria, or tuberculosis have been accused of ignoring the global reach of corporate responsibility. Marketers must also take into account the long-term effects of their decisions and the well-being of future generations. Manufacturing processes that negatively affect the environment or that use up natural energy resources are easy targets for criticism.

There are several methods through which marketers can help their companies behave in socially responsible ways. Chapter 1 discussed cause marketing as one channel through which companies can

COURTESY OF HITACHI, LTD.

Hitachi developed new technologies to help the environment. Its new water-purification processes ensure the availability of clean water—clean enough for a trout.

promote social causes—and at the same time benefit by linking their people and products to worthy undertakings. Socially responsible marketing involves campaigns that encourage people to adopt socially beneficial behaviors, whether they be safe driving, eating more nutritious food, or improving the working conditions of people half a world away. Not only can campaigns like these help society, but they can affect the firm's bottom line as well.

MARKETING AND ECOLOGY

Ecology—the relationship between organisms and their natural environments—has become a driving force in influencing the ways in which businesses operate. Many industry and government leaders rank the protection of the environment as the biggest challenge facing today's corporations. From water pollution, waste disposal, and acid rain to depletion of the ozone layer and global warming, environmental issues affect everyone. They influence all areas of marketing decision making from product planning to public relations, spanning such topics as planned obsolescence, pollution control, recycling waste materials, and resource conservation.

DuPont has adopted the goal of owning businesses that can sustain themselves forever without depleting natural resources. After pledging to reduce waste, emissions, and energy usage, the industrial company that once was known for its poor record on pollution has gone even further. It recently spun off its oil-and-gas unit, Conoco, to buy Pioneer Hi-Bred International, which produces seeds for growing food and renewable manufacturing materials such as corn that can be manufactured into T-shirts. DuPont's corporate vice president for safety, health, and the environment, Paul Tebo, says the firm asks the following question about all its strategic decisions: "How do you bring the economics together with the environmental and the societal needs so that they are all part of your business strategies?" The unanswered question for DuPont is how much employees, consumers, and investors will be impressed by its new mission. But, says Tebo, "the closer we can align with social values, the faster we'll grow."[45]

In creating new-product offerings that respond to consumer demands for convenience by offering extremely short-lived products, such as disposable diapers, ballpoint pens, razors, and cameras, marketers occasionally find themselves accused of intentionally offering products with limited durability—in other words, of practicing **planned obsolescence.** In addition to convenience-oriented items, other products become obsolete when rapid changes in technology create superior alternatives. In the computer industry, upgrades that make products obsolete are the name of the game. In response to the mounting piles of obsolete computers, which amount to nearly 2 million tons of trash a year, Dell began a program to recycle computers from any manufacturer, not just those bearing the Dell name. For a small fee, the company will have a carrier pick up the equipment and deliver it to environmentally safe recycling centers or donate still-useful computer equipment to economically disadvantaged people and organizations. The program saves the environment from added pollution and potentially cancer-causing chemicals such as lead, cadmium, beryllium, and flame retardants.[46]

Lawmakers in California, Massachusetts, Nebraska, and South Carolina have proposed legislation to force manufacturers to take back "e-waste"—used PCs and other technology products that contain toxic chemicals.[47]

Public concern about pollution of such natural resources as water and air affects some industries, such as pharmaceuticals or heavy-goods manufacturing, more than others. However, the marketing system annually generates billions of tons of packaging materials such as glass, metal, paper, and plastics that add to the world's growing piles of trash and waste. Recycling such materials, as Dell does for computers, for reuse is another important aspect of ecology. Recycling can benefit society by saving

Air pollution is turning Mother Nature prematurely gray.

Irv Kupcinet (1912–2003)
American newspaper columnist

natural resources and energy as well as by alleviating a major factor in environmental pollution—waste disposal.

The impact of powerful, highly creative promotional messages on changing consumer attitudes was never demonstrated more powerfully than in Figure 3.10. First introduced over 30 years ago by advertising agency Marstellar Inc. for the Ad Council, the industry's public service group, a Native American—the very symbol of dignity and respect for the natural world—is brought to tears by pollutants in the air, water, and land. The message made the image of Iron Eyes Cody, the tear-shedding model for the ad, an advertising icon and shamed Americans into accepting responsibility for their environment.[48]

figure 3.10

Iron Eyes Cody: Teaching Generations of Americans to Become Concerned about Their Environment

As the saying goes, one person's trash is another's treasure. Yokohama Metals mines used cell phones, digging out the gold, platinum, and silver embedded there. It takes 125,000 phones to produce a single gold bar worth $10,000. Swedish-owned Metech International turns discarded computer hardware into gold. In just one year, the firm recovered 120,000 ounces of gold worth $35 million, as well as other precious metals including silver, platinum, and palladium.[49]

The disposal of nuclear waste is an ongoing public safety issue. Nevada recently lost its long fight against government plans to open a national storage site in the bowels of isolated Yucca Mountain, about 100 miles outside Las Vegas. The September 11 terrorist attacks gave supporters of the proposed national repository an unexpected boost. Housed at more than 100 power plants nationwide, radioactive materials pose a considerable national security risk as possible terrorist targets. Supporters of the Nevada storage site also argue that Yucca Mountain is critical to building America's nuclear-power capacity—the means through which the nation may one day meet its own energy needs.[50]

Many companies respond to consumers' growing concern about ecological issues through **green marketing**—production, promotion, and reclamation of environmentally sensitive products. In the green marketing revolution of the early 1990s, marketers were quick to tie their companies and products to ecological themes. The organic food and beverage market, for instance, is expected to grow between $12 billion and $13 billion by 2007, according to the Natural Marketing Institute. "Up to 60 percent of the population [is] willing to buy organic products," says Holly Givens, communication director of the Organic Trade Association.[51]

green marketing Production, promotion, and reclamation of environmentally sensitive products.

1. Define *social responsibility.*
2. Can the government mandate socially responsible practices?
3. What is green marketing?

Strategic Implications of Marketing in the 21st Century

MANAGEMENT of the nation's businesses is affected by and must respond to a large number of important trends that are shaping business in the 21st century. The marketing decisions businesses make will influence and be influenced by changes in the competitive, political-legal, economic, technological, and social-cultural environments. Marketing ethics and social responsibility will continue to play important roles in business transactions in your hometown and around the globe.

As the Internet and the rapid changes in technology that it represents are fully absorbed into the competitive environment in coming years, competition will become even more intense than it is today. Much of the competition will result from innovations in technology and scientific discoveries. Business in the 21st century will be propelled by information technologies and sustained by creativity and entrepreneurial activity. Biotechnology—an industry whose growth was fueled in response to terrorist threats of biological warfare—is still in its infancy. It is expected to explode in the next decade. Scientists will be able to create materials atom by atom, replicating much that nature can do and more.

In the 20th century economy, the major industrial sectors included retail, financial services, and manufacturing. But today, those sectors frequently do not fit the networked economy. The idea of what it means to be a retail company will change in five years when a billion people are logged on to the Internet. The bundling of services on the Internet will bypass many of the financial services we take for granted today. For example, when a 14-year-old buys a digital CD off the Internet, digital cash will be transferred from her hard drive to that of the recording artist, thereby eliminating the need for a bank or credit-card company. Money will eventually be relegated to encrypted numbers on disk drives and digital wallets.

Dynamic growth cannot be left entirely to self-regulation. The next 10 years will produce a plethora of rules and regulations to control the marketing environments that will force businesses to change aspects of their operations. For example, new legislation to control dangerous emissions that deplete the ozone layer will lead to energy-efficient manufacturing processes and a new wave of alternative energy automobiles.

Consumers will feel the impact of environmental changes in every aspect of their lives. The new century is ushering in new generations of consumers who expect high-quality, low-cost products readily available on demand. To succeed, every company will be forced to build relationships to attract and retain loyal customers.

Underlying all the changes in the business environments and marketing mix elements is a requirement for companies to act ethically and in socially responsible ways. Marketers will have to go beyond what is legally right and wrong by integrating ethical behavior in all of their actions. Forward-looking companies will reap the benefits tomorrow of socially responsible behavior today. ◆◆◆

Briefly Speaking

At this moment, America's greatest economic need is higher ethical standards—standards enforced by strict laws and upheld by responsible business leaders. There is no capitalism without conscience; there is no wealth without character.

George W. Bush (b. 1946)
43rd president of the United States

REVIEW OF CHAPTER OBJECTIVES

Identify the five components of the marketing environment.

The five components of the marketing environment are (1) *the competitive environment*—the interactive process that occurs in the marketplace as competing organizations seek to satisfy markets; (2) *the political-legal environment*—the laws and interpretations of laws that require firms to operate under competitive conditions and to protect consumer rights; (3) *the economic environment*—environmental factors resulting from business fluctuations and resulting variations in inflation rates and employment levels; (4) *the technological environment*—applications to marketing of knowledge based on discoveries in science, inventions, and innovations; and (5) *the social-cultural environment*—the component of the marketing environment consisting of the relationship between the marketer and society and its culture.

1.1. Briefly describe each of the five components of the marketing environment. Give an example of each.
1.2. What is the relationship between the political and the legal environments?

2 Explain the types of competition marketers face and the steps necessary for developing a competitive strategy.

Three types of competition exist: (1) direct competition among marketers of similar products; (2) competition among goods or services that can be substituted for one another; and (3) competition among all organizations that vie for the consumer's purchasing power. To develop a competitive strategy, marketers must answer the following questions: (1) Should we compete? The answer depends on the firm's available resources and objectives as well as its expected profit potential; (2) If so, in what markets should we compete? This question requires marketers to make product, pricing, distribution, and promotional decisions that give their firm a competitive advantage; (3) How should we compete? This question requires marketers to make the technical decisions involved in setting a comprehensive marketing strategy.

2.1. Explain the types of competition marketers face.
2.2. What steps must marketers complete to develop a competitive strategy?

③ Describe how government and other groups regulate marketing activities and how marketers can influence the political-legal environment.

Marketing activities are influenced by federal, state, and local laws that require firms to operate under competitive conditions and to protect consumer rights. Government regulatory agencies such as the Federal Trade Commission enforce these laws and develop procedures for identifying and correcting unfair marketing practices. Public and private consumer interest groups and industry self-regulatory groups also affect marketing activities. Marketers may seek to influence public opinion and legislative actions through advertising, political action committees, and political lobbying.

3.1. Government regulation in the U.S. has evolved in four general phases. Identify each phase and give an example of laws enacted during that time.

3.2. Give an example of a federal law affecting:
   a. product strategy
   b. pricing strategy
   c. distribution strategy
   d. promotional strategy

3.3. Explain the methods the Federal Trade Commission uses to protect consumers. Which of these methods seems the most effective to you?

④ Outline the economic factors that affect marketing decisions and consumer buying power.

The primary economic factors are (1) the stage in the business cycle, (2) inflation and deflation, (3) unemployment, (4) income, and (5) resource availability. All are vitally important to marketers because of their effects on consumers' willingness to buy and consumers' perceptions regarding changes in the marketing mix variables.

4.1. What major economic factors affect marketing decisions?

4.2. Explain how each of these forces produces its effect on these decisions.

⑤ Discuss the impact of the technological environment on a firm's marketing activities.

The technological environment consists of applications to marketing of knowledge based on discoveries in science, inventions, and innovations. This knowledge can provide marketing opportunities: It results in new products and improves existing ones, and it is a frequent source of price reductions through new production methods or materials. Technological applications also pose a threat because they can make existing products obsolete overnight. The technological environment demands that marketers continually adapt to change, since its scope of influence reaches into consumers' lifestyles, competitors' products, industrial users' demands, and government regulatory actions.

5.1. Identify the ways in which the technological environment affects marketing activities. Cite examples.

5.2. What is the role of research and development in private industry?

⑥ Explain how the social-cultural environment influences marketing.

The social-cultural environment relates to the attitudes of members of society toward goods and services as well as pricing, promotion, and distribution strategies. It influences the general readiness of society to accept new marketing ideas. It also has an impact on legislation regulating business and marketing. While the social-cultural environment affects all domestic marketing decisions, it is an even more prevalent force in influencing international marketing strategy. Society demands that business be concerned with the quality of life. Consumerism is the social force within the environment designed to aid and protect the consumer by exerting legal, moral, and economic pressures on business. Consumer rights include the following: (1) the right to choose freely, (2) the right to be informed, (3) the right to be heard, and (4) the right to be safe.

6.1. Identify the ways in which the social-cultural environment affects marketing activities. Cite examples.

6.2. What are the consumers' rights, and how do they affect marketers?

⑦ Describe the role of marketing in society and identify the two major social issues in marketing.

Marketing operates in an environment external to the firm, building relationships with customers, employees, vendors, the government, and society as a whole. These relationships have a significant effect on the relative degree of success the firm achieves. The two critical social issues in marketing are marketing ethics and social responsibility. Marketing ethics describes the marketer's standards of conduct and moral values. Social responsibility is the marketer's acceptance of the obligation to consider profit, consumer satisfaction, and societal well-being of equal value when evaluating the performance of the firm.

7.1. What is marketing ethics?

7.2. Describe the ethical problems related to:
   a. marketing research
   b. product strategy
   c. distribution strategy
   d. promotional strategy
   e. pricing strategy

7.3. What is social responsibility? Give an example.

(8) Identify the four levels of the social responsibility pyramid.

The four dimensions of social responsibility are (1) *economic*—to be profitable, the foundation upon which the other three levels of the pyramid rest; (2) *legal*—to obey the law, society's codification of right and wrong; (3) *ethical*—to do what is right, just, and fair and to avoid wrongdoing; (4) *philanthropic*—to be a good corporate citizen, contributing to the community and improving quality of life.

8.1. Identify each of the four dimensions of social responsibility.
8.2. Which two dimensions have emerged most recently?

MARKETING TERMS YOU NEED TO KNOW

environmental scanning 79
environmental management 79
competitive environment 80
time-based competition 82
political-legal environment 84
economic environment 89
demarketing 92
technological environment 93
social-cultural environment 95
consumerism 96
consumer rights 96
marketing ethics 98
social responsibility 102
green marketing 107

OTHER IMPORTANT MARKETING TERMS

strategic alliance 79
monopoly 80
deregulation movement 80
oligopoly 80
competitive strategy 82
switchless reseller 89
business cycle 89
inflation 91
unemployment 91
discretionary income 92
planned obsolescence 106

PROJECTS AND TEAMWORK EXERCISES

1. Find examples of how marketers in your community might meet each of the following responsibilities:
   a. economic
   b. legal
   c. ethical
   d. philanthropic
2. Choose two competing marketers with which you are familiar (through using their products, employment experiences, or other means). List all the ways in which they compete and describe what you believe to be the competitive strategy of each.
3. Classify the following laws as (a) assisting in maintaining a competitive environment, (b) assisting in regulating competitors, (c) regulating specific marketing activities, or (d) deregulating industries. Justify your classifications and identify the marketing mix variable(s) most affected by each law.
   a. Children's Online Privacy Protection Act
   b. Robinson-Patman Act
   c. Airline Security Act
   d. Telecommunications Act
4. Should the U.S. impose regulations on the advertising of alcoholic beverages? Working in small groups, have one team present the argument for regulation and the other present the counterargument.
5. Can monopoly ever be a good thing? What goods or services do you think might best be provided by a monopolist? Defend your answer.
6. What types of firms or industries do you think are best able to weather economic downturns? Research one such firm or industry in your community and compare its marketing strategy during recession and during recovery. How much do the two strategies differ?
7. Some service firms such as hotels, airlines, and theaters deal with resource availability by trying to even out consumer demand for their offerings over time. List as many examples as you can think of that firms like this can use to limit demand.
8. Cite two examples of instances in which the technological environment has produced positive benefits for marketers. Give two instances of the harmful effect of the technological environment on a firm's marketing operations.
9. Identify a critical social issue confronting your local community. In teams, research all sides of the issue via newspapers, on the Internet, or through contacting local activist groups and reviewing their literature. How does this issue affect marketers in your area? Provide specific examples. Describe your findings in either a written or an oral presentation.
10. Do you think firms that market products for children have any special ethical responsibilities when they advertise? Why or why not? Find two examples of marketing campaigns that appear to support your position and two that do not.

APPLYING CHAPTER CONCEPTS

1. Firms that have been convicted of negligence are often required to pay restitution as well as punitive damages. Costs can climb into the billions of dollars, but the U.S. Supreme Court recently ruled (in the case against Exxon Mobil Corp. arising out of the 1989 Exxon *Valdez* oil spill) that the ratio of punitive to actual damages should not exceed 9 to 1. Identify a recent award for punitive damages against a negligent firm. To whom is the money to be paid? Who gains and who loses in this case?
2. Thousands of salaried employees who have been asked to work overtime without pay are now filing class-action suits, demanding millions of dollars in overtime for which their employers say they are not eligible. The lawsuits allege that the workers' jobs were improperly classified, are not "creative," and are therefore eligible for the extra pay. Radio Shack and Starbucks have already been ordered to pay hundreds of millions in back pay. What are some of the economic implications for a firm facing a possible compensation award? What effect could such judgments have on Radio Shack's and Starbucks' competitors?
3. Emissions standards for motorcycles take effect in 2006 under rules adopted by the Environmental Protection Agency. There were no previous emissions controls for motorcycles at all, but even under the new laws, "dirt" bikes (for off-road use) will be exempt, and manufacturers producing fewer than 3,000 vehicles a year will have an extra two years to comply. The new standards will add about $75 to the average cost of a motorcycle according to the EPA, but $250 according to the Motorcycle Industry Council. Why do you think motorcycle makers have not adopted voluntary emissions standards? Should they have done so? Why or why not?
4. Suppose you and a friend want to start a company that markets frozen fish dinners. What are some of the questions about the competitive environment that you would like to have answered before you begin production? How will you determine whom your customers are likely to be? How will you reach them?

ETHICS EXERCISE

Some retail firms protect their inventory against theft by locking their premises after hours even though maintenance and other workers are inside the stores working all night. Employees have charged that they are forbidden to leave the premises during work hours and that during an emergency, such as illness or injury, precious time is lost waiting for a manager to arrive who is authorized to unlock the doors. Although workers could open an emergency exit, in some cases they claim that they will be fired for doing so. Employers assert that managers with keys are on the premises (or minutes away) and that locking employees in ensures their own safety as well as cutting down on costly "shrinkage."

1. Under what circumstances, if any, do you think locking employees in at night is appropriate?
2. If you feel this practice is appropriate, what safeguards do you think should be put into effect? What responsibilities do employers and employees have in such circumstances?

'netWork EXERCISES

1. **Developing a competitive strategy**. Choose a well-known consumer products company such as Gillette (**http://www.gillette.com**) or Procter and Gamble (**http://www.pg.com**). Select one of the company's products and analyze how the firm answered each of the key questions when developing its competitive strategy for the product you selected.
2. **Direct to consumer drug advertising**. A controversial issue is whether or not pharmaceutical manufacturers are too aggressive in advertising prescription drugs directly to consumers. Using Google or another Internet search engine, search for recent articles and studies on direct to consumer drug advertising. What are the ethical issues confronting pharmaceutical manufacturers, the medical community, and government regulators?
3. **Social responsibility.** Many firms highlight their activities to promote social responsibility. Visit the Web sites of Nike (**http://www.nike.com**), Patagonia (**http://www.patagonia.com**) and Starbucks (**http://www.starbucks.com**). Write a report summarizing activities each firm uses to promote social responsibility. Speculate how promoting social responsibility ties in with the company's overall marketing strategy.

Note: Internet Web addresses change frequently. If you don't find the exact sites listed, you may need to access the organization's or company's home page and search from there or use a search engine such as Google.

INFOTRAC CITATIONS AND EXERCISES

Record: A117535105
A Future with Nowhere to Hide? This connectedness may lead toward a future where our cell phones track us like FedEx packages, sometimes when we're not aware.
Steven Levy.
Newsweek, June 7, 2004 p76

Abstract: Privacy issues are among the most serious concerns facing marketers and consumers in the technology age. The invasion of privacy that accompanies technological advances such as electronic commerce and radio-frequency identification (RFID) places marketers in a precarious position. Businesses eager to improve marketing services by generating detailed profiles of individual consumers walk a fine line between good practice and grave ethics violations. For certain, technology is a double-edged sword, and the wireless boom has particularly sharp edges. The idea of shedding wires and cables is exhilarating: People can go anywhere and still maintain intimate contact with work, play, and personal relationships. But the same persistent connectedness may lead to a future in which cell phones tag and track the public like FedEx packages, sometimes voluntarily and sometimes without the public knowing it.

1. What is *marketing ethics,* and why is it important in the business world?
2. How might a solid understanding of ethics help marketers anticipate and prevent ethical dilemmas before they happen?
3. In what ways could marketers benefit from using cell phones or other wireless devices to track the geographical movements and electronic transactions of individual consumers? Do you think such total access constitutes serious privacy violations? Explain your answer.

Ethics Quiz Answers

Quiz is on page 100.

1. 34% said personal e-mail on company computers is wrong
2. 37% said using office equipment for schoolwork is wrong
3. 49% said playing computer games at work is wrong
4. 54% said Internet shopping at work is wrong
5. 61% said it's unethical to blame your error on technology
6. 87% said it's unethical to visit pornographic sites at work
7. 33% said $25 is the amount at which a gift from a supplier or client becomes troubling, while 33% said $50, and 33% said $100
8. 35% said a $50 gift to the boss is unacceptable
9. 12% said a $50 gift from the boss is unacceptable
10. 70% said it's unacceptable to take the $200 football tickets
11. 70% said it's unacceptable to take the $120 theater tickets
12. 35% said it's unacceptable to take the $100 food basket
13. 45% said it's unacceptable to take the $25 gift certificate
14. 40% said it's unacceptable to take the $75 raffle prize
15. 11% reported they lied about sick days
16. 4% reported they have taken credit for the work or ideas of others

CASE 3.1 Is Detroit Losing the Race to Hybrids?

U.S. drivers have been known to wait weeks for a new car that has just the right set of options or paint color they want. But suddenly, they're lining up for a Japanese car with a brand-new kind of engine designed to protect the environment, the Toyota Prius.

Toyota has been developing the hybrid engine, which relies on computer technology to blend a gas engine with a battery-powered electric motor, for years. In fact, the second generation of Prius, with an advance order of 10,000 autos and publicity surrounding actor Leo DiCaprio's decision to buy one, resulted in a six-month waiting list for one of the 47,000 units made in 2004. Named *Motor Trend*'s Car of the Year, the $21,000 hybrid won praise from drivers and engineers alike. "At first they [consumers] think it's going to have relatively little power, a lot of compromises in performance," says Paul Anecharico, general sales manager at Bill Kidd's Toyota in Maryland. "When they drive the car they find that's not the case, and they are overwhelmed by the performance." And John Hanson, national manager of corporate communications at Toyota, says, "We're begging for more product."

With a wider, longer body and a lot more interior space, the new Prius offers a comfortable ride with twice the mileage of other midsize cars—about 55 miles per gallon. It's faster, cleaner, and safer than the earlier model. Size, power, and its clean-running engine are the focus of Toyota's marketing efforts for the car, which should recover its development costs and start earning money for the company in a few years if it continues to sell at the current rate.

Honda has already produced its Civic hybrid, priced at about $20,000 and getting 40 to 45 miles per gallon. But where are the U.S. manufacturers? Ford Motor Co. was the first and may be the only U.S. firm to dive into the hybrid market. Its first-generation Escape, already delayed once, will be the first hybrid SUV on the road if all goes as planned. Priced at about $26,000, the Escape will get about 40 miles per gallon. But Toyota's hybrid SUV, the RX400H, could be on the market first, giving the Japanese automaker a big sales lead in the marketplace as well as in the technology of the hybrid engine. "If Toyota succeeds," says a hybrid expert at a rival automaker, "they're going to have a 10- to 15-year head start."

Where are the other U.S. automakers? Despite rising oil prices, DaimlerChrysler appears to be sticking with diesel engines, counting on technological improvements, while General Motors is banking on hydrogen-powered cars. Toyota sees hybrid-engine technology as here to stay. In contrast, GM believes hybrids are a step on the way to hydrogen-powered vehicles. It is leading the way with its Hy-Wire, a still-experimental model with an electric motor powered by hydrogen fuel cells and highly responsive computer-aided hand controls like those on aircraft. The Hy-Wire is a long way from market, however. Its fuel cells cost about $50,000 per car, 10 times more than is feasible for a production-line car, and they power a trip of only 80 miles.

Questions for Critical Thinking

1. What differences do you think marketers at Ford, DaimlerChrysler, General Motors, and Japanese firms Honda and Toyota see in the economic and technological environments they face?
2. Do you think Toyota has chosen an effective strategy for its competitive environment? Why or why not?

Sources: Richard J. Newman, "Red-Hot and Green," *U.S. News & World Report,* February 23/March 1, 2004, p. D6; Ron Amadon, "Honda Civic Hybrid," *CBS Market Watch*, January 24, 2004, http://cbs.marketwatch.com; John Tayman, "It's Easy Being Green," *Business 2.0*, December 2003, pp. 132–135; Larry Armstrong, "Green—and Red-Hot, Too," *BusinessWeek*, December 1, 2003, p. 116; Sholnn Freeman, "Toyota's Prius Hybrid Named *Motor Trend*'s 'Car of the Year,'" *The Wall Street Journal*, November 26, 2003, p. D3; Kathleen Kerwin with David Welch, "Detroit Is Missing the Boat," *BusinessWeek*, October 27, 2003, pp. 44–46; Lillie Guyer, "$2.50 a Gallon Gas? Not a Problem," *Advertising Age*, April 14, 2003, p. S-6.

VIDEO CASE 3.2 Green Mountain Coffee Roasters

The written case on Green Mountain Coffee appears on page VC-4. The recently filmed Green Mountain Coffee video is designed to expand and highlight the concepts in this chapter and the concepts and questions covered in the written video case.

chapter 4

E-Commerce: Marketing in the Digital Age

chapter objectives

1. Define e-commerce and give examples of each function of the Internet.
2. Describe how marketers use the Internet to achieve their firm's objectives.
3. Explain how online marketing benefits organizations, marketers, and consumers.
4. Identify the goods and services marketed most often on the Internet and the demographic characteristics of the typical online shopper.
5. Identify the primary online marketing channels.
6. Explain how marketers use interactive tools as part of their online marketing strategies.
7. Discuss how an effective Web site can enhance customer relationships.
8. Describe how to measure the effectiveness of online marketing efforts.

SPORTS MEMORABILIA GO ONLINE

You might be surprised to learn that no less than 10 vintage baseball trading cards have sold for over $100,000 each in recent public auctions. But you probably wouldn't be surprised to learn that the record-shattering sale among them took place on the world's leading online auction site, eBay. The winning bid on one of the rarest and most famous cards in baseball history, the Honus Wagner T-206 card of 1909 (a 1- × 2.5-inch lithograph now encased in a plastic slab) bearing the likeness of the Hall of Fame Pittsburgh Pirates shortstop, sold to a southern California businessman for $1.265 million.

Why bid such a jaw-dropping amount for a cardboard collectible, the type of item that you or your brother may have collected a hundred or more of—and may still have (assuming your mother didn't throw them out during one of her periodic cleanups of your bedroom)? Supply and demand play major roles in the explanation; the card sponsor played an even bigger one.

Although baseball cards have long been associated with bubblegum, they were originally used as part of a corporate marketing push to sell tobacco products. According to legend, Wagner had the tobacco card pulled off the market because

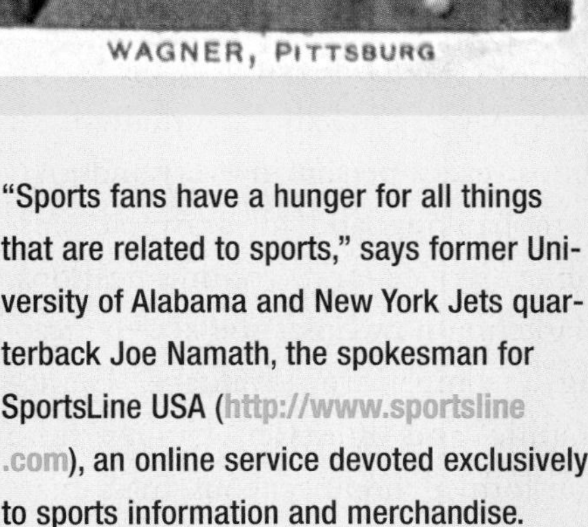

he neither smoked nor chewed tobacco—and did not like the image the card portrayed to children. American Tobacco Co. complied with his request and pulled his card from general circulation shortly after release. At least 58 of these cards are in circulation today, but the only known mint-condition card is the one sold on eBay.

Sports memorabilia have always been a big business, but since they began to move online a few years ago, the trade in them has become even bigger, faster, and more widespread. A recent marketing research survey cosponsored by ESPN and Buy.com found that accessing sports information was the top reason for searching the Internet among young men, so the burgeoning trade in signed baseballs, bats, and torn, dirty uniforms has apparently set up shop in the right place.

Around the world, there are about 17 million collectors of sports items, and they account for more than $2 billion in sales every year. Some believe the collecting mania first gathered steam in the 1980s when rookie cards of such baseball luminaries as Don Mattingly and Roger Clemens found a big market and were followed by equally successful football, basketball, and hockey cards. New card manufacturers sprang up, and a circuit of consumer shows for collectors developed as fans indicated their interest in—and willingness to pay for—cards, autographs, and memorabilia related to current and retired stars. The value of items associated with legendary players like Mickey Mantle and Babe Ruth skyrocketed; for instance, Mantle's used glove from about 1960 was auctioned at Sotheby's in 1999. Billy Crystal bought it for nearly $240,000. Collectors' conventions boast guests like Muhammad Ali, Cal Ripken Jr., Shaquille O'Neal, and Magic Johnson, who sign autographs and shmooze with fans. Longtime card collectors nodded their heads in agreement at the words of President George W. Bush, who hosted a White House luncheon for Baseball Hall of Famers: "It's kind of like having your baseball card collection spread out in real life."

Because they are cheap to produce and are printed in quantity, trading cards make up the bulk of items traded by collectors. But all kinds of items are bought and sold, including game uniforms, signed balls, bats, gloves, hockey pucks, basketball shoes, hats, and even an entire basketball court. Card manufacturer Upper Deck bought the Utah Jazz home court in a private sale. "Sports fans have a hunger for all things that are related to sports," says former University of Alabama and New York Jets quarterback Joe Namath, the spokesman for SportsLine USA (http://www.sportsline.com), an online service devoted exclusively to sports information and merchandise.

Autographs are treasured, and autographed items are worth much more than those without a famous player's scrawl. Missing a signature? Go online. One firm, http://www.steinersports.com, will accept shipment of the collectible you already own for signing by otherwise elusive—but still living—heroes, at a cost of $750 to $1,700. But forgeries abound, and the FBI has conducted more than one "sting" operation. These operations go by names like Operation Foul Ball and Operation Bullpen, the latter sparked by former San Diego Padres outfielder Tony Gwynn's realization that all his signatures on baseballs and photos in the team's gift shop had been forged. Some sports memorabilia experts believe that

© KIT KITTLE/ CORBIS

nearly four of every five autographed products sold online are forgeries, and a whole new industry has sprung up to authenticate signatures using special bar codes, biometric devices, and decoding software.

Buyers need to be wary, especially when purchasing online, and the market can be fickle. After all, says Bill Mastro of http://www.mastronet.com—one of the world's largest online sports memorabilia auction sites—"disposable income is what's spent on this stuff, and let's face it, we're not selling open-heart surgery here. We're selling baseball cards." Still, the surge in interest shows no signs of abating. eBay has dozens of Web pages devoted to its brisk trade in autographs, equipment, uniforms, cards, photos, and other collectibles from every sport and team imaginable and then some. The Web site also offers helpful information about autograph authentication, tips for buyers, and tips for sellers. Rival sites with similar features abound. So whether you're looking for a vintage baseball card, an autographed football helmet, or a Madrid Réal jersey signed by superstar David Beckham, the Internet is a good place to start.[1]

Chapter Overview

DRAMATIC societal and economic changes in global economies during the last 10 years have grabbed the attention of almost every person in every industry, from banking and air travel to customer service and communications. Marketing now holds the key to creating a competitive advantage. Demographic and lifestyle changes have transformed homogeneous mass markets into much more personalized, even one-to-one interactions. Deregulation, rapid technological changes, and the relative stability of its economy have made the U.S. a world leader in e-commerce.

During the past 10 years, marketing has become the cutting-edge tool for success on the Internet. Profit-seeking organizations are not the only beneficiaries of the Internet; organizations of all kinds are beginning to emphasize marketing's role in achieving set goals. Colleges and universities, charities, museums, symphony orchestras, and hospitals now employ the marketing concept discussed in Chapter 1: providing customers the goods and services they want to buy when they want to buy them.[2] Marketing continues to perform its function of bringing buyers and sellers together, and now it does this faster and more efficiently than ever before.

With just a few ticks of the clock and a few clicks of a mouse, the Internet revolutionizes every aspect of life. New words have emerged—such as streaming video, Wi-Fi, blog, Internet, extranet, and intranet—and old words have new meanings never imagined a few years ago: Web, Net, surfer and server, banner and browser, online and offline. E-business has turned virtual reality into reality. With a computer and a telephone, a virtual marketplace is open 24 hours, 7 days a week to provide almost anything anywhere to anyone, including clothes, food, information, entertainment, and medicine. You can pay your cell phone bill, make travel reservations, post a résumé at an employment bulletin board, or even buy a used car—perhaps at a lower price than you could in person.

And here lies a major explanation for the success of e-commerce: Consumers like it so much that entire industries have changed the way they conduct their marketing and business practices. The furor over file sharing of music is transforming the music industry and increasing buyer flexibility as more and more firms offer legal downloads of high-demand songs. The movie industry is not far behind. Travel has undergone an Internet makeover as well. Expedia.com is now the largest leisure travel agency in the world, but its success has come at a price to some brick-and-mortar travel agencies that have been forced to close their doors. A major factor in Dell's ranking as the leading computer maker is that it built its sales and manufacturing efforts around the Internet. Financial institutions, from mortgage companies to stock brokerage firms,

Briefly Speaking

On the day of the race, a lot of people want you to sign something just before you get in the car so that they can say they got your last autograph.

A. J. Foyt (b. 1935)
American auto racer

have discovered the power of the Internet. Online-based mortgage company Lending Tree is growing at a rate of 70 percent a year, while E*Trade is posting its largest profits ever. E*Trade is no longer just an online brokerage; it is now the 62nd largest bank in the U.S.

Internet marketers can reach individual consumers or target organizations worldwide through a vast array of computer and communications technologies. In a few short years, more than a half million companies large and small have been connected to electronic marketing channels. The value of consumer goods and services sold online is growing much faster than overall retail sales. For instance, during a recent holiday shopping period, U.S. consumers spent more than $17 billion online, an increase of over 20 percent from the prior year.[3]

This chapter examines the nature of electronic business and commerce and explores the many ways it is transforming marketing. After defining e-commerce and e-marketing, the chapter proceeds with a discussion of the Internet and the World Wide Web. It further explains the transition of industrial economies to electronic economies, the benefits online marketing provides, and the challenges it presents. Some recent successes and failures are described. We also look at the buyers and sellers who populate the Web and how marketers build online relationships with customers. Next, we discuss the various digital marketing tools and the ways marketers use Web sites to achieve organizational goals. Finally, we examine the potential of online marketing and the challenges associated with achieving that potential.

© JEFF ZARUBA

The widespread use of the Internet—and the need to stay connected with the home office as well as with family members—has led hotel chains like Marriott's Residence Inns to provide high-speed Internet access as a service to their business and vacationing guests.

WHAT IS E-COMMERCE?

1 Define e-commerce and give examples of each function of the Internet.

A number of terms have been used to describe marketing activities that take place on the Internet or through such electronic tools as smart phones and interactive kiosks. Among the most popular is **electronic commerce**, or **e-commerce** (also referred to as *e-business*)—targeting customers by collecting and analyzing business information, conducting customer transactions, and maintaining online relationships with customers by means of telecommunications networks. E-commerce provides a foundation for launching new businesses, extending the reach of existing companies, and building and retaining customer relationships.

The e-commerce component of particular interest to marketers is **electronic marketing (e-marketing)**, the strategic process of creating, distributing, promoting, and pricing goods and services to a target market over the Internet or through such **digital tools** as tablet PCs and Apple's Bluetooth technology that enable short-range wireless connections between desktop and notebook

electronic commerce (e-commerce) Targeting customers by collecting and analyzing business information, conducting customer transactions, and maintaining online relationships with customers by means of computer networks.

electronic marketing (e-marketing) Strategic process of creating, distributing, promoting, and pricing goods and services to a target market over the Internet or through digital tools.

APPLE COMPUTER, INC.

More than 50 million songs were purchased—at 99 cents each—in the six months following the launch of Apple's iTunes Web site. Despite increased competition, songs were downloaded at the rate of 2.5 million every week, and Apple ranked as the leading legitimate music download service. A recent promotion with Pepsi resulted in an additional million songs being given away.

computers.[4] E-marketing is the means by which e-commerce is achieved. It encompasses such activities as:

1. Legally downloading songs from Apple Computer's iTunes Web site.
2. Buying a used laptop computer on the online auction site eBay.
3. Accessing the online version of *BusinessWeek* through your college's wireless computer network to complete a class research assignment.
4. Researching new car models on Edmunds.com and getting price quotes from several local dealers.

The application of these electronic tools to 21st century marketing has the potential to greatly reduce costs and increase customer satisfaction by increasing the speed and efficiency of marketing interactions. Just as e-commerce is a major function of the Internet, e-marketing is an integral component of e-commerce.

A closely related but somewhat narrower term than e-marketing is online marketing. While electronic marketing can involve noncomputer digital technologies ranging from DVDs to smart phones, online marketing refers to marketing activities that connect buyers and sellers electronically through interactive computer systems.

digital tools Electronic technologies used in e-commerce, including fax machines, personal digital assistants (PDAs) like Bluetooth, smart phones, and DVDs.

E-commerce offers countless opportunities for marketers to reach consumers. This radical departure from traditional brick-and-mortar operations provides the following benefits to contemporary marketers, as shown in Table 4.1.

1. *Global reach.* The Net eliminates the geographic protections of local business. eBay, for instance, is now the nation's largest used car dealer.[5] Buyers and sellers throughout the country meet in this virtual used car marketplace where over $7 billion worth of used cars are bought and sold annually.
2. *One-to-one marketing (personalization).* Only a handful of Dell computers are waiting for customers at any one time. The production process begins when an order is received and ends a day or two later when the PC is shipped to the customer. Not only does this approach better satisfy customer needs, but it also sharply reduces the amount of inventory Dell has to carry.[6]
3. *Interactive marketing.* Customers and suppliers negotiate prices online in much the same manner as they do at a local flea market or car dealership. The result is the creation of an ideal product at the right price that satisfies both parties.
4. *Right-time marketing.* Online retailers, such as Amazon.com and Buy.com, can provide products when and where customers want them.
5. *Integrated marketing.* The Internet enables the coordination of all promotional activities and communications to create a unified, customer-oriented promotional message.

In addition to the benefits listed here, there is increasing evidence that an effective online presence improves the performance of traditional operations. For instance, a study by e-commerce research firm Jupiter Media Metrix found that half of all online visitors use a retailer's Web site primarily for research before buying a product in the retailer's physical store.[7]

MARKETING Concept Check

1. Define *e-commerce.* Distinguish between e-commerce and e-marketing.
2. List three examples of e-marketing.
3. What are the major benefits of e-marketing?

table 4.1 *E-Commerce Capabilities*

CAPABILITY	DESCRIPTION	EXAMPLE
Global reach	The ability to reach anyone connected to a PC anywhere in the world.	eBay—the online auction site—links buyers and sellers throughout the world.
One-to-one marketing	Creating products to meet customer specifications, also called personalization.	Lands' End offers online shoppers custom-made shirts, slacks, and jeans.
Interactive marketing	Buyer–seller communications through such channels as the Internet and interactive kiosks.	Best Buy stores have a "Computer Creation Station" that lets customers design and order custom-made personal computers.
Right-time marketing	The ability to provide a product at the exact time needed.	UPS customers can place service orders online and track shipments 24/7.
Integrated marketing	Coordination of all promotional activities to produce a unified, customer-focused promotional message.	Southwest Airlines use the slogans "A Symbol of Freedom" and "You're Now Free to Move around the Country" in both online and offline promotions.

INTERACTIVITY AND E-COMMERCE

The e-commerce approach to buying and selling has been embraced by millions worldwide because it offers substantial benefits over traditional marketing practices. The two-way, back-and-forth communications enable marketers to supply the precise items desired by their customers. At the same time, purchasers can continue to refine their product specifications until they find a purchase opportunity that fills their precise needs.

One of the largest online retailers is Amazon.com. Like many other successful Internet marketers, it uses a concept called **interactive marketing.** This approach, which consists of buyer-seller communications in which the customer controls the amount and type of information received from a marketer, has been used by marketers for over a decade. Point-of-sale brochures and coupon dispensers located in supermarkets are simple forms of interactive marketing. However, when digital tools such as the Internet are included in interactive marketing efforts, the results are infinitely improved for sellers and buyers alike.

interactive marketing Buyer–seller communications in which the customer controls the amount and type of information received from a marketer through such channels as the Internet and virtual reality kiosks.

Say, for example, you've decided to address your love for specialty coffees by purchasing an espresso machine. All you need is a computer and an Internet connection. You don't have to get in the car and drive to the mall. You can evaluate used machine alternatives by checking eBay listings; you can use Google or another search engine to identify online retailers of new machines; or you can log onto Yahoo! Shopping. This Web site allows you not only to research different models but also to compare prices among dozens of online sellers. You can then place your order and have the product shipped to you. But successful online retailers such as Amazon.com or Lands' End don't stop there. You can sign in with the retailer, permanently registering your shipping and credit-card information. Based on your past purchases and personal preferences, many retailers will even send you personalized recommendations of new products. These companies want you to feel that your shopping experience is as personal as it would have been at a traditional store.

THE INTERNET

Although two-way communications between buyers and sellers describe most personal sales and have been taking place electronically since the invention of the telephone, the Golden Age of interactivity began a few decades ago. Its beginnings can be traced to the creation of the **Internet (Net),** a global collection of computer networks linked together for the purpose of exchanging data and information. The Net originally served scientists and government researchers, but it has since evolved into a multifaceted and popular medium of communication for individual households and business users. Users

Internet (Net) Worldwide network of interconnected computers that lets anyone with access to a personal computer send and receive images and data anywhere.

The Net is a 10.5 on the Richter scale of economic change.

Nicholas Negroponte (b. 1945)

American writer and director of the MIT Media Laboratory

intranet Internal corporate network that allows employees within an organization to communicate with each other and gain access to corporate information.

extranet Secure network accessible through a Web site by external customers or organizations for electronic commerce. It provides more customer-specific information than a public site.

can exchange data with other computer users around the world in formats from simple text to graphic images to *streaming video* that allows longer—or live—images to be watched as they download to a computer.

Growth of the Internet

In the last decade, the number of active Internet users in the United States grew dramatically from less than 20 million to over 132 million today. Worldwide, the number of active Internet users exceeds 300 million.[8] While some of the novelty has worn off, the Internet has become a significant presence in the daily lives of a majority of Americans.[9]

Intranets and Extranets

Internet technologies provide a platform for **intranets,** internal corporate networks that allow employees within a firm to communicate with each other and gain access to corporate information. **Extranets,** on the other hand, are corporate networks that allow communication between a firm and selected customers, suppliers, and business partners outside the firm. Companies that use both extranets and intranets benefit even further from online communication. Retail giant Wal-Mart uses an extranet called Retail Link to communicate with its 11,000-plus suppliers. Suppliers can access a variety of sales and inventory data. Retail Link helps both Wal-Mart and its suppliers manage inventory more efficiently and improves communications.

THE WORLD WIDE WEB

The Internet provides an efficient way to find and share information, but initially, most people outside universities and government agencies found it difficult to use. This changed in 1989, when Tim Berners-Lee at the European Laboratory for Particle Physics in Geneva, Switzerland, developed the **World Wide Web.** Originally thought of as an internal document-management system, the Web quickly grew to become a collection of hundreds of thousands of interlinked computers, called Web servers, that function together within the Internet. These computers are located all over the world and

figure 4.1

A Typical Day on the Web

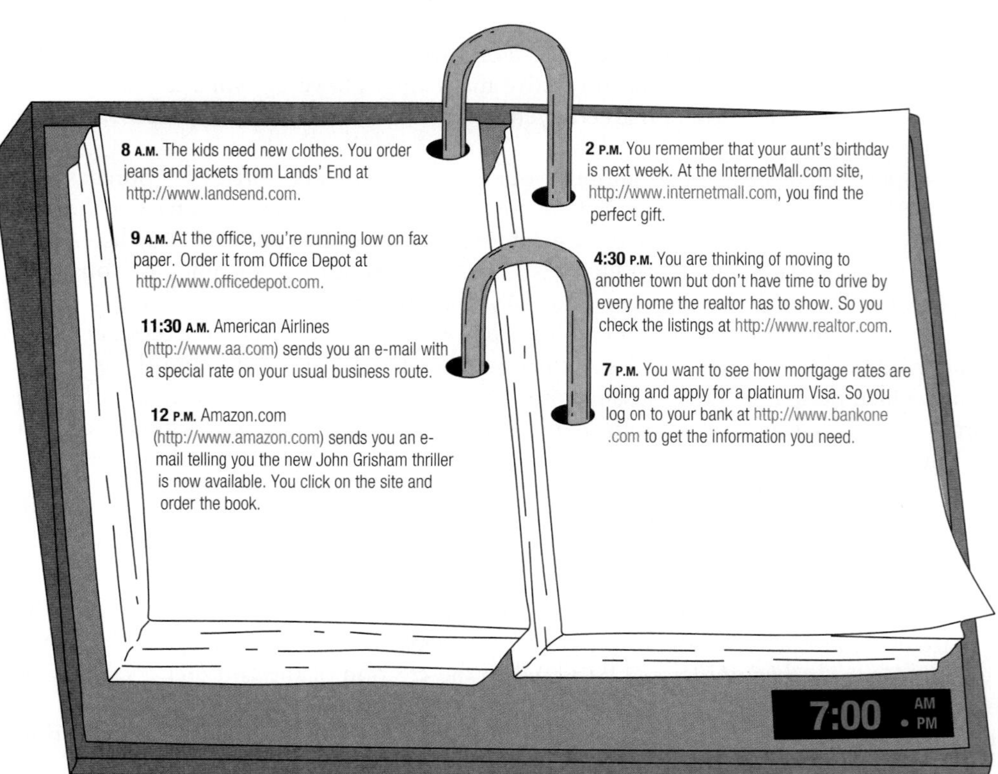

rely on high-speed Internet circuits and software to allow users to hop from server to server, providing the illusion that the Web is one big computer. The Web, along with the development of specialized software called Web browsers—such as Netscape and Microsoft Internet Explorer—made the Internet accessible to millions of users worldwide.

The Web can handle so much information in so many different media that it has become a revolutionary means for marketers to reach consumers in their target markets and for two-way communications between sellers and potential customers. Over half of regular Internet users have purchased at least one product online. Millions of other visitors, though not actually buying online, use the Web to help them make purchasing decisions.

How do people use the Web? Figure 4.1 illustrates how a typical consumer might spend time online during a day. Many of these interactions occur as a means of communicating—such as sending electronic mail or posting messages on electronic bulletin boards. Still other interactions involve gathering information about airfares, gifts for friends or family members, a new home, a mortgage, or a credit card. Still other interactions—such as an REI outdoor clothing purchase or an order for printer supplies from Office Depot—would be considered electronic commerce. The Web's entertainment function might be performed when a Web visitor reads reviews of a best-selling book on BN.com or watches a "trailer" for an upcoming movie on Quicktime.com.

FOUR WEB FUNCTIONS

As Figure 4.2 shows, there are four primary functions of the Web: communication, information, entertainment, and e-commerce. Let's consider the role of each in contemporary marketing.

Communication

For both households and businesses, one of the most popular applications of the Internet in the U.S. is e-mail. In fact, e-mails now outnumber regular mail (often referred to as *snail mail*) by more than

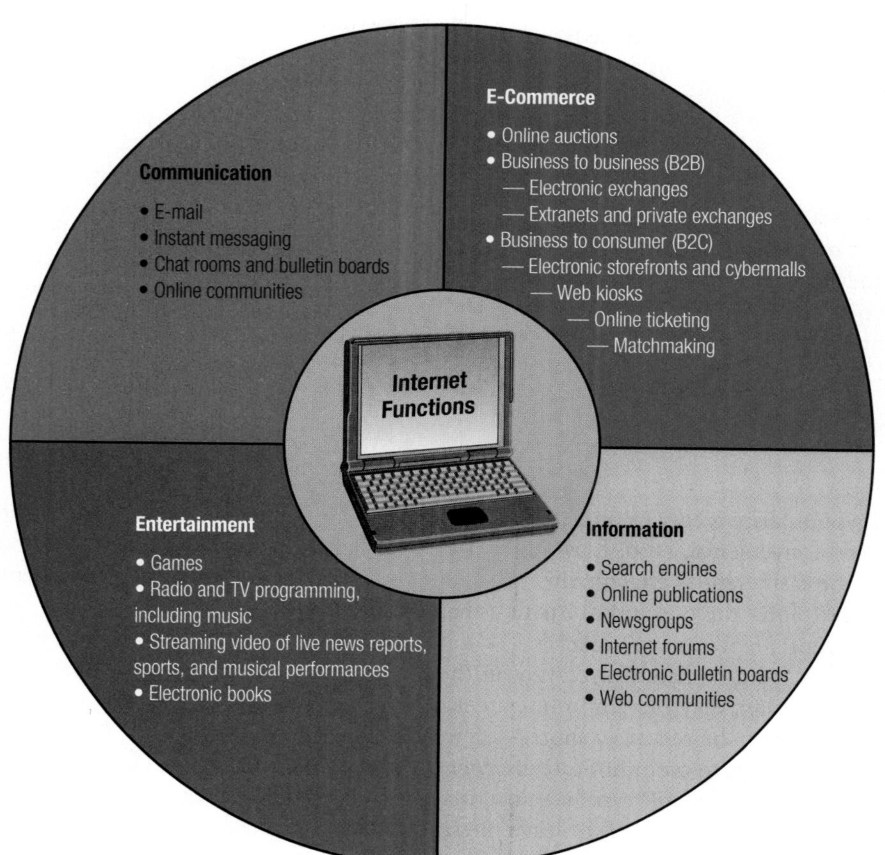

figure 4.2
Four Functions of the Internet

ETIQUETTE TIPS

FOR MARKETING PROFESSIONALS

E-Mail and Fax Etiquette

BECAUSE it's so fast and informal, communicating by e-mail or fax is almost like talking. It's all too easy to forget not only that both these media are more permanent than conversation but also that the traditional rules of written correspondence apply to them. Here are a few important suggestions.

FOR E-MAIL

1. Include a subject line in your message so the recipient knows before opening it whether the matter is urgent and what the e-mail is about.
2. If you're angry, write your message offline and wait 24 hours to calm down and reconsider before sending it.
3. Avoid typing your message in all caps; that's interpreted online as shouting and is never appropriate in a business setting.
4. Be sparing with emoticons (smiley faces and the like) in business mail. Remember that subtlety is often lost in electronic mail.
5. Before you click "Send," proofread your message for errors, make sure you've actually attached your attachment, and double-check that you're sending the message to the right person.

FOR FAX

1. Attach a cover sheet (or a label or template on the first page of your message) indicating the name and fax number of the recipient, your name and fax number, the number of pages you're sending, a number to call in case of transmission problems, and the subject of the message.
2. Avoid using a fax for lengthy documents that can be sent by overnight service instead.
3. Check the time zone of your recipient before sending. Someone who works at home will appreciate getting faxes only during his or her own business hours.
4. Make sure the print on your original is dark, large, and clear.

FOR BOTH E-MAIL AND FAX

1. Avoid e-mail and fax transmissions when the information is sensitive, confidential, personal, or legal in nature. Remember that both these forms of communication can easily be read and copied by others.
2. Tell the recipient what you need in the way of a reply—an acknowledgment that your message was received? A written response? Action within a certain time frame?
3. Avoid forwarding jokes, petitions, chain letters, and other junk mail at work. Such transmissions add to the growing problem of *spam.*
4. As a courtesy to your reader, keep your message short. If the matter under discussion is long or complex, consider a meeting or phone call instead.

Sources: "Fax Etiquette," http://www.sciandtech.com/, accessed January 3, 2005; http://etiquette.tips4me.com, accessed January 3, 2005; "Internet Etiquette," *Heritage Bank Newsletter,* July/August 2003; Shelly Golly, "Fax Etiquette," http://www.stenograph.com, Winter 2002.

ten to one. Its popularity is easy to understand: E-mail is simple to use, travels quickly, and can be read at the receiver's convenience. Also, files—such as Microsoft Excel spreadsheets or Adobe Photoshop pictures—can be easily sent as attachments to e-mail messages. The "Etiquette Tips for Marketing Professionals" box explores the dos and don'ts of e-mail and fax communication.

instant messaging E-mail service that allows for the immediate exchange of short messages between online users.

A more recent adaptation of e-mail is **instant messaging.** With this application, when someone sends a message, it is immediately displayed on the recipient's computer screen. As sender and recipient reply to one another, they can communicate in real time. However, unlike regular e-mail messages, instant messages have to be relatively short—a few sentences at the most.

Other popular ways to communicate are *chat rooms* and *bulletin boards.* These methods provide a forum in which a group of people can share information. When someone sends a message, it is displayed for all to see. Users join chat sessions, or leave messages on bulletin boards, on topics that interest them. The resulting online communities are not only personally satisfying but can become an important force for business. Many companies sponsor such communication as part of their overall customer service. For instance, Whole Latte Love's Web site—an online coffee retailer—contains a bulletin board for each of the major products it sells. Customers can post questions on the appropriate product bulletin board. Replies are posted by both Whole Latte Love employees and other customers. Recent postings include where to buy replacement parts for an old espresso machine and the right way to clean a coffee machine.

Information

For many users, getting information is one of the main reasons they go online. Internet users can begin by consulting commercial search engines—such as Google or Ask Jeeves—which search for information on topics entered by the user. Or they may visit the online editions of publications and news organizations like *The New York Times,* the BBC, CNN, or *Forbes.* Government sites provide a wealth of free data in the public domain. One of the most visited Web sites is that of the U.S. Census Bureau. Another fast-growing area of the Internet consists of sites providing online educational services. One of every three U.S. colleges and universities now offer some sort of accredited degree online.

Entertainment

Internet users find lots of entertainment online, including everything from concert Webcasts to online gaming. Online providers of entertainment can offer competitive prices, speed, and boundless services. Games, radio programming, and movie and music clips, to name just a few entertainment options, are available online. Some content is free, with the costs borne by advertising, and other content is available for a fee. Apple Computer's popular iTunes service charges users 99 cents for each song downloaded.[10] Manufacturers of video game consoles—Microsoft, Nintendo, and Sony—appear convinced that online gaming is the next big thing for video games. Microsoft's Xbox game console has an Ethernet port that allows users to easily connect to the Internet. An Ethernet cable, attached to a port, is a common method of connecting a computer or other device to the Web or to another computer network. New consoles coming from Nintendo and Sony within the next couple of years are expected to have a similar feature.

Entertainment on the Internet has raised numerous legal and ethical issues, including questions relating to copyrighted materials. The well-documented case of the recording industry versus Napster is but one example. A court ruled that Napster's free music download service was a clear violation of copyright and effectively shut the company down. Napster has reemerged offering a fee-based music download service similar to Apple's iTunes. Copyright and other legal and ethical issues, however, are unlikely to chase entertainment off the Internet.

MLB.COM

Baseball fans who can't get enough of the game now have the option of watching or listening to over 100 games a week with a subscription to MLB.com. The live broadcasts make it possible for Major League Baseball to increase overall revenues by providing live broadcasts of most baseball games to distant fans.

E-Commerce

Today, e-commerce is the primary function of the Web. According to recent statistics, four of every five Web sites are devoted to some aspect of e-commerce. Almost every organization has some sort of Web presence, from multinational corporations to individual entrepreneurial ventures and from sellers of goods to service providers. Organizations ranging from not-for-profits like the American Cancer Society and the Boston Symphony Orchestra to world-famous for-profit jewelry retailer Tiffany's are vying for space on the Web and for "eyeballs"—in short, consumers' attention.

The Web facilitates marketing activities, including buying and selling goods and services, building relationships, increasing overall market size (number of customers, annual revenues, and geographic coverage), and reducing marketing costs by replacing intermediaries with direct distribution channels. This chapter focuses on the e-commerce function of the Internet since it fuels the growth of electronic marketing. The Web, the most popular area of the Internet, has

figure 4.3

Online Matchmaking for Fun and Profit

DONAT/ WALD COMPANY

become an integral part of the lives of most consumers both in the U.S. and in other highly developed nations.

Most people generally think of the Web as a giant cybermall of retail stores selling millions of goods online. However, service providers are also important participants in e-commerce. These include entertainment sites; online specialists in auto rentals, lodging, and air travel; real estate sales and rental sites; and providers of financial services. Traditional banks—such as Wachovia—and brokerage firms—like Fidelity Investments—have greatly expanded their online services. In addition, many new online service providers are rapidly attracting customers who want to do more of their own banking and investment trading on whatever time and day that suits them. Airlines, too, have discovered the power of the Web. Southwest Airlines sells over half of its tickets online, leading the industry in sales via this low-cost channel.[11]

Figure 4.3 describes a growing online commercial presence: matchmaking. The dating scene, like flea markets, is one of those fragmented marketplaces where the Internet can shine. After all, it offers speed, anonymity, and the ability to connect vast numbers of buyers and sellers. By requiring each subscriber to complete a 29-dimension compatibility matching system, eHarmony.com attempts to improve the quality of its matches and enhance customer satisfaction. This growing online segment, led by industry pioneer Match.com, is discussed in depth in Case 4.1.

The Web also provides tremendous opportunities for business-to-business (B2B) e-commerce. Currently, an estimated one-third of all B2B transactions take place online, amounting to over $2 trillion annually. The online penetration of B2B e-commerce will grow to more than 40 percent of B2B sales by 2006.[12] These sales are spread out across thousands of businesses. The number of U.S. businesses engaged in B2B e-commerce will grow to more than 90 percent within the next year or two. Cisco Systems, IBM, and Intel are among the firms that generate billions of dollars in online sales revenues each year.

Needless to say, however, not every e-commerce idea has worked out. The online landscape is littered with dozens of dot.com failures. Figure 4.4 describes some of the most notorious dot.com busts. Moreover, some of the growth and profitability projections about the Internet and e-commerce, made in the 1990s, turned out to have been overly optimistic. The first decade of the 21st century is seeing a resurgence of e-commerce, although at a much less hectic pace than during the 1990s.

ACCESSING THE INTERNET

In the same way an explorer relies on a compass and map to seek out a desired destination, marketers and their customers must depend on navigation instruments to locate Web sites and find relevant information in a database. The basic pathway for going online is through an **Internet service provider (ISP).** An ISP, such as Earthlink and MSN, provides direct access to the Internet for both individual consumers and business users. ISP giants such as America Online (AOL) let the user access the Internet through their own specially designed online sites. These sites can be thought of as doors opening to a giant communications center called the Internet.

Internet service provider (ISP) Organization that provides access to the Internet via a telephone, satellite TV service, or cable TV network.

Most Internet users still connect via phone lines using a dial-up connection. Dial-up connections, however, are gradually being replaced by much faster broadband connections. Today, more than 30 million U.S. households have opted for a broadband ISP connection.[13] The two most common types are DSL (which stands for *digital subscriber line* and connects via telephone lines) and cable modems.

A growing number of cell phones offer at least a limited ability to access the Internet. Around 6 million U.S. cell phone users currently use their devices to regularly surf the Web.[14] So-called *smart phones,* which are a combination of a cell phone and a handheld computer, make it even easier to access

figure 4.4

Five Notorious Dot.Com Busts

NAME	WHAT IT DID	WHY IT FAILED
iHarvest.com	Company offered a browser plug-in that allowed users to store copies of Web pages.	Both Netscape and Internet Explorer already have the same feature; why would anyone pay for something they could get for free?
Furniture.com	Online furniture store.	Since UPS and FedEx wouldn't ship large, bulky items—like furniture—products were shipped using much more expensive common carriers; shipping costs often exceeded cost of product.
Kozmo.com	Single movie rental service; movies messengered to your front door.	Costs overwhelmed revenues; no way the business model could make money.
SwapIt.com	People could trade in used CDs and video games, receiving "swap-it bucks" that they could use to buy other people's used CDs and videos.	Could make money only on shipping and handling charges; people mostly "sold" CDs and videos no one else wanted to buy.
MySpace.com	Gave away free disk space on company servers for people and businesses to store files.	Tried to make money by selling ads; when that didn't work, the company started charging for the service. Only 6,000 out of the company's 9 million customers were willing to pay for the service.

Source: "Fiercely Stupid," *Newsweek,* http://www.newsweek.com, accessed March 19, 2004.

the Internet and to send and receive e-mail. Sales of smart phones are expected to exceed 20 million units by 2007.[15]

Wireless Internet access is possible at an increasing number of locations, including airports, hotels, public libraries, college campuses, and even the local Starbucks. McDonald's has recently tested the concept in about 300 restaurants in the San Francisco, Seattle, Chicago, and New York areas. **Wi-Fi**—short for **wireless fidelity**—cuts the Internet plug-in cord by offering mobile online users wireless Internet access—even at 30,000 feet. Already, airlines such as Lufthansa and British Airways are offering this feature at both flat-rate and metered pricing. Flights lasting under three hours currently cost a flat rate of $14.95 or $7.95 for the first half hour, plus 25 cents for every additional minute.[16] Connecting to the Internet while away from home or office has never been easier.

Wi-Fi (wireless fidelity) Wireless Internet access.

Within a matter of months, mobile Internet users will have an alternative to Wi-Fi without having to search for prewired "hot spots" in airports, coffee shops, and other locations. Verizon Wireless is already offering a new high-speed technology that wirelessly connects a laptop, Primary Domain Controller (PDC), or cell phone in San Diego and Washington, D.C., and will expand to the 100 largest markets in the U.S. by 2007. All it takes is a special software program and a Verizon modem for the PC card slot. The monthly service fee, currently a pricey $80, is expected to drop to around $50 a month—about the same price as wired broadband connections.[17]

The early gateways for Internet access were basically **search engines.** Over time, these Internet entrances became portals by adding shopping services and software applications like e-mail and online calendars to their site contents. In addition to AOL, Earthlink, and MSN, portals include Terra Lycos and Yahoo! A more recent trend is the creation of portals built around specific services or communities. These include ESPN, CNN.com, and CBS Market Watch. Their aim is to draw in Web surfers and keep their interest with specific types of content or transactions.

In addition to serving as gateways for Internet access, portals are pushing to become the grand entrance for consumer business. At present, most portal revenue comes from advertising or subscriber fees. Online shopping generates only a small percentage of portal site revenue, but this percentage is increasing. Yahoo!, for instance, offers a virtual mall consisting of hundreds of stores. Stores pay Yahoo! rent for the "real estate" on Yahoo's shopping pages.

1. **Explain interactive marketing.**
2. **Distinguish between an intranet and an extranet.**
3. **List the four functions of the Web and give an example of each.**

GETTY IMAGES.

Verizon Wireless, the nation's largest wireless network, is well known for its service quality and customer service levels. Its new EV-DO (short for Evolution-Data Optimized) offers wireless broadband connections that can be used just about anywhere—even in a car or on a street—in the nation's 100 largest markets.

E-COMMERCE AND THE ECONOMY

The early years of the 21st century are witnessing the change from a century-old industrial economy to its electronic successor—an economy based on information, the Internet, and other related online technologies. Many people see e-commerce as a major component of growth for most of the 21st century. Each year since the Web first opened for commercial activity in 1993, the impact of e-commerce on both consumers and businesses has continued to grow. By 2010, e-commerce will comprise over 5 percent of total U.S. gross domestic product.[18] Moreover, the Brookings Institution estimates that annual productivity gains resulting from e-commerce will reach $450 billion by 2006.[19]

The Web is now used by small, previously unheard-of companies as well as large, multinational corporations. Consider the following successful examples of e-commerce:

1. More than 70,000 students are currently taking courses online at the University of Phoenix. The Web has helped the for-profit institution become the largest private college in the United States.[20]
2. FreshDirect—an online supermarket—now has annual revenues exceeding $100 million. It will likely become the first Web-based supermarket to turn a profit.[21]
3. The Boston Symphony Orchestra's Web site attracts over 7,000 visitors a day and online ticket sales today exceed $4 million annually. The orchestra credits the Web for a dramatic increase in the number of young concertgoers and season ticket subscribers.[22]
4. More than 64 million Americans used the Internet last year to get travel information. Forty-two million people booked their travel arrangements online, spending an average of $2,600 each.[23]

(2) Describe how marketers use the Internet to achieve their firm's objectives.

But conducting business successfully and profitably on the Net requires more than creating a Web site. State-of-the-art graphics, audio and video, and pages of information do not spell success any more than fancy business cards or company brochures do. A Web site must provide a platform for communication between organizations, customers, and suppliers. Businesses now hold auctions for utility suppliers, banks partner with computer companies, and music groups sell directly from their Web sites to their fans. New businesses and new ways of conducting business on the Web have contributed to overall economic growth. The following sections in this chapter describe the current state of business-to-business (B2B) e-commerce.

BUSINESS-TO-BUSINESS ONLINE MARKETING

The FedEx Web site is not designed to be flashy. There are no fancy graphics or streaming video clips, just lots of practical information to assist the firm's customers. The site enables customers to check rates, compare services, schedule package pickups and deliveries, track shipments, and order needed shipping supplies. This information is vital to FedEx's customers, most of whom are businesses. Customers access the site thousands of times a day.

Unlike the business-to-consumer (B2C) segment of the online market, B2B interactions involve professional buyers and sellers—people whose performances are evaluated by their purchasing and selling decisions. Consequently, B2B marketing usually does not need the same glitz and glamour as the B2C segment.

Although most people are familiar with such B2C online marketers as Amazon.com and eBay, B2C transactions are dwarfed by their B2B counterparts, which buy and sell both business services and commodities like paper, plastics, chemicals, and office supplies. B2B e-commerce transactions stand at

Global online auction site eBay offers an alternative marketing channel for both the B2B and B2C markets. Peak utilization on the site has increased 29-fold since 1999, with major new growth coming from France, the UK, China, and India.

$2.4 trillion according to Forrester Research. By some estimates, 80 percent of all e-commerce activity involves B2B transactions.[24]

Early B2B e-commerce typically consisted of a company setting up a Web site and offering products to any buyer willing to make online purchases. More recently, businesses are buying and selling through **electronic exchanges,** Web-based marketplaces that cater to a specific industry's needs. An example of an electronic exchange is FreeMarkets, where suppliers compete for the business of organizational buyers who might be purchasing anything from gears to printed circuit boards. FreeMarkets was founded by Glen Meakem, a former General Electric executive. Meakem understood that manufacturers spend roughly $5 trillion each year on industrial parts and that the purchase process for these items is usually very inefficient. He developed a system whereby suppliers promise to deliver parts on standardized schedules, with identical payment terms and inventory arrangements. The only variable is price. FreeMarkets consults with buyers and screens suppliers so that, by the time an auction takes place, each is familiar with the process. The auction itself usually takes less than an hour. In addition to its auction services, FreeMarkets also offers a wide range of other Web-based products designed to improve procurement efficiency. Royal Mail—Britain's public mail system—estimates that it saves around $4 million annually using FreeMarkets products.[25]

One of Fujitsu sales VP Don McMahan's least pleasant tasks involves haggling with reluctant buyers as he tries to get rid of hundreds of refurbished high-end Fujitsu scanners. In the past, he might have simply turned to traditional third-party liquidators to find buyers for this excess inventory. Today, however, he turns to eBay. Within 12 months after first contacting the online giant, McMahan had sold all 700 scanners he posted on his Fujitsu Scanner Outlet site. Most of his eBay customers are small businesses that he couldn't have reached through his regular sales channels.[26]

Not all B2B exchanges have succeeded, however. The "Marketing Miss" box discusses the problems of online exchanges.

As noted earlier, B2B e-commerce totals around $2.4 trillion worldwide and should continue to grow rapidly in the coming years. The U.S. is expected to remain the largest market for B2B e-commerce, with transactions increasing at an annual rate of around 68 percent. However, B2B e-commerce is expected to grow even faster in Western Europe (increasing at an annual rate of 91 percent) and the Asia-Pacific region, where B2B e-commerce transactions are expected to increase at an annual rate of over 100 percent during the next several years.[27]

Durable goods manufacturers alone account for almost half of all B2B e-commerce sales. Wholesalers of business products such as office supplies, electronic goods, and scientific equipment are a close second in B2B e-commerce market share. Even though they still provide many of their services in person, professionals such as doctors, attorneys, and accountants are finding new ways to use the Internet to reach existing and potential clients as well as communicate with others in their fields.

Companies large and small have developed the systems and software necessary to make B2B online marketing a reality. Many have even created new business units to serve the needs of customers and suppliers online. While there are many small, start-up companies in this industry, larger, more established firms also have a significant presence. IBM, for instance, provides e-commerce services to hundreds of other companies. E-commerce services generate over $30 billion annually in revenue for IBM, more than a third of the computer giant's total revenue.[28] While most people consider Amazon.com to be just an online retailer, the company has also established itself as a major e-commerce services company that provides software and related services to a wide variety of other businesses.[29]

An important objective of online as well as offline marketing is to enable current and potential customers to quickly distinguish the firm and its products from competitive offerings. Purchasing managers can search the Web looking for the best deals on everything from office supplies to plastics, selecting from hundreds of different vendors throughout the world. But what about the vendors themselves? How do they position themselves on the Web so that corporate buyers notice them, let alone make a purchase? Most online marketers begin by listing their firms with Internet Yellow Pages such as Verizon's SuperPages.com, which operate just like their printed counterparts. A purchasing manager can look up "laser printer supplies" at the SuperPages.com Web site and get listings of relevant sites. Many industries have their own online references, such as the *Thomas Register of American Manufacturers.*

It also goes without saying that online marketers need to make sure that their firms are listed with the major search engines, such as Google (shown in Figure 4.5). But that is often not enough. A single search for an item—say, steel—could yield thousands of sites, many of which might not even be relevant. To overcome this problem, online marketers pay search engines fees to have their Web sites or ads pop up after a computer user enters certain words into the search engine or to make sure that their firms' listing appears toward the top of the search results.[30] This is called **search marketing.**

Successful online B2B marketers serve their customers by thinking like a buyer. They interview their regular customers to learn more about exactly how these customers use the Internet and where they find the information needed in making purchase decisions. This information can be used to devise

marketing miss Why Are Online Exchanges Dying?

Background. Less than a decade ago, Internet experts were predicting that one of the most popular uses of the Internet would be B2B exchanges: auction houses for purchasing parts, raw materials, and other components used in construction, retail, and the biotech industry. It didn't exactly turn out that way.

The Marketing Problem. Business buyers and purchasing agents needed to be sold on the idea that technology could help them find suppliers faster, improve on traditional distribution channels, and reduce prices without lowering quality or product availability or adding to delivery times. Suppliers would have to accept the fact that the lowest bidders would end up with most of the business.

The Outcome. According to the *California Management Review,* of about 15,000 business-to-business exchanges that were launched on the Web, just over two of every five remain. Some have consoli-

strategies that attract new customers and improve relationships with existing ones.

Benefits of B2B Online Marketing

The advantages of business-to-business online marketing strategies over traditional methods of connecting buyers and sellers are only beginning to be realized. Online marketers can find new markets and customers. In addition, cost savings are realized in almost every aspect of the online firm's marketing strategy as electronic marketing replaces the traditional approach. Finally, online marketing greatly reduces the time involved in reaching target markets. Many business writers label e-commerce as *easy commerce,* because online marketing tools allow the direct exchange of information, such as order fulfillment and customer service, in a seamless fashion without the involvement of marketing intermediaries. Communicating with suppliers, customers, and distributors over the Web can be more cost-effective and efficient than letters, phone calls, faxes, and personal sales calls.

figure 4.5

An Example of Search Marketing

DES JENSON/BLOOMBERG NEWS/LANDOV

The number of Web sites continues to increase, with most of the growth from the launch of new commercial sites. A *home page* creates a company's online storefront where existing and potential customers go for product and company information. A site should capture the personality of the company and serve as an effective public relations tool. The Web enhances an organization's operations by reducing distances and removing time zones and political boundaries. Both not-for-profit and profit-seeking organizations are enjoying these benefits. For instance, the state of North Carolina has recently instituted a program called *NC E-Procurement.* The program combines the use of Internet technology with traditional procurement practices to streamline the purchasing process and reduce costs. State and local governmental agencies, public schools, and state-supported colleges and universities can use the system to purchase a variety of products from state-approved vendors. According to the Web site, "E-Procurement has reduced prices for goods and services through volume discounts, and also enables administrative and operational cost savings by streamlining processing and interactions with vendors/suppliers." One North Carolina county reported saving over 30 percent on printer supplies by using E-Procurement.[31]

ONLINE CONSUMER MARKETING

Just as e-commerce is a major function of the Internet, online marketing is an integral component of e-commerce. For years, catalog clothing retailer Lands' End generated virtually all of its orders by

dated and others have simply disappeared. One exception is in electronic components, where about two-thirds of the original online exchanges are still in operation, offering hard-to-find and liquidated items to an industry in which personal relationships with vendors are less important than they are elsewhere. Transportation sites have also survived, including freight-matching services and other kinds of collaboration among shippers.

Lessons Learned. Many suppliers weren't happy with the pressure to come in with the lowest bid each time a long-term satisfied buyer decided to make a new purchase. And many buyers clung to an "If it ain't broke . . . " philosophy, preferring to cultivate long-term relationships with their suppliers. These B2B purchasers are likely to be slow to change business processes that seem to be working. Purchasing agents didn't see enough benefits from the online exchanges to abandon suppliers they knew. Says one consultant in B2B marketing, "The keys to success begin and end with customers—it is Marketing 101."

Sources: David Hannon, "Exchanges Are Dead, but Collaboration Is Not," *Purchasing,* November 20, 2003; Cara Cannella, "Why Online Exchanges Died," *Inc.,* August 2003, p. 28; Arundhati Parmar, "A Focus on Services Helps Revive B-to-B E-Exchanges," *Marketing News,* September 2, 2002, p. 21.

telephone or mail. A few years ago, the company decided to turn to online marketing to boost sales and reduce costs. As shown in Figure 4.6, Lands' End marketers alert consumers to its new online services, such as its virtual model that allows consumers to "try on" clothes before they buy. Online customers can communicate with customer service representatives in real time. Two customers can even shop on the site simultaneously—just as if they were shopping together in a brick-and-mortar store. As the following sections explain, both consumers and marketers alike enjoy the benefits of online marketing.

Online marketing is inherently interactive marketing. It obviously expands the reach of marketers in connecting with consumers, but to be effective, it must be part of an overall marketing strategy before it can create value for customers. A point to remember is that just as quickly as a firm can rise to become a star in cyberspace, if its online site is not launched properly and operated efficiently, it can just as quickly burn out. Many of the notorious dot.com busts described in Figure 4.4 failed to properly launch or efficiently operate their Web sites.

Another point to remember is that there are basically two types of B2C Web sites: shopping sites and informational sites. Williams-Sonoma has a shopping site. Customers can view product information and place orders online. By contrast, Toyota's Web site is informational only. Consumers can view detailed product information, compare financing alternatives, and even request a price quote from a local dealer. They *cannot,* however, buy a new car online.

③ Explain how online marketing benefits organizations, marketers, and consumers.

Consumers who shop online can point to a number of advantages to online marketing. Figure 4.7 shows the results of a recent survey in which consumers were asked to list the reasons they shopped online during a recent holiday shopping period. The perceived benefits for online shoppers fall into three categories: lower prices, convenience, and personalization. Marketers should ensure that their Web sites offer consumers these basic advantages over traditional shopping experiences. In addition, Web sites should provide high levels of security and privacy, be easy to navigate, and supply information that consumers can use in making product comparisons and purchase decisions. Moreover, it is

figure 4.6
Lands' End Web Site

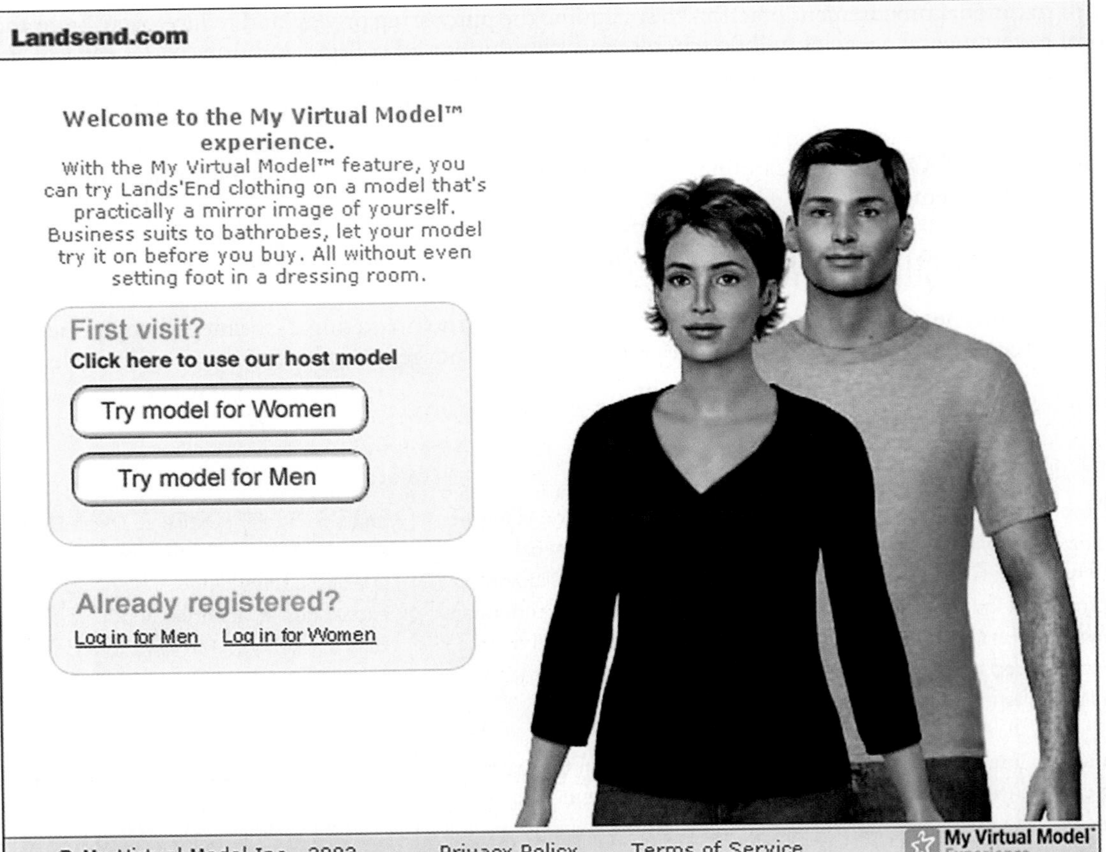

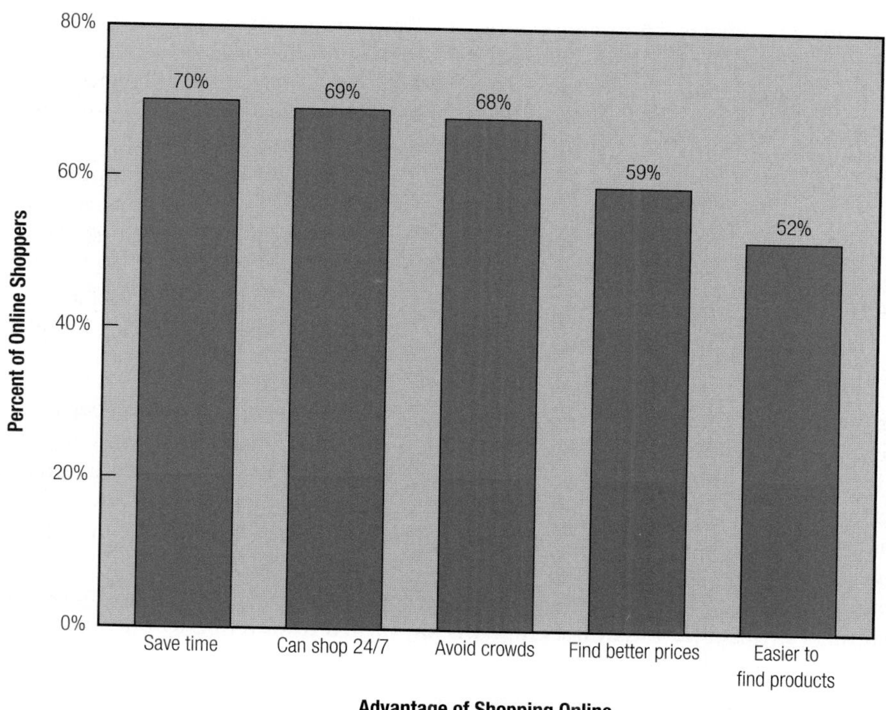

Note: Online shoppers were asked to list all of the reasons they choose to shop online.
Source: Robyn Greenspan, "E-Tailers Will See Green," Click Z Network, http://www.clickz.com, accessed March 9, 2004. Reprinted with permission.

figure 4.7
Reasons for Shopping Online

important for e-tailers to listen to their customers and be willing to make changes to their Web sites based on this feedback.

Lower Prices

Many products cost less online. Many of the best deals on airfares and hotels, for instance, can often be found at travel sites on the Internet. If you call Delta Airlines' toll-free number, before speaking to an agent a recorded voice invites you to visit Delta.com "where lower fares may be available." Visitors to BN.com—the online store of bookseller Barnes & Noble—find many best sellers discounted by up to 40 percent. At the traditional stores, best sellers are marked down by only 30 percent. It comes as no surprise to anyone who has ever searched the Web for the best price for software or a newly issued CD that almost 60 percent of Web shoppers cited lower prices as a motivation for shopping online.[32]

The Web is an ideal method for savvy shoppers to compare prices from dozens—even hundreds—of sellers. Online shoppers can compare features and prices at their leisure, without being pressured by a salesperson or having to conform to the company's hours of operation. One of the newer e-commerce tools, **bots,** aids consumers in comparison shopping. Bots—short for robots—are search programs that check hundreds of sites, gather and assemble information, and bring it back to the sender. Say, for instance, you're in the market for a new computer monitor. At Shopping.com, you can specify the type and size of monitor you're looking for, and the Web site displays a list of the highest ranked monitors and the e-tailer offering the best price on each, along with estimated taxes and shipping expenses. The Web site even ranks the e-tailers by customer experience and tells you whether or not a particular model is in stock.

bot Search program that checks hundreds of sites, gathers and assembles information, and brings it back to the sender.

Convenience

A second factor influencing the growth of online purchases is shopper convenience. Included in their convenience expectations are an easy-to-use Web site and convenient return policies.

Cybershoppers can order goods and services from around the world at any hour of the day or night. Most e-tailers allow customers to register their credit-card and shipping information for quick use in making future purchases. Users are required to select a user name and password. Registered customers are asked to type in their password when they place another order. E-tailers typically send an e-mail message confirming an order and the amount charged to the buyer's credit card. Another e-mail is sent once the product is shipped, along with a number the customer can use to track the order through the delivery process.

Many Web sites will design customized products to match individual customer requirements. Nike offers online shoppers the opportunity to customize a running shoe, personalizing such features as the outsole, the amount of cushioning, and the width. The personalized shoe costs about $10 more than buying a comparable—but not custom—shoe off the shelves of the local Nike retailer. Shoppers are also able to personalize men's and women's dress pants and men's dress shirts at Landsend.com.

Personalization

While electronic marketing often operates with little or no human interaction, cyberspace marketers know how important personalization is to the quality of the shopping experience. Customer satisfaction is greatly affected by the marketer's ability to offer service tailored to many individual customers. But each person expects not only a certain minimum level of customer service but also specific types of service that fit his or her needs in making a particular purchase. Consequently, most leading online retailers currently offer customized features on their Web sites.

The early years of e-commerce saw Web marketers casting their nets broadly in an effort to land as many customers as possible. Today, the emphasis has turned toward one-to-one marketing, creating loyal customers who are likely to make repeat purchases. How does personalized marketing work online? Say you buy a book at Amazon.com and register with the site. The site will welcome you back for your next purchase by name. Using special software that analyzes your previous purchases, it will also suggest several other books you might like. You even have the option of receiving periodic e-mails from Amazon.com informing you of new products that relate to previous purchases or to topics you have specified. Many other leading e-tailers offer similar types of personalized marketing.

BENEFITS OF ONLINE CONSUMER MARKETING

Many of the same benefits achieved by B2B online marketers are also realized by marketers of consumer products who rely on the Web in their businesses. As Figure 4.8 indicates, marketers can use their Web sites to build strong relationships, reduce costs, increase efficiency, create a more level playing field, and achieve a global presence.

Relationship Building

Building relationships with consumers is crucial to the success of both offline and online marketing. As an earlier section explained, personalization is an important component of online relationship building. If a shopper visits a Web site that sells accessories and buys a dress and a purse, the next time she visits the site, she may be greeted with an attractive ad showing a belt or shoes that can be coordinated with her previous purchase. In this way, marketers create a one-to-one shopping experience that often leads to enhanced customer satisfaction levels and repeat purchases. Brand loyalty forms a part of many offline relationships that can be transferred to online sites. In fact, customers expect Web sites to emulate the traditional retail world. They like being greeted when they enter a store or a Web site.

figure 4.8

Benefits of B2C Online Marketing

Small businesses, with even smaller budgets, can use the Internet to find customers in unexpected places and build relationships with them. Proving that the Internet acts as a great equalizer, small car-rental firms with names like L&M, E-Z, and U.-Save account for nearly half of total bookings through Orbitz in Orlando. Vacationers account for an increasing share of the car-rental business—and a one-day rental price of less than $35, versus $66 through Avis, is sufficient to entice thrifty consumers to shift to the unknown brands.[33]

The Internet is the most exciting development in my professional career.

John F. Welch Jr. (b. 1935)
retired Chairman and CEO, General Electric

Rick Brown, president of Newspaper Collectors Society of America, holds online auctions to sell historic papers to collectors. A few years ago, he sold a 19th century receipt from a drugstore in Canton, Maine. Ordinarily, this would not be a big seller, but it proved highly desirable to residents of Canton who were establishing a local historical society. Another antiques dealer had difficulty at first selling a 1903 bicycle-parts catalog from France, but it sold quickly after French collectors discovered the dealer's Web site.[34] Once customers have received quick and efficient service from online dealers, they often return in search of other rare objects for which they might be looking.

Customer service is the key to building strong customer relationships in both traditional and online marketing. Because the Web has the power to create instant two-way communications between companies and their customers, many people get a good feeling about shopping online, believing that someone is on the other end with immediate answers to their questions and solutions to their problems. Unfortunately, this is still an area where improvements are needed: a quick, personalized response to e-mail questions from current and potential customers. A recent survey revealed that it takes merchants a long 25 hours on average to send personalized responses to e-mail questions. Laura Freeman, president of e-tailing group, inc., noted that while customer service performance has generally improved, e-tailers "must remain vigilant in the overall customer service as it will significantly impact their brand."[35]

Increased Efficiency

For large corporations and small businesses, sales made entirely through a Web site typically generate much greater profit margins than sales from traditional channels such as catalogs, retail outlets, or phone centers. However, even if the sale does not close online, marketers who educate their customers online ultimately save money and increase sales productivity because salespeople no longer have to spend their time answering routine questions.

Cost Reductions

Marketers have found that e-commerce can markedly reduce the costs of starting and operating a business. Scott Smith, manager of inventory at Ace Hardware, says that since his company installed a Web-enabled collaborative-commerce program, the cost of picking goods off warehouse shelves has fallen about 18 percent, and inventory receiving costs dropped by 20 percent.[36]

A More Level Playing Field

Minority business owners believe that the anonymity provided by the Internet has allowed them to succeed on their own merits in a world where discrimination still exists. Roosevelt Gist, an African-American car dealership owner, reports that some white customers would ask for another salesperson when he would approach them in the showroom. Today, Gist is still in the car business but in cyberspace. He runs AutoNetwork.com, an online forum for researching, buying, and selling cars. The site hosts thousands of visitors a month, none of whom has had the chance to prejudge Gist on the basis of race.[37]

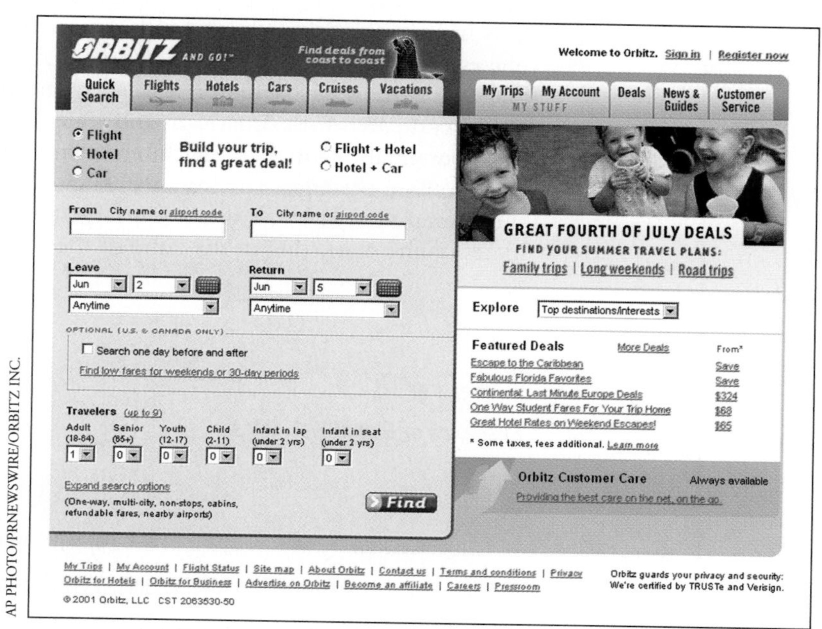

AP PHOTO/PRNEWSWIRE/ORBITZ INC.

Travel sites like Orbitz, Expedia.com, and Travelocity make it possible for travelers to search for convenient, lowest cost airfares, hotel accommodations, and auto rentals without paying additional fees for travel agency services.

ONLINE MARKETING IS INTERNATIONAL MARKETING

Another advantage to both online business-to-consumer and business-to-business marketers is the Internet's global reach, enabling inexpensive communication with consumers in faraway places. A U.S. marketer who wants to contact consumers in Australia, for example, may find overnight mail or long-distance telephone rates prohibitive, but the low cost and speed of such online marketing tools as fax machines and e-mail make global marketing a reality. More than one-third of Australian households have computers, and the typical Australian spends more time accessing Web pages than anyone except Americans.

Culture can prove to be a barrier that hampers online marketing overseas, however. Marketers, particularly those in Asia, face such barriers. Today, most e-commerce sites are still in English, which often restricts access by Asian consumers. Moreover, many Asian consumers are less familiar and comfortable with catalog or telephone purchases than shoppers in North America. Consequently, they are more reluctant to accept online shopping as a safe and secure way of purchasing products. On the other hand, Asia is an attractive market for online marketers. The number of Internet users in Asia is growing rapidly. China, for instance, now has more regular Internet users than any other country in the world except the U.S.[38]

Even though over 100 million Europeans were online in 2005, they use the Internet for shopping much less than American consumers. The European wired set is much more likely to value the Internet as a way to work from home, catch up on local politics, choose vacation destinations, and take courses. Even in Norway, Sweden, and Denmark, where Net penetration is Europe's highest at around half of all households, e-commerce often takes a backseat to such uses as e-mail and information services.

In the increasingly global business environment, e-commerce allows companies like Pacific Internet and Europe Online to create a regional framework for business transactions. Pacific Internet joined with Internet Initiative and Sumitomo (both based in Japan) and the Hong Kong Supernet, using Hong Kong and Singapore as hubs. Figure 4.9 lists a sampling of international Web sites that call the world their domestic market. Marketers must not forget that although the Internet has no geographic boundaries, countries do. Issues of infrastructure, economy, legal restrictions, and politics all come into play when marketers try to enter international markets. While astute marketers think globally, they should also remember that e-commerce is a local experience in each country.

Even though e-commerce is growing rapidly, global online commerce still lags behind the pace of online marketing in the U.S. Web advertising revenues in Europe will not reach current U.S. levels for at least another five years. Some countries have infrastructure barriers. For instance, most telephone calls in Europe, including local calls, are metered and charged based on the length of the call, which makes it much more expensive for European consumers to spend time on the Internet if they use a dial-up connection. Moreover, a smaller percentage of Europeans use broadband connections to get online compared with Americans and Canadians. Nevertheless, most marketers recognize the tremendous potential of international Internet markets, and many are scrambling to expand their international online presence. For instance, eBay currently operates over 20 different country-specific Web sites. Amazon.com UK is one of the largest e-commerce Web sites in Europe, and Yahoo! Japan dominates online marketing in the Land of the Rising Sun.

figure 4.9

Examples of Global Web Sites

http://netsprint.pl	Polish version of Infoseek.
http://us.starmedia.com	Spanish- and Portuguese-language Star Media Network.
http://homeuol.com.br	Universo Online, the largest Internet portal serving Brazil.
http://www.sina.com.tw	Sinanet.com, which targets the more than 60 million Chinese living outside China and Taiwan.
http://www.sify.com	Sify.com, offering users of Indian ancestry "all the India you want to know."

SECURITY AND PRIVACY ISSUES

Consumers worry that information about them will become available to others without their permission. In fact, issues relating to privacy and security are still considered impediments to the growth of e-commerce. Half of all online shoppers abandon their shopping carts before completing their transactions. A significant factor in this interruption of the consumer purchase process, according to a survey by the research firm WebTrends, is that shoppers feel Web sites ask for too much personal information.[39]

Consumers are particularly concerned about the safety of credit-card information. Concern about the privacy of credit-card numbers has led to the use of secure payment systems. To add to those security systems, e-commerce sites require passwords as a form of authentication—that is, to determine that the person using the site is actually the one authorized to have access to the account. Within the last couple of years, **electronic signatures** have become a quick way to enter into legal contracts, such as home mortgages and insurance policies, online. With an e-signature, an individual obtains a form of electronic identification and installs it in his or her Web browser. Signing the contract involves looking up and verifying the buyer's identity with this software.

electronic signature Electronic approval of a document that has the same status as a written signature.

Thanks to automatic data collection methods called *cookies,* online marketers are able to follow the electronic trails Web users leave as they move from one Web site to another. As a result, these marketers have considerable information about the buying and viewing habits of online visitors. Not only do cookies make it possible to post pop-up ads about products relevant to the user's recent Web site visits, but they also have the potential of invading a computer user's privacy. Newer *spyware* programs are another growing problem. Like cookies, these spyware programs track what computer users do online, can adjust their Web browser setting, and can turn their computers into Internet advertising generators, all without the users' knowledge. Web surfers often unwittingly download spyware programs when downloading other programs or files or even when visiting certain Web sites.[40]

Most consumers want assurances that any information they provide won't be sold to others without their permission. In response to these concerns, online merchants have been taking steps to protect consumer information. Many Internet companies have signed on with Internet privacy organizations like TRUSTe. By displaying the TRUSTe logo on their Web sites, they indicate that they have promised to disclose how they collect personal data and what they do with the information. Prominently displaying a privacy policy is an effective way to build customers' trust. As Figure 4.10 describes, global credit-card issuer Visa has added *Verified by Visa,* a special password verification number that must be entered prior to the purchase of online products—a service designed to protect Visa cards from unauthorized online use.

A policy is only as good as the company publishing it, though. Consumers have no assurances about what happens if a company is sold or goes out of business. Now-defunct Toysmart.com promised customers that it would never share their personal data with a third party. But when the company landed in bankruptcy court, it considered selling its database, one of its most valuable assets. And Amazon.com has told customers openly that if it or part of its business is purchased at some point, its database would be one of the transferred assets.[41]

Such privacy features may become a necessary feature of Web sites if consumer concerns continue to grow. They also may become legally necessary. The states and federal government are getting involved. Already in the U.S., the Children's Online Privacy Protection Act (COPPA) requires that Web sites targeting children younger than 13 years of age obtain "verifiable parental consent" before collecting any data that could be used to identify or contact individual users, including names and e-mail addresses. Threatened with legal action by the Federal Trade Commission, Toysmart.com agreed to honor its privacy policy and not sell any portion of its database except under severe restrictions.[42] Moreover, a bill recently introduced in the

figure 4.10

Visa: Helping to Safeguard Online Purchases from Unauthorized Use

COURTESY OF VISA

1. Which is larger, B2B e-commerce or B2C e-commerce?
2. What are some of the benefits of B2B e-marketing?
3. List the reasons many consumers prefer shopping online.

U.S. Senate would make it illegal to use the Internet to install programs on a user's computer without consent. Oregon Senator Ron Wyden, one of the bill's sponsors, argues that "computer users should have the security of knowing their privacy isn't being violated by software parasites that have secretly burrowed into their hard drives."[43]

WHO ARE THE ONLINE BUYERS AND SELLERS?

As the growth of e-commerce continues, it becomes easier to use and much broader in consumer appeal. Over the past five years, online retail sales have more than tripled to an estimated $65 billion. This figure is expected to increase to almost $120 billion by 2008. Presently, an estimated 30 percent of the population shops online. By 2008, one of every two American consumers will make purchases online.[44]

ONLINE BUYERS

The Pew Internet and American Life Project regularly collects and analyzes data about Americans' Internet usage, including online buying behavior. A recent report paints the following picture of online buyers:

1. Three of every five Internet users purchase products online. This translates into more than 67 million online buyers. Since 2000, the number of online buyers has increased by more than 63 percent.
2. On a typical day, about 6 million Americans buy a product online, double the number of online purchasers at the turn of the century.
3. Internet users with higher levels of education, higher household incomes, and those living in urban or suburban areas are more likely to purchase products online. For instance, three of every four Internet users living in households with annual incomes exceeding $75,000 use online channels to buy products. By contrast, less than half of users living in households with annual incomes of $30,000 or less have tried shopping online.
4. Three of every five white Internet users purchase products online compared with around 58 percent of Hispanic Internet users and 45 percent of African-American Internet users.
5. Prior to the 21st century, most online shoppers were male. Today, women are just as likely as men to purchase products online.
6. Younger consumers are still more likely to purchase products online compared to older consumers.[45]

While the typical Internet user is still relatively young, highly educated, urban, and more affluent, there is evidence that the demographics of online buyers will continue to change. Those shopping online will be older, less affluent, and more diverse ethnically; in other words, online consumers will look more and more like offline consumers in the coming years. An important factor explaining these expected trends is online experience. Research shows that as people's level of comfort with online functions such as e-mail and research increases, their willingness to make online purchases also increases. Younger, more affluent Americans have, on average, more Internet experience. As Internet usage among members of other demographic groups catches up, their online shopping activity should also increase. Therefore, marketers need to constantly study the changing composition of their customer base and develop new strategies to reflect the changing demographics of online buyers. The "Solving an Ethical Controversy" box discusses one problem with online transactions—Internet piracy.

Why are they picking on me? My stomach is all in knots.

Brianna LaHara (b. 1991)

New York honors student (on being among the first to be sued by the record industry for sharing music on the Internet; her mother settled the lawsuit for $2,000)

Solving an Ethical Controversy

FIGHTING INTERNET PIRACY: ARE ALL MEANS FAIR?

ONLINE file sharing is here to stay, and although free sharing of copyrighted music, motion pictures, and printed materials is illegal because it violates the copyrights held by recording artists, authors, publishers, music companies, and motion picture studios, both free and fee-collecting sites are multiplying rapidly. They are even listening to their consumers; the fee-based sites are foregoing expensive subscriptions and knocking prices down to less than $1 a song. Wal-Mart currently charges 88 cents per downloaded song, and that bargain may be driven further downward when Dell enters the market. Illegal sharing has dropped thanks to both cheap new services that are above the law and the aggressive pursuit of pirates by the Recording Industry Association of America (RIAA) under the 1998 Digital Millennium Copyright Act.

Despite a setback in the courts that prevents it from forcing Internet providers like Verizon to divulge the names of individual users suspected of piracy, the RIAA continues to file lawsuits against listeners it identifies by their unique "Internet protocol" numbers. It remains willing to reach out-of-court settlements, like those it settled for an average of $3,000 in its first round of suits against nearly 400 people, including schoolchildren and grandmothers.

ARE MUSIC COMPANIES PURSUING PIRATES WITH APPROPRIATE MEANS?

PRO

1. Free file sharing violates copyright law and deprives musicians and other artists of the income they've earned through their work.
2. There are no other controls on the use of the Internet for illegal file sharing, so the RIAA has to act on its own behalf or lose revenue.

CON

1. Twelve-year-olds who download a few songs have no criminal intent and do not profit from using the files.
2. The RIAA should use its resources to help make music files more accessible and affordable instead of fighting the inevitable.

SUMMARY

More than a million U.S. music lovers are believed to have deleted music content from their hard drives since the RIAA's first wave of lawsuits, but according to the Internet research firm Big Champagne, "There has been no net decline in the number of people doing [file swapping] or the number of files being traded." Kazaa, a completely distributed peer-to-peer file-sharing service, has been used to download more than 300 million songs and has spawned a handful of similar services. Meanwhile, "We're not going to just sit and do no enforcement while the courts are figuring out the Verizon case," says RIAA senior vice president Mitch Glazier.

Sources: Jeff Howe, "File-sharing Is, Like, Totally Uncool," *Wired,* May 2004, pp. 133, 135; Damien Cave, "Don't Blame Kazaa," *Rolling Stone,* April 29, 2004, pp. 17–18; Larry Armstrong, "E-Tune Shopping," *BusinessWeek,* March 29, 2004, pp. 108–109; Peter Lewis, "Drop a Quarter in the Internet," *Fortune,* March 22, 2004, pp. 56, 58; Damien Cave, "How to Get It Online," *Rolling Stone,* February 5, 2004, pp. 16–17; David McGuire, "RIAA Sues Song-Swapping Suspects," *The Washington Post,* January 21, 2004, http://www.washingtonpost.com; Scarlet Pruitt, "Are the RIAA's Lawsuits Working?" *PCWorld.com,* January 5, 2004.

Marketers must also continually be aware of the ways in which e-commerce is changing customers. For one thing, online marketing reaches people who do not normally watch television and read magazines. For another, online marketing is educating consumers in ways that traditional marketing cannot—by offering more information (often personalized) more rapidly than a retail salesperson, product brochure, or 30-second television commercial. Customers are more knowledgeable, and sometimes more demanding, than they used to be. Once consumers discover how easy it is to learn about wines at winespectator.com, they may be disappointed with the wine-shopping experience in a supermarket or liquor store.

Figure 4.11
Popular Products Sold Online

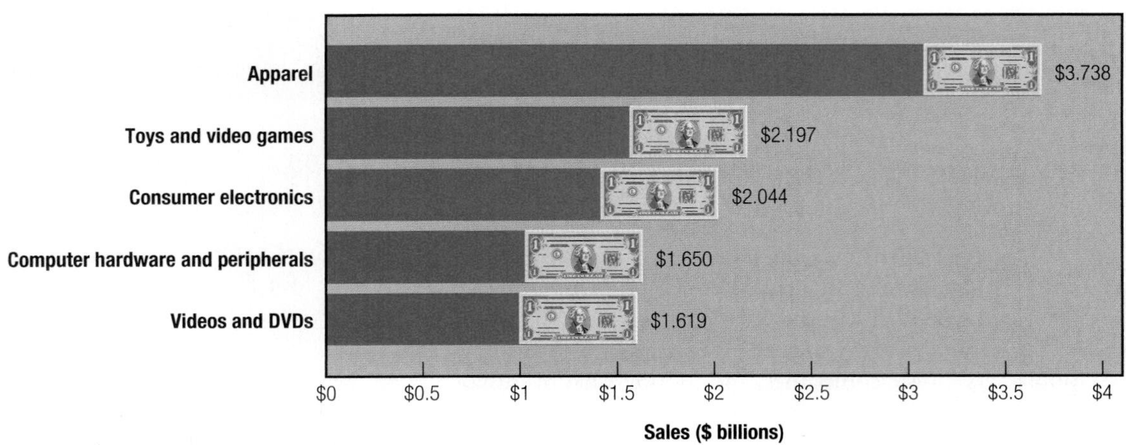

Source: Laura Rush, "Women, Comparison Shopping Helps Boost E-Commerce Holiday Revenues," Click Z Network, http://www.clickz.com, accessed March 9, 2004. Reprinted with permission.

ONLINE SELLERS

(4) **Identify the goods and services marketed most often on the Internet and the demographic characteristics of the typical online shopper.**

Realizing that customers would have little or no opportunity to rely on many of the sense modes—smelling the freshness of direct-from-the-oven bread, touching the soft fabric of a new cashmere sweater, or squeezing fruit to assess its ripeness—early online sellers focused on offering products that consumers were familiar with and tended to buy frequently, such as books and music. Other popular early online offerings included computer hardware and software and airline tickets.

Figure 4.11 lists the five most popular products sold online during a recent two-month holiday shopping period. The data show how the B2C market has changed in recent years. A few years ago, books, music, and airline tickets were the most popular items sold online. Today, it's apparel, toys and video games, and consumer electronics. In fact, online clothing sales are growing at an annual rate of more than 40 percent.[46]

MARKETING Concept Check

1. **In what ways are the demographics of the typical online shopper changing? What factor explains these demographic trends?**
2. **How is e-commerce changing consumer behavior?**
3. **List the top-selling products online.**

In the coming years, online sales of apparel, prescription drugs, and home products will continue to grow rapidly as the demographics of Internet users change. Since women—who spend more money on apparel than men do—will continue to become a larger and larger share of Internet users, online apparel sales are likely to stay hot. Similarly, as the population of online users over 55 grows, so will the online sales of prescription drugs. Kitchen products, small appliances, and large appliances—which typically are bought more frequently by women and older consumers—will also experience strong growth in the next few years.[47]

INTERACTIVE MARKETING CHANNELS

(5) **Identify the primary online marketing channels.**

Both manufacturers and marketing intermediaries frequently turn to online channels to market their goods and services. Want to buy a new suit for an upcoming job interview? Check http://www.josbank.com. Need a student loan for next year? Visit http://www.lendingtree.com. Want to find a cheap airfare to Colorado to go skiing over spring break? Check http://www.expedia.com.

Each of these marketers—and thousands more like them—has turned to online marketing as a faster, less expensive, and more efficient alternative to traditional retail stores. As Figure 4.12 shows, businesses deciding to market their products online can do so through one or a combination of primary online alternatives: company Web sites, online advertisements on other sites, and as a part of online communities. Other interactive marketing links include Web kiosks, smart cards, and virtual coupons and samples.

COMPANY WEB SITES

Virtually all online marketers have their own Web site that offers general information, electronic shopping, and promotions such as games, contests, and online coupons. Type in the firm's Internet address, and the Web site's home page will appear on your computer screen.

Two types of company Web sites exist. Many firms have established **corporate Web sites** to increase their visibility, promote their goods and services, and provide information for other interested parties. Rather than selling products directly, these sites attempt to build customer goodwill and assist channel members in their marketing efforts. For example, the Web site for Levi's jeans offers product information and a chance to view recent commercials. Consumers who want to buy jeans can then link to the Web sites of retailers such as Kohl's and JCPenney.

Although **marketing Web sites**—the second type of company Web sites—often include information about company history, products, locations, and finances, their goal is to increase purchases by site visitors. For instance, Starbucks' Web site contains all of the information traditionally found on a corporate Web site, but it also includes an online store selling everything from coffee to espresso machines. Many marketing Web sites try to engage consumers in interactions that will move them closer to a demonstration, trial visit, purchase, or other marketing outcome. Some marketing Web sites, such as Sony.com, are quite complex. Visitors can link to pages for Sony Pictures Entertainment (with movie trailers and sweepstakes), Sony Music (audio and video clips plus news about recordings), and Sony Online Entertainment (online games plus information about games and gaming systems), among other possibilities.

figure 4.12

Online Marketing Channels

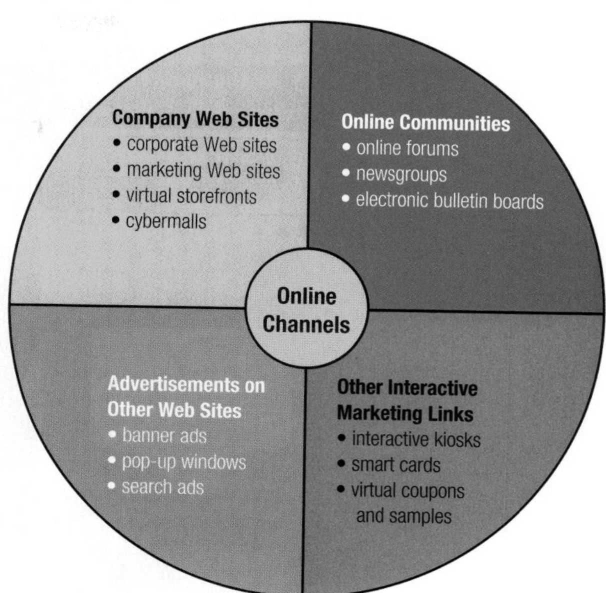

corporate Web sites Web sites that seek to build customer goodwill and supplement other sales channels rather than to sell goods and services.

marketing Web sites Web sites whose primary objective is to increase purchases by online visitors.

Electronic Storefronts and Cybermalls

Clicking http://www.harleydavidson.com takes you on a virtual visit to this popular motorcycle company. This **electronic storefront** is just what its name implies—a virtual store where customers can view and order merchandise much like shopping at traditional retail establishments. The Harley-Davidson online shopper is offered a store finder, electronic forms for ordering a catalog or subscribing to promotional e-mail, a store directory, thousands of online items, and secure online shopping. The shopper is offered a variety of shipping options, including same day delivery in certain markets.

electronic storefront Online store where customers can view and order merchandise much like window shopping at traditional retail establishments.

Whether a supplement to existing retail outlets or as a virtual replacement, electronic storefronts can offer marketers a number of advantages. These include the ability to expand operations in different cities, states, or countries without the major capital investments typically required for such growth. There is also evidence that an electronic storefront can enhance the performance of brick-and-mortar operations. In addition, virtual stores provide great flexibility since the business is open 24 hours a day, thus removing time-zone barriers. Inventory locations can be centralized, and orders can be filled promptly. Moreover, the image of the electronic storefront is controlled by the quality, creativity, and originality of the Web site and the ability of the Web marketers to offer customer satisfaction.

Online shopping got off to a rocky start. Many of the original e-tailers went out of business, and those that survived learned some hard lessons about how to satisfy customers. While many of the surviving e-tailers have successful brick-and-mortar operations, such as Talbots.com and llbean.com, a few, such as Amazon.com and Buy.com, exist only in cyberspace.

A common approach is to group electronic storefronts into **cybermalls,** some of which can link as many as 400 participating online retailers. Like concrete shopping malls, cybermalls typically feature a popular national retailer with high customer traffic as an anchor tenant. Other stores included in the mall are selected to produce a good match of merchandise offerings for the shopper. The operators of cybermalls charge each individual storefront operator a fee—either a flat monthly charge or a sliding scale based on the number of visits to the storefront. Cybermalls are also operated by the major Internet portals and ISPs. In fact, two of the world's largest cybermalls are operated by AOL and Yahoo!.

cybermall Group of virtual stores planned, coordinated, and operated as a unit for online shoppers.

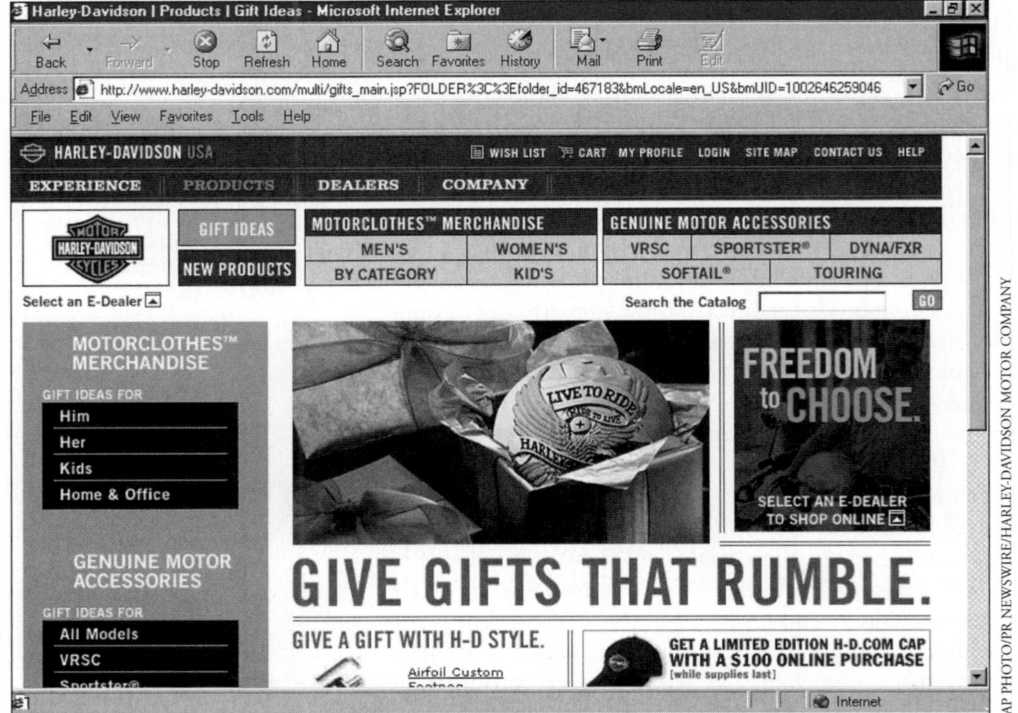

AP PHOTO/PR NEWSWIRE/HARLEY-DAVIDSON MOTOR COMPANY

Electronic storefronts have become virtual malls, where customers can view and order merchandise. These storefronts often contain other information consumers may be interested in, such as fun facts, company histories, and investor information.

ADVERTISING ON OTHER WEB SITES

Rather than relying completely on their Web sites to attract buyers, online marketers frequently expand their reach in the marketplace by placing ads on sites their prospective customers are likely to visit. **Banner ads,** the most common form of Internet advertising, are typically small strip messages placed in high-visibility areas of frequently visited Web sites. **Pop-up ads** are separate windows that pop up. An example of a banner ad is shown in Figure 4.13. As noted earlier in the chapter, another type of online advertising gaining in popularity is so-called search marketing. Firms pay search engines, such as Google, a fee to have their ads or Web site pop up after a computer user enters certain words into the search engine.

Many online marketers advocate using a variety of online and offline advertising combined with other forms of interactive promotion for better results. Lands' End created its "My Virtual Model" interactive tool to give customers a way of "trying on" clothes and accessories while sitting at their computers. The customer enters some basic information—such as height, weight, and hair color—and the software creates a customized model. The model can even be saved for future use. The firm's marketers also use ads placed on popular Web sites and portals to target its customer base as well as send out e-mails to customers advertising new products or promotions.

ONLINE COMMUNITIES

In addition to such direct channels as marketing merchandise through a firm's Web site, many firms use Internet forums, newsgroups, electronic bulletin boards, and Web communities that appeal to people who share common interests. All of these approaches take advantage of the communication power of the Internet which, as noted earlier, is still a main reason people go online. Members congregate online and exchange views and information on topics of interest. These communities may be organized for commercial or noncommercial purposes.

Online communities can take several forms, but all offer specific advantages to users and marketers alike. *Online forums,* for instance, are Internet discussion groups located on commercial online services. Users log in and participate by sending comments and questions or receiving information from other forum members. Forums may operate as electronic bulletin boards, as libraries for storing

figure 4.13
Examples of Banner Ads in the Right-Hand Column

information, or even as a type of classified ad directory. Marketers often use forums to ask questions and exchange information with customers. Adobe, which designs software such as Acrobat and Photoshop, operates a "user-to-user" forum on its Web site as a support community for its customers. Customers who share common personal and professional interests can congregate, exchange industry news and practical product tips, share ideas, and equally important, create publicity for Adobe products.

Newsgroups are noncommercial Internet versions of forums. Here people post and read messages on specific topics. Tens of thousands of newsgroups are on the Internet, and the number continues to rise. **Electronic bulletin boards** are specialized online services that center on a specific topic or area of interest. For instance, mountain bikers might check online bulletin boards to find out about the latest equipment, new places to ride, or current weather conditions in popular biking locations. While newsgroups resemble two-way conversations, electronic bulletin boards are more like announcements. Marketers often place banner or pop-up ads on newsgroups and electronic bulletin boards.

electronic bulletin board Specialized online service that provides information on a specific topic or area of interest.

Online communities are not limited to consumers. They also facilitate business-to-business marketing. Participating in extranets or business communities like Farms.com helps small businesses develop relationships that transcend the former limits of their real-world, local communities. Using the Internet to build communities helps companies find other organizations to benchmark against, including suppliers, distributors, and competitors that may be interested in forming an alliance. Business owners who want to expand internationally frequently seek advice from other members of their online community.

OTHER INTERACTIVE MARKETING LINKS

6 Explain how marketers use interactive tools as part of their online marketing strategies.

A variety of high-tech interactive tools are used by today's e-marketers to reach targeted market segments. These buyer–seller links include interactive kiosks, smart cards, virtual coupons and samples, and blogs. **Web kiosks** are freestanding computers, often located in retail showrooms or shopping centers. They are versatile multimedia devices that deliver information on demand. Shoppers can stop by a kiosk and get discount coupons or product information. Web kiosks are a marriage of traditional kiosks and Internet connections. Officially dubbed "in store, Web-assisted selling," the goals of these kiosks are to keep customers from leaving empty-handed and provide new levels of selection, especially for customers who may not otherwise have Internet access.

Web kiosk Small, freestanding computer, often located in a store, that provides consumers with Internet connections to a firm and its goods and services.

Some Web kiosks can even take the place of online shopping. For instance, CompUSA stores have "Software To Go" kiosks that let customers download their software with or without the assistance of a salesperson. The customer's unique software CD is ready in just a few minutes and has all instructions for use on the CD itself, so that customers don't have to store the boxes and packaging associated with traditional software purchases. "Software To Go" kiosks allow CompUSA to compete

GETTY IMAGES

Electronics retailer CompUSA has joined the likes of e-marketers by adding "Software To Go" kiosks in its stores. These kiosks offer quick downloading of customer-specific software. This saves the customer time compared with Web downloads and has the added benefit of having less packaging and marketing materials than does traditionally packaged software.

with direct sellers of traditionally packaged software, as well as with Internet software, which can take a long time to download.

Another e-commerce innovation involves **smart cards**—plastic cards similar to credit cards that are embedded with computer chips that store personal and financial information. To buy an item, the card is inserted into a card scanner or reader, which electronically debits the purchase amount. The card can be "reloaded" periodically with cash from a checking or savings account. Some believe that smart cards are the first step toward electronic currency—a system of exchange in which a consumer can set up accounts at Web sites and transfer money into the accounts.

Although smart cards have been popular in Europe and Asia for years, they have been slow to catch on in the U.S. A few years ago, Target became the first major retailer to offer customers a smart credit card. This special Visa card contained a computer chip that allowed users to download coupons off the Internet, or inside the store, and then use the coupons when making purchases at Target. Recently, however, Target announced that it would phase out the smart card and replace it with regular Visa cards due to disappointing demand and use. Some believe that Target's decision will dampen the growth of smart-card technology in the United States, at least in the near term.[48]

Recently, many traditional direct marketing companies began going online with **virtual coupon** and **online sample** offerings. Customers can find virtual coupons on their PCs by such criteria as business name, location, and keyword and can download them on a home computer. Online consumers can also register to have coupons e-mailed directly to them. ValPak Direct Marketing Systems, a longtime leader in the paper coupon industry, now offers the online equivalent at its Web site, http://www.valpak.com.

Other Web sites offer free product samples. The Freesite.com and All-free-samples.com are but two Web sites that list and provide links to companies offering free samples of their products.

smart card Multipurpose card embedded with computer chips that store personal and financial information, such as credit-card data, health records, and driver's license numbers.

blog (short for Web log) Web page that serves as a publicly accessible personal journal for individuals and, in more and more instances, for marketers.

A relatively new promotional technique utilizes traditionally nonmarketing Web pages called blogs. A **blog** (short for *Web log*) is a Web page that serves as a publicly accessible personal journal for an individual. Typically updated daily, these hybrid diary/guide sites are read by a U.S. blog market estimated at 1.6 million keyboard tappers. Unlike e-mail and instant messaging, blogs let readers post comments and ask questions aimed at the author (called a "blogger"). Long a favorite medium for humorists, fledgling writers, enthusiasts, and people with an ax to grind, blogs received considerable publicity during the 2004 presidential primaries with the unexpected success of *Blog for America* in raising funds for former presidential candidate Howard Dean. Not surprisingly, hundreds of marketers began looking for ways to incorporate this approach in their online marketing efforts.

Random House's Crown Publishing now sends books to bloggers for review. Nokia sent a small group of bloggers its 3650 model camera phone to try out and then write about. So far, the most extensive campaign was conducted by Dr Pepper/Seven Up for its new flavored-milk drink, Raging Cow, aimed at a target audience of 18- to 24-year-olds. In this instance, the "writer" was a cow that had tired of white milk, broken out of its barn, and left on a countrywide tour, pleading with readers to break out of their own white-milk habit in favor of the new product. Raging Cow marketers were pleased with the results—and the amazingly low cost of this form of *stealth marketing.* Although Web log readers make up only about 1 in 25 members of the online community, Dr Pepper spent only $35,000 on the blog marketing effort.[49]

MARKETING Concept Check

1. Explain the differences between a corporate Web site and a marketing Web site.
2. Explain how electronic bulletin boards can help companies effectively market their products.
3. What is a Web kiosk? A smart card? A blog?

CREATING AN EFFECTIVE WEB PRESENCE

(7) Discuss how an effective Web site can enhance customer relationships.

One of the preliminary tasks of starting a business or entering a new market is performing marketing research. Marketers evaluate every proposed e-commerce venture to ensure it benefits the firm by cutting costs, improving customer satisfaction, and increasing revenues. To have a successful e-commerce business, it is also essential that marketing activities remain customer-oriented. Other areas that must be assessed include the competitive environment and the costs of updating the firm's technological infrastructure. An effective Internet strategy should create sustainable shareholder value by increasing profits, accelerating growth, reducing time-to-market for products, improving customer service, and improving the public perception of the organization.

BUILDING AN EFFECTIVE WEB SITE

Most Web experts agree: "It is easier to build a bad Web site than a good one." To be effective, a firm's strategies must focus on building relationships through the use of company Web sites. Because of the high costs associated with going online, marketers must get the highest possible return on their Web site investments. Building an effective Web site involves three basic steps:

1. establish a mission for the company's site
2. identify the purpose of the site
3. satisfy customer needs and wants through a clear site design

The first step is to *establish a mission* for the site. A site mission involves the creation of a statement that explains the organization's overall goals. Without a mission to guide decision makers, the technology will be aimless. Dell, the world's largest computer maker, describes its mission in three clicks: to make it easier for customers to do business with it, to reduce the cost of business for both Dell and its customers, and to enhance the computer maker's relationships with its customers.

Next, marketers must *identify the purpose* of the site. Is it primarily to provide information or entertainment, or is it solely intended to connect buyers and sellers? Priceline.com, which auctions such travel-related services as airline tickets and hotel rooms, operates by the phrase "Name your price" and prominently displays this phrase throughout its Web site. Visitors know exactly what they are supposed to do. In addition, marketers should educate themselves—not so much about the details of technology but about how Web sites enhance customer communications and how those communications benefit the company.

Briefly Speaking

In designing a Web site, it helps to be self-effacing. For example, you'll get more feedback from a button labeled "Click here to criticize the site" than from one labeled "E-mail us with your comments."

Jim Sterne

American Internet-marketing specialist

Marketers should also be clear about how the purpose of the site fits in with the company's overall marketing strategy. For instance, Mattel, well known for producing and marketing toys such as Barbie, Cabbage Patch dolls, and Matchbox cars, sells most of its products in toy stores and toy departments of other retailers, like Target and Wal-Mart. The company wants an Internet presence, but it would generate ill will among its traditional channel members by cutting the retailers out of this important source of revenue if it sold toys online to consumers. Mattel cannot afford to lose the goodwill and purchasing power of these giant retailers. So the company sells only specialty products online, such as the pricey American Girl dolls that are not carried in most retail stores.

Finally, *identifying—and satisfying—customer needs and wants* is critical to marketers both online and offline. However, online marketers must consider how their strategies will need to be adjusted to continue satisfying customers through online transactions. Well-designed Web sites are straightforward, provide security and privacy, and most important, are easy to navigate. Successful sites follow accepted Internet conventions and familiar screen layouts so customers do not get lost on the site. They also use the right color combinations. Many organizations outsource their Internet services entirely, from building Web sites to designing intranets and extranets.

MANAGING A WEB SITE

Once a site is up and running, it has to be managed effectively. Marketers must update the site frequently by flagging new merchandise and services and eliminating items that did not sell well and references to past events. Some marketers recommend avoiding dates on Net pages so the site always appears current. Web site management involves constant attention not only to content but to technical presentation. Frequent software updates may be necessary to take advantage of new technologies that permit increasing levels of customer interaction. Marketers should also monitor the costs associated with Web sites. Profitability has still been erratic. If costs exceed revenues, they should reevaluate whether the site is meeting expected goals or whether changes need to be implemented to boost its effectiveness.

Amazon.com, one of the world's first and largest e-tailers, found profitability elusive. Consequently, it kept tinkering with its Web site. It expanded its offerings from books and music to electronics, toys, and housewares. Moreover, the firm entered into alliances with other retailers to further broaden its product offerings. Amazon.com was also the first commercial site to use software that could analyze a customer's purchases and suggest other related items—a terrific way of targeting a market. To keep up with future technology needs, Amazon.com acquired Junglee Corp., a developer of comparison-shopping technologies, and PlanetAll, a computerized register of customer information ranging from addresses to birthdays. Amazon.com marketers use this personalized marketing tool to send e-mail reminders to customers. And it appears to be working; profits continue to grow for the giant online business.

(8) Describe how to measure the effectiveness of online marketing efforts.

MEASURING THE EFFECTIVENESS OF ONLINE MARKETING

How does a company gauge the return from investing in a Web site? Measuring the effectiveness of a Web site is a tricky process that often depends on the purpose of the site. Figure 4.14 lists several popular measures of effectiveness. Profitability is relatively easy to measure in firms that generate revenues directly from online product orders, advertising, or subscription sales. However, a telephone order resulting from an ad on a Web site still shows the sale as a phone sale, not a Web site sale, even though the order originated at the site. Similarly, a customer who researches a product online before buying it at a retail store is not considered an online customer.

click-through rate The percentage of people presented with a Web banner ad who click it.

conversion rate The percentage of visitors to a Web site who make a purchase.

For many companies, revenue is not a major Web site objective. Only about 15 percent of large companies use their Web sites to generate revenue; the rest use them to showcase their products and to offer information about their organizations. For such companies, success is measured by increased brand awareness and brand loyalty, which presumably translates into greater profitability offline.

Some standards guide efforts to collect and analyze traditional consumer purchase data, such as how many Florida residents purchased Toyota Highlanders the previous year, watched this year's Super Bowl, or tried Subway's new low-carb wraps during the 12 months following their introduction. Still, the Internet presents several challenges for marketers. Although information sources are getting better, it is difficult to be sure how many people use the Internet, how often, and what they actually do online.

figure 4.14

Measures of Web Site Effectiveness

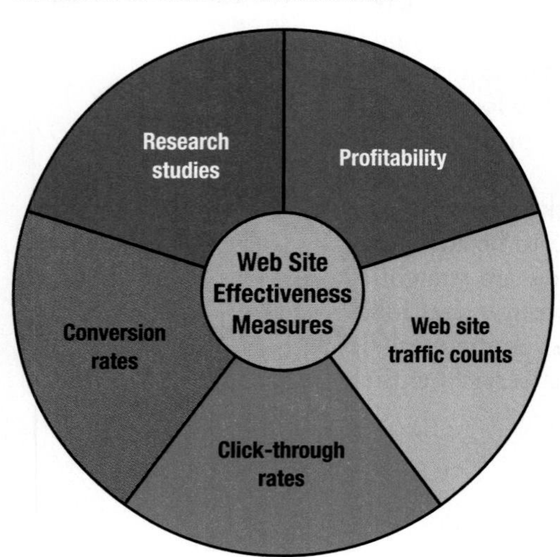

Some Web pages display counters that measure the number of visits. However, the counters can't tell whether someone has spent time on the page or skipped over it on the way to another site or whether that person is a first-time or repeat viewer.

Advertisers typically measure the success of their ads in terms of **click-through rate,** meaning the percentage of people presented with a banner ad who click it, thereby linking to a Web site or a pop-up page of information related to the ad. The average click-through rate is about three-fifths of 1 percent. Even though this rate is still lower than the 1.0 to 1.5 percent response rate for direct-mail advertisements, the click-through rate has been rising steadily over the past two years, leading to a 49 percent increase in online advertising volume.[50]

As e-commerce gains popularity, new models for measuring its effectiveness are being developed. A basic measurement is the **conversion rate,** the percentage of Web site visitors who make purchases. A conversion rate of 3 to 5 percent is considered average by today's standards. A company can use its advertising cost, site traffic, and conversion rate data to find out the cost to capture each customer. For instance, a company that spends $10,000 to attract 5,000 visitors to a Web site with a 4 percent conversion rate is obtaining 200 transactions (.04 × 5,000). It spent $10,000 for those 200 transactions, so the advertising cost is $50 per transaction, meaning each of those customers cost $50 to acquire through the advertising campaign.

E-marketers work on boosting their conversion rates by ensuring their sites download quickly, are easy to use, and deliver on their promises. Coremetrics—an e-commerce consulting firm—is helping Sharper Image gain a better understanding of why customers abandon their electronic shopping carts prior to completing purchases and of customer response to special offers. This information will help the firm improve site navigation and merchandising. According to Susan Fischer, vice president of Internet operations at Sharper Image, "The challenge is how to make the site more fun and easy to use while also increasing sales conversion rates."[51]

Besides measuring click-through and conversion rates, companies can study samples of consumers. Research firms such as Comscore and Relevant Knowledge recruit panels of computer users to track Internet site performance and evaluate Web activity. This service works in much the same way that television rating firm AC Nielsen—a major marketing research firm—monitors television audiences. The WebTrends service provides information on Web site visitors, including where they come from, what they see, and how many "hits," or visits to the site, are logged during different times of the day. Other surveys of Web users investigate their brand awareness and their attitudes toward Web sites and brands.

1. List the three steps involved in building an effective Web site.
2. Identify the key issues associated with properly managing a Web site.
3. Explain conversion rate.

Strategic Implications of Marketing in the 21st Century

THE future is bright for marketers who continue to take advantage of the tremendous potential of e-commerce. Online channels that seem cutting edge today will be eclipsed within the next decade by newer technologies, some of which haven't been invented yet. First and foremost, e-commerce empowers consumers. For instance, already a significant percentage of auto buyers show up at a dealership armed with information on dealer costs and option packages—information they obtained online. And the percentage of informed car buyers is only going to increase. This trend isn't about being market led or customer focused; it is about consumer control. Some argue that the Internet represents the ultimate triumph of consumerism.

Since the end of World War II, a fundamental shift in the retailing paradigm has occurred—from Main Street to malls to superstores. Each time the paradigm shifted, a new group of leaders emerged. The old leaders often missed the early warning signs because they were easy to ignore. When the first Wal-Mart stores and Home Depots appeared, how many really understood what the impact of superstores and so-called category killers would be on supply chain management? Similarly, marketers must understand the potential impact of the Web.

Initially, some experts predicted the death of traditional retailing. This hasn't happened yet, and it may never happen. Rather, what has occurred has been a marketing evolution for organizations that embrace Internet technologies as essential parts of their marketing strategies. E-commerce is fueled by information; marketers who effectively use the wealth of data available will not only survive but thrive in cyberspace. ◆◆◆

REVIEW OF CHAPTER OBJECTIVES

① Define e-commerce and give examples of each function of the Internet.

E-commerce involves targeting customers by collecting and analyzing business information, conducting customer transactions, and maintaining online relationships with customers by means of computer networks such as the Internet. The four main functions of the Internet are communications (such as e-mail), information (searching commercial and government sites), entertainment (such as online music), and e-commerce (such as selling products on a company Web site).

1.1. Give two or three examples of e-marketing. What are the main benefits of e-marketing?

1.2. Of the four functions of the Internet, which is the most popular? Which of the four is the fastest growing?

② Describe how marketers use the Internet to achieve their firm's objectives.

A Web site can provide a platform for communications between organizations, customers, and suppliers. It can distinguish a firm and its merchandise from competitive offerings. The Web site can be used to interview customers to find out how they use the Internet and where they find information needed to make purchase decisions. This information can help devise strategies to attract new customers and improve relationships with existing ones.

2.1. What are some of the advantages of online marketing in B2B transactions? What are some of the major challenges?

2.2. What is search marketing? Give an example.

③ Explain how online marketing benefits organizations, marketers, and consumers.

Online marketers can find new markets and customers who could not have been served adequately using traditional techniques. They also produce cost savings in every area of the marketing mix. Online marketing greatly reduces the time involved in reaching target markets. Online marketing tools allow the direct exchange of information in a seamless fashion without the involvement of marketing intermediaries. The benefits online shoppers obtain from Web purchases include lower prices, convenience, and personalization. Marketers can use their Web sites to build strong relationships, reduce costs, increase efficiency, and achieve a global presence.

3.1. What is a *bot*? How do consumers use bots to find lower prices online?

3.2. Distinguish between a shopping Web site and an informational Web site. Give an example of each.

3.3. What is considered to be the major impediment to the future growth in online shopping? How have marketers responded to this challenge?

④ Identify the goods and services marketed most often on the Internet and the demographic characteristics of the typical online shopper.

Traditionally, online users tended to live in urban areas, earn more than $75,000 per year, and have college degrees. However, in recent years, the typical Internet user has gotten older and less affluent. Also, as many women shop online as men. All of these trends mean that the typical online shopper is looking more and more like the average consumer. The most popular goods and services sold online include toys and games, computer hardware, and apparel. As the demographics of online shoppers change, so too will the mix of items sold online. For instance, as the average age of Internet users rises, so will the online sales of prescription drugs.

4.1. Why have the demographics of online shoppers changed in recent years? Which demographic group currently has the lowest percentage of Internet users shopping online?

4.2. What other products will likely see rapid online sales growth given current demographic trends?

⑤ Identify the primary online marketing channels.

The primary online marketing channels include company Web sites, online advertisements on other Web sites, and online communities. Company Web sites can be either corporate sites (containing general product and financial information) or marketing sites (sites that enable e-commerce). Online advertisements on other Web sites consist of either banner ads or pop-up ads. Both types of advertisements contain links to the firm's Web site. Online communities consist of online forums, electronic bulletin boards, and newsgroups.

5.1. Explain the differences between corporate Web sites and marketing Web sites. Which is more common?

5.2. How do marketers use online communities to build customer relationships?

6 Explain how marketers use interactive tools as part of their online marketing strategies.

Marketers reach targeted segments of their markets using a variety of interactive tools. Web kiosks deliver information and coupons on demand. Smart cards are used as a form of electronic currency for payment. Virtual coupons and online sample offerings can be downloaded from Web sites to home computers. Used correctly, blogs can be an effective way to get the word out about new products and reach a difficult-to-attract audience.

6.1. How does a Web kiosk operate? Where are they typically located?
6.2. What is a smart card? In what parts of the world are smart cards most widely used?

7 Discuss how an effective Web site can enhance customer relationships.

An effective Web site is customer oriented and follows three basic steps: Establish a mission for the company's site, identify the purpose of the site, and satisfy customer needs and wants through clear site design. Well-designed Web sites are straightforward, provide security and privacy, and are easy to navigate. Sites must also be carefully maintained and should be kept up to date. Marketers should always be aware of the cost of a Web site relative to the revenue it generates.

7.1. Explain how to establish a mission statement for a company's Web site. What should the mission statement convey?
7.2. Discuss what a clearly designed Web site should look like.

8 Describe how to measure the effectiveness of online marketing efforts.

Some of the first steps online marketers use to measure the effectiveness of their Web efforts included counting hits and page views. More sophisticated measures of Web site effectiveness include click-through rates and conversion rates. Click-through rates are the number of viewers that click the link. The conversion rate calculates the advertising cost per visitor.

8.1. What is considered an average click-through rate? Has this average increased or decreased in recent years?
8.2. Explain the difference between a click-through rate and a conversion rate. Why is the conversion rate considered a better measure of the effectiveness of a Web site?
8.3. Assume a company spends $100,000 to attract 25,000 visitors to its Web site. If the conversion rate is 5 percent, how much did the company spend to acquire each customer?

MARKETING TERMS YOU NEED TO KNOW

electronic commerce (e-commerce) 117
electronic marketing (e-marketing) 117
digital tools 118
interactive marketing 119
Internet (Net) 119
intranet 120
extranet 120
instant messaging 122
Internet service provider (ISP) 124
Wi-Fi (wireless fidelity) 125
bot 131
electronic signature 135
corporate Web sites 139
marketing Web sites 139
electronic storefront 139
cybermall 139
electronic bulletin board 141
Web kiosk 141
smart card 142
blog 142
click-through rate 144
conversion rate 144

OTHER IMPORTANT MARKETING TERMS

World Wide Web 120
search engine 125
electronic exchange 127
search marketing 128
banner ads 140
pop-up ads 140
virtual coupon 142
online sample 142

PROJECTS AND TEAMWORK EXERCISES

1. Explain how online marketing benefits the following organizations:
   a. USA Cycling
   b. The National Audubon Society
   c. Ohio State University
   d. Starbucks
2. In small teams, research the benefits of purchasing the following products online:
   a. computer monitors
   b. plane tickets
   c. men's business wear
   d. highly popular DVDs
3. Assume your team is assigned the task of developing the Web site for a large online clothing retailer that also has brick-and-mortar stores. Research the demographic trends in Web users and online shoppers. How should your company respond? What changes should be made to the virtual storefront? To the brick-and-mortar stores?
4. How can marketers use the concept of community to add value to their products? Give a real-world example of each of the types of communities discussed in the chapter.
5. Working with a small group, assume your group designs e-commerce Web sites. Identify a local company that operates with little or no online presence. Outline a proposal that explains the benefits to the firm of either going online or significantly expanding its online presence. Sketch out what the firm's Web site should look like and the functions it should perform.
6. Many consumers are reluctant to purchase online products that are perishable or that consumers typically like to touch, feel, or smell before buying. Suggest ways a Web marketer might be able to reduce this reluctance.
7. Working with a partner, identify and visit at least 10 different e-commerce Web sites. These sites can be either B2C or B2B sites. Which of these sites, in your opinion, have the highest and lowest conversion rates? Explain your choices and suggest some ways the conversion rates of all 10 sites could be improved.
8. Identify a local company that has an extensive online presence. Arrange to interview the person in charge of the company's Web site. Ask him or her the following questions:
   a. How was the Web site developed?
   b. Did the company develop the site in-house or did it outsource the task?
   c. How often does the company make changes to the site?
   d. In the opinion of the company, what are the advantages and disadvantages of going online?
9. Most colleges and universities use the Web for marketing purposes. Visit your college or university's Web site and identify how it uses the Web to market its services to prospective students and other interested parties, such as college sports fans. Suggest ways in which your college or university could improve its Web site.
10. Government and Internet service providers have begun to aggressively target spam—the popular name for junk e-mail. Working in a small group, research the current state of spam restrictions. Some marketers worry that efforts to reduce spam will make it more difficult for them to use e-mail to market their products and may hurt the growth of e-commerce. Do you agree or disagree? Why?

APPLYING CHAPTER CONCEPTS

1. Check several Internet auction sites and determine the current price of an autographed baseball by the following athletes:
   a. Hank Aaron
   b. Barry Bonds
   c. Joe DiMaggio
   d. Derek Jeter
   e. Willie Mays
   f. Babe Ruth

   Prepare a list of reasons for the marked variations in autograph values of different players.
2. How are the profiles of online buyers and sellers changing? What are some of the strategic implications of these shifts to online marketers?
3. Some marketers argue that search marketing is a more effective means of using the Web to advertise than traditional pop-up or banner ads. Research search marketing. What are some benefits of using search marketing?
4. Assume consumer adoption of broadband technology doesn't grow as expected. What are some of the implications for B2C e-commerce? How should marketers respond?
5. Assume you work for a domestic company that markets its products throughout the world. Its current online presence outside the U.S. is limited. Outline some steps the company should take to expand its online presence internationally and increase the volume of international e-commerce transactions.

ETHICS EXERCISE

One of the lingering impediments to e-commerce revolves around privacy concerns. Virtually all Web sites collect user data. Internet service providers, for example, have the ability to track where users go on the Web and store that information. Those arguing that additional privacy laws and regulations are needed claim that users never know exactly what information is being collected nor when it is being collected. Moreover, there is no means for determining whether Web sites are following their own privacy policies. On the other hand, some argue that current laws and regulations are adequate because they make it illegal for firms to misrepresent their privacy policies or fail to disclose material information. Further, there is no evidence that Internet companies are quietly passing on "material" customer information to outside parties. Aside from the strictly legal issues, Web privacy raises a number of ethical issues as well.

Assume your company collects and stores personal information about its online customers. The company's privacy policy allows the company to give limited amounts of that information to "selected" third parties.

1. Is this policy, in your opinion, appropriate and adequate? What ethical issues does your company's policy raise?
2. How would you change the privacy policy to reflect your ethical concerns?
3. From strictly an economic perspective, is the company's existing policy adequate and appropriate?

'netWork EXERCISES

1. **Search marketing.** To see how search marketing works, go to the Google Web site (http://www.google.com). Enter as your search term the name of a fairly standard product such as plastic fasteners, aluminum trusses, or DRAM memory chips. Note the search results. The companies whose sites are listed first or listed in the "sponsored link" section pay Google for this privilege. Based on your experience, do you agree or disagree with the statement that search marketing is a more cost-effective means of Web-based advertising? Explain your answer.
2. **Using a shopping bot.** Visit two of the large cybermalls on the Web such as Shopping.com (http://www.shopping.com) or the Yahoo! shopping site (http://shopping.yahoo.com). Enter the name of a product you are interested in purchasing. Evaluate the results. How many featured merchants offer your product? How much do prices vary? Is there sufficient information—such as information on shipping charges and customer ratings—to help you make an informed decision? Which of the two cybermalls did you prefer? Why?
3. **Trends in Web usage worldwide.** One source of statistics on the Web is Click Z Network (http://www.clickz.com). Go to the statistics section of the Click Z Web site and read the most recent report on international Web traffic.
   a. Which five countries, other than the United States, have the highest number of regular Internet users?
   b. Which countries have experienced the fastest growth in regular Internet users over the past year?
   c. List two or three other interesting facts about trends in worldwide Internet usage.

Note: Internet Web addresses change frequently. If you don't find the exact sites listed, you may need to access the organization's or company's home page and search from there or use a search engine such as Google.

INFOTRAC CITATIONS AND EXERCISES

Record: A116357369
Bidding drives keyword prices up; as big search engines become more popular, marketers turn to more affordable players.
Carol Krol.
B to B, May 3, 2004 v89 i5 p1

Abstract: As the primary gateways to the World Wide Web, search engines are becoming the center of attention in the world of Internet marketing. Search-related Web sites such as Google, Overture, and Ask Jeeves create exciting opportunities for marketers hoping to increase sales and generate brand exposure. The recent development of paid search, the keyword-based advertising method used at search engines, has attracted marketers because of its precision target-marketing capabilities and measurable results. However, as the cost of paid search continues to swell, especially at the most popular search portals, budget-conscious marketers are turning to less expensive search portals to get the most bang for their advertising buck.

1. Of the four primary functions of the Web listed in your text, which is most closely associated with search engines such as Google and Ask Jeeves? How often do you use search engines when browsing the Web?
2. Read the article and briefly explain how marketers pay for search listings. Why has the price of search marketing skyrocketed, causing some marketers to use second- and third-tier search engines such as Looksmart and FindWhat, for which keywords cost less?
3. Can marketers expect to get the same results when making media buys at more affordable search Web sites? Why or why not?

CASE 4.1

Match.com: The Love Algorithm

Matchmaking has a long and venerable history, and now it has a new partner—the Internet. Online dating brings in more revenue than any other legitimate Web content, beating out both digital music and business and investment advice. It has come a long way since 1995, when industry pioneer Match.com got under way. Still the leader, Match accounts for about 55 percent of the industry's approximately $300 million in revenue and has brought online dating a long way from the slightly seedy desperation once associated with personal ads in the print media. Match ventured into new territory, determined to remake the dating business from a marketing niche tainted with social stigma into a smart new way for time-challenged singles to connect with compatible people. "We decided early on that we would introduce the category and not just Match.com," explains the company's vice president of romance. To prove that being single is no longer something to be ashamed of, the company took the word "single" off its home page and has introduced a continuous flow of improvements and innovations in service. Nothing remains new in this highly competitive business for long, however; good ideas are very quickly copied on the dozens of rival sites that have sprung up. And the market is big enough now for companies to begin targeting subgroups, defining singles by age, interests, religious beliefs, ethnic group, and even pets.

Like its competitors—which include AmericanSingles.com, Friendster, Spring Street Networks, Yahoo! Personals, and specialized sites eHarmony, 8minuteDating, LatinSingles.com, and the personals pages at trendy magazine Web site Salon.com—Match charges users about $25 a month to subscribe. Though it can't verify any of the information subscribers post in their profiles, Match does screen all messages for code words like "discreet," which is often used to signal an affair as opposed to a dating relationship. Members can post pictures of themselves and view those of others; search for dates by using criteria like age, income, and hobbies; and contact each other through chat features, e-mail, or instant messaging. What happens after that is up to the individuals, of course, but Match is working hard to try to refine members' ability to find a good match beyond these fairly rough criteria. Disappointments are still common. One Match member who is gay was recently matched with his own profile, for example.

What everyone in the business would like to find is the so-called *killer app,* that elusive programming algorithm that could more or less guarantee that matched couples would click in person. Personality tests seem to offer the highest potential, but creating one that's quick, easy, and fun but also works has proven difficult. Match boasts a 10-minute questionnaire that purports to divine the respondent's strongest traits, such as "You have an insatiable curiosity" or "You can get so caught up in a conversation that you talk more than most." According to Match management, more than a million people have already taken the quiz, despite the fact that it is not yet sophisticated enough to match respondents up with one another based on the results.

But Match is betting that since online dating has become more than acceptable as a way of meeting people, things can only get better. In the near future, "it'll feel very universal," says president Tim Sullivan. "It will be quite a natural thing to be using Match in some way." The company has already given away untold baseball caps and matchbooks as wedding favors for couples who met on the site and went on to marry. Those couples represent a minority, but Match's consultant Mark Thomson says, "Maybe we won't be really good at predicting who to marry, but this is a good way to get you to date the right people."

Questions for Critical Thinking

1. Match.com admits that about 140,000 members left the site in one recent year, but the reason was that "they found the person they were seeking there." Do you think an online dating service can suffer from being too successful? Why or why not? How can it ensure a flow of new members to replace those who no longer need its services?
2. Industry observers have noted that in contrast to the information-poor listings in personals columns ("SWM seeks 30-ish SWF"), postings to online dating sites can offer a great deal of information about a potential date. Even so, about 10 percent of Internet personals users are not single, according to a recent Nielsen/NetRatings study. How much responsibility should a site like Match.com accept for the validity of the content its members provide to one another? What kind of safeguards do you think are possible? Appropriate?

3. One of the problems Match.com faces as a result of being the industry leader is having the biggest database of singles on the Internet, which means users can sometimes be inundated by responses to sort through. How can Match ensure that its size remains an advantage and market its resources to best advantage?

Sources: Gwendolyn Bounds, "In Search of Single Men—Must Have Pulse," *The Wall Street Journal,* March 9, 2004, pp. B1, B4; Jennifer Egan, "Love in the Time of No Time," *The New York Times Magazine,* November 23, 2003; Anna Mulrine, "Love.com," *U.S. News & World Report,* September 29, 2003, pp. 52–58; Susan Orenstein, "The Love Algorithm," *Business 2.0,* August 2003, pp. 117–121.

VIDEO CASE 4.2 Job-Hunting in the Digital Age: Monster.com

The written case on Monster.com appears on page VC-5. The recently filmed Monster.com video is designed to expand and highlight the concepts in this chapter and the concepts and questions covered in the written video case.

Talking about Marketing Careers with Eric Stisser, Director of Corporate Sales and Marketing for the St. Louis Rams

A widely repeated truism is that no city can truly claim the title of "major city" unless it has one or more major league sports teams. If you accept such a statement, then St. Louis qualifies easily. In fact, local and regional fans in the Midwest support the Cardinals (baseball), the Blues (hockey), and the Rams (football) so enthusiastically that *Sporting News* recently named St. Louis "North America's Best Sports City." Rival sports publication *ESPN The Magazine* followed up by bestowing to St. Louis the title "Ultimate Sports City."

The St. Louis Rams are one of professional football's oldest and most storied franchises. The Rams were the first to win an NFL championship in three different cities: Cleveland, Los Angeles, and St. Louis. They were also the first team to move to the West, beginning a trend that would spill over to other professional sports and continue for decades. The franchise was founded in Cleveland in 1937 but made its name after a 1946 move to Los Angeles, where it spent almost 50 years. St. Louis welcomed the Rams in 1995 and cheered them to a historic victory over the Tennessee Titans in Super Bowl XXXIV. Today, the Rams are an integral part of the greater St. Louis community and a major entertainment source for area residents. Although much of their history may be in L.A., the Rams continue to build a strong reputation for themselves throughout the Midwest.

Joining us in assessing the Rams' recent successes in assembling a winning team and building a well-run organization is Eric Stisser, the team's director of corporate sales and marketing. He agreed to participate in a brief Q&A session on sports, business, and marketing as they relate to building and retaining a successful organization.

ERIC STISSER, DIRECTOR OF CORPORATE SALES AND MARKETING FOR THE ST. LOUIS RAMS

PHOTO: COURTESY OF ERIC STISSER

BOONE & KURTZ: Eric, you've got a job that thousands of our readers would give their eyeteeth for: applying your marketing knowledge and experience in the world of sport. Tell us a little about your background.

I completed my undergraduate degree at DePauw University in Indiana, where I was a communications major. My first job out of college was as director of admissions at Lake Forest Academy, a private prep school in Lake Forest, Illinois. I was responsible for the selling and marketing of the school via student recruitment. My duties entailed managing the admissions process and the financial aid budget. I also was an assistant coach in football, basketball, and baseball.

Due to my passion for sports, I knew I wanted to make a full-time career out of it. I had done my winter-term internship in college at the ESPN headquarters as a production assistant. After a few years at Lake Forest Academy, I joined the League Office of the Continental Basketball Association, which was in St. Louis at the time. The CBA was the minor league of the NBA, and I was the assistant director of business development and marketing. I was responsible for selling national corporate sponsorships and TV packages.

A few years later I was fortunate to join the Rams as a sales executive. The past six years I have gone from sales executive to executive sales manager before becoming director of corporate sales and marketing two years ago. While working for the Rams, I also received my executive MBA from Washington University in St. Louis.

I really stress to kids in school how important it is to stay in touch with people. Send a handwritten thank-you note and make a follow-up phone call. When I was working for the CBA, I met the VP of sales and marketing for the Rams at a conference and I kept in touch. That's basically how I got my job. Don't hound folks, but stay in touch and tactfully keep your name out there with personal touches that will make someone remember you.

BOONE & KURTZ: Tell us about the Rams' "front office," focusing specifically on marketing.

The Rams' front office has two main divisions: the football side and the business administration side. The football division entails the players, coaches, scouts, and media relations. The business division deals with finance, operations, community relations, ticketing, and sales and marketing. I report to the vice president of sales and marketing. Our staff consists of about 10 people. We are the revenue arm for the Rams; we sell and manage the 125 corporate suites and 65 corporate sponsors. Sales executives mainly work on selling sponsorships and suites, while account executives manage the business relationships and the day-to-day detail work.

During the season we do a lot of "hand holding," working on contract fulfillment. The business for the season has been finalized, and we have to deliver and activate the partnerships. We do a great deal of client entertainment during the season—inviting them to our marketing suite for home games; taking clients on the team plane for away games; and hosting corporate events at our team training facility, Rams Park. From a selling standpoint, during the season our focus really turns to renewal business for the following season.

My busiest selling time is February to August; that's when we're out "pounding the pavement," trying to get everything renewed and sold for the next season.

BOONE & KURTZ: After 10 years, the Rams appear to have settled in well in St. Louis—a city with an outstanding reputation for enthusiastic, supportive fans. Tell us a little about your fans.

For the Rams' 10th season in St. Louis, we geared up for our 10th anniversary celebration. We were really excited about this season after 10 years here, and we thanked the fans and the city. In the time we've been here, we've had four division titles, two Super Bowl appearances, and one Super Bowl victory.

I would say our fan base goes about 100 miles north into southern Illinois, and 100 miles south and west in Missouri. But our main fan base is in the St. Louis metro area.

The Rams have a higher-income season-ticket base, being an early team to offer PSLs [personal seat licenses] to fans. [PSLs are a separate charge for season-ticket buyers that allow them lifetime rights to buying season tickets.] This type of demo draws the interest of corporate sponsors who want to develop relationships with our passionate, higher-income clientele.

BOONE & KURTZ: At the same time, competitors like the Cardinals, the Blues, college sports, and numerous major one-time sporting events all compete with the Rams for the entertainment dollars of fans and corporate support. How do you go about creating and maintaining good relationships that will translate into customer loyalty so that fans—and business support—keep coming back?

The Cardinals and Blues are certainly competitors, and we have working relationships with the teams and share clients in this midsized market of about 3 million. We are very well supported by the fans, but we also leverage the power of the NFL brand. Football is far and away the number-one sport in America, in terms of viewers and revenue sharing. That's the good thing about the NFL; they work hard to "level the playing field," so we don't have the problems of other sports with a real disparity in team payrolls. NFL teams share ticket and merchandising revenue. The NFL caps salaries at $80 million on players, and we all get the same check for merchandise revenue, whether you're number 2 or number 30. The power of the NFL is huge for us. It's a unique brand; with 10 home games a season, each game is an event. These marquis events create a real value and ROI [return on investment] for sponsorships.

BOONE & KURTZ: We are aware of the NFL's long-standing record of generous community support, and we read with considerable interest the current "Rams Community Report" posted on your Web site. Describe a few examples of your community outreach or volunteer activities designed to give back to the community. In what ways does the organization benefit from such activities? Given their busy schedules of long daily practices and weekly games, is it difficult to motivate Rams team members to participate in such activities?

We have a community relations department whose mission it is to reach out to the community. This entails planning community events, supporting various charity auctions by supplying autographed items, and, most importantly, donating monies to various organizations through the Rams Foundation. The department works closely with the players implementing appearances out in the community, working with inner-city kids in the flag football program; in the Rams literacy reading and writing program; or visiting patients in the local hospitals.

The players are very interested in getting involved, and they play a key role in what we do in the community.

BOONE & KURTZ: Tell us a little about sales and marketing planning by the Rams. Who is involved? What sort of time horizon is used when you develop marketing plans? And how is it integrated with the overall business plan?

We don't do a tremendous amount of traditional marketing of the team; we're sold out, which is a great situation. We don't do media "blitzes" like other teams have to do, but we do some *presence marketing,* a handful of bus shelters, a few billboards with team slogans. This year was all about the 10th anniversary and building on that.

A lot of the marketing campaign is done through the community, trying to encourage the city of St. Louis to get involved. An example of this is the United Way campaign, which we do with billboards and community events, encouraging people to give back to the community.

BOONE & KURTZ: The NFL has jumped on the technology bandwagon, and every team has high-tech Internet sites up and running full of commentary, stats, rosters, and schedules.

Our Web site helps us with CRM [customer relationship management]. Through this we can get to know the preferences of our customers. We utilize our site in a big way. The sponsorship revenue comes from ad banners and elements like the FedEx forum, where fans can chat live or participate in the Rams trivia section. This way we can build a Rams fan club; we capture fans' interest and then use e-mail "blasts" to keep them updated and to keep in constant contact. Fans can go online and express their opinions.

Sponsors like Domino's and MasterCard can offer our Web site users and other fans special deals on products and promotions. Also, the Rams merchandise pro shop does a tremendous amount of sales on our Web site.

BOONE & KURTZ: By now, our readers have probably recognized that a great way of getting their foot in the door career-wise would be to complete an internship with an organization like the Rams. But they also realize that you must receive hundreds of internship applications every year. What advice would you give our readers about how to increase the chances that their application will receive serious consideration?

We do get hundreds of résumés each year, and it may sound like a cliché, but I would just say, get involved. Get involved with the athletic department at your school. See if you can sell tickets or hand out programs. Approach minor-league teams during your summers and see if you can help in any way. We get a lot of résumés that say, "I'm a big fan." Everyone is a fan. We need to see some sports-related experience. It doesn't have to be with a team; try to intern with businesses that are involved with sports marketing, like Wilson, Gatorade, Visa, Nike, etc.

Get involved, get involved, get involved, whenever and wherever you can.

The Meeting Place for U.S. Soccer Fans

PHOTO: COURTESY OF WIREIMAGES.COM

Major League Soccer (MLS) began its second decade with high hopes of growing into a world-class professional soccer league that American sports fans would love. Not only has the quality of play made positive strides on the MLS teams around the country, but media coverage is also expanding, momentum is building, and the marketing MLS employs has become ever more sophisticated.

As the league gradually expands from its original roster of 10 teams (5 of which are in the country's top 10 Hispanic markets), more fans can attend games in or near their home cities, and more spots are available for American and international soccer stars to fill. Exhibition games and international tournaments, in addition to 30 season matches per team, provide plenty of opportunities for showcasing exciting young players and, MLS hopes, for captivating and rewarding spectacles to thrill the young tech-savvy fans the league wants to attract. This year, 19 of every 20 MLS games can be seen live on television, and during its first eight seasons, almost 22 million MLS fans attended the games in person. Those who are already fans of European soccer also fall within MLS's intended market because American stars like Carlos Boccanegra and Brian McBride have impressed the world while playing on teams for England, and international players like Andreas Herzog (Austria) and Amado Guevara (Honduras) have in turn been signed by MLS teams like the New York MetroStars. The teenage phenom Freddy Adu—currently the youngest player on any major sports team—has an appeal all his own.

From its inception in 1993, MLS has vowed to follow five guiding principles:

1. to become the meeting place for U.S. soccer fans
2. to reflect inclusiveness and diversity
3. to stay young in attitude, style, and fan profile
4. to express and evoke passion for soccer
5. to be the inspirational destination point for today's soccer-playing youth

The league's overarching goals continue to be the establishment of soccer as a viable business, entertainment property, and institution in the U.S. and "to become the world's most competitive and prestigious soccer league."

Currently, the U.S. has about 80 million soccer fans. Even given the size of that number, soccer lags well behind baseball and football as the nation's favorite sport. And despite the presence of world-class players like Mia Hamm and Brandi Chastain, the professional women's soccer league collapsed after only a few seasons. The causes were many, but poor attendance at the games was one of them. Among the many challenges MLS faces is the difficulty of turning on millions of families who think of soccer as another youth activity whose attraction fades after high school, if not sooner. With powerful new broadcast partners such as ABC, ESPN, ESPN2, Fox Sports World, and HDnet, MLS hopes to turn youth players into young fans and keep them focused on soccer by making it easy to follow favorite teams and players from week to week. For the first time, "Soccer Saturday" is now broadcast in a regular Saturday afternoon time slot.

MLS is also pinning high hopes on new stadiums being built around the country that are designed for and dedicated to soccer. With plans to expand to as many as 20 teams in the future, the league will need venues for play, and cities from Atlanta to Oklahoma City have stated their interest in having an MLS team in their area. The Home Depot Center opened in Los Angeles as the home stadium of both the MLS Galaxy and the Chivas USA expansion team from Mexico. The Frisco Sports and Entertainment Center is near completion in Dallas, home of the Dallas Burn. A 25,000-seat arena for the Chicago Fire has been announced as well, to be funded by the suburban community of Bridgeview. Denver, Washington, D.C., and New Jersey are also promising spots for future new facilities.

Questions for Critical Thinking

1. How well do you think MLS has identified its target customer? Who is that customer?
2. Do MLS's five guiding principles include an ethical component? If so, what is it, and what values does it encompass?
3. Before they can fall in love with MLS, fans must fall in love with soccer. How can MLS help make that happen?
4. What factors do you think MLS considers in choosing the cities to which it will expand with new teams?

Sources: "About MLS," http://www.mlsnet.com, accessed September 2, 2004; Grant Wahl, "Football vs. Fútbol," *Sports Illustrated,* July 5, 2004, pp. 68–72; Ridge Mahoney, "In MLS Cities, Much Adu about Freddy," *USA Today,* June 9, 2004, p. C8; Kelly Whiteside, "WUSA's Shutdown Jolts Players," *USA Today,* September 16, 2003, p. 3C; Marc Connolly, "Soccer-Only Stadiums Counted on as Arenas for Profit," *USA Today,* September 11, 2003, p. 3C.

part 2

UNDERSTANDING BUYERS AND MARKETS

chapter 5 Consumer Behavior

chapter 6 Business-to-Business (B2B) Marketing

chapter 7 Serving Global Markets

PHOTO: COURTESY OF WIREIMAGES.COM

chapter 5

Consumer Behavior

chapter objectives

① Distinguish between customer behavior and consumer behavior.

② Explain how marketers classify behavioral influences on consumer decisions.

③ Describe cultural, group, and family influences on consumer behavior.

④ Explain each of the personal determinants of consumer behavior: needs and motives, perceptions, attitudes, learning, and self-concept theory.

⑤ Distinguish between high-involvement and low-involvement purchase decisions.

⑥ Outline the steps in the consumer decision process.

⑦ Differentiate among routinized response behavior, limited problem solving, and extended problem solving by consumers.

CATERING TO THE LONG-DISTANCE FAN

Do you "root, root, root for the home team," or are you one of the millions of fans who identify with a team from out of town? A recent research study commissioned by Major League Baseball revealed that more than half its fans root for a team that plays somewhere else, a sea change from the days when sports teams lived and died by the loyalty of their hometown fans. The avid devotion of long-distance fans in baseball, football, basketball, hockey, and other sports is remarkable, and sports marketers are eager to tap into their strong brand loyalty.

Fortunately, sophisticated new technology makes it possible for long-distance fans to keep up with their favorite teams through a wide variety of home media. For instance, college football and basketball games are sometimes available on pay per view cable channels and some radio stations. If you enjoy radio coverage of sports, a Seattle Internet company offers subscriptions to radio broadcasts of any major league baseball team for $11.95 a season. Wireless updates of games in progress are available, too; for example, Nextel has a deal with the National Hockey League that brings fans

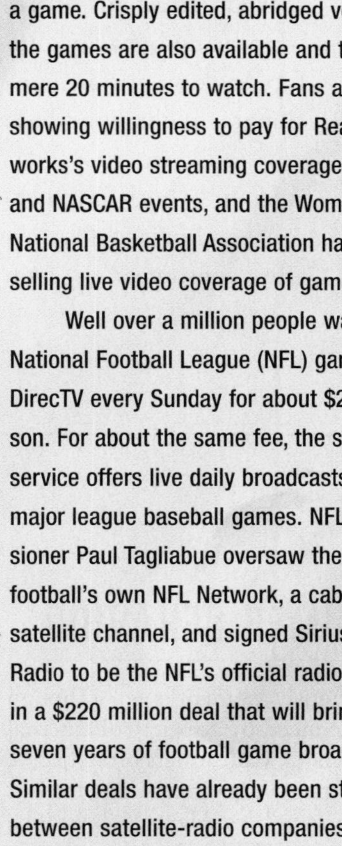

continuous updates on their cell phones. Live Internet broadcasts of thousands of baseball games reach about 1 million fans per season via MLB.com, which charges $3 a game. Crisply edited, abridged versions of the games are also available and take a mere 20 minutes to watch. Fans are also showing willingness to pay for RealNetworks's video streaming coverage of golf and NASCAR events, and the Women's National Basketball Association has begun selling live video coverage of games online.

Well over a million people watch National Football League (NFL) games on DirecTV every Sunday for about $200 a season. For about the same fee, the satellite service offers live daily broadcasts of most major league baseball games. NFL commissioner Paul Tagliabue oversaw the launch of football's own NFL Network, a cable and satellite channel, and signed Sirius Satellite Radio to be the NFL's official radio network in a $220 million deal that will bring fans seven years of football game broadcasts. Similar deals have already been struck between satellite-radio companies and the National Basketball Association and National Hockey League. Cable channel ESPN brings more than 65 different sports, including baseball, basketball, hockey, golf, international soccer matches, and college and professional football, to nearly 90 million households.

If you insist on traveling, of course, there are custom sports travel packages that can be purchased, promising the fan an unforgettable vacation with a major sports event as the centerpiece. And for those who prefer to buy their souvenirs from home, virtually every team has a Web site with merchandise offerings, online ticket purchase options, and upbeat team reports geared for the fans. "We're doing [Internet] business in 36 states," says a marketing executive for San Francisco's baseball Giants, and 20 percent of the activity on the team's online ticket exchange, where fans swap unused tickets, comes from out-of-towners. Ticket exchanges are also popular with other sports teams, including New York's football Jets and Giants and basketball's Seattle SuperSonics. The online swap sites allow faraway fans to pick up tickets for the times they'll be in town and help subscribers, whether near or far, justify the cost of hanging on to their season tickets year after year whether they can attend every game or not. The professional hockey league even helps teams sell seats to local fans who want to cheer for the opposition.

Major League Baseball's chief executive of advanced media sums up the opportunity that far-flung fans' loyalty offers to sports marketers. "These fans have always been there. We're just going after them like never before."[1]

Chapter Overview

WHY do fans develop loyalty to a certain team? Why do people prefer one brand of soda over another? Because the answers directly affect every aspect of the marketing strategy, from product development to pricing and promotion, finding them is the goal of every marketer. It requires an understanding of customer behavior, the process by which consumers and business-to-business buyers make purchase decisions. **Customer behavior** includes both individual consumers who buy goods and services for their own use and organizational buyers who purchase business products.

1. Distinguish between customer behavior and consumer behavior.
2. Explain how marketers classify behavioral influences on consumer decisions.

A variety of influences affect both individuals buying items for themselves and personnel purchasing products for their firms. This chapter focuses on individual purchasing behavior, which applies to all of us. **Consumer behavior** is the process through which the ultimate buyer makes purchase decisions from toothbrushes to autos to vacations. Chapter 6 will shift the focus to business buying decisions.

The study of consumer behavior builds on an understanding of human behavior in general. In their efforts to understand why and how consumers make buying decisions, marketers borrow extensively from the sciences of psychology and sociology. The work of psychologist Kurt Lewin, for example, provides a useful classification scheme for influences on buying behavior. Lewin's proposition is

$$B = f(P,E)$$

This statement means that behavior (B) is a function (f) of the interactions of personal influences (P) and pressures exerted by outside environmental forces (E).

The statement is usually rewritten to apply to consumer behavior as follows:

$$B = f(I,P)$$

Consumer behavior (B) is a function (f) of the interactions of interpersonal influences (I)—such as culture, friends, classmates, coworkers, and relatives—and personal factors (P)—such as attitudes, learning, and perception. In other words, inputs from others and an individual's psychological makeup affect his or her purchasing behavior. Before looking at how consumers make purchase decisions, we first consider how both interpersonal and personal factors affect consumers. ◆◆◆

Briefly Speaking

A [fan] is a person who sits forty rows up in the stands and wonders why a seventeen-year-old kid can't hit another seventeen-year-old kid with a ball from forty yards away . . . and then he goes out to the parking lot and can't find his car.

Chuck Mills (b. 1928)
American college football coach

customer behavior Mental and physical activities that occur during selection and purchase of a product.

consumer behavior Mental and physical activities of individuals who actually use the purchased goods and services.

INTERPERSONAL DETERMINANTS OF CONSUMER BEHAVIOR

You don't make purchase decisions in a vacuum. You might not be consciously aware of it yet, although you will be after this course, but every buying decision you make is influenced by a variety of external and internal factors. This section focuses on external, interpersonal influences. Consumers often decide to buy goods and services based on what they believe others expect of them. They may want to project positive images to peers or to satisfy the unspoken desires of family members. Figure 5.1 lists the reasons people gave for buying new products in a recent survey. Marketers recognize three broad categories of interpersonal influences on consumer behavior: cultural, social, and family influences.

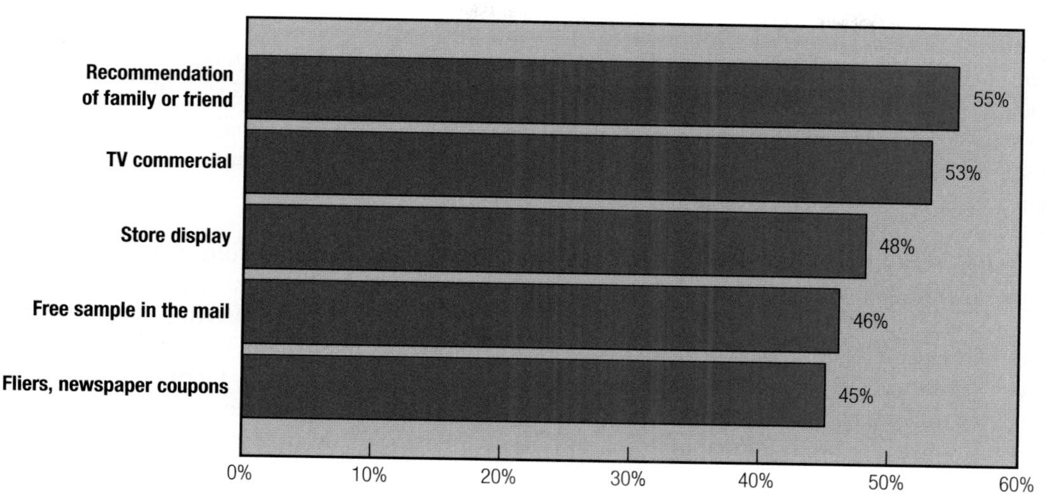

Source: Data from a survey conducted by InsightExpress for Schneider & Associates/Stagnito Communications of 1,001 respondents, as cited in "USA Today Snapshot," *USA Today*, February 16, 2004, p. B1.

figure 5.1
Why People Buy New Products

CULTURAL INFLUENCES

(3) **Describe cultural, group, and family influences on consumer behavior.**

Culture can be defined as the values, beliefs, preferences, and tastes handed down from one generation to the next. Culture is the broadest environmental determinant of consumer behavior. Marketers need to understand its role in consumer decision making, both in the U.S. and abroad. They must also monitor trends in cultural values as well as recognize changes in these values.

culture Values, beliefs, preferences, and tastes handed down from one generation to the next in a society.

Marketing strategies and business practices that work in one country may be offensive or ineffective in another. Strategies may even have to be varied from one area of a country to another. Retailers as different as Japanese auto giant Nissan and Texas-based ice cream maker Blue Bell Creameries are tailoring their marketing campaigns to appeal to the rapidly growing Hispanic market. Nissan is running its first Quest minivan ads aimed specifically at Hispanics after finding that one of every two buyers in the Southwest is Hispanic. The carmaker is being joined in its foray into the Hispanic market by a host of other advertisers new to Spanish-language television, including Target, Old Navy, and Visa. Kellogg and Procter & Gamble are adding new products and brands to their existing Spanish-language advertising campaigns. Blue Bell, a family-owned company, sells its 98 flavors of popular Blue Bell brand ice cream in just 14 southern states. The firm has also developed special flavors like *tres leches con fresas* (three-milks cake with strawberries) and *naranja y piña* (orange puree with crushed pineapple) specifically for the Hispanic markets in Texas and Florida.[2]

Core Values in U.S. Culture

Some cultural values change over time, but basic core values do not. The work ethic and the desire to accumulate wealth are two core values in American society. Even though the typical family structure and family members' roles have shifted in recent years, American culture still emphasizes the importance of family and home life. This value has been further strengthened in the wake of the events of September 11. Other core values include education, individualism, freedom, youthfulness, activity, humanitarianism, efficiency, and practicality. Each of these values influences consumer behavior.

Values that change over time also have their effects. The Internet has created a generation of globally aware teens who have access to a greater diversity of information and products. They also have considerable purchasing power. Consumer electronics giant Sony recognizes the importance of this group and plans to make extra efforts to build loyal consumers among them. One strategy is to develop and use a comprehensive consumer database to make frequent contact with teens. According to the company's Consumer Segment Marketing Division's mission, the goal is to "develop an intimate understanding of Sony's end consumers . . . from cradle to grave."[3]

International Perspective on Cultural Influences

Cultural differences are particularly important for international marketers. Marketing strategies that prove successful in one country often cannot extend to other international markets because of cultural variations. Europe is a good example, with many different languages and a wide range of lifestyles and product preferences. Even though the continent is becoming a single economic unit as a result of the expansion of the European Union and the widespread use of the euro as currency, cultural divisions continue to define multiple markets.

Sometimes cultural differences can work to a marketer's advantage. Despite the growing desire of Chinese manufacturers to increase the reach of their own brands in their vast home markets, a recent survey showed that young Chinese shoppers perceive Western brands as trendsetting and strongly favor names like Coca-Cola, Nike, and Disney over local competitors like athletic goods maker Li Ning or Happy Valley amusement parks. Most of the respondents to the survey identified themselves as strongly nationalistic, but they "do not see any direct relationship between patriotism and buying national brands over international ones," according to a research firm that participated in the study.[4]

Subcultures

subcultures Smaller groups within a society that have their own distinct characteristics and modes of behavior, defined by ethnicity, race, region, age, religion, gender, social class, or profession.

Cultures are not homogeneous entities with universal values. Each culture includes numerous **subcultures**—groups with their own distinct modes of behavior. Understanding the differences among subcultures can help marketers develop more effective marketing strategies.

The U.S., like many nations, is composed of significant subcultures that differ by ethnicity, nationality, age, rural versus urban location, religion, and geographic distribution. The Southwestern lifestyle emphasizes casual dress, outdoor entertaining, and active recreation. Mormons refrain from buying or using tobacco and liquor. Orthodox Jews purchase and consume only kosher foods. Understanding these and other differences among subcultures contributes to successful marketing of goods and services.

America's ethnic mix is changing. By 2050, ethnic and racial minority groups will constitute half the U.S. population.[5] Marketers need to be sensitive to these changes and to the differences in shopping patterns and buying habits among ethnic segments of the population. Businesses can no longer succeed by selling one-size-fits-all products; they must consider consumer needs, interests, and concerns when developing their marketing strategies.

figure 5.2

Ethnic and Racial Minorities as a Percentage of the Total U.S. Population

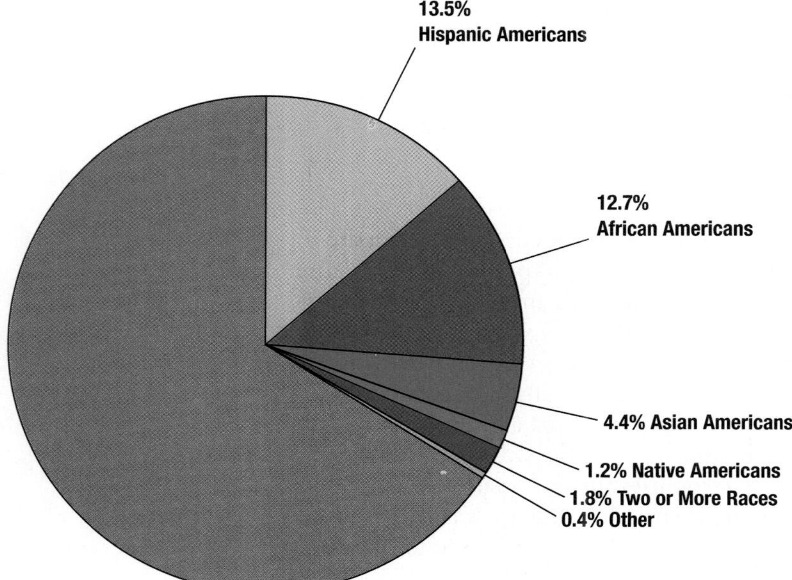

Source: Data from the U.S. Census Bureau, in Haya El Nasser, "Census Numbers Show Jump from 2000 Tally," *USA Today*, June 19, 2003, pp. 1A, 2A.

Hispanics, for example, now make up nearly 14 percent of the U.S. population, and nearly one-third of Hispanic Americans are under age 18. By 2050, their share of the U.S. population will almost double—to 24 percent.[6] The youngest members of this group have made Nickelodeon's bilingual show *Dora the Explorer* the No. 2 preschool show on commercial television. Meanwhile, Hispanics buy 15 percent of all movie tickets sold in the U.S., and—thanks in part to an explosion of Latin music into mainstream pop—they are also making up a growing portion of the radio audience. Circulation of Time Inc.'s *People en Español* has doubled in a few years to make it the top-selling Spanish-language magazine in the U.S. Yet Hispanics are a highly varied group whose members can differ markedly depending on what country or region they are from.[7]

Marketing concepts may not always cross cultural boundaries without changes. For example, new immigrants may not be familiar with cents-off coupons and contests. Marketers may need to provide specific instructions when targeting such promotions to these groups.

According to the U.S. Census Bureau, the three largest and fastest growing U.S. ethnic subcultures are Hispanics, African Americans, and Asians. Figure 5.2 shows the proportion of the U.S. population made up of minority groups. Although no ethnic or racial subculture is entirely homogeneous, researchers have found that each of these three ethnic segments has identifiable consumer behavior profiles.

Hispanic-American Consumers Marketers face several challenges in appealing to Hispanic consumers. The nearly 40 million Hispanics in the U.S. are not a homogeneous group. They come from a wide range of countries, each with its own culture. Two-thirds come from Mexico, one in seven is Central and South American, one in twelve is Puerto Rican, and nearly 4 percent are Cuban.[8] Cultural differences among these segments often affect consumer preferences.

The term *Hispanic* is a broad concept that includes a wide spectrum of national identities. "There are white, black, and brown Hispanics," notes Esteban Torres, a former congressman from California. "You are what you think you are." Even the word *Hispanic* is not universal; Puerto Ricans and Dominicans in New York and Cubans in southern Florida refer to themselves as Hispanic, but many Mexican and Central Americans in the southwestern U.S. prefer to be called Latinos.

More important than differences in national origin are differences in **acculturation,** or the degree to which newcomers have adapted to U.S. culture. Acculturation plays a vital role in consumer behavior. For instance, marketers should not assume that all Hispanics understand Spanish. By the third generation after immigration, most Hispanic Americans speak only English.

Hispanics can be divided into three major acculturation groups:

- *Largely unacculturated Hispanics* (about 28 percent of the U.S. Hispanic population) were typically born outside the U.S. and have lived in the country for less than 10 years. They tend to have the lowest income of the three groups and depend almost exclusively on Spanish-language media.
- *Partially acculturated Hispanics* (approximately 59 percent) were born in the U.S. or have lived there for more than 10 years. Most are bilingual, speaking English at work and Spanish at home. Many are middle income, and marketers can reach them through both Spanish- and English-language media.
- *Highly acculturated Hispanics* (13 percent) enjoy the highest income of the three groups. Usually born and raised in the U.S., they are English speaking but retain many Hispanic cultural values and traditions.[9]

Research reveals several other important points:

- The Hispanic market is large and fast growing. Already the U.S. is home to the fifth largest Hispanic population in the world; only the populations of Argentina, Colombia, Mexico, and Spain are bigger.
- Hispanics tend to be young, with a median age of 25 compared with a median age of 35 for the general U.S. population.
- Hispanic consumers are geographically concentrated in the following states: California, Florida, New Mexico, New York, and Texas. In fact, 42 percent of New Mexico's population is Hispanic. Almost half of all Hispanics living in the U.S. reside in five cities: Chicago, Los Angeles, Miami, New York, and San Francisco.

Hispanics tend to have larger households than non-Hispanics, making them good customers for products sold in bulk. They spend more on their children than do parents in other subcultures, especially on clothing. Hispanics also place great importance on keeping in touch with relatives in other countries, making them excellent customers for phone cards, air travel, and wire transfers of money. In addition, Hispanics make more visits to pizza and chicken chain restaurants than do general-market consumers and bring along with them a larger group of family members and friends.

African-American Consumers One U.S. resident in eight is African American. The growing African-American market offers a tremendous opportunity for marketers who understand its buying patterns. A recent study shows African-American buying power rose 73 percent during the past decade, compared with 57 percent for U.S. consumers in general.

Family structures may differ for African-American consumers. The median age of the typical African-American household is about five years younger than that of the average white family. This creates differences in preferences for clothing, music, cars, and many other products. Also, African-American women are twice as likely as non–African-American women to make the majority of purchase decisions for their households.

The Ariel/Schwab Black Investor Survey, sponsored in part by Charles Schwab & Co., Inc., revealed that many African-American investors feel insecure about their investment knowledge and do not fully trust financial advisors. Perhaps as a result, African Americans tend to invest more conservatively than other groups. They are more likely to choose real estate and life insurance as investments and are less likely to put their money in the stock market. However, the survey found that the number of high-income African Americans who invest in the stock market rose 30 percent since 1998, while stock ownership among whites rose only 4 percent.

Schwab used this information to design investment programs for African Americans. The company teamed up with the Coalition of Black Investors to sponsor nationwide investment seminars at beginner, intermediate, and advanced levels. Schwab is also actively recruiting new stockbrokers at conferences hosted by professional groups, such as the National Association of Black Accountants, National Association of Black MBAs, and Blacks in Government, just to name a few. To date, more than 4,500 people have attended Schwab's seminars.[10]

As with any other subculture, it is important for marketers to avoid approaching all African-American consumers in the same way; demographic factors such as age, language, and educational level must be considered. Some African Americans are recent immigrants, and others are descended from families who have lived in the U.S. for generations. They are members of every economic group—from the well-to-do to poverty stricken. John Bryant founded Operation Hope in an effort to attract banks and other businesses to south central Los Angeles to revitalize the area and the minorities—including African Americans—who lived there. Because of the organization's efforts, today two Starbucks coffee shops and a Sony Theater operate in the neighborhood. Still other African Americans occupy the upper levels of economic class. Oprah Winfrey's *O, The Oprah Magazine*, reaches a wealthier group of readers (including both African Americans and whites) than does her daily talk show. *O* readers earn an average annual income of $63,000 and generally prefer upscale brands like Lexus, Donna Karan, and Coach. The magazine enjoyed the most successful magazine launch ever and now has 2.5 million regular readers and more than $140 million a year in revenues.[11]

Adidas considers African Americans a critical market segment for its success. The company hopes to reach the segment with this advertisement.

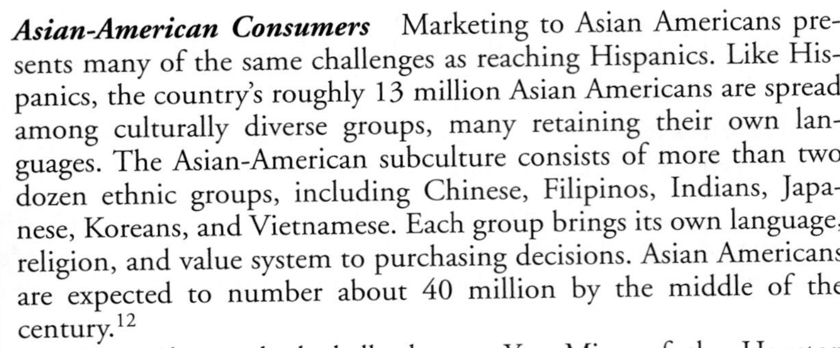

Asian-American Consumers Marketing to Asian Americans presents many of the same challenges as reaching Hispanics. Like Hispanics, the country's roughly 13 million Asian Americans are spread among culturally diverse groups, many retaining their own languages. The Asian-American subculture consists of more than two dozen ethnic groups, including Chinese, Filipinos, Indians, Japanese, Koreans, and Vietnamese. Each group brings its own language, religion, and value system to purchasing decisions. Asian Americans are expected to number about 40 million by the middle of the century.[12]

Three Chinese basketball players—Yao Ming of the Houston Rockets, Wang Zhizhi of the Los Angeles Clippers, and Mengke Bateer of the Toronto Raptors—have become superstars in Asian-American communities, creating a surge of interest in NBA games and prompting the league to create a marketing campaign that specifically targets Asian-American audiences.[13] Special events and community outreach form part of the campaign, along with supplements created for the two most popular Chinese publications in the U.S.

SOCIAL INFLUENCES

Every consumer belongs to a number of social groups. A child's earliest group experience comes from membership in a family. As children grow older, they join other groups such as friendship groups, neighborhood groups, school groups, and organizations such as Girl Scouts, Boys' and Girls' Clubs, and Little League. Adults are also members of various groups at work and in the community.

Group membership influences an individual's purchase decisions and behavior in both overt and subtle ways. Every group establishes certain norms of behavior. **Norms** are the values, attitudes, and behaviors that a group deems appropriate for its members. Group members are expected to comply with these norms. Members of the Nature Conservancy, National Rifle Association, American Medical Association, and the local country club tend to adopt their organization's norms of behavior. Norms can even affect nonmembers. Individuals who aspire to membership in a group may adopt its standards of behavior and values.

Differences in group status and roles can also affect buying behavior. **Status** is the relative position of any individual member in a group; **roles** define behavior that members of a group expect of individuals who hold specific positions within that group. Some groups (such as Rotary Club or Lion's Club) define formal roles, and others (such as friendship groups) impose informal expectations. Both types of groups supply each member with both status and roles; in doing so, they influence that person's activities—including his or her purchase behavior.

The Internet provides an opportunity for individuals to form and be influenced by new types of groups. Usenet mailing lists and chat rooms allow groups to form around common interests. Some of these online "virtual communities" can develop norms and membership roles similar to those found in real-world groups. For example, to avoid criticism, members must observe rules for proper protocol in posting messages and participating in chats.

The Asch Phenomenon

Groups often influence an individual's purchase decisions more than is realized. Most people tend to adhere in varying degrees to the general expectations of any group that they consider important, often without conscious awareness of this motivation. The surprising impact of groups and group norms on individual behavior has been called the **Asch phenomenon,** named after social psychologist S. E. Asch, who through his research first documented characteristics of individual behavior.

Asch found that individuals would conform to majority rule, even if that majority rule went against their beliefs. The Asch phenomenon can be a big factor in many purchase decisions, from major choices such as buying a house or car to deciding whether to buy a pair of shoes on sale.

Reference Groups

Discussion of the Asch phenomenon raises the subject of **reference groups**—groups whose value structures and standards influence a person's behavior. Consumers usually try to coordinate their purchase behavior with their perceptions of the values of their reference groups. The extent of reference-group influence varies widely among individuals. Strong influence by a group on a member's purchase requires two conditions:

reference groups People or institutions whose opinions are valued and to whom a person looks for guidance in his or her own behavior, values, and conduct, such as family, friends, or celebrities.

1. The purchased product must be one that others can see and identify.
2. The purchased item must be conspicuous; it must stand out as something unusual, a brand or product that not everyone owns.

Reference-group influence would significantly affect the decision to buy a Jaguar, for example, but it would have little or no impact on the decision to purchase a loaf of bread. The status of the individual within a group produces three subcategories of reference groups: a membership group to which the person actually belongs, such as a political party; an aspirational group with which the person desires to associate; and a dissociative group with which the individual does not want to be identified.

Children are especially vulnerable to the influence of reference groups. They often base their buying decisions on outside forces such as what they see on television, opinions of friends, and fashionable products among adults. Advertising, especially endorsements by celebrities, can have much bigger impacts on children than on adults, in part because children want so badly to belong to aspirational groups.

A father is a banker provided by nature.

French proverb

Reference-group influences appear in other countries as well. Many young people in Japan aspire to American culture and values. Buying products decorated with English words and phrases—even if inaccurate—helps them achieve this feeling.

Social Classes

W. Lloyd Warner's research identified six classes within the social structures of both small and large U.S. cities: the upper-upper, lower-upper, upper-middle, and lower-middle classes, followed by the working class and lower class. Class rankings are determined by occupation, income, education, family background, and residence location. Note, however, that income is not always a primary determinant; pipe fitters paid at union scale earn more than many college professors, but their purchase behavior may be quite different. Thus, marketers are likely to disagree with the adage that "a rich man is a poor man with more money."

Family characteristics, such as the occupations and incomes of one or both parents, have been the primary influences on social class. As women's careers and earning power have increased over the past few decades, marketers have begun to pay more attention to their position as influential buyers.

People in one social class may aspire to a higher class and therefore exhibit buying behavior common to that class rather than to their own. For example, middle-class consumers often buy items they associate with the upper classes. Although the upper classes themselves account for a very small percentage of the population, many more consumers treat themselves to prestigious products, such as antique carpets or luxury cars, as illustrated in Figure 5.3.

opinion leaders Trendsetters who purchase new products before others in a group and then influence others in their purchases.

Opinion Leaders

In nearly every reference group, a few members act as **opinion leaders.** These trendsetters are likely to purchase new products before others in the group and then share their experiences and opinions via word of mouth. As others in the group decide whether to try the same products, they are influenced by the reports of opinion leaders.

figure 5.3

A Product for Those Aspiring to a Higher Social Class

Generalized opinion leaders are rare; instead, individuals tend to act as opinion leaders for specific goods or services based on their knowledge of and interest in those products. Their interest motivates them to seek out information from mass media, manufacturers, and other sources and, in turn, transmit this information to associates through interpersonal communications. Opinion leaders are found within all segments of the population.

Information about goods and services sometimes flows from the Internet, radio, television, and other mass media to opinion leaders and then from opinion leaders to others. In other instances, information flows directly from media sources to all consumers. In still other instances, a multistep flow carries information from mass media to opinion leaders and then on to other opinion leaders before dissemination to the general public. Figure 5.4 illustrates these three types of communication flow.

Some opinion leaders influence purchases by others merely through their own actions, which is particularly true in the case of fashion decisions. When actress Sarah Jessica Parker began wearing a horseshoe necklace studded with diamonds during her television series *Sex in the City*, the necklace style suddenly became the rage among women and girls of all ages. Jewelry manufacturers reproduced the necklace in a variety of materials, ranging from platinum and diamonds to silvertone metal and crystals.

FAMILY INFLUENCES

Most people are members of at least two families during their lifetimes—the ones they are born into and those they eventually form later in life. The family group is perhaps the most important determinant of consumer behavior because of the close, continuing interactions among family members. Like other groups, each family typically has norms of expected behavior and different roles and status relationships for its members.

The traditional family structure consists of a husband, wife, and children. However, according to the U.S. Census Bureau, this structure has been steadily changing over the last century. In 1900, 80 percent of households were headed by married couples; today, only 53 percent are. A century ago, half of all households consisted of extended families, with six or more people living under one roof; today, only 10 percent of such households exist. Today, three of every five married women and 69 percent of single women work outside the home, as compared with 6 percent of married women and 44 percent of single women in the year 1900.[14] These statistics have important implications for marketers because they indicate a change in who makes buying decisions. Still, marketers describe the role of each spouse in terms of these four categories:

1. *Autonomic role* is seen when the partners independently make equal numbers of decisions. Personal-care items would fall into the category of purchase decisions each would make for him- or herself.
2. *Husband-dominant role* occurs when the husband usually makes certain purchase decisions. Buying a life insurance policy is a typical example.
3. *Wife-dominant role* has the wife making most of certain buying decisions. Children's clothing is a typical wife-dominant purchase.
4. *Syncratic role* refers to joint decisions. The purchase of a house follows a syncratic pattern.

figure 5.4

Alternative Channels for Communications Flow

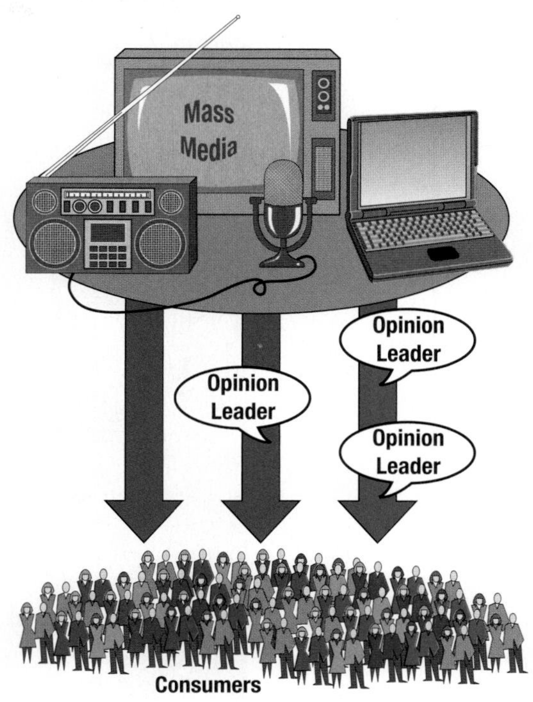

figure 5.5

French's: Emphasizing the Well-Known Brand on a Variety of Products Appealing to Busy Households

The emergence of the two-income family has changed the role of women in family purchasing behavior. Today, women have more say in large-ticket family purchases such as automobiles and computers. Studies of family decision making have also shown that households with two wage earners are more likely than others to make joint purchasing decisions. Members of two-income households often do their shopping in the evening and on weekends.

Shifting family roles have created new markets for timesaving goods and services. The desire to save time is not new. As early as 1879, Heinz advertised its ready-made ketchup "for the blessed relief of mother and other women of the household"—but it has taken on new urgency as growing numbers of parents juggle multiple roles: raising families, building careers, and managing household operations. This time crunch explains the growing market for home-meal replacement, as more and more grocery stores prepare and sell complete meals to go. As Figure 5.5 shows, even condiments are taking new forms. The maker of French's mustard also offers a variety of garnishes to enliven quick meals and, at the bottom of the ad, refers to a Web site "for more fun tips and recipes."

Children and Teenagers in Family Purchases

As parents have become busier, they have delegated some family purchase decisions to children, specifically teenagers. Children learn

Children often influence what their parents buy. Cereal is a classic example.

Briefly Speaking

Happy is the child whose father died rich.

Anonymous

about the latest products and trends because they watch so much television and cruise the Internet, often becoming the family experts on what to buy. As a result, children have gained sophistication and assumed new roles in family purchasing behavior.[15]

Children and teenagers represent a huge market—over 50 million strong—and they influence what their parents buy, from cereal to automobiles. Marketers are so aware of the $175 billion of household spending this market segment controls that Procter & Gamble has tapped some 280,000 teens aged 13 to 19 to sample and endorse its products. Using coupons, product samples, and the cachet of being in the know about what's new, the company has built an effective, and unpaid, sales force. Known as Tremor, the project helps P&G promote its brands like Pantene shampoo, CoverGirl cosmetics, and Pringles potato chips. Word-of-mouth marketing spreads from the Tremor group's members to their peers via cell phone, e-mail, instant messaging, chat rooms, sleepovers, and conversations at school, parties, and athletic fields.[16]

1. **List the interpersonal determinants of consumer behavior.**
2. **What is a subculture?**
3. **Describe the Asch phenomenon.**

Even after they grow up, children continue to play roles in family consumer behavior, often by recommending products to their parents. Advertisers try to influence these relationships by showing adult children interacting with their parents.

4 Explain each of the personal determinants of consumer behavior: needs and motives, perceptions, attitudes, learning, and self-concept theory.

PERSONAL DETERMINANTS OF CONSUMER BEHAVIOR

Consumer behavior is affected by a number of internal, personal factors in addition to interpersonal ones. Each individual brings unique needs, motives, perceptions, attitudes, learned responses, and self-concepts to buying decisions. This section looks at how these factors influence consumer behavior.

NEEDS AND MOTIVES

Individual purchase behavior is driven by the motivation to fill a perceived need. A **need** is an imbalance between the consumer's actual and desired states. A person who recognizes or feels a significant or urgent need then seeks to correct the imbalance. Marketers attempt to arouse this sense of urgency by making a need "felt" and then influencing consumers' motivation to satisfy their needs by purchasing specific products.

need Imbalance between a consumer's actual and desired states.

Motives are inner states that direct a person toward the goal of satisfying a felt need. The individual takes action to reduce the state of tension and return to a condition of equilibrium.

motive Inner state that directs a person toward the goal of satisfying a need.

Maslow's Hierarchy of Needs

Psychologist Abraham H. Maslow developed a theory that characterized needs and arranged them into a hierarchy. Maslow identified five levels of needs, beginning with physiological needs and progressing to the need for self-actualization. A person must at least partially satisfy lower-level needs, according to Maslow, before higher needs can affect behavior. In developed countries, where relatively large per-capita incomes allow most people to satisfy the basic needs on the hierarchy, higher-order needs may be more important to consumer behavior. Table 5.1 illustrates products and marketing themes designed to satisfy needs at each level.

Physiological Needs Needs at the most basic level concern essential requirements for survival, such as food, water, shelter, and clothing. The Coca-Cola Co. promotes its Dasani bottled water with the slogan "Can't live without it," emphasizing that it satisfies physiological needs.

Safety Needs Second-level needs include security, protection from physical harm, and avoidance of the unexpected. To gratify these needs, consumers may buy disability insurance or security devices. State Farm Insurance appeals to these needs by saying, "Like a good neighbor State Farm is there."

Social/Belongingness Needs Satisfaction of physiological and safety needs leads a person to attend to third-level needs—the desire to be accepted by people and groups important to that individual. To

table 5.1 ***Marketing Strategies Based on Maslow's Hierarchy of Needs***

PHYSIOLOGICAL NEEDS	*Products*	Vitamins, herbal supplements, medicines, food, exercise equipment, fitness clubs
	Marketing themes	Pepcid antacid—"Just one and heartburn's done"; Puffs facial tissues—"A nose in need deserves Puffs indeed"; Ocean Spray cranberry juice—"Crave the wave"
SAFETY NEEDS	*Products*	Cars and auto accessories, burglar alarm systems, retirement investments, insurance, smoke and carbon-monoxide detectors, medicines
	Marketing themes	Fireman's Fund Insurance—"License to get on with it"; American General Financial Group—"Live the life you've imagined"; Volvo—"Protect the body. Ignite the soul."
BELONGINGNESS	*Products*	Beauty aids, entertainment, clothing, cars
	Marketing themes	Old Navy clothing—"Spring Break from coast to coast"; Washington Mutual banks—"More human interest"; TJ Maxx clothing store—"You should go"
ESTEEM NEEDS	*Products*	Clothing, cars, jewelry, hobbies, beauty spa services
	Marketing themes	Lexus automobiles—"The relentless pursuit of perfection"; Van Cleef & Arpels—"The pleasure of perfection"; Accutron watches—"Perhaps it's worthy of your trust"; Jenn-Air kitchen appliances—"The sign of a great cook"
SELF-ACTUALIZATION	*Products*	Education, cultural events, sports, hobbies, luxury goods, technology, travel
	Marketing themes	Gatorade—"Is it in you?"; DePaul University—"Turning goals into accomplishments"; Dodge cars and trucks—"Grab life by the horns"; Southwest Airlines—"You are now free to move about the country"

figure 5.6

Harley-Davidson's Appeal to Self-Actualization Needs

satisfy this need, people may join organizations and buy goods or services that make them feel part of a group. BMW appeals to the desire to be accepted into a high socioeconomic group by using the tag line, "'Someday' just arrived" to describe its new leasing program, which makes the expensive automobiles more available for those with less income.

Esteem Needs People have a universal desire for a sense of accomplishment and achievement. They also wish to gain the respect of others and even to exceed others' performance once lower-order needs are satisfied. Lexus automobiles reinforce their drivers' esteem needs with their advertising, which touts the company's "relentless pursuit of perfection."

Self-Actualization Needs At the top rung of Maslow's ladder of human needs is people's desire to realize their full potential and to find fulfillment by expressing their unique talents and capabilities. Companies specializing in exotic adventure vacations aim to satisfy consumers' needs for self-actualization. Other travel providers, such as Smithsonian Study Tours, offer specialized educational trips that appeal to consumers' desires for a meaningful experience as well as a vacation. Elderhostel tailors similar trips for baby boomers and seniors. These trips usually involve an informal course of study—whether it's cooking, history, anthropology, or golf. As Figure 5.6 shows, Harley-Davidson appeals to self-actualization needs with the tag line, "After a lifetime of no's, see what a yes feels like. It's time to ride."[17]

Maslow noted that a satisfied need no longer motivates a person to act. Once the physiological needs are met, the individual moves on to pursue satisfaction of higher-order needs. Consumers are periodically motivated by the need to relieve thirst and hunger, but their interests soon return to focus on satisfaction of safety, social, and other needs in the hierarchy. People may not always progress through the hierarchy; they may fixate on a certain level. For example, some people who lived through the Great Depression were continually worried about money afterward.

Critics have pointed out a variety of flaws in Maslow's reasoning. For example, some needs can be related to more than one level, and not every individual progresses through the needs hierarchy in the same order; some bypass social and esteem needs and are motivated by self-actualization needs. However, the hierarchy of needs continues to occupy a secure place in the study of consumer behavior.

marketing hit — Bread Makers Responding to a Double-Wide Nation

Background. Nearly one in three Americans is obese, defined as being overweight by 30 percent of ideal body weight. The increasing size of U.S. consumers has created an unexpected marketing opportunity for companies like furniture maker Steelcase, which markets a desk chair that can hold up to 500 pounds, and Goliath Casket Co., which offers a triple-wide coffin. On the other hand, increased public awareness of the health consequences of obesity puts some food manufacturers, particularly bakers whose products are rich in carbs, on the spot.

The Challenge. The bread industry faces unprecedented changes in the way its products are made, packaged, labeled, and sold. With more than 28 percent of adult consumers currently cutting back on carbohydrates such as white flour and sugar, counting calories, and reading nutrition labels, bread marketers in particular must meet their immediate needs for low-carbohydrate products while trying to be prepared for the possibility that the low-carb craze could vanish as quickly as it appeared. Billions of dollars could be made or lost. For instance, about 40 percent of U.S. consumers ate less bread in a recent year. "Our products have an image problem," says the pres-

PERCEPTIONS

Perception is the meaning that a person attributes to incoming stimuli gathered through the five senses—sight, hearing, touch, taste, and smell. Certainly, a buyer's behavior is influenced by his or her perceptions of a good or service. Only recently have researchers come to recognize that people's perceptions depend as much on what they want to perceive as on the actual stimuli. It is for this reason that Neiman Marcus and Godiva chocolates are perceived so differently from Wal-Mart and Hershey, respectively.

perception Meaning that a person attributes to incoming stimuli gathered through the five senses.

A person's perception of an object or event results from the interaction of two types of factors:

1. stimulus factors—characteristics of the physical object such as size, color, weight, and shape
2. individual factors—unique characteristics of the individual, including not only sensory processes but also experiences with similar inputs and basic motivations and expectations

Perceptions of food are highly individual. Consumers' recent preoccupation with carbohydrates has changed their perception of the nutritional value of bread, as the "Marketing Hit" feature shows.

Consumers' perceptions that they should avoid carbohydrates, a belief largely shaped in part by the popular Atkins diet, have led to the creation of a new category of "low-carb" foods.

Perceptual Screens

The average American is constantly bombarded by marketing messages. According to the Food Marketing Institute, a typical supermarket now carries 30,000 different packages, each serving as a miniature billboard vying to attract consumers' attention. Over 6,000 commercials a week are aired on network TV. Prime-time TV shows carry more than 15 minutes of advertising every hour. Thousands of businesses have set up Web sites to tout their offerings. Marketers have also stamped their messages on everything from popcorn bags in movie theaters to airsickness bags on planes.

Marketing clutter has caused consumers to ignore many promotional messages. People respond selectively to messages that manage to break through their **perceptual screens**—the mental filtering processes through which all inputs must pass.

All marketers struggle to determine which stimuli evoke responses from consumers. They must learn how to capture a customer's attention

ident of the Wheat Foods Council. But it is difficult to make lower carbohydrate bread products that retain good taste and texture.

The Strategy. Bread makers like Great Harvest Bread Co. are introducing low-carb bread in their franchise outlets, and Panera, the bakery café, has rolled out three. George Weston Bakeries (maker of Arnold bread) and Flowers Baking Group are following suit, and Interstate Bakeries, which makes Wonder Bread, is also creating a low-carb alternative. A coalition of bakers, retailers, and suppliers to the bakery industry have formed a National Bread Leadership Council that hopes to restore public confidence in bread as a healthy food and in particular to educate Americans about its real place in such popular diets as the Atkins Nutritional Approach. Doing Atkins correctly rules out only highly processed, bleached white flour breads, bagels, and rolls, but grains remain a key component of federal diet guidelines.

The Outcome. Panera reports that it is losing about 2 to 3 percent in sales each month due to the low-carb trend, and consumption of wheat flour dropped from 147 to 137 pounds per person in a recent year. But if the industry can avoid underestimating the latest trend and restore bread to its position as a healthy food, breadbaskets may begin to reappear on tables around the country and hamburger chains will offer fewer bunless burgers.

Sources: "The Kiplinger Monitor: Low-Carb Lifestyle," *Kiplinger's*, May 2004, p. 26; Matthew Boyle, "Atkins World," *Fortune*, January 12, 2004, pp. 94–104; Brian Grow and Gerry Khermouch, "The Low-Carb Food Fight Ahead," *BusinessWeek*, December 22, 2003, p. 48; Bruce Horovitz, "Two Fast-Food Chains Give Buns the Boot," *USA Today*, December 15, 2003, p. 1B; Nanci Hellmich, "Low-Carb Foods Leading Many Dieters Astray," *USA Today*, December 10, 2003, p. 14D; David Sharp, "Low-Carb Diets Slice Business at Bakers," *USA Today*, November 10, 2003, p. 9B.

© PHOTOPIA

Word-of-mouth marketing helped the* Harry Potter *books leap to success when they were first published.

long enough to read an advertisement, listen to a sales representative, or react to a point-of-purchase display. In general, marketers seek to make a message stand out and gain the attention of prospective customers.

One way to break through clutter is to run large ads. Doubling the size of an ad in printed media increases its attention value by about 50 percent. Advertisers use color to make newspaper ads contrast with the usual black-and-white graphics, providing another effective way to penetrate the reader's perceptual screen. Other methods for enhancing contrast include arranging a large amount of white space around a printed area or placing white type on a dark background. Vivid illustrations and photos can also help to break through clutter in print ads.

Color is so suggestive, in fact, that its use on product packaging and logos is often the result of a long and careful process of selection. Red is attention getting, for instance, and orange has been shown to stimulate appetite. Blue is associated with water, which is why cleaning products are often blue, and brown denotes strength and stability, as highlighted in ads for United Parcel Service. Green connotes low-fat or healthy food products like the Healthy Choice brand.[18]

The psychological concept of closure also helps marketers create a message that stands out. *Closure* is the human tendency to perceive a complete picture from an incomplete stimulus. Advertisements that allow consumers to do this often succeed in breaking through perceptual screens. During a Kellogg campaign promoting consumption of fruit with cereal, the company emphasized the point by replacing the letters *ll* in Kellogg with bananas. In a campaign featuring a 25-cent coupon offer, Kellogg reinforced the promotional idea by replacing the letter *o* in the brand name with the image of a quarter.

Word-of-mouth marketing can be a highly effective way of breaking through consumers' perceptual screens. Take the early *Harry Potter* books. Although the series featuring the orphaned English schoolboy who is sent to wizardry school is now a huge international success, early popularity of the first two books was based on word of mouth. Before U.S. marketers even got wind of the bespectacled young wizard from England, kids were requesting the books at their local bookstores, reading them, and passing them along to friends.

A new tool that marketers are exploring is the use of virtual reality. Some companies have created presentations based on virtual reality that display marketing messages and information in a three-dimensional format. Eventually, experts predict, consumers will be able to tour resort areas via virtual reality before booking their trips or to walk through the interiors of homes they are considering buying via virtual reality. Virtual reality technology may allow marketers to penetrate consumer perceptual filters in a way not currently possible with other forms of media.

With selective perception at work screening competing messages, it is easy to see the importance of marketers' efforts in developing brand loyalty. Satisfied customers are less likely to seek information about competing products. Even when competitive advertising is forced on them, they are less apt than others to look beyond their perceptual filters at those appeals. Loyal customers simply tune out information that does not agree with their existing beliefs and expectations.

Subliminal Perception

Almost 50 years ago, a New Jersey movie theater tried to boost concession sales by flashing the words *Eat Popcorn* and *Drink Coca-Cola* between frames of actress Kim Novak's image in the movie *Picnic.* The messages flashed on the screen every five seconds for a duration of one three-hundredth of a second each time. Researchers reported that these messages, though too short to be recognizable at the conscious level, resulted in a 58 percent increase in popcorn sales and an 18 percent increase in Coke sales. After the findings were published, advertising agencies and consumer protection groups became intensely interested in **subliminal perception**—the subconscious receipt of incoming information.

Subliminal advertising is aimed at the subconscious level of awareness to circumvent the audience's perceptual screens. The goal of the original research was to induce consumer purchases while keeping consumers unaware of the source of the motivation to buy. All later attempts to duplicate the test findings, however, have been unsuccessful.

Although subliminal advertising has been universally condemned as manipulative, it is exceedingly unlikely that it can induce purchasing except by people already inclined to buy. Three reasons ensure that this fact will remain true:

1. Strong stimulus factors are required just to get a prospective customer's attention.
2. Only a very short message can be transmitted.
3. Individuals vary greatly in their thresholds of consciousness. Messages transmitted at the threshold of consciousness for one person will not be perceived at all by some people and will be all too apparent to others. The subliminally exposed message, "Drink Coca-Cola," may go unseen by some viewers, while others may read it as "Drink Pepsi-Cola," "Drink Cocoa," or even "Drive Slowly."

Despite early fears, research has shown that subliminal messages cannot force receivers to purchase goods that they would not consciously want without the messages.

In recent years, subliminal communication has spread to programming for self-help tapes. These tapes play sounds that listeners hear consciously as relaxing music or ocean waves; subconsciously, imperceptibly among the other sounds, they hear thousands of subliminal messages. Americans spend millions of dollars a year on subliminal tapes that are supposed to help them stop smoking, lose weight, or achieve a host of other goals. Unfortunately, the National Research Council recently concluded that the subliminal messages do little to influence personal behavior.

ATTITUDES

Perception of incoming stimuli is greatly affected by attitudes. In fact, a consumer's decision to purchase an item is strongly based on his or her attitudes about the product, store, or salesperson.

Attitudes are a person's enduring favorable or unfavorable evaluations, emotions, or action tendencies toward some object or data. As they form over time through individual experiences and group contacts, attitudes become highly resistant to change. Sometimes it takes a possible health threat to change consumers' attitudes. Some people avoided eating beef after the first U.S. case of mad cow disease was discovered, as outlined in the "Solving an Ethical Controversy" feature.

attitudes Person's enduring favorable or unfavorable evaluations, emotions, or action tendencies toward some object or idea.

Because favorable attitudes likely affect brand preferences, marketers are interested in determining consumer attitudes toward their offerings. Numerous attitude-scaling devices have been developed for this purpose.

Attitude Components

An attitude has cognitive, affective, and behavioral components. The *cognitive* component refers to the individual's information and knowledge about an object or concept. The *affective* component deals with feelings or emotional reactions. The *behavioral* component involves tendencies to act in a certain manner. For example, in deciding whether to shop at a warehouse-type food store, a consumer might obtain information about what the store offers from advertising, trial visits, and input from family, friends, and associates (cognitive component). The consumer might also receive affective input by listening to others about their shopping experiences at this type of store. Other affective information might lead the person to make a judgment about the type of people who seem to shop there—whether they represent a group with which he or she would like to be associated. The consumer may ultimately decide to buy some canned goods, cereal, and bakery products there but continue to rely on a regular supermarket for major food purchases (behavioral component).

All three components maintain a relatively stable and balanced relationship to one another. Together, they form an overall attitude about an object or idea.

Changing Consumer Attitudes

Since a favorable consumer attitude provides a vital condition for marketing success, how can a firm lead prospective buyers to adopt such an attitude toward its products? Marketers have two choices: (1) attempt to produce consumer attitudes that will motivate purchase of a particular product or (2) evaluate existing consumer attitudes and then make the product features appeal to them.

Solving an Ethical Controversy

ASSURING CONSUMERS THE BEEF SUPPLY IS SAFE

MAD cow disease is a fatal brain disorder in cows caused by an unknown agent. Humans who eat meat infected with bone or spinal tissue can develop a similar disease, a variation of a rare and fatal brain disorder that has killed over 150 people worldwide. The disease-causing agent cannot be killed by cooking or freezing, and disinfectants used to kill bacteria and viruses have no effect. The U.S. Department of Agriculture (USDA) prohibits the import of meat, feed, and by-products from Europe, where mad cow disease first appeared. It also mandates inspections and testing for signs of any neurological disease in domestic cattle, including all that appear sick or cannot walk—so-called downer cows. Mad cow disease was discovered in a single dairy cow in Washington State, and meat from the cow and 19 others that were slaughtered with it was sold by several stores and restaurants in California before managers heard of the recall. Some grocery chains notified their customers of the recall, but others did not. A media frenzy began, worrying beef consumers. And 50 countries worldwide slammed the door on U.S. beef imports.

IS THE U.S. FOOD INDUSTRY DOING ENOUGH TO PROTECT CONSUMERS AND IMPORTERS FROM MAD COW DISEASE?

PRO

1. The discovery of a single case of mad cow disease indicates that the government's testing is adequate and the food industry is doing all it can to comply with the law.
2. After initial hesitation, U.S. consumption of beef rebounded, although foreign exports of U.S. beef have still suffered.

CON

1. Because it is fatal and preventable, even one case of mad cow disease is too many. The disease has a long incubation period; some seemingly healthy animals in Europe have later tested positive for mad cow disease.
2. Some private beef producers have offered to test 100 percent of their cows to reassure the public that their beef is safe, but the USDA does not allow such private testing for the disease.

SUMMARY

Currently, no test is available for mad cow disease that can be done on live animals, and although research continues, such a test may not be available for some time. Some are calling for increased preventive testing and better animal tracking and labeling systems to prevent future cases. Following recommendations of an international scientific review panel, the USDA decided to expand its testing 10-fold of animals over an 18-month period—to include more than 200,000 animals that appear sick or are considered at high risk for the disease and 20,000 older animals sent to slaughter that appear healthy. Japan is still insisting on 100 percent testing before it will open its doors to U.S. beef again, and most of the other 50 countries continue their ban on U.S. beef. The debate still rages among critics, who want all cattle tested.

Sources: "Mad Cow Disease Still Hurting U.S. Beef Exports," *ABC Rural News*, April 12, 2004, http://www.abc.net.au; "Beef Firm Faces Perplexing Resistance to Mad Cow Tests," *USA Today*, March 26, 2004, http://news.yahoo.com; Ira Dreyfuss, "Government Expands Mad Cow Testing," *Associated Press*, March 16, 2004, http://story.news.yahoo.com; Maura Kelly, "Democrat U.S. Senate Candidates Want More Done to Prevent Mad Cow Disease," *The Mercury News*, February 23, 2004, http://www.mercurynews.com; Benjamin Ortiz, "State Senators Target Secrecy on Tainted Beef," *The Sacramento Bee*, February 20, 2004, http://www.sacbee.com; Craig C. Freudenrich, "How Mad Cow Disease Works," http://science.howstuffworks.com/mad-cow-disease.htm, accessed February 23, 2004; "Mad Cow Case Causes Drop in Beef Prices," *Associated Press*, February 19, 2004; Nicholas K. Geranios, "Researchers Struggle with Mad-Cow Test," Associated Press, February 18, 2004; Ira Dreyfuss and Randy Fabi, "Lawmakers Urge Big Increase in Mad Cow Testing," *Reuters Limited*, February 17, 2004.

If consumers view an existing good or service unfavorably, the seller may choose to redesign it or offer new options. American automakers have struggled for years to change consumers' attitudes about the way American cars are built, perform, and look. General Motors has spent decades—and millions—working to overcome quality problems and has succeeded in many areas. But sales of its Hummer H2 have dropped from their early peak, with consumers complaining about poor rear-window visibility, a cramped interior, cheap workmanship, and especially poor gas mileage—about 11 to 13 miles per gallon. The H2 SUT and the H3 will focus on satisfying complaints with plusher interiors and improved gas mileage as well as broadening the Hummer's appeal to a whole new market segment, drivers under 40 who like its rugged personality.[19]

Modifying the Components of Attitude

Attitudes frequently change in response to inconsistencies among the three components. The most common inconsistencies result when new information changes the cognitive or affective components of an attitude. Marketers can work to modify attitudes by providing evidence of product benefits and by correcting misconceptions. Marketers may also attempt to change attitudes by engaging buyers in new behavior. Free samples, for instance, can change attitudes by getting consumers to try a product.

Sometimes new technologies can encourage consumers to change their attitudes. Some people, for example, are reluctant to purchase clothing by mail order because they are afraid it will not fit properly. To address these concerns, e-retailer Lands' End (now part of Sears) introduced a "virtual model" feature on its Web site. People who visit the site answer a series of questions about height, body proportions, and hair color, and the software creates a three-dimensional figure reflecting their responses. Consumers can then adorn the electronic model with Lands' End garments to get an idea of how various outfits might look on them. Of course, for the electronic model to be correct, shoppers must enter information about their bodies accurately instead of simply relying on their perception of themselves.

LEARNING

Marketing is concerned as seriously with the process by which consumer decisions change over time as with the current status of those decisions. **Learning,** in a marketing context, refers to immediate or expected changes in consumer behavior as a result of experience. The learning process includes the component of **drive,** which is any strong stimulus that impels action. Fear, pride, desire for money, thirst, pain avoidance, and rivalry are examples of drives. Learning also relies on a **cue**—that is, any object in the environment that determines the nature of the consumer's response to a drive. Examples of cues are a newspaper advertisement for a new Thai restaurant—a cue for a hungry person—and a Shell sign near an interstate highway—a cue for a motorist who needs gasoline.

learning Knowledge or skill that is acquired as a result of experience, which changes consumer behavior.

A **response** is an individual's reaction to a set of cues and drives. Responses might include reactions such as purchasing Frontline flea and tick prevention for pets, dining at Pizza Hut, or deciding to enroll at a particular community college or university.

A man who carries a cat by the tail learns something he can learn in no other way.

Mark Twain (1835–1910)
American author

Reinforcement is the reduction in drive that results from a proper response. As a response becomes more rewarding, it creates a stronger bond between the drive and the purchase of the product, likely increasing future purchases by the consumer. Reinforcement is the rationale that underlies frequent-buyer programs, which reward repeat purchasers for their loyalty. These programs may offer points for premiums, frequent-flyer miles, and the like. AAdvantage is American Airlines's frequent-flyer program. Figure 5.7 shows the Web site for the airline, which contains a link to its AAdvantage program.

Applying Learning Theory to Marketing Decisions

Learning theory has some important implications for marketing strategists, particularly those involved with consumer packaged goods. Marketers must find a way to develop a desired outcome such as repeat purchase behavior gradually over time. **Shaping** is the process of applying a series of rewards and reinforcements to permit more complex behavior to evolve.

Both promotional strategy and the product itself play a role in the shaping process. Marketers want to motivate consumers to become regular buyers of certain merchandise. Their first step in getting consumers to try the product might be to offer a free-sample package that includes a substantial discount coupon for the next purchase. This example uses a cue as a shaping procedure. If the item performs well, the purchase response is reinforced and followed by another inducement—the coupon.

The second step is to entice the consumer to buy the item with little financial risk. The discount coupon enclosed with the free sample prompts this action. Suppose the package that the consumer purchases has still another, smaller discount coupon enclosed. Again, satisfactory product performance and the second coupon provide reinforcement.

The third step is to motivate the person to buy the item again at a moderate cost. A discount coupon accomplishes this objective, but this time the purchased package includes no additional coupon. The only reinforcement comes from satisfactory product performance.

figure 5.7

American Airlines: Providing Reinforcement for Customer Loyalty

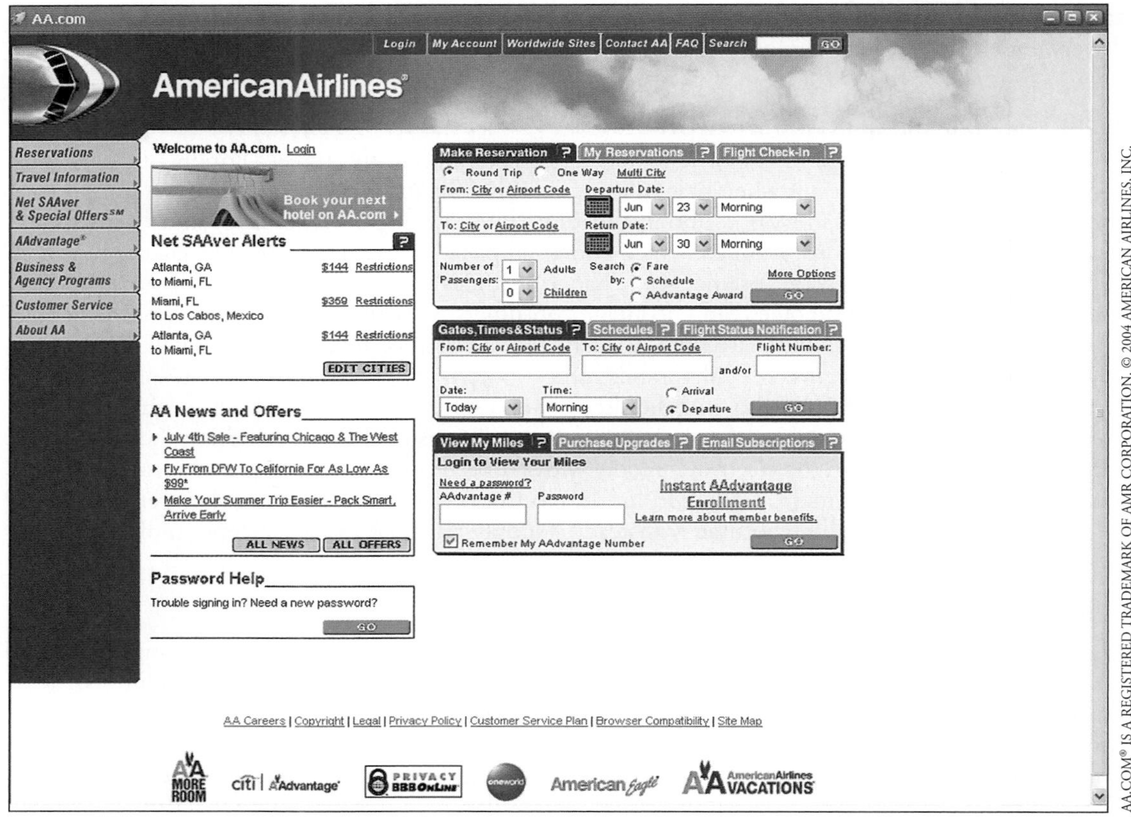

The final test comes when the consumer decides whether to buy the item at its true price without a discount coupon. Satisfaction with product performance provides the only continuing reinforcement. Repeat purchase behavior is literally shaped by effective application of learning theory within a marketing strategy context.

SELF-CONCEPT THEORY

self-concept Person's multifaceted picture of himself or herself.

The consumer's **self-concept**—a person's multifaceted picture of himself or herself—plays an important role in consumer behavior. Say a young woman views herself as bright, ambitious, and headed for a successful marketing career. She'll want to buy attractive clothes and jewelry to reflect that image of herself. Say an older man views himself as young for his age; he may purchase a sports car and stylish clothes to reflect his self-concept.

The concept of self emerges from an interaction of many of the influences—both personal and interpersonal—that affect buying behavior. The individual's needs, motives, perceptions, attitudes, and learning lie at the core of his or her conception of self. In addition, family, social, and cultural influences affect self-concept. Interestingly, we convey many aspects of our self-concept, intentionally or not, through body language, as the accompanying "Etiquette Tips for Marketing Professionals" feature explains.

It is only in our decisions that we are important.

Jean-Paul Sartre
(1905–1980)
French philosopher, dramatist, and novelist

A person's self-concept has four components: real self, self-image, looking-glass self, and ideal self. The *real self* is an objective view of the total person. The *self-image*—the way an individual views himself or herself—may distort the objective view. The *looking-glass self*—the way an individual thinks others see him or her—may also differ substantially from self-image because people often choose to project different images to others than their perceptions of their real selves. The *ideal self* serves as a personal set of objectives, since it is the image to which the individual aspires. In purchasing goods and services, people are likely to choose products that move them closer to their ideal self-images.

1. **Identify the personal determinants of consumer behavior.**
2. **What are the human needs categorized by Abraham Maslow?**
3. **How do perception and learning differ?**

ETIQUETTE TIPS

FOR MARKETING PROFESSIONALS

Communicating through Body Language

NOT long ago, a U.S. Customs inspector noticed that a suspect whose car was being searched had laid down in the back of the patrol car, occasionally peering out the window with wide eyes. Only afterward, when a liquid explosive was discovered in the suspect's trunk, did the inspector realize that the man's body language was a perfect expression of fear. Knowing how dangerous the jar of explosives was and seeing the agents handling it and twirling its contents around, the suspect had assumed they were all about to be blown to pieces.

Few of us will ever have such a desperate need to interpret someone else's body language. But some commonsense understanding of the ways in which your posture and gestures "speak" to others can help you in many professional situations. After all, experts in the science of body language say that more than half of what we communicate is nonverbal and that the body "doesn't know how to lie." Its most expressive parts are the lips, the fingertips, and the hands.

The following 12 suggestions are designed to assist you in making appropriate body language a valuable component of your communications skills.

1. Practice a firm handshake; this conveys confidence.
2. Beware of someone who turns palm downward over yours while shaking hands; it indicates a controlling personality.
3. Keep your hands open and avoid clenching them into fists; openness suggests receptiveness.
4. Avoid covering your mouth with your hand when you speak; this conveys nervousness.
5. Train yourself not to fidget, touch your nose or eye, or tug your ear when you speak; these all indicate untruthfulness.
6. Make eye contact; it establishes trust. Fail to make eye contact and you lose credibility and a chance to connect. "Eyes are perhaps the most underutilized but most powerful parts of the body when it comes to being a persuasive communicator," says Dan Broden of Ketchum's Communications Training Network.
7. Cross your legs at the ankles if you must cross them at all; it won't cut off your circulation or make you look defensive.
8. Note that "steepled" fingers, placing your fingers and thumbs together in a triangle while listening, indicate that you are giving someone who is speaking your full attention.
9. Avoid folding your arms across your chest; it makes you look defensive.
10. Keep your hands off your hips; that suggests combativeness.
11. Avoid clasping your hands behind your back; it indicates you are defensive. Relaxed hands indicate an openness to communication.
12. Try making a video of yourself and see how you can improve your body language to convey confidence, honesty, and willingness to listen to others.

Sources: Mindy Charski, "Body of Evidence," *AdWeek*, May 10, 2004, p. 54; Sue Morem, "Body Language in a Job Interview," http://www.careerknowhow.com, accessed February 23, 2004; "How to Read Body Language," http://sd.essortment/com, accessed February 23, 2004; Debbie O'Halloran, "How to Use Body Language in an Interview," IrishJobs.ie, accessed at http://www.exp.ie/advice/bodylanguage.html, February 23, 2004; Richard Conniff, "Reading Faces," *Smithsonian*, January 2004, pp. 44–50.

THE CONSUMER DECISION PROCESS

5 Distinguish between high-involvement and low-involvement purchase decisions.

Consumers complete a step-by-step process in making purchasing decisions. The length of time and the amount of effort they devote to a particular purchasing decision depend on the importance of the desired item to the consumer.

Purchases with high levels of potential social or economic consequences are said to be **high-involvement purchase decisions.** Buying a new car or deciding where to go to college are two examples of high-involvement decisions. Routine purchases that pose little risk to the consumer are **low-involvement decisions.** Purchasing a candy bar from a vending machine is a good example.

COURTESY OF KRAFTMAID CABINETRY, INC.

House remodeling requires considerable expense and time for homeowners. Kitchens, which are packed from floor to ceiling and wall to wall with cabinets and fixtures, are one of the most expensive rooms to remodel. So, they require many high-involvement purchase decisions.

Consumers generally invest more time and effort in buying decisions for high-involvement products than in those for low-involvement products. A home buyer will visit a number of listings, compare asking prices, apply for a mortgage, have the selected house inspected, and even have friends or family members visit the home before signing the final papers. Few buyers invest that much effort in choosing between Nestlé's and Hershey's candy bars. Believe it or not, though, they will still go through the steps of the consumer decision process—but on a more compressed scale.

Figure 5.8 shows the six steps in the consumer decision process. First, the consumer recognizes a problem or unmet need and then searches for goods or services that will fill that need and evaluates the alternatives before making a purchase decision. The next step is the actual purchase act. After completing the purchase, the consumer evaluates whether he or she made the right choice. Much of marketing involves steering consumers through the decision process in the direction of a specific item.

Consumers apply the decision process in solving problems and taking advantage of opportunities. Such decisions permit them to correct differences between their actual and desired states. Feedback from each decision serves as additional experience in helping guide subsequent decisions.

PROBLEM OR OPPORTUNITY RECOGNITION

During the first stage in the decision process, the consumer becomes aware of a significant discrepancy between the existing situation and a desired situation. Perhaps the consumer realizes that there is little food in the refrigerator. By identifying the problem—an empty refrigerator—the consumer can resolve it with a trip to the grocery store. Sometimes the problem is more specific. The consumer might have a full refrigerator but no mustard or mayonnaise with which to make sandwiches. This problem requires a solution as well.

(6) Outline the steps in the consumer decision process.

Suppose the consumer is unhappy with a particular purchase—say, a brand of cereal. Or maybe he or she wants a change from the same old cereal every morning. This is the recognition of another type of problem or opportunity—the desire for change.

figure 5.8

Integrated Model of the Consumer Decision Process

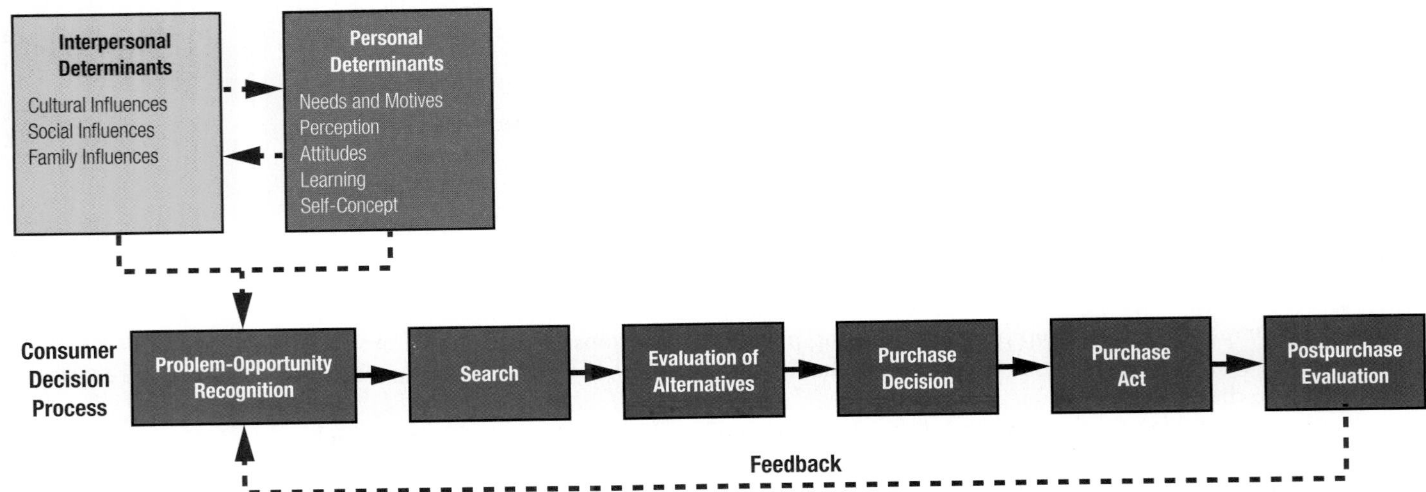

Source: Roger Blackwell, Paul W. Miniard, and James F. Engel, *Consumer Behavior,* 10th Edition (Mason, OH: South-Western, 2004).

What if our consumer just got a raise at work? He or she might want to try some of the prepared gourmet take-home dinners offered by the local supermarket. These dinners are more expensive than the groceries our consumer has purchased in the past, but now they are within financial reach. The marketer's main task during this phase of the decision-making process is to help prospective buyers identify and recognize potential problems or needs. This task may take the form of advertising, promotions, or personal sales assistance. A supermarket employee might suggest appetizers or desserts to accompany our grocery shopper's gourmet take-home dinner.

SEARCH

During the second step in the decision process, the consumer gathers information about the attainment of a desired state of affairs. This search identifies alternative means of problem solution. High-involvement purchases may elicit extensive information searches, whereas low-involvement purchases require little search activity.

The search may cover internal or external sources of information. An internal search is a mental review of stored information relevant to the problem situation. Maybe the consumer recalls past experiences with or observations of a certain type of product. Or perhaps it is the recollection of a commercial or magazine advertisement. On an external search, the consumer gathers information from outside sources, which may include family members, friends, associates, store displays, sales representatives, brochures, and product-testing publications such as *Consumer Reports*. The Internet has become a popular source of information as well. Since conducting an external search requires time and effort, consumers often use an internal search to make purchase decisions.

The search identifies alternative brands for consideration and possible purchase. The number of alternatives that a consumer actually considers in making a purchase decision is known in marketing as the **evoked set.** In some searches, consumers already know of the brands that merit further consideration; in others, their external searches develop such information. The number of brands included in the evoked set vary depending on both the situation and the person. For example, an immediate need might limit the evoked set, while someone who has more time to make a decision might expand the evoked set to choose from a broader range of options.

evoked set Number of alternatives that a consumer actually considers in making a purchase decision.

Consumers now choose among more alternative products than ever before. This variety can confuse and complicate the analysis necessary to narrow the range of consumer choices. Instead of comparing one or two brands, a consumer often faces a dizzying array of brands and subbrands. Products that once included only one or two categories—regular coffee versus decaffeinated—are now available in many different forms—cappuccino, latté, tall skinny latté, flavored coffee, espresso, and iced coffee, just to name a few possibilities.

Please find me a one-armed economist so we will not always hear "on the other hand."

Herbert Hoover (1874–1964)

31st president of the United States

Marketers try to influence buying decisions during the search process by providing persuasive information about their offerings in a format useful to consumers. As discussed earlier, marketers encounter a difficult challenge in breaking through the clutter that distracts customers. The marketer must find creative ways to penetrate a consumer's evoked set of alternatives.

EVALUATION OF ALTERNATIVES

The third step in the consumer decision process is to evaluate the evoked set of options identified during the search step. Actually, it is difficult to completely separate the second and third steps because some evaluation takes place as the search progresses; consumers accept, discount, distort, or reject incoming information as they receive it.

The outcome of the evaluation stage is the choice of a brand or product in the evoked set or possibly a decision to renew the search for additional alternatives, should all those identified during the initial search prove unsatisfactory. To complete this analysis, the consumer must develop a set of evaluative criteria to guide the selection. **Evaluative criteria** are the features that a consumer considers in choosing among alternatives. These criteria can either be objective facts (government tests of an automobile's miles-per-gallon rating) or subjective impressions (a favorable view of DKNY clothing). Common evaluative criteria include price, brand name, and country of origin. Evaluative criteria can also vary with the consumer's age, income level, social class, and culture. Auto shoppers planning to select one of the so-called "retro" cars introduced in recent years may include such popular models as the Chrysler PT Cruiser or the recent entry by BMW of the British Morris MiniCar popularized in the Austin Powers movies.

evaluative criteria Features that a consumer considers in choosing among alternatives.

Test-driving a new car is part of the evaluation stage in the consumer decision process.

Porsche reinforces the quality of its cars—and its customers' satisfaction with their purchases.

Marketers attempt to influence the outcome of this stage in three ways. First, they try to educate consumers about attributes that they view as important in evaluating a particular class of goods. They also identify which evaluative criteria are important to an individual and attempt to show why a specific brand fulfills those criteria. Finally, they try to induce a customer to expand the evoked set to include the product being marketed.

A travel agent might ask a client about the family's travel budget and recreational preferences. The agent might also explain the differences between two destinations that the client had not considered, pointing out important considerations, such as weather and activities. Finally, the agent might suggest other destinations or resorts to increase the client's range of choices.

PURCHASE DECISION AND PURCHASE ACT

The search and alternative evaluation stages of the decision process result in the eventual purchase decision and the act of making the purchase. At this stage, the consumer has evaluated each alternative in the evoked set based on his or her personal set of evaluative criteria and narrowed the alternatives down to one.

The consumer then decides the purchase location. Consumers tend to choose stores by considering characteristics such as location, price, assortment, personnel, store image, physical design, and services. In addition, store selection is influenced by the product category. Some consumers choose the convenience of in-home shopping via telephone or mail order rather than traveling to retail stores to complete transactions. Marketers can smooth the purchase decision and purchase act phases by helping customers arrange for financing or delivery.

POSTPURCHASE EVALUATION

The purchase act produces one of two results. The buyer feels either satisfaction at the removal of the discrepancy between the existing and desired states or dissatisfaction with the purchase. Consumers are generally satisfied if purchases meet their expectations.

Sometimes, however, consumers experience some postpurchase anxieties called **cognitive dissonance.** This psychologically unpleasant state results from an imbalance among a person's knowledge, beliefs, and attitudes. A consumer may experience dissonance after choosing a particular automobile over several other models when some of the rejected models have desired features that the chosen one does not provide.

Dissonance is likely to increase (1) as the dollar values of purchases increase, (2) when the rejected alternatives have desirable features that the chosen alternatives do not provide, and (3) when the purchase decision has a major effect on the buyer. In other words, dissonance is more likely with high-involvement purchases than with those that require low involvement. The consumer may attempt to reduce dissonance by looking for advertisements or other information to support the chosen alternative or by seeking reassurance from acquaintances who are satisfied purchasers of the product. The individual may also avoid information that favors a rejected alternative. Someone who buys a Toyota is likely to read Toyota advertisements and avoid Nissan and Honda ads.

Marketers can help buyers reduce cognitive dissonance by providing information that supports the chosen alternative. Automobile dealers recognize the possibility of "buyer's remorse" and often follow up purchases with letters or telephone calls from dealership personnel offering personal attention to any customer problems. Advertisements that stress customer satisfaction also help reduce cognitive dissonance.

cognitive dissonance Imbalance between beliefs and attitudes that occurs after an action or decision is taken, such as a purchase.

A final method of dealing with cognitive dissonance is to change product options, thereby restoring the cognitive balance. The consumer may ultimately decide that one of the rejected alternatives would have been the best choice and vows to purchase that item in the future. Marketers may capitalize on this with advertising campaigns that focus on the benefits of their products or with tag lines that say something like, "If you're unhappy with them, try us."

CLASSIFYING CONSUMER PROBLEM-SOLVING PROCESSES

7 **Differentiate among routinized response behavior, limited problem solving, and extended problem solving by consumers.**

As mentioned earlier, the consumer decision processes for different products require varying amounts of problem-solving efforts. Marketers recognize three categories of problem-solving behavior: routinized response, limited problem solving, and extended problem solving.[20] The classification of a particular purchase within this framework clearly influences the consumer decision process.

Routinized Response Behavior

Consumers make many purchases routinely by choosing a preferred brand or one of a limited group of acceptable brands. This type of rapid consumer problem solving is referred to as **routinized response behavior.** A routine purchase of a regular brand of soft drink is an example. The consumer has already set evaluative criteria and identified available options. External search is limited in such cases, which characterize extremely low-involvement products.

routinized response behavior Rapid consumer problem solving in which no new information is considered; the consumer has already set evaluative criteria and identified available options.

Limited Problem Solving

Consider the situation in which the consumer has previously set evaluative criteria for a particular kind of purchase but then encounters a new, unknown brand. The introduction of a new shampoo is an example of a **limited problem-solving** situation. The consumer knows the evaluative criteria for the product, but he or she has not applied these criteria to assess the new brand. Such situations demand moderate amounts of time and effort for external searches. Limited problem solving is affected by the number of evaluative criteria and brands, the extent of external search, and the process for determining preferences. Consumers making purchase decisions in this product category are likely to feel involvement in the middle of the range.

limited problem solving Situation in which the consumer invests some small amount of time and energy in searching for and evaluating alternatives.

Extended Problem Solving

Extended problem solving results when brands are difficult to categorize or evaluate. The first step is to compare one item with similar ones. The consumer needs to understand the product features before evaluating alternatives. Most extended problem-solving efforts involve lengthy external searches. High-involvement purchase decisions usually require extended problem solving.

extended problem solving Situation that involves lengthy external searches and long deliberation; results when brands are difficult to categorize or evaluate.

1. List the steps in the consumer decision process.
2. What are evaluative criteria?
3. Describe cognitive dissonance.

Strategic Implications of Marketing in the 21st Century

MARKETERS who plan to succeed with today's consumers will understand how their potential market behaves. Consider the new generation spawned by the tragic events of September 11 and the ensuing war on terrorism, during which consumers tended to engage in cocooning, or staying close to home.

Cultural influences will play a big role in marketers' relationships with consumers, particularly as firms conduct business on a global scale but also as they try to reach diverse populations in the U.S. In addition, family characteristics are changing—more women are in the workforce—which forecasts a change in the way families make purchasing decisions. Perhaps the most surprising shift in family spending is the amount of power—and money—children and teenagers now wield in the marketplace. These young consumers are becoming more and more involved, and in some cases know more about certain products, like electronics, than their parents do, and very often influence purchase decisions. This holds true even with high-involvement purchases like the family auto.

Marketers will constantly work toward changing or modifying components of consumers' attitudes about their products to gain a favorable attitude and purchase decision. Finally, they will refine their understanding of the consumer decision process and use their knowledge to design effective marketing strategies.

REVIEW OF CHAPTER OBJECTIVES

1 Distinguish between customer behavior and consumer behavior.

The term *customer behavior* refers to both individual consumers and organizational buyers. By contrast, consumer behavior refers to the buyer behavior of individual consumers only.

1.1. What is the difference between customer behavior and consumer behavior? Give an example of each.

2 Explain how marketers classify behavioral influences on consumer decisions.

The behavioral influences on consumer decisions are classified as either personal or interpersonal. These categories resulted from the work of Kurt Lewin, who developed a general model of behavior that can be adapted to consumer behavior.

2.1. How do personal and interpersonal determinants of consumer behavior differ?
2.2. What are some core values of U.S. culture?

3 Describe cultural, group, and family influences on consumer behavior.

Cultural influences, such as the work ethic or the desire to accumulate wealth, are those that come from society. Core values may vary from culture to culture. Group or social influences include social class, opinion leaders, and reference groups with which consumers may want to be affiliated. Family influences may come from parents, grandparents, or children.

3.1. Why is an understanding of subcultures important to marketers?
3.2. What are the three largest ethnic and racial minorities in the U.S.?
3.3. How do reference groups differ from opinion leaders?

④ Explain each of the personal determinants of consumer behavior: needs and motives, perceptions, attitudes, learning, and self-concept theory.

A need is an imbalance between a consumer's actual and desired states. A motive is the inner state that directs a person toward the goal of satisfying a need. Perception is the meaning that a person attributes to incoming stimuli gathered through the five senses. Attitudes are a person's enduring favorable or unfavorable evaluations, emotions, or action tendencies toward something. In self-concept theory, a person's view of himself or herself plays a role in purchasing behavior. In purchasing goods and services, people are likely to choose products that move them closer to their ideal self-images.

4.1. Identify and briefly describe Maslow's hierarchy of needs. How can marketers use this hierarchy to create successful marketing efforts?

4.2. What are perceptual screens? What strategies might marketers use to break through them?

4.3. How does a consumer's self-concept influence that person's buying behavior?

⑤ Distinguish between high-involvement and low-involvement purchase decisions.

Purchases with high levels of potential social or economic consequences are called high-involvement purchase decisions. Examples include buying a new car or home. Routine purchases that pose little risk to the consumer are called low-involvement purchase decisions. Choosing a candy bar or a newspaper are examples.

5.1. Differentiate between high-involvement products and low-involvement products.

5.2. Categorize each of the following as a high- or low-involvement product: shampoo, computer, magazine, car, snack food, entertainment system.

⑥ Outline the steps in the consumer decision process.

The consumer decision process consists of six steps: problem or opportunity recognition, search, alternative evaluation, purchase decision, purchase act, and postpurchase evaluation. The time involved in each stage of the decision process is determined by the nature of the individual purchases.

6.1. Identify and briefly describe the six steps in the consumer decision process. Cite an example of each step.

6.2. What makes cognitive dissonance increase? How do consumers attempt to reduce it?

⑦ Differentiate among routinized response behavior, limited problem solving, and extended problem solving by consumers.

Routinized response behavior refers to repeat purchases made of the same brand or limited group of items. Limited problem solving occurs when a consumer has previously set criteria for a purchase but then encounters a new brand or model. Extended problem solving results when brands are difficult to categorize or evaluate. High-involvement purchase decisions usually require extended problem solving.

7.1. Give examples of each type of consumer problem solving: routinized response, limited problem solving, and extended problem solving.

MARKETING TERMS YOU NEED TO KNOW

customer behavior 158
consumer behavior 158
culture 159
subcultures 160
reference groups 163
opinion leaders 164

need 167
motive 167
perception 169
attitudes 171
learning 173
self-concept 174

evoked set 177
evaluative criteria 177
cognitive dissonance 178
routinized response behavior 179
limited problem solving 179
extended problem solving 179

OTHER IMPORTANT MARKETING TERMS

acculturation 161
norms 163
status 163
roles 163
Asch phenomenon 163
perceptual screen 169
subliminal perception 170
drive 173
cue 173
response 173
reinforcement 173
shaping 173
high-involvement purchase decision 175
low-involvement purchase decision 175

PROJECTS AND TEAMWORK EXERCISES

1. Choose a classmate to be your partner. Separately, list what you think the core values for your culture are. Then compare your two lists. Which values are similar? Which are different? What influences do you think have created the differences?
2. Think about your participation in family purchases. How much influence do you have on your family's decisions? Has this influence changed over time? Why or why not? Describe your experience with a recent family purchase to the class.
3. With another student, create a one-page advertisement using stimuli such as color or size designed to evoke a response from consumers. Present your ad to the class for their responses. Do they think it is effective? Why or why not?
4. Select a print advertisement and identify its cognitive, affective, and behavioral components as well as your attitude toward the advertisement. Discuss the advertisement with your class.
5. Find an advertisement that makes use of self-concept theory to promote its product. Write a brief description of how the ad plays on self-image, looking-glass self, or the ideal self to promote the product, or present your findings to the class.
6. Think about the last major purchase you made (or imagine one you would like to make). Find several ads that would appeal to you during the search phase of your purchase decision process and several that you would avoid or overlook after your purchase due to cognitive dissonance. How do these ads differ from one another? Is one set more effective or more informative than the other? Report your findings about this comparison to the class.
7. Choose a partner and select a consumer product like toothpaste or detergent. Working separately, write a short list of statements that express your positive and/or negative attitudes toward the product and brand you selected. Exchange your lists and write a new list indicating how you would respond to your partner's attitudes as a marketer, either by changing negative attitudes or reinforcing positive ones. Share your lists with the class.
8. Advertising on the Internet is still in its infancy. Have you ever responded to a banner or pop-up ad? Why or why not? What good or service did you buy? Prepare a list of qualities that you think characterize successful Internet advertising and share it with the class.
9. Are you an opinion leader in any group to which you belong or for any specific type of good or service? Do you know someone who is? Write a description of an opinion leader you know (or of yourself in this role) and emphasize the qualities and actions that make others defer to that leader's opinion.
10. Suppose you were making a buying decision about an expensive item like an entertainment center. What characteristics of your self-concept, if any, do you think would come into play in this decision? Make a list of these and suggest characteristics of the product that relate to them.

APPLYING CHAPTER CONCEPTS

1. Create a marketing diary. Write down every marketing message you are aware of over the next 24 hours (make a special effort to lower your perceptual screen and record as many messages as possible). Indicate the product, the medium, the type of purchase (low or high involvement), and the type of appeal using Maslow's needs as a guide. Also try to note how the message attempted to bridge your perceptual screen. Which ones were most successful and why? Summarize your findings and report them to the class.
2. Create a consumption diary. Make a note each time you purchase something during the next 48 hours, whether large or small. Write down what kind of purchase decision you made: a routinized response, limited problem solving, or extended problem solving. Indicate whether you used any or all the steps in the consumer decision process and whether you experienced any cognitive dissonance after the purchase. Try to note whether your purchase was a response to a personal or interpersonal determinant of consumer behavior. Do you notice any patterns in your purchase decisions? What do they tell you about the kinds of decisions you most frequently make?
3. Think about a purchase with which you have had a negative experience. Perhaps an item did not perform according to your expectations or a service was not all it promised to be.

What would have to change for you to try this good or service again? Compose a marketing message—a print or radio ad, a script for a short television commercial, a flyer, or other form of your choice. Use the piece to demonstrate what it would take for the marketer to change your negative attitude about the product.

4. Suppose you are responsible for helping to market a new product like hybrid cars or wireless Internet or a new service like printable electronic postage. Do a little research on such an offering and prepare a profile of the ideal opinion leader for the offering. Describe the leader in as much realistic detail as you can and describe in general terms how you would find and reach him or her. Present your profile to the class.

ETHICS EXERCISE

Marketing directly to children has become a controversial strategy, particularly on television, because so many programs are aimed at the very young. Some critics think that many ads directed at children mislead and take advantage of children's inability to distinguish fantasy from reality. Marketers say that parents whose children ask for what they see advertised can still say no if they don't wish to buy. Research some articles that illustrate both sides of this issue. Then select a specific children's product (a toy, game, movie, or food or candy, for instance) and observe the seller's marketing strategy (ads, commercials, coupons, contests, and so on).

1. Do any characteristics of the campaign support the idea that advertising to children should be carefully regulated?
2. Write a report about your observations, explain why you came to the conclusion you did, and cite your research.

'netWork EXERCISES

1. **Consumer decision process**. Assume you're in the market for a motor vehicle. Follow the first three steps in the consumer decision process model shown in the text (problem-opportunity recognition, search, and evaluation of alternatives). Use the Web to aid in your decision process. Relevant Web sites include those from auto manufacturers, such as GM (http://www.gm.com) and Honda (http://www.honda.com), as well as independent auto sites, such as Edmunds (http://www.edmunds.com), MSN's auto site (http://autos.msn.com), and *Consumer's Guide* (http://www.consumersguide.com). Compare and contrast your results with those of a friend.
2. **Maslow's hierarchy of needs**. As noted in the chapter, different products are designed to satisfy different needs, although many products can satisfy multiple needs. Pick five well-known products and visit the product's or manufacturer's Web site. Based on the way the information is presented on the Web site, which of Maslow's needs do you think the product is trying to satisfy? Is it trying to satisfy more than one? Are you surprised by any of your findings?
3. **Targeting the Hispanic consumer**. Hispanics make up a growing percentage of American consumers. Procter & Gamble is one of many companies that has aggressively targeted Hispanic consumers. Visit the P&G Web site (http://www.pg.com) and prepare a report summarizing P&G's efforts to target this important consumer segment.

Note: Internet Web addresses change frequently. If you don't find the exact sites listed, you may need to access the organization's or company's home page and search from there or use a search engine such as Google.

INFOTRAC CITATIONS AND EXERCISES

Record: A117521616
Shopping.com Puts the Shopper First by Launching Smart Buy.
PR Newswire, June 2, 2004

Abstract: Shopping.com is a leading online comparison shopping service that helps consumers make informed purchase decisions by enabling them to find items; compare products, prices, and stores; and buy from among thousands of online merchants. The company recently launched Smart Buy, a consumer-friendly feature that helps shoppers find the lowest price quickly and easily from trusted stores.

1. List the steps in the consumer decision process.
2. Which particular step—or steps—of the consumer decision process does Shopping.com help consumers with most? How does it do so?
3. Distinguish between high-involvement and low-involvement purchase decisions. Which type of purchase decision do you think is most typical of the purchases made at online shopping sites, and why?

CASE 5.1

Cabela's: Marketing to the Consumer Who Hates to Shop

Some marketers would be happy just to get "I hate to shop" consumers into their stores. But Cabela's, the sporting goods retailer, doesn't draw only a few reluctant—and mostly male—shoppers from a few miles away into its eight stores. It has made those stores into blockbuster destinations around the country.

The Michigan store, for example, is the largest tourist attraction in the state. Six million people visit every year, more than visited New York City to shop in a typical year. The Cabela's store in Minnesota is second only to the Mall of America for tourist-drawing power in that state. The Sidney, Nebraska, store has revitalized the once-depressed town of 6,000, where not even Wal-Mart has opened an outlet. About 150 miles from Denver, Sidney now boasts new restaurants, hotels, and other businesses that cater to Cabela's visitors and shoppers, and it has 200 more jobs than residents. It's also Nebraska's second-largest tourist attraction. "The economic-development impact of Cabela's is off the charts," says Sidney's city manager.

Cabela's began as a catalog marketer in 1961 and opened its first retail store, in Sidney, 30 years later. At the time, says president Jim Cabela, "We didn't expect the store to make any money." Jim and his brother, company chairman Dick Cabela, intended the store merely to showcase the catalog's decoys, lures, lines, reels, boots, camouflage, dog shoes, tents, boats, fishing vests, archery bows, ammunition, and every other kind of hunting and fishing equipment an outdoorsman would want, along with dozens and dozens of new, used, and antique guns. With that purpose in mind, they spent lavishly on furnishing the retail outlet, covering the selling floor with museum-caliber wildlife displays and about 400 stuffed trophies worth tens of thousands of dollars, arrayed in realistic action poses amid authentically decorated settings. Four massive aquariums, holding 8,000 gallons apiece, showcase a variety of freshwater fish. There was even a kennel and a corral for the horses and dogs of hunters who dropped by to shop while hunting.

Like its competitor, Bass Pro Shops, which also maintains both retail and catalog operations, Cabela's competes well with discount houses but offers its customers the advantage of a much deeper selection, especially of more expensive items. "I'd have to go to two or three different stores to find all the brands they have at Cabela's," says Jason Gies, who drove 150 miles to visit Cabela's and purchase a rare used Remington shotgun there. The huge variety of items, the wildlife displays, and the carefully selected gift and clothing offerings for women and children all encourage shoppers to stay for hours, filling their carts with merchandise. Whole families, as well as hunting or fishing buddies and busloads of schoolchildren, come to spend the morning, the afternoon, or even the entire day. Shoppers generally find what they're looking for.

Another way in which Cabela's caters to its typical customer—the man who hates crowds and shopping—is by offering top-notch service. The stores are staffed with plenty of knowledgeable employees, who must pass thorough tests on the merchandise sold in the stores. And offerings in the clothing departments compete well with the styles and prices found in upscale department stores, some of which are hard to find in the rural areas Cabela's favors. "Cabela's is the only place around that has classy clothing," says one female shopper in the Sidney store.

Cabela's has discovered that rural shoppers will drive for miles to enjoy a little ambiance, good service, and stylish clothes. The wife of Wyoming resident John Brown has convinced him to shop only twice in his 35-year marriage. But when it comes to Cabela's, he says, "I'm like a kid in a candy store here."

Questions for Critical Thinking

1. What are some of the perceptual barriers Cabela's has overcome in the customers in its retail stores? How has it done so?
2. How do you think family or social influences affect reluctant male shoppers who visit Cabela's?
3. Do you think Cabela's in-store shopping experience satisfies any of the needs in Maslow's hierarchy? Which ones and why?

Sources: Laurie Lee Dovey, "Cabela's: Outfitting America," *America's 1st Freedom*, March 2004, pp. 40–41, 55; company Web site, **http://www.cabelas.com**, accessed February 23, 2004; Kevin Helliker, "Rare Retailer Scores by Targeting Men Who Hate to Shop," *The Wall Street Journal*, December 17, 2002, p. A1.

VIDEO CASE 5.2 Vida Wellness Spa Wishes You Well

The written case on Vida Wellness Spa appears on page VC-6. The recently filmed Vida Wellness Spa video is designed to expand and highlight the concepts in this chapter and the concepts and questions covered in the written video case.

chapter 6

Business-to-Business (B2B) Marketing

chapter objectives

1. Explain each of the components of the business-to-business (B2B) market.
2. Describe the major approaches to segmenting business-to-business (B2B) markets.
3. Identify the major characteristics of the business market and its demand.
4. Discuss the decision to make, buy, or lease.
5. Describe the major influences on business buying behavior.
6. Outline the steps in the organizational buying process.
7. Classify organizational buying situations.
8. Explain the buying center concept.
9. Discuss the challenges of and strategies for marketing to government, institutional, and international buyers.

RAWLINGS AND MAJOR LEAGUE BASEBALL: THEY FIT LIKE BALL IN GLOVE

The sport referred to as America's favorite pastime has had its share of glory and scandal, sometimes all in the same year. Mark McGwire beat Roger Maris's home-run record. At a critical point in the end-of-season playoffs, a hapless Cubs fan mistakenly caught a ball in play. After years of denying allegations that he gambled on baseball, Pete Rose came clean. The smell of scandal followed the San Francisco Giants and New York Yankees, where sluggers Barry Bonds, Jason Giambi, and Gary Sheffield, along with other pros, were alleged to have received steroids and human growth hormones. Despite the enormous player salaries and high-priced tickets, fans keep coming back to the ballpark.

One other component of the game remains constant: the baseball. All major league baseballs are manufactured by Rawlings in a single plant kept under tight security in Costa Rica. This is because Rawlings has an exclusive agreement with Major League Baseball (MLB) to provide the league with all its official baseballs.

DAVID MAXWELL/EPA/LANDOV

This type of relationship between two businesses is an important aspect of today's marketing environment. In this relationship, Rawlings must satisfy two customers—Major League Baseball and the players themselves. According to the agreement, the balls must be made to exact specifications. Each official ball weighs 5 to 5.25 ounces and measures 9 to 9.25 inches in circumference. It is covered in cowhide and hand-stitched with a thread that is 88 inches long. The core of the ball is a cork sphere a bit smaller than a Ping-Pong ball. Several layers of wool yarn are wrapped around the core in a room that is so secure it is off-limits to almost everyone except those who work there. All of the balls must be manufactured exactly the same way. Any alteration could affect the performance of the ball, the players, and the outcome of a game. "We're not trying to reinvent the wheel every year," says Rawlings president Howard Keene, "we're just trying to keep the wheel in the middle of the road." But in one year not too long ago, balls seemed to be flying off bats faster and farther than ever. After a close examination of the balls and the manufacturing process, it was determined that there was no difference in that year's balls.

A few years later, Major League Baseball entered a new five-year agreement with Rawlings, naming Rawlings the exclusive "official baseball" of the minor leagues. Now Rawlings—a division of K2 Inc.—supplies baseballs to both levels. "We are very proud of our long-standing relationship with Major League Baseball," noted Richard J. Heckman, chairman and CEO of K2 Inc. "Rawlings's long-term commitment to baseball, especially through its involvement in youth projects . . . is a critical element to the continuing growth of the game," noted baseball commissioner Bud Selig. Comments like these signify a strong relationship between the two organizations. In fact, Rawlings has been the exclusive supplier of baseballs to the 30 teams that make up the American and National major leagues since 1976. In 1985, the firm was awarded the contract for uniforms as well. And it is the official supplier of baseballs to the National Collegiate Athletic Association (NCAA).

The renewed contract to produce balls for Major League Baseball resulted in a new exterior design: the silhouetted batter logo along with the signature of MLB commissioner Bud Selig. Despite the new design however, Rawlings and MLB reassured players and fans alike that the properties of the baseballs remained unchanged. And for all those fans who fail to catch a fly ball drifting into the stands, it's a simple matter to purchase an official ball on the Rawlings Web site. All it takes is a click of the mouse and $14.99.[1]

Chapter Overview

We are all aware of the consumer marketplace. As consumers, we're involved in purchasing needed items almost every day of our lives. In addition, we can't help noticing the barrage of marketing messages aimed at us through a variety of media. But the business-to-business marketplace is, in fact, significantly larger. U.S. companies pay more than $300 billion each year just for office and maintenance supplies. Government agencies contribute to the business-to-business market even further; the Department of Defense budget for one recent year was nearly $400 billion.[2] Worldwide business-to-business commerce conducted over the Internet now totals more than $2 trillion.[3] Whether conducted through face-to-face transactions, via telephone, or over the Internet, business marketers each day deal with complex purchasing decisions involving multiple decision makers. They range from simple reorders of previously purchased items to complex buys for which materials are sourced from all over the world. As illustrated by the opening vignette, they involve the steady building of relationships between organizations such as Rawlings and Major League Baseball. Customer satisfaction and customer loyalty are major factors in the development of these long-term relationships.

This chapter discusses buying behavior in the business or organizational market. **Business-to-business,** or **B2B, marketing** deals with organizational purchases of goods and services to support production of other products, to facilitate daily company operations, or for resale. But you ask, "How do I go about distinguishing between consumer purchases and B2B transactions?" Actually, it's pretty simple. Just ask yourself two questions:

1. Who is buying the good or service?
2. Why is the purchase being made?

Consumer buying involves purchases made by people like you and me. We purchase items for our own use and enjoyment—and not for resale. By contrast, B2B purchases are made by businesses, government, and marketing intermediaries to be resold, combined with other items to create a finished product for resale, or used up in the day-to-day operations of the organization. So answer the two questions—"Who is buying?" and "Why?"—and you have the answer.

Briefly Speaking

When you're hitting the ball, it comes at you looking like a grapefruit. When you're not, it looks like a black-eyed pea.

George Scott (b. 1944)
American professional baseball player

business-to-business (B2B) marketing Organizational sales and purchases of goods and services to support production of other products, for daily company operations, or for resale.

NATURE OF THE BUSINESS MARKET

Firms usually sell fewer standardized products to organizational buyers than to ultimate consumers. Whereas you might purchase a cell phone for your personal use, a company generally has to purchase an entire communications system—which involves greater customization, more decision making, and usually more decision makers. So the buying and selling process becomes more complex. Customer service is extremely important to B2B buyers. Advertising plays a much smaller role in the business market than in the consumer market, although advertisements placed in business magazines or trade publications are common. Business marketers advertise primarily to announce new products, to enhance their company image and presence, and to attract potential customers who would then deal directly with a salesperson. The ad for the Linux NetWare application in Figure 6.l is directed at retail organizations that might be interested in purchasing the application for office use.

Personal selling plays a much bigger role in business markets than in consumer markets, distribution channels are shorter, customer relationships tend to last longer, and purchase decisions can involve multiple decision makers. All of these factors would probably apply in the case of the Canon copier. Table 6.1 compares the marketing practices commonly used in both B2B and consumer-goods marketing.

Like final consumers, an organization purchases products to fill needs. However, its primary need—meeting the demands of its own customers—is similar from firm to firm. A manufacturer buys raw materials such as wood pulp, fabric, or grain to create the company's product. A wholesaler or retailer buys the manufactured products—paper, clothing, or cereal—to resell. Mattel buys everything from plastic to paints to produce its toys; Wal-Mart buys finished toys to sell to the public. Companies also buy services from other businesses. A firm may purchase law and accounting services, an office cleaning service, a call center service, and a recruiting service. Kelly Services is a temporary staffing firm that has been in business since 1946. Kelly screens and provides temporary staff for a wide range of industries, including education, finance, health care, automotive, scientific, and information technology. The firm currently serves 200,000 business customers in 26 countries.[4] Institutional purchasers such as government agencies and nonprofit organizations buy things to meet the needs of their constituents, whether it is Humvees or food.

figure 6.1

B2B Purchases: Business Office Products

COURTESY OF IBM

Environmental, organizational, and interpersonal factors are among the many influences in B2B markets. Budget, cost, and profit considerations all play parts in business buying decisions. In addition, the business buying process typically involves complex interactions among many people. An organization's goals must also be considered in the B2B buying process. Later sections of the chapter will explore these topics in greater detail.

Some firms focus entirely on business markets. For instance, Hoechst sells chemicals to manufacturers that use them in a variety of products. Advanced Micro Devices makes flash memory chips for the cellular phone and Internet-provider markets. Computer Associates, Oracle, and Sybase are software vendors specializing in business applications. Other firms sell to both consumer and business markets. Netscape, best known for giving its Navigator Web browser to consumers, actually gets about 80 percent of its revenues from corporate customers. It offers a complete line of sophisticated networking software for companies like 3M and Chrysler. Note also that marketing strategies developed in consumer marketing are often appropriate for the business sector, too. Final consumers are often the end users of products sold into the business market and, as explained later in the chapter, can influence the buying decision.

The B2B market is diverse. Transactions can range from orders as small as a box of paper clips or copy-machine toner for a home-based business to transactions as large as thousands of parts for an

table 6.1 **Comparing Business-to-Business Marketing and Consumer Marketing**

	BUSINESS-TO-BUSINESS MARKETING	CONSUMER MARKETING
Product	Relatively technical in nature, exact form often variable, accompanying services very important	Standardized form, service important but less than for business products
Promotion	Emphasis on personal selling	Emphasis on advertising
Distribution	Relatively short, direct channels to market	Product passes through a number of intermediate links en route to consumer
Customer Relations	Relatively enduring and complex	Comparatively infrequent contact, relationship of relatively short duration
Decision-Making Process	Diverse group of organization members makes decision	Individual or household unit makes decision
Price	Competitive bidding for unique items, list prices for standard items	List prices

TANNEN MAURY/BLOOMBERG NEWS/LANDOV

Commercial markets include corporations like Sara Lee, which purchases wheat that it then uses as an ingredient in its breads.

automobile manufacturer or massive turbine generators for an electric power plant. As mentioned earlier, businesses are also big purchasers of services, such as telecommunications, computer consulting, and transportation services. Four major categories define the business market: (1) the commercial market, (2) trade industries, (3) government organizations, and (4) institutions.

(1) **Explain each of the components of the business-to-business (B2B) market.**

COMPONENTS OF THE BUSINESS MARKET

commercial market Individuals and firms that acquire products to support, directly or indirectly, production of other goods and services.

trade industries Retailers or wholesalers that purchase products for resale to others.

reseller Marketing intermediaries that operate in the trade sector.

The **commercial market** is the largest segment of the business market. It includes all individuals and firms that acquire products to support, directly or indirectly, the production of other goods and services. When Hewlett-Packard buys computer chips from Intel, when Sara Lee purchases wheat to mill into flour for an ingredient in its breads, and when a plant supervisor orders lightbulbs and cleaning supplies for a factory in Tennessee, these transactions all take place in the commercial market. Some products aid in the production of other items (the computer chips). Others are physically used up in the production of a good or service (the wheat). Still others contribute to the firm's day-to-day operations (the maintenance supplies). The commercial market includes manufacturers, farmers, and other members of resource-producing industries, construction contractors, and providers of such services as transportation, public utilities, financing, insurance, and real-estate brokerage.

The second segment of the organizational market, **trade industries,** includes retailers and wholesalers, known as **resellers,** who operate in this sector. Most resale products, such as clothing, appliances, sports equipment, and automobile parts, are finished goods that the buyers sell to final consumers. In other cases, the buyers may complete some processing or repackaging before reselling the products. A retail meat market may purchase a side of beef and then cut individual pieces for its customers. Lumber dealers and carpet retailers may purchase in bulk and then provide quantities and sizes to meet customers' specifications. In addition to resale products, trade industries buy computers, display shelves, and other products needed to operate their businesses. These goods, as well as maintenance items, and specialized services such as scanner installation, newspaper inserts, and radio advertising all represent organizational purchases. Stephen and Michael Maharam, fourth-generation owners of textile company Maharam, sell office textiles to businesses for lining cubicles or covering office chairs. The two brothers have steered the century-old company into new markets as well. They've revived archival patterns by famous furniture designers Charles and Ray Eames and teamed up with current designers to produce new furniture and accessory lines sold to consumers through upscale retailers.[5]

The government category of the business market includes domestic units of government—federal, state, and local—as well as foreign governments. This important market segment makes a wide variety of purchases, ranging from highways to social services. The primary motivation of government purchasing is to provide some form of public benefit, such as national defense or pollution control. But government agencies have also become creative when it comes to selling—local police departments and state and federal agencies are selling unclaimed shipments, confiscated goods, and unclaimed items found in safe-deposit boxes on eBay. Lucky bidders might be able to buy a custom yacht, a fancy watch, or DVDs through an Internet auction.[6]

Institutions, both public and private, are the fourth component of the business market. This category includes a wide range of organizations, such as hospitals, churches, skilled care centers, colleges and universities, museums, and not-for-profit agencies. Some institutions—such as in higher education—must rigidly follow standardized purchasing procedures, but others have less formal buying practices. Business-to-business marketers often benefit by setting up separate divisions to sell to institutional buyers.

B2B MARKETS: THE INTERNET CONNECTION

While consumers' use of Internet markets receives the bulk of public attention, more than 90 percent of all Internet sales are B2B transactions.[7] Many business-to-business marketers have set up private portals that allow their customers to buy needed items. Service and customized pages are accessed through passwords provided by B2B marketers. Online auctions and virtual marketplaces offer other ways for buyers and vendors to connect with each other over the Internet.

During the early Internet boom, start-up companies rushed to connect buyers and sellers without considering basic marketing principles such as targeting their market and making sure to fulfill customers' needs. As a result, many of these companies failed. But the companies that survived—and new firms that have learned lessons from the mistakes of the old—have established a much stronger marketing presence. For instance, they recognize that their business customers have a lot at stake and expect greater value and utility from the goods and services they purchase. One study recommends that firms who want to build an Internet B2B business should stress "enhancing—not replacing—traditional industry relationships."[8]

The Internet also opens up foreign markets to sellers. One such firm, a cotton exchange called The Seam, survived the Internet boom and bust and is now expanding overseas—in particular, to China. "You have to look at China," explains Kevin Brinkley, vice president for marketing and business at The Seam. "There's so much tied up in world consumption and production [of cotton] that is tied up there that you have to consider it." The firm is also considering expansion into Brazil.[9]

DIFFERENCES IN FOREIGN BUSINESS MARKETS

As The Seam moves into other countries, its marketers must consider the fact that foreign business markets may differ due to variations in government regulations and cultural practices. The Seam began its efforts in China by discussing with government officials how the firm can be involved with the China National Cotton Exchange.[10] Some business products need modifications to succeed in foreign markets. In Australia, Japan, and Great Britain, for instance, motorists drive on the left side of the road. Automobiles must be modified to accommodate such differences.

Business marketers must be willing to adapt to local customs and business practices when operating abroad. They should also research cultural preferences. Factors as deceptively simple as the time of a meeting and methods of address for associates can make a difference. A company even needs to consider what ink colors to use for documents because colors can have different meanings in different countries.

1. Define *B2B marketing.*
2. What is the commercial market?

② Describe the major approaches to segmenting business-to-business (B2B) markets.

SEGMENTING B2B MARKETS

Business-to-business markets include wide varieties of customers. So, marketers must identify the different market segments they serve. By applying market segmentation concepts to groups of business customers, a firm's marketers can develop a strategy that best suits a particular segment's needs. The overall process of segmenting business markets divides markets based on different criteria, usually organizational characteristics and product applications. Among the major ways to segment business markets are demographics (size), customer type, end-use application, and purchasing situation.

SEGMENTATION BY DEMOGRAPHIC CHARACTERISTICS

As with consumer markets, demographic characteristics define useful segmentation criteria for business markets. For example, firms can be grouped by size, based on sales revenues or number of employees. Marketers may develop one strategy to reach *Fortune* 500 corporations with complex purchasing procedures and another strategy for small firms where decisions are made by one or two people. To win their business, American Express created its Small Business Services unit, providing information and assistance for entrepreneurs and small-business owners. The ability to print fast, high-quality color is a desired goal in business, regardless of the size of the business. FedEx serves businesses of all sizes but focuses on small businesses in the ad in Figure 6.2.

SEGMENTATION BY CUSTOMER TYPE

Another useful segmentation approach groups prospects according to type of customer. Marketers can apply this concept in several ways. They can group customers by broad categories—manufacturer, service provider, government agency, not-for-profit organization, wholesaler, or retailer—and also by industry. These groups may be further divided using other segmentation approaches discussed in this section.

customer-based segmentation Dividing a business-to-business market into homogeneous groups based on buyers' product specifications.

Customer-based segmentation is a related approach often used in the business-to-business marketplace. Organizational buyers tend to have much more precise—and complex—requirements for goods and services than ultimate consumers do. As a result, business products often fit narrower market segments than consumer products do. This fact leads some firms to design business goods and services to meet detailed buyer specifications. Pasadena-based Tetra Tech FW, Inc., provides a variety of environmental services, including technology development, design, engineering, and remediation for organizations around the world. Because the company's customers include government agencies as well as private firms—and because customers' needs are different—Tetra Tech FW offers a range of programs to suit each type of customer. For instance, the firm provides consulting services for utilities, helps communities clean up polluted water sources, and even conducts missions to clear public and private sites of unexploded ordnance.[11]

figure 6.2
Targeting Small Businesses

North American Industrial Classification System (NAICS)

In the 1930s, the U.S. government set up a uniform system for subdividing the business marketplace into detailed segments. The Standard Industrial Classification (SIC) system standardized efforts to collect and report information on U.S. industrial activity.

SIC codes divided firms into broad industry categories: agriculture, forestry, and fishing; mining and construction; manufacturing; transportation, communication, electric, gas, and sanitary services; wholesale trade; retail trade; finance, insurance, and real-estate services; public administration; and nonclassifiable establishments. The system assigned each major category within these classifications its own two-digit number. Three-digit and four-digit numbers further subdivided each industry into smaller segments.

For almost 70 years, B2B marketers used SIC codes as a tool for segmenting markets and identifying new customers. The system, however, became outdated with implementation of the North American Free Trade Agreement (NAFTA). Each NAFTA member—the U.S., Canada, and Mexico—had its own system for measuring business activity. The new North American Free Trade Area required a joint classification system that would allow marketers to compare business sectors among the member nations. In effect, marketers required a segmentation tool they could use across borders. The **North American Industrial Classification System (NAICS)** replaced the SIC and provides more detail than was previously available. NAICS created new service sectors to better reflect the economy of the 21st century. They include information; health care and social assistance; and professional, scientific, and technical services.

North American Industrial Classification System (NAICS) Classification used by NAFTA countries to categorize the business marketplace into detailed market segments.

Table 6.2 demonstrates the NAICS system for the wholesale motor vehicle trade. NAICS uses six digits, compared with the four digits used in the SIC. The first five digits are fixed among the members of NAFTA. The sixth digit can vary among U.S., Canadian, and Mexican data. In short, the sixth digit accounts for specific data needs of each nation.[12]

SEGMENTATION BY END-USE APPLICATION

A third basis for segmentation, **end-use application segmentation,** focuses on the precise way in which a business purchaser will use a product. For example, a printing equipment manufacturer may serve markets ranging from a local utility to a bicycle manufacturer to the U.S. Department of Defense. Each end use of the equipment may dictate unique specifications for performance, design, and price. Praxair, a supplier of industrial gases, for example, might segment its markets according to user. Steel and glass manufacturers might buy hydrogen and oxygen, while food and beverage manufacturers need carbon dioxide. Praxair also sells krypton, a rare gas, to companies that produce lasers, lighting, and thermal windows. Many small- and medium-sized companies also segment markets according to end-use application. Instead of competing in markets dominated by large firms, they concentrate on specific end-use market segments.

end-use application segmentation Segmenting a business-to-business market based on how industrial purchasers will use the product.

SEGMENTATION BY PURCHASE CATEGORIES

Firms have different structures for their purchasing functions, and B2B marketers must adapt their strategies according to those organizational buyer characteristics. Some companies designate centralized purchasing departments to serve the entire firm, and others allow each unit to handle its own buying. A supplier may deal with one purchasing agent or several decision makers at various levels. Each of these structures results in different buying behavior.

When the buying situation is important to marketers, they typically consider whether the customer has made previous purchases or if this is the customer's first order. Since Staples has renewed its focus on small-business customers, the firm's marketers want to reach out to potential new customers by informing them about the addition of 450 products that are geared toward their needs. Once these new customers become established, marketers can focus on continuing to provide office solutions, setting up reorder programs, sending out reminders, and providing other services.[13]

Increasingly, businesses that have developed **customer relationship management (CRM)** systems—strategies and tools that reorient an entire organization to focus on satisfying customers—are

table 6.2 **NAICS Classifications for the Wholesale Vehicle Trade**

42	Old SIC Code and new NAICS Code for Broad Category	Wholesale Trade
421	Subdivision of Wholesale Trade	Wholesale Trade, Durable Goods
4211	Further subdivision of Wholesale Trade	Motor Vehicle and Motor Vehicle Parts and Supplies Wholesalers
42111	Subdivision of Motor Vehicle Wholesalers	Automobile and other Motor Vehicle Wholesalers
421110	Subdivision including Country Code	Automobile and other Motor Vehicle Wholesalers in U.S. Industry

Source: NAICS, U.S. Census Bureau, http://www.census.gov/epcd/www/naics.html.

1. What are the four major ways marketers segment business markets?
2. What is the NAICS?

able to segment customers in terms of the stage of the relationship between the business and the customer. A B2B company, for example, might develop different strategies for newly acquired customers than it would for existing customers to which it hopes to cross-sell new products. Similarly, building loyalty among satisfied customers requires a different approach than developing programs to "save" at-risk customer relationships. CRM will be covered in more depth in Chapter 10.

CHARACTERISTICS OF THE B2B MARKET

3 Identify the major characteristics of the business market and its demand.

Businesses that serve both B2B and consumer markets must understand the needs of their customers. However, several characteristics distinguish the business market from the consumer market: (1) geographic market concentration, (2) the sizes and numbers of buyers, (3) purchase decision procedures, and (4) buyer–seller relationships. The next sections consider how these traits influence business-to-business marketing.

GEOGRAPHIC MARKET CONCENTRATION

The U.S. business market is more geographically concentrated than the consumer market. Manufacturers converge in certain regions of the country, making these areas prime targets for business marketers. For example, the midwestern states that make up the East North Central region—Ohio, Indiana, Michigan, Illinois, and Wisconsin—lead the nation in manufacturing concentration, followed by the Middle Atlantic and the South Atlantic regions.

Certain industries locate in particular areas to be close to customers. Firms may choose to locate sales offices and distribution centers in these areas to provide more attentive service. It makes sense that the Washington, D.C., area is favored by companies that sell to the federal government.

In the automobile industry, suppliers of components and assemblies frequently build plants close to their customers. Ford recently established a first-of-its-kind campus for suppliers near its Chicago assembly plant. The campus allows suppliers to produce or assemble products close to the plant, reducing costs, controlling parts inventory, and increasing flexibility.[14] As Internet-based technology continues to improve, allowing companies to transact business even with distant suppliers, business markets may become less geographically concentrated. Much of government spending, for example, is now directed through the Internet.

SIZES AND NUMBERS OF BUYERS

In addition to geographic concentration, the business market features a limited number of buyers. Marketers can draw on a wealth of statistical information to estimate the sizes and characteristics of business markets. The federal government is the largest single source of such statistics. Every five years, it conducts both a *Census of Manufacturers* and a *Census of Retailing and Wholesaling*, which provide detailed information on business establishments, output, and employment. Many government units and trade organizations also operate Web sites that contain helpful information.

COURTESY OF FORD MOTOR COMPANY

Ford Motor Company's Chicago Assembly Plant has a nearby campus for its suppliers. The Chicago Manufacturing Campus is currently home to nine Ford suppliers, plus logistics and tool supply firms.

Many buyers in limited-buyer markets are large organizations. The international market for jet engines is dominated by three manufacturers: United Technology's Pratt & Whitney unit, General Electric, and Rolls-Royce. These firms sell engines to

Boeing and the European consortium, Airbus Industrie. These aircraft manufacturers compete for business from passenger carriers like Northwest Airlines, British Airways, KLM, and Singapore Airlines, along with cargo carriers such as DHL, Federal Express, and United Parcel Service.

Trade associations and business publications provide additional information on the business market. Private firms such as Dun & Bradstreet publish detailed reports on individual companies. These data serve as a useful starting point for analyzing a business market. Finding data in such a source requires an understanding of the NAICS, which identifies much of the available statistical information.

THE PURCHASE DECISION PROCESS

To market effectively to other organizations, businesses must understand the dynamics of the organizational purchase process. Suppliers who serve business-to-business markets must work with multiple buyers, especially when selling to larger customers. Decision makers at several levels may influence final orders, and the overall process is more formal and professional than the consumer purchasing process. Purchasers typically require a longer time frame because B2B involves more complex decisions. Suppliers must evaluate customer needs and develop proposals that meet technical requirements and specifications. Also, buyers need time to analyze competing proposals. Often, decisions require more than one round of bidding and negotiation, especially for complicated purchases.

Briefly Speaking

I would rather have a million friends than a million dollars.

Edward V. Rickenbacker (1890–1973)
American aviator

BUYER–SELLER RELATIONSHIPS

An especially important characteristic of B2B marketing is the relationship between buyers and sellers. These relationships are often more complex than consumer relationships, and they require superior communications among the organizations' personnel. Satisfying one major customer may mean the difference of millions of dollars to a firm.

Relationship marketing involves developing long-term, value-added customer relationships. A primary goal of business-to-business relationships is to provide advantages that no other vendor can provide—for instance, lower price, quicker delivery, better quality and reliability, customized product features, or more favorable financing terms. For the business marketer, providing these advantages means expanding the company's external relationships to include suppliers, distributors, and other organizational partners. It also includes managing internal relationships between departments. Pitney Bowes recently helped St. Jude Children's Research Hospital develop a program called Arrival Package Tracking and Delivery Management. When a package arrives at the hospital via a delivery service like FedEx or the U.S. Postal Service, it can be tracked internally until it reaches its final destination—whether the recipient is a patient or a staff member.[15]

Close cooperation, whether through informal contacts such as the business dinner described in the "Etiquette Tips for Marketing Professionals" box or under terms specified in contractual partnerships and strategic alliances, enables companies to meet buyers' needs for quality products and customer service. This holds true both during and after the purchase process. Goodyear, which equips law enforcement vehicles with its Goodyear Eagle tires, uses its advertising to promote its customers' objectives, thus building the buyer–seller relationship. Tetra Tech FW, mentioned earlier, has formal Client Service Quality and Shared Vision programs, which are designed to engage customers in continuous communication leading to customer satisfaction.[16]

Relationships between for-profit and nonprofit organizations are just as important as those between two commercial organizations. Figure 6.3 illustrates Minor League Baseball's commitment to helping the ALS foundation raise money for and awareness of this debilitating disease. Often referred to as "Lou Gehrig's Disease," ALS is a progressive nerve disease that affects the nerves in the brain and spinal cord. The Minor League's support helps the ALS foundation in its search for a cure for the disease.

figure 6.3

Building a Relationship between Two Organizations

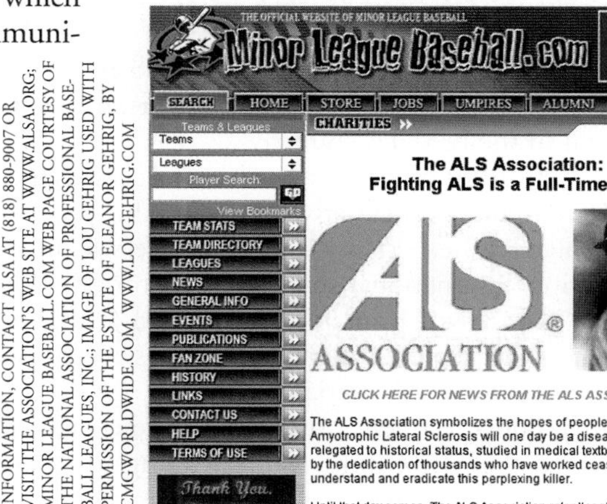

THE ALS ASSOCIATION IS THE ONLY NATIONAL NOT-FOR-PROFIT VOLUNTARY HEALTH ORGANIZATION DEDICATED SOLELY TO THE FIGHT AGAINST ALS. FOR MORE INFORMATION, CONTACT ALSA AT (818) 880-9007 OR VISIT THE ASSOCIATION'S WEB SITE AT WWW.ALSA.ORG; MINOR LEAGUE BASEBALL.COM WEB PAGE COURTESY OF THE NATIONAL ASSOCIATION OF PROFESSIONAL BASEBALL LEAGUES, INC.; IMAGE OF LOU GEHRIG USED WITH PERMISSION OF THE ESTATE OF ELEANOR GEHRIG, BY CMGWORLDWIDE.COM, WWW.LOUGEHRIG.COM

ETIQUETTE TIPS

FOR MARKETING PROFESSIONALS

Make Your Next Business Dinner a Marketing Success

KEEP your elbows off the table. Put your napkin on your lap. Don't leave your spoon in your empty ice cream dish. You have a business dinner coming up, and you are frantically trying to remember everything your parents told you about good table manners. Relax. It isn't so hard if you keep in mind that the goal of good manners is to make yourself and everyone around you feel comfortable. And the goal of a business dinner is business. Let's assume that the dinner is at a nice restaurant, and you are meeting your boss and two or three customers representing another company. Here are a few tips from the experts that will make you seem like a pro:

1. Arrive on time. You don't want either your boss or your customers waiting for you. Greet everyone cordially, shake hands, and reintroduce yourself to customers if necessary.
2. Let your boss indicate the seating plan at the table. If there are men and women in the group, it is customary to alternate male–female around the table.
3. If others in your party order alcoholic drinks, it is appropriate for you to do so—but never have more than one. If they do not, order water, iced tea, or the like. Your boss is the host and will probably ask the server to take your customers' orders for both food and drink first.
4. When you order, don't order the most expensive dish on the menu. And don't order a meal that is tricky or messy to eat—like lobster or spaghetti. Likewise, don't order something that takes a long time to prepare or that will be brought to the table flaming. You want your attention focused on your customers, not your meal.
5. You may eat bread, corn on the cob, a hamburger, or sandwich with your fingers, but most food should be eaten with a knife and fork, including French fries and even pizza, unless you are in a very casual setting.
6. Everyone makes mistakes now and then. Instead of calling attention to a faux pas, move past it as quickly as possible. If you drop cutlery on the floor, quietly signal the server and ask to have it replaced.
7. Let your boss lead the conversation, but if it seems to break into pairs, be sure to talk with whomever you are sitting next to, even if you don't know the person well. Focus the conversation on the other person by asking his or her outlook on the business or industry in which he or she works.
8. If your boss is hosting the dinner, he or she will pay for the meal. If you are hosting, it is your job to do so. A credit card is the most discreet method. Add a tip of at least 18 to 20 percent for your server.

Sources: Jason Lambert, "Dinner Etiquette," *ArticleInsider.com*, http://www.etiquetteandimage.com, accessed February 6, 2004; "Business Etiquette Answers," *Career Center*, http://www.collegeview.com/career/, accessed February 6, 2004; "Dining Etiquette," http://etiquette.tips4me.com, accessed January 23, 2004; Kimball Payne, "Crash Course in Business Manners; Don't Reach for That Extra Roll," *Knight Ridder/Tribune Business News*, March 29, 2003, http://www.hotel-online.com.

EVALUATING INTERNATIONAL BUSINESS MARKETS

Business purchasing patterns differ from one country to the next. Researching these markets poses a particular problem for B2B marketers. Of course, as explained earlier, NAICS is correcting this problem in the NAFTA countries.

In addition to quantitative data such as the size of the potential market, companies must also carefully weigh its qualitative features. This process involves considering cultural values, work styles, and generally, the best ways to enter overseas markets. For example, after winning its effort to fly into China, international shipper UPS promoted the introduction of its first flights with media briefings, TV advertising, print and billboard ads, and direct mail. The messages are delivered using Chinese characters that represent such attributes as speed and reliability. The company's Web site uses Mandarin.

Liftomatic Materials Handling, a small company that makes equipment to handle barrels on factory floors, estimates that the Chinese market accounts for a quarter of its revenue. The company found that the Chinese are unwilling to invest in new products without having seen them demonstrated, so Liftomatic depends heavily on in-person or video demonstrations. Trade shows, print advertising, and a Chinese-enabled Web site all aim to improve communications between the American company and its Chinese customers.[17]

In today's international marketplace, companies often practice **global sourcing**, which involves contracting to purchase goods and services from suppliers worldwide. This practice can result in substantial cost savings. FedEx, for example, estimates that it saves over 30 percent on the prices of computer hardware and software by soliciting bids worldwide. Applica is a business-to-business company that manufactures small appliances such as irons and hair dryers for large retailers like Wal-Mart. Applica uses Internet-based technology to link sales data from Wal-Mart directly to the factory floor in Mexico, where irons are made to order. By connecting manufacturing operations directly with customer sales, Applica is able to slash inventories while producing in low-cost regions of the world.[18]

global sourcing Purchasing goods and services from suppliers worldwide.

Global sourcing requires companies to adopt a new mind-set; some must even reorganize their operations. Among other considerations, businesses sourcing from multiple multinational locations should streamline the purchase process and minimize price differences due to labor costs, tariffs, taxes, and currency fluctuations. U.S.-based General Motors took advantage of global sourcing when it developed its new Saab models, as described in the "Marketing Hit" feature.

1. Why is geographic segmentation important in the B2B market?
2. In what ways is the buyer–seller relationship important in B2B marketing?
3. What is global sourcing?

BUSINESS MARKET DEMAND

The previous section's discussion of business market characteristics demonstrated considerable differences between marketing techniques for consumer and business products. Demand characteristics also differ in these markets. In business markets, the major categories of demand include derived demand, joint demand, inelastic demand, volatile demand, and inventory adjustments. Figure 6.4 summarizes these different categories of business market demand.

DERIVED DEMAND

The term **derived demand** refers to the linkage between demand for a company's output and its purchases of resources such as machinery, components, supplies, and raw materials. The demand for

derived demand Demand for a resource that results from demand for the goods and services that are produced by that resource.

marketing hit: The New Saab Is No Sob Story

Background. It was a gamble. When General Motors plunked down $125 million to buy the half of Saab that it didn't already own, skeptics raised their eyebrows. Saab had lost money during 8 of the previous 10 years and was continuing to leak financial fuel.

The Challenge. GM needed a new car to compete with BMW, Audi, and Mercedes in the premium small-car market, and it would have cost $750 million or more to develop a whole new model from scratch. After taking ownership of Saab, GM had to figure out how to come out with a new model in a little more than a year.

The Strategy. To meet a tight time schedule and to save costs, GM decided to skip most of the time-consuming process of designing an entirely new platform by adapting an existing one from a sister automobile. GM engineers found what they were looking for when they turned to Fuji Heavy Industries, which also happens to make the four-wheel-drive Subarus. (GM owns 20 percent of Fuji.) Within 15 months, they came up with a design for the new 9-2X. Shortly after that, they announced a new Saab SUV 9-7X. The 9-2X is built on a Subaru platform; the 9-7X is on the Chevy Trailblazer chassis.

The Outcome. Ad campaigns for the new Saab models appeared several months before the vehicles themselves rolled off the assembly line. GM marketers hope that they will sell as fast as GM and Fuji worked together to come up with a competitive new car.

Sources: Saab Web site, http://www.saab.com, accessed March 2, 2004; David Welch and Kathleen Kerwin, "Detroit Tries It the Japanese Way," *BusinessWeek*, January 26, 2004, pp. 76–77; Joann Muller, "Global Motors," *Forbes*, January 12, 2004, pp. 62–68.

figure 6.4

Categories of Business Market Demand

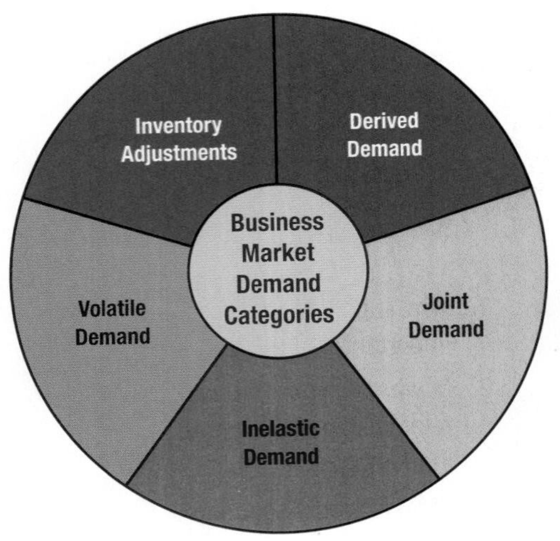

computer microprocessor chips is *derived* from the demand for personal computers. If more businesses and individuals buy new computers, the demand for chips increases; if fewer computers are sold, the demand for chips decreases. In recent years, worldwide slowdowns in sales of personal computers reduced demand for chips. In response, chipmaker Intel slashed prices of its high-end Pentium 4 processors in half. But as demand for computers in existing U.S. markets and in new markets such as Asia began to turn around, so did demand for Intel's products. Intel was ready for the comeback with new products such as the Pentium M processor and a Wi-Fi chip. Intel also came out with a major update to the Pentium 4 based on its 90-nanometer Prescott core.[19]

Organizational buyers purchase two general categories of business products: capital items and expense items. Derived demand ultimately affects both. Capital items are long-lived business assets that must be depreciated over time. *Depreciation* is an accounting term that refers to charging a portion of a capital item's cost as a deduction against the company's annual revenue for purposes of determining its net income. Examples of capital items include major installations such as new manufacturing plants, office buildings, and computer systems.

Expense items, in contrast, are items consumed within short time periods. Accountants charge the cost of such products against income in the year of purchase. Examples of expense items include the supplies necessary to operate the business, ranging from paper clips to machine lubricants.

joint demand Demand for a product that depends on the demand for another product used in combination with it.

COURTESY OF THE CATTLEMEN'S BEEF BOARD

After the mad cow disease scare in the U.S., foreign imports of beef in several countries were banned temporarily. While many expected the scare to affect consumer consumption, recent research shows that U.S. consumption was not affected. The beef industry uses ads like this one to stimulate demand for its products.

VOLATILE DEMAND

Derived demand creates volatility in business market demand. Assume that the sales volume for a gasoline retailer is increasing at an annual rate of 5 percent. Now suppose that the demand for this gasoline brand slows to a 3 percent annual increase. This slowdown might convince the firm to keep its current gasoline pumps and replace them only when market conditions improve. In this way, even modest shifts in consumer demand for a gasoline brand would greatly affect the pump manufacturer.

JOINT DEMAND

Another important influence on business market demand is **joint demand,** which results when the demand for one business product is related to the demand for another business product used in combination with the first item. Both lumber and concrete are required to build most homes. If the lumber supply falls, the drop in housing construction will most likely affect the demand for concrete. Another example is the joint demand for electrical power and large turbine engines. If consumers decide to conserve power, demand for new power plants drops, as does the demand for components and replacement parts for turbines.

INELASTIC DEMAND

Inelastic demand means that demand throughout an industry will not change significantly due to a price change. If the price of lumber drops, a construction firm will not necessarily buy more lumber from its suppliers unless another factor—such as lowered mortgage interest rates—causes more consumers to purchase new homes.

INVENTORY ADJUSTMENTS

inelastic demand Demand that, throughout an industry, will not change significantly due to a price change.

Adjustments in inventory and inventory policies can also affect business demand. Assume that manufacturers in a particular industry consider a 60-day supply of raw materials the optimal inventory level. Now suppose that economic conditions or other factors induce these firms to increase their inventories to a 90-day supply. The change will bombard the raw-materials supplier with new orders.

Further, **just-in-time (JIT)** inventory policies seek to boost efficiency by cutting inventories to absolute minimum levels and by requiring vendors to deliver inputs as the production process needs them. JIT allows companies to better predict which supplies they will require and the timing for when they will need them, markedly reducing their costs for production and storage. Widespread implementation of JIT has had a substantial impact on organizations' purchasing behavior. Firms that practice JIT tend to order from relatively few suppliers. In some cases, JIT may lead to **sole sourcing** for some items—in other words, buying a firm's entire stock of a product from just one supplier. Electronic data interchange (EDI) and quick-response inventory policies have produced similar results in the trade industries. The latest inventory trend, **JIT II,** leads suppliers to place representatives at the customer's facility to work as part of an integrated, on-site customer–supplier team. Suppliers plan and order in consultation with the customer. This streamlining of the inventory process improves control of the flow of goods.

Although inventory adjustments are critical in manufacturing processes, they are equally vital to wholesalers and retailers. Perhaps nowhere is inventory management more complex than at Wal-Mart, the largest retailer in the world, with more than $250 billion in sales per year. With no signs of slowing down, suppliers such as Procter & Gamble and Unilever—giants themselves—work closely with Wal-Mart to monitor and adjust inventory as necessary. "One of the reasons why P&G and Wal-Mart have had such a positive relationship is that they both are strongly data-driven," explains one former senior P&G executive. Other suppliers, such as Remington, Revlon, and Hershey Foods, generate at least 20 percent of their total income from Wal-Mart, so inventory management is critical for those companies as well.[20]

1. How does derived demand create volatile demand?
2. Give an example of joint demand.
3. How might JIT II strengthen marketing relationships?

THE MAKE, BUY, OR LEASE DECISION

4 Discuss the decision to make, buy, or lease.

Before a company can decide what to buy, it should decide whether to buy at all. Organizational buyers must figure out the best way to acquire needed products. In fact, a firm considering the acquisition of a finished good, component part, or service has three basic options:

1. Make the good or provide the service in-house.
2. Purchase it from another organization.
3. Lease it from another organization.

Manufacturing the product itself, if the company has the capability to do so, may be the best route. It may save a great deal of money if its own manufacturing division does not incur costs for overhead that an outside vendor would otherwise charge.

On the other hand, most firms cannot make all of the business goods they need. Often, it would be too costly to maintain the necessary equipment, staff, and supplies. Therefore, purchasing from an outside vendor is the most common choice. Hewlett-Packard manufactures 23 different types of color printers to meet nearly any business need—from affordable color laser printers to high-performance inkjets. Its wide array of products, coupled with its track record of 20 years supplying businesses, has made it a leader in the B2B printer market. Companies can also look outside their own plants for goods and services that they formerly produced in-house, a practice called *outsourcing* that the next section will describe in more detail.

In some cases, however, a company may choose to lease inputs. This option spreads out costs compared with lump-sum costs for up-front purchases. The company pays for the use of equipment

GETTY IMAGES NORTH AMERICA

Hewlett-Packard has supplied more than 290 million printers to meet business needs over its 20-year history. The company's printers generate crisp color images to meet many personal and professional needs.

for a certain time period. A small business may lease a copier for a few years and make monthly payments. At the end of the lease term, the firm can buy the machine at a prearranged price or replace it with a different model under a new lease. This option can provide useful flexibility for a growing business, allowing it to easily upgrade as its needs change.

Companies can also lease sophisticated computer systems and heavy equipment. For example, some airlines prefer to lease airplanes rather than buy them outright because short-term leases allow them to adapt quickly to changes in passenger demand.

THE RISE OF OUTSOURCING AND OFFSHORING

Chances are, if you dial a call center for a firm like America Online, your call will be answered by someone in India. Accenture and IBM have an information technology presence there as well. For those U.S.-based firms that want to remain closer to home but take advantage of the benefits of locating some of their operations overseas, Mexico and Canada are attractive locations. In today's highly competitive marketplace, firms look outside the U.S. to improve efficiency and cut costs on just about everything from mailroom management, customer service, human resources, and accounting to information technology, manufacturing, and distribution. **Outsourcing,** using outside vendors to produce goods and services formerly produced in-house or in-country, is a trend that continues to rise. Businesses outsource for several reasons: (1) they need to reduce costs to remain competitive; (2) they need to improve the quality and speed of software maintenance and development; (3) outsourcing has begun to offer greater value than ever before.[21]

outsourcing Using outside vendors to produce goods and services formerly produced in-house.

Outsourcing allows firms to concentrate their resources on their core business. It also allows access to specialized talent or expertise that does not exist within the firm. The most frequently outsourced business functions include information technology (IT) and human resources. Many hospitals and managed-care organizations spend more than a third of their IT budgets on outsourced consulting and support services.[22] Although the majority of outsourcing is done by North American–based companies, the practice is rapidly becoming commonplace in Asia, Europe, and Central America. In the U.S., a firm called Paychex is one of the largest national providers of payroll, human resource, and benefits outsourcing solutions for other companies, with nearly a half-million clients. Most of Paychex's customers are small to medium-sized firms, but the company also has a division called Major Market Services, which handles larger corporations.[23]

Software is now a $200 billion-a-year industry in the U.S. But many firms are now outsourcing their business to other countries, in particular India. Some experts believe IT outsourcing to India will grow as much as 30 percent in one year. One reason is the cost of labor—a starting call center operator or a programmer with a college degree will earn around $10,000 a year. Another reason is the large pool of highly educated, English-speaking workers. In addition, there is currently a shortfall of tech students in the U.S. Microsoft CEO Stephen A. Ballmer warns, "The U.S. is number 3 in the world and falling behind quickly number 1 [India] and number 2 [China] in terms of computer-science graduates."[24]

Although the language barrier in China is still an obstacle for U.S. and European companies considering outsourcing, experts note that Eastern Europe is becoming an increasingly popular outsourcing location. Giants such as Boeing, BMW, General Motors, Siemens, and Nortel contract small programming firms in Bulgaria, while IBM, Hewlett-Packard, Oracle, and Alcatel have support centers or software labs in Romania. German software powerhouse SAP AG has a Bulgarian research lab with 180 engineers who write Java software for SAP's innovative products around the world. "There is an exceptionally high level of talent in Eastern Europe," says Kasper Rorsted, managing director for Europe, Middle East, and Africa at Hewlett-Packard.[25]

Despite the current trend, several analysts say that U.S. programmers can be as successful if not more successful than their overseas counterparts if they master the people skills required to build relationships with business customers. Firms are looking for people who can manage teams that may be scattered around the world.[26]

Outsourcing can be a smart strategy if a company chooses a vendor that can provide high-quality products and perhaps at a lower cost than could be achieved on the company's own. This priority allows the outsourcer to focus on its core competencies. Successful outsourcing requires companies to carefully oversee contracts and manage relationships. Some vendors now provide performance guarantees to assure their customers that they will receive high-quality services that meet their needs.

Fidelity Investments offers companies outsourcing services for human resource and benefits needs.

In recent years, a political firestorm has been ignited by a different form of outsourcing: the movement of high-wage jobs from the United States to lower-cost overseas locations, a business practice referred to as **offshoring**. This relocation of business processes to a lower-cost location can involve production offshoring or services offshoring. China has emerged as the preferred destination for production offshoring, while India has emerged as the dominant player in services offshoring.

offshoring Movement of high-wage jobs from the U.S. to lower-cost overseas locations.

Business leaders argue that global businesses must continually work to achieve the lowest possible costs in order to remain competitive. After the state of Indiana cancelled a $15 million contract to upgrade its computer system because workers from India would have been working on the government job, Stuart Anderson, executive director at a Washington-based think tank devoted to trade issues, pointed out that no Indiana company had even bid on the job. "It doesn't make sense that taxpayers in Indiana, for example, should have to pay more for services so people in Florida or somewhere else can get more jobs." But Washington state respresentative Sandra Romero introduced a bill banning non-U.S. workers from state jobs in response to requests from state employees. "They're very concerned," she said. "How can state employees compete with 50-cents-an-hour employees in overseas markets like India, for example?"[29]

When I am president, and with your help, we're going to repeal every benefit, every loophole, every reward that entices any Benedict Arnold company or CEO to take the money and the jobs overseas and stick the American people with the bill.

John Kerry (b. 1943)

2004 presidential candidate (on receiving an endorsement from the AFL-CIO)

PROBLEMS WITH OUTSOURCING AND OFFSHORING

Outsourcing and offshoring are not without their downsides. Many companies discover that their cost savings are less than vendors sometimes promise. Also, companies that sign multiyear contracts may find that their savings drop after a year or two. When proprietary technology is an issue, outsourcing raises security concerns. Similarly, companies that are protective of customer data and relationships may think twice about entrusting functions like customer service to outside sources.

In some cases, outsourcing and offshoring can reduce a company's ability to respond quickly to the marketplace, or it can slow efforts in bringing new products to market. Suppliers who fail to deliver goods promptly or provide required services can adversely affect a company's reputation with its customers. General Electric had to delay the introduction of a new washing machine because of a contractor's production problems.[27]

Another major danger of outsourcing and offshoring is the risk of losing touch with customers. When telecom giant Sprint realized that customer data from its outsourced technology providers was not being put to work fast enough, the company decided to pull the plug on its outside vendors. In their place, customized customer relationship management (CRM) software was able to pull data on more than 10 million business accounts, saving Sprint $1 million in the first year.[28]

Outsourcing and offshoring are controversial topics with unions, especially in the auto industry, as the percentage of component parts made in-house has steadily dropped. These practices can create conflicts between nonunion outside workers and in-house union employees, who fear job loss. Management initiatives to outsource jobs can lead to strikes and plant shutdowns. Even if it does not lead to disruption in the workplace, outsourcing and offshoring can have a negative impact on employee morale and loyalty.

MARKETING Concept Check

1. **Identify two potential benefits of outsourcing.**
2. **Identify two potential problems with outsourcing.**

5 **Describe the major influences on business buying behavior.**

THE BUSINESS BUYING PROCESS

Suppose that CableBox, Inc., a hypothetical manufacturer of television decoder boxes for cable TV service providers, decides to upgrade its manufacturing facility with $1 million in new automated assembly equipment. Before approaching equipment suppliers, the company must analyze its needs, determine goals that the project should accomplish, develop technical specifications for the equipment, and set a budget. Once it receives vendors' proposals, it must evaluate them and select the best one. But what does *best* mean in this context? The lowest price or the best warranty and service contract? Who in the company is responsible for such decisions?

The business buying process is more complex than the consumer decision process. Business buying takes place within a formal organization's budget, cost, and profit considerations. Furthermore, B2B and institutional buying decisions usually involve many people with complex interactions among individuals and organizational goals. To understand organizational buying behavior, business marketers require knowledge of influences on the purchase decision process, the stages in the organizational buying model, types of business buying situations, and techniques for purchase decision analysis.

INFLUENCES ON PURCHASE DECISIONS

B2B buying decisions react to various influences, some external to the firm and others related to internal structure and personnel. In addition to product-specific factors such as purchase price, installation, operating and maintenance costs, and vendor service, companies must consider broader environmental, organizational, and interpersonal influences.

Environmental Factors

Environmental conditions such as economic, political, regulatory, competitive, and technological considerations influence business buying decisions. CableBox may wish to defer purchases of the new equipment in times of slowing economic activity. During a recession, sales to cable companies might drop because households hesitate to spend money on cable service. The company would look at the derived demand for its products, possible changes in its sources of materials, employment trends, and similar factors before committing to such a large capital expenditure.

Political, regulatory, and competitive factors also come into play in influencing purchase decisions. Passage of a law freezing cable rates would affect demand, as would an introduction of a less expensive decoder box by a competitor. Finally, technology plays a role in purchase decisions. A few years ago, cable-ready televisions decreased demand for set-top boxes, and smaller, more powerful satellite dishes have cut into the market for cable TV, reducing derived demand. But customers still need the boxes to access premium channels and movies, even with digital service. CableBox can benefit from technological advances, too. As more homes want fast Internet connections, adding cable modems to its product line may present a growth opportunity.

Organizational Factors

Successful business-to-business marketers understand their customers' organizational structures, policies, and purchasing systems. A company with a centralized procurement function operates differently from one that delegates purchasing decisions to divisional or geographic units. Trying to sell to the local store when head office merchandisers make all the decisions would clearly waste salespeople's time. Buying behavior also differs among firms. For example, centralized buying tends to emphasize long-term relationships, whereas decentralized buying focuses more on short-term results. Personal selling skills and user preferences carry more weight in decentralized purchasing situations than in centralized buying.

How many suppliers should a company patronize? Because purchasing operations spend over half of each dollar their companies earn, consolidating vendor relationships can lead to large cost savings. However, a fine line separates maximizing buying power from relying too heavily on a few suppliers. Many companies engage in **multiple sourcing**—purchasing from several vendors. Spreading orders ensures against shortages if one vendor cannot deliver on schedule. However, dealing with many sellers can be counterproductive and take too much time. Each company must set its own criteria for this decision.

Interpersonal Influences

Many people may influence B2B purchases, and considerable time may be spent obtaining the input and approval of various organization members. Both group and individual forces are at work here. When committees handle buying, they must spend time to gain majority or unanimous approval. Also, each individual buyer brings to the decision process individual preferences, experiences, and biases.

Tell me who's your friend and I'll tell you who you are.

Russian proverb

Business marketers should know who will influence buying decisions in an organization for their products and should know each of their priorities. To choose a supplier for an industrial press, for example, a purchasing manager and representatives of the company's production, engineering, and quality control departments may jointly decide on a supplier. Each of these principals may have a different point of view that the vendor's marketers must understand.

Boise Cascade, in collaboration with a training company, ran a marketing campaign to encourage companies to use its catalog and online service as a single source for office supplies. A color flyer was included with its direct-mail catalog, which reached 300,000 potential business buyers. The flyer was designed to appeal to Boise's end users—administrative assistants. A focal point of the campaign was an online personality assessment that allowed catalog users to gain a better understanding of themselves and their coworkers by "color-typing" their personalities. Then it gave tips on how best to work with other color types. The flyer was so popular that administrative assistants passed it around the office, along with the Boise catalog, creating an informal network of people who influenced the purchase of office supplies. In addition, an interactive quiz on the Boise Web site won more new customers through pass-along e-mails.[30]

To effectively address the concerns of all people involved in the buying decision, sales personnel must be well versed in the technical features of their products. They must also interact well with employees of the various departments involved in the purchase decision. Sales representatives for medical products—traditionally called "detailers"—frequently visit hospitals and doctors' offices to discuss the advantages of their new products and leave samples with clinical staff. Representatives for IBM would most likely try to talk with staff who would potentially use its Linux application, which is advertised in Figure 6.5.

figure 6.5

Appealing to Users

COURTESY OF IBM

The Role of the Professional Buyer

Many large organizations attempt to make their purchases through systematic procedures employing professional buyers. In the trade industries, these buyers, often referred to as **merchandisers,** are responsible for securing needed products at the best possible prices. Nordstrom has buyers for shoes and clothing that will ultimately be sold to consumers. Ford has buyers for components that will be incorporated into its cars and trucks. A firm's purchasing or merchandising unit devotes all of its time and effort in determining needs, locating and evaluating alternative suppliers, and making purchase decisions.

Purchase decisions for capital items vary significantly from those for expense items. Firms often buy expense items routinely with little delay. Capital items, however, involve major fund commitments and usually undergo considerable review.

One way in which a firm may attempt to streamline the buying process is through **systems integration,** or centralization of the procurement function. One company may designate a lead division to handle all purchasing. Another firm may choose to designate a major supplier as the systems integrator. This vendor then assumes responsibility for dealing with all of the suppliers for a project and for presenting the entire package to the buyer. In trade industries, this vendor is sometimes called a **category captain.**

A business marketer may set up a sales organization to serve national accounts that deals solely with buyers at geographically concentrated corporate headquarters. A separate field sales organization may serve buyers at regional production facilities.

Corporate buyers often use the Internet to identify sources of supplies. They view online catalogs and Web sites to compare vendors' offerings and to obtain product information. Some use Internet exchanges to extend their supplier networks.

(6) Outline the steps in the organizational buying process.

MODEL OF THE ORGANIZATIONAL BUYING PROCESS

An organizational buying situation takes place through a sequence of activities. Figure 6.6 illustrates an eight-stage model of an organizational buying process. The additional steps arise because business purchasing introduces new complexities that do not affect consumers. Although not every buying situation will require all these steps, this figure provides a good overview of the whole process.

Stage 1: Anticipate or Recognize a Problem/Need/Opportunity and a General Solution

Both consumer and business purchase decisions begin when the recognition of problems, needs, or opportunities triggers the buying process. Perhaps a firm's computer system has become outdated or an account representative demonstrates a new service that could improve the company's performance. Companies may decide to hire an outside marketing specialist when their sales stagnate.

The problem may be as simple as needing to provide a good cup of coffee to a firm's employees. "These people needed to be caffeinated, and when they left the office to get coffee, it was lost billable hours," says Nick Lazaris, CEO of Keurig, a firm that sells a patented coffee machine to corporations.[31]

figure 6.6

Stages in the B2B Buying Process

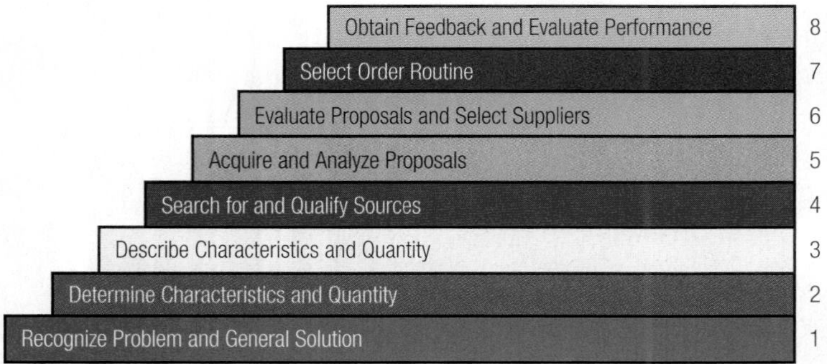

Source: Based on Michael D. Hutt and Thomas W. Speh, *Business Marketing Management: A Strategic View of Industrial and Organizational Markets,* 8th edition (Mason, OH: South-Western, 2004).

Stage 2: Determine the Characteristics and Quantity of a Needed Good or Service

The coffee problem described in Stage 1 translated into a service opportunity for Keurig. The small firm was able to offer a coffee system that would brew one perfect cup of coffee at a time, according to the preferences of each employee. PricewaterhouseCoopers became one of Keurig's first customers, followed by other accounting firms, law practices, and medical offices.[32]

Stage 3: Describe Characteristics and the Quantity of a Needed Good or Service

After determining the characteristics and quantity of needed products, B2B buyers must translate these ideas into detailed specifications. PricewaterhouseCoopers and subsequent customers told Keurig that they wanted a foolproof, individual coffee maker. The Keurig system supplies a plastic K-cup containing ground coffee that the individual simply places in the coffee maker—no measuring of water or coffee is required. Out comes the perfect cup of coffee.[33] Firms could easily base the quantity requirements of the Keurig system on the number of coffee-drinking employees they have or the amount of space they occupy.

Stage 4: Search for and Qualify Potential Sources

Both consumers and businesses search for good suppliers of desired products. The choice of a supplier may be relatively straightforward—since there was no other machine like it, PricewaterhouseCoopers had no trouble selecting the Keurig coffee system. Other searches may involve more complex decision making. A company that wants to buy a group life and health insurance policy, for example, must weigh the varying provisions and programs of many different vendors.

Stage 5: Acquire and Analyze Proposals

The next step is to acquire and analyze suppliers' proposals, which are often submitted in writing. If the buyer is a government or public agency, this stage of the purchase process may involve competitive bidding. During this process, each marketer must develop its bid, including a price, that will satisfy the criteria determined by the customer's problem, need, or opportunity. While competitive bidding is less common in the business sector, a company may follow the practice to purchase nonstandard materials, complex products, or products that are made to its own specifications.

Stage 6: Evaluate Proposals and Select Suppliers

Next in the buying process, buyers must compare vendors' proposals and choose the one that seems best suited to their needs. Proposals for sophisticated equipment, such as a large computer networking system, can include considerable differences among product offerings, and the final choice may involve trade-offs.

Price is not the only criterion for the selection of a vendor. Relationship factors like communications and trust may also be important to the buyer. Other issues include reliability, delivery record, time from order to delivery, quality, and order accuracy.

Recently, United Airlines broke its decades-long pact with The Coca-Cola Company and decided to switch to Pepsi as its in-flight soft-drink supplier. While the financial package was a key motivator, the two companies also explored ways in which the partnership could benefit their businesses. Marketing sessions for flight attendants and soft-drink promotions with air tickets as prizes are among the strategies designed to strengthen the relationship between PepsiCo and United.[34]

Stage 7: Select an Order Routine

Once a supplier has been chosen, buyer and vendor must work out the best way to process future purchases. Ordering routines can vary considerably. Most orders will, however, include product descriptions, quantities, prices, delivery terms, and payment terms. Today, companies have a variety of options for submitting orders: written documents, phone calls, faxes, or electronic data interchange.

Stage 8: Obtain Feedback and Evaluate Performance

At the final stage, buyers measure vendors' performances. Sometimes this judgment may involve a formal evaluation of each supplier's product quality, delivery performance, prices, technical knowledge, and overall responsiveness to customer needs. At other times, vendors may be measured according to whether they have lowered the customer's costs or reduced its employees' workloads. In general, bigger firms are more likely to use formal evaluation procedures, while smaller companies lean toward informal evaluations. Regardless of the method used, buyers should tell vendors how they will be evaluated.

Keurig has received the best kind of feedback on its coffee system—more than 12,000 people in two years asked the firm to start making a home version of its coffee maker. In addition, Keurig has begun licensing its technology to coffee roasters such as Vermont-based Green Mountain, which now owns a 40 percent stake in the company. And professional reviews of the Keurig system? "It's fast,

COURTESY OF J.D. POWER AND ASSOCIATES

J.D. Power and Associates conducts studies on customer satisfaction in various industries—among them automotive, telecommunications, health care, and other business products and services. Lanier, a document management company, received a No. 1 ranking two years in a row (tied in 2003) for customer satisfaction from J.D. Power and Associates.

simple, and does a really good job," remarks Den Davids, cofounder of CoffeeReview.com, an online coffee-rating service.[35]

Sometimes firms rely on independent organizations to gather quality feedback and summarize results. J.D. Power and Associates conducts research and provides information to a variety of firms so that they can improve the quality of their goods and services.

CLASSIFYING BUSINESS BUYING SITUATIONS

As discussed earlier, business buying behavior responds to many purchasing influences such as environmental, organizational, and interpersonal factors. This buying behavior also involves the degree of effort that the purchase decision demands and the levels within the organization where it is made. Like consumer behavior, marketers can classify B2B buying situations into three general categories, ranging from least to most complex: (1) straight rebuying, (2) modified rebuying, and (3) new-task buying. Business buying situations may also involve reciprocity. The following sections look at each type of purchase.

Straight Rebuying

The simplest buying situation is a **straight rebuy,** a recurring purchase decision in which a customer reorders a product that has satisfied needs in the past. The buyer already likes the product and terms of sale, so the purchase requires no new information. The buyer sees little reason to assess competing options and so follows a routine repurchase format. A straight rebuy is the business market equivalent of routinized response behavior in the consumer market. Purchases of low-cost items such as paper clips and pencils for an office are typical examples of straight rebuys. Reorders of coffee from Keurig would also be straight rebuys.

Marketers who maintain good relationships with customers by providing high-quality products, superior service, and prompt delivery can go a long way toward ensuring straight rebuys.

7 Classify organizational buying situations.

Modified Rebuying

In a **modified rebuy,** a purchaser is willing to reevaluate available options. Buyers may see some advantage in looking at alternative offerings within their established purchasing guidelines. They might take this step if their current supplier has let a rebuy situation deteriorate because of poor service or delivery performance. Price, quality, and innovation differences can also provoke modified rebuys. Modified rebuys resemble limited problem solving in consumer markets.

B2B marketers want to induce current customers to make straight rebuys by responding to all of their needs. Competitors, on the other hand, try to lure those buyers away by raising issues that will convince them to reconsider their decisions.

New-Task Buying

The most complex category of business buying is **new-task buying**—first-time or unique purchase situations that require considerable effort by the decision makers. The consumer market equivalent of new-task buying is extended problem solving. A recent copy-intensive ad from Hewlett-Packard gave a detailed explanation of how Hewlett-Packard will help solve the problem of information storage, despite the complexities of shrinking budgets, reduced staff, and the difficulties of predicting future storage needs.

A new-task buy often requires a purchaser to carefully consider alternative offerings and vendors. A company entering a new field must seek suppliers of component parts that it has never before purchased. When Linksys decided to start making a four-port router for consumers who wanted higher speed Internet connections from their home—but who didn't want to pay the going rate of $500 for a system—the firm had to buy new components for the product.[36] This new-task buying would require several stages, each yielding a decision of some sort. These decisions would include developing product requirements, searching out potential suppliers, and evaluating proposals. Information requirements and decision makers can complete the entire buying process, or they may change from stage to stage.

Reciprocity

Reciprocity—a practice of buying from suppliers that are also customers—is a controversial practice in a number of procurement situations. An office equipment manufacturer may favor a particular supplier of component parts if the supplier has recently made a major purchase of the manufacturer's products. Reciprocal arrangements traditionally have been common in industries featuring homogeneous products with similar prices, such as the chemical, paint, petroleum, rubber, and steel industries.

Reciprocity suggests close links among participants in the organizational marketplace. It can add to the complexity of B2B buying behavior for new suppliers who are trying to compete with preferred vendors. Although buyers and sellers enter into reciprocal agreements in the U.S., both the Department of Justice and the Federal Trade Commission view them as attempts to reduce competition. Outside the U.S., however, governments may take more favorable views of reciprocity. Business-to-business buyers in Canada, for instance, see it as a positive, widespread practice. In Japan, close ties between suppliers and customers are common.

value analysis
Systematic study of the components of a purchase to determine the most cost-effective approach.

vendor analysis
Assessment of supplier performance in areas such as price, back orders, timely delivery, and attention to special requests.

ANALYSIS TOOLS

Two tools that help professional buyers in improving purchase decisions are value analysis and vendor analysis. **Value analysis** examines each component of a purchase in an attempt to either delete the item or replace it with a more cost-effective substitute. Airplane designers have long recognized the need to make planes as light as possible. Value analysis supports using DuPont's synthetic material Kevlar in airplane construction because it weighs less than the metals it replaces. The resulting fuel savings are significant for the buyers in this marketplace.

Vendor analysis carries out an ongoing evaluation of a supplier's performance in categories such as price, EDI capability, back orders, delivery times, liability insurance, and attention to special requests. In some cases, vendor analysis is a formal process. Some buyers use a checklist to assess a vendor's performance. A checklist quickly highlights vendors and potential vendors that do not satisfy the purchaser's buying requirements.

1. Identify the three major factors that influence purchase decisions.
2. Why does the organizational buying process contain more steps than the consumer buying process?
3. What are the four classifications of business buying situations?

THE BUYING CENTER CONCEPT

(8) Explain the buying center concept.

The buying center concept provides a vital model for understanding B2B buying behavior. A company's **buying center** encompasses everyone who is involved in any aspect of its buying activity. A buying center may include the architect who designs a new research laboratory, the scientist who works in the facility, the purchasing manager who screens contractor proposals, the chief executive officer who makes the final decision, and the vice president for research who signs the formal contracts for the project. Buying center participants in any purchase seek to satisfy personal needs, such as participation or status, as well as organizational needs. A buying center is not part of a firm's formal organizational structure. It is an informal group whose composition and size vary among purchase situations and firms.

buying center
Participants in an organizational buying action.

BUYING CENTER ROLES

Buying center participants play different roles in the purchasing decision process. Users are the people who will actually use the good or service. Their influence on the purchase decision may range from negligible to extremely important. **Users** sometimes initiate purchase actions by requesting products, and they may also help develop product specifications. Users often influence the purchase of office equipment. Office Depot knows this. Recently, the company redesigned its office supply stores to make them more attractive to shoppers. The new layout includes a Business Solutions Center, where potential customers can learn about computers and other office equipment they are likely to use on the job. There is also an enhanced Copy and Print Center that offers specialized business services.[37]

Gatekeepers control the information that all buying center members will review. They may exert this control by distributing printed product data or advertisements or by deciding which salespeople will speak to which individuals in the buying center. A purchasing agent might allow some salespeople to see the engineers responsible for developing specifications but deny others the same privilege. The office manager for a medical group may decide whether to accept and pass along sales literature from a visiting sales representative.

Influencers affect the buying decision by supplying information to guide evaluation of alternatives or by setting buying specifications. Influencers are typically technical staff such as engineers or quality control specialists. Sometimes a buying organization hires outside consultants, such as architects, who influence its buying decisions.

The **decider** chooses a good or service, although another person may have the formal authority to do so. The identity of the decider is the most difficult role for salespeople to pinpoint. A firm's buyer may have the formal authority to buy, but the firm's chief executive officer may actually make the buying decision. Alternatively, a decider might be a design engineer who develops specifications that only one vendor can meet.

The **buyer** has the formal authority to select a supplier and to implement the procedures for securing the good or service. The buyer often surrenders this power to more influential members of the organization, though. The purchasing manager often fills the buyer's role and executes the details associated with a purchase order.

B2B marketers face the task of determining the specific role and the relative decision-making influence of each buying center participant. Salespeople can then tailor their presentations and information to the precise role that an individual plays at each step of the purchase process. Business marketers have found that their initial—and in many cases, most extensive—contacts with a firm's purchasing department often fail to reach the buying center participants who have the greatest influence, since these people may not work in that department at all.

Consider the selection of meeting and convention sites for trade or professional associations. The primary decision maker could be an association board or an executive committee, usually with input from the executive director or a meeting planner; the meeting planner or association executive might choose meeting locations, sometimes with input from members; finally, the association's annual-meeting committee or program committee might make the meeting location selection. Because officers change annually, centers of control may change from year to year. As a result, destination marketers and hotel operators are constantly assessing how an association makes its decisions on conferences.

INTERNATIONAL BUYING CENTERS

Two distinct characteristics differentiate international buying centers from domestic ones. First, marketers may have trouble identifying members of foreign buying centers. In addition to cultural differences in decision-making methods, some foreign companies lack staff personnel. In less developed countries, line managers may make most purchase decisions.

Second, a buying center in a foreign company often includes more participants than U.S. companies involve. International buying centers employ from 1 to 50 people, with 15 to 20 participants being commonplace. Global B2B marketers must recognize and accommodate this greater diversity of decision makers.

International buying centers can change in response to political and economic trends. Many European firms once maintained separate facilities in each European nation to avoid tariffs and customs delays. When the European Union lowered trade barriers between member nations, however, many companies closed distant branches and consolidated their buying centers. The Netherlands has been one of the beneficiaries of this trend.

Still, marketers who are flexible and quick to respond to change can get a jump on the competition in foreign markets if they can readily identify the decision maker in the process. Victor Tsao of Linksys signed a major deal when he learned that the head of a Taiwanese manufacturing company was visiting his California town. He invited the executive to a meeting at 10:30 on a Saturday night, during which the two men discussed a new design for a small-business computer device. They decided on a square shape with silver and gray for the colors. By Monday, the design and the deal were finalized—before either company's competitors ever got wind of the conversation.[38]

TEAM SELLING

To sell effectively to all members of a firm's buying center, many vendors use **team selling,** combining several sales associates or other staff to assist the lead account representative in reaching all those who influence the purchase decision. Fibre Containers, a company that sells corrugated paperboard for making boxes, considers team selling particularly helpful in building chemistry between the buyer and seller. If a salesperson learns that a prospect's two biggest concerns are box design and payment schedules, a meeting that includes a designer and the finance person can help develop a relationship of trust.[39]

Team selling may be extended to include members of the seller firm's own supply network into the sales situation. Consider the case of small resellers of specialized computer applications whose clients require high levels of product knowledge and access to training. By working with its supply network—for example, by forming alliances with suppliers to provide training or ongoing service to end clients—resellers are able to offer a higher degree of support.

1. Identify the five roles that people in the buying center play.
2. What are some of the problems that U.S. marketers face in dealing with international buying centers?

DEVELOPING EFFECTIVE BUSINESS-TO-BUSINESS MARKETING STRATEGIES

A business marketer must develop a marketing strategy based on a particular organization's buying behavior and on the buying situation. Clearly, many variables affect organizational purchasing decisions. This section examines three market segments whose decisions present unique challenges to B2B marketers: units of government, institutions, and international markets. Finally, it summarizes key differences between consumer and business marketing strategies.

CHALLENGES OF GOVERNMENT MARKETS

9 Discuss the challenges of and strategies for marketing to government, institutional, and international buyers.

Government agencies—federal, state, and local—together make up the largest customer in the U.S. Over 85,000 government units buy a wide variety of products, including office supplies, furniture, concrete, vehicles, grease, military aircraft, fuel, and lumber, to name just a few. In addition to U.S.-based agencies, marketers have opportunities to provide goods and services to federally funded projects and units around the world, as discussed in the "Solving an Ethical Controversy" box.

To compete effectively, business marketers must understand the unique challenges of selling to government units. One challenge results because government purchases typically involve dozens of interested parties who specify, evaluate, or use the purchased goods and services. These parties may or may not work within the government agency that officially handles a purchase.

Government purchases are also influenced by social goals, such as minority subcontracting programs. Government entities such as the U.S. Postal Service strive to maintain diversity in their suppliers, often making a special effort to purchase goods and services from small firms and companies owned by minorities and women. The government also relies on its prime suppliers to subcontract to minority businesses.[40]

Contractual guidelines create another important influence in selling to government markets. The government buys products under two basic types of contracts: fixed-price contracts, in which seller and buyer agree to a set price before finalizing the contract, and cost-reimbursement contracts, in which the government pays the vendor for allowable costs, including profits, incurred during performance of the contract. Each type of contract has advantages and disadvantages for B2B marketers. Although the fixed-price contract offers more profit potential than the alternative, it also carries greater risks from unforeseen expenses, price hikes, and changing political and economic conditions.

Government Purchasing Procedures

Many U.S. government purchases go through the General Services Administration (GSA), a central management agency involved in areas such as procurement, property management, and information

Solving an Ethical Controversy

WHO GETS THE CONTRACTS TO REBUILD IRAQ?

AFTER the U.S. war with Iraq, companies—and countries—scrambled to offer their services to rebuild Iraq's roads, schools, hospitals, transportation and communications systems, and other infrastructure. Because Iraq also has vast oil resources, many companies were interested in being part of the country's reconstruction. However, the U.S. federal government controlled the process as a gatekeeper for the awarding of contracts, and it had its own ideas about who should be allowed to bid. Initially, President George W. Bush announced that only companies based in countries that had actively supported the war would be eligible for these lucrative contracts—which would exclude France and Germany. Later, he modified the U.S. position.

SHOULD COUNTRIES THAT DID NOT SUPPORT OR PARTICIPATE IN THE WAR BE EXCLUDED FROM MAJOR CONTRACTS INVOLVED IN REBUILDING IRAQ?

PRO

1. The U.S. and its coalition partners made the sacrifice in terms of lives and financial resources to bring down the regime of Saddam Hussein. So firms based in those countries should receive preferential treatment when contracts are awarded.
2. The U.S. government has already pledged $87 billion to help rebuild Iraq. U.S.-based firms are best equipped to work with U.S. government agencies like USAID to provide the goods and services Iraq needs to rebuild its infrastructure.

CON

1. If countries such as France and Germany are excluded, then competition among companies is reduced, and Iraq as a customer may not receive the goods and services that could best meet its people's needs.
2. Most of the 63 countries on the list of eligible partners do not have the resources to offer significant aid to Iraq, so the U.S. will win most of the contracts by default.

SUMMARY

The rebuilding of an entire country is likely to take years, with the efforts of many companies and government agencies. The entire process will also have political overtones both in the U.S. and around the world. Marketers who want to be involved will have to be aware of the challenges of international *and* institutional markets and make their way carefully among various roadblocks.

Sources: "Six Companies Await Contracts to Rebuild Iraq Power System," *Forbes,* January 27, 2004, http://www.forbes.com; Sue Pleming, "U.S. Softens Stand on Who Can Get Iraq Contracts," *Reuters Limited,* January 6, 2004, http://in.news.yahoo.com; Mark Gongloff, "Iraq Rebuilding Contracts Awarded," *CNNMoney,* March 25, 2003, http://money.cnn.com.

resources management. The GSA buys goods and services for its own use and for use by other government agencies. In its role as, essentially, the federal government's business manager, it purchases billions of dollars worth of products. The Defense Logistics Agency (DLA) serves the same function for the Department of Defense.

By law, most federal purchases must be awarded on the basis of bids, or written sales proposals, from vendors. As part of this process, government buyers develop specifications—detailed descriptions of needed items—for prospective bidders. U.S. government purchases must comply with the Federal Acquisition Regulation (FAR), a 30,000-page set of standards originally designed to cut red tape in government purchasing. FAR standards have been further complicated by numerous exceptions issued by various government agencies. Numerous additional restrictions are designed to prevent overspending, corruption, and favoritism. Because they provide services to various federal government agencies like the Department of Energy, Environmental Protection Agency, and Department of Defense, large environmental engineering firms like MACTEC, Tetra Tech FW, and Weston Solutions typically have procurement and contract specialists on staff. These specialists stay current with FAR standards and conduct internal quality assurance and control programs to make sure these standards are followed by their companies.

Recent reforms have attempted to speed purchasing and increase flexibility. They include an increased reliance on fast, easy-to-use, prenegotiated contracts with multiple vendors; elimination of detailed specifications for readily available commercial products; paperwork reduction; and the use of government-issued credit cards to make small buys. As an indicator of the government's success in making its acquisition system more responsive and effective, consider the following sample of what the GSA purchased for the New York and Pentagon relief efforts within days of the September 11, 2001, terrorist attacks: 65,000 protective suits, 5,000 face masks, 3,000 respirators, 400 vehicles, 250 cell phones, 2,000 computers, 300 fax machines, and more than 1,200 items of office equipment.[41]

State and local government purchasing procedures resemble federal procedures. Most states and many large cities have created buying offices similar to the GSA. Detailed specifications and open bidding are common at this level as well. Many state purchasing regulations typically give preference to in-state bidders.

Government spending patterns may differ from those in private industry. Because the federal government's fiscal year runs from October 1 through September 30, many agencies spend much of their procurement budgets in the fourth quarter, from July 1 to September 30. They hoard their funds to cover unexpected expenditures, and if they encounter no such problems, they find themselves with money to spend in late summer. Companies understand this system and keep their eyes on government bulletins, so they can bid on the listed agency purchases, which often involve large amounts of money.

Online with the Federal Government

Like their colleagues in the private sector, government procurement professionals are streamlining purchasing procedures with new technology. Rather than paging through piles of paper catalogs and submitting handwritten purchase orders, government buyers now prefer online catalogs that help them to compare competing product offerings. In fact, vendors find business with the government almost impossible unless they embrace electronic commerce.

Vendors can sell products to the federal government through three electronic options. Web sites provide a convenient method of exchanging information for both parties. Government buyers locate and order products, paying with a federally issued credit card, and the vendors deliver the items within about a week. Another route is through government-sponsored electronic ordering systems, which help standardize the buying process. GSA Advantage, shown in Figure 6.7, allows federal employees to order products directly over the Internet at the preferred government price. The Electronic Posting System sends automatic notices of opportunities to sell to the government to more than 29,000 registered vendors. The Phoenix Opportunity System, set up by the Department of Commerce, provides a similar service for minority-owned companies. A pilot program at the Treasury is testing an electronic check-payment system to speed up the settling of vendor invoices.

Despite these advances, many government agencies remain less sophisticated than private-sector businesses. The Pentagon, for instance, is still coping with procurement procedures that were developed over the last 50 years. However, it is introducing a streamlined approach to defense contracting that reduces the time necessary to develop specifications and select suppliers. Spurred by the events of 9/11, the Department of Defense has taken a leading role in reinventing the federal procurement system. The government expenditures on upgrading technology are expected to grow by 65 percent before 2010.[42]

CHALLENGES OF INSTITUTIONAL MARKETS

Institutions constitute another important market. Institutional buyers include a wide variety of organizations, such as schools, hospitals, libraries, foundations, clinics, churches, and not-for-profit agencies.

Institutional markets are characterized by widely diverse buying practices. Some institutional purchasers behave like government purchasers because laws and political considerations determine their buying procedures. Many of these institutions, such as schools and prisons, may even be managed by government units.

Buying practices can differ between institutions of the same type. In a small hospital, the chief dietitian may approve all food purchases, while in a larger medical facility, food purchases may go through a committee consisting of the dietitian and a business manager, purchasing agent, and cook. Other hospitals may belong to buying groups, perhaps health maintenance organizations or local hospital cooperatives. Still others may contract with outside firms to prepare and serve all meals.

Within a single institution, multiple-buying influences may affect decisions. Many institutions, staffed by professionals such as physicians, nurses, researchers, and instructors, may also employ purchasing managers or even entire purchasing departments. Conflicts may arise among these decision

figure 6.7
Goods and Services Sold Online to the U. S. Government

makers. Professional employees may prefer to make their own purchase decisions and resent giving up control to the purchasing staff. This conflict can force a business marketer to cultivate both professionals and purchasers. A detailer for a pharmaceutical firm must convince physicians and nurses of the value to patients of a certain drug while simultaneously convincing the hospital's purchasing department that the firm offers competitive prices, good delivery schedules, and prompt service. Baxter Healthcare, a large manufacturer of health-care products including vaccines, medication delivery systems, transfusion therapies, and the like, must maintain relationships with the hospitals, doctors' groups, and other health-care centers that it serves as well as its suppliers. The firm's marketers must anticipate customers' needs, ensure quality, and determine delivery schedules to successfully fulfill purchases.[43]

Group purchasing is an important factor in institutional markets because many of the organizations join cooperative associations to pool purchases for quantity discounts. Universities may join the Education and Institutional Purchasing Cooperative; hospitals may belong to regional associations; and chains of profit-oriented hospitals like HCA Healthcare can also negotiate quantity discounts. Central headquarters staff usually handles purchasing for all members of such a chain.

Diverse practices in institutional markets pose special challenges for B2B marketers. They must maintain flexibility in developing strategies for dealing with a range of customers, from large cooperative associations and chains to midsize purchasing departments and institutions to individuals. Buying centers can work with varying members, priorities, and levels of expertise. Discounts and effective distribution functions play important roles in obtaining—and keeping—institutions as customers.

CHALLENGES OF INTERNATIONAL MARKETS

To sell successfully in international markets, business marketers must consider buyers' attitudes and cultural patterns within areas where they operate. In Asian markets, a firm must maintain a local presence to sell products. Personal relationships are also important to business deals in Asia. Companies that want to expand globally often need to establish joint ventures with local partners. International marketers must also be poised to respond to shifts in cultural values.

Local industries, economic conditions, geographic characteristics, and legal restrictions must also be considered in international marketing. Many local industries in Spain specialize in food and wine; therefore, a maker of forklift trucks might market smaller vehicles to Spanish companies than to German firms, which require bigger, heavier trucks to serve the needs of that nation's large automobile industry.

Remanufacturing—production to restore worn-out products to like-new condition—can be an important marketing strategy in a nation that cannot afford to buy new products. Developing countries often purchase remanufactured factory machinery, which costs 35 to 60 percent less than new equipment.

Foreign governments represent another important business market. In many countries, the government or state-owned companies dominate certain industries, such as construction and other infrastructure sales. Additional examples include airport and highway construction, telephone system equipment, and computer networking equipment. Sales to a foreign government can involve an array of regulations. Many governments, like that of the U.S., limit foreign participation in their defense programs. Joint ventures and countertrade are common, as are local content laws, which mandate domestic production of a certain percentage of a business product's components.

Strategic Implications of Marketing in the 21st Century

TO develop marketing strategies for the B2B sector, marketers must first understand the buying practices that govern the segment they are targeting, whether it is the commercial market, trade industries, government, or institutions. Similarly, when selling to a specific organization, strategies must take into account the many factors that influence purchasing. B2B marketers must identify people who play the various roles in the buying decision. They must also understand how these members interact with one another, other members of their own organizations, and outside vendors. Marketers must be careful to direct their marketing efforts to their organization, to broader environmental influences, and to individuals, who operate within the constraints of the firm's buying center. ◆◆◆

REVIEW OF CHAPTER OBJECTIVES

① Explain each of the components of the business-to-business (B2B) market.

The B2B market is divided into four segments: the commercial market, trade industries, governments, and institutions. The commercial market consists of individuals and firms that acquire products to be used, directly or indirectly, to produce other goods and services. Trade industries are organizations, such as retailers and wholesalers, that purchase for resale to others. The primary purpose of government purchasing, at federal, state, and local levels, is to provide some form of public benefit. The fourth segment, institutions, includes a diverse array of organizations, such as hospitals, schools, museums, and not-for-profit agencies.

1.1. Which is the largest segment of the business market?
1.2. What role does the Internet play in the B2B market?
1.3. What role do resellers play in the B2B market?

② Describe the major approaches to segmenting business-to-business (B2B) markets.

Business markets can be segmented by (1) demographics, (2) customer type, (3) end-use application, and (4) purchasing situation. The North American Industrial Classification System (NAICS) helps further classify types of customers.

2.1. How is customer-based segmentation beneficial to B2B marketers?
2.2. Describe segmentation by purchasing situation.

③ Identify the major characteristics of the business market and its demand.

The major characteristics of the business market are geographic concentration, size and number of buyers, purchase decision procedures, and buyer–seller relationships. The major categories of demand are derived demand, joint demand, inelastic demand, volatile demand, and inventory adjustments.

3.1. How do the sizes and numbers of buyers affect B2B marketers?
3.2. Why are buyer–seller relationships so important in B2B marketing?
3.3. Give an example of each type of demand.

④ Discuss the decision to make, buy, or lease.

Before a company can decide what to buy, it must decide whether to buy at all. A firm has three options: (1) make the good or service in-house; (2) purchase it from another organization; or (3) lease it from another organization. Companies may outsource goods or services formerly produced in-house and shift high-wage jobs from the U.S. to lower-wage locations—a process known as offshoring. Each option has its benefits and drawbacks, including cost and quality control.

4.1. For what reasons might a firm choose an option other than making a good or service in-house?
4.2. Why is outsourcing on the rise?
4.3. How is offshoring different from outsourcing?

⑤ Describe the major influences on business buying behavior.

B2B buying behavior tends to be more complex than individual consumer behavior. More people and time are involved, and buyers often seek several alternative supply sources. The systematic nature of organizational buying is reflected in the use of purchasing managers to direct such efforts. Major organizational purchases may require elaborate and lengthy decision-making processes involving many people. Purchase decisions typically depend on combinations of such factors as price, service, certainty of supply, and product efficiency.

5.1. What are some of the environmental factors that may influence buying decisions?
5.2. Identify organizational factors that may influence buying decisions.
5.3. Describe the role of the professional buyer.

⑥ Outline the steps in the organizational buying process.

The organizational buying process consists of eight general stages: (1) anticipate or recognize a problem/need/opportunity and a general solution; (2) determine characteristics and quantity of needed good or service; (3) describe characteristics and quantity of needed good or service; (4) search for and qualify potential sources; (5) acquire and analyze proposals; (6) evaluate proposals and select supplier(s); (7) select an order routine; and (8) obtain feedback and evaluate performance.

6.1. Why are there more steps in the organizational buying process than in the consumer buying process?
6.2. Explain why feedback between buyers and sellers is important to the marketing relationship.

⑦ Classify organizational buying situations.

Organizational buying situations differ. A straight rebuy is a recurring purchase decision in which a customer stays with an item that has performed satisfactorily. In a modified rebuy, a purchaser is willing to reevaluate available options. New-task buying refers to first-time or unique purchase situations that require considerable effort on the part of the decision makers. Reciprocity involves buying from suppliers that are also customers.

7.1. Give an example of a straight rebuy and a modified rebuy.
7.2. Why is new-task buying more complex than the first two buying situations?

⑧ Explain the buying center concept.

The buying center includes everyone who is involved in some fashion in an organizational buying action. There are five buying center roles: users, gatekeepers, influencers, deciders, and buyers.

8.1. In the buying center, who is a marketer likely to encounter first?
8.2. In the buying center, who has the formal authority to make a purchase?
8.3. What is the purpose of team selling?

⑨ Discuss the challenges of and strategies for marketing to government, institutional, and international buyers.

A government purchase typically involves dozens of interested parties. Social goals and programs influence government purchases. Many U.S. government purchases involve complex contractual guidelines and often require detailed specifications and a bidding process.

Institutional markets are challenging because of their diverse buying influences and practices. Group purchasing is an important factor, since many institutions join cooperative associations to get quantity discounts. An institutional marketer must be flexible enough to develop strategies for dealing with a range of customers. Discounts and effective distribution play an important role.

An effective international business marketer must be aware of foreign attitudes and cultural patterns. Other important factors include economic conditions, geographic characteristics, legal restrictions, and local industries.

9.1. Describe some of the factors that direct U.S. government purchases.

9.2. Why are institutional markets particularly challenging?

9.3. Describe some of the challenges faced by international business marketers.

MARKETING TERMS YOU NEED TO KNOW

business-to-business (B2B) marketing 188
commercial market 190
trade industries 190
reseller 190
customer-based segmentation 192
North American Industrial Classification System (NAICS) 193
end-use application segmentation 193
global sourcing 197
derived demand 197
joint demand 198
inelastic demand 198
outsourcing 200
offshoring 201
value analysis 207
vendor analysis 207
buying center 207

OTHER IMPORTANT MARKETING TERMS

customer relationship management (CRM) 193
just-in-time (JIT)/just-in-time II (JIT II) 199
sole sourcing 199
multiple sourcing 203
merchandisers 204
systems integration 204
category captain 204
straight rebuy 206
modified rebuy 206
new-task buying 206
reciprocity 207
user 207
gatekeeper 208
influencer 208
decider 208
buyer 208
team selling 209
remanufacturing 212

PROJECTS AND TEAMWORK EXERCISES

1. In small teams, research the buying process through which your school purchases the following products:
   a. lab equipment for one of the science labs
   b. the school's telecommunications system
   c. food for the cafeteria
   d. furniture for the dormitories

   Does the buying process differ for any of these products? If so, how?
2. As a team or individually, choose a commercial product, such as computer chips, flour for baking, paint, or equipment, and research and analyze its foreign market potential. Report your findings to the class.
3. In pairs or individually, select a firm in your area and ask to interview the person who is in charge of purchasing. In particular, ask the person about the importance of buyer–seller relationships in his or her industry. Report your findings to the class.
4. In pairs, select a business product in one of two categories—capital or expense—and determine how derived demand will affect the sales of the product. Create a chart showing your findings.
5. As a team, research a firm such as Microsoft or Boeing to learn how it is using outsourcing and/or offshoring. Then report on what you think the benefits and drawbacks to the firm might be.
6. Imagine that you and your teammates are buyers for a firm such as Starbucks, Dick's Sporting Goods, Marriott, or another firm you like. Map out a logical buying process for a new-task purchase for your organization.
7. Form a team to conduct a hypothetical team selling effort for the packaging of products manufactured by a food company such as Kraft or General Mills. Have each team member cover a certain concern, such as package design, delivery, and payment schedules. Present your marketing effort to the class.
8. Conduct further research into the U.S. government's awarding of contracts to businesses who want to provide goods and services for the rebuilding of Iraq. Who seems to have the largest contracts and for what types of services? Which countries are represented? What types of challenges do these firms face?
9. Find an advertisement with marketing messages targeted for an institutional market. Analyze the ad to determine how the marketer has segmented the market, who in the buying center might be the target of the ad, and what other marketing strategies may be apparent.
10. In teams, research the practice of remanufacturing of business products like factory machinery for foreign markets. What challenges do marketers of such products face?

APPLYING CHAPTER CONCEPTS

1. Imagine that you are a wholesaler for dairy products such as yogurt and cheese, which are produced by a cooperative of small farmers. Describe what steps you would take to build relationships with both the producers—farmers—and retailers such as supermarkets.
2. Describe an industry that might be segmented by geographic concentration. Then identify some of the types of firms that might be involved in that industry. Keep in mind that these companies might be involved in other industries as well.
3. Imagine that you are in charge of making the decision to lease or buy a fleet of automobiles for the limousine service for which you work. What factors would influence your decision and why?
4. Do you think online selling to the federal government benefits marketers? What might be some of the drawbacks to this type of selling?

ETHICS EXERCISE

Suppose you work for a well-known local restaurant, and a friend of yours is an account representative for a supplier of restaurant equipment. You know that the restaurant owner is considering upgrading some of the kitchen equipment. Although you have no purchasing authority, your friend has asked you to arrange a meeting with the restaurant owner. You have heard unflattering rumors about this supplier's customer service.

1. Would you arrange the meeting between your friend and your boss?
2. Would you mention the customer-service rumors either to your friend or your boss?
3. Would you try to influence the purchase decision in either direction?

'netWork EXERCISES

1. **American Express Small Business Network**. American Express offers a service it calls Open, which provides financing and other services to small businesses. Visit the American Express Web site and click "Small Business." Make a list of four or five services—both financial and nonfinancial—offered through Open. Make sure to note what American Express considers a "small business."

   http://www.americanexpress.com
2. **Census data**. The Census Bureau is a major source of statistics for marketers. Go to the Census Bureau's Web site and click "Business." Select the most recent *Survey of Manufacturers* you can find. Prepare a brief report summarizing how marketers could use some of the data in the *Survey* to help segment the B2B market. What are some advantages and limitations of using census data?

   http://www.census.gov
3. **Selling to Wal-Mart**. Wal-Mart Stores is the world's largest retailer and has approximately 11,000 different suppliers. Assume your company would like to begin selling products to Wal-Mart. Go to the Wal-Mart Stores Web site and click "Supplier Information." Read the information on supplier standards and prepare a brief report on what you learned.

   http://www.walmartstores.com

Note: Internet Web addresses change frequently. If you don't find the exact sites listed, you may need to access the organization's or company's home page and search from there or use a search engine such as Google.

INFOTRAC CITATIONS AND EXERCISES

Record: A116357402
Marketers use data to help cross-selling.
Christine Blank.
B to B, May 3, 2004 v89 i5 p43

Abstract: More marketers are realizing the value of using customer databases to cross-sell products and services to current customers, particularly across channels. However, in the business-to-business industry, a majority of marketers still do not have an overall picture of whom their customers are and which channels they buy from. Before marketers can use databases to cross-sell effectively, they must be able to properly identify customers and target the executives responsible for making purchasing decisions.

1. According to your text, what is the *buying center concept,* and what are the five different buying center roles in the purchasing decision process?
2. Why is it difficult for business-to-business marketers to know whom their customers are and identify the decision makers and purchasers within an organization?
3. According to the article, what can marketers do to become more successful at selling to other business organizations?

CASE 6.1 Siebel and Sun Microsystems Keep Their Customers Satisfied

It's one thing to talk about customer satisfaction; it is another thing to achieve it. To achieve superior satisfaction among its business customers, marketers at two software companies, Siebel Systems and Sun Microsystems, have come up with an old-fashioned method: Let them talk with each other.

Both companies have instituted reference programs for their B2B customers, in which designated customers who are already satisfied with the services they receive are willing to communicate with potential or new customers. At both Sun and Siebel, suitable customers are nominated—usually by the salespeople who know them best. Then these customers are contacted and asked whether they would like to participate in a reference program. If they decline, that's fine. If they accept, they have a number of options with regard to how they want to participate. They might be willing to take calls or accept visits from prospective customers of Sun or Siebel; they might participate in a customer roundtable or breakfast; they could do speaking engagements or media tours. In addition, they are likely to meet with Sun or Siebel executives on a regular basis for updates. EMI Industries recently hosted calls and granted interviews to trade publications about its experiences with Siebel. Target participated in an ad campaign for Sun. How does this help get Sun's message across? "An ad that says 'Target saves a certain amount per year' means more than just saying, 'Retailers save,'" explains Sun's Aaron Cohen, senior program manager.

The reference relationship benefits everyone. "A reference program is a great way to manage and monitor the health of your customers," notes Pamela Evans, senior director of customer programs and corporate marketing at Siebel. "You're able to track your reference activity, and recognize and reward the customers who are making a significant contribution for you." Customers benefit from greater exposure, such as appearing in ad campaigns. And potential customers get the information they need in a credible manner. However, Michael Reagan, president of the National Association of Sales Professionals, warns that companies should not wear out their welcome with customers that have volunteered for the reference program. "If they say they're doing too many [references], find out if that's burnout from the number of references . . . or if there's a problem with the relationship. You need to have other means of measuring, such as customer satisfaction questionnaires." Pamela Evans also advises against enrolling too many customers too soon in the program, suggesting that it's better to establish a long-term relationship first.

In the end, the reference program is all about relationships. With a reference program, "you understand your users. It increases their satisfaction, and your revenues, when you're keeping in close contact with the customers in your reference program," says Evans.

Questions for Critical Thinking

1. In what ways do the reference programs create added value for Siebel's and Sun Microsystems' B2B customers?
2. How might the reference programs help Siebel and Sun Microsystems predict demand for their products?

Sources: Siebel Web site, http://www.siebel.com, accessed February 9, 2004; Sun Microsystems Web site, http://www.sun.com, accessed February 9, 2004; Catherine Arnold, "Reference Programs Keep B-to-B Customers Satisfied," *Marketing News,* August 18, 2003, pp. 4–5.

VIDEO CASE 6.2 Technomic Helps Businesses Serve Good Food

The written case on Technomic, Inc. appears on page VC-7. The recently filmed Technomic, Inc. video is designed to expand and highlight the concepts in this chapter and the concepts and questions covered in the written video case.

chapter 7

Serving Global Markets

chapter objectives

① Describe the importance of international marketing from the perspectives of the individual firm and the nation.

② Identify the major components of the environment for international marketing.

③ Outline the basic functions of GATT, WTO, NAFTA, the proposed FTAA, and the European Union.

④ Compare the alternative strategies for entering international markets.

⑤ Differentiate between a global marketing strategy and a multidomestic marketing strategy.

⑥ Describe the alternative marketing mix strategies used in international marketing.

⑦ Explain the attractiveness of the U.S. as a target market for foreign marketers.

MANCHESTER UNITED TRIES TO SCORE WITH SOCCER IN AMERICA

Parents all over the U.S. are learning how to yell "Offsides!" at the ref just as knowledgeably as they jeer "Safe!" at the umpire. Youth soccer has grown rapidly to become nearly as popular as Little League baseball, and it appeals to boys and girls equally, filling ball fields every weekend and raising American awareness of the world's most beloved sport.

About 28 million Americans play soccer (known as "football" to the rest of the world). A whole new generation of young players is growing up with the game, and a recent survey by the Sporting Goods Manufacturing Association (SGMA) reports that the number of high school varsity soccer players has increased 85 percent since 1990. Nearly half those players are female. Soccer relies on speed and skill more than on physical aggression, and in contrast to such big-league sports as basketball, football, and rugby, player size isn't a big constraint and equipment needs are minimal. So you might imagine that professional soccer is poised to sweep the U.S. with the same passionate fever that grips Europeans, Latin Americans, and Asians devoted to the game.

But you would be wrong. Except for the youth leagues springing up in every community, soccer has never really caught on in America. With game attendance low, the men's professional league is struggling financially, and the women's professional league, founded in the aftermath of the U.S.'s thrilling 1999 Women's World Cup victory, folded despite the presence of international stars like Mia Hamm and Brandi Chastain. "I think soccer in the U.S. is a participation sport and not a spectator sport," says one sports marketing consultant.

But if the consultant thinks soccer isn't a spectator sport, he needs to look at the TV ratings. Ask "What's the sporting event with the highest ratings?" of a local sports fan and you'll likely get this knee-jerk response: "The Super Bowl, of course." But the 150 million viewers who tune in the annual NFL championship are dwarfed by the World Cup audience. The most recent battle for soccer bragging rights between Germany and Brazil drew 1.1 billion.

Where homegrown professional soccer organizations have failed, however, invaders from England are hoping to succeed. Perhaps the most lucrative and powerful sports franchise in the world, the Manchester United club (known as Man U) has already completed its first American tour, playing exhibition matches to sold-out stadiums and looking for corporate investors, and it plans to return for repeat performances. In fact, it must return—and it must succeed—because it has nearly saturated its European and Asian markets.

Operating with a sophisticated business model and running debt-free, Man U, a publicly traded company, boasts 53 million fans worldwide and earns annual revenues of over $260 million. It has highly profitable partnerships with multinational firms Pepsi, Budweiser, and Nike, which is paying $450 million over 13 years for the right to design and supply Man U's clothing and equipment. Nike will also take over Man U's merchandising operations, helping the club expand its global reach. Man U routinely sells out the 67,700-seat stadium it built and owns. It sells branded merchandise such as mugs, bedsheets, souvenirs, and clothing in its retail store, by mail order, and online. The team even has its own TV network, with 75,000 paying subscribers who receive game highlights and player interviews over four channels seven days a week. It has an online auction business and a string of new restaurants (called Red Café) in locations as far away as Singapore. It even sells Man U–branded credit cards and offers financial services such as mortgages, insurance, and consumer loans. Says the club's marketing director, Peter Draper, "We are trying to package loyalty and affinity."

Despite the loss of its biggest star, the charismatic, golden-haired midfielder David Beckham, whom the club traded to the Spanish team Réal Madrid for $40 million, Man U is confident it can leverage its enormous brand recognition to crack the U.S. market. Maggie English, a London fan of the world's most popular team, says, "I have traveled all over Europe to support them. I went eight years without missing a game. I went to Turkey three times for the day and Russia once for the day to see them play." Gillette, with about 60 percent of its sales outside the United States, recently signed the European soccer superstar to a $10 million global endorsement deal for its razors. Beckham, who already has lucrative global gigs with Pepsi, Adidas, and Vodafone, is rapidly moving into the multimillion-dollar sports marketing territory once limited to Michael Jordan and Tiger Woods.

Without Beckham, and with only exhibition soccer, televised matches devoid of halftime shows, and branded merchandise to tempt them, how fervently will Americans finally embrace soccer? Time will tell. In the meantime, Major League Soccer has shown new life in recent years, securing a network deal for broadcasts each Saturday during the season. In addition, D.C. United outbid Man U and signed teenage soccer phenom Freddy Adu. While Adu, now a U.S. citizen who immigrated from Ghana in 1997, may not be another Beckham, he is considered the world's best young player and the youngest player at the top level of pro team sports in the U.S. in over a century. With a $500,000 contract and a $1 million endorsement deal with Nike, he is also one of the richest.[1]

Chapter Overview

U.S. and foreign companies, including those based in the European Union, are crossing national boundaries in unprecedented numbers in search of new markets and profits. International trade now accounts for at least 25 percent of the U.S. gross domestic product (GDP), compared with 5 percent 30 years ago. Figure 7.1 shows the top 10 nations with which the U.S. trades. Those 10 countries account for nearly 70 percent of U.S. imports and two-thirds of U.S. exports.

International trade can be divided into two categories: **exporting,** marketing domestically produced goods and services abroad, and **importing,** purchasing foreign goods and services. International trade is vital to a nation and its marketers for several reasons. It expands markets, makes production and distribution economies possible, allows companies to explore growth opportunities in other nations, and makes them less dependent on economic conditions in their home nations. Many also find that global marketing and international trade can help them meet customer demand, reduce costs, and provide valuable information on potential markets around the world.

For North American marketers, international trade is especially important because the U.S. and Canadian economies represent a mature market for many products. Outside North America, however, it is a different story. Economies in many parts of sub-Saharan Africa, Asia, Latin America, Europe, and the Middle East are growing rapidly. This opens up new markets for U.S. products as consumers in these areas have more money to spend and as the need for American goods and services by foreign companies expands. Exports of high-tech capital goods account for more than one-third of U.S total exports worldwide—the largest segment at a whopping $291 billion.[2] International trade also builds employment. The United Nations estimates that 65,000 transnational corporations are operating today, with more than 850,000 foreign affiliates. Those affiliates account for about 54 million employees.[3] Your next job, in fact, might involve global marketing, since export-related jobs play an important role in the U.S. economy.

Briefly Speaking

Manchester United are the Yankees of soccer. It's probably the Yankees on steroids.

Randy Bernstein
owner, Premier Partnerships sports consultancy

International marketers carefully evaluate the marketing concepts described in earlier chapters. However, transactions that cross national borders involve additional considerations. For example, different laws, varying levels of technological capability, economic conditions, cultural and business norms, and consumer preferences often require new strategies. Companies that want to market their products worldwide must reconsider each of the marketing variables (product, distribution, promotion, and price) in terms of the global marketplace. To succeed in global marketing, today's marketers answer questions such as: How do our products fit into a foreign market? How can we turn potential threats into opportunities? Which strategic alternatives will work in global markets?

Many of the answers to these questions can be

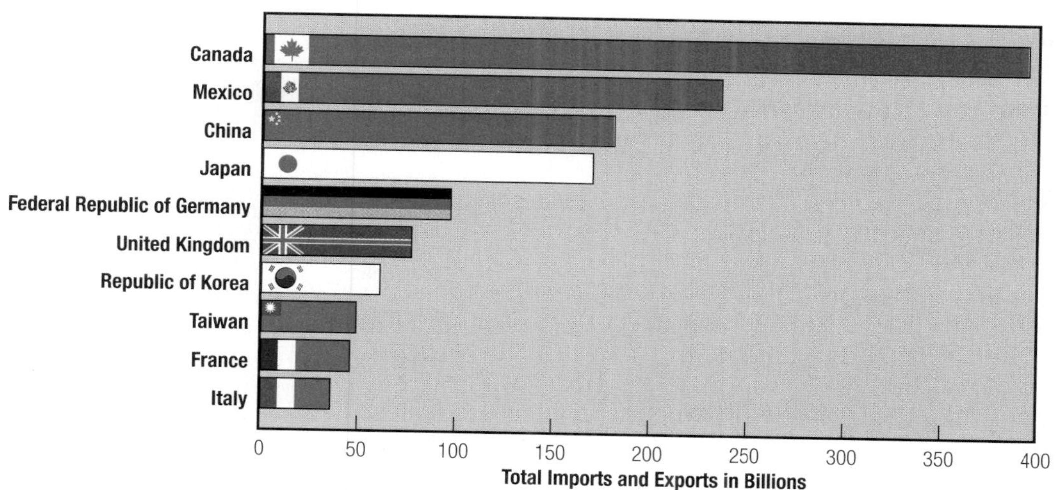

Source: Data from the U.S. Census Bureau, "Top Ten Countries with Which the U.S. Trades," December 2004, http://www.census.gov.

figure 7.1

Top 10 U.S. Trading Partners

exporting Marketing domestically produced goods and services in foreign countries.

importing Purchasing foreign goods, services, and raw materials.

found by studying techniques used by successful international marketers. This chapter first considers the importance and characteristics of the global marketplace. It then examines the international marketing environment, the trend toward multinational economic integration, and the steps that most firms take to enter the global marketplace. Next, the importance of developing an international marketing mix is discussed. The chapter closes with a look at the U.S. as a target market for foreign marketers. ◆◆◆

THE IMPORTANCE OF GLOBAL MARKETING

1 **Describe the importance of international marketing from the perspectives of the individual firm and the nation.**

As the list of the world's 10 largest corporations shown in Table 7.1 reveals, half of these companies are headquartered in the U.S. For most U.S. companies—both large and small—global marketing is rapidly becoming a necessity. The demand for foreign products in the fast-growing economies of Pacific Rim and other Asian nations offers one example of the benefits of thinking globally. In a recent year, U.S. exports to Asia rose 37 percent to about $200 billion—almost twice its exports to Europe. This surge is partly because Asian consumers believe American goods are higher quality and a better value than those made in their own countries. International marketers recognize how the slogan "Made in the USA" yields tremendous selling power throughout the world. As a result, overseas sales are important revenue sources for many U.S. firms.

Over the last two decades, U.S. exports have grown an average of 10 percent each year, with the No. 1 export during this time period being agricultural products. Other products included among the top five U.S. exports are electrical machinery, computers and office equipment, general industrial machinery, and motor vehicle parts. Among the leading U.S. firms in terms of the portion of their revenues generated from exports are Boeing, Intel, Motorola, Caterpillar, and Sun Microsystems.

Wal-Mart currently ranks as the world's largest private employer (1.5 million people) and largest retailer (annual sales are 50 percent greater than Target, Sears, Costco, and Kmart combined). And although it recently passed longtime leaders ExxonMobil and General Motors as America's largest corporation, its sights are clearly aimed at global dominance. The retail giant is currently devoting billions of dollars in expansion efforts abroad in Great Britain, the European mainland, Japan, and South America. After some early stumbles with foreign languages, customs, and regulations, the Bentonville, Arkansas-based company is beginning to gain its stride overseas, planning to open almost one store a day this year. Propelled by its highly sophisticated global inventory management and a passion for

table 7.1 The World's 10 Largest Marketers Ranked by Sales

RANK	COMPANY	COUNTRY OF ORIGIN
1	Wal-Mart Stores	United States
2	ExxonMobil	United States
3	General Motors	United States
4	Royal Dutch/Shell Group	Netherlands
5	British Petroleum (BP)	United Kingdom
6	Ford Motor Co.	United States
7	DaimlerChrysler	Germany
8	Toyota Motor Corp.	Japan
9	General Electric	United States
10	Mitsubishi	Japan

Source: Data from "The Global 2000: 2003," *Forbes,* July 3, 2003, http://www.forbes.com.

offering consumers a widening choice of products at the lowest possible price, the retail giant accounts for 10 percent of U.S. imports from China.[4]

The rapid globalization of business and the boundless nature of the Internet have made it possible for every marketer to become an international marketer. However, becoming an Internet international marketer is not necessarily easy. While larger firms have the advantage of more resources and wider distribution systems, smaller companies can build Web sites for as little as a few hundred dollars and can bring products to market quickly. Beth and Lou Drucker began their wedding supplier referral service in 1996 with $3,000. Recently, the couple took their business online at http://www.newyorkmetroweddings.com. The site was an instant hit and remains so, with about 300,000 visitors per month. Within 12 months, the company tripled in size.[5]

Just as some firms depend on foreign and Internet sales, others rely on purchasing raw materials abroad as input for their domestic manufacturing operations. A North Carolina furniture manufacturer may depend on purchases of South American mahogany, while 21st century furniture retailers are taking advantage of increased Chinese-made styling and quality and their traditionally low prices. The top five U.S. imports are computers and office equipment, crude oil, clothing, telecommunications equipment, and agricultural products.

SERVICE AND RETAIL EXPORTS

Manufacturing no longer accounts for the lion's share of annual production output in the U.S. Today, three of every five dollars included in the nation's gross domestic product (GDP) comes from services—banking, entertainment, business and technical services, retailing, and communications. Only about 40 percent of annual output is derived from the manufacturing sector. This profound shift from a largely manufacturing to a largely service economy is also reflected in the nation's exports.

In addition to agricultural products and manufactured goods, the U.S. is the world's largest exporter of services and retailing. Of the approximately $290 billion in annual U.S. service exports, over half comes from travel and tourism—money spent by foreign nationals visiting the U.S. Tourism is the third largest U.S. industry, contributing $430 billion to the economy each year, and is responsible for creating more than $6 billion in travel and tourism-related jobs. With 102 million tourists per year, the U.S. ranks second only to China in visitors. By 2020, tourists will spend $2 trillion during their international travels. Vacation marketers look to attract and serve customers on a global basis. The Hilton HHonors® program allows travelers to earn both hotel points and airline miles for the same stay at more than 2,500 Hilton Family hotels worldwide—including Hilton®, Conrad®, Doubletree®, Embassy Suites Hotels®, Hampton Inn®, Hampton Inn & Suites®, Hilton Garden Inn®, Hilton Grand Vacations Club®, Homewood Suites by Hilton®, and Scandic hotels.[6]

The most profitable U.S. service exports are business and technical services, such as engineering, financial, computing, legal services, insurance, and entertainment.[7] Worldwide Internet services revenues grew an enormous 71 percent to almost $8 billion during a recent 12-month period.

The financial services industry, already a major presence outside North America, is expanding globally via the Internet. Nearly half the world's active Web population visits a finance Web site at least once a month, with online stock trading and banking leading the way. And more than one of every four Europeans with Internet access currently banks online. By 2005, nearly 60 million French, German, British, Italian, and Spanish consumers were banking online.[8] A glance at the increasing number of foreign companies listed on the New York Stock Exchange illustrates the importance of global financial services.

A number of global service exporters are household names in the U.S.: American Express, AT&T, Citigroup, Disney, and Allstate Insurance. Many earn a substantial percentage of their revenues from international sales. Others are smaller firms, such as the many software firms that have found overseas markets receptive to their products. Still others are nonprofit organizations such as the United States Postal Service, which is attempting to increase overall revenues by operating a worldwide delivery service, as illustrated in Figure 7.2. The service competes with for-profit firms like DHL, UPS, and Federal Express.

The entertainment industry is another major service exporter. Movies, TV shows, and music groups often travel to the ends of the earth to entertain their audiences. Almost a century of exposure to U.S.-made films, television programs, and more recently, music video clips has made international viewers more familiar with American culture and geography than any other nation on earth. However, some markets are more receptive to American entertainment than others depending on their own culture and language barriers. India and some Asian countries have their own entertainment industries, complete with stars, and are likely to be less interested in American entertainers and products.

COURTESY OF HILTON HOSPITALITY, INC.

The global coverage and international reputation of the Hilton name combine to generate additional sales revenues in the U.S. and around the world as both business and vacation travelers from the U.S. and other countries select accommodations for their stays. The 160 upscale Doubletree Hotels, Suites, Resorts, and Clubs, all members of the Hilton Family of Hotels, offer different services to meet specific traveler needs, including a health club, complete meeting and banquet facilities, and other luxury amenities. In addition, guests can earn airline miles and hotel points with the Hilton HHonors guest reward program. These added values are designed to enhance customer loyalty through rewards for heavy users.

U.S. retailers, ranging from Victoria's Secret, Foot Locker, and The Gap to Office Depot and Costco, are opening stores around the world at rapid paces. Amway Corp. opened about 100 retail outlets in China after its traditional direct-sales method was banned by the government, and the marketer of household and personal care products is generating annual sales of $700 million from its Chinese customers. Krispy Kreme has opened its first British store on the premises of Harrod's department store and plans to open 25 more shops over the next few years. Starbucks' expansion into hundreds of stores in Germany, Spain, Britain, and Japan has been aggressive if not yet profitable. Still, the firm opened its first French café in Paris in 2004. And McDonald's 3,800 stores in Japan are fine-tuning their appeal to young professionals with a rotating menu of more sophisticated offerings like ratatouille burgers, smoked beef sandwiches with onions and tomatoes, and tofu burgers.[9]

BENEFITS OF GOING GLOBAL

Besides generating additional revenue, firms expand their operations outside their home country to gain other benefits, including new insights into consumer behavior, alternative distribution strategies, and advance notice of new products. By setting up foreign offices and production facilities, marketers may encounter new products, new approaches to distribution, or clever new promotions that they may

figure 7.2

The U.S. Postal Service's Global Delivery Service: Competing with For-Profit Marketers by Offering Customers Speedy Global Coverage and Competitive Prices

be able to apply successfully in their domestic market or in other international markets.

Global marketers are typically well positioned to compete effectively with foreign competitors. A major key to achieving success in foreign markets is a firm's ability to adapt its products to local preferences and culture. Toyota Motor Corp. recently had to withdraw magazine and newspaper ads it ran during a marketing campaign in China for its Prado Land Cruiser SUV. Stone lions in the ads were "intended to reflect Prado's imposing presence," but they reminded some of lions flanking a bridge near Beijing where Japan's invasion of China began in 1937. And the word *Prado* can translate into "rule by force" or "overbearing" in Chinese.[10]

Since firms must perform the marketing functions of buying, selling, transporting, storing, standardizing and grading, financing, risk taking, and obtaining market information in both domestic and global markets, some may question the wisdom of treating international marketing as a distinct subject. After all, international marketing is marketing; a firm performs the same functions and works toward the same objectives in both domestic and international marketing. As the chapter will explain, however, both similarities and differences influence strategies for international and domestic marketing.

1. Why has global marketing become a necessity for U.S. firms?
2. What are some of the major goods and services the U.S. exports?
3. List three benefits of going global.

THE INTERNATIONAL MARKETPLACE

Today, it is rare to find a U.S. firm that never ventures outside its domestic market. Even if it focuses almost entirely on the domestic market, which is huge in its own right, it may look overseas for raw materials or component parts or it may face foreign competition in its home market. In addition, since most domestic marketers maintain a Web site, they may receive product inquiries or orders from international purchasers who located their home page.

Those who venture abroad may find the international marketplace far different from the domestic one they are accustomed to. Market sizes, buyer behavior, and marketing practices all vary. To be successful, international marketers must do their homework, capitalize on similarities, and carefully evaluate all market segments in which they expect to compete.

MARKET SIZE

From the dawn of civilization until the 1800s, world population grew to about 1 billion people. It almost doubled by 1900, and today, over 6 billion people inhabit the planet. According to Census Bureau projections, world population will increase to nearly 8 billion by 2025. Ninety-six percent of the increase in world population occurs in less-developed regions such as Africa, Asia, and Latin America. Population growth rates in affluent countries, however, have slowed to 0.4 percent annually—one-fifth the annual growth of less-developed countries. What this all means is that, over the next quarter-century, firms will have to adapt their goods and services to meet the needs and wants of growing numbers of young consumers in developing countries.

One-fifth of the world's population—1.2 billion people—lives in China. Africa is growing fastest at 2.8 percent a year, followed by Latin America at 1.9 percent and Asia at 1.7 percent. Average birthrates are dropping around the world due to family planning efforts, but death rates are declining even more rapidly and people are living longer. Although African birthrates are still high—six children per woman—European birthrates have fallen considerably, with couples averaging only one or two children.[11] All this information is important to marketers as they try to target these markets for their goods and services.

The global marketplace is increasingly an urban one. Today, almost 50 percent of its people live in large cities. As a result, city populations are swelling: 39 cities currently have a population of 5 million or more. Mexico City, whose influx of residents has surpassed the population of both London and Tokyo, currently ranks as the world's largest city. The Mexican capital city is expected to grow to 31 million by 2010. Increased urbanization will expand the need for transportation, housing, machinery, and services.

The growing size and urbanization of the international marketplace do not necessarily mean all foreign markets offer the same potential. Another important influence on market potential is a nation's economic development stage. In a subsistence economy such as Nepal or Sudan, most people engage in agriculture and earn low incomes, supporting few opportunities for international trade of any magnitude. In a newly industrialized country, such as Brazil or South Korea, growth in manufacturing creates demand for consumer products and industrial goods such as high-tech equipment. Industrial nations, including the U.S., Japan, and countries in Western Europe, trade manufactured goods and services among themselves and export to less-developed countries. Although these wealthy countries account for just a small percentage of the world's population, they produce over half its output.

As a nation develops, an increasingly affluent, educated, and cosmopolitan middle class emerges. India's middle class includes nearly 300 million people, a number larger than the entire U.S. population. India's processed-food producers and marketers are now facing global competition as a result of economic reforms and market liberalization. But marketers in India must overcome an underdeveloped **infrastructure**, the underlying foundation for modern life and efficient marketing that includes transportation and communications networks, banking, utilities, and public services. In addition, cultural differences and language barriers frequently exist. On the other end of the scale is Japan, a highly industrialized, educated country with a sophisticated infrastructure that includes such high-speed transportation modes as the bullet train. As Figure 7.3 shows, efficient transportation systems are essential components of the infrastructures of Japan, the U.S., and other highly industrialized countries.

infrastructure Nation's basic system of transportation networks, communications systems, and energy facilities.

DIGITAL VISION

figure 7.3

Efficient Transportation Systems: Important Component of a Nation's Infrastructure

International marketers see much growth in middle-income households occurring in the booming East Asian economies such as China, Malaysia, Singapore, South Korea, and Thailand, as well as in Mexico, South America, and sub-Saharan Africa. These new middle-class consumers have both the desire for consumer goods, including luxury and leisure goods and services, and money to pay for them. Many Chinese firms that have traditionally served as manufacturers for Western brand-name products are now poised to take advantage of the growing markets at home with brand names of their own. See the "Marketing Hit" feature for their story.

BUYER BEHAVIOR

Buyer behavior differs among nations and often among market segments within a country. Marketers must carefully match their marketing strategies to local customs, tastes, and living conditions. Even the Coca-Cola Co. can't go to the bank on its name alone in foreign countries. In Japan, for instance, sales of Coke have recently declined, and as the Japanese population ages, Coke may continue to lose customers.[12] Still, Coke commands about half the global soft-drink market and generates 60 percent of its sales from international markets by varying its product emphasis in different parts of the world. In Japan, it heavily promotes Leaf, a new canned-tea product that has become a hot seller there. The reason for the shift: Soft drinks make up only 20 percent of nonalcoholic beverage sales in Japan.[13]

Meanwhile, the U.S. video store Blockbuster decided to shut down all 24 of its stores in Hong Kong. Citing high operating costs, Blockbuster may also jettison plans to enter the Chinese market due to rampant video piracy and the spread of bootleg copies that sell for less than a dollar.[14] Piracy is difficult to control overseas and is fueled in part by a technologically sophisticated market eager for the newest films and video games.

Differences in buying patterns require marketing executives to complete considerable research before entering a foreign market. Sometimes the marketer's own organization or a U.S.-based research firm can provide needed information. In other cases, only a foreign-based marketing research organization can tell marketers what they need to know. Regardless of who conducts the research, investigators must focus on six different areas before advising a company to enter a foreign market:

1. *Demand.* Do foreign consumers need the company's good or service?
2. *Competitive environment.* How do supplies currently reach the market?
3. *Economic environment.* What is the state of the nation's economic health?

marketing hit: Made—and Branded—in China

Background. China already serves as a high-quality, low-cost outsourcing location for manufacturers based in other nations—for instance, 30 percent of the world's microwaves are made there under 80 different foreign brand names—but the next step for its marketers is to develop China's own brands. With a rapidly growing middle class, China offers big opportunities at home as well as abroad.

The Challenge. Even though Chinese-made goods fill American store shelves, Chinese marketers have yet to establish a truly global brand. You probably aren't using a Lenovo personal computer or a Ningbo Bird cell phone, and chances are you've never heard of Haier appliances. In addition to the lack of global awareness of Chinese brands, many Chinese firms find they must overcome an image problem. They must change customer perceptions of low quality while maintaining low prices and building reputations based on product performance and customer service. They also face tough competition at home from both domestic and foreign brands, and many are not experienced at developing expansion plans or anticipating the changing needs of customers thousands of miles away. Realizing the difficulty of building a brand in a country where intellectual property is not protected adequately, Chinese companies traditionally have stayed at home—and competed on price. Their approach to global markets has been to attach foreign brands on products they produce for international marketers.

4. *Social-cultural environment.* How do cultural factors affect business opportunities?
5. *Political-legal environment.* Do any legal restrictions complicate entering the market?
6. *Technological environment.* To what degree are technological innovations used by consumers in the market?

1. What characteristics of the international marketplace differ from the domestic markets in the U.S.?
2. Define *infrastructure.*
3. What are the six different areas that marketers must study before advising their company to enter a foreign market?

THE INTERNATIONAL MARKETING ENVIRONMENT

(2) Identify the major components of the environment for international marketing.

As in domestic markets, the environmental factors discussed in Chapter 3 have a powerful influence on the development of international marketing strategies. Marketers must pay close attention to changing demand patterns as well as competitive, economic, social-cultural, political-legal, and technological influences when they venture abroad.

INTERNATIONAL ECONOMIC ENVIRONMENT

A nation's size, per-capita income, and stage of economic development determine its prospects as a host for international business expansion. Nations with low per-capita incomes may be poor markets for expensive industrial machinery but good ones for agricultural hand tools. These nations cannot afford the technical equipment that powers an industrialized society. Wealthier countries may offer prime markets for many U.S. industries, particularly those producing consumer goods and services and advanced industrial products.

But some less-industrialized countries are growing fast. India and China, for example, may rival the U.S. in world economic importance in a generation or two. Although per-capita income in the U.S. is eight times that of China and about eleven times that of India, both those countries have much larger populations, which partially offsets the per-capita numbers. Their ability to import technology and foreign capital, as well as to train scientists and engineers and invest in research and development,

The economic dominance of the U.S. is already over. What is emerging is a world economy. India is becoming a powerhouse very fast.

Peter F. Drucker (b. 1909)
American business philosopher

The Strategy. Chinese firms are moving away from their traditional—but profitable—role as the manufacturing link in the supply chains of foreign firms. Today, they are not only developing their own labels but also offering high quality, low prices, warranties, and after-sale service. TCL International Holdings Ltd., a manufacturer of branded televisions for foreign multinationals, sends repair technicians on motorcycles within 24 hours of customer complaints and offers loaner TVs during service.

In addition to developing their own brands, several Chinese firms are buying midsize foreign companies, brands and all. Techtronic Industries manufactured Dirt Devil vacuums for U.S.-based Royal Appliance Manufacturing Co.; it now owns both Royal and the Dirt Devil brand. Other Chinese firms are winning exclusive licenses, such as Hong Kong's Moulin International Holdings Ltd., which makes Benetton eyeglass frames and has rights to Revlon, Reebok, and Nikon brands as well.

The Outcome. Firms like TCL, Konka Group Ltd., and Sichuan Chang-hong Electric Co. are moving aggressively into nearby markets in Southeast Asia. In Malaysia, for instance, Chinese brands have recently tripled their share of the market for DVDs and 29-inch TVs. China exported more than $23 billion of goods to Southeast Asia in 2002, a 27 percent jump over 2001. Observers predict that as Chinese firms gain market share and experience, they will begin to earn the benefits of their own low-cost manufacturing. "If a Chinese company comes in at a low price," says one electronics industry analyst, "that puts more pressure on everything. It has raised the bar of competition, without a doubt."

Sources: Thomas Hout and Jim Hemerling, "China's Next Great Thing," *Fast Company*, March 2004, pp. 31–32; Clay Chandler, "TV's Mr. Big," *Fortune*, February 9, 2004, pp. 84–88; Gabriel Kahn, "After Years behind the Scenes, Chinese Join the Name Game," *The Wall Street Journal*, December 26, 2003, p. A1; Cris Prystay, "Can China Sell the World on Its Own Labels?" *The Wall Street Journal*, December 18, 2003, p. B1.

ensures that their growth will be rapid and their income gaps with the U.S. will close quickly. China currently exports about $100 billion more goods and services a year to the U.S. than it imports. In 2006, it is expected to pass the U.S. and become No. 1 in Web users with 153 million Chinese online. The nation is currently scrambling to begin automobile production to meet the demands of a growing middle class almost as large as the entire U.S. population. Both India and China have enjoyed higher rates of economic growth in recent years than the U.S., and some analysts project that by mid-century, an integrated Asian economy could account for about half the world's GDP.[15]

Infrastructure, discussed earlier, is another important economic factor to consider when planning to enter a foreign market. An inadequate infrastructure may constrain marketers' plans to manufacture, promote, and distribute goods and services in a particular country. People living in countries blessed by navigable waters often rely on them as inexpensive, relatively efficient alternatives to highways, rail lines, and air transportation. Thai farmers use their nation's myriad rivers to transport their crops. Their boats even become retail outlets in so-called floating markets like the one located outside the capital city of Bangkok.

Marketers expect developing economies to have substandard utility and communications networks. China encountered numerous problems in establishing a 21st century communications industry infrastructure. The Chinese government's answer was to bypass the need for landline telephone connections by leapfrogging technologies and moving directly to cell phones. By 2007, China is expected to have 500 million cell phone users. But Chinese cell phone users pay only a nickel a minute, one of the cheapest rates in the world.[16]

The health-care infrastructure of many developing countries is also a concern for international marketers and their employees. The NetJets message in Figure 7.4 reassures business executives who fly this private airline that emergency medical help will be available to them anywhere in the world, an important consideration in countries with less-developed medical infrastructures.

Briefly Speaking

There have been many definitions of hell, but for the English the best definition is that it is a place where the Germans are the police, the Swedish are the comedians, the Italians are the defence force, Frenchmen dig the roads, the Belgians are the pop singers, the Spanish run the railways, the Turks cook the food, the Irish are the waiters, the Greeks run the government, and the common language is Dutch.

David Frost (b. 1939)

English author and TV-show host

figure 7.4

Overcoming Concerns about Infrastructure: Private Airline NetJets Offers Medical Assistance to Passengers in Developing Nations

COURTESY OF NETJETS, INC.

Changes in exchange rates can also complicate international marketing. An **exchange rate** is the price of one nation's currency in terms of another country's currency. Fluctuations in exchange rates can make a nation's currency more valuable or less valuable compared with those of other nations. Americans traveling to Europe were directly affected by these shifts when they exchanged dollars for euros, only to learn that the currently strong euro meant that it cost more and more dollars to purchase the European currency. As a result, Europe became a more expensive place for Americans to visit—either as tourists or business travelers. Vacation travel patterns began to change, as U.S. travelers increasingly selected domestic destinations or visited neighbors Canada, Mexico, or the island nations of the Caribbean where exchange rates had remained constant or where U.S. currency was accepted at hotels, restaurants, and other local retailers.

At the beginning of this century, most members of the European Union switched to the euro as the replacement to their traditional schillings, francs, and liras. The long-range idea behind the new currency is that switching to a single currency will strengthen Europe's competitiveness in the global marketplace.[17] Russian and many Eastern European currencies are considered *soft currencies* that cannot be readily converted into such hard currencies as the dollar, euro, or Japanese yen. International marketers doing business in these countries may resort to barter, accepting such commodities as oil or timber as payment for exports.

INTERNATIONAL SOCIAL-CULTURAL ENVIRONMENT

Before entering a foreign market, marketers should study all aspects of that nation's culture, including language, education, religious attitudes, and social values. The French love to debate and are comfortable with frequent eye contact. In China, humility is a prized virtue, colors have special significance, and it is insulting to be late. Swedes value consensus and do not use humor in negotiations.[18] The "Etiquette Tips for Marketing Professionals" box offers more

ETIQUETTE TIPS — FOR MARKETING PROFESSIONALS

When in Rome . . .

THE stakes are high when you're trying to make a good impression abroad and aren't sure how business customs differ from those at home. Gesturing too much with your hands in Thailand may draw ridicule, and in Canada, the right gesture made the wrong way, like the victory sign (index and middle fingers outstretched) with palm facing inward instead of outward, will be considered rude. The best preparation is a thorough study of the country you will visit, its culture, and its customs.

Here are a few examples of little things that can matter a lot.

IN CHINA

1. Remember that clocks, straw sandals, handkerchiefs, and the colors white, blue, and black are associated with death and should not be used as gifts.
2. Taste everything you are served, as a courtesy, but eat sparingly, as there may be several courses.
3. Remember that making appointments and being on time are extremely important.
4. Present and receive business cards with both hands, and carry a card case for any cards you are given.

IN SOUTH AFRICA

1. Dress well in public for your host's sake.
2. Remember that gift giving in business is not the norm.
3. Keep in mind that handshakes vary among different ethnic groups.
4. Be prepared for a poolside barbecue—called a *braaivleis*—when dining at the home of a white South African.

IN BRAZIL

1. Dress conservatively for business but avoid wearing yellow and green together (these are the colors of the Brazilian flag).
2. Make business appointments at least two weeks in advance.
3. Remember that touching arms, elbows, and backs is very common.
4. Be on time for business meetings in large cities like Rio and São Paulo, but expect casual chatting first and wait for your host to introduce business topics.

Wherever you go, remember that U.S. customs and practices are not the worldwide norm. Honor and dignity are so important in Asian cultures that some workers have committed suicide upon being fired, Donald Trump style, from their jobs. And even the most established customs can change with time. Saunas, attended naked by Finnish men, were long considered the place where most business deals were made. But since they are closed to women, saunas may now be losing their hold on decision making and advancement in Finland.

Sources: "International Business Etiquette and Manners," http://www.cyborlink.com, accessed February 9, 2004; Jennifer Bensko Ha, "Board Meeting at 4; Nudity Required," *Fortune,* October 6, 2003, p. 30; "Global Firing Etiquette," *Sales & Marketing Management,* September 2003, p. 18.

examples of cultural differences that arise in business dealings abroad—and how easy it is to offend clients, business partners, and others when you are unaware of these differences.

Language plays an important role in international marketing. Table 7.2 lists the world's 10 most frequently spoken languages. Marketers must make sure not only to use the appropriate language (or languages) for a country but also ensure that the message is correctly translated and conveys the intended meaning. Abbreviations and slang words and phrases may also cause misunderstandings when marketing abroad. Among the most humorous—and disastrous—language faux pas by marketers are product slogans that are carelessly translated, such as Kentucky Fried Chicken's "Finger lickin' good," which was translated into Chinese as "Eat your fingers off," and Perdue Farms, Inc.'s "It takes a tough man to make a tender chicken," which in Spanish became, "It takes a sexually excited man to make a chicken affectionate."[19]

exchange rate Price of one nation's currency in terms of another country's currency.

table 7.2 *The World's Most Frequently Spoken Languages*

RANK	LANGUAGE	NUMBER OF SPEAKERS
1	Mandarin (Chinese)	1 billion +
2	English	508 million
3	Hindustani	497 million
4	Spanish	392 million
5	Russian	277 million
6	Arabic	246 million
7	Bengali	211 million
8	Portuguese	191 million
9	Malay-Indonesian	159 million
10	French	129 million

Source: Data from "The Ten Most Widely Spoken Languages in the World," http://www.soyouwanna.com, accessed January 13, 2004.

INTERNATIONAL TECHNOLOGICAL ENVIRONMENT

More than any innovation since the telephone, Internet technology has made it possible for both large and small firms to be connected to the entire world. The Internet transcends political, economic, and cultural barriers, reaching to every corner of the globe. It has made it possible for traditional brick-and-mortar retailers to add new e-commerce channels. It also assists developing nations in becoming competitive with industrialized nations.

The Internet is truly a global medium that allows seamless communications and business transactions between individual consumers and multinational companies. It is critical that 21st century marketers understand how the Web is reshaping social and cultural values.

Technology presents challenges for international marketers that extend beyond the Internet and other telecommunications innovations. A major issue involving food marketers competing in Europe is genetic reengineering. Although U.S. grocery shelves are filled with foods grown with genetically modified organisms (GMOs), most Americans are unaware they are eating GMO foods because no labeling disclosures are required. In Britain and other European countries, where GMO foods are often referred to as "frankenfoods," the story is quite different. Activists are pushing for labeling laws to inform shoppers that these foods are "not naturally grown" or to ban them altogether. Marketers of agricultural commodities and packaged goods are already taking actions in response to these concerns. Gerber recently reformulated its baby foods to remove all ingredients containing GMOs.[20]

The new trade routes of the [21st century] are laser flashes and satellite beams. The cargo is not silk or spices, but technology, information, and ideas.

Renato Ruggiero (b. 1930)

Italian-born director general, World Trade Organization

INTERNATIONAL POLITICAL-LEGAL ENVIRONMENT

Global marketers must continually stay abreast of laws and trade regulations in each country in which they compete. Political conditions often influence international marketing as well. Political unrest in places like the Middle East, Afghanistan, Africa, Eastern Europe, Spain, and South America sometimes results in acts of violence, such as destruction of a firm's property or even deaths from bombings or other terrorist acts. As a result, many Western firms have set up internal **political risk assessment (PRA)** units or turned to outside consulting services to evaluate the political risks of the marketplaces in which they operate. In addition, the fall of communism and the transformation of state-dominated industries into privately owned and managed profit-seeking enterprises have been accompanied by a trend toward freer trade among nations.

The political environment also involves labor conditions in different countries. Chinese officials do not respond well to labor unrest, particularly when it spills into the streets in protest. Only a few years ago, government officials jailed labor activist Zhang Shangguang for 10 years for "endangering state security." In 2002, tens of thousands of factory workers surrounded government buildings, demanding that city officials resign because of unpaid employment benefits and back pay. In the past, protests like these were likely to provoke government tactics such as rounding people up, arresting them, silencing them with bribes, and the like. But China's global economic successes are resulting in changes. Constitutional changes that permit more of the freedoms and flexibility of private enterprise are now being considered by the Chinese government. Although these steps are promising, an uncertain climate continues to exist for foreign businesses and investors in many international markets. Still, many choose to pursue their investment in such a large potential market. The situation "hasn't deterred us," says Michael Dell, founder and chairman of Dell Inc. "We [understand] the risk."[21]

The legal environment for U.S. firms operating abroad results from three forces: (1) international law, (2) U.S. law, and (3) legal requirements of host nations. International law emerges from the treaties, conventions, and agreements that exist among nations. The U.S. has many **friendship, commerce, and navigation (FCN) treaties** with other governments. These agreements set terms for various aspects of commercial relations with other countries, such as the right to conduct business in the treaty partner's domestic market. Other international business agreements concern worldwide standards for various products, patents, trademarks, reciprocal tax treaties, export control, international air travel, and international communications.

© LON C. DIEHL/PHOTOEDIT

Many Europeans view the protests against foods grown with genetically modified organisms (GMOs) as an extension of the growing demand for organic foods—both in Europe and the U.S. Although more expensive to produce because they require more intensive use of human resources, organic foods grown without synthetic pesticides or chemicals are the fastest-growing segment of both the U.S. and European grocery industries. In 2006, they accounted for 10 percent of total grocery sales in the U.S.

Since the 1990s, Europe has pushed for mandatory **ISO (International Organization for Standardization) certification**—internationally recognized standards that ensure a company's goods, services, and operations meet established quality levels. The organization has two sets of standards: The ISO 9000 series of standards sets requirements for quality in goods and services; the ISO 14000 series sets standards for operations that minimize harm to the environment. Today, many U.S. companies follow these certification standards as well. The International Monetary Fund, another major player in the international legal environment, lends foreign exchange to nations that require it to conduct international trade. These agreements facilitate the entire process of world marketing. However, there are no international laws for corporations—only for governments. So marketers include special provisions in contracts, such as which country's courts have jurisdiction.

The second dimension of the international legal environment, U.S. law, includes various trade regulations, tax laws, and import/export requirements that affect international marketing. One important law, the Export Trading Company Act of 1982, exempts companies from antitrust regulations so that they can form export groups that offer a variety of products to foreign buyers. The law seeks to make it easier for foreign buyers to connect with U.S. exporters. A controversial 1996 law, the Helms-Burton Act, tried to impose trade sanctions against Cuba. Under this law, U.S. corporations and citizens can sue foreign companies and their executives for using expropriated U.S. assets to do business in Cuba. The Foreign Corrupt Practices Act, which makes it illegal to bribe a foreign official in an attempt to solicit new or repeat sales abroad, has had a major impact on international marketing. The act also mandates that adequate accounting controls be installed to monitor internal compliance. Violations can result in a $1 million fine for the firm and a $10,000 fine and five-year imprisonment for the individuals involved. This law has been controversial, mainly because it fails to clearly define what constitutes bribery. The 1988 Trade Act amended the law to include more specific statements of prohibited practices.

Finally, legal requirements of host nations affect foreign marketers. International marketers generally recognize the importance of obeying these legal requirements since even the slightest violation

Solving an Ethical Controversy

MUST AMERICANS ALWAYS PAY MORE FOR PRESCRIPTION DRUGS?

IT is technically illegal to import prescription medications into the U.S. for personal use, but for many years, the Food and Drug Administration (FDA) has overlooked the fact that large numbers of chronically ill or elderly patients—in particular, people living near the Canadian border—have been saving hundreds or even thousands of dollars a year by getting their prescriptions filled abroad. With U.S. drug prices running at two or more times the amount people pay in other countries, and with U.S. drug companies routinely raising those prices even higher, the trickle of drugs from Canada in particular has recently turned into a flood. A recent comparison of retail prices for a three-month supply of Pfizer's Lipitor was $275.97 at Drugstore.com, compared with $179.90 at Rx/North.com of Canada. The price disparity grew for Celebrex: $255.98 at Walgreens.com and $122.90 from CanaRx. Kytril, an antinausea drug, costs $120 a dose in the U.S. and $31 in Canada. As one American whose wife's cancer treatment required Kytril said, "We are not fighting over vacation fares. It's about sustaining life."

Why such a price disparity? Most Western nations other than the U.S. regulate the price of prescriptions, either through direct price controls or through government-driven cost-containment activities. In Canada, a federal board sets price ceilings on patented drugs; then each province adds downward price pressure by capping reimbursements. The pharmaceutical industry's position: Since huge research and development (R&D) outlays go into major drug discoveries, someone has to foot the bill. And as *Fortune* business writer Roger Parloff puts it, "greed might be a factor too."

SHOULD AMERICANS BE ALLOWED TO BENEFIT FROM THE LOWER DRUG PRICES AVAILABLE IN OTHER COUNTRIES?

PRO

1. The sophisticated drug approval agencies of industrialized countries like Canada ensure that the imported drugs are genuine, safe, and unspoiled. As Minnesota's Republican governor, Tim Pawlenty, responded to the FDA's safety concerns, "Show me the dead Canadians."
2. U.S. pharmaceutical companies price their drugs exorbitantly high to offset money they would have made from sales in other countries—if they didn't have price controls. But U.S. consumers who need medication to survive shouldn't have to bear the burden of this situation.

CON

1. Drug companies plough their profits back into sophisticated R&D operations that make new "miracle" drugs possible in the first place.
2. Imported drugs are easy to counterfeit or water down; despite the numerous checks by U.S. and Canadian inspectors at every stage in the supply chain, they remain potentially unsafe.

SUMMARY

The FDA hasn't filed suits against any mayors, governors, or retirees—recognizing such moves as guaranteed PR fiascoes. However, the agency is actively pursuing people who have begun businesses to facilitate the importation of drugs from Canada, often shutting down their operations. Pfizer, the nation's No. 1 drugmaker, recently cut off two Canadian wholesalers that it said were supplying retailers who sell to Americans. Importers are fighting back with plenty of popular support, and even some U.S. local governments—including Springfield, Massachusetts, Montgomery, Alabama, and Westchester County, New York—have set up prescription plans to help their employees and retirees (as well as the local health-care budgets) benefit from lower prices abroad. Meanwhile, Congress struggles with legislation intended to ban the federal government from doing likewise. Several other drug manufacturers have threatened to join Pfizer and cease shipments to Canadian pharmacies and Internet sites that sell in the U.S. market. Some observers feel the controversy will at least force a change in the drug industry's "outmoded" business model.

Sources: "Drug Prices: A New Covenant?" *BusinessWeek,* May 10, 2004, pp. 46–47; Richard C. Morais, "Pssst . . . Wanna Buy Some Augmentin?" *Forbes,* April 12, 2004, pp. 112–116; Roger Parloff, "The New Drug War," *Fortune,* March 8, 2004, pp. 144–156; Brian Grow, "Is He a Hero or an Outlaw?" *BusinessWeek,* November 17, 2003, pp. 135–139; Julie Appleby, "Firm Fights for Canadian Drugs," *USA Today,* October 7, 2003, p. 3B; Alex Markels, "A Prescription for Controversy," *U.S. News & World Report,* October 6, 2003, pp. 50–51.

could set back the future of international trade. Marketers must navigate a maze of international and foreign laws pertaining to conducting business on the Internet. Most European laws governing e-commerce focus on consumer privacy.

Legal requirements of host countries can create unexpected hurdles. Under new city laws in Beijing, China's capital city, all companies must remove advertising signs that have been posted in pavement or on rooftops. That includes McDonald's famous golden arches, which have risen above Beijing for the past decade. McDonald's has been a huge success in Beijing, particularly with children and teens. But middle-aged and elderly Chinese citizens often view the fast-food chain as a victory of capitalism over traditional Chinese cooking. And city officials, intent on sprucing up Beijing's image by the time it hosts the 2008 Summer Olympics, have decided that the arches "are not in harmony with the surroundings and affect the architectural ambience." Cai Weiqian, deputy general manager of Beijing McDonald's, is concerned about the effects of the new regulation on his business. "Seventy percent of our business comes from people who see our signs," he argues. "Fast food is an instant consumption, and sign-boards are important to attract customers." But a Chinese official in the public relations office of Beijing McDonald's demurs. "We are a law-abiding company. Since the city government has adjusted its rules, we will follow the new regulations."[22]

Sometimes marketing challenges arise because of laws in effect in the U.S. The "Solving an Ethical Controversy" feature describes a highly controversial and widely publicized situation in which prescription drug consumers are receiving some unexpected help with their medical expenses from entrepreneurs who are testing the boundaries of American law.

TRADE BARRIERS

Assorted trade barriers also affect global marketing. These barriers fall into two major categories: **tariffs**—taxes levied on imported products—and administrative, or nontariff, barriers. Some tariffs impose set taxes per pound, gallon, or unit; others are calculated according to the value of the imported item. Administrative barriers are more subtle than tariffs and take a variety of forms such as customs barriers, quotas on imports, unnecessarily restrictive standards for imports, and export subsidies. Because the GATT and WTO agreements (discussed later in the chapter) eliminated tariffs on many products, countries frequently use nontariff barriers to boost exports and control the flows of imported products. The U.S. and other nations are constantly negotiating tariffs and other trade agreements. A free trade agreement between the U.S. and Guatemala, El Salvador, Nicaragua, and Honduras was recently signed after last-minute hurdles about textiles were overcome. The deal, which phases out all trade barriers among the participants over the next 10 years, is the sixth such agreement the U.S. has signed; the others cover Mexico and Canada (NAFTA), Israel, Jordan, Chile, and Singapore.[23]

tariff Tax levied against imported goods.

Tariffs

The U.S. has long been the champion of free trade throughout the world, but recently, with shrinking economies of industrialized foreign nations and a growing number of developing countries that are struggling to stabilize their economies, U.S. legislators have been pressured to protect domestic industries from troubles abroad. But moves designed to protect business at home are often a double-edged sword. They also frequently end up penalizing domestic consumers because prices typically rise under protectionist regulations. For example, the U.S. recently slapped a 30 percent import tax on frozen orange juice concentrate; duties on imported glassware, porcelain, and china as high as 38 percent; rubber boots and shoes, 20 percent; luggage, 16 percent; and canned tuna, 12.5 percent. While this may or may not create a competitive environment for domestic producers, it seldom reduces product prices for the consumer.

Tariffs can be classified as either revenue or protective tariffs. **Revenue tariffs** are designed to raise funds for the importing government. Most early U.S. government revenue came from this source. **Protective tariffs,** which are usually higher than revenue tariffs, are designed to raise the retail price of an imported product to match or exceed that of a similar domestic product. Some countries use tariffs in a selective manner to discourage certain consumption practices and thereby reduce access to their local markets. For example, the U.S. has tariffs on luxury items like Rolex watches and Russian caviar. In 2002, the U.S. imposed tariffs on steel imports "to give our domestic industry an opportunity to restructure and consolidate and become stronger and more competitive," said a White House spokesperson. But the tariffs were recently lifted when the World Trade Organization ruled that they violated global trade agreements. The WTO has also authorized the European Union and Japan to retaliate with penalties on citrus fruits, apparel, rice, and apples exported from the U.S.[24]

In 1988, the U.S. passed the Omnibus Trade and Competitiveness Act to remedy what it perceived as unfair international trade conditions. Under the so-called Super 301 provisions of the law, the U.S. can now single out countries that unfairly impede trade with U.S. domestic businesses. If these countries do not open their markets within 18 months, the law requires retaliation in the form of U.S. tariffs or quotas on the offenders' imports into this country.

Some nations limit foreign ownership in the business sectors. Tariffs also can be used to gain bargaining clout with other countries, but they risk adversely affecting the fortunes of domestic companies. In recent years, scores of trading nations have agreed to abolish tariffs on 500 high-technology products such as computers, software, fax machines, and related goods. Elimination of these tariffs means as much as $100 million in annual savings to communications giants like IBM.

Administrative Barriers

In addition to direct taxes on imported products, governments may erect a number of other barriers ranging from special permits and detailed inspection requirements to quotas on foreign-made items in an effort to stem the flow of imported goods—or halt them altogether. European shoppers pay about twice the price for bananas that North Americans pay. The reason for these high prices? Through a series of import license controls, Europe allows fewer bananas to be imported than people want to buy. Even worse, the European countries set up a system of quotas designed to support banana growing in former colonies in Africa and Asia, which restricts imports from Latin American countries.

import quotas Trade restrictions that limit the number of units of certain goods that can enter a country for resale.

Other forms of trade restrictions include import quotas and embargoes. **Import quotas** limit the number of units of products in certain categories that can cross a country's border. The quota is supposed to protect domestic industry and employment and to preserve foreign exchange, but it doesn't always work that way. Since the late 1950s, the U.S. has had quotas affecting the apparel industry—whether they involve certain textiles or the manufacturing of the clothes themselves. However, foreign companies often find loopholes in the quota systems and wind up not only with huge profits but also plenty of jobs for their own workers.

The ultimate quota is the **embargo**—a complete ban on the import of a product. Since 1960, the U.S. has maintained an embargo against Cuba in protest of Fidel Castro's dictatorship and policies such as expropriation of property and disregard for human rights. Not only do the sanctions prohibit Cuban exports (cigars and sugar are the island's best-known products) to enter the country, but they also apply to companies that profit from property that Cuba's communist government expropriated from Americans following the Cuban revolution.[25] However, many leading U.S. executives oppose the embargo. They know that they are losing the opportunity to develop the Cuban market while foreign rivals establish production and marketing facilities there.

Other administrative barriers include **subsidies.** Airbus, the French, German, British, and Spanish aircraft consortium, often comes under attack from U.S. trade officials because it is so heavily subsidized. The Europeans, on the other hand, argue that Boeing and Lockheed Martin benefit from research done by NASA, the Pentagon, and other U.S. agencies. And still another way to block international trade is to create so many regulatory barriers that it is almost impossible to reach target markets. The European Union, for example, enforces more than 2,700 different sets of trade requirements by states, counties, cities, and insurance providers. Indian law contains even more complex requirements.

Foreign trade can also be regulated by exchange control through a central bank or government agency. **Exchange control** means that firms that gain foreign exchange by exporting must sell foreign currencies to the central bank or other foreign agency, and importers must buy foreign currencies from the same organization. The exchange control authority can then allocate, expand, or restrict foreign exchange according to existing national policy.

DUMPING

The practice of selling a product in a foreign market at a price lower than what it commands in the producer's domestic market is called **dumping.** Critics of free trade often argue that foreign governments give substantial support to their own exporting companies. Government support may permit

© DOAN BAO CHAU/ AP

U.S. producers are not the only businesses struggling to meet foreign competition. Sales of Vietnamese toy producer Nguyen Van Nham's handcrafted tin toys have suffered recently because of a flood of mass-produced plastic Chinese imports. But increased tourism in Vietnam has helped steady the market for the brightly painted ships, animals, and other toys he produces with his family.

these firms to extend their export markets by offering lower prices abroad. In retaliation for this kind of interference with free trade, the U.S. adds import tariffs to products that foreign firms dump on U.S. markets to bring their prices in line with those of domestically produced products. However, businesses often complain that charges of dumping must undergo a lengthy investigative and bureaucratic procedure before the government assesses import duties. U.S. firms that claim dumping threatens to hurt their business can file a complaint with the U.S. International Trade Commission (ITC), which—on average—rejects about half the claims it receives.

U.S. shrimpers recently filed a complaint with the U.S. International Trade Commission and the Department of Commerce asking for protection from six countries they say are dumping seafood in the U.S. market. Imports from the six countries—Thailand, Vietnam, China, India, Brazil, and Ecuador—have climbed 28 percent in the last few years and now make up three-quarters of the U.S.'s annual shrimp imports. The U.S. shrimping industry is seeking tariffs between 57 and 267 percent. Complicating the issue are claims that foreign shrimp producers use methods that would not be environmentally acceptable in the U.S. and the fact that U.S. shrimp producers are already receiving federal subsidies to combat falling prices for their catch.[26]

1. What is an exchange rate?
2. What does ISO 9000 and 14000 certification represent?
3. What is a tariff?

MULTINATIONAL ECONOMIC INTEGRATION

free trade area Region in which participating nations agree to the free trade of goods among themselves, abolishing tariffs and trade restrictions.

A noticeable trend toward multinational economic integration has developed over the six decades since the end of World War II. Multinational economic integration can be set up in several ways. The simplest approach is to establish a **free trade area** in which participating nations agree to the free trade of

We are all internationalists now, whether we like it or not.

Tony Blair (b. 1953)

British prime minister

goods among themselves, abolishing all tariffs and trade restrictions. A **customs union** establishes a free trade area plus a uniform tariff for trade with nonmember nations. A **common market** extends a customs union by seeking to reconcile all government regulations affecting trade. Despite the many factors in its favor, not everyone is enthusiastic about free trade, particularly Americans who hear news reports of U.S. jobs being outsourced to lower wage nations such as Bangladesh, China, India, and Bulgaria and worry that their jobs may be affected. So it is important to consider both sides of the issue. Although productivity and innovation are said to grow more quickly with free trade, American workers face pay-cut demands and potential job loss as more companies move their operations overseas.[27]

③ Outline the basic functions of GATT, WTO, NAFTA, the proposed FTAA, and the European Union.

GATT AND THE WORLD TRADE ORGANIZATION

The **General Agreement on Tariffs and Trade (GATT)**, a 117-nation trade accord that has sponsored several rounds of major tariff negotiations, substantially reducing worldwide tariff levels, celebrated its 50th birthday in 1997. In 1994, a seven-year series of GATT conferences, called the Uruguay Round, culminated in one of the biggest victories for free trade in decades. The new accord's reduction of trade barriers helped the U.S. economy grow by $1 trillion and created some 2 million new jobs.

The Uruguay Round reduced average tariffs by one-third, or more than $700 billion. Among its major victories were the following:

- reduction of farm subsidies, which opened vast new markets for U.S. exports
- increased protection for patents, copyrights, and trademarks
- inclusion of services under international trading rules, creating opportunities for U.S. financial, legal, and accounting firms
- phasing out import quotas on textiles and clothing from developing nations, a move that cost textile workers thousands of jobs when their employers moved many of these domestic jobs to lower wage countries, but benefited U.S. retailers and consumers because these quotas hiked clothing prices by $15 billion a year

General Agreement on Tariffs and Trade (GATT) International trade accord that has helped reduce world tariffs.

World Trade Organization (WTO) Organization that replaces GATT, overseeing GATT agreements, making binding decisions in mediating disputes, and reducing trade barriers.

A key outcome of the GATT talks was establishment of the **World Trade Organization (WTO)**, a 136-member organization that succeeds GATT. The WTO oversees GATT agreements, mediates disputes, and continues the effort to reduce trade barriers throughout the world. Unlike GATT, WTO decisions are binding.

To date, however, the WTO has made only slow progress toward its major policy initiatives—liberalizing world financial services, telecommunications, and maritime markets. Trade officials have not agreed on the direction for the WTO. Its activities have focused more on complaint resolution than on removing global trade barriers. The U.S. has been the most active plaintiff in WTO dispute courts. Recently, the WTO announced a decision about U.S. tax breaks and software bundling for companies like Microsoft and Boeing, which have significant operations overseas, essentially granting the European Union permission to impose billions of dollars in punitive tariffs on U.S. imports. However, both the European Union and the U.S. immediately engaged in discussions to resolve the situation and avert a trade war, which would have been harmful to both.[28]

Big differences between developed and developing areas create a major roadblock to WTO progress. These conflicts became apparent at the first WTO meeting in Singapore in the late 1990s. Asian nations want trade barriers lifted on their manufactured goods, but they also want to protect their own telecommunications companies. In addition, they oppose monitoring of corruption and labor practices by outsiders. The U.S. wants free trade for telecommunications, more controls on corruption, and establishment of international labor standards. Europe wants standard rules on foreign investments and removal of profit repatriation restrictions but is not as concerned with worker rights.

China is the world's largest nation, with an economy that has grown 10 percent annually for the last two decades. As a market, it holds the promise of enormous potential for exporters. But China's exports show less than 2 percent annual growth as a result of the multitude of barriers and red tape that make it extremely difficult for foreign firms to operate there. Recently, however, the release of trade rights allowed new enterprises to engage in importing and exporting, and the nation was admitted to the WTO.

THE NAFTA ACCORD

A heated controversy continues a decade after the passage of the **North American Free Trade Agreement (NAFTA),** an agreement between the U.S., Canada, and Mexico that removes trade restrictions among the three nations over a 14-year period. Proponents claim that NAFTA has been good for the American economy; critics charge that U.S. and Canadian workers have lost their jobs to cheap Mexican labor. The NAFTA accord brings together more than 415 million people and a combined gross domestic product of $7.9 trillion, making it by far the world's largest free trade zone.

North American Free Trade Agreement (NAFTA) Accord removing trade barriers among Canada, Mexico, and the United States.

The NAFTA accord was approved despite serious concerns about job losses from the relatively high-wage industries in the U.S. and Canada as manufacturers relocated their production facilities in lower wage Mexico. However, NAFTA supporters point out that the availability of cheap labor has allowed the prices of some goods to drop, leaving Americans with more money to spend and stimulating the economy.[29]

To date, NAFTA seems to have succeeded in promoting greater trade between the U.S. and Mexico, and it actually boosted jobs and cut inflation without hurting wages. Trade among the three countries more than doubled—from $291 billion to $678 billion—during the past 10 years. Although China receives more headlines for its international trade importance to the U.S., the nation's first and second largest trading partners are on either side of our borders. U.S. businesses export nearly four times more to them than to China and Japan and 75 percent more than to the European Union. In addition, Canada and Mexico supply the U.S. with 36 percent of its energy imports. Canada has long been the U.S.'s leading trade partner.[30]

But nine of every ten dollars in Mexican exports are shipped to the U.S., and its recent recession has had an impact on the Mexican economy. Exports of electronics, textiles, chemicals, and auto parts dropped sharply. Not surprisingly, Mexico's unskilled labor is now more expensive than China's, so companies are looking to Asia for production facilities. Despite the fact that China was admitted to the WTO, Mexico lagged in forming a bilateral trade agreement with that country, and some analysts think that Mexico may lose its natural advantage as a manufacturing center for North America to China.[31]

Recently, the U.S. signed a free trade agreement with Chile—the first between the U.S. and a South American country—which went into effect in 2004. It immediately eliminated tariffs on more than 85 percent of trade between the two nations. Other trade barriers are being phased out over a 12-year period. Total trade between the U.S. and Chile amounts to roughly $6.5 billion annually. This pact is a step toward a comprehensive Free Trade Area of the Americas.

THE FREE TRADE AREA OF THE AMERICAS

NAFTA was the first step toward creating a **Free Trade Area of the Americas (FTAA),** stretching the length of the entire Western Hemisphere, from Alaska's Bering Strait to Cape Horn at South America's southern tip, encompassing 34 countries, a population of 800 million, and a combined gross domestic product of more than $11 trillion. The FTAA would be the largest free trade zone on earth and would offer low or nonexistent tariffs, streamlined customs, and no quotas, subsidies, or other barriers to trade. In addition to the U.S., Canada, and Mexico, countries expected to be members of the proposed FTAA include Argentina, Brazil, Chile, Colombia, Ecuador, Guatemala, Jamaica, Peru, Trinidad and Tobago, Uruguay, and Venezuela. The U.S. is a staunch supporter of the FTAA, which still has many hurdles to overcome as countries wrangle for conditions that are most favorable to them.

Free Trade Area of the Americas (FTAA) Proposed free trade area stretching the length of the entire Western Hemisphere and designed to extend free trade benefits to additional nations in North, Central, and South America.

THE EUROPEAN UNION

The best-known example of a multinational economic community is the **European Union (EU).** As Figure 7.5 shows, 25 countries make up the EU: Finland, Sweden, Denmark, the United Kingdom, Ireland, the Netherlands, Belgium, Germany, Luxembourg, France, Austria, Italy, Greece, Spain, Portugal, Hungary, Poland, the Czech Republic, the Slovak Republic, Slovenia, Estonia, Latvia, Lithuania, Malta, and Cyprus.[32] With a total population of approximately 500 million people, the EU forms a huge common market.

European Union (EU) Customs union that is moving in the direction of an economic union by adopting a common currency, removing trade restrictions, and permitting free flow of goods and workers throughout the member nations.

The goal of the EU is to eventually remove all barriers to free trade among its members, making it as simple and painless to ship products between England and Spain as it is between New Jersey and

figure 7.5

The 25 Members of the European Union

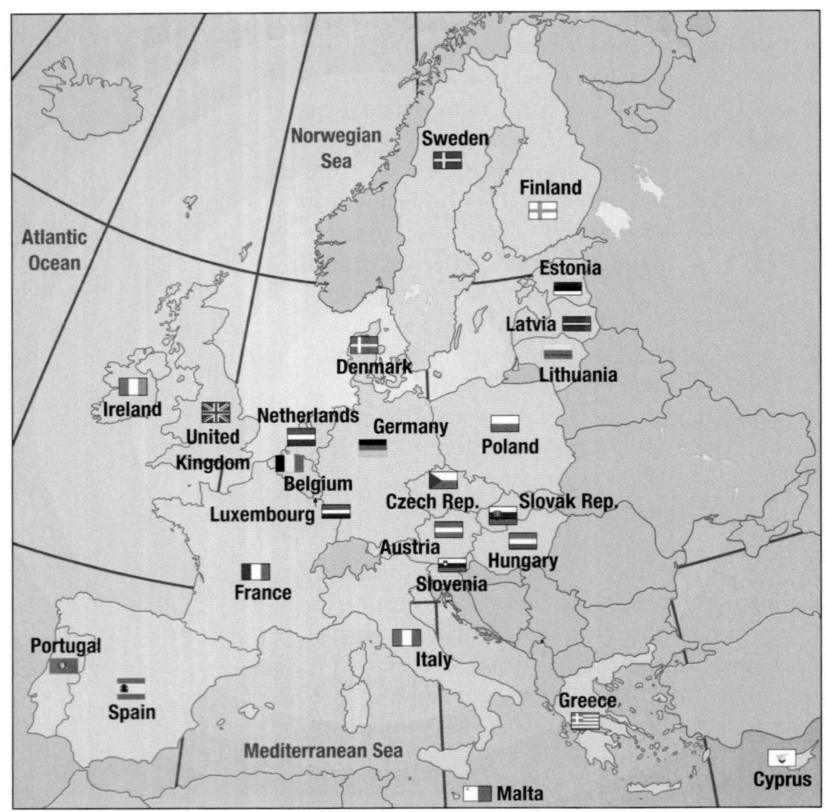

Pennsylvania. Also involved is the standardization of regulations and requirements that businesses must meet. Instead of having to comply with 25 sets of standards and 25 different currencies, companies will have fewer to deal with. This simplification should lower the costs of doing business in Europe by allowing firms to take advantage of economies of scale.

In some ways, the EU is making definite progress toward its economic goals. We have already seen that it is drafting standardized eco-labels to certify that products are manufactured according to certain environmental standards as well as creating guidelines governing marketers' uses of customer information. Marketers can also protect trademarks throughout the entire EU with a single application and registration process through the Community Trademark (CTM), which simplifies doing business and eliminates having to register with each member country. It is, however, sometimes difficult to obtain approval for trademark protection.

Yet marketers still face challenges when selling their products in the EU. Customs taxes differ, and there is no uniform postal system. Mail between countries can often be extremely slow. In fact, the Federation of European Direct Marketing is pushing for modernization and integration of postal systems. Using one toll-free number for several countries will not work, either, because each country has its own telephone system for codes and numbers. Furthermore, when the euro was introduced by the European Union, three EU nations decided to retain their own national currencies, at least temporarily.

Mexico has successfully negotiated a trade agreement with the EU that makes it easier for European companies to set up their operations in Mexico, which benefits EU companies by giving them the same privileges enjoyed by the U.S. and Canada and brings new investors to Mexico.

1. **What is the World Trade Organization (WTO)?**
2. **What countries are parties to the NAFTA accord?**
3. **What is the goal of the European Union (EU)?**

Briefly Speaking

A day will come when you, France; you, Russia; you, Italy; you, England; you, Germany—all of you nations of the continent—will, without losing your distinctive qualities, be blended into a European fraternity . . .

Victor Hugo (1802–1885)

French poet, novelist, and dramatist

GOING GLOBAL

As we move further into the 21st century, globalization will affect almost every industry and every individual throughout the world. Traditional marketers who decide to take their firms global may do so because they already have strong domestic market shares or their target market is too saturated to offer any substantial growth. Sometimes, by evaluating key indicators of the marketing environment, marketers can move toward globalization at an optimal time. Zippo, the family-owned lighter company headquartered in Bradford, Pennsylvania, has spent the past half-century scouting new markets for its durable products as the number of U.S. smokers has steadily declined and cheaper, disposable butane lighters cut into Zippo sales. Today, 60 percent of Zippo's $140 million annual sales comes from overseas. Even though the durable lighter sells for more than $30—a third of a monthly paycheck for the average Chinese—Zippo has become a status symbol among China's 320 million smokers. To reduce the sale of made-in-China knockoffs, Zippo's promotions emphasize how to look for the marks of an authentic Zippo, such as each lighter's serial number, and to purchase them from major department stores. And while Zippo's long-stemmed multipurpose lighters sold in the U.S. are made in China, the classic lighter is produced in Bradford. In this case, the label "Made in America" is worth a premium.[33]

A critical task facing international marketers is developing strategies for successfully entering new foreign markets. Figure 7.6 identifies six reasons that companies cite for going global.

Most large firms—and many smaller businesses—already participate in global commerce, and virtually every domestic marketer, large or small, recognizes the need to investigate whether to market its products overseas. It is not an easy step to take, requiring careful evaluation and preparation.

figure 7.6

Why Marketers Decide to Go Global

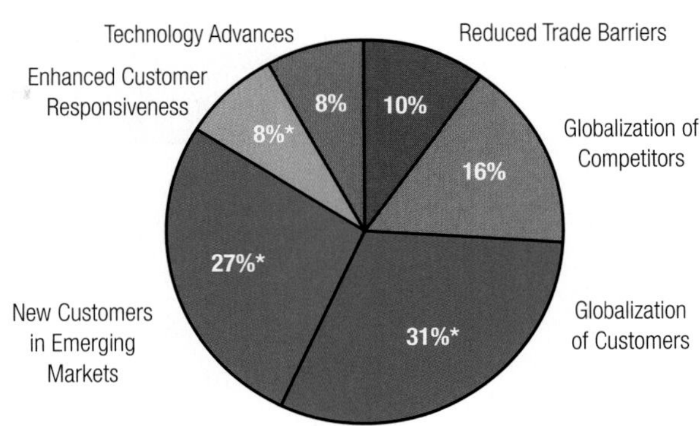

Source: Data from "Shaping the Value Chain for Outstanding Performance," PricewaterhouseCoopers survey of 200 leading European businesses.

FIRST STEPS IN DECIDING TO MARKET GLOBALLY

The first step toward successful global marketing is to secure top management's support. Without the enthusiasm and support of senior executives, export efforts are likely to fail. The advocate for going global must explain and promote the potential of foreign markets and facilitate the global marketing process.

The next step is to research the export process and potential markets. The U.S. Department of Commerce sponsors a toll-free hotline that describes the various federal export programs currently available. Trade counselors at 68 district offices offer export advice, computerized market data, and names of contacts in over 60 countries. Some services are free, and others are available at a reasonable cost. Table 7.3 describes four important sources for marketers who want to analyze foreign markets.

STRATEGIES FOR ENTERING INTERNATIONAL MARKETS

4 Compare the alternative strategies for entering international markets.

Once marketers have completed their research, they may choose from among three basic strategies for entering international markets: importing and exporting; contractual agreements like franchising, licensing, and subcontracting; and international direct investment. As Figure 7.7 shows, the level of risk and the firm's degree of control over international marketing increase with greater involvement. Firms often use more than one of these entry strategies. L.L. Bean subcontracts with a Japanese company to handle its product returns, and it also maintains a direct investment in several Japanese retail outlets in partnership with Matsushita.

table 7.3 Sources for Analyzing Foreign Markets

SOURCE	DESCRIPTION
U.S. Department of Commerce	Maintains the National Trade Data Bank (market reports on foreign demand for specific products), produces catalogs and video shows, and participates in trade shows.
The Green Book	Published by the American Management Association, this guide lists all market research firms and those with international capabilities.
Esomar	The European Society of Opinion and Market Research maintains a worldwide listing by company.
U.S. Department of State	Offers commercial guides compiled by local embassies to almost every country in the world.

figure 7.7

Levels of Involvement in International Marketing

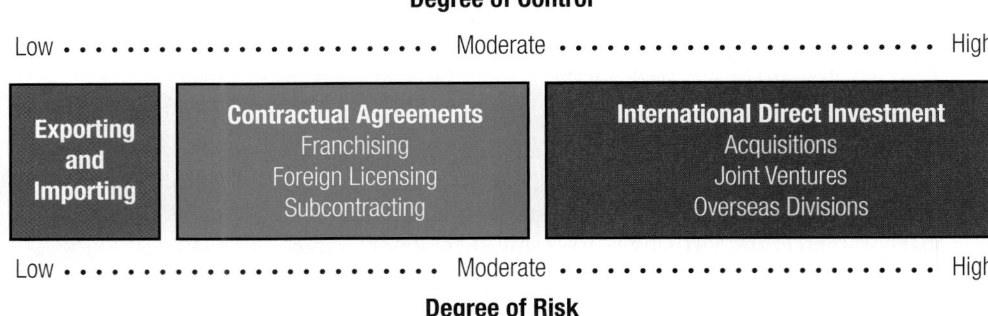

A firm that brings in goods produced abroad to sell domestically or to be used as components in its products is an importer. In making import decisions, the marketer must assess local demand for the product, taking into consideration factors such as the following:

- ability of the supplier to maintain agreed-to quality levels
- capability of filling orders that might vary considerably from one order to the next
- response time in filling orders
- total costs—including import fees, packaging, and transportation—in comparison with costs of domestic suppliers

Exporting, another basic form of international marketing, involves a continuous effort in marketing a firm's merchandise to customers in other countries. Many firms export their products as the first step in reaching foreign markets. Success in exporting often encourages them to try other entry strategies.

First-time exporters can reach foreign customers through one or more of three alternatives: export-trading companies, export-management companies, or offset agreements. An export-trading company (ETC) buys products from domestic producers and resells them abroad. While manufacturers lose control over marketing and distribution to the ETC, it helps them export through a relatively simple and inexpensive channel, in the process providing feedback about the overseas market potential of their products.

The second option, an export-management company (EMC), provides the first-time exporter with expertise in locating foreign buyers, handling necessary paperwork, and ensuring that its goods meet local labeling and testing laws. However, the manufacturer retains more control over the export process when it deals with an EMC than if it were to sell the goods outright to an export-trading company. Smaller firms can get assistance with administrative needs such as financing and preparation of proposals and contracts from large EMC contractors.

The final option, entering a foreign market under an offset agreement, teams a small firm with a major international company. The smaller firm essentially serves as a subcontractor on a large foreign project. This entry strategy provides new exporters with international experience, supported by the assistance of the primary contractor in such areas as international transaction documentation and financing.

CONTRACTUAL AGREEMENTS

As a firm gains sophistication in international marketing, it may enter contractual agreements that provide several flexible alternatives to exporting. Both large and small firms can benefit from these methods. Franchising and foreign licensing, for example, are good ways to take services abroad. Subcontracting may set up either production facilities or services. Sponsorships are another form of international contractual marketing agreements.

Franchising

A **franchise** is a contractual arrangement in which a wholesaler or retailer (the franchisee) agrees to meet the operating requirements of a manufacturer or other franchiser. The franchisee receives the right to sell the products and use the franchiser's name as well as a variety of marketing, management, and other services. Fast-food companies such as McDonald's have been active franchisers around the world.

One advantage of franchising is risk reduction by offering a proven concept. Standardized operations typically reduce costs, increase operating efficiencies, and provide greater international recognizability. However, the success of an international franchise depends on its willingness to balance standard practices with local customer preferences. McDonald's, Pizza Hut, and Domino's are all expanding into India with special menus that feature lamb, chicken, and vegetarian items, in deference to Hindu and Muslim customers who do not eat beef and pork.

BLOOMBERG NEWS/LANDOV

As every international traveler knows, Oak Brook, Illinois-headquartered McDonald's has expanded its franchised fast-food operations around the globe. In recent years, the restaurant chain—traditionally known for its appeal to kids and young adults—has attempted to expand its market by attracting more adult diners to both its domestic and international restaurants. For this segment, the focus is on taste.

Foreign Licensing

A second method of going global through the use of contractual agreements is **foreign licensing.** Such an agreement grants foreign marketers the right to distribute a firm's merchandise or use its trademark, patent, or process in a specified geographic area. These arrangements usually set certain time limits, after which agreements are revised or renewed.

Licensing offers several advantages over exporting, including access to local partners' marketing information and distribution channels and protection from various legal barriers. Because licensing does not require capital outlays, many firms, both small and large, regard it as an attractive entry strategy. Like franchising, licensing allows a firm to quickly enter a foreign market with a known product or concept. The arrangement also may provide entry into a market that government restrictions close to imports or international direct investment.

franchise Contractual arrangement in which a wholesaler or retailer agrees to meet the operating requirements of a manufacturer or other franchiser.

foreign licensing Agreement that grants foreign marketers the right to distribute a firm's merchandise or to use its trademark, patent, or process in a specified geographic area.

Subcontracting

A third strategy for going global through contractual agreements is **subcontracting,** in which the production of goods or services is assigned to local companies. Using local subcontractors can prevent mistakes involving local culture and regulations. Manufacturers might subcontract with a local company to produce their goods or use a foreign distributor to handle their products abroad or provide customer service. Manufacturing within the country can provide protection from import duties and may be a lower cost alternative that makes it possible for the product to compete with local offerings. Sears subcontracts with local manufacturers in Mexico and Spain to produce many of the products—especially clothing—sold in its department stores.

INTERNATIONAL DIRECT INVESTMENT

Another strategy for entering global markets is international direct investment in foreign firms, production, and marketing facilities. As the world's largest economy, the U.S.'s foreign direct investment inflows and outflows—total of American firm investments abroad and foreign firm investments in the U.S.—are one-third greater than Germany's and twice as much as Japan's, its two largest competitors. By the beginning of this century, U.S. direct investment abroad was nearly $2.2 trillion, with a high number of acquisitions in the United Kingdom, the Netherlands, and Canada. On the other hand, foreign direct investment in the U.S. had grown to over $2.1 trillion. Three of every four dollars of foreign investment in the U.S. came from Europe and Canada.[34]

Although high levels of involvement and high-risk potential are characteristics of investments in foreign countries, firms choosing this method often have a competitive advantage. Direct investment can take several forms. A company can acquire an existing firm in a country where it wants to do business, or it can set up an independent division outside its own borders with responsibility for production and marketing in a country or geographic region. Recently, European firms have been acquiring U.S. companies as a way to enter the American marketplace. Foreign sales offices, overseas marketing subsidiaries, and foreign offices and manufacturing facilities of U.S. firms all involve direct investment. Motorola has had offices in Israel since 1964 and continues to strengthen its presence in the Middle East.

Companies may also engage in international marketing by forming joint ventures, in which they share the risks, costs, and management of the foreign operation with one or more partners. These partnerships join the investing companies with nationals of the host countries. While some companies choose to open their own facilities overseas, others share with their partners. Service companies often find that joint ventures provide the most efficient way to penetrate a market.

Although joint ventures offer many advantages, foreign investors have encountered problems in several areas throughout the world, especially in developing economies. Lower trade barriers, new technologies, lower transport costs, and vastly improved access to information mean that many more partnerships will be involved in international trade.

MARKETING Concept Check

1. **What are the three basic strategies for entering international markets?**
2. **What is a franchise?**
3. **What rights does foreign licensing grant?**

FROM MULTINATIONAL CORPORATION TO GLOBAL MARKETER

multinational corporation Firm with significant operations and marketing activities outside its home country.

A **multinational corporation** is a firm with significant operations and marketing activities outside its home country. Examples of multinationals include General Electric, Siemens, and Mitsubishi in heavy electrical equipment, and Timex, Seiko, and Citizen in watches. Since they first became a force in international business in the 1960s, multinationals have evolved in some important ways. First, these companies are no longer exclusively U.S. based. Today, it is as likely for a multinational to be based in Japan, Germany, or Great Britain as in the U.S. Second, multinationals no longer think of their foreign operations as mere outsourcing appendages that carry out the design, production, and engineering ideas conceived at home. Instead, they encourage constant exchanges of ideas, capital, and technologies among all the multinational operations.

Multinationals often employ huge foreign workforces relative to their American staffs. Over half of all Ford and IBM personnel are located outside the U.S. These workforces are no longer seen merely as sources of cheap labor. On the contrary, many multinationals center technically complex activities in locations throughout the world. Texas Instruments does much of its research, development, design, and manufacturing in East Asia. In fact, it is increasingly common for U.S. multinationals to bring product innovations from their foreign facilities back to the States.

Multinationals have become global corporations that reflect the interdependence of world economies, the growth of international competition, and the globalization of world markets. An increasing number of acquisitions include U.S. multinationals as targets for takeover. In one recent year, Germany's Deutsche Bank acquired Bankers Trust; British Petroleum took over Amoco; and Chrysler became part of Germany's Daimler-Benz.

1. What is a multinational corporation?
2. What are two ways in which multinationals have changed since the 1960s?

(5) Differentiate between a global marketing strategy and a multidomestic marketing strategy.

DEVELOPING AN INTERNATIONAL MARKETING STRATEGY

In developing a marketing mix, international marketers may choose between two alternative approaches: a global marketing strategy or a multidomestic marketing strategy. A **global marketing strategy** defines a standard marketing mix and implements it with minimal modifications in all foreign markets. This approach brings the advantage of economies of scale to production and marketing activities. Procter & Gamble (P&G) marketers follow a global marketing strategy for Pringles potato chips, its leading export brand. P&G sells one product with a consistent formulation in every country. Unlike Frito-Lay's Cheetos snacks, which come in flavors geared to local tastes, P&G meets 80 percent of worldwide demand with only six flavors of Pringles. The brand relies on one package design throughout the world. This standardized approach saves money since it allows large-scale production runs and reinforces the brand's image. Also, similar advertising around the world builds brand awareness by featuring the slogan, "Once you pop, you can't stop." P&G intends all of these tactics to build strong global brand equity for Pringles.

global marketing strategy Standardized marketing mix with minimal modifications that a firm uses in all of its domestic and foreign markets.

multidomestic marketing strategy Application of market segmentation to foreign markets by tailoring the firm's marketing mix to match specific target markets in each nation.

A global marketing perspective can effectively market some goods and services to segments in many nations that share cultures and languages. This approach works especially well for products with strong, universal appeal such as McDonald's, luxury items like Rolex watches, and high-tech brands like Microsoft. Global advertising outlets, such as international editions of popular consumer and business magazines and international transmissions of TV channels such as CNN, MTV, and the CNBC financial network, help marketers deliver a single message to millions of global viewers. International satellite television channels such as StarTV reach 260 million Asian viewers through a host of sports, news, movie, music, and entertainment channels programmed in eight languages.

A global marketing strategy can be highly effective for luxury products that target upscale consumers everywhere. Marketers of diamonds and luxury watches, for instance, typically use advertising with little or no copy—just a picture of a beautiful diamond or watch with the name discreetly displayed at the bottom.

A major benefit of a global marketing strategy is its low cost to implement. Most firms, however, find it necessary to practice market segmentation outside their home markets and tailor their marketing mixes to fit the unique needs of customers in specific countries. This **multidomestic marketing strategy** assumes that differences between market characteristics and competitive situations in certain nations require firms to customize their marketing decisions to effectively reach individual marketplaces. (This strategy is sometimes mistakenly called *multinational* marketing. In fact, a multinational corporation may combine both strategies in its international marketing plans.) Many marketing experts believe that most products demand multidomestic marketing strategies to give them realistic global marketing appeal. Cultural, geographic, language, and other differences simply make it impractical to send one message to many countries. Specific situations may allow marketers to standardize some parts of the marketing process but customize others.

COURTESY OF PROCTER & GAMBLE

This Spanish-language ad for Tide detergent promotes Tide's universally recognized qualities: quick dissolving power ("even in cold water") and stain removing strength.

Even Procter & Gamble, famed for its one-size-fits-all global marketing strategy, had to create a multidomestic marketing strategy for its Tide detergent in China. The firm's typical pricing approach of designing superior products and then setting prices slightly above local offerings proved to be a hurdle that many Chinese households—two-thirds of them earning less than $25 per month—could not overcome. So P&G switched to a tiered pricing strategy, offering its Tide Clean White for 23 cents compared with Tide Triple Action at 33 cents. Clean White doesn't offer such benefits as stain removal and fragrance, but it costs less to make. This way, P&G was able to offer Tide detergents at different prices for different market segments.[35]

6 **Describe the alternative marketing mix strategies used in international marketing.**

INTERNATIONAL PRODUCT AND PROMOTIONAL STRATEGIES

International marketers can choose from among five strategies for selecting the most appropriate product and promotion strategy for a specific foreign market: straight extension, promotion adaptation, product adaptation, dual adaptation, and product invention. As Figure 7.8 indicates, the strategies center on whether to extend a domestic product and promotional strategy into international markets or adapt one or both to meet the target market's unique requirements.

A firm may follow a one-product, one-message straight extension strategy as part of a global marketing strategy, like Pepsi Cola's. This strategy permits economies of scale in production and marketing. Also, successful implementation creates universal recognition of a product for consumers from country to country.

Briefly Speaking

Hong Kong will take your breath away.

Tourism ad headline commissioned before the SARS outbreak and cancelled soon afterward

Other strategies call for product adaptation, promotion adaptation, or both. While bicycles, motorcycles, and outboard motors primarily form part of the market for U.S. recreational vehicles, they may represent important basic transportation modes in other nations. Consequently, producers of these products may adapt their promotional messages even if they sell the product without changes. Mattel Inc. recently discovered that it can sell its blonde, blue-eyed Barbie dolls just as well in Asia as it does in the U.S., thanks to the rapid expansion of cable and satellite television channels that expose millions of children around the world to the same iconic figures, in the same way that movies and the Internet do. The ad campaign for Rapunzel Barbie, with her ankle-length blonde locks, was broadcast around the world in 35 different languages, and Mattel's Barbie Web site features eight language options, but the doll is the same everywhere.[36]

Sometimes international marketers must change both the product and the promotional message in a dual adaptation strategy to meet the unique needs of specific international markets. As part of its overall efforts to adapt to local tastes, Coca-Cola marketers developed new drink flavors. In Turkey, the firm now offers a pear-flavored drink, and in Germany, consumers are treated to a berry-flavored Fanta. These and other new flavors are designed to appeal to the tastes of people in different countries.[37]

Finally, a firm may select product invention to take advantage of unique foreign market opportunities. To match user needs in developing nations, an appliance manufacturer might introduce a hand-powered washing machine even though such products became obsolete in industrialized countries years ago.

Although Chapter 12 discusses the idea of branding in greater detail, it is important to note here the importance of a company's recognizable name, image, product, or even slogan around the world.

figure 7.8

Alternative International Product and Promotional Strategies

Promotion Strategy \ Product Strategy	Same Product	Product Adaptation	New Product
Same Promotion	**Straight Extension** Wrigley's gum Coca-Cola Eastman Kodak cameras and film	**Product Adaptation** Campbell's soup Exxon gasoline	**Product Invention** Nonelectric sewing machines Manually operated washing machines
Different Promotion	**Promotion Adaptation** Bicycles/motorcycles Outboard motors	**Dual Adaptation** Coffee Some clothing	

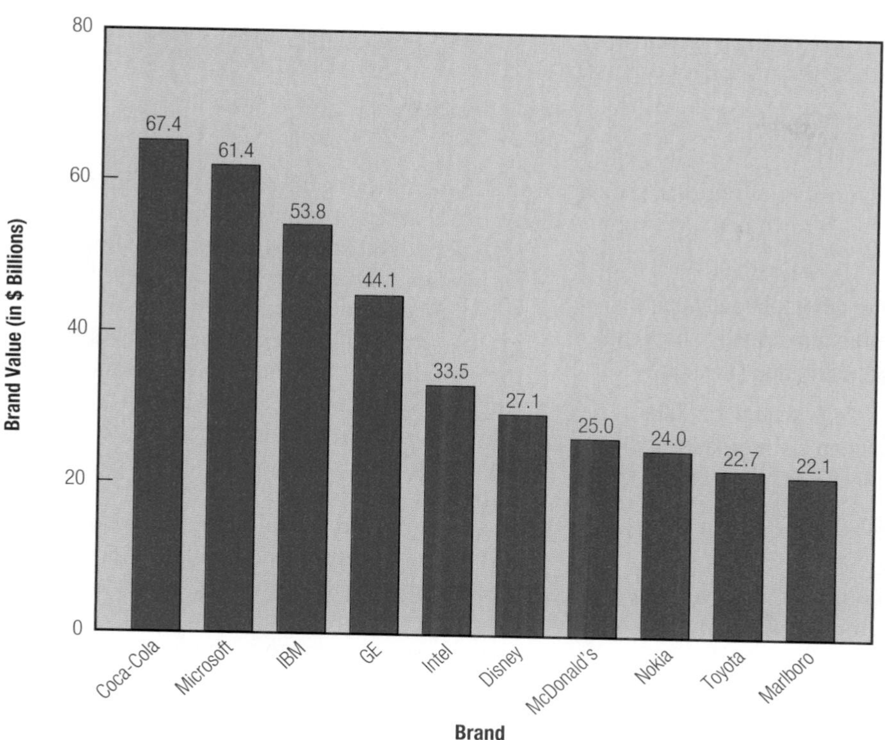

figure 7.9

The World's 10 Most Valuable Brands

Source: Data from "The World's 10 Most Valuable Brands," *BusinessWeek,* August 4, 2003, http://www.businessweek.com.

Figure 7.9 identifies the world's 10 most valuable brands as rated by Interbrand. Other than Mercedes and Nokia, all are brands owned by U.S.-based companies.[38]

INTERNATIONAL DISTRIBUTION STRATEGY

Distribution is a vital aspect of overseas marketing. Marketers must set up proper channels and anticipate extensive physical distribution problems. Foreign markets may offer poor transportation systems and warehousing facilities—or none at all. International marketers must adapt promptly and efficiently to these situations to profit from overseas sales.

A distribution decision involves two steps. First, the firm must decide on a method of entering the foreign market. Second, it must determine how to distribute the product within the foreign market through that entry channel.

PRICING STRATEGY

Pricing can critically affect the success of an overall marketing strategy for foreign markets. Considerable competitive, economic, political, and legal constraints often limit pricing decisions. Global marketers can succeed if they thoroughly understand these requirements.

Companies must adapt their pricing strategies to local markets and change them when conditions change. Until recently, foreign shipments carried premium prices without assurance that the package would be delivered on time in good condition—or even delivered at all. After the air freight and overnight-delivery services boomed in the 1980s, delivery became more reliable, but costs to many areas were exorbitant. To compete in this crowded market without losing market share, the United States Postal Service (USPS) began advertising International Express Mail services to over 175 countries at set delivery rates. Global Priority Mail, for example, provides prompt delivery to over 30 key business countries for as little as four dollars.

An important development in pricing strategy for international marketing has been the emergence of commodity marketing organizations that seek to control prices through collective action. The

Organization of Petroleum Exporting Countries (OPEC) is a good example of this kind of collective export organization, and many others exist.[39]

countertrade Form of exporting whereby goods and services are bartered rather than sold for cash.

COUNTERTRADE

In a growing number of nations, the only way a marketer can gain access to foreign markets is through **countertrade**—a form of exporting in which a firm barters products rather than selling them for cash. Less-developed nations sometimes impose countertrade requirements when they lack sufficient foreign currency to attain goods and services they want or need from exporting countries. These countries allow sellers to exchange their products only for domestic products as a way to control their balance-of-trade problems.

1. What is the difference between a global marketing strategy and a multidomestic marketing strategy?
2. What two steps should marketers take in making an international distribution decision?
3. What is countertrade?

Countertrade became popular two decades ago, when companies wanted to conduct business in Eastern European countries and the former Soviet Union. Those governments did not allow exchanges of hard currency, so this form of barter facilitated trade. PepsiCo made one of the largest countertrades ever when it exchanged $3 billion worth of Pepsi Cola for Russian Stolichnaya vodka, a cargo ship, and tankers from the former Soviet Union.

Estimating the actual volume of countertrade as a percentage of world trade is difficult, but the American Countertrade Association puts the figure at about 25 percent. Countertraders include large multinational firms like General Electric and PepsiCo. Almost half of the *Fortune* 500 companies now practice countertrade in response to increasing global competition. Although countertrade is still growing at about 10 percent a year, its rate of increase has slowed.

7 Explain the attractiveness of the U.S. as a target market for foreign marketers.

THE U.S. AS A TARGET FOR INTERNATIONAL MARKETERS

Foreign marketers regard America as an inviting target. It offers a large population, high levels of discretionary income, political stability, a generally favorable attitude toward foreign investment, and a relatively well-controlled economy.

Among the best-known industries in which foreign manufacturers have established U.S. production facilities is automobiles. Most of the world's leading auto companies have built assembly facilities in the U.S.: Honda, Hyundai, and Mercedes-Benz in Alabama, BMW in South Carolina, Toyota in Kentucky, Nissan and Honda in Tennessee, Mississippi, and Ohio.

SUZI ALTMAN/BLOOMBERG NEWS/LANDOV

Foreign car manufacturers have taken advantage of U.S. consumers' desire for foreign cars by locating many new assembly plants in the U.S. Here, the first car rolls off the line at the new Nissan plant in Canton, Mississippi.

Many foreign executives are transforming their companies' mission statements to reflect their move toward globalization. Fusao Sekiguchi, president and CEO of Venture Safenet, a Japanese firm that provides professional engineers to companies on a temporary basis, wants to expand his company's reach around the world. "With the chance of developing this company profile, I am also in hope of sharing useful business hints with investors who are interested in the Japanese human resource market, as well as looking forward to all the opportunities of expanding my business to a global scale," he writes in an open letter on the firm's Web site.[40] Sekiguchi expanded his reach to America when the racehorse he owned, Fusaichi Pegasus, won the Kentucky Derby a few years ago.

As we discussed earlier, foreign investment continues to grow in the U.S. Foreign multinationals will probably continue to invest in U.S. assets as they seek to produce goods locally and control distribution channels. Major U.S. companies owned by foreign firms include Random House, *Family Circle* and *Inc.* magazines, and Arista Records, all owned by Bertelsmann AG (Germany); Pillsbury, Green Giant, and Heublein, owned by Grand Metropolitan (UK), and Ralph Lauren and Maybelline, owned by L'Oréal (France). European firms poured $950 billion into the U.S. in a recent 12-month period, accounting for three-fourths of all foreign direct investment that year.[41]

1. **What characteristics of the U.S. make it an inviting target for foreign marketers?**
2. **Is foreign investment in the U.S. expected to grow or to decline?**

Strategic Implications of Marketing in the 21st Century

THIS first decade of the new century is marking a new era of truly global marketing, where nearly every marketer can become a global marketer. The previous eras of domestic markets are largely being relegated to niche marketing. The Internet has played a major role in these changes in the traditional marketing practices of the last century. Marketers in both small, localized firms and giant businesses need to reevaluate the strengths and weaknesses of current marketing practices and realign their plans to meet the new demands of the information age.

Marketers are the pioneers in bringing new technologies to developing nations. Their successes and failures will determine the direction global marketing will take and the speed with which it will be embraced. Actions of international marketers will influence every component of the marketing environments: competitive, economic, social-cultural, political-legal, and technological.

The greatest competitive advantages will belong to those marketers who capitalize on the similarities of their target markets and adapt to the differences. In some instances, the actions of marketers today help determine the rules and regulations of tomorrow.

Marketers need flexible and broad views of an increasingly complex customer. Goods and services will become more customized as they are introduced in foreign markets. New and better products in developing markets will create and maintain relationships for the future. Specialization will once again be a viable business concept. Marketing has just entered a new frontier of limitless opportunities. Much like the first voyages into space, the world looks more different than anyone could have ever imagined.

REVIEW OF CHAPTER OBJECTIVES

① Describe the importance of international marketing from the perspectives of the individual firm and the nation.

International marketing expands a company's market, allows firms to grow, and makes them less dependent on their own country's economy for success. For the nation, global trade provides a source of needed raw materials and other products not available domestically in sufficient amounts, opens up new markets to serve with domestic output, and converts countries and their citizens into partners in the search for high-quality products at the lowest possible prices. Companies find that global marketing and international trade can help them meet customer demand, reduce certain costs, provide information on markets around the world, and increase employment.

1.1. Why is international trade important for North American marketers?

1.2. Why is it important for marketers in developing and newly industrialized nations?

② Identify the major components of the environment for international marketing.

The major components of the international environment are competitive, economic, social-cultural, political-legal, and technological.

2.1. How does the international marketplace differ from the domestic marketplace?

2.2. Explain each of the three forces that drive the legal environment for U.S. firms operating abroad.

2.3. Identify the two major categories of trade barriers to global marketing. Give an example of each.

3 Outline the basic functions of GATT, WTO, NAFTA, the proposed FTAA, and the European Union.

The General Agreement on Tariffs and Trade is a 117-nation accord that has substantially reduced tariffs. The World Trade Organization oversees GATT agreements, mediates disputes, and tries to reduce trade barriers throughout the world. The North American Free Trade Agreement removes trade restrictions among Canada, Mexico, and the U.S. The proposed Free Trade Area of the Americas is a free trade area covering the entire Western Hemisphere. The European Union is a customs union whose goal is to remove all barriers to free trade among its members.

3.1. Describe briefly the following trade agreements:
   a. GATT
   b. WTO
   c. NAFTA
   d. FTAA
   e. European Union

3.2. Identify the NAFTA member countries.

3.3. In what parts of Europe are the 10 newest members of the EU located?

4 Compare the alternative strategies for entering international markets.

Several strategies are available to marketers, including exporting, importing, franchising, foreign licensing, subcontracting, and direct investment.

4.1. Describe importing and exporting as strategies for entering international markets.

4.2. Describe the advantages of franchising, foreign licensing, and subcontracting. Which might be the best strategy for a chain of moderately priced hotels to enter a foreign market?

5 Differentiate between a global marketing strategy and a multidomestic marketing strategy.

A global marketing strategy defines a standard marketing mix and implements it with minimal modifications in all foreign markets. A multidomestic marketing strategy requires firms to customize their marketing decisions to reach individual marketplaces.

5.1. Define global marketing strategy and multidomestic marketing strategy.

5.2. What are the pros and cons of each?

6 Describe the alternative marketing mix strategies used in international marketing.

Product and promotional strategies include the following: straight extension, promotion adaptation, product adaptation, dual adaptation, and product invention. Marketers may also choose among distribution, pricing, and countertrade strategies.

6.1. Explain the five product and promotional strategies used in international marketing and give an example of each.

6.2. What is countertrade? Why is the practice growing in popularity?

7 Explain the attractiveness of the U.S. as a target market for foreign marketers.

The U.S. has a large population, high levels of discretionary income, political stability, a favorable attitude toward foreign investment, and relatively controlled economic ills.

7.1. Why is the U.S. an attractive target for foreign marketers?

MARKETING TERMS YOU NEED TO KNOW

exporting 220
importing 220
infrastructure 225
exchange rate 228
tariff 233
import quota 234
free trade area 235
General Agreement on Tariffs and Trade (GATT) 236
World Trade Organization (WTO) 236
North American Free Trade Agreement (NAFTA) 237
Free Trade Area of the Americas (FTAA) 237
European Union (EU) 237
franchise 241
foreign licensing 241
multinational corporation 242
global marketing strategy 243
multidomestic marketing strategy 243
countertrade 246

OTHER IMPORTANT MARKETING TERMS

political risk assessment (PRA) 230
friendship, commerce, and navigation (FCN) treaties 231
ISO (International Organization for Standardization) certification 231
revenue tariff 233
protective tariff 233
embargo 234
subsidy 234
exchange control 234
dumping 234
customs union 236
common market 236
subcontracting 241

PROJECTS AND TEAMWORK EXERCISES

1. Imagine that you and a classmate are marketers for one of the following companies: AT&T, Amazon.com, Starbucks, Apple Computer, Burger King. Or select one of your own. Decide whether your company will expand internationally by entering the market in either Mexico, India, or China. Then write a brief outline describing the issues that your company must consider, based on the six areas of demand, competition, economy, political-legal, social-cultural, and technology.
2. Assume that you work for Domino's Pizza, which already has 3,000 outlets in more than 46 countries. With a classmate, identify a country that Domino's has not yet reached and write a brief plan for entering that country's market. Then create a print ad for that market (you can write the ad copy in English). It may be helpful to visit Domino's Web site for some ideas.
3. Assume that you are a marketer for a highly recognizable company like IBM, Old Navy, or Nike. Decide whether you think a global marketing strategy or a multidomestic strategy would be better for your product. Then create a print ad for your product reflecting your decision.
4. Beijing, China's capital city, is slated to host the 2008 Summer Olympics. By yourself or with a classmate, identify a company that might benefit from promoting its goods or services at the Beijing Olympics. Describe which strategy you would use: straight extension, product or promotion adaptation, dual adaptation, or product invention.
5. Imagine that you are a consultant for one of the following businesses. Write a proposal to the marketers for that company that could help the firm enter the U.S. market.
   a. a chain of Japanese restaurants
   b. a chain of European theme parks
   c. a South American music producer
   d. a manufacturer of Australian outdoor clothing and gear
6. Your company is a successful manufacturer of cell phones that you would like to market to Europe. The slogan for your U.S. ad campaign is, "We put the world in your hands." Prepare a plan for ensuring that your ads translate accurately into Dutch, German, Greek, Italian, Norwegian, Polish, Portuguese, and Spanish.
7. A foreign firm asks for your help in deciding whether to market its line of men's toiletries in the U.S. What questions about the U.S. market would you try to answer for the firm, and what answers do you think your research would provide?
8. Research a recent case of dumping not mentioned in the text. Write a report about the product(s) and issues involved in the case, including any resolution to date.
9. Some members of the EU have not yet adopted the organization's common currency, the euro. Select one of these countries (Denmark, Sweden, or Great Britain) and prepare a written report summarizing the reasons the government has elected to keep its own currency. Include any possible effects it might have on participation in free trade with other EU members.
10. Research the current status of the FTAA and summarize your findings in a brief report.

APPLYING CHAPTER CONCEPTS

1. Few elements in the international marketing environment are more difficult to overcome than the unexpected, such as the recent outbreaks of SARS (severe acute respiratory syndrome) and bird flu in several Asian countries. With foreign and domestic consumers all staying away from the affected areas, business suffered and marketing plans were curtailed or even halted. Suppose your company is in the travel industry. How can it protect itself from the effects of such unanticipated events? What elements would you include in a contingency plan for your firm?
2. The EU has its own antitrust arm, known as the European Commission, which recently warned Microsoft Corp. about alleged abuses in the way it markets some of its software products and which has the power to force the software maker to disclose some of its proprietary software and pay fines. What legal powers do you think economic communities like the EU should have? List those you think are appropriate and give your reasons.
3. Genetically modified (GM) food products face tough hurdles in Europe, where a five-year moratorium on new approvals of modified crops and food is reaching its end. Outline the

arguments for and against GM products. What environmental factors in the international marketplace are at play in this debate?

4. Cheap—and illegal—copies of pirated popular films like *The Lord of the Rings: The Return of the King* are often available for sale in Asia within days of their worldwide theatrical release. Firms in the entertainment industry have so far had little success in stopping the flow of these copies into consumers' hands. Do you think multinational economic communities should be more effective at combating piracy? Why or why not? What actions could they take?

ETHICS EXERCISE

One argument in favor of allowing dumping is that it sometimes provides the best or only market for small suppliers from poor countries. Without the ability to sell their products so cheaply, the argument goes, some farmers and fishermen would be destitute. Meanwhile, domestic suppliers, who may even be protected by government price supports, make a more than adequate living and have access to all the legal help they need to keep dumped products off the market.

1. Do you think dumping should be illegal? Why or why not?
2. Does your answer change if the dumped products are perishable so that if they had to be shipped to another destination to avoid dumping, they would spoil and their suppliers would earn nothing?

'netWork EXERCISES

1. **EU expansion.** The European Union (EU) expanded significantly in 2004 adding 10 Central and Eastern European nations and former Soviet republics. Visit the EU's U.S. Web site (http://www.eurunion.org) and prepare a brief report outlining the purposes of the EU and the benefits of EU membership. List some of the challenges you feel an expanded and stronger EU poses for marketers in this country.
2. **International promotion strategies.** Visit the Web sites of two international consumer-products companies, one based in the United States (such as Gillette) and one based outside the U.S. (such as Unilever). Review the sites carefully and prepare two lists. On the first list, note two or three differences in the promotional strategies you found between the companies' products sold in the U.S. and those sold in other countries. The second list should record two or three similarities among promotional strategies used by the companies in different countries. Did you find any differences between the U.S. and non-U.S. company?
3. **Rapidly growing international markets.** Visit the Web site of the United Nations Statistics Division (http://unstats.un.org). Click "National Accounts." The site contains several projections on the economic growth of individual nations. Review the projections. Which five countries are expected to experience the fastest economic growth (GDP and personal income) over the next 10 years? Which five countries are expected to experience the fastest population growth over the next 10 years? Write a brief report to a global consumer products company outlining how it can take advantage of these trends.

Note: Internet Web addresses change frequently. If you don't find the exact sites listed, you may need to access the organization's or company's home page and search from there or use a search engine such as Google.

INFOTRAC CITATIONS AND EXERCISES

Record: A116229609
The Trouble with Freedom. Jeffrey E. Garten.
Newsweek International, May 10, 2004 p45

Abstract: While the global story of the 1990s was the opening of economies around the world, the bigger theme for this decade is the deepening and maturing of democratic movements. Both trends are cause for cheer, but the two may not reinforce one another, especially in the next several years. In fact, the flowering of democracy may actually slow economic globalization even as it makes trade more inclusive and more equitable over time.

1. According to the article, why might the growth of democracy around the world slow the expansion of international trade in the short term? Do you agree with that assessment? Why or why not?
2. What are the major components of the international marketing environment according to your text? List one component of the international marketing environment that the expansion of democracy may affect, and give an example from the article.

CASE 7.1 MTV Updates Its Global Strategy

Everyone thinks we have a great job [at MTV] but we spend all of our time thinking, thinking. All the time trying to reinvent ourselves. We have to stay in touch with our audience without getting older." Those are the words of MTV Network International's creative director, Cristián Jofré. They reflect MTV's marketing commitment to understanding its environment by keeping ahead of the trends, continually "reinventing" its popular cable music programming and extended product lines. MTV, a unit of Viacom, is extremely good at reinventing itself, and it recently reinvented its international marketing strategy as well.

Its U.S. market is nearly saturated, but internationally, there is still room for growth. In fact, Viacom's management believes that MTV's foreign operations can provide up to 40 percent of its revenue over the next several years. MTVNI, the parent network of MTV, already reaches more than 380 million subscribers in 166 countries. MTV alone consists of 37 channels broadcast in 17 different languages. In the past, its international programming focused specifically on local markets, which helped its global operations grow so rapidly that 80 percent of all MTV viewers are outside the U.S. MTV Russia, for instance, developed a show called *12 Angry Viewers,* in which intellectuals discuss music videos, and a Brazilian backpack travel show is hosted by a popular Brazilian model. For its cricket-crazy viewers, MTV India features a comedy show called *Silly Point,* in which characters demonstrate the use of cricket gear in everyday life.

But while it has been successful, MTV's strategy of customizing programming for individual markets was also expensive. The average production costs between $200,000 and $350,000 for each half-hour episode. As the MTV program director in Germany says, "Almost every month we'd come up with an idea and say, 'Wow, this is a great idea but we can't afford it.'" The shift in strategy will allow the international operation, MTVNI, to develop shows that can play in more than one overseas market and thus to create programming with wide international appeal that crosses borders easily.

Among the pilot shows under development are a UK program called *Heroes,* which features pop stars interviewing their personal idols. Kelly Osbourne chats with Deborah Harry (lead singer of the 1980s band Blondie), for instance. Another pilot is called *TimeZone* and will host music performances and interviews in five locations around the world. *Mash* will blend two videos together once copyright issues have been cleared, and it has the backing of a $75 million sponsorship deal with Motorola Inc.

Under the new strategy, MTVNI's national managers will still make local programming decisions. But program developers in various international markets will be able to cooperate in developing shows that readily appeal to more than one audience, and they will have a centralized pool of money (increased by "tens of millions" of dollars) with which to work. Although such cooperation isn't entirely new—many of MTV's U.S. shows have been adapted for foreign audiences, for instance—the strategy is expected to allow for more animated programming, which is normally very expensive to develop. *Famous Last Minutes,* an animated show about the imagined last moments in the lives of famous rock stars, is in the pilot stage.

To complement its new global programming strategy, MTVNI will also expand into other operations aimed at the youth audience. It has acquired a 50 percent share in a French video game cable channel and hopes to add more such deals.

Questions for Critical Thinking

1. How do you think the global reach of the Internet has affected the youth market at which MTV is aimed? Does this make it more or less difficult to devise programming that crosses borders? Why?
2. What should MTVNI do to ensure that cultural traditions and varying styles of humor don't negatively affect any of its new international programming?

Sources: "About Viacom," http://www.viacom.com, accessed February 9, 2004; "Highlights," MTV International Web site, http://www.mtv.com, accessed February 9, 2004; "Cristián Jofré Wants His MTV," http://www.brandchannel.com, February 2, 2004; Charles Goldsmith, "MTV Seeks Global Appeal," *The Wall Street Journal*, July 21, 2003, p. B1.

VIDEO CASE 7.2 Doc Martens Makes Strides around the World

The written case on Doc Martens appears on page VC-9. The recently filmed Doc Martens video is designed to expand and highlight the concepts in this chapter and the concepts and questions covered in the written video case.

Talking about Marketing Careers with Roger Curtis, Vice President of Marketing and Sales for California Speedway

Traditionally stereotyped as a rural, largely southeastern sport, NASCAR continues to challenge these stereotypes as it expands to every corner of the nation. The same thrills that attracted hundreds of thousands of fans to major Nextel Cup races are also drawing huge crowds to tracks in New York (Watkins Glen), Michigan (Michigan International Speedway), New Hampshire (New Hampshire International Speedway), and Chicago (Chicagoland Speedway), and to a host of western locations such as Las Vegas, Denver, Phoenix, Texas, and California.

Just 46 miles east of Los Angeles and about 100 miles north of San Diego, the D-shaped oval of the California Speedway draws huge crowds to major races in all three NASCAR circuits—the Nextel Cup, Busch, and Craftsman Truck races—as well as the Indy Racing League. The track seats over 91,000, including skyboxes and luxury boxes, and parking lots surround the speedway.

Although in the entertainment and sports industries, facilities such as California Speedway, Carnegie Hall, Fenway Park, and Green Bay's Lambeau Field are referred to as *venues,* they operate much like other retail locations. To learn more about such facilities and their target markets, we visited with Roger Curtis, vice president of marketing and sales for California Speedway.

BOONE & KURTZ: Have you always been interested in racing, or was it an acquired taste? What school and work experiences led you to the California Speedway?

Being from Indiana, home of the Indianapolis 500, I grew up with racing. Sprint car, Formula One, NASCAR, Indy car racing. About the only kind of racing I didn't go to was drag racing. I'm certainly not a mechanic or a gear head either.

In high school there was a big push for math and science, and even though I knew I really didn't like math and science, that's what everyone told you to study. I started at Purdue University in nuclear engineering, but then I switched to marketing and got my degree from Indiana State University. After college I had a few internships with music companies in the Los Angeles area and then worked for a music company in North Carolina before I decided I wanted to get into motor sports. I started out working for free, volunteering and helping out wherever I could. It was mostly about getting my face out there and proving myself. I was literally on my own; I worked for no money, no expenses. These sorts of unofficial internships allowed me to hone my skills and build my network. Motor sports are hard to break into. Everyone who's a fan thinks they can be in the business. I had to really prove myself and finally got a break when one of my connections led to my first job in the industry. From there, I had to really work my way up from the bottom. It was tough; I was making hundreds of calls before anyone would even agree to see a presentation. This is a very difficult business to break into and to stay in unless you are willing to put in the extra effort.

ROGER CURTIS, VICE PRESIDENT OF MARKETING AND SALES FOR CALIFORNIA SPEEDWAY

PHOTO: COURTESY OF ROGER CURTIS

BOONE & KURTZ: In addition to generating revenue from sponsors like Gatorade, Carl's Jr., Pepsi, and Toyota; track rentals; merchandise sales through your online store; and at least six driving/riding schools, including the Richard Petty Driving Experience, much of your revenues are generated from ticket sales, parking, and concessions generated by hosting major racing weekends. Tell us a little bit about these events. How is marketing a race different than a traditional product or service?

The structure of racing is different from other sports. Think of NASCAR as the NFL. Then the Indy Racing League is like Major League Baseball. These are all sanctioning bodies in racing. The racing teams would be the Colts or the Bears or the Rams. California Speedway is the stadium that the "game" is played in. But the contestants aren't limited to just two teams. Not at all. In fact, all 43 teams in "the league" compete at the same time. The sanctioning bodies, teams, and tracks are all doing their own thing: trying to get their own sponsorships. You get some interesting conflicts. One of them for us is Coke and Pepsi. Coca-Cola is an official sponsor of NASCAR and some of the racing teams. Pepsi is the official soft drink of California Speedway. These sorts of anomalies are always present.

Motor sports marketing is incredibly different from marketing in other sports. There's no revenue sharing like there is in the NFL; it's really every man for himself.

BOONE & KURTZ: Who makes up the front office of California Speedway?

We're unique in that our marketing and sales department really includes everything: ticket sales, public relations, advertising, promotions, corporate sales, client services. We're structured differently than other tracks. At the end of the day, we're all about selling tickets. No matter what we do, either directly or in a roundabout way, the end game is getting the name out there and selling tickets. Therefore, we're all under the same marketing and sales umbrella.

From what I know about "stick and ball" sports, they're very "siloed." They have separate silos for public relations, advertising, and ticket sales. It's hard to have a fully integrated sales plan when you're so divided

Our product's like milk: When the race is over, the milk is sour and you have to throw out the tickets you didn't sell. You have a finite amount of time, and you have to sell the product or it goes bad. It's definitely not your standard marketing setup. There's no day-to-day continuity for the product. You have one shot a year at each race, and then it's gone. It makes it very difficult sometimes because you can't change plans midstream.

BOONE & KURTZ: Describe your target market. How do the track and NASCAR in general determine who the audience is?

NASCAR demographics tell us the NASCAR fan base is divided about 60/40 between men and women, so it's pretty broad. We've got baby boomers all the way through Generation X and Y in there. Out east and even in the Midwest, NASCAR has a more mature image and they are able to really market to all these groups with one generic message. Out here in Los Angeles, it's a really unique situation because the awareness of NASCAR is not as advanced. There's more to do out here; it's the largest media market in the country, and we really need multiple unique marketing plans to match the various audiences—which is difficult and very expensive. It's the most difficult marketing challenge I've ever had in my life.

BOONE & KURTZ: With so many attractions in Greater Los Angeles, how does the California Speedway compete for a share of the entertainment market?

There's a lot more competition for the entertainment dollar. I think southern California is ahead of the bell curve in some ways. There's a population and demographic shift going on out here—you've got 14 million people out here, immigrants, transplants, natives all at various ages, incomes, etc. Then you throw in the huge variety of choices that these various groups have: going to the desert, the mountains, the beaches, baseball, basketball, college sports, amusement parks, their kids' activities. Everything is competition for us. Even traffic can make a big difference. People sit in traffic all week and might not want to deal with traffic to get to the track on a weekend. Racing fans out here are just as loyal and rabid as in other parts of the country; there just aren't as many of them because the market isn't as mature. We're really fighting that and working with NASCAR to do some fundamental marketing to get awareness of NASCAR up before getting to the track's goal of converting awareness to sales. Our current task is the epitome of the AIDA model.

BOONE & KURTZ: Built in 1997, the track is relatively new. How does it compare to other tracks, and is this newness an asset to your marketing team?

In our location we need every advantage we can get. When this facility was built, no expense was spared—from the palm trees to the awnings on the ticket office, it's a spectacular facility and it is kept up very well. We spend more than other tracks on maintenance because fans here expect that level of quality in the facility. They don't compare California Speedway with other tracks back east. For them, it's how does it compare to Angels Stadium? How does it compare to Disneyland? To Sea World? We have to live up to a different standard out here. For us, marketing and sales are also the operations department, guest services, parking and traffic, and concessions. The marketing and sales department has to bring in the people, but operations is also responsible for making sure that they have a great experience, whether it is a clean restroom or a quality hot dog at the concession stand. These things will eventually affect our renewal rate. Even the guy cutting the grass is involved in marketing and sales. At the end of the day, everyone plays a role in sales.

Can MLS Speak the International Language?

With 20 million Asian fans for one team alone—Britain's famed Manchester United—European soccer seems to have successfully cracked the world sports market. By recruiting popular Asian players, forming alliances with local Asian clubs, and marketing team merchandise such as logo clothing and souvenirs, European teams are building enthusiasm for their brands everywhere they go. Even the less well-known clubs, such as Stockport County of the U.K., have found fans abroad who are sometimes more committed than those at home. "People will travel for four days to watch us in China," says Stockport's international marketing manager. And Man U (as it's known to its fans) has found an enthusiastic following in the U.S., packing stadiums for its annual series of summer exhibition games.

But despite the international success of some teams, European teams are not all making huge profits. About two dozen English teams have teetered near bankruptcy, and Italy's teams are famous for the speed at which their cash inflow flows out again. Revenues from broadcasting and sponsorship deals are often spent on player salaries; unlike the National Football League and a number of other professional sports in the U.S., there is no salary cap. Taxes are also high, and compliance with government regulations is often costly. To some observers, it seems that rich teams get better and more profitable by buying up top players, while poor teams and those that slip in the crucial divisional rankings continue to slide because they have to cut good players they no longer can afford. Being shifted down from the top division, which is based on its win–loss record, can cost a European team millions of dollars a year in broadcasting fees and other revenue.

Major League Soccer (MLS) is not immune to these problems as it tries to expand its global reach beyond the United States. When the U.S. national team plays in the World Cup, the most prestigious and highly anticipated competition in soccer, the attention and publicity make more people around the world aware of American players and the MLS teams from which many of them come. Signing international players to U.S. team rosters can help draw foreign fans. But with Europe's teams already well established abroad, and China making plans to restart its own national league, competition for fans abroad will continue to be tough—and expensive. There is money to be made in merchandising, licensing, and sponsorships, but the fan base must be built first.

Meanwhile, MLS has been facing another sort of competition, within its very borders. Hispanic fans have attended more than 50 professional Mexican soccer matches played in the U.S. each year, packing stadiums and lining up to greet the players enthusiastically on arrival. "Major League Soccer would love to have a crowd like this," said a representative of a Mexican soccer promotion agency. And it's probably true. One of the two money-losing teams that recently folded was a Miami team that had been launched with the intent of helping to bring American soccer to a growing Hispanic market. To counter the threat to this lucrative market, MLS is creating an expansion franchise spun off from what may be Mexico's most popular team, the Guadalajara Chivas. "A lot of Mexican-Americans have been supporting Chivas all their lives," says team owner Jorge Vergara, who claims there are more than 10 million U.S. fans of the homegrown Mexican club. Vergara and MLS are hoping the new team, Los Angeles–based Chivas USA, will win these fans over even though, under MLS rules, it will not be able to match the Mexican team's boast that it has never signed a non-Mexican player. The expansion team plans to include as many Mexican nationals on its player roster as regulations allow and fill remaining slots with green-card holders, players under 25, and even some U.S. players.

MLS commissioner Don Garber says, "In the global culture, the universal language is soccer. That's the sweet spot. If it weren't for . . . globalization, we wouldn't have the opportunity we have today."

Questions for Critical Thinking

1. Why do you think Asian fans travel for hours or days to attend a soccer match when European teams are on tour?
2. Can MLS teams share the success of English teams that are more popular abroad than they are at home? Should that be their goal? Why or why not?
3. Are European teams doing a good job of serving their world market? Why or why not?
4. Do you think U.S. fans of Mexico's Chivas team will become fans of the MLS spinoff, Chivas USA? Why or why not?

Sources: Jack Ewing with Laura Cohn, "Can Soccer Be Saved?" *BusinessWeek*, July 19, 2004, pp. 46–48; Grant Wahl, "Football v. Fútbol," *Sports Illustrated*, July 5, 2004, pp. 68–72; L. Jon Wertheim, "The Whole World Is Watching," *Sports Illustrated*, June 14, 2004, pp. 73–86; Martha Mendoza, "Mexican Pro Soccer Draws U.S. Fans," *Marketing News*, April 15, 2004, p. 22; Michael Freedman, "Madness of Crowds," *Forbes 2000*, April 12, 2004, pp. 120–128; Amy Rosewater, "Manchester United Leads Soccer Invasion," *USA Today*, July 22, 2003, p. 3C.

part 3

TARGET MARKET SELECTION

chapter 8 Marketing Research, Decision Support Systems, and Sales Forecasting

chapter 9 Market Segmentation, Targeting, and Positioning

chapter 10 Relationship Marketing, Customer Relationship Management (CRM), and One-to-One Marketing

PHOTO: COURTESY OF WIREIMAGES.COM

chapter 8

Marketing Research, Decision Support Systems, and Sales Forecasting

chapter objectives

1. Describe the development of the marketing research function and its major activities.
2. Explain the steps in the marketing research process.
3. Distinguish between primary and secondary data and identify the sources of each type.
4. Explain the different sampling techniques used by marketing researchers.
5. Identify the methods by which marketing researchers collect primary data.
6. Explain the challenges of conducting marketing research in global markets.
7. Outline the most important uses of computer technology in marketing research.
8. Explain how the use of information technology, particularly marketing decision support systems (MDSSs), can enhance and refine market research and its impact on decision making.
9. Identify the major types of forecasting methods.

CHARLOTTE NBA TEAM HUNTS A NEW IDENTITY

Creating an identity for a new sports team is no stroll down the court. The process involves thousands of hours of work and hundreds of thousands of dollars in marketing research. The new NBA expansion team in Charlotte, North Carolina, already received favorable publicity by being the first team with African-American majority ownership. Media mogul Robert L. Johnson, founder of Black Entertainment Television and publisher of *Jet* magazine, purchased the franchise rights to the team for an estimated $300 million. Once the NBA's board of governors approved the deal, club executives began their drive to establish the team's identity—not only a name but a logo, team colors, and uniform—a complete package attractive enough to make the public forget all about the recently departed Hornets franchise, which team owners took to New Orleans.

The previous franchise's tenure from 1988 until 2002 was an immediate success. For the first nine years of its existence, it played before sellouts at every home game. Its top-selling teal and purple pinstriped uniforms and all-star players like Alonzo Mourning and Larry Johnson made the Hornets the pride of Charlotte. But fans grew

disenchanted as the owner failed to re-sign his stars and voted against his request for a public bond issue to build a new arena. And shortly thereafter, the team moved to the Big Easy.

Because the public's acceptance and support were so critical to the start of the new team, marketers began to research the team's identity with the local community by forming the Charlotte Regional Sports Commission to search for a name. In a "Help Name the Team" campaign, the researchers received more than 1,250 suggestions. To narrow the choices, researchers set up focus groups of Charlotte-area residents and business and civic leaders. During three rounds, the groups helped researchers reduce the names to 85, to 25, and then to the final 10. The 10 finalists were then presented to a representative group of Charlotteans—as a "sanity check" to head off unforeseen disaster, as one researcher put it. The three finalists were the Charlotte Flight (drawing on North Carolina's famous Wright brothers' legacy), the Charlotte Dragons (a fantasy nickname with appeal to young people), and the Charlotte Bobcats (a wild animal that is common in the Carolinas). Team executives took it from there, selecting the Bobcats because of the predator's athleticism and ferocity.

Next came selection of the team colors and logo. A team's logo and colors are important components of total team revenues. Successful merchandise sales add to the pool of money coming from ticket sales, luxury suite rentals, corporate sponsorships, food and beverage sales, and parking. All of these funds are funneled into recouping the cost of the franchise and retaining talented players to make the team competitive from year to year. Bobcat staff researchers concentrated on selecting team colors and hired an outside marketing research firm, Gameplan Branding Group, to work on the logo design. Both research teams started with every NBA and WNBA team logo and all their colors. After reviewing the colors, the club's researchers noticed that very few teams used orange in their logos or uniforms, and none used it as the dominant color. Cary Mitchell, a clothing designer who had worked for such high-profile sports figures as Tiger Woods, Ken Griffey Jr., LeBron James, and Yao Ming, was called in to consult and agreed that orange was a hot new clothing color. It also didn't hurt that team owner Johnson had studied at both the University of Illinois and Princeton, schools whose teams feature orange in their uniforms. After the selection of Bobcat Orange, the team picked complementary colors of blue, black, and silver.

The logo consultants developed several sketches of bobcats with basketballs and had them plastered on their office walls, with Post-it Notes pointing to various features. The Bobcat's ears alone were redrawn several times, until they had the look of a cat ready to pounce on its prey. But the forward-facing initial sketches looked too static to represent a fast-paced basketball team. So, to provide the illusion of speed and ferocity, the team decided on a springing bobcat profile.

Has the team's new identity captured the public's imagination? Response to date has been positive. The team's long-term success on the court and in attracting fans will ultimately determine the fate of the Bobcats, but marketing researchers will be there to work hand in hand with executives to take the pulse of the Charlotte sports fans. As adjustments are needed, they'll get back to work.[1]

Chapter Overview

CREATING a distinct image in consumers' minds is a difficult task for any business but particularly so for a new sports franchise like the Charlotte Bobcats. As we saw in the opening story, the team's marketers used a variety of methods to gain fan input, create a team identity, and align the team with its community.

Marketing research is the process of collecting and using information for marketing decision making. Data comes from a variety of sources. Some results come from well-planned studies designed to elicit specific information. Other valuable information comes from sales force reports, accounting records, and published reports. Still other data emerges from controlled experiments and computer simulations. Marketing research, by presenting pertinent information in a useful format, aids decision makers in analyzing data and in suggesting possible actions.

This chapter discusses the marketing research function. Marketers use research to understand their customers, target customer segments, and develop long-term customer relationships—all keys to profitability. Information collected through marketing research underlies much of the material on market segmentation discussed in the following chapter. Clearly, the marketing research function is the primary source of the information needed to make effective marketing decisions. This chapter also explains how marketing research techniques are used to make accurate sales forecasts, a critical component of marketing planning. The use of decision support systems is also discussed, as is their vast impact on market research decision making and planning.

Briefly Speaking

America is good at three things: basketball, making war, and buying stuff.

Watts Wacker
American futurist, author, and chairman, FirstMatter

marketing research Process of collecting and using information for marketing decision making.

THE MARKETING RESEARCH FUNCTION

Before looking at how marketing research is conducted, we must first examine its historical development, the people and organizations it involves, and the activities it entails. Since an underlying purpose of the research is to find out more about consumers, it is clear that research is central to effective customer satisfaction and customer relationship programs. Media technologies such as the Internet and virtual reality are opening up new channels through which researchers can tap into consumer information.

1 **Describe the development of the marketing research function and its major activities.**

DEVELOPMENT OF THE MARKETING RESEARCH FUNCTION

More than 125 years have passed since advertising pioneer N. W. Ayer conducted the first organized marketing research project in 1879. A second important milestone in the development of marketing research occurred 32 years later, when Charles C. Parlin organized the nation's first commercial research department at Curtis Publishing Co., publisher of *The Saturday Evening Post.*

Parlin got his start as a marketing researcher by counting soup cans in Philadelphia's garbage. Here is what happened. Parlin, an ad salesman, was trying to convince the Campbell Soup Co. to advertise in *The Saturday Evening Post.* Campbell Soup resisted, believing that the *Post* reached primarily working-class readers, who preferred to make their own soup. Campbell Soup marketers were targeting higher income people who could afford to pay for the convenience of soup in a can. To prove Campbell wrong, Parlin began counting soup cans in the garbage collected from different neighborhoods. His research revealed that working-class families bought more canned soup than wealthy households, who had servants to cook for them. Campbell Soup soon became a regular *Saturday Evening Post* client. It is interesting to note that garbage remains a good source of information for marketing researchers even today. Prior to the recent cutbacks in food service, some airlines studied the leftovers from onboard meals to determine what to serve passengers.

Most early research gathered little more than written testimonials from purchasers of firms' products. Research methods became more sophisticated during the 1930s as the development of statistical techniques led to refinements in sampling procedures and greater accuracy in research findings.

In recent years, advances in computer technology have significantly changed the complexion of marketing research. Besides accelerating the pace and broadening the base of data collection, computers have aided marketers in making informed decisions about problems and opportunities. Simulations, for example, allow marketers to evaluate alternatives by posing what-if questions. Marketing researchers at many consumer goods firms simulate product introductions through computer programs to determine whether to risk real-world product launches or even to subject products to test marketing. We are only beginning to see the impact of marketing decision support systems (MDSSs), which allow marketing researchers to transform data into useful information.

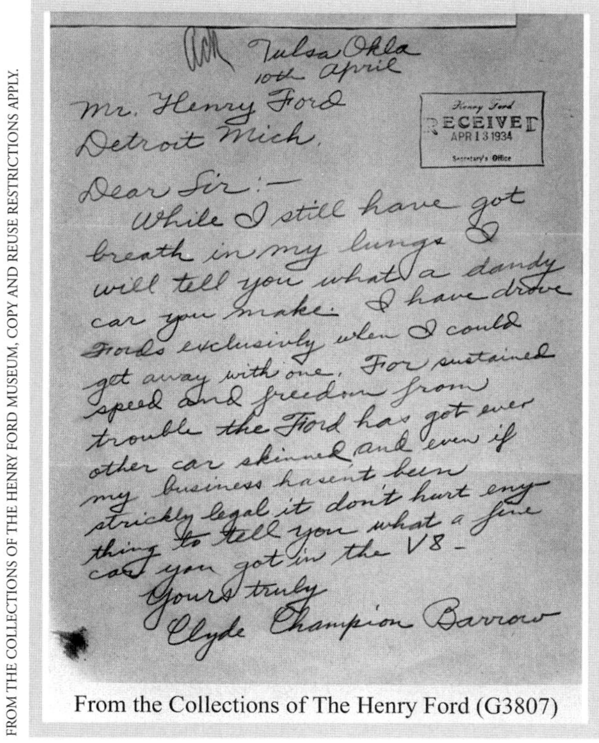
Tulsa Okla
10th April

Mr. Henry Ford
Detroit Mich.

Henry Ford
RECEIVED
APR 13 1934
Secretary's Office

Dear Sir:—
While I still have got breath in my lungs I will tell you what a dandy car you make. I have drove Fords exclusivly when I could get away with one. For sustained speed and freedom from trouble the Ford has got ever other car skinned and even if my business hasen't been strickly legal it don't hurt eny thing to tell you what a fine car you got in the V8 -

Yours truly
Clyde Champion Barrow

From the Collections of The Henry Ford (G3807)

This testimonial letter from a satisfied "customer"—allegedly written by Clyde Barrow of the infamous Bonnie and Clyde gang of the 1930s—was received by Henry Ford before the two gangsters were shot by law enforcement officers on May 23, 1934.

WHO CONDUCTS MARKETING RESEARCH?

The size and organizational form of the marketing research function are usually tied to the structure of the company. Some firms organize research units to support different product lines, brands, or geographic areas. Others organize their research functions according to the types of research they need performed, such as sales analysis, new-product development, advertising evaluation, or sales forecasting.

Many firms outsource their research needs and depend on independent marketing research firms. These independent organizations might specialize in handling just part of a larger study, such as conducting consumer interviews. Firms can also contract out entire research studies.

Marketers usually decide whether to conduct a study internally or through an outside organization based on cost. Another major consideration is the reliability and accuracy of the information collected by an outside organization. Because collecting marketing data is what these outside organizations do full time, the information they gather is often more thorough and accurate than that collected by less experienced in-house staff. Often, an outside marketing research firm can provide technical assistance and expertise not available within the company's marketing department. Interaction with outside suppliers also helps to ensure that a researcher does not conduct a study only to validate a favorite viewpoint or preferred option.

Marketing research companies range in size from sole proprietorships to national and international firms such as ACNielsen, Information Resources Inc., and Arbitron. They can be classified as syndicated services, full-service suppliers, or limited-service suppliers depending on the types of services they offer to clients. Some full-service organizations are also willing to take on limited-service activities.

Briefly Speaking

You can give people responsibility and authority, but without information they are helpless. Knowledge is the ultimate power tool.

Bill Gates (b. 1954)
cofounder, Microsoft Corp.

Syndicated Services

An organization that regularly provides a standardized set of data to all customers is called a **syndicated service.** Mediamark Research Inc., for example, operates a syndicated product research service based on personal interviews with adults regarding their exposure to advertising media. Clients include advertisers, advertising agencies, magazines, newspapers, broadcasters, and cable TV networks.

Full-Service Research Suppliers

An organization that contracts with clients to conduct complete marketing research projects is called a **full-service research supplier.** JRP Marketing Research Services Inc., whose promotional message is shown in Figure 8.1, is a full-service firm specializing in brand strategies and in building customer loyalty. A full-service supplier becomes the client's marketing research arm, performing all of the steps in the marketing research process (discussed later in this chapter).

figure 8.1

Full-Service Marketing Research Firm

Limited-Service Research Suppliers

A marketing research firm that specializes in a limited number of activities, such as conducting field interviews or performing data processing, is called a **limited-service research supplier.** Working almost exclusively for major movie studios, Nielsen National Research Group specializes in testing promotional materials for and marketing of motion pictures. The firm also prepares studies to help clients develop advertising strategies and to track awareness and interest. Syndicated services can also be considered a type of limited-service research supplier.

CUSTOMER SATISFACTION MEASUREMENT PROGRAMS

In their marketing research, firms often focus on tracking the satisfaction levels of current customers. But some marketers have gained valuable insights by tracking the dissatisfaction that led customers to abandon certain products for those of competitors. Some customer defections are only partial; customers may remain somewhat satisfied with a business but not completely satisfied. Such attitudes could lead them to take their business elsewhere. Studying the underlying causes of customer defections, even partial defections, can be useful for identifying problem areas that need attention. Confidata, whose promotional message is featured in Figure 8.2, uses interviews and telephone verification to find out exactly how satisfied consumers will be with a firm's products.

figure 8.2

Research Designed to Assess Levels of Customer Satisfaction

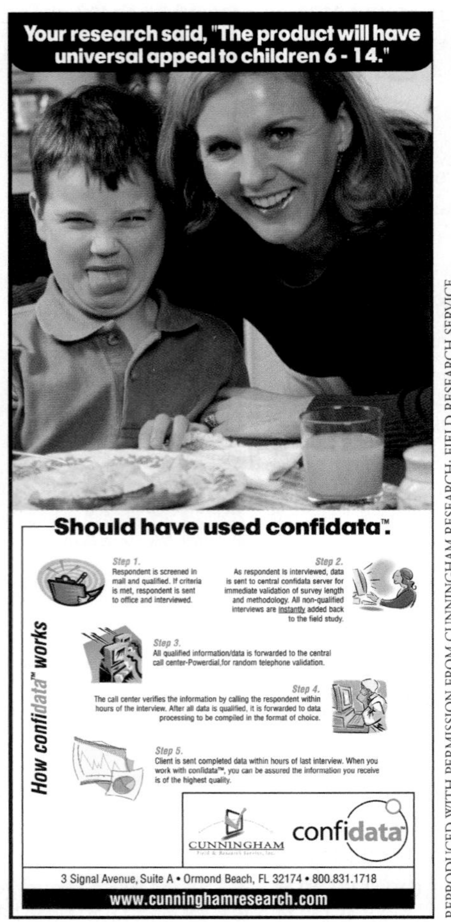

1. Identify the different classifications of marketing research suppliers and explain how they differ from one another.
2. What research methods can be used to measure customer satisfaction?

THE MARKETING RESEARCH PROCESS

(2) **Explain the steps in the marketing research process.**

As discussed earlier, business executives rely on marketing research to provide the information they need to make effective decisions regarding their firm's current and future activities. The chances of making good decisions improve when the right information is provided at the right time during decision making. To achieve this goal, marketing researchers often follow the six-step process shown in Figure 8.3. In the initial stages, researchers define the problem, conduct exploratory research, and formulate a hypothesis to be tested. Next, they create a design for the research study, followed by the collection of needed data. Finally, researchers interpret and present the research information. The following sections take a closer look at each step of the marketing research process.

DEFINE THE PROBLEM

A popular anecdote advises that well-defined problems are half solved. A well-defined problem permits the researcher to focus on securing the exact information needed for the solution. Clearly defining the question that research needs to answer increases the speed and accuracy of the research process.

Researchers must carefully avoid confusing symptoms of a problem with the problem itself. A symptom merely alerts marketers that a problem exists. For example, suppose that a maker of frozen pizzas sees its market share drop from 8 to 5 percent in six months. The loss of market share is a symptom of a problem the company must solve. To define the problem, the firm must look for the underlying causes of its market share loss.

A logical starting point in identifying the problem might be to evaluate the firm's target market and marketing mix elements. Suppose, for example, a firm has recently changed its promotional strategies. Research might then seek to answer the question "What must we do to improve the effectiveness of our marketing mix?" The firm's marketers might also look at possible environmental changes. Perhaps a new competitor entered the firm's market. Decision makers will need information to help answer the question "What must we do to distinguish our company from the new competitor?"

When McDonald's started making minor changes to some of its basic recipes in a recent cost-cutting campaign, unheeded customer complaints set off an 11-month decline in sales. The company experienced its first loss since becoming a publicly traded firm more than 35 years before. Its new CEO, the late James Cantalupo, told the company's senior managers, "If you're confused about what this is about, let me make it clear: This is about our customers." Cantalupo's passion for understanding customers by listening to their opinions boiled down to a simple rule: "I made it a policy never to leave a store without talking to a customer." Cantalupo extended that policy companywide, sending 900 employees out to stores on fact-finding missions to identify problems. He made a separate survey of repeat customers and hired outside survey firms to troubleshoot as well. Soon McDonald's had focused on the problem and improved the quality of its food. Within a couple of years, sales began to rise and the company's stock price more than doubled.[2]

figure 8.3

The Marketing Research Process

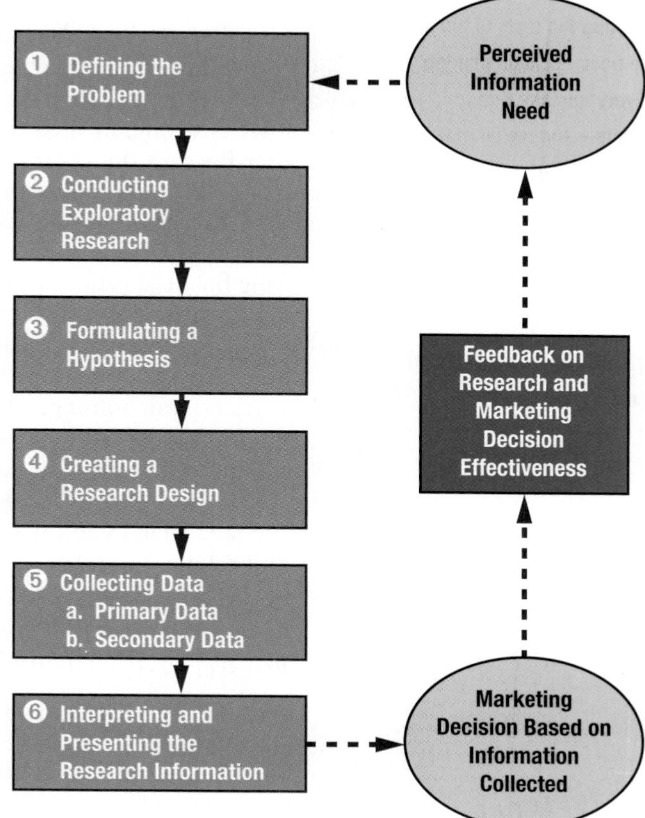

CONDUCT EXPLORATORY RESEARCH

Once a firm has defined the question it wants to answer, researchers can begin exploratory research. **Exploratory research** seeks to discover the cause of a specific problem by discussing the problem with informed sources both within and outside the firm and by examining data from other information sources. Marketers at Macaroni Grill, for example, might talk with their wholesalers, retailers, and customers. Executives might also ask for input from the sales force or look for overall market clues.

In addition to talking with employees, exploratory research can include evaluation of company records, such as sales and profit analyses, and available competitive data. Marketing researchers often refer to internal data collection as situation analysis. The term *informal investigation* is often used for exploratory interviews with informed persons outside the researchers' firms.

Using Internal Data

Marketers can find valuable data in their firm's own internal records. Typical sources of internal data are sales records, financial statements, and marketing cost analyses. Marketers analyze sales performance records to gain an overall view of company efficiency and to find clues to potential problems. Easily prepared from company invoices or a computer database system, this **sales analysis** can provide important details to management. The study typically compares actual and expected sales based on a detailed sales forecast by territory, product, customer, and salesperson. Once the sales quota—the level of expected sales to which actual results are compared—has been established, it is a simple process to compare actual results with expected performance.

Briefly Speaking

When I was a kid, I used to imagine animals running under my bed. I told my dad, and he solved the problem quickly. He cut the legs off my bed.

Lou Brock (b. 1939)
American baseball player

exploratory research Process of discussing a marketing problem with informed sources both within and outside the firm and examining information from secondary sources.

Briefly Speaking

Getting the facts is the key to good decision making. Every mistake that I made—and we all make mistakes—came because I didn't take the time. I didn't drive hard enough. I wasn't smart enough to get the facts.

Charles F. Knight (b. 1936)
chairman, Emerson Electric

Other possible breakdowns for sales analysis separate transactions by customer type, product, sales method (mail, telephone, or personal contact), type of order (cash or credit), and order size. Sales analysis is one of the least expensive and most important sources of marketing information available to a firm. Anheuser-Busch has crafted a highly accurate method of amassing sales data about its own and competitors' products. Called BudNet, the closely guarded process relies on distributors' drivers and sales reps to input an incredible amount of detail about beer sales, shelf stock, and displays at thousands of outlets around the country. The company collects the data daily for an up-to-the-minute picture of what's selling, in what quantities and package types, and backed by what kind of promotions. "Anheuser-Busch is the smartest in figuring out how to use [the data]," says one industry analyst, and indeed, the company forecasts the themes and images in its ads, and even its new-product development strategies, based on the data it collects through BudNet.[3]

Accounting data, as summarized in the firm's financial statements, can be another good tool for identifying financial issues that influence marketing. Using ratio analysis, researchers can compare performance in current and previous years against industry benchmarks. These exercises may hint at possible problems, but only more detailed analysis would reveal specific causes of indicated variations.

A third source of internal information is *marketing cost analysis*—evaluation of expenses for tasks such as selling, warehousing, advertising, and delivery to determine the profitability of particular customers, territories, or product lines. Firms often examine the allocation of costs to products, customers, and territories. Marketing decision makers then evaluate the profitability of particular customers and territories on the basis of the sales produced and the costs incurred in generating those sales.

Like sales analysis and financial research, marketing cost analysis is most useful when it provides information linked to other forms of marketing research. A later section of this chapter will address how computer technologies can accomplish these linkages and move information among a firm's units.

FORMULATE A HYPOTHESIS

After defining the problem and conducting an exploratory investigation, the marketer needs to formulate a **hypothesis**—a tentative explanation for some specific event. A hypothesis is a statement about the relationship among variables that carries clear implications for testing this relationship. It sets the stage for more in-depth research by further clarifying what researchers need to test.

Not all studies test specific hypotheses. However, a carefully designed study can benefit from the rigor introduced by developing a hypothesis before beginning data collection and analysis.

The great tragedy of science is the slaying of a beautiful hypothesis by an ugly fact.

Thomas H. Huxley (1825–1895)
British biologist and educator

CREATE A RESEARCH DESIGN

To test hypotheses and find solutions to marketing problems, a marketer creates a **research design,** a master plan or model for conducting marketing research. In planning a research project, marketers must be sure that the study will measure what they intend to measure. A second important research design consideration is the selection of respondents. Marketing researchers use sampling techniques (discussed later in the chapter) to determine which consumers to include in their studies.

Some of the nation's biggest food companies employ a simple research design to test new products. They offer items to Wal-Mart first. The nation's largest retailer doesn't charge producers a fee—called a *slotting fee*—to stock their merchandise. Then, if the item sells at Wal-Mart, other retailers will take notice and drop their slotting fees.[4]

3 **Distinguish between primary and secondary data and identify the sources of each type.**

secondary data Previously published information.

primary data Information collected specifically for the investigation at hand.

COLLECT DATA

Marketing researchers gather two kinds of data: secondary data and primary data. **Secondary data** is information from previously published or compiled sources. Census data is an example. **Primary data** refers to information collected for the first time specifically for a marketing research study. An example of primary data is statistics collected from a survey that asks current customers about their preferences for product improvements.

Secondary data offers two important advantages: (1) It is almost always less expensive to gather than primary data, and (2) researchers usually spend less time to locate and use secondary data. A research study that requires primary data may take three to four months to complete, while a researcher can often gather secondary data in a matter of days.

Solving an Ethical Controversy

DID TEST RESULTS GO BETTER WITH COKE?

WHEN Atlanta-based Coca-Cola Company tried to persuade Burger King that Frozen Coke was a big enough seller to merit a national promotional campaign, Burger King wanted proof. So Coca-Cola selected a test city—Richmond, Virginia—and scheduled a two-week test that offered a free Frozen Coke with every Value Meal. Initial results were disappointing, so a Coke executive distributed $9,000 of his own money for buying Value Meals to a Boys & Girls Club in the area, through a consultant who said he represented Burger King.

The Coca-Cola Company presented the inflated test results to Burger King, and a cooperative national promotional campaign for Frozen Coke was launched. The manipulation of the test came to light months afterward during a routine audit, but it was not revealed to Burger King until later still and caused The Coca-Cola Company enormous public embarrassment.

DOES FALSIFICATION OF RESEARCH UNDERMINE THE ENTIRE MARKETING RESEARCH INDUSTRY?

PRO

1. If companies are willing to manipulate their research results, no one can trust any marketing information.
2. Actions like Coca-Cola's also undermine trust between business partners, who rely on market information to shape their cooperative efforts.

CON

1. This was an isolated incident that resulted from bad judgment by a single executive under pressure.
2. The bad publicity that The Coca-Cola Company received, coupled with its ongoing legal troubles related to the fraud, should discourage other marketers from falsifying data.

SUMMARY

Burger King announced it would withdraw Frozen Coke from its 8,400 restaurants but later decided it would reconsider. The two firms have since reached a settlement, in which the Atlanta firm will pay Burger King and its franchisees millions of dollars. The U.S. Department of Justice and the Securities and Exchange Commission are conducting investigations about this and other possible improprieties in marketing research.

Sources: "Coca-Cola Gets Grand Jury Subpoenas in Fraud Investigation," *Atlanta Business Chronicle,* February 27, 2004, http://www.bizjournals.com/atlanta; Elliot Blair Smith and Theresa Howard, "Whistle-blower Settles with Coke," *USA Today,* October 8, 2003, p. B2; Christina Cheddar Berk, "Executive at Coke Gives Up His Post in Scandal's Wake," *The Wall Street Journal,* August 26, 2003, p. B4; Chad Terhune, "How Coke Officials Beefed Up Results of Marketing Test," *The Wall Street Journal,* August 20, 2003, p. A1; Theresa Howard, "Burger King, Coke Deal May Reach $20M," *USA Today,* August 13, 2003, p. B3.

Secondary data does have limitations that primary data does not. First, published information can quickly become obsolete. A marketer analyzing the population of various areas may discover that even the most recent census figures are already out of date because of rapid growth and changing demographics. Second, published data collected for an unrelated purpose may not be completely relevant to the marketer's specific needs. For example, census data will not reveal the brand preferences of consumers.

Although research to gather primary data can cost more and take longer, the results can provide richer, more detailed information than secondary data offers. The choice between secondary and primary data is tied to cost, applicability, and effectiveness. In reality, many marketing research projects combine secondary and primary data to fully answer marketing questions. This chapter examines specific methods for collecting both secondary and primary data in later sections. As the "Solving an Ethical Controversy" feature illustrates, however, the collection of data should not be influenced in any way to yield results that marketers want to hear.

figure 8.4

The Research Report and Presentation: Linking the Study to the Research User

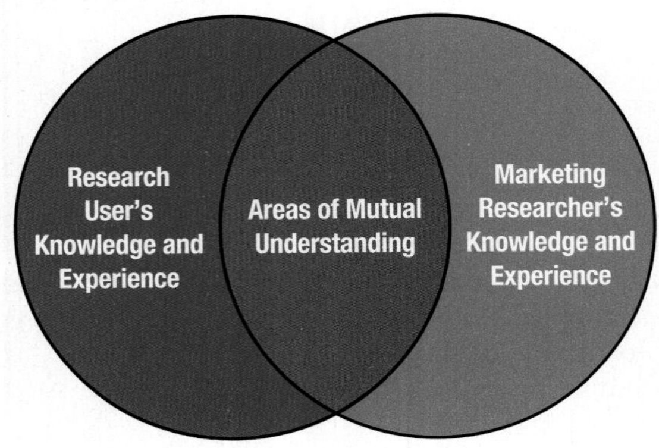

INTERPRET AND PRESENT RESEARCH INFORMATION

The final step in the marketing research process is to interpret the findings and present them to decision makers in a format that allows managers to make effective judgments. As Figure 8.4 illustrates, possible differences in interpretations of research results may occur between marketing researchers and their audiences due to differing backgrounds, levels of knowledge, and experience. Both oral and written reports should be presented in a manner designed to minimize such misinterpretations.

Marketing researchers and research users must cooperate at every stage in the research process. Too many studies go unused because management fears restrictions on usefulness of the results once they hear lengthy discussions of research limitations or unfamiliar terminology. Marketing researchers must remember to direct their reports toward management and not to other researchers. They should spell out their conclusions in clear and concise terms that can be put into action. Reports should confine technical details of the research methods to an appendix, if they are included at all. By presenting research results to all key executives at a single sitting, researchers can ensure that everyone will understand the findings. Decision makers can then quickly reach consensus on what the results mean and what actions are to be taken.[5]

1. What are the six steps in the marketing research process?
2. What is the goal of exploratory research?
3. Distinguish between primary and secondary data.

MARKETING RESEARCH METHODS

Briefly Speaking

When you are drowning in numbers, you need a system to separate the wheat from the chaff.

Anthony Adams (b. 1940)

vice president, Campbell Soup Co.

Clearly, data collection is an integral part of the marketing research process. One of the most time-consuming parts of collecting data is determining what method the marketer should use to obtain the data. This section discusses the most commonly used methods by which marketing researchers find both secondary and primary data.

SECONDARY DATA COLLECTION

Secondary data comes from many sources. The overwhelming quantity of secondary data available at little or no cost challenges researchers to select only data that is relevant to the problem or issue being studied.

Secondary data consists of two types: internal and external data. Internal data, as discussed earlier, includes sales records, product performance reviews, sales force activity reports, and marketing cost reports. External data comes from a variety of sources, including government records, syndicated research services, and industry publications. Computerized databases provide access to vast amounts of data from both inside and outside an organization. The following sections on government data, private data, and online sources focus on databases and other external data sources available to marketing researchers.

Government Data

The federal government is the nation's most important source of marketing data. Census data provides the most frequently used government statistics. A census of population is conducted every 10 years and is made available at no charge in local libraries, on computer disks, and through the Internet. The Bureau of the Census also conducts a periodic census of housing, population, business, manufacturers, agriculture, minerals, and governments.

The U.S. Census of Population contains a wealth of valuable information for marketers. It breaks down the population by very small geographic areas, making it possible to determine population traits by city block or census tract in large cities. It divides the populations of nonmetropolitan areas into block-numbering areas (BNAs). The BNAs and census tracts are important for marketing analysis because they highlight populations with similar traits, avoiding diversity within political boundaries such as county lines. This data helps marketers such as local retailers and shopping center developers gather vital information about customers in an immediate neighborhood without spending time or money to conduct comprehensive surveys. The Census Bureau uses a variety of statistical techniques to group households into homogeneous clusters of people who have similar lifestyles and spending habits and who listen to similar kinds of broadcast media.

Marketing researchers find even more valuable resources in the government's computerized mapping database called the TIGER system, for Topographically Integrated Geographic Encoding and Referencing system. This system overlays topographic features such as railroads, highways, and rivers with census data such as household income figures. TIGER data is available on DVD, making the Census Bureau one of the first federal agencies to use this technology to publish huge amounts of digital data. The DVDs contain both database management software and mapping software, making TIGER data highly accessible to marketers.[6]

Marketers often get other information from the federal government, such as the following:

- *Monthly Catalog of the United States Government Publications* and *Statistical Abstract of the United States*, published annually
- *Survey of Current Business*, updated monthly
- *County and City Data Book*, typically published every three years, providing data on each county and city of over 25,000 residents

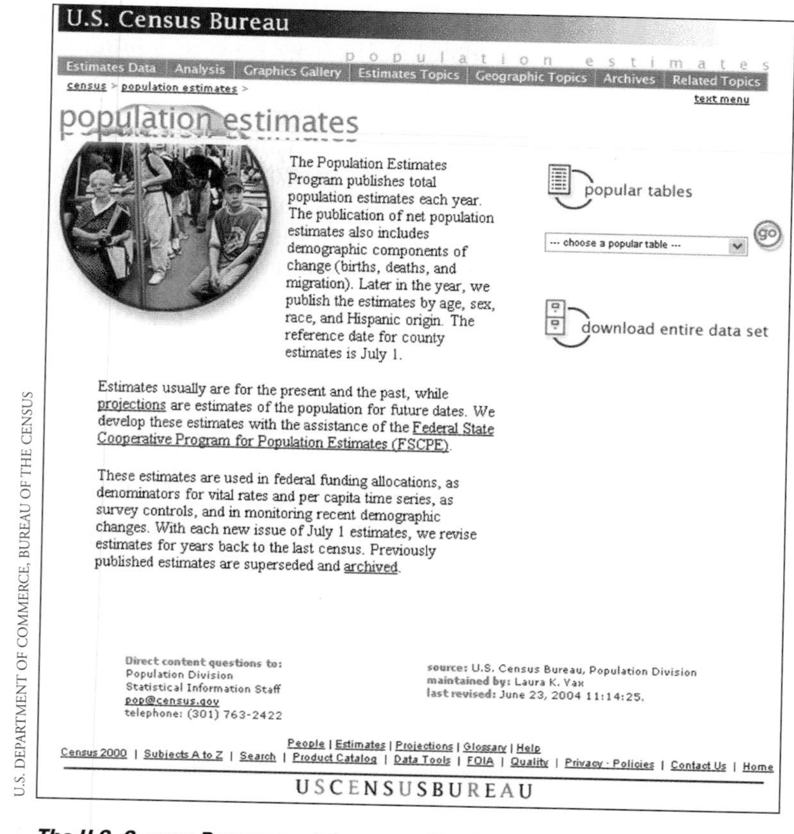

U.S. DEPARTMENT OF COMMERCE, BUREAU OF THE CENSUS

The U.S. Census Bureau contains a wealth of data—from current population estimates and projections, to shifts in population growth for states and counties, to information on ages, sex, and ethnic and racial makeup of population segments. Marketers can use such secondary data to learn more about their customers.

State and city governments serve as additional important sources of information on employment, production, and sales activities. In addition, university bureaus of business and economic research frequently collect and disseminate valuable information.

Private Data

Many private organizations provide information for marketing decision makers. A trade association may be an excellent source of data on activities in a particular industry. Gale Publishing's *Encyclopedia of Associations,* available in many libraries, can help marketers track down trade associations that may have data pertinent to their company. Also, the advertising industry continuously collects data on audiences reached by various media.

Business and trade magazines also publish a wide range of valuable data. Ulrich's *Guide to International Periodicals,* another common library reference, can point researchers in the direction of trade publications that conduct and publish industry-specific research. General business magazines can also be good sources. *Sales & Marketing Management,* for instance, publishes an annual *Survey of Media Markets* that combines statistics for population, effective buying income (EBI), and retail sales into buying power indexes that indicate each geographic market's ability to buy.

Since few libraries carry specialized trade journals, the best way to gather data from them is either directly from the publishers or through online periodical databases like Dialog's *ABI/Inform,* available at many libraries, or CompuServe's *Knowledge Index*. Increasingly, trade publications maintain Web home pages that allow archival searches. Larger libraries can often provide directories and other publications that can help researchers find secondary data. For instance, Find/SVP's *FindEx, the Directory of Market Research Reports, Studies, and Surveys* lists a tremendous variety of completed research studies that are available for purchase.

Several national firms offer information to businesses by subscription. *Roper Starch Worldwide* is a global database service with continuing data on consumer attitudes, life stages, and behavior information for 30 countries. Roper also provides *Starch Readership Reports* that measure more than 20,000 ads in 400 magazines.

Electronic systems that scan UPC bar codes speed purchase transactions, and they also provide data used for inventory control, ordering, and delivery. Scanning technology is widely used by grocers and other retailers, and marketing research companies, such as ACNielsen and Information Resources Inc., store this data in commercially available databases. These scanner-based information services track consumer purchases of a wide variety of UPC-coded products. Retailers can use this information to target customers with the right merchandise at the right time.

ACNielsen SalesNet uses the Internet to deliver scanner data quickly to clients. Data is processed as soon as it is received from supermarkets and is then forwarded to marketing researchers so they can perform more in-depth analysis. At the same time, Nielsen representatives summarize the data in both graphic and spreadsheet form and post it on the Internet for immediate access by clients.

Online Sources of Secondary Data

The tools of cyberspace sometimes simplify the hunt for secondary data. Hundreds of databases and other sources of information are available online, both through the Internet and through commercial services such as America Online. A well-designed, Internet-based marketing research project can cost less yet yield faster results than offline research. For instance, toy building-block marketer Lego needed to make a quick decision on rereleasing some of its classic sets. The company posted a bulletin board at Lego.com, inviting its 2 million monthly visitors to share opinions and to comment on their favorite Lego classics. Using software from Recipio, results were gathered and analyzed in real time. Within two weeks, the company had the information it needed. Almost 40 percent of respondents aged 18 and under—Lego's "sweet spot" target market—favored rereleasing Guarded Inn and Metroliner. Within six weeks, Metroliner sales topped the annual sales of comparable Lego sets.[7]

A recent survey reported that more than 70 percent of marketing research firms currently conduct some form of Internet research, up from 50 percent a year earlier. Today, industry experts estimate that about half of all marketing research could easily be done online.[8]

The Internet has spurred the growth of research aggregators—companies that acquire, catalog, reformat, segment, and then resell premium research reports that have already been published. Aggregators put valuable data within reach of marketers who lack the time or the budget to commission custom research. Since Web technology makes their databases easy to search, aggregators are able to compile detailed, specialized reports quickly and cost-effectively.[9]

Internet search tools such as Google and Yahoo! can find specific sites that are rich with information. Discussion groups may also provide information and insights that can help answer some marketing questions. Additionally, a post to a chat room or newsgroup may draw a response that uncovers previously unknown sources of secondary data. Usenet, the largest newsgroup network, boasts 500 million messages posted since 1995. Unlike chat-room postings, these opinions are unsolicited and uncensored. Online services like Survey.com and PlanetFeedback gather data from multiple sources, organized according to demographic, industry, product, or multiple other characteristics.

Briefly Speaking

With so much information now online, it is exceptionally easy to simply dive in and drown.

Alfred Glossbrenner
American author

Researchers must, however, carefully evaluate the validity of information they find on the Internet. People without in-depth knowledge of the subject matter may post information in a newsgroup. Similarly, Web pages might contain information that has been gathered using questionable research methods. The phrase *caveat emptor* (let the buyer beware) should guide evaluation of secondary data on the Internet.

SAMPLING TECHNIQUES

4 Explain the different sampling techniques used by marketing researchers.

sampling Process of selecting survey respondents or research participants.

Before undertaking a study to gather primary data, researchers must first identify which participants to include in the study. **Sampling** is the process of selecting survey respondents or research participants. It is one of the most important aspects of research design because if a study fails to involve consumers who accurately reflect the target market, the research is likely to yield misleading conclusions.

The total group of people that the researcher wants to study is called the **population** or **universe.** For a political campaign study, the population would be all eligible voters. For research about a new lipstick line, it might be all women in a certain age bracket. The sample is a representative group chosen from this population. Researchers rarely gather information from a study's total population, resulting in a census. Unless the total population is small, the costs of a census are simply too high.

Samples can be classified as either probability samples or nonprobability samples. A **probability sample** is one that gives every member of the population a chance of being selected. Types of probability samples include simple random samples, stratified samples, and cluster samples.

probability sample Sample that gives every member of the population a known chance of being selected.

In a **simple random sample,** every member of the relevant universe has an equal opportunity of selection. The draft lottery of the Vietnam era is an example. The days of the year were drawn and set into an array. The placement of a person's birthday in this list determined his likelihood of being called for service. In a **stratified sample,** randomly selected subsamples of different groups are represented in the total sample. Stratified samples provide efficient, representative groups that are relatively homogeneous for a certain characteristic for such studies as opinion polls, in which groups of individuals share various divergent viewpoints. In a **cluster sample,** researchers select a sample of subgroups (or clusters) from which they draw respondents. Each cluster reflects the diversity of the whole population being sampled. This cost-efficient type of probability sample is widely used when the entire population cannot be listed or enumerated.

In contrast, a **nonprobability sample** relies on personal judgment somewhere in the selection process. In other words, researchers decide which particular groups to study. Types of nonprobability samples are convenience samples and quota samples. A **convenience sample** is a nonprobability sample selected from among readily available respondents; this sample is often called an *accidental sample* because those included just happen to be in the place where the study is being conducted. Mall intercept surveys and TV call-in opinion polls are good examples. Marketing researchers sometimes use convenience samples in exploratory research but not in definitive studies. A **quota sample** is a nonprobability sample that is divided to maintain the proportion of certain characteristics among different segments or groups as is seen in the population as a whole. In other words, each field worker is assigned a quota that specifies the number and characteristics of the people to contact. It differs from a stratified sample, in which researchers select subsamples by some random process; in a quota sample, they hand-pick participants. An example would be a survey of owners of imported autos that includes two Hyundai owners, six Honda owners, and four Volvo owners.

nonprobability sample Sample that involves personal judgment somewhere in the selection process.

PRIMARY RESEARCH METHODS

(5) **Identify the methods by which marketing researchers collect primary data.**

Marketers use a variety of methods for conducting primary research, as Figure 8.5 shows. The principal methods for collecting primary data are observation, surveys, and controlled experiments. The choice among these methods depends on the issues under study and the decisions that marketers need to make. In some cases, researchers may decide to combine techniques during the research process.

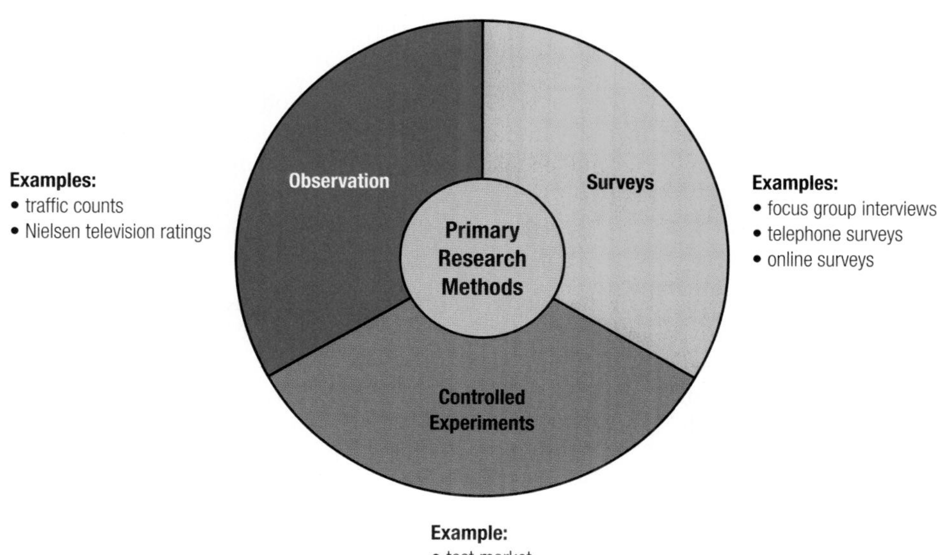

figure 8.5

Types of Primary Research

Observation Method

In observational studies, researchers view the overt actions of subjects being studied. Marketers trying to understand how consumers behave in certain situations find observation to be a useful technique. Observation tactics may be as simple as counting the number of cars passing by a potential site for a fast-food restaurant or checking the license plates at a shopping center near a state line to determine where shoppers live.

Technological advances provide increasingly sophisticated ways for observing consumer behavior. The television industry relies on data from people meters, which are electronic remote-control devices that record the TV-viewing habits of individual household members to measure the popularity of TV shows. Traditional people meters require each viewer to press a button each time he or she turns on the TV, changes channels, or leaves the room.

Marketers have long worried that some viewers do not bother to push people meter buttons at appropriate times, skewing research findings. In response, Arbitron recently tested a portable people meter (PPM) that participants keep with them at all times. Throughout the day, the PPM picks up and stores codes embedded in radio and TV programming. At night, the participant puts the PPM into a docking station, from which the data is uploaded to Arbitron. The PPM even has a built-in motion detector to ensure that it is not abandoned midtest.[10]

Nielsen Media Research has also introduced a new electronic meter to capture demographic data about television viewers, replacing the combination of set-top meters and paper-and-pencil diaries it used for the past 50 years. The new method also allows the company to double sample sizes for more accurate reporting.[11]

Videotaping consumers in action is also gaining acceptance as a research technique. Cookware manufacturers may videotape consumers cooking in their own kitchens to evaluate how they use their pots and pans. A toothbrush manufacturer asked marketing research firm E-Lab to videotape consumers brushing their teeth and using mouthwash in its quest to develop products that would leave behind the sensation of cleanliness and freshness.

TiVo, the digital video recording service, is pioneering a method of collecting data about its viewers, from which it filters out any identifying information to keep the data anonymous. The company does not store any individual's viewing record, and viewers can opt out of the data collection process if they wish. TiVo receives a steady stream of information from its viewers, and it plans to begin selling the data to the television industry through a partnership with Nielsen Media Research.[12]

In an effort to understand what makes younger consumers tick, a trend-forecasting firm called Look-Look has recruited an army of about 20,000 people aged 14 to 30 who send in a constant stream of information by instant messaging and pagers. These handpicked "field correspondents" also upload images from their digital cameras that record events like parties, concerts, and sporting events. And the information flow goes both ways. "Because we've built this huge network," says founder Sharon Lee, "we have the capability to test [a] hypothesis with any kind of sample size that we want and get an immediate response. Yes, this is happening, or no, it isn't."[13]

Interpretative Research

Another type of primary research is **interpretative research,** a method in which a researcher observes a customer or group of customers in their natural setting and interprets their behavior based on an understanding of the social and cultural characteristics of that setting. We discuss interpretative research in more detail later.

interpretative research Observational research method developed by social anthropologists in which customers are observed in their natural setting and their behavior is interpreted based on an understanding of social and cultural characteristics; also known as *ethnography,* or "going native."

Survey Method

Observation alone cannot supply all of the desired information. Researchers must ask questions to get information on attitudes, motives, and opinions. It is also difficult to get exact demographic information—such as income levels—from observation. To discover this information, researchers can use either interviews or questionnaires. Good listening skills are critical to interviewers, as the "Etiquette Tips for Marketing Professionals" box discusses.

Telephone Interviews

Telephone interviews are a quick and inexpensive method for obtaining a small quantity of relatively impersonal information. Simple, clearly worded questions are easy for interviewers to pose over the

ETIQUETTE TIPS — FOR MARKETING PROFESSIONALS

How to Be a Good Listener

MARKETING research survey techniques such as personal interviews call for very good listening skills. Review this checklist of pointers and remember that the rules of mindful listening, like all forms of good business etiquette, are always in effect.

1. Have only one conversation at a time. In a face-to-face conversation, make eye contact to indicate your undivided attention. In a phone conversation, act just as if the other person were in the room with you. No secret checking of e-mail while on the phone!
2. Listen without speaking until the other person is finished. Don't interrupt or finish people's sentences for them.
3. Avoid changing the subject; the other person is likely to interpret this as a signal that you haven't been paying attention and don't think the conversation is important.
4. Confirm that you've heard and understood the other person's message. Rephrase and repeat it, or ask questions to clarify.
5. Take notes of the conversation, particularly if it's an important one in which you are setting marketing budgets, sales force schedules, or other obligations.
6. Respect the confidentiality of privileged information.
7. In personal interviews, note the other person's body language. If someone doesn't meet your eye, mumbles, or hesitates, the person may be uncomfortable with the topic.
8. Try to be aware of messages you may be sending with your own unconscious gestures (smile, don't cross your arms, and don't loom over someone who is seated).
9. Finally, always think before you speak.

In any conversation, listening is one-half of the equation. In fact, conversations can often be most useful and interesting if one listens more than one speaks. It is always a good idea to keep this old adage in mind: "If you think you're talking too much, you probably are."

Sources: "Are You a Good Listener?" http://www.effectivemeetings.com/productivity/, accessed March 22, 2004; "How to Be a Good Listener," University of Nebraska Cooperative Extension, http://extension.unl.edu/welfare/listener.htm, accessed March 22, 2004; "Be a Good Listener!" http://www.jobstreet.com.my/career/jobs123/tips16.htm, accessed March 22, 2004; "How to Be a Good Listener," http://vt.essortment.com/howtobeagood_rvlz.htm, accessed March 22, 2004.

phone and are effective at drawing appropriate responses. Telephone surveys have relatively high response rates, especially with repeated calls; calling a number once yields a response rate of 50 to 60 percent, but calling the same number five times raises the response rate to 85 percent. To maximize responses and save costs, some researchers use computerized dialing and digitally synthesized voices that interview respondents.

However, phone surveys have several drawbacks. Most important, about 44 percent of all people now invited to take part in them refuse, compared with only 15 percent 20 years ago. Their reasons include concern for data privacy, a negative association of phone surveys with telemarketing, and the lack of financial rewards for participating.[14] The national Do Not Call Registry excludes calls made for research purposes.[15]

Many respondents are hesitant to give personal characteristics about themselves over the telephone. Results may be biased by the omission of typical households where adults are off working during the day. Other households, particularly market segments such as single women and physicians, are likely to have unlisted numbers. While computerized random dialing can give access to unlisted numbers, it is restricted in several states.

The popularity of caller-ID systems to screen unwanted calls is another obstacle for telephone researchers. Some legal experts believe caller-ID violates the caller's right to privacy; in one case, Pennsylvania State courts ruled it unconstitutional. Still, state laws on caller-ID vary. Some require vendors to offer a blocking service to callers who wish to evade the system. The Harris Interactive promotional message in Figure 8.6 highlights the problems marketers face in obtaining responses from a

The more the data banks record about each one of us, the less we exist.

Marshall McLuhan (1911–1980)

Canadian communications theorist

figure 8.6

Problems in Using the Telephone for Marketing Research Interviews

representative sample of respondents using phone surveys: consumer perception of intrusion into their privacy and the number of consumers in the national Do Not Call Registry.

Other obstacles restrict the usefulness of telephone surveys abroad. In areas where telephone ownership is rare, survey results will be highly biased. Telephone interviewing is also difficult in countries that lack directories, charge landline telephone customers on a per-minute basis, or where call volumes congest limited phone line capacity.

Personal Interviews

The best means for obtaining detailed information about consumers is usually the personal interview since the interviewer can establish rapport with respondents and explain confusing or vague questions. In addition to contacting respondents at their homes or workplaces, marketing research firms can conduct interviews in rented space in shopping centers, where they gain wide access to potential buyers of the merchandise they are studying. These locations sometimes feature private interviewing space, videotape equipment, and food-preparation facilities for taste tests. As mentioned earlier, interviews conducted in shopping centers are typically called **mall intercepts.** Downtown retail districts and airports provide other valuable locations for marketing researchers.

Focus Groups

focus group Simultaneous personal interview of a small group of individuals, which relies on group discussion about a certain topic.

Marketers also gather research information through the popular technique of focus group interviews. A **focus group** brings together 8 to 12 individuals in one location to discuss a subject of interest. Unlike other interview techniques that elicit information through a question-and-answer format, focus groups usually encourage a general discussion of a predetermined topic. Focus groups can provide quick and relatively inexpensive insight into consumer attitudes and motivations. Within days of the September 11 terrorist attacks, Southwest Airlines was able to roll out a campaign that reflected the changed mood of the American public. Focus groups were a key technique used to quickly evaluate consumer attitudes toward the airlines in the wake of the attacks. Figure 8.7 lists some of the ways in which focus groups help marketers capture information.

In a focus group, the leader, or moderator, typically begins by explaining the purpose of the meeting and suggesting an opening topic. The moderator's main purpose, however, is to stimulate interaction among group members to encourage their discussion of numerous points. The moderator may occasionally interject questions as catalysts to direct the group's discussion. The moderator's job is difficult, requiring preparation and group facilitation skills.

Focus group sessions often last one or two hours. Researchers usually record the discussion on tape, and observers frequently watch through a one-way mirror. Some research firms also allow clients to view focus groups in action through videoconferencing systems.

Focus groups are a particularly valuable tool for exploratory research, developing new-product ideas, and preliminary testing of alternative marketing strategies. They can also aid in the development of well-structured questionnaires for larger scale research.

Focus groups do have drawbacks, however. Some researchers fear that the focus group setting is sterile and unnatural and may not produce honest responses to questions. Participants may, for example, feel a need to identify with other members of the group and so provide less than truthful answers. Other researchers feel that the sample sizes are too small to be truly representative of larger population groups. Still others question the consistency of the interviewing process.[16]

Researchers are finding ways to re-create the focus group environment over the Internet. With experienced moderators who have the technical skills to function fluently online, it is possible to gain valuable qualitative information at a fraction of the cost it takes to run a traditional focus group session.

Research firm Greenfield Online used an online focus group to test reactions to a redesigned Web site for Captain Morgan Original Spiced Rum. Participants "gathered" in Greenfield's private chat room. A moderator posed questions and responded to answers on one side of a split screen, while participants typed their comments on the other side. How can researchers tell whether online participants are being truthful? Greenfield staff members cross-checked participants' answers to earlier screening questionnaires against the information they entered later when they registered for the database. The company then cross-checked a second time before the focus group began and found substitutes for respondents whose answers appeared inconsistent. Figure 8.8 highlights SurveySite's expertise in online marketing research.

GroupSpark is a new program that uses a network of laptop computers to accept and tabulate the response of focus group participants. The method has been particularly successful in eliminating the awkwardness some people (especially teenagers) feel in group settings by offering anonymity that allows people to be more truthful, which saves time and money for marketers.[17]

figure 8.7

Focus Groups: Insights into Consumer Perceptions

Mail Surveys

Although personal interviews can provide very detailed information, cost considerations usually prevent an organization from using personal interviews in a large-scale study. A mail survey can be a cost-effective alternative. Mail surveys can provide anonymity that may encourage respondents to give candid answers. They can also help marketers track consumer attitudes through ongoing research and sometimes provide demographic data that may be helpful in market segmentation.

Mail questionnaires do, however, have several limitations. First, response rates are typically much lower than for personal interviews. Second, because researchers must wait for respondents to complete and return questionnaires, mail surveys usually take a considerably longer time to conduct. A third limitation is that questionnaires cannot answer unanticipated questions that occur to respondents as they complete the forms. In addition, complex questions may not be suitable for a mail questionnaire. Finally, unless they gather additional information from nonrespondents through other means, researchers must worry about possible bias in the results stemming from differences between respondents and nonrespondents.

Researchers try to minimize these limitations by carefully developing and pretesting questionnaires. Researchers can boost response rates by keeping questionnaires short and by offering incentives—discount coupons or a dollar bill—to respondents who complete and return the survey documents.

Fax Surveys

The low response rates and long follow-up times associated with mail surveys have spurred interest in the alternative of faxing survey documents. In some cases, faxes may supplement mail surveys; in others, they may be the primary method for contacting respondents. Because millions of households do not have fax machines, securing a representative sample of respondents is a difficult undertaking in fax surveys of final consumers. As a result, most of these surveys focus on business-related research studies.

Online Surveys and Other Internet-Based Methods

The growing population of Internet users has spurred researchers to conduct online surveys. Using the Web, they are able to speed the survey process, increase sample sizes, ignore geographic boundaries, and dramatically reduce costs. While a standard research project can take up to eight weeks to complete, a thorough online project may take two

figure 8.8

Benefits of Online Focus Groups

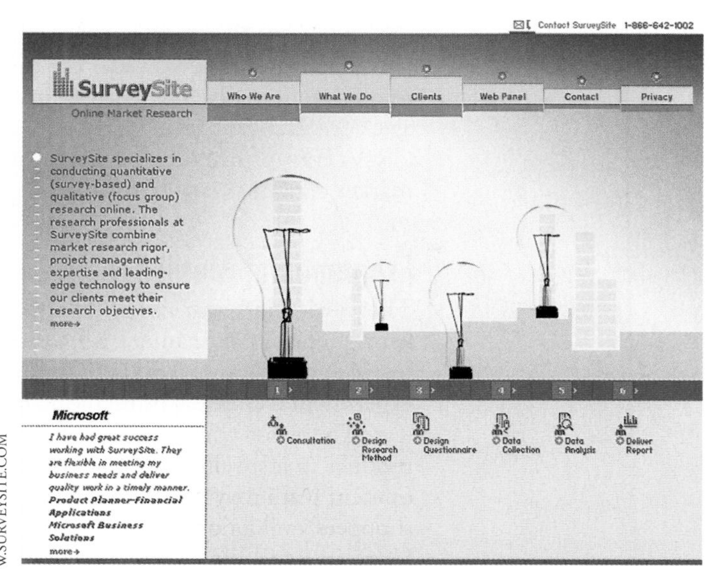

Decision Analyst conducts worldwide Internet research with panels in areas such as consumer behavior, technology, business, medicine, and the construction industry.

weeks or less. Less intrusive than telephone surveys, online research allows participants to respond at their leisure. The novelty and ease of answering online may even encourage higher response rates. Additional questions and longer responses have only a slight effect, if any, on an online study's cost, enabling researchers to gather more detailed information than through traditional mail surveys. Furthermore, since online research is already in digital form, it generally requires less preparation—such as keyboarding into a database—before analysis.[18]

Businesses are increasingly including questionnaires on their Web pages to solicit information about consumer demographics, attitudes, and comments and suggestions for improving goods and services or improving marketing messages. Marketers are also experimenting with electronic bulletin boards as an information-gathering device. On a password-protected Web site, moderators pose questions to selected respondents—usually just 15 to 25—over a predetermined period of time. Respondents have a chance to try out new products and are able to submit feedback at their leisure. Unlike focus group sessions, there are no group dynamics, so some researchers feel that these responses are more truthful. Bulletin boards are particularly effective when targeting respondents who are unable to commit to real-time group sessions or for topics that are highly sensitive or complex.[19]

The growth of the Internet is creating a need for new research techniques to measure and capture information about Web-site visitors. At present, no industrywide standards define techniques for measuring Web use. Some sites ask users to register before accessing the pages; others merely keep track of the number of "hits" or number of times a visitor accesses a page. Marketers have tried to place a value on a site's "stickiness" (longer lasting site visits) as a means of measuring effectiveness. Others use "cookies," which, as Chapter 4 explained, are electronic identifiers deposited on viewers' computers, to track click-through behavior—the paths users take as they move through the site. However, since some consumers change their Internet service providers frequently, and special software is available to detect and remove them, cookies have lost some of their effectiveness.

Some software can monitor the overall content that a person is viewing and display banner advertisements likely to be of interest. For example, a search using the keyword "car" might call up a banner ad for General Motors or Ford. CMG Information Services offers a service called Engage.Knowledge, which collects profiles of Web users from numerous sites and organizes the data into 800 categories, including sports and hobbies. Researchers can use this information to develop marketing strategies. The popularity of video games has led to the emergence of a new advertising platform, "advergames." YaYa LLC streams three-dimensional console-quality games over the Internet. Also, net surfers may receive promotional e-mail that invites them to play a Honda-sponsored racing game, driving a replica of a new-model car through an exciting virtual racetrack. The game being a marketing research tool in disguise, players must register before starting their engines—submitting details of their age, address, occupation, and hobbies. They are rewarded with free entry into a contest to win a Honda CR-V. Four of five users register—and many pass the game along to friends. Of course, Honda gains market data on a key demographic group—potential young car buyers. [20]

Experimental Method

The third—and least-used—method for collecting primary data is the **controlled experiment.** A marketing research experiment is a scientific investigation in which a researcher controls or manipulates a test group (or groups) and compares the results with those of a control group that did not receive the experimental controls or manipulations.

The most common use of this method by marketers is **test-marketing,** or introducing a new product in a specific area and then observing its degree of success. Up to this point, a product development team may have gathered feedback from focus groups. Other information may have come from shoppers' evaluations of competing products. Test-marketing is the first stage at which the product performs in a real-life business environment.

Test-marketing introduces a new product supported by a complete marketing campaign to a selected city or TV coverage area. Marketers look for a location with a manageable size, where residents match their target market's demographic profile. After the test has been under way for a few months and sales and market share in the test market have been calculated, marketers can estimate the product's likely performance in a full-scale rollout.

Anheuser-Busch test-marketed its low-carbohydrate Michelob Ultra in Denver, Tucson, and central Florida. Enthusiastic response led to an earlier-than-expected national rollout. Teaser ads, featuring the famous Michelob red ribbon, promise that the new brand will make diet-conscious consumers "look at beer in a whole new light."[21]

Some firms omit test-marketing and move directly from product development to full-scale production. These companies cite three problems with test-marketing:

1. Test-marketing is expensive. A firm can spend more than $1 million depending on the size of the test-market city and the cost of buying media to advertise the product.
2. Competitors quickly learn about the new product. By studying the test market, competitors can develop alternative strategies.
3. Some products are not well suited to test-marketing. Few firms test-market long-lived, durable goods such as cars because of the major financial investments required for their development, the need to establish networks of dealers to distribute the products, and requirements for parts and servicing.

Companies that decide to skip the test-marketing process can choose several other options. A firm may simulate a test-marketing campaign through computer-modeling software. By plugging in data on similar products, it can develop a sales projection for a new product. Another firm may offer an item in just one region of the U.S. or in another country, adjusting promotions and advertising based on local results before going to other geographic regions. Another option may be to limit a product's introduction to only one retail chain to carefully control and evaluate promotions and results.

CONDUCTING INTERNATIONAL MARKETING RESEARCH

6 **Explain the challenges of conducting marketing research in global markets.**

As corporations expand globally, they need to gather correspondingly more knowledge about consumers in other countries. Although marketing researchers follow the same basic steps for international studies as for domestic ones, they often face some very different challenges.

U.S. organizations can tap many secondary resources as they research global markets. One major information source is the U.S. government, particularly the Department of Commerce. The Department of Commerce regularly publishes two useful reports, *Foreign Economic Trends and Their Implications for the United States* (semiannual) and *Overseas Business Reports* (annual), that discuss marketing activities in more than 100 countries. The Department of State offers commercial guides to almost every country in the world, compiled by the local embassies. Other government sources include state trade offices, small-business development centers, and U.S. embassies in various nations.

When conducting international research, companies must be prepared to deal with both language issues—communicating their message in the most effective way—and cultural issues—capturing local citizens' interests while avoiding missteps that could unintentionally offend them. Companies also need to take a good look at a country's business environment, including political and economic conditions, trade regulations affecting research studies and data collection, and the potential for short- and long-term growth. Many marketers recommend tapping local researchers to investigate foreign markets.

Businesses may need to adjust their data collection methods for primary research in other countries because some methods do not easily transfer across national frontiers. Face-to-face interviewing, for instance, remains the most common method for conducting primary research outside the U.S.

While mail surveys are a common data collection method in developed countries, they are useless in many other nations because of low literacy rates, unreliable mail service, and a lack of address lists. Telephone interviews may also not be suitable in other countries, especially those where many people do not have phones. Focus groups can be difficult to arrange because of cultural and social factors. In Latin American countries, for example, highly educated consumers make up a sought-after and opinionated minority, but they have little time to devote to lengthy focus group discussions. Middle- to lower-income Latin Americans may not be accustomed to articulating their opinions about prod-

figure 8.9

Marketing Research on a Global Scale

ucts and grow reticent in the presence of others, whereas in some countries where violence and kidnapping are common, affluent consumers are reluctant to attend any meetings with strangers.[22]

A growing number of international research firms offer experience in conducting global studies. For example, Focus World International, featured in Figure 8.9, promises specialized attention to research projects around the world.

INTERPRETATIVE RESEARCH

We mentioned earlier that interpretative research was a method that observes a customer or group of customers in their natural settings and then interprets their behavior based on an understanding of social and cultural characteristics of that setting. Interpretative research has attracted considerable interest in recent years. Developed by social anthropologists as a method for explaining behavior that operates below the level of conscious thought, interpretative research can provide insights into consumer behavior and the ways in which consumers interact with brands. The researcher first spends an extensive amount of time studying the culture, and for that reason, the studies are often called *ethnographic* studies. The word *ethnographic* means that a researcher takes a cultural perspective of the population being studied. For that reason, interpretative research is often used to interpret consumer behavior within a foreign culture, where language, ideals, values, and expectations are all subject to different cultural influences. But ethnographic research is also used domestically by looking at the consumer behavior of different groups of people.

1. What are the major methods of collecting secondary data?
2. What are the major methods of collecting primary data?
3. What is the most common method of primary data collection outside the U.S.?

Interpretative research focuses on understanding the meaning of a product or the consumption experience in a consumer's life.[23] Its methods capture consumers interacting with products in their environment—in other words, capturing what they actually do, not what they say they do. Typically, subjects are filmed in specific situations, such as socializing with friends in a bar for research into beverage consumption, or for extended periods of time for paid participants. Paid participants are followed by a videographer, who records the day-to-day movements and interactions of people. Miller Brewing Co. hired an ethnographic research team from Ogilvy & Mather, one of the world's largest advertising agencies, to observe how young men related to each other and its product, Miller Lite. After extensive study across the U.S., the researchers found that Miller Lite was preferred by groups of men, while its competitor, Bud Lite, was sold more often to individual males. That insight helped Miller design a new advertising campaign to target its market.[24]

Marketers have found plenty of other interpretative research applications. Frontier Airlines asked some of its passengers whether it could observe their behavior at Denver International Airport. It discovered that parents really enjoyed showing their children the airline's fleet, with its distinctive tailfins featuring cats, rabbits, and foxes. While focus groups had shown that the painted animals helped people identify the airline, their real popularity had gone unnoticed until the study was conducted. This observation led to a marketing campaign with computer-animated animals interacting in cocktail-party situations. As one marketer says, interpretative research is "the difference between sitting you in a room and asking you about your coffee habits and following you around for a week to see how you really drink coffee."[25]

Cost is an issue in interpretative research. This type of study takes time and money—a typical project lasts four to six weeks and costs in the neighborhood of $50,000 to $100,000.[26] Because of its expense, interpretative research is used only when a company needs detailed information about how consumers use its products.

1. How is interpretative research typically conducted?
2. When should ethnographic research be employed?

COMPUTER TECHNOLOGY IN MARKETING RESEARCH

7 Outline the most important uses of computer technology in marketing research.

In a world of rapid change, the ability to quickly gather and analyze business intelligence can create a substantial strategic advantage. As noted earlier, computer databases provide a wealth of data for marketing research, whether they are maintained outside the company or designed specifically to gather important facts about its customers. Chapter 10 will explore how companies are leveraging internal databases and customer relationship management technology as a means of developing long-term relationships with customers. This section addresses important uses of computer technology related to marketing research: marketing information systems (MISs), marketing decision support systems (MDSSs), data mining, business intelligence, and competitive intelligence.

MARKETING INFORMATION SYSTEMS (MISs)

In the past, many marketing managers complained that their information problems resulted from too much rather than too little information. Reams of data were difficult to use and not always relevant. At times, information was almost impossible to find. Modern technological advances have made constraints like these obsolete.

A **marketing information system (MIS)** is a planned, computer-based system designed to provide decision makers with a continuous flow of information relevant to their areas of responsibility. A component of the organization's overall management information system, a marketing information system deals specifically with marketing data and issues.

A well-constructed MIS serves as a company's nerve center, continually monitoring the market environment—both inside and outside the organization—and providing instantaneous information. Marketers are able to store data for later use, classify and analyze that data, and retrieve it easily when needed.

MARKETING DECISION SUPPORT SYSTEMS (MDSSs)

8 Explain how the use of information technology, particularly marketing decision support systems (MDSSs), can enhance and refine market research and its impact on decision making.

A **marketing decision support system (MDSS)** consists of software that helps users quickly obtain and apply information in a way that supports marketing decisions. Taking MIS one step further, it allows managers to explore and make connections between such varying information as the state of the market, consumer behavior, sales forecasts, competitors' actions, and environmental changes. MDSSs consist of four main characteristics: interactive, investigative, flexible, and accessible. An MDSS can create simulations or models to illustrate the likely results of changes in marketing strategies or market conditions.

While an MIS provides raw data, an MDSS develops this data into information useful for decision making. For example, an MIS might provide a list of product sales from the previous day. A manager could use an MDSS to transform this raw data into graphs illustrating sales trends or reports estimating the impacts of specific decisions, such as raising prices or expanding into new regions.

marketing decision support system (MDSS) Marketing information system component that links a decision maker with relevant databases and analysis tools.

DATA MINING

Data mining is the process of searching through computerized data files to detect patterns. It focuses on identifying relationships that are not obvious to marketers—in a sense, answering questions that marketing researchers may not even have thought to ask. The data is stored in a huge database called a *data warehouse*. Software for the marketing decision support system is often associated with the data warehouse and is used to mine data. Once marketers identify patterns and connections, they use this intelligence to check the effectiveness of different strategy options.

Data mining is an efficient way to sort through huge amounts of data and to make sense of that data. It helps marketers create customer profiles, pinpoint reasons for customer loyalty or the lack thereof, analyze the potential returns on changes in pricing or promotion, and forecast sales. Wal-Mart, for example, mines its point-of-sale data for insights into shoppers' buying habits. By examining data, the retailer can tell which products are purchased together and drive up sales of both items through store placement or special offers.[27] Data mining also offers considerable advantages in the hotel industry, banking, utilities, and many others and holds the promise of providing answers to such specific strategic questions as, "Which clients are most likely to respond to our latest marketing campaign?"[28]

Advances in data mining applications allow for real-time analysis of data flows. NonObvious Relationship Awareness (NORA) software from Systems Research & Development (SRD) was devised to help casinos identify nonobvious relationships between data from multiple sources. For example, using real-time analysis, the software might discover that a job applicant shares a telephone number with a known criminal and issue an immediate alert to the hiring manager. Given an unexpected boost due to the September 11 terrorist attacks, NORA recently received funding from the CIA to create plug-ins that would help identify potential terrorists. Using streaming technology that scans data in real time, the software might discover that a passenger buying a ticket at an airline counter recently purchased controlled explosive materials. An alert would go out before the passenger could board a plane.[29]

Briefly Speaking

Torture the data long enough, and they will confess anything.

Anonymous

BUSINESS INTELLIGENCE

Business intelligence is the process of gathering information and analyzing it to improve business strategy, tactics, and daily operations. Using advanced software tools, marketers gather information from both within and outside the organization. Business intelligence can thus tell the firm how its own sales department is doing or what its top competitors are up to.

The key is not only gathering the information but also getting it into a form that employees can make sense of and use for decision making and strategizing. Software to help users collect, aggregate, and create reports with outside information available on the Web from such databases as, say, Dun & Bradstreet is just beginning to become available. One program from IBM, called WebFountain, looks for information about consumer responses to new products by delving into chat rooms, advertising sites, competitors' Web sites, and news sites. Then it creates a report for marketers about how the product is being received.[30] WebFountain can also help banks identify fraud suspects; Citibank has signed up as the first user of this application.[31] The "Marketing Hit" box describes another application of business intelligence at Ben & Jerry's.

marketing hit — Ben & Jerry's Seeks Intelligence in Ice Cream

Background. Ben & Jerry's, the Vermont ice cream maker, produces nearly 200,000 pints of ice cream every day. It distributes its high-quality, all-natural products through supermarkets, grocery and convenience stores, restaurants, and several hundred franchised "scoop shops" around the U.S. The company's success depends to a large extent on knowing what its customers like or dislike about its dozens of exotic ice cream flavors like Chunky Monkey and Cherry Garcia. Much of that information comes from owners of the scoop shops.

The Challenge. Ben & Jerry's needed to help its franchised shop owners manage the information they gathered from the 7,000 to 10,000 monthly transactions they handled during their peak ice cream selling season. As one marketing research executive said, having data you can't use is "like having a bank account with millions of dollars in it but no ATM card. If you can't get it out and can't make it work for you, then it is not really useful."

The Strategy. Ben & Jerry's employs a new business intelligence tool, a software package called MICROS RES3000. This program allows the company to analyze not only sales data but also labor costs and other related information almost in real time and from any location. An information lag of about six weeks has been reduced to under 15 minutes.

The Outcome. "Instead of reacting to 'old' data," says Ben & Jerry's director of retail operations, "we'll receive fresh, real-time data, which we can collect and view anywhere in the world. This immediacy of information permits us to make better decisions faster and gives our valued franchisees real tools for success."

Sources: "No More Rocky Roads for Ben & Jerry's," *RetailSystems.com*, March 1, 2004, http://www.retailsystems.com; "Ben & Jerry's Scoop Shops to Dish Out Near Real-Time Sales Data," company press release, February 24, 2004, http://biz.yahoo.com; Julie Schlosser, "Looking for Intelligence in Ice Cream," *Fortune*, March 17, 2003, pp. 114–120.

COMPETITIVE INTELLIGENCE

Competitive intelligence is a form of business intelligence that focuses on finding information about competitors using published sources, interviews, observations by salespeople and suppliers in the industry, government agencies, public filings such as patent applications, and other secondary sources including the Internet. Its aim is to uncover the specific advantages a competitor has, such as new-product launches, new features in existing goods or services, or new marketing or promotional strategies. Even a competitor's advertising can provide clues. Marketers use competitive intelligence to make better decisions that strengthen their own competitive strategy in turn.

1. Distinguish between an MIS and an MDSS.
2. What is data mining?
3. Describe the process of collecting business intelligence.

SALES FORECASTING

(9) Identify the major types of forecasting methods.

A basic building block of any marketing plan is a **sales forecast,** an estimate of a firm's revenue for a specified future period. Sales forecasts play major roles in new-product decisions, production scheduling, financial planning, inventory planning and procurement, distribution, and human-resource planning. An inaccurate forecast may lead to incorrect decisions in each of these areas. Marketing research techniques are used to deliver effective sales forecasts. A sales forecast is also an important tool for marketing control because it sets standards against which to measure actual performance. Without such standards, no comparisons can be made.

sales forecast Estimate of company revenue for a specified future period.

Planners rely on short-run, intermediate, and long-run sales forecasts. A short-run forecast usually covers a period of up to one year, an intermediate forecast covers one to five years, and a long-run forecast extends beyond five years. Although sales forecasters use an array of techniques to predict the future—ranging from computer simulations to studying trends identified by futurists—their methods fall into two broad categories: qualitative and quantitative forecasting.

It's tough to make predictions, especially about the future.

Yogi Berra (b. 1925)
American baseball player

Qualitative forecasting techniques rely on subjective data that reports opinions rather than exact historical data. **Quantitative forecasting** methods, by contrast, use statistical computations such as trend extensions based on past data, computer simulations, and econometric models. As Table 8.1 shows, each method has benefits and limitations. Consequently, most organizations use a combination of both techniques.

QUALITATIVE FORECASTING TECHNIQUES

Planners apply qualitative forecasting methods when they want judgmental or subjective indicators. Qualitative forecasting techniques include the jury of executive opinion, Delphi technique, sales force composite, and survey of buyer intentions.

Jury of Executive Opinion

The technique called the **jury of executive opinion** combines and averages the outlooks of top executives from such areas as marketing, finance, production, and purchasing. Top managers bring the following capabilities to the process: experience and knowledge about situations that influence sales, open-minded attitudes toward the future, and awareness of the bases for their judgments. This quick and inexpensive method generates good forecasts for sales and new-product development. It works best for short-run forecasting.

jury of executive opinion Qualitative sales forecasting method that assesses the sales expectations of various executives.

Delphi Technique

Like the jury of executive opinion, the **Delphi technique** solicits opinions from several people, but it also gathers input from experts outside the firm, such as academic researchers, rather than relying completely on company executives. It is most appropriately used to predict long-run issues, such as technological breakthroughs, that could affect future sales and the market potential for new products.

Delphi technique Qualitative sales forecasting method that gathers and redistributes several rounds of anonymous forecasts until the participants reach a consensus.

table 8.1 ***Benefits and Limitations of Various Forecasting Techniques***

TECHNIQUES	BENEFITS	LIMITATIONS
Qualitative Methods		
Jury of executive opinion	Opinions come from executives in many different departments; quick; inexpensive	Managers may lack sufficient knowledge and experience to make meaningful predictions
Delphi technique	Group of experts can accurately predict long-term events such as technological breakthroughs	Time-consuming; expensive
Sales force composite	Salespeople have expert customer, product, and competitor knowledge; quick; inexpensive	Inaccurate forecasts may result from low estimates of salespeople concerned about their influence on quotas
Survey of buyer intentions	Useful in predicting short-term and intermediate sales for firms that serve only a few customers	Intentions to buy may not result in actual purchases; time-consuming; expensive
Quantitative Methods		
Market test	Provides realistic information on actual purchases rather than on intent to buy	Alerts competition to new-product plans; time-consuming; expensive
Trend analysis	Quick; inexpensive; effective with stable customer demand and environment	Assumes the future will continue the past; ignores environmental changes
Exponential smoothing	Same benefits as trend analysis, but emphasizes more recent data	Same limitations as trend analysis, but not as severe due to emphasis on recent data

The Delphi technique works as follows: A firm selects a panel of experts and sends each a questionnaire relating to a future event. After combining and averaging the answers, the firm develops another questionnaire based on these results and sends it back to the same people. The process continues until it identifies a consensus. Although firms have successfully used Delphi to predict future technological breakthroughs, the method is both expensive and time-consuming.

Sales Force Composite

sales force composite Qualitative sales forecasting method based on the combined sales estimates of the firm's salespeople.

The **sales force composite** technique develops forecasts based on the belief that organization members closest to the marketplace—those with specialized product, customer, and competitive knowledge—offer the best insights concerning short-term future sales. It typically works from the bottom up. Management consolidates salespeople's estimates first at the district level, then at the regional level, and finally nationwide to obtain an aggregate forecast of sales that reflects all three levels.

The sales force composite approach has some weaknesses, however. Since salespeople recognize the role of their sales forecasts in determining sales quotas for their territories, they are likely to make conservative estimates. Moreover, their narrow perspectives from within their limited geographic territories may prevent them from considering the impact on sales of trends developing in other territories, forthcoming technological innovations, or the major changes in marketing strategies. Consequently, the sales force composite gives the best forecasts in combination with other techniques.

It is important not to ignore forecasts that are uncongenial.

Jib Fowles

professor of communications, University of Houston–Clear Lake

Survey of Buyer Intentions

A **survey of buyer intentions** gathers input through mail-in questionnaires, online feedback, telephone polls, and personal interviews to determine the purchasing intentions of a representative group of present and potential customers. This method suits firms that serve limited numbers of customers but often proves impractical for those with millions of customers. Also, buyer surveys gather useful information only when customers willingly reveal their buying intentions. Moreover, customer intentions do not necessarily translate into actual purchases. These surveys may help a firm to predict short-run or intermediate sales, but they employ time-consuming and expensive methods.

QUANTITATIVE FORECASTING TECHNIQUES

Quantitative techniques attempt to eliminate the subjectiveness of the qualitative methods. They include such methods as market tests, trend analysis, and exponential smoothing.

Test Markets

One quantitative technique, the test market, frequently helps planners in assessing consumer responses to new-product offerings. The procedure typically begins by establishing one or more test markets to gauge consumer responses to a new product under actual marketplace conditions. Market tests also permit experimenters to evaluate the effects of different prices, alternative promotional strategies, and other marketing mix variations by comparing results among different test markets.

The primary advantage of market tests is the realism that they provide for the marketer. On the other hand, these expensive and time-consuming experiments may also communicate marketing plans to competitors before a firm introduces a product to the total market.

Trend Analysis

Trend analysis develops forecasts for future sales by analyzing the historical relationship between sales and time. It implicitly assumes that the collective causes of past sales will continue to exert similar influences in the future. When historical data is available, planners can quickly and inexpensively complete trend analysis. Software programs can calculate the average annual increment of change for the available sales data. This average increment of change is then projected into the future to come up with the sales forecast. So, if the sales of a firm have been growing $15.3 million on average per year, this amount of sales could be added to last year's sales total to arrive at next year's forecast.

Of course, trend analysis cannot be used if historical data is not available, as in new-product forecasting. Also, trend analysis makes the dangerous assumption that future events will continue in the same manner as the past. Any variations in the determinants of future sales will cause deviations from the forecast. In other words, this method gives reliable forecasts during periods of steady growth and stable demand. If conditions change, predictions based on trend analysis may become worthless. For this reason, forecasters have applied more sophisticated techniques and complex, new forecasting models to anticipate the effects of various possible changes in the future.

trend analysis Quantitative sales forecasting method that estimates future sales through statistical analyses of historical sales patterns.

exponential smoothing Quantitative forecasting technique that assigns weights to historical sales data, giving the greatest weight to the most recent data.

Exponential Smoothing

A more sophisticated method of trend analysis, the **exponential smoothing** technique, weighs each year's sales data, giving greater weight to results from the most recent years. Otherwise, the statistical approach used in trend analysis is applied here. For example, last year's sales might receive a 1.5 weight, while sales data from two years ago could get a 1.4 weighting. Exponential smoothing is considered the most commonly used quantitative forecasting technique.

1. Describe the jury of executive opinion.
2. What is the Delphi technique?
3. How does the exponential smoothing technique forecast sales?

Strategic Implications of Marketing in the 21st Century

MARKETING research can help an organization develop effective marketing strategies. Approximately 75 percent of new products eventually fail to attract enough buyers to remain viable. Why? A major reason is the seller's failure to understand market needs.

Consider, for example, the hundreds of dot-com companies that went under. A characteristic shared by all of those failing businesses is that virtually none of them was founded on sound marketing research. Very few used marketing research techniques to evaluate product potential, and even fewer studied consumer responses after the ventures were initiated. While research might not have prevented every dot-com meltdown, it may have helped a few of those businesses survive the waning economy in which they were launched.[32]

Marketing research ideally matches new products to potential customers. Marketers also conduct research to analyze sales of their own and competitors' products, to gauge the performance of existing products, to guide the development of promotional campaigns and product enhancements, and to develop and refine products. All of these activities enable marketers to fine-tune their marketing strategies and reach customers more effectively and efficiently.

Marketing researchers have at their disposal a broad range of techniques with which to collect both quantitative and qualitative data on customers, their lifestyles, behaviors, attitudes, and perceptions. Vast amounts of data can be rapidly collected, accessed, interpreted, and applied to improve all aspects of business operations. Because of customer relationship management technology, that information is no longer generalized to profile groups of customers—it can be analyzed to help marketers understand each and every customer. ◆◆◆

REVIEW OF CHAPTER OBJECTIVES

① Describe the development of the marketing research function and its major activities.

Marketing research, or the collection and use of information in marketing decision making, reached a milestone when Charles C. Parlin, an advertising space salesperson, counted empty soup cans in Philadelphia's trash in an effort to convince the Campbell Soup Company to advertise in *The Saturday Evening Post.* Today, the most common marketing research activities are (1) determining market potential, market share, and market characteristics and (2) conducting sales analyses and competitive product studies. Most large companies now have internal marketing research departments. However, outside suppliers still remain vital to the research function. Some perform the complete research task, while others specialize in a limited area or provide specific data services.

1.1. Outline the development and current status of the marketing research function.
1.2. What role did Charles Parlin play in the development of marketing research?
1.3. What are the differences between full-service and limited-service research suppliers?

② Explain the steps in the marketing research process.

The marketing research process can be divided into six specific steps: (1) defining the problem, (2) conducting exploratory research, (3) formulating hypotheses, (4) creating a research design, (5) collecting data, and (6) interpreting and presenting the research information. A clearly defined problem focuses on the researcher's search for relevant decision-oriented information. Exploratory research refers to information gained outside the firm. Hypotheses, tentative explanations of specific events, allow researchers to set out specific research designs—that is, the series of decisions that, taken together, comprise master plans or models for the conduct of the investigations. The data-collection phase of the marketing research process can involve either or both primary (original) and secondary (previously published) data. After the data is collected, researchers must interpret and present it in a way that will be meaningful to management.

2.1. List and explain the steps in the marketing research process.
2.2. Trace a hypothetical study through the stages in this process.

③ Distinguish between primary and secondary data and identify the sources of each type.

Primary data can be collected by the firm's own researchers or by independent marketing research companies. Three principal methods of primary data collection are: observation, survey, or experiment. Secondary data can be classified as either internal or external. Sources of internal data include sales records, product evaluation, sales force reports, and records of marketing costs. Sources of external data include the government and private sources, such as business magazines. Both external and internal data can also be obtained from computer databases.

3.1. Distinguish between primary and secondary data.
3.2. When should researchers collect each type of data?
3.3. What kind of information of use to marketers is available from the government?

④ Explain the different sampling techniques used by marketing researchers.

Samples can be categorized as either probability samples or non-probability samples. A probability sample is one in which every member of the population has a known chance of being selected. Probability samples include simple random samples, in which every item in the relevant universe has an equal opportunity to be selected; stratified samples, which are constructed such that randomly selected subsamples of different groups are represented in the total sample; and cluster samples, in which geographic areas are selected from which respondents are drawn. A nonprobability sample is arbitrary and does not allow application of standard statistical tests. Nonprobability sampling techniques include convenience samples, in which readily available respondents are picked, and quota samples, which are divided so that different segments or groups are represented in the total sample.

4.1. What is sampling?

4.2. Explain the differences between probability and nonprobability samples and identify the various types of each.

⑤ Identify the methods by which marketing researchers collect primary data.

Observation data is gathered by observing consumers via devices such as people meters or videotape. Survey data can be collected through telephone interviews, mail or fax surveys, personal interviews, focus groups, or a variety of online methods. Telephone interviews provide over half of all primary marketing research data. They give the researcher a fast and inexpensive way to get small amounts of information but generally not detailed or personal information. Personal interviews are costly but allow researchers to get detailed information from respondents. Mail surveys are a means of conducting national studies at a reasonable cost; their main disadvantage is potentially inadequate response rates. Focus groups elicit detailed, qualitative information that provides insight not only into behavior but also into consumer attitudes and perceptions. Online surveys and other online methods can yield fast responses but face obstacles such as the adequacy of the probability sample. The experimental method creates verifiable statistical data through the use of test and control groups to reveal actual benefits from perceived benefits.

5.1. Distinguish among surveys, experiments, and observational methods of primary data collection. Cite examples of each method.

5.2. Define and give an example of each of the methods of gathering survey data. Under what circumstances should researchers choose a specific approach?

5.3. Describe the experimental method of collecting primary data and indicate when researchers should use it.

⑥ Explain the challenges of conducting marketing research in global markets.

Many resources are available to help U.S. organizations research global markets. Government resources include the Department of Commerce, state trade offices, small-business development centers, and foreign embassies. Private companies, such as marketing research firms and companies that distribute research from other sources, are another resource. Electronic networks offer online international trade forums, in which marketers can establish global contacts.

6.1. How does the process of international marketing research compare with domestic marketing research?

⑦ Outline the most important uses of computer technology in marketing research.

Important uses of computer technology in marketing research include (1) a marketing information system (MIS)—a planned, computer-based system designed to provide managers with a continuous flow of information relevant to their specific decision-making needs and areas of responsibility; (2) a marketing decision support system (MDSS)—a marketing information system component that links a decision maker with relevant databases and analysis tools; (3) data mining—the process of searching through consumer information files or data warehouses to detect patterns that guide marketing decision making; (4) business intelligence—the process of gathering information and analyzing it to improve business strategy, tactics, and daily operations; and (5) competitive intelligence—the form of business intelligence that focuses on finding information about competitors using published sources, interviews, observations by salespeople and suppliers in the industry, government agencies, public filings such as patent applications, and other secondary methods including the Internet.

7.1. Distinguish among marketing information systems, marketing decision support systems, and data mining. Cite examples of each.

7.2. What is the goal of data mining and how can marketers use it?

7.3. Describe business intelligence.

⑧ Explain how the use of information technology, particularly marketing decision support systems (MDSSs), can enhance and refine market research and its impact on decision making.

A marketing decision support system (MDSS) is a marketing information system component that not only links a decision maker to relevant information, but also provides important enhancements in the area of analysis. MDSSs consist of four main characteristics: interactive, investigative, flexible, and accessible. MDSSs help decision makers to apply the data that has been gathered in useful and relevant ways. Decision makers can use the information and data gathered to create a simulation or a model that illustrates likely results. These visual images such as graphs and charts illustrate the connection between the data and what is likely to happen in a given scenario. This is an invaluable tool in deciding on marketing strategies or in understanding market conditions.

8.1. What is a marketing decision support system (MDSS)?
8.2. What are the four characteristics of MDSSs?
8.3. How do MDSSs help decision makers decide on market strategies and understand market conditions?

⑨ Identify the major types of forecasting methods.

There are two categories of forecasting methods: (1) Qualitative methods are more subjective since they are based on opinions rather than exact historical data. They include the jury of executive opinion, the Delphi technique, the sales force composite, and the survey of buyer intentions. (2) Quantitative methods include test markets, trend analysis, and exponential smoothing.

9.1. Contrast qualitative and quantitative sales forecasting methods.

MARKETING TERMS YOU NEED TO KNOW

marketing research 258
exploratory research 261
secondary data 262
primary data 262
sampling 266
probability sample 267
nonprobability sample 267
interpretative research 268
focus group 270
marketing decision support system (MDSS) 275
sales forecast 277
jury of executive opinion 277
Delphi technique 277
sales force composite 278
trend analysis 279
exponential smoothing 279

OTHER IMPORTANT MARKETING TERMS

syndicated service 259
full-service research supplier 259
limited-service research supplier 260
sales analysis 261
hypothesis 262
research design 262
population (universe) 266
simple random sample 267
stratified sample 267
cluster sample 267
convenience sample 267
quota sample 267
mall intercept 270
controlled experiment 272
test-marketing 272
marketing information system (MIS) 275
data mining 275
qualitative forecasting 277
quantitative forecasting 277
survey of buyer intentions 278

PROJECTS AND TEAMWORK EXERCISES

1. ACNielsen offers data collected by optical scanners from the United Kingdom, France, Germany, Belgium, the Netherlands, Austria, Italy, and Finland. This scanner data tracks sales of UPC-coded products in those nations. In small teams, imagine that you are Nielsen clients in the U.S. One team might be a retail chain, another an Internet company, and still another a toy manufacturer. Discuss the types of marketing questions this data might help you answer. Share your list with other teams.
2. Set up two class teams to debate the use of the Internet to research new domestic markets. What other research options are available?
3. Today, one in three new homes sold in America is likely to be a manufactured home. New manufactured homes are built using higher quality materials than those of the past. As a result, the market for manufactured homes has grown to include more affluent buyers. Alabama-based Southern Energy Homes tries to appeal to upscale buyers by custom-building its homes according to customer specifications. What type of data and information should Southern Energy gather through its ongoing marketing intelligence to predict demand for its products? Would primary or secondary methods work best? Name some specific secondary sources of

data that Southern Energy might study to find useful business intelligence.

4. Discuss some of the challenges Pizza Hut might face in conducting marketing research in potential new international markets. What types of research would you recommend the company use in choosing new countries for expansion?
5. Which sales forecasting technique(s) are most appropriate for each of the following products? Prepare your arguments in pairs or teams:
   a. Post Shredded Wheat breakfast cereal
   b. No Doubt rock group
   c. Kinko's copy shops
   d. *Time* magazine
6. Assume you are responsible for launching a new family of skincare products for teens, with separate product lines for males and females. You would like to collect primary data from a sampling of each market before you prepare your marketing campaign. Let one team make the case for using a focus group and another team devise a plan supporting the use of an online chat room. Present the class with the benefits of each method and the ways in which each team plans to overcome its method's possible shortcomings. Now take this project one step further by having a classroom discussion on whether a decision support system could enhance the data collected from each method. How could an MDSS make the data more useful?
7. Interpretative research offers marketing researchers many possibilities, including the opportunity to improve product features such as packaging for food or over-the-counter medication that is difficult for seniors or the disabled to open. List some other ways in which you think this observation method can help make existing product offerings more appealing or more useful to specific kinds of users. What kind of products would you choose, and how would you test them?
8. Use the Internet to research the details of the national Do Not Call Registry and prepare a report outlining what it does and does not allow marketers to do. Research the effects of the registry to date. Do you think the public understands the purpose of the registry? Why or why not, and if not, what do you think marketers can do to clarify it?
9. McDonald's conducts extensive marketing research for all its new products, including new menu items for its overseas stores. Due to cultural and other differences and preferences, the company cannot often extrapolate its results from one country to another. For instance, Croque McDo fried ham-and-cheese sandwiches are unlikely to be as popular in the U.S. as they are in France, which invented the *croque monsieur* sandwich on which McDonald's product is based. Can you think of any other kinds of firms that share this limitation on global applications of their research? In contrast, what sorts of questions *could* multinational firms answer on a global basis? Why?
10. Outdoor advertising, including billboards, ads on bus shelters, and shopping mall displays, accounts for only a tiny portion of the $110 billion spent on advertising in a typical year in the U.S. ACNielsen is giving global positioning devices to 700 Chicagoans so it can track how many times they pass by specially coded billboards in the city. List some other ways you can think of to research the effectiveness of outdoor advertising (choose a specific location if you like) and cite the pros and cons of each.

APPLYING CHAPTER CONCEPTS

1. Some companies are broadening their markets by updating classic products to appeal to younger people's tastes and preferences. For example, Wrigley's has introduced two new Juicy Fruit flavors that it hopes will duplicate the success of Altoids and Mountain Dew in becoming revitalized and popular brands. What primary and secondary market information would you want to have if you were planning to reinvigorate an established brand in each of the following categories? Where and how would you obtain the information?
   a. household cleaner
   b. moist packaged cat food
   c. spray starch
   d. electrical appliances
2. Marketers sometimes collect primary information by using so-called *mystery shoppers* who visit stores anonymously (as if they were customers) and take note of such critical factors as store appearance and ambiance, items in stock, and quality of service including waiting time and courtesy of employees. (The CEO of Staples has gone on mystery shopper trips and sometimes asked his mother to make similar trips.) Prepare a list of data that you would want to obtain from a mystery shopper surveying a chain of gas stations in your area. Devise a format for inputting the information that combines your need to compile the data electronically and the researcher's need to remain "undercover" while visiting the stores.
3. Select a sales forecasting method (or combination of methods) for each of the following information needs and explain why you chose it.
   a. estimates of next quarter's raw materials needs from the managers of production, purchasing, distribution, and warehousing
   b. prediction of next year's sales based on last year's figures
   c. prediction of next year's sales based on weighted data from the last five years
   d. expected sales categorized by district and by region
   e. estimated product usage for the next year by representative consumers
   f. probable consumer response to a new product
   g. a consensus estimate from a panel of experts
4. The Internet provides ready access to secondary market information but is also a portal to an almost limitless store of primary information via message boards, chat rooms, e-mail questionnaires, newsgroups, and Web site registration forms. What are some specific drawbacks of each of these methods for obtaining primary information from customers?

ETHICS EXERCISE

Consumer groups sometimes raise objections to marketers' methods of collecting primary data from customers. They object to such means as product registration forms; certain types of games, contests, or product offers; and "cookies" and demographic questionnaires on company Web sites. Marketers believe that such tools offer them an easy way to collect market data. Most strictly control the use of such data and never link identifying information with consumers' financial or demographic profiles. However, the possibility of abuse or error always exists.

Research the code of ethics of the American Marketing Association (AMA) and pay particular attention to the guidelines for use of the Internet in marketing research.

1. How effectively do you think most corporate Web sites inform visitors about the use of "cookies" on the sites? (Check the Web sites of a few large consumer-products companies, for example.) Do you think marketers could or should improve their performance in protecting site visitors' privacy in this regard, and if so how?
2. Do you think it violates the code of ethics if marketers compile a mailing list based on warranty and product registration cards and use it to distribute new-product information? Why or why not? Does your opinion change if the company also sends list members special discount offers and private sale notices?

'netWork EXERCISES

1. **Focus groups.** Visit the following Web site, which describes how a focus group should be conducted. Read through the guidelines and prepare a summary you can use during a class discussion of the topic.
   http://www.managementhelp.org/grp_skll/focusgrp/focusgrp.htm
2. **Marketing research on the Web.** As noted in the chapter, many organizations find it efficient and effective to use the Web when conducting marketing research. Go to the following Web site, **http://www.decisionanalyst.com/online.asp**, and make a list of the advantages of Web-based marketing research.
3. **Online data sources.** There is an enormous amount of statistical data available online, much of which can be obtained for free. To give you an idea of the scope of data available online, go to the main Web page for the *Statistical Abstract of the United States* (**http://www.census.gov/prod/www/statistical-abstract-us.html**). Click the most recent year and answer the following questions:
   a. Under the Population section, what is the current population of the United States? What is the projected population of the United States in 10 years?
   b. Under the Population section, what are the five largest metropolitan areas in the United States? What are the five fastest growing metropolitan areas? Which metropolitan areas have the highest percentage of Hispanic residents?
   c. Under the Labor Force, Employment, and Earnings section, what is the average annual earnings for workers with four-year college degrees? Has the gap between the average annual earnings of high school and college graduates narrowed or widened in recent years?

Note: Internet Web addresses change frequently. If you don't find the exact sites listed, you may need to access the organization's or company's home page and search from there or use a search engine such as Google.

INFOTRAC CITATIONS AND EXERCISES

Record: A116286722
Nielsen tracks new boys club. Ben Fritz.
Daily Variety, April 12, 2004 v283 i5 p1(2)

Abstract: A television industry confounded by a 7.7 percent decline in 18- to 34-year-old male TV viewership recorded this past fall season has taken steps to find the reason for this flagging interest. Nielsen Entertainment and video game publisher Activision have partnered to expand audience research in the video game sector and, as a first move, have conducted a poll on the TV viewing habits of young men. Results of the survey reinforce what industry analysts suspected: There's a greater affinity among young males for video games, and this is challenging other forms of entertainment.

1. Read the article and briefly summarize the study conducted on the television and gaming habits of young men. Do you think the results of the study explain the recent decline in TV viewing among males aged 18 to 34? Why or why not?
2. Why might Nielsen Entertainment and Activision have chosen to use a survey poll for their study instead of using other research methods?
3. Why is the advertising industry particularly interested in the results of this research study? How do advertisers plan to capitalize on the growing popularity of video games, according to the article?

CASE 8.1 Marketing Research Goes to the Movies

It was bound to happen—Hollywood has discovered the power of the Internet. In the past, studios would test-screen films with random audiences a few months before release, showing them free at malls, say, and then gathering reactions from viewers. Afterward that information would sometimes send writers, directors, and actors back to work to film revised scenes, new scenes, alternative endings, and even dramatic plot changes. Test screenings have fallen out of favor lately, sometimes because of fear of negative word of mouth about an unfinished picture and sometimes because tight schedules don't allow time for making any changes. And test screenings cost money that studios sometimes don't want to spend on films that are already over budget. But this doesn't mean that writers, directors, and backers don't want audience feedback.

Some films are screened privately, as *Spider-Man* was. But the reactions of friends and colleagues might not reflect unbiased opinion. Aside from industry efforts, movie fans have colonized the Internet, setting up fan sites and message boards for popular films well before they opened. *Lord of the Rings* fans opened multiple sites to trade information, rumors, and opinions for more than five years, starting during the production phase and including the three years over which the trilogy of movies was released. Dozens of other films spawned similar sites, though perhaps none as long-lived.

At first, much of the information on sites like SuperHeroHype.com, Aintitcool.com, and DarkHorizons.com came from people in the industry who had access to film sets and inside information. Film companies soon realized they couldn't easily control what reached the public from these sources and put nondisclosure clauses in all their employment contracts. Now, despite their lingering fears that Web sites will become nothing more than portals to stolen copies of new films, studios are realizing that an important new opportunity exists for give-and-take on the Internet. For instance, when fans of the popular comic-book superhero The Hulk learned that his movie incarnation might not be wearing the character's trademark purple pants in the Ang Lee film, they took to the Internet to vent their frustration and protest. Marvel Studios chief Avi Arad and Lee listened, and The Hulk was properly costumed.

Other filmmakers and studios are responding also. New Line Cinema, for instance, set up its own *Lord of the Rings* Web site and cooperated with major fan site theonering.net, offering exclusive information and news in exchange for a promise that the site would not host any unauthorized material. The partnership has been a success for fans and studio alike, and *Rings* director Peter Jackson even participated in online chats on the site, which drew 20 million visits a month at its peak.

Of course, some filmmakers' fears about the Internet are well founded. Sometimes copies of films are leaked and downloaded. Negative reviews of new films have appeared on the Internet before release, but whether they alone are responsible for flops like *Gigli* is debatable. So perhaps the lesson for Hollywood is just to make better movies.

In the meantime, the Internet fan base is thriving. One film, *The Yank*, sported a fan site before a foot of film had even been shot. Could there be a better way to build an audience?

Questions for Critical Thinking

1. Do you think filmmakers and film companies should actively cultivate the Internet community? Why or why not? What possible advantages and drawbacks could such a strategy have?
2. Find an upcoming film that has an official Web site. What features does the site have? Which ones are designed to deliver information to the public and which are designed to capture information? How successful do you think this site will prove to be as a marketing research tool? Why?
3. How can filmmakers control the information that appears on the Internet? Should they take these steps? Why or why not?

Sources: Scott Bowles, "Fans Use Their Muscle to Shape the Movie," *USA Today*, June 20–22, 2003, pp. 1A, 2A; Ty Burr, "Web Buzz Control Is Hollywood's Newest Mission," *Boston Globe*, July 24, 2003; Tom King, "Hollywood Previews Go Private," *The Wall Street Journal*, April 26, 2002, p. W9.

VIDEO CASE 8.2 Teenage Research Unlimited Has the True Story on Teens

The written case on Teenage Research Unlimited appears on page VC-10. The recently filmed Teenage Research Unlimited video is designed to expand and highlight the concepts in this chapter and the concepts and questions covered in the written video case.

chapter 9

Market Segmentation, Targeting, and Positioning

chapter objectives

1. Identify the essential components of a market.
2. Outline the role of market segmentation in developing a marketing strategy.
3. Describe the criteria necessary for effective segmentation.
4. Explain each of the four bases for segmenting consumer markets.
5. Identify the steps in the market segmentation process.
6. Discuss four basic strategies for reaching target markets.
7. Summarize the types of positioning strategies.
8. Explain the reasons for positioning and repositioning products.

ARTE MORENO: AN ANGEL TO MAJOR LEAGUE BASEBALL

Every guy's dream is to own a baseball team," said Arturo "Arte" Moreno several years ago, when he purchased the Anaheim Angels from the Walt Disney Co. for $180 million. Now that his dream has come true, Moreno is working doubly hard to make it a success as well. Success in Major League Baseball means winning on two different fields: against other teams and with the fans. Moreno, baseball's first Hispanic team owner—whose college major was marketing—has his work cut out for him. The Angels have had trouble attracting fans, partly because they live and play in the shadow of the colorful Los Angeles Dodgers. But Moreno's supporters believe that he can lure a special group of consumers to Edison International Field in Anaheim, California: Hispanic fans. After all, 43 percent of Anaheim's residents speak Spanish; in nearby Santa Ana, that percentage rises to 74 percent. In all, an estimated 6.5 million Hispanics live in the Los Angeles area—all of whom are potential fans.

Moreno asserts that his preference is to appeal to everyone in the Los Angeles area—not just Hispanics. "We want to target everyone interested in going to a ball game," he explains. "We don't want to put up any barriers." He is determined to create value—and ultimately, loyalty—for his fans. One of his first moves was to slash beer prices at the Angels' park, a popular decision. He also dropped ticket prices and made other concession items more affordable for the average working fan. Monday through Thursday, right-field bleacher seats now cost only $5, and four hot dogs, a liter of Coke (including cups and ice), and a giant popcorn go for $16. This brings an evening of entertainment—including a meal—for a family of four to $50. Most people agree that is a major league bargain. "I want to be able to create a family atmosphere that is reasonably priced," notes Moreno. "That way we expand our overall audience." Moreno also focuses on turning kids into satisfied customers. Recently, he redefined the ticket age for a child as anyone under 18 years old instead of under 12. "You get me the kids in here," says Moreno, "and I'll get you a fan base that will last for a long, long time."

GETTY IMAGES

But Moreno is also taking actions specifically aimed at drawing Hispanics into the park. "This year almost a third of our [marketing] budget is devoted to the Hispanic market," says Kevin Uhlich, the Angels' vice president. Moreno plans to have more Angels' games broadcast in Spanish, and he has already signed several big-name Hispanic players: pitchers Bartolo Colon (four years for $51 million) and Kelvim Escobar (three years for $18.75 million) and outfielders Jose Guillen (two years for $6 million) and Vladimir Guerrero (five years for $70 million). During negotiations, Moreno was the only team owner who discussed his terms in Spanish with Colon and also translated for Guerrero at the press conference announcing his contract signing. Guerrero's agent believes that Moreno's understanding of his own language and culture was a serious factor in Guerrero's decision to sign with the Angels.

Despite the media focus on Moreno's heritage, as well as the significant Hispanic population as a potential consumer base, Moreno himself believes in the fundamental marketing principle of satisfying his customers—no matter who they are. He wants to give them a good value and have them enjoy the game. He also knows that he is running a business. "You know, it's a fun business. It's *supposed* to be fun," says Moreno. He hopes that everyone else thinks so too.[1]

Chapter Overview

EACH of us is unique. We come from different backgrounds, live in different households, and have different interests and goals. You and your best friend may shop at different stores, listen to different music, play different sports, and take different courses in college. Suppose you like baseball, but your best friend prefers hockey. Marketers for all kinds of sports events, ranging from table tennis to professional bowling tournaments, want to capture your interest as well as that of your friends. Arte Moreno, owner of the Anaheim Angels, hopes you will want to attend one of his team's games, listen to it on the radio, or watch on television. He hopes you will encourage your friends to attend as well and that you will visit the concession stands for food and souvenirs. Your interests and needs, your lifestyle and income, the city where you live, and your age all contribute to your willingness to become a sports fan. All of these factors make up a market. A **market** is composed of people with sufficient purchasing power, authority, and willingness to buy. And marketers must use their expertise to understand the market for a good or service, whether it's tickets for a baseball game—or a hot dog with mustard.

market Group of people with sufficient purchasing power, authority, and willingness to buy.

target market Group of people to whom a firm decides to direct its marketing efforts and ultimately its goods and services.

Many markets include consumers with different lifestyles, backgrounds, and income levels. Nearly everyone buys toothpaste, but that does not mean every consumer has the same lifestyle, background, or income. So it is unusual for a single marketing mix strategy to attract all sectors of a market. By identifying, evaluating, and selecting a target market to pursue, such as consumers who prefer toothpaste made with all-natural ingredients or those who want an extra-whitening formula, marketers are able to develop more efficient and effective marketing strategies. On the other hand, some products—such as luxury sports cars or fly fishing supplies—are intended for a more specific market. In either case, the **target market** for a product is the specific segment of consumers most likely to purchase a particular product.

Marketing now takes place on a global basis more than ever, incorporating many target markets. To identify those markets, marketers must determine useful ways for segmenting different populations and communicating with them successfully. This chapter discusses useful ways to accomplish this, explaining the steps of the market segmentation process and surveying strategies for reaching target markets. Finally, it looks at the role of positioning in developing a marketing strategy. ◆◆◆

Briefly Speaking

The most beautiful thing in the world is a ballpark filled with people.

Bill Veeck (1914–1986)
American baseball team owner

① **Identify the essential components of a market.**

consumer products Products bought by ultimate consumers for personal use.

business products Goods and services purchased for use either directly or indirectly in the production of other goods and services for resale.

TYPES OF MARKETS

Products are usually classified as either consumer products or business products. **Consumer products** are bought by ultimate consumers for personal use, such as cell phones or fashion magazines. **Business products** are goods and services purchased for use either directly or indirectly in the production of other goods and services for resale. Most goods and services purchased by individual consumers, such as DVDs, cookbooks, or restaurant meals, are considered consumer products. Rubber and raw cotton are examples of items generally purchased by manufacturers and are, therefore, classified as business products. Goodyear buys rubber to manufacture tires; textile manufacturers such as Burlington Industries convert raw cotton into cloth.

However, in many cases, a single product can serve different uses. Tires purchased for the family car constitute consumer products. But tires purchased by General Motors to be mounted on its Chevy Suburban are business products because they become part of another product destined for resale. Or a product that was once a business product might be modified for consumer use, and vice versa. A line of professional cookware sold to restaurants—a business product—could be adapted by its manufacturer to become a line of cookware for home use—a consumer product. If you want to determine the classification of items, just think about who is going to buy the product and why or how the product will be used. The bottle of mouthwash you buy at the supermarket is a consumer product, but if a large hotel chain purchases large quantities of the same mouthwash from a wholesaler, it becomes a business product.

1. Distinguish between a consumer product and a business product.
2. Give another example of a product that could serve both markets.

THE ROLE OF MARKET SEGMENTATION

(2) Outline the role of market segmentation in developing a marketing strategy.

There are 6.3 billion people in the world today, nearly 300 million of whom live in the U.S.[2] In today's business world, there are too many variables in consumer needs, preferences, and purchasing power to attract all consumers with a single marketing mix. That's not to say that firms must actually change products to meet the needs of different market segments—although they often do—but they must attempt to identify the factors that affect purchase decisions and then group consumers according to the presence or absence of these factors. Finally, they adjust marketing strategies to meet the needs of each group.

market segmentation Division of the total market into smaller, relatively homogeneous groups.

Consider motor vehicles. Unlike a century ago, when Henry Ford pronounced that customers could order any color of car they liked—as long as it was black—today there is a make, model, and color for every taste and budget. But auto manufacturers need to adjust their messages for different markets. And savvy marketers are looking toward markets that show growth, such as the U.S. Hispanic population, which is now the largest ethnic group in the country, and aging baby boomers, whose needs for goods and services are already changing. Nissan Motor Company targets its Hispanic-American customers with ads in Spanish like the one in Figure 9.1.

The division of the total market into smaller, relatively homogeneous groups is called **market segmentation.** Both profit-oriented and not-for-profit organizations practice market segmentation.

(3) Describe the criteria necessary for effective segmentation.

CRITERIA FOR EFFECTIVE SEGMENTATION

Segmentation doesn't automatically guarantee success in the marketing arena; instead, it is a tool for marketers to use. Its effectiveness depends on the following four basic requirements.

First, the market segment must present measurable purchasing power and size. A perfect example is women. With jobs, incomes, and decision-making power, women consumers represent a hefty amount of purchasing power. Women make up half the potential market for many new electronic products. In fact, in one recent year, women actually spent more than men—$55 billion of the $96 billion spent on electronics gear.[3] Lowe's home improvement chain recognizes the importance of women to its success. Armed with research showing that women initiate more than 80 percent of home improvement projects—especially large ones such as remodeling a kitchen or adding a bathroom—the chain refocused its marketing efforts to target women. Lowe's has made its stores more comfortable for browsing, with wide aisles, clear signs to direct shoppers, and call buttons that customers can use to summon a salesperson. The company also stocks more appliances and home décor items—from Laura Ashley paints to Pergo laminate floors to Jacuzzi tubs. Such efforts have rebuilt the company's reputation, and its competitiveness, in the home improvement retail market.[4]

Second, marketers must find a way to promote effectively and to serve the market segment. Since

figure 9.1

Nissan: Serving the Hispanic-American Market

AP PHOTO/KOJI SASAHARA

figure 9.2

Women: An Increasingly Important Market for Consumer Electronics

women are more likely than men to think twice about a technology purchase—and often care about style and color as well as functionality—marketers need to find different ways to appeal to women. Although a recent electronics industry survey revealed that three of every four women complained about salespeople who either ignored them or dealt with them in a condescending manner, Evins Communications technology director Catherine Markman is convinced that nearly any electronic device could be sold to women with the right kind of marketing. Some companies have taken this advice to heart: Sharp redesigned its flat-panel TVs—along with its advertising—to appeal to women. Instead of concentrating on sports channels, Sharp now promotes its AQUOS TVs, shown in Figure 9.2, on Lifetime and the Food Network, as well as in home decorating magazines like *Traditional Home.* "When it came to consumer electronics, we noticed that the female population was being ignored a bit," admits Sharp's vice president of marketing.[5]

Third, marketers must then identify segments that are sufficiently large to give them good profit potential. If women—who make up more than half the U.S. population—are now spending $55 billion a year on electronics purchases, there is plenty of profit potential for the electronics industry. Radio Shack reports that women now comprise 40 percent of its customer base—up from 20 percent seven years ago. So Radio Shack is hiring more female store managers; about 1,000 of its 7,000 stores are managed by women.[6]

And fourth, the firm must aim for segments that match its marketing capabilities. Targeting a large number of small markets can be an expensive, complex, and inefficient strategy, so smaller firms may decide to stick with a particular niche, or target market. To compete for women's business, Tri-City Electronics Inc., an upscale North Carolina–based audio-video retailer, installed a children's play area so that moms could shop freely and replaced its high-tech, industrial atmosphere with a cozier, homier feel. The store owners even offered a tour of their own home, where the products were in use. They report that sales to women have been climbing steadily following the changes.[7]

MARKETING Concept Check

1. **Define *market segmentation.***
2. **Identify the four criteria for effective segmentation.**

SEGMENTING CONSUMER MARKETS

Market segmentation attempts to isolate the traits that distinguish a certain group of consumers from the overall market. An understanding of the group's characteristics—such as age, gender, geographic location, income, and buying patterns—plays a vital role in developing a successful marketing strategy. In most cases, marketers seek to pinpoint a number of factors affecting buying behavior in the target segment. Marketers in the travel industry consider employment trends, changes in income levels and buying patterns, age, lifestyle, and other factors when promoting their goods and services. To boost flagging attendance at its theme parks, Disney World has been advertising to adults who are "empty nesters" and groups of friends instead of focusing entirely on families with young children. In their efforts to attract new students, colleges and universities are affected by the number of graduating high school seniors and also by changing attitudes toward the value of a college education and trends in enrollment of older adults. Marketers rarely identify totally homogeneous segments, in which all potential customers are alike; they always encounter some differences among members of a target group. But they must be careful to ensure that their segments accurately reflect consumers.

(4) Explain each of the four bases for segmenting consumer markets.

In the next sections, we discuss the four common bases for segmenting consumer markets: geographic segmentation, demographic segmentation, psychographic segmentation, and product-related segmentation. These segmentation approaches can give important guidance for marketing strategies, provided they identify significant differences in buying behavior.

GEOGRAPHIC SEGMENTATION

Marketers have long practiced **geographic segmentation**—dividing an overall market into homogeneous groups on the basis of their locations. Geographic location does not ensure that all consumers in a location will make the same buying decisions, but this segmentation approach does help identify some general patterns. The 295 million people who live in the U.S. are not scattered evenly across the country. Instead, they are concentrated in major metropolitan areas. New York is the largest U.S. city, with 8 million citizens. Los Angeles is a distant second, with 3.6 million.[8] Figure 9.3 shows populations of the 10 largest cities in the U.S.

geographic segmentation Division of an overall market into homogeneous groups based on their locations.

The five states with the most residents are California (34 million), Texas (21 million), New York (19 million), Florida (16 million), and Illinois (12 million). By contrast, only about 1 million people live in New Hampshire and Maine with about half that number living in Vermont.[9]

A look at the worldwide population distribution illustrates why so many firms are pursuing customers around the globe. China and India both have more than 1 billion people. As in the U.S., much of the population lives in urban environments. The two metropolitan areas with the world's largest populations, Tokyo and Mexico City, dwarf New York City.[10]

Population size alone, however, may not be reason enough for a business to expand into a specific country. Businesses also need to look at a wide variety of economic variables. Some businesses may decide to combine their marketing efforts for countries that share similar population and product-use patterns instead of treating each country as an independent segment. This grouping is taking place with greater frequency throughout the European Union as the currency and trade laws of the 25 member nations are unified.

While population numbers indicate the overall size of a market, other geographic indicators such as job growth can also give useful guidance to marketers depending on the type of products they sell. Automobile manufacturers might segment geographic regions by household income because it is an important factor in the purchase of a new car.

Geographic areas also vary in population migration patterns. The most recent census data indicated that 40 million Americans lived in a different home than they had a year earlier—over half of them moving for such "housing-related reasons" as a desire for a better house or apartment or to own rather than rent.[11] U.S. census data also indicate two major population shifts: migration toward the Sunbelt states of the Southeast and Southwest and toward the West. In recent years, the West has experienced the fastest growth at 19.7 percent, with the South just behind at 17.3 percent. Nevada has had the highest growth of an individual state at 66 percent.[12] And although you may not have heard of

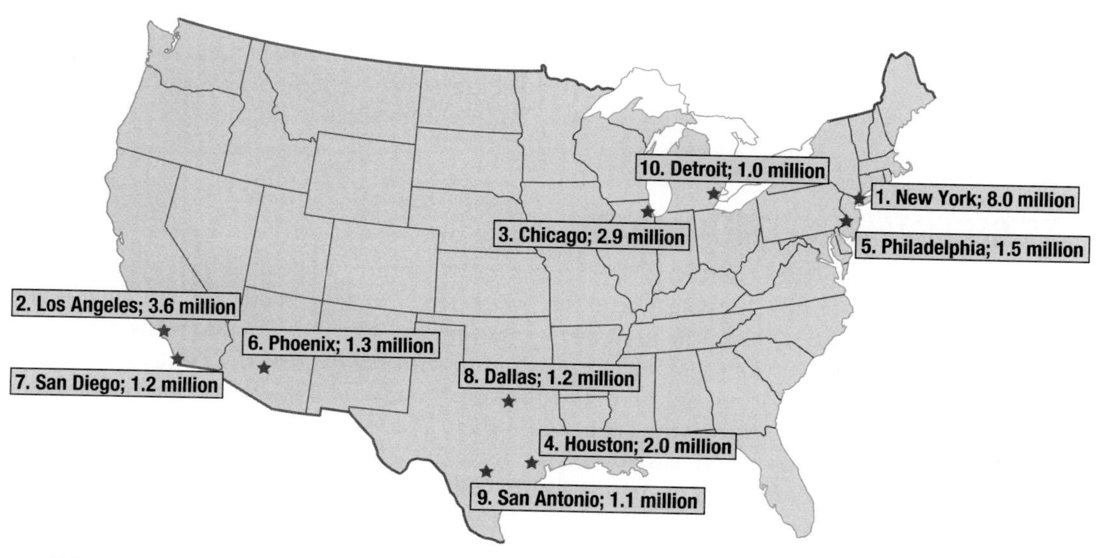

Source: U.S. Census Bureau, http://www.census.gov, accessed March 8, 2004.

figure 9.3

The 10 Largest Cities in the U.S.

Gilbert, Arizona, this suburb of Phoenix has grown nearly 25 percent in two years.[13] Researchers expect these trends to continue. Between now and 2020, the states expected to experience the fastest population growth are Nevada, Hawaii, California, and Washington.[14] However, it is important to note another trend: People who leave the East Coast aren't necessarily jumping to the West, and vice versa. New Yorkers tend to gravitate to the South or even just to Connecticut or New Jersey. Californians tend to move to other western states instead of coming East.[15]

The move from urban to suburban areas after World War II created a need to redefine the urban marketplace. This trend radically changed cities' traditional patterns of retailing and led to decline in many downtown shopping areas—although recent trends have been toward the revitalization of downtown areas. Subsequently, traditional city boundaries became almost meaningless for marketing purposes.

In an effort to respond to these changes, the government now classifies urban data using three categories.

- The category of **core based statistical area (CBSA)** became effective in 2000 and refers collectively to metropolitan and micropolitan statistical areas. Each CBSA must contain at least one urban area with a population of 10,000 or more. Each metropolitan statistical area must have at least one urbanized area of 50,000 or more inhabitants. Each micropolitan statistical area must have at least one urban cluster with a population of at least 10,000 but less than 50,000.
    - A **metropolitan statistical area** is a freestanding urban area with a population in the urban center of at least 50,000 and a total metropolitan statistical area population of 100,000 or more. Buyers in metropolitan statistical areas exhibit social and economic homogeneity. They usually border on nonurbanized counties. Examples include Rochester, New York; Odessa-Midland, Texas; and Kalamazoo-Battle Creek, Michigan.
    - A **micropolitan statistical area** is an area that has at least one town of 10,000 to 49,999 people—and it can have several of these—and proportionally few of its residents commuting to outside the area. In 2000 the government counted 567 such micropolises in the continental U.S. Examples of micropolises include Granbury, Texas; Marion, Ohio; Alamogordo, New Mexico; and Yazoo City, Mississippi.
- The category of **consolidated metropolitan statistical area (CMSA)** includes the country's 25 or so urban giants such as Detroit-Ann Arbor-Flint, Michigan; Los Angeles-Riverside-Orange County, California; and Philadelphia-Wilmington-Atlantic City. (Note that in the third example, three states are involved—Pennsylvania, Delaware, and New Jersey.) A CMSA must include two or more primary metropolitan statistical areas, discussed next.
- A **primary metropolitan statistical area (PMSA)** is an urbanized county or set of counties with social and economic ties to nearby areas. PMSAs are identified within areas of 1-million-plus populations. Olympia, Washington, is part of the Seattle-Tacoma-Bremerton PMSA. Bridgeport, Connecticut, is part of the New York-Northern New Jersey-Long Island PMSA, and Riverside-San Bernardino, California, is a PMSA within the Los Angeles-Riverside-Orange County PMSA.[16]

USING GEOGRAPHIC SEGMENTATION

Demand for some categories of goods and services can vary according to geographic region, and marketers need to be aware of how these regions differ. Marketers of major brands are particularly interested in defining their **core regions,** the locations where they get 40 to 80 percent of their sales.

Residence location within a geographic area is an important segmentation variable. City dwellers often rely on public transportation and may find they get along fine without automobiles, whereas those who live in the suburbs or rural areas depend on their personal vehicles. Also, those who live in the suburbs spend more on lawn and garden care products than do people in the city.

Climate is another important segmentation factor. Consumers in chilly northern states, for example, eat more soup than people who live in warmer southern markets. But here's a surprise—they also eat a great deal of ice cream! Homeowners in warm climates—who are also located in the suburbs—

are likely to be interested in the promotional message for outdoor awnings in Figure 9.4.

Geographic segmentation provides useful distinctions when regional preferences or needs exist. A consumer might not want to invest in a snow blower or flood insurance but may *have* to because of the location of his or her home. But it's important for marketers not to stop at geographic location as a segmentation method because distinctions among consumers also exist within a geographic location. Consider those who relocate from one region to another for work or family reasons. They may bring with them their preferences from other parts of the country. Using multiple segmentation variables is probably a much better strategy for targeting a specific market.

figure 9.4

Geographic Segmentation: The Importance of Suburban Homeowners' Buying Habits

DURASOL SYSTEMS, INC.

GEOGRAPHIC INFORMATION SYSTEMS (GISs)

Super Bowl Sunday is more than a sporting event—it is also the single biggest sales day of the year for a pizza company like Domino's. On that day alone, Domino's delivers 900,000 pizzas around the nation. The firm has built its reputation as the No. 1 pizza delivery company in the world, which means that its delivery system must be as streamlined and efficient as possible. Delivery companies traditionally planned their routes by using statistical databases, maps, and reports. These sources do provide valuable information but not in a format that is quick and easy to use. So Domino's invested in a geographic information system. Once used mainly by the military, **geographic information systems (GISs)** are computer systems that assemble, store, manipulate, and display data by their location. GISs simplify the job of analyzing marketing information by relating data to their locations. The result is a geographic map overlaid with digital data about consumers in a particular area. A growing number of companies benefit from using a GIS to locate new outlets, assign sales territories, plan distribution centers—and map out the most efficient delivery routes. Although the earliest geographic information systems were prohibitively expensive for all but the largest companies, recent technological advances have made GIS software available at a much lower cost, increasing usage among smaller firms. Marketing researchers agree, however, that firms have not yet realized the full potential of GIS technology.

geographic information systems (GISs) Computer systems that assemble, store, manipulate, and display data by their location.

1. Under what circumstances are marketers most likely to use geographic segmentation?
2. What is a geographic information system (GIS)?

DEMOGRAPHIC SEGMENTATION

The most common method of market segmentation—**demographic segmentation**—defines consumer groups according to demographic variables such as gender, age, income, occupation, education, household size, and stage in the family life cycle. This approach is also called *socioeconomic segmentation*. Marketers review vast quantities of available data to complete a plan for demographic segmentation. One of the primary sources for demographic data in the U.S. is the Bureau of the Census. Marketers can obtain many of the Census Bureau's statistics online at http://www.census.gov. The following discussion considers the most commonly used demographic variables. Keep in mind, however, that while demographic segmentation is helpful, it can also lead to stereotyping—a preconception about a group of people—which can alienate a potential market or cause marketers to miss a potential market altogether. The idea is to use segmentation as a starting point, not as an end point.[17]

demographic segmentation Division of an overall market into homogeneous groups based on variables such as gender, age, income, occupation, education, sexual orientation, household size, and stage in the family life cycle; also called *socioeconomic segmentation*.

SEGMENTING BY GENDER

Gender is an obvious variable that helps define the markets for certain products. But segmenting by gender can be tricky. In some cases, the segmenting is obvious—lipstick for women, facial shaving

REBECCA COOK/REUTERS/LANDOV

Market segmentation often falls along gender lines. Auto manufacturers such as Dodge have begun considering women's preferences in the design of their cars.

products for men. But in recent years, the lines have increasingly blurred. As the roles, interests, and preferences of men and women have changed, so have their product needs. So marketers of cars and trucks, power tools, jewelry, and skincare products have had to change the way they segment their markets. When it comes to home improvement products, ranging from a new sink to a new sofa, men and women tend to share purchasing responsibility. "What we are seeing is the democratization of the household and a blur of traditional roles," notes Christopher Camps, marketing director for This Old House Ventures, which conducted a marketing survey of home improvement purchase decisions. "It clearly proves there have been preconceptions that don't reflect the current marketplace. . . . The goal is to make sure we're speaking to the marketplace as it exists today."[18]

Some companies successfully market the same—or similar—products to both men and women. Gillette markets its disposable razor Slim Twist in two colors—one for men, one for women—but it's the same razor nonetheless. "The only difference is the color," says a company product specialist.[19] Even books are marketed differently to men and women. A recent ad for the latest Harry Potter book, shown in Figure 9.5, is meant to appeal to women's appreciation for clothing and sense of style.

Auto manufacturers have begun to pay far more attention to the purchasing influence of women. Not only do they now target women in their advertising, but they also consider women's preferences in the design of vehicles. The Dodge Caravan appeals to young, active women with busy schedules because of such items as stow-and-go seating, a preference chosen by women and communicated to Dodge. According to the U.S. Census Bureau, 55 percent of mothers in the workforce have infant children, which means they are juggling work and family and are likely to spend many hours driving.[20]

SEGMENTING BY AGE

Age is another variable that marketers use to segment their markets. As with gender, age seems like an easy distinction to make—baby food for babies, retirement communities for seniors. But also like gender, the distinctions become blurred as consumers' roles and needs change and as age distribution shifts and projected changes in each group take place. St. Joseph's baby aspirin is no longer marketed just to parents for their infants; now it is also marketed to middle-aged and senior consumers as an aid in the prevention of heart disease.

School-age children—and those who are even younger—exert considerable influence over family purchases, as marketers are keenly aware, particularly in the area of food. One study showed that a 30-second commercial could influence the food choices of children as young as age two.[21] Breakfast cereals, snack foods, beverages, and desserts of all kinds are designed to attract the attention of children—who in turn try to persuade their families to purchase them.

Now let's look in more depth at three age groups whose characteristics have proved to be of particular importance to marketers. Those segments are teens, baby boomers, and seniors.

Tweens and Teens

Tweens—also called *preteens*—and teens are a rapidly growing market. According to Teenage Research Unlimited, the purchases that the average teen makes—or influences—add up to about $116 a week. Multiply that by 52, and you have over $6,000 per year.[22] This figure includes not only purchases teens may make themselves but also family purchases—such as cars or DVD players—that teens may influence. As a group, tweens and teens spend more than $150 billion themselves annually on everything from snacks to clothing to electronics.[23] This group, commonly referred to as Generation Y, isn't as cynical about advertising as their older counterpart—Generation X, those born between 1966 and

1976—seems to be. In fact, says Anne Zehren, publisher of *Teen People,* "They like being marketed to. They like that someone's paying attention to them."[24]

Marketers for cell phone companies like Boost Mobile and Virgin Mobile USA are actively targeting the millions of teens who have—or want—their own cell phones. But instead of following traditional marketing methods, these two companies have found innovative ways to reach their consumers. They sell through surf shops and music stores, they don't make credit checks or require binding contracts, and they allow teens to purchase prepaid chunks of airtime through outlets like 7-Eleven and Target. Virgin also offers a popular feature called "rescue ring," with which customers can schedule an incoming call at a particular time—so they can exit from a boring date or meeting. Industry watchers are impressed. "Boost and Virgin have done a phenomenal job reaching Gen Y," says David Morrison, president of Twenty-something Inc., a youth-marketing consulting firm. "They are just nailing it."[25]

Other firms that have had success marketing to teens include Avon, Old Navy, Gap, and even auto manufacturers such as Ford and Toyota. You will read about Scion, Toyota's new car aimed at Gen Y, in the case at the end of this chapter. The Coca-Cola Company has recently opened teen lounges in Chicago and Los Angeles—called Coke Red Lounges—where teens can go to watch music videos, listen to their favorite CDs, play video games, and of course, drink Coke. In Britain, the firm launched myCokeMusic.com, a Web site where teens can legally download more than half a million songs. And in Spain, where older Gen Yers tend to live with their parents, Coke offers a Web site where they can build their own virtual apartment.[26]

figure 9.5

Gender Segmentation: Stylish Women Who Read

AP PHOTO/PR NEWSWIRE/SCHOLASTIC CORPORATION

Marketers can learn from a sociological concept called the **cohort effect,** the tendency of members of a generation to be influenced and bound together by significant events occurring during their key formative years, roughly 17 to 22 years of age. These events help to define the core values of the age group that eventually shape consumer preferences and behavior. For seniors, who are discussed later in this section, the event would be World War II or Korea because many were in this age bracket at the time of those wars. Marketers have already labeled people who were in the 17 to 22 age bracket at the time of the September 11, 2001, terrorist attacks the **9/11 Generation.** Clearly, this group's previous priorities and values have changed, and those changes will become more evident as time passes.

Baby Boomers

Baby boomers—people born between 1946 and 1965—are a popular segment to target because of their numbers. More than two of every five U.S. adults were born in this period. The values of this age group were influenced both by the Vietnam War era and the career-driven era that followed, as well as the civil rights and women's movements.

Baby boomers are a lucrative segment for thousands of marketers. Baby boomers over the age of 50 will have a total disposable income of $1 trillion within the next few years, which is why businesses are trying to woo this group. Different subgroups within this generation complicate segmentation and targeting strategies. Some boomers put off having children until their 40s, while others their age have already become grandparents. Boomer grandparents are healthier and more physically active than their own grandparents were, and they expect to take an active role in their grandchildren's lives. When buying toys, for instance, they often purchase items that focus on a shared experience—games they can play with their grandchildren or craft sets they can assemble together. Because they are healthy and active, they enjoy adventure travel. Firms like Overseas Adventure Travel, which once designed its trips to South America and Africa for younger travelers, now target older baby boomers and even seniors who have the time, interest, and money for such travel.[27]

figure 9.6

MasterCard: Appealing to Baby Boomers' Nostalgia for Music

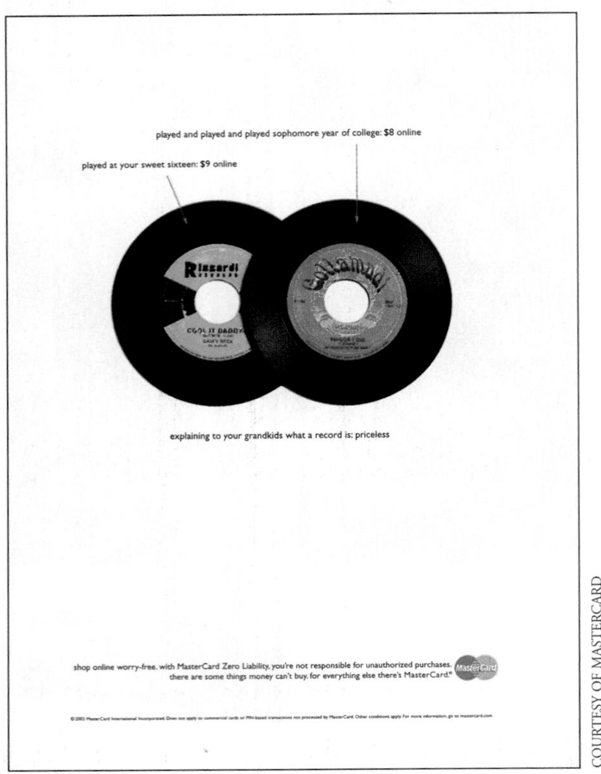

COURTESY OF MASTERCARD

Nostalgic references that remind baby boomers of their own childhood and adolescence are a popular way to target this segment. The MasterCard ad in Figure 9.6 appeals to baby boomer nostalgia about music.

Seniors

Marketers also recognize a trend dubbed *the graying of America.* By 2025, one American in five will be over age 65. As Americans continue to live longer, the median age of the U.S. population has dramatically increased. The current median age is now 35.2 years, up from 32.8 years a decade ago.[28] And the average life expectancy in the U.S. has increased for both genders to age 74 for men and to age 79 for women.[29] In addition, people aged 65 can expect to live an average of nearly 18 more years. Explanations for these increases in life spans include better medicines and healthier lifestyles.[30]

Because they are healthier and are living longer, seniors want marketers to know that they are more active. During a recent focus group, Amazon Advertising president Millie Olson noticed that the female participants became annoyed when they were shown health-care ads portraying older women taking walks or sitting around the house. Olson herself said she'd prefer to see ads for arthritis medication portraying women working out at the gym, "not silver-haired couples walking along the beach with a golden retriever."[31]

In the U.S., heads of households aged 55-plus control about three-quarters of the country's total financial assets. Their discretionary incomes and rates of home ownership are higher than those of any other age group. They account for about 40 percent of new car sales and most of the travel dollars spent. These numbers show why many marketers should target this group. Some refer to these prosperous consumers as WOOFs—Well-Off Older Folks. Although many seniors do live on modest, fixed incomes, those who are well off financially have both time and money to spend on leisure activities and luxury items.[32]

Traditionally, one way marketers have targeted seniors is through the senior discount, whether it's for a cup of coffee at McDonald's or a pass at the ski slopes. But with more seniors living longer and collecting these discounts, some companies are rolling them back. However, not all marketers agree with this cost-cutting approach because seniors do make up such a large group of potentially loyal customers.

SEGMENTING BY ETHNIC GROUP

According to the Census Bureau, America's racial and ethnic makeup is changing. Because of comparatively high immigration and birthrates among some minority groups, the Census Bureau projects that by 2050, only half of the population will belong to the formerly white majority, and Hispanics will comprise nearly a quarter of the U.S. population, at 103 million.[33] Figure 9.7 shows the current breakdown of minority populations in the U.S.

The three largest and fastest growing racial/ethnic groups are Hispanics, African Americans, and Asian Americans. From a marketer's perspective, it is important to note that spending by these groups is rising at a faster pace than for U.S. households in general.

Hispanics and African Americans

Hispanics and African Americans are currently the largest racial/ethnic minority groups in the U.S., with Hispanics edging out African Americans at nearly 40 million, according to the most recent census data.[34] The Hispanic population's growth rate is four times that of the African-American population and nine times the growth rate of whites. During the 1990s, nearly 2 million people immigrated to the U.S. from Mexico alone. Census projections predict that Hispanics will continue to widen their lead over African Americans.[35] Just as important for marketers, U.S. Hispanics' disposable income has increased by nearly a third over a two-year period—to $652 billion in a recent year—double the rate of the rest of the population.[36]

Many marketers have focused their efforts on the Hispanic population in the U.S. during the last few years, from fast-food restaurants to retailers to Major League Baseball (MLB), as described in the chapter-opening example. The Florida Marlins, Los Angeles Dodgers, and Arizona Diamondbacks regularly broadcast their games in Spanish. The Diamondbacks designate five nights a week as Hispanic nights, with special T-shirts and other promotions.[37] Although MLB has made a significant effort to attract more Hispanic fans, one survey shows that Hispanics between the ages of 18 and 64 cite football as their favorite sport, with the Olympics, boxing, and basketball following. Major League Baseball falls into fifth place.[38]

figure 9.7

Breakdown of U.S. Minority Populations

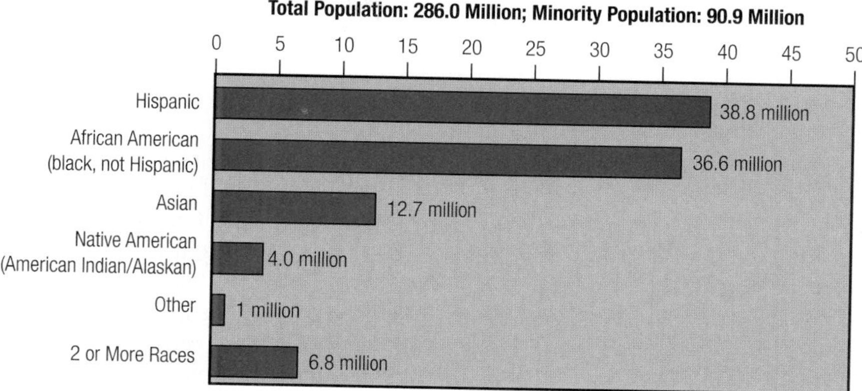

Source: "Hispanics, Asians Continuing Explosive Population Growth," http://www.usatoday.com, June 14, 2004.

Marketers of various products continue to try to reach Hispanics. Hallmark has launched a line of 2,500 greeting cards targeted for the Hispanic market, and Blockbuster now has bilingual signs and stocks more Spanish-language videos in its San Francisco stores.[39]

About $2 billion is spent each year on advertising to the Hispanic market, a figure that experts predict will continue to grow. "The Hispanic market isn't some separate country," says Luis Garcia, founder of an ad agency for the Hispanic market. "It's part of the overall marketplace."[40] Procter & Gamble tops the list of advertisers to the Hispanic market, followed by Philip Morris, General Motors, AT&T, and McDonald's. Johnson Publishing, publisher of *Ebony* and *Jet* magazines, is the top advertiser to African-American markets, with Procter & Gamble, General Motors, Johnson & Johnson, and L'Oréal following.[41]

Critics warn against stereotyping when trying to reach these two large and lucrative markets. However, messages that some people find acceptable may be offensive to others. African-American comedienne Diane Amos has been pitching Pine-Sol to consumers for nearly a decade. She calls people "honey" and has a sassy attitude. Some experts believe she portrays a stereotype of the African-American working-class woman. Others believe she relates well to consumers. "[Diane] is seen as likable, hard-working, assertive, and witty," argues Mary O'Connell, a company spokesperson. "We strongly disagree that she is in any way stereotypical."[42] Marketers whose goal is to build long-lasting relationships with consumers need to consider these issues carefully.

COURTESY OF WAL-MART

The Hispanic-American market is extremely important for firms like Wal-Mart to develop because this ethnic group is the largest in the U.S. Wal-Mart hopes that families like this one will become satisfied customers. To welcome them, Wal-Mart advertises in Spanish.

Asian Americans

Although Asian Americans represent a smaller segment than either the African-American or Hispanic populations, they are the second fastest growing segment of the U.S. population. The Census Bureau, which includes Pacific Islanders in its Asian segment, estimates that this group will grow to 23 million by 2020. Asian Americans are an attractive target for marketers because they also have the fastest growing income. Their average income per household is considerably higher than that of any other ethnic group, including whites.[43]

Most of us are immigrants from someplace.

Arturo "Arte" Moreno
(b. 1946)
owner of the Anaheim Angels Major League Baseball club

The Asian-American population is concentrated in fewer geographic areas than are other ethnic markets. One-half of Asians live in the West, and 95 percent live in metropolitan areas.[44] Companies can lower their costs of reaching Asian-American consumers by advertising in appropriate local markets rather than on a national scale. Honda's first Asian-American advertising campaign, called "Calligraphy," was launched in Los Angeles.

Native Americans

Another important minority group is Native Americans, whose current population numbers about 4 million, or 1.2 percent of the total U.S. population. In addition to the Great Plains, South, and Southwest tribes, such as the Cherokee, Choctaw, and Navajo, the Census Bureau also includes Alaska native tribes, such as the Inuit and Tlingit, in this population segment. The Native-American population is growing at double the rate of the U.S. population in general—an increase of 26 percent over a decade. Four of ten Native Americans live in the West, and three in ten live in the South. Eleven states (listed in descending order) include 62 percent of the Native-American population: California, Oklahoma, Arizona, Texas, New Mexico, New York, Washington, North Carolina, Michigan, Alaska, and Florida.[45] As a group, Native Americans tend to be younger than the population as a whole, with a median age of 27.

Native-American household incomes have been gaining ground in recent years—with a median income of $31,800, almost tied with Hispanics' median at $31,700. They own nearly 200,000 businesses nationwide, with more than $34 billion in revenues.[46] Native groups have begun to establish economic and political clout, which marketers take seriously. Their business ownership has extended to large entertainment centers like Foxwoods—a huge resort and casino in Connecticut that is owned and operated by the Mashantucket Pequot Tribal Nation (Pequot means "the fox people"). Thousands of tourists visit Foxwoods each year to stay in the 1,400 guest rooms and suites, play golf, enjoy live entertainment, and gamble. The entertainment centers that Native Americans own often are economic dynamos in some of the more rural locations in which they operate. Nationwide, nearly 300 tribally owned casinos generate revenues of close to $15 billion per year.[47] In addition to entertainment and gaming centers, the San Manuel Band of Mission Indians in California, for instance, has holdings that include a restaurant in Pasadena, two office buildings in Irvine, a water-bottling plant in Highland, and a Marriott Residence Inn in Washington, D.C.[48]

People of Mixed Race

U.S. residents completing census forms now have the option of identifying themselves as belonging to more than one racial category. Marketers need to be aware of this change. In some ways, it benefits marketers by making racial statistics more accurate. On the other hand, marketers may find it difficult to compare the new statistics with data from earlier censuses. The "Solving an Ethical Controversy" box discusses whether the collection of racial and ethnic data is even appropriate or whether it is in fact an invasion of privacy.

SEGMENTING BY FAMILY LIFE CYCLE STAGES

Still another form of demographic segmentation employs the stages of the **family life cycle**—the process of family formation and dissolution. The underlying theme of this segmentation approach is that life stage, not age per se, is the primary determinant of many consumer purchases. As people move from one life stage to another, they become potential consumers for different types of goods and services.

An unmarried person setting up an apartment for the first time is likely to be a good prospect for inexpensive furniture and small home appliances. This consumer probably must budget carefully, ruling out expenditures on luxury items. On the other hand, a young single person who is still living at home will probably have more money to spend on goods such as sporting and entertainment equipment, personal-care items, and clothing. As couples marry, their consumer profiles change. Couples without children are frequent buyers of personalized gifts, power tools, furniture, and homes. Eating out and travel may also be part of their lifestyles.

The birth of a first child changes any couple's consumer profile considerably; parents must buy cribs, changing tables, baby clothes, baby food, car seats, and similar products. Parents usually spend less on the children who follow the first because they have already bought many essential items for the

Solving an Ethical Controversy

WHAT KIND OF INFORMATION SHOULD MARKETERS COLLECT?

A CRITICAL part of a marketer's job is to collect information about existing and potential customers. But at what point does this information gathering cross the line to become an invasion of people's privacy? The debate over whether colleges, governments, and other organizations should be allowed to collect racial and ethnic data on individuals has reached a heated level.

IS THE COLLECTION OF RACIAL AND ETHNIC DATA AN INVASION OF AN INDIVIDUAL'S PRIVACY?

PRO

1. Collecting such data serves no positive purpose in most cases and may in fact lead to stereotyping or prejudiced behavior on the part of organizations that receive the data.
2. Racial and ethnic data do not necessarily provide an accurate picture of a person. "We are just too diverse as . . . Americans to have a simple race box to tell the government who we are," argued one student in an interview for *The Wall Street Journal.*

CON

1. People can always opt not to offer racial or ethnic data to organizations.
2. Such data can help not-for-profit and for-profit organizations serve their customers better. A firm that has some information on the ethnic background of its customers may be able to provide sales representatives who speak a certain language or products that better suit customers' tastes.

SUMMARY

In California, a proposition to ban state and local governments from collecting racial and ethnic data was rejected by voters. However, some researchers argue that without such information, it is more difficult to prove discrimination in hiring or workplace promotions by companies, governments, or other organizations.

Sources: "Racial Privacy Initiative," http://www.racialprivacy.org, accessed February 9, 2004; "Racial Privacy Initiative Defeated," *MSNBC,* October 7, 2003, http://www.msnbc.com; Robert Tomsho, "Some Seek Ban on Collection of Ethnic Data," *The Wall Street Journal,* June 30, 2003, pp. B1, B4; Michael S. Victoroff, MD, "Medically, Race Means Nothing," *Managed Care Magazine,* April 2002, http://www.managedcaremag.com.

first child. Today, the average woman gives birth to fewer children than she did a century ago and usually waits until she is older to have them. Although the average age for American women to have their first child is 25, many women wait much longer, often into their 30s and even 40s.[49] This means that, if they work outside the home, older women are likely to be more established financially with more money to spend.

Families typically spend the most during the years their children are growing—on everything from housing, food, and clothing to braces and college. Thus, they often look to obtain value wherever they can. Marketers can create satisfied and loyal customers among this group by giving them the best value possible. The ad for metal roofing in Figure 9.8 seeks to persuade consumers that an investment in one roof will last them throughout most of their life cycle stages.

Once the children are grown and on their own—or at least off to college—married couples enter the "empty nest" stage. Empty nesters may have the disposable incomes necessary to purchase premium products once college tuitions and mortgages are paid off. They may travel more, eat out more often, redecorate the house, or go back to school themselves. They may treat themselves to a new and more luxurious car or buy a vacation home.[50] In later years, empty nesters may decide to sell their homes and become customers for retirement or assisted living communities. They may require home-care services or more health-care products as well.

One trend noted by researchers in the past decade is an increase in the number of grown children who have returned home to live with their parents. Called "boomerangs," some of these grown children bring along families of their own. Another trend is the growing number of grandparents who care for grandchildren on a regular basis—making them customers all over again for baby and child products such as toys, food, and safety devices.

figure 9.8

Segmenting by Family Life Cycle Stage

METAL ROOFING ALLIANCE/COPACINO & FUJIKADO

SEGMENTING BY HOUSEHOLD TYPE

The first U.S. census in 1790 found an average household size of 5.8 persons. Today, that number is below 3. The U.S. Department of Commerce cites several reasons for the trend toward smaller households: lower fertility rates (including the decision to have fewer children or no children at all), young people's tendency to postpone marriage, the frequency of divorce, and the ability and desire of many people to live alone.

Today's U.S. households represent a wide range of diversity. They include households with a married couple and their children; households that are blended through divorce or loss of a spouse and remarriage; those headed by a single parent, same-sex parents, or grandparents; couples without children; groups of friends; and single-person households.

Couples without children may be young or old. If they are seniors, their children may have already grown and flown the nest. According to the U.S. Census Bureau, some older couples are choosing to live together rather than get married because they prefer to keep their finances separate and because they could lose valuable health or pension benefits if they married.[51] Currently, nearly 1 million such couples live together.[52] Couples who are younger and do not have children are considered attractive to marketers because they often have high levels of income to spend. These couples typically eat out often, take expensive vacations, and buy luxury cars.

Same-sex couples who share households—with or without children—are on the rise. According to the Urban Institute, 22 percent of gay couples and 34 percent of lesbian couples are now raising children.[53] While the controversy over same-sex marriage and civil unions rages, more and more companies have begun offering domestic-partner benefits for same-sex couples. Approximately three in ten large companies now provide such benefits.[54]

Two great forces, aging and diversity, have rendered the traditional categories in many cases irrelevant.

Robert Lang

director of the Metropolitan Institute at Virginia Tech

People live alone for a variety of reasons—sometimes by choice and sometimes by necessity such as divorce or widowhood. In response, marketers have modified their messages and their products to meet the needs of single-person households. Food industry manufacturers are downsizing products, offering more single-serve foods ranging from soup to macaroni and cheese.

SEGMENTING BY INCOME AND EXPENDITURE PATTERNS

Part of the earlier definition of *market* described people with purchasing power. Not surprisingly, then, a common basis for segmenting the consumer market is income. Marketers often target geographic areas known for the high incomes of their residents. Or they might consider age or household type when determining potential buying power. The ad for Princess Cruises in Figure 9.9 targets consumers who can afford a luxury vacation.

Engel's Laws

How do expenditure patterns vary with income? Over a century ago, Ernst Engel, a German statistician, published what became known as **Engel's laws**—three general statements based on his studies of the impact of household income changes on consumer spending behavior. According to Engel, as household income increases, the following will take place:

1. A smaller percentage of expenditures go for food.
2. The percentage spent on housing and household operations and clothing remains constant.
3. The percentage spent on other items (such as recreation and education) increases.

Are Engel's laws still valid? Recent studies say yes, with a few exceptions. Researchers note a steady decline in the percentage of total income spent on food, beverages, and tobacco as income increases.

Although high-income families spend greater absolute amounts on food items, their purchases represent declining percentages of their total expenditures compared with low-income families. The second law remains partly accurate. However, it is important to note that the percentage of fixed expenditures for housing and household operations has increased over the past 30 years so that an average two-income family of today is actually worse off than the average one-income family of three decades ago.[55] And the percentage spent on clothing rises with increased income because of choice. The third law remains true, with the exception of medical and personal-care costs, which appear to decline as a percentage of increased income.

Engel's laws can help marketers target markets at all income levels. It is interesting to note that, regardless of the economic environment, consumers still buy luxury goods and services. One reason is that some companies now offer their luxury products at different price levels. Mercedes-Benz has its lower priced C-class models, while Tiffany sells a $100 Elsa Peretti sterling silver pendant with chain. Both of these firms continue to offer their higher priced items as well but have chosen to broaden their market by serving consumers whose incomes might be somewhat lower than those who are considered truly wealthy.[56]

figure 9.9

Princess Cruise Lines Targets People with Significant Disposable Incomes

COURTESY OF PRINCESS CRUISES

DEMOGRAPHIC SEGMENTATION ABROAD

Marketers often face a difficult task in obtaining the data necessary for demographic segmentation abroad. Many countries do not have scheduled census programs. For instance, the most recent count of the Dutch population is now over two decades old. Germany skipped counting from 1970 to 1987, and France conducts a census about every seven years. By contrast, Japan and Canada conduct censuses every five years; however, the mid-decade assessments are not as complete as the end-of-decade counts.

Also, some foreign data include demographic divisions not found in the U.S. census. Canada collects information on religious affiliation, for instance. On the other hand, some of the standard segmentation data for U.S. markets are not available abroad. Many nations do not collect income data. Great Britain, Japan, Spain, France, and Italy are examples. Similarly, family life cycle data are difficult to apply in global demographic segmentation efforts. Ireland acknowledges only three marital statuses—single, married, and widowed—while Latin-American nations and Sweden count their unmarried cohabitants.

One source of global demographic information is the International Programs Center (IPC) at the U.S. Bureau of the Census. The IPC provides a searchable online database of population statistics for many countries on the Census Bureau's Web page. Another source is the United Nations, which sponsors national statistical offices that collect demographic data on a variety of countries. In addition, private marketing research firms can supplement government data.

1. What are the categories of demographic segmentation?
2. Explain why the cohort effect is important to marketers.
3. Why would a marketer be interested in understanding a person's family life cycle stage?

PSYCHOGRAPHIC SEGMENTATION

Marketers have traditionally referred to geographic and demographic characteristics as the primary bases for dividing consumers into homogeneous market segments. Still, they have long recognized the need for fuller, more lifelike portraits of consumers in developing their marketing programs. As a result, psychographic segmentation can be a useful tool for gaining sharper insight into consumer purchasing behavior.

WHAT IS PSYCHOGRAPHIC SEGMENTATION?

psychographic segmentation Division of a population into groups that have similar psychological characteristics, values, and lifestyles.

Psychographic segmentation divides a population into groups that have similar psychological characteristics, values, and lifestyles. Lifestyle refers to a person's mode of living; it describes how an individual operates on a daily basis. Consumers' lifestyles are composites of their individual psychological profiles, including their needs, motives, perceptions, and attitudes. A lifestyle also bears the mark of many other influences, such as family, job, social activities, and culture. One expression of lifestyle is body art, as discussed in the "Etiquette Tips for Marketing Professionals" box.

The most common method for developing psychographic profiles of a population is to conduct a large-scale survey that asks consumers to agree or disagree with a collection of several hundred AIO statements. These **AIO statements** describe various activities, interests, and opinions. The resulting data allow researchers to develop lifestyle profiles. Marketers can then develop a separate marketing strategy that closely fits the psychographic makeup for each lifestyle segment.

Marketing researchers have conducted psychographic studies on hundreds of goods and services, ranging from beer to air travel. Hospitals and other health-care providers use such studies to assess consumer behavior and attitudes toward health care in general, to learn the needs of consumers in particular marketplaces, and to determine how consumers perceive individual institutions. Many businesses turn to psychographic research in an effort to learn what consumers in various demographic and geographic segments want and need.

VALS2

A quarter century ago, the research and consulting firm SRI International developed a psychographic segmentation system called VALS. The name stands for "values and lifestyles," and the original VALS format categorized consumers by their opinions regarding social issues. A decade later, SRI revised the system to link it more closely with consumer buying behavior. The revised system, VALS2, is based on two key concepts: resources and self-motivation. **VALS2** divides consumers into eight psychographic categories. Figure 9.10 details the profiles for these categories and their relationships.

figure 9.10

The VALS2 Network

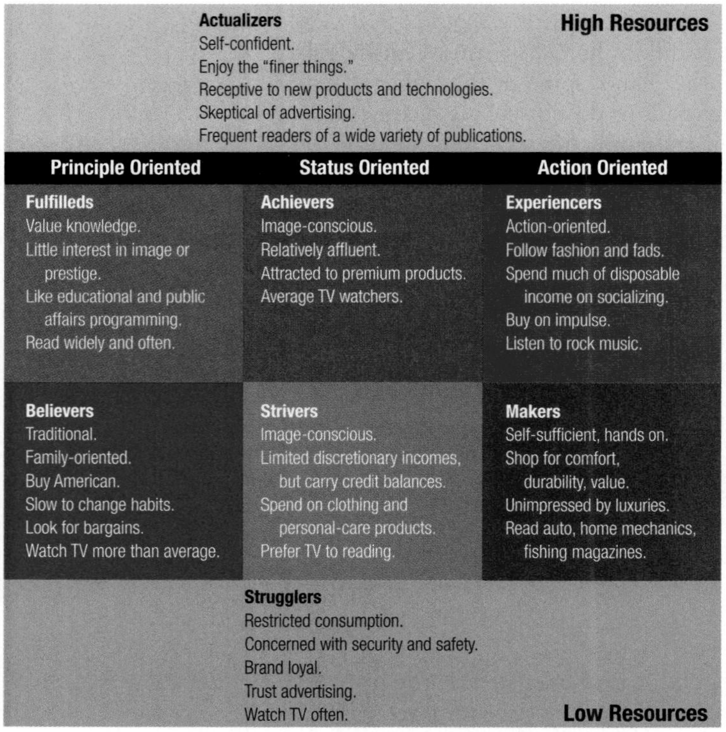

High Resources

Actualizers
Self-confident.
Enjoy the "finer things."
Receptive to new products and technologies.
Skeptical of advertising.
Frequent readers of a wide variety of publications.

Principle Oriented	Status Oriented	Action Oriented
Fulfilleds Value knowledge. Little interest in image or prestige. Like educational and public affairs programming. Read widely and often.	**Achievers** Image-conscious. Relatively affluent. Attracted to premium products. Average TV watchers.	**Experiencers** Action-oriented. Follow fashion and fads. Spend much of disposable income on socializing. Buy on impulse. Listen to rock music.
Believers Traditional. Family-oriented. Buy American. Slow to change habits. Look for bargains. Watch TV more than average.	**Strivers** Image-conscious. Limited discretionary incomes, but carry credit balances. Spend on clothing and personal-care products. Prefer TV to reading.	**Makers** Self-sufficient, hands on. Shop for comfort, durability, value. Unimpressed by luxuries. Read auto, home mechanics, fishing magazines.

Strugglers
Restricted consumption.
Concerned with security and safety.
Brand loyal.
Trust advertising.
Watch TV often.

Low Resources

Source: Copyright by SRI Consulting. All rights reserved. Unauthorized reproduction prohibited. VALS2 is a trademark of SRI International.

The VALS network chart in the figure displays differences in resources as vertical distances, and self-orientation is represented horizontally. The resource dimension measures income, education, self-confidence, health, eagerness to buy, and energy level. Self-orientations divide consumers into three groups: principle-oriented consumers who have a set of ideas and morals—principles—that they live by; status-oriented consumers who are influenced by what others think; and action-oriented consumers who seek physical activity, variety, and adventure.

SRI has created several specialized segmentation systems based on this approach. GeoVALS, for instance, estimates the percentage of each VALS type in each U.S. residential zip code. JapanVALS was developed to help companies understand Japanese consumers, and iVALS focuses on Internet sites and users. SRI uses the VALS2 segmentation information in conjunction with marketers in consulting projects and on a subscriber basis. Product, service, and media data are available by VALS-types from companies' databases.

Other tools available include LifeMatrix, developed by RoperASW and Mediamark Research. LifeMatrix crunches the numbers on hundreds of personal variables that include political views, religious affiliations, and social attitudes and comes up with 10 psychographic cat-

ETIQUETTE TIPS — FOR MARKETING PROFESSIONALS

Body Art: Beauty Is in the Eye of the Beholder

"DON'T judge a book by its cover." You have heard that expression many times, but you also know that your outward personal style—your hair, your clothing, your jewelry—is an expression of who you are. Perhaps at some point, you decided to include a tattoo or body piercing as part of your style. Is this body art appropriate for the business world? Will showing off your nose ring or flower tattoo affect your chances of getting a job? Here are a few points to consider:

1. The Equal Employment Opportunity Commission (EEOC) guarantees that your civil liberties in the workplace are protected, which means that a potential employer cannot discriminate against a person's race, color, religion, age, national origin, or gender. However, an employer does have the right to impose a dress code that may prohibit body art. Policies will naturally vary from company to company—a large food manufacturer is likely to have a different policy from that of a New York–based clothing design firm.
2. Even if a firm does not have a written policy about body art, it may be a good idea to leave that tongue ring at home or wear a jacket over your shoulder tattoo until you know what the company expects. In one survey, four of five respondents said they thought piercings in places other than ears looked unprofessional; three-fourths said that visible tattoos were unprofessional as well. In the same survey, 42 percent of managers said their opinion of a job candidate would be lowered by visible body art, but 44 percent said they had body art themselves!

Keep in mind that while most companies celebrate diversity and individual creativity, they need to be sure that their marketers accurately represent their customers. If you're headed out on the road as part of the marketing staff for a rock group, that's one thing. But if you are planning a career as a marketer for an upscale hotel chain, visible body art may not be welcomed by your employer. So, unless you are absolutely certain that body art is welcome on the job—and approved by your customers—hide it.

Sources: Regina M. Robo, "Body Art in the Workplace," *Salary.com,* http://www.salary.com/advice, accessed February 9, 2004; "Tattoos and Body Piercing Survey," *Vault,* http://www.vault.com, accessed February 9, 2004; Mielikki Ong, "Body Art Gains Acceptance in Once-Staid Workplace," *CareerJournal.com,* September 8, 2003, http://www.careerjournal.com.

egories that reflect today's lifestyles. Depending on your own variables, you might be a "priority parent" or "tribe wired." LifeMatrix subdivides the categories even further, making conclusions about personality traits such as "caring" or "altruistic."[57]

PSYCHOGRAPHIC SEGMENTATION OF GLOBAL MARKETS

As JapanVALS suggests, psychographic profiles can cross national boundaries. Roper Starch Worldwide, a marketing research firm, recently surveyed 7,000 people in 35 countries. From the resulting data, Roper identified six psychographic consumer segments that exist in all 35 nations, although to varying degrees:

- *Strivers*, the largest segment, value professional and material goals more than the other groups. One-third of the Asian population and one-fourth of Russians are strivers. They are slightly more likely to be men than women.
- *Devouts* value duty and tradition. While this segment comprises 22 percent of all adults, they are most common in Africa, the Middle East, and developing Asia. They are least common in Western Europe and developed Asian countries. Worldwide, they are more likely to be female.

figure 9.11

Appealing to Intimates and Fun Seekers

COURTESY OF CENTEX DESTINATION PROPERTIES

- *Altruists* emphasize social issues and societal well-being. Comprising 18 percent of all adults, this group shows a median age of 44 and a slightly higher percentage of women. Altruists are most common in Latin America and Russia.
- *Intimates* value family and personal relationships. They are divided almost equally between males and females. One American or European in four would be categorized as intimates, but only 7 percent of consumers in developing Asia fall into this category.
- *Fun seekers*, as you might guess from their name, focus on personal enjoyment and pleasurable experiences. They comprise 12 percent of the world's population, with a male–female ratio of 54 to 46. Many live in developed Asia.
- *Creatives*, the smallest segment, account for just 10 percent of the global population. This group seeks education, technology, and knowledge, and their male–female ratio is roughly equal. Many creatives live in Western Europe and Latin America.

Roper researchers note that some principles and core beliefs apply to more than one psychographic segment. For example, consumers in all 35 countries cite "family" as one of their five most important values, and "protecting the family" ranks as one of the top ten.[58]

USING PSYCHOGRAPHIC SEGMENTATION

No one suggests that psychographic segmentation is an exact science, but it does help marketers quantify aspects of consumers' personalities and lifestyles to create goods and services for a target market. Psychographic profile systems like those of Roper and SRI can paint useful pictures of the overall psychological motivations of consumers. These profiles produce much richer descriptions of potential target markets than other techniques can achieve. The enhanced detail aids in matching a company's image and product offerings with the types of consumers who use its products. Ed Keller, president of RoperASW, describes how psychographic segmentation helps refine marketers' profiles of their customers. Keller asserts that if a car manufacturer uses only demographic data to study a market, it can probably identify what kind of car a consumer will buy 18 percent of the time. But "when you combine people's attitudes, behaviors, life stages and values, you can predict 82 percent of the time what car a person will buy next."[59]

Identifying which psychographic segments are most prevalent in certain markets helps marketers plan and promote more effectively. Often, segments overlap. The ad for Canopy Walk in Figure 9.11 would probably appeal to intimates and fun seekers.

Psychographic segmentation is a good supplement to segmentation by demographic or geographic variables. For example, marketers may have access to each consumer type's media preferences in network television, cable television, radio format, magazines, and newspapers. As Ed Keller explained earlier, psychographic studies may then refine the picture of segment characteristics to give a more elaborate lifestyle profile of the consumers in the firm's target market. A psychographic study could help marketers of goods and services in New York predict what kinds of products consumers would be drawn to. During uncertain economic times—and in the wake of the terrorist attacks of September 11—there was an increase in luxury buying. "I feel like nothing's promised anymore," explained one 40-year-old female New Yorker. "We don't know if we're going to have jobs. So I've decided to live for now." In response, this consumer took several exotic trips and began dining out more often with friends.[60]

MARKETING Concept Check

1. **What is psychographic segmentation?**
2. **Name the eight psychographic categories of VALS2.**

PRODUCT-RELATED SEGMENTATION

Product-related segmentation involves dividing a consumer population into homogeneous groups based on characteristics of their relationships to the product. This segmentation approach can take several forms:

product-related segmentation Division of a population into homogeneous groups based on their relationships to the product.

1. segmenting based on the benefits that people seek when they buy a product
2. segmenting based on usage rates for a product
3. segmenting according to consumers' brand loyalty toward a product

SEGMENTING BY BENEFITS SOUGHT

This approach focuses on the attributes that people seek and the benefits they expect to receive from a good or service. It groups consumers into segments based on what they want a product to do for them.

Consumers who quaff Starbucks premium coffees are not just looking for a dose of caffeine. They are willing to pay extra to savor a pleasant experience, one that makes them feel pampered and appreciated. Women who work out at Curves want to look their best and feel healthy. Pet owners who feed their cats and dogs Science Diet believe that they are giving their animals a great tasting, healthy pet food.

Even if a business offers only one product line, however, marketers must remember to consider product benefits. Two people may buy the same product for very different reasons. A box of Arm & Hammer baking soda could end up serving as a refrigerator freshener, a toothpaste substitute, an antacid, or a deodorizer for a cat's litter box.

SEGMENTING BY USAGE RATES

Marketers may also segment a total market by grouping people according to the amounts of a product that they buy and use. Markets can be divided into heavy-user, moderate-user, and light-user segments. The **80/20 principle** holds that a big percentage of a product's revenues—maybe 80 percent—comes from a relatively small, loyal percentage of total customers—perhaps 20 percent. The 80/20 principle is sometimes referred to as "Praedo's Law." Although the percentages need not exactly equal these figures, the general principle often holds true: Relatively few heavy users of a product can account for much of its consumption.

Depending on their goals, marketers may target heavy, moderate, or light users as well as nonusers. A company may attempt to lure heavy users of another product away from their regular brands to try a new brand. Nonusers and light users may be attractive prospects because other companies are ignoring them. Usage rates can also be linked to other segmentation methods such as demographic and psychographic segmentation.

SEGMENTING BY BRAND LOYALTY

A third product-related segmentation method groups consumers according to the strength of the brand loyalty they feel toward a product. A classic example of brand loyalty segmentation is airline frequent-flyer programs. Originally targeted at heavy users—business travelers—frequent-flyer programs now help to tie even occasional travelers to specific airlines. The success of these programs has resulted in similar efforts in the hotel industry, bookstores, and elsewhere. Airlines also try to develop loyalty by increasing seat size, offering in-flight entertainment, and serving more destinations. Other companies attempt to segment their market by developing brand loyalty over a period of time, through consumers' stages of life. Children whose parents dress them in Baby Gap clothes may grow up to wear Gap Kids and Gap clothing.

USING MULTIPLE SEGMENTATION BASES

Segmentation is a tool that can help marketers increase their accuracy in reaching the right markets. Like other marketing tools, segmentation is probably best used in a flexible manner—for instance,

1. List some products for which marketers might want to segment by the benefits consumers seek.
2. What is the 80/20 principle?

combining geographic and demographic segmentation techniques or dovetailing product-related segmentation with segmentation by income and expenditure patterns. The important point to keep in mind is that segmentation is a tool to help marketers get to know their potential customers better and ultimately satisfy their needs with the appropriate goods and services.

THE MARKET SEGMENTATION PROCESS

To this point, the chapter has discussed various bases on which companies segment markets. But how do marketers decide which segmentation base—or bases—to use? Firms may use a management-driven method, in which segments are predefined by managers based on their observation of the behavioral and demographic characteristics of likely users. Or they may use a market-driven method, in which segments are defined by asking customers which attributes are important. Then marketers follow a four-stage process.

5 Identify the steps in the market segmentation process.

DEVELOP A RELEVANT PROFILE FOR EACH SEGMENT

After identifying promising segments, marketers should understand the customers in each one. This in-depth analysis of customers helps managers accurately match customers' needs with the firm's marketing offers. The process must identify characteristics that both explain the similarities among customers within each segment and account for differences among segments.

The task at this stage is to develop a profile of the typical customer in each segment. Such a profile might include information about lifestyle patterns, attitudes toward product attributes and brands, product-use habits, geographic locations, and demographic characteristics.

FORECAST MARKET POTENTIAL

In the second stage, market segmentation and market opportunity analysis combine to produce a forecast of market potential within each segment. Market potential sets the upper limit on the demand that competing firms can expect from a segment. Multiplying by market share determines a single firm's maximum sales potential. This step should define a preliminary go or no-go decision from management because the total sales potential in each segment must justify resources devoted to further analysis.

An example of a segment that shows tremendous market potential is U.S. children ages 4 to 12. Aggregate spending by consumers in this age group or on their behalf doubled every decade between the 1960s and 1980s and tripled during the 1990s to reach its current level of $24 billion a year. Thirty years ago, children spent most of their money on candy. Today, only one-third is spent on food and beverages; the rest goes toward clothing and entertainment.

FORECAST PROBABLE MARKET SHARE

Once market potential has been estimated, a firm must forecast its probable market share. Competitors' positions in targeted segments must be analyzed, and a specific marketing strategy must be designed to reach these segments. These two activities may be performed simultaneously. Moreover, by settling on a marketing strategy and tactics, a firm determines the expected level of resources it must commit—that is, the costs it will incur to tap the potential demand in each segment.

Kinko's, now a key part of FedEx, currently has more than 1,200 photocopying outlets in 10 countries. The company used to be viewed, and used to view itself, as simply a copy shop at which customers could get quick turnaround for their reports, flyers, or manuscripts. But Gary Kusin, CEO of the company, made a trip around the U.S. to talk to customers and learned that they are now looking "more for ongoing business partners. They want to know that they can partner with us for digital solutions for bigger jobs." So Kusin and his managers needed to figure out how to meet these needs and capture as much of this segment of the market as possible. "Right now," he says, "the biggest service we can sell is competence: the ability to listen to our customers, to understand their problems, and to apply our knowledge to come up with creative solutions."[61]

SELECT SPECIFIC MARKET SEGMENTS

The information, analysis, and forecasts accumulated throughout the entire market segmentation decision process allow management to assess the potential for achieving company goals and to justify committing resources in developing one or more segments. Demand forecasts, together with cost projections, determine the profits and the return on investment (ROI) that the company can expect from each segment. Marketing strategy and tactics must be designed to reinforce the firm's image, yet keep within its unique organizational capabilities.

At this point in the analysis, marketers weigh more than monetary costs and benefits; they also consider many difficult-to-measure but critical organizational and environmental factors. The firm may lack experienced personnel to launch a successful attack on an attractive market segment. Similarly, a firm with 60 percent of the market faces possible legal problems with the Federal Trade Commission if it increases its market concentration. This assessment of both financial and nonfinancial factors is a difficult but vital step in the decision process.

1. Identify the four stages of the process of market segmentation.
2. Why is forecasting important to market segmentation?

STRATEGIES FOR REACHING TARGET MARKETS

(6) Discuss four basic strategies for reaching target markets.

Marketers spend a lot of time and effort in developing strategies that will best match their firm's product offerings to the needs of particular target markets. An appropriate match is vital to the firm's marketing success. Marketers have identified four basic strategies for achieving consumer satisfaction: undifferentiated marketing, differentiated marketing, concentrated marketing, and micromarketing.

UNDIFFERENTIATED MARKETING

A firm may produce only one product or product line and promote it to all customers with a single marketing mix; such a firm is said to practice **undifferentiated marketing,** sometimes called *mass marketing*. Undifferentiated marketing was much more common in the past than it is today.

undifferentiated marketing Market strategy that focuses on producing a single product and marketing it to all customers; also called *mass marketing*.

While undifferentiated marketing is efficient from a production viewpoint, the strategy also brings inherent dangers. A firm that attempts to satisfy everyone in the market with one standard product may suffer if competitors offer specialized units to smaller segments of the total market and better satisfy individual segments. In fact, firms that implement strategies of differentiated marketing, concentrated marketing, or micromarketing may capture enough small segments of the market to defeat another competitor's strategy of undifferentiated marketing.

DIFFERENTIATED MARKETING

Firms that promote numerous products with differing marketing mixes designed to satisfy smaller segments are said to practice **differentiated marketing.** By providing increased satisfaction for each of many target markets, a company can produce more sales by following a differentiated marketing strategy than undifferentiated marketing would generate. Oscar Mayer, a marketer of a variety of meat products, practices differentiated marketing. It increased its sales by introducing a new product—Lunchables—aimed at children. In general, however, differentiated marketing also raises costs. Production costs usually rise because additional products and variations require shorter production runs and increased setup times. Inventory costs rise because more products require added storage space and increased efforts for record keeping. Promotional costs also rise because each segment demands a unique promotional mix.

differentiated marketing Market strategy that focuses on producing several products and pricing, promoting, and distributing them with different marketing mixes designed to satisfy smaller segments.

Despite higher marketing costs, however, an organization may be forced to practice differentiated marketing to remain competitive. The travel industry now recognizes the need to target smaller groups of travelers with specialized interests. Elderhostel, for instance, targets seniors with specialized trips that may focus on history, hiking, golf, cooking, or other special interests. Old Sturbridge Village in Massachusetts targets people who are interested in American history.

CONCENTRATED MARKETING

concentrated marketing Focusing marketing efforts on satisfying a single market segment; also called *niche marketing*.

Rather than trying to market its products separately to several segments, a firm may opt for a concentrated marketing strategy. With **concentrated marketing** (also known as **niche marketing**), a firm focuses its efforts on profitably satisfying only one market segment. This approach can appeal to a small firm that lacks the financial resources of its competitors and to a company that offers highly specialized goods and services. Kohl's, JCPenney, and Wal-Mart all sell children's clothing, but Hot Topic is aimed straight at tweens and teens who want the hottest (or coolest) alternative trends in fashion and accessories. Hot Topic is a retailer with nearly 500 stores across the country staffed by workers who look just like their customers—wearing rock T-shirts, white makeup, long vinyl coats, chain belts, and lots and lots of black. Teens who don't like the typical preppy stuff love Hot Topic, whose fashions and atmosphere are based on the latest alternative music.[62]

General Motors is pursuing a concentrated marketing strategy—something it had avoided in the past. On the company's drawing board and soon to be in showrooms are the Pontiac Solstice sports car, another yet-unnamed sport coupe concept car, the Chevrolet HHR retro-style wagon, and the Chevy Nomad small wagon. GM is betting that its new strategy will draw in new buyers—and boost the company's image and profits.[63]

But along with its benefits, concentrated marketing has its dangers. Since the strategy ties a firm's growth to a specific segment, sales can suffer if new competitors appeal successfully to the same target. Furthermore, errors in forecasting market potential or customer buying habits lead to severe problems, particularly if the firm has spent substantially on product development and promotion.

MICROMARKETING

micromarketing Targeting potential customers at very narrow, basic levels, such as by zip code, specific occupation, or lifestyle—possibly even individuals themselves.

The fourth targeting strategy, still more narrowly focused than concentrated marketing, is **micromarketing,** which involves targeting potential customers at a very basic level, such as by zip code, specific occupation, or lifestyle. Ultimately, micromarketing can target even individuals themselves. The salesperson at your favorite clothing boutique may contact you when certain merchandise that she thinks you might like arrives at the store. The Internet may allow marketers to make micromarketing even more effective. By tracking specific demographic and personal information, marketers can send e-mail directly to individual consumers who are most likely to buy their products. If you purchase a book via Amazon.com, the company will offer to send you e-mail notices about other books that may be of interest.

But micromarketing, like niche marketing, can become too much of a good thing if companies spend too much time, effort, and marketing dollars to unearth a market that is too small and specialized to be profitable. In addition, micromarketing may cause a company to lose sight of other reachable markets.

Put all your eggs in one basket, and watch the basket.

Mark Twain (1835–1910)
American author

SELECTING AND EXECUTING A STRATEGY

Although most organizations adopt some form of differentiated marketing, no single best choice suits all firms. Any of the alternatives may prove most effective in a particular situation. The basic determinants of a market-specific strategy are (1) company resources, (2) product homogeneity, (3) stage in the product life cycle, and (4) competitors' strategies.

A firm with limited resources may have to choose a concentrated marketing strategy. Small firms may be forced to select small target markets because of limitations in their sales force and advertising budgets. On the other hand, an undifferentiated marketing strategy suits a firm selling items perceived by consumers as relatively homogeneous. Marketers of grain, for example, sell standardized grades of generic products rather than individual brand names. Some petroleum companies implement undifferentiated marketing to distribute their gasoline to the mass market.

The firm's strategy may also change as its product progresses through the stages of the life cycle. During the early stages, undifferentiated marketing might effectively support the firm's effort to build initial demand for the item. In the later stages, however, competitive pressures may force modifications in products and in the development of marketing strategies aimed at segments of the total market.

The strategies of competitors also affect the choice of a segmentation approach. A firm may encounter obstacles to undifferentiated marketing if its competitors actively cultivate smaller segments. In such instances, competition usually forces each firm to adopt a differentiated marketing strategy.

Having chosen a strategy for reaching their firm's target market, marketers must then decide how best to position the product. The concept of **positioning** seeks to put a product in a certain position, or place, in the minds of prospective buyers. Marketers use a positioning strategy to distinguish their firm's offerings from those of competitors and to create promotions that communicate the desired position.

(7) **Summarize the types of positioning strategies.**

positioning Placing a product at a certain point or location within a market in the minds of prospective buyers.

To achieve this goal, marketers follow a number of positioning strategies. Possible approaches include positioning a product according to the following categories:

1. *Attributes*—Ads for Talbot's line of women's clothing claim, "It's a classic." The Chevy Tahoe is "Like a rock."
2. *Price/quality*—Chelsea House furniture likes to be "Reflecting a graceful way of living."
3. *Competitors*—Hidden Valley Ranch says, "We made it first. We made it right."
4. *Application*—Whirlpool wants to "Wash your world clean."
5. *Product user*—Crane's makes its stationery "for the writer somewhere in each of us."
6. *Product class*—The diamond industry claims, "A diamond is forever."

(8) **Explain the reasons for positioning and repositioning products.**

Whatever strategy they choose, marketers want to emphasize a product's unique advantages and to differentiate it from competitors' options. With the influx of new discount airlines, each of these airlines needs to do more than simply position itself as a discounter offering lower prices than the larger, more expensive airlines. Thus, Song differentiates itself by offering 24 free channels of live satellite TV, audio stations, and multiplayer video games delivered to in-seat monitors. JetBlue offers five free snack options.[64]

A **positioning map** provides a valuable tool in helping managers position products by graphically illustrating consumers' perceptions of competing products within an industry. Marketers can create a competitive positioning map from information solicited from consumers or from their accumulated knowledge about a market. A positioning map might present two different characteristics—price and perceived quality—and show how consumers view a product and its major competitors based on these traits. The hypothetical positioning map in Figure 9.12 compares selected retailers based on possible perceptions of the prices and quality of their offerings.

Sometimes changes in the competitive environment force marketers to **reposition** a product—changing the position it holds in the minds of prospective buyers relative to the positions of competing products. Marketers at Bertucci's restaurants, which are famous for their brick-oven pizza, made a bold move when they decided to downplay the chain's signature food and emphasize instead more expensive dinners like seafood, veal, and pork. The decision was made because the chain had experienced a drop in pizza sales and marketers wanted to appeal to a broader market instead of focusing only on pizza customers. To introduce the menu changes, the company ran television and radio ads with the slogan, "Everybody eats when they come to our house."[65]

Repositioning may even be necessary for already-successful products or firms. The "Marketing Miss" box discusses a problem

Hidden Valley Ranch positions itself against its competitors when it says, "We made it first. We made it right."

figure 9.12

Hypothetical Positioning Map for Selected Retailers

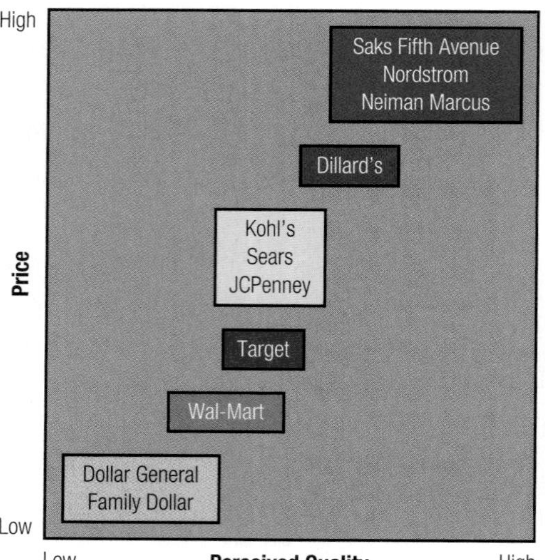

clothing retailer Brooks Brothers encountered when it tried to reposition itself as a casual clothier. When eBay realized the potential for marketing high-end fashion on its auction site, the firm had to reposition itself away from its original image as the clearinghouse for vintage pottery and collectible Barbies. So the firm hired Constance White, a former fashion journalist, to begin forging relationships with fashion wholesalers and designers. In addition, eBay redesigned its fashion Web pages to appear more attractive and upscale. In one day, eBay now gets 53,000 keyword searches for Louis Vuitton and 34,000 searches for Prada. Rare or otherwise highly desirable items sometimes appear, including the Hermès Birkin bag. The average starting bid for the Hermès is $10,000.[66]

1. **Explain the difference between undifferentiated and differentiated marketing strategies.**
2. **What are the benefits of concentrated marketing?**
3. **What are the four determinants of a market-specific strategy?**

marketing miss Who Buys the Pants in the Family?

Background. Men's spending on their own clothes has decreased steadily for several years. Male consumers still buy the garments they really need—underwear, sleepwear, and athletic shoes. But sales statistics gathered by the apparel industry show that most men just couldn't care less about buying clothes or shoes other than sneakers.

The Marketing Problem. Marketers of men's clothes have been searching for ways to get men into their stores to buy their products. Men usually venture into a store only when they need something specific, and they make their purchase and leave. They don't browse or shop for recreation the way women do. "We've found that men tend to shop less than women and thus have fewer pieces in their wardrobes," noted one retail expert. "At the same time, though, they choose quality over quantity." So clothiers have to find new reasons to get men into their stores.

The Outcome. After straying into casual wear—without success—Brooks Brothers has repositioned itself according to its original image as an upscale, dressier clothier. "We're going dressy again with a lot more offerings in suits," says spokesperson Geri Corrigan. Levi Strauss introduced a discount line of jeans and men's apparel and met with sluggish sales—competitors promoted their own discount goods so aggressively that Levi's Signature line stalled. Discount retailer Target has decided to cut back on men's apparel and commit floor space instead to food offerings. Gadzooks, a teen retailer, has opted to drop its male clothing line altogether.

Lessons Learned. Brooks Brothers may have learned the old adage, "If it ain't broke, don't fix it." Other retailers have realized that marketing to men—who profess not to care about clothes—may be more difficult than marketing to the changing tastes of women. But men's clothing marketers could probably take their cue from fashion expert Alan Flusser: "The basic premise of male dressing is to draw the observer to the wearer's face. That's what you communicate with. You don't want clothes to distract from it; you want them to enhance it." According to the experts, men really want clothes to be simple, comfortable, and practical. That's their position on fashion.

Sources: Mark Ganem, "Blazer Sharp," *The Shuttle Sheet,* March 2004, p. 12; Alice Z. Cuneo, "Levi's Struggles to Peddle Signature to Men," *Advertising Age,* December 1, 2003, p. 12; Lorrie Grant, "Real Men Don't Buy Clothes," *USA Today,* July 7, 2003, p. B6; "It's Not Just the Suit, It's How You Wear It," *Black Enterprise,* March 2003, http://www.findarticles.com.

Strategic Implications of Marketing in the 21st Century

To remain competitive, today's marketers must accurately identify potential customers. They can use a variety of methods to accomplish this, from segmenting markets by gender to segmenting by geographic location. The trick is to figure out the best combination of methods for segmentation to identify the most lucrative, long-lasting potential markets. Marketers must also remain flexible, responding to markets as they change—for instance, following a generation as it ages or reaching out to new generations by revamping or repositioning products.

The greatest competitive advantage will belong to firms that can pinpoint and serve markets without segmenting them to the point where they are too small or specialized to garner profits. Marketers who can reach and communicate with the right customers have a greater chance of attracting and keeping those customers than marketers who are searching for the wrong customers in the wrong place. ◆◆◆

REVIEW OF CHAPTER OBJECTIVES

1 Identify the essential components of a market.

A market consists of people and organizations with the necessary purchasing power, willingness, and authority to buy. Consumer products are purchased by the ultimate consumer for personal use. Business products are purchased for use directly or indirectly in the production of other goods and services. Certain products may fall into both categories.

1.1. Give an example of a consumer product. Give an example of a business product.
1.2. Could either of the products you just cited find a market in the opposite category as well? Explain.

2 Outline the role of market segmentation in developing a marketing strategy.

Market segmentation is the process of dividing a total market into several homogeneous groups. It is used in identifying a target market for a good or service. Segmentation is the key to deciding a marketing strategy.

2.1. What types of organizations use market segmentation?

3 Describe the criteria necessary for effective segmentation.

Effective segmentation depends on these four basic requirements: (1) The segment must have measurable purchasing power and size; (2) marketers can find a way to promote to and serve the market; (3) marketers must identify segments large enough for profit potential; and (4) the firm can target a number of segments that match its marketing capabilities.

3.1. Describe a market that would most likely provide measurable purchasing power and size.
3.2. Why would a smaller firm decide to stick with a particular niche market instead of targeting a broader segment?

4 Explain each of the four bases for segmenting consumer markets.

Consumer markets may be divided on the basis of geographic, demographic, psychographic, or product-related segmentation approaches. Geographic segmentation divides the overall market into homogeneous groups according to population locations. Demographic segmentation classifies the market into groups based on characteristics such as age, gender, and income level. Psychographic segmentation uses behavioral profiles developed from analyses of consumers' activities, opinions, interests, and lifestyles to identify market segments. Product-related segmentation involves dividing a population into groups based on characteristics of the consumers' relationship to the product, including benefits, usage rates, and brand loyalty.

4.1. In addition to population size, what other geographic indicators might affect a firm's decision to use geographic segmentation?
4.2. Why do marketers pay so much attention to teens and tweens?
4.3. What is VALS2?
4.4. What are the three types of product-related segmentation?

5 Identify the steps in the market segmentation process.

Market segmentation is the division of markets into relatively homogeneous groups. Segmentation follows a four-step sequence: (1) developing user profiles; (2) forecasting the overall market potential; (3) estimating market share; and (4) selecting specific market segments.

5.1. Why is it important for marketers to follow a specific process when engaging in market segmentation?

6 Discuss four basic strategies for reaching target markets.

Four strategies are (1) undifferentiated marketing, which uses a single marketing mix; (2) differentiated marketing, which produces numerous products, each with its own mix; (3) concentrated marketing, which directs all the firm's marketing resources toward a small segment; and (4) micromarketing, which targets potential customers at basic levels, such as zip code or occupation.

6.1. What are the benefits and drawbacks of differentiated marketing?
6.2. Under what circumstances might a firm use micromarketing?

7 Summarize the types of positioning strategies.

Positioning strategies include positioning a good or service according to attributes, price/quality, competitors, application, product user, and product class.

7.1. How do marketers choose which type of positioning strategy is best for their products?
7.2. What is a positioning map?

8 Explain the reasons for positioning and repositioning products.

Positioning helps create a memorable impression of a product in a consumer's mind and is used to differentiate a product from competitors' products. Changes in the competitive environment may require repositioning to maintain or even grab more of the market share.

8.1. In addition to increased competition, what other factors might cause a firm to reposition a product?

MARKETING TERMS YOU NEED TO KNOW

market 288
target market 288
consumer products 288
business products 288
market segmentation 289
geographic segmentation 291
geographic information system (GIS) 293
demographic segmentation 293
psychographic segmentation 302
product-related segmentation 305
undifferentiated marketing 307
differentiated marketing 307
concentrated marketing 308
micromarketing 308
positioning 309

OTHER IMPORTANT MARKETING TERMS

core based statistical area (CBSA) 292
metropolitan statistical area 292
micropolitan statistical area 292
consolidated metropolitan statistical area (CMSA) 292
primary metropolitan statistical area (PMSA) 292
core region 292
cohort effect 295
9/11 Generation 295
baby boomers 295
family life cycle 298
Engel's laws 300
AIO statements 302
VALS2 302
80/20 principle 305
niche marketing 308
positioning map 309
repositioning 309

PROJECTS AND TEAMWORK EXERCISES

1. On your own or with a partner, choose a product that could serve both business and consumer markets. Create a chart with the headings "business" and "consumer" to show specific ways in which your product could serve each one.
2. Choose your favorite participant or spectator sport. Consider snowboarding, soccer, figure skating, golf, bicycle racing, or something else. Identify the different market segments for your sport. Then write a brief plan for selecting a segmentation strategy for the sport.
3. Once you have selected a segmentation strategy for your sport, try out your idea on your targeted market. If you selected young teens, interview one or two to see if they are interested in the sport. If you selected people who live in the suburbs or in a specific part of the country, try to talk with someone who represents your market. Present your findings to the class.
4. Find an advertisement that uses product-related segmentation as part of its strategy for reaching consumers. Present the ad to the class, identifying specific aspects of the ad, such as segmenting by benefits sought, segmenting by usage rates, or segmenting by brand loyalty.
5. Identify a product that you or someone you know uses that is either niche marketed or micromarketed. Do you believe the product could reach a wider audience? Why or why not?
6. With a partner, comb through various media to find an example of each type of positioning for goods or services. Discuss your findings with the rest of the class.
7. On your own or with a classmate, select one of the following products. Decide how it should be positioned and then come up with a slogan that reflects this positioning. You can review the examples given in the chapter. Create a print advertisement that uses your slogan.
   a. refrigerator
   b. restaurant that serves low-carb meals
   c. cell phone service
   d. motorcycle
8. Now create a positioning map for your product.
9. Now create a chart showing the ways you might reposition your product as it moves through the various product life cycle stages.
10. With a partner, choose a product that you believe might benefit from repositioning—whether it's a favorite food (such as pizza or tacos), a form of entertainment (such as a theme park or radio station), a type of automobile, or some electronic equipment. Identify ways in which marketers might reposition the product.

APPLYING CHAPTER CONCEPTS

1. Create a description of your family as a market segment using geographic and demographic factors.
2. Select one of the following products and explain how you would use segmentation by income and expenditure patterns to determine your targeted market.
   a. golf resort
   b. MP3 player
   c. supermarket frozen dinners
   d. amusement park
3. Which of the six Roper Starch Worldwide psychographic consumer segments do you represent? Why?
4. Why do marketers use less undifferentiated marketing today? Describe a situation in which undifferentiated marketing might actually be advantageous.
5. Think of a product that really reminds you of your childhood—a particular candy bar, a toy, a television show, or the like. Describe how you would reposition that product to appeal to children now.

ETHICS EXERCISE

Imagine that you work for a major department store located in the suburb of a large city that wants to reach new customers—both in surrounding towns and in the city. A coworker claims that he or she has access to ethnic data on people who live in these locations. The data might help your store know whom to target with special mailings or in-store promotions.

1. Would you accept and use the data? Why or why not?
2. Would you inform your supervisor that you had access to the data? Why or why not?
3. If you declined the data, what alternative methods might you use to target your market?

'netWork EXERCISES

1. **Geographic segmentation.** As discussed in the chapter, the U.S. Census Bureau is an important source of data used by marketers to make decisions concerning geographic segmentation of their products. Visit the Census Bureau Web site (http://www.census.gov). Click "People" and then "Estimates." Review the projections needed to answer the following questions:
   a. Which metropolitan statistical areas (MSAs) are expected to grow the fastest over the next few years?
   b. Which age groups are expected to grow the fastest (slowest) over the next few years?
   c. How many new housing units will be built in the next decade?
2. **How companies segment their markets.** Visit the Web sites of Ford Motor Company (http://www.ford.com) and Procter & Gamble (http://www.pg.com). How does each company segment its markets (such as geographic, product-related, or demographic)? Does the company use more than one method of product segmentation?
3. **Segmenting by brand loyalty.** Visit the Guinness Brewing Company's Web store (http://www.guinness-webstore.com). Prepare a brief report on how Guinness uses its Web store to build brand loyalty. Pick another company you have heard of and visit its Web site. How does this company use its Web site to enhance brand loyalty?

Note: Internet Web addresses change frequently. If you don't find the exact sites listed, you may need to access the organization's or company's home page and search from there or use a search engine such as Google.

INFOTRAC CITATIONS AND EXERCISES

Record: A116931596
Cosmetic changes beyond skin deep.
Christine Bittar.
Brandweek, May 17, 2004 v45 i20 p20(2)

Abstract: At the time Unilever sold its Elizabeth Arden unit in 2000, the aging cosmetics firm was woefully behind on the latest trends. Its conservative makeup colors were consistently out of step with fashion, while its perfume launches, such as Elizabeth Taylor's White Diamonds, reinforced a brand image unappealing to younger audiences—no surprise given that a majority of Elizabeth Arden consumers were women in their 60s. That was then. The recent buzz in the industry is that Elizabeth Arden is again growing its cosmetics business and returning youth and vitality to the brand—the cosmetics marketer is even garnering a celebrity following that includes fashion mavens Kate Beckinsale, Kirsten Dunst, and Sarah Jessica Parker.

1. What is *repositioning,* and why do marketers reposition products?
2. What negative perceptions of Elizabeth Arden cosmetics led marketers to reposition the brand?
3. List at least two recent developments at Elizabeth Arden that have helped revitalize the brand's image. Why do you think these changes have been effective?

CASE 9.1 Scion: Toyota's Next Generation

The new generation of drivers doesn't want to look like their parents tooling down the road. They wouldn't be caught dead in a wagon or a minivan, and even an SUV brings up images of carting the entire soccer team around town. They want something new and different, something a little edgy, a car that represents who they are. But the steep price tag of a Hummer is out of reach for those who are just joining the workforce. So Toyota has come up with a new car for the Gen Y driver—and a marketing campaign to go with it.

It's called the Scion. It comes in two models, xA and xB. The xA is "tough, sleek, and ready to roll," according to the colorful marketing brochure that also uses phrases such as "a serious sound system" and "what moves you." The xB looks like a shoebox on wheels. In fact, it is so weird looking it's almost cute—at the very least, you'll cross the street to take a second look at one parked along the curb. Scions arrive in the U.S. as bare bones and go through customization that includes funky side panel decorations and flared fenders once they are ordered. The idea is to make each car as unique as the buyer who purchases it. Both Scion models are affordable—starting around $14,000—which is key for the 65 million Americans who were born between 1977 and 1995 and are just getting their licenses or entering the workforce. Because about 3.5 million Gen Y consumers get their driver's licenses each year, automakers are swarming around them in an effort to grab their attention and develop a relationship that will turn into brand loyalty over time.

Toyota *doesn't* want Gen Y's parents—the aging baby boomers—to buy this car. They have positioned the Scion so it is practically hidden from the older generation. That's because Toyota marketers have already had a bit of bad luck with building and marketing cars to younger drivers—their parents bought the cars instead. That was the case with the Echo, a small sedan with excellent reliability and fuel efficiency, topped off by a low sticker price—about $11,000. The more recent Matrix—a small wagon starting at around $15,000—has appealed more to baby boomers and young families than the Gen Y crowd it was intended for. So Toyota marketers have stayed away from mainstream advertising. Instead, they have concentrated on nontraditional ways of getting their message to their intended consumers.

The Scion's brochure, which focuses on youth and lifestyle, looks like a music-industry magazine—it is filled with urban graffiti art; profiles of Scion salespeople, artists, and hip-hop stars; advertisements for other products like *URB* magazine; listings for Scion promotional events such as the Scion Screening Series; and an invitation to check out the Scion Web site. The brochure even comes with a CD that has a music mix, movie trailers, Scion event footage—and some information about the cars. Instead of inviting Gen Y consumers directly into the showroom, Toyota marketers have taken the Scion to locations where younger drivers hang out. They have parked it outside coffee shops near college campuses and in parking lots at the beach. They have invited staffers at hip-hop fashion magazines like *Yellow Rat Bastard* to test-drive Scions and talk about the experience.

Ultimately, for the Scion to be a success, Gen Y drivers will have to get behind the wheel themselves and plunk down their hard-earned cash. Initial sales figures show that the median age of an xB purchaser is 33—which is 14 years younger than the average Toyota owner. Meanwhile, if a few baby boomers wander in to the showroom and flip through the brochure, the Toyota salesperson won't chase them away.

Questions for Critical Thinking

1. If Toyota were to broaden its target market for Scion, which segment or segments might the firm include?
2. How would you describe Toyota's positioning strategy for the Scion?

Sources: "Toyota's Scion: It's Cheap, Cute, Built to Hold Gen Y," *Newsday.com,* February 6, 2004, http://www.newsday.com; "Scion," Toyota brochure, Summer/Fall 2003; Michael V. Copeland, "Hits & Misses," *Business 2.0,* September 2003, p. 92; Bob Garfield, "Toyota Finds Attractive Effort to Push the Plug-Ugly Scion," *Advertising Age,* August 4, 2003, p. 29; Sholan Freeman and Norihiko Shirouzo, "Toyota's Gen Y Gamble," *The Wall Street Journal,* July 30, 2003, p. B1; Daren Fonda, "Baby, You Can Drive My Car," *Time,* June 30, 2003, pp. 46–48.

VIDEO CASE 9.2 Orange Glo Cleans Up the Marketplace

The written case on Orange Glo, International appears on page VC-11. The recently filmed Orange Glo, International video is designed to expand and highlight the concepts in this chapter and the concepts and questions covered in the written video case.

chapter 10

Relationship Marketing, Customer Relationship Management (CRM), and One-to-One Marketing

chapter objectives

1. Contrast transaction-based marketing with relationship marketing.
2. Identify and explain the four basic elements of relationship marketing as well as the importance of internal marketing.
3. Identify each of the three levels of the relationship marketing continuum.
4. Explain how firms can enhance customer satisfaction and how they build buyer–seller relationships.
5. Discuss how marketers use grassroots and viral marketing in their one-to-one marketing efforts.
6. Explain customer relationship management (CRM) and the role of technology in building customer relationships.
7. Describe the buyer–seller relationship in business-to-business marketing, and identify the four different types of business partnerships.
8. Describe how business-to-business marketing incorporates national account selling, electronic data interchange, vendor-managed inventories (VMI), CPFaR, managing the supply chain, and creating alliances.
9. Identify and evaluate the most common measurement and evaluation techniques within a relationship marketing program.

THE WOMEN'S NATIONAL BASKETBALL ASSOCIATION (WNBA) REBOUNDS

Starting up a professional sports league isn't easy. If you stay around even a few seasons, you can call yourself a success, and at least when you hit the floor, the rink, or the field, you'll go down fighting. Starting a *women's* professional sports league is even tougher. Getting spectators to come to the games, winning the trust of sponsors, and turning spectators into loyal fans in a culture that has traditionally celebrated men's professional sports is a huge challenge. But slowly, year after year, the Women's National Basketball Association has grown stronger. People are watching, particularly women, and they are buying tickets to the games. A J.D. Power and Associates survey reveals that 78 percent of the people who attend WNBA games are women, half of whom bring their families along. A few WNBA stars have emerged—Lisa Leslie, Sheryl Swoopes, Rebecca Lobo, and Sue Bird aren't quite household names yet, but they have a following. It has been only 10 years since WNBA players shot their first baskets, but the organization is building a base of loyal followers.

And marketers have noticed. Recently, Procter & Gamble signed a three-year sponsorship deal with the WNBA that includes several big brands—Herbal Essences, Head & Shoulders, Secret, Swiffer, Cascade, Cheer, and Joy. Under the agreement, P&G will advertise during WNBA telecasts on ABC, ESPN2, Oxygen, and NBA TV. The basketball league will schedule player appearances, post signs promoting P&G products at games, and ensure a P&G presence on WNBA.com and at the annual All-Star Game. Fans will hear the "Herbal Essences Halftime Report" and the presentation of the "Dish and Assist Award by Cascade." P&G will feature the WNBA in some of its retail promotions as well. "This deal allows both of our companies to reach a strong female audience base," notes Mary Reiling Spencer, vice president of marketing partnerships for the WNBA. Val Ackerman, WNBA president, concurs. "I believe that women's sports are increasingly being recognized as a way for companies to emotionally connect with fans and consumers in a way that's very unique as an advertising medium," she explains.

Meanwhile, in Connecticut, another relationship is being forged. The Mohegan Sun casino and arena—which has hosted all kinds of entertainment acts ranging from bull riding to arena football, from comedian Rich Little to pop diva Cher—has bought a WNBA team. The Native American–owned entertainment organization paid $10 million for the Orlando team and converted it to the Connecticut Sun. Mohegan Sun marketers think the move is good business. It's a way to reach out to families with entertainment for all age groups. And it's a way to let more people know about Mohegan Sun. "There's nothing that gets you media exposure, local or national, like sports," says Paul Munick, who presides over Mohegan Sun's sports and entertainment and who is now the Connecticut Sun president. "It gets your name out there."

As the WNBA continues to grow, it must manage its relationships both on and off the court—with players, fans, and an increasing number of organizations that see an opportunity to reach their own target market through agreements with the WNBA. One market that the WNBA has made an effort to reach is the gay and lesbian community. The league has already advertised in gay and lesbian media and conducted ticket promotions that have proved successful. However, WNBA president Val Ackerman notes that the league wants to reach a broad spectrum of consumers and businesses. With the slogan "This Is Who I Am," the league hopes to appeal to every potential fan's individuality, including men as well as women. "A league like ours uses a dual marketing approach," says Ackerman. "We bring in many women, but it's important to sell the basketball side because we do attract men." All the fans, men and women alike, want to see a great game—and the WNBA intends to keep coming up with the jump shots.[1]

Chapter Overview

As the experiences of the WNBA demonstrate, marketing revolves around relationships not only with customers but with everyone involved in creating a product and bringing it to market. The shift away from **transaction-based marketing,** which focuses on short-term, one-time exchanges, to customer-focused relationship marketing is one of the most important trends in marketing today. Companies recognize that they cannot prosper simply by identifying and attracting new customers; to succeed, they must build loyal, mutually beneficial relationships with both new and existing customers, suppliers, distributors, and employees. This strategy benefits the bottom line because retaining customers costs much less than acquiring new ones. Building and managing long-term relationships between buyers and sellers are the hallmark of relationship marketing. **Relationship marketing** is the development, growth, and maintenance of cost-effective, high-value relationships with individual customers, suppliers, distributors, retailers, and other partners for mutual benefit over time.

Relationship marketing is based on promises: the promise of low prices, the promise of high quality, the promise of prompt delivery, the promise of superior service. A network of promises—within the organization, between the organization and its supply chain, and between buyer and seller—determines whether a relationship will grow. A firm is responsible for ensuring it keeps or exceeds the agreements it makes, with the ultimate goal of achieving customer satisfaction.

Briefly Speaking

People in the States used to think that if girls were good at sports their sexuality would be affected. Being feminine meant being a cheerleader, not being an athlete. The image of women is changing now. You don't have to be pretty for people to come and see you play. At the same time, if you're a good athlete, it doesn't mean you're not a woman.

Martina Navratilova (b. 1956)
American tennis player

This chapter examines the reasons organizations are moving toward relationship marketing and customer relationship management, explores the impact this move has on producers of goods and services and their customers, and looks at ways to evaluate customer relationship programs.

transaction-based marketing Buyer and seller exchanges characterized by limited communications and little or no ongoing relationship between the parties.

relationship marketing Development and maintenance of long-term, cost-effective relationships with individual customers, suppliers, employees, and other partners for mutual benefit.

① **Contrast transaction-based marketing with relationship marketing.**

THE SHIFT FROM TRANSACTION-BASED MARKETING TO RELATIONSHIP MARKETING

Since the Industrial Revolution, most manufacturers have run production-oriented operations. They have focused on making products and then promoting them to customers in the hope of selling enough to cover costs and earn profits. The emphasis has been on individual sales or transactions. In transaction-based marketing, buyer and seller exchanges are characterized by limited communications and little or no ongoing relationships. The primary goal is to entice a buyer to make a purchase through such inducements as low price, convenience, or packaging. The goal is simple and short term: Sell something—now.

Some marketing exchanges remain largely transaction based. In residential real estate sales, for example, the primary goal of the agent is to make a sale and collect a commission. While the agent may seek to maintain the appearance of an ongoing buyer–seller relationship, in most cases, the possibility of future transactions is limited. The best an agent can hope for is to represent the seller again in a subsequent real-estate deal that may be several years down the line or, more likely, to gain positive referrals to other buyers and sellers.

Today, many organizations have embraced an alternative approach. Relationship marketing views customers as equal partners in buyer–seller transactions. By motivating customers to enter a long-term relationship in which they repeat purchases or buy multiple brands from the firm, marketers obtain a clearer understanding of customer needs over time. This process leads to improved products or customer service, which pays off through increased sales and lower marketing costs. In addition, marketers have discovered that it is less expensive to retain satisfied customers than it is to attract new ones or to repair damaged relationships.

The move from transactions to relationships is reflected in the changing nature of the interactions between customers and sellers. In transaction-based marketing, exchanges with customers are generally sporadic and in some instances disrupted by conflict. As interactions become relationship oriented, however, conflict changes to cooperation, and infrequent contacts between buyers and sellers become ongoing exchanges.

As Figure 10.1 illustrates, relationship marketing emphasizes cooperation rather than conflict between all of the parties involved. This ongoing collaborative exchange creates value for both parties and builds customer loyalty. Customer relationship management goes a step further and integrates the customer's needs into all aspects of the firm's operations and its relationships with suppliers, distributors, and strategic partners. It combines people, processes, and technology with the long-term goal of maximizing customer value through mutually satisfying interactions and transactions.

figure 10.1

Forms of Buyer–Seller Interactions on a Continuum from Conflict to Cooperation

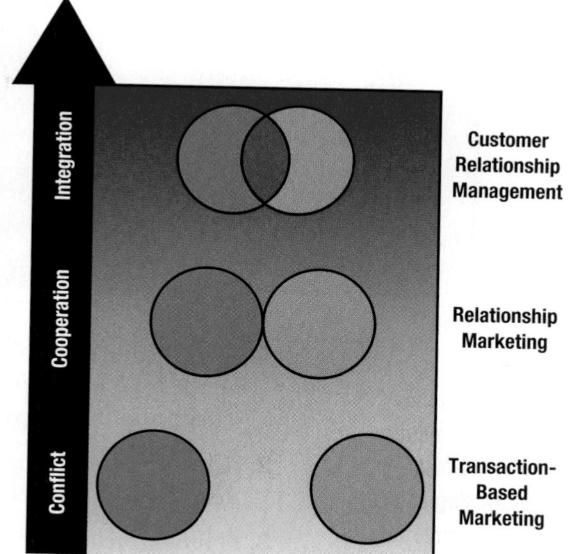

Twenty-first century marketers now understand they must do more than simply create products and then sell them. With so many goods and services to choose from, customers look for added value from their marketing relationships. In the past, consumers viewed banks as a place to keep their money until they needed it; a typical bank customer might have a certificate of deposit, a savings account, and a checking account, which represented transactions. Today's banking industry revolves around relationships, including those involving mortgages, retirement savings, and credit cards in addition to traditional checking and savings accounts. Recently, Wilmington, Delaware-based banking giant MBNA Corporation announced that it would add American Express cards to its existing credit-card offerings, which include MasterCard and Visa. The new offering gives MBNA customers more choice, cements relationships, and makes MBNA more competitive.[2]

Table 10.1 summarizes the differences between the narrow focus of transaction marketing and the much broader view that relationship marketing takes. The customer–seller bonds developed in a relationship marketing partnership last longer and cover a much broader scope than those developed in transaction marketing. Customer contacts are generally more frequent. A companywide emphasis on customer service contributes to customer satisfaction.

table 10.1 ***Comparing Transaction-Based Marketing and Relationship Marketing Strategies***

CHARACTERISTIC	TRANSACTION MARKETING	RELATIONSHIP MARKETING
Time orientation	Short-term	Long-term
Organizational goal	Make the sale	Emphasis on retaining customers
Customer service priority	Relatively low	Key component
Customer contact	Low to moderate	Frequent
Degree of customer commitment	Low	High
Basis for seller–customer interactions	Conflict manipulation	Cooperation; trust
Source of quality	Primarily from production	Companywide commitment

Source: Adapted from Martin Cristopher, Adrian Payne, and David Ballantyne, *Relationship Marketing* (Oxford, UK: Butterworth Heinemann Ltd., 1993), p. 4.

figure 10.2

Integrating Quality and Customer Service with Other Marketing Mix Elements to Create and Maintain a Relationship Marketing Focus

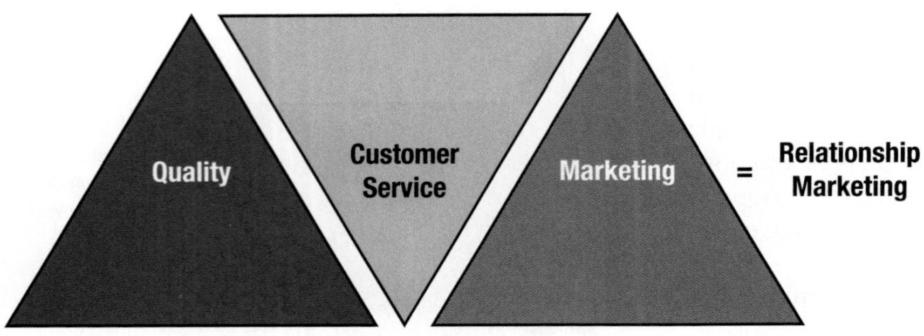

ELEMENTS OF RELATIONSHIP MARKETING

To build long-term customer relationships, marketers need to place customers at the center of their efforts. Figure 10.2 shows the need to blend quality and customer service with traditional elements of the marketing mix. When a company integrates customer service and quality with marketing, the result is a relationship marketing orientation.

But how do firms achieve these long-term relationships? They build them with four basic elements.

(2) **Identify and explain the four basic elements of relationship marketing as well as the importance of internal marketing.**

1. They gather information about their customers. Database technology, discussed later in this chapter, helps a company identify current and potential customers with selected demographic, purchase, and lifestyle characteristics.
2. They analyze the data they have collected and use it to modify their marketing mix to deliver differentiated messages and customized marketing programs to individual consumers.
3. Through relationship marketing, they monitor their interactions with customers. They are then able to assess the customer's level of satisfaction or dissatisfaction with their service. Marketers can also calculate the cost of attracting one new customer and figure out how much profit that customer will generate during the relationship. Information is fed back, and they are then able to seek ways to add value to the buyer–seller transaction so that the relationship will continue.
4. With customer relationship management (CRM) software, they use intimate knowledge of customers and customer preferences to orient every part of the organization, including both its internal and external partners, toward building a unique company differentiation that is based on strong, unbreakable bonds with customers. Sophisticated technology and the Internet help make that happen.[3]

INTERNAL MARKETING

internal marketing Managerial actions that help all members of the organization understand and accept their respective roles in implementing a marketing strategy.

The concepts of customer satisfaction and relationship marketing are usually discussed in terms of **external customers**—people or organizations that buy or use a firm's goods or services. But marketing in organizations concerned with customer satisfaction and long-term relationships must also address **internal customers**—employees or departments within the organization whose success depends on the work of other employees or departments. A person processing an order for a new piece of equipment is the internal customer of the salesperson who completed the sale, just as the person who bought the product is the salesperson's external customer. Although the order processor might never directly encounter an external customer, his or her performance can have a direct impact on the overall value the firm is able to deliver.

Internal marketing involves managerial actions that enable all members of an organization to understand, accept, and fulfill their respective roles in implementing a marketing strategy. Good internal customer satisfaction helps organizations to attract, select, and retain outstanding employees who appreciate and value their role in the delivery of superior service to external customers. Consider how Cleveland-based National City Corp. enriched the banking experience for its customers—and its staff. In one program, the bank upgraded its offerings to customers while offering a major employee training program that focused on service through its internal management development center National City Institute. Within the first year, 3,000 employees—a tenth of the workforce—graduated. New hires now receive three weeks of training, rather than three days. Salary increases and major investments in technology also served to boost employee morale and loyalty and create a positive attitude that translates to enhanced customer service.[4]

The team that trusts—their leader and each other—is more likely to be successful.

Mike Krzyzewski (b. 1947)

basketball coach, Duke University

Employee knowledge and involvement are important goals of internal marketing. Companies that excel at satisfying customers typically place a priority on keeping employees informed about corporate goals, strategies, and customer needs. Employees must also have the necessary tools to address customer requests and problems in a timely manner. Companywide computer networks aid the flow of communications between departments and functions. Several companies—like Harley-Davidson—also include key suppliers on their networks to speed and ease communication of all aspects of business from product design to inventory control.

Employee satisfaction is another critical objective of internal marketing. Employees can seldom, if ever, satisfy customers when they themselves are unhappy. Dissatisfied employees are likely to spread negative word-of-mouth messages to relatives, friends, and acquaintances, and these reports can affect purchasing behavior. Satisfied employees buy their employer's products, tell friends and families how good the customer service is, and ultimately send a powerful message to customers. In an industry that has suffered tremendous setbacks in the past few years, Southwest Airlines has maintained an upbeat outlook among employees as well as profitability. In the wake of the terrorist attacks of September 11, 2001, other airlines laid off hundreds of employees and several went into bankruptcy. But Southwest didn't furlough a single employee and remained profitable throughout hard times. The airline continues to fly 5.5 million travelers to their destinations each month. How do they do it? "Listen, we have an incredible *esprit de corps* here," explains CEO Jim Parker. "It's like the Marine Corps. The intangibles have always been more important than the tangibles. Plus we run this company to prepare ourselves for the bad times, which always come in the business."[5]

Kyocera knows the importance of satisfying employees by allowing them to work more efficiently.

1. What are the major differences between transaction-based marketing and relationship marketing?
2. Why is internal marketing important to a firm?

THE RELATIONSHIP MARKETING CONTINUUM

(3) Identify each of the three levels of the relationship marketing continuum.

Like all other interpersonal relationships, buyer–seller relationships function at a variety of levels. As an individual or firm progresses from the lowest level to the highest level on the continuum of relationship marketing, as shown in Table 10.2, the strength of commitment between the parties grows.

table 10.2 ***Three Levels of Relationship Marketing***

CHARACTERISTIC	LEVEL 1	LEVEL 2	LEVEL 3
Primary bond	Financial	Social	Structural
Degree of customization	Low	Medium	Medium to high
Potential for sustained competitive advantage	Low	Moderate	High
Examples	American Airlines's AAdvantage program	Harley-Davidson's Harley Owners Group (HOG)	Federal Express's PowerShip Program

Source: Adapted from information in Leonard L. Berry, "Relationship Marketing of Services—Growing Internet, Emerging Perspectives," *Journal of the Academy of Marketing Science,* Fall 1995, p. 240.

figure 10.3

The First Level of Relationship Marketing

The likelihood of a continuing, long-term relationship grows as well. Whenever possible, marketers want to move their customers along this continuum, converting them from Level 1 purchasers, who focus mainly on price, to Level 3 customers, who receive specialized services and value-added benefits that may not be available from another firm.

FIRST LEVEL: FOCUS ON PRICE

Interactions at the first level of relationship marketing are the most superficial and the least likely to lead to a long-term relationship. In the most prevalent examples of this first level, relationship marketing efforts rely on pricing and other financial incentives to motivate customers to enter into buying relationships with a seller. The General Motors MasterCard rewards cardholders with credits for every dollar charged toward purchases of GM products. McDonald's sometimes offers two Big Macs for the price of one. CleanSweep Homewood Suites offers a "spring cleaning" vacation weekend. Guests who take a suite for four days receive coupons from ServiceMaster Clean and MerryMaids so that their homes are spotless when they return.[6]

Although these programs can be attractive to users, they may not create long-term buyer relationships. Because the programs are not customized to the needs of individual buyers, they are easily duplicated by competitors. When McDonald's runs its two-for-one special on Big Macs, Burger King may respond with a similar offer on its Whopper sandwiches. Within three years after American Airlines introduced its AAdvantage frequent-flyer program, some 23 other airlines enacted similar programs. Today, consumers expect frequent-flyer rewards from airlines and no longer consider them something special. The lesson is that it takes more than a low price or other financial incentives to create a long-term relationship between buyer and seller. Consider the Toyota ad in Figure 10.3. Although the tag line, "all this and change back from your $20,000," appeals to consumers' desire for a good price, the ad also points out many other benefits derived from the Camry. So, while a low price might entice consumers to test-drive the car, the relationship will ultimately be built on other factors.

SECOND LEVEL: SOCIAL INTERACTIONS

As buyers and sellers reach the second level of relationship marketing, their interactions develop on a social level—one that features deeper and less superficial links than the financially motivated first level. Sellers have begun to learn that social relationships with buyers can be very effective marketing tools. Customer service and communication are key factors at this stage.

Social interaction can take many forms. The owner of a local shoe store or dry cleaner might chat with customers about local events. An art gallery may host a reception for artists and customers. The service department of an auto dealership might call a customer after a repair to see whether the customer is satisfied or has any questions. An investment firm might send holiday cards to all its customers. Virgin Radio established a VIP club that sends targeted e-mails to customers, telling them about concerts and other music events in their geographic area. "We wanted to be able to tie in promotions, competitions, and advertising to areas," says James Cridland of Virgin Radio. "Now we're not only in a position to tell someone that [musical group] Coldplay are touring, we can actually send an e-mail to them telling when the group will play at the venues nearest to them."[7]

THIRD LEVEL: INTERDEPENDENT PARTNERSHIP

At the third level of relationship marketing, relationships are transformed into structural changes that ensure buyer and seller are true business partners. As buyer and seller work more closely together, they develop a dependence on one another that continues to grow over time.

Although car manufacturers do not sell through the Internet, their Web strategies are structured to develop leads and provide support for dealers. By advertising on independent research sites like Kel-

Solving an Ethical Controversy

WHEN IS A CLOSE RELATIONSHIP TOO CLOSE?

MANAGING customer relationships is vital to the success of any firm. In the auto industry, the relationship between manufacturer and dealer can be a bumpy road, and sometimes it becomes a wreck. Dealers are essentially entrepreneurs who have invested millions of their own dollars in their businesses. They depend on manufacturers to provide high-quality products, training, and support. Because of their own investment—and the fact that manufacturers don't always meet their needs—they believe they should be free to sell as many different brands of vehicles as they want. But manufacturers such as Chrysler disagree. In a highly competitive market, Chrysler does not want its dealers selling non-Chrysler products on the same lot. The automaker is now demanding exclusive dealership agreements. Chrysler has announced that dealers who sell non-Chrysler products will not be eligible for its prestigious Five Star designation.

SHOULD AUTO MANUFACTURERS BE ABLE TO DICTATE WHICH BRANDS THEIR DEALERS MAY SELL?

PRO

1. The automobile market is so competitive that manufacturers and dealers must work as closely together as possible to gain an edge. This may mean excluding sales of imports and other competing brands. "Today, the imports are not just niche players," explains Chrysler CEO Dieter Zetsche. "If we get that competition out of our showrooms, it is a significant opportunity for sales growth."
2. Combining Chrysler product lines such as Jeep and Dodge will create stronger, more profitable, more loyal dealerships. The move gives consumers a consistent choice and should ultimately create loyal Chrysler customers.

CON

1. Car dealers invest a great deal of time and money in their own businesses, and they should be free to choose the products they feel will best meet the needs of their customers and will be the most profitable.
2. The high sales standards established by Chrysler are "causing us to have to compete against ourselves," says one dealer. Instead of selling the cars that consumers want, dealers claim, they are being forced to push certain models to meet sales quotas.

SUMMARY

Although automakers clearly must find ways to attract car buyers who become loyal to their brand, they must also manage their relationships with dealers. Because competition from foreign manufacturers such as Toyota and Honda is so strong, U.S. automakers like Chrysler are attempting to tighten the reins on its dealers. "We want our best dealers focused on our product lines," says Gary Dilts, Chrysler senior vice president of sales. And they don't want to see any other car names in Chrysler showrooms.

Sources: Jason Stein, "Chrysler Group Sticks with Its High Sales Bar," *Automotive News*, February 9, 2004, http://infotrac-college.thomsonlearning.com; Mary Connelly and Rick Kranz, "Chrysler Group Demands Stand-Alones; Dealerships Will Lose Five-Star Rating if Not in Compliance," *Automotive News*, February 2, 2004, http://infotrac-college.thomsonlearning.com; Dale Buss, "Wheeling and Dealing," *Sales & Marketing Management*, February 2004, pp. 36–39, 70.

ley Blue Book (http://www.kbb.com) or Carmax.com (http://www.carmax.com), manufacturers such as Saturn entice browsers to their sites. Since Web shoppers cannot be cornered by a salesperson before they are ready to buy, some customers find Web research a less stressful process than walking into a showroom. At the carmaker's site, customers can configure the exact car they want to buy, feature by feature. Saturn offers price and affordability calculators that help buyers figure out monthly payments. Saturn buyers can then find their local dealer and continue the sales process there at the price quoted on the Web site. In this way, both the manufacturer and the dealer benefit from the sale, and customers get the cars they want at a fair price.[8] However, sometimes the relationship between partners such as auto manufacturers and dealers can become *too* close, as discussed in the "Solving an Ethical Controversy" box.

1. **Identify the three levels of the marketing relationship.**
2. **Which level is the most complicated? Why?**

figure 10.4

Three Steps to Measure Customer Satisfaction

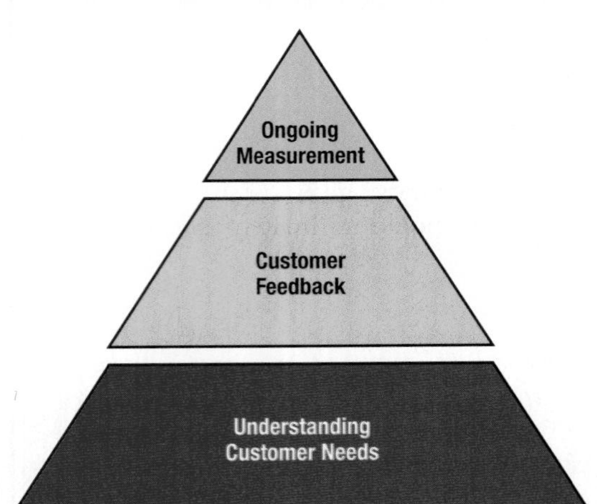

ENHANCING CUSTOMER SATISFACTION

Marketers monitor customer satisfaction through various methods of marketing research. As part of an ongoing relationship with customers, marketers must continually measure and improve how well they meet customer needs. As Figure 10.4 shows, three major steps are involved in this process: understanding customer needs, obtaining customer feedback, and instituting an ongoing program to ensure customer satisfaction.

UNDERSTANDING CUSTOMER NEEDS

Knowledge of what customers need, want, and expect is a central concern of companies focused on building long-term relationships. This information is also a vital first step in setting up a system to measure **customer satisfaction.** Marketers must carefully monitor the characteristics of their product that really matter to customers. They also must remain constantly alert to new elements that might affect satisfaction.

④ Explain how firms can enhance customer satisfaction and how they build buyer–seller relationships.

Satisfaction can be measured in terms of the gaps between what customers expect and what they perceive they have received. Such gaps can produce favorable or unfavorable impressions. Goods or services may be better or worse than expected. If they are better, marketers can use the opportunity to create loyal customers. Aetna's promotional message in Figure 10.5 lets consumers know that the firm probably provides more services than they thought.

If goods or services are worse than expected, a company may lose enough customers to wind up in bankruptcy. Sometimes it is simply a matter of failing to provide the products that consumers want, as in the case of toy retailer FAO Schwarz, which filed for bankruptcy. The store, which concentrated on high-end, hard-to-find, or classic toys, lost much of its market share to mass retailers such as Wal-Mart and Toys 'R' Us partly because it didn't have the popular items that consumers were seeking.[9] However, by examining the gaps between what customers expect and what they receive, companies like FAO Schwarz can often return to the marketplace.

To avoid unfavorable gaps, marketers need to keep in touch with the needs of current and potential customers. They must look beyond traditional performance measures and explore the factors that determine purchasing behavior to formulate customer-based missions, goals, and performance standards.

figure 10.5

Aetna: Assuring Customers They Get More Than They Expect

OBTAINING CUSTOMER FEEDBACK AND ENSURING CUSTOMER SATISFACTION

The second step in measuring customer satisfaction is to compile feedback from customers regarding present performance. Increasingly, marketers try to improve customers' access to their companies by including toll-free 800 numbers or Web site addresses in their advertising. Most firms rely on reactive methods of collecting feedback. Rather than solicit complaints, they might, for example, monitor Usenet and other online discussion groups as a means of tracking customer comments and attitudes about the value received. Some companies hire mystery shoppers, who visit or call businesses posing as customers, to evaluate the service they receive. Their unbiased appraisals are usually conducted semiannually or quarterly to monitor employees, diagnose problem areas in customer service, and measure the impact of employee training.

United Kingdom–based Virgin Radio uses its Web site to obtain feedback, just as it uses its VIP club to target its customers. Listeners can log on to rate music programs and tell DJs what they want to hear;

they can also vote on the "Most Wanted" list to help determine nightly programs. This direct feedback gives the station a current assessment of its listeners' musical tastes and helps marketers tailor the programming to its customers' needs.[10]

Any method that makes it easier for customers to complain actually benefits a firm. Customer complaints offer firms the opportunity to overcome problems and prove their commitment to service. People often have greater loyalty to a company after a conflict has been resolved than if they had never complained at all.

Many organizations also use proactive methods to assess customer satisfaction, including visiting, calling, or mailing out surveys to clients to find out their level of satisfaction. Xerox gathers information by mailing approximately 60,000 customer satisfaction surveys per month to its customers, and AT&T's Universal Credit Card division calls 2,500 customers every month to measure quality in the company's nine most important areas of service performance. Pizza Hut calls 50,000 customers each week to ask about their experiences at the restaurant chain's units. The chef at a local restaurant may appear among diners to ask them whether they are enjoying their meal. The owner of a small clothing store may ask customers what they think of the window display.

1. How is customer satisfaction measured?
2. Identify two ways that marketers may obtain customer feedback.

BUILDING BUYER–SELLER RELATIONSHIPS

Marketers of consumer goods and services have discovered that they must do more than simply create products and then sell them. With a dizzying array of products to choose from, many customers are seeking ways to simplify both their business and personal lives, and relationships provide a way to do this.

One reason consumers form continuing relationships is their desire to reduce choices. Through relationships, they can simplify information gathering and the entire buying process as well as decrease the risk of dissatisfaction. They find comfort in brands that have become familiar through their ongoing relationships with companies. Such relationships may lead to more efficient decision making by customers and higher levels of customer satisfaction.

A key benefit to consumers in long-term buyer–seller relationships is the perceived positive value they receive. Relationships add value because of increased opportunities for frequent customers to save money through discounts, rebates, and similar offers; via special recognition from the relationship programs; and through convenience in shopping. Figure 10.6 illustrates how American Express seeks to encourage consumers to become cardmembers—by offering a wide range of opportunities to redeem reward points.

Marketers should also understand why consumers end relationships. Computerized technologies and the Internet have made consumers better informed than ever before by giving them unprecedented abilities to compare prices, merchandise, and customer service. If they perceive that a competitor's product or customer service is better, customers may switch loyalties. Music retailer Tower Records fell into bankruptcy partly because it couldn't compete with music downloads from the Internet and partly because it couldn't compete with the prices of discounters like Best Buy.[11] Many consumers dislike feeling that they are locked into a relationship with one company, and that is reason enough for them to try a competing item next time they buy. Some customers simply become bored with their current providers and decide to sample the competition.

HOW MARKETERS KEEP CUSTOMERS

One of the major forces driving the push from transaction-based marketing to relationship marketing is the realization that retaining customers is far more profitable than losing them. Customers usually enable a firm to generate more profits with each additional year of the relationship.

A good example of this is the Marriott Rewards program, which now boasts more than 17 million members. Members spend an average of 2.5 times more at Marriott hotels than nonmembers and

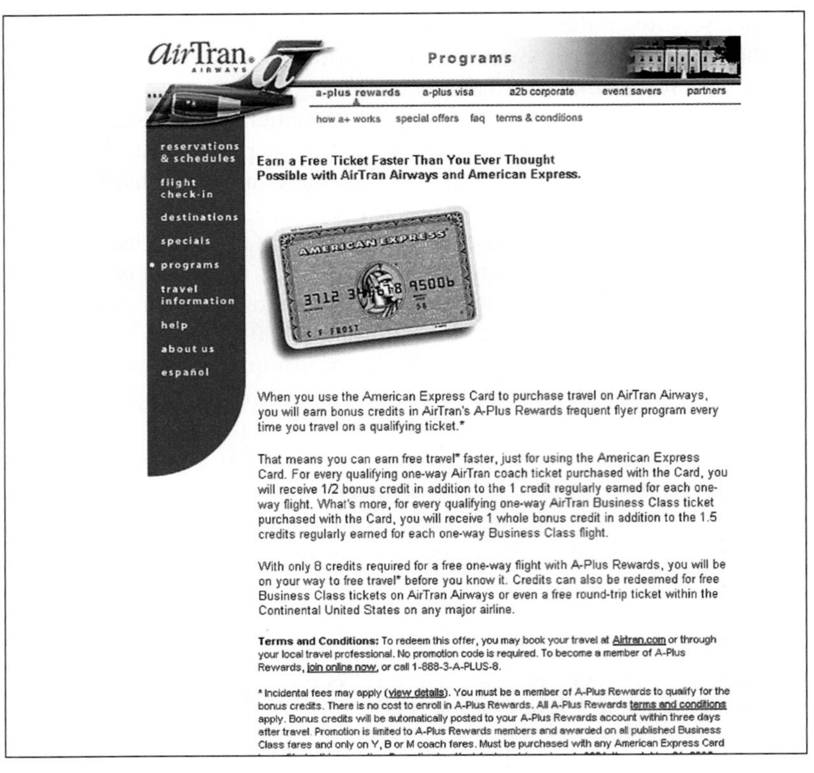

figure 10.6

American Express Rewards Program: Adding Value by Increasing Customer Opportunities to Earn Points

WWW.AIRTRAN.COM

account for 40 percent of Marriott's total sales. Members have over 250 reward options, earning airline miles or points toward hotel stays and merchandise. They can receive 33 percent savings through Marriott Rewards Pointsavers, and during certain time periods, they may earn double Marriott rewards or double upgrade points with Hertz. Marriott also offers a special Marriott Visa Signature card and elite membership benefits.[12]

frequency marketing Frequent buyer or user marketing programs that reward customers with cash, rebates, merchandise, or other premiums.

Programs like Marriott's are an example of **frequency marketing.** These programs reward top customers with cash, rebates, merchandise, or other premiums. Buyers who purchase an item more often earn higher rewards. Frequency marketing focuses on a company's best customers with the goal of increasing their motivation to buy even more of the same or other products from the seller.

Many different types of companies use frequency programs, from fast-food restaurants to retail stores, telecommunications companies, and travel firms. Popular programs include airline frequent-flyer programs, such as United Airlines's Mileage Plus, and retail programs, such as Hallmark's Gold Crown Card.

The Internet is proving a fertile medium for frequency-marketing initiatives. Borrowing from the airlines' frequent-flyer model, Harrah's Casino has created a Web-based program to reward frequent gamblers. Loyalty cards are swiped on the casino floor to monitor time spent at slot machines or card tables and to total up the sums gambled. A Web site allows members to view their points and learn how to earn more benefits as they gamble their way up to platinum or diamond status. The program also identifies which so-called high rollers yield the highest profits.[13]

affinity marketing Marketing effort sponsored by an organization that solicits responses from individuals who share common interests and activities.

In addition to frequency programs, companies use **affinity marketing** to retain customers. Each of us holds certain things dear. Some may feel strongly about Eastern Michigan University, while others admire the Green Bay Packers or the New York Yankees. These examples, along with an almost unending variety of others, are subjects of affinity programs. An affinity program is a marketing effort sponsored by an organization that solicits involvement by individuals who share common interests and activities. With affinity programs, organizations create extra value for members and encourage stronger relationships. Some companies, like On Demand Business Software, provide the technology to other firms for creating and monitoring affinity programs.[14]

Affinity credit cards are a popular form of this marketing technique. The sponsor's name appears prominently in promotional materials, on the card itself, and on monthly statements. For example, the National Association for Female Executives, a professional networking organization, offers qualified members a Gold Visa or MasterCard with no first-year fee and with low interest rates. A not-for-profit organization such as a charity or educational institution, like the Smithsonian Institution, may sponsor a card if the issuer donates a percentage of user purchases to the group.

Not all affinity programs involve credit cards. KETC, the St. Louis public television station, thanks members who contribute more than $50 annually with a card that entitles them to discounts at participating restaurants. Private banks in Europe and Great Britain often hold special events such as wine tastings or art shows to which they invite their wealthiest clients. When it hosted one such event, Investec Private Bank in London invited Nelson Mandela to speak.[15]

DATABASE MARKETING

The use of information technology to analyze data about customers and their transactions is referred to as **database marketing**. The results form the basis of new advertising or promotions targeted to carefully identified groups of customers. Database marketing is a particularly effective tool for building relationships because it allows sellers to sort through huge quantities of data from multiple sources on the buying habits or preferences of thousands or even millions of customers. Companies are then able to track buying patterns, develop customer relationship profiles, customize their offerings and sales promotions, and even personalize customer service to suit the needs of targeted groups of customers. Properly used, databases can help companies in several ways, including these:

database marketing Use of software to analyze marketing information, identifying and targeting messages toward specific groups of potential customers.

- identifying their most profitable customers
- calculating the lifetime value of each customer's business
- creating a meaningful dialogue that builds relationships and encourages genuine brand loyalty
- improving customer retention and referral rates
- reducing marketing and promotion costs
- boosting sales volume per customer or targeted customer group

Where do organizations find all the data that fill these vast marketing databases? Everywhere! Credit-card applications, software registration, and product warranties all provide vital statistics of individual customers. Cash register scanners, customer opinion surveys, and sweepstakes entry forms may offer not just details of name and address but information on preferred brands and shopping habits. Web sites offer free access in return for personal data, allowing companies to amass increasingly rich marketing information.

Illinois-based Central DuPage Health—an independent network of health-care organizations and services—needed to centralize information about its patients. So the firm built a database tracking system for its call center that could automatically match a caller's name with the same name throughout the entire system. Once it began offering round-the-clock call-in service, customer satisfaction increased dramatically. In addition, patients told family and friends about the prompt, personal service they received. Once the system was thoroughly evaluated, Central DuPage Health learned that through physician and nursing referrals alone, the database had saved the company $800,000.[16]

Nonprofit organizations, including government agencies, benefit from database marketing as well. Both the U.S. Marine Corps and the Air Force use databases compiled by Merkle Direct Marketing to identify potential recruits. Databases can target candidates by such criteria as age and education. For instance, the Air Force requires its physician recruits to be between the ages of 20 and 58 and to have a medical degree or be in the process of earning one. When a candidate calls an 800 number or logs on to the Air Force Web site, Merkle software tracks the individual's age, education level, geographic location, interests, and other data for recruiters.[17]

Interactive television promises to deliver even more valuable data—information on real consumer behavior and attitudes toward brands. Linked to digital television, sophisticated set-top boxes like TiVo and Replay TV are already able to collect vast amounts of data on television viewer behavior, organized in incredible detail. Once the technology makes its way into more homes, marketers will have firsthand knowledge of what kind of programming and products their targeted customers want. In addition, rather than using television to advertise to the masses, they will be able to talk directly to those viewers most interested in their products. At a click of a button, viewers will be able to skip ads, but they'll also be able to click to a full-length infomercial on any brand that captures their interest.[18]

As database marketing has become more complex, a variety of software tools and services enable marketers to target consumers more and more narrowly while enriching their communications to selected groups. After all, a huge collection of data isn't valuable unless it can be turned into information that is useful to a firm's marketers. **Application service providers (ASPs)** assist marketers by providing software when it is needed to capture, manipulate, and analyze masses of consumer data. One type of software collects data on product specifications and details, which marketers can use to isolate products that best meet a customer's needs. This would be particularly important in dealing with business products that are expensive and require high involvement in making a purchase decision.[19] Convio provides such database services to nonprofit organizations that are trying to cultivate a wider base of members and supporters. Convio supplies software and online services designed to help groups like Farm Aid, Easter Seals, the American Diabetes Association, Mothers Against Drunk Driving, Avon Foundation, museums, and other organizations identify and communicate with contributors. "Providing emergency assistance to family farms requires donations throughout the year, and it's equally important for consumers to keep farmers in mind every time they shop for food," remarks Wendy Matusovich, Farm Aid's director of development. "It's a huge advantage to use Convio's tools for e-mail, online fundraising, and Web site content management. Now we'll be able to efficiently communicate and sustain relationships with hundreds of thousands of consumers 365 days a year."[20]

Firms can also use database marketing to rebuild customer relationships that may have lapsed. When *The Toronto Globe and Mail* gathered data on its advertisers, the paper discovered that 2,900 of them had advertised in the past but for some reason had stopped. Since the newspaper sales force didn't want to contact these advertisers because they were now unprofitable, marketers hired a telemarketing firm to reestablish contact and learn why these customers had stopped advertising. Marketers gained two things by conducting the survey: (1) They found out why the customers had stopped advertising and could then address any problems related to the paper, and (2) they brought in $2.9 million more in advertising revenues just by making the calls.[21]

one-to-one marketing Program that is customized to build long-term relationships with customers, one at a time.

ONE-TO-ONE MARKETING

As discussed in Chapter 1, **one-to-one marketing** is a marketing program that is customized to build long-term relationships with customers—one at a time. IBM launched a one-to-one marketing campaign that its CEO Samuel J. Palmisano called "eBusiness on demand." Under the program, business customers could purchase exactly enough computer power to take care of a job and then increase the power temporarily at times of peak demand. A tax preparer might purchase an increase just before April 15; a Florida resort might purchase an increase for January and February.[22] In the promotional message in Figure 10.7, Japanese electronics giant NEC offers network support for businesses like hotels that want to track individual customer preferences.

Marketers use a variety of tools to identify their company's best customers, communicate with them, and increase their loyalty. Databases and frequency programs are helpful, but marketers are always coming up with new ways to engage in one-to-one marketing. Silk Soymilk marketers didn't shy away from the idea of appealing to the relatively small number of consumers who couldn't drink milk because they couldn't digest it. Company head Steve Demos came up with the idea of using the carton itself to send the message directly to lactose-intolerant consumers by depicting the soy milk flowing into a cereal bowl. Some marketing experts warned Demos that this wouldn't work, but he went ahead. Today, an estimated one in twelve U.S. households purchases Silk at mainstream supermarkets across the country.[23]

Sony Music offers its business customers an opportunity to create custom CDs to be sold to consumers in their own outlets, such as catalogs and retail stores. Companies that have taken advantage of this offering include Old Navy, Pottery Barn, Target, Williams-Sonoma, and Banana Republic. Shoppers who visit a Williams-Sonoma store,

figure 10.7

NEC: Offering Support for One-to-One Marketing

USED BY PERMISSION, NEC CORPORATION

order through the catalog, or shop online can purchase a custom CD with classic jazz tunes like "April in Paris," "Blue Sky," and "Jersey Bounce." Pottery Barn customers can pick up a holiday CD with "Deck the Halls," "My Favorite Things," and the overture to "The Nutcracker."[24]

(5) Discuss how marketers use grassroots and viral marketing in their one-to-one marketing efforts.

As one-to-one marketing evolves, marketers have begun to explore opportunities for grassroots marketing and viral marketing. **Grassroots marketing** involves connecting directly with existing and potential customers through nonmainstream channels. The grassroots approach involves marketing strategies that are unconventional, nontraditional, not by the book, and extremely flexible. Grassroots marketing is sometimes characterized by a relatively small budget and lots of legwork, but its hallmark is the ability to develop long-lasting, individual relationships with loyal customers.[25] To get consumers interested in the sport of baseball in Germany, ITMS Sports used a grassroots marketing approach in conjunction with Major League Baseball that established a "Play Ball!" program for more than 1 million German schoolchildren.[26] Another marketing firm, Alliance, developed the Hanes Fashion Police campaign, which sent the Hanes "Panty Line Patrol" around in trucks to hand out free samples of Hanes's Body Enhancers to women who wanted to try the new product.[27]

With **viral marketing,** firms let satisfied customers get the word about products out to other consumers—like a spreading virus. "We like to let our customers do the talking for us," explains Amber Kozler, director of fund raising for Metz & Associates, which owns several Krispy Kreme franchises in Pittsburgh.[28] The Internet has become the hottest medium for viral marketing because video clips or games containing advertising can be passed rapidly from user to user.[29] Mazda North America uses online videos that it hopes will create a buzz about its upcoming models. Consumers can pass the videos—which Mazda marketers hope will be highly entertaining—around online. "If you hit it right, it spreads like wildfire," says David Sanabria, group manager of relationship marketing at Mazda.[30]

1. What is a frequency marketing program?
2. What are the benefits of database marketing?
3. Describe two forms of one-to-one marketing.

CUSTOMER RELATIONSHIP MANAGEMENT

(6) Explain customer relationship management (CRM) and the role of technology in building customer relationships.

Emerging from—and closely linked to—relationship marketing, **customer relationship management (CRM)** is the combination of strategies and technologies that empowers relationship programs, reorienting the entire organization to a concentrated focus on satisfying customers. Made possible by technological advances, it leverages technology as a means to manage customer relationships and to integrate all stakeholders into a company's product design and development, manufacturing, marketing, sales, and customer service processes.

customer relationship management (CRM) Combination of strategies and tools that drives relationship programs, reorienting the entire organization to a concentrated focus on satisfying customers.

CRM represents a shift in thinking for everyone involved with a firm—from the CEO down through and encompassing all other key stakeholders, including suppliers, dealers, and other partners. All recognize that solid customer relations are fostered by similarly strong relationships with other major stakeholders. Since CRM goes well beyond traditional sales, marketing, or customer service functions, it requires a top-down commitment and must permeate every aspect of a firm's business. Technology makes that possible by allowing firms—regardless of size and no matter how far-flung their operations—to manage activities across functions, from location to location, and among their internal and external partners.

BENEFITS OF CRM

CRM software systems are capable of making sense of the vast amounts of customer data that technology allows firms to collect. After several years of trying to patch together its existing technology to automate functions like customer service and sales lead management, IBM decided to seek a CRM solution. A custom-created software application was implemented at IBM's 26 customer service centers and connected employees worldwide. The impact was huge and immediate: Most customer inquiries were quickly and efficiently resolved, and the number of abandoned calls fell dramatically. Since customer service personnel spent significantly less time with each call, IBM was able to handle the same volume of calls with 450 fewer people.[31]

Another key benefit of customer relationship management systems is that they are able to simplify complex business processes while keeping the best interests of customers at heart. Biotechnology company Amgen worked with Siebel Systems to come up with CRM software that would make it easier for doctors to manage complicated trials of new drugs. The software is able to keep digital logs of each trial as well as each patient's progress. Not only is Amgen able to receive more reliable test results, but physicians get paid faster and are more willing to take part in new trials. Moreover, administration for the trials takes Amgen staff only a fifth of the time it took in the past. Here, a commitment to improve relationships with doctors has led to improved efficiency and real cost savings.[32]

Selecting the right CRM software system can be critical to the success of a firm's entire CRM program. A firm may choose to buy a system from a company like Siebel or Oracle or rent hosted CRM applications through Web sites like Salesforce.com or Salesnet. Purchasing a customized system can cost a firm millions of dollars and take months to implement, while hosted solutions—rented through a Web site—are cheaper and quicker to get up and running. But purchasing a system allows a firm to expand and customize, whereas hosted systems are more limited. Experienced marketers also warn that it is easy to get mired in a system that is complicated for staff. Solucient, shown in Figure 10.8, is a CRM system that markets itself as simple and easy to use.

This was the case at Cingular Wireless, which spent $10.5 million on a customized system from Siebel. But no one on the sales force understood how to use it. So together, Siebel and Cingular streamlined the program, silencing the extra unneeded bells and whistles, and now the Cingular sales staff is comfortable using the new system.[33]

Software solutions are just one component of a successful CRM initiative. The most effective companies approach customer relationship management as a complete business strategy, in which people, processes, and technology are all organized around delivering superior value to customers. Successful CRM systems share the following qualities:

- They are results driven. The firm must decide on specific goals and benefits before attempting to implement a CRM strategy.
- They are implemented from the top down. Top level executives must be committed to changing the firm to a new focus on customers.
- They require investment in companywide training so people know how to use their new tools.
- They communicate effectively across functions. Effective customer relationship management depends on cross-disciplinary teams that work together to solve customer problems.
- They are streamlined. A concentrated focus on the customers allows firms to weed out wasteful business practices.
- They involve end users in the creation of software solutions. Input from employees, suppliers, distributors, and any other partners who will use the systems is essential. This encourages everyone to support the transition to customer relationship management.
- They constantly seek improvement. By tracking and measuring results, firms are able to continuously improve relationships with customers.[34]

Once the groundwork has been laid, technology solutions drive firms toward a clearer understanding of each customer and his or her needs.

figure 10.8

Solucient: Simplifying CRM Systems

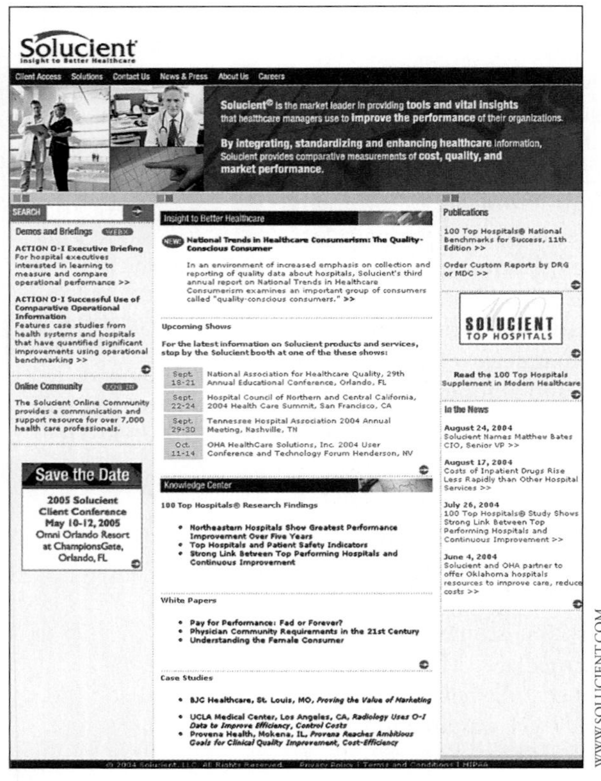

WWW.SOLUCIENT.COM

PROBLEMS WITH CRM

CRM is not a magic wand. The strategy needs to be thought out in advance, everyone in the firm must be committed to it, and everyone must understand how to use it. If no one can put the system to work—as happened at Cingular Wireless—it is an expensive mistake. The

CRM system must do what the firm needs it to do. For instance, many CRM systems provide historical analyses, summarizing data such as consumer preferences in the past. They can tell marketers who their best customers were last month or last week, but not who will be the best next month. So it is important for firms to implement an application that can take historical data and create models that predict future patterns. Projections help marketers understand their customers, develop targeted offers, implement marketing messages in real time, match specific offers to specific individuals, and monitor results.[35]

Experts explain that failures with CRM often result from companies approaching it as a software project rather than a business strategy. "CRM is not a technology; it's not an application," argues Joe Outlaw of Stamford, Connecticut-based technology research firm Gartner Inc. "It's a business strategy around interacting with your customers in a way that brings them more value and is more profitable to you."[36] Other experts warn that firms should avoid using CRM to explore uncharted territory; instead, they suggest that marketers use it to solve problems that are well defined.[37] The founders of California-based medical electronics supplier Inland Empire Components had two failures with CRM systems before trying their third—which they hope will be their last. The first two services were not able to deliver the type of system that Ron and Dana Jiron needed to run their business. So they turned to a third. "We need to have better software so we can provide services for our customers to bring us into line with what we aspire to," says Ron Jiron. "We want to be like the big guys." An effective CRM strategy should be able to help small companies succeed "like the big guys."[38]

MANAGING VIRTUAL RELATIONSHIPS

"Ninety-nine percent of my clients have never been to my office," says Damian Bazadona, who runs his own marketing consulting firm, Situation Marketing. While this wouldn't work for a dental practice, a hair salon, or a restaurant, **virtual relationships**—links between businesses and customers that are developed without person-to-person contact—are becoming more and more common. Virtual relationships exist in both business-to-consumer and business-to-business marketplaces. Managing them so that they result in long-term customer satisfaction and loyalty requires some creativity on the part of marketers.

Damian Bazadona uses the Internet to establish and maintain his links. He posts samples of his work online for prospective customers to review and responds to e-mails rapidly. "I'm as proactive as possible about staying in touch with clients," he says. Neil Fishman of phone-messaging company HoldCom has 6,000 clients worldwide. He actually makes his virtual relationships part of his marketing presentation. "We always say, it's more efficient for you to [receive service] via phone, e-mail, and our Web site," he explains to clients. He shows them how much more quickly and cheaply he can get their work done this way.

Some firms like to get away from technology once in a while in their communications with customers. SecureWorks, an Internet security products provider, makes sure that its clients receive phone calls and signed letters because "letters and phone calls help keep the relationship personal," says Tyler Winkler, senior vice president of sales. Sherry Carnahan of Total Office Inc. sends clients signed birthday and holiday cards.[39]

RETRIEVING LOST CUSTOMERS

Customers defect from an organization's goods and services for a variety of reasons. They might be bored, they might move away from the region, they might not need the product anymore, or they might have tried—and preferred—competing products. An increasingly important part of an effective CRM strategy is **customer winback,** the process of rejuvenating lost relationships with customers. Figure 10.9 illustrates the yearly defection rates for some industries, including Internet service providers (22 percent) and clothing catalogs (25 percent).[40]

In many cases, a relationship gone sour can be sweetened again with the right approach. "You really don't want to fire a customer if you can help it," says Lynn Daniel, president of consulting firm The Daniel Group. As part of a CRM strategy, marketers should look at the mix of products they are offering—and make changes if necessary. North Carolina-based Environmental Inks conducted an audit of its numerous products and realized it was offering its customers too many choices. So marketers decided to reduce the number. Gary Nance, chief operating officer of the company, met with

figure 10.9

Annual Customer Defection Rates

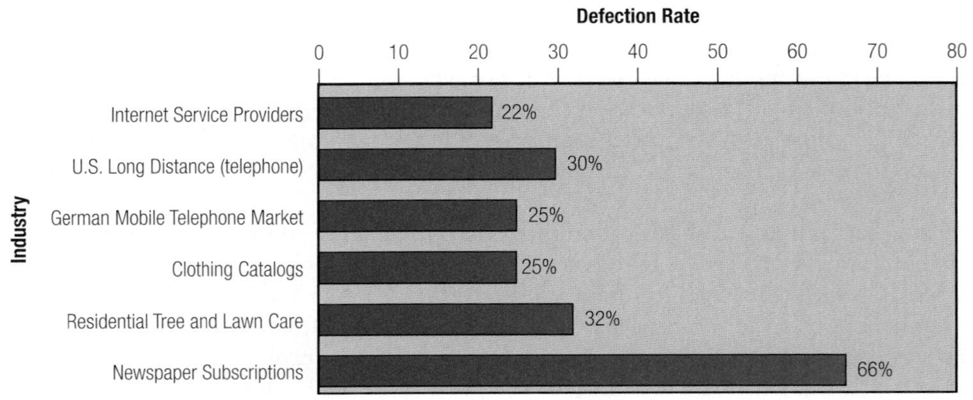

Source: Data from Jacquelyn S. Thomas, Robert C. Blattberg, and Edward J. Fox, "Recapturing Lost Customers," *Journal of Marketing Research,* vol. XLI (February 2004), pp. 31–45.

his long-term customers to explain the changes. Some opted to find other suppliers, but most stayed with Environmental Inks—and are now more profitable to the firm.[41]

Other firms may need to change some of their processes to win back customers or make them more profitable to a seller. By focusing sales staff on his *least* lucrative customers, Curt Tueffert turned some important customer relationships around when he was vice president of sales at a technology firm. "They felt they were getting more service from this new arrangement, and some of them began to order more product," Tueffert recalls.[42]

1. **Define *customer relationship management.***
2. **What are the two major types of CRM systems?**
3. **Describe two steps a firm can take to rejuvenate a lost relationship.**

7 **Describe the buyer–seller relationship in business-to-business marketing, and identify the four different types of business partnerships.**

BUYER–SELLER RELATIONSHIPS IN BUSINESS-TO-BUSINESS MARKETS

Customer relationship management, one-to-one marketing, and relationship marketing are not limited to consumer goods and services. Building strong buyer–seller relationships is a critical component of business-to-business marketing as well.

Business-to-business marketing involves an organization's purchase of goods and services to support company operations or the production of other products. Buyer–seller relationships between companies involve working together to provide advantages that benefit both parties. These advantages might include lower prices for supplies, quicker delivery of inventory, improved quality and reliability, customized product features, and more favorable financing terms.

partnership Affiliation of two or more companies that assist each other in the achievement of common goals.

A **partnership** is an affiliation of two or more companies that assist each other in the achievement of common goals. Partnerships cover a wide spectrum of relationships from informal cooperative purchasing arrangements to formal production and marketing agreements. In business-to-business markets, partnerships form the basis of relationship marketing.

A variety of common goals motivate firms to form partnerships. Companies may want to protect or improve their positions in existing markets, gain access to new domestic or international markets, or quickly enter new markets. Expansion of a product line—to fill in gaps, broaden the product line, or differentiate the product—is another key reason for joining forces. Other motives include sharing resources, reducing costs, warding off threats of future competition, raising or creating barriers to entry, and learning new skills.

CHOOSING BUSINESS PARTNERS

How does an organization decide which companies to select as partners? The first priority is to locate firms that can add value to the relationship—whether through financial resources, contacts, extra manufacturing capacity, technical know-how, or distribution capabilities. The greater the value added, the greater the desirability of the partnership. In many cases, the attributes of each partner complement those of the other; each firm brings something to the relationship that the other party needs but cannot provide on its own. Other partnerships join firms with similar skills and resources to reduce costs.

Organizations must share similar values and goals for a partnership to succeed in the long run. Walt Disney Records forged a partnership with Kellogg Cereals that builds sales of Disney CDs while moving newer cereal brands like Mickey's Magix, Buzz Blasts, and Hunny B's off grocery store shelves. Free on-the-pack sampler CDs encourage families to buy the cereals, and $2-off coupons for full-length CDs spur sales at Disney. Since both marketers target the same group of customers—families with young children—the ongoing campaign succeeds in generating excitement for two distinct products in a single promotion.[43]

One of our ironclad rules is "Never do business with anybody you don't like." If you don't like somebody, there's a reason. Chances are it's because you don't trust him and you're probably right. I don't care who he is or what guarantees you get—cash in advance or whatever. If you do business with somebody you don't like, sooner or later you'll get screwed.

Harry V. Quadracci (1936–2002)

American entrepreneur; founder of Quad/Graphics

TYPES OF PARTNERSHIPS

Companies form four key types of partnerships in business-to-business markets: buyer, seller, internal, and lateral partnerships. This section briefly examines each category.

In a **buyer partnership,** a firm purchases goods and services from one or more providers. When Northrop Grumman was asked to prepare a design bid for the next-generation unmanned airplane for the U.S. military, its top engineer turned to Tacit Knowledge Systems, the designer of a software application called ActiveNet, which is used to locate people with the right skills to take on a job. Pharmaceutical firm Aventis called on Tacit to provide the software necessary to help recruit the best volunteers for clinical trials for a new drug designed to treat multiple sclerosis.[44] When a company assumes the buyer position in a relationship, it has a unique set of needs and requirements that vendors must meet to make the relationship successful. While buyers want sellers to provide fair prices, quick delivery, and high quality levels, a lasting relationship often requires more effort. To induce a buyer to form a long-term partnership, a supplier must also be responsive to the purchaser's unique needs, as Tacit is with both Aventis and the Pentagon decision makers.

Seller partnerships set up long-term exchanges of goods and services in return for cash or other consideration. Sellers, too, have specific needs as partners in ongoing relationships. Most prefer to develop long-term relationships with their partners. Sellers also want prompt payment.

The importance of **internal partnerships** is widely recognized in business today. The classic definition of the word *customer* as the buyer of a good or service is now more carefully defined in terms of external customers. However, customers within an organization also have their own needs. Internal partnerships are the foundation of an organization and its ability to meet its commitments to external entities. If the purchasing department selects a parts vendor that fails to ship on the dates required by manufacturing, production will halt, and products will not be delivered to customers as promised. As a result, external customers will likely seek other more reliable suppliers. Without building and maintaining internal partnerships, an organization will have difficulty meeting the needs of its external partnerships.

Lateral partnerships include strategic alliances with other companies or with not-for-profit organizations and research alliances between for-profit firms and colleges and universities. The relationship focuses on external entities—such as customers of the partner firm—and involves no direct buyer-seller interactions. Strategic alliances are discussed in a later section of this chapter.

COBRANDING AND COMARKETING

Two other types of business marketing relationships include cobranding and comarketing. **Cobranding** joins together two strong brand names, perhaps owned by two different companies, to sell a product. The automotive world is packed with cobranded vehicles, as described in the "Marketing Hit" feature. A car buyer can pick up the Columbia Edition of the Jeep Liberty and wear home a new Columbia ski jacket in the bargain. Subaru and L.L. Bean have a multiyear agreement in which Subaru becomes the official car of the outdoor retail giant, featured at L.L. Bean stores and in its catalogs.

cobranding Cooperative arrangement in which two or more businesses team up to closely link their names on a single product.

figure 10.10

***A Comarketing Effort Involving* SpongeBob Squarepants**

L.L. Bean is now the official outfitter to Subaru, which sells Bean's clothing with Subaru branding at Subaru dealerships.

comarketing Cooperative arrangement in which two businesses jointly market each other's products.

In a **comarketing** effort, two organizations join together to sell their products in an allied marketing campaign. A classic example involves movies. A recent *SpongeBob Squarepants Movie* benefited from $100 million in marketing support from Nickelodeon's marketing partners, including Mattel, Mitsubishi, Burger King, Kellogg, candymaker Perfetti Van Melle USA, and even the Cayman Islands, as illustrated in Figure 10.10.

marketing hit: Carmakers Pitch to the Gay Community

Background. In the past couple of years, companies have begun to recognize that gays and lesbians represent a true market. Together, they spend about $600 billion a year on goods and services. Marketers who make the time and effort to understand and try to meet the needs of these consumers may very well gain a jump on the competition.

The Challenge. Marketers need to identify the needs and wants of the gay and lesbian community, whose own diversity intersects with other market segments in terms of age, income, gender, household type, ethnic background, and the like. Then they need to find ways to forge lasting relationships with this group of consumers.

The Strategy. Targeting the more affluent members of the gay and lesbian community, several years ago, Subaru launched an ad campaign starring tennis legend Martina Navratilova. Ford, Jaguar, Volvo, and Land Rover followed suit with advertisements in gay and lesbian publications. Cadillac rolled into the game with a splashy advertisement for its SRX sport utility vehicle in *The Advocate,* a well-known gay publication. And in a major cobranding move, carsdirect.com teamed up with PlanetOut, in which planetout.com would carry content and sell ads for the auto dealers represented by carsdirect.com.

The Outcome. "Brand allegiance is one of the big selling points of the gay market," notes advertising executive John Nash. So attracting the attention of gay and lesbian consumers, understanding their needs as car buyers, and meeting them goes a long way toward developing loyal customers.

Sources: William C. Symonds, "The Gay Marriage Dividend," *BusinessWeek,* May 24, 2004, p. 50; Jean Halliday, "Cadillac Takes Tentative Step Toward Targeting Gay Market," *Advertising Age,* February 2, 2004, p. 8; Christine L. Romero, "Valley Hosts Gay Chambers," *The Arizona Republic,* April 10, 2003, p. D1; Jean Halliday, "Carsdirect.com Deal Links with PlanetOut," *Advertising Age,* September 9, 2002, p. 25.

SpongeBob appeals to everyone—kids, parents, and those in between—which is why such a wide range of companies came on board the marketing campaign. Perfetti launched a limited-edition SpongeBob Airheads candy, while the Cayman Islands were marketed as a "real" Bikini Bottom—the setting for *SpongeBob.* "*SpongeBob* really skews from 2 to 80, and a third of the products are sold to adults," noted one Nickelodeon marketer.[45]

1. **What are the four key types of business marketing partnerships?**
2. **Distinguish between cobranding and comarketing.**

IMPROVING BUYER–SELLER RELATIONSHIPS IN BUSINESS-TO-BUSINESS MARKETS

Organizations that know how to find and nurture partner relationships, whether through informal deals or contracted partnerships, can enhance revenues and increase profits. Partnering often leads to lower prices, better products, and improved distribution, resulting in higher levels of customer satisfaction. Partners who know each other's needs and expectations are more likely to satisfy them and forge stronger long-term bonds. Often, partnerships can be cemented through personal relationships, no matter where firms are located. See the "Etiquette Tips for Marketing Professionals" feature for guidelines on gift giving.

In the past, business relationships were conducted primarily in person, over the phone, or by mail. Today, businesses are using the latest electronic, computer, and communications technology to link up, sometimes managing virtual relationships as described earlier. E-mail, the Internet, and other telecommunications services allow businesses to communicate anytime and anyplace. Chapter 4 discussed the business role of the Internet in detail. The following sections explore other ways that buyers and sellers cooperate in business-to-business markets.

NATIONAL ACCOUNT SELLING

8 Describe how business-to-business marketing incorporates national account selling, electronic data interchange, vendor-managed inventories (VMI), CPFaR, managing the supply chain, and creating alliances.

Some relationships are more important than others due to the large investments at stake. Large manufacturers such as Procter & Gamble or Clorox pay special attention to the needs of major retailers such as Wal-Mart and Target. Manufacturers use a technique called **national account selling** to serve their largest, most profitable customers. The cluster of supplier offices in northwestern Arkansas—near Wal-Mart's home office—suggests how national account selling might be implemented.

The advantages of national account selling are many. By assembling a team of individuals to serve just one account, the seller demonstrates the depth of its commitment to the customer. The buyer–seller relationship is strengthened as both collaborate to find solutions that are mutually beneficial. Finally, cooperative buyer–seller efforts can bring about dramatic improvements in both efficiency and effectiveness for both partners. These improvements find their way to the bottom line in the form of decreased costs and increased profits.

BUSINESS-TO-BUSINESS DATABASES

As noted earlier, databases are indispensable tools in relationship marketing. They are also essential in building business-to-business relationships. Using information generated from sales reports, scanners, and many other sources, sellers can create databases that help guide their own efforts and those of buyers who resell products to final users.

ELECTRONIC DATA INTERCHANGE

electronic data interchange (EDI) Computer-to-computer exchanges of invoices, orders, and other business documents.

Technology has transformed the ways in which companies control their inventories and replenish stock. Gone are the days when a retailer would notice stocks were running low, call the vendor, check prices, and reorder. Today's **electronic data interchanges (EDIs)** automate the entire process. EDI involves computer-to-computer exchanges of invoices, orders, and other business documents. It allows

ETIQUETTE TIPS

FOR MARKETING PROFESSIONALS

It's the Thought That Counts: Dealing with Gifts and Greetings

MOST of us want to share the holiday spirit, whether we're celebrating Christmas or Kwanzaa, Hanukkah or Ramadan. We want to acknowledge a significant birthday, express sorrow when a loved one is lost, and send congratulations for a promotion or graduation. As marketers, our world continues to grow smaller as more and more firms engage in business outside the U.S. Not everyone celebrates the same holidays—or other occasions—in the same manner. If you aren't a world traveler, how do you know when or what to give as a gift? Here are some tips from the experts.

1. In China, the color white is the symbol of death, so a gift should never be wrapped in white paper, even if it is a wedding or baby gift. On the other hand, red wrapping paper or ribbon implies wishes for good luck and happiness. The Lunar New Year is one of China's biggest holidays—gifts and warm wishes are appreciated.
2. Cows are revered as sacred in India, so a gift made of leather would be offensive. Fruit and sweets are good gifts for your Indian customers or colleagues—even better if they are wrapped in bright colors, which are considered lucky.
3. In Japan, gift giving takes place on many occasions, including a visit to someone's home. Packages should always be gift-wrapped, but not in red paper, which symbolizes blood. Knives, scissors, or letter openers are poor choices because they represent suicide. But gourmet food, expensive sweets, good-quality coffee or tea, or small luxury items like tea towels or soaps are good house gifts. Present your gift with both hands, bowing low as you do so. If a Japanese customer sends you a gift, be sure to send a return gift as your "thank you"—which should be about half the value of the gift you received.
4. Middle Eastern cultures have strict rules about gift giving—they are also generous. If you admire something in your Arab customer's office, home, or store, most likely you'll receive it as a gift—so be careful when admiring expensive items! Don't offer food, which is considered an insult to a host. But glassware, crystal, nature artwork, and items displaying craftsmanship are always appreciated. As in Japan, gifts are presented with both hands. If you receive a gift, don't tear it open—gifts are not opened in the presence of the giver.

Are you discouraged or intimidated? Don't be. Some gifts are appropriate almost anywhere, anytime. "Our pens write in any language," said George S. Parker, founder of the Parker Pen Company. In fact, a high-quality pen is an excellent business gift for almost any occasion in any country. Other business items, such as diaries or handcrafted business card holders, make good gifts as well. You'll be fine if you do a little homework on the customs of your customers and colleagues—and always remember to say thank you when you are on the receiving end.

Sources: "International Business Etiquette and Manners," http://www.cyborlink.com, accessed February 9, 2004; Kamala Thiagaraja, "The International Language of Holiday Gifts," *Women in Business*, November–December 2002, http://0-newfirstsesarch.oclc.org.lrc.cod.edu:80; Cynthia Grosso, "Etiquette: A Guide for Giving," *Charleston School of Protocol and Etiquette*, December 9, 2002, http://www.charlestonschoolofprotocol.com.

firms to reduce costs and improve efficiency and competitiveness. Retailers like Wal-Mart, Dillard's, and Lowe's all require vendors to use EDI as a core **quick-response merchandising** tool. Quick-response merchandising is a just-in-time strategy that reduces the time merchandise is held in inventory, resulting in substantial cost savings. An added advantage of EDI is that it opens new channels for gathering marketing information that is helpful in developing long-term business-to-business relationships.

vendor-managed inventory (VMI) Inventory management system in which the seller—based on an existing agreement with a buyer—determines how much of a product is needed.

VENDOR-MANAGED INVENTORY

The proliferation of electronic data interchange and the constant pressure on suppliers to improve response time have led to another way for buyers and sellers to do business. **Vendor-managed inventory (VMI)** has replaced buyer-managed inventory in many instances. It is an inventory management system in which the seller—based on an existing agreement with the buyer—determines how much of a product a buyer needs and automatically ships new supplies to that buyer.

Sears collaborates with its appliance vendors to manage inventory in its 900 stores nationwide. Supply-chain management software collects data both from Sears's vendor network and across multiple stores. The application alerts Sears to any potential shortages or overstocks before they have a chance to create a problem. Since vendors also have access to information in the system, they have the opportunity to resolve possible issues, thereby maintaining good relationships with the buyer. While the system currently manages only Sears's appliance vendor relationships, the company expects that if rolled out to Sears's entire vendor network, it could result in inventory savings of tens of millions of dollars.[46]

Some firms have modified VMI to an approach called **collaborative planning, forecasting, and replenishment (CPFaR).** This approach is a planning and forecasting technique involving collaborative efforts by both purchasers and vendors. Consumer packaged goods giant Unilever has begun to implement CPFaR with some of its retailers, and there have been slow but steady benefits. Retailers experienced tangible benefits first in the form of inventory reduction. Unilever experienced fewer tangible benefits, such as a better understanding of its customers' supply chains, more effective linking of organizations, and greater opportunities for alliances. But Unilever expects those benefits to grow over time. Firms that choose a CPFaR approach need to establish a solid plan, start small, choose appropriate collaboration partners, and make sure that relationships between supply chains and sales groups are maintained. They also need to stick with it long enough to reap the benefits.[47]

MANAGING THE SUPPLY CHAIN

Good relationships between businesses require careful management of the **supply chain,** sometimes called the *value chain*, which is the entire sequence of suppliers that contribute to the creation and delivery of a product. This process affects both upstream relationships between the company and its suppliers and downstream relationships with the product's end users. The supply chain is discussed in greater detail in Chapter 13.

supply chain Sequence of suppliers that contribute to the creation and delivery of a good or service.

Effective supply-chain management can provide an important competitive advantage for a business marketer that results in the following:

- increased innovation
- decreased costs
- improved conflict resolution within the chain
- improved communication and involvement among members of the chain

By coordinating operations with the other companies in the chain, boosting quality, and improving its operating systems, a firm can improve speed and efficiency. Because companies spend considerable resources on goods and services from outside suppliers, cooperative relationships can pay off in many ways. Ariba, whose promotional message appears in Figure 10.11, offers companies a variety of strategies for managing the supply chain.

BUSINESS-TO-BUSINESS ALLIANCES

Strategic alliances are the ultimate expression of relationship marketing. A **strategic alliance** is a partnership formed to create a competitive advantage. These more formal long-term partnership arrangements improve each partner's supply-chain relationships and enhance flexibility in operating in today's complex and rapidly changing marketplace. The size and location of strategic partners are not important. Strategic alliances include businesses of all sizes, of all kinds, and in many locations; it is what each partner can offer the other that is important.

Companies can structure strategic alliances in two ways. Alliance partners can establish a new business unit in which each takes an ownership position. In such a joint venture, one partner might own 40 percent, while the other owns 60 percent. Alternatively, the partners may decide to form a cooperative relationship that is less formal and does not involve ownership—for example, a joint new-product design team. The cooperative alliance can operate more flexibly and can change more easily as

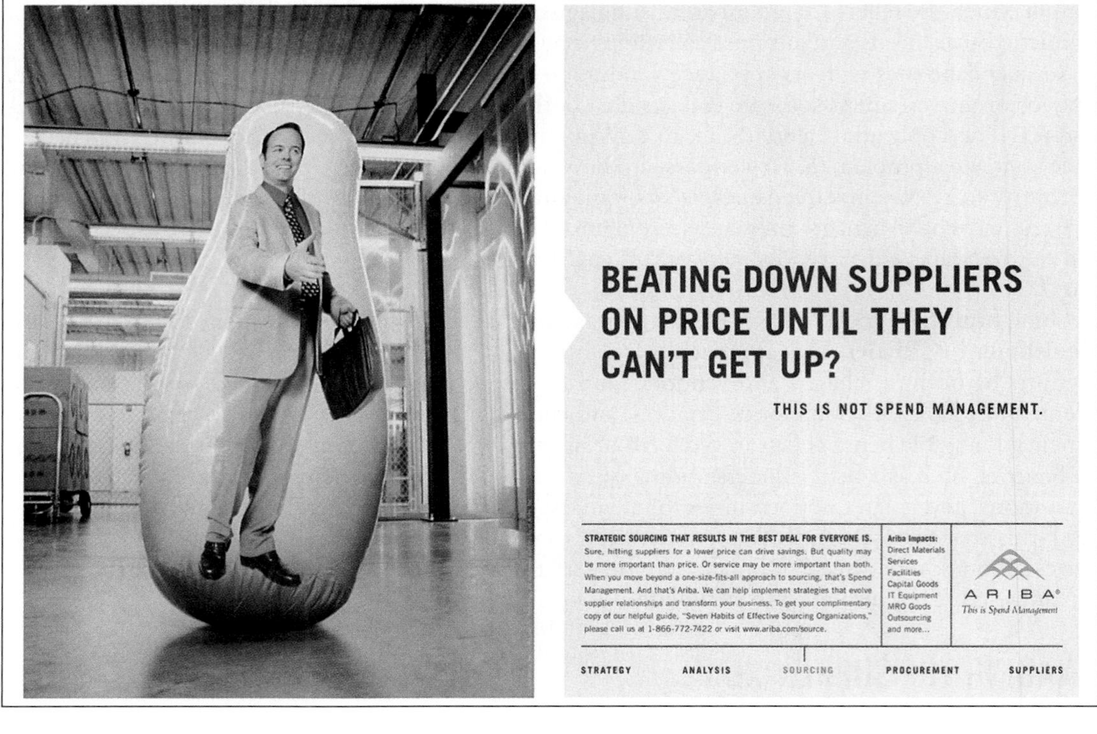

figure 10.11

The Importance of Managing the Supply Chain

table 10.3 ***Resources and Skills That Partners Contribute to Strategic Alliances***

RESOURCES		SKILLS
Patents	Customer base	Marketing skills
Product lines	Marketing resources	• Innovation and product development
Brand equity	• Marketing infrastructure	• Positioning and segmentation
Reputation	• Sales force size	• Advertising and sales promotion
• For product quality	Established relationship with:	Manufacturing skills
• For customer service	• Suppliers	• Miniaturization
• For product innovation	• Marketing intermediaries	• Low-cost manufacturing
Image	• End-use customers	• Flexible manufacturing
• Companywide	Manufacturing resources	Planning and implementation skills
• Business unit	• Location	R&D skills
• Product line/brand	• Size, scale economies, scope economies, excess capacity, newness of plant and equipment	Organizational expertise, producer learning, and experience effects
Knowledge of product-market		
	Information technology and systems	

Source: Adapted from P. Rajan Varadarajan and Margaret H. Cunningham, "Strategic Alliances: A Synthesis of Conceptual Foundations," *Journal of the Academy of Marketing Science,* Fall 1995, p. 292.

market forces or other conditions dictate. In either arrangement, the partners agree in advance on the skills and resources, such as those listed in Table 10.3, that each will bring into the alliance to achieve their mutual objectives and gain a competitive advantage.

Companies form many types of strategic alliances. Some create horizontal alliances between firms at the same level in the supply chain; others define vertical links between firms at adjacent stages. The firms may serve the same or different industries. Alliances can involve cooperation among rivals who are market leaders or between a market leader and a follower.

Strategic alliances can also be domestic or international. SkyTeam is an international airline network that includes Delta Airlines, Aeromexico, Alitalia, Air France, CSA Czech Airlines, and Korean Air. A recent global advertising campaign, "Caring Hands," is built around the consumer and focuses on amenities offered to passengers.[48]

1. **Name three technologies businesses can use to improve buyer–seller relationships in B2B markets.**
2. **What are the benefits of effective supply-chain management?**

EVALUATING CUSTOMER RELATIONSHIP PROGRAMS

9 **Identify and evaluate the most common measurement and evaluation techniques within a relationship marketing program.**

One of the most important measures of relationship marketing programs, whether in consumer or business-to-business markets, is the **lifetime value of a customer.** This can be defined as the revenues and intangible benefits such as referrals and customer feedback that a customer brings to the seller over an average lifetime, less the amount the company must spend to acquire, market to, and serve the customer. Long-term customers are usually more valuable assets than new ones because they buy more, cost less to serve, refer other customers, and provide valuable feedback. The "average lifetime" of a customer relationship depends on industry and product characteristics. Customer lifetime for a consumer product like microwave pizza may be very short, while that for an automobile or computer will last longer.

lifetime value of a customer Revenues and intangible benefits, such as referrals and customer feedback, that a customer brings to the seller over an average lifetime, less the amount the company must spend to acquire, market to, and service the customer.

For a simple example of a lifetime value calculation, assume that a Chinese takeout restaurant determines that its average customer buys dinner twice a month at an average cost of $25 per order over a lifetime of five years. That business translates this calculation to revenues of $600 per year and $3,000 for five years. The restaurant can calculate and subtract its average costs for food, labor, and overhead to arrive at the per-customer profit. This figure serves as a baseline against which to measure strategies to increase the restaurant's sales volume, customer retention, or customer referral rate.

Another approach is to calculate the payback from a customer relationship, or the length of time it takes to break even on customer acquisition costs. Assume that an Internet service provider spends $75 per new customer on direct mail and enrollment incentives. Based on average revenues per subscriber, the company takes about three months to recover that $75. If an average customer stays with the service 32 months and generates $800 in revenues, the rate of return is nearly 11 times the original investment. Once the customer stays past the payback period, the provider should make a profit on that business.

In addition to lifetime value analysis and payback, companies use many other techniques to evaluate relationship programs, including:

- tracking rebate requests, coupon redemption, credit-card purchases, and product registrations
- monitoring complaints and returned merchandise and analyzing why customers leave
- reviewing reply cards, comment forms, and surveys
- monitoring "click-through" behavior on Web sites to identify why customers stay and why they leave

These tools give the organization information about customer priorities so that managers can make changes to their systems, if necessary, and set appropriate, measurable goals for relationship programs.

A hotel chain may set a goal of improving the rate of repeat visits from 44 to 52 percent. A mail-order company may want to reduce time from 48 to 24 hours to process and mail orders. If a customer survey reveals late flight arrivals as the No. 1 complaint of an airline's passengers, the airline might set an objective of increasing the number of on-time arrivals from 87 to 93 percent.

Companies large and small are able to implement technology to aid in measuring the value of customers and the return on investment from expenditures developing customer relationships. They are able to choose from among a growing number of software products, many of which are tailored to specific industries or flexible enough to suit companies of varying sizes.

MARKETING
Concept Check

1. **Define the term *lifetime value of a customer.***
2. **Why are customer complaints valuable to evaluating customer relationship programs?**

Strategic Implications of Marketing in the 21st Century

A FOCUS on relationship marketing helps companies create better ways to communicate with customers and develop long-term relationships. This focus challenges managers to develop strategies that closely integrate customer service, quality, and marketing functions. By leveraging technology—both through database marketing and through customer relationship management applications—companies can compare the costs of acquiring and maintaining customer relationships with the profits received from these customers. This information allows managers to evaluate the potential returns from investing in relationship marketing programs.

Relationships include doing business with consumers as well as partners, such as vendors, suppliers, and other companies. Partners can structure relationships in many different ways to improve performance, and these choices vary for consumer and business markets. In all marketing relationships, it is important to build shared trust. For long-term customer satisfaction and success, marketers must make—and keep—their promises.

REVIEW OF CHAPTER OBJECTIVES

① Contrast transaction-based marketing with relationship marketing.

Transaction-based marketing refers to buyer–seller exchanges characterized by limited communications and little or no ongoing relationships between the parties. Relationship marketing is the development and maintenance of long-term, cost-effective relationships with individual customers, suppliers, employees, and other partners for mutual benefit.

1.1. Describe the benefits of relationship marketing.

② Identify and explain the four basic elements of relationship marketing as well as the importance of internal marketing.

The four basic elements are database technology, database marketing, monitoring relationships, and customer relationship management (CRM). Database technology helps identify current and potential customers. Database marketing analyzes the information provided by the database. Through relationship marketing, a firm monitors each relationship. With CRM, the firm orients every part of the organization toward building a unique company with an unbreakable bond with customers. Internal marketing involves activities within the company designed to assist all employees toward meeting their roles in the marketing strategy.

2.1. How does database technology help firms build relationships with customers?
2.2. What types of factors might the firm monitor in its relationships?

③ Identify each of the three levels of the relationship marketing continuum.

The three levels of the relationship marketing continuum are: (1) focus on price, (2) social interaction, and (3) interdependent partnership. At the first level, marketers use financial incentives to attract customers. At the second level, marketers engage in social interaction with buyers. At the third level, buyers and sellers become true business partners.

3.1. Give an example of a marketing relationship at the first level.
3.2. Describe a type of social interaction at the second level.

4 Explain how firms can enhance customer satisfaction and how they build buyer–seller relationships.

Marketers monitor customer satisfaction through various methods of marketing research. They look to understand what customers want—including what they expect—from goods or services. They also obtain customer feedback through means such as toll-free numbers and Web sites. Then they use this information to improve. Firms build buyer–seller relationships through frequency marketing programs, affinity marketing, database marketing, and one-to-one marketing.

4.1. What is an affinity marketing program?
4.2. What is an application service provider (ASP)? How does it work?

5 Discuss how marketers use grassroots and viral marketing in their one-to-one marketing efforts.

One-to-one marketing is a marketing program that is customized to build long-term relationships with customers—one at a time. Grassroots marketing involves connecting directly with existing and potential customers through nonmainstream channels, often characterized by small budgets and lots of legwork. In viral marketing, marketers let satisfied customers pass information directly to other consumers.

5.1. Distinguish between grassroots marketing and viral marketing.
5.2. How do grassroots and viral marketing support an overall one-to-one marketing approach?

6 Explain customer relationship management (CRM) and the role of technology in building customer relationships.

Customer relationship management is the combination of strategies and technologies that empowers relationship programs, reorienting the entire organization to a concentrated focus on satisfying customers. Made possible by technological advances, it leverages technology as a means to manage customer relationships and to integrate all stakeholders into a company's product design and development, manufacturing, marketing, sales, and customer service processes. CRM allows firms to manage vast amounts of data from multiple sources to improve overall customer satisfaction. The most effective companies approach CRM as a complete business strategy in which people, processes, and technology are all organized around delivering superior value to customers. A recent outgrowth of CRM is virtual relationships, in which buyers and sellers rarely, if ever, meet face-to-face.

6.1. Describe at least four qualities of a successful CRM system.
6.2. Describe the potential problems with CRM.
6.3. Explain how marketers manage virtual relationships.

7 Describe the buyer–seller relationship in business-to-business marketing, and identify the four different types of business partnerships.

By developing buyer–seller relationships, companies work together for their mutual benefit. Advantages may include lower prices for supplies, faster delivery of inventory, improved quality or reliability, customized product features, or more favorable financing terms. The four different types of business partnerships are buyer, seller, internal, and lateral. Regardless of the type of partnership, partners usually share similar values and goals that help the alliance endure over time. Two other types of business marketing relationships include cobranding and comarketing.

7.1. Describe each of the four types of business partnerships.
7.2. Give an example of cobranding and comarketing.

8 Describe how business-to-business marketing incorporates national account selling, electronic data interchange, vendor-managed inventories, CPFaR, managing the supply chain, and creating alliances.

National account selling assists firms in forming a strong commitment with key buyers, resulting in improvements in efficiency and effectiveness for both parties. The use of electronic data interchanges allows firms to reduce costs and improve efficiency and competitiveness. Vendor-managed inventory (VMI) is a system in which sellers can automatically restock to previously requested levels. The collaborative planning, forecasting, and replenishment (CPFaR) approach bases plans and forecasts on collaborative seller–vendor efforts. Managing the supply chain provides increased innovation, decreased costs, conflict resolution, and improved communications. Strategic alliances can help both partners gain a competitive advantage in the marketplace.

8.1. What is the difference between VMI and CPFaR? What are the advantages of each?
8.2. Why is it important for a firm to manage the relationships along its supply chain?
8.3. What is the most important factor in a strategic alliance?

(9) Identify and evaluate the most common measurement and evaluation techniques within a relationship marketing program.

The effectiveness of relationship marketing programs can be measured using several methods. In the lifetime value of a customer, the revenues and intangible benefits that a customer brings to the seller over an average lifetime, less the amount the company must spend to acquire, market to, and service the customer, are calculated. With this method, a company may determine its costs to service each customer and develop ways to increase profitability. The payback method calculates how long it takes to break even on customer acquisition costs. Other measurements include tracking rebates, coupons, and credit-card purchases; monitoring complaints and returns; and reviewing reply cards, comment forms, and surveys. These tools give the organization information about customer priorities so managers can make changes to their systems and set measurable goals.

9.1. Explain how a firm goes about evaluating the lifetime value of a customer.

MARKETING TERMS YOU NEED TO KNOW

transaction-based marketing 318
relationship marketing 318
internal marketing 320
frequency marketing 326
affinity marketing 326
database marketing 327
one-to-one marketing 328
customer relationship management (CRM) 329
partnership 332
cobranding 333
comarketing 334
electronic data interchange (EDI) 335
vendor-managed inventory (VMI) 336
supply chain 337
lifetime value of a customer 339

OTHER IMPORTANT MARKETING TERMS

external customer 320
internal customer 320
employee satisfaction 321
customer satisfaction 324
interactive television 327
application service providers (ASPs) 328
grassroots marketing 329
viral marketing 329
virtual relationships 331
customer winback 331
business-to-business marketing 332
buyer partnership 333
seller partnership 333
internal partnership 333
lateral partnership 333
national account selling 335
quick-response merchandising 336
collaborative planning, forecasting, and replenishment (CPFaR) 337
strategic alliance 337

PROJECTS AND TEAMWORK EXERCISES

1. With a teammate, choose one of the following companies. Create a plan to attract customers at the first level of the relationship marketing continuum—price—and move them to the next level with social interactions. Present your plan to the class.
   a. amusement or theme park
   b. health spa
   c. manufacturer of surfboards or snowmobiles
   d. manufacturer of cell phones
2. By yourself or with a classmate, ask a local business if you can design a brief survey to obtain customer feedback about the business. Then hand out the survey at the business location. Be sure to keep your survey short and to the point, so it can be completed quickly and easily.
3. With a teammate, select a business with which you are familiar and design a frequency marketing program for the firm.

4. With a teammate, design a grassroots or viral marketing campaign for the company you selected in project 3. Present your campaign to the class.
5. A hotel chain's database has information on guests that includes demographics, number of visits, and room preferences. Describe how the chain can use this information to develop several relationship marketing programs. How can it use a more general database to identify potential customers and to personalize its communications with them?
6. Select a local business enterprise. Find out as much as you can about its customer base, marketing strategies, and internal functions. Consider whether a customer relationship management focus would help the enterprise's competitive position. Argue your position in class.
7. Choose one of the following businesses and create a plan describing how you would manage virtual relationships in this business. Explain why you think you would be successful.
   a. online travel agency
   b. data storage service
   c. insurance agency
   d. firm that ships lobsters and other seafood around the country
8. Suppose you and a classmate were hired by a local independent bookstore to help its owner win back customers lost to a large bookstore chain. Design a plan to win back the store's lost customers and rebuild those relationships. Present your plan in class.
9. Choose a company that makes great stuff—something you really like, whether it is designer handbags, electronics equipment, the tastiest ice cream flavors, or the best jeans. Now, come up with a partner for your firm that you think would make a terrific strategic alliance. Write a plan for your alliance, explaining why you made the choice, what you want the two firms to accomplish, and why you think the alliance will be successful.
10. With a teammate, interview a local business owner to find out what methods he or she uses to evaluate customer relationships. You might discover that the businessperson uses very systematic techniques or perhaps just talks to customers. Either way, you will learn something valuable. Discuss your findings in class.

APPLYING CHAPTER CONCEPTS

1. Suppose you were asked to be a marketing consultant for a restaurant that specializes in a regional cuisine, such as Tex-Mex, Cuban specialties, New England clambake, or the like. The owner is concerned about employee satisfaction. When you visit the restaurant, what clues would you look for to determine employee satisfaction? What questions might you ask employees?
2. What types of social interaction might be appropriate—and effective—for a local bank to engage in with its customers?
3. What steps might a music retailer take to win back its lost customers?
4. Explain why a large firm like General Mills might use national account selling to strengthen its relationship with a chain of supermarkets in the Midwest.
5. Why is it important for a company to calculate the lifetime value of a customer?

ETHICS EXERCISE

Suppose you work for a firm that sells home appliances such as refrigerators, microwaves, and clothes washers and dryers. Your company has been slowly losing customers, but no one seems to know why. Employee morale is sliding as well. You believe that the company is run by honest, dedicated owners who want to please their customers. One day, you overhear an employee quietly advising a potential customer to shop at another store. You realize that your firm's biggest problem may be lack of employee satisfaction—which is leading to external customer loss.

1. Would you approach the employee to discuss the problem?
2. Would you ask the employee why he or she is turning customers away?
3. What steps do you think your employer could take to turn the situation around?

'netWork EXERCISES

1. **Customer relationship management software.** GoldMine is one of several customer relationship management (CRM) software products currently available. Visit the GoldMine Web site (**http://www.frontrange.com/goldmine/**). Review three of the case studies listed on the Web site. How did each of these organizations use CRM software to build and maintain customer relationships?
2. **Loyalty marketing programs.** Airlines, hotel chains, and rental car companies were among the first to introduce loyalty marketing programs that are designed to reward frequent customers. Customer loyalty programs have since expanded to a wide variety of other companies. Visit the Web sites of several retailers such as Amazon.com (**http://www.amazon.com**), L.L. Bean (**http://www.llbean.com**), and Williams-Sonoma (**http://www.williams-sonoma.com**). In what ways do these companies attempt to reward frequent customers?
3. **Relationship marketing.** You've probably heard of Swiffer®, a brand of cleaning products. Visit the Swiffer® product Web site (**http://www.swiffer.com**) and identify five ways in which the brand's marketers have applied the principles of relationship marketing discussed in the chapter.

Note: Internet Web addresses change frequently. If you don't find the exact sites listed, you may need to access the organization's or company's home page and search from there or use a search engine such as Google.

INFOTRAC CITATIONS AND EXERCISES

Record: A113985335
Plastic That Pays Back: Reward cards help you spend more at your favorite stores. Should you bite? *Barbara Kiviat.*
Time, March 15, 2004 v163 i11 p94

Abstract: Credit-card issuers, aware that consumers are more attracted to favorite brands than to them, have come up with a strategy to help bridge the loyalty gap. Knowing that consumers consistently flock to brands such as Avon, Barnes & Noble, and Amazon, card companies now offer credit cards that entice customers by giving them payback rewards to spend on preferred brands such as Starbucks, Gap, and Delta Air.

1. Why do marketers feel the need to create incentive programs that award special benefits and perks to customers for using a product?
2. Read the article and explain how cobranded credit cards can offer greater benefits to consumers. Would you be more likely to use a cobranded credit card instead of a regular one? Why or why not?
3. How do credit-card companies benefit from offering special rewards bonuses to customers, and why might customers need to exercise caution with these cards?

CASE 10.1 Hilton Is OnQ with Customers

Information is power. It can help marketers understand their customers, meet their needs, and even anticipate future needs. It can help firms communicate better with suppliers and partners. And it can help organizations manage their customer relationships. Technology like Hilton Hotels' new OnQ system is designed to provide marketers with the information they need to gain an edge over the competition and create loyal customers.

Hilton Hotels is a big company. The firm owns several well-known, branded hotel chains in addition to the Hilton brand—Hampton Inn, Homewood Suites by Hilton, Embassy Suites, Hilton Garden Inn, and Conrad. Some of these hotels cater to business travelers, others to leisure travelers. In all, there are 2,100 hotels, 1,700 of which are franchises. Communication among all of these enterprises is key to creating a unified marketing message. OnQ is technology that integrates several major business functions—property management, reservations, customer relationship management (CRM), and back-office systems such as accounting and purchasing. "We believe having consistent technology across all brands and key customer touch points is the essential ingredient necessary to establish guest satisfaction and loyalty within our family of hotel brands," explains Tim Harvey, Hilton's chief information officer.

OnQ is so sophisticated it is actually simple. The system creates a database of information about customers that is consistent throughout the organization, which includes 200,000 employees at call centers and hotels. It also supports the HHonors loyalty program—a frequency marketing program that has 16 million customer members. Because all of the data are compiled and streamlined in a single program, staffers such as customer service representatives or front-desk personnel can retrieve the information they need rapidly to help customers on the spot. It also individualizes the experience for customers. "CRM for us means the customer really matters," says Harvey. "We want people in our organization to realize that what is important is to treat customers consistently, one customer at a time, 365 days a year, no matter where we touch them. We want to enable our employees to delight guests." So a business customer who happens to be traveling with his or her family during the weekend gets the same treatment in either circumstance—at any one of the Hilton hotels.

OnQ also helps Hilton marketers tailor marketing messages to certain segments of their guest population. But Harvey emphasizes that the true purpose of OnQ is to serve customers. "Marketing and upselling programs are in the scheme of things," he explains, "but companies tend to get too enamored with this type of software and neglect the basics. What's important to us is that we make a difference in guest service and really give customers what they want."

Finally, there is the issue of promises made, promises kept, and trust. OnQ helps Hilton make and keep its promises to customers, building trust over the long term. "There's a certain level of trust between Hilton and our customers," says Harvey. "And this system gives us the ability to consistently provide the type of service that earns a customer's trust."

Questions for Critical Thinking

1. How might OnQ promote internal marketing throughout the Hilton organization?
2. Identify three specific ways Hilton staff could use OnQ to enhance customer service and enhance customer satisfaction.

Sources: "Hilton Hotels Corp. Takes Lead with OnQ," *Hotels Magazine,* August 2003, **http://www.hotelsmag.com**; Esther Shein, "Hilton Hotels CIO Talks OnQ," *CIO Update,* July 15, 2003, **http://www.cioupdate.com**; Reid A. Paul, "Hilton Is OnQ," *Hospitality Technology Magazine,* June 2003, **http://www.htmagazine.com**; Martin Schneider, "Eight Brands, One Customer," *Destination CRM,* May 9, 2003, **http://www.destinationcrm.com**.

VIDEO CASE 10.2 International Flavors & Fragrances Makes Marketing Personal

The written case on International Flavors & Fragrances appears on page VC-12. The recently filmed International Flavors & Fragrances video is designed to expand and highlight the concepts in this chapter and the concepts and questions covered in the written video case.

Talking about Marketing Careers with Michael McCullough, Executive Vice President and Chief Marketing Officer of the Miami Heat

EXCITEMENT filled the air as we arrived at Miami Heat headquarters to meet with Michael McCullough, the NBA team's executive vice president and chief marketing officer. A blockbuster trade had just been announced that landed superstar Shaquille O'Neal in Miami. The "Shaq Attack" was returning to the Sunshine State.

Head coach Stan Van Gundy and his staff were already at work revising their plans for the new season to exploit the strengths of O'Neal's massive 7'1", 300-plus-pound presence. An obvious possibility is to throw the ball into the low post to O'Neal, who is always double-teamed, and who can then shoot or dish the ball off to his teammates for open shots. As Van Gundy points out, "We've gone from being totally a perimeter team . . . that ran a lot of pick-and-rolls and brought guys off screens . . . to now having a primarily post-up team, so there has been a lot of change in terms of our system."

The front office was equally busy in revising their marketing and other business plans to capitalize on Shaq's presence.

BOONE & KURTZ: The Heat's big news of late is the "man in black," Shaquille O'Neal. How does the addition of this high-profile celebrity and outstanding athlete affect this year's marketing plans?

Our marketing plan "before Shaq" was a sales-driven model. We concentrated mostly on ticket sales. But the first rumors about Shaq made the phones really start ringing, and once it was official the phones exploded. Ticket sales have been phenomenal; we've sold more season tickets than ever before. Because of this sellout situation our focus has changed from sales to renewal, retention, and service. We've been able to redirect sales and advertising and beef up communications with season-ticket holders, especially first-time season-ticket holders. We want to treat everyone as a brand-new ticket holder and ensure that they are always reminded of the value

MICHAEL MCCULLOUGH, EXECUTIVE VICE PRESIDENT AND CHIEF MARKETING OFFICER OF THE MIAMI HEAT

PHOTO: COURTESY OF MICHAEL MCCULLOUGH

of holding those tickets. Now our ads are more about the brand and selling merchandise, the Web site, and enhancing the experience.

Shaq is his own entity, and having him as a presence on the team adds another layer to the checks and balances we go through with ads, graphics, etc. We have to communicate with Shaq's people; when you have someone of that caliber, there are extra steps you have to go through.

BOONE & KURTZ: Tell us a little about your background and how your sports marketing career began.

I was a college basketball player for Utah State University on a basketball scholarship. I majored in political science with a business minor, and, after college, I spent four years working in retail management and buying. I worked at a department store, going through the long training program. I was still playing pretty competitive ball on a part-time basis. That's how I met an executive for the NBA's Sacramento Kings, who said he might have a position in promotions/marketing/sales. With the Kings, I did a little bit of everything. I must have been doing a good job, though, because within a few months I was promoted to director of broadcasting. From there I went on to work for the NBA league office as a broadcasting coordinator. At that time the NBA had only 27 teams, and I worked with each of the teams on their local broadcasts and also with NBC and TNT on the nationally televised games.

Later on, I was contacted by the new owners of the Kings to come back as vice president of marketing and broadcasting, which I did for some time. I was in charge of sponsorships, marketing, and promotion—everything but finance and trading players. Then a headhunter contacted me about a position with the Miami Heat, which ultimately resulted in the position I currently hold. My current position is fairly similar to my previous job in Sacramento, but now I'm not responsible for ticket sales. My work deals with all the aspects of the game experience that touch the public. We're the front line between the Heat and the public: the public face of the franchise.

The best thing about sports is that people are passionate, whether it's good or bad. You can always strike up a conversation. As a marketer you get to find out what people think of your product. You can really gauge the public pulse just by wearing a Miami Heat T-shirt. Other fields just don't have that.

BOONE & KURTZ: Describe a typical day in the life of the Heat's chief marketing officer.

There's really no such thing as a typical day. No two days are the same because of all the different areas I am in charge of. I have a lot of phone calls each day, and then there are meetings, both scheduled and impromptu. We are always brainstorming or finalizing or changing a project. Today I reviewed a movie trailer with our ad agency, and then dealt with some employee issues. Then we went over some graphics for a mailing to season-ticket holders and began work on the season-ticket renewal program. The season hasn't even started yet, and we are already working on the following year. My days really vary; tomorrow will be different from today, but that's the good part about this job.

BOONE & KURTZ: Miami is one of the most bilingual cities in the United States. How do the Heat's marketing strategies address this duality?

The Hispanic community is a big part of what we do here. We're really focused on reaching them and ingratiating ourselves with them, letting these folks know they are important to us before expecting them to commit money to our product. Before we ran any advertising directed to the Hispanic community, we had players participate in philanthropic efforts in that community so they could see how involved the team is. Most things we do, we do in both English and Spanish. We have Spanish-language radio broadcasts and are currently pursuing Spanish TV broadcasts of the games. We've found that the majority of Spanish speakers want to get their sports information in English, but we still provide it in Spanish as well. The Spanish media is involved in everything we do; they're at our events and get copies of our press releases. We're very dialed into the Hispanic community, which used to be mostly Cuban in South Florida but now is expanding to include other Latin American groups and others.

Although we do not have any Spanish-speaking players on the team, many of our staff are bilingual: broadcasters, Heat Dancers, the Xtreme Team (our gymnastics/dunking team). They can carry the message in Spanish. Also, DJs for the FM radio stations in the area speak Spanglish, a combination of English and Spanish. You might hear a Spanish-language song and then a Nelly song. Our players can go on radio shows and speak English to the DJs and still be understood. They can mingle with the Hispanic community in that way. We also have a Chinese player, Wang Zhizhi, and we've utilized him to engage the Asian community, which is small in South Florida but growing.

BOONE & KURTZ: Miami is such a dynamic, culturally diverse city that draws tourists from the world. But the attractions—more than in any NBA city other than, possibly, L.A. and New York—also compete with sporting events for the visitor's time and dollars. After all, the Miami resident—or visitor—has so many choices, ranging from hanging at the beach and clubbing to deep-sea fishing and shopping. Do your marketing plans address means of encouraging visitors to include a night with the Heat as part of their vacation?

Miami is the 17th-largest media market in the country, but it's something like the second smallest market to have all four professional sports teams: baseball, basketball, football, and hockey. In addition, we also have the University of Miami football team, which around here is viewed basically as a professional sport. In addition to the sports competition, we have a major competitive strength in the form of beautiful weather during the winter. Because of our location, we get a lot of celebrities at our games. We always try to get them on camera and talk to them during the game; it really enhances the experience of seeing a game when you get to see P. Diddy or Jennifer Lopez at the same game. People want to see celebs and have a taste of the nightlife, and we try to cater to this excitement.

BOONE & KURTZ: By now, our readers have recognized that a great way of getting their foot in the door career-wise would be to complete an internship with an organization like the Heat. But they also realize that you must receive hundreds of internship applications every year. What advice would you give our readers about how to increase the chances that their application will receive serious consideration?

Like most sports teams, we live on interns. A lot of our team members started as interns. Our interns really do a lot; there are no coffee-making interns here.

A good intern is willing to do almost anything. In today's world, marketers need to be well rounded, so I suggest that students take what they can get, even if it's in an unrelated field. If there's a team or industry or sport you're interested in, take the position that's available. I really encourage interns to just make themselves available.

As an intern, meet as many people as possible. Make the most of it: Come in early, stay late. And make sure that you do what you're assigned to do very well. Impress people! You don't have to spend your career there, and it may not be for you, but you'll be getting a wide range of experience. And what you do for one team is pretty transferable.

Does MLS Need a Superhero?

What will it take to make Americans finally fall in love with soccer and make all Major League Soccer's dreams come true? Could it be an untested teenager from Ghana with the unlikely name of Freddy Adu?

PHOTO: COURTESY OF WIREIMAGES.COM

Adu—like golf's teenage sensation Michelle Wie and the NBA's LeBron James—is the latest in a line of very young sports stars to catch the public eye. Only 14 and a naturalized U.S. citizen when he signed a two-year $1 million total contract to become the highest paid player in the MLS, Adu has been hailed as a gifted player, perhaps with the potential to become the greatest in the world. No less an authority than the legendary Brazilian player Pélé, who himself made his soccer debut at 17, says Adu will be very much in the spotlight as his first few seasons unfold. "Now things will become more difficult," Pélé warned Adu. "People will start looking at you. Coaches will look at you. The crowd will ask for more."

Whether or not Adu will live up to the hype and the promise, maturing into a brilliant competitor, there's little doubt that he is already having a huge impact on how deeply MLS pushes soccer into the American psyche. "Freddy has the potential to bring soccer almost for the first time into the public's consciousness. Soccer in the United States isn't really part of the culture. What it needs, I think, is a superhero, and he clearly could be it," says Nike chairman Phil Knight. (Nike has signed Adu to a $1 million endorsement contract.) And in assessing Adu's first season in the professional ranks, at least one sportswriter noted that "his marketing impact has been significant." In fact, teams that played against Adu's club, DC United, have experienced season attendance highs and even sellouts when he appears. "He's created a buzz in every city he's been to, and here in Chicago it's no exception," said the general manager of the Chicago Fire.

Suzy Christopher, senior director of marketing for the Columbus Crew, was impressed not only by the fact that Adu's appearance resulted in a sold-out stadium but by the number of new fans he attracted. "It was amazing to talk to guests who knew nothing of soccer . . . He received so much publicity that people came to see him . . . It was a wonderful opportunity for guests to sample our product."

Although a world-class player, especially one with a unique story like Adu's, could lure soccer fans of all ages, there's also little doubt that a good part of his appeal at the moment will be among the sport's younger market segment. More than 17 million Americans play soccer, and the vast majority are kids. MLS has been providing them with plenty of opportunities to meet with the eager and personable Adu, to read and hear about him, and to see pictures and interviews. The designated star-to-be adds another layer to MLS's existing strategy for targeting the youth market. That effort includes youth development programs and camps associated with many MLS teams, along with plans for partnerships with youth soccer organizations around the country to form summer camps, training clinics, sponsored competitions, awards and recognition programs, opportunities to meet MLS players, autograph sessions, and special teams and leagues. Some of the new soccer stadiums MLS is building, such as the complex in Frisco, Texas, will include fields and facilities designated for youth soccer.

While Adu's presence can only enhance these existing efforts, there's no magic solution to the problem of capturing the youth market and holding on to it as its members mature. Says DC United's general manager Kevin Payne, "We know we still have to work hard to sell tickets and do all the other things to make this business work, and so do the other teams."

MLS is also working hard at developing relationships with its fans. Through the youth training programs many of its teams operate (which are open to male and female youth players and their coaches), as well as through fan clubs, online team newsletters, an e-mail address for fans to contact the league, and even online team message boards, the league keeps the lines of communication and commitment open. Whether their favorite team is winning or losing, MLS wants soccer fans of all ages to feel like part of the family.

Questions for Critical Thinking

1. Do you think MLS can use Freddy Adu's youth to help target its younger market segment effectively? Why or why not? What are some possible pitfalls of relying on his appeal?
2. Do you think that supporting youth soccer is a good strategy for relationship marketing? Why or why not? How many market segments does this strategy target and which ones are they?
3. What additional strategies can MLS use to appeal to the youth segment of its market?
4. What kind of marketing information should MLS be gathering as it reaches out to the youth market? How can it conduct this marketing research?

Sources: "Youth Soccer," Major League Soccer Web site, http://www.mlsnet.com, accessed August 2, 2004; Lang Whitaker, "You Better Recognize," *Sports Illustrated,* August 2, 2004, http://sportsillustrated.cnn.com; Don Garber, "The State of the League Address," July 30, 2004, http://www.mlsnet.com; Cheryl Holladay, "Major League Soccer Camp under Way at Houghton Lake," *The Houghton Lake Resorter,* July 29, 2004, http://www.houghtonlakeresorter.com; Jerry Lindquist, "Kid Power," *Richmond Times-Dispatch,* July 21, 2004, http://www.timesdispatch.com; Ridge Mahoney, "In MLS Cities, Much Adu about Freddy," *USA Today,* June 9, 2004, p. C8; Ridge Mahoney, "United GM Says Rookie Is Meeting Expectations," *USA Today,* June 9, 2004, p. C8.

part 4

PRODUCT DECISIONS

chapter 11 Product and Service Strategies

chapter 12 Category and Brand Management, Product Identification, and New-Product Development

chapter 11

Product and Service Strategies

chapter objectives

1. Define the term *product* and distinguish between goods and services and how they relate to the goods–services continuum.
2. Explain the importance of the service sector in today's marketplace.
3. List the classifications of consumer goods and services and briefly describe each category.
4. Describe each of the types of business goods and services.
5. Explain how quality is used by marketers as a product strategy.
6. Explain why firms develop lines of related products.
7. Describe the way marketers typically measure product mixes and make product mix decisions.
8. Explain the concept of the product life cycle and identify the different stages.
9. Describe how a firm can extend a product's life cycle.

THE NEW ANGLE ON FISHING

If you think of fishing as something you did from a rowboat at summer camp, from the flimsy dock of a rented cottage, or from the bank of a lazy stream, think again. Fishing is now one of the biggest outdoor sports in the nation—an estimated 44 million Americans participate in recreational fishing. And it is also big business—U.S. anglers buy more than $2 billion in fishing tackle alone each year. BASS, the largest fishing organization in the world, has hooked 600,000 members in its first three decades. It hosts the $6 Million Bassmaster Tournament Trail and the Bassmaster Classic; publishes *Bassmaster Magazine, Guns & Gear Magazine, BASS Times, Bassmaster Tour Magazine*, and *Fishing Tackle Retail Magazine;* produces a weekly TV show; has initiated the "catch-and-release" fish conservation program; and has helped support legislation generating millions of dollars annually for state fisheries. That's just one organization. Then there's the Women's Bass Fishing Association, the American Bass Anglers, and others. Retailers from L.L. Bean to Bass Pro Shops to Cabella's are ready to outfit beginners and advanced fishermen alike with clothing, tackle, boats, and organized trips to the best fishing spots around the world. Today's fishing marketplace is a long way from the kinked line tied to a stick with a red and white bobber floating on the water. Millions of avid anglers are intent on spending their dollars on the quest to reel in the big one.

Meeting the needs of the fishing population requires understanding the target market and developing effective strategies to offer the goods and services that fishing customers want. In addition to offering new products, marketers may look for ways to increase the number of users of existing products. Wal-Mart carries an extensive line of the latest and tried-and-true fishing gear—everything from rods and reels, to trolling motors, to high-tech global positioning system fish finders. Bass Pro Shops, another leader in the retail fishing industry, also offers more than rods and reels. Each of the company's 20 Outdoor World stores offers boats, campers, gear, and clothing for all kinds of outdoor activities, including fishing. It also offers a unique shopping experience that becomes an event. The stores—which take up nearly 300,000 square feet—are popular tourist attractions. They feature their own fishtanks, restaurants, and video arcades. The firm operates its own resort in the Ozarks and offers organized hunting and fishing trips. In this way, Bass Pro Shops create an entire fishing experience for the beginner or the advanced sports person, the amateur or the professional.

JASON SEALOCK, FLW OUTDOORS

The BASS organization surveys its membership to learn more about people who like to fish. One recent survey showed that the average BASS member is 51 years old, attended or graduated from college, has an annual income of $66,000, and spends nearly $2,000 a year on fishing equipment. The greatest number of BASS members live in Texas, Florida, and California. This information helps BASS and related organizations develop goods and services, from lures to tournaments, to satisfy the fishing public. Why do they take fishing so seriously? Because, according to BASS research, the millions of sport fishermen in the U.S. have created a $116 billion sport fishing industry, with $75 billion spent on freshwater fishing alone.

Professional tours are another facet of today's sport fishing, and several organizations arrange events in the U.S. and abroad. The Wal-Mart FLW Tour is a huge draw among sport fishermen. Its tournaments around the U.S. are televised on the Outdoor Life Network, and avid fans can buy DVDs of the events. Working with such companies as Chevrolet, Castrol, Evinrude, and Energizer, the FLW Tour's championship tournament—often called the Super Bowl of fishing—brings together the 48 top bass anglers from the U.S. and Japan. The winner takes home a cool $500,000 out of a total purse of $1.5 million. Competitors travel throughout the southern states in search of big fish and big prizes.

The fishing industry is an excellent example of not-for-profit organizations and commercial firms working together to bring goods and services to consumers. In addition, many of these organizations are customers of each other—advertisers, suppliers, retailers, manufacturers, and service providers. So business-to-business marketing takes place as well. No matter where you live, no matter how old you are, no matter what your household income is, the fishing industry has something to offer you. That's an accomplishment that any industry would like to achieve.[1]

Chapter Overview

WE'VE discussed how marketers conduct research to determine unfilled needs in their markets, how customers behave during the purchasing process, and how firms expand their horizons overseas. Now our attention shifts to a company's **marketing mix,** the blend of four elements of a marketing strategy—product, distribution, promotion, and price—to satisfy the target market. This chapter focuses on how firms select and develop the goods and services they offer, starting with planning which products to offer. The other variables of the marketing mix—distribution channels, promotional plans, and pricing decisions—must accommodate the product strategy selected.

marketing mix Blending of the four strategy elements—product, distribution, promotion, and pricing—to fit the needs and preferences of a specific target market.

Marketers develop strategies to promote both tangible goods and intangible services. Any such strategy begins with investigation, analysis, and selection of a particular target market, and it continues with the creation of a marketing mix designed to satisfy that segment. But while the designs of tangible goods and intangible services both intend to satisfy consumer wants and needs, their marketing efforts may be vastly different.

Briefly Speaking

It has always been my private conviction that any man who pits his intelligence against a fish and loses has it coming.

John Steinbeck (1902–1968)
American novelist

This chapter examines both the similarities and the differences in marketing goods and services. It then presents basic concepts—product classifications, development of product lines, and the product life cycle—that marketers apply in developing successful products. Finally, the chapter discusses product deletion and product mix decisions.

1 **Define the term *product* and distinguish between goods and services and how they relate to the goods–services continuum.**

product Bundle of physical, service, and symbolic attributes designed to satisfy a customer's wants and needs.

WHAT IS A PRODUCT?

At first, you might think of a product as an object you hold in your hand. But that doesn't take into account the idea of a service as a product. Nor does it consider the idea of what the product is used for. So a television is more than a box with a screen and a remote control. It's really a means of providing entertainment—your favorite movies, news programs, or reality shows. Marketers acknowledge this broader conception of product; they realize that people buy *want satisfaction* rather than objects. You might feel a need for a television to satisfy a want for entertainment. You might not know a lot about how the machine itself works, but you understand the results. If you are entertained by watching TV, then your wants are satisfied. If, however, the television is working just fine but you don't like the programming offered, you may need to satisfy your desire for entertainment by changing your cable service or purchasing satellite service. Each of those services is a product.

Marketers think in terms of a product as a compilation of package design and labeling, brand name, price, availability, warranty, reputation, image, and customer-service activities that add value for the customer. Consequently, a **product** is a bundle of physical, service, and symbolic attributes designed to satisfy a customer's wants and needs.

1. **Define the term *product*.**
2. **Why is want satisfaction so important to marketers?**

service Intangible task that satisfies the needs of consumer and business users.

WHAT ARE GOODS AND SERVICES?

Services are intangible products. A general definition identifies **services** as intangible tasks that satisfy the needs of consumer and business users. But you can't hold a service in your hand the way you can

figure 11.1

The Goods–Services Continuum

goods, which are tangible products that customers can see, hear, smell, taste, or touch like the television just described. Most service providers cannot transport or store their products; customers simultaneously buy and consume these products, like haircuts, car repairs, and visits to the dentist. One way to distinguish services from goods is the **goods–services continuum,** as shown in Figure 11.1.

good Tangible product that customers can see, hear, smell, taste, or touch.

This spectrum helps marketers to visualize the differences and similarities between goods and services.[2] A car is a pure good, but the dealer may also offer repair and maintenance services or include the services in the price of a lease. The car falls at the pure good extreme of the continuum because the customer values the repair service less than the car itself. A dinner at an exclusive restaurant is a mix of goods and services because it combines the physical goods of exquisitely prepared food and an extensive selection of wine with the intangible services of experienced wait staff, elegant surroundings, and often a visit to your table by a well-known chef who inquires about your satisfaction with the meal. At the other extreme, a hair styling salon provides the pure services of haircuts and tinting, manicures and pedicures, massages, waxing, as well as airbrush tanning. But it may also sell high-end personal-care products, candles, or aromatherapy products. The salon's customers, though, value the care products less than the quality of the services that improve their appearance.

You can begin to see the diversity of services. Services can be distinguished from goods in several ways:

1. *Services are intangible.* Services do not have physical features that buyers can see, hear, smell, taste, or touch prior to purchase. Service firms essentially ask their customers to buy a promise. In the promotional message in Figure 11.2, Cigna offers customers the promise to take care of them if they become injured.

2. *Services are inseparable from the service providers.* Consumer perceptions of a service provider become their perceptions of the service itself. A spotless house will give you the impression that a house cleaning service is excellent; a dirty house will give a negative impression of the cleaning service.

3. *Services are perishable.* Providers cannot maintain inventories of their services. During times of peak demand, prices may rise, only to fall drastically when demand declines. For instance, hotels often raise room rates during special events and lower them to normal levels when the events are over. Airlines do the same with their peak, shoulder, and off-peak prices on international flights.

4. *Companies cannot easily standardize services.* However, many firms are trying to change this. Most fast-food chains promise that you'll get your meal within a certain number of minutes and that it will taste the way you expect it to. With few exceptions, they also offer the same menu at all their restaurants.

5. *Buyers often play important roles in the creation and distribution of services.* Service transactions frequently require interaction between buyer and seller at the production and distribution

figure 11.2

Cigna: The Promise of Peace of Mind

stages. While some restaurant chains are attempting to standardize to meet customers' expectations, others are striving to customize, involving consumers in decisions about how food is prepared or presented—which is a service in itself. According to the National Restaurant Association, 70 percent of restaurant diners customize their orders.[3]

6. *Service quality shows wide variations.* New York City's posh Le Cirque and your local Pizza Hut are both restaurants. Their customers, however, experience considerably different cuisine, physical surroundings, service standards, and prices.

1. What are the primary differences between goods and services?
2. Give examples of a good and service you have used during the past month.

Keep in mind that a product often blurs the distinction between services and goods. Avis is a service that provides rental cars, which are goods. Lenscrafters provides eye examinations—services from optometrists—while also selling eyeglasses and contact lenses (goods).

2 Explain the importance of the service sector in today's marketplace.

IMPORTANCE OF THE SERVICE SECTOR

You would live a very different life without service firms to fill many needs. You could not place a phone call, log on to the Internet, flip a switch for electricity, or even take a college course if organizations did not provide such services. During an average day, you probably use many services without much thought, but these products play an integral role in your life.

The service sector makes a crucial contribution to the U.S. economy in terms of both products and jobs. Two of *Fortune*'s top 10 most admired U.S. companies are pure service firms—Southwest Airlines and Federal Express. But the other eight firms provide highly regarded services in conjunction with the goods they sell—Wal-Mart, Berkshire Hathaway, General Electric, Dell, Microsoft, Johnson & Johnson, Starbucks, and IBM.[4]

The U.S. service sector now makes up more than two-thirds of the economy; its annual growth rate recently reached a six-year high, compared with much slower growth in nonservice jobs.[5] According to the U.S. Census Bureau, the nearly 16 million people who work in professional and business services alone make up 1 of every 20 U.S. employees and represent more than 1 in 10 of all businesses; none of these figures includes workers in other service industry sectors, which range from health care to construction.[6]

Services also play a crucial role in the international competitiveness of U.S. firms. While the U.S. runs a continuing trade deficit in goods, it has maintained a trade surplus in services for every year since 1970. However, although some economists think that more precise measurements of service exports would reveal an even larger surplus, others worry about the effect of **offshoring** service jobs such as customer-service call centers to developing nations like India. Already, some companies are using the issue of offshoring service as part of their marketing message. E-Loan Inc., an online lender, lets customers choose whether to have their applications processed in India or in the U.S. If they choose the U.S., the application takes longer. That's because Wipro, the Indian firm that provides workers for E-Loan and other companies, has a larger staff. E-Loan believes that allowing its customers the choice makes good, ethical marketing sense.[7]

Observers cite several reasons for the growing importance of services, including consumer desire for speed and convenience and technological advances that allow firms to fulfill this demand. Services that involve wireless communications, data backup and storage, and even meal preparation for busy families are on the rise. Consumers are also looking to advisors to help plan for a financially secure future and insurance to protect their homes and families. The promotional message for American Family Insurance in Figure 11.3 offers consumers the secure feeling that their lives are protected from almost any type of disaster.

Most service firms emphasize marketing as a significant activity for two reasons. First, the growth potential of service transactions represents a vast marketing opportunity. Second, the environment for services is changing. For instance, increased competition is forcing traditional service industries to differentiate themselves from their competitors. Providing superior service is one way to develop long-term customer relationships and compete more effectively. As we discussed earlier, one-to-one and relationship marketing are just two of the ways service firms can develop and solidify their customer relationships.

1. Identify two reasons that services are important to the U.S. economy and business environment.
2. Why do service firms emphasize marketing?

figure 11.3

Property Insurance: An Important Part of the Service Sector

CLASSIFYING GOODS AND SERVICES FOR CONSUMER AND BUSINESS MARKETS

A firm's choices for marketing a good or service depend largely on the offering itself and on the nature of the target market. Product strategies differ for consumer and business markets. **Consumer products** (sometimes called *B2C products*) are those destined for use by ultimate consumers, while business or **B2B products** (also called *industrial* or *organizational products*) contribute directly or indirectly to the output of other products for resale. Marketers further subdivide these two major categories into more specific categories, as discussed in this section.

It is important to note that some products fall into both categories. A case in point is prescription drugs. Traditionally, pharmaceutical companies marketed prescription drugs to doctors, who then made the purchase decision for their patients by writing the prescription. Thus, the medications could be classified as a business product. However, many drug companies now advertise their products in consumer-oriented media, including magazines and television. In fact, in a recent year, pharmaceutical giant Merck spent a whopping $135.5 million on advertising for its anti-inflammatory drug Vioxx, which included TV spots featuring Olympic figure-skating champion Dorothy Hamill.[8] As patients have begun to behave more like customers, they are more likely to take the initiative in requesting prescriptions for certain medications they have seen advertised in the media, such as Nexium, Alavert, and Aricept. As these prescription drugs lose their patents and become over-the-counter medications like Claritin did, they complete the transition to become consumer products.[9]

consumer product
Product destined for use by ultimate consumers.

business-to-business (B2B) product
Product that contributes directly or indirectly to the output of other products for resale; also called industrial or organizational product.

TYPES OF CONSUMER PRODUCTS

The most widely used product classification system focuses on the buyer's perception of a need for the product and his or her buying behavior. However, **unsought products** are marketed to consumers who may not yet recognize any need for them. Examples of unsought products are long-term-care insurance and funeral services. Figure 11.4 takes this classification to another level by suggesting to pet owners that they need veterinary insurance for their pets.

However, relatively few products fall into the unsought category. Most consumers recognize their own needs for various types of consumer purchases and actively seek them, so the customer buying behavior variations are the key to distinguishing the various categories. The most common classification scheme for sought products divides consumer goods and services into three groups based on customers' buying behavior: convenience, shopping, and specialty. Figure 11.5 illustrates samples of these three categories, together with the unsought classification.

3 List the classifications of consumer goods and services and briefly describe each category.

convenience products
Goods and services that consumers want to purchase frequently, immediately, and with minimal effort.

Convenience Products

Convenience products refer to goods and services that consumers want to purchase frequently, immediately, and with minimal effort. Milk, bread, and soft drinks are examples of these products, as are

figure 11.4

An Unsought Product

chewing gum, candy, and most vending-machine items. Convenience services include 24-hour quick-stop stores, walk-in hair salons, copy shops, dry cleaners, and one-hour photo processing.

Marketers further subdivide the convenience category into impulse items, staples, or emergency items. **Impulse goods and services** are purchased on the spur of the moment, such as a visit to a car wash or a pack of gum tossed in at the register. Some marketers have even come up with ways to make impulse shopping on the Internet attractive. Marc Malaga, founder of GiftBaskets.com, a site that provides gift and food baskets, flowers, and other gifts, decided to set up a special Gift Emergency Center on his Web site's home page. Consumers can order such items as a Grand Gourmet Basket, Junk Food Fantasy, or Lovely Lilies by 1:00 P.M. Eastern time Monday through Friday and be assured that they will be delivered the same day. These last-minute items don't come cheap—they range in price from about $40 to $125. But they fulfill an immediate need for both goods and services.[10] Yahoo! has a similar service on its home page. Consumers can order last-minute gifts for Mother's Day, Valentine's Day, or any special occasion. Consumers who might otherwise have accessed another Web site or gone to the store can conveniently click on Yahoo!'s gift site instead.

Staples are convenience goods and services that consumers constantly replenish to maintain a ready inventory; gasoline, toothpaste, and dry cleaning are good examples. Marketers spend many hours and dollars creating messages for consumers about these products, partly because there are so many competitors.

Emergency goods and services are bought in response to unexpected and urgent needs. A snow blower purchased during a snowstorm and a visit to a hospital emergency room to treat a broken ankle

figure 11.5

Classification of Consumer Products

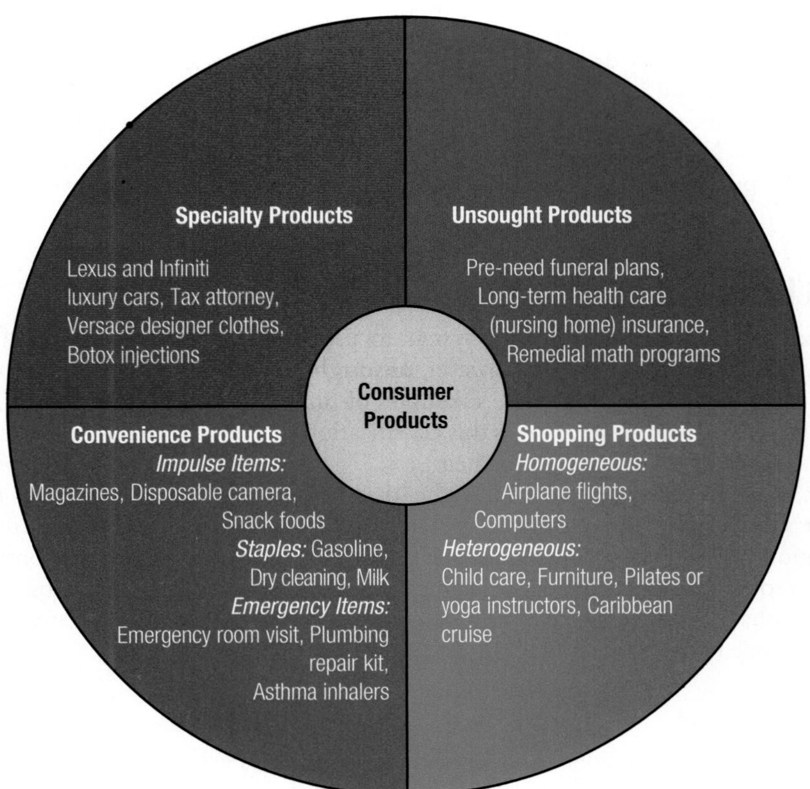

are examples. Depending on your viewpoint, the products offered by Yahoo!'s and Giftbaskets' last-minute gifts could also fall into this category!

Since consumers devote little effort to convenience product purchase decisions, marketers must strive to make these exchanges as simple as possible. Store location can boost a convenience product's visibility. Marketers compete vigorously for prime locations, which can make all the difference between a consumer choosing one gas station, vending machine, or dry cleaner over another.

In addition, location *within* a store can make the difference between success and failure of a product, which is why manufacturers fight so hard for the right spot on supermarket shelves. Typically, the larger and more powerful grocery manufacturers such as Sara Lee, Kellogg, and General Mills get the most visible spots. Kraft Foods has 8 or 10 special displays in many supermarkets. Brands like Miracle Whip, Ritz crackers, Philadelphia cream cheese, Kool-Aid, and Oreo cookies all belong to Kraft—and enjoy prime shelf space. But visibility to consumers comes at a price, often through a practice called **slotting allowances,** or slotting fees, money paid by producers to retailers to guarantee display of their merchandise. According to retailers, the purpose of slotting allowances is to cover their losses if products don't sell. A typical slotting allowance for one product in a single supermarket can run anywhere from $2,300 to $21,770. A nationwide roll-out of a new product can cost a manufacturer as much as $1.5 million to $2 million in slotting fees. The Federal Trade Commission (FTC) estimates that each year more than $9 billion is paid in slotting fees for new products. The high cost of these controversial fees means that it is very difficult for small or local businesses that make products such as salsa, yogurt, and even milk to get their goods on the shelves of large supermarkets, even if consumers want the products. Although the FTC and U.S. General Accounting Office have attempted to end the practice, thus far no significant action has been taken.[11]

Shopping Products

In contrast to the purchase of convenience items, consumers buy **shopping products** only after comparing competing offerings on such characteristics as price, quality, style, and color. Shopping products typically cost more than convenience purchases. This category includes tangible items such as clothing, furniture, and appliances as well as services such as child care, home remodeling, auto repairs, and insurance. The purchaser of a shopping product lacks complete information prior to the buying trip and gathers information during the buying process. Consumers who want to learn more about upscale women's clothier Chico's, shown on the right side of Figure 11.6, can visit a retail store or the company's Web site.

shopping products Products that consumers purchase after comparing competing offerings.

Several important features distinguish shopping products: physical attributes, service attributes such as warranties and after-sale service terms, prices, styling, and places of purchase. A store's name and reputation have considerable influence on people's buying behavior. The personal selling efforts of salespeople also provide important promotional support.

Buyers and marketers treat some shopping products, such as refrigerators and washing machines, as relatively homogeneous products. To the consumer, one brand seems largely the same as another. Marketers may try to differentiate homogeneous products from competing products in several ways. They may emphasize price and value, or they may attempt to educate buyers about less obvious features that contribute to a product's quality, appeal, and uniqueness.

Other shopping products seem heterogeneous because of basic differences among them. Examples include furniture, physical-fitness training, vacations, and clothing. Differences in features often separate competing heterogeneous shopping products in the minds of consumers. Perceptions of style, color, and fit can all affect consumer choices.

Specialty Products

Specialty products offer unique characteristics that cause buyers to prize those particular brands. They typically carry high prices, and many represent well-known brands. Examples of specialty goods include Hermès scarves, Gucci leather goods, Ritz-Carlton resorts, Tiffany jewelry, and Rolls-Royce automobiles. Specialty services include professional services such as financial, legal, and medical services.

specialty products Products that offer unique characteristics that cause buyers to prize those particular brands.

Purchasers of specialty goods and services know exactly what they want—and they are willing to pay accordingly. These buyers begin shopping with complete information, and they refuse to accept substitutes. Because consumers are willing to exert considerable effort to obtain specialty products, pro-

figure 11.6

Examples of a Convenience (Impulse) Product and a Shopping Product

ducers can promote them through relatively few retail locations. In fact, some firms, like Kabana, a designer and maker of exclusive jewelry, as shown in Figure 11.7, intentionally limit the range of retailers that carry their products to add to their cachet.

Both highly personalized service by sales associates and image advertising help marketers promote specialty items. Because these products are available in so few retail outlets, advertisements frequently list their locations or give toll-free telephone numbers that provide customers with this information.

It is important to note that in recent years some makers of specialty products, such as Coach handbags and Donna Karan clothing, have broadened their market by selling some of their goods through company-owned discount outlets. But these stores nearly always carry items from previous years' inventory. The stores attract consumers who want to own specialty items but who cannot or do not wish to pay their high prices.

CLASSIFYING CONSUMER SERVICES

Like tangible goods, services are also classified based on the convenience, shopping, and specialty products categories. But added insights can be gained by examining several factors that are unique to classifying services. Service firms may serve consumer markets, business markets, or both. A firm offering architectural services may design either residential or commercial buildings or both. A cleaning service may clean houses, offices, or both. In addition, services can be classified as equipment based or people based. A car wash is an equipment-based service, whereas a law office is people based. Marketers may ask themselves any of these five questions to help classify certain services:

1. What is the nature of the service?
2. What type of relationship does the service organization have with its customers?
3. How much flexibility is there for customization and judgment on the part of the service provider?
4. Do demand and supply for the service fluctuate?
5. How is the service delivered?[12]

A marketer attempting to classify the activities of a boarding kennel would answer these questions in one way; a marketer evaluating a lawn care service would come up with different answers. For example, customers would bring their pets to the kennel to receive service, while the lawn care staff would travel to customers' homes to provide service. Workers at the kennel are likely to have closer interpersonal relationships with pet owners—and their pets—than lawn care workers, who might not meet their customers at all. A marketer assessing demand for the services of a ski resort or a food concession at the beach is likely to find fluctuations by season. And a dentist has flexibility in making decisions about a patient's care, whereas a delivery service must arrive with a package at the correct destination, on time.

figure 11.7

Diamond Jewelry: A Specialty Product

APPLYING THE CONSUMER PRODUCTS CLASSIFICATION SYSTEM

The three-way classification system of convenience, shopping, and specialty goods and services helps to guide marketers in developing a successful marketing strategy. Buyer behavior patterns differ for the three types of purchases. For example, classifying a new food item as a convenience product leads to insights about marketing needs in branding, promotion, pricing, and distribution decisions. Table 11.1 summarizes the impact of this classification system on the development of an effective marketing mix.

The classification system, however, also poses a few problems. The major obstacle in implementing this system results from the suggestion that all goods and services must fit within one of the three categories. Some fit neatly into one category, but others share characteristics of more than one category.

For example, how would you classify the purchase of a new automobile? Before classifying the expensive good, which is handled by a few exclusive dealers in the area as a specialty product, con-

table 11.1 **Marketing Impact of the Consumer Products Classification System**

	CONVENIENCE PRODUCTS	SHOPPING PRODUCTS	SPECIALTY PRODUCTS
Consumer Factors			
Planning time involved in purchase	Very little	Considerable	Extensive
Purchase frequency	Frequent	Less frequent	Infrequent
Importance of convenient location	Critical	Important	Unimportant
Comparison of price and quality	Very little	Considerable	Very little
Marketing Mix Factors			
Price	Low	Relatively high	High
Importance of seller's image	Unimportant	Very important	Important
Distribution channel length	Long	Relatively short	Very short
Number of sales outlets	Many	Few	Very few; often one per market area
Promotion	Advertising and promotion by producer	Personal selling and advertising by both producer and retailer	Personal selling and advertising by both producer and retailer

sider other characteristics. New car buyers often shop extensively among competing models and dealers before deciding on the best deal. Think of the categorization process in terms of a continuum representing degrees of effort expended by consumers. At one end of the continuum, they casually pick up convenience items; at the other end, they search extensively for specialty products. Shopping products fall between these extremes. In addition, car dealers may offer services, both during and after the sale, that play a big role in the purchase decision. On this continuum, the new car purchase might appear between the categories of shopping and specialty products but closer to specialty products.

A second problem with the classification system emerges because consumers differ in their buying patterns. One person may make an emergency visit to the dentist because of a toothache, while another may extensively compare prices and office hours before selecting a dentist. But one buyer's impulse purchase does not make dental services a convenience item. Marketers classify goods and services by considering the purchase patterns of the majority of buyers.

(4) Describe each of the types of business goods and services.

TYPES OF BUSINESS PRODUCTS

Business buyers are professional customers. Their job duties require rational, cost-effective purchase decisions. For instance, General Mills applies much of the same purchase decision process to buying flour that Pillsbury does.

The classification system for business products emphasizes product uses rather than customer buying behavior. B2B products generally fall into one of six categories for product uses: installations, accessory equipment, component parts and materials, raw materials, supplies, and business services.[13] Figure 11.8 illustrates the six types of business products.

Installations

The specialty products of the business market are called **installations.** This classification includes major capital investments for new factories and heavy machinery and for telecommunications sys-

figure 11.8

Classification of Business Products

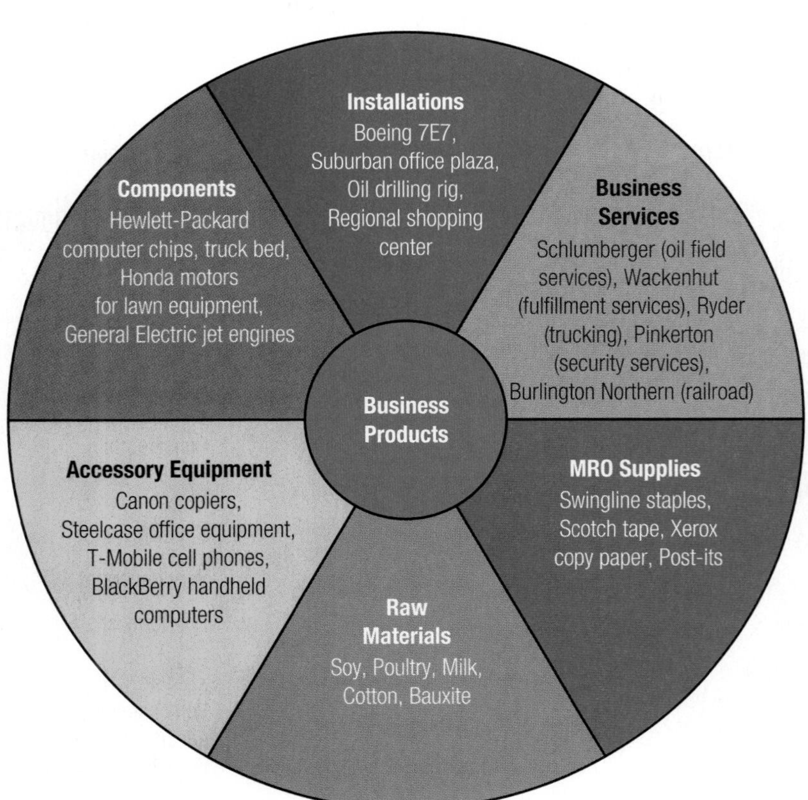

tems. Purchases of new Boeing 7E7 Dreamliner airplanes for All Nippon Airways and locomotives for Burlington Northern are considered installations.

Since installations last for long periods of time and their purchases involve large sums of money, they represent major decisions for organizations. Negotiations often extend over several months and involve numerous decision makers. Vendors often provide technical expertise along with tangible goods. Representatives who sell custom-made equipment work closely with buying firms' engineers and production personnel to design the most satisfactory products possible.

Price typically does not dominate purchase decisions for installations. A purchasing firm buys such a product for its efficiency and performance over its useful life. The firm also wants to minimize breakdowns. Downtime is expensive because the firm must pay employees while they wait for repairs on the machine. Installations are major investments often designed specifically for the purchasers, like the large equipment provided to businesses by United Technologies, illustrated in Figure 11.9.

Training of the buyer's workforce to operate the equipment correctly, along with significant after-sale service, is usually also involved. As a result, marketers of these systems typically focus their promotional efforts on employing highly trained sales representatives, often with technical backgrounds. Advertising, if the firm uses it at all, emphasizes company reputation and directs potential buyers to contact local sales representatives.

Most installations are marketed directly from manufacturers to users. Even a one-time sale may require continuing contacts for regular product servicing. Some manufacturers prefer to lease extremely expensive installations to customers rather than sell the items outright, and they assign personnel directly to the lessees' sites to operate or maintain the equipment.

Accessory Equipment

Only a few decision makers may participate in a purchase of **accessory equipment**—capital items that typically cost less and last for shorter periods than installations. Although quality and service exert important influences on purchases of accessory equipment, price may significantly affect these decisions. Accessory equipment includes products such as power tools, computers, PDAs, and cell phones. Although these products are considered capital investments and buyers depreciate their costs over several years, their useful lives generally are much shorter than those of installations.

Marketing these products requires continuous representation and dealing with the widespread geographic dispersion of purchasers. To cope with these market characteristics, a wholesaler—often called an industrial distributor—might be used to contact potential customers in its own geographic area. Customers usually do not require technical assistance, and a manufacturer of accessory equipment often can distribute its products effectively through wholesalers.

Advertising is an important component in the marketing mix for accessory equipment, as illustrated in Figure 11.10. Sony promotes several cutting-edge technologies in its new notebook PC, including wireless connectivity, sleek design that accommodates Intel's Centrino mobile technology, and the capacity to burn CDs and edit photos.

figure 11.9

Business Installations

figure 11.10

Advertising Accessory Equipment

Component Parts and Materials

Whereas business buyers use installations and accessory equipment in the process of producing their own final products, **component parts and materials** represent finished business products of one producer that become part of the final products of another producer. Milwaukee-based Johnson Controls has supplied automobile seats to car manufacturers for years. Now the company has teamed up with Philips Electronics to deliver in-car DVD entertainment systems. The products made and sold by these two firms become part of the completed autos sold by the auto manufacturers. Some fabricated materials, such as flour, undergo further processing before becoming part of finished products. Textiles, paper pulp, and chemicals are also examples of component parts and materials.

Purchasers of component parts and materials need regular, continuous supplies of uniform-quality products. They generally contract to purchase these items for set periods of time. Marketers commonly emphasize direct sales, and satisfied customers often become regular buyers. Wholesalers sometimes supply fill-in purchases and handle sales to smaller purchasers.

Raw Materials

Farm products, such as beef, cotton, eggs, milk, poultry, and soybeans, and natural products, such as coal, copper, iron ore, and lumber, constitute **raw materials.** These products resemble component parts and materials in that they become part of the buyers' final products.

Most raw materials carry grades determined according to set criteria, assuring purchasers of the receipt of standardized products of uniform quality. As with component parts and materials, vendors commonly market raw materials directly to buying organizations, typically according to contractual terms. Wholesalers are increasingly involved in purchasing raw materials from foreign suppliers.

Price is seldom a deciding factor in a raw materials purchase since the costs are often set at central markets, determining virtually identical transactions among competing sellers. Purchasers buy raw materials from the firms they consider best able to deliver the required quantities and qualities.

Supplies

If installations represent the specialty products of the business market, operating supplies are its convenience products. **Supplies** constitute the regular expenses that a firm incurs in its daily operations. These expenses do not become part of the buyer's final products.

Supplies are also called **MRO items** because they fall into three categories: (1) maintenance items, such as brooms, filters, and lightbulbs; (2) repair items, such as nuts and bolts used in repairing equipment; and (3) operating supplies, such as fax paper, Post-it Notes, and pencils.

A purchasing manager regularly buys operating supplies as a routine job duty. Wholesalers often facilitate sales of supplies due to the low unit prices, the small order size, and the large number of potential buyers. Since supplies are relatively standardized, heavy price competition frequently keeps costs under control. However, a business buyer spends little time making decisions about these products. Exchanges of products frequently demand simple telephone or EDI orders or regular purchases from a sales representative of a local wholesaler.

Business Services

business services Intangible products that firms buy to facilitate their production and operating processes.

The **business services** category includes the intangible products that firms buy to facilitate their production and operating processes. Examples of business services are financial services, leasing and rental services that supply equipment and vehicles, insurance, security, legal advice, and consulting. As mentioned earlier, many service providers sell the same services to both consumers and organizational buyers—telephone, gas, and electric, for example—although service firms may maintain separate marketing groups for the two customer segments.

Organizations also purchase many adjunct services that assist their operations but are not essentially a part of the final product. W.R. Grace purchases Polycom's videoconferencing and collaboration solutions for use in real-time collaboration. According to the promotional message in Figure 11.11, Polycom's system saved W.R. Grace $1.8 million in a single year. Although Polycom's services are not a part of W.R. Grace's final products, they are essential to the firm's operations.

Price may strongly influence purchase decisions for business services. The buying firm must decide whether to purchase a service or provide that service internally. This decision may depend on how frequently the firm needs the service and the specialized knowledge required to provide it.

Purchase decision processes vary considerably for different types of business services. A firm may purchase window-cleaning services through a routine and straightforward process similar to that for buying operating supplies. By contrast, a purchase decision for highly specialized environmental engineering advice requires complex analysis and perhaps lengthy negotiations similar to those for purchases of installations. This variability of the marketing mix for business services and other business products is outlined in Table 11.2.

The buying and selling of business products often involve alliances among different types of firms. As mentioned earlier, Johnson Controls formed a relationship with Philips Electronics to deliver in-car DVD systems. Akamai Technologies has relationships with 750 hardware and software vendors to provide services to its customers.

1. What are the three major classifications of consumer products?
2. Identify three factors marketers should consider in classifying consumer services.
3. What are the six main classifications of business products?

figure 11.11

Collaborative Communications for a Dispersed Workforce: Valuable Productivity Enhancer

table 11.2 ***Marketing Impact of the Business Products Classification System***

FACTOR	INSTALLATIONS	ACCESSORY EQUIPMENT	COMPONENT PARTS AND MATERIALS	RAW MATERIALS	SUPPLIES	BUSINESS SERVICES
Organizational Factors						
Planning time	Extensive	Less extensive	Less extensive	Varies	Very little	Varies
Purchase frequency	Infrequent	More frequent	Frequent	Infrequent	Frequent	Varies
Comparison of price and quality	Quality very important	Quality and price important	Quality important	Quality important	Price important	Varies
Marketing Mix Factors						
Price	High	Relatively high	Low to high	Low to high	Low	Varies
Distribution channel length	Very short	Relatively short	Short	Short	Long	Varies
Promotion method	Personal selling by producer	Advertising	Personal selling	Personal selling	Advertising by producer	Varies

5 Explain how quality is used by marketers as a product strategy.

QUALITY AS A PRODUCT STRATEGY

No matter how a product is classified, nothing is more frustrating to a customer than having a new item break after just a few uses or having it not live up to expectations. The cell phone that hisses static at you unless you stand still or the seam that rips out of your new jacket aren't life-altering experiences, but they do leave an impression of poor quality that likely will lead you to make different purchases in the future. Then there's the issue of service quality—the department store that seems to have no salespeople or the computer help line that leaves you on hold for 20 minutes.

Quality is a key component to a firm's success in a competitive marketplace. The efforts to create and market high-quality goods and services have been referred to as **total quality management (TQM)**. TQM expects all of a firm's employees to continually improve products and work processes with the goal of achieving customer satisfaction and world-class performance. This means that engineers design products that work, marketers develop products that people want, and salespeople deliver on their promises. Managers are responsible for communicating the goals of total quality management to all staff members and for encouraging workers to improve themselves and take pride in their work. Of course, achieving maximum quality is easier said than done, and the process is never complete.

total quality management (TQM) Continuous effort to improve products and work processes with the goal of achieving customer satisfaction and world-class performance.

Fast is fine, but accuracy is everything.

Wyatt Earp (1849–1929)

American lawman, gambler, and gunfighter

WORLDWIDE QUALITY PROGRAMS

Although the movement began in the U.S. in the 1920s as an attempt to improve product quality by improving the manufacturing process, it was during the 1980s that the quality revolution picked up speed in U.S. corporations. The campaign to improve quality found leadership in large manufacturing firms like Ford, Xerox, and Motorola that had lost market share to Japanese competitors. Smaller companies that supplied parts to large firms then began to recognize quality as a requirement for success. Today, commitment to quality has spread to service industries, not-for-profit organizations, government agencies, and educational institutions.

As part of the national quality improvement campaign, Congress established the Malcolm Baldrige National Quality Award in 1987 to recognize excellence in quality management. Named after late Secretary of Commerce Malcolm Baldrige, the award is the highest national recognition for quality that a U.S. company can receive. The award works toward promoting quality awareness, recognizing quality achievements of U.S. companies, and publicizing successful quality strategies.

The quality movement is also strong in European countries. The European Union's **ISO 9002** (formerly ISO 9000) standards define international criteria for quality management and quality assurance. These standards were originally developed by the International Organization for Standardization in Switzerland to ensure consistent quality among products manufactured and sold throughout the nations of the European Union (EU). The standards now include criteria for systems of management as well. Many European companies require suppliers to complete ISO certification, which is a rigorous 14-month process, as a condition of doing business with them. The U.S. member body of ISO is the American National Standards Institute.

BENCHMARKING

Firms often rely on an important tool called **benchmarking** to set performance standards. The purpose of benchmarking is to achieve superior performance that results in a competitive advantage in the marketplace. A typical benchmarking process involves three main activities: identifying manufacturing or business processes that need improvement, comparing internal processes to those of industry leaders, and implementing changes for quality improvement.

Benchmarking requires two types of analyses: internal and external. Before a company can compare itself with another, it must first analyze its own activities to determine strengths and weaknesses. This assessment establishes a baseline for comparison. External analysis involves gathering information about the benchmark partner to find out why the partner is perceived as the industry's best. A comparison of the results of the analysis provides an objective basis for making improvements.

ETIQUETTE TIPS — FOR MARKETING PROFESSIONALS

Telephone Manners: Hello, Goodbye, and in Between

YOU'VE probably never thought about how you answer the phone—it's just second nature. But in business, the way you speak on the phone not only creates an impression for callers but can actually make or break a sale, a deal, or a relationship. So it is important to be aware of how others perceive your phone etiquette. Here are a few tips from the experts to make your telephone conversations proceed smoothly:

1. When you answer the phone, state your name and the name of your firm clearly. Ask how you can help the caller. If you are answering another person's line, state his or her name, then identify yourself.
2. If you are calling someone, state your name and the name of your firm and ask to speak with the person you want to contact. If an assistant offers to take a message, politely leave a brief message indicating the reason for your call.
3. Be an active listener during a phone conversation. The other person can't see you nod your head or smile, so be sure to offer an occasional "I understand" or "Yes" or "Let me see if I can help you." This way, the other person is reassured that you are listening.
4. Toward the end of the call, try to recap the important points such as, "I'll see you at the conference on Friday," or "I will get back to you on Tuesday morning," or "I understand your problem with this product, and I will correct it for you." Even if the conversation has become a bit strained, try to end it on a positive note. Thank the person for his or her time, regardless of who called whom.
5. When you are talking with someone about business matters, be considerate of the other person's time—it is a workday, and he or she probably has many other things to handle. Make your call informative and short without being abrupt or rude.

Telephone etiquette plays a large role in customer service activities as well as other strategies involved in bringing services to the marketplace. A friendly voice, a pleasant attitude, and a willingness to be helpful can go a long way toward cementing marketing relationships over the phone lines.

Sources: "Business Telephone Etiquette for Success," *PageWise,* http://ny.essortment.com/businesstelepho_rtli.htm, accessed April 2, 2004; Marilyn Ledgerwood, "Telephone Etiquette," *PageWise,* http://mt.essortment.com/telephoneetique_rbpa.htm, accessed April 2, 2004; "Telephone Manners," http://www.salary.com/advice/layouthtmls/advl_display_nocat_Ser83_Par176.html, accessed April 2, 2004.

QUALITY OF SERVICES

A buyer's perception of the quality of the service he or she has purchased is usually determined during the **service encounter**—the point at which the customer and service provider interact. Employees such as bank tellers, cashiers, and customer-service representatives have a powerful impact on their customers' decision to return or not. You might pass the word to your friends about the friendly wait staff at a local breakfast eatery, the slow cashiers at a local supermarket, or the huge scoops of ice cream you got at the nearby ice cream stand. Those words form powerful marketing messages about the services you received. Tips on how to enhance the service encounter on the phone are provided by the "Etiquette Tips for Marketing Professionals" feature.

Service quality refers to the expected and perceived quality of a service offering, and it has a huge effect on the competitiveness of a company. Recently, budget airline JetBlue ranked No. 1 in quality among U.S. air carriers, largely because it arrived punctually 86 percent of the time—although the leather seats and individual satellite TVs didn't hurt either. The same survey noted that the low-cost carriers ranked above the industry average for quality, while the traditional airlines ranked below. "The low-fare carriers are definitely solid in their ability to attract passengers, and it shows in the market share that they're gaining," concluded Dean Headley, Wichita State University marketing professor and coauthor of the survey.[14]

service quality Expected and perceived quality of a service offering.

figure 11.12

Providing Assurance and Empathy as a Means of Enhancing Service Quality

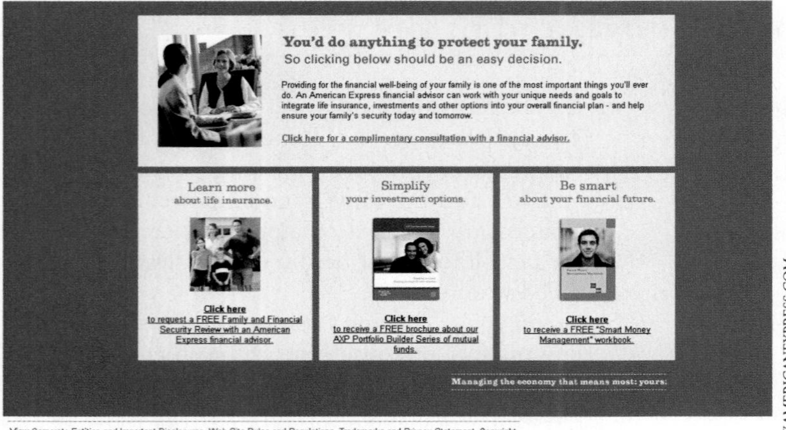

WWW.AMERICANEXPRESS.COM

Service quality is determined by five variables:

1. *Tangibles*, or physical evidence. A tidy office and clean uniform are examples.
2. *Reliability*, or consistency of performance and dependability. UPS emphasizes its dependability in its ads.
3. *Responsiveness*, or the willingness and readiness of employees to provide service. A salesperson who asks, "How may I help you?" is an example.
4. *Assurances,* or the confidence communicated by the service provider. "(We'll) help insure your family's security today and tomorrow," states the promotional message for American Express Financial Advisors in Figure 11.12.
5. *Empathy*, or the service provider's efforts to understand the customer's needs and then individualize the service. "Managing the economy that means most: yours," empathizes American Express.

If a gap exists between the level of service that customers expect and the level they think they have received, it can be favorable or unfavorable, as described in the "Solving an Ethical Controversy" feature. If you get a larger steak than you expected or your plane arrives ahead of schedule, the gap is favorable, and you are likely to try that service again. But if your steak is tiny, cold, and overcooked or your train is two hours late, the gap is unfavorable, and you will probably find another restaurant or mode of transportation next time. General Motors has struggled to close gaps in its OnStar service, which was originally touted as a travel-changing technology. At its launch, OnStar marketers excitedly predicted that motorists would be able to connect to a call center, a wireless network, and the Internet, where they could chat with customers, check their stocks, and book tickets for the theater. However, GM has since discovered that drivers don't want to be more distracted than they already are, and even if they want the service, they don't want to pay a premium for it. OnStar just doesn't create the value for consumers that GM thought it would. So marketers have begun to redefine the service as a safety feature instead of a high-tech convenience, with ads depicting stranded motorists communicating with OnStar operators who reassure them that help is on the way. The new marketing effort may close the gap, and OnStar may become a valuable service.[15]

1. **What is TQM?**
2. **What are the five variables of service quality?**

DEVELOPMENT OF PRODUCT LINES

product line Series of related products offered by one company.

(6) **Explain why firms develop lines of related products.**

Few firms today market only one product. A typical firm offers its customers a **product line**—that is, a series of related products. Although Yum! Brands, illustrated in Figure 11.13, concentrates its business in the casual dining and take-out restaurant industry, the company is subdivided into five highly recognized restaurants, or product lines: Kentucky Fried Chicken (chicken), Long John Silver's (seafood), Pizza Hut (pizza), Taco Bell (Mexican), and A&W Root Beer (root beer and hamburgers).

The motivations for marketing complete product lines rather than concentrating on a single product include the desire to grow, enhancing the company's position in the market, optimal use of company resources, and exploiting the product life cycle. Large companies such as Kraft Foods, Clorox, and General Mills have the resources to develop and market an entire mix of product lines. The following subsections examine each of the first three reasons. The final reason, exploiting the stages of the product life cycle, is discussed in the main section that focuses on strategic implications of the product life cycle concept.

Solving an Ethical Controversy

MTV'S SUPER BOWL DISASTER: WHO IS RESPONSIBLE?

IF you didn't see it, you certainly heard about it. Janet Jackson's breast-baring performance during the MTV-produced halftime show of the 2004 Super Bowl garnered more news than the results of the game itself—which was won by the New England Patriots. The incident sparked criticism from groups across the nation, including the NFL, CBS (which aired the game and the show), and the Federal Communications Commission (FCC). Advertisers AOL and PepsiCo weighed in with negative reactions. "I am outraged at what I saw during the halftime show of the Super Bowl," said FCC chairman Michael Powell. "Like millions of Americans, my family and I gathered around the television for a celebration. Instead, that celebration was tainted by a classless, crass and deplorable stunt. Our nation's children, parents, and citizens deserve better." In a statement after the incident, both Janet Jackson and Justin Timberlake took responsibility for their actions.

SHOULD MTV BE HELD RESPONSIBLE FOR THE CONTENT OF ITS SUPER BOWL HALFTIME SHOW?

PRO

1. As the producer, MTV must take responsibility for hiring the two performers and for their subsequent behavior.
2. A story posted on MTV's Web site before the game promised "shocking moments" during the Jackson–Timberlake performance. Although executives claimed to be surprised by the specific incident, the entire show was not geared toward family viewing.

CON

1. MTV had nothing to do with the incident—the two performers claimed responsibility for the incident, which was not part of the planned performance.
2. There are far more revealing images on television than this particular incident, including *Survivor* contestant Richard Hatch's nudity and the frequent suggestive scenes on programs like *The Bachelor.* MTV should not be held to a different standard in its programming.

SUMMARY

The debate over who is responsible—and what should be done about it—continues. Within days after the Super Bowl, networks instituted tape delays of several seconds for live broadcasts to prevent a similar occurrence. Major advertiser PepsiCo stated that it would consider pulling out of next year's Super Bowl if it did not receive reassurance that this would never happen again. But MTV might not get another chance, anyway—Fox Sports immediately put in a bid to produce upcoming shows. In the end, the NFL will decide who gets to entertain the fans.

But the federal government is not settling for apologies and promises of better conduct in the future. It has taken swift action in the form of stiffer fines—up to $500,000 per incident—and possible suspension of broadcast licenses for repeated violations. Worried about the legal consequences and public opinion, major TV and radio networks began reviewing their programming and clamping down on anything even remotely controversial. What is the balance between decency and infringement of free speech? Time will tell.

Sources: Eric Gillin and Greg Lindsay, "The New Puritanism," *Advertising Age,* April 5, 2004, pp. 1, 34–35; Sarah McBride, "Clear Channel Dumps Stern after Big Fine," *The Wall Street Journal,* April 9, 2004, pp. B1–B2; Jeffry Bartash, "Broadcast-Indecency Penalties Ok'd," *CBS Marketwatch,* March 11, 2004, http://cbs.marketwatch.com; Super Bowl Web site, http://www.superbowl.com, accessed April 4, 2004; "Janet Jackson Super Bowl Flash Sparks Outrage," *ABC News Online,* February 3, 2004, http://www.abc.net.au; Ann Oldenburg, "A Cultural Clash," *USA Today,* February 3, 2004, p. 1.

DESIRE TO GROW

A company limits its growth potential when it concentrates on a single product, even though the company may have started that way, as retailer L.L. Bean did with its single style of work boots called Maine Hunting Shoes. Now the company sells a complete line of work boots for men, women, and children, not to mention other types of boots, along with apparel, outdoor and travel gear, home furnishings, and even products for pets. The company, which has grown into a large mail-order and online retailer

figure 11.13

Yum! Brands' Product Lines

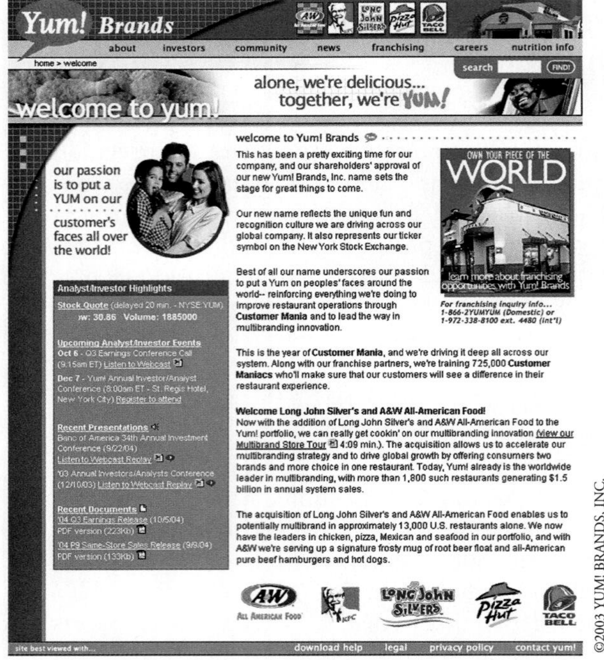

with a flagship store in Freeport, Maine, is now nearly a century old. It is unlikely that the company would have grown to its current size if the successors of Leon Leonwood Bean had stuck to manufacturing and selling a single style of his original Maine Hunting Shoes.[16]

ENHANCING THE COMPANY'S POSITION IN THE MARKET

A company with a line of products often makes itself more important to both consumers and marketing intermediaries than a firm with only one product. A shopper who purchases a tent often buys related camping items. For instance, L.L. Bean now offers a wide range of products so that consumers can completely outfit themselves for outdoor activities or travel. They can purchase hiking boots, sleeping bags and tents, fishing gear, duffel bags, kayaks and canoes, snowshoes and skis, as well as clothing for their adventures. In addition, the firm offers its Outdoor Discovery Schools programs, which teach customers the basics of kayaking, fly-fishing, and other sports directly related to the products they purchase from L.L. Bean. Few would know about Bean if the company only sold its original boots. Business buyers often expect a firm that manufactures a particular product to offer related items as well.[17]

OPTIMAL USE OF COMPANY RESOURCES

By spreading the costs of its operations over a series of products, a firm may reduce the average production and marketing costs of each product. Hospitals have taken advantage of idle facilities by adding a variety of outreach services. Many now operate health and fitness centers that, besides generating profits themselves, also feed customers into other hospital services. For example, a blood pressure check at the fitness center might result in a referral to a staff physician.

1. **List the four reasons for developing a product line.**
2. **Cite an example of a product line from a company with which you are familiar.**

THE PRODUCT MIX

(7) **Describe the way marketers typically measure product mixes and make product mix decisions.**

product mix Assortment of product lines and individual product offerings that a company sells.

A company's **product mix** is the assortment of product lines and individual product offerings that the company sells. The right blend of product lines and individual products allows a firm to maximize sales opportunities within the limitations of its resources. Marketers typically measure product mixes according to width, length, and depth.

PRODUCT MIX WIDTH

The *width* of a product mix refers to the number of product lines the firm offers. As Table 11.3 shows, Johnson & Johnson offers a broad line of retail consumer products in the U.S. market, as well as business-to-business products to the medical community. Consumers can purchase over-the-counter medications, nutritional products, dental care products, and first-aid products among others. Health-care professionals can obtain prescription drugs, medical and diagnostic devices, and wound treatments. Cordis Corporation, owned by Johnson & Johnson, introduced its PALMAZ-SCHATZ® Balloon Expandable Stent back in 1994, revolutionizing the treatment of coronary artery disease in hospitals throughout the United States. It has since launched a series of improved, more flexible stents, including one for small vessels, which help keep clogged arteries open following balloon angioplasty. This is just one of many examples of B2B that provides both a profit to the company and help to the community at large.

table 11.3 Johnson & Johnson's Mix of Health-Care Products

ALLERGY, COLDS, FLU	NUTRITIONALS	SKIN AND HAIR CARE	DENTAL CARE	MEDICAL DEVICES AND DIAGNOSTIC EQUIPMENT FOR HOSPITALS
Motrin pain reliever	Lactaid digestive aid	Aveeno lotions	ACT fluoride rinse	Three-dimensional cardiac mapping and navigation equipment
Tylenol pain reliever	Splenda artificial sweetener	Clean & Clear facial cleansers and toners	REACH dental floss	Laparoscopic and open surgery stapling devices
Simply Cough cough syrup	Viactiv calcium supplement	Johnson's Baby Shampoo	STIM-U-DENT plaque remover	Orthopedic joint replacement products
		Neutrogena soaps and shampoos	REACH toothbrushes	MAMMOTOME® Breast Biopsy System

Source: Company Web site, http://www.jnj.com/product/categories, accessed May 5, 2004.

PRODUCT MIX LENGTH

The *length* of a product mix refers to the number of different products a firm sells. Table 11.3 identifies some of the hundreds of health-care products offered by Johnson & Johnson. Some of J&J's most recognizable brands are Band-Aid, Motrin, Tylenol, and Neutrogena.

PRODUCT MIX DEPTH

Depth refers to variations in each product that the firm markets in its mix. Johnson & Johnson's Band-Aid brand bandages come in a variety of shapes and sizes, including Finger-Care Tough Strips, Flexible Fabric for elbows and knees, and Advance Healing Blister bandages.

PRODUCT MIX DECISIONS

Establishing and managing the product mix have become increasingly important marketing tasks. Adding depth, length, and width to the product mix requires careful thinking and planning—otherwise a firm can end up with too many products, including some that don't sell well. To evaluate a firm's product mix, marketers look at the effectiveness of its depth, length, and width. Has the firm ignored a viable consumer segment? It may improve performance by increasing product line depth to offer a product variation that will attract the new segment. Can the firm achieve economies in its sales and distribution efforts by adding complementary product lines to the mix? If so, a wider product mix may seem appropriate. Does the firm gain equal contributions from all products in its portfolio? If not, it may decide to lengthen or shorten the product mix to increase revenues. Legendary gunmaker Smith & Wesson evaluated its product mix and recently announced a new offering: a line of furniture and other home décor items under a new brand called Crossings. If that seems like an odd choice for a gunmaker, the company disagrees. "The products reflect the heritage that Smith & Wesson has long been associated with," explains a company spokesperson. Crossings products are designed with a rustic look intended to evoke images of the American Old West. Consumers can purchase a genuine cowboy boot lamp or a branding iron in the shape of an armadillo that can actually be used to brand things such as a leather briefcase or steaks on the grill.[18]

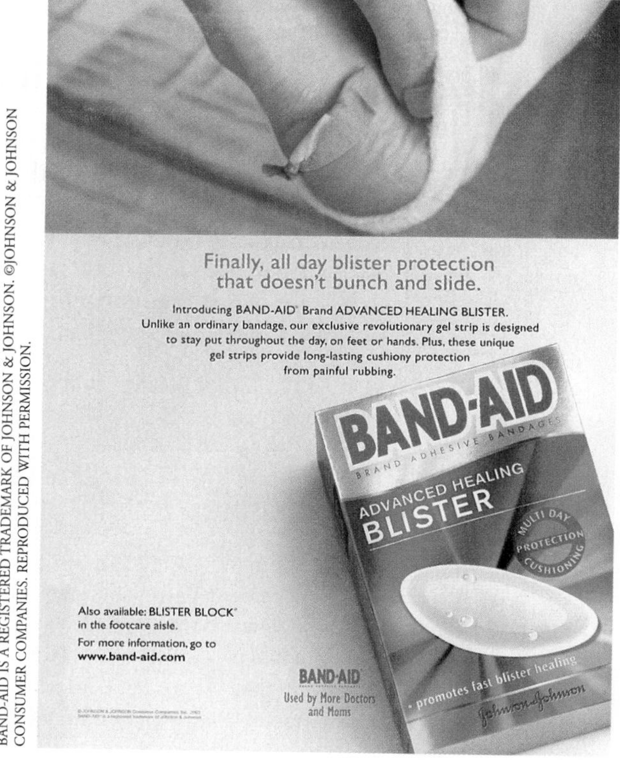

Johnson & Johnson creates depth in its product mix with variations on its original Band-Aid brand bandages.

Another way to add to the mix is to purchase product lines from other companies. Or a firm can acquire entire companies through mergers or acquisitions. A few years ago, Sears, Roebuck & Co. acquired the mail-order firm Lands' End in order to reestablish its general mail-order presence. Sears originally began as a mail-order firm but stopped publishing its "Big Book" catalog. Instead of starting it back up again, the firm decided to acquire Lands' End, which already had a successful product mix and a loyal following.

A firm should assess its current product mix for another important reason: to determine the feasibility of a line extension. A **line extension** adds individual offerings that appeal to different market segments while remaining closely related to the existing product line. Coach, well known for its upscale, traditional handbags, recently decided to extend its line by offering watches, hats, shoes, sunglasses, coats, and even straw beach mats with Coach's letter "C" logo. In addition to extending the line, the company has decided to add some depth to the product mix with hipper styles, shapes, and colors in its handbags. Customers love the new products, including the trendy new Hamptons Weekend tote, a straw-and-leather basket that comes in red, white, black, and baby blue. "These bags are art!" exclaims Coach chairman and CEO, Lew Frankfort.[19]

The marketing environment also plays a role in a marketer's evaluation of a firm's product mix. In the case of Coach, the social-cultural environment had shifted so that consumers were looking for more casual, contemporary styles than Coach had been offering. And although Coach launched some of the designs to appeal to younger customers, older consumers love them as well. Birkenstock faced a similar challenge when the firm decided to update its image for younger consumers who wanted trendier styles. Without offending its loyal customers—who still wanted the company's traditional offerings—Birkenstock introduced a new line of shoes, as described in the "Marketing Hit" feature.

Careful evaluation of a firm's current product mix can also help marketers in making decisions about brand management and new-product introductions. Chapter 12 will examine the importance of branding, brand management, and the development and introduction of new products.

1. Define *product mix.*
2. How do marketers typically measure product mixes?
3. What are line extensions?

(8) Explain the concept of the product life cycle and identify the different stages.

THE PRODUCT LIFE CYCLE

product life cycle Progression of a product through introduction, growth, maturity, and decline stages.

Products, like people, pass through stages as they age. Successful products progress through four basic stages: introduction, growth, maturity, and decline. This progression, known as the **product life cycle,** is shown in Figure 11.14. The product life cycle concept applies to products or product categories within an industry, not to individual brands. For instance, camera cell phones are currently in the introductory stage but rapidly moving to the growth stage. Digital cameras are now in the growth stage, while traditional film cameras in the U.S. are in decline. There is no set schedule or time frame for a particular stage of the life cycle. Some products pass through certain stages rapidly, while others

marketing hit — Birkenstocks: They're Not Just for Hippies Anymore

Background. For decades, Birkenstocks have been associated with tree hugging, political rallies, and flower power. The clunky, cork-soled sandals whose insides admittedly looked like cat litter were considered by many to be so ugly they were cute. But loyal followers, who swear they are comfortable, have kept wearing them and wearing them—indeed, Birks just don't wear out.

The Challenge. In recent years, Birkenstock has decided to look for ways to update its image, capitalize on its product's endurance, attract new customers—and encourage existing customers to buy a new pair or two.

The Strategy. Birkenstock has teamed up with industrial architect Yves Behar to come up with a new line of shoes called Footprints: The Architect Collection. The new designs are intended to appeal to upscale, urban consumers who are "looking for something edgy and out there, new and different," says Footprints owner Lance De St. Croix. The first spring collection has eight styles for women and six

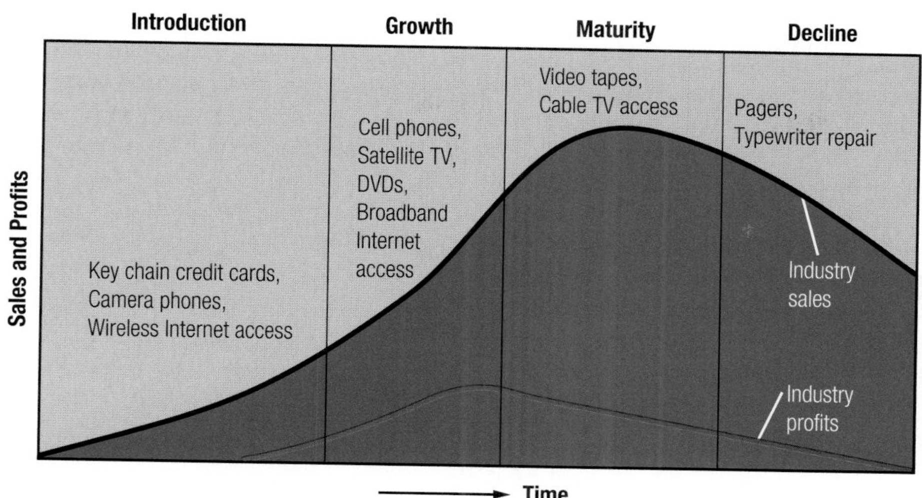

figure 11.14

Stages in the Product Life Cycle

move more slowly. DVD players have shot through the introductory stage, while the Segway human transporter seems to be stuck in the introductory stage.

INTRODUCTORY STAGE

During the **introductory stage** of the product life cycle, a firm works to stimulate demand for the new market entry. Products in this stage might bring new technology to a product category. Since the product is unknown to the public, promotional campaigns stress information about its features. Additional promotions try to induce distribution channel members to carry the product. In this phase, the public becomes acquainted with the item's merits and begins to accept it.

Competition brings out the best in products and the worst in people.

David Sarnoff (1891–1971)
founder and president of RCA

Recent examples of new products whose introductory stage has been successful include DVD players and camera phones. By slashing prices almost immediately, manufacturers of DVD players got consumers to try them at little or no risk, so the new product virtually shot through the introductory stage into the growth stage. A year or two later, camera cell phones, which were introduced first in Japan and then in the U.S., caught on so fast that spokespeople for Nokia announced that most new phones would subsequently contain built-in cameras. Nokia, which is the largest cell phone maker in the world, introduced six new phone models in two months, all with cameras. Although the phones were initially priced as high as $399, within a year Bellevue, Washington-based wireless service provider T-Mobile announced that it would give a camera phone to consumers who subscribed to its service.[20]

Technical problems and financial losses are common during the introductory stage as companies fine-tune product design and spend money on advertising. Everyone remembers early problems with the Internet—jammed portals, order fulfilling glitches, dot-coms that went bust. But DVD players and camera phones have experienced few of these setbacks. Although the photos taken by camera phones lack the clarity of full-featured cameras, new models will eventually catch up. And consumers don't

for men in new colors of suede and leather. Behar has designed "sculpted, fluid" lines for the shoes, making them less clunky than the original shoes. In fact, they hardly look like Birkenstocks at all. That is why industry watchers believe it is important for Birkenstock to market the new shoes separately from the old. "Birkenstock has a strong, loyal customer base who will always support the brand," says industry expert James Wright. "As long as they don't go too far out there, they will be able to fall back on that base."

The Outcome. Supporters of the new line of shoes say that the company has done a good job of creating an updated design without sacrificing Birk quality. And the company has been meticulous in separating the old from the new. "We knew we were launching a new brand and product line," says marketing director Patrick Hull. The new line of shoes even has its own Web site at http://www.footprints.com. And the Architect Collection has started to draw the attention of consumers who want up-to-date styles and don't mind paying the price. The new Birks aren't cheap; prices hover around $245. The older designs range from about $60 to $100. But if it catches on, the new collection could add as much as $50 million each year to company revenues.

Sources: Company Web site, http://www.birkenstock.com, accessed April 2, 2004; *Footprints* catalog, Spring 2004; Sandra O'Loughlin, "Hip Shoes, Not Just for Hippies," *Brandweek,* November 3, 2003, pp. 18–20; "Birkenstock Image Shakes 1960s-Era Image with New Shoe Line," *Knight Ridder/Tribune Business News,* February 25, 2003, http://infotrac-college.thomsonlearning.com.

seem to mind this, perhaps because they are still enjoying the novelty of taking pictures with their phones. But another problem has cropped up—the issue of privacy. Camera phones are already so widespread that they have been banned from fitness centers, schools, and similar venues because officials fear that someone might post photos from the locker room or other private areas on the Internet.[21]

GROWTH STAGE

Sales volume rises rapidly during the **growth stage** as new customers make initial purchases and early buyers repurchase the product, such as DVD players and camera phones. The growth stage usually begins when a firm starts to realize substantial profits from its investment. Word-of-mouth reports, mass advertising, and lowered prices all encourage hesitant buyers to make trial purchases of products like flat-panel LCD televisions and computer monitors. Although these screens are still more expensive than conventional ones, increased manufacturing capacity has slashed production cost 40 percent in the last couple of years, making them much more affordable—and attractive—to consumers. Industry analysts expect flat-panel LCDs to outnumber traditional screens soon.[22]

Flat-screen TVs will soon be supplanted by laptop and cell phone displays that provide a realistic and compelling 3-D image. Sanyo Electric will soon begin marketing these screens for use as billboards or in the offices of product designers, neurosurgeons, and other specialists willing to pay the expected $20,000 price tags for these systems. As was the case for both flat-screens and DVD players, prices should fall dramatically once mass production begins. Before long, you may find yourself talking to 3-D projections when you make a phone call.[23]

Customer needs have an unsettling way of not staying satisfied for very long.

Karl Albrecht

American business consultant and author

However, the growth stage may also bring new challenges for marketers. Inevitably, success attracts competitors, who rush into the market with similar offerings. An item that built enviable market share during the introductory stage may suddenly lose sales to competitive products. To compete effectively, a firm may need to make improvements and changes to a product during this stage. Additional spending on promotion and distribution may also be necessary.

MATURITY STAGE

Sales of a product category continue to grow during the early part of the **maturity stage,** but eventually, they reach a plateau as the backlog of potential customers dwindles. By this time, many competitors have entered the market, and the firm's profits begin to decline as competition intensifies.

At this stage in the product life cycle, differences between competing products diminish as competitors discover the product and promotional characteristics most desired by customers. Available supplies exceed industry demand for the first time. Companies can increase their sales and market shares only at the expense of competitors, so the competitive environment becomes increasingly important.

In the maturity stage, heavy promotional outlays emphasize any differences that still separate competing products, and brand competition intensifies. Some firms try to differentiate their products by focusing on attributes such as quality, reliability, and service. Others focus on redesign or other ways of extending the product life cycle. Zippo, illustrated in Figure 11.15, launched a new promotional campaign emphasizing the quality and reliability of its 70-year-old product *and* a new product design.

As competition intensifies, competitors tend to cut prices to attract new buyers. Although a price cut may seem the easiest method for boosting purchases, it is also one of the simplest moves for competitors to duplicate. Reduced prices decrease revenues for all firms in the industry, unless the lower prices stimulate enough new purchases to offset the loss in revenue on each unit sold. Interestingly, Zippo decided not to reduce its prices. Consumers can purchase a Zippo lighter for around $12.95 for conventional models or splurge for a collectible style at $3,000. Competing disposables run around $2.[24]

figure 11.15

Using Promotion—and Product Extensions—to Extend the Maturity Stage of the Product Life Cycle

DECLINE STAGE

In the **decline stage** of a product's life, innovations or shifts in consumer preferences bring about an absolute decline in industry sales. Dial telephones became touch-tone phones, which evolved to portable phones, which are now being replaced by conventional cell phones, which in turn are being replaced by camera phones.

Notice that the decline stage of an old product often coincides with the growth stage for a new entry. This is true of VCRs and DVD players. DVD players are rapidly replacing VCRs, meaning that DVDs are replacing VHS tapes. Most industry watchers predict that recording capacity will be built into every DVD player in the near future, rendering VCRs just about obsolete.[25]

As sales fall, profits for the product category decline, sometimes actually becoming negative. This downward trend forces firms to cut prices further in a bid for the dwindling market. Companies gradually drop the declining items from their product lines and search for alternatives. Signaling the end of an era, Kodak recently announced that it would stop selling most of its film-based cameras. The firm will still market its traditional 35mm film and its Advantix brand film, along with disposable cameras. Kodak will also continue to sell several of its film-based cameras to markets in China, India, Eastern Europe, and Latin America, where sales of traditional cameras and film remain strong. But in the decade since the introduction of the digital camera, U.S. sales of film-based cameras have declined steadily to the point where digital cameras are now outselling traditional cameras. Despite the move, Kodak is not getting out of the camera business; instead, the firm is focusing on the digital era.[26] The next section discusses potential strategies for extending the life cycle of a product.

The numerous benefits of digital cameras—predevelopment analysis of photo quality and the ability to erase poor shots, as well as simplicity and lower prices on self-developing film devices—are readily apparent to almost everyone. Within the space of a few years, they have turned the traditional film camera into a dinosaur.

The traditional product life cycle differs from fad cycles. Fashions and fads profoundly influence marketing strategies. Fashions are currently popular products that tend to follow recurring life cycles. For example, bell-bottom pants that were popular in the 1960s and 1970s have returned as flares or boot-cut pants. In contrast, fads are products with abbreviated life cycles. Most fads experience short-lived popularity and then quickly fade, although some maintain residual markets among certain segments. Mood rings and Pet Rocks are examples of fads.

1. Identify the four stages of the product life cycle.
2. During which stage or stages are products likely to attract the most new customers?

EXTENDING THE PRODUCT LIFE CYCLE

9 Describe how a firm can extend a product's life cycle.

Marketers usually try to extend each stage of the life cycles for their products as long as possible. Product life cycles can stretch indefinitely as a result of decisions designed to increase the frequency of use by current customers, increase the number of users for the product, find new uses, or change package sizes, labels, or product quality.

INCREASING FREQUENCY OF USE

During the maturity stage, the sales curve for a product category reaches a maximum point if the competitors exhaust the supply of potential customers who previously had not made purchases. However, if current customers buy more frequently than they formerly did, total sales will rise even though no new buyers enter the market.

For instance, consumers buy some products during certain seasons of the year. Marketers can boost purchase frequency by persuading these people to try the product year round. For decades, most people used sunscreen only during warm and sunny seasons of the year. With greater warnings about the risks of sun damage and skin cancer, however, companies now advertise the benefits of using sun-

Mars Inc. increases frequency of use for its M&Ms by offering holiday editions like this one for Easter.

screen year round. In another change, Mars Inc. now releases special-edition M&Ms for different holidays, including Halloween and Easter.

INCREASING THE NUMBER OF USERS

A second strategy for extending the product life cycle seeks to increase the overall market size by attracting new customers who previously have not used the product. Marketers may find their products in different stages of the life cycle in different countries. This difference can help firms extend product growth. Items that have reached the maturity stage in the U.S. may still be in the introductory stage somewhere else.

In recent years, the Walt Disney Company has spent time and money on advertising its theme parks to attract adults in addition to young families. Television commercials portray empty nesters taking off to Disney World for a second honeymoon once their children are grown. And the dairy industry's "Got Milk?" campaign is aimed at all sorts of nontraditional milk drinkers—anyone other than children or pregnant women—in an attempt to increase the number of people who drink milk.

The video game industry is seeking to expand its customer base by not only attracting young, new users but by keeping middle-aged users who started playing in their teens. Electronic Arts, the largest U.S. video game maker, releases new versions of existing games such as "Madden's NFL Football" year after year to attract new users who are curious about the technological upgrades. It also develops games with more complicated plot lines—unlike the typical sports game—because those games attract players over the age of 35. One middle-aged industry watcher and game player says, "When I was in my early 20s, it was socially unacceptable to be playing video games. My parents thought I was a moron. Now the socially acceptable age for gamers is about 6 to 40."[27]

FINDING NEW USES

Finding new uses for a product is an excellent strategy for extending a product's life cycle. New applications for mature products include oatmeal as a cholesterol reducer, antacids as a calcium supplement, and aspirin for promoting heart health.

WD-40 has always been used to clean metal parts, remove squeaks from springs and door hinges, and dissolve rust. But in a recent marketing effort, the WD-40 company conducted a survey to find the top 2,000 uses for its product. Some of the 300,000 responses were practical, others hilarious. One person sprays it on a snow shovel to keep snow from sticking. Another used WD-40 to extricate a python stuck in the exhaust pipe of a public bus. So WD-40 took its survey to the states—all 50 of them. Launching the Great State Debate, the company asked users from each state to submit their favorite uses for WD-40. Marketers then awarded each state a No. 1 use. New York's award-winning use is protecting the Statue of Liberty from the elements. Pennsylvania's is keeping the Liberty Bell from squeaking. With this kind of loyalty, WD-40 isn't dissolving from the marketplace anytime soon. That would cause distress to many consumers, including the 60,000 members of the WD-40 Fan Club.[28]

1. **Provide an example of a product whose life cycle was extended either by increasing its frequency of use or by attracting new users.**
2. **Go to the supermarket and find an example of a product packaged for use at home or away from home.**

CHANGING PACKAGE SIZES, LABELS, OR PRODUCT QUALITY

Many firms try to extend their product life cycles by introducing physical changes in their offerings. Alternatively, new labels or changes in product size can lengthen a product's life cycle. Food marketers have brought out small packages designed to appeal to one-person households and extra-large containers for customers who want to buy in bulk. Other firms offer their products in convenient packages for use away from home or for use at the office.

PRODUCT DELETION DECISIONS

To avoid wasting resources promoting unpromising products, marketers must sometimes prune product lines and eliminate marginal products, as Kodak has done. Marketers typically face this decision during the late maturity and early decline stages of the product life cycle. Periodic reviews of weak products should justify either eliminating or retaining them.

A firm may continue to carry an unprofitable item to provide a complete line for its customers. For example, while most grocery stores lose money on bulky, low-unit-value items such as salt, they continue to carry these items to meet shopper demand.

Shortages of raw materials sometimes prompt companies to discontinue production and marketing of previously profitable items. Alcoa discontinued making its brand of aluminum foil due to such a shortage. A firm may even drop a profitable item that fails to fit into its existing product line. Some of these products return to the market carrying the names of other firms that purchase these "orphan brands" from the original manufacturers.

1. Find an example of a product that has been discontinued and investigate why it was deleted from its company's product line.

Strategic Implications of Marketing in the 21st Century

MARKETERS who want their businesses to succeed will continue to develop new goods and services to attract and satisfy customers. They will engage in continuous improvement activities, focusing on quality and customer service. And they will continually evaluate their company's mix of products.

Marketers everywhere are constantly developing new and better products that fit their firm's overall strategy. High-tech innovations such as camera phones and DVDs are one area in which new products quickly replace old ones. Marketers are sometimes faced with the dilemma of lagging sales for formerly popular products. They must come up with ways to extend the lives of certain products to extend their firms' profitability and sometimes must recognize and delete those that no longer meet expectations.

REVIEW OF CHAPTER OBJECTIVES

① Define the term *product* and distinguish between goods and services and how they relate to the goods–services continuum.

Marketers define a product as the bundle of physical, service, and symbolic attributes designed to satisfy customers' wants and needs. Goods are tangible products that customers can see, hear, smell, taste, or touch. Services are intangible tasks that satisfy the needs of customers. Goods represent one end of a continuum, and services represent the other.

1.1. What is the goods–services continuum?
1.2. What are the six identifiable characteristics of services?

② Explain the importance of the service sector in today's marketplace.

The service sector makes a crucial contribution to the U.S. economy in terms of products and jobs. The U.S. service sector now makes up more than two-thirds of the economy. Services have grown because of consumers' desire for speed, convenience, and technological advances.

2.1. How do services play a role in the international competitiveness of U.S. firms?
2.2. Why do service firms emphasize marketing as a significant activity?

③ List the classifications of consumer goods and services and briefly describe each category.

Consumer products—both goods and services—are classified as convenience products (frequently purchased items), shopping products (products purchased after comparison), and specialty products (those that offer unique characteristics that consumers prize).

3.1. Identify three types of convenience products and give an example of each.
3.2. List three or four characteristics on which consumers may base their comparisons of shopping products.

④ Describe each of the types of business goods and services.

Business products are classified as installations (major capital investments), accessory equipment (capital items that cost less and last for shorter periods than installations), component parts and materials (finished business products of one producer that become part of the final products of another producer), raw materials (natural resources such as lumber, beef, or cotton), supplies (the regular expenses that a firm incurs in daily operations), and business services (the intangible products that firms buy to facilitate their production and operating processes).

4.1. How do raw materials differ from component parts and materials?
4.2. What are the three categories of supplies?

⑤ Explain how quality is used by marketers as a product strategy.

Many companies use total quality management (TQM) in an effort to encourage all employees to participate in producing the best goods and services possible. Companies may also participate in ISO 9002 certification or benchmarking to evaluate and improve quality. Consumers often evaluate service quality on the basis of tangibles, reliability, responsiveness, assurance, and empathy, so marketers of service firms strive to excel in all of these areas.

5.1. What is total quality management (TQM)?
5.2. Why is ISO 9002 important for U.S. firms that want to conduct business abroad?
5.3. What are the five variables used to determine the quality of services?

⑥ Explain why firms develop lines of related products.

Companies usually produce several related products rather than individual ones to achieve the objectives of growth, optimal use of company resources, and increased company importance in the market, and to make optimal use of the product life cycle.

6.1. How do product lines help enhance a company's position in the market?

⑦ Describe the way marketers typically measure product mixes and make product mix decisions.

Marketers must decide the right width, length, and depth of product lines. Width is the number of product lines. Length is the number of products a company sells. Depth refers to the number of variations of a product available in a product line. Marketers evaluate the effectiveness of all three elements of the product mix. They may purchase product lines from other companies or extend the product line if necessary. Firms may also acquire entire companies and their product lines through mergers and acquisitions.

7.1. Why is it important for marketers to evaluate the product mix?

⑧ Explain the concept of the product life cycle and identify the different stages.

The product life cycle outlines the stages that a product goes through during its "life," including introduction, growth, maturity, and decline.

8.1. When does a product reach the growth stage?
8.2. What can a marketer do once a product reaches the decline stage?

⑨ Describe how a firm can extend a product's life cycle.

Marketers can extend the product life cycle by increasing frequency of use or number of users, finding new uses for the product, or changing package size, label, or quality. If none of these is successful, a firm may decide to delete a product from its line.

9.1. What are two ways to increase the number of users of a product?
9.2. Identify two ways of changing packaging.

MARKETING TERMS YOU NEED TO KNOW

marketing mix 352
product 352
service 352
good 353
consumer product 355
business-to-business (B2B) product 355
convenience product 355
shopping product 357
specialty product 357
business services 362
total quality management (TQM) 364
service quality 365
product line 366
product mix 368
product life cycle 370

OTHER IMPORTANT MARKETING TERMS

goods–services continuum 353
offshoring 354
unsought products 355
impulse goods and services 356
staples 356
emergency goods and services 356
slotting allowances 357
installations 360
accessory equipment 361
component parts and materials 362
raw materials 362
supplies 362
MRO items 362
ISO 9002 364
benchmarking 364
service encounter 365
line extension 370
introductory stage 371
growth stage 372
maturity stage 372
decline stage 373

PROJECTS AND TEAMWORK EXERCISES

1. Locate an advertisement that catches your attention. Then describe where you believe the product falls on the goods–services continuum and explain why. Create a chart showing the product features that you think belong in the goods category and the services category.
2. Keep a consumer journal for a week. List all of the services you purchase during that week. Share your results with the class. Do some classmates use more services than others? If this is the case, discuss the reasons.
3. The next time you go grocery shopping, keep a list of all the convenience products you buy. When you get home, make a chart showing which of these products are impulse, staple, and emergency goods.
4. Choose a specialty good that you have purchased or might be interested in purchasing. Visit the manufacturer's Web site to learn more about the processes that go into bringing the product to market. Then list as many business products—goods and services—as you think the company might rely on to get your product to market.
5. Consider a customer-service experience you have had in the last month or so. Was it positive or negative? Describe your experience to the class and then discuss how the firm might improve the quality of its customer service—even if it is already positive.
6. With a classmate, visit the Web site of a company that interests you—say, Nike, Sony, Timberland, or Toyota. "Measure" the company's product mix according to width, length, and depth. If the firm is small, you can list all of its products or product lines. If it is large, try to identify the product lines and give a few examples of individual products.
7. With your classmate, come up with a plan for further extending one of the firm's product lines. Describe the strategy you would recommend for extending the line as well as new products that might be included.
8. For the product you selected in 6, create an ad reflecting your strategy for extending the product's life cycle.
9. With a classmate, choose a product that you believe has reached either the maturity or decline stage—say, sandals or dial-up Internet service. Together, come up with a possible strategy for extending the life cycle of your product.
10. Find an advertisement that reflects a change in packaging. Discuss it with the class. Do you think the advertisement is effective? Why or why not?

APPLYING CHAPTER CONCEPTS

1. Draw a line representing the goods–services continuum. Then place each of the following along the continuum. Briefly explain your decision.
   a. Google
   b. eBay
   c. Starbucks coffee
   d. L'Oréal shampoo
2. Think of a shopping product you purchased in the last six months. Describe your thought process during the purchase, including which attributes you used in comparison to competitors. Have you been satisfied with your purchase? Why or why not?
3. Why is the service encounter so important to a firm's relationships with its customers? When is a service gap favorable? When is it unfavorable?
4. Why is it important for even a small company to consider developing a line of products rather than a single product?

ETHICS EXERCISE

Your behavior as a marketer for a company that provides services to consumers is extremely important to your firm's success. Your organization has recently received an opportunity to outsource its customer-services operations overseas. This move will not only improve efficiency but also dramatically cut labor costs, allowing your company to develop new services and ultimately enter new markets. In a marketing meeting, the argument grows heated over whether customers should be told that the new service representatives are located in another country.

1. Do you believe that customers should be informed of the change? Why or why not?
2. If the firm's executives decide that, as a marketing strategy, customers should not be told about the change, would you adhere to the strategy? Why or why not?

'netWork EXERCISES

1. **Slotting allowances.** Visit the two Web sites listed below and read the reports published on each site on slotting allowances in the supermarket industry. Answer the following questions:
   a. What are slotting allowances?
   b. How much are slotting allowances?
   c. Why are they used?
   d. Are slotting allowances unfair to small manufacturers?
   e. Are they anticompetitive?

   http://www.fmi.org/media/bg/slottingfees2002.pdf

   (To view this report you need to have Adobe Acrobat or Adobe Reader. You can download Adobe Reader for free from the Adobe Web site: http://www.adobe.com.)

   http://www.ftc.gov/opa/2003/11/slottingallowances.htm
2. **Consumer product classifications.** Visit the Web site of a well-known consumer products company such as Gillette (http://www.gillette.com), Procter & Gamble (http://www.pg.com), or Unilever (http://www.unilever.com). Make a list of the company's consumer products. Classify each product as either a convenience, shopping, or specialty product. Choose two products from your list. In which phase of the product life cycle is each product? Be prepared to defend your answer.
3. **Managing the product life cycle.** While you may not have heard of Church & Dwight Company, you likely know the name of its famous product, Arm and Hammer baking soda, which has been around for over 150 years. Visit the product's Web site (http://www.armandhammer.com) and click "Our History." Review the history of the product and make a list of the ways in which the company has effectively managed the product's life cycle. Bring your list to class so you can participate in a class discussion of the product life cycle.

Note: Internet Web addresses change frequently. If you don't find the exact sites listed, you may need to access the organization's or company's home page and search from there or use a search engine such as Google.

INFOTRAC CITATIONS AND EXERCISES

Record: A116678199

A stunning success for embedded—Electronic intelligence turns Taser into a weapon of choice. Charles J. Murray.

Electronic Engineering Times, May 17, 2004 p1

Abstract: When Taser International applied embedded intelligence to its lowly stun gun product, it had no idea that the move would reverse its fortunes and catapult the Scottsdale, Arizona, company into the national spotlight. The combination of signal processing and a shaped-pulse output profile made the Taser gun smaller, more efficient, and more desirable for law enforcement agencies. As a result of the product redesign, law enforcement agencies have been snapping up the new Tasers at unprecedented rates, making Taser International one of the big success stories on Wall Street in recent years.

1. Read the article and explain why the Taser product wasn't selling well prior to its recent redesign. How did the improvements make the product more appealing to law enforcement agencies?
2. At what stage of the product life cycle is the stun gun? Explain.
3. What are some potential problems that could threaten the continued success of the Taser gun at this stage in its development?

CASE 11.1 Kevlar: A Product in Search of a Need

Sometimes products are discovered by accident. Sometimes they are developed as a solution to a particular problem. Other times they are invented for one purpose but wind up being used for an entirely different one. That's what happened in the case of Kevlar.

In 1964, DuPont chemists Stephanie Kwolek and Herbert Blades were asked by their managers to try to come up with the company's next big-selling high-performance fiber. While that may seem like a huge assignment, Kwolek and Blades were undaunted. Within a year, the lab had developed a flameproof, lightweight fiber intended to reinforce the treads of radial tires. At the time, there was already a fear of a global energy shortage, and DuPont anticipated a need for lightweight tires that would help conserve fuel. However, when the new product was introduced, the auto industry wasn't interested. Although some Kevlar is used in tires, the industry instead developed the cheaper steel-belted radials.

Despite the rejection of Kevlar for its intended use, the product did make quiet inroads in a number of markets. Over the years, Kevlar has been used in the manufacture of everything from kayaks and skis to ropes that secured the airbags in the landing apparatus of the Mars Pathfinder—not to mention motorcycle apparel, sailing gear, automobile brake pads, and the ropes used to moor large U.S. Navy vessels. Kevlar has proved its strength and versatility, as well as its value to DuPont in the business marketplace. But suddenly, this mature product has been given new life—by saving the lives of others. It has also attracted a lot of publicity.

During the conflict in Iraq, more than 100,000 British and American soldiers and journalists have been outfitted with bulletproof vests and helmets made of Kevlar. Although there is no exact count, military watchers estimate that several hundred of these individuals have been spared death or severe injury by the Kevlar products. "It is one of the most significant pieces of military equipment ever invented," notes David Nelson, deputy product manager of clothing and equipment for the U.S. Army. In addition, about 3,000 police officers around the U.S. who wear the vests and helmets have been saved. Kevlar is so effective because it is five times stronger than steel, with half the density (and weight) of fiberglass.

Stephanie Kwolek is gratified that her invention is saving lives, despite the fact that she does not receive any royalties for her product because she was a full-time employee when she made the discovery. She enjoys meeting the soldiers and police officers whose lives have been saved by Kevlar. "It's a gratifying experience to have had such an impact on the world," she says. But DuPont isn't stopping here. The firm intends to extend the life of this miracle product in a whole host of new ways, partly through technological advances. Alexa Dembek, global business manager for DuPont's life protection division, explains, "There have been many innovations since that molecule was discovered. . . . The basic molecule has not changed, but the technology that allows that molecule to realize its full potential continues to advance."

Part of DuPont's new strategy for the product includes marketing to home builders an add-on storm room made of Kevlar-reinforced wall panels. This would appeal to homeowners who live in areas of the country where hurricanes and tornadoes are common. It appears as though Kevlar still has a long life ahead.

Questions for Critical Thinking

1. Kevlar has reached the maturity stage in its life cycle, and DuPont has already begun to take steps to extend its life. In addition to finding new uses for the product, what other strategies might DuPont employ?
2. How important do you think quality is as a product strategy for DuPont?

Sources: DuPont Web site, http://www.dupont.com/kevlar, accessed May 3, 2004; James A. Bacon, "Still Going Strong," *Greater Richmond Catalyst,* January 29, 2004, http://www.richmondcatalyst.com; Jon Swartz and Edward Iwata, "Invented to Save Gas, Kevlar Now Saves Lives," *USA Today,* April 16, 2003, pp. B1–B2.

VIDEO CASE 11.2 Curves: A New Angle on Fitness

The written case on Curves, International appears on page VC-13. The recently filmed Curves, International video is designed to expand and highlight the concepts in this chapter and the concepts and questions covered in the written video case.

chapter 12

Category and Brand Management, Product Identification, and New-Product Development

chapter objectives

1. Explain the benefits of category and brand management.
2. Identify the different types of brands.
3. Explain the strategic value of brand equity.
4. Discuss how companies develop strong identities for their products and brands.
5. Identify and briefly describe each of the four strategies for new-product development.
6. Describe the consumer adoption process.
7. List the stages in the process for developing new products.
8. Explain the relationship between product safety and product liability.

TEAMING UP TO MARKET MERCHANDISE FEATURING COLLEGE LOGOS

Which college or university currently sells the most licensed merchandise in the U.S.? It's the Big Ten's University of Michigan. Rounding out the top five are North Carolina, Notre Dame, Texas, and Oklahoma. Many brand names are associated with sports: Nike, Adidas, Calloway, Wilson, Reebok, Champion, and Russell Athletic are just a few. But the real winners are clothing and gear emblazoned with team mascots and logos, and those college logos are brands, too.

If you've ever purchased or worn anything with the name, logo, or mascot of your school, you probably know that college mer-

AP PHOTO/SUE OGROCKI

chandise is a big business built around what have become, in effect, brand names. Although manufacturers and retailers had unrestricted use of college logos and trademarks for many years, schools began to register their trademarks so that they could not be used without payment of royalties. Hundreds of schools now have established lucrative licensing programs that often help to keep their athletic departments financially self-sufficient, an important benefit given the rising costs and decreased funding many campuses face. Nearly half of Division 1A schools administer these programs on their own, while the remainder use independent licensing agencies. One advantage of the agencies is that they are better able to ensure national distribution of the school's products.

A school's sports team doesn't even have to be a winner to profit from licensing its brand. There's a growing market for so-called *rivalry merchandise,* in which schools competing in tournaments put their logos or mascots on the same clothing or other item, promoting both the winner and the loser of their most significant contest. Even though the loser's mascot is usually shown being crushed or throttled, both schools usually want to promote the rivalry—and they share the revenue, although the loser usually gets less because fans of the winning school buy more items.

Getting into the brand-name marketing business has been a financial boon for schools. With students and sports fans spending millions of dollars every year on hats, sweatshirts, sports jerseys, mugs, glassware, license plate frames, scarves, pennants, candles, T-shirts, picture frames, jewelry, and collectibles, schools are able to earn hundreds of thousands and even millions of dollars from their brand-licensing agreements with equipment makers like Nike, Reebok, and others.[1]

Chapter Overview

BRANDS play a huge role in our lives. We try certain brands for all kinds of reasons: on recommendations from friends, because we want to associate ourselves with the images possessed by certain brands, or because we remember colorful advertisements. We develop loyalty to certain brands and product lines for varying reasons as well—quality of a product, price, and habit are a few examples. This chapter examines the way companies make decisions about developing and managing the products and product lines that they hope will become consumer necessities. Developing and marketing a product and product line and building a desired brand image are costly propositions. To protect its investment and maximize the return on it, a specialized marketer called a *category manager*, who is responsible for an entire product line, must carefully nurture both existing and new products.

This chapter focuses on two critical elements of product planning and strategy. First, it looks at how firms build and maintain identity and competitive advantage for their products through branding. Second, it focuses on the new-product planning and development process. Effective new-product planning and meeting the profit responsibility that a category manager has for a product line require careful preparation. The needs and desires of consumers change constantly, and successful marketers manage to keep up with—or stay just ahead of—those changes.

Briefly Speaking

The man who uses Calloway golf clubs, drives a Jaguar, and wears Ralph Lauren apparel makes a statement about his identity. He is a man separate and apart from the man who uses a Penn fishing reel, drives a Dodge Durango, and wears Levi's.

Laurence Vincent
American author

MANAGING BRANDS FOR COMPETITIVE ADVANTAGE

1 **Explain the benefits of category and brand management.**

brand Name, term, sign, symbol, design, or some combination that identifies the products of one firm while differentiating them from the competition's.

Think of the last time you went shopping for groceries. As you moved through the store, chances are your recognition of various brand names influenced many of your purchasing decisions. Perhaps you chose Colgate toothpaste over competitive offerings or loaded Heinz ketchup into your cart instead of the store brand. Walking through the snack food aisle, you might have reached for Smartfood popcorn or Lay's potato chips without much thought.

Marketers recognize the powerful influence that products and product lines have on customer behavior, and they work to create strong identities for their products and protect them. Branding is the process of creating that identity. A **brand** is a name, term, sign, symbol, design, or some combination that identifies the products of one firm while differentiating these products from competitors' offerings. The designer Tommy Hilfiger has built an instantly recognizable brand around his own name, as illustrated in Figure 12.1.

As you read this chapter, consider how many brands you are aware of—both those you are loyal to and those you have never tried or have tried and abandoned. Table 12.1 shows some selected brands, brand names, and brand marks. Satisfied buyers respond to branding by making repeat purchases of the same product because they identify the item with the name of its producer. One buyer might derive satisfaction from an ice cream bar with the brand name Dove; another might derive the same satisfaction from one with the name Ben & Jerry's.

BRAND LOYALTY

Brands achieve widely varying consumer familiarity and acceptance. A snowboarder might insist on a Burton snowboard, but the same consumer might show little loyalty to particular brands in another product category such as tissue paper. Marketers measure brand loyalty in three stages: brand recognition, brand preference, and brand insistence.

figure 12.1

Tommy Hilfiger: Promoting a Well-Known Brand

Brand recognition is a company's first objective for newly introduced products. Marketers begin the promotion of new items by trying to make these items familiar to the public. Advertising offers one effective way for increasing consumer awareness of a brand. Glad is a familiar brand in U.S. kitchens, and it drew on customers' recognition of its popular sandwich bags and plastic wraps when it recently introduced a new plastic food wrap that seals around items with just the press of a finger.

brand recognition Consumer awareness and identification of a brand.

Other tactics for creating brand recognition include offering free samples or discount coupons for purchases. Once consumers have used a product, seen it advertised, or noticed it in stores, it moves from the unknown to the known category, which increases the probability that some of those consumers will purchase it.

At the second level of brand loyalty, **brand preference,** buyers rely on previous experiences with the product when choosing it, if available, over competitors' products. You may prefer Steve Madden shoes or Sean John clothes to other brands and buy their new lines as soon as they are offered. If so, those products have established brand preference.

brand preference Consumer reliance on previous experiences with a product to choose that product again.

Brand insistence, the ultimate stage in brand loyalty, leads consumers to refuse alternatives and to search extensively for the desired merchandise. A product at this stage has achieved a monopoly position with its consumers. Although many firms try to establish brand insistence with all consumers, few achieve this ambitious goal. Companies that offer specialty or luxury goods and services, such as Tiffany diamonds or Lexus automobiles, are more apt to achieve this status than those that offer mass-marketed goods and services.

brand insistence Consumer refusals of alternatives and extensive search for desired merchandise.

table 12.1 ***Selected Brands, Brand Names, and Brand Marks***

Brand type	Dr. Pepper or Canada Dry ginger ale
Private brand	Sam's Choice beverage (Wal-Mart) or ACE brand tools
Family brand	RAID insect sprays or Progresso soups
Individual brand	Tide or Clorox
Brand name	Life or Cheese Nips
Brand mark	Colonel Sanders for KFC or Mr. Peanut for Planters

Solving an Ethical Controversy

COUNTERFEITERS: IS IT WORTH THE FIGHT TO STOP THEM?

MILLIONS of counterfeit goods are produced every year. It's estimated that about 10 percent of all perfumes and toiletries and 12 percent of toys and sporting goods on the market are fakes and that criminal and terrorist organizations, which are behind many of the world's counterfeiting operations, are making about $500 billion on sales of phony products every year. Shoes, perfumes, watches, appliances, stereos, car parts, food, prescription drugs, alcohol, sportswear, designer clothing, toys, cosmetics, and even champagne are frequent targets of counterfeiters, as are CDs, cassettes, videotapes, and DVDs.

The International Anticounterfeiting Coalition estimates that the jobs, taxes, and sales lost to counterfeiters every year amount to more than $200 billion, and most *Fortune* 500 companies are each spending between $2 and $4 million annually in the fight against fakes. But no one sees an end to counterfeiting. Not all countries have signed on to copyright protection treaties, and continuing attempts to get them to police illegal operations have met with limited success. Also, technologies of various kinds are making it easier all the time to produce and market bogus branded goods.

SHOULD COMPANIES CONTINUE TO INVEST MORE AND MORE IN TRYING TO PREVENT COUNTERFEITING OF THEIR BRANDS?

PRO

1. Counterfeit drugs, for example, can be tainted and therefore dangerous, and other counterfeit goods are often shoddy and unreliable.
2. These knock-offs carrying well-respected brand names are often poor imitations of the real item, and their presence in the marketplace is likely to cause irreparable harm to the overall image of the legitimate products carrying the brand.

CON

1. Counterfeiters will always find an easy market for bargain-priced goods and so will never give up.
2. The effort of fighting counterfeiters is very hard for foreign firms, unless they can secure the cooperation of local authorities in stamping out this problem.

SUMMARY

Some firms are forming alliances with retailers to try to prevent counterfeit products from reaching the market, and law enforcement agents all over the world continue to stage raids on facilities of suspected counterfeiters. The fight shows no sign of slackening; makers of genuine branded goods have jobs, revenue, and reputations at stake. In the meantime, in a lot of countries, it's a matter of let the buyer beware. Consumers are advised to buy only from reputable merchants, to be suspicious of a "steal" (it usually *is* one), to inspect goods and packaging carefully before buying, and to be particularly careful about bargains offered on the Internet.

Sources: Sarah McBride, "The Hunt for Movie Pirates," *The Wall Street Journal,* April 12, 2004, pp. B1, B3; Erwin Lemuel G. Oliva, "Canon Seeks Alliance with Vendors vs. Counterfeit Goods," *Inquirer News Service,* http://www.inq7.net, April 20, 2004; "How Can I Protect Myself from Counterfeit Goods?" *BBC,* http://www.bbc.co.uk, accessed April 17, 2004; "Psst. Wanna Real Rolex?" *The Economist,* http://www.economist.com, January 22, 2004; Michael Wilson, "2 Chinatown Stores Raided in Counterfeit-Goods Sweep," *The New York Times,* http://www.nytimes.com, December 3, 2003; Timothy W. Maier, "Counterfeit Goods Pose Real Threat," *Insight,* http://www.insightmag.com, October 30, 2003; Matthew Benjamin, "A World of Fakes," *U.S. News & World Report,* July 14, 2003, pp. 46–47.

One problem facing many brand names is the persistence of counterfeiting. See the accompanying "Solving an Ethical Controversy" feature for some questions about how far to carry the fight against fakes.

(2) **Identify the different types of brands.**

TYPES OF BRANDS

Companies that practice branding classify brands in many ways: private, manufacturer's or national, family, and individual brands. In making branding decisions, firms weigh the benefits and disadvantages of each type of brand.

Some firms, however, sell their goods without any efforts at branding. These items are called **generic products.** They are characterized by plain labels, little or no advertising, and no brand names. Common categories of generic products include food and household staples. These no-name products were first sold in Europe at prices as much as 30 percent below those of branded products. This product strategy was introduced in the U.S. a quarter century ago. The market shares for generic products increase during economic downturns but subside when the economy improves. However, many consumers do request generic substitutions for certain brand-name prescriptions at the pharmacy whenever they are available.

generic products
Products characterized by plain labels, no advertising, and the absence of brand names.

Manufacturers' Brands versus Private Brands

Manufacturers' brands, also called *national brands*, define the image that most people form when they think of a brand. A **manufacturer's brand** refers to a brand name owned by a manufacturer or other producer. Well-known manufacturers' brands include Hewlett-Packard, Kodak, Pepsi Cola, Dell, and Heinz. In contrast, many large wholesalers and retailers place their own brands on the merchandise they market. The brands offered by wholesalers and retailers are usually called **private brands** (or private labels). Although some manufacturers refuse to produce private label goods, most regard such production as a way to reach additional market segments. Wal-Mart offers many private label products at its stores, including its Sam's Choice cola and Old Roy dog food.

manufacturer's brand
Brand name owned by a manufacturer or other producer.

Private brands and generic products expand the number of alternatives available to consumers. As Figure 12.2 illustrates, JCPenney sells its own brand of jeans and sportswear under the Arizona brand name.[2]

The growth of private brands has paralleled that of chain stores in the U.S. Manufacturers not only sell their well-known brands to stores but also put the store's own label on similar products. Such leading manufacturers as Westinghouse, Armstrong Rubber, and Heinz generate ever-increasing percentages of their total incomes by producing goods for sale under retailers' private labels.

One arena in which private label branding is gaining new ground is personal computers. After watching sales of big-name PCs stumble, retailers such as Best Buy and RadioShack have begun stocking their shelves with their own private label computers. Best Buy started by selling a line of PCs designed for teenagers who mostly play games. The PCs come in fluorescent colors instead of black or silver, and kids are attracted to them.

figure 12.2
JCPenney: Use of Private Brands

Captive Brands

The nation's major discounters—such as Wal-Mart, Target, and Kmart—have come up with a spin-off of the private label idea. So-called **captive brands** are national brands that are sold exclusively by a retail chain. Captive brands typically provide better profit margins than private labels. Kmart's captive brands include Martha Stewart paints, linens, and home furnishings. Similarly, Wal-Mart sells General Electric small appliances, even though these items are actually made by other manufacturers that purchased the GE brand to use on small appliances.

Family and Individual Brands

family brand Single brand name that identifies several related products.

A **family brand** is a single brand name that identifies several related products. For example, KitchenAid markets a complete line of appliances under the KitchenAid name, and Johnson & Johnson offers a line of baby powder, lotions, plastic pants, and baby shampoo under its name. All Pepperidge Farm products, from bread to rolls to cookies, carry the Pepperidge Farm brand.

The Internet is all about branding. It's more important here than it is offline. People have to remember your name and type it in. There are no Golden Arches or Coke cans to remind them.

Mark Brier
Amazon.com executive

Alternatively, a manufacturer may choose to market a product under an **individual brand,** which uniquely identifies the item itself, rather than promoting it under the name of the company or under an umbrella name covering similar items. Lever Brothers, for example, markets Aim, Close-Up, and Pepsodent toothpastes; All and Wisk laundry detergents; Imperial margarine; Caress, Dove, Lifebuoy, and Lux bath soaps; and Shield and Lever 2000 deodorant soaps. PepsiCo's Quaker Oats unit markets Aunt Jemima breakfast products, Gatorade beverages, and Celeste Pizza. Individual brands cost more than family brands to market because the firm must develop a new promotional campaign to introduce each new product to its target market. Distinctive brands are extremely effective aids in implementing market segmentation strategies, however.

On the other hand, a promotional outlay for a family brand can benefit all items in the line. For example, products like motorcycles, lawn mowers, snow blowers, and all-terrain vehicles, shown in Figure 12.3, gain immediate recognition as part of the well-known Honda family brand. Family brands also help marketers introduce new products to both customers and retailers. Since supermarkets stock thousands of items, they hesitate to add new products unless they are confident they will be in demand.

Family brands should identify products of similar quality, or the firm risks harming its overall product image. If Rolls-Royce marketers were to place the Rolls name on a low-end car or a line of discounted clothing, they would severely tarnish the image of the luxury car line. Conversely, Lexus,

figure 12.3
Products Marketed by Honda Using a Family Brand

"AND YOU THOUGHT WE ONLY MADE CARS" ADVERTISEMENT IS COURTESY OF AMERICAN HONDA MOTOR CO., INC.

Infiniti, and Mercedes-Benz put their names on luxury sport-utility vehicles to capitalize on their reputations and to enhance the acceptance of the new models in a competitive market.

Individual brand names should, however, distinguish dissimilar products. PepsiCo's Quaker Oats division markets dog food under the Ken-L Ration brand name but uses Puss 'n Boots for its cat food items. Kimberly-Clark markets two different types of diapers under its Huggies and Pull-Ups names. Procter & Gamble offers fruit drinks under its Sunny Delight name; laundry detergent under Cheer, Tide, and other brands; and dishwasher detergent under Cascade.

BRAND EQUITY

(3) **Explain the strategic value of brand equity.**

As individuals, we often like to say that our strongest asset is our reputation. The same is true of organizations. A brand can go a long way toward making or breaking a company's reputation. A strong brand identity backed by superior quality offers important strategic advantages for a firm. First, it increases the likelihood that consumers will recognize the firm's product or product line when they make purchase decisions. Second, a strong brand identity can contribute to buyers' perceptions of product quality. Branding can also reinforce customer loyalty and repeat purchases. A consumer who tries a brand and likes it will probably look for that brand on future store visits. All of these benefits contribute to a valuable form of competitive advantage called *brand equity.*

Brand equity refers to the added value that a certain brand name gives to a product in the marketplace. Brands with high equity confer financial advantages on a firm because they often command comparatively large market shares and consumers may pay little attention to differences in prices. Studies have also linked brand equity to high profits and stock returns.

brand equity Added value that a respected, well-known brand name gives to a product in the marketplace.

In global operations, high brand equity often facilitates expansion into new markets. Currently, Coca-Cola is the most valuable—and most recognized—brand in the world.[3] Similarly, Disney's brand equity allows it to market its goods and services in Europe and Japan—and now China. What makes a global brand powerful? According to Interbrand Corp., which measures brand equity in dollar values, a strong brand is one that has the power to increase a company's sales and earnings. A global brand is generally defined as one that sells at least 20 percent outside its home country, as Coca-Cola does. Interbrand's top 10 global brands include Microsoft, Disney, McDonald's, and IBM.[4]

The right name is an advertisement in itself.

Claude C. Hopkins (1866–1932)

American advertising pioneer

The global advertising agency Young & Rubicam (Y&R) developed another brand equity system called the *Brand Asset Valuator*. Y&R interviewed more than 90,000 consumers in 30 countries and collected information on over 13,000 brands to help create this measurement system. According to Y&R, a firm builds brand equity sequentially on four dimensions of brand personality. These four dimensions are differentiation, relevance, esteem, and knowledge:

- *Differentiation* refers to a brand's ability to stand apart from competitors. Brands like Porsche and Victoria's Secret stand out in consumers' minds as symbols of unique product characteristics.
- *Relevance* refers to the real and perceived appropriateness of the brand to a big consumer segment. A large number of consumers must feel a need for the benefits offered by the brand. Brands with high relevance include AT&T and Hallmark.
- *Esteem* is a combination of perceived quality and consumer perceptions about the growing or declining popularity of a brand. A rise in perceived quality or in public opinion about a brand enhances a brand's esteem. But negative impressions reduce esteem. Brands with high esteem include Starbucks and Honda.
- *Knowledge* refers to the extent of customers' awareness of the brand and understanding of what a good or service stands for. Knowledge implies that customers feel an intimate relationship with a brand. Examples include Jell-O and Band-Aid.[5]

Unfortunately, even brands with high equity can lose their luster for a variety of reasons. It may occur because of perceived or real defects in a product that become public knowledge, as in the case of the Bridgestone/Firestone tires installed on Ford's Explorer SUVs. Or it may be because of a court battle, as in the case of Microsoft's antitrust struggles. Starbucks, the fastest growing brand on *BusinessWeek*/Interbrand's annual list of top 100 brands, has enjoyed double-digit growth in the U.S. but lags overseas, where competition and start-up costs are high and where consumers are less interested in the "Starbucks experience."[6]

THE ROLE OF CATEGORY AND BRAND MANAGEMENT

Because of the tangible and intangible value associated with strong brand equity, marketing organizations invest considerable resources and effort in developing and maintaining these dimensions of brand personality. Traditionally, companies assigned the task of managing a brand's marketing strategies to a **brand manager.** Recently, companies have been reevaluating the effectiveness of brand management and changing the system in a variety of ways. General Motors has decided to eliminate brand managers in favor of marketing director positions, largely because of duplication. The company found that it was spending time, money, and effort in separate divisions to come up with essentially the same car.[7]

category management Product management system in which a category manager—with profit and loss responsibility—oversees a product line.

Today, major consumer goods companies have adopted a strategy called **category management,** in which a category manager oversees an entire product line. Unlike traditional product managers, category managers have profit responsibility for their product group. These managers are assisted by associates usually called "analysts." Part of this shift was initiated by large retailers, which realized they could benefit from the marketing muscle of large grocery and household goods producers like Kraft and Procter & Gamble.

As a result, producers began to focus their attention on in-store merchandising instead of mass-market advertising. A few years ago, Kraft reorganized its sales force so that each representative was responsible for a retailer's needs instead of pushing a single brand. Kraft now has a "customer manager" for each major grocery chain in a city or region. Technology also plays a role in Kraft's strategy. A software application called Three-Step Category Builder allows managers to tear apart a product category, analyze all its related data, and create a new management plan in two days. The software presents the plan in a few easy-to-read charts that the manager can show to the retailer. "It shouldn't take more than 15 minutes to explain," says Christopher Hogan, technology chief of Kraft's sales division. Kraft then recommends everything from which products the retailer should carry to where they should be positioned.[8]

Like many marketing functions, category management can often require the collaboration of colleagues within and outside the manufacturer. Meetings are still the most frequent method for sharing business ideas. See the "Etiquette Tips for Marketing Professionals" feature for ideas about how to improve your business meeting skills.

1. What is a brand?
2. How are generic products different from branded products?
3. What is brand equity?

(4) Discuss how companies develop strong identities for their products and brands.

PRODUCT IDENTIFICATION

Organizations identify their products in the marketplace with brand names, symbols, and distinctive packaging. Almost every product that is distinguishable from another gives buyers some means of identifying it. Sunkist Growers, for instance, stamps its oranges with the name Sunkist. Iams stamps a paw print on all of its pet food packages. For nearly 100 years, Prudential Insurance Co. has used the Rock of Gibraltar as its symbol. Choosing how to identify the firm's output represents a major strategic decision for marketers.

BRAND NAMES AND BRAND MARKS

brand name Part of a brand consisting of words or letters that form a name that identifies and distinguishes a firm's offerings from those of its competitors.

A name plays a central role in establishing brand and product identity. The American Marketing Association defines a **brand name** as the part of the brand consisting of words or letters that form a name that identifies and distinguishes the firm's offerings from those of its competitors. The brand name is, therefore, the part of the brand that people can vocalize. Firms can also identify their brands by brand marks. A **brand mark** is a symbol or pictorial design that distinguishes a product. In Figure 12.4, Saturn is the brand name, and the red and blue design is the brand mark that distinguishes Saturn from its competitors.

Effective brand names are easy to pronounce, recognize, and remember. Short names, such as Nike, Ford, and Bounty, meet these requirements. Marketers try to overcome problems with easily mispronounced brand names by teaching consumers the correct pronunciations. For example, early advertisements for the Korean carmaker Hyundai explained that the name rhymes with *Sunday.*

ETIQUETTE TIPS

FOR MARKETING PROFESSIONALS

How to Run a Business Meeting

DESPITE the prevalence of electronic communications in business, meetings will never go away. There is probably no more efficient way to deliver information to, or get agreement from, a group than a well-run meeting, and marketing professionals are sure to attend their share with clients and colleagues. Here are a few tips for making your meetings successful.

IF YOU'RE RUNNING THE MEETING

1. Set appropriate goals. The best meetings are short (under an hour), so if you have a lot to accomplish, you might want to have more than one meeting to cover everything.
2. Distribute an agenda with time frames before the meeting. An agenda not only lets you plan your time—and ensure that you get to all the necessary points—but also lets the attendees know what to expect so they can prepare. Stick to the agenda, and start and finish at the designated times.
3. Keep attendees informed. In addition to the agenda, participants need to know why their presence is necessary and how they will benefit from attending. Make sure you let them know so you can ensure their cooperation.

IF YOU'RE ATTENDING THE MEETING

4. Let the meeting organizer know whether or not you will attend. If attendance will be poor, the meeting might have to be rescheduled.
5. Come early and come prepared. Don't be late, and bring information you will be asked to share as well as something to take notes with.
6. Avoid interrupting when others are speaking, either by speaking yourself or by having your phone or pager go off. Hold or forward your calls so you can listen attentively throughout the meeting.
7. Keep your questions and comments brief and to the point. This guarantees you'll be heeded when you do speak, and it helps the meeting end on time.
8. Maintain your cool. Don't allow yourself to become angry or upset at other participants, and don't fidget or lose your concentration. It distracts others, particularly those who are speaking.
9. Be prepared to stay for the entire meeting. Leaving early is disruptive and rude.
10. Follow up after the meeting, promptly completing any tasks you've been assigned.

Meetings are an important part of any successful business career. Understanding how to facilitate a well-run meeting and understanding how to participate properly in a meeting led by someone else are important skills to obtain. The tips presented here will help you start your career with a better understanding of how best to handle meeting situations successfully.

Sources: Jared Sandberg, "A Survival Guide for Office Meetings: Bring Your Own Toys," *The Wall Street Journal*, May 19, 2004, p. B1; "Three Easy Steps to a Well-Run Meeting," *Strategic Communications*, http://www.strategiccomm.com, accessed April 17, 2004; Gary M. Smith, "Eleven Commandments for Business Meeting Etiquette," *Society for Technical Communication*, http://www.stc.org, accessed April 17, 2004; Vadim Kotelnikov and Ten3 East-West, "Effective Meetings," *The Business e-Coach*, http://www.1000ventures.com, accessed April 17, 2004; John Eckberg, "Mind Your Meeting Etiquette," *The Cincinnati Enquirer*, http://www.enquirer.com, December 23, 2003.

A brand name should also give buyers the correct connotation of the product's image. The name Lunchables for Oscar Mayer's prepackaged lunches suggests a convenient meal that can be eaten anywhere. Discover suggests a credit card that allows treasure hunting. Chevy's Trail Blazer represents adventure and ruggedness.

A brand name must also qualify for legal protection. The Lanham Act of 1946 states that registered trademarks must not contain words or phrases in general use, such as *automobile* or *suntan lotion*. These generic words actually describe particular types of products, and no company can claim exclusive rights to them.

figure 12.4

Saturn's Brand Name and Logo Featured on a Lands' End Gift Tote Bag

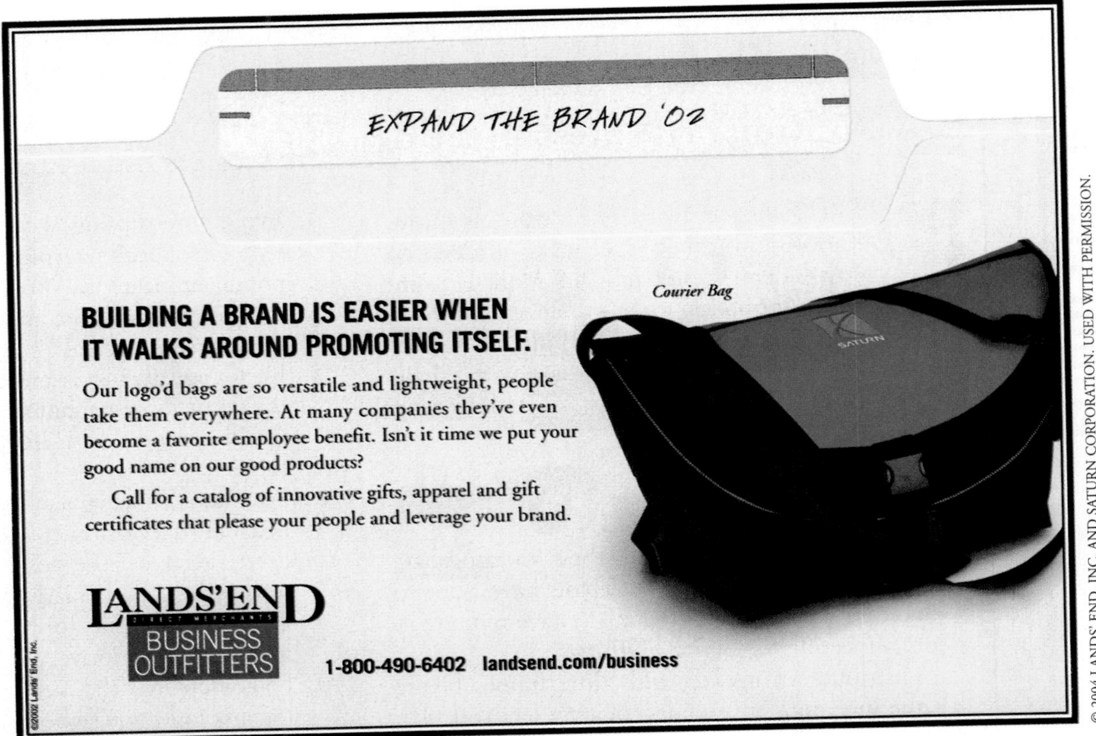

Marketers feel increasingly hard-pressed to coin effective brand names, as multitudes of competitors rush to stake out brand names for their own products. Some companies register names before they have products to fit the names to prevent competitors from using them. Few, however, have found as memorable a name for their product as Louisiana pharmacist George Boudreaux, whose highly successful diaper rash cream is called Boudreaux's Butt Paste. "If I had called it George's Diaper Rash Ointment," Boudreaux asked a reporter, "would we be talking now?"[9]

marketing miss — SPAM versus Spam: Who Will Win?

Background. SPAM (uppercase letters) is the trademark of a canned meat product produced by Hormel Foods Co. It's been around for decades and was a frequent, if not particularly popular, food ration for the U.S. armed forces during World War II. On the other hand, spam (lowercase letters) is that annoying junk mail that makes up half or more of all e-mail being sent today. The name originated in a Monty Python skit in which a group of Vikings in a restaurant sang "Spam, spam, spam, spam . . ." endlessly and in increasingly louder tones. What could be more annoying? Well, unsolicited e-mail.

The Marketing Problem. While unsolicited ads are even less popular than canned meat, Hormel marketers don't want anyone to confuse the two. The e-mail variety of spam has quickly become even better known than the branded food product, and the name is undoubtedly here to stay. It has even been incorporated into the names of some software products designed to get rid of unwanted messages.

The Outcome. Hormel's Web site includes a full explanation of the origins of both names and advises visitors of the proper spelling of

When a class of products becomes generally known by the original brand name of a specific offering, the brand name may become a descriptive generic name. If this occurs, the original owner loses exclusive claim to the brand name. The generic names nylon, aspirin, escalator, kerosene, and zipper started as brand names. Other generic names that were once brand names include cola, yo-yo, linoleum, and shredded wheat. See the accompanying "Marketing Miss" feature to appreciate what the makers of SPAM are up against when it comes to protecting their brand name.

Marketers must distinguish between brand names that have become legally generic terms and those that seem generic only in many consumers' eyes. Consumers often adopt legal brand names as descriptive names. Jell-O, for instance, is a brand name owned exclusively by General Foods, but many consumers casually apply it as a descriptive name for gelatin desserts. Similarly, many people use the term Kleenex to refer to facial tissues. English and Australian consumers use the brand name Hoover as a verb for vacuuming. Xerox is such a well-known brand name that people frequently—though incorrectly—use it as a verb to mean photocopying. To protect its valuable trademark, Xerox Corp. has created advertisements explaining that Xerox is a brand name and registered trademark and should not be used as a verb.

Briefly Speaking

The brand is the amusement park. The product is the souvenir.

Nicholas Graham

founder and CUO (Chief Underpants Officer), Joe Boxer, Inc.

TRADEMARKS

Businesses invest considerable resources in developing and promoting brands and brand identities. The high value of brand equity encourages firms to take steps in protecting the expenditures they invest in their brands.

A **trademark** is a brand for which the owner claims exclusive legal protection. A trademark should not be confused with a trade name, which identifies a company. The Coca-Cola Company is a trade name, but Coke is a trademark of the company's product. Some trade names duplicate companies' brand names. For example, Stride Rite is the children's shoe brand name of Stride Rite Corporation.

trademark Brand for which the owner claims exclusive legal protection.

Protecting Trademarks

Trademark protection confers the exclusive legal right to use a brand name, brand mark, and any slogan or product name abbreviation. It designates the origin or source of a good or service. The character of Mr. Clean shown in Figure 12.5 is a trademarked symbol.

Frequently, trademark protection is applied to words or phrases, such as *Bud* for Budweiser or *the Met* for the New York Metropolitan Opera. For example, the courts upheld Budweiser's trademark in

each. It also carefully avoids using the word *spam* as much as possible and instead refers to "unsolicited commercial e-mail," or UCE. The site concludes, "Ultimately, we are trying to avoid the day when the consuming public asks, 'Why would Hormel Foods name its product after junk e-mail?'"

Lessons Learned. There is no way to guarantee that your product's name will not some day be transformed into a generic term, as nylon and zipper were. If the name has negative connotations, as spam does, sometimes the best defense is change. It's happened before. In the early 1980s, marketers of a popular diet candy named Ayds at first fought the encroachment of AIDS on its brand equity, proclaiming, "Let the disease change its name." But eventually, they realized that the battle was a losing one and chose a new name. The future will show how long Hormel can hang on.

Sources: "SPAM and the Internet," http://www.spam.com/ci/ci_in.htm, accessed April 17, 2004; Amit Asaravala and Bill Lubinger, "Hormel's Spam Aims to Stand Tall over Its Lower-case Nemesis," *Mobile Register*, December 28, 2003, p. 3E; "Tomorrow's Menu: Spam, Spam, Spam," *Wired News*, http://www.wired.com/news, December 11, 2003.

figure 12.5

Mr. Clean: Trademark of the Famous Household Cleaner

Owens Corning uses the color pink as part of its trade dress. In fact, the company has registered the color as a trademark to distinguish its insulation from competitors'.

one case, ruling that an exterminating company's slogan "This Bug's for You" infringed on Budweiser's rights.

Firms can also receive trademark protection for packaging elements and product features such as shape, design, and typeface. U.S. law has fortified trademark protection in recent years. The Federal Trademark Dilution Act of 1995 gives a trademark holder the right to sue for trademark infringement even if other products using its brand are not particularly similar or easily confused in the minds of consumers. The infringing company does not even have to know that it is diluting another's trademark. The act also gives a trademark holder the right to sue if another party imitates its trademark.

The Internet may be the next battlefield for trademark infringement cases. Some companies are attempting to protect their trademarks by filing infringement cases against companies using similar Internet addresses.

Trade Dress

Visual cues used in branding create an overall look sometimes referred to as **trade dress.** These visual components may be related to color selections, sizes, package and label shapes, and similar factors. For example, McDonald's golden arches, Merrill Lynch's bull, and the yellow of Shell's seashell are all part of these products' trade dress. Owens Corning has registered the color pink to distinguish its insulation from the competition. A combination of visual cues may also constitute trade dress. Consider a Mexican food product that uses the colors of the Mexican flag: green, white, and red.

Trade dress disputes have led to numerous courtroom battles. In one widely publicized case, Kendall-Jackson Vineyards and Winery sued Ernest & Julio Gallo Winery Inc., claiming that the bottle design used for Gallo's Turning Leaf Chardonnay was too similar to its Kendall's Vintner's Reserve Chardonnay bottle. Kendall-Jackson lost in court, but this case suggests the importance that firms assign to trade dress.[10]

DEVELOPING GLOBAL BRAND NAMES AND TRADEMARKS

Cultural and language variations make brand-name selection a difficult undertaking for international marketers; an excellent brand name or symbol in one country may prove disastrous in another. Iranian detergent producer Paxan Corp., for example, might have a hard time marketing its laundry detergent Barf to English-speaking countries. (In Iran, *barf* means "snow.")[11] A firm marketing a product in multiple countries must also decide whether to use a single brand name for universal promotions or tailor names to individual countries. Most languages contain *o* and *k* sounds, so *okay* has become an international word. Most languages also have a short *a,* so Coca-Cola, Kodak, and Texaco work as effective brands abroad. Figure 12.6 shows the most popular global brand name.

Trademarks that are effective in their home countries may do less well in other cultures. Perhaps the world's most dubious brand name at the moment is attached to a line of clothing recently launched by one of Osama bin Laden's relatives, Yeslam Binladin. Yeslam Binladin applied for trademark protection for the Bin Ladin clothing label in Switzerland several months before the

DANIEL ACKER/BLOOMBERG NEWS/LANDOV

Figure 12.6

Coca-Cola: The World's Most Valuable Brand

tragedies of September 11, 2001. In spite of the events, he decided to push ahead with his line. Yeslam is from a different branch of the family (the surnames are spelled slightly differently), and his Saudi family is well respected in the Middle East, where it controls a $5 billion construction conglomerate, the Saudi Binladin Group. So Yeslam hopes to counteract negative impressions of the Bin Ladin brand name with a positive one. The clothing line will appear first in the Arab world, then in Europe, and much later in the U.S. Yeslam wants to donate a portion of the profits from the clothing line to a charitable foundation in Switzerland. Gaining worldwide acceptance for the label will undoubtedly be an uphill battle. "It's not that the sins of the fathers should fall on the shoulders of the children, or that one brother should be blamed for the actions of another," explains Mario Boselli, head of Italy's fashion trade organization. "But I can't see how someone could ever try to exploit this type of notoriety."[12]

PACKAGING

A firm's product strategy must also address questions about packaging. Like its brand name, a product's package can powerfully influence buyers' purchase decisions.

Marketers are applying increasingly scientific methods to their packaging decisions. Rather than experimenting with physical models or drawings, more and more package designers work on special computer graphics that create three-dimensional images of packages in thousands of colors, shapes, and typefaces. Another software program helps marketers design effective packaging by simulating the displays shoppers see when they walk down supermarket aisles. Companies conduct marketing research to evaluate current packages and to test alternative package designs. Kellogg, for example, tested its Nutri-Grain cereal package—as well as the product itself—before launching the product into the market.

A package serves three major objectives: (1) protection against damage, spoilage, and pilferage; (2) assistance in marketing the product; and (3) cost effectiveness. Let's briefly consider each of these objectives.

Protection against Damage, Spoilage, and Pilferage

The original objective of packaging was to offer physical protection for the merchandise. Products typically pass through several stages of handling between manufacturing and customer purchases, and a package must protect its contents from damage. Furthermore, packages of perishable products must protect the contents against spoilage in transit and in storage until purchased by the consumer. The American Plastics Council developed an advertising campaign to promote the benefits of using plastics in food packaging, asserting that plastic bottles, wraps, and containers reduce the chance of food contamination and that tamper-resistant plastic seals provide product safety assurance.

Fears of product tampering have forced many firms to improve package designs. Over-the-counter medicines are sold in tamper-resistant packages covered with warnings informing consumers not to purchase merchandise without protective seals intact. Many grocery items and light-sensitive products are packaged in tamper-resistant containers as well. Products in glass jars, like spaghetti sauce and jams, often come with vacuum-depressed buttons in the lids that pop up the first time the lids are opened.

Likewise, many packages offer important safeguards for retailers against pilferage. Shoplifting and employee theft cost retailers several billion dollars each year. To limit this activity, many packages feature oversized cardboard backings too large to fit into a shoplifter's pocket or purse. Efficient packaging that protects against damage, spoilage, and theft is especially important for international marketers, who must contend with varying climatic conditions and the added time and stress involved in overseas shipping.

H.J. Heinz completely redesigned its packaging to make its product easier to use. Customers routinely turned ketchup bottles upside down to get the last bit out of the bottle. So a smart package designer fixed the problem.

Assistance in Marketing the Product

The proliferation of new products, changes in consumer lifestyles and buying habits, and marketers' emphasis on targeting smaller market segments have increased the importance of packaging as a promotional tool. Many firms are addressing consumer concerns about protecting the environment by designing packages made of biodegradable and recyclable materials. To demonstrate serious concern regarding environmental protection, Procter & Gamble, Coors, McDonald's, BP Chemical, and other firms have created ads that describe their efforts in developing environmentally sound packaging.

In a grocery store where thousands of different items compete for notice, a product must capture the shopper's attention. Marketers combine colors, sizes, shapes, graphics, and typefaces to establish distinctive trade dress that sets their products apart from the products of competitors. Packaging can help establish a common identity for a group of items sold under the same brand name. Like the brand name, a package should evoke the product's image and communicate its value.

Packages can also enhance convenience for the buyers. Pump dispensers, for example, facilitate the use of products ranging from mustard to insect repellent. Squeezable bottles of honey and ketchup make the products easier to use and store. Packaging provides key benefits for convenience foods such as meals and snacks packaged in microwavable containers, juice drinks in aseptic packages, and frozen entrees and vegetables packaged in single-serving portions. Because tests show that corks in wine bottles have a failure rate between 3 and 15 percent, resulting in tainted or degraded wine, a longstanding tradition in the wine industry is beginning to change. Argyle Winery of Dundee, Oregon, recently began using screw caps—previously viewed as a telltale symbol of low-priced wines of inferior quality—on its entire production of Pinot Noir. Other winemakers are experimenting with synthetic cork and stainless steel seals that are also tamper proof, and although the trend is still controversial, many feel that for wine meant to be aged less than 10 years, popping traditional corks may become a ritual of the past.[13]

Some firms increase consumer utility with packages designed for reuse. Empty peanut butter jars and jelly jars have long doubled as drinking glasses. Parents can buy bubble bath in animal-shaped plastic bottles suitable for bathtub play. Packaging is a major component in Avon's overall marketing strategy. The firm's decorative, reusable bottles have even become collectibles.

Cost-Effective Packaging

Although packaging must perform a number of functions for the producer, marketers, and consumers, it must do so at a reasonable cost. Sometimes changes in the packaging can make packages both cheaper and better for the environment. Compact disc manufacturers, for instance, once packaged music CDs in two containers, a disc-sized plastic box inside a long, cardboard box that fit into the record bins in stores. Consumers protested against the waste of the long boxes, and the recording industry finally agreed to eliminate the cardboard outer packaging altogether. Now CDs come in just the plastic cases, and stores display them in reusable plastic holders to discourage theft.

Labeling

Labels were once a separate element that was applied to a package; today, they are an integral part of a typical package. Labels perform both promotional and informational functions. A **label** carries an item's brand name or symbol, the name and address of the manufacturer or distributor, information about the product's composition and size, and recommended uses. The right label can play an important role in attracting consumer attention and encouraging purchases.

Consumer confusion and dissatisfaction over such descriptions as giant economy size, king size, and family size led to the passage of the Fair Packaging and Labeling Act in 1966. The act requires that a label offer adequate information concerning the package contents and that a package design facilitate value comparisons among competing products.

The Nutrition Labeling and Education Act of 1990 imposes a uniform format in which food manufacturers must disclose nutritional information about their products. In addition, the Food and Drug Administration (FDA) has mandated design standards for nutritional labels that provide clear guidelines to consumers about food products. The FDA has also tightened definitions for loosely used terms like light, fat free, lean, and extra lean, and it mandates that labels list the amounts of fat, sodium, dietary fiber, calcium, vitamins, and other components in typical servings. The latest ruling requires food manufacturers to include on nutritional labels the total amount of trans fats—hydrogenated oils that improve texture and freshness but contribute to high levels of cholesterol—in each product.[14]

Labeling requirements differ elsewhere in the world. In Canada, for example, labels must provide information in both French and English. The type and amount of information required on labels also vary among nations. International marketers must carefully design labels to conform to the regulations of each country in which they market their merchandise.

The **Universal Product Code (UPC)** designation is another important aspect of a label or package. Introduced in 1974 as a method for cutting expenses in the supermarket industry, UPCs are numerical bar codes printed on packages. Optical scanner systems read these codes, and computer systems recognize items and print their prices on cash register receipts. Although UPC scanners are costly, they permit both considerable labor savings over manual pricing and improved inventory control. The Universal Product Code is also a major asset for marketing research. However, many consumers feel frustrated when only a UPC is placed on a package without an additional price tag because they do not always know how much an item costs if the price labels are missing from the shelf. With the advent of radio frequency ID tags—electronic chips which carry encoded product identification—UPC bar codes will probably go the way of the dinosaur.

BRAND EXTENSIONS

Some brands become so popular that marketers may decide to use them on unrelated products in pursuit of instant recognition for the new offerings. The strategy of attaching a popular brand name to a new product in an unrelated product category is known as **brand extension.** This practice should not be confused with **line extensions,** which refers to new sizes, styles, or related products. A brand extension, in contrast, carries over from one product nothing but the brand name. In establishing brand extensions, marketers hope to gain access to new customers and markets by building on the equity already established in their existing brands.

brand extension Strategy of attaching a popular brand name to a new product in an unrelated product category.

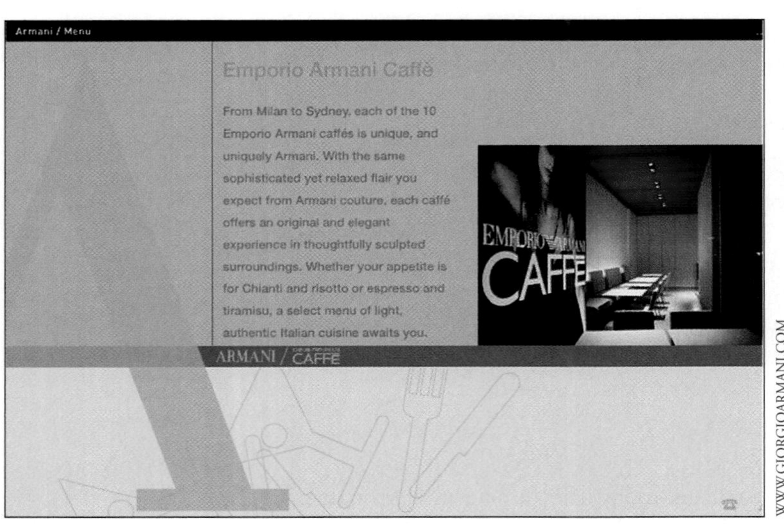

Giorgio Armani, best known for his designer clothing, has recently begun extending his brand by opening cafes around the world.

Fashion designer Giorgio Armani has branched out from his original line of designer clothing into Armani perfumes, cosmetics, eyewear, watches, accessories, chocolates, flowers, and even furniture. He also recently extended the Armani brand to include restaurants and cafés in Paris, London, Milan, and New York. There is even an Armani nightclub. Most recently, Armani's company has begun a $1 billion hotel partnership with Dubai's Emaar Properties, in which the designer will oversee designs for 10 new luxury hotels and four resorts to be built over the next several years.[15]

BRAND LICENSING

A growing number of firms have authorized other companies to use their brand names. As we saw in the opening story, even colleges have licensed their logos and trademarks. This practice, known as **brand licensing,** expands a firm's exposure in the marketplace, much as a brand extension does. The brand name's owner also receives an extra source of income in the form of royalties from licensees, typically 4 to 8 percent of wholesale revenues.

Brand experts note several potential problems with licensing, however. Brand names do not transfer well to all products. In addition, if a licensee produces a poor-quality product or an item ethically incompatible with the original brand, the arrangement could damage the reputation of the brand.

Even highly successful brands can run into licensing problems. A 13-year-old licensing lawsuit that could have cost Walt Disney Co. as much as $1 billion was recently thrown out of court. The suit was brought by Stephen Slesinger Inc., a family-owned company that controls some Winnie the Pooh merchandising rights it licenses to the entertainment giant. Slesinger has received more than $80 million from the license with Disney in the last 20 years—Winnie the Pooh merchandise outsells Mickey Mouse items, generating billions for Disney—but the company claimed that Disney had underpaid royalties during that period. It plans to appeal the court's decision, but Disney claims the items named in the suit—DVDs, tapes, and computer software—are not covered under the original licensing contract.[16]

1. Distinguish between a brand name and a trademark.
2. What are the three purposes of packaging?
3. Describe brand extension and brand licensing.

NEW-PRODUCT PLANNING

As its offerings enter the maturity and decline stages of the product life cycle, a firm must add new items to continue to prosper. Regular additions of new products to the firm's line help to protect it from product obsolescence.

New products are the lifeblood of any business, and survival depends on a steady flow of new entries. Some new products may implement major technological breakthroughs. Other new products simply extend existing product lines. In other words, a new product is one that either the company or the customer has not handled before. Only about 10 percent of new-product introductions bring truly new capabilities to consumers.

5 Identify and briefly describe each of the four strategies for new-product development.

PRODUCT DEVELOPMENT STRATEGIES

A firm's strategy for new-product development varies according to its existing product mix and the match between current offerings and the firm's overall marketing objectives. The current market positions of products also affect product development strategy. Figure 12.7 identifies four alternative development strategies as market penetration, market development, product development, and product diversification.

A **market penetration strategy** seeks to increase sales of existing products in existing markets. Firms can attempt to extend their penetration of markets in several ways. They may modify products, improve product quality, or promote new and different ways to use products. Packaged goods marketers often pursue this strategy to boost market share for mature products in mature markets. Product positioning often plays a major role in such a strategy.

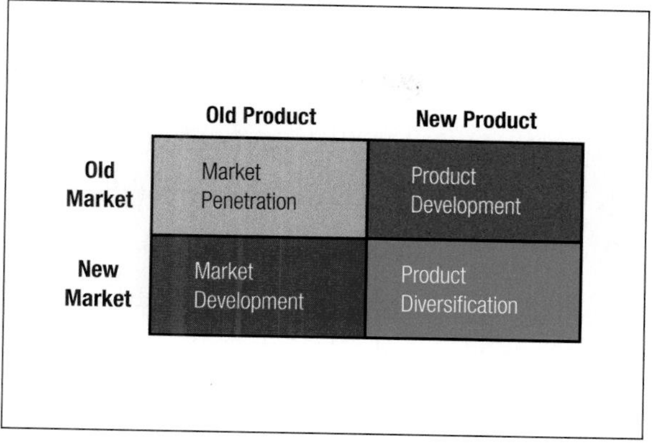

figure 12.7

Alternative Product Development Strategies

Product positioning refers to consumers' perceptions of a product's attributes, uses, quality, and advantages and disadvantages relative to competing brands. Marketers often conduct marketing research studies to analyze consumer preferences and to construct product positioning maps that plot their products' positions in relation to those of competitors' offerings. Procter & Gamble, long known for its premium-priced consumer goods, has developed a less-costly formulation of its Crest toothpaste for the Chinese market. Also, the company bought Clairol, bringing under its corporate umbrella that company's lower priced shampoos. P&G is also reviewing the pricing of its existing products to ensure that their most expensive products are in line with local consumer demands.[17]

A **market development strategy** concentrates on finding new markets for existing products. Market segmentation, discussed in Chapter 9, provides useful support for such an effort. Bank of America has succeeded in developing a new market by targeting Asian residents in San Francisco with special television commercials aimed at Chinese, Korean, and Vietnamese consumers.

The strategy of **product development** refers to the introduction of new products into identifiable or established markets. A few years ago, Nike decided to enter the golf market by creating a new division called Nike Golf and introducing its first new golf products—branded golf balls. Although the company stumbled at first by targeting casual and budget-oriented players, the firm's marketers quickly changed gears and went after more skilled players who were willing to purchase premium balls. Today, Nike Golf's market share amounts to between 8 and 10 percent of the entire golf ball market of $800 million. With that success, the company decided to introduce its golf clubs, which it spent two years developing. Nike began by offering drivers and later introduced a complete range of clubs.[18]

Firms may also choose to introduce new products into markets in which they have already established positions to try to increase overall market share. These new offerings are called *flanker brands*. The fragrance industry uses this strategy extensively when it develops scents that are related to their most popular products. The flanker scents are related in both their smell and their names. Clinique's popular Happy cologne, for example, has a sister flanker brand called Happy Heart. Flanker brands in the fragrance industry have generated retail sales on the order of $200 million.[19]

Finally, a **product diversification strategy** focuses on developing entirely new products for new markets. Some firms look for new target markets that complement their existing markets; others look in completely new directions. Dell, the top PC maker, has begun marketing its own brand of consumer electronics, selling flat-screen TVs and MP3 players on its Web site and even offering an online music downloading store. The company follows many of its computer-firm competitors into the consumer electronics market, not only because PC sales are slowing but also because music, movies, and photos are increasingly relying on digital technology. Says president Kevin Rollins, "How many new products can Dell add to its portfolio? Where does it end? We think there's a somewhat limitless number of products and services we could get into."[20]

In selecting a new-product strategy, marketers should keep in mind an additional potential problem: **cannibalization.** Any firm wants to avoid investing resources in a new-product introduction that will adversely affect sales of existing products. A product that takes sales from another offering in the same product line is said to cannibalize that line. A company can accept some loss of sales from existing products if the new offering will generate sufficient additional sales to warrant its investment in its development and market introduction.

6 Describe the consumer adoption process.

adoption process Stages that consumers go through in learning about a new product, trying it, and deciding whether to purchase it again.

THE CONSUMER ADOPTION PROCESS

In the **adoption process,** consumers go through a series of stages from first learning about the new product to trying it and deciding whether to purchase it regularly or to reject it. These stages in the consumer adoption process can be classified as follows:

1. *Awareness.* Individuals first learn of the new product, but they lack full information about it.
2. *Interest.* Potential buyers begin to seek information about it.
3. *Evaluation.* They consider the likely benefits of the product.
4. *Trial.* They make trial purchases to determine its usefulness.
5. *Adoption/Rejection.* If the trial purchase produces satisfactory results, they decide to use the product regularly.[21]

Marketers must understand the adoption process to move potential consumers to the adoption stage. Once marketers recognize a large number of consumers at the interest stage, they can take steps to stimulate sales by moving these buyers through the evaluation and trial stages. Johnson & Johnson enhanced the evaluation and trial of its disposable contact lenses by offering free trial pairs to consumers. Time Warner's America Online mails its Internet-access software and offers a free one-month membership to computer owners who are not AOL members. From time to time, you may receive free samples of breakfast cereals, snack foods, cosmetics, or shampoos in the mail. These companies are encouraging you to try their products in the hope that you will eventually adopt them.

ADOPTER CATEGORIES

consumer innovator People who purchase new products almost as soon as the products reach the market.

First buyers of new products, the so-called **consumer innovators,** are people who purchase new products almost as soon as these products reach the market. Later adopters wait for additional information and rely on the experiences of initial buyers before making trial purchases. Consumer innovators welcome innovations in each product area. Some computer users, for instance, rush to install new software immediately after each update becomes available. Some physicians pioneered the uses of new pharmaceutical products for their AIDS patients.

A number of studies about the adoption of new products have identified five categories of purchasers based on relative times of adoption. These categories, shown in Figure 12.8, are consumer innovators, early adopters, early majority, late majority, and laggards.

diffusion process Process by which new goods or services are accepted in the marketplace.

While the adoption process focuses on individuals and the steps they go through in making the ultimate decision of whether to become repeat purchasers of the new product or to reject it as a failure to satisfy their needs, the **diffusion process** focuses on all members of a community or social system. The focus here is on the speed at which an innovative product is accepted or rejected by all members of the community.

figure 12.8

Categories of Adopters Based on Relative Times of Adoption

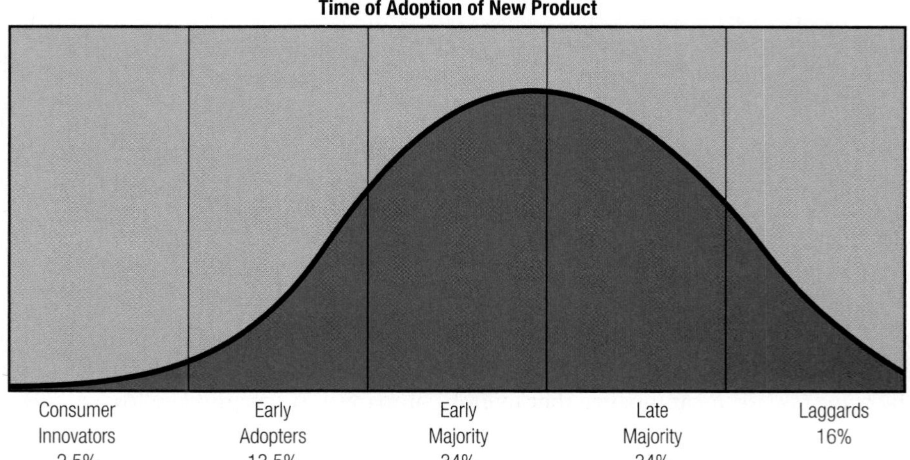

Figure 12.8 shows the diffusion process as following a normal distribution from a small group of early purchasers (called *innovators*) to the final group of consumers (called *laggards*) to make trial purchases of the new product. A few people adopt at first and then the number of adopters increases rapidly as the value of the product becomes apparent. The adoption rate finally diminishes as the number of potential consumers who have not adopted, or purchased, the product diminishes. Typically, innovators make up the first 2.5 percent of buyers who adopt the new product; laggards are the last 16 percent to do so. Figure 12.8 excludes those who never adopt the product.

IDENTIFYING EARLY ADOPTERS

It's no surprise that identifying consumers or organizations that are most likely to try a new product can be vital to a product's success. By reaching these buyers early in the product's development or introduction, marketers can treat these adopters as a test market, evaluating the product and discovering suggestions for modifications. Since early purchasers often act as opinion leaders from whom others seek advice, their attitudes toward new products quickly spread to others. Acceptance or rejection of the innovation by these purchasers can help forecast its expected success. Several auto companies, including Honda and Ford, have developed gasoline-electric vehicles for the consumer market. These hybrid vehicles use a combination of gasoline and electric batteries to get superior gas mileage and send fewer exhaust emissions into the air. But although Honda and Ford got their vehicles to market first, Toyota tried an entirely different marketing approach in attempting to gain a competitive edge. While Honda and Ford targeted environmentalists and consumers who are concerned about clean air, Toyota aimed its first promotional efforts at consumer innovators and early adopters. The ads for its new Prius mentioned its environmentally friendly features, but they focused on consumers who wanted to be the first on their block to have one of these unique cars.[22]

A large number of studies have established the general characteristics of first adopters. These pioneers tend to be younger, have higher social status, are better educated, and enjoy higher incomes than other consumers. They are more mobile than later adopters and change both their jobs and addresses more often. They also rely more heavily than later adopters on impersonal information sources; more hesitant buyers depend primarily on company-generated promotional information and word-of-mouth communications.

Rate of Adoption Determinants

Frisbees progressed from the product introduction stage to the market maturity stage in a period of six months. By contrast, the U.S. Department of Agriculture tried for 13 years to convince corn farmers to use hybrid seed corn, an innovation capable of doubling crop yields. Five characteristics of a product innovation influence its adoption rate:

1. *Relative advantage.* An innovation that appears far superior to previous ideas offers a greater relative advantage—reflected in terms of lower price, physical improvements, or ease of use—and increases the product's adoption rate.

2. *Compatibility.* An innovation consistent with the values and experiences of potential adopters attracts new buyers at a relatively rapid rate. Investors who are already comfortable with making transactions online would probably be attracted to Lycos's LiveCharts, which offers live, real-time streaming charts showing the activity of stocks.

3. *Complexity.* The relative difficulty of understanding the innovation influences the speed of acceptance. In most cases, consumers move slowly in adopting new products that they find difficult to understand or use. Farmers' cautious acceptance of hybrid seed corn illustrates how long an adoption can take.

4. *Possibility of trial use.* An initial free or discounted trial of a good or service means that adopters can reduce their risk of financial or social loss when they try the product. A coupon for a free item or a free night's stay at a hotel can accelerate the rate of adoption.

5. *Observability.* If potential buyers can observe an innovation's superiority in a tangible form, the adoption rate increases. In-store demonstrations or even advertisements that focus on the superiority of a product can encourage buyers to adopt a product.

Marketers who want to accelerate the rate of adoption can manipulate these five characteristics at least to some extent. An informative promotional message about a new allergy drug could help consumers overcome their hesitation in adopting this complex product. Effective product design can emphasize an item's advantages over the competition. Everyone likes to receive something for free, so giving away small samples of a new product lets consumers try it at little or no risk. In-home demonstrations or trial home placements of items such as furniture or carpeting can achieve similar results. Marketers must also make positive attempts in ensuring the innovation's compatibility with adopters' value systems.

ORGANIZING FOR NEW-PRODUCT DEVELOPMENT

A firm needs to be organized in such a way that its personnel can stimulate and coordinate new-product development. Some companies contract with independent design firms to develop new products. Many assign product-innovation functions to one or more of the following entities: new-product committees, new-product departments, product managers, and venture teams.

New-Product Committees

The most common organizational arrangement for activities in developing a new product is to center these functions in a new-product committee. This group typically brings together experts in such areas as marketing, finance, manufacturing, engineering, research, and accounting. Committee members spend less time conceiving and developing their own new-product ideas than reviewing and approving new-product plans that arise elsewhere in the organization. The committee might review ideas from the engineering and design staff or perhaps from marketers and salespeople who are in constant contact with customers.

Since members of a new-product committee hold important jobs in the firm's functional areas, their support for any new-product plan likely foreshadows approval for further development. However, new-product committees in large companies tend to reach decisions slowly and maintain conservative views. Sometimes members may compromise so they can return to their regular responsibilities.

New-Product Departments

Many companies establish separate, formally organized departments to generate and refine new-product ideas. The departmental structure overcomes the limitations of the new-product committee system and encourages innovation as a permanent full-time activity. The new-product department is responsible for all phases of a development project within the firm, including screening decisions, developing product specifications, and coordinating product testing. The head of the department wields substantial authority and typically reports to the chief executive officer, chief operating officer, or a top marketing executive.

Product Managers

A **product manager** is another term for a brand manager, a function mentioned earlier in the chapter. This marketer supports the marketing strategies of an individual product or product line. Procter & Gamble, for instance, assigned its first product manager in 1927, when it made one person responsible for Camay soap.

Product managers set prices, develop advertising and sales promotion programs, and work with sales representatives in the field. In a company that markets multiple products, product managers fulfill key functions in the marketing department. They provide individual attention for each product and support and coordinate efforts of the firm's sales force, marketing research department, and advertising department. Product managers often lead new-product development programs, including creation of new-product ideas and recommendations for improving existing products.

However, as mentioned earlier in the chapter, companies such as Procter & Gamble and General Mills have either modified the product manager structure or done away with it altogether in favor of a category management structure. Category managers have profit and loss responsibility, which is not characteristic of the product management system. This change has largely come about because of customer preference, but it can also benefit a manufacturer by avoiding duplication of some jobs and competition among the company's own brands and its managers.

Venture Teams

A **venture team** gathers a group of specialists from different areas of an organization to work together in developing new products. The venture team must meet criteria for return on investment, uniqueness of product, serving a well-defined need, compatibility of the product with existing technology, and strength of patent protection. Although the organization sets up the venture team as a temporary entity, its flexible life span may extend over a number of years. When purchases confirm the commercial potential of a new product, an existing division may take responsibility for that product, or it may serve as the nucleus of a new business unit or of an entirely new company.

Some marketing organizations differentiate between venture teams and task forces. A new-product task force assembles an interdisciplinary group working on temporary assignment through their functional departments. Its basic activities center on coordinating and integrating the work of the firm's functional departments on a specific project.

Unlike a new-product committee, a venture team does not disband after every meeting. Team members accept project assignments as major responsibilities, and the team exercises the authority it needs to both plan and implement a course of action. To stimulate product innovation, the venture team typically communicates directly with top management, but it functions as an entity separate from the basic organization.

1. Who are consumer innovators?
2. What characteristics of a product innovation can influence its adoption rate?
3. What is the role of a venture team in new-product development?

THE NEW-PRODUCT DEVELOPMENT PROCESS

Once a firm is organized for new-product development, it can establish procedures for moving new-product ideas to the marketplace. Developing a new product is often time-consuming, risky, and expensive. Usually, firms must generate dozens of new-product ideas to produce even one successful product. In fact, the failure rate of new products averages 80 percent. Products fail for a number of reasons, including inadequate market assessments, lack of market orientation, poor screening and project evaluation, product defects, and inadequate launch efforts. And these blunders cost a bundle: Firms invest nearly half of the total resources devoted to product innovation on products that become commercial failures.

A new product is more likely to become successful if the firm follows a six-step development process shown in Figure 12.9: (1) idea generation, (2) screening, (3) business analysis, (4) development, (5) test marketing, and (6) commercialization. Of course, each step requires decisions about whether to proceed further or abandon the project. And each step involves a greater financial investment.

(7) List the stages in the process for developing new products.

Traditionally, most companies have developed new products through phased development, which follows the six-step process in an orderly sequence. Responsibility for each phase passes first from product planners to designers and engineers, to manufacturers, and finally to marketers. The phased development method can work well for firms that dominate mature markets and can develop variations on existing products. But with rapid changes in technology and markets, many companies feel pressured to speed up the development process.

This time pressure has encouraged many firms to implement accelerated product development programs. These programs generally consist of teams with experts from design, manufacturing, marketing, and sales who carry out development projects from idea generation to commercialization.

figure 12.9

Steps in the New-Product Development Process

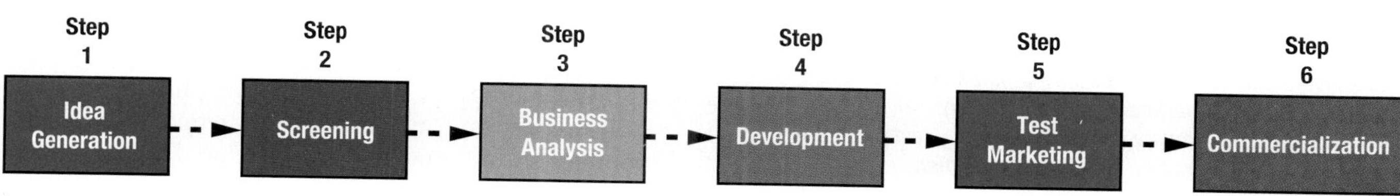

This method can reduce the time needed to develop products because team members work on the six steps concurrently rather than in sequence. Wyeth was able to bring its antidepressant Effexor to market in just two years—half the usual time it takes to develop and launch such a drug—by using such a team.[23]

Whether a firm pursues phased development or parallel product development, all phases can benefit from planning tools and scheduling methods such as the program evaluation and review technique (PERT) and the critical path method (CPM). These techniques, originally developed by the U.S. Navy in connection with construction of the Polaris missile and submarine, map out the sequence of each step in a process and show the time allotments for each activity. Detailed PERT and CPM flowcharts help marketers to coordinate all activities entailed in the development and introduction of new products.

In introducing its golf clubs described earlier in the chapter, Nike followed its own patented business strategy that includes a systematic product introduction, extensive endorsement by golf tour professionals—including Tiger Woods—and a new-product budget of up to $100 million, with a $35 million marketing budget. The financial outlays illustrate the importance of planning.[24]

IDEA GENERATION

New-product development begins with ideas from many sources: suggestions from customers, the sales force, research-and-development specialists, competing products, suppliers, retailers, and independent inventors. Some top executives are beginning to recognize the value of keeping their eyes, ears, and minds open to ideas from employees at all levels of the firm. Susan Lyne, president of ABC Entertainment, says, "My top priority is getting the younger, creative people at the network to feel comfortable speaking up. . . . We need to find the gaps in our schedule, identify categories of viewers that we're missing, and force everyone to address those needs as we read the material coming in."[25]

Makeovers are not just the stuff of reality TV. Products get image makeovers, too. When Georgia-Pacific improved its Brawny paper towels, its marketers also completely revamped the look of its Brawny man. The company tested the new clean-shaven look to be sure it had a winner.

SCREENING

Screening separates ideas with commercial potential from those that cannot meet company objectives. Some organizations maintain checklists of development standards in determining whether a project should be abandoned or considered further. These checklists typically include factors such as product uniqueness, availability of raw materials, and the proposed product's compatibility with current product offerings, existing facilities, and present capabilities. The screening stage may also allow for open discussions of new-product ideas among different parts of the organization.

BUSINESS ANALYSIS

A product idea that survives the initial screening must then pass a thorough business analysis. This stage consists of assessing the new product's potential market, growth rate, and likely competitive strengths. Marketers must evaluate the compatibility of the proposed product with organizational resources.

Concept testing subjects the product idea to additional study prior to its actual development. This important aspect of a new product's business analysis represents a marketing research project that attempts to measure consumer attitudes and perceptions about the new-product idea. Focus groups and in-store polling can contribute effectively to concept testing. When Georgia-Pacific Corp. revamped its Brawny© paper towels, it not only budgeted $500 million for production upgrades to improve the product but also took a long hard look at the lumberjack on all the Brawny© packaging. Was it time to drop the character? Consumer testing among females showed wholehearted approval of the Brawny man, so he, too, underwent a makeover that started with consumers using digital images to create their ideal vision of his look. Said a partner at the design firm that helped create the new lumberjack, "We took what [consumers] had seen and blown up in their heads. They wanted him to be real, but not too real. They didn't want to be reminded of someone they dated, or the guy down the street."[26]

The screening and business analysis stages generate extremely important information for new-product development because they (1) define the proposed product's target market and customers' needs and wants and (2) determine the product's financial and technical requirements. Firms that are willing to invest money and time during these stages tend to be more successful at generating viable ideas and creating successful products.

DEVELOPMENT

Financial outlays increase substantially as a firm converts an idea into a visible product. The conversion process is the joint responsibility of the firm's development engineers, who turn the original concept into a product, and of its marketers, who provide feedback on consumer reactions to the product design, package, color, and other physical features. Many firms implement computer-aided design systems to streamline the development stage, and prototypes may go through numerous changes before the original mock-up becomes a final product.

TEST MARKETING

As discussed in Chapter 8, many firms test market their new-product offerings to gauge consumer reaction. After a company has developed a prototype, it may decide to test market it to measure consumer reactions under normal competitive conditions. Test marketing's purpose is to verify that the product will perform well in a real-life business environment. If the product does well, the company can proceed to commercialization. If it flops, the company can decide to fine-tune certain features and reintroduce it or pull the plug on the project altogether. Industries that rely heavily on test marketing are snack foods, automobiles, and movies. Of course, even if a product tests well and reaches the commercialization stage, it may still take a while to catch on with the general public.

Briefly Speaking

Product testing should not be the basis for introducing a new product because 90 percent of the failures have had successful product test results.

Richard H. Buskirk
American educator

COMMERCIALIZATION

When a new-product idea reaches the commercialization stage, it is ready for full-scale marketing. Commercialization of a major new product can expose the firm to substantial expenses. It must establish marketing strategies, fund outlays for production facilities, and acquaint the sales force, marketing intermediaries, and potential customers with the new product.

When Nike was ready to launch its drivers, wedges, and irons, the company unveiled them at the PGA Merchandise Show in Orlando, Florida. Several golf pros, including John Cook, Michael Campbell, and David Duval, used the clubs in successful tournament play. And Nike signed a multimillion-dollar endorsement deal with golf star Tiger Woods.[27] All of this was part of the commercialization process.

1. Where can ideas for new products come from?
2. What is concept testing?
3. What happens in the commercialization stage?

PRODUCT SAFETY AND LIABILITY

8 Explain the relationship between product safety and product liability.

A product can fulfill its mission of satisfying consumer needs only if it ensures safe operation. Manufacturers must design their products to protect users from harm. Products that lead to injuries, either directly or indirectly, can have disastrous consequences for their makers. **Product liability** refers to the responsibility of manufacturers and marketers for injuries and damages caused by their products. Chapter 3 discussed some of the major consumer protection laws that affect product safety. These laws include the Flammable Fabrics Act of 1953, the Fair Packaging and Labeling Act of 1966, the Poison Prevention Packaging Act of 1970, and the Consumer Product Safety Act of 1972.

Federal and state legislation play a major role in regulating product safety. The Poison Prevention Packaging Act requires drug manufacturers to place their products in packaging that is child resistant yet accessible to all adults, even ones who have trouble opening containers. The Consumer Product Safety Act created a powerful regulatory agency—the Consumer Product Safety Commission (CPSC). This agency has assumed jurisdiction over every consumer product category except food, automobiles, and a few other products already regulated by other agencies. The CPSC has the authority to ban products without court hearings, order recalls or redesigns of products, and inspect production facilities. It can charge managers of negligent companies with criminal offenses. The CPSC is especially watchful of products aimed at babies and young children.

The federal Food and Drug Administration (FDA) must approve food, medications, and health-related devices such as wheelchairs. The FDA can also take products off the market if concerns arise about the safety of these products.

The number of product liability lawsuits filed against manufacturers has skyrocketed in recent years. Although many of these claims reach settlements out of court, juries have decided on many others, sometimes awarding multimillion-dollar settlements. This threat has led most companies to step up efforts to ensure product safety. Safety warnings appear prominently on the labels of such potentially hazardous products as cleaning fluids and drain cleaners to inform users of the dangers of these products, particularly to children. Changes in product design have reduced the hazards posed by such products as lawn mowers, hedge trimmers, and toys. Product liability insurance has become an essential element for any new or existing product strategy. Premiums for this insurance have risen alarmingly, however, and insurers have almost entirely abandoned some kinds of coverage.

Regulatory activities and the increased number of liability claims have prompted companies to sponsor voluntary improvements in safety standards. Safety planning is now a vital element of product strategy, and many companies now publicize the safety planning and testing that go into the development of their products. Volvo, for example, is well known for the safety features it designs into its automobiles, and consumers recognize that fact when they decide to purchase a Volvo.

1. What is the role of the Consumer Product Safety Commission (CPSC)?
2. What safety issues come under the jurisdiction of the Food and Drug Administration (FDA)?

Strategic Implications of Marketing in the 21st Century

MARKETERS who want to see their products reach the marketplace successfully have a number of options for developing them, branding them, and developing a strong brand identity among consumers and business customers. The key is to integrate all of the options so that they are compatible with a firm's overall business and marketing strategy and ultimately the firm's mission. As marketers consider ideas for new products, they need to be careful not to send their companies in so many different directions as to dilute the identities of their brands, making it nearly impossible to keep track of what their companies do well. Category management can help companies develop a consistent product mix with strong branding, while at the same time meeting the needs of customers. Looking for ways to extend a brand without diluting it or compromising brand equity is also an important marketing strategy. Finally, marketers must continue to work to produce high-quality products that are also safe for all users.

REVIEW OF CHAPTER OBJECTIVES

1 Explain the benefits of category and brand management.

Category management is beneficial to a business because it gives direct responsibility for creating profitable product lines to category managers and their product group. Consumers respond to branding by making repeat purchases of favored goods and services. Therefore, managing brands and categories of brands or product lines well can result in a direct response from consumers, increasing profits and revenues for companies and creating consumer satisfaction. Brand and category managers can also enhance relationships with business customers such as retailers.

1.1. What stages do consumers go through in achieving the ultimate brand loyalty?

2 Identify the different types of brands.

A generic product is an item characterized by a plain label, no advertising, and no brand name. A manufacturer's brand is a brand name owned by a manufacturer or other producer. Private brands are brand names placed on products marketed by a wholesaler or retailer. A family brand is a brand name that identifies several related products. An individual brand is a unique brand name that identifies a specific offering within a firm's product line to avoid grouping it under a family brand.

2.1. Identify and briefly describe the different types of brands.

3 Explain the strategic value of brand equity.

Brand equity provides a competitive advantage for a firm because consumers are more likely to buy a product that carries a respected, well-known brand name. Brand equity also smoothes the path for global expansion.

3.1. Why is brand equity so important to companies?

4 Discuss how companies develop strong identities for their products and brands.

Effective brands communicate to a buyer an idea of the product's image. Trademarks, brand names, slogans, and brand icons create an association that satisfies the customer's expectation of the benefits that using or having the product will yield.

4.1. What are the characteristics of an effective brand name?
4.2. What role does packaging play in helping create brand loyalty and brand equity?

5 Identify and briefly describe each of the four strategies for new-product development.

The success of a new product can result from four product development strategies: (1) market penetration, in which a company seeks to increase sales of an existing product in an existing market; (2) market development, which concentrates on finding new markets for existing products; (3) product development, which is the introduction of new products into identifiable or established markets; and (4) product diversification, which focuses on developing entirely new products for new markets.

5.1. Describe the different product development strategies.

6 Describe the consumer adoption process.

In the adoption process, consumers go through a series of stages from learning about the new product to trying it and deciding whether to purchase it again. The stages are called awareness, interest, evaluation, trial, and adoption/rejection.

6.1. What are the five stages of the consumer adoption process?
6.2. Describe an instance in which you went through those stages to reach a decision about whether to accept or reject a product.

7 List the stages in the process for developing new products.

The six-step process includes: (1) idea generation, (2) screening, (3) business analysis, (4) development, (5) test marketing, and (6) commercialization. These steps may be performed sequentially or, in some cases, concurrently.

7.1. Describe the different ways companies can organize to develop new products.
7.2. List the six steps in the new-product development process.

⑧ Explain the relationship between product safety and product liability.

Product safety refers to the goal of manufacturers to create products that can be operated safely and will protect consumers from harm. Product liability is the responsibility of marketers and manufacturers for injuries and damages caused by their products. There are major consumer protection laws in place to protect consumers from faulty products.

8.1. Do you think strict regulations about product safety help or hurt marketers of products? Explain your answer.

MARKETING TERMS YOU NEED TO KNOW

brand 382
brand recognition 383
brand preference 383
brand insistence 383
generic products 385
manufacturer's brand 385
family brand 386
brand equity 387
category management 388
brand name 388
trademark 391
brand extension 395
adoption process 398
consumer innovator 398
diffusion process 398

OTHER IMPORTANT MARKETING TERMS

private brand 385
captive brand 386
individual brand 386
brand manager 388
brand mark 388
trade dress 392
label 395
Universal Product Code (UPC) 395
line extension 395
brand licensing 396
market penetration strategy 397
product positioning 397
market development strategy 397
product development 397
product diversification strategy 397
cannibalization 397
product manager 400
venture team 401
concept testing 402
product liability 403

PROJECTS AND TEAMWORK EXERCISES

1. Locate an advertisement for a product that illustrates an especially effective brand name, brand mark, packaging, and overall trade dress. Explain to the class why you think this product has a strong brand identity.
2. With a classmate, go shopping in the grocery store for a product that you think could benefit from updated or new package design. Then sketch out a new package design for the product, identifying and explaining your changes as well as your reasons for the changes. Bring the old package and your new package design to class to share with your classmates.
3. What category of consumer adopter best describes you? Do you follow the same adoption pattern for all products, or are you an early adopter for some and a laggard for others? Create a graph or chart showing your own consumer adoption patterns for different products.
4. With a classmate, choose a firm that interests you and together generate some ideas for new products that might be appropriate for the company. Test your ideas out on each other and then on your classmates. Which ideas make it past the first stage? Which don't? Why?
5. Consider the steps in the new-product development process. Do you think this process accounts for products that come into being by chance or accident? Why or why not? Defend your answer.
6. With a classmate, visit a couple of supermarkets and look for generic products. How many did you find and in what product categories? Are there any products you think could be successfully marketed as generics that are not now? Why do you think they would be successful?
7. Which product labels do you read? Over the next several days, keep a brief record of the labels you check while shopping. Do you read nutritional information when buying food products? Do you check care labels on clothes before you buy them? Do you read the directions or warnings on a product you haven't used before? Make notes about what

influenced your decision to read or not read the product labels. Did you feel they provided enough information, too little, or too much?

8. Some brands achieve customer loyalty by retaining an air of exclusivity and privilege, even though that often comes along with high price tags. Louis Vuitton, the maker of luxury leather goods, is one such firm. "You buy into the dream of Louis Vuitton," says one loyal customer. "We're part of a sect, and the more they put their prices up, the more we come back. They pull the wool over our eyes, but we love it." What kind of brand loyalty is this, and how does Vuitton achieve it?
9. Make a list of all the different brands of bottled water you can identify. Visit a grocery store, look at print ads, or note television advertising to make your list. How do the producers of bottled water turn this commodity item into a branded product? How does each differentiate its brand from all the others?
10. As the owner of a huge food business, Philip Morris is more than just a cigarette maker. Eager to make a new start in the wake of damaging lawsuits brought by smokers, the company changed its name to Altria. What associations do you think this name is intended to convey? Do you think it will help improve the company's image? Why or why not?

APPLYING CHAPTER CONCEPTS

1. With smoking bans in effect in many places, Zippo Manufacturing, maker of the well-known lighters, is looking for ways to license its brand name to makers of products like grills, torches, space heaters, and fireplaces. Do you think this is a good strategy for Zippo? Why or why not? Identify another well-known product that you think would profit from a licensing strategy. What kind of companies would make good licensing partners for this firm? Do you think the strategy would be successful? Why or why not?
2. General Mills and several other major food makers have begun producing organic foods. But they have deliberately kept their brand names off the packaging of these new products, thinking that the kind of customer who goes out of his or her way to buy organic products is unlikely to trust multinational brands. Other companies, however, like Heinz, PepsiCo, and Tyson Foods, are betting that their brand names will prove to be persuasive in the $11 billion organic foods market. Which strategy do you think is more likely to be successful? Why?
3. After the terrorist attacks of 9/11, an ad hoc task force of DDB Worldwide advertising professionals in 17 countries set out to discover what people abroad thought of the United States. In the course of their research, they developed the concept of "America as a Brand," urged U.S. corporations with overseas operations to help "restore" positive impressions of Brand America around the world, and urged the U.S. to launch Al Hurra as an alternative to the popular Al Jazeera network. Do you think foreigners' perception of a country and its culture can be viewed in marketing terms? Why or why not?
4. Brand names contribute enormously to consumers' perception of a brand. One writer has argued that alphanumeric brand names, such as the Toyota RAV4, Jaguar's X-Type sedan, the Xbox game console, and the GTI from Volkswagen, can translate more easily overseas than "real" names like Golf, Jetta, Escalade, and Eclipse. What other advantages and disadvantages can you think of for each type of brand name? Do you think one type is preferable to the other? Why?

ETHICS EXERCISE

As mentioned in the chapter, some analysts predict that bar codes may soon be replaced by a wireless technology called *radio frequency identification* (*RFID*). RFID is a system of installing tags containing tiny computer chips on, say, supermarket items. These chips automatically radio the location of the item to a computer network where inventory data are stored, letting store managers know not only where the item is at all times but also when and where it was made and its color and size. Proponents of the idea believe RFID will cut costs and simplify inventory tracking and reordering. It may also allow marketers to respond quickly to shifts in demand, avoid under- and overstocking, and reduce spoilage by automatically removing outdated perishables from the shelves. Privacy advocates, however, think the chips provide too much product-preference information that might be identified with individual consumers. In the meantime, Wal-Mart has announced plans to ask its top suppliers to begin using the new technology on products stocked by the giant retailer.

1. Do you think RFID poses a threat to consumer privacy? Why or why not?
2. Do you think the technology's possible benefits to marketers outweigh the potential privacy concerns? Are there also potential benefits to consumers, and if so, what are they?
3. How can marketers reassure consumers about privacy concerns if RFID comes into widespread use?

'netWork EXERCISES

1. **Leveraging a brand name.** Visit the Web site of one of the upscale car manufacturers such as BMW (http://www.bmwusa.com) or Lexus (http://www.lexus.com). List several ways the manufacturer is attempting to leverage its brand name. Bring the list with you to class so you can participate in a class discussion on the subject.
2. **Product safety.** As noted in the chapter, the Consumer Product Safety Commission (CPSC) has safety jurisdiction over most consumer products, with the exception of foods, drugs, and automobiles. Visit the commission's Web site (http://www.cpsc.gov). Review current product recalls and answer the following questions:
   a. Do certain types of products appear on the recall list more frequently than others?
   b. Was the recall voluntary—meaning the firm agreed to recall the product—or was it involuntary—meaning the firm was ordered by the CPSC to recall the product?
   c. What did the recall involve (repair or replacement)?
   d. Why was the product recalled?
3. **Patents.** Visit the Web site of the U.S. Patent and Trademark Office (http://www.uspto.gov). Review the patent application procedure. Note how much it costs to apply for a patent, how the patent application is evaluated, the benefits of a patent, and the length of time a patent is valid. Prepare a brief report to your class on the patent application process.

Note: Internet Web addresses change frequently. If you don't find the exact sites listed, you may need to access the organization's or company's home page and search from there or use a search engine such as Google.

INFOTRAC CITATIONS AND EXERCISES

Record: A117464132
Scent of a Doll: Barbie's First Fragrance.
Kristin Finn.
WWD, May 28, 2004 p4

Abstract: If Britney Spears can have her own special line of beauty fragrances, why not Barbie? Spanish beauty and fragrance company Puig has teamed up with toy manufacturer Mattel to launch a signature fragrance and body spray collection under the Barbie brand name. Marketers claim that Barbie is the ultimate scent for "girls of all ages," capturing the essence of what it is like to be fun, feminine, and stylish. The fragrance—a nice complement to the successful Barbie Apparel clothing line—will be available in 1.3-oz. and 2.5-oz. bottles for around $15 to $20. And, no surprise, the glass bottle with the blonde bombshell's image comes in the signature color of Barbie pink.

1. Why do companies like Mattel develop various related products instead of focusing on a single product?
2. What is a *brand extension,* and how does it relate to the new Barbie signature fragrance?
3. Do you think it was a smart business decision for Mattel to extend the Barbie brand to beauty and fashion apparel products for girls? Why or why not?
4. Can you think of other product categories that might succeed as extensions of the Barbie brand? List one and explain your reasoning.

CASE 12.1 What Will Become of the Box?

Did you eat breakfast this morning? If you're like many consumers today, you probably answered no. Or even if you ate breakfast, it's less and less likely that you sat down at your kitchen table and ate a leisurely bowl of cereal. About half of all Americans now either skip the day's first meal or eat it on the run, opting for yogurt, pastry, a nutrition bar, or a prepared or frozen meal or sandwich consumed on the way to work or school.

Nutritionists may cringe, but it's cereal manufacturers who are really worried. The $6.9 billion market for cold cereal is in a state of near stagnation, and efforts to revive the category have to overcome not just a simple preference for plain or frosted flakes but an enormous shift in lifestyles and eating habits that seems to have passed this mature food category by.

Cereal makers have already tried price cuts, price promotions, and even price wars. They've introduced new products and new flavors, added fruit, promoted cereal as a weight-loss option, and launched multimillion-dollar ad campaigns. They've created partnerships with stores like Target to tie well-known brands like Trix, Cheerios, and Lucky Charms to kids' clothing and with companies like Revlon to create promotions linking Special K to lip-care products. They've entered licensing agreements with Nickelodeon, the WB, DreamWorks SKG, Disney, and the Cartoon Network, teaming up with the Grinch, Spider Man, the Flintstones, and the Simpsons. Adult cereal brands have forged partnerships with high-tech firms and now give away CDs, DVDs, and frequent flier miles. Still, 10 of the top 15 cereal brands are losing money, and overall sales growth has stalled for at least five years. There's no question that quicker and more convenient substitutes are growing faster than traditional dry cereals.

Many industry experts offer ideas for reviving interest in a bowl of cereal and milk. They suggest promoting cereal as a healthy meal or snack for any time of the day, not just breakfast. (That might even include a vegetable-based product to serve with tomato juice instead of milk.) They propose cobranding cereal with fruit brands like Del Monte or Chiquita and producing packages of cereal with packets of fruit tucked inside. They urge cereal makers to reconsider a "Got Milk?" type of campaign. But perhaps the most interesting suggestion is to simply reinvent the whole concept of cereal by repackaging it.

Suggestions for thinking outside the cereal box range from bagging individual servings in zippered plastic bags to using metalized bag linings, as potato chip makers have long done. Other packaging options include cereals in sleeves like the kind crackers come in, a milk-and-cereal combination with a long shelf life, vacuum-packed cereal in containers like coffee cans, and transparent easy-to-pour containers like the ones that some juice brands use. Currently being tested is a canister with a three-way spout that allows consumers to mix and match different options, such as three different brands or three different flavors or textures of the same brand.

Of course, cereal bars are already growing in popularity and, ironically, are among the many breakfast options competing with the 150-plus current varieties of traditional cereal products. Realistically, says one Kellogg's executive, there is no "single silver bullet that will solve the issues we face today." So, what are you having for breakfast tomorrow?

Questions for Critical Thinking

1. One industry consultant argues that cereal companies should be focusing on new-product innovations instead of on ways to repackage the same old products. Do you agree? Why or why not? Support your answer with evidence from the case or from your reading of the chapter.
2. How can cereal manufacturers reposition their brands in light of today's hectic lifestyles and even changes in eating habits (like carb avoidance as advocated by the Atkins diet)? What would it take for you to perceive dry cereal as a convenient and healthy food? How do you think companies like Kellogg's could use your answer to persuade the general public?

Sources: William A. Roberts Jr., "A Cereal Star," *Prepared Foods,* **http://www.preparedfoods.com**, November 25, 2003; "The U.S. Market for Food Bars: Cereal, Snacks, Sports, Meal Replacement," report of *Global Information, Inc.,* **http://www.the-infoshop.com**, September 2003; Sonia Reyes, "What Will Become of the Box?" *Brandweek,* January 27, 2003, pp. 24–28; "Cereal Bars: Major Markets Outlook to 2006," *Food Info Net,* **http://www.foodinfonet.com**, January 15, 2003.

VIDEO CASE 12.2 Everything Is Beautiful at L'Oréal

The written case on L'Oréal appears on page VC-15. The recently filmed L'Oréal video is designed to expand and highlight the concepts in this chapter and the concepts and questions covered in the written video case.

part 4

marketer's minute

Talking about Marketing Careers with David Abrutyn, Senior Vice President of IMG Consulting

FOLLOWING a varied career in sports marketing, David Abrutyn found himself holding a senior position at the world's premier sports and lifestyle management and marketing company. IMG began when legendary founder Mark McCormack teamed up with Arnold Palmer to apply his legal and business skills with Palmer's golfing prowess. From that beginning the Cleveland-based IMG has expanded beyond the U.S. with offices in major cities around the globe. Along the way, it expanded its services to include creation of special events, representation of nonsports celebrities such as fashion models and musicians, and major television and Internet operations.

BOONE & KURTZ: David, tell us a little bit about yourself. What academic and work experience led you to become a senior executive at IMG?

I graduated from the University of Hartford, where I majored in marketing. I went to work for the Washington Capitals of the National Hockey League, where I had been an intern. I was able to turn that experience into a full-time opportunity. I spent almost three full seasons with the Capitals in their sales and marketing department when I found out from a friend about a sports business publication opportunity, which sounded interesting. I spent the next five years helping to launch and grow *Sports Business Daily,* which has since celebrated its 10th anniversary. I liked working in the publishing and sports marketing arena, but I wanted to get back to the core marketing function. I got a job with the NHL Corporate Marketing Group, working with league advertisers and helping them leverage their relationships with the NHL. Most of my work has been from the business perspective, allowing me to utilize my background in marketing and business development. From the NHL it was a clear transition to IMG.

DAVID ABRUTYN, SENIOR VICE PRESIDENT OF IMG CONSULTING

PHOTO: COURTESY OF DAVID ABRUTYN

BOONE & KURTZ: Many readers may not know what is involved in marketing an individual, be it an athlete or a supermodel. What goes into an average day's work as an IMG exec?

Marketing an athlete includes all of the traditional elements of sports business, including negotiating their contracts and/or endorsements, but it also extends well beyond that to include a lot of services that many outside our industry may not recognize. They include managing and protecting their interests; helping them to establish a public persona or image; providing cross-marketing opportunities with other clients; exploring multimedia opportunities, including television and the Internet; and also managing their schedules to meet their needs for a private personal life. I've worked across the board, from my team days to today at IMG Consulting where we work with the companies investing in sponsorships in general and, at times, athletes, so my understanding of marketing an athlete is born from experience. We work with athletes in the same way that we might work with a product or brand.

Be it a tennis player or a golfer, the talent they possess and their personality are what matter when it comes to designing a marketing plan—especially the character traits they have. People become aware of an athlete based on his or her performance on the field or the course. We have to figure out how to translate their performance and their personality into corporate America. In terms of sponsorships, we have to find out what's important to the athlete/model: what they like to do, what they're interested in, identifying their favorite charities, etc. The affiliations need to be believable. Athlete sponsorship is more of a risk because it's personality driven. We capitalize on the athletes' personal styles. And the corporate alliances will also be built on those styles, so it has to be authentic.

BOONE & KURTZ: In marketing we talk a lot about the *product,* but in sports marketing the product is a little bit more difficult to define. How would you describe IMG's product?

IMG has many products and clients, and the product changes depending on the area of business. In terms of talent representation, we're known as the company that represents the marquis athletes and models like Pete Sampras, Tiger Woods, and Naomi Campbell. It's a *Jerry Maguire*-esque view of representation. Our world-class talent includes publishers, writers, musical artists, and models as well as athletes. Our special events are also a product. On average, IMG is involved with about 11 events a day around the world. Whether these events are a made-for-television program, a world's strongest man competition, or the Christmas-tree-lighting ceremony at Rockefeller Center in New York, these events are of great value to some segment of the public. We're also involved in world-class television programs, with the major focus being on sports.

What I worry about on a day-to-day basis is sponsorship marketing in our consulting division. We work with mostly *Fortune 100* companies as expert consultants to help their overall marketing programs by using sponsorship marketing, which has become much more of a driver on the overall sponsorship mix than what it has been in the past.

BOONE & KURTZ: Along the same lines, management and marketing are not IMG's only strong suits: TWI, IMG's television division, and TWI Interactive, its Internet division, are leaders in their fields. How can one organization keep up in so many different markets?

In order to be as successful as IMG has been, you need to hire quality people with the skill sets in the right areas. IMG has always hired the best, from the beginning when Mark [McCormack] was just getting started to our current Internet and TV divisions. These people have the knowledge base and expertise in the field in which they work, but they also have a general idea of what other IMG employees do, which is where the importance of communication factors in. This allows all of our divisions to excel, because we have the right people in the right jobs, working together for our clients.

BOONE & KURTZ: How has IMG changed since the death in 2003 of the firm's founder Mark McCormack?

Anytime a company loses its founder and core visionary, there is always going to be a great impact because of the loss of that personality. The top people in our organization have been here for many, many years, and the experience of our core management team has filtered into all the divisions of our company. IMG is quick to adapt, so in the past few years we've been working on streamlining our operations and building sustainable growth; we don't want to be stagnant. While we are building on Mark's vision, we are also adapting to the current marketplace needs. IMG may be leaner and hungrier than it once was, but I think it's a good structure, focused on accountability and the entrepreneurial spirit, which is the key to IMG's success.

BOONE & KURTZ: IMG has clients who range from professional sports teams to Victoria's Secret models. How much of the firm's current work is actually done with athletes?

Although sports are what IMG is best known for, music and entertainment are becoming increasingly important. Today, sports are more of a subset of entertainment than an entity of its own. Many athletes today market themselves in an entertainment environment. We remain focused on these growth areas, and we'll definitely have a role in the entertainment arena in the future. TV is also a big driver, but TV programming doesn't have the same recognition with people that saying you represent Tiger Woods does. However, IMG is the largest producer of sports programming in the world.

BOONE & KURTZ: Golf is a huge industry in the United States today. Millions of amateurs play it, and millions of viewers tune in to watch the pros out on the links. IMG represents about half of the world's top 20 golfers. How important is golf to IMG's bottom line?

Golf is a major driver of the sports economy. We have a strong position in the world of golf. IMG was founded on a base of golf, and Mark expanded beyond that into other key areas: football in Europe, U.S. football, etc. This vision has enabled us to grow to be the largest entertainment and sports marketing company in the world. We're involved in the key drivers of the business across the board. As we are adapting to the marketplace, we grow in tandem with the sports and entertainment world. Golf remains a growth sport, so our business continues to be strong in that area. Ultimately, our main goal is to connect companies to consumers and people to athletes, and that's how IMG built the business.

BOONE & KURTZ: You began by mentioning the importance of your internship in launching your career in sports marketing. Your comments have been echoed by other sports marketing professionals we have interviewed for the book. But we also realize that you must receive hundreds of internship applications every year. What advice would you give our readers about how to increase the chances that their applications will receive serious consideration?

We have a fairly structured summer internship program, and most interns are grad students or beginning their junior or senior year in college and looking for exposure to our industry. We're looking for people with a strong educational background and an interest or education in the field they're trying to get into. And whether it's sales or accounting or marketing, we definitely look for personality. Interns need to possess the ability to communicate both in writing and in person. This skill is even more important today than it was five years ago. You should be able to write an articulate e-mail or letter; it's become a lost art. There is something about demonstrating an ability to communicate that I find to be extremely important, particularly in marketing. In a business where perception means a lot, our people need to be perceived as the best, especially as they communicate within our industry and with our clients.

We also look for resourceful people. Everyone knows somebody or knows how to find somebody. You need to show that you are resourceful enough to get yourself noticed. It's a highly competitive industry, and IMG looks for people who stand out.

MLS Finds Fertile New Ground

Major League Soccer has seen some market growth and some success, and there's no doubt that soccer's U.S. profile is rising, partly as a result of its savvy broadcast deals, which bring games to fans' homes all season long. But attendance at games is still lower than it could be, and with expansion teams and new soccer-specific stadiums on the drawing board, MLS will have to continue to market soccer with effective marketing strategies and new appeals aimed at drawing increased numbers of fans to enjoy this intangible "product."

A new MLS team based in Utah has been announced, and an expansion team is being introduced in California that will capitalize on the popularity of the renowned Mexican team, the Guadalajara Chivas. Called Chivas USA, the spin-off club will feature a number of popular Mexican players on its roster. The Los Angeles location means a first for MLS: two MLS teams in the same city. Team owner Jorge Vergara is optimistic about his new team's future. "We have more than 10 million Chivas followers in this country," he said in reference to the Mexican team from which the U.S. team is being spun off. "A lot of Mexican-Americans have been supporting Chivas all their lives. . . . Our followers are already here."

MLS commissioner Don Garber echoes the sentiment. "It was so obvious," he said of the plan to create Chivas USA, "that you smacked yourself in the head and said, 'Why didn't we do this in 1996?'" For those fans who may worry that the new team will simply be a farm team for the powerhouse Mexican original, Vergara is reassuring. The new venture is simply too expensive to serve as a farm team for the famed Guadalajara Chivas. Grassroots recruiting efforts are under way to identify promising U.S. players, and team management says it is committed to keeping its players in the U.S.

As for the new Utah team, it will play in an existing stadium at first, but there are plans to build a new soccer stadium for the Salt Lake City club within the next few years. After all, the facilities used are key ingredients for both the player and fan experience. "The future of soccer in the United States is soccer-specific stadiums," says Robert Contiguglia, president of the U.S. Soccer Federation. Contiguglia sees such stadiums as "the footprint for the sport in the United States in the future," and MLS has already completed two, the Columbus Crew Stadium and the Home Depot Center (where Chivas USA will also play). More construction will follow, and not only in Utah. With plans to expand by two teams a year to a total of 18 or 20 (double the original 10 teams), MLS may soon have new homes in cities such as Cleveland, Houston, Philadelphia, Rochester, and San Antonio, all of which are eager to host professional soccer teams.

Another big drawing card for MLS is the popularity of Mexican soccer among the Hispanic populations of many U.S. cities. Soccer United Marketing (SUM), MLS's sister organization, has had great success bringing Mexican teams to the U.S. for sellout tournaments and exhibition matches that are also aired on Fox Sports en Español. One game, a tournament final, earned the cable network its highest ever prime-time ratings. With its 40 million Hispanics, the U.S. is a popular place to play for Mexican players. "There are so many people here rooting for us. They're fans, and they don't get to see us play very often, but we love to come," says Mexico's star goalie Moises Muñoz. "In Mexico, we are born as soccer fans," agrees one fan who now lives in California.

If MLS can just borrow a little of that enthusiasm, perhaps the seats in those new stadiums will begin to fill up.

Questions for Critical Thinking

1. MLS is planning on adding teams and building new stadiums. What other kinds of new product planning do you think it can effectively do?
2. If professional soccer is having difficulty filling stadiums with its existing teams, do you think it is a wise product decision to expand the league? Why or why not? If not, what other product strategies would you recommend?
3. How can MLS use the popularity of Mexican soccer to increase the market for its U.S. teams?
4. Do you think MLS is protecting its brand of U.S.-based soccer sufficiently with the addition of the Chivas USA team? Why or why not?

Sources: "About MLS," Major League Soccer Web site, http://www.mlsnet.com, accessed September 2, 2004; Rod Zundel, "Major League Soccer Comes to SLC," KSL TV, http://tv.ksl.com/index.php?nid=5&sid=106400, July 14, 2004; Grant Wahl, "Football vs. Fútbol," *Sports Illustrated,* July 5, 2004, pp. 68–72; Martha Mendoza, "Mexican Pro Soccer Draws U.S. Fans," *Marketing News,* April 15, 2004, p. 22; Marc Connolly, "Soccer-Only Stadiums Counted on as Arenas for Profit," *USA Today,* September 11, 2003, p. 3C.

part 5

DISTRIBUTION DECISIONS

chapter 13 Marketing Channels and Supply Chain Management

chapter 14 Direct Marketing and Marketing Resellers: Retailers and Wholesalers

PHOTO: COURTESY OF WIREIMAGES.COM

chapter 13

Marketing Channels and Supply Chain Management

chapter objectives

1. Describe the types of marketing channels and the roles they play in marketing strategy.
2. Outline the major channel strategy decisions.
3. Describe the concepts of channel management, conflict, and cooperation.
4. Identify and describe the different vertical marketing systems.
5. Explain the roles of logistics and supply-chain management in an overall distribution strategy.
6. Identify the major components of a physical distribution system.
7. Compare the major modes of transportation.
8. Discuss how transportation intermediaries and combined transportation modes can improve physical distribution.
9. Identify and briefly describe the different types of warehousing.

SWOOSH! NIKE'S BID FOR CHANNEL DOMINANCE

When Nike was founded in 1972, its shoes were sold in small tennis and running shoe stores. When the first Foot Locker opened in 1975 as a unit of Woolworth's, the store's buyers weren't interested in Nike's shoes because they were considered unknown and unbranded. But as Foot Locker began to evolve into a nationwide chain of athletic shoe stores—the first of its kind—Nike persisted, and the two saw how they could work together to benefit both parties. For 30 years, Nike and Foot Locker worked as partners. Over the years, Nike's stylish product lines and its innovative and catchy ads built consumer demand for its shoes. In turn, Nike made Foot Locker its highest priority retailer, guaranteeing an ample supply of its hottest shoes. Nike had the best display space in Foot Locker stores, while Foot Locker received a 14 percent discount on advance

orders of Nike products. The enduring relationship between the two seemed to illustrate the best possible outcome of supply-chain management. Together, the two companies are credited with creating today's $16 billion wholesale market for branded athletic footwear.

Then came the split. Several years ago, Foot Locker CEO Matt Serra resisted Nike's strict terms prohibiting his company from discounting shoes. Nike also required its retailers, including Foot Locker, to carry unproven styles to receive shipments of the more desirable shoes. Serra announced that Foot Locker would cut its orders from Nike by 15 to 25 percent. Nike responded with an even unkinder cut, slashing shipments of the shoe company's high-demand brands by 40 percent, meaning that consumers could not find the Nike shoes they wanted at Foot Locker stores. During the dispute, Foot Locker seemed to have the most to lose. The retailer had relied on Nike ads to drive consumers into its stores; now they were shopping elsewhere. Nike began to market its products to smaller, hipper boutiques as well as other mall-based retailers like Finish Line and FootAction.

Following months of a feud to determine exactly which of the two giants would reign as the top dog in the athletic shoe channel—including an unsuccessful meeting between Foot Locker's Matt Serra and Nike's founder and CEO Phil Knight—the dispute between the two companies began to cool. It became apparent that both companies were losing sales. In addition to Foot Locker's losses, Nike recorded a 10 percent drop in domestic sales as a result of the split. "You can safely say it negatively impacted both companies," says one industry analyst. So Nike made a peace offering, announcing that it would resume shipments of its high-end shoes to Foot Locker, as well as marketing a new line of shoes called "20 Pack" exclusively to the retail chain. Consumers can now shop for their favorite styles with the "swoosh" logo at Foot Locker. As for future relationships between the two companies, "They're the two biggest guys in the business," observes Al Kingsley of the Greenway Group, a large Foot Locker shareholder. "They have to work together."[1]

Chapter Overview

DISTRIBUTION—moving goods and services from producers to customers—is the second marketing mix variable and an important marketing concern. Although eye-catching design and creative promotion may motivate consumers to purchase a product, these practices are useless if consumers cannot buy the product when and where they want it. Distribution strategy has two critical components: (1) marketing channels and (2) logistics and supply-chain management.

distribution Movement of goods and services from producers to customers.

marketing (distribution) channel System of marketing institutions that enhances the physical flow of goods and services, along with ownership title, from producer to consumer or business user.

logistics Process of coordinating the flow of information, goods, and services among members of the distribution channel.

A **marketing channel**—also called a **distribution channel**—is an organized system of marketing institutions and their interrelationships that enhances the physical flow and ownership of goods and services from producer to consumer or business user. The choice of marketing channels should support the firm's overall marketing strategy. By contrast, **logistics** refers to the process of coordinating the flow of information, goods, and services among members of the marketing channel. **Supply-chain management** is the control of activities of purchasing, processing, and delivery through which raw materials are transformed into products and made available to final consumers. Efficient logistical systems support customer service, enhancing customer relationships—an important goal of any marketing strategy.

A key aspect of logistics is physical distribution, which covers a broad range of activities aimed at efficient movement of finished goods from the end of the production line to the consumer. Although some marketers use the terms *transportation* and *physical distribution* interchangeably, these terms do not carry the same meaning. **Physical distribution** extends beyond transportation to include such important decision areas as customer service, inventory control, materials handling, protective packaging, order processing, transportation, warehouse site selection, and warehousing.

Briefly Speaking

There is no finish line.

Nike Corporation motto

Well-planned marketing channels and effective logistics and supply-chain management provide ultimate users with convenient ways for obtaining the goods and services they desire. This chapter discusses the activities, decisions, and marketing intermediaries involved in managing marketing channels and logistics. Chapter 14 looks at other players in the marketing channel: retailers, direct marketers, and wholesalers. ◆◆◆

supply-chain management Control of the activities of purchasing, processing, and delivery through which raw materials are transformed into products and made available to final consumers.

physical distribution Broad range of activities aimed at efficient movement of finished goods from the end of the production line to the consumer.

THE ROLE OF MARKETING CHANNELS IN MARKETING STRATEGY

① **Describe the types of marketing channels and the roles they play in marketing strategy.**

A firm's distribution channels play a key role in its overall marketing strategy because these channels provide the means by which the firm makes the goods and services available to ultimate users. Channels perform four important functions. First, they facilitate the exchange process by reducing the number of marketplace contacts necessary to make a sale. Suppose you want to buy a new camera. You spot an ad for a new Panasonic Lumix digital camera like the one in Figure 13.1. The ad prompts you to check the Panasonic Web site, where you'll find out more about the camera and connect with a local dealer. The dealer forms part of the channel that brings you, a potential buyer, and Panasonic, the seller, together to complete the exchange process. It's important to keep in mind that all channel members benefit when they work together; when they begin to disagree, or compete directly with each other as Nike and Foot Locker did, everyone loses.

Distributors adjust for discrepancies in the market's assortment of goods and services via a process known as *sorting,* the second channel function. A single producer tends to maximize the quantity it makes of a limited line of goods, while a single buyer needs a limited quantity of a wide selection of merchandise. Sorting alleviates such discrepancies by channeling products to suit both the buyer's and the producer's needs.

The third function of marketing channels involves standardizing exchange transactions by setting expectations for products, and it involves the transfer process itself. Channel members tend to standardize payment terms, delivery schedules, prices, and purchase lots among other conditions. Standardization helps make the transactions efficient and fair. However, sometimes standardization can create problems for certain channel members. Recently, Wal-Mart agreed to soften its firm stance against price increases by manufacturers who claimed that the hikes were justified to cover the rising costs of raw materials. However, a Wal-Mart spokesperson insisted that the retailer had not changed its overall strategy toward pricing. "We remain committed to selling for less," she said. By cooperating with its suppliers, Wal-Mart was able to give them a break without sacrificing value for consumers.[2]

The final marketing channel function is to facilitate searches by both buyers and sellers. Buyers search for specific goods and services to fill their needs, while sellers attempt to learn what buyers want. Channels bring buyers and sellers together to complete the exchange process.

figure 13.1

Marketing Channels: Linking Buyers and Sellers

© SHIZOV KAMBAYASHI/AP WIDE WORLD PHOTO

Literally hundreds of distribution channels exist today, and no single channel best serves the needs of every company. Instead of searching for the best channel for all products, a marketing manager must analyze alternative channels in light of consumer needs to determine the most appropriate channel or channels for the firm's goods and services.

Marketers must remain flexible because channels may change over time. Today's ideal channel may prove inappropriate in a few years. Or the way a company uses that channel may change. Nike, well known for its presence in retail stores, recently hired R/GA, a small advertising agency, to improve its Internet presence. The firm devised several online marketing efforts for separate Nike Web sites, including nike.com (the company's global site), nikegoddess.com (for women), nikelab.com (an interactive tour of products), and others. "For a lot of companies, the idea of using the Web is to copy and paste a commercial onto their Web site," notes Rei Inamoto of R/GA. "But Nike is smart enough to realize that the Web as a medium is a different channel."[3]

The following sections examine the diverse types of channels available to marketers. They look at the decisions marketers must make to develop an effective distribution strategy that supports their firm's marketing objectives.

1. **Distinguish between a marketing channel and logistics.**
2. **What four functions do marketing channels perform?**

TYPES OF MARKETING CHANNELS

The first step in selecting a marketing channel is determining which type of channel will best meet both the seller's objectives and the distribution needs of customers. Figure 13.2 depicts the major channels available to marketers of consumer and business goods and services.

Most channel options involve at least one **marketing intermediary.** A marketing intermediary (or *middleman*) is an organization that operates between producers and consumers or business users. Retailers and wholesalers are both marketing intermediaries. A retail store owned and operated by someone other than the manufacturer of the products it sells is one type of marketing intermediary. A **wholesaler** is an intermediary that takes title to the goods it handles and then distributes these goods

Relationships are fragile things and require as much care in handling as any other fragile and precious thing.

Anonymous

figure 13.2
Alternative Marketing Channels

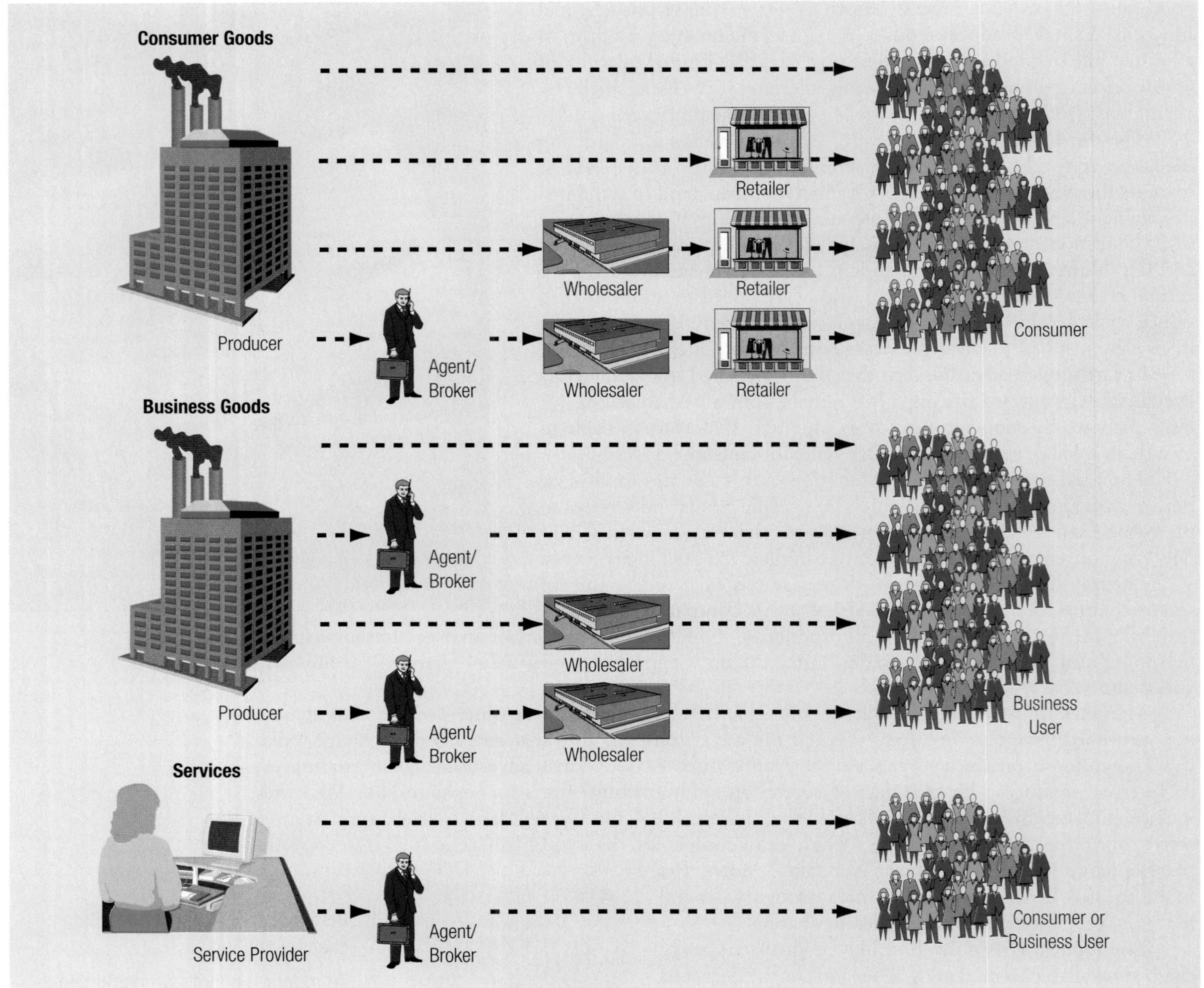

to retailers, other distributors, or sometimes end consumers. Although some analysts believed that the Internet would ultimately render many intermediaries obsolete, that hasn't happened. In fact, resellers like CDW Computer Centers are thriving. CDW, launched by entrepreneur Michael Krasny two decades ago, is now the largest reseller of computer gear in the country. Much of the company's success is due to its high level of customer service. "Despite all the bold statements by the dotcoms a few years ago, the personal touch still matters," says CEO John Edwardson.[4]

A short marketing channel involves few intermediaries. By contrast, a long marketing channel involves many intermediaries working in succession to move goods from producers to consumers. Business products usually move through short channels due to geographic concentrations and comparatively few business purchasers. Service firms market primarily through short channels because they sell intangible products and need to maintain personal relationships within their channels. Not-for-profit organizations also tend to work with short, simple, and direct channels. Any marketing intermediaries in such channels usually act as agents, such as independent ticket agencies or fund-raising specialists.

DIRECT SELLING

The simplest and shortest marketing channel is a direct channel. A **direct channel** carries goods directly from a producer to the business purchaser or ultimate user. This channel forms part of **direct selling,** a marketing strategy in which a producer establishes direct sales contact with its product's final users. Direct selling is an important option for goods that require extensive demonstrations in convincing customers to buy.

Direct selling plays a significant role in business-to-business marketing. Most major installations, accessory equipment, and even component parts and raw materials are sold through direct contacts between producing firms and final buyers. Firms such as Xerox that market items to other businesses often develop and maintain large sales forces to call on potential customers. A recent Xerox ad reported that by using its company-wide work processes, retailer Dillard's saved $1.6 billion. It then gives a toll-free phone number to contact a Xerox sales rep.

figure 13.3

Pampered Chef: Direct Selling in the Consumer Goods Market

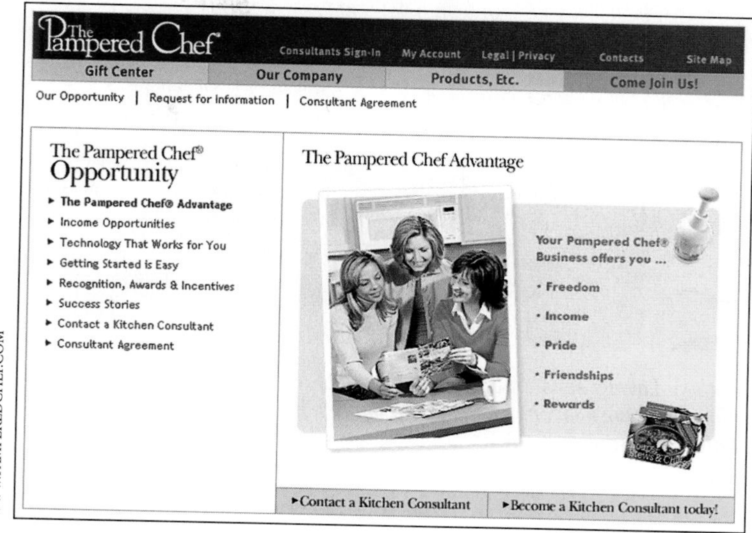

WWW.PAMPEREDCHEF.COM

Direct selling is also important in consumer goods markets. Direct sellers such as Avon, Pampered Chef, illustrated in Figure 13.3, and Longaberger Baskets sidestep competition in store aisles by developing networks of independent representatives who sell their products directly to consumers. Many of these companies practice a direct selling strategy called the *party plan,* originally popularized by Tupperware. A seller attends a gathering at a host customer's home to demonstrate products and take orders.

direct channel Marketing channel that moves goods directly from a producer to the business purchaser or ultimate user.

The Internet provides another direct selling channel for both B2B and B2C purchases. Dell sells computers and computer parts directly to businesses, government agencies, and individual consumers. It builds computers to customer specifications, configured for processor speed, hard drive size, and monitor type. Dell is able to cut overhead and save customers money at the same time. Today, the nation's leading PC maker sells more than $31 billion worth of computers each year via telephone and the Internet.

CHANNELS USING MARKETING INTERMEDIARIES

Although direct channels allow simple and straightforward marketing, they are not practical in every case. Some products serve markets in different areas of the country or world or have large numbers of potential end users. Other categories of goods rely heavily on repeat purchases. The producers of these goods may find more efficient, less expensive, and less time-consuming alternatives to direct channels by using marketing intermediaries. This section considers five channels that involve marketing intermediaries.

Producer to Wholesaler to Retailer to Consumer

The traditional channel for consumer goods proceeds from producer to wholesaler to retailer to user. This method carries goods between literally thousands of small producers with limited lines and local retailers. A firm with limited financial resources will rely on the services of a wholesaler that serves as an immediate source of funds and then markets to hundreds of retailers. On the other hand, a small retailer can draw on a wholesaler's specialized distribution skills. In addition, many manufacturers hire their own field sales representatives to service retail accounts with marketing information. Wholesalers may then handle the actual sales transactions.

Producer to Wholesaler to Business User

Similar characteristics in the organizational market often attract marketing intermediaries to operate between producers and business purchasers. The term *industrial distributor* commonly refers to intermediaries in the business market that take title to the goods.

© AP WIDE WORLD PHOTO/RIC FELD

Retailer Lowe's sells thousands of products to consumers. While much of Lowe's inventory, including lumber, is purchased directly from the producer, many other items have passed through other marketing intermediaries.

Producer to Agent to Wholesaler to Retailer to Consumer

In markets served by many small companies, a unique intermediary—the agent—performs the basic function of bringing buyer and seller together. An agent may or may not take possession of the goods but never takes title. The agent merely represents a producer by seeking a market for its products or a wholesaler (which does take title to the goods) by locating a supply source.

Producer to Agent to Wholesaler to Business User

Like agents, brokers are independent intermediaries who may or may not take possession of goods but never take title to these goods. Agents and brokers also serve the business market when small producers attempt to market their offerings through large wholesalers. Such an intermediary, often called a **manufacturers' representative,** provides an independent sales force to contact wholesale buyers. A kitchen equipment manufacturer may have its own manufacturer's representatives to market its goods, for example.

Producer to Agent to Business User

For products sold in small units, only merchant wholesalers can economically cover the markets. A merchant wholesaler is an independently owned wholesaler that takes title to the goods. By maintaining regional inventories, this wholesaler achieves transportation economies, stockpiling goods and making small shipments over short distances. For a product with large unit sales, however, and for which transportation accounts for a small percentage of the total cost, the producer-agent-business user channel is usually employed. The agent in effect becomes the producer's sales force, but bulk shipments of the product reduce the intermediary's inventory management function.

DUAL DISTRIBUTION

dual distribution Network that moves products to a firm's target market through more than one marketing channel.

Dual distribution refers to movement of products through more than one channel to reach the firm's target market. Nordstrom, for instance, has a three-pronged distribution system, selling through stores, catalogs, and the Internet. Marketers usually adopt a dual distribution strategy either to maximize their firm's coverage in the marketplace or to increase the cost effectiveness of the firm's marketing effort. For instance, automobile parts manufacturers promote products through both direct sales forces and independent salespeople. The cost-effectiveness goal, on the other hand, might lead a manufacturer to assign its own sales force to sell in high-potential territories while relying on manufacturers' representatives (independent, commissioned salespeople) in lower volume areas.

REVERSE CHANNELS

While the traditional concept of marketing channels involves the movement of goods and services from producer to consumer or business user, marketers should not ignore **reverse channels**—channels designed to return goods to their producers. Reverse channels have gained increased importance with rising prices for raw materials, increasing availability of recycling facilities, and passage of additional antipollution and conservation laws. Purchase a new set of tires, and you'll find a recycling charge for disposing of the old tires. The intent is to halt the growing litter problem of illegal tire dumps. If you live in New Jersey, the state requires businesses and households to separate their trash to aid recycling.

Some reverse channels move through the facilities of traditional marketing intermediaries. In states that require bottle deposits, retailers and local bottlers perform these functions in the soft-drink industry. For other products, manufacturers establish redemption centers, develop systems for rechanneling products for recycling, and create specialized organizations to handle disposal and recycling.

Other reverse channel participants include community groups that organize cleanup days and develop recycling and waste disposal systems. Timberland actually gives its employees paid time off to participate in programs that involve cleaning up parks, schools, and other public places.

Reverse channels also handle product recalls and repairs. An appliance manufacturer might send recall notices to the buyers of a washing machine. An auto manufacturer might send notices to car owners advising them of a potential problem and offering to repair it at no cost through local dealerships.

1. Give an example of direct selling.
2. Describe the traditional channel for consumer goods.
3. Why would marketers use a dual distribution strategy?
4. What is a reverse channel?

CHANNEL STRATEGY DECISIONS

2 Outline the major channel strategy decisions.

Marketers face several strategic decisions in choosing channels and marketing intermediaries for their products. Selecting a specific channel is the most basic of these decisions. Marketers must also resolve questions about the level of distribution intensity, assess the desirability of vertical marketing systems, and evaluate the performance of current intermediaries.

SELECTION OF A MARKETING CHANNEL

Consider the following questions: What characteristics of a franchised dealer network make it the best channel option for a company? Why do operating supplies often go through both agents and merchant wholesalers before reaching their actual users? Why would a firm market a single product through multiple channels? Marketers must answer many such questions in choosing marketing channels.

A variety of factors affect the selection of a marketing channel. Some channel decisions are dictated by the marketplace in which the company operates. In other cases, the product itself may be a key variable in picking a marketing channel. Finally, the marketing organization may base its selection of channels on its size and competitive factors.

Market Factors

Channel structure reflects a product's intended markets, either for consumers or business users. Business purchasers usually prefer to deal directly with manufacturers (except for routine supplies or small accessory items), but most consumers make their purchases from retailers. Marketers often sell products that serve both business users and consumers through more than one channel.

Other market factors also affect channel choice, including the market's needs, its geographic location, and its average order size. To serve a concentrated market with a small number of buyers, a direct channel offers a feasible alternative. But in serving a geographically dispersed potential market in which customers purchase small amounts in individual transactions—the conditions that characterize the consumer goods market—distribution through marketing intermediaries makes sense.

Product Factors

Product characteristics also guide the choice of an optimal marketing channel strategy. Perishable goods, such as fresh fruit and vegetables, milk, and the Tropicana orange juice in Figure 13.4, move through short channels. Trendy or seasonal fashions, such as swimsuits and ski wear, are also examples.

figure 13.4

Short Marketing Channels: Characteristics of Perishable Products

figure 13.5

Long Marketing Channels: Characteristics of Products with Low Unit Costs

© PHOTOPIA

Vending machines represent another short channel. Typically, you can buy a bag of M&Ms, Wise potato chips, or a Coke from a vending machine. But how about a car? In France, you can do it—almost. At the DaimlerChrysler Smart car plant in France, a customer selects a vehicle, a salesperson pushes a button, and the car is mechanically transferred from its on-site storage unit to a viewing station. If the customer and salesperson are satisfied with the car, accessories, and the price quote, the sale is completed. Yes, there is one intermediary—but all the other employees traditionally associated with car buying, such as greeters and closers, are eliminated. "It is a simple, efficient way of selling cars," explains Scott Keogh, general manager of Smart USA, which is developing a similar facility in the U.S.[5]

Complex products such as custom-made installations and computer equipment are often sold directly to ultimate buyers. In general, relatively standardized items that are also nonperishable pass through comparatively long channels. Products with low unit costs, like the Friskies cat food in Figure 13.5, typically travel through long channels.

Organizational and Competitive Factors

Companies with strong financial, management, and marketing resources feel less need for help from intermediaries. A financially strong manufacturer can hire its own sales force, warehouse its own goods, and extend credit to retailers or consumers. A weaker firm must rely on marketing intermediaries for these services.

A firm with a broad product line can usually market its products directly to retailers or business users since its own sales force can offer a variety of products. High sales volume spreads selling costs over a large number of items, generating adequate returns from direct sales. Single-product firms often view direct selling as unaffordable.

The manufacturer's desire for control over marketing its products also influences channel selection. Some manufacturers choose to sell their products only at their own stores. Manufacturers of specialty or luxury goods like scarves from Hermès and watches from Rolex strictly limit the number of retailers that can carry their products.

Businesses that explore new marketing channels must be careful to avoid upsetting their channel intermediaries. In the past decade, conflicts frequently arose as companies began to establish an Internet presence in addition to traditional outlets. Today, firms look for new ways to handle both without damaging relationships. Still, some firms feel compelled to develop new marketing channels to remedy inadequate promotion of their products by independent marketing intermediaries.

Recently, Home Depot launched a marketing campaign through direct-response TV, running ads for its private-label Husky power washer and the Ryobi tool kit on national cable networks like CNN and Discovery Channel. "Retailers using DRTV is something that is becoming more prevalent," says Greg Sarnow, founder of the Direct Response Academy. "Sears has been doing it for about 10 years. It is a growing model because of the fact that you do get that awareness and sale all in one."[6]

Table 13.1 summarizes the factors that affect the selection of a marketing channel. The table also examines the effect of each factor on the channel's overall length.

DETERMINING DISTRIBUTION INTENSITY

Another key channel strategy decision is the intensity of distribution. *Distribution intensity* refers to the number of intermediaries through which a manufacturer distributes its goods in a particular market. Optimal distribution intensity should ensure adequate market coverage for a product. Adequate market coverage varies depending on the goals of the individual firm, the type of product, and

table 13.1 *Factors Influencing Marketing Channel Strategies*

	CHARACTERISTICS OF SHORT CHANNELS	CHARACTERISTICS OF LONG CHANNELS
Market factors	Business users	Consumers
	Geographically concentrated	Geographically dispersed
	Extensive technical knowledge and regular servicing required	Little technical knowledge and regular servicing not required
	Large orders	Small orders
Product factors	Perishable	Durable
	Complex	Standardized
	Expensive	Inexpensive
Organizational factors	Manufacturer has adequate resources to perform channel functions	Manufacturer lacks adequate resources to perform channel functions
	Broad product line	Limited product line
	Channel control important	Channel control not important
Competitive factors	Manufacturer feels satisfied with marketing intermediaries' performance in promoting products	Manufacturer feels dissatisfied with marketing intermediaries' performance in promoting products

the consumer segments in its target market. In general, however, distribution intensity varies along a continuum with three general categories: intensive distribution, selective distribution, and exclusive distribution.

Intensive Distribution

An **intensive distribution** strategy seeks to distribute a product through all available channels in a trade area. Because Nabisco practices intensive distribution for many of its products, you can pick up a box of Wheat Thins just about anywhere, including supermarkets, convenience stores, and large drugstore chains. Usually, an intensive distribution strategy suits items with wide appeal across broad groups of consumers.

intensive distribution Distribution of a product through all available channels.

Selective Distribution

In another market coverage strategy, **selective distribution,** a firm chooses only a limited number of retailers in a market area to handle its line. Italian fashion designers Dolce & Gabbana promote the exclusivity of their designs by selecting just the right markets to carry their goods. Such an arrangement helps to control price cutting since relatively few dealers handle the firm's line. By limiting the number of retailers, marketers can reduce total marketing costs while establishing strong working relationships within the channel. Moreover, selected retailers often agree to comply with the company's strict rules for advertising, pricing, and displaying its products. **Cooperative advertising,** in which the manufacturer pays a percentage of the retailer's advertising expenditures and the retailer prominently displays the firm's products, can be utilized for mutual benefit, and marginal retailers can be avoided. Where service is important, the manufacturer usually provides training and assistance to the dealers it chooses.

selective distribution Distribution of a product through a limited number of channels.

Exclusive Distribution

When a producer grants exclusive rights to a wholesaler or retailer to sell its products in a specific geographic region, it practices **exclusive distribution.** The automobile industry provides a good example of exclusive distribution. A city with a population of 40,000 may have a single Ford dealer. Exclusive distribution agreements also govern marketing for some major appliance and apparel brands.

exclusive distribution Distribution of a product through a single wholesaler or retailer in a specific geographic region.

Auto dealerships often have exclusive distribution rights in their local markets. And that exclusiveness can enhance a car's desirability in consumers' minds. Chrysler's powerful and stylish new 300 is turning heads and building sales as a performance alternative to other vehicles.

Marketers may sacrifice some market coverage by implementing a policy of exclusive distribution. However, they often develop and maintain an image of quality and prestige for the product. If it's harder to find a Kate Spade handbag, the item seems more valuable. In addition, exclusive distribution limits marketing costs since the firm deals with a smaller number of accounts. In exclusive distribution, producers and retailers cooperate closely in decisions concerning advertising and promotion, inventory carried by the retailers, and prices.

Legal Problems of Exclusive Distribution

Exclusive distribution presents potential legal problems in three main areas: exclusive dealing agreements, closed sales territories, and tying agreements. Although none of these practices is illegal per se, all may break the law if they reduce competition or tend to create monopolies, as discussed in the "Solving an Ethical Controversy" feature.

As part of an exclusive distribution strategy, marketers may try to enforce an **exclusive dealing agreement,** which prohibits a marketing intermediary (a wholesaler or, more typically, a retailer) from handling competing products. Producers of high-priced shopping goods, specialty goods, and accessory equipment often require such agreements to assure total concentration on their own product lines. Such contracts violate the Clayton Act only if the producer's or dealer's sales volumes represent a substantial percentage of total sales in the market area. While exclusive distribution is legal for companies first entering a market, such agreements violate the Clayton Act if used by firms with a sizable market share seeking to bar competitors from the market.

Producers may also try to set up **closed sales territories** to restrict their distributors to certain geographic regions. Although the distributors gain protection from rival dealers in their exclusive territories, they sacrifice any opportunities in opening new facilities or marketing the manufacturers' products outside their assigned territories. The legality of a system of closed sales territories depends on whether the restriction decreases competition. If so, it violates the Federal Trade Commission Act and provisions of the Sherman and the Clayton Acts.

The legality of closed sales territories also depends on whether the system imposes horizontal or vertical restrictions. Horizontal territorial restrictions result from agreements between retailers or wholesalers to avoid competition among sellers of products from the same producer. Such agreements consistently have been declared illegal. However, the U.S. Supreme Court has ruled that vertical territorial restrictions—those between producers and wholesalers or retailers—may meet legal criteria. The ruling gives no clear-cut answer, but such agreements likely satisfy the law in cases where manufacturers occupy relatively small parts of their markets. In such instances, the restrictions may actually increase competition among competing brands; the wholesaler or retailer faces no competition from other dealers carrying the manufacturer's brand, so it can concentrate on effectively competing with other brands.

The third legal question of exclusive distribution involves **tying agreements,** which allow channel members to become exclusive dealers only if they also carry products other than those that they want to sell. In the apparel industry, for example, an agreement might require a dealer to carry a comparatively unpopular line of clothing to get desirable, fast-moving items. Tying agreements violate the Sherman Act and the Clayton Act when they reduce competition or create monopolies that keep competitors out of major markets.

You can do away with middlemen, but you can't do away with the functions they perform.

American business saying

WHO SHOULD PERFORM CHANNEL FUNCTIONS?

A fundamental marketing principle governs channel decisions. A member of the channel must perform certain central marketing functions. Responsibilities of the different members may vary, however. Although independent wholesalers perform many functions for manufacturers, retailers, and other wholesaler clients, other channel members could fulfill these roles instead. A manufacturer might bypass

Solving an Ethical Controversy

TICKETMASTER: WHO PAYS THE PRICE?

JUST about everyone who has ever booked entertainment tickets online or even over the phone has dealt with Ticketmaster at one time or another. Over the years, the world's largest ticketing company, which sells more than 95 million tickets valued at $4 billion each year, has generated its share of controversy. It has many of the characteristics of a monopoly, and performers and audiences alike agree that the ticketing agency's fees are excessive. A decade ago, the rock group Pearl Jam asked Congress to investigate Ticketmaster's practices. More recently, the jam band String Cheese Incident sued the agency for alleged antitrust violations because an exclusive agreement between Ticketmaster and concert venues prohibited the group from selling tickets to its own concerts—with much lower service charges.

DO EXCLUSIVE AGREEMENTS GIVE TICKETMASTER TOO MUCH CONTROL OVER TICKET SALES TO MAJOR ENTERTAINMENT EVENTS?

PRO

1. The exclusive agreements allow Ticketmaster to set any price it wants, creating less value for consumers.
2. The agreements also block performers from profiting from their own work. "We've come to a point where Ticketmaster is not allowing us to get tickets available to our own shows," argues String Cheese bassist Keith Moseley. "Our supply of tickets has essentially dried up to the point where we can barely stay in business."

CON

1. Consumers can try to bypass Ticketmaster by visiting the box office of a venue and seeing whether they have tickets available for purchase directly. Ticketmaster allots a limited number of tickets to be sold independently.
2. Ticketmaster claims that the service fees are "the cost of doing business" and that the agency provides services to consumers—such as e-mailing fans when their favorite band is coming to town—that performers do not.

SUMMARY

According to several experts, Ticketmaster's fees may total up to 50 percent of the face value of a ticket. Ticketmaster prints and distributes tickets exclusively for 89 percent of the top 50 event arenas in the U.S. Recently, Ticketmaster announced that it would begin auctioning off tickets on eBay. The firm will not be subject to antiscalping rules because it is making first-time sales instead of reselling. Speaking of String Cheese's attempt to tackle Ticketmaster, a representative for the Grateful Dead asks, "Who's got a better right to sell String Cheese's tickets than String Cheese?"

Sources: "Buying Concert Tickets at Ticketmaster.com Was Easy, but Their Fees Are High," *Epinions.com*, http://www.epinions.com, accessed April 17, 2004; Steve Knopper, "Ticketmaster under Attack," *Rolling Stone*, September 18, 2003, pp. 21–22; "New World in Concert Tickets," *CBSNews.com*, September 1, 2003, http://www.cbsnews.com; Jillian Helmer, "Ticketmaster Is Out of Control," *Columbia Chronicle Online*, April 22, 2002, http://www.cchronicle.com.

its wholesalers by establishing regional warehouses, maintaining field sales forces, serving as sources of information for retail customers, or arranging details of financing. For years, auto manufacturers have operated credit units that offer new-car financing; some have even established their own banks.

An independent intermediary earns a profit in exchange for providing services to manufacturers and retailers. This profit margin is low, however, ranging from 1 percent for food wholesalers to 5 percent for durable goods wholesalers. Manufacturers and retailers could retain these costs, or they could market directly and reduce retail prices—but only if they could perform the channel functions and match the efficiency of the independent intermediaries.

To grow profitably in a competitive environment, an intermediary must provide better service at lower costs than manufacturers or retailers can provide for themselves. In this case, consolidation of channel functions can represent a strategic opportunity for a company.

1. **Identify four major factors in selecting a marketing channel.**
2. **What is the fundamental marketing principle governing channel decisions?**

(3) Describe the concepts of channel management, conflict, and cooperation.

CHANNEL MANAGEMENT AND LEADERSHIP

Distribution strategy does not end with the choice of a channel. Manufacturers must also focus on channel management by developing and maintaining relationships with the intermediaries in their marketing channels. Positive channel relationships encourage channel members to remember their partners' goods and market them. Manufacturers also must carefully manage the incentives offered to induce channel members to promote their products. This effort includes weighing decisions about pricing, promotion, and other support efforts that the manufacturer performs.

Increasingly, marketers are managing channels in partnership with other channel members. Effective cooperation allows all channel members to achieve goals that they could not achieve on their own. Keys to successful management of channel relationships include the development of high levels of coordination, commitment, and trust between channel members.

Not all channel members wield equal power in the distribution chain, however. The dominant member of a marketing channel is called the **channel captain.** This firm's power to control a channel may result from its control over some type of reward or punishment to other channel members, such as granting an exclusive sales territory or taking away a dealership. Power might also result from contractual arrangements, specialized expert knowledge, or agreement among channel members about their mutual best interests.

channel captain Dominant and controlling member of a marketing channel.

All things being equal, people will do business with a friend. All things being unequal, people will still do business with a friend.

Mark McCormack (1930–2003)

American sports agent and founder, IMG Sports Management

In the grocery industry, food producers once were considered channel captains. Today, however, the power has shifted to the retail giants. Kroger, Albertson's, and Safeway operate 6,500 supermarkets nationwide. These three chains also own smaller stores, food warehouse stores, department stores, and even jewelry stores. Manufacturers who want to get their products on the shelves and properly marketed have to pay slotting fees, described in Chapter 11, to do so. It is the retailer who decides what goes on the shelf, where, and for how long.[7]

Wal-Mart is also a well-known channel captain. In fact, the retailer accounts for 18 to 20 percent of total sales of several large manufacturers, including Dial Corp., Clorox Co., Revlon, Hershey Foods, and Procter & Gamble. Interestingly, Wal-Mart does not charge slotting fees in its stores.[8]

CHANNEL CONFLICT

Marketing channels work smoothly only when members cooperate in well-organized efforts to achieve maximum operating efficiencies. Yet channel members often perform as separate, independent, and even competing forces. Two types of conflict—horizontal and vertical—may hinder the normal functioning of a marketing channel.

Horizontal Conflict

Horizontal conflict sometimes results from disagreements among channel members at the same level, such as two or more wholesalers or two or more retailers, or among marketing intermediaries of the same type, such as two competing discount stores or several retail florists. More often, horizontal conflict causes sparks between different types of marketing intermediaries that handle similar products. Netflix, which recently began advertising its DVD rental service on network television, competes with Blockbuster and other movie rental firms as well as Hollywood studios—some of which own a stake in Netflix. A relative newcomer to the business, Netflix has gained significant competitive ground.[9]

Vertical Conflict

Vertical relationships may result in frequent and severe conflict. Channel members at different levels find many reasons for disputes, as when retailers develop private brands to compete with producers' brands or when producers establish their own retail stores or create mail-order operations that compete with retailers. Producers may annoy wholesalers and retailers when they attempt to bypass these intermediaries and sell directly to consumers. In one well-publicized case, Levi Strauss suspended attempts to sell through its own Web site following complaints from enraged retailers. In other instances, retailers may anger suppliers by requesting concessions suppliers believe are unfair. Slotting fees, mentioned earlier, have generated controversy for many years.

Recently, a group of U.S. furniture manufacturers filed a petition to prohibit Chinese furniture makers from "dumping" similar goods into the American marketplace for less than the cost of making the product. Furniture retailers, however, defended the practice because it helps keep consumer prices lower. The disagreement has caused conflict between furniture manufacturers and retailers.[10]

The Grey Market

Another type of channel conflict results from activities in the grey market. As U.S. manufacturers license their technology and brands abroad, they sometimes find themselves in competition in the U.S. market against versions of their own brands produced by overseas affiliates. These **grey goods,** goods produced for overseas markets often at reduced prices, enter U.S. channels through the actions of unauthorized foreign distributors. While licensing agreements usually prohibit foreign licensees from selling in the U.S., no such rules inhibit their distributors.

Because of the disproportionately high cost of medications in the U.S., many consumers turn to Canada to fill prescriptions. They can do this online or by traveling to Canada. Although it is technically illegal to import drugs, some authorities have made exceptions for "personal use." In New Hampshire and Illinois, governors have openly supported the right of American consumers to buy prescription drugs in Canada. However, U.S. pharmaceutical companies and other critics warn that quality control is uncertain when consumers cross the border to buy their medications.[11]

Briefly Speaking

I am not a combative person. My long experience has taught me to resolve conflict by raising the issues before I or others burn their boats.

Sir Alistair Grant (1937–2000)

Scottish business executive; chairman of Scottish & Newcastle

ACHIEVING CHANNEL COOPERATION

The basic antidote to channel conflict is effective cooperation among channel members. Cooperation is best achieved when all channel members regard themselves as equal components of the same organization. The channel captain is primarily responsible for providing the leadership necessary to achieve this kind of cooperation.

Samsung Electronics is committed to achieving channel cooperation to have its products reach as many North American homes and offices as possible. The company launches nearly 200 new products every year, including a new cell phone every two weeks. It depends on sales from its retail partners but supports them with research, data, customer leads, and sales help so they can take advantage of the quick shifts in the marketplace.[12]

1. What is a channel captain?
2. Compare and contrast the two types of channel conflict.

VERTICAL MARKETING SYSTEMS

4 **Identify and describe the different vertical marketing systems.**

Efforts to reduce channel conflict and improve the effectiveness of distribution have led to the development of vertical marketing systems. A vertical marketing system (VMS) is a planned channel system designed to improve distribution efficiency and cost effectiveness by integrating various functions throughout the distribution chain.

vertical marketing system (VMS) Planned channel system designed to improve distribution efficiency and cost effectiveness by integrating various functions throughout the distribution chain.

A vertical marketing system can achieve this goal through either forward or backward integration. In **forward integration,** a firm attempts to control downstream distribution. For example, a manufacturer might set up a retail chain to sell its products. **Backward integration** occurs when a manufacturer attempts to gain greater control over inputs in its production process. A manufacturer might acquire the supplier of a raw material the manufacturer uses in the production of its products. Backward integration can also extend the control of retailers and wholesalers over producers that supply them.

A VMS offers several benefits. First, it improves chances for controlling and coordinating the steps in the distribution or production process. It may lead to the development of economies of scale that ultimately saves money. A VMS may also let a manufacturer expand into profitable new businesses. However, a VMS also involves some costs. A manufacturer assumes increased risk when it takes control of an entire distribution chain. Manufacturers may also discover that they lose some flexibility in responding to market changes.

Marketers have developed three categories of VMSs: corporate systems, administered systems, and contractual systems. These categories are outlined in the sections that follow.

CORPORATE AND ADMINISTERED SYSTEMS

corporate marketing system VMS in which a single owner operates the entire marketing channel.

administered marketing system VMS that achieves channel coordination when a dominant channel member exercises its power.

contractual marketing system VMS that coordinates channel activities through formal agreements among participants.

When a single owner runs organizations at each stage of the marketing channel, it operates a **corporate marketing system.** Phillips auctioneers runs a corporate marketing system. An **administered marketing system** achieves channel coordination when a dominant channel member exercises its power. Even though Goodyear sells its tires through independently owned and operated dealerships, it controls the stock that these dealerships carry. Other examples of channel captains leading administered channels include McKesson, Sears, and Costco.

CONTRACTUAL SYSTEMS

Instead of common ownership of intermediaries within a corporate VMS or the exercising of power within an administered system, a **contractual marketing system** coordinates distribution through formal agreements among channel members. In practice, three types of agreements set up these systems: wholesaler-sponsored voluntary chains, retail cooperatives, and franchises.

Wholesaler-Sponsored Voluntary Chain

Sometimes an independent wholesaler will try to preserve a market by strengthening its retail customers through a wholesaler-sponsored voluntary chain. The wholesaler adopts a formal agreement with its retailers to use a common name and standardized facilities and to purchase the wholesaler's goods. The wholesaler may even develop a line of private brands to be stocked by the retailers. This practice often helps smaller retailers compete with rival chains—and strengthens the wholesaler's position as well.

IGA (Independent Grocers' Alliance) Food Stores is a good example of a voluntary chain. Other wholesaler-sponsored chains include Associated Druggists, Sentry Hardware, and Western Auto. Since a single advertisement promotes all the retailers in the trading area, a common store name and similar inventories allow the retailers to save on advertising costs.

Retail Cooperative

In a second type of contractual VMS, a group of retailers establishes a shared wholesaling operation to help them compete with chains. This is known as a **retail cooperative.** The retailers purchase ownership shares in the wholesaling operation and agree to buy a minimum percentage of their inventories from this operation. The members typically adopt a common store name and develop common private brands. Ace Hardware is an example of a retail cooperative.

Franchise

A third type of contractual vertical marketing system is the **franchise,** in which a wholesaler or dealer (the franchisee) agrees to meet the operating requirements of a manufacturer or other franchiser. Franchising is a huge and growing industry. More than 3,000 U.S. companies distribute goods and services through systems of franchised dealers, and numerous firms also offer franchises in international markets. Table 13.2 shows the 20 fastest growing franchises in the U.S.

Franchise owners pay anywhere from several thousand to more than a million dollars to purchase and set up a franchise. Typically, they also pay a royalty on sales to the franchising company. In exchange for these initial and ongoing fees, the franchise owner receives the right to use the company's brand name as well as services such as training, marketing, advertising, and volume discounts. Major franchise chains justify the steep price of entry since it allows new businesses to sell winning brands. But if the brand enters a slump or the corporation behind the franchise makes poor strategic decisions, franchisees are often hurt.

1. What are vertical marketing systems (VMSs)? Identify the major types.
2. Identify the three types of contractual marketing systems.

table 13.2 ***The Top 20 Fastest Growing Franchises***

RANK	COMPANY	RANK	COMPANY
1	Subway	11	RE/MAX International Inc.
2	Curves	12	Jackson Hewitt Tax Service
3	7-Eleven	13	Choice Hotels International
4	Kumon Math & Reading Centers	14	WSI Internet (business Internet consulting)
5	Jan-Pro Franchising International (commercial cleaning)	15	Dunkin' Donuts
6	The Quizno's Franchise Co.	16	Action International (business coaching, consulting, and training)
7	Jani-King	17	Baskin-Robbins USA Co.
8	Coverall Cleaning Concepts (commercial cleaning)	18	Great Clips
9	Liberty Tax Service	19	Rezcity.com (online local guides and travel store)
10	Jazzercise Inc.	20	The UPS Store

Source: Data from "The Race Goes to the Swift," *Entrepreneur,* February 2004, p. 80.

LOGISTICS AND SUPPLY CHAIN MANAGEMENT

(5) Explain the roles of logistics and supply-chain management in an overall distribution strategy.

Pier 1 imports its eclectic mix of items from 600 vendors in 55 countries, and more than 80 percent come from small companies. If high-demand items or seasonal products are late into its warehouses or are shipped in insufficient quantities, the company misses opportunities to deliver popular shopping choices at its 700 retail stores and risks losing ground to competitors such as Pottery Barn and Crate & Barrel.

The situation facing Pier 1 Imports illustrates the importance of logistics. Careful coordination of Pier 1's supplier network, its shipping processes, and its inventory control is the key to its continuing success. Even so, Pier 1's rivals have managed to sell through, or turn, their inventory faster. So Pier 1's logistics team is implementing a new electronic monitoring system to improve the efficiency of moving goods from one place to another.[13] In addition, the retailer must maintain relationships with people in different countries such as China. The "Etiquette Tips for Marketing Professionals" feature discusses ways to build positive relationships with Chinese business partners.

Effective logistics requires proper supply-chain management, the control of activities of purchasing, processing, and delivery through which raw materials are transformed into products and made available to final consumers. The **supply chain,** also known as the *value chain,* is the complete sequence of suppliers and activities that contribute to the creation and delivery of goods and services. The supply chain begins with the raw-material inputs for the manufacturing process of a product and then proceeds to the actual production activities. The final link in the supply chain is the movement of finished products through the marketing channel to customers. Each link of the chain benefits the consumers as raw materials move through manufacturing to distribution. The chain encompasses all activities that enhance the value of the finished goods, including design, quality manufacturing, customer service, and delivery. Customer satisfaction results directly from the perceived value of a purchase to its buyer.

To manage the supply chain, businesses must look for ways to maximize customer value in each activity they perform. Supply-chain management takes place in two directions: upstream and downstream, as illustrated in Figure 13.6. **Upstream management** involves managing raw materials, inbound logistics, and warehouse and storage facilities. **Downstream management** involves managing finished product storage, outbound logistics, marketing and sales, and customer service.

Companies choose a variety of methods for managing the supply chain. Dell founder Michael Dell says that the keys to his company's success are online sales and automation. "Over 90 percent of

ETIQUETTE TIPS — FOR MARKETING PROFESSIONALS

Developing Relationships with Supply Chain Contacts in China

NEVER has the old saying "it's a small world" been more appropriate than it is today. Large and small companies are growing far beyond national boundaries so that marketers and other businesspeople must develop relationships with people across the globe. Because many supply chains now originate in China, it is important for U.S. marketers to do their best to understand Chinese values and customs to ensure smooth relationships with various suppliers located in China. If that sounds foreign to you, here are a few tips from the experts to help you get started:

1. Before you make initial direct contact with a businessperson in China, try to obtain a personal introduction from someone else. Relationships and personal connections are very important in China.
2. If you are scheduling a trip to China, be sensitive to Chinese holidays and traditions. Businesses are closed during Chinese New Year, May Day, and National Day, among others.
3. Always be prompt for appointments and meetings. Being late is considered a serious insult.
4. Address a business colleague in China with his or her title and last name, or use "Mr.," "Miss," or "Madam." Note that most married Chinese women retain their own family names for business. Never refer to someone as "Comrade."
5. You may greet a Chinese person with a slight bow, nod of the head, or handshake.
6. Do not be discouraged if the person you meet does not smile or seem openly friendly. It is customary for people in China to hide their feelings.
7. If a Chinese businessperson hands you a personal business card, accept it with both hands according to tradition.
8. Allow a business meeting to begin with small talk about the weather or recent travels and then build toward more serious subjects. Be patient. You are building trust with your Chinese colleagues.

Sources: "Making Contacts" and "Business Meetings," *Business-in-Asia.com,* http://www.business-in-china.net, accessed April 17, 2004; "OCBC Says Doing Business in China Is Still a Challenge," *ChannelNewsAsia.com,* April 15, 2004, http://www.channelnewsasia.com; Peter P. W. Chen, "Appointment Alert!" *Executive Planet,* http://www.executiveplanet.com, May 25, 2003.

figure 13.6

The Supply Chain of a Manufacturing Company

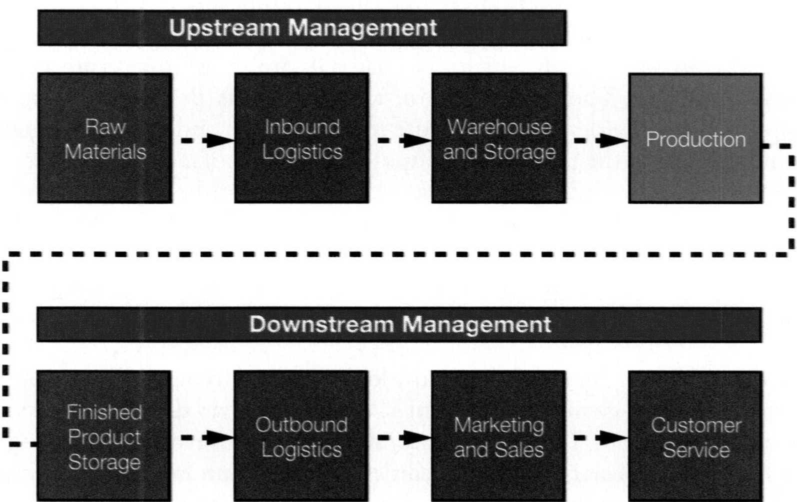

Source: Adapted from Figure 2.2, Ralph M. Stair and George W. Reynolds, *Principles of Information Systems,* 6th ed. Boston: Course Technology, © 2003.

Menlo Worldwide provides a variety of services to help other businesses manage their supply chains.

our supply-chain transactions are machine-to-machine transactions," he claims. Dell concedes that "you have to put some sort of human framework in there," but he insists that his firm's costs would skyrocket if all transactions were handled over the phone by operators.[14] IBM has recently overhauled its supply chain, as described in the "Marketing Hit" feature.

Logistical management plays a major role in giving customers what they need when they need it and thus is central in the supply chain. Another important component of this chain, *value-added service,* adds some improved or supplemental service that customers do not normally receive or expect. The following sections examine methods for streamlining and managing logistics and the supply chain as part of an overall distribution strategy.

Briefly Speaking

Be prepared for all possible instances of demand, whenever and wherever they may occur.

Michael Dell (b. 1965)
founder, Dell Inc.

RADIO FREQUENCY IDENTIFICATION (RFID)

One tool that marketers are using to help manage logistics is **radio frequency identification (RFID)** technology. With RFID, a tiny chip with identification information that can be read by a radio frequency scanner from a distance is placed on an item. These chips are already widely used in tollway pass transmitters, allowing drivers to zip through toll booths without stopping or rolling

radio frequency identification (RFID) Technology that uses a tiny chip with identification information that can be read by a scanner using radio waves from a distance.

marketing hit — IBM Overhauls Its Supply Chain

Background. Imagine trying to overhaul a system so huge and cumbersome you don't know where to start. It's like bringing down a mammoth with a peashooter. But IBM's supply chain has been a mammoth for decades, eating up the profits and spewing out costs in the billions.

The Challenge. "You cannot hope to thrive in the information technology industry if you are a high-cost, slow-moving company," says IBM's chief executive, Samuel J. Palmisano. "Supply chain is one of the new competitive battlegrounds. We are committed to being the most efficient and productive player in our industry." That's where Robert Moffatt, head of IBM's Integrated Supply Chain division, comes in.

The Strategy. Moffatt and his associates have adopted an "end-to-end" approach to cutting costs and improving efficiency along the supply chain. That means evaluating everything from the cost of raw materials to the delivery of inventory. Specifically, the ISC division has made recommendations as broad as redesigning products to save on shipping costs, reusing certain parts, and cutting the give-aways. Moffatt hopes to integrate the end-to-end approach into every aspect of IBM's business. In addition, Moffatt is trying to win new consulting business for his division.

The Outcome. IBM recently reported saving more than $5 billion in supply-chain costs in a single year. CEO Palmisano then gave Moffatt new orders: Save another $400 million. Moffatt was happy to oblige. "The thing that I'm most proud of, if you look at what IBM has been doing," says Moffatt, "besides having some pretty laudable financial results, we've been able to gain a share in every one of the key categories of the marketplace that we participate in."

Sources: David Drickhamer, "Supply-Chain Superstars," *Industry Week,* January 5, 2004, http://www.industryweek.com; Daniel Lyons, "Back on the Chain Gang," *Forbes,* October 13, 2003, pp. 114–123; Scott Campbell, "IBM Optimized Supply Chain Leads to Channel Efficiencies," *CRN,* April 11, 2003, http://www.crn.com.

down their windows. They are also embedded in employee ID cards that workers use to open office doors without keys. But businesses such as retail giant Wal-Mart, manufacturers Gillette and Procter & Gamble, credit-card firms MasterCard and American Express, along with German retailer Metro AG are eagerly putting the technology to wider use; they say it will speed deliveries, make consumer bar codes obsolete, and provide marketers with valuable information about consumer preferences.

Wal-Mart is pushing its biggest suppliers to attach RFID tags to pallets and cases of products ranging from Coca-Cola to Dove soap, saying that the technology will vastly improve its ability to track inventory and keep the right amount of products in stock. Some industry analysts estimate that the technology could save the Arkansas-based retailer $8 billion over the next few years.[15] In Germany, Metro AG is using the same technology to track inventory with handheld devices.[16]

After initial concerns about consumer privacy as well as technical problems when Gillette and Wal-Mart planned to have a chip embedded in each product—instead of on cases or pallets—both companies decided to focus on managing inventory flow instead of attempting to track consumer behavior.[17]

MasterCard and American Express have both launched trials of their "contactless" credit cards using RFID. Instead of swiping a card through a slot, the consumer only has to hold it near a special scanner for the sale to go through—and the consumer still receives a paper receipt. "In some instances, it's faster than cash," says Betsy Foran-Owens, a vice president at MasterCard. "You're eliminating the fumble factor."[18]

ENTERPRISE RESOURCE PLANNING

Software is an important aspect of logistics management and the supply chain. Consider the case of Mott's, the applesauce people. Their ideal production plan is developed from enterprise resource planning (ERP) software sold by SAP, the largest German software producer. An **enterprise resource planning (ERP) system** is an integrated software system that consolidates data from among the firm's units. Roughly two-thirds of ERP system users are manufacturers concerned with production issues such as sequencing and scheduling.

As valuable as it is, ERP and its related software aren't always perfect. For example, ERP failures were blamed for Hershey's inability to fulfill all of its candy orders during a recent Halloween period, when a fall-off in sales was blamed on a combination of shipping delays, inability to fill orders, and partial shipments while candy stockpiled in warehouses. The nation's major retailers were forced to shift their purchases to other candy vendors.

LOGISTICAL COST CONTROL

In addition to enhancing their products by providing value-added services to customers, many firms are focusing on logistics for another important reason: to cut costs. Distribution functions currently represent almost half of a typical firm's total marketing costs. To reduce logistical costs, businesses are reexamining each link of their supply chains to identify activities that do not add value for customers. By eliminating, reducing, or redesigning these activities, they can often cut costs and boost efficiency. As just described, new technologies such as RFID can save businesses millions—or even billions—of dollars, as in the case of Wal-Mart.

Because of increased security requirements in recent years, businesses involved in importing and exporting have faced a major rise in logistical costs. The Department of Homeland Security required these companies to submit detailed safety reports and then suggested ways to improve security on incoming and outgoing ships as well as at ports. Many businesses have already received security surcharges, and these costs are likely to continue to rise. Some are seeking to control increases by joining the Customs-Trade Partnership Against Terrorism, which certifies its members as safe port users, making them exempt from lengthy inspections of cargo, ships, and warehouses.[19]

Third-Party Logistics

Some companies try to cut costs and offer value-added services by outsourcing some or all of their logistics functions to specialist firms. The **third-party (contract) logistics firms** specialize in handling logistical activities for their clients. TRW Aeronautical Systems won a contract to provide supply-chain management systems to South African Airways Technical. The third-party logistics firm manages overhaul and repair of avionics and engine control parts for a fleet of Boeing jets.[20]

Through such outsourcing alliances, producers and logistical service suppliers cooperate in developing innovative, customized systems that speed goods through carefully constructed manufacturing and distribution pipelines. Although many companies have long outsourced transportation and warehousing functions, today's alliance partners use similar methods to combine their operations.

1. List some ways companies are streamlining their supply chains.
2. Identify three methods for managing logistics.

PHYSICAL DISTRIBUTION

6 Identify the major components of a physical distribution system.

A firm's physical distribution system is an organized group of components linked according to a plan for achieving specific distribution objectives. It contains the following elements:

1. *Customer service.* What level of customer service the distribution activities should support.
2. *Transportation.* How the firm should ship its products.
3. *Inventory control.* How much inventory the firm should maintain at each location.
4. *Protective packaging and materials handling.* How the firm can package and efficiently handle goods in the factory, warehouse, and transport terminals.
5. *Order processing.* How the firm should handle orders.
6. *Warehousing.* Where the distribution system will locate stocks of goods and the number of warehouses the firm should maintain.

All of these components function in interrelated ways. Decisions made in one area affect efficiency in others. The physical distribution manager must balance each component so that the system avoids stressing any single aspect to the detriment of overall functioning. A firm might decide to reduce transportation costs by shipping its products by less costly—but slow—water transportation. But slow deliveries would likely force the firm to maintain higher inventory levels, raising those costs. This mismatch between system elements often leads to increased production costs. So balancing the components is crucial.

Perhaps nowhere is the physical distribution balance more vital than in military operations. One organization, the Defense Logistics Agency, has provided most of the food and fuel to U.S. military troops in Iraq. In fact, DLA moves 4.6 million different items from one place to another. "We've gotten out of the business of warehousing huge mountains of inventories, but we still manage small hills of critical and high-demand items," says Leonard Petrucelli, chief of DLA's Contingency Plans and Operations. "We ensure the supplies are delivered straight to where the customer wants them—whether that's an office in Virginia, a pier in Kuwait, or an airfield inside Iraq."[21]

THE PROBLEM OF SUBOPTIMIZATION

Logistics managers seek to establish a specified level of customer service while minimizing the costs of physically moving and storing goods. Marketers must first decide on their priorities for customer service and then figure out how to fulfill those goals by moving goods at the best cost. Meshing together all the physical distribution elements is a huge challenge that firms don't always meet.

Suboptimization results when the managers of individual physical distribution functions attempt to minimize costs, but the impact of one task on the others leads to less than optimal results. Imagine a hockey team composed of record-holding players. Unfortunately, despite the individual talents of the players, the team fails to win a game. This is an example of suboptimization. The same thing can happen at a company when each logistics activity is judged by its own accomplishments instead of the way it contributes to the overall goals of the firm. Suboptimization often happens when a firm introduces a new product that may not fit easily into its current physical distribution system.

figure 13.7

Allocation of Physical Distribution Expenditures

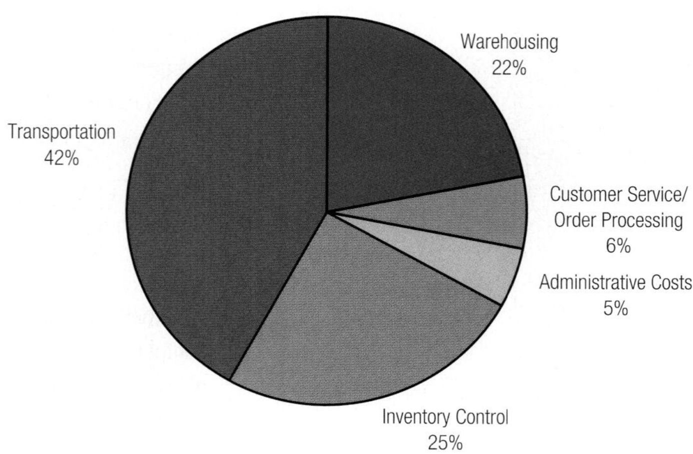

Source: These estimates were provided by Dr. Julie Gentry, Logistics Faculty, University of Arkansas–Fayetteville.

Effective management of the physical distribution function requires some cost trade-offs. By accepting relatively high costs in some functional areas to cut costs in others, managers can minimize their firm's total physical distribution costs. Of course, any reduction in logistical costs should support progress toward the goal of maintaining customer-service standards.

CUSTOMER-SERVICE STANDARDS

Customer-service standards state the goals and define acceptable performance for the quality of service that a firm expects to deliver to its customers. Many Internet retailers survive through their ability to ship within hours of receiving an order. A restaurant might set a standard that requires all customers to receive their meals within 10 minutes of ordering. A supermarket might set a standard that all the produce it sells has been picked within the week.

Designers of a physical distribution system begin by establishing acceptable levels of customer service. These designers then assemble physical distribution components in a way that will achieve this standard at the lowest possible total cost. As shown in Figure 13.7, this overall cost breaks down into five components: (1) transportation, (2) warehousing, (3) customer service/order processing, (4) administrative costs, and (5) inventory control.

Briefly Speaking

Timely service, like timely gifts, is doubled in value.

George MacDonald
(1824–1905)
Scottish novelist, poet, and clergyman

TRANSPORTATION

The transportation industry has been largely deregulated. Deregulation has been particularly important for motor carriers, railroads, and air carriers. Many transporters are now free to develop unique solutions to shippers' needs. Before deregulation, no truck carrier served all 48 contiguous U.S. states. Today, more than 4,000 carriers have that authority. In addition, the trucking industry now operates far more efficiently than it did under government regulation; many carriers have reduced empty mileage by two-thirds.

Typically adding 10 percent to the cost of a product, transportation and delivery expenses represent the largest category of logistics-related costs for most firms. Also, for many items—particularly perishable ones such as fresh fish or produce—transportation makes a central contribution to satisfactory customer service.

Many logistics managers have found that the key to controlling their shipping costs is careful management of relationships with shipping firms. Freight carriers use two basic rates: class and commodity rates. A class rate is a standard rate for a specific commodity moving between any pair of destinations. A carrier may charge a lower commodity rate, sometimes called a special rate, to a favored shipper as a reward for either regular business or a large-quantity shipment. Railroads and inland water carriers frequently reward customers in this way.

In addition, the railroad and motor carrier industries sometimes supplement this rate structure with negotiated, or contract, rates. In other words, the two parties finalize terms of rates, services, and other variables in a contract.

Classes of Carriers

Freight carriers are classified as common, contract, and private carriers. **Common carriers,** often considered the backbone of the transportation industry, provide transportation services as for-hire carriers to the general public. The government still regulates their rates and services, and they cannot conduct their operations without permission from the appropriate regulatory authority. Common carriers move freight via all modes of transport.

Contract carriers are for-hire transporters that do not offer their services to the general public. Instead, they establish contracts with individual customers and operate exclusively for particular industries, such as the motor freight industry. These carriers operate under much looser regulations than common carriers.

Private carriers do not offer services for hire. These carriers provide transportation services solely for internally generated freight. As a result, they observe no rate or service regulations. The Interstate Commerce Commission (ICC), a federal regulatory agency, permits private carriers to operate as common or contract carriers as well. Many private carriers have taken advantage of this rule by operating their trucks fully loaded at all times.

© DWAYNE NEWTON/PHOTOEDIT

UPS is a large common carrier that serves business customers as well as consumers.

Major Transportation Modes

7 Compare the major modes of transportation.

Logistics managers choose among five major transportation alternatives: railroads, motor carriers, water carriers, pipelines, and air freight. Each mode has its own unique characteristics. Logistics managers select the best options for their situations by matching the situation features to their specific transportation needs.

Railroads

Railroads continue to control the largest share of the freight business as measured by ton-miles. The term *ton-mile* indicates shipping activity required to move one ton of freight one mile. Rail shipments quickly rack up ton-miles because this mode provides the most efficient way for moving bulky commodities over long distances. Rail carriers generally transport huge quantities of coal, chemicals, grain, nonmetallic minerals, lumber and wood products, and automobiles. Union Pacific's promotional message in Figure 13.8 emphasizes the long history that railroads have delivering goods throughout the U.S.

THE TIES THAT BIND A NATION.

It's 33,000 miles of timber and steel that connect America—from Portland to New Orleans, from Chicago to Los Angeles. It's the backbone of our economy and in turn, the backbone of our nation. Most importantly, it's 47,000 men and women who every day transport the raw materials and finished goods that keep our country moving.

BUILDING AMERICA™ UNION PACIFIC

www.up.com

figure 13.8

Railroads: Efficient Delivery of Products Nationwide

The railroads have improved their service standards through a number of innovative concepts, such as unit trains, run-through trains, **intermodal operations,** and double-stack container trains. Unit trains carry much of the coal, grain, and other high-volume commodities shipped, running back and forth between single loading points (such as a mine) and single destinations (such as a power plant) to deliver a single commodity. Run-through trains bypass intermediate terminals to speed up schedules. They work similar to unit trains, but a run-through train may carry a variety of commodities.

intermodal operations Combination of transport modes such as rail and highway carriers (piggyback), air and highway carriers (birdyback), and water and air carriers (fishyback) to improve customer service and achieve cost advantages.

In piggyback operations, one of the intermodal operations, highway trailers and containers ride on railroad flatcars, thus combining the long-haul capacity of the train with the door-to-door flexibility of the truck. A double-stack container train pulls special rail cars equipped with bathtub-shaped wells so they can carry two containers stacked on top of one another. By nearly doubling train capacity and slashing costs, this system offers enormous advantages to rail customers.

Motor Carriers

About 80 percent of all goods in the U.S. ride on trucks at some point. The trucking industry has grown dramatically over recent decades and is expected to grow by 25 percent in the next 10 years to keep up with demand.[22] Trucking offers some important advantages over the other transportation modes, including relatively fast shipments and consistent service for both large and small shipments. Motor carriers concentrate on shipping manufactured products, while railroads typically haul bulk shipments of raw materials. Motor carriers, therefore, receive greater revenue per ton shipped, since the cost for shipping raw materials is higher than for shipping manufactured products.

Technology has also improved the efficiency of trucking. Many trucking firms now track their fleets via satellite communications systems, and in-truck computer systems allow drivers and dispatchers to make last-minute changes in scheduling and delivery. The Internet is also adding new features to motor carrier services.

Some private fleets function as rolling assembly plants that pick up semifinished products from manufacturers, assemble them en route, and deliver the finished goods to customers, increasing overall service and customer satisfaction. Arizona-based distributor Pinacor, for example, partners with New Jersey–based Lucent Technologies to perform final testing and configuration of Lucent's telecommunications systems. Pinacor's ability to assume these final manufacturing steps reduces product lead time dramatically, from an average of 30 to 45 days to about 10 days.[23]

Water Carriers

Two basic types of transport methods move products over water: inland or barge lines and oceangoing, deepwater ships. Barge lines efficiently transport bulky, low unit value commodities such as grain, gravel, lumber, sand, and steel. A typical lower Mississippi River barge line may stretch more than a quarter-mile across. Large ships also operate on the Great Lakes, transporting materials such as iron ore from Minnesota and harvested grain for the market. These lake carrier ships range in size from roughly 400 to more than 1,000 feet in length.

Oceangoing ships carry a growing stream of containerized freight between ports around the world. New supertankers from global companies like Maersk Sealand are the size of three football fields, almost doubling the capacity of other vessels. At full capacity, the ships can cut the cost of shipping a container across the Pacific by a fifth. Shippers that transport goods via water carriers incur very low costs compared with the rates for other transportation modes. Standardized modular shipping containers maximize savings by limiting loading, unloading, and other handling.

Ships often carry large, refrigerated containers called "reefers" for transporting everything from fresh produce to medical supplies. These containers, along with their nonrefrigerated counterparts, improve shipping efficiency because they can easily be removed from a ship and attached to trucks or trains. Maersk Sealand, shown in Figure 13.9, is one of the largest shipping firms in the world and owns more than 1 million containers.[24] Although shipping by water has traditionally been less expensive than other modes of transportation, as explained earlier, costs for this mode have increased dramatically because of tightened security measures.

Pipelines

Although the pipeline industry ranks third after railroads and motor carriers in ton-miles transported, many people scarcely recognize its existence. More than 214,000 miles of pipelines crisscross the U.S.

© MACDUFF EVERTON/CORBIS

figure 13.9

Containerized Shipping: Increasing Efficiency in the Supply Chain

in an extremely efficient network for transporting natural gas and oil products. Oil pipelines carry two types of commodities: crude (unprocessed) oil and refined products, such as gasoline, jet fuel, and kerosene. In addition, one so-called *slurry pipeline* carries coal in suspension after it has been ground up into a powder and mixed with water. The Black Mesa Pipeline, owned by Union Pacific, moves the coal 290 miles from northern Arizona into southern Nevada.

Although pipelines offer low maintenance and dependable methods of transportation, a number of characteristics limit their applications. They have fewer locations than water carriers, and they can accommodate shipments of only a small number of products. Finally, pipelines represent a relatively slow method of transportation; liquids travel through this method at an average speed of only three to four miles per hour.

Air Freight

International water carriers still transport many low-value products or heavy mass-market goods such as automobiles, but more and more international shipments travel by air. The significant growth in shipping volume handled by air carriers such as DHL will probably continue as freight carriers seek to satisfy increased customer demand for fast delivery. Although 80 percent of the world's overnight air deliveries take place in the U.S., international demand for overnight air-freight service is soaring by 18 percent every year. Already more than 1.3 million 24-hour deliveries are made daily outside the U.S.[25]

Comparing the Five Modes of Transport

Table 13.3 compares the five transportation modes on several operating characteristics. Although all shippers judge reliability, speed, and cost in choosing the most appropriate transportation methods, they assign varying importance to specific criteria when shipping different goods. For example, while motor carriers rank highest in availability in different locations, shippers of petroleum products frequently choose the lowest ranked alternative, pipelines, for their low cost.

Examples of types of goods most often handled by the different transports include the following:

- *Railroads.* Lumber, iron, steel, coal, automobiles, grain, chemicals
- *Motor carriers.* Clothing, furniture, fixtures, lumber, plastic, food, leather, machinery

table 13.3 Comparison of Transport Modes

MODE	SPEED	DEPENDABILITY IN MEETING SCHEDULES	FREQUENCY OF SHIPMENTS	AVAILABILITY IN DIFFERENT LOCATIONS	FLEXIBILITY IN HANDLING	COST
Rail	Average	Average	Low	Low	High	Average
Water	Very slow	Average	Very low	Limited	Very high	Very low
Truck	Fast	High	High	Very extensive	Average	High
Pipeline	Slow	High	High	Very limited	Very low	Low
Air	Very fast	High	Average	Average	Low	Very high

- *Water carriers.* Fuel, oil, coal, chemicals, minerals, petroleum products
- *Pipelines.* Oil, diesel fuel, jet fuel, kerosene, natural gas
- *Air carriers.* Flowers, technical instruments, machinery, high-priced specialty products, direct-to-consumer e-commerce goods

8 Discuss how transportation intermediaries and combined transportation modes can improve physical distribution.

Freight Forwarders and Supplemental Carriers

Freight forwarders act as transportation intermediaries, consolidating shipments to gain lower rates for their customers. The transport rates on less-than-truckload (LTL) and less-than-carload (LCL) shipments often double the per-unit rates on truckload (TL) and carload (CL) shipments. Freight forwarders charge less than the highest rates but more than the lowest rates. They profit by consolidating shipments from multiple customers until they can ship at TL and CL rates. The customers gain two advantages from these services: lower costs on small shipments and faster delivery service than they could achieve with their own LTL and LCL shipments.

In addition to the transportation options reviewed so far, a logistics manager can ship products via a number of auxiliary, or supplemental, carriers that specialize in small shipments. These carriers include bus freight services, United Parcel Service, FedEx, DHL International, and the U.S. Postal Service.

Intermodal Coordination

Transportation companies emphasize specific modes and serve certain kinds of customers, but they sometimes combine their services to give shippers the service and cost advantages of each. *Piggyback* service, mentioned in the section on rail transport, is the most widely used form of intermodal coordination. *Birdyback* service, another form of intermodal coordination, sends motor carriers to pick up a shipment locally and deliver that shipment to local destinations; an air carrier takes it between airports near those locations. *Fishyback* service sets up a similar intermodal coordination system between motor carriers and water carriers.

Intermodal transportation generally gives shippers faster service and lower rates than either mode could match individually because each method carries freight in its most efficient way. However, intermodal arrangements require close coordination between all transportation providers.

Recognizing this need, multimodal transportation companies have formed to offer combined activities within single operations. Piggyback service generally joins two separate companies—a railroad and a trucking company. A multimodal firm provides intermodal service through its own internal transportation resources. Shippers benefit because the single service assumes responsibility from origin to destination. This unification prevents disputes over which carrier delayed or damaged a shipment.

9 Identify and briefly describe the different types of warehousing.

WAREHOUSING

Products flow through two types of warehouses: storage and distribution warehouses. A storage warehouse holds goods for moderate to long periods in an attempt to balance supply and demand for producers and purchasers. For example, controlled atmosphere—also called *cold storage*—warehouses in Yakima and Wenatchee, Washington, serve nearby apple orchards. By contrast, a distribution warehouse assembles and redistributes goods, keeping them moving as much as possible. Many distribution warehouses or centers physically store goods for less than 24 hours before shipping them to customers.

Logistics managers have attempted to save on transportation costs by developing central distribution centers. A manufacturer might send a single, large, consolidated shipment to a break-bulk center—a central distribution center that breaks down large shipments into several smaller ones and delivers them to individual customers in the area. Many Internet retailers use break-bulk distribution centers.

Wal-Mart operates an enormous distribution network of 146 distribution centers around the world, with 103 U.S. centers and 43 centers overseas. The firm plans to open even more centers. The result is that delivery trucks have to travel shorter distances to stores to make deliveries. "If you can cut a day of lead time out of the supply chain of a company the size of Wal-Mart, that's big bucks," explains Ted Wade, a former vice president of logistics for Wal-Mart.[26]

Automated Warehouse Technology

Logistics managers can cut distribution costs and improve customer service dramatically by automating their warehouse systems. Although automation technology represents an expensive investment, it can provide major labor savings for high-volume distributors such as grocery chains. A computerized system might store orders, choose the correct number of cases, and move those cases in the desired sequence to loading docks. This kind of warehouse system reduces labor costs, worker injuries, pilferage, fires, and breakage.

Warehouse Locations

Every company must make a major logistics decision when it determines the number and locations of its storage facilities. Two categories of costs influence this choice: (1) warehousing and materials handling costs and (2) delivery costs from warehouses to customers. Large facilities offer economies of scale in facilities and materials handling systems; per-unit costs for these systems decrease as volume increases. Delivery costs, on the other hand, rise as the distance from warehouse to customer increases. As just mentioned, Wal-Mart continues to work to increase the number of warehouse locations to reduce distance and cost.

Warehouse location also affects customer service. Businesses must place their storage and distribution facilities in locations from which they can meet customer demands for product availability and delivery times. They must also consider population and employment trends. For example, the rapid growth of metropolitan areas in the southern and western U.S. has caused some firms to open more distribution centers in these areas.

INVENTORY CONTROL SYSTEMS

Inventory control captures a large share of a logistics manager's attention because companies need to maintain enough inventory to meet customer demand without incurring unneeded costs for carrying excess inventory. Some firms attempt to keep inventory levels under control by implementing just-in-time (JIT) production. Others are beginning to use RFID technology, discussed earlier in this chapter.

Companies such as Costco have shifted responsibility—and costs—for inventory control from retailers back to individual manufacturers. Costco gives Kimberly-Clark access to individual store sales data. Kimberly-Clark uses the information to track inventory levels of its diapers and other products and replenishes stocks as needed. **Vendor-managed inventory (VMI)** systems like this are based on the assumption that suppliers are in the best position to spot understocks or surpluses, cutting costs along the supply chain that can be translated into lower prices at the checkout.

ORDER PROCESSING

Like inventory control, order processing directly affects the firm's ability to meet its customer-service standards. A company may have to compensate for inefficiencies in its order processing system by shipping products via costly transportation modes or by maintaining large inventories at many expensive field warehouses.

Order processing typically consists of four major activities: (1) conducting a credit check; (2) keeping a record of the sale, which involves tasks such as crediting a sales representative's commission account; (3) making appropriate accounting entries; and (4) locating orders, shipping them, and adjusting inventory records. A stockout occurs when an order for an item is not available for shipment. A firm's order processing system must advise affected customers of a stockout and offer a choice of alternative actions.

As in other areas of physical distribution, technological innovations improve efficiency in order processing. Many firms are streamlining their order processing procedures by using e-mail and the Internet. Outdoor-gear retailer REI, for example, pushes customers toward Web ordering, its least costly fulfillment channel, in its catalogs, store receipts, signs, mailers, and membership letters.

PROTECTIVE PACKAGING AND MATERIALS HANDLING

Logistics managers arrange and control activities for moving products within plants, warehouses, and transportation terminals, which together compose the **materials handling system.** Two important concepts influence many materials handling choices: unitizing and containerization.

Unitizing combines as many packages as possible into each load that moves within or outside a facility. Logistics managers prefer to handle materials on pallets (platforms, generally made of wood, on which goods are transported). Unitizing systems often lash materials in place with steel bands or shrink packaging. A shrink package surrounds a batch of materials with a sheet of plastic that shrinks after heating, securely holding individual pieces together. Unitizing promotes efficient materials handling because each package requires minimal labor to move. Securing the materials together also minimizes damage and pilferage.

Logistics managers extend the same concept through **containerization**—combining several unitized loads. A container of oil rig parts, for example, can be loaded in Tulsa and trucked to Kansas City, where rail facilities place the shipment on a high-speed run-through train to New York City. There, the parts are loaded on a ship headed to Saudi Arabia.

In addition to the benefits outlined for unitizing, containerization also markedly reduces the time required to load and unload ships. Containers limit in-transit damage to freight because individual packages pass through few handling systems en route to purchasers.

1. Identify the five distribution objectives.
2. What are the major modes of transportation?

Strategic Implications of Marketing in the 21st Century

SEVERAL factors, including the burgeoning e-commerce environment, are driving changes in channel development, logistics, and supply-chain management. As the Internet continues to revolutionize the ways manufacturers deliver goods to ultimate consumers, marketers must find ways to promote cooperation between existing dealer, retailer, and distributor networks while harnessing the power of the Web as an alternative channel. This system demands not only delivery of goods and services faster and more efficiently than ever before but also superior service to Web-based customers.

In addition, increased product proliferation—grocery stores typically stock almost 50,000 different items—demands logistics systems that can manage multiple brands delivered through multiple channels. And those channels must be finely tuned to identify and rapidly rectify problems such as retail shortfalls or costly overstocks. The trend toward leaner retailing, in which the burden of merchandise tracking and inventory control is switching from retailers to manufacturers, means that to be effective, logistics and supply-chain systems must result in cost savings.

REVIEW OF CHAPTER OBJECTIVES

1 Describe the types of marketing channels and the roles they play in marketing strategy.

Marketing (distribution) channels are the systems of marketing institutions that enhance the physical flow of goods and services, along with ownership title, from producer to consumer or business user. In other words, they help bridge the gap between producer or manufacturer and business customer or consumer. Types of channels include direct selling, selling through intermediaries, dual distribution, and reverse channels. Channels perform four functions: facilitating the exchange process, sorting, standardizing exchange processes, and facilitating searches by buyers and sellers.

1.1. Define *marketing channel.* What is its alternative name?
1.2. What is the role of marketing intermediaries?
1.3. Give an example of a reverse channel.

2 Outline the major channel strategy decisions.

Decisions include selecting a marketing channel and determining distribution intensity. Selection of a marketing channel may be based on market factors, product factors, organizational factors, or competitive factors. Distribution may be intensive, selective, or exclusive.

2.1. What are some of the market factors affecting channel selection?
2.2. What are some of the product factors?
2.3. Describe some of the problems of exclusive distribution.

3 Describe the concepts of channel management, conflict, and cooperation.

Manufacturers must practice channel management by developing and maintaining relationships with the intermediaries in their marketing channels. The channel captain is the dominant member of the channel. Horizontal and vertical conflict can arise when there is disagreement among channel members. Cooperation is best achieved when all channel members regard themselves as equal components of the same organization.

3.1. Describe horizontal and vertical conflict.
3.2. What is the grey market?

4 Identify and describe the different vertical marketing systems.

A vertical marketing system (VMS) is a planned channel system design to improve distribution efficiency and cost effectiveness by integrating various functions throughout the distribution chain. This may be achieved by forward integration or backward integration. Options include a corporate marketing system, operated by a single owner; an administered marketing system, run by a dominant channel member; and contractual marketing systems, based on formal agreements among channel members.

4.1. Describe forward and backward integration.
4.2. Identify some benefits and drawbacks to franchising.

5 Explain the roles of logistics and supply-chain management in an overall distribution strategy.

Effective logistics requires proper supply-chain management. The supply chain begins with raw materials, proceeds through actual production, and then continues with the movement of finished products through the marketing channel to customers. Supply-chain management takes place in two directions: upstream and downstream. Tools that marketers use to streamline and manage logistics include radio frequency identification (RFID), enterprise resource planning (ERP), and logistical cost control.

5.1. Give examples of upstream and downstream management.
5.2. What is the difference between upstream and downstream supply-chain management?
5.3. What is RFID and how is it used?
5.4. Why is logistical cost control important?

6 Identify the major components of a physical distribution system.

Physical distribution involves a broad range of activities concerned with efficient movement of finished goods from the end of the production line to the consumer. As a system, physical distribution consists of six elements: (1) customer service, (2) transportation, (3) inventory control, (4) materials handling and protective packaging, (5) order processing, and (6) warehousing. These elements are interrelated and must be balanced to create a smoothly functioning distribution system and to avoid suboptimization.

6.1. Why is it important for a manager to balance each of the major components of a physical distribution system?
6.2. What is suboptimization?

⑦ Compare the major modes of transportation.

Railroads rank high on flexibility in handling products; average on speed, dependability in meeting schedules, and cost; and low on frequency of shipments. Motor carriers are relatively high in cost but rank high on speed, dependability, shipment frequency, and availability in different locations. Water carriers balance their slow speed, low shipment frequency, and limited availability with lower costs. The special nature of pipelines makes them rank relatively low on availability, flexibility, and speed, but they are also low in cost. Air transportation is high in cost but offers very fast and dependable delivery schedules.

7.1. What recent events have had a major effect on water carriers?
7.2. What type(s) of transportation might a firm use to ship fresh flowers?

⑧ Discuss how transportation intermediaries and combined transportation modes can improve physical distribution.

Transportation intermediaries facilitate movement of goods in a variety of ways, including piggyback, birdyback, and fishyback services—all forms of intermodal coordination. Methods such as unitization and containerization facilitate intermodal transfers.

8.1. How does the unification provided by multimodal transportation companies benefit shippers?
8.2. Identify the major forms of intermodal transportation.

⑨ Identify and briefly describe the different types of warehousing.

Products flow through two types of warehouses: storage and distribution. A storage warehouse holds goods for moderate to long periods of time, whereas a distribution warehouse assembles and redistributes goods quickly. Warehouse location can affect distribution costs.

9.1. Identify the two categories of costs associated with the selection of warehouse location.

MARKETING TERMS YOU NEED TO KNOW

distribution 416
marketing (distribution) channel 416
logistics 416
supply-chain management 416
physical distribution 416
direct channel 419
dual distribution 420
intensive distribution 423
selective distribution 423
exclusive distribution 423
channel captain 426
vertical marketing system (VMS) 427
corporate marketing system 428
administered marketing system 428
contractual marketing system 428
radio frequency identification (RFID) 431
intermodal operations 436

OTHER IMPORTANT MARKETING TERMS

marketing intermediary (middleman) 417
wholesaler 417
direct selling 419
manufacturers' representative 420
reverse channel 420
cooperative advertising 423
exclusive dealing agreement 424
closed sales territory 424
tying agreement 424
grey goods 427
forward integration 427
backward integration 427
retail cooperative 428
franchise 428
supply chain 429
upstream management 429
downstream management 429
enterprise resource planning (ERP) system 432
third-party (contract) logistics firm 432
suboptimization 433
customer-service standards 434
common carriers 434
contract carriers 434
private carriers 435
vendor-managed inventory (VMI) 439
materials handling system 440
containerization 440

PROJECTS AND TEAMWORK EXERCISES

1. Imagine a vending machine that would charge more for soft drinks during hot weather. The Coca-Cola Company has tested such a device. What is your opinion of a temperature-sensitive vending machine? How do you think customers would react? Research the conclusion of this test.
2. The traditional channel for consumer goods runs from producer to wholesaler to retailer to user. With a classmate, select a product from the following list (or choose one of your own) and create a chart that traces its distribution system.
   a. pair of L.L. Bean work boots
   b. meal at Taco Bell
   c. DVD player
   d. bottle of Odwalla juice
3. Identify, draw, and explain a reverse channel with which you are personally familiar.
4. On your own or with a classmate, visit the Web site of one of the following companies (or choose one of your own) to learn more about its products and its choice of marketing channels. Then determine which factors—market, product, organizational, and/or competitive—influenced the selection of the distribution channels. Discuss your findings in class.
   a. 3M
   b. Travelocity
   c. Yamaha
   d. Old Navy
5. How might e-commerce lead to channel conflict? What type of channel conflict could result from e-commerce? Suggest a resolution to this conflict. Form two teams and discuss channel conflict from the perspectives of different channel members.
6. One recent Halloween, children were disappointed because Hershey was unable to stock retailers' shelves with supplies of chocolate candy. In small groups, research this distribution and logistics failure. What went wrong? What lessons does this offer for future distribution strategies?
7. Choose one of the franchises listed in Table 13.2 and visit the Web site of that company. Based on what you can learn about its contractual marketing system as well as other information about its products, logistics, supply-chain management, and physical distribution system, would you be interested in purchasing a franchise from this company? Why or why not? Present your findings in class.
8. For the company you selected in project 7, create a chart outlining the physical distribution objectives for your franchise.
9. Suggest the most appropriate method for transporting the products listed here. Defend your choices.
   a. iron ore
   b. oil-field equipment
   c. natural gas
   d. cherries
   e. lumber
10. Wal-Mart continues to build distribution centers to get products into stores faster and at lower cost. Visit Wal-Mart's Web site and research other articles on the Web to learn more about the system.

APPLYING CHAPTER CONCEPTS

1. Tupperware recently decided to break from its tradition of selling products only through private parties and instead place its goods in retail stores. Marketers thought that customers would love having easier access to their favorite Tupperware products. The result? Sales slumped badly. Why do you think this marketing channel switch affected Tupperware sales the way it did?
2. A firm that begins selling its products over the Internet directly to consumers may create channel conflict with retailers with whom it has existing agreements. Describe a solution to this problem.
3. Franchising has become an increasingly popular business enterprise for all kinds of marketers. Why do you think this is the case? What are the benefits and drawbacks to franchising?
4. Imagine that you are a marketer for Nike or Foot Locker, the firms described at the beginning of the chapter. What mode of transportation would you select for your products?

ETHICS EXERCISE

The Internet has created a whole new channel for delivering marketing messages as well as products. While it has opened doors to new markets for small and large businesses, it has also created opportunities for entrepreneurs like Scott Richter, whose firm, OptinRealBig.com, sends out several hundred million unsolicited e-mails every day—in other words, spam. "We're a powerhouse in the e-mail marketing world," claims Richter. "I stand up for what I do." But Paul Judge, chief technology officer for the e-mail security firm CipherTrust Inc., doesn't think Richter's business is so admirable. "Last year, commercial spam cost U.S. corporations $10 billion in U.S. dollars," he argues.[27]

1. Do you think businesspeople like Richter serve a legitimate marketing function? Why or why not?
2. Should federal legislation be enacted to reduce or eliminate spam? Why or why not?

'netWork EXERCISES

1. **Distribution channels.** Visit the Web site of Specialized Bicycle Components (http://www.specialized.com). What channels does Specialized use to distribute its products? Make a list of the ways in which Specialized avoids channel conflict and bring the list to class for a class discussion on the topic.
2. **Maritime statistics.** Go to the Web site of the U.S. Maritime Administration (http://www.marad.dot.gov). Click "Publications & Statistics." There you will find a variety of statistical reports. Access the most recent reports you can find to answer the following questions:
   a. What was the total amount of waterborne commerce shipped into, out of, and within the United States? Has the amount of waterborne commerce increased in recent years? What percentage of waterborne commerce was carried by U.S. flag carriers?
   b. What five countries ship the most containerized cargo to and from the United States?
   c. What are the 10 largest container ports in the U.S.?
3. **Vendor-managed inventory.** Visit the following Web site to learn more about vendor-managed inventory (http://www.vendormanagedinventory.com). Review the definition of vendor-managed inventory, how a vendor-managed inventory program should be set up, the benefits of vendor-managed inventory, and some of the problems with a vendor-managed inventory system. Prepare a brief oral report on the subject that you can present to your class.

Note: Internet Web addresses change frequently. If you don't find the exact sites listed, you may need to access the organization's or company's home page and search from there or use a search engine such as Google.

INFOTRAC CITATIONS AND EXERCISES

- **Record:** CJ119206678
Distribution warehouses vital to Tulsa, Okla.-area commerce. *Tom Droege.*
Knight Ridder/Tribune Business News, July 13, 2004 pITEM04195169

Abstract: Tulsa, Oklahoma, is shaping up to become a major distribution hub in the United States, as Wal-Mart, Hodges, and United Warehouse have moved into the neighborhood with sprawling new multimillion-dollar warehouses. The cavernous distribution centers will house everything from lawn mowers and beer to paper and chocolate-chip cookies, as growing numbers of trucking fleets carry on the nonstop trafficking of inventories from warehouse shelves to various points around the country.

1. What is warehousing's role in logistics and supply-chain management? How does it make physical distribution more efficient and cost effective?
2. In the article, the claim is made that manufacturers consider distribution warehouses a "necessary evil." Explain why that is the case.
3. Why might Tulsa, Oklahoma, be a good geographic location for distribution warehouses in the United States?

CASE 13.1

BAX to the Future: How a Logistics Firm Has Survived and Grown

The terrorist attacks of September 11, 2001, wars in Afghanistan and Iraq, and the resulting tightened security have all had a huge impact on the supply chain of many industries. Today's marketplace conditions are complicated and volatile, which means that global companies must find new ways to manage all aspects of their supply channels, including their physical distribution systems. That's where BAX Global comes in. With 40 logistics centers in 20 countries and 500 offices in 123 countries, BAX offers a wide range of supply-chain services to its customers.

BAX provides other businesses with all the traditional services associated with logistics management, including transportation, storage, documentation, order assembly, packaging, and distribution. However, the company goes much further than that. BAX marketers work with their business customers to figure out how BAX can help its customers reduce costs and time, increase efficiency, and create and monitor ways to measure performance. For physical distribution, BAX operates a huge fleet of planes and trucks with real-time tracking, so customers have access at all times to the status of their products.

All of this does not come easily in the current marketing environment. When recent homeland security measures created more demands on logistics firms to keep goods flowing so that compliance with import/export regulations didn't completely shut down manufacturing operations, BAX Global figured out a way. "Security used to be a paragraph at the bottom of a [contract proposal]," explains Jerry Levy, vice president of marketing for BAX Global. "Now companies, especially electronics companies, want a full disclosure of your security knowledge and procedures, along with security requirements, in any country where they do business. They say they want expedited deliveries to keep inventory levels low, but on the other side they want flawless compliance of security procedures." That's not easy. In addition, as more and more firms expand into markets in developing countries, they are looking toward firms like BAX to provide services to make up for a lack of infrastructure in those countries. "People want financial, purchasing, order fulfillment, warehousing, and sales support, not just transport services," says Levy.

So BAX gives customers what they want by building security procedures right into the entire operational schedule. "That way, it doesn't cost more for clients," says Pete Cheviot, director of corporate security for BAX Global. BAX's program includes security measures both for its customers' products and against terrorism. With its DIRECTSHIP program, customers can reduce supply-chain time by skipping distribution centers and shipping directly to customers. BAX's electronic documentation capability provides preclearance. "A pre-alert process is integrated into the operation," explains Levy. This means that any potential problems can be handled en route, and customers have access to information about their shipments at all times through MyBAX, the firm's extranet. BAX considers itself a strategic partner to its customers and strives for nothing less than 100 percent customer satisfaction. That makes for a powerful supply-chain strategy.

Questions for Critical Thinking

1. As a third-party logistics firm, how does BAX Global help its customers achieve their own goals?
2. BAX Global has set its customer service standards at 100 percent. Describe additional steps the firm might take to achieve this.

Sources: "BAX Global," *Inbound Logistics,* http://www.inboundlogistics.com, accessed April 17, 2004; "BAX Forwarder Network Enhances Its Wholesale Airport-to-Airport Services with Online Shipping Tools," *PR Newswire,* February 9, 2004, http://www.prnewswire.com; "Fast Forwarding," *Fortune,* September 1, 2003, pp. S2–S5.

VIDEO CASE 13.2

1-800-Flowers.com: Great Gifts by Phone or Online

The written case on 1-800-Flowers appears on page VC-16. The recently filmed 1-800-Flowers video is designed to expand and highlight the concepts in this chapter and the concepts and questions covered in the written video case.

chapter 14

Direct Marketing and Marketing Resellers: Retailers and Wholesalers

chapter objectives

1. Explain the wheel of retailing.
2. Explain how retailers select target markets.
3. Show how the elements of the marketing mix apply to retailing strategy.
4. Explain the concepts of retail convergence and scrambled merchandising.
5. Identify the functions performed by wholesaling intermediaries.
6. Outline the major types of independent wholesaling intermediaries and the appropriate situations for using each.
7. Compare the basic types of direct marketing and nonstore retailing.
8. Explain how much the Internet has altered the wholesaling, retailing, and direct marketing environments.

REI: THE RETAILER WITH 2 MILLION OWNERS

Recreational Equipment Inc. (REI) is an unusual retailer. It is organized as a cooperative, which means that every year it shares its profits with member-customers who have paid a one-time fee of $15 to join the REI cooperative. The firm believes this return supports its efforts to preserve natural resources in the communities in which its stores are located. Founded as a cooperative in 1938 by Seattle-area rock and mountain climbers who were looking for quality gear and equipment, REI now has almost 2 million members in 24 states. In addition to its 66 retail stores, REI generates sales through its catalog and its online store and earns about $735 million in sales each year. Nonmembers can shop at any of REI's retail outlets or its Web site, of course, but in

©DAVID SAMUEL ROBBINS/CORBIS

addition to their profit shares, members get special offers, discounts, and other benefits.

REI specializes in top brands of outdoor gear and sells its own exclusive line as well. Its commitment to the local community is evident in its donations of outdoor gear to youth groups dedicated to teaching kids about enjoying and protecting the environment. The firm's 6,000 employees are encouraged to contribute as well—REI gives them equipment and time off to enjoy outdoor challenges, and it relies on their experience to make them more knowledgeable associates when they return. Customers can try out equipment right in the stores, many of which are enormous. The San Francisco store takes in 37,000 square feet of space and includes a water-filter testing station, a testing rock for buyers of hiking boots, a display of camping tents, and gear rental and repair departments. The outlet in Seattle has a huge climbing wall, indoor bike trails for testing the merchandise, camp stove demonstration tables, and in-store clinics. The company also sponsors sports and trekking trips that feature hiking, cycling, canoeing, camping, and climbing for various groups. REI makes all the travel arrangements and supplies trusted guides and tour operators.

Consistently voted one of the 100 best companies to work for in the U.S., REI donates a portion of its profits each year to the support of conservation, outdoor recreation, and environmental stewardship. Recipients of the grants, which recently totaled $1.8 million a year, are nominated by employees. Asked how REI differs from a traditional retailer, president and CEO Dennis Madsen replied, "The biggest difference is that the customer and the investor are the same."[1]

Chapter Overview

IN exploring how today's retailing sector operates, this chapter introduces many examples that explain the combination of activities involved in selling goods to ultimate consumers, as REI does in its efforts to attract people who are interested in enjoying and preserving the outdoors. Then the chapter discusses the role of wholesalers and other intermediaries who deliver goods from the manufacturers into the hands of retailers or other intermediaries. Finally, the chapter looks at nonstore retailing. Direct marketing, a channel consisting of direct communication to consumers or business users, is a major form of nonstore retailing. It includes not just direct mail and telemarketing but direct-response advertising, infomercials, and Internet marketing. The chapter concludes by looking at a less pervasive but growing aspect of nonstore retailing, automatic merchandising.◆◆◆

Briefly Speaking

Because it's there.

George H. L. Mallory (1886–1924)

English mountain climber (explaining why he wanted to climb Mt. Everest)

RETAILING

retailing Activities involved in selling merchandise to ultimate consumers.

Retailers are the marketing intermediaries who are in direct contact with ultimate consumers. **Retailing** describes the activities involved in selling merchandise to these consumers. Retail outlets serve as contact points between channel members and ultimate consumers. In a very real sense, retailers represent the distribution channel to most consumers since a typical shopper has little contact with manufacturers and virtually no contact with wholesaling intermediaries. Retailers determine locations, store hours, number of sales personnel, store layouts, merchandise selections, and return policies—factors that often influence the consumers' images of the offerings more strongly than consumers' images of the products themselves. Both large and small retailers perform the major channel activities: creating time, place, and ownership utilities.

When I walk into a grocery store and look at all the products you can choose, I say, "My God! No king ever had anything like I have in my grocery store today."

Bill Gates (b. 1954)

founder, Microsoft Corp.

Retailers act as both customers and marketers in their channels. They sell products to ultimate consumers, and at the same time, they buy from wholesalers and manufacturers. Because of their critical location in the marketing channel, retailers often perform a vital feedback role. They obtain information from customers and transmit that information to manufacturers and other channel members.

EVOLUTION OF RETAILING

The development of retailing illustrates the marketing concept in operation. Early retailing in North America can be traced to the establishment of trading posts, such as the Hudson Bay Company, and to pack peddlers who carried their wares to outlying settlements. The first type of retail institution, the general store, stocked a wide range of merchandise that met the needs of an isolated community or rural area. Supermarkets appeared in the early 1930s in response to consumers' desire for lower prices. In the 1950s, discount stores delivered lower prices in exchange for reduced services. The emergence of convenience food stores in the 1960s satisfied consumer demand for fast service, convenient locations, and expanded hours of operation. The development of off-price retailers in the 1980s and 1990s reflected consumer demand for brand-name merchandise at prices considerably lower than those of traditional retailers. In recent years, Internet-enabled retailing has increased in influence and importance.

(1) **Explain the wheel of retailing.**

wheel of retailing Hypothesis that each new type of retailer gains a competitive foothold by offering lower prices than current suppliers charge; the result of reducing or eliminating services.

A key concept, known as the **wheel of retailing** theory, attempts to explain the patterns of change in retailing. According to the wheel of retailing, a new type of retailer gains a competitive foothold by offering customers lower prices than current outlets charge and maintains profits by reducing or eliminating services. Once established, however, the innovator begins to add more services, and its prices gradually rise. It then becomes vulnerable to new low-price retailers that enter with minimum services—and so the wheel turns. The retail graveyard is littered with former giants like W.T. Grant, Montgomery Ward, the original Sears catalog, and catalog retailers such as Service Merchandise.

Many major developments in the history of retailing appear to fit the wheel's pattern. Early department stores, chain stores, supermarkets, discount stores, hypermarkets, and catalog retailers all emphasized limited service and low prices. Most of these retailers gradually increased prices as they added services.

Some exceptions disrupt this pattern, however. Suburban shopping centers, convenience food stores, and vending machines never built their appeals around low prices. Still, the wheel pattern has been a good indicator enough times in the past to make it an accurate indicator of future retailing developments.

1. What is retailing?
2. Explain the wheel of retailing concept.

RETAILING STRATEGY

Like manufacturers and wholesalers, a retailer develops a marketing strategy based on the firm's goals and strategic plans. The organization monitors environmental influences and assesses its own strengths and weaknesses in identifying marketing opportunities and constraints. A retailer bases its key decisions on two fundamental steps in the marketing strategy process: (1) selecting a target market and (2) developing a retailing mix to satisfy the chosen market. The retailing mix specifies merchandise strategy, customer-service standards, pricing guidelines, target market analysis, promotion goals, location/distribution decisions, and store atmosphere choices. The combination of these elements projects a desired retail image. Retail image communicates the store's identity to consumers. Kohl's, for instance, counts on its trendy, contemporary image to attract consumers. As Figure 14.1 points out, components of retailing strategy must work together to create a consistent image that appeals to the store's target market.

One retailer that has emphasized a retail image consistent with its luxury products is Lexus. Lexus dealerships pamper customers with amenities such as marble bathrooms, gourmet deli sandwiches and salads, carpeted lounges with easy chairs, and TVs and magazines. A New Jersey dealership even has an indoor golf driving range, and in Las Vegas, you can get a manicure while you wait. All of these features reinforce the premium image of Lexus's cars, providing customers with a positive message about the brand.[2]

(2) Explain how retailers select target markets.

SELECTING A TARGET MARKET

A retailer starts to define its strategy by selecting a target market. Factors that influence the retailer's selection are the size and profit potential of the market and the level of competition for its business. Retailers pore over demographic, geographic, and psychographic profiles to segment markets. In the end, most retailers identify their target markets in terms of certain demographics.

The importance of identifying and targeting the right market is dramatically illustrated by the erosion of department store retailing. While mall anchor stores like Sears and JCPenney fight to hold on to customers, stand-alone store Target, known for its chic but cheap casual clothes, has solidified its niche. The store attracts style-conscious consumers with fashionable lines under its own designer labels, like cosmetics from Kashuk, apparel from Mossimo Giannulli, and sleek kitchenware from Michael Graves. The trendy but affordable lines draw shoppers with conservative tastes away from traditional department stores.[3]

Deep-discount chains like Family Dollar Stores or Dollar General, with their less glamorous locations and low-price merchandise crammed into narrow aisles, target lower income bargain hunters. Attracted by cents-off basics like shampoo, cereal, or laundry detergent, customers typically pick up higher margin goods—toys or chocolates—on their way to the checkout.[4]

figure 14.1

Components of Retail Strategy

By broadening its product lines and adding services that appeal to women as well as men, hardware chain Lowe's hopes to hammer archrival Home Depot. Wide aisles, clean presentation, friendly service, and a broad selection of high-end merchandise, such as Laura Ashley paints, have boosted the store's popularity with female shoppers, who now account for half of all home improvement store customers.[5]

After identifying a target market, a retailer must then develop marketing strategies to attract these chosen customers to its stores or Web site. The following sections discuss tactics for implementing different strategies.

3 Show how the elements of the marketing mix apply to retailing strategy.

MERCHANDISING STRATEGY

A retailer's merchandising strategy guides decisions regarding the items it will offer. A retailer must decide on general merchandise categories, product lines, specific items within lines, and the depth and width of its assortments. Target stores, for example, offer customers a wide variety of merchandise, from apparel to personal care, home décor, and automotive products. But to compete as the upscale alternative to Wal-Mart, Target has rolled out a chain of combination food and general merchandise stores called SuperTarget. As part of its plan to bring fashion to food, the retailer has expanded its categories. Its *planogram*—a computerized diagram of how to exhibit selections of merchandise within each store—now includes gourmet-brand pastas and sauces, produce, and fresh-baked goods.[6]

To develop a successful merchandise mix, a retailer must weigh several priorities. First, it must consider the preferences and needs of its previously defined target market, keeping in mind that the competitive environment influences these choices. The retailer must also consider the overall profitability of each product line and product category.

Category Management

As mentioned in Chapter 12, a popular merchandising strategy is *category management,* in which a category manager oversees an entire product line for both vendors and retailers and is responsible for the profitability of the product group. Category management seeks to improve the retailer's product category performance through more coordinated buying, merchandising, and pricing. Rather than focusing on the performance of individual brands, such as Flex shampoo or Kleenex tissue, category management evaluates performance according to each product category. Laundry detergent, skin-care products, and paper goods, for example, are each viewed as individual profit centers, and different category managers supervise each group. Those that underperform are at risk of being dropped from inventory, regardless of the strength of individual brands. To improve their profitability, for example, some department stores have narrowed their traditionally broad product categories to eliminate high-overhead, low-profit lines like toys, appliances, and furniture.

The Battle for Shelf Space

As discussed in Chapter 13, large-scale retailers are increasingly taking on the role of channel captain within many distribution networks. Some have assumed traditional wholesaling functions, while others dictate product design and specifications to manufacturers. The result is a shift in power from the manufacturers of top-selling brands to the retailer who makes them available to customers.

Adding to the pressure is the increase in the number of new products and variations on existing products. To identify the varying items within a product line, retailers refer to a specific product offering as a **stockkeeping unit (SKU)**. Within the skin-care category, for example, each facial cream, body moisturizer, and sunscreen in each of a variety of sizes and formulations is a separate SKU. The proliferation of new SKUs has resulted in a fierce battle for space on store shelves.

stockkeeping unit (SKU) Offering within a product line such as a specific size of liquid detergent.

Increasingly, major retailers, such as Sears and JCPenney, make demands in return for providing shelf space. They may, for example, seek pricing and promotional concessions from manufacturers as conditions for selling their products. Retailers also routinely require that manufacturers participate in their electronic data interchange (EDI) and quick-response systems. Manufacturers unable to comply may find themselves unable to penetrate the marketplace.

Slotting allowances, described in Chapter 11, are just one of the range of nonrefundable fees grocery retailers receive from manufacturers to secure shelf space for new products. A manufacturer can pay a retailer as much as $21,000 per item just to get its new products displayed on store shelves.[7]

Other fees include failure fees (imposed if a new product does not meet sales projections), annual renewal fees (a "pay to stay" inducement for retailers to continue carrying brands), trade allowances, discounts on high-volume purchases, survey fees for research done by the retailers, and even fees to allow salespeople to present new items.

CUSTOMER-SERVICE STRATEGY

Some stores build their retailing strategy around heightened customer services for shoppers. Gift wrapping, alterations, return privileges, bridal registries, consultants, interior design services, delivery and installation, and perhaps even electronic shopping via store Web sites are all examples of services that add value to the shopping experience. A retailer's customer-service strategy must specify which services the firm will offer and whether it will charge customers for these services. Those decisions depend on several conditions: store size, type, and location; merchandise assortment; services offered by competitors; customer expectations; and financial resources. Netflix, the successful Internet video rental firm, offers a wide assortment of movies by mail and eliminated late fees. For more on the Netflix story, see the "Marketing Hit" feature.

The basic objective of all customer services focuses on attracting and retaining target customers, thus increasing sales and profits. Some services—such as convenient restrooms, lounges, and complimentary coffee—enhance shoppers' comfort. Other services are intended to attract customers by making shopping easier and faster than it would be without the services. Some retailers, for example, offer child-care services for customers. At Kroger's and other supermarket chains, a self-scanning device lets customers avoid the cashier's line—and the wait involved—by checking out their own groceries.

A customer-service strategy can also support efforts in building demand for a line of merchandise. Despite the trend toward renovation, redecorating, and do-it-yourself home projects, Home Depot was experiencing slowing sales until its recent decision to revamp its own stores, improve customer service, and upgrade its marketing efforts. As the promotional message in Figure 14.2 shows, the company offers customers decorating assistance. Home Depot is now seeing its best growth in years, assuring its customers that "You can do it; we can help."[8]

Consumers are statistics. Customers are people.

Stanley Marcus (1905–2002)
American merchant

marketing hit — Netflix: Movies by Mail

Background. Movie fans spend over $8 billion a year on films rented from retail stores like Blockbuster and Hollywood Video. The process of going to the store, picking out the DVD or cassette, taking it home, and playing it hasn't changed much in 20 years. In the not-too-distant future, all consumers will have access to video-on-demand technology from cable and satellite companies that lets them watch any film or TV show they want whenever they want, making rentals a thing of the past. But in the meantime, somewhere between Blockbuster and the future, there's Netflix.

The Challenge. Launched in 1999, Netflix wanted to provide "the world's best movie service," an alternative to giants like Blockbuster but with greater convenience to the consumer and, most important, no late fees. Getting customers comfortable with the idea of using the postal service and the Internet to order films, and to maintain a list of desired films, was an early challenge, as was making the labor-intensive service as efficient as possible.

The Strategy. Subscribers to the service pay a monthly fee to rent as many films as they want, posting their "wish list" to Netflix's Web site (there are about 18,000 titles to choose from). They receive the three movies at the top of their list and then get each subsequent film each time they return a viewed selection, using the postage-paid envelope provided. Subscribers can keep up to three movies at a time for as long as they choose, and the company's distribution has improved enough to make overnight delivery available to 80 percent of the U.S. population.

The Outcome. Netflix has become a very profitable company, with projected revenues of $500 million in one recent year, more than 10 times its revenues of just five years earlier. Its subscriber list is climbing, too, now reaching 1.3 million people. But competition from Wal-Mart and Blockbuster—who have launched similar rent-by-mail departments—is already threatening.

Sources: Frank Ahrens, "NetFlix Faces Rivals, Cable Competition," *The Washington Post*, April 17, 2004, p. E01; Rick Aristotle Munarriz, "Netflix Not Done," *The Motley Fool*, April 16, 2004, http://www.fool.com; Martin Peres and Nick Wingfield, "Blockbuster Set to Offer Movies by Mail," *The Wall Street Journal*, February 11, 2004, pp. D1, D4; Jon Swartz, "For Netflix, It's So Far, So Good," *USA Today*, October 15, 2003, p. 3B.

figure 14.2

Home Depot: Catering to Do-It-Yourselfers

PRICING STRATEGY

Prices reflect a retailer's marketing objectives and policies. They also play a major role in consumer perceptions of a retailer. Consumers realize, for example, that when they enter a Gucci boutique in Milan, New York, or Tokyo, they will find such expensive products as $275 suede pumps and $1,500 boar-hide briefcases. Customers of the retail chain Everything's $1.00 expect a totally different type of merchandise; true to the name, every product in the store bears the same low price.

Markups and Markdowns

The amount that a retailer adds to a product's cost to set the final selling price is the **markup.** The amount of the markup typically results from two marketing decisions:

1. *The services performed by the retailer.* Other things being equal, stores that offer more services charge larger markups to cover their costs.
2. *The inventory turnover rate.* Other things being equal, stores with a higher turnover rate can cover their costs and earn a profit while charging a smaller markup.

A retailer's markup exerts an important influence on its image among present and potential customers. In addition, the markup affects the retailer's ability to attract shoppers. An excessive markup may drive away customers; an inadequate markup may not generate sufficient income to cover costs and return a profit. Retailers typically state markups as percentages of either the selling prices or the costs of the products.

markup Amount that a retailer adds to the cost of a product to determine its selling price.

Saks Fifth Avenue is an upscale retailer. Customers know they can find a huge selection of the latest fashions—"everything but closet space"—at its stores.

Marketers determine markups based partly on their judgments of the amounts that consumers will pay for a given product. When buyers refuse to pay a product's stated price, however, or when improvements in other items or fashion changes reduce the appeal of current merchandise, a retailer must take a **markdown.** The amount by which a retailer reduces the original selling price—the discount typically advertised for a sale item—is the markdown. Markdowns are sometimes used to evaluate merchandisers. For example, a department store might base its evaluations of buyers partly on the average markdown percentages for the product lines for which they are responsible.

markdown Amount by which a retailer reduces the original selling price of a product.

The formulas for calculating markups and markdowns are provided on pages 000–000 in the "Financial Analysis in Marketing" appendix at the end of the text.

LOCATION/DISTRIBUTION STRATEGY

Retail experts often cite location as a potential determining factor in the success or failure of a retail business. A retailer may choose to locate at an isolated site, in a central business district, or in a planned shopping center. The location decision depends on many factors, including the type of merchandise, the retailer's financial resources, characteristics of the target market, and site availability.

Briefly Speaking

The universe is really big. It's even bigger than Wal-Mart.

Richard Belzer (b. 1944)
American comedian

In recent years, many localities have become saturated with stores. As a result, some retailers have reevaluated their location strategies. A chain may close individual stores that do not meet sales and profit goals. Other retailers have experimented with nontraditional location strategies. McDonald's now operates stores in hospitals, military bases, amusement parks, train stations, and gasoline stations.

Locations in Planned Shopping Centers

Over the past several decades, retail trade has shifted away from traditional downtown retailing districts and toward suburban shopping centers. A **planned shopping center** is a group of retail stores designed, coordinated, and marketed to shoppers in a geographic trade area. Together, the stores provide a single convenient location for shoppers as well as free parking. They facilitate shopping by maintaining uniform hours of operation, including evening and weekend hours.

planned shopping center Group of retail stores planned, coordinated, and marketed as a unit.

There are five main types of planned shopping centers. The smallest, the *neighborhood shopping center,* is likely to consist of a group of smaller stores, such as a drugstore, a dry cleaner, a card and gift shop, and perhaps a hair-styling salon. This kind of center provides convenient shopping for 5,000 to 50,000 shoppers who live within a few minutes' commute. It contains 5 to 15 stores, and the product mix is usually confined to convenience items and some limited shopping goods.

A *community shopping center* serves 20,000 to 100,000 people in a trade area extending a few miles from its location. It contains anywhere from 10 to 30 retail stores, with a branch of a local department store or some other large store as the primary tenant. In addition to the stores found in a neighborhood center, a community center probably encompasses more stores featuring shopping goods, some professional offices, a branch bank, and perhaps a movie theater or supermarket. Community shopping centers typically offer ample parking, and tenants often share some promotion costs. With the advent of stand-alone big-box retailers, some community shopping centers have declined in popularity. Some department stores are also moving away from the strategy of locating in shopping centers and opting for freestanding stores, such as the new Bloomingdale's that opened in New York's trendy SoHo neighborhood recently. "Off-mall is easier to shop and closer to where you live," says one industry observer. Other stores like Sears and JCPenney are planning to open more off-mall stores as well.[9]

A *regional shopping center* is a large facility with at least 400,000 square feet of shopping space. Its marketing appeal usually emphasizes major department stores with the power to draw customers, supplemented by as many as 200 smaller stores. A successful regional center needs a location within 30 minutes' driving time of at least 250,000 people. A regional center—or a superregional center like Minnesota's Mall of America—provides a wide assortment of convenience, shopping, and specialty goods, plus many professional and personal service facilities.

A *power center,* usually located near a regional or superregional mall, brings together several huge specialty stores, such as Toys "R" Us, Home Depot, or Bed, Bath, and Beyond, as stand-alone stores in a single trading area. Rising in popularity during the 1990s, power centers offered value because they were able to underprice department stores while providing a huge selection of specialty merchandise. Heated competition from cost-cutter Wal-Mart and inroads from more upscale discounters like Target and Kohl's are currently reducing the drawing power of these centers.

CHARLES NYE/THE INDIANAPOLIS STAR

Lifestyle centers are a hot trend in retailing these days. This center at Jefferson Pointe in Fort Wayne, Indiana, offers 650,000 square feet of shopping paradise, with upscale stores such as Ann Taylor, Chico's, and Talbots.

Recently, a fifth type of planned center has emerged, known as a *lifestyle center.* This retailing format seeks to offer a combination of shopping, movie theaters, stages for concerts and live entertainment, decorative fountains and park benches in greenways, and restaurants and bistros in an attractive outdoor environment. At around 300,000 to 1 million square feet, the centers are large, but they seek to offer the intimacy and easy access of neighborhood village retailing with a fashionable cachet. Convenience, safety, and pleasant ambiance are also part of the appeal. Here, there are usually no big anchor stores but rather a mix of just the right upscale tenants—Williams-Sonoma, Eddie Bauer, Banana Republic, Ann Taylor, Pottery Barn, and Restoration Hardware, for instance. About 80 lifestyle centers are currently operating or opening in suburbs around the nation as well as in cities like Tacoma and New York, and some include office parks, townhouses, and condominiums. Well-heeled customers are currently flocking to them.[10]

The opening of a new retail store is sometimes marked with celebrations such as receptions or parties. See the accompanying "Etiquette Tips for Marketing Professionals" feature for some guidelines about creating invitations for events that combine business with socializing.

Retail analysts believe that the "malling of America" has reached the saturation point. There are 20 square feet of retail space per capita, up by more than a third over a 15-year period. As upscale shoppers migrate to newer lifestyle centers or to the Internet, the malls have begun to shift away from traditional department store anchors. Some are turning to high-traffic draws like Target or Kohl's, but this puts specialty retailers like Gap or Banana Republic in a tough spot. Taking their lead from the popularity of lifestyle centers, others seek to combine shopping with entertainment; malls are adding carousels, rock-climbing walls, movie theaters, and large food courts. For example, Minnesota's Mall of America promotes its shopping center as a "shopping and fun destination," complete with an amusement park, a spa, an aquarium, and nightclubs and restaurants. Still others, such as the Market Place Mall in Champaign-Urbana, Illinois, emphasize customer service: well-padded playgrounds for toddlers, comfortable lounges for their parents, and luxurious restrooms equipped with infant changing rooms and nursing rooms with rocking chairs. Some malls hire concierges to help customers locate hard-to-find gifts and order theater tickets; others may offer valet parking, gift-wrap services, and parking-lot shuttle buses.[11]

PROMOTIONAL STRATEGY

To establish store images that entice more shoppers, retailers use a variety of promotional techniques. Through its promotional strategy, a retailer seeks to communicate to consumers information about its stores—locations, merchandise selections, hours of operation, and prices. If merchandise selection changes frequently to follow fashion trends, advertising is typically used to promote current styles effectively. In addition, promotions help retailers attract shoppers and build customer loyalty.

Innovative promotions can pay off in unexpected ways. IKEA China used the interiors of the elevators in 20 Beijing apartment buildings to demonstrate to residents how small apartments can be inexpensively transformed into comfortable living spaces. The elevators were covered with floor-to-ceiling posters picturing ingeniously styled and decorated apartments, and the elevator operators gave out IKEA catalogs to their passengers. "It's a strategic decision to go where the competition isn't," said IKEA's worldwide marketing communications manager.[12]

National retail chains often purchase advertising space in newspapers, on radio, and on television. Like many retail chains, Best Buy promotes its stores through advertising circulars in local and regional Sunday newspapers as well as in ads such as the one shown in Figure 14.3. Other retailers are experimenting with promoting over the Internet. Sometimes a well-chosen store location aids promotion;

ETIQUETTE TIPS — FOR MARKETING PROFESSIONALS

Dos and Don'ts of Business Invitations

ENTERTAINING is a part of business and marketing, and one that should be fun for the guest and the host. When you are planning a business reception or a party—perhaps to celebrate the opening of a new retail location for your firm—here are some simple rules about invitations that can help ensure the success of your event:

1. Always send a written invitation on company stationery.
2. Include the date, the time, the location, and the purpose of the event or celebration. If there is a guest of honor, give his or her name.
3. If the event is outside normal business hours, specify what kind of dress will be appropriate.
4. If the guests are traveling any distance or the location is unfamiliar, include reliable directions, a map, and an estimate of the travel time required.
5. Send your invitations at least two weeks in advance.
6. Request that guests RSVP (the abbreviation for *répondez s'il vous plaît*—"please reply" in French). This is particularly important if you need to order food or giveaways and the number of guests must be established ahead of time.
7. If you only need to know who is not attending, your invitation should read, "Regrets only."
8. In either case (RSVP or Regrets only), make sure your name, address, phone number, and e-mail address appear on the invitation.
9. If guests are permitted to bring other guests (spouse or date), be sure to specify this on the invitation.
10. If guests need to know anything about parking arrangements you've made (valet parking or prepaid or reserved spaces, for instance), make sure the invitation specifies.

Following these guidelines can make your guests feel comfortable and you feel at ease. Even more important, they can help make your event a success.

Sources: Phyllis Cambria and Patty Sachs, "Executive Etiquette: Tips for Entertaining for Business," http://www.partyplansplus.com, accessed April 17, 2004; "How to Write an Invitation," entertaining.about.com, accessed April 17, 2004; Lydia Ramsey, "Etiquette: Responding to Invitations Promptly Isn't Just Good Etiquette, It's Good Business," http://www.savannahnow.com, June 1, 2003.

this is why dollar stores like California-based 99¢ Only Stores tend to locate on major streets leading to a large competitor, such as Wal-Mart.

Retailers also try to combine advertising with in-store merchandising techniques that influence decisions at the point of purchase. Victoria's Secret's flagship store in New York is leading the way for all the chain's outlets with a new design that locates the beauty department in the center of the store. The purpose is to encourage customers to linger there while browsing through the store's lingerie offerings. "Relocating beauty to the center was a critical move," says the chain's vice president. "If you want to buy something, you have to go through there."[13]

A friendly, well-trained, and knowledgeable salesperson plays a vital role in conveying the store's image to consumers and in persuading shoppers to buy. To serve as a source of information, a salesperson must possess extensive knowledge regarding credit policies, discounts, special sales, delivery terms, layaways, and returns. To increase store sales, the salesperson must persuade customers that the store sells what those customers need. To this end, salespeople should receive training in selling up and suggestion selling.

By *selling up,* salespeople try to persuade customers to buy higher priced items than originally intended. For example, an automobile salesperson might convince a customer to buy a more expensive model than the car that the buyer had initially considered. Of course, the practice of selling up must always respect the constraints of a customer's real needs. If a salesperson sells customers something that they really do not need, the potential for repeat sales dramatically diminishes.

Another technique, *suggestion selling,* seeks to broaden a customer's original purchase by adding related items, special promotional products, or holiday or seasonal merchandise. Here, too, the sales-

figure 14.3

Best Buy: Promoting Electronics That Attract Young Consumers

COURTESY OF BEST BUY. ©2002–2004 BEST BUY.

person tries to help a customer recognize true needs rather than unwanted merchandise. Beauty advisers in upscale department stores are masters of suggestion selling.

Just as knowledgeable and helpful sales personnel can both boost sales and set retailers apart from competitors, poor service influences customers' attitudes toward a retailer. Increasing customer complaints about unfriendly, inattentive, and uninformed salespeople have prompted many retailers to intensify their attention to training and motivating salespeople. Saks Fifth Avenue retrained all its sales associates after discovering that they were often making snap judgments about who was a customer prospect and why. "Customers felt that their service level was based on their appearances, including their race," says the president of the firm that created the training program for Saks. Diversity and sensitivity training are now credited with at least $1 million in increased sales for the first full year the training program was in effect.[14]

Sometimes advertising attempts to take the place of salespeople. The prescription drug industry has supplemented the sales calls it makes to physicians with advertisements aimed at patients; see the "Solving an Ethical Controversy" feature.

STORE ATMOSPHERICS

While store location, merchandise selection, customer service, pricing, and promotional activities all contribute to a store's consumer awareness, stores also project their personalities through **atmospherics**—physical characteristics and amenities that attract customers and satisfy their shopping needs. Atmospherics include both a store's exterior and interior décor.

A store's exterior appearance, including architectural design, window displays, signs, and entryways, helps to identify the retailer and attract its target market shoppers. The Saks Fifth Avenue script logo on a storefront and McDonald's golden arches are exterior elements that readily identify these retailers. Other retailers design eye-catching exterior elements aimed at getting customers' attention. Life-size cartoon figures seem poised in midflight over the entrance to the Warner Brothers outlet in San Diego's Horton Plaza Shopping Center, drawing customer interest.

The interior décor of a store should also complement the retailer's image, respond to customers' interests, and most important, induce shoppers to buy. Interior atmospheric elements include store layout, merchandise presentation, lighting, color, sounds, scents, and cleanliness. At Sam's Club or Costco, for instance, merchandise is stacked high on pallets to emphasize the chains' rock-bottom pricing and no-frills approach and to encourage customers to buy in bulk. Low, low prices and unexpected deals on selected upscale merchandise draw customers in. The strategy has been so successful that Sam's Club is extending it to appeal to small-business owners with staple items they need as well as "treasure hunt" items for their personal needs.[15]

Appliance maker Maytag is convinced that atmospherics can play a major role in its intense competition from Asian imports and lower priced models sold by Home Depot and Sears. Shopping for appliances can be an intimidating experience. The products are usually shown in bunches where their differences are difficult to compare. And there's no way to try out the item. But it's a different scene in 100 independently owned Maytag stores, where functioning Maytag kitchens containing a sink, cooktop, refrigerator, microwave, trash compactor, two ranges, and a built-in double oven await shoppers who are invited to "try before you buy." Potential washer-dryer purchasers can do a load of laundry; people interested in the new range can bake a sheet of cookies. They can also listen to a dishwasher to determine whether it really is as quiet as advertised. And it's working. Maytag spokesperson Ruth Cain is a big fan of the store makeovers: "The environment lets us showcase the product. It has worked in terms of sales."[16]

When designing the interior and exterior of a store, the fact that many people shop for reasons other than just purchasing needed products must be taken into account. Other common reasons for

Solving an Ethical Controversy

ASK YOUR DOCTOR—OR NOT?

THE practice of advertising prescription drugs directly to consumers, encouraging them to "ask your doctor" to prescribe them for patient use, has been controversial from the start. It has been under scrutiny in the wake of an FDA survey indicating that while some physicians find the ads neutral or mildly positive, nearly half feel pressure from their patients as a result of the ads. Other research showed that 9 of 10 drugs requested most often by patients were those advertised directly to consumers and that most physicians prefer to be the sole source of drug information needed by their patients.

SHOULD DRUG MARKETERS BE PERMITTED TO ADVERTISE PRESCRIPTION DRUGS DIRECTLY TO CONSUMERS?

PRO

1. Such advertising supplies consumers with valuable information about new drugs and their uses and side effects.
2. While consumers may ask their doctors for the advertised drugs, doctors still make the medical decision about whether the patient should take them or not.

CON

1. The print and television ads are paid for by increases in the price of the drugs.
2. If the drugs are safe and effective, doctors will prescribe them anyway without being pressured by their patients to do so.

SUMMARY

Government regulations require that the negative side effects of advertised prescription drugs be given the same amount of space and be printed in the same type size as the benefits. Advertised prescription drugs do tend to be the most expensive in their categories. But drug companies are no longer allowed to offer physicians cash or expensive gifts in return for prescribing their products. And in the meantime, legislation to limit prescription drug advertising continues to be proposed.

Sources: "Payers, Pending Legislation, Provide More Focus on Impact of DTC Ads on Drug Costs," *Drug Cost Management Report,* October 10, 2003, accessed at http://www.findarticles.com; Rich Thomaselli, "DTC Ads Influence Majority of Consumers, Say Doctors," *Advertising Age,* January 20, 2003; Julie Appleby, "Feds Warn Drugmakers: Gifts to Doctors May Be Illegal," *USA Today,* October 2, 2002, p. A1.

shopping include escaping the routine of daily life, avoiding weather extremes, fulfilling fantasies, and socializing with family and friends. Retailers expand beyond interior design to create welcoming and entertaining environments that draw shoppers. H&M, a cheap-chic chain from Sweden that is making inroads on U.S. markets, plays loud rap music in its three-level store in New York and constantly changes its huge selection of brightly colored clothes.[17]

1. What is an SKU?
2. What are the two components of a markup?
3. What are store atmospherics?

TYPES OF RETAILERS

Since new types of retailers continue to evolve in response to changes in consumer demand, a universal classification system for retailers has yet to be devised. Certain differences do, however, define several categories of retailers: (1) forms of ownership, (2) shopping effort expended by customers, (3) services provided to customers, (4) product lines, and (5) location of retail transactions.

As Figure 14.4 points out, most retailing operations fit in different categories. A 7-Eleven outlet may be classified as a convenience store (category 2) with self-service (category 3) and a relatively broad

figure 14.4

Bases for Categorizing Retailers

product line (category 4). It is both a store-type retailer (category 5) and a member of a chain (category 1).

CLASSIFICATION OF RETAILERS BY FORM OF OWNERSHIP

Perhaps the easiest method for categorizing retailers is by ownership structure, distinguishing between chain stores and independent retailers. In addition, independent retailers may join wholesaler-sponsored voluntary chains, band together to form retail cooperatives, or enter into franchise agreements with manufacturers, wholesalers, or service-provider organizations. Each type of ownership has its own unique advantages and strategies.

Chain Stores

Chain stores are groups of retail outlets that operate under central ownership and management and handle the same product lines. Chains have a major advantage over independent retailers in economies of scale. Volume purchases allow chains to pay lower prices than their independent rivals must pay. Since a chain may encompass hundreds of retail stores, it can afford extensive advertising, sales training, and sophisticated computerized systems for merchandise ordering, inventory management, forecasting, and accounting. Also, the large sales volume and wide geographic reach of a chain may enable it to advertise in a variety of media, including television and national magazines.

Independent Retailers

The U.S. retailing structure supports a large number of small stores, many medium-size stores, and a small number of large stores. Even though only 12 percent of the almost 2.7 million retail establishments earn annual sales of $1 million or more, those large operators account for almost three-quarters of all retail sales in the U.S. On the other hand, over half of all stores generate yearly sales below $500,000. According to the U.S. Department of Commerce, independent retailers account for about 43 percent of all retail sales.

Independent retailers compete with chains in a number of ways. The traditional advantage of independent stores is friendly, personalized service. Cooperatives offer another strategy for independents. For instance, cooperatives like Ace Hardware and Valu-Rite Pharmacies help independents compete with chains by providing volume buying power as well as advertising and marketing programs.

CLASSIFICATION BY SHOPPING EFFORT

Another classification system is based on the reasons consumers shop at particular retail outlets. This approach categorizes stores as convenience, shopping, or specialty retailers.

Convenience retailers focus their marketing appeals on accessible locations, long store hours, rapid checkout service, and adequate parking facilities. Local food stores, gasoline stations, and dry cleaners fit this category.[18]

Shopping stores typically include furniture stores, appliance retailers, clothing outlets, and sporting goods stores. Consumers usually compare prices, assortments, and quality levels at competing outlets before making purchase decisions. Consequently, managers of shopping stores attempt to differentiate their outlets through advertising, in-store displays, well-trained and knowledgeable salespeople, and appropriate merchandise assortments.

Specialty retailers combine carefully defined product lines, services, and reputations in attempts to convince consumers to expend considerable effort to shop at their stores. Examples include Neiman Marcus, Lord & Taylor, and Nordstrom.

CLASSIFICATION BY SERVICES PROVIDED

Another category differentiates retailers by the services they provide to customers. This classification system consists of three retail types: self-service, self-selection, or full-service retailers.

Target illustrates a self-service store, while Safeway grocery stores and A&P Future Stores are examples of self-selection stores. Both categories sell convenience products that people can purchase frequently with little assistance. In the clothing industry, catalog retailer Lands' End is a self-selection store but one whose commitment to customer satisfaction is paramount, as the promotional message in Figure 14.5 demonstrates. Full-service retailers such as Neiman Marcus focus on fashion-oriented merchandise, backed by a complete array of customer services.

figure 14.5

Lands' End Commitment: The Customer Is King

CLASSIFICATION BY PRODUCT LINES

Product lines also define a set of retail categories and the marketing strategies appropriate for firms within those categories. Grouping retailers by product lines produces three major categories: specialty stores, limited-line retailers, and general merchandise retailers.

Specialty Stores

A *specialty store* typically handles only part of a single product line. However, it stocks this portion in considerable depth or variety. Specialty stores include a wide range of retail outlets: Examples include fish markets, grocery stores, men's and women's shoe stores, and bakeries. Although some specialty stores are chain outlets, most are independent small-scale operations. They represent perhaps the greatest concentration of independent retailers who develop expertise in one product area and provide narrow lines of products for their local markets.

Specialty stores should not be confused with specialty products. Specialty stores typically carry convenience and shopping goods. The label *specialty* reflects the practice of handling a specific, narrow line of merchandise. For example, Lady Foot Locker is a specialty store that offers a wide selection of name-brand athletic footwear, apparel, and accessories made specifically for women.

Limited-Line Retailers

Customers find a large assortment of products within one product line or a few related lines in a **limited-line store.** This type of retail operation typically develops in areas with a large enough population to sufficiently support it. Examples of limited-line stores are IKEA (home furnishings and housewares) and Wickes (furniture). These retailers cater to the needs of people who want to select from complete lines in purchasing particular products.

A unique type of limited-line retailer is known as a **category killer.** These stores offer huge selections and low prices in single product lines. Stores within this category—for example, Best Buy; Borders Books; Bed, Bath, and Beyond; and Home Depot—are among the most successful retailers in the nation. Popular in the 1990s, category killers at first took business away from general merchandise discounters, which were not able to compete in selection or price. Recently, however, expanded merchandise and aggressive cost cutting by warehouse clubs and by Wal-Mart have turned the tables. Competition from Internet companies that are able to offer unlimited selection and speedy delivery has also taken customers away. While they still remain a powerful force in retailing, category killers are not invulnerable.[19]

General Merchandise Retailers

General merchandise retailers, which carry a wide variety of product lines that are all stocked in some depth, distinguish themselves from limited-line and specialty retailers by the large number of product lines they carry. The general store described earlier in this chapter is a primitive form of a general merchandise retailer. This category includes variety stores, department stores, and mass merchandisers such as discount stores, off-price retailers, and hypermarkets.

Variety Stores

A retail outlet that offers an extensive range and assortment of low-price merchandise is called a *variety store.* Less popular today than they once were, many of these stores have evolved into or given way to other types of retailers such as discount stores or hybrid combinations of drugstores and variety stores, such as Walgreen's and RiteAid. The nation's variety stores now account for less than 1 percent of all retail sales. However, variety stores remain popular in other parts of the world. Many retail outlets in Spain and Mexico are family-owned variety stores.

Department Stores

In essence, a **department store** is a series of limited-line and specialty stores under one roof. By definition, this large retailer handles a variety of merchandise, including men's, women's, and children's clothing and accessories; household linens and dry goods; home furnishings; and furniture. It serves as a one-stop shopping destination for almost all personal and household products. Chicago's Marshall Field's is a classic example.

Department stores built their reputations by offering wide varieties of services, such as charge accounts, delivery, gift wrapping, and liberal return privileges. As a result, they incur relatively high operating costs, averaging about 45 to 60 percent of sales.

Department stores have faced intense competition over the past several years. Relatively high operating costs have left them vulnerable to retailing innovations such as discount stores, Internet retailers, and hypermarkets. In addition, department stores' traditional locations in downtown business districts have suffered from problems associated with limited parking, traffic congestion, and population migration to the suburbs.

Department stores have fought back in a variety of ways. Many have closed certain sections, such as electronics, in which high costs kept them from competing with discount houses and category killers. They have added bargain outlets, expanded parking facilities, and opened major branches in regional shopping centers. Marketers have attempted to revitalize downtown retailing in many cities by modernizing their stores, expanding store hours, making special efforts to attract the tourist and convention trade, and serving the needs of urban residents.

To increase profits, Lord & Taylor displays fewer sale signs, and its flagship Manhattan store boasts a new restaurant run by a well-known chef. The store has also stocked up on youthful products and high-end brands like Kate Spade and Rebecca Taylor, cutting down on its inventory of moderate-priced labels seen in other stores. "We are getting back to our specialty store roots," said CEO Jane Elfers.[20]

Mass Merchandisers

Mass merchandising has made major inroads into department store sales by emphasizing lower prices for well-known brand-name products, high product turnover, and limited services. A **mass merchandiser** often stocks a wider line of items than a department store but usually without the same depth of assortment within each line. Discount houses, off-price retailers, hypermarkets, and catalog retailers are all examples of mass merchandisers.

Discount Houses A **discount house** charges low prices and offers fewer services. Early discount stores sold mostly appliances. Today, they offer soft goods, drugs, food, gasoline, and furniture.

By eliminating many of the "free" services provided by traditional retailers, these operations can keep their markups 10 to 25 percent below those of their competitors. Some of the early discounters have since added services, stocked well-known name brands, and boosted their prices. In fact, many now resemble department stores.

A discount format that is gaining strength is the *warehouse club.* Costco, BJ's, and Wal-Mart's Sam's Club are the largest warehouse clubs in the U.S. These no-frills, cash-and-carry outlets offer consumers access to name-brand products at deeply discounted prices. Selection at warehouse clubs includes everything from gourmet popcorn to fax machines to peanut butter to luggage and sunglasses sold in vast warehouselike settings. Attracting business away from almost every retailing segment, warehouse clubs now even offer fresh food and gasoline. Customers must be members to shop at warehouse clubs.

Off-Price Retailers Another version of a discount house is an *off-price retailer.* This kind of store stocks only designer labels or well-known brand-name clothing at prices equal to or below regular wholesale prices and then passes the cost savings along to buyers. While many off-price retailers are located in outlets in downtown areas or in freestanding buildings, a growing number are concentrating in *outlet malls*—shopping centers that house only off-price retailers.

Inventory at off-price stores changes frequently as buyers take advantage of special price offers from manufacturers selling excess merchandise. Off-price retailers such as Loehmann's, Marshall's, Stein Mart, and T.J. Maxx also keep their prices below those of traditional retailers by offering fewer services. Off-price retailing has been well received by today's shoppers.

© A. RAMEY/PHOTOEDIT

Wal-Mart's Supercenters offer a vast array of products—including several different fast food options.

Hypermarkets and Supercenters Another innovation in discount retailing is the creation of *hypermarkets*—giant one-stop shopping facilities that offer wide selections of grocery and general merchandise products at discount prices. Store size determines the major difference between hypermarkets and supercenters. Hypermarkets typically fill up 200,000 or more square feet of selling space, about a third larger than most **supercenters.** At Meijer stores, for example, Michigan, Ohio, and Indiana consumers can buy food, hardware, soft goods, building materials, auto supplies, appliances, and prescription drugs in locations averaging 245,000 square feet. When Meijer customers finish shopping, they can visit a restaurant, beauty salon, barber shop, bank branch, or bakery within the facility. Fred Meyer on the West Coast is another hypermarket approach. By contrast, the supercenter format is used by Wal-Mart, Kmart, and Target.

Showroom and Warehouse Retailers These retailers send direct mail to their customers and sell the advertised goods from showrooms that display samples. Back-room warehouses fill orders for the displayed products. Low prices are important to catalog store customers. To keep prices low, these retailers offer few services, store most inventory in inexpensive warehouse space, limit shoplifting losses, and handle long-lived products such as luggage, small appliances, gift items, sporting equipment, toys, and jewelry.

CLASSIFICATION OF RETAIL TRANSACTIONS BY LOCATION

Although most retail transactions occur in stores, nonstore retailing serves as an important marketing channel for many products. In addition, both consumer and business-to-business marketers rely on nonstore retailing to generate orders or requests for more information that may result in future orders.

Direct marketing is a broad concept that includes direct mail, direct selling, direct response retailing, telemarketing, Internet retailing, and automatic merchandising. The last sections of this chapter will consider each type of nonstore retailing.

4 Explain the concepts of retail convergence and scrambled merchandising.

RETAIL CONVERGENCE AND SCRAMBLED MERCHANDISING

Many traditional differences no longer distinguish familiar types of retailers, rendering any set of classifications less useful. **Retail convergence,** whereby similar merchandise is available from multiple retail outlets distinguished by price more than any other factor, is blurring distinctions between types of retailers and the merchandise mix they offer. A few years ago, a customer looking for a fashionable coffeepot might have headed straight for Williams-Sonoma or Starbucks. Today, she's just as likely to pick one up at Target or Wal-Mart, where she can check out new spring fashions and stock up on paper goods. Gap is no longer pitted only against Eddie Bauer or American Eagle Outfitters but against designer-label brands at department stores and Kohl's, too. Grocery stores compete with Wal-Mart.[21]

retail convergence A situation in which similar merchandise is available from multiple retail outlets, resulting in the blurring of distinctions between type of retailer and merchandise offered.

Scrambled merchandising—in which a retailer combines dissimilar product lines in an attempt to boost sales volume—has also muddied the waters. Drugstores not only fill prescriptions but offer cameras, cards, housewares, magazines, and even small appliances. Convenience retailer 7-Eleven recently began offering such services as bill payment, payroll check cashing, money wiring, and ticket

scrambled merchandising Retailing practice of combining dissimilar product lines to boost sales volume.

1. How do we classify retailers by form of ownership?
2. Categorize retailers by shopping effort and by services provided.
3. List several ways to classify retailers by product line.

purchasing through in-store terminals hooked up to the Web. Goods ordered through the system are delivered to the store for later pickup.[22]

WHOLESALING INTERMEDIARIES

wholesaler Channel intermediary that takes title to goods it handles and then distributes these goods to retailers, other distributors, or B2B customers.

wholesaling intermediary Comprehensive term that describes wholesalers as well as agents and brokers.

5 **Identify the functions performed by wholesaling intermediaries.**

Recall from Chapter 13 that several distribution channels involve marketing intermediaries called **wholesalers.** These firms take title to the goods they handle and sell those products primarily to retailers or to other wholesalers or business users. They sell to ultimate consumers only in insignificant quantities if at all. **Wholesaling intermediaries,** a broader category, include not only wholesalers but also agents and brokers, who perform important wholesaling activities without taking title to the goods.

FUNCTIONS OF WHOLESALING INTERMEDIARIES

As specialists in certain marketing functions, as opposed to production or manufacturing functions, wholesaling intermediaries can perform these functions more efficiently than producers or consumers. The importance of these activities results from the utility they create, the services they provide, and the cost reductions they allow.

Creating Utility

Wholesaling intermediaries create three types of utility for consumers. They enhance time utility by making products available for sale when consumers want to purchase them. They create place utility by helping to deliver goods and services for purchase at convenient locations. They create ownership (or possession) utility when a smooth exchange of title to the products from producers or intermediaries to final purchasers is complete. Possession utility can also result from transactions in which actual title does not pass to purchasers, as in rental-car services.

Wholesaler CDW offers high-tech products to business, government, and educational buyers.

Providing Services

Table 14.1 lists a number of services provided by wholesaling intermediaries. The list clearly indicates the marketing utilities—time, place, and possession utility—that wholesaling intermediaries create or enhance. These services also reflect the basic marketing functions of buying, selling, storing, transporting, providing market information, financing, and risk taking.

Of course, many types of wholesaling intermediaries provide varying services, and not all of them perform every service listed in the table. Producer-suppliers rely on wholesaling intermediaries for distribution and selection of firms that offer the desired combinations of services. In general, however, the critical marketing functions listed in the table form the basis for any evaluation of a marketing intermediary's efficiency. The risk-taking function affects each service of the intermediary.

Synnex Information Technologies of Fremont, California, markets computer-related products and peripherals, and it also offers warehousing and trucking capabilities that help lower overhead for retail customers. Inventory management, next-day delivery, financing, and technical service support are among the menu of services the company offers.[23]

Lowering Costs by Limiting Contacts

When an intermediary represents numerous producers, it often cuts the costs of buying and selling. The transaction economies are illus-

table 14.1 **Wholesaling Services for Customers and Producer-Suppliers**

SERVICE	BENEFICIARIES OF SERVICE: Customers	BENEFICIARIES OF SERVICE: Producer-Suppliers
Buying Anticipates customer demands and applies knowledge of alternative sources of supply; acts as purchasing agent for customers.	Yes	No
Selling Provides a sales force to call on customers, creating a low-cost method for servicing smaller retailers and business users.	No	Yes
Storing Maintains warehouse facilities at lower costs than most individual producers or retailers could achieve. Reduces risk and cost of maintaining inventory for producers.	Yes	Yes
Transporting Customers receive prompt delivery in response to their demands, reducing their inventory investments. Wholesalers also break bulk by purchasing in economical carload or truckload lots, then reselling in smaller quantities, thereby reducing overall transportation costs.	Yes	Yes
Providing Marketing Information Offers important marketing research input for producers through regular contacts with retail and business buyers. Provides customers with information about new products, technical information about product lines, reports on competitors' activities and industry trends, and advisory information concerning pricing changes, legal changes, and so forth.	Yes	Yes
Financing Grants credit that might be unavailable for purchases directly from manufacturers. Provides financing assistance to producers by purchasing products in advance of sale and by promptly paying bills.	Yes	Yes
Risk Taking Evaluates credit risks of numerous, distant retail customers and small-business users. Extends credit to customers that qualify. By transporting and stocking products in inventory, the wholesaler assumes risk of spoilage, theft, or obsolescence.	Yes	Yes

trated in Figure 14.6, which shows five manufacturers marketing their outputs to four different retail outlets. Without an intermediary, these exchanges create a total of 20 transactions. Adding a wholesaling intermediary reduces the number of transactions to 9.

United Stationers is a wholesaler of everything from paper clips to fax machines to discount chains, independent stores, and Internet resellers. While big-box retailers buy in bulk directly from manufacturers, they are able to order low-volume specialty goods faster and more efficiently from United Stationers. Through Web-enabled orders, mom-and-pop stores have access to more than 35,000 items, delivered either to the store or directly to customers overnight. Positioning itself as a one-stop warehousing, logistics, and distribution network, the company recently expanded beyond its office-products roots by establishing a new janitorial supply unit.[24]

TYPES OF WHOLESALING INTERMEDIARIES

6 **Outline the major types of independent wholesaling intermediaries and the appropriate situations for using each.**

Various types of wholesaling intermediaries operate in different distribution channels. Some provide wide ranges of services or handle broad lines of goods, while others specialize in individual services, goods, or industries. Figure 14.7 classifies wholesaling intermediaries by two characteristics: ownership and title flows (whether title passes from manufacturer to wholesaling intermediary). The three basic ownership structures are as follows: (1) manufacturer-owned facilities, (2) independent wholesaling

figure 14.6

Transaction Economies through Wholesaling Intermediaries

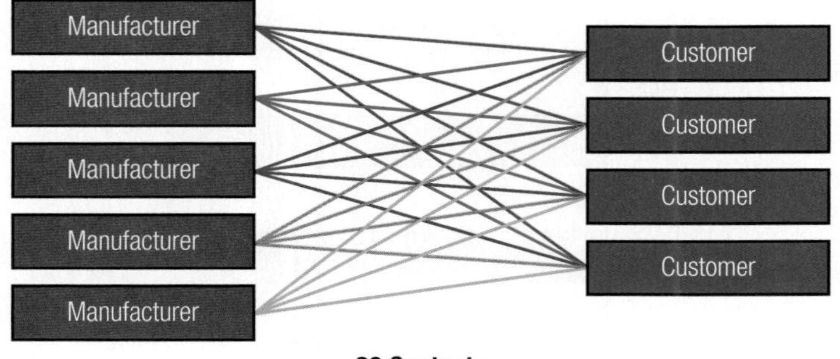

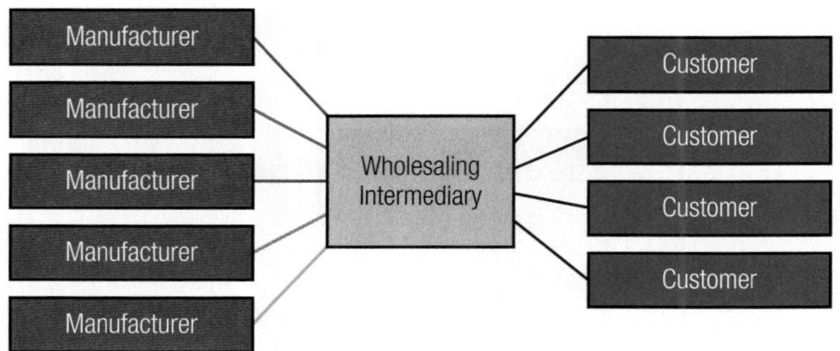

intermediaries, and (3) retailer-owned cooperatives and buying offices. The two types of independent wholesaling intermediaries are merchant wholesalers, which take title of the goods, and agents and brokers, which do not.

Manufacturer-Owned Facilities

Several reasons lead manufacturers to distribute their goods directly through company-owned facilities. Some perishable goods need rigid control of distribution to avoid spoilage; other goods require complex installation or servicing. Some goods need aggressive promotion. Goods with high-unit values allow profitable sales by manufacturers directly to ultimate purchasers. Manufacturer-owned facilities include sales branches, sales offices, trade fairs, and merchandise marts.

A *sales branch* carries inventory and processes orders for customers from available stock. Branches provide a storage function like independent wholesalers and serve as offices for sales representatives in their territories. They are prevalent in marketing channels for chemicals, commercial machinery and equipment, motor vehicles, and petroleum products.

A *sales office,* in contrast, does not carry inventory, but it does serve as a regional office for a manufacturer's sales personnel. Locations close to the firm's customers help limit selling costs and support active customer service. For example, numerous sales offices in the Detroit suburbs serve the area's automobile industry.

A *trade fair* (or trade exhibition) is a periodic show at which manufacturers in a particular industry display their wares for visiting retail and wholesale buyers. For example, the Internet World Conference sponsors an enormous trade exhibition that brings together over 600 companies to demonstrate their latest Internet technology.

A *merchandise mart* provides space for permanent showrooms and exhibits, which manufacturers rent to market their goods. One of the world's largest merchandise marts is Chicago's Merchandise Mart Center, a 7-million-square-foot complex that hosts more than 30 seasonal buying markets each year.

Independent Wholesaling Intermediaries

Many wholesaling intermediaries are independently owned. These firms fall into two major categories: merchant wholesalers and agents and brokers.

Merchant Wholesalers

A **merchant wholesaler** takes title to the goods it handles. Merchant wholesalers account for roughly 60 percent of all sales at the wholesale level. Further classifications divide these wholesalers into full-function or limited-function wholesalers, as indicated in Figure 14.7. Synnex, mentioned in the previous section, is a merchant wholesaler.

A full-function merchant wholesaler provides a complete assortment of services for retailers and business purchasers. Such a wholesaler stores merchandise in a convenient location, allowing customers to make purchases on short notice and minimizing inventory requirements. The firm typically maintains a sales force that calls on retailers, makes deliveries, and extends credit to qualified buyers. Full-function wholesalers are common in the drug, grocery, and hardware industries. In the business-goods market, full-function merchant wholesalers (often called *industrial distributors*) sell machinery, inexpensive accessory equipment, and supplies.

A **rack jobber** is a full-function merchant wholesaler who markets specialized lines of merchandise to retailers. A rack jobber supplies the racks, stocks the merchandise, prices the goods, and makes regular visits to refill shelves.

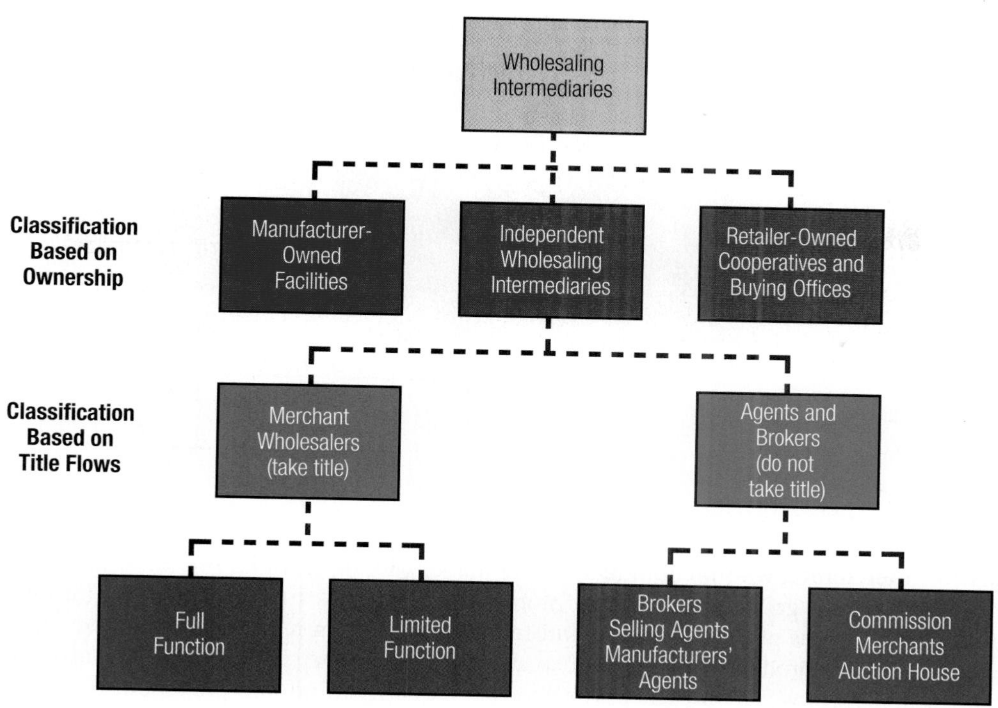

figure 14.7
Major Types of Wholesaling Intermediaries

Limited-function merchant wholesalers fit into four categories: cash-and-carry wholesalers, truck wholesalers, drop shippers, and mail-order wholesalers. Limited-function wholesalers serve the food, coal, lumber, cosmetics, jewelry, sporting goods, and general merchandise industries.

A *cash-and-carry wholesaler* performs most wholesaling functions except for financing and delivery. Although feasible for small stores, this kind of wholesaling generally is unworkable for large-scale grocery stores. Today, cash-and-carry operations typically function as departments within regular full-service wholesale operations. Cash-and-carry wholesalers are commonplace outside the U.S., such as in the United Kingdom.

A **truck wholesaler,** or **truck jobber,** markets perishable food items such as bread, tobacco, potato chips, candy, and dairy products. Truck wholesalers make regular deliveries to retailers, perform sales and collection functions, and promote product lines.

A **drop shipper** accepts orders from customers and forwards these orders to producers, which then ship the desired products directly to customers. Although drop shippers take title to goods, they never physically handle or even see the merchandise. These intermediaries often operate in industries selling bulky goods that customers buy in large lots. Coal and lumber would be examples.

A **mail-order wholesaler** is a limited-function merchant wholesaler who distributes physical or online catalogs as opposed to sending sales representatives to contact retail, business, and institutional customers. Customers then make purchases by mail, phone, or online. Such a wholesaler often serves relatively small customers in outlying areas. Mail-order operations mainly exist in the hardware, cosmetics, jewelry, sporting goods, and specialty food lines as well as in general merchandise.

Table 14.2 compares the various types of merchant wholesalers and the services they provide. Full-function merchant wholesalers and truck wholesalers rank as relatively high-cost intermediaries due to the number of services they perform, while cash-and-carry wholesalers, drop shippers, and mail-order wholesalers provide fewer services and set lower prices since they incur lower operating costs.

Agents and Brokers

A second group of independent wholesaling intermediaries, agents and brokers, may or may not take possession of the goods they handle, but they never take title. They normally perform fewer services than merchant wholesalers, working mainly to bring together buyers and sellers. Agents and brokers fall into five categories: commission merchants, auction houses, brokers, selling agents, and manufacturers' representatives (reps).

table 14.2 ***Comparison of the Types of Merchant Wholesalers and Their Services***

		LIMITED-FUNCTION WHOLESALER			
SERVICE	**Full-Function**	**Cash-and-Carry**	**Truck**	**Drop Shipper**	**Mail-Order**
Anticipates customer needs	Yes	Yes	Yes	No	Yes
Carries inventory	Yes	Yes	Yes	No	Yes
Delivers	Yes	No	Yes	No	No
Provides market information	Yes	Rarely	Yes	Yes	No
Provides credit	Yes	No	No	Yes	Sometimes
Assumes ownership risk by taking title	Yes	Yes	Yes	Yes	Yes

Commission merchants, who predominate in the markets for agricultural products, take possession when producers ship goods such as grain, produce, and livestock to central markets for sale. Commission merchants act as producers' agents and receive agreed-upon fees when they make sales. Since customers inspect the products and prices fluctuate, commission merchants receive considerable latitude in marketing decisions. The owners of the goods may specify minimum prices, but the commission merchants sell these goods at the best possible prices. The commission merchants then deduct their fees from the sales proceeds.

An *auction house* gathers buyers and sellers in one location and allows potential buyers to inspect merchandise before submitting competing purchase offers. Auction house commissions typically reflect specified percentages of the sales prices of the auctioned items. Auctions are common in the distribution of tobacco, used cars, artworks, livestock, furs, and fruit. The Internet has led to a new type of auction house that connects customers and sellers in the online world. A well-known example is eBay, which auctions a wide variety of products in all price ranges.

broker Agent wholesaling intermediary who does not take title to or possession of goods in the course of its primary function, which is to bring together buyers and sellers.

Brokers work mainly to bring together buyers and sellers. A broker represents either the buyer or the seller, but not both, in a given transaction, and the broker receives a fee from the client when the transaction is completed. Intermediaries that specialize in arranging buying and selling transactions between domestic producers and foreign buyers are called *export brokers.* Brokers operate in industries characterized by large numbers of small suppliers and purchasers, such as real estate, frozen foods, and used machinery. Since they provide one-time services for sellers or buyers, they cannot serve as effective channels for manufacturers seeking regular, continuing service. A firm that seeks to develop a more permanent channel might choose instead to use a selling agent or manufacturer's agent.

A **selling agent** typically exerts full authority over pricing decisions and promotional outlays, and it often provides financial assistance for the manufacturer. Selling agents act as independent marketing departments because they can assume responsibility for the total marketing programs of client firms' product lines. Selling agents mainly operate in the coal, lumber, and textiles industries. For a small, poorly financed, production-oriented firm, such an intermediary might prove the ideal marketing channel.

manufacturers' representative Agent wholesaling intermediary who represents manufacturers of related but noncompeting products and who receives a commission on each sale.

While a manufacturer may deal with only one selling agent, a firm that hires **manufacturers' representatives** often delegates marketing tasks to many of these agents. Such an independent salesperson may work for a number of firms that produce related, noncompeting products. Manufacturers' reps are paid on a commission basis, such as 6 percent of sales. Unlike selling agents, who may contract for exclusive rights to market a product, manufacturers' agents operate in specific territories. They may develop new sales territories or represent relatively small firms and those firms with unrelated lines.

When inventor Jane McKittrick first launched Earth Bud-Eze, an innovative range of tools that eased the strains of many gardening tasks, the products—sold largely at state fairs—were modestly successful. But when McKittrick enlisted the expertise of Marshall Associates, a manufacturers' rep group with extensive contacts in the hardware and gardening markets, sales skyrocketed. The start-up product line was even able to penetrate mass merchants nationwide.[25]

table 14.3 ***Services Provided by Agents and Brokers***

SERVICE	Commission Merchant	Auction House	Broker	Manufacturers' Agent	Selling Agent
Anticipates customer needs	Yes	Sometimes	Sometimes	Yes	Yes
Carries inventory	Yes	Yes	No	No	No
Delivers	Yes	No	No	Sometimes	No
Provides market information	Yes	Yes	Yes	Yes	Yes
Provides credit	Sometimes	No	No	No	Sometimes
Assumes ownership risk by taking title	No	No	No	No	No

The importance of selling agents in many markets has declined because manufacturers want better control of their marketing programs than these intermediaries allow. In contrast, the volume of sales by manufacturers' agents has more than doubled and now accounts for 37 percent of all sales by agents and brokers. Table 14.3 compares the major types of agents and brokers on the basis of the services they perform.

RETAILER-OWNED COOPERATIVES AND BUYING OFFICES

Retailers may assume numerous wholesaling functions in an attempt to reduce costs or provide special services. Independent retailers sometimes band together to form buying groups that can achieve cost savings through quantity purchases. Other groups of retailers establish retailer-owned wholesale facilities by forming cooperative chains. Large chain retailers often establish centralized buying offices to negotiate large-scale purchases directly with manufacturers.

1. **What is a wholesaler? How does it differ from a wholesaling intermediary?**
2. **How do wholesaling intermediaries help sellers lower costs?**
3. **Differentiate between agents and brokers.**

DIRECT MARKETING AND OTHER NONSTORE RETAILING

(7) Compare the basic types of direct marketing and nonstore retailing.

Although most retail transactions occur in stores, nonstore retailing is an important marketing channel for many products. Both consumer and business-to-business marketers rely on nonstore retailing to generate leads or requests for more information that may result in future orders.

Direct marketing is a broad concept that includes direct mail, direct selling, direct-response retailing, telemarketing, Internet retailing, and automatic merchandising. Direct and interactive marketing expenditures amount to hundreds of billions of dollars in yearly purchases. The last sections of this chapter consider each type of nonstore retailing.

direct marketing Direct communications, other than personal sales contacts, between buyer and seller, designed to generate sales, information requests, or store or Web site visits.

DIRECT MAIL

Direct mail is a major component of direct marketing. It comes in many forms, ranging from sales letters, postcards, brochures, booklets, catalogs, and house organs (periodicals published by organizations to cover internal issues) to video and audio cassettes. Both not-for-profit and profit-seeking organizations make extensive use of this distribution channel.

Direct mail offers several advantages such as the ability to select a narrow target market, achieve intensive coverage, send messages quickly, choose from various formats, provide complete information, and personalize each mailing piece. Response rates are measurable and higher than other types of advertising. In addition, direct mailings stand alone and do not compete for attention with magazine articles and television programs. On the other hand, the per-reader cost of direct mail is high, effectiveness depends on the quality of the mailing list, and some consumers object strongly to direct mail, considering it "junk mail."

Direct mail marketing relies heavily on database technology in managing lists of names and in segmenting these lists according to the objectives of the campaign. Recipients get targeted materials, often personalized with their names within the ad's content.

Catalogs are a popular form of direct mail, with more than 10,000 different consumer specialty mail-order catalogs—and thousands more for business-to-business sales—finding their way to almost every mailbox in the U.S. In a typical year, mail-order catalogs generate almost $40 billion in consumer sales and $24 billion in business-to-business sales. Catalogs can be a company's only or primary sales method. Spiegel, L.L. Bean, and Coldwater Creek are well-known examples. Brick-and-mortar retailers like Bloomingdale's and Macy's also distribute catalogs. Web retailers, too, have discovered that catalogs stimulate sales. Exotic goods e-tailer eZiba.com used a catalog to expand its customer base beyond young, Web-savvy clientele to older shoppers. Amazon has recently mailed a catalog of home and garden products, while Yahoo! is testing direct mail offers for its range of premium pay services.[26]

New technologies are changing catalog marketing. Today's catalogs can be updated quickly, providing consumers with the latest information and prices. CD-ROM catalogs allow marketers to display products in three-dimensional views and can include video sequences of product demonstrations. Following terrorist scares in which letters laced with anthrax were sent through the mail, direct marketers responded by combining e-mail marketing and direct mail. E-mails alerted customers that catalogs or direct mail packages were coming through the postal service, easing concerns over mail from unknown sources.[27]

DIRECT SELLING

Through direct selling, manufacturers completely bypass retailers and wholesalers. Instead, they set up their own channels to sell their products directly to consumers. Avon, Pampered Chef, Dell, and party-plan marketers like Tupperware are all direct sellers. This channel was discussed in detail in Chapter 13.

DIRECT-RESPONSE RETAILING

Customers of a direct-response retailer can order merchandise by mail or telephone, by visiting a mail-order desk in a retail store, or by computer or fax machine. The retailer then ships the merchandise to the customer's home or to a local retail store for pickup.

Many direct-response retailers rely on direct mail, such as catalogs, to create telephone and mail-order sales and to promote in-store purchases of products featured in the catalogs. Additionally, some firms, such as Lillian Vernon, make almost all of their sales through catalog orders. Mail-order sales have grown about 10 percent a year in recent years, about twice the rate of retail store sales.

Direct-response retailers are increasingly reaching buyers through the Internet and through unique catalogs. Lillian Vernon supplements its general merchandise catalogs with specialty catalogs of children's products and personalized gifts. As the Web page in Figure 14.8 shows, the Lillian Vernon Web site offers six different online catalogs from which customers may choose to shop. Jackson and Perkins holiday season catalogs offer a variety of plants for gift giving. Nordstrom, long known for the fashion selection in its retail stores, also offers consumers thousands of products through its catalogs and Web site.

Direct-response retailing also includes home shopping, which runs promotions on cable television networks to sell merchandise through telephone orders. One form of home shopping has existed

figure 14.8

Lillian Vernon: A Direct Response Marketer Offering General Merchandise and Specialty Children's Products

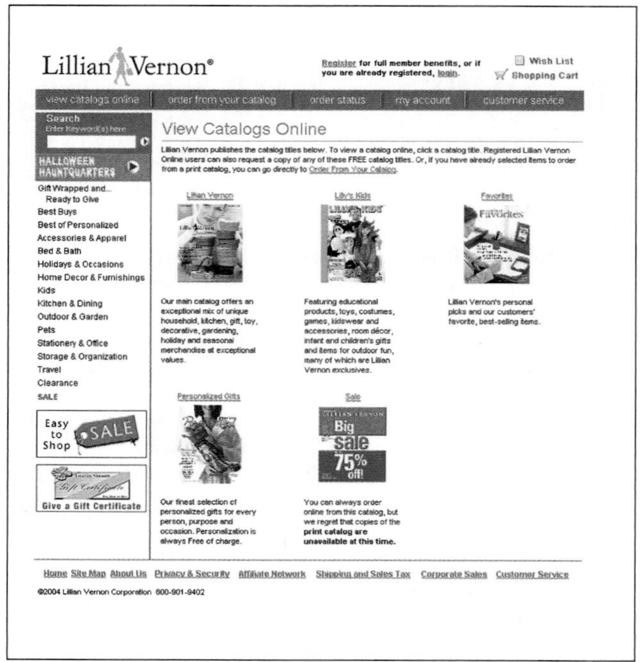

WWW.LILLIANVERNON.COM

for years—*infomercials* that run for at least 30 minutes. Such products as K-Tel Records and Veg-O-Matic vegetable slicers have been featured on these commercials. More recently, TV networks like Home Shopping Network have successfully focused exclusively on providing shopping opportunities. Programming ranges from extended commercials to call-in shows to game-show formats. Shoppers call a toll-free number to buy featured products, and the retailer ships orders directly to their homes.

TELEMARKETING

Telemarketing refers to direct marketing conducted entirely by telephone. It is the most frequently used form of direct marketing. It provides marketers with a high return on their expenditures, an immediate response, and the opportunity for personalized two-way conversations. Telemarketing is discussed in further detail in Chapter 17.

INTERNET RETAILING

8 Explain how much the Internet has altered the wholesaling, retailing, and direct marketing environments.

Internet-based retailers sell directly to customers via virtual storefronts on the Web. They usually maintain little or no inventory, ordering directly from vendors to fill customer orders received via their Web sites. In recent years, conventional retailers have anxiously watched the rise—and then the demise—of many poorly planned, financed, and marketed Internet-based retailers. During the dot.com bust, 130 e-tailers failed. Even early successes like Ezshop, an online home furnishings retailer, eventually ran aground. Traditional retailers, using the Web to support brick-and-mortar stores—the so-called brick-and-click retailers—have had much better staying power. Gap, Best Buy, and Lands' End, for example, have succeeded in extending their expertise to the Web. Office Depot credits its success to its solid brand name, its low-cost buying strategies, and most important, its extensive distribution network—customers can pick up purchases they initiate on the Web at local Office Depot outlets.[28] Chapter 4 discussed Internet retailing and other forms of e-commerce in more detail.

AUTOMATIC MERCHANDISING

The world's first vending machines dispensed holy water for five-drachma coins in Egyptian temples around 215 B.C. This retailing method has grown rapidly ever since; today, about 4.7 million vending machines sell approximately $25 billion in convenience goods to Americans.

While in the past U.S. vending machines have been limited to snacks, soft drinks, and lottery tickets, Japanese consumers use automatic merchandising for everything from fresh sushi to new underwear. Recently, U.S. marketers have begun to realize the potential of this underused marketing tool. As technological advances and credit-card payments make it easier to sell high-cost items, vending machines offering $15 movie soundtracks are popping up in movie-theater lobbies, while Underwear to Go offers boxer shorts in pop-up aluminum cans.[29]

1. What is direct marketing?
2. What is direct mail?

Strategic Implications of Marketing in the 21st Century

As the Internet revolution steadily becomes a way of life—both for consumers and for the businesses marketing goods and services to them—technology will continue to transform the ways in which retailers, wholesalers, and direct marketers connect with customers.

In the retail sector, the unstoppable march toward lower and lower prices has forced retailers from Neiman Marcus to dollar stores to reevaluate everything from their logistics and supply networks to their profit margins. Many have used the power of the Internet to strengthen such factors as store image, the merchandising mix, customer service, and the development of long-term relationships with customers.

Though manufacturers first anticipated that Internet technology would enable them to bypass such intermediaries as wholesalers and agents, bringing them closer to the customer, the reality is quite different. Successful wholesalers have been able to establish themselves as essential links in the supply, distribution, and customer-service network. By leveraging technology, they have been able to carve out new roles, providing such expert services as warehousing or fulfillment to multiple retail clients.

The Internet has empowered direct marketers by facilitating ever more sophisticated database segmentation. Traditional catalog and direct mail marketers have integrated Internet sites, Web advertising, and e-mailing programs into a cohesive targeting, distribution, and repeat-buying strategy.

Briefly Speaking

If you're not doing Internet business, then you're in the Dark Ages, and you're going to be left behind.

John Chambers (b. 1948)
CEO, Cisco Systems

REVIEW OF CHAPTER OBJECTIVES

(1) Explain the wheel of retailing.

The wheel of retailing is the hypothesis that each new type of retailer gains a competitive foothold by offering lower prices than current suppliers and maintains profits by reducing or eliminating services. A recent example is Sears, which continues to struggle to compete against higher-end department stores on the one hand and Target on the other. Sears is having difficulty finding an alternative niche for its stores.

1.1. Find some examples of retailers that demonstrate the concept of the wheel of retailing. Explain the stages they went through and are in currently.

(2) Explain how retailers select target markets.

A retailer starts to define its strategy by selecting a target market. The target market dictates, among other things, the product mix, pricing strategy, and location strategy. Retailers deal with consumer behavior at the most complicated level, and a clear understanding of the target market is critical. Strategies for selecting target markets include merchandising, customer services, pricing, location/distribution, and promotional strategies.

2.1. How do retailers identify target markets?
2.2. Explain the major strategies by which retailers reach their target markets.

(3) Show how the elements of the marketing mix apply to retailing strategy.

A retailer must first identify a target market and then develop a product strategy. Next, it must establish a customer-service strategy. Retail pricing strategy involves decisions on markups and markdowns. Location is often the determining factor in a retailer's success or failure. A retailer's promotional strategy and store atmosphere play important roles in establishing a store's image.

3.1. Explain the importance of a retailer's location to its strategy.
3.2. Why are store atmospherics so important to retailers?

(4) Explain the concepts of retail convergence and scrambled merchandising.

Retail convergence is the coming together of shoppers, goods, and prices, resulting in the blurring of distinctions between types of retailers and the merchandise mix they offer. Similar selections are available from multiple sources and are differentiated mainly by price. Scrambled merchandising refers to retailers' practice of carrying dissimilar product lines in an attempt to generate additional sales volume. Retail convergence and scrambled merchandising have made it increasingly difficult to classify retailers.

4.1. What is retail convergence?
4.2. Define *scrambled merchandising.* Why has this practice become so common in retailing?

5 Identify the functions performed by wholesaling intermediaries.

The functions of wholesaling intermediaries include creating utility, providing services, and lowering costs by limiting contacts.

5.1. What is a wholesaling intermediary?
5.2. Describe the activities it performs.

6 Outline the major types of independent wholesaling intermediaries and the appropriate situations for using each.

Independent wholesaling intermediaries can be divided into two categories: merchant wholesalers and agents and brokers. The two major types of merchant wholesalers are full-function merchant wholesalers, such as rack jobbers, and limited-function merchant wholesalers, including cash-and-carry wholesalers, truck wholesalers, drop shippers, and mail-order wholesalers. Full-function wholesalers are common in the drug, grocery, and hardware industries.

Limited-function wholesalers are sometimes used in the food, coal, lumber, cosmetics, jewelry, sporting goods, and general merchandise industries. Agents and brokers do not take title to the products they sell; this category includes commission merchants, auction houses, brokers, selling agents, and manufacturers' reps. Companies seeking to develop new sales territories, firms with unrelated lines, and smaller firms use manufacturers' reps. Commission merchants are common in the marketing of agricultural products. Auction houses are used to sell tobacco, used cars, livestock, furs, and fruit. Brokers are prevalent in the real estate, frozen foods, and used machinery industries.

6.1. Distinguish among the different types of manufacturer-owned wholesaling intermediaries. What conditions might suit each one?
6.2. What is a broker's main function?
6.3. How are brokers paid for their work?

7 Compare the basic types of direct marketing and nonstore retailing.

Direct marketing is a distribution channel consisting of direct communication to a consumer or business recipient. It generates orders and sales leads that may result in future orders. Since direct marketing responds to fragmented media markets and audiences, growth of customized products, and shrinking network broadcast audiences, marketers consider it an important part of their planning efforts. While most U.S. retail sales take place in stores, such nonstore retailing activities as direct mail, direct selling, direct-response retailing, telemarketing, Internet retailing, and automatic merchandising are important in marketing many types of goods and services.

7.1. Differentiate between direct selling and direct-response retailing. Cite examples of both.
7.2. What are the advantages of Internet retailing?

8 Explain how much the Internet has altered the wholesaling, retailing, and direct marketing environments.

The Internet has affected everything from how supply networks operate to how relationships are formed with customers. Successful wholesalers have carved out a niche as a source of expertise offering faster, more efficient, Web-enabled distribution and fulfillment. The Internet has allowed retailers to enhance their merchandising mix and their customer service by, among other things, giving them access to much broader selections of goods. Direct marketers have merged their traditional catalog or direct mail programs with an Internet interface that allows for faster, more efficient, and more frequent contact with customers and prospects.

8.1. In what ways has the Internet changed direct-response retailing?
8.2. Define *automatic merchandising* and explain its role in U.S. retailing today and in the future.

MARKETING TERMS YOU NEED TO KNOW

retailing 448
wheel of retailing 448
stockkeeping unit (SKU) 450
markup 452
markdown 453
planned shopping center 453
retail convergence 461
scrambled merchandising 461
wholesaler 462
wholesaling intermediary 462
broker 466
manufacturers' representative 466
direct marketing 467

OTHER IMPORTANT MARKETING TERMS

atmospherics 456
convenience retailer 458
specialty retailer 458
limited-line store 459
category killer 459
general merchandise retailer 459
department store 460
mass merchandiser 460
discount house 460
supercenter 461
merchant wholesaler 464
rack jobber 464
truck wholesaler (truck jobber) 465
drop shipper 465
mail-order wholesaler 465
commission merchant 466
selling agent 466

PROJECTS AND TEAMWORK EXERCISES

1. Research and then classify each of the following retailers:
   a. Circuit City
   b. Petite Sophisticates
   c. Limited
   d. Ethan Allen Galleries
   e. Macy's
2. In small groups, visit a local Wal-Mart store and observe such aspects as product placement, shelf placement, inventory levels on shelves, traffic patterns, customer service, and checkout efficiency. Discuss what makes Wal-Mart the world's most successful retailer.
3. Target has become known for trendy clothes and stylish housewares, all readily available in spacious stores at reasonable prices. With your team, visit a local Target store or the company's Web site and compare its product selection to your local hardware store and/or a department store. Make a list of each store's advantages and disadvantages, including convenience, location, selection, service, and general prices. Do any of their product lines overlap? How are they different from each other? Which would your team members visit most often?
4. In pairs, match each industry with the most appropriate type of wholesaling intermediary.

_____ hardware	a. drop shipper
_____ perishable foods	b. truck wholesaler
_____ lumber	c. auction house
_____ wheat	d. full-function merchant wholesaler
_____ used cars	e. commission merchant

5. In teams, develop a retailing strategy for an Internet retailer. Identify a target market and then suggest a mix of merchandise, promotion, service, and pricing strategies that would help a retailer to reach that market via the Internet. What issues must Internet retailers address that do not affect traditional store retailers?
6. With a classmate, visit two or three retail stores that compete with one another in your area and compare their customer-service strategies. (You might wish to visit each store more than once to avoid making a snap judgment.) Select at least 10 criteria and use them to assess each store. How do you think each store sees its customer-service strategy as fitting into its overall retailing strategy? Present your findings in detail to the class.
7. Visit a department store and compare at least two departments' pricing strategies based on the number of markdowns you find and the size of the discount. What, if anything, can you conclude about the success of each department's retailing strategy?
8. Think of a large purchase you make on a nonroutine basis, such as a new winter coat or expensive clothing for a special occasion. Where will you shop for such items? Will you travel out of your way? Will you go to the nearest shopping center? Will you look on the Internet? Once you have made your decision, describe any strategies used by the retailer that led you to this decision. What would make you change your mind about where to shop for this item?
9. Outlet malls are a growing segment of the retail market. Visit a local outlet mall or research one on the Internet. What types of stores are located there? How do the product selection and price compare with typical stores?
10. Torrid is a national chain of about 50 stores that feature clothing for plus-size women. Recommend an appropriate retailing strategy for this type of retailer.

APPLYING CHAPTER CONCEPTS

1. Talbots made its name as a retailer of classic sportswear for women, but it has recently expanded its target market to include men and children. Men, however, typically don't enjoy shopping for clothes, and children shop with their parents. Visit http://talbots.com and assess how well Talbots is reaching men through its Web site. Do you think Talbots' target market is still women who shop for the men in their lives? Why or why not? How can Talbots widen its appeal on the Internet?
2. Several major retailers have begun to test the extreme markdown strategy that lies behind popular "dollar" stores like Dollar General and Family Dollar Stores. Kroger, A&P, and Wal-Mart are all opening sections in selected stores that feature items from snacks to beauty supplies priced at $1. Is this experiment simply a test of pricing strategy? What else might motivate these retailers to offer such deep discounts?
3. When Tower Records filed for bankruptcy, it was only one symptom of the general decline of the retail music store. Industry analysts blame everything from music downloading programs to changes in consumers' tastes. Most, however, feel that music stores will somehow remain viable. What are some changes that these retailers could make in their merchandising, customer service, pricing, location, and other strategies to try to reinvent their business?
4. From its earliest days, Starbucks has placed great value on its unique atmospherics. With unified store designs that allowed for customized décor at individual locations, the company sought to create a distinctive social experience that went beyond the purchase of a mere cup of coffee. Visit a Starbucks in your area and note what contributes to this experience. Is it really "unique"? Why or why not? If you can, compare the store you visit to another retail food or coffee shop (or even another Starbucks). How are they different? Similar? What contributes to the atmospherics in each location?

ETHICS EXERCISE

As the largest company in the world, with 1.4 million employees worldwide and about $257 billion in sales in one recent year, Wal-Mart has become big and powerful enough to influence the national economy. It is responsible for 10 percent of total U.S. imports from China and for about 12 percent of U.S. productivity gains since the late 1990s. Some observers believe Wal-Mart is also responsible for the low U.S. inflation rates of recent years. However, its unbeatable buying power and efficiency have forced many local stores to close when Wal-Mart opens a new store in their area, and tax breaks may mean there are no net increases in jobs or tax revenue from new outlets either. Some communities have protested, and even blocked, new store openings.

1. Do you think a store as powerful as Wal-Mart should be allowed to open new outlets wherever it wants? Why or why not?
2. Wal-Mart is selective about what it sells, refusing, for instance, to carry music or computer games with mature ratings, magazines with content that it considers too adult, or a popular morning-after pill. Because of its sheer size, these decisions can become influential in the culture. Do you think this is a positive or negative effect of the growth of this retailer? Why?
3. Some economists fear what might happen to the U.S. economy if Wal-Mart has a bad year (so far it has had 41 years of nonstop growth). Should retailers have that much influence on the economy? Why or why not?

'netWork EXERCISES

1. **Convenience as a retailing strategy.** Starbucks offers customers something it calls a Starbucks Card. It is an electronic debit card that allows customers to make purchases online or at most Starbucks retail locations without having to carry cash or use a credit card. Visit the Starbucks Web site (**http://www.starbucks.com**) and click "Card." Review the features of the Starbucks Card. Write a report summarizing the benefits of the card to both customers and Starbucks, and how the card fits into Starbucks' overall retailing strategy. Identify another retailer that also uses convenience as a retailing strategy.
2. **Elements of a retailing strategy.** REI is one of the nation's largest retailers of outdoor equipment and clothing. Visit REI's Web site (**http://www.rei.com**) and answer the following questions regarding REI's retailing strategy:
   a. How does the REI adventure page appeal to the company's target market?
   b. Part of REI's retailing strategy is to show its commitment to community service to its target market. What types of community services can you find information about on the Web site and how do these community service projects further REI as a retailer?
3. **Retailing statistics.** The U.S. Census Bureau reports regularly on U.S. retail sales. Visit the Web site listed below, access the most recent Retail Sales report you can find, and answer the following questions:
   a. What is the current level of retail sales in the U.S.?
   b. By how much have retail sales grown over the past month and past year?
   c. Which categories are growing the fastest? Which categories are growing the slowest?
   d. Do you see any evidence of a seasonal pattern in retail sales?

   http://www.census.gov/mrts/www/mrts.html

Note: Internet Web addresses change frequently. If you don't find the exact sites listed, you may need to access the organization's or company's home page and search from there or use a search engine such as Google.

INFOTRAC CITATIONS AND EXERCISES

Record: A119386878
Mass Retailers Find Custom Clothing Fits Them Just Fine. *Cate T Corcoran.*
WWD, July 14, 2004 p10

Abstract: For most women, finding attractive, affordable clothing that fits can be a challenge. Once the factory took over in the clothing industry, good fit and customized individuality went out of fashion. Mass production, while effective at producing large quantities of products for the greatest number of people, compromises fit for quantity—especially when it comes to women's apparel. Fortunately, help is on the way. Advanced computer technology is making it possible for retailers to offer mass customization and personalization of women's apparel. Retailers long frustrated in their pursuit of delivering mass quantity *and* personal fit may have discovered their own Holy Grail. Through the combined use of electronic questionnaires and Internet retailing, companies such as Lands' End and JCPenney are building profitable custom clothing programs for women, and industry observers expect other retailers to follow their lead.

1. Why do you think Lands' End made a strategic decision to offer custom-fit clothing after this merchandise option had become virtually nonexistent among retailers? How might customization in the apparel sector affect the trend of *retail convergence* discussed in the chapter?
2. Read the article and write a brief profile on consumers that prefer custom-fitting clothing. What makes these particular consumers attractive to retailers?
3. Why do you think some retailers might decide not to get into the business of offering custom clothing?

CASE 14.1 Costco Challenges Mighty Wal-Mart

Costco Wholesale Corp., the big national warehouse club based in Issaquah, Washington, is highly profitable. The company is worth about $42 billion, which makes it only about 20 percent the size of Wal-Mart, but it ranks as one of the larger company's biggest competitors.

Sam's Club, the warehouse arm of Wal-Mart, was founded the same year as Costco (1983) and has 532 stores in the U.S. compared to 312 Costco outlets, but the average Costco store earns nearly twice as much revenue as the average Sam's Club ($112 million compared to $63 million).

Costco has carved out its market by appealing not so much to bargain hunters with moderate budgets but to more sophisticated urban shoppers who look for the "new luxury." They appreciate bargains on expensive name brands and "treasure hunt" items, but they also don't mind buying money-saving private-label commodities like paper towels, detergent, and vitamins in bulk from stacked pallets in the store's cavernous, no-frills environment. Small-business owners make up a large portion of Costco customers. "We understood that small-business owners, as a rule, are the wealthiest people in a community," says chairman Jeff Brotman. "So they would not only spend significant money on their businesses, they'd spend a lot on themselves if you gave them quality and value. . . . You couldn't entice a wholesale customer with 20-pound tins of mayonnaise; you had to romance him with consumer goods." Costco's customers pay a small annual fee for a membership card that allows them to shop there; the annual renewal rate is an impressive 86 percent.

Costco doesn't offer unlimited choices. But by stocking fewer items and reducing the number of sizes, brands, and colors it carries, the company streamlines its distribution process and turns over inventory faster. Thanks to its large volume and its ability to attract affluent customers (who return to the store an average of 11.4 times a year), Costco is able to offer prestigious brands like Titleist, Cuisinart, and Levi's, labels that wouldn't ordinarily want to annoy their full-price retail customers by striking a deal with a discounter.

Costco sees itself as an innovator in retailing. Among the goods and services it offered before Sam's Club did were the sale of fresh meat and produce and of its own premium private-label brand (Kirkland Signature). Costco also started selling gasoline before Sam's Club did and is now one of the largest independent gasoline retailers in the state of California. Costco has 61 stores in Canada, and Sam's has recently opened four there with more to come.

The two firms also differ in their employment practices. Wal-Mart pays an average of about $11.50 an hour; Costco pays nearly $16. Wal-Mart offers its health plan to fewer than half its workers; Costco covers over 80 percent of its workers and pays 92 percent of their healthcare costs. Wal-Mart's employee turnover rate is 21 percent a year; Costco's is 6 percent, the lowest in the retailing industry. Some Wall Street observers want Costco to cut its employment costs to increase profits, but Costco has consistently high productivity, and its labor and overhead costs are less than 10 percent of sales (Sam's Club's costs are 17 percent). Says Costco's CEO Jim Sinegal, "Paying your employees well is not only the right thing to do but it makes for good business."

Questions for Critical Thinking

1. Sam's Club is adding more upscale merchandise, including pricey jewelry. Do you think it can successfully capture many of the "new luxury" buyers in Costco's target market? Why or why not?
2. From the case or from your own experience, how would you characterize Costco's merchandising strategy? Its customer-service strategy? Its pricing and location/distribution strategies? Its atmospherics?

Sources: Stanley Holmes and Wendy Zellner, "The Costco Way," *BusinessWeek,* April 12, 2004, pp. 76–77; Christine Frey, "Costco's Love of Labor: Employees' Well-being Key to Its Success," *Seattle Post-Intelligencer,* May 29, 2004, **http://seattlepi.nwsource.com**; John Helyar, "The Only Company Wal-Mart Fears," *Fortune,* November 24, 2003, pp. 158–166; Kate Berry, "No Frills Fills: Discounter Costco Gaining Larger Share of Gas Market," *Los Angeles Business Journal,* April 7, 2003, accessed at **http://www.findarticles.com**.

VIDEO CASE 14.2 Westfield Group Creates a Shopper's Paradise

The written case on The Westfield Group appears on page VC-17. The recently filmed The Westfield Group video is designed to expand and highlight the concepts in this chapter and the concepts and questions covered in the written video case.

Talking about Marketing Careers with Jennifer Gardner, Director of Sales for the Cincinnati Reds

RECENT seasons have carried the label "Rebuilding Year" for Major League Baseball's Cincinnati Reds. Following a year in which the team lost 93 of 161 games, player payroll was slashed to $43 million—sixth lowest in the majors—and the fans' refrain "Wait 'til Next Year" was heard to describe what they expected from the Reds' performance. After all, some sports publications had picked Cincinnati to finish dead last in their division. Everyone agreed that the new park, the Great American Ball Park, which opened in 2003, was one of the best places to play—and watch—a game in the league, but the team simply needed more experience before becoming a contender.

But June arrived, and the Reds found themselves breathing rarified air: first place in the NL Central with the best record in the National League. Although no one really expected it to last in a rebuilding year, for longtime fans it was fun to reminisce about the glory years of the Big Red Machine, a period during the 1970s in which Cincinnati became the first National League team in over 50 years to win back-to-back world championships. But even the most diehard fan realized that such comparisons were unfair ones. With players like Sean Casey, Danny Graves, and Barry Larkin, the current team has several stars, but few teams could ever compare to Sparky Anderson's collection of all-stars—a team that included such Hall of Fame candidates as Johnny Bench, George Foster, Joe Morgan, and Pete Rose.

Joining us in reminiscing about the Reds' glory years—and their recent success in assembling a winning team—is Jennifer Gardner, the team's director of sales. She agreed to participate in a brief Q&A session on sports, business, and marketing as they relate to building and retaining a successful organization.

JENNIFER GARDNER, DIRECTOR OF SALES FOR THE CINCINNATI REDS

PHOTO: COURTESY OF JENNIFER GARDNER

BOONE & KURTZ: How did your college background and early career decisions lead you to the Cincinnati Reds?

I have a bachelor's in communications from the University of Dayton and a master's from Miami University in speech communications. I graduated in 1994 and still didn't know exactly what I wanted to do. I had a background in sports; my dad coached for the Bengals for 15 years, so I had pretty much grown up with the NFL. I had also played sports all my life. I got a job with a small sports marketing firm in Cincinnati that handled marketing for the U.S. Open, and I sold hospitality tents and tables.

I wanted to get my foot in the door with the Bengals, so I took an internship in public relations, which wasn't exactly what I wanted to do. I didn't really like it, but while I was there, I realized they had a need for someone to help with sales for the new stadium. I helped sell suites and season tickets before the new stadium opened, which gave me the background that took me to the Reds.

BOONE & KURTZ: *Director of sales* sounds like a very important position in the Reds organization. Tell us a little about what you are directly involved with as far as sales goes.

I oversee season-ticket sales, group sales, and luxury sales, which include club seats and suites. I make sure we're proactively selling accounts as well as servicing our current accounts.

BOONE & KURTZ: You've been involved with ticket sales in two major professional sports. Was the activity similar in both sports, or was one more difficult than the other?

Ticket sales for baseball is definitely challenging. I've worked in football as well, and it's the difference between 10 home games and 81. In baseball if you lose a game, you have 161 others. There's also a lot of competition, especially in the fall. People start thinking about football, and it's harder to keep them interested in baseball.

BOONE & KURTZ: You've got a great new facility, the Great American Ball Park, that would rival any location this side of Mall of America. It's 2 years old, has a stunning view of the Ohio River beyond the outfield fences and the Cincinnati skyline immediately behind home plate. No wonder that visiting teams and fans are calling it one of the most beautiful parks in America. How has this helped you in your job?

Our facility definitely has helped us. There was such anticipation when it was being built. People were really ready, especially because the Bengals' stadium had opened a few years before.

It has really helped sales to have more categories of seats to sell. We have suites, but we also have diamond seats, scout seats, club seats, and regular seats. Because of their great location, we offer scout seats to the general public when they aren't occupied by Major League scouts.

BOONE & KURTZ: Back in 1996 when Cincinnati voters approved the half-cent sales tax increase to underwrite the stadium's construction, they specified that it should be baseball only and the Bengals stadium should be separate and built for football. How does the fact that it's baseball only and seats only 42,036 help you in attracting fans?

The new stadium is much more of an intimate setting, and all the seats are dedicated to baseball. Our ticket sales have definitely increased, and there is more of a draw to see it. The old stadium had 60,000 seats; it was so big, and the outfield seats were not made to watch baseball. In the new stadium every seat is actually tilted toward home plate. The whole stadium was designed to watch baseball.

BOONE & KURTZ: In efforts to provide an additional source of revenue, newly constructed stadiums for both Major League Baseball and the NFL have included huge increases in the number of luxury seats. In football, the Washington Redskins, which *Forbes* magazine recently valued at $1.1 billion—the most valuable NFL franchise—leads the league with an amazing 234 suites. The Reds have come a long way with 61 suites at Great American Ball Park. Are you responsible for leasing these suites? How do suite leases differ from the sale of individual and season tickets?

The number of suites is definitely an improvement over the 20 suites in the old stadium. Our suites have great amenities, great catering—they're an excellent experience for the companies who own them. All but three of our suites are sold, and most of them were sold back in 2000 before the park even opened.

Suite sales is very different from season-ticket sales. Suite owners pay the lease as well as the ticket portion for the suite, which comes to about $80,000 to $150,000 a year. We also have long-term agreements (five-, seven-, or ten-year contracts) with suite owners, which differs from season tickets, which are for one year only. Suites are a very high-end purchase, but owners are getting a lot for their money. They can entertain up to 16 people per game, with seats inside and outside, and the amenities include everything from catering to private bathrooms.

BOONE & KURTZ: We read about problems in major sports like baseball, basketball, and hockey resulting from rapidly escalating player salaries—and how much those involved with these sports envy the approach of the NFL in initiating a so-called *hard* salary cap that limits players' salaries to 65 percent of revenues. Could you give our readers a brief summary of how a Major League Baseball team makes money?

Teams make money in a number of ways. Every team is different. We bring in money with merchandise sales at the ballpark as well as marketing sponsorships, ticket sales, concessions, and TV and radio rights. Fox Sports and Clear Channel pay us a lot of money to broadcast our games.

Baseball recently started doing revenue sharing; each of the 30 teams puts money in the pot. It's still only local revenue, and it's a small portion. It hasn't had the impact of the NFL revenue sharing, but it's a place to start evening out larger-market teams with smaller-market teams who don't make as much locally.

BOONE & KURTZ: After reading about how the Houston Astros scrambled to replace the original name of their new baseball park—Enron Field—with a less controversial name—Minute Maid Park—it struck us that Great American Ball Park is a great name for the home of the Reds. Tell us a little about the sale of naming rights to Great American Insurance Co.—price, term of the lease. Also, what does Great American Insurance receive from this agreement?

Carl Lindner, the team's owner, also owns the company. It's a corporate name, but it doesn't sound corporate. It's a great name—it sounds very American, very patriotic—so it's a great deal for us. We gave them a lot more for their money: signage, sponsorships, and perks for their employees.

BOONE & KURTZ: In the world of professional sports, who you know is everything. You were lucky enough to have an "in" in the business. What do you suggest to our readers who may be interested in trying to break into pro sports?

I would say networking is the number-one key. The only reason I got an internship was because I knew people. Also, be flexible with your expectations. You may not get what you want right away. I did an internship in PR, although that wasn't my interest, because I knew it would get my foot in the door. You're also not going to get a lot of money right away. The people who are doing the best and excelling are those who love what they do and are willing to sacrifice some for it. We do pay our interns—we started paying them recently—but it is only the minimum.

In terms of internships, I would say it's important to start early, while you're in college. In the past few years, I've heard that a lot of teams only take people while they are in school. If you get started after your sophomore year, the team you intern for may ask you back for the next year. If you are around long enough and make yourself valuable, they will want to keep you around.

MLS Delivers the Goods

In the world of sports, the supply chain holds a unique meaning that has little to do with moving manufactured goods into customers' hands. Rather, like soccer itself, supply-chain issues play themselves out in the game—in the fans' experience of the match, whether at the stadium or at home, watching the game on television, listening to it on the radio, or even picking up live audio and video feeds on the Internet. Inputs required to deliver the intangible product to fans are important—uniforms, equipment, food and drink, and people who deliver the myriad services for players and fans at a soccer game—but the key focus is on the entertainment aspects of this service and the various delivery channels.

Over the league's short history, attendance figures first rose, then briefly fell, and have recently climbed again. Average attendance now compares well with the size of crowds in other soccer-playing countries—even Brazil, whose national team is a five-time World Cup winner. MLS management is relying on soccer-specific stadiums to help grow attendance even more.

To improve sight lines for fans, as well as to provide better playing surfaces, clubhouses, and other facilities for players, MLS plans to increase the number of soccer-specific stadiums around the country. Smaller and more intimate than the football and baseball fields where many teams are currently housed, soccer-specific stadiums include Columbus Crew Stadium (Ohio), the first arena constructed just for an MLS team, and Home Depot Center, home of the L.A. Galaxy and the expansion team Chivas USA, in Carson, California. Both have the wide playing fields and cozy atmosphere that fans and players appreciate and that make attending a match a significant entertainment experience. Owning soccer stadiums also allows the teams to retain all the revenue from ticket sales, not only for home games but also for special events like the MLS All-Star Game, the Women's World Cup, and the MLS Cup Final.

Television audiences have been increasing as well. MLS signed broadcast deals with ABC and ESPN2 to broadcast nearly all regular-season games, all-star games, and Cup games for the next several seasons. Most matches will be broadcast live in the popular "Soccer Saturday" time slot; the others will be shown with tape delays. MLS also purchased American broadcast and sponsorship rights to the FIFA (Fédération Internationale de Football Association) Men's World Cups up through 2006 and the most recent Women's World Cup, which was relocated to the U.S. from China after the SARS outbreak. Broadcasts of these premier matches allowed MLS to use cross-marketing and promotion to integrate U.S. soccer with the most highly anticipated soccer events in the world. In fact, the league's television ratings were up almost 25 percent following the broadcast of the recent Men's World Cup. As one MLS spokesperson pointed out, "The fact that people are watching all across the country says the interest isn't just local."

MLS has launched a service called "Sights and Sounds," which offers free live Internet audio and video feeds as well as archived footage of most televised games. Many MLS games are covered by local radio stations, and some teams offer their own Internet audio streams of these game commentaries. Quite a few are delivered in both English and Spanish; the Chicago Fire offers a Polish broadcast, and Radio Korea aired 10 home games of the L.A. Galaxy. A few MLS teams have weeknight radio shows featuring player interviews and call-in segments, and the New England Revolution has a weekly live Internet talk show. So, however fans prefer to experience soccer, MLS hopes to provide a generous array of exciting options.

Questions for Critical Thinking

1. MLS believes that soccer matches become more significant and enjoyable events in smaller stadiums. How or why do you think the size of the venue contributes to the fans' ultimate experience of the game?
2. What other factors influence the experience of attending a game in person? Which of these are under the league's control, and what do you think MLS can do to ensure they are of the highest quality?
3. Do you think hard-core soccer fans would enjoy experiencing a soccer match over the radio or Internet? Why or why not? Do you think these media are a good way to introduce new fans to the sport? Why or why not?
4. Do you agree with MLS management that linking the league to U.S. broadcasts of world-class events like the World Cup will generate more interest in American teams? Why or why not?

Sources: "United States," http://www.socceraudio.com/USA.htm, accessed September 1, 2004; "Major League Soccer," http://www.fact-index.com, accessed August 27, 2004; Ridge Mahoney "In MLS Cities, Much Adu about Freddy," *USA Today,* June 9, 2004, p. C8; "MLS Announces Return of 'Soccer Saturday,'" http://www.rhinossoccer.com, February 19, 2004; Amy C. Sims, "Pro Soccer Kicks Up U.S. Fanbase," *Fox News,* October 25, 2002, http://www.foxnews.com; "MLS Acquires FIFA World Cup Television Rights through 2006," http://www.sweetspotsoccer.com, January 2, 2002.

PHOTO: COURTESY OF WIREIMAGES.COM

part 6

PROMOTIONAL DECISIONS

chapter 15	Integrated Marketing Communications
chapter 16	Advertising and Public Relations
chapter 17	Personal Selling and Sales Promotion

PHOTO: COURTESY OF WIREIMAGES.COM

chapter 15

Integrated Marketing Communications

chapter objectives

1. Explain how integrated marketing communications relates to the development of an optimal promotional mix.
2. Describe the communication process and how it relates to the AIDA concept.
3. Explain how the promotional mix relates to the objectives of promotion.
4. Identify the different elements of the promotional mix and explain how marketers develop an optimal promotional mix.
5. Describe the role of sponsorships and direct marketing in integrated marketing communications.
6. Contrast the two major alternative promotional strategies.
7. Explain how marketers budget for and measure the effectiveness of promotion.
8. Discuss the value of marketing communications.

TOUR DE LANCE

When the U.S. Postal Service (USPS) decided to sponsor bicycle racing in 1996, the sport was uncomplicated. Its relatively uncrowded field of competitors was sponsored—given financial support—by generally unknown industrial firms such as commercial bakers and cement manufacturers. The USPS liked the sport's emphasis on teamwork and endurance and hoped that some of those qualities would help to burnish the postal service's somewhat damaged reputation at a time when competitors like DHL, UPS, and FedEx were capturing huge shares of its overnight and package-delivery markets. Its marketing specialists were aware of cycling's popularity in Europe and felt that sponsorship of Lance Armstrong's team would help their effort to increase their international business. So the USPS signed a sponsorship agreement with Armstrong, who had just lost his French sponsor because of his cancer diagnosis, to lead its pro team for $215,000 a year plus bonuses. The relationship would continue for an almost unprecedented length in the sport: a total of nine years before ending in 2005. And as the saying goes, the rest is history.

Still recovering from cancer at the time he was contacted by the postal service, Armstrong has since gone on to win the Tour de

France, the world's most prestigious and most grueling bicycle race, six times in a row. He has written a best-selling autobiography and seen his annual income soar to $16 million. And just as important to Armstrong, he's been credited not only with inspiring millions of people around the world in families touched by cancer but also with salvaging the good name of the postal service. "Lance has completely changed the meaning of 'going postal,'" according to a USPS spokesperson.

It's estimated that the USPS received about $19 million in free advertising a year just from backing Armstrong and his team for the past nine years. This is despite the fact that nearly all the races in which the team competes take place abroad. Almost half a million U.S. households tuned in to watch the most recent Tour. Armstrong's team now has about 20 sponsors, of which the Discovery Channel, his new title sponsor, is by far the most heavily committed at about $10 million a year, an amount similar to what USPS paid. As part of the new agreement, Armstrong will serve as spokesman on the cable company's various networks, including The Discovery Channel, The Learning Channel, Animal Planet, and others. The agreement, in effect for 2005–2007, also calls for Lance to ride in the 2006 Tour.

AP PHOTO/PETER DEJONG

With such a string of almost unbelievable successes (Armstrong had suffered from and beaten testicular, lung, and brain cancer), and with so much positive exposure for the USPS, how could there be a downside to this story? But the success of the Armstrong racing team might in fact begin to discourage potential sponsors for rival teams, who see little hope of winning as long as Lance is in the race. His string of victories is so stunning that charges of illegal performance enhancers (typically called *doping*) follow him throughout each Tour. But he has been drug-tested regularly by cycling's governing bodies and declared clean following an extensive two-year French law-enforcement probe of drug use in cycling. When the subject comes up in interviews, Armstrong's face gets a relaxed, cool look: "I'll have the peace of heart, the peace of mind, the peace of soul of knowing I did it the hard way."

Sponsors of lesser teams began to reconsider their commitments, and one team sponsored by a German clothing chain collapsed into insolvency. The International Cycling Union now requires teams with shaky finances to prove that riders are being paid on time. The Amaury Sports Organization, which plans the Tour de France every year, is considering reducing the number of teams in the top tier to 15 from the current 30, on the grounds that if there are fewer teams competing, they will all have more secure financial backing.

Armstrong's commitment to the sport of cycling remains firm. He overcame the problems and weaknesses that made his fifth race the most challenging one to date—he took a spill and suffered from dehydration. He came back stronger and more dominant than ever. His drive to win is obvious. In his words, "When I was sick, I didn't want to die. When I race I don't want to lose. Dying and losing; it's the same thing." As long as he's winning, can any marketer with an eye on the European market really lose by sponsoring him and his team?[1]

Chapter Overview

TWO of the four components of the marketing mix—product and distribution strategies—were discussed in previous chapters. The three chapters in Part 6 analyze the third marketing mix variable—promotion. **Promotion** is the function of informing, persuading, and influencing the consumer's purchase decision.

This chapter introduces the concept of integrated marketing communications, briefly describes the elements of a firm's promotional mix—personal and nonpersonal selling—and explains the characteristics that determine the success of the mix. Next, we identify the objectives of promotion and describe the importance of developing promotional budgets and measuring the effectiveness of promotion. Finally, we discuss the importance of the business, economic, and social aspects of promotion. Chapter 16 covers advertising, public relations, and other nonpersonal selling elements of the promotional mix, including sponsorships and guerilla advertising. Chapter 17 completes this part of the book by focusing on personal selling and sales promotion.

promotion
Communication link between buyers and sellers. Function of informing, persuading, and influencing a consumer's purchase decision.

marketing communications
Messages that deal with buyer–seller relationships.

integrated marketing communications (IMC)
Coordination of all promotional activities to produce a unified, customer-focused promotional message.

Throughout *Contemporary Marketing,* special emphasis has been given to new information that shows how technology is changing the way marketers approach *communication,* the transmission of a message from a sender to a receiver. Consumers receive **marketing communications**—messages that deal with buyer–seller relationships—from a variety of media, including television, radio, magazines, direct mail, and the Internet. Marketers can broadcast an ad on the Web to mass markets or design a customized appeal targeted to a small market segment. Each message the customer receives from any source represents the brand, company, or organization. A company needs to coordinate all these messages for maximum total impact and to reduce the likelihood the consumer will completely tune them out.

To prevent this loss of attention, marketers are turning to **integrated marketing communications (IMC)**, which coordinates all promotional activities—media advertising, direct mail, personal selling, sales promotion, public relations, and sponsorships like Nike's sponsorship contract with Tiger Woods and the USPS's nine-year relationship with Lance Armstrong's racing team—to produce a unified, customer-focused promotional message. IMC is a broader concept than marketing communications and promotional strategy. It uses database technology to refine the marketer's understanding of the target audience, segment this audience, and select the best type of media for each segment.

This chapter shows that IMC involves not only the marketer but also all other organizational units that interact with the consumer. Marketing managers set the goals and objectives of the firm's promotional strategy in accordance with overall organizational objectives and marketing goals. Based on these objectives, the various elements of the promotional strategy—personal selling, advertising, sales promotion, direct marketing, publicity, and public relations—are formulated into an integrated communications plan. This plan becomes a central part of the firm's total marketing strategy to reach its selected market segments. The feedback mechanism, including marketing research and field reports, completes the system by identifying any deviations from the plan and suggesting improvements.

Life is like riding a bicycle. You don't fall off unless you stop pedaling.

Claude D. Pepper (1900–1989)
U.S. senator

INTEGRATED MARKETING COMMUNICATIONS

① Explain how integrated marketing communications relates to the development of an optimal promotional mix.

Stop and think for a moment about all the marketing messages you receive in a single day. You click on the television for the morning news, and you see plenty of commercials. Listen to the car radio on the way to work or school, and you can sing along with the jingles. You get catalogs, coupons, and flyers in the mail. People even leave promotional flyers under your car's windshield wiper while it sits in the parking lot. When you log on to your computer, you're deluged with banner and pop-up ads and even marketing-related e-mail. Marketers know that you are receiving many types of communication. They know they need to compete for your attention. So they look for ways to reach you in a coordinated manner through integrated marketing communications.

Successful marketers use the marketing concept and relationship marketing to develop customer-oriented marketing programs. The customer is at the heart of integrated marketing communications. An IMC strategy begins not with the organization's goods and services but with consumer wants or needs and then works in reverse to the product, brand, or organization. It sends receiver-focused rather than product-focused messages.

Rather than separating the parts of the promotional mix and viewing them as isolated components, IMC looks at these elements from the consumer's viewpoint: as information about the brand, company, or organization. Even though the messages come from different sources—sales presentations, word of mouth, TV, radio, newspapers, billboards, direct mail, coupons, public relations, and online services—consumers may perceive them as "advertising" or a "sales pitch." IMC broadens promotion to include all the ways a customer has contact with an organization, adding to traditional media and direct mail such sources as package design, store displays, sales literature, and online and interactive media. Unless the organization takes an integrated approach to present a unified, consistent message,

Briefly Speaking

Make it simple. Make it memorable. Make it inviting to look at. Make it fun to read.

Leo Burnett (1891–1971)

founder, Leo Burnett advertising agency

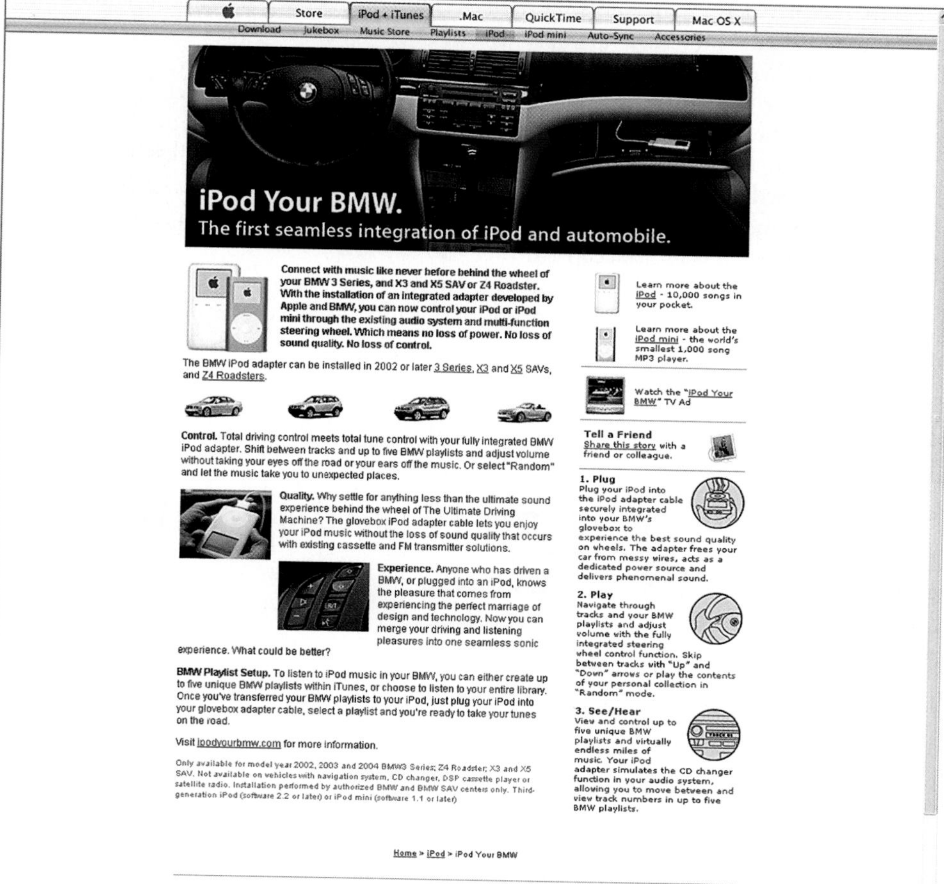

WWW.APPLE.COM/IPOD/BMW

figure 15.1

Joint Integrated Marketing Promotion by BMW and Apple Computer, Inc.

it may send conflicting information that confuses consumers. Figure 15.1 illustrates how two organizations—a computer manufacturer and an automaker—recently joined together to create a unified marketing campaign for music downloads.

Today's business environment is characterized by many diverse markets and media, creating both opportunities and challenges. The success of any IMC program depends on identifying the members of an audience and understanding what they want. Without accurate, current information about existing and potential customers, their purchase histories, needs, and wants, marketers may send the wrong message. But they cannot succeed simply by improving the quality of the messages or by sending more of them. IMC must not only deliver messages to intended audiences but also gather responses from them. Databases and interactive marketing are important IMC tools that help marketers collect information from customers and then segment markets according to demographics and preferences. Marketers can then design specialized communications programs to meet the needs of each segment.

Art museums often face an uphill battle when it comes to attracting more visitors. It's even harder, sometimes, for television networks to get viewers to sit down and watch programming about art. But A&E Network met the challenge in promoting its special "Biography" series, *The Impressionists,* with a successful IMC campaign. Working in conjunction with the Civic Entertainment Group in New York, A&E contacted dozens of art museums around the country whose regular visitors and membership base matched the demographic profiles of A&E's viewers. A&E then supplied the museums with a "Fundraiser in a Box" promotional kit, complete with a 20-minute preview of the series, a customized media release and invitations, a handbook for producing fund-raising events (with special tips on French catering and music), a coupon for purchasing cheese and crackers, and two cases of Turning Leaf wine supplied by Gallo Wines. The museums loved it—and so did their visitors, who then tuned in to watch *The Impressionists.* A&E reported a viewing audience of 2.7 million households, which was 32 percent higher than its prime-time average for that month.[2]

Despite low wages, Hispanic immigrants send about $10 million a year home to Latin America. Half of this total goes to Mexico. Both U.S. banking giants Citibank and Bank of America are aggressively marketing such financial assistance as money-transfer services to the 10 million U.S. households they refer to as "the unbanked": people without bank accounts. The money-transfer market, currently dominated by Western Union and other remittance companies such as MoneyGram, appeared to reflect a banking services need that could serve the immigrant market and result in many Hispanic households graduating to checking accounts, credit cards, and even mortgages.

In addition to traditional TV, print, radio, and out-of-home messages, Citibank sponsors free community-based screenings of Mexican films. Bank of America offers a SafeSend card used to send money back home with a special feature that lets recipients in Mexico load funds on a debit card and spend them wherever Visa is accepted.[3]

The increase in media options provides more ways to give consumers product information; however, it can also create information overload. Marketers have to spread available dollars across frag-

Te hablamos en el mismo idioma en el que sueñas.

Citibank Access Account | Servicio en español.

This Citibank message for its money-transfer Access Account card tells consumers, "We speak to you in the language you dream in."

mented media markets and a wider range of promotional activities to achieve their communication goals. Mass media such as TV ads, while still useful, are no longer the mainstays of marketing campaigns. In 1960, a marketer could reach about 90 percent of U.S. consumers by advertising on the three major TV networks. Today, these network ads reach fewer than 60 percent. Audiences are also more fragmented. So to reach desired groups, organizations are turning to niche marketing by advertising in special-interest magazines; by purchasing time on cable TV channels to target consumers with sports, family, science, history, comedy, and women's interests; by reaching out through telecommunications like the Internet; and by sponsoring events and activities. Without an IMC program, marketers frequently encounter problems within their own organizations because separate departments have authority and responsibility for planning and implementing specific promotional mix elements.

The coordination of an IMC program often produces a competitive advantage based on synergy and interdependence among the various elements of the promotional mix. With an IMC strategy, marketers can create a unified personality for the product or brand by choosing the right elements from the promotional mix to send the message. At the same time, they can develop more narrowly focused plans to reach specific market segments and choose the best form of communication to send a particular message to a specific target audience. IMC provides a more effective way to reach and serve target markets than less coordinated strategies.

IMPORTANCE OF TEAMWORK

IMC requires a big-picture view of promotion planning, a total strategy that includes all marketing activities, not just promotion. Successful implementation of IMC requires that everyone involved in every aspect of promotion—public relations, advertising, personal selling, and sales promotion—function as a team. They must present a consistent, coordinated promotional effort at every point of customer contact with the organization. This way, they save time, money, and effort. They avoid duplication of efforts, increasing marketing effectiveness and reducing costs. Teamwork involves both in-house resources and outside vendors. It involves marketing personnel; members of the sales force who deal with wholesalers, retailers, and organizational buyers; and customer-service representatives. A firm gains nothing from a terrific advertisement featuring a great product, an informational Web site, and an 800 toll-free number if unhelpful salespeople frustrate customers when they answer the phones. The company must train its representatives to send a single positive message to consumers and also to solicit information for the firm's customer database. As Figure 15.2 illustrates, the successful launch of

figure 15.2

Chrysler Crossfire: Using a Web Site and a Toll-free Number in an IMC Campaign

the Chrysler Crossfire used an IMC campaign that combined advertising, dealership displays and promotional materials, a special Web site, and a toll-free telephone number for one-to-one communications between potential purchasers and Chrysler marketers.

IMC also challenges the traditional role of the advertising agency. A single agency may no longer fulfill all a client's communications requirements, including traditional advertising and sales promotions, interactive marketing, database development, direct marketing, and public relations. To best serve client needs, an agency must often assemble a team with members from other companies.

ROLE OF DATABASES IN EFFECTIVE IMC PROGRAMS

With the explosive growth of the Internet during the past 10 years, marketers have been given the power to gather more information faster and to organize it more easily than ever before in history. By sharing this detailed knowledge appropriately among all relevant parties, a company can lay the foundation for a successful IMC program.

The move from mass marketing to a customer-specific marketing strategy—a characteristic of online marketing—requires not only a means of identifying and communicating with the firm's target market but also information regarding important characteristics of each prospective customer. As discussed in Chapter 10, organizations can compile different kinds of data into complete databases with customer information, including names and addresses, demographic data, lifestyle considerations, brand preferences, and buying behavior. This information provides critical guidance in designing an effective IMC strategy that achieves organizational goals and finds new opportunities for increased sales and profits.

Direct sampling is another method frequently used to quickly obtain customer opinions regarding a particular firm's goods and services. If you've ever received a free sample of bath soap, aspirin, or even a newspaper in your mailbox, you've been the recipient of direct sampling. Companies such as Illinois-based Snyder Communications use databases to target these promotions to certain consumers for their marketing clients. They might target a particular ethnic audience, such as Hispanic consumers, or they might focus on a particular age group, such as aging baby boomers.

1. What is promotion?
2. What is marketing communications?
3. How is integrated marketing communications (IMC) different from both promotion and marketing communications?

(2) Describe the communication process and how it relates to the AIDA concept.

THE COMMUNICATION PROCESS

When you have a conversation with someone, do you wonder whether the person understood your message? Do you worry that you might not have heard the person correctly? Marketers have the same concerns—when they send a message to an intended audience or market, they want to make sure it gets through clearly and persuasively. That is why the communication process is so important to marketing. The top portion of Table 15.1 shows a general model of the communication process and its application to promotional strategy. The **sender** acts as the source in the communication system as he or she seeks to convey a **message** (a communication of information, advice, or a request) to a receiver. An effective message accomplishes three tasks:

1. It gains the receiver's attention.
2. It achieves understanding by both receiver and sender.
3. It stimulates the receiver's needs and suggests an appropriate method of satisfying them.

Table 15.1 also provides several examples of promotional messages. Although the types of promotion may vary from a highly personalized sales presentation to such nonpersonal promotions as television advertising and dollar-off coupons, each goes through every stage in the communications process.

Written communications can be even more difficult because immediate feedback is not available. For some tips on how to achieve clear communication in your own written marketing messages, see the accompanying "Etiquette Tips for Marketing Professionals" feature.

table 15.1 **Relating Promotion to the Communication Process**

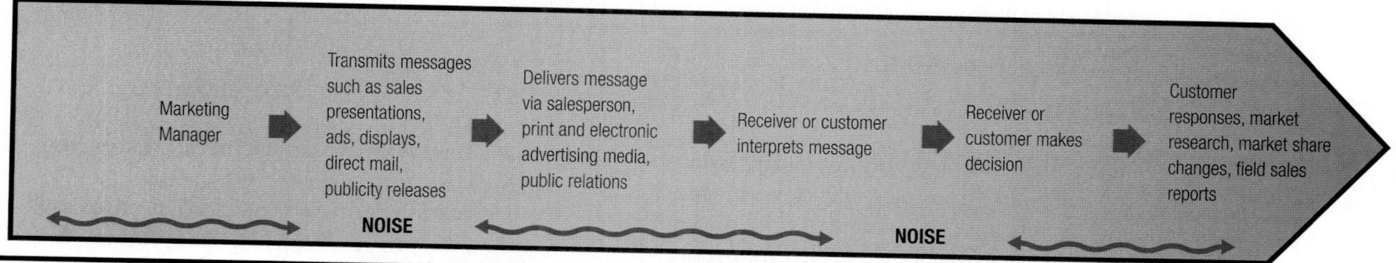

Type of Promotion	Sender	Encoding by Sender	Channel	Decoding by Receiver	Response	Feedback
Personal selling	IBM e-solutions networking system	Sales presentation on new applications of system	IBM sales representative	Office manager and employees discuss sales presentation and those of competing suppliers.	Order is placed for IBM e-solutions system installation.	Customer asks about a second system for subsidiary company.
Dollar-off coupon (sales promotion)	Kellogg's Special K cereal	Coupons prepared by Kellogg's marketing department and advertising agency	Coupon insert in Sunday newspaper	Newspaper reader sees coupon for Special K cereal and saves it.	Special K is purchased by consumer using coupon.	Kellogg researchers see increase in market share.
Television advertising	Styx River Water World	Advertisement developed by Styx River's advertising agency featuring the new park rides	Network television ads during program with high percentages of viewers under 20 years old	Teens and young adults see ad and decide to try out the new park.	Water World tickets are purchased.	Customers purchase season ticket packages for Water World.

The three tasks just listed are related to the **AIDA concept** (attention-interest-desire-action), the steps consumers take in reaching a purchase decision. First, the promotional message must gain the potential consumer's attention. It then seeks to arouse interest in the good or service. At the next stage, it stimulates desire by convincing the would-be buyer of the product's ability to satisfy his or her needs. Finally, the sales presentation, advertisement, or sales promotion technique attempts to produce action in the form of a purchase or a more favorable attitude that may lead to future purchases.

AIDA concept Steps through which an individual reaches a purchase decision: attention, interest, desire, and action.

The message must be **encoded,** or translated into understandable terms, and transmitted through a communications channel. **Decoding** is the receiver's interpretation of the message. The receiver's response, known as **feedback,** completes the system. Throughout the process, **noise** (in such forms as ineffective promotional appeals, inappropriate advertising media, or poor radio or television reception) can interfere with the transmission of the message and reduce its effectiveness.

The marketer is the message sender in Table 15.1. He or she encodes the message in the form of sales presentations, advertising, displays, or publicity releases. The **channel** for delivering the message may be a salesperson, a public relations outlet, a Web site, or one of the numerous advertising media. Decoding is often the most troublesome step in marketing communications because consumers do not always interpret promotional messages in the same way that senders do. Since receivers usually decode messages according to their own frames of reference or experiences, a sender must carefully encode a message in a way that matches the frame of reference of the target audience. Consumers today are bombarded daily by hundreds of sales messages through many media channels. This communications traffic can create confusion as noise in the channel increases. Since the typical shopper will choose to process only a few messages, ignored messages waste communications budgets.

The AIDA concept is also vital to online marketers. It is not enough to say a Web site has effective content or high response rates. Marketers must know just how many "eyeballs" are looking at the site, how often they come to view a message, and what they are examining. Most important, they must find out what consumers do besides just look. The bottom line is that if nobody is responding to a Web site, it might as well not exist. According to Bill White, vice president of sales for financial services site The Motley Fool, "A few years ago, advertisers just wanted to get on the Internet. Today it's all about return on investment (ROI)."[4] Experts advise attracting users' attention by including people in

ETIQUETTE TIPS

FOR MARKETING PROFESSIONALS

How to Write an Effective Letter

LIKE marketing communications, business letters are designed to convey information and generate a response. Despite the increased informality of today's workplace, some important rules still apply to the writing of business letters. Since they go a long way toward ensuring that you get your message across, a quick review of a few basics should pay off for you later on.

1. Include all the standard parts of a business letter. These begin with your complete address (including phone number, e-mail, and Web addresses) and the complete address of the person to whom you are writing. Also include the date and a subject line ("RE: Your order of January 12") if it will help the reader. Begin with a greeting ("Dear Ms. Austin:").
2. Indent new paragraphs, and make sure you use each paragraph to convey a single point.
3. Write clearly and concisely, getting to the point and stating what you need or expect in the way of a response. ("Please call me to confirm that you will attend the meeting.")
4. Use the appropriate style of a business letter—cordial formality—whether you are writing to inquire, to complain, to express thanks, or to inform. Contractions ("it's, I'm, we'll") are acceptable, but avoid jargon and technical terms unless you are sure your reader understands them.
5. Use "I," "we," and "you" to make your writing personal and to avoid the passive voice. Say, "I will send you the storyboards" instead of "The storyboards will be sent to all our clients."
6. If you are enclosing something, such as an agenda, a check, or a contract, mention it in the letter. ("Enclosed is the list of air dates you requested.")
7. Avoid needless gratitude (you don't need to say "thank you" in a letter of complaint, for instance), but if it is appropriate, thank the reader for his or her time or attention.
8. Close the letter appropriately with a simple phrase such as "Sincerely yours."
9. Sign neatly.
10. Remember that appearances count, and proof your letter carefully. Use the spell-check feature on your word processor, but check the contents yourself to make certain that such typographic errors as writing "may" instead of "my" are not included. Such inaccuracies are typically ignored by spell checkers. Check particularly for the proper spelling of the names of people and companies.

It is always a good idea to remember that writing a business letter is just like writing any other form of written communication. Prepare in advance for the writing, know what you are to write about, and have all the information you need close by. Write the letter and then put it aside for a few hours or even a day. Once you've stepped away from it for a while, go back and review the letter. At this time, you will be able to decide if you've clearly conveyed your message in the best manner possible.

Sources: Genevieve Thiers, "How to Write a Business Letter," http://Pa.essortment.com/howtowriteb_rtxy.htm, accessed December 15, 2004; "Business Letter Writing," http://www.business-letter-writing.com, accessed December 15, 2004; "Writing@CSU: Writing Guide," http://writing.colostate.edu, accessed December 15, 2004.

advertisements and other communications in addition to new content and formats. Marketers at iwon.com alternate the sizes of their customers' ads as well as balance the types of ads that appear on the site. Ad sales increased 37 percent during the following year as a result of greater response to diverse messages.[5]

Feedback, the receiver's response to the message, provides a way for marketers to evaluate the effectiveness of the message and tailor their responses accordingly. Feedback may take the form of attitude changes, purchases, or nonpurchases. In some instances, organizations use promotion to create favorable attitudes toward their goods or services in the hope of future purchases. Other promotional communications have the objective of directly stimulating consumer purchases. Marketers using infomercials that urge the viewer to call a toll-free number to place orders for music collections, the latest fitness fad, or other products can easily measure their success by counting the number of calls they receive that result in orders.

Even nonpurchases may serve as feedback to the sender. Failure to purchase may result from ineffective communication in which the receivers do not believe or—worse yet—even remember the message. Alternatively, the message may have failed to persuade the receiver that the firm's goods or services are superior to those of its competitors. Marketers frequently gather feedback through such techniques as marketing research studies and field sales reports. For an example of how important such feedback can be, see the accompanying "Marketing Miss" feature about Gap Inc.

Noise represents interference at some stage in the communication process. It may result from disruptions such as transmissions of competing promotional messages over the same communications channel, misinterpretation of a sales presentation or advertising message, receipt of the promotional message by the wrong person, or random events such as people conversing or leaving the room during a television commercial. Noise can also result from distractions within an advertising message itself.

Noise can be especially problematic in international communications. Disruption often results from too many competing messages. Italian television channels, for instance, broadcast all advertisements during a single half-hour slot each night. Noise might stem from differences in technology, such as a bad telephone connection, or from poor translations into other languages. Nonverbal cues, such as body language and tone of voice, are important parts of the communication process, and cultural differences may lead to noise and misunderstandings. For example, in the U.S., the round o sign made with the thumb and first finger means "okay." However, in Mediterranean countries, it means "zero" or "the worst." A Tunisian interprets this same sign as "I'll kill you," and to a Japanese it means "money."

Perhaps the most misunderstood language for U.S. marketers is English. It is often said that each of the 74 English-speaking nations is separated by a common language. The following examples illustrate how easy it can be for marketers to make mistakes in English-language promotional messages:

- *Underpants:* pants (Britain), underdaks (Australia)
- *Police:* bobby (Britain), garda (Ireland), Mountie (Canada), police wallah (South Asia)
- *Porch:* stoep (South Africa), gallery (Caribbean)

"Be comfortable with who you are" reads the headline on the Hush Puppies poster. Are they mad? If people were comfortable with who they were, they'd never buy any products other than the ones they needed, and then where would the advertising industry be?

Mark Edwards
British journalist

marketing miss — How the Gap Lost Its Groove

Background. Under the leadership of former CEO Mickey Drexler, Gap became a quick hit and grew to be worth $6.8 million as part of a fashion merchandising powerhouse that also includes Old Navy and Banana Republic. But then Gap's grip on what made fashion tick for the youth market faltered, and it racked up 29 consecutive months of declining sales. As a result, Drexler was forced to resign.

The Marketing Problem. Most fashion buying decisions at Gap were made by Drexler, who famously relied on his gut instincts about what was going to be the next hot thing. The company conducted little systematic research, and the marketing message was fairly uniform across all segments. As long as Gap guessed right, both the retail chain and its CEO looked like a trend leader. But when it missed a trend or promoted a look that didn't catch on, it was left with merchandise to spare.

The Outcome. Under its new CEO Paul Pressler, Gap relied more on research, such as focus groups and other consumer research, as well as on extensive surveys of its own staff about what customers want to wear. It's offering fewer styles but targeting and segmenting its customers more carefully, tailoring its marketing messages differently for men and for women, for instance. It's also looking for the right mix of four main style categories that it calls basics, essentials, style items, and trendy clothes for its most adventurous customers. Brighter colors are on the way, backed by trendy commercials with popular celebrity spokespeople like Madonna and Missy Elliott.

Lessons Learned. Although some fashion-industry analysts argue that consumers don't know what they want until they see it, it pays to remain close to the customer, asking about preferences and listening to and evaluating the answers. Gut instinct can work for a time, given luck, but it usually isn't enough to build a long-term relationship with customers no matter how fickle their fashion sense may be.

Sources: Company Web site, http://www.gapinc.com, accessed December 14, 2004; Diane Brady, "Trying Not to Be a Fashion Victim," *BusinessWeek,* October 6, 2003, pp. 112–113; Amy Merrick, "Worse for the Wear," *The Wall Street Journal* classroom edition, May 2003, http://www.wsjclassroomedition.com.

- *Bar:* pub (Britain), hotel (Australia), boozer (Australia, Britain, New Zealand)
- *Bathroom:* loo (Britain), dunny (Australia), lav (Britain, South Africa)
- *Ghost or monster:* wendigo (Canada), duppy (Caribbean), taniwha (New Zealand)
- *Barbecue:* braai (South Africa), barbie (Australia)
- *Pickup truck:* bakkie (South Africa), ute (Australia), utility vehicle (New Zealand)

Faulty communications can be especially risky on a global level, where noise can lead to some interesting misinterpretations. Here are three recent international examples:

- *On a sign in a Bucharest hotel lobby:* The lift is being fixed for the next day. During that time, we regret that you will be unbearable.
- *From a Japanese information booklet about using a hotel air conditioner:* Cooles and Heates: If you want just condition of warm in your room, please control yourself.
- *In an Acapulco hotel:* The manager has personally passed all the water served here.

1. What are the three tasks accomplished by an effective message?
2. What is the AIDA concept?
3. Briefly relate the communication process to promotional strategy.

③ Explain how the promotional mix relates to the objectives of promotion.

OBJECTIVES OF PROMOTION

What specific tasks should promotion accomplish? The answers to this question seem to vary as much as the sources consulted. Generally, however, marketers identify the following objectives of promotion:

1. Provide information to consumers and others.
2. Increase demand.
3. Differentiate a product.
4. Accentuate a product's value.
5. Stabilize sales.

figure 15.3

Schick: Offering Product Information and Benefits to Consumers

PROVIDE INFORMATION

The traditional function of promotion was to inform the market about the availability of a particular good or service. In fact, marketers still direct much of their current promotional efforts at providing product information to potential customers. An advertisement for a musical performance typically provides information about the performer, time, and place. A commercial for a theme park offers information about rides, location, and admission price. Information can also help differentiate a product from its competitors by focusing on its features or benefits. The promotional message in Figure 15.3 provides consumers with information on the Quattro shaver's two skin-conditioning strips and four blades, which provide the benefit of a close shave.

In addition to traditional print and broadcast advertising, marketers often distribute a number of high-tech, low-cost tools to give consumers product information. One such tool, the information-packed videocassette or CD, is currently used for products ranging from cosmetics to automobiles to exercise equipment. In fact, one college recently sent videos to alumni in an attempt to increase attendance at their upcoming reunion. A 10-minute video costs about $1.50 to duplicate and send (not including production costs), compared with

$8 or more for a full-color brochure. Consumers are more likely to regard the video or CD as a novelty that stands out from other promotions, so they are less likely to consider them junk mail and throw them out. In fact, 9 of every 10 recipients take the time to view them. In some cases, response rates are as high as 49 percent and returns on investment exceed 1,000 percent. These figures translate into substantial profits for companies involved in videocassette and CD promotions.

Many companies also send CDs containing software that provides information about or sampling of a good or service. Music companies and Internet service providers such as AOL are regular users of this promotional technique.

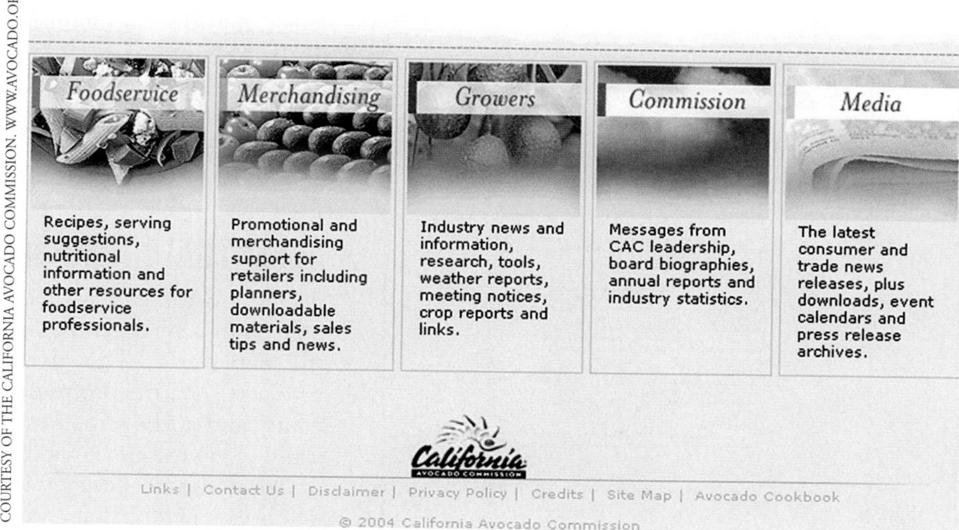

The California Avocado Commission spends more than $10 million annually to promote national awareness, interest, and increased purchases of one of the state's most prized delicacies.

INCREASE DEMAND

Most promotions pursue the objective of increasing demand for a product. Some promotions are aimed at increasing **primary demand,** the desire for a general product category such as HDTVs or DVD players. Last year, $700 million was spent on advertising and sales promotions on agricultural commodities ranging from milk and produce to cotton. Funded by fees called agricultural marketing "checkoffs" levied on the sale of these products, the objective of these expenditures is to increase sales of the entire product category, not focus on individual brands.[6] Primary-demand promotions are also typical for firms holding exclusive patents on significant product improvements and for marketers who decide to expand overseas, creating new markets for their products in other parts of the world. When Procter & Gamble first introduced its Pampers disposable diapers in Hungary, most parents were using overpants with paper inserts to diaper their babies. So early Pampers television ads focused on generating interest in the novel product.

More promotions, however, are aimed at increasing **selective demand,** the desire for a specific brand. PepsiCo, for instance, wants consumers to choose its lemon-lime soft drink brand, Sierra Mist. To help jump-start sales, it has tied Sierra Mist to the promotion of the popular film *Shrek 2,* uses radio ads containing sound bites from old comedy routines, and ran a $10 million promotion with cable channel Comedy Central, offering big prizes like 42-inch plasma TVs and sets of Comedy Central DVDs. The overriding theme of the promotions, according to Pepsi's vice president of marketing for flavored soft drinks, is comedy. "We felt that comedy was an ownable property for Sierra Mist. No one else is doing it."[7]

DIFFERENTIATE THE PRODUCT

A frequent objective of the firm's promotional efforts is **product differentiation.** Homogeneous demand for many products results when consumers regard the firm's output as virtually identical to its competitors' products. In these cases, the individual firm has almost no control over marketing variables

figure 15.4

Pella: Differentiating Its Windows by Offering Window Fashion Options

WWW.PELLA.COM.

such as price. A differentiated demand schedule, in contrast, permits more flexibility in marketing strategy, such as price changes.

At first glance, windows from one company may seem about the same as those from any other. But Pella seeks to differentiate its windows by demonstrating its built-in remote-control window blinds. Figure 15.4 shows the promotional message of Pella's window fashion options.

Surveys focusing on the Internet experience often list pop-up ads as the most annoying online experience. So marketers at Atlanta-based EarthLink came up with an idea: offer subscribers software to block them. Although the 4.9 million subscribers to the U.S.'s No. 3 Internet service provider sound like small change in an industry dominated by industry giant AOL, EarthLink based its recent market growth strategy on offering a solution to the estimated 4.8 billion ads that pop up on computer screens worldwide every month.[8]

ACCENTUATE THE PRODUCT'S VALUE

Promotion can explain the greater ownership utility of a product to buyers, thereby accentuating its value and justifying a higher price in the marketplace. This objective benefits both consumer and business products. A firm's promotional messages must build brand image and equity and at the same time deliver a "call to action." Advertising typically offers reasons a good or service fits into the consumer's lifestyle. Today, consumers everywhere value their time; the challenge for marketers is to demonstrate how their products will make their lives better.

Best Western and Shell recently teamed up in a "Sleep and Win" promotion in which Best Western hotel guests received a scratch-and-win card offering one of 15 Jaguars and Ford Explorers, free or discounted room nights, or gas coupons redeemable at more than 10,000 Shell stations. Ramada countered with a "Getaway for Life Sweepstakes" in which guests staying at Ramada Inns had a chance to win an annual weeklong vacation at any Ramada for life.[9]

1. How does promotion help provide information to consumers?
2. What effect can promotion have on demand? on sales?
3. What does it mean to differentiate a product through promotion?

STABILIZE SALES

For the typical firm, sales are not uniform throughout the year. Sales fluctuations may result from cyclical, seasonal, or irregular demand. Stabilizing these variations is often an objective of promotional strategy. Coffee sales, for example, follow a seasonal pattern, with purchases and consumption increasing during the winter months. To stimulate summer sales of Sanka brand decaffeinated coffee, General Foods created ads that include a recipe for instant iced coffee, promoting it as a refreshing, caffeine-free summer beverage. Hotels and motels often seek to supplement high occupancy during the week from business travelers by promoting special weekend packages with lower room rates. Some firms sponsor sales contests during slack periods that offer prizes to sales personnel who meet goals.

4 Identify the different elements of the promotional mix and explain how marketers develop an optimal promotional mix.

promotional mix Subset of the marketing mix in which marketers attempt to achieve the optimal blending of the elements of personal and nonpersonal selling to achieve promotional objectives.

ELEMENTS OF THE PROMOTIONAL MIX

Like the marketing mix, the promotional mix requires a carefully designed blend of variables to satisfy the needs of a company's customers and achieve organizational objectives. The **promotional mix** works like a subset of the marketing mix, with its product, distribution, promotion, and pricing elements. With the promotional mix, the marketers attempt to create an optimal blend of various elements to achieve promotional objectives. The components of the promotional mix are personal selling and nonpersonal selling, including advertising, sales promotion, direct marketing, public relations, and guerilla marketing.

Personal selling, advertising, and sales promotion usually account for the bulk of a firm's promotional expenditures. However, direct marketing, guerilla marketing, sponsorships, and public relations also contribute to integrated marketing communications. Later sections of this chapter examine the use of guerilla marketing, sponsorships, and direct marketing, and Chapters 16 and 17 present detailed discussions of the other elements. This section defines the elements and reviews their advantages and disadvantages.

personal selling Interpersonal influence process involving a seller's promotional presentation conducted on a person-to-person basis with the buyer.

PERSONAL SELLING

Personal selling is the oldest form of promotion, dating back as far as the beginning of trading and commerce. Traders vastly expanded both market sizes and product varieties as they led horses and camels along the Silk Road from China to Europe roughly between 300 B.C.E. and A.D. 1600, conducting personal selling at both ends. Personal selling may be defined as a seller's promotional presentation conducted on a person-to-person basis with the buyer. This direct form of promotion may be conducted face-to-face, over the telephone, through videoconferencing, or through interactive computer links between the buyer and seller. Today, about 14 million people in the U.S. are employed in personal selling, and the average sales call costs about $300.

nonpersonal selling Promotion that includes advertising, sales promotion, direct marketing, guerilla marketing, and public relations—all conducted without being face-to-face with the buyer.

NONPERSONAL SELLING

Nonpersonal selling includes advertising, product placement, sales promotion, direct marketing, guerilla marketing, and public relations. Advertising and sales promotion are usually regarded as the most important forms of nonpersonal selling. About one-third of marketing dollars spent on nonpersonal selling activities are allocated for media advertising; the other two-thirds fund trade and consumer sales promotions.

advertising Any paid, nonpersonal communication through various media about a business firm, not-for-profit organization, product, or idea by a sponsor identified in a message that is intended to inform or persuade members of a particular audience.

Advertising

Advertising is any paid, nonpersonal communication through various media about a business firm, not-for-profit organization, product, or idea by a sponsor identified in a message that is intended to inform or persuade members of a particular audience. It is a major promotional mix component for thousands of organizations. Mass consumption and geographically dispersed markets make advertising particularly appropriate for marketing goods and services aimed at large audiences likely to respond to the same promotional messages.

Advertising primarily involves the mass media, such as newspapers, television, radio, magazines, and billboards, but also includes electronic and computerized forms of promotion such as Web commercials, CDs and videotapes, and video screens in supermarkets. The rich potential of the Internet as an advertising channel to reach millions of people one at a time has attracted the attention of companies large and small, local and international. In fact, some forms of advertising are becoming ubiquitous, as the accompanying "Solving an Ethical Controversy" feature suggests.

The codfish lays ten thousand eggs,

The homely hen lays one.

The codfish never cackles

To tell you what she's done.

And so we scorn the codfish,

While the humble hen we prize.

Which only goes to show you

That it pays to advertise.

Anonymous

Product Placement

Product placement is a form of nonpersonal selling in which the marketer pays a motion picture or television program owner a fee to display his or her product prominently in the film or show. The practice gained attention more than two decades ago in the movie *E.T.: The Extra-Terrestrial* when Elliott, the boy who befriends E.T., lays out a trail of Reese's Pieces for the extraterrestrial to follow, to draw the alien from his hiding place. Product sales for Reese's Pieces candies went through the roof. (Interestingly, this was not the moviemaker's first choice of candy; Mars turned down the opportunity to have its M&Ms appear in the film.) Fees charged to marketers for such placements have grown significantly since then, and most studios employ specialists to market them to relevant product suppliers.

Few product placement deals involve the product as much as the Lincoln Navigator in the recent comedy *Johnson Family Vacation.* Ford's marketing goal was to showcase the redesigned SUV and highlight its dual role as a family vehicle that also appeals to a younger crowd. As Ford brand entertainment manager Miles Romero points out, "We sell the Navigator to a range of people, a lot of rap stars and

Solving an Ethical Controversy

CAPTIVE ADVERTISING

Ads are everywhere, and sometimes you can't avoid them. Marketers are working harder than ever to reach consumers who increasingly rely on TiVo to tune out mainstream ads running on cable and network TV with the flick of a switch on their remote. Using a strategy called *captive advertising,* marketers are placing ads in office elevators, stores, movie theaters, cabs and buses, golf courses, and even on the telephone. When you're "on hold," you're likely to be hit with advertising messages that you can't hang up on without losing your place in the queue of calls waiting to be answered. Montreal-based Zoom Media places audio ads triggered by infrared motion detectors in the restrooms of trendy restaurants. The head of the firm's U.S. operations sums up the appeal of his advertising approach this way: "The base appeal of this trend is that the audience can't opt out."

A recent class-action suit was brought against Loews Cineplex Entertainment Group, alleging that the company gives false start times for films because it screens the ads first instead.

SHOULD CAPTIVE ADVERTISING BE REGULATED?

PRO

1. It is becoming intrusive and annoying.
2. In cases like the showing of ads before a feature film, the practice is actually deceptive.

CON

1. Research shows the ads are effective.
2. Most consumers don't really mind them.

SUMMARY

Marketers show no signs of backing away from their increasing commitment to captive advertising. The market for ads in movie theaters alone is worth about $250 million a year, and although this form of advertising is particularly difficult for viewers to avoid, many survey respondents in the coveted 12- to 24-year age groups say they don't really mind the ads. That might be because other research shows most audiences generally tune them out after the first couple of minutes.

Sources: American Indoor Advertising, "Advertising to a Captive Audience," http://www.indoorads.com/, accessed May 15, 2004; Chester Dawson, "Coming Soon: More Big-Screen Ads," *BusinessWeek,* July 14, 2003, p. 44; Michele Orecklin, "Captive Marketing: There's No Escape," *Time* special "Inside Business" section, June 2003; "A Silly Lawsuit on Cinema Ads," editorial, *Advertising Age,* March 3, 2003, p. 22; Wayne Friedman, "Cinema-Ad Lawsuit Could Chill Business," *Advertising Age,* February 24, 2003, p. 4.

celebrities, as well as yuppies and families." As Figure 15.5 shows, the SUV, in which much of the on-screen action occurs, even has a character name: Mr. Hip-Hop.[10]

Sales Promotion

sales promotion Marketing activities other than personal selling, advertising, guerilla marketing, and public relations that stimulate consumer purchasing and dealer effectiveness.

Sales promotion consists of marketing activities other than personal selling, advertising, guerilla marketing, and public relations that stimulate consumer purchasing and dealer effectiveness. This broad category includes displays, trade shows, coupons, contests, samples, premiums, product demonstrations, and various nonrecurring, irregular selling efforts. Sales promotion provides a short-term incentive, usually in combination with other forms of promotion, to emphasize, assist, supplement, or otherwise support the objectives of the promotional program. Restaurants, including those that serve fast food, often place certain items on the menu at a lower price "for a limited time only." Advertisements may contain coupons for free or discounted items for a specified period of time. Or companies may conduct sweepstakes for prizes such as new cars or vacations, which may even be completely unrelated to the products the companies are selling.

Movie promotional tie-ins are a classic example. However, many companies that used to be involved with sales promotions, advertising, and tie-ins with movies are finding that they no longer get

figure 15.5
Product Placement: Displaying Products in Motion Pictures and Television Programs

the return they were hoping for. Taco Bell, which lost money on promotions tied to recent releases in the six-film *Star Wars* series, recently decided to abandon movie characters and focus its promotion on featuring expanded menu offerings. "It's less risky than tying in with a movie that may or may not be a hit—or might not help your product, even if it is," explains vice president Amy Sherwood.[11]

Sales promotion geared to marketing intermediaries is called **trade promotion.** Companies spend about as much on trade promotion as on advertising and consumer-oriented sales promotion combined. Trade promotion strategies include offering free merchandise, buyback allowances, and merchandise allowances along with sponsorship of sales contests to encourage wholesalers and retailers to sell more of certain products or product lines.

Direct Marketing

Another element in a firm's integrated promotional mix is **direct marketing,** the use of direct communication to a consumer or business recipient designed to generate a response in the form of an order (direct order), a request for further information (lead generation), or a visit to a place of business to purchase specific goods or services (traffic generation). While many people equate direct marketing with direct mail, this promotional category also includes telephone marketing (telemarketing), direct-response advertising and infomercials on television and radio, direct-response print advertising, and electronic media.

direct marketing Direct communications, other than personal sales contacts, between buyer and seller, designed to generate sales, information requests, or store or Web site visits.

Public Relations and Publicity

Public relations refer to a firm's communications and relationships with its various publics. These publics include customers, suppliers, stockholders, employees, the government, the general public, and the society in which the organization operates. Public relations programs can conduct either formal or informal contacts. The critical point is that every organization, whether or not it has a formally organized program, must be concerned about its public relations.

public relations Firm's communications and relationships with its various publics.

Publicity is the marketing-oriented aspect of public relations. It can be defined as nonpersonal stimulation of demand for a good, service, person, cause, or organization through unpaid placement of significant news about it in a published medium or through a favorable presentation of it on the radio, television, or stage. Compared with personal selling, advertising, and even sales promotion, expenditures for public relations are usually low in most firms. Since companies do not pay for publicity, they have less control over the publication by the press or electronic media of good or bad company news. But this often means that consumers find this type of news source more believable than if the information were disseminated directly by the company. Of course, bad publicity can damage a company's reputation and diminish brand equity.

Sometimes bad publicity can have unintended consequences. The furor over singer Janet Jackson's "wardrobe malfunction" during the Super Bowl halftime show did more than fail to boost sales of her just-released album. It also spurred both congressional hearings and a federal investigation of indecency and, in response to threats by the Federal Trade Commission to levy large fines on future violators, prompted Clear Channel Communications to fire its highly publicized shock-jock Howard Stern.[12]

Guerilla Marketing

guerilla marketing Unconventional, innovative, and low-cost marketing techniques designed to get consumers' attention in unusual ways.

Guerilla marketing uses unconventional, innovative, and low-cost techniques to attract consumers' attention. It is a relatively new approach used by marketers whose firms are underfunded for a full marketing program. Many of these firms can't afford the huge costs involved in the orthodox media of print and broadcasting, so they need to find an innovative, low-cost way to reach their market. But some large companies, like PepsiCo, engage in guerilla marketing as well. It launched Code Red, a cherry-flavored extension of the Mountain Dew line. After focus group interviews revealed that young, urban, and ethnic consumers—especially Hispanics—preferred cherry-flavored beverages and liked the name Code Red more than other suggested alternatives, PepsiCo's ad agency came up with a rap radio jingle called "Crack the Code" and placed ads in hip-hop magazines *Vibe* and the *Source.* Despite the difficulty of standing out in an already saturated soft-drink market, PepsiCo marketers avoided mass marketing and stuck to guerilla marketing. Soon Code Red became the fifth most popular soft drink sold in convenience stores. Charles Taylor-Hines, PepsiCo's director of urban and ethnic marketing, explained the success of Code Red this way: "With the urban youth audience, you really have to gain street credibility first, and you can't do that with a typical mass-marketing campaign."[13]

Toyota Motor Co. turned to guerilla marketing when it decided to target its new Scion to first-car buyers in their 20s. The company handed out branded merchandise carrying the scion.com Web address at public events, and during the first six weeks of the product launch, 158,000 people configured their own Scion online. Also included in the nationwide rollout were "street teams" who drove around in Scions and passed out promotional items at small gatherings of between 300 and 1,000 people. The company's marketers hoped to develop a closer relationship with its potential customers that way. Toyota also sponsored an "Installation" art tour, Scion Hot Import Nights at car customization events, and a Scion DJ Contest in various cities across the U.S. The goal of these efforts was to attract attention and create a buzz among consumers for the new vehicle.[14]

Guerilla marketers often use the Internet and other technology such as cell phones to reach customers one on one. In a campaign to promote its Above the Rim brand of basketball shoes and apparel, Reebok International created a "Whodunit?" online mystery game. Participants had to figure out which of four seasoned NBA players had bested a rookie opponent with their slick moves. The Web site periodically posted clues such as a sneaker print or handprint on its virtual basketball court. People who solved the mystery were entered in a sweepstakes to view the filming of a new Above the Rim TV commercial. Reebok marketers reported that traffic to their site doubled during the promotion, and 97,000 people participated in the game. Better yet, the online visitors spent nearly one-third more time at the site than nonparticipants—raising the brand's visibility, which was the goal of the campaign.[15]

The results of guerilla marketing can be funny and outrageous—even offensive to some people. But they almost always get consumers' attention. Some guerilla marketers stencil their company and product names anywhere graffiti might appear. Street artists are hired to plaster company and product logos on blank walls or billboards. Ethical issues of cluttering public spaces aside, the messages do seem to draw interest.

As Table 15.2 indicates, each type of promotion has both advantages and shortcomings. Although personal selling entails a relatively high per-contact cost, it involves less wasted effort than do nonpersonal forms of promotion such as advertising. Personal selling often provides more flexible promotion than the other forms because the salesperson can tailor the sales message to meet the unique needs—or objections—of each potential customer.

The major advantages of advertising come from its ability to create instant awareness of a good, service, or idea; build brand equity; and deliver the marketer's message to mass audiences for a relatively low cost per contact. Major disadvantages include the difficulty in measuring advertising effectiveness and high media costs. Sales promotions, by contrast, can be more accurately monitored and measured than advertising, produce immediate consumer responses, and provide short-term sales increases. Direct marketing gives potential customers an action-oriented choice, permits narrow audi-

table 15.2 **Comparison of the Six Promotional Mix Elements**

	PERSONAL SELLING	ADVERTISING	SALES PROMOTION	DIRECT MARKETING	PUBLIC RELATIONS	GUERILLA MARKETING
Advantages	Permits measurement of effectiveness Elicits an immediate response Tailors the message to fit the customer	Reaches a large group of potential consumers for a relatively low price per exposure Allows strict control over the final message Can be adapted to either mass audiences or specific audience segments	Produces an immediate consumer response Attracts attention and creates product awareness Allows easy measurement of results Provides short-term sales increases	Generates an immediate response Covers a wide audience with targeted advertising Allows complete, customized, personal message Produces measurable results	Creates a positive attitude toward a product or company Enhances credibility of a product or company	Is low cost Attracts attention because it is innovative Is less cluttered with competitors trying the same thing
Disadvantages	Relies almost exclusively upon the ability of the salesperson Involves high cost per contact	Does not permit totally accurate measurement of results Usually cannot close sales	Is nonpersonal in nature Is difficult to differentiate from competitors' efforts	Suffers from image problem Involves a high cost per reader Depends on quality and accuracy of mailing lists May annoy consumers	May not permit accurate measurement of effect on sales Involves much effort directed toward non-marketing-oriented goals	May not reach as many people If the tactics are too outrageous, they may offend some people

ence segmentation and customization of communications, and produces measurable results. Public relations efforts such as publicity frequently offer substantially higher credibility than other promotional techniques. Guerilla marketing efforts can be innovative—and highly effective—at a low cost to marketers with limited funds, as long as the tactics are not too outrageous, but it is more difficult to reach people. The marketer must determine the appropriate blend of these promotional mix elements to effectively market the firm's goods and services.

1. **What is the promotional mix?**
2. **Differentiate between personal and nonpersonal selling.**
3. **How does publicity differ from public relations?**
4. **Why do marketers sometimes use guerilla marketing?**

SPONSORSHIPS

5 Describe the role of sponsorships and direct marketing in integrated marketing communications.

One of the hottest trends in promotion during the past 10 years offers marketers the ability to integrate several elements of the promotional mix. Commercial sponsorships of an event or activity apply personal selling, advertising, sales promotion, and public relations in achieving specific promotional goals. These sponsorships, which link events with sponsors and with media ranging from TV and radio to print and the Internet, have become a $30 billion worldwide business.

sponsorship
Event/sponsor relationship in which an organization provides funds or in-kind resources to an event or activity in exchange for a direct association with that event or activity.

As illustrated in the chapter opener, **sponsorship** occurs when an organization provides money or in-kind resources to an event or activity in exchange for a direct association with that event or activity. The sponsor purchases two things: (1) access to the activity's audience and (2) the image associated with the activity. Sponsorships typically involve advertising that includes print and broadcast ads, direct mail and sales promotion, publicity in the form of media coverage of the event, and personal selling at the event itself. They also involve relationship marketing, bringing together the event, its participants, the sponsoring firms, and their channel members and major customers. Marketers underwrite varying levels of sponsorships depending on the amount their companies wish to spend and the types of events.

SPONSORSHIP SPENDING

Global marketers have flocked to sponsorships as a means of reaching an increasingly segmented audience to leverage the equity of celebrities and sporting and entertainment events. In addition, an army of e-commerce firms found sponsorships to be a quick way to enhance—and in many cases, initiate—brand awareness. Sponsorships also provide a platform through which sports and entertainment properties can expand their programs and attract new partners. Even utilities and pharmaceutical firms that sell over-the-counter medication and prescription drugs are also increasing their activities. U.S. sponsorship spending on a national level—including sports, festivals, fairs, and touring attractions—reached a whopping $11 billion last year.[16]

These included not only big spenders like Anheuser-Busch and PepsiCo at events like the Olympics and the World Cup but also sponsors like New Balance Athletic Shoe Inc. and Domino's Pizza, which spend more modestly at smaller venues. Domino's, for instance, recently served as the exclusive pizza vendor for the World Ultimate Championships in Hawaii, generating double the business impact the company expected and solid brand exposure as well. New Balance sponsors many small walking and running races around the country as well as statewide amateur sports festivals in Maine and Massachusetts.[17]

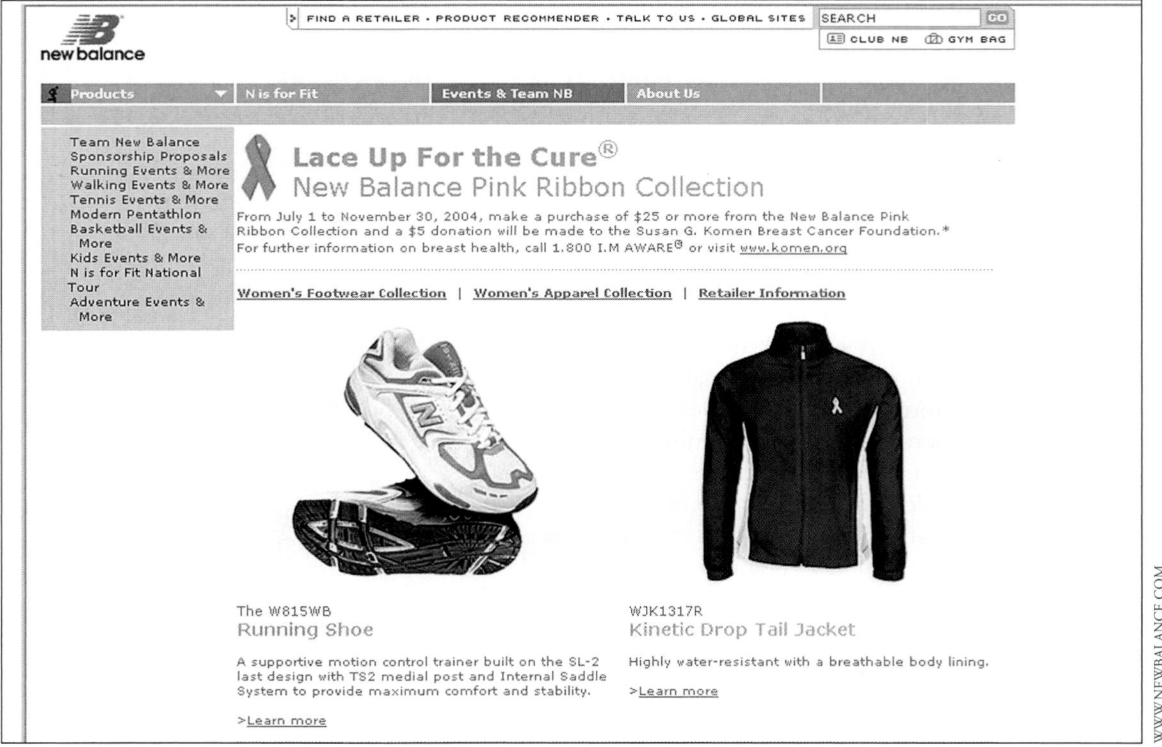

Sporting events often draw sponsors to fund their expenses. New Balance Shoes, Inc. sponsors many walking and running races around the United States, and they also donate money to the Susan G. Komen Breast Cancer Foundation through the sale of their "Pink Ribbon" collection of running gear.

Nowhere is sponsorship more prevalent than at sports events, and college sports draw particular interest from sponsors. The Coca-Cola Co. recently beat out archrival PepsiCo by inking an 11-year $500 million agreement with the National Collegiate Athletic Association and CBS to advertise and promote its products during NCAA championships. The sponsorship fee tripled the amount PepsiCo was paying.[18]

GROWTH OF SPONSORSHIPS

Commercial sponsorship of sporting and cultural events is not a new phenomenon. Aristocrats in ancient Rome sponsored gladiator competitions and chariot races featuring teams that were often supported financially by competing businesses. Over 2,000 years ago, wealthy Athenians underwrote drama, musical, and sporting festivals. Craft guilds in 14th century England sponsored plays (occasionally insisting that the playwrights insert "plugs" for their lines of work in the scripts). In the U.S. during the 1880s, local baseball teams were frequently sponsored by streetcar companies.

Sponsorship as a promotional alternative has grown rapidly over the past three decades. During this period, corporate sponsorship spending has increased faster than promotional outlays for advertising and sales promotion. Several factors have influenced the growth of commercial sponsorships:

- Government restrictions on tobacco and alcohol advertising and the growing reluctance of newspaper and magazine publishers to accept print ads for alcoholic beverages and tobacco products have led marketers to seek alternative promotional media. Although NASCAR ended its 31-year relationship with RJR Tobacco as title sponsor of the Winston Cup Series in 2003 when it selected wireless communications giant Nextel as title sponsor of the Nextel Cup series, it is seriously considering ending its ban on alcoholic beverage companies as team sponsors.
- Escalating costs of traditional advertising media make commercial sponsorships cost-effective promotional alternatives.
- Additional opportunities resulting from diverse leisure activities, as well as the increasing array of sporting events featured on television and in newspapers and magazines, allow marketers to target specific audiences.
- Greater media coverage of sponsored events allows sponsors to gain improved exposure from their investment.
- Global marketers recognize sponsorship as an effective way to reach an international audience in a manner that is universally understood.
- The proven effectiveness of a sponsorship that is properly planned and executed can generate productive marketing contacts. Sponsorships also represent alternatives to the increased clutter associated with advertising and direct mail.

The most puzzling thing about TV is the steady advance of the sponsor across the line that has always separated news from promotion, entertainment from merchandizing. The advertiser has assumed the role of originator and the performer has gradually been eased into the role of peddler.

E. B. White (1899–1985)
American author and editor

It is important to note that today's sponsorships cover a broad base, including events and programs that fall into the category of socially responsible activities. Companies and nonprofit organizations may sponsor reading programs, child-care programs, programs to help small or minority-owned businesses get started, as well as humanitarian programs like the Make-a-Wish Foundation® and cultural events such as free classical concerts.

HOW SPONSORSHIP DIFFERS FROM ADVERTISING

Even though sponsorship spending and traditional advertising spending represent forms of nonpersonal selling, their differences outnumber their similarities. Chief among these differences are the sponsor's degree of control versus that of advertising, the nature of the message, audience reaction, and measurements of effectiveness.

Marketers have considerable control over the quantity and quality of market coverage when they advertise. Sponsors, on the other hand, must rely on signs to present their messages. Also, they have little control of sponsored events beyond matching the audiences to profiles of their own target markets. In addition, sponsorship is a mute, nonverbal medium since the message is delivered in association with an activity possessing its own personality in the eyes of its audience. By contrast, a traditional

TV exposure is so important to our program and so important to this university that we will schedule ourselves to fit the medium. I'll play at midnight, if that's what TV wants.

Paul W. "Bear" Bryant (1913–1983)

American college football coach

advertisement allows the marketer to create an individual message containing an introduction, a theme, and a conclusion.

Audiences react differently to sponsorship as a communications medium than to other media. The sponsor's investment provides a recognizable benefit to the sponsored activity that the audience can appreciate. As a result, sponsorship is often viewed more positively than traditional advertising. Some marketers have tried to take advantage of this fact by practicing **ambush marketing,** in which a firm that is not an official sponsor tries to link itself to a major international event, such as the Olympics or a concert tour by a musical group. While it might be tempting to assume that smaller firms with limited marketing budgets would be most likely to engage in ambush marketing, this is not always the case. At a recent World Cup soccer match, television cameras panned hordes of cheering spectators wearing caps bearing the Samsung logo. Samsung was not the official sponsor for the match; its competitor Philips Electronics was.[19] While passing out logo-bearing hats is not illegal, some ambush practices clearly are. If a nonsponsor used the Olympic rings in an advertisement, the ad would be an illegal use of a trademark.

ASSESSING SPONSORSHIP RESULTS

To assess the results of sponsorships, marketers utilize some of the same techniques by which they measure advertising effectiveness. However, the differences between the two promotional alternatives often necessitate some unique research techniques as well. A few corporate sponsors attempt to link expenditures to sales. Kraft General Foods, for example, evaluates the effectiveness of its NASCAR sponsorship by comparing Country Time lemonade sales in the races' core southeastern U.S. markets with sales in other markets. Other sponsors measure improved brand awareness and image as effectiveness indicators; they conduct traditional surveys before and after the events to secure this information. Still other sponsors measure the impact of their event marketing in public relations terms. Typically, a researcher will count press clippings featuring a sponsor's name or logo and then translate this number into equivalent advertising costs.

Despite the impressive visibility of special events like soccer's World Cup and football's Super Bowl, these events do not necessarily lead directly to increased sales. Marketers want their brands to be associated with characteristics of the sporting event such as speed, accuracy, precision, and teamwork. They want to be included in the weeklong publicity that surrounds the $2.5 million they spend for each 30-second ad. Ideally, viewers will then argue that their ads were among the best for several days after the event.

1. Define *sponsorship.*
2. What are some factors that have speeded the growth of commercial sponsorships?

DIRECT MARKETING

Few promotional mix elements are growing as fast as direct marketing. Overall media spending for direct marketing initiatives such as interactive electronic media, direct mail, telemarketing, infomercials, and direct-response advertising totals more than $1.7 trillion a year.[20] Both business-to-consumer and business-to-business marketers rely on this promotional mix element to generate orders or sales leads (requests for more information) that may result in future orders. Direct marketing also helps increase store traffic—visits to the store or office to evaluate and perhaps purchase the advertised goods or services.

Direct marketing opens new international markets of unprecedented size. Electronic marketing channels have become the focus of direct marketers, and Web marketing is international marketing. Even direct mail and telemarketing will grow outside the U.S. as commerce becomes more global. Consumers in Europe and Japan are proving to be responsive to direct marketing. But most global marketing systems remain undeveloped, and many are almost dormant. The growth of international direct marketing is being spurred by marketing operations born in the U.S.

Direct marketing communications pursue goals beyond creating product awareness. Marketers want direct marketing to persuade people to place an order, request more information, visit a store, call a toll-free number, or respond to an e-mail message. In other words, successful direct marketing should prompt consumers to take action. Since direct marketing is interactive, marketers can tailor individual responses to meet consumers' needs. They can also measure the effectiveness of their efforts more easily than with advertising and other forms of promotion. Direct marketing is a very powerful tool that helps organizations win new customers and enhance relationships with existing ones.

The growth of direct marketing parallels the move toward integrated marketing communications in many ways. Both respond to fragmented media markets and audiences, growth in customized products, shrinking network broadcast audiences, and the increasing use of databases to target specific markets. Lifestyles also play a role because today's busy consumers want convenience and shopping options that save them time.

Databases are an important part of direct marketing. Using the latest technology to create sophisticated databases, a company can select a narrow market segment and find good prospects within that segment based on desired characteristics. Marketers can cut costs and improve returns on dollars spent by identifying customers who are most likely to respond to messages and by eliminating others from their lists who are not likely to respond. In fact, mining information about customers is a trend boosted by the growth of e-commerce. DNA software from Austin, Texas-based Smart Technologies can create profiles of customers, suppliers, and business partners by analyzing their movements on a Web site.

DIRECT MARKETING COMMUNICATIONS CHANNELS

As Figure 15.6 indicates, direct marketing uses many different media forms. Each works best for certain purposes, although marketers often combine two or more media in one direct marketing program. As long as it complies with current "do not call" regulations, a company might start with telemarketing to screen potential customers and then follow up by sending more material by direct mail to those who are interested.

DIRECT MAIL

direct mail Communications in the form of sales letters, postcards, brochures, catalogs, and the like conveying messages directly from the marketer to the customer.

As the amount of information about consumer lifestyles, buying habits, and wants continues to mount, direct mail has become a viable channel for identifying a firm's best prospects. Marketers gather information from internal and external databases, surveys, personalized coupons, and rebates that require responses. **Direct mail** is a critical tool in creating effective direct-marketing campaigns. It comes in many forms, ranging from sales letters, postcards, brochures, booklets, catalogs, and *house organs* (periodicals issued by organizations) to CDs, videotapes, and audiocassettes.

Direct mail offers advantages such as the ability to select a narrow target market, achieve intensive coverage, send messages quickly, choose from various formats, provide complete information, and personalize each mailing piece.

Response rates are measurable and higher than other types of advertising. In addition, direct mailings stand alone and do not compete for attention with magazine ads and radio and TV commercials. On the other hand, the per-reader cost of direct mail is high, effectiveness depends on the quality of the mailing list, and some consumers object strongly to what they consider "junk mail."

The anthrax scares following the 9/11 terrorist attacks caused a real disruption in many direct mail marketing efforts. According to a survey conducted by the Direct Marketing Association, one-third of all consumers were treating their mail with at least some suspicion. Some companies, such as the B2B software maker Commerce One, decided to abandon its traditional direct mail programs in favor of e-mail and, for its current customers, telemarketing. "Normally we would have used direct mail," explained vice president Bill Fraine. "But I don't think people are opening their mail." Still other mailers switched from letter-type mailings to postcards. Although the anthrax scare that followed the September 11 terrorist attacks disrupted the direct mail portion of the Nissan Altima IMC campaign

figure 15.6

Direct Marketing Sales by Media Category

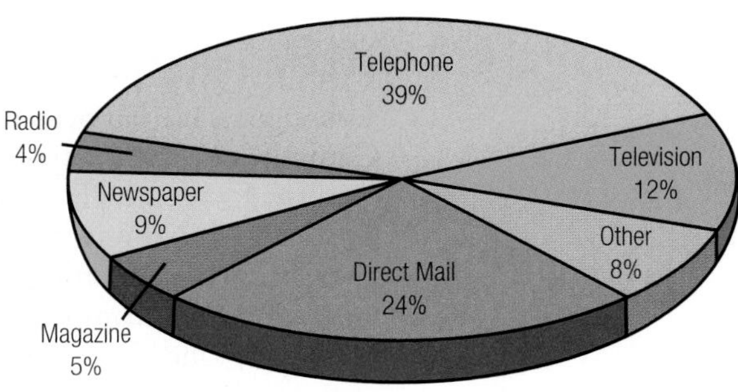

Note: Percentages do not total to 100 percent due to rounding.

Source: Data from the Direct Marketing Association, cited in Jack Feuer and David Kaplan, "A New Day for Direct Response: Once All but Ignored by Major Agencies, the Category Has Become a Media Hot Spot," *Adweek*, September 15, 2003.

because the firm sent unsolicited packages to prospective customers, marketers at Foot-Smart turned the problem into an opportunity. With the assistance of Caroline Ernst, director of e-commerce at the health-care products firm, they contacted customers in advance to alert them that the new Foot-Smart catalog was in the mail. As a result of this advance message, Foot-Smart saw a 20 percent increase in sales.[21]

CATALOGS

Catalogs have been a popular form of direct mail in the U.S. since the late 1800s. More than 10,000 different general and special-interest mail-order catalogs for household purchasers—and thousands more for business-to-business sales—find their way into almost every U.S. mailbox. In a typical year, they generate over $57 billion in consumer sales and $36 billion in business-to-business sales. On any given day, you might find a catalog from Patagonia, Crate & Barrel, Office Depot, Title IX, or Birkenstock in your mailbox. Catalogs fill so many segments that you could probably order just about anything you need for any facet of your life from a catalog.

Home improvement chain Home Depot recently entered the direct mail market by issuing its first-ever holiday catalog. The catalog featured 250 holiday items, ranging from power tools to small appliances, and is part of the retailer's expansion into other marketing channels. Similar to its stores, which provide do-it-yourselfers with classes on home improvement, the catalog also provided tips and ideas for home decorating.[22]

Many companies, such as L.L. Bean, Sears, and its Lands' End subsidiary, built their businesses and created a well-known image through their catalogs. More recently, however, catalog companies have expanded into Web sites, and some firms that traditionally depended totally on catalog orders have even opened retail stores to strengthen brand awareness and increase sales and market share. (Sears discontinued its catalog in favor of its retail stores but continued to use specialty catalogs and later bought Wisconsin-based catalog retailer Lands' End.) Sophisticated electronic technologies are changing catalog marketing. Today's catalogs can be updated quickly, providing consumers with the latest information and prices. CD-ROM catalogs allow marketers to display products in three-dimensional views and include video sequences of product demonstrations.

Most consumers have made at least some catalog purchases, but others—such as those who live in rural areas with little or no access to retail stores, shoppers seeking more variety than they can find at local retail stores, and busy professionals who do not have time to spend wandering store aisles—depend on them for much of their shopping needs. Although many consumers like to receive direct mail, others object to unsolicited communications. Some catalog companies do not understand their customers' needs and wants but instead send loads of catalogs to millions of people whether or not they want them. The 21st century consumer is time-pressed and overloaded with information. To help consumers escape the barrage of mail stuffed into their boxes, the Direct Marketing Association established its Mail Preference Service. This consumer service sends name removal forms to people who do not wish to receive direct mail advertising.[23]

TELEMARKETING

Although its use has been limited by a number of "do not call" restrictions enacted by the Federal Trade Commission, telemarketing remains the most frequently used form of direct marketing. It provides marketers with a high return on their expenditures, an immediate response, and the opportunity for personalized two-way conversations. In addition to business-to-consumer direct marketing, business-to-business telemarketing is another form of direct customer contact. Marketers at Xerox and long-distance telephone companies use telemarketing to develop sales leads. **Telemarketing** refers to direct marketing conducted entirely by telephone, and it can be classified as either outbound or inbound contacts. Outbound telemarketing involves a sales force that uses only the telephone to contact customers, reducing the cost of making personal visits. The customer initiates inbound telemarketing, typically by dialing a toll-free number that firms provide for customers to use at their convenience to obtain information and/or make purchases. Like direct mail, telemarketing taps into databases to target calls based on customer characteristics like family income, number of children, and home ownership.

New predictive dialer devices improve telemarketing's efficiency and reduce costs by automating the dialing process to skip busy signals and answering machines. When the dialer reaches a human voice, it instantaneously puts the call through to a salesperson. This technology is often combined with a print advertising campaign that features a toll-free number for inbound telemarketing.

Because recipients of both consumer and business-to-business telemarketing calls often find them annoying, the Federal Trade Commission passed a *Telemarketing Sales Rule* in 1996. The rule curtailed abusive telemarketing practices by establishing allowed calling hours (between 8 A.M. and 9 P.M.) and regulating call content. Companies must clearly disclose details of any exchange policies, maintain lists of people who do not want to receive calls, and keep records of telemarketing scripts, prize winners, customers, and employees for two years. This regulation was recently strengthened by the passage of amendments, creating the national *Do Not Call Registry.* The new rules prohibit telemarketing calls to anyone who has registered his or her phone number, restrict the number and duration of telemarketing calls generating dead air space with use of automatic dialers, crack down on unauthorized billing, and require telemarketers to transmit their caller ID information. Violators can be fined as much as $11,000 per occurrence. Exempt from these rules, however, are current customers, charities, opinion pollsters, and political candidates.

Unwanted telemarketing calls are intrusive, they are annoying, and they're all too common. When Americans are sitting down to dinner, or a parent is reading to his or her child, the last thing they need is a call from a stranger with a sales pitch.

George W. Bush (b. 1946)

43rd president of the United States (announcing implementation of the national Do Not Call Registry)

DIRECT MARKETING VIA BROADCAST CHANNELS

Broadcast direct marketing can take three basic forms: brief direct-response ads on television or radio, home shopping channels, and infomercials. Direct-response spots typically run 30, 60, or 90 seconds and include product descriptions and toll-free telephone numbers for ordering. Often shown on cable television and independent stations and tied to special-interest programs, broadcast direct marketing usually encourages viewers to respond immediately by offering them a special price or a gift if they call within a few minutes of an ad's airing. Radio direct-response ads also provide product descriptions and addresses or phone numbers to contact the sellers. However, radio often proves expensive compared with other direct marketing media, and listeners may not pay close enough attention to catch the number or may not be able to write it down because they are driving a car, which accounts for a major portion of radio listening time.

Home shopping channels like Quality Value Convenience (QVC), Home Shopping Network (HSN), and ShopNBC represent another type of television direct marketing. Broadcasting around the clock, these channels offer consumers a variety of products, including jewelry, clothing, skincare, home furnishings, computers, cameras, kitchen appliances, and toys. In essence, home shopping channels function like on-air catalogs. The channels also have Web sites that consumers can browse through to make purchases. In both cases, customers place orders via toll-free telephone numbers and pay for their purchases by credit card.

Infomercials are 30-minute or longer product commercials that resemble regular television programs. Because of their length, infomercials do not get lost as easily as 30-second commercials can, and they permit marketers to present their products in more detail. But they are usually shown at odd hours, and people often watch only portions of them. Think of how many times you have channel-surfed past an infomercial for Bow-flex, Victoria Principal's skincare line, or Ronco's rotisserie. Infomercials do provide toll-free telephone numbers so that viewers can order products or request more information. Although infomercials incur higher production costs than prime-time 30-second ads on national network TV, they generally air on less expensive cable channels and in late-night time slots on broadcast stations.

ELECTRONIC DIRECT MARKETING CHANNELS

Anyone who has ever logged on to the Web is abundantly aware of the growing number of commercial advertisements that now clutter their computer screen. Web advertising is a recurring theme throughout this text, corresponding to its importance as a component of the promotional mix. In fact, Chapter 4 explained the vital role e-commerce now plays in contemporary marketing practices. By 2006, Web companies will likely sell $8 billion in advertising, and that number grows with each new application of electronic technology.

Web advertising, however, is only one component of electronic direct marketing. E-mail direct marketers have found that traditional practices used in print and broadcast media are easily adapted to electronic messaging. You may be receiving periodic e-mail notices from your computer or software manufacturer about new products, special offers, software upgrades, or security patches that are

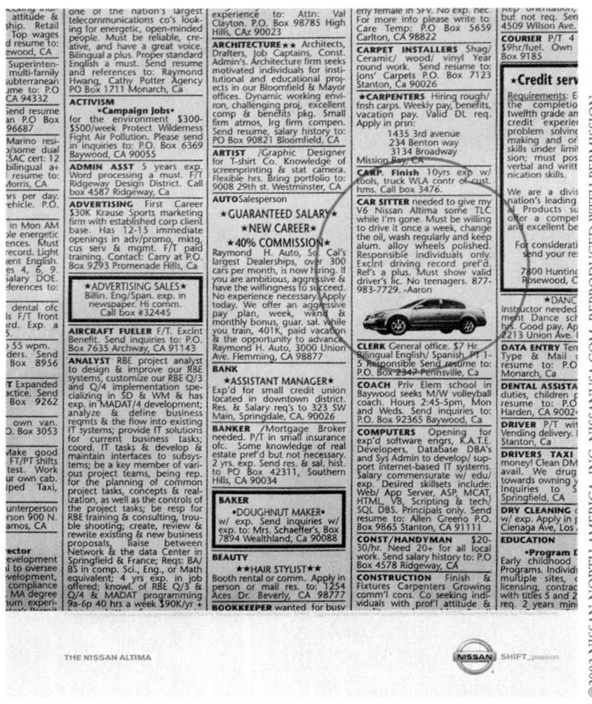

This Nissan promotional message attracts customers' attention by simulating a newspaper classified ad. Here the company is requesting a "car sitter" for its popular Nissan V6 Altima while the owner is away.

available. Antivirus program makers routinely provide new downloads with the latest protection via the Web and notify you by e-mail. Experts agree that the basic rules for online direct marketing mirror those of traditional practices. Any successful offline direct marketing campaign can be applied to e-mail promotions.

Electronic media deliver data instantly to direct marketers and help them track customer buying cycles quickly. As a result, they can place customer acquisition programs online for about 50 to 80 percent less than the cost of traditional programs. In the early years of the Internet, the most common products sold by online marketers were books, music CDs, wine, and gourmet foods. Today, however, there seems to be no limit to the variety of goods and services available to online shoppers. In fact, consumer-to-consumer sales through auction sites are quickly becoming the most popular avenue for direct online sales.

OTHER DIRECT MARKETING CHANNELS

Print media like newspapers and magazines do not support direct marketing as effectively as do Web marketing and telemarketing. However, print media and other traditional direct marketing channels are still critical to the success of all electronic media channels. Magazine ads with toll-free telephone numbers enhance inbound telemarketing campaigns. Companies can place ads in magazines or newspapers, include reader-response cards, or place special inserts targeted for certain market segments within the publications.

Kiosks provide another outlet for electronic sales. Verizon telecommunications customers in the western and eastern U.S. can pay their phone bills at Vcom electronic kiosks at their local 7-Eleven stores while they grab a cup of coffee or the daily newspaper. The purpose of these installations is to give customers who do not have Internet access at home the convenience and flexibility of online transactions. The kiosks offer ATM capabilities and touch-screen financial services such as check cashing and money-order purchasing 24 hours a day as well as the ability to view and pay their bills and view their phone service account. And customers can conduct their business in either English or Spanish.[24]

1. **Name at least five direct marketing channels.**
2. **What is direct mail?**
3. **Describe the most common electronic direct marketing channels.**

DEVELOPING AN OPTIMAL PROMOTIONAL MIX

By blending advertising, personal selling, sales promotion, and public relations to achieve marketing objectives, marketers create a promotional mix. Since quantitative measures are not available to determine the effectiveness of each mix component in a given market segment, the choice of an effective mix of promotional elements presents one of the marketer's most difficult tasks. Several factors influence the effectiveness of a promotional mix: (1) the nature of the market, (2) the nature of the product, (3) the stage in the product life cycle, (4) the price, and (5) the funds available for promotion.

NATURE OF THE MARKET

The marketer's target audience has a major impact on the choice of a promotion method. When a market includes a limited number of buyers, personal selling may prove a highly effective technique. However, markets characterized by large numbers of potential customers scattered over sizable geographic areas may make the cost of contact by personal salespeople prohibitive. In such instances, extensive use of advertising often makes sense. The type of customer also affects the promotional mix. Personal selling works better in a target market made up of industrial purchasers or retail and wholesale buyers than in a target market consisting of ultimate consumers. Similarly, pharmaceutical firms use large sales forces to sell prescription drugs directly to physicians and hospitals, but they also advertise to promote over-the-counter and prescription drugs for the consumer market. So, the drug firm must switch its promotional strategy from personal selling to consumer advertising based on the market it is targeting.

The Coca-Cola Co. and PepsiCo have both faced the need to change their market offerings in the face of changing consumer desires. Both companies are still big media spenders—Coca-Cola's annual advertising spending approaches $200 million, and PepsiCo spends well over $120 million.[25] Because baby boomers and seniors aren't drinking the amount of cola they once did, the cola giants are focusing on younger target markets. But changes in their traditional promotional mixes were necessary to reach these consumer groups. PepsiCo has run a highly successful series of splashy ads with pop star Beyoncé Knowles and did promotional tie-ins with Apple's new iTunes online music store and the WB television network through a summer concert series.[26] Both companies have addressed consumer demands for new drinks by focusing on new items: bottled water brands Aquafina and Dasani as well as a stable of noncarbonated drinks. PepsiCo has created a 100-person sales force to sell its noncarbonated drinks, such as Gatorade and Lipton iced teas.

NATURE OF THE PRODUCT

A second important factor in determining an effective promotional mix is the product itself. Highly standardized products with minimal servicing requirements usually depend less on personal selling than do custom products with technically complex features or requirements for frequent maintenance. Consumer products are more likely to rely heavily on advertising than are business products. PepsiCo, for instance, wants to keep up the momentum that's gathering behind its Sierra Mist soft drink brand. "We're completely investing in the brand," says Cie Nicholson, vice president of flavors for Pepsi-Cola North America. "We're not taking [our] foot off the gas." That means increasing spending on media advertising from $35 million the year it launched to $51 million during the first nine months of last year. Sierra Mist, seen in Figure 15.7, may have only 1 percent of the carbonated soft drink market, but that's nothing to sneeze at. It's right behind 7Up in the $6.5 billion lemon-lime product category.[27]

Promotional mixes vary within each product category. In the B2B market, for example, installations typically rely more heavily on personal selling than does marketing of operating supplies. In contrast, the promotional mix for a convenience product is likely to involve more emphasis on manufacturer advertising and less on personal selling. On the other hand, personal selling plays an important role in the promotion of shopping products, and both personal and nonpersonal selling are important in the promotion of specialty items. A personal-selling emphasis is also likely to prove more effective than other alternatives in promotions for products involving trade-ins.

STAGE IN THE PRODUCT LIFE CYCLE

The promotional mix must also be tailored to the product's stage in the product life cycle. In the introductory stage, both nonpersonal and personal selling are used to acquaint marketing intermediaries and final consumers with the merits of the new product. Heavy emphasis on personal selling helps inform the marketplace of the merits of the new good or service. Salespeople contact marketing intermediaries to secure interest in and commitment to handling the newly introduced item.

figure 15.7

The Refreshment of Sierra Mist's Lemon-Lime Flavor: Promotion Focusing on the Nature of the Product

WWW.SIERRAMIST.COM

figure 15.8

McDonald's Dollar Menu: Promotion Based on Price

USED WITH PERMISSION FROM MCDONALD'S CORPORATION

Trade shows are frequently used to inform and educate prospective dealers and ultimate consumers about its merits over current competitive offerings. Advertising and sales promotion are also used during this stage to create awareness, answer questions, and stimulate initial purchases.

As the good or service moves into the growth and maturity stages, advertising gains relative importance in persuading consumers to make purchases. Marketers continue to direct personal-selling efforts at marketing intermediaries in an attempt to expand distribution. As more competitors enter the marketplace, advertising begins to stress product differences to persuade consumers to purchase the firm's brand. In the maturity and early decline stages, firms frequently reduce advertising and sales promotion expenditures as market saturation is reached and newer products with their own competitive strengths begin to enter the market.

Mature products often require creative promotions to keep the product in the mind of the consumer. That's the case with Coke and Pepsi, as described earlier. Pepsi recently entered a partnership with Dell to run a technology-oriented Black History Month promotion, with merchandising displays in about 1,500 stores in the South and on the East Coast. Ten $10,000 college scholarships were offered in a sweepstakes, and other prizes included Dell computers, software, and Pepsi 12-packs. Premium giveaways included calendars and posters designed by African-American artists, and a section of the Pepsi Web site featured sweepstakes entry forms, the calendar and poster artwork with information about the artists, and information about African-American history. Second-year participation in the program was double the first, with more than 167,000 entries in the sweepstakes and 15 percent growth in sales volume for Pepsi.[28]

PRICE

The price of an item is the fourth factor that affects the choice of a promotional mix. Advertising dominates the promotional mixes for low-unit-value products due to the high per-contact costs in personal selling. These costs make the sales call an unprofitable tool in promoting most lower value goods and services. Advertising, in contrast, permits a low promotional expenditure per sales unit because it reaches mass audiences. McDonald's features the affordability of its Dollar Menu items in the promotional message "Get a lot for a little, every day" in Figure 15.8. For low-value consumer goods, such as chewing gum, soft drinks, and snack foods, advertising is the most feasible means of promotion. Even shopping products can be sold at least partly on the basis of price. On the other hand, consumers of high-priced items like luxury cars expect lots of well-presented information from qualified salespeople. High-tech direct marketing promotions like CDs and videocassettes, CD-ROMs, fancy brochures, and personal selling by informed, professional salespeople appeal to these potential customers.

1. How do the nature of the market and the nature of the product affect the choice of an optimal promotional mix?
2. What role does the product life cycle play in designing an appropriate promotional mix?
3. Why do low-priced goods rely heavily on advertising in the promotional mix?

FUNDS AVAILABLE FOR PROMOTION

A real barrier in implementing any promotional strategy is the size of the promotional budget. A single 30-second television commercial during the Super Bowl telecast costs an advertiser $2.5 million. While millions of viewers may see the commercial, making the cost per contact relatively low, such an expenditure exceeds the entire promotional budgets of thousands of firms, a catch-22 dilemma that at least partially explains how guerilla marketing got its start. And if a company wants to hire a celebrity to advertise its goods and services, the fee can run into the millions of dollars a year. Sometimes no amount of money is enough to win

table 15.3 Factors Influencing Choice of Promotional Mix

	Emphasis	
	PERSONAL SELLING	ADVERTISING
Nature of the market		
Number of buyers	Limited number	Large number
Geographic concentration	Concentrated	Dispersed
Type of customer	Business purchaser	Ultimate consumer
Nature of the product		
Complexity	Custom-made, complex	Standardized
Service requirements	Considerable	Minimal
Type of good or service	Business	Consumer
Use of trade-ins	Trade-ins common	Trade-ins uncommon
Stage in the product life cycle	Often emphasized at every stage; heavy emphasis in the introductory and early growth stages in acquainting marketing intermediaries and potential consumers with the new good or service	Often emphasized at every stage; heavy emphasis in the latter part of the growth stage, as well as the maturity and early decline stages, to persuade consumers to select specific brands
Price	High unit value	Low unit value

celebrity participation, however. Advertisers are still asking the remaining members of the rock group The Doors to allow one of their songs to be used as background music for a commercial. But staying true to the wishes of late lead singer Jim Morrison, the group continues to refuse all offers, even a bid of $1.5 million from Apple Computer to use "When the Music's Over."[29] Table 15.3 summarizes the factors that influence the determination of an appropriate promotional mix.

PULLING AND PUSHING PROMOTIONAL STRATEGIES

6 **Contrast the two major alternative promotional strategies.**

Marketers may implement essentially two promotional alternatives: a pulling strategy or a pushing strategy. A **pulling strategy** is a promotional effort by the seller to stimulate final-user demand, which then exerts pressure on the distribution channel. When marketing intermediaries stock a large number of competing products and exhibit little interest in any one of them, a firm may have to implement a pulling strategy to motivate them to handle its product. In such instances, this strategy is implemented with the objective of building consumer demand so that consumers will request the product from retail stores. Advertising and sales promotion often contribute to a company's pulling strategy.

pulling strategy Promotional effort by the seller to stimulate final-user demand, which then exerts pressure on the distribution channel.

In contrast, a **pushing strategy** relies more heavily on personal selling. Here the objective is promoting the product to the members of the marketing channel rather than to final users. To achieve this goal, marketers employ cooperative advertising allowances to channel members, trade discounts, personal selling efforts by salespeople, and other dealer supports. Such a strategy is designed to gain marketing success for the firm's products by motivating representatives of wholesalers and/or retailers to spend extra time and effort promoting the products to customers. About half of manufacturers' promotional budgets are allocated for cash incentives used to encourage retailers to stock their products.

pushing strategy Promotional effort by the seller directed to members of the marketing channel rather than final users.

Timing also affects the choice of promotional strategies. The relative importance of advertising and selling changes during the various phases of the purchase process. Prior to the actual sale, advertising usually is more important than personal selling. However, one of the primary advantages of a successful advertising program is the support it gives the salesperson who approaches the prospective buyer for the first time. Selling activities are more important than advertising at the time of purchase.

Personal selling provides the actual mechanism for closing most sales. In the postpurchase period, advertising regains primacy in the promotional effort. It affirms the customer's decision to buy a particular good or service and—as pointed out in Chapter 5—reminds him or her of the product's favorable qualities by reducing any cognitive dissonance that might occur.

The promotional strategies used by auto marketers illustrate this timing factor. Car, truck, and SUV makers spend heavily on consumer advertising to create awareness before consumers begin the purchase process. At the time of their purchase decisions, however, the personal-selling skills of dealer salespeople provide the most important tools for closing sales. Finally, advertising is used frequently to maintain postpurchase satisfaction by citing awards such as *Motor Trend*'s Car of the Year and results of J.D. Power's customer-satisfaction surveys to affirm buyer decisions.

MARKETING Concept Check

1. What is a pulling strategy?
2. What is a pushing strategy?

7 Explain how marketers budget for and measure the effectiveness of promotion.

BUDGETING FOR PROMOTIONAL STRATEGY

Promotional budgets may differ not only in amount but also in composition. Business-to-business marketers generally invest larger proportions of their budgets in personal selling than in advertising, while the reverse is usually true of most producers of consumer goods. Cannondale Associates, a leading U.S. sales and marketing consulting firm, conducts an annual survey of trade promotion spending in different industries. Figure 15.9 shows estimated 2005 allocations of promotional budgets by consumer packaged-goods manufacturers.

Evidence suggests that sales initially lag behind promotional expenses for structural reasons—funds spent filling up retail shelves, boosting low initial production, and supplying buyer information. This fact produces a threshold effect in which few sales may result from substantial initial investments in promotion. A second phase might produce sales proportionate to promotional expenditures—the most predictable range. Finally, promotion reaches the area of diminishing returns where an increase in promotional spending fails to produce a corresponding increase in sales.

For example, an initial expenditure of $40,000 may result in sales of 100,000 units for a consumer goods manufacturer. An additional $10,000 expenditure during the second phase may generate sales of 30,000 more units, and another $10,000 may produce sales of an additional 35,000 units. The cumulative effect of the expenditures and repeat sales will have generated increasing returns from the promotional outlays. However, as the advertising budget moves from $60,000 to $70,000, the marginal productivity of the additional expenditure may fall to 28,000 units. At some later point, the return may actually become zero or negative as competition intensifies, markets become saturated, and marketers employ less expensive advertising media.

figure 15.9

Allocation of Promotional Budgets for Consumer Packaged Goods

TRADE PROMOTION SPENDING AS A PERCENTAGE OF TOTAL PROMOTIONAL BUDGET — 2005 ESTIMATE

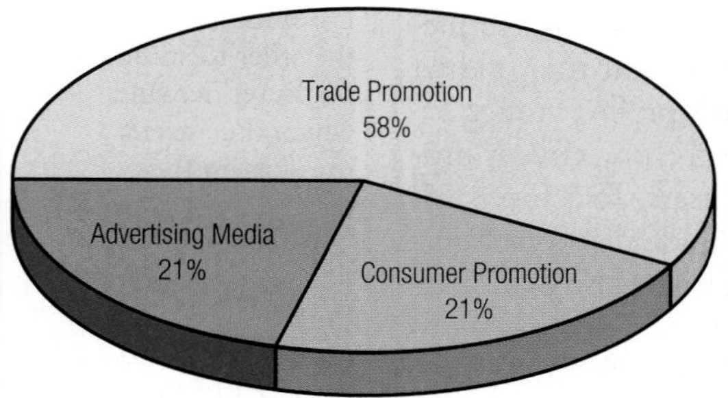

SOURCE: Data from Donnelley Marketing and Accenture Analysis, "Capturing and Sustaining Value Opportunities in Trade Promotion," accessed at the Accenture Web site, April 5, 2004, http://www.accenture.com. © 2004 Accenture. All rights reserved.

The ideal method of allocating promotional funds would increase the budget until the cost of each additional increment equals the additional incremental revenue received. In other words, the most effective allocation procedure increases promotional expenditures until each dollar of promotional expense is matched by an additional dollar of profit. This procedure—referred to as marginal analysis—maximizes the input's productivity. The difficulty arises in identifying the optimal point, which requires a precise balance between marginal expenses for promotion and the resulting marginal receipts. Traditional methods used for creating a promotional budget include the percentage-of-sales and fixed-sum-per-unit methods, along with techniques for meeting the competition and achieving task objectives. Each method is briefly examined in Table 15.4.

The **percentage-of-sales method** is perhaps the most common way of establishing promotional budgets. The percentage can be based on sales either from some past period (such as the previous year) or forecasted for a future period (the current year). While this plan is appealingly simple, it does not effectively support the achievement of basic promotional objec-

table 15.4 *Promotional Budget Determination*

METHOD	DESCRIPTION	EXAMPLE
Percentage-of-sales method	Promotional budget is set as a specified percentage of either past or forecasted sales.	"Last year we spent $10,500 on promotion and had sales of $420,000. Next year we expect sales to grow to $480,000, and we are allocating $12,000 for promotion."
Fixed-sum-per-unit method	Promotional budget is set as a predetermined dollar amount for each unit sold or produced.	"Our forecast calls for sales of 14,000 units, and we allocate promotion at the rate of $65 per unit."
Meeting competition method	Promotional budget is set to match competitor's promotional outlays on either an absolute or relative basis.	"Promotional outlays average 4 percent of sales in our industry."
Task-objective method	Once marketers determine their specific promotional objectives, the amount (and type) of promotional spending needed to achieve them is determined.	"By the end of next year, we want 75 percent of the area high school students to be aware of our new, highly automated fast-food prototype outlet. How many promotional dollars will it take, and how should they be spent?"

tives. Arbitrary percentage allocations can't provide needed flexibility. In addition, sales should depend on promotional allocation rather than vice versa.

The **fixed-sum-per-unit method** differs from budgeting based on a percentage of sales in only one respect: It allocates a predetermined amount to each sales or production unit. This amount can also reflect either historical or forecasted figures. Producers of high-value consumer durable goods, such as automobiles, often use this budgeting method.

Another traditional budgeting approach, **meeting competition,** simply matches competitors' outlays, either in absolute amounts or relative to the firms' market shares. But this method doesn't help a company gain a competitive edge. A budget that is appropriate for one company may not be appropriate for another.

The **task-objective method** develops a promotional budget based on a sound evaluation of the firm's promotional objectives. As a result, it attunes its allocation of funds to modern marketing practices. The method has two steps:

1. The firm's marketers must define realistic communication goals that they want the promotional mix to achieve. Say that a firm wants to achieve a 25 percent increase in brand awareness. This step quantifies the objectives that promotion should attain. These objectives in turn become integral parts of the promotional plan.
2. Then the company's marketers determine the amount and type of promotional activity required for each objective that they have set. Combined, these units become the firm's promotional budget.

A crucial assumption underlies the task-objective approach: Marketers can measure the productivity of each promotional dollar. That assumption explains why the objectives must be carefully chosen, quantified, and accomplished through promotional efforts. Generally, budgeters should avoid general marketing objectives such as, "We want to achieve a 5 percent increase in sales." A sale is a culmination of the effects of all elements of the marketing mix. A more appropriate promotional objective might be, "We want to achieve an 8 percent response rate from a targeted direct mail advertisement."

Promotional budgeting always requires difficult decisions. Still, recent research studies and the spread of computer-based models have made it a more manageable problem than it used to be.

1. **Compare the percentage-of-sales method of promotional budgeting with the fixed-sum-per-unit method.**
2. **Briefly describe setting a promotional budget by meeting the competition.**
3. **What is the task-objective budgeting method?**

MEASURING THE EFFECTIVENESS OF PROMOTION

It is widely recognized that part of a firm's promotional effort is ineffective. John Wanamaker, a leading 19th century retailer, expressed the problem this way: "Half the money I spend on advertising is wasted; the trouble is I don't know which half."

Evaluating the effectiveness of a promotion today is a far different exercise in marketing research than it was even a few decades ago. For years, marketers depended on store audits conducted by large organizations like ACNielsen. Other research groups conducted warehouse withdrawal surveys of shipments to retail customers. These studies were designed to determine whether sales had risen as a direct result of a particular promotional campaign. During the 1980s, the introduction of scanners and automated checkout lanes completely changed marketing research. For the first time, retailers and manufacturers had a tool to obtain sales data quickly and efficiently. The problem was that the collected data was used for little else other than determining how much of which product was bought at what price and at what time.

By the 1990s, marketing research entered another evolutionary period with the advent of the Internet. Now marketing researchers can delve into each customer's purchase behavior, lifestyle, preferences, opinions, and buying habits. All of this information can also be obtained in a matter of seconds. The next section explains the impact of electronic technologies on measuring promotional effectiveness. However, marketers today still depend on two basic measurement tools: direct sales results tests and indirect evaluations.

Most marketers would prefer to use a **direct sales results test** to measure the effectiveness of promotion. Such an approach would reveal the specific impact on sales revenues for each dollar of promotional spending. This type of technique has always eluded marketers, however, due to their inability to control other variables operating in the marketplace. A firm may receive $20 million in additional sales orders following a new $1.5 million advertising campaign, but the market success may really have resulted from the products benefiting from more intensive distribution as more stores decide to carry them or price increases for competing products rather than from the advertising outlays.

Marketers often encounter difficulty isolating the effects of promotion from those of other market elements and outside environmental variables. **Indirect evaluation** helps researchers to concentrate on quantifiable indicators of effectiveness, such as recall (how much members of the target market remember about specific products or advertisements) and readership (size and composition of a message's audience). The basic problem with indirect measurement is the difficulty in relating these variables to sales. Will the fact that many people read an ad lead directly to increased sales?

Marketers need to ask the right questions and understand what they are measuring. Promotion to build sales volume produces measurable results in the form of short-term returns, but brand-building programs and efforts to generate or enhance consumers' perceptions of value in a product, brand, or organization cannot be measured over the short term.

MEASURING ONLINE PROMOTIONS

The latest challenge facing marketers is how to measure the effectiveness of electronic media. Early attempts at measuring online promotional effectiveness involved counting hits (user requests for a file) and visits (pages downloaded or read in one session). But as Chapter 4 explained, it takes more than counting "eyeballs" to measure online promotional success. What matters is not how many times a Web site is visited but how many people actually buy something. Traditional numbers that work for other media forms are not necessarily relevant indicators of effectiveness for a Web site. For one thing, the Web combines both advertising and direct marketing. Web pages effectively integrate advertising and other content, such as product information, that may often prove to be the page's main—and most effective—feature. For another consideration, consumers generally choose the advertisements they want to see on the Net, whereas traditional broadcast or print media automatically expose consumers to ads.

One way that marketers measure performance is by incorporating some form of direct response into their promotions. This technique also helps them to compare different promotions for effectiveness and rely on facts rather than opinions. Consumers may say they will try a product when responding to a survey question yet not actually buy it. A firm may send out three different direct mail offers in the same promotion and compare response rates from the groups of recipients receiving each alternative. An offer to send for a sample may generate a 75 percent response rate, coupons might show a 50 percent redemption rate, and rebates might appeal to only 10 percent of the targeted group.

The two major techniques for setting Internet advertising rates are cost per impression and cost per response (click-throughs). **Cost per impression** is a measurement technique that relates the cost of an ad to every thousand people who view it. In other words, anyone who sees the page containing the banner or other form of ad creates one impression. This measure assumes that the site's principal purpose is to display the advertising message. **Cost per response (click-throughs)** is a direct marketing technique that relates the cost of an ad to the number of people who click it. Measurement based on click-throughs assumes that those who click an ad want more information and, therefore, consider the ad valuable. Both rating techniques have merit. Site publishers point out that click-through rates are influenced by the creativity of the ad's message. Advertisers, on the other hand, point out that the Web ad has value to those who click it for additional information.

1. What is the direct sales results test?
2. What is indirect evaluation?
3. What are two major ways of setting Internet advertising rates?

THE VALUE OF MARKETING COMMUNICATIONS

(8) Discuss the value of marketing communications.

The nature of marketing communications is changing as new formats transform the traditional idea of an advertisement or sales promotion. Sales messages are now placed subtly, or not so subtly, in movies and television shows, blurring the lines between promotion and entertainment and changing the traditional definition of advertising. Messages show up at the beach in the form of skywriting, in restrooms, on stadium turnstiles, buses, and even police cars.

Despite new tactics by advertisers, promotion has often been the target of criticism. Some people complain that it offers nothing of value to society and simply wastes resources. Others criticize promotion's role in encouraging consumers to buy unnecessary products that they cannot afford. Many ads seem to insult people's intelligence or offend their sensibilities, and they criticize the ethics—or lack thereof—displayed by advertisers and salespeople. Although 43 percent of U.S. teens surveyed report they like "a lot" the American Legacy Foundation "Truth" antismoking ads funded by $1.8 billion from the $246 billion settlement reached in 1998 between 46 state attorneys general and tobacco companies, many consumers worry that even antismoking ads are not only ineffective but also unethical in even mentioning smoking.[30]

Briefly Speaking

You can tell the ideals of a nation by its advertising.

Norman Douglas (1862–1952)
British author

New forms of promotion are considered even more insidious because marketers are designing promotions that bear little resemblance to paid advertisements. Many of these complaints cite issues that constitute real problems. Some salespeople use unethical sales tactics. Some product advertising hides its promotional nature or targets consumer groups that can least afford the advertised goods or services. Many television commercials do, in fact, contribute to the growing problem of cultural pollution. One area that has sparked both criticism and debate is promotion aimed at children.

While promotion can certainly be criticized on many counts, it also plays a crucial role in modern society. This point is best understood by examining the social, business, and economic importance of promotion.

SOCIAL IMPORTANCE

We live in a diverse society characterized by consumer segments with differing needs, wants, and aspirations. What one group finds tasteless may be quite appealing to another. But diversity is one

figure 15.10

Promotional Message Addressing an Important Social Concern: Absent Fathers

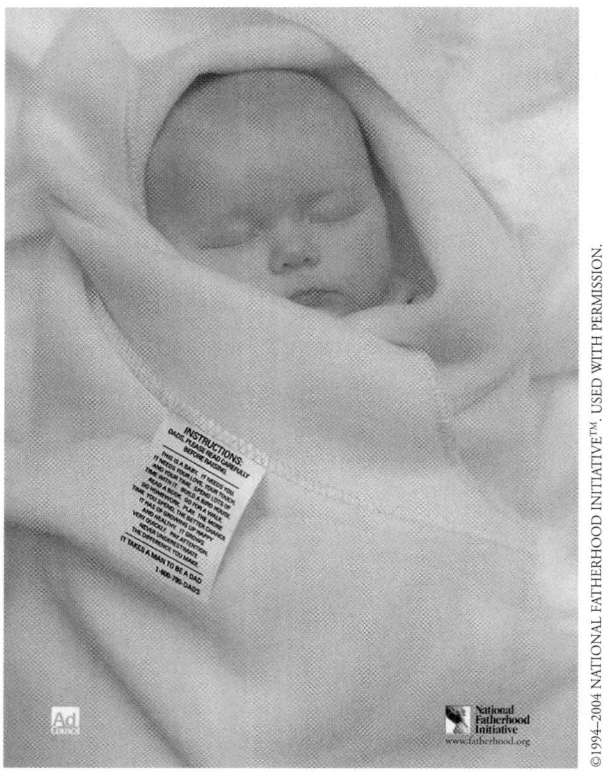

of the benefits of living in our society because it offers us many choices and opportunities. Promotional strategy faces an averaging problem that escapes many of its critics. The one generally accepted standard in a market society is freedom of choice for the consumer. Consumer buying decisions eventually determine acceptable practices in the marketplace, which is why consumers who criticize cigarette ads may also agree that it is acceptable for them to appear.

Promotion has also become an important factor in campaigns aimed at achieving social objectives, such as stopping drug abuse or supporting national parks. The mission of the 11-year-old National Fatherhood Initiative (NFI) is to improve the well-being of children by increasing the proportion of children growing up with involved, responsible, and committed fathers. Advertising agencies donate their expertise in creating **public service announcements (PSAs)** aimed at promoting such important causes as stopping drug abuse or supporting national parks. A good example of a PSA is the message shown in Figure 15.10, which is designed to educate and inspire all people, especially fathers, about their importance in a child's life and the negative outcomes of father's absence on their children. As the tag on the blanket states, "It takes a man to be a Dad."

Promotion performs an informative and educational task crucial to the functioning of modern society. As with everything else in life, what is important is how promotion is used rather than whether it is used.

BUSINESS IMPORTANCE

Promotional strategy has become increasingly important to both large and small business enterprises. The well-documented, long-term increase in funds spent on promotion certainly attests to management's faith in the ability of promotional efforts to encourage attitude changes, brand loyalty, and additional sales. It is difficult to conceive of an enterprise that would not attempt to promote its good or service in some manner. Most modern institutions simply cannot survive in the long run without promotion. Business must communicate with its publics.

Nonbusiness enterprises also recognize the importance of promotional efforts. The U.S. government spends about $300 million a year on advertising and ranks 36th among all U.S. advertisers. The Canadian government is the leading advertiser in Canada, promoting many concepts and programs. Religious organizations have acknowledged the importance of promotional channels to make their viewpoints known to the public at large.

ECONOMIC IMPORTANCE

Briefly Speaking

Early to bed, early to rise, work like hell, and advertise.

Laurence J. Peter (1919–1990)
American author

Promotion has assumed a degree of economic importance if for no other reason than because it provides employment for millions of people. More important, however, effective promotion has allowed society to derive benefits not otherwise available. For example, the criticism that promotion costs too much isolates an individual expense item and fails to consider its possible beneficial effects on other categories of expenditures.

Promotional strategies increase the number of units sold and permit economies of scale in the production process, thereby lowering the production costs for each unit of output. Lower unit costs allow lower consumer prices, which in turn make products available to more people. Similarly, researchers have found that advertising subsidizes the information contents of newspapers and the broadcast media. In short, promotion pays for many of the enjoyable entertainment and educational opportunities in contemporary life as it lowers product costs.

Strategic Implications of Marketing in the 21st Century

WITH the incredible proliferation of promotional messages in the media, today's marketers—who are also consumers themselves—must find new ways to reach customers without overloading them with unnecessary or unwanted communications. Guerilla marketing has emerged as an effective strategy for large and small companies, but ambush marketing has raised ethical concerns. Product placement has gained in popularity, but if movies and television shows become jammed with brands, marketers will have to find yet another venue for their messages. In addition, it is difficult to overstate the impact of the Internet on the promotional mix of 21st century marketers. Small companies are on the Web, and big businesses are there as well. Even individual entrepreneurs have found a lucrative new launch pad for their enterprises. But even though cyberspace marketing has been effective in business-to-business transactions and, to a lesser extent, for some types of consumer purchases, a major source of Internet revenues is advertising. The Net has ads for almost every good or service imaginable. Not surprisingly, annual online advertising revenues for these Web sites have passed the $1 billion mark.

Integrating marketing communications into an overall consumer-focused strategy that meets a company's promotional and business objectives has become more and more critical in the busy global marketplace. Chapter 16 will examine specific ways marketers can use advertising and public relations to convey their messages; then Chapter 17 will discuss personal selling, sales force management, and sales promotion in the same manner. ◆◆◆

REVIEW OF CHAPTER OBJECTIVES

① Explain how integrated marketing communications relates to the development of an optimal promotional mix.

Integrated marketing communications (IMC) refers to the coordination of all promotional activities to produce a unified, customer-focused promotional message. Developing an optimal promotional mix involves selecting the personal and nonpersonal selling strategies that will work best to deliver the overall marketing message as defined by IMC.

1.1. Define *integrated marketing communications (IMC)*.
1.2. Discuss the importance of teamwork in achieving a successful IMC effort.

② Describe the communication process and how it relates to the AIDA concept.

In the communication process, a message is encoded and transmitted through a communications channel; then it is decoded, or interpreted by the receiver; finally, the receiver provides feedback, which completes the system. The AIDA concept (attention-interest-desire-action) explains the steps through which a person reaches a purchase decision after being exposed to a promotional message. The marketer sends the promotional message, and the consumer receives and responds to it via the communication process.

2.1. Describe the three tasks an effective promotional message accomplishes. How are these tasks related to the AIDA concept?

③ Explain how the promotional mix relates to the objectives of promotion.

The objectives of promotion are to provide information, stimulate demand, differentiate a product, accentuate the value of a product, and stabilize sales. The promotional mix, which is the blend of numerous variables intended to satisfy the target market, must fulfill the overall objectives of promotion.

3.1. Identify and briefly describe the five objectives of promotion.

4 Identify the different elements of the promotional mix and explain how marketers develop an optimal promotional mix.

The different elements of the promotional mix are personal selling and nonpersonal selling (advertising, product placement, sales promotion, direct marketing, and public relations). Guerilla marketing is frequently used by marketers with limited funds and firms attempting to attract attention for new-product offerings with innovative promotional approaches. Marketers develop the optimal mix by considering the nature of the market, the nature of the product, the stage in the product life cycle, price, and funds available for promotion.

4.1. State whether you think each of the following would benefit most from personal or nonpersonal selling and explain why. If you think a product would benefit from both, explain your answer.
   a. new juice-based performance drink
   b. home security system designed for small homes and apartments
   c. complete skincare system
   d. exercise equipment

5 Describe the role of sponsorships and direct marketing in integrated marketing communications.

Sponsorship, which occurs when an organization provides money or in-kind resources to an event or activity in exchange for a direct association with the event or activity, has become a hot trend in promotion. The sponsor purchases access to an activity's audience and the image associated with the activity, both of which contribute to the overall promotional message being delivered by a firm. Direct marketing involves direct communication between a seller and a B2B or final customer. It includes such promotional methods as telemarketing, direct mail, direct-response advertising and infomercials on TV and radio, direct-response print advertising, and electronic media.

5.1. In what ways does sponsorship differ from advertising?
5.2. What are the goals of direct marketing?
5.3. Why do you think direct marketing has gained in popularity among marketers?

6 Contrast the two major alternative promotional strategies.

The two major strategies are pushing and pulling. In a pulling strategy, marketers attempt to stimulate final-user demand, which then exerts pressure on the distribution channel. In a pushing strategy, marketers attempt to promote the product to channel members rather than final users. To do this, they rely heavily on personal selling.

6.1. Do you think marketers can ever use both pushing and pulling strategies for the same product? Explain.

7 Explain how marketers budget for and measure the effectiveness of promotion.

Marketers may choose among several methods for determining promotional budgets, including percentage-of-sales, fixed-sum-per-unit, meeting competition, or task-objective, which is considered the most flexible and most effective. Today, marketers use either direct sales results tests or indirect evaluation to measure effectiveness. Both methods have their benefits and drawbacks because of the difficulty of controlling variables.

7.1. What is the most effective method for developing a promotional budget? Why?
7.2. What are the six major factors that influence the effectiveness of a promotional mix?
7.3. Identify and briefly describe the two methods marketers use today for measuring the effectiveness of promotion. What are the benefits and drawbacks of each?

8 Discuss the value of marketing communications.

Despite a number of valid criticisms, marketing communications provide socially important messages, are important to businesses, and contain economic importance. As with every communication in society, it is important to consider how promotion is used rather than whether it is used at all.

8.1. Describe your own criticisms of some marketing communications. Then discuss the ways in which you think marketing communications are valuable.

MARKETING TERMS YOU NEED TO KNOW

promotion 482
marketing communications 482
integrated marketing communications (IMC) 482
AIDA concept 487
promotional mix 492
personal selling 493
nonpersonal selling 493
advertising 493
sales promotion 494
direct marketing 495
public relations 495
guerilla marketing 496
sponsorship 498
direct mail 501
pulling strategy 507
pushing strategy 507

OTHER IMPORTANT MARKETING TERMS

sender 486
message 486
encoding 487
decoding 487
feedback 487
noise 487
channel 487
primary demand 491
selective demand 491
product differentiation 491
product placement 493
trade promotion 495
publicity 495
ambush marketing 500
telemarketing 502
home shopping channel 503
infomercial 503
percentage-of-sales method 508
fixed-sum-per-unit method 509
meeting competition 509
task-objective method 509
direct sales results test 510
indirect evaluation 510
cost per impression 511
cost per response (click-throughs) 511
public service announcements (PSAs) 512

PROJECTS AND TEAMWORK EXERCISES

1. Select a print advertisement that catches your attention and analyze it according to the AIDA concept (attention-interest-desire-action). Identify features of the ad that catch your attention, pique your interest, make you desire the product, and spur you toward a purchase. Present your findings to the class.
2. With a classmate, locate up to five print ads that illustrate each of the five objectives of promotion (an ad might fulfill more than one objective). Present the ads to the class, identifying the objectives fulfilled in each.
3. With a classmate, choose a good or service that you feel could benefit from guerilla marketing. Imagine that you have a limited promotional budget and come up with a plan for a guerilla approach. Outline several ideas and explain how you plan to carry them out. Present your plan to the class.
4. Evaluate two or three pieces of direct mail that you have received lately. Which items caught your attention and at least made you save the mailing? Which items did you toss in the trash without even opening or considering beyond an initial glance? Why?
5. With a classmate, choose one of the products listed here or select another that interests you. Then, keeping in mind your objectives for promotion, write an outline for an infomercial for the product. Present your infomercial to the class.
   a. piece of exercise equipment
   b. line of cosmetics
   c. top-of-the-line backyard grill
   d. personal shopping service
6. Select any two stages of the product life cycle and create a print ad for the same product in each of the two stages. You can focus on either the graphics, the ad copy, or both, but your ads should take the product's life cycle stage into account in identifiable ways.
7. Take a careful look at a direct mail catalog (one you regularly receive or any other). Who is the audience for the products being advertised, and what immediate response is the marketer seeking? How does the catalog overcome the image problem of direct marketing?
8. Identify a corporate sponsorship for a cause or program in your area, or find a local company that sponsors a local charity or other organization. What do you think the sponsor is gaining from its actions (be specific)? What does the sponsored organization receive? Do you think this sponsorship is good for your community? Explain.
9. Why do you think prescription drug companies now advertise directly to consumers on television and in publications like *Time* and *People* magazines, instead of strictly in medical trade journals read by doctors, as in the past? What kind of demand are the companies trying to generate (primary or selective), and how would you characterize their strategy (push or pull)? Find such an ad to support your answer.
10. What are some of the advantages and disadvantages of using a celebrity spokesperson to promote a product or service? Compare two or more different ad campaigns that rely on the endorsement of sports stars like LeBron James and 15-year-old golf phenom Michelle Wie and list similarities, differences, and pros and cons.

APPLYING CHAPTER CONCEPTS

1. Advertisements that run in movie theaters before the featured film are becoming more common and more elaborate. Sometimes they are even embedded in blocks of specially created "content." Consider the placement of such ads with particular films (for instance, soft drinks might be advertised before films targeted to teen audiences or sports cars with films aimed at young men). In what ways is it similar to the placement of product ads in print media? What are some of the advantages and disadvantages of these ads?
2. Toyota is marketing its new Solara model primarily to women with specially targeted media and outdoor advertising and an online auction for a breast-cancer research fund. Design

a promotional plan for a new line of women's golf clothes, including whatever balance of nonpersonal selling tools you think will be most effective. Explain your choices.

3. Product placement has grown tremendously and some critics might even say brand names are so commonplace in hit films and TV shows that viewers no longer notice them. Imagine that you are given the task of placing your product, a household cleaner. Make a list of the current or upcoming films and shows that you think would be good targets for your efforts, and draft a brief plan for ways the product could realistically appear in them.
4. McDonald's recently changed the theme of its ad campaign from "We love to see you smile" to "I'm lovin' it," and the new theme is accompanied by new promotions involving music, sports, fashion, and entertainment—as well as major changes in the company's menu. Although polls indicated that customers were somewhat resistant to the change, the fast-food giant believes that the old theme didn't appeal to young adults as much as the new one will. What promotional messages do you think the two slogans convey? Do you agree with McDonald's assessment of their effectiveness in reaching the young adult market? Why or why not?

ETHICS EXERCISE

Pop-up ads, those unsolicited messages that sometimes pop onto your computer screen and block the site or information you're looking for until you close or respond to them, are inexpensive to produce and cost nearly nothing to send. But they are so annoying to some computer users that dozens of special programs have been written to block them from appearing on the screen during Internet use.

1. Do you think that because they are unsolicited, pop-up ads are also intrusive? Are they an invasion of privacy? Explain your reasoning.
2. Do you consider the use of pop-up ads to be unethical? Why or why not?

'netWork EXERCISES

1. **Guerilla marketing**. Visit the Web site listed below. Review and summarize the article on guerilla marketing. Take your summary to class so you can contribute to a class discussion on the topic.

   http://www.efuse.com/Grow/guerilla .marketing.html
2. **Promotional mix.** Visit three or four prominent e-commerce retailers, including at least one that has brick-and-mortar stores in addition to its online store. Write a brief report comparing and contrasting the promotional mix used by each retailer.
3. **AIDA**. Visit the Web sites of at least two online retailers—such as L.L. Bean (**http://www.llbean.com**), Barnes & Noble (**http://www.bn.com**), or one of your favorites. Write a brief report explaining how the companies have succeeded in applying the AIDA (attention-interest-desire-action) concept discussed in the chapter.

Note: Internet Web addresses change frequently. If you don't find the exact sites listed, you may need to access the organization's or company's home page and search from there or use a search engine such as Google.

INFOTRAC CITATIONS AND EXERCISES

- **Record:** A117865137

  The emotional side of Sears: Retailer finds a hit with extreme home makeover. Scott H. Wright.

  Do-It-Yourself Retailing, June 2004 v186 i6 p8(1)

Abstract: Do-it-yourself home improvement has finally made it to prime-time television—and Sears is getting in on the act. Sears, Roebuck and Co., the multiline retailer once famous for catalog-based marketing, is the sole home-improvement sponsor for *Extreme Makeover: Home Edition,* ABC's popular reality TV show that sends teams of professional designers, carpenters, subcontractors, and construction workers to restore hopelessly dilapidated homes—all in one week's time. The sponsorship is important as Sears seeks to expand its presence within a booming home-improvement sector dominated by giants such as Lowe's and Home Depot.

1. What is *sponsorship,* and how does it differ from advertising?
2. How does Sears benefit from its sponsorship of *Extreme Makeover: Home Edition*?
3. Define *product placement,* and explain how it relates to the various home-improvement tools, furnishings, and appliances seen on ABC's reality TV show.

CASE 15.1 IMC Strategy Launches New $20 Bill

They say you have to spend money to make money. Apparently, you also have to spend money to give money away. The U.S. Department of the Treasury recently launched a $30 million global marketing campaign to introduce the public to the colorful new $20 bill. The integrated campaign included the hiring of a Hollywood talent agency and a public relations firm to work on product placement opportunities in the media.

Product placement for U.S. currency?

The new bill, with a redesigned portrait of Andrew Jackson and the addition of peach, blue, and yellow to the familiar institutional green, was featured on TV game shows *Jeopardy* and *Wheel of Fortune,* college football broadcasts, and as part of the storylines of several prime-time shows. Other promotional efforts were also staged. Wal-Mart aired a public service announcement about the new bill on its in-house satellite network. A special informational Web site was set up at **http://www.moneyfactory.com**. Pepperidge Farm promoted the new bill on its Goldfish crackers packaging and ran a contest offering a trip to Washington, D.C., as the grand prize.

Advertising wasn't left to chance. Paid TV ads showed people celebrating when clerks handed them the new bill. Print ads reassured the public that the new bills and the old bills were worth the same and would be equally valuable "for good." The ads also pointed out features and characteristics of the new design that make the colorful 20s harder to counterfeit.

The redesign effort is the first in a series of money makeovers being undertaken by the U.S. Treasury. New 50s and 100s are being rolled out as well. But since the $20 bill has become the most frequently used, especially since the advent of ATMs, it has also been a favorite among counterfeiters, who are all too adept at using digital technology that defies detection by all but the sharpest eyes. So the 20 was the first bill to be given a new look and a starring role in a full-scale marketing campaign.

With an estimated $43 million in counterfeit notes passing into circulation every year, the U.S. government was anxious to reassure the public about the legitimacy of the new 20s. About $19 billion worth of them have been produced, at a slightly higher cost than the old ones: 7.5 cents per bill. "These are the most secure notes the U.S. government has ever produced," said Mark Olson of the Federal Reserve System. The safety features of the new bill include an engrained watermark image, an embedded plastic strip, and color-shifting ink.

The main goal of the government's campaign, of course, is "public education, to build awareness and trust," according to a spokesperson for the Bureau of Engraving and Printing, which actually produces the bills. (A similar campaign heralded the arrival of the euro a few years back.) Will the public accept it? Will counterfeiters hate it? Whatever the outcome, history has been made. The new $20 bill marks the first time in nearly 100 years that U.S. currency has featured a color other than green or black. And it's the first time money has been the subject of a marketing campaign.

Questions for Critical Thinking

1. What characteristics of an IMC campaign does the government's currency rollout have? What traits or elements are missing?
2. One critic of the campaign pointed out that the government had no real need to "sell" people on the new $20 bill, since consumers can't really choose whether to use it or not. Why do you think the campaign was undertaken? What was its real purpose? Explain your answer.

Sources: "U.S. Currency Milestones," **http://www.exchangerate.com**, accessed May 28, 2004; Rob Walker, "The Money Pitch," *Slate,* October 27, 2003; "The Color of Money," *U.S. News & World Report,* October 13, 2003, p. 54; Gordon T. Anderson, "Peach $20s Landing," *CNNMoney,* October 9, 2003; Theresa Howard, "As Seen on TV: New $20 Bill," *USA Today,* October 6, 2003, p. B2; Claire Atkinson, "New Hollywood Star: The $20 Bill," *Advertising Age,* November 15, 2003, p. 3.

VIDEO CASE 15.2 Jimmy John's Sandwich Shops Give Customers Something to Chew On

The written case on Jimmy John's Gourmet Sandwiches appears on page VC-18. The recently filmed Jimmy John's Gourmet Sandwiches video is designed to expand and highlight the concepts in this chapter and the concepts and questions covered in the written video case.

chapter 16

Advertising and Public Relations

chapter objectives

1. Identify the three major advertising objectives and the two basic categories of advertising.
2. List the major advertising strategies.
3. Describe the process of creating an advertisement.
4. Identify the major types of advertising appeals and discuss their uses.
5. List and compare the major advertising media.
6. Outline the organization of the advertising function and the role of an advertising agency.
7. Explain the roles of cross promotions, public relations, publicity, and ethics in an organization's promotional strategy.
8. Explain how marketers assess promotional effectiveness.

THE DARK SIDE OF CELEBRITY ENDORSEMENTS

Marketers invest considerable money and effort in lining up celebrity spokespeople for their companies. The reason is clear: To borrow for their brands some of the glamour and goodwill attached to sports, film, and TV stars. Sports figures "have a level of popularity that helps make the brand compelling," says one industry executive.

The strategy certainly isn't foolproof. Executives at Nike were horrified by a recent Masters tournament snafu in which the collar of winner Tiger Woods's Nike golf shirt visibly wilted in the hot, humid air. It was the "best and worst moment of my life," said Nike Golf's director of apparel.

But the sports apparel and equipment giant's chagrin over a limp collar was nothing compared with the dismay many a marketer has felt when a highly paid spokesperson's reputation becomes tarnished or his or her impact otherwise diminishes. Nike, for

AP WIDE WORLD PHOTO/PAUL SANCYA

instance, has earmarked $192 million for contracts with world-class athletes, including the very young—such as soccer superstar Freddy Adu and basketball phenom LeBron James. Other Nike spokespeople under contract include Mia Hamm, whose team folded when the U.S. women's soccer league went out of business, and track star Marion Jones, who was investigated for steroid use.

Retirement can reduce a spokesperson's visibility and thus his or her effectiveness. Nike is coping with the retirement of NBA star Michael Jordan by building "Team Jordan," which includes Jason Kidd (New Jersey Nets), Gary Payton (Lakers), Warren Sapp (Tampa Bay Buccaneers), Derek Jeter (Yankees), and Carmelo Anthony (Denver Nuggets). Rounding out the team is jazz saxophonist Mike Phillips. The concept of the team was developed when Jordan signed with Nike in 1997, and part of its purpose is to expand endorsements beyond athletic wear and into casual clothing. "People are just as comfortable seeing Michael on the cover of *GQ* as on the cover of *SI*," says the president of Jordan Brand. "He has that mix of style and sport, and that means we can take the brand to other categories."

NBA star Kobe Bryant, another Nike endorser with a contract worth $45 million, has admitted adultery and faced rape charges. Bryant also held lucrative contracts with The Coca-Cola Co. and McDonald's, both of which have replaced him with other sports figures in their recent advertising. McDonald's simply let Bryant's contract expire, and the soft-drink giant replaced him with LeBron James.

Even if they don't face criminal charges, some athletes lose their marketability by showing poor judgment or disloyalty. Baseball superstar Sammy Sosa's reputation suffered after he was suspended for using a corked bat in one game, six-time Tour de France champion Lance Armstrong continues to deny allegations of doping, and the number of athletes who have run afoul of the law continues to climb.

But some advertisers are not afraid of the "bad boy" image that some athletes cultivate. And if the endorsement gets too uncomfortable for the firm, most endorsement contracts include a morals clause that allows the marketer to end the relationship if the spokesperson is convicted of a crime, for instance. Many observers believe such clauses will be getting tighter in the future.[1]

Chapter Overview

FROM the last chapter, you already know that the nonpersonal elements of promotion include advertising and public relations. Thousands of organizations rely on nonpersonal selling in developing their promotional mixes and integrated marketing communications strategies. Advertising is the most visible form of nonpersonal promotion, and marketers often use it together with sales promotion (discussed in the next chapter) to create effective promotional campaigns. Television is probably the most obvious medium for nonpersonal selling dollars. But theater advertising is a major ad component in Europe, and Regal Entertainment, the large U.S. movie theater chain, took in $70 million in on-screen advertising in a single 12-month period.[2]

Marketers seeking excitement for new-product launches have recently paid as much as $3 million to have the Rolling Stones perform at a single event. And pop music icon Beyoncé Knowles has signed multimillion-dollar endorsement deals for L'Oréal beauty and hair care products, Pepsi, and Tommy Hilfiger Toiletries for a perfume line.[3]

This chapter begins with a discussion of the types of advertising and explains how advertising is used to achieve a firm's objectives. It then considers alternative advertising strategies and the process of creating an advertisement. Next we provide a detailed look at various advertising media channels, from television and radio to print advertising and direct mail to outdoor and interactive media. The chapter then focuses on the importance of public relations, publicity, and cross promotions. Alternative methods of measuring the effectiveness of both online and offline nonpersonal selling are examined. We conclude the chapter by exploring current ethical issues relating to nonpersonal selling.

Briefly Speaking

The professional celebrity, male and female, is the crowning result of the star system of a country that makes a fetish of competition. In America, this system is carried to the point where a man who can knock a small white ball into a series of holes in the ground with more efficiency than anyone else thereby gains social access to the President of the United States.

C. Wright Mills
(1916–1962)
American sociologist

ADVERTISING

advertising
Paid, nonpersonal communication through various media about a business firm, not-for-profit organization, product, or idea by a sponsor identified in a message that is intended to inform or persuade members of a particular audience.

Twenty-first century advertising is closely related to integrated marketing communications (IMC) in many respects. While IMC involves a message dealing with buyer–seller relationships, **advertising** consists of paid nonpersonal communication through various media with the purpose of informing or persuading members of a particular audience. Advertising is used by marketers to reach target markets with messages designed to appeal to business firms, not-for-profit organizations, or ultimate consumers.

While the ability of the Internet to make every marketer a global marketer has become a truism, America remains home to most of the world's leading advertisers. General Motors, Time Warner, Procter & Gamble, Pfizer, and Ford Motor Co. are five of the top advertisers in the world, each spending more than $2 billion annually—an average of almost $6 million a day—on U.S. advertising.[4]

Advertising spending varies among industries as well as companies. The cosmetics industry is widely known for pouring dollars into advertising, as is the auto manufacturing industry. Among the newcomers of top U.S. advertisers are telecommunications companies. Verizon, AT&T, Sprint, and Cingular Wireless all ranked in the top 10 U.S. megabrands for ad spending, with a combined total of $3.2 billion in U.S. advertising spending.[5]

As previous chapters have discussed, the emergence of the marketing concept, with its emphasis on a companywide consumer orientation, boosted the importance of integrated marketing communications. This change in turn expanded the role of advertising. Today, a typical consumer is exposed to

figure 16.1

Pepsi and Strawberries: Product and Institutional Advertising

hundreds of advertising messages each day. Advertising provides an efficient, inexpensive, and fast method of reaching the ever-elusive, increasingly segmented consumer market. Its current role rivals those of sales promotion and personal selling. In fact, advertising has become a key ingredient in the effective implementation of the marketing concept.

As a profession advertising is young; as a force it is as old as the world. The first four words ever uttered, "Let there be light," constitute its charter. All nature is vibrant with its impulse.

Bruce Barton (1886–1967)

American author and advertising executive

TYPES OF ADVERTISING

Advertisements fall into two broad categories: product advertising and institutional advertising. **Product advertising** is nonpersonal selling of a particular good or service. This is the type of advertising the average person usually thinks of when talking about most promotional activities. The Pepsi ad in Figure 16.1 featuring celebrity Beyoncé Knowles is intended to encourage soft-drink purchasers to choose this brand over other available alternatives. **Institutional advertising,** in contrast, promotes a concept, an idea, a philosophy, or the goodwill of an industry, company, organization, person, geographic location, or government agency. This term has a broader meaning than *corporate advertising,* which is typically limited to nonproduct advertising sponsored by a specific profit-seeking firm.

product advertising Nonpersonal selling of a particular good or service.

institutional advertising Promotion of a concept, idea, philosophy, or goodwill of an industry, company, organization, person, geographic location, or government agency.

Institutional advertising is often closely related to the public relations function of the enterprise. The second ad in Figure 16.1 plays up the bright color of strawberries and includes copy that promotes the health benefits of eating them. Its ultimate objective is to persuade consumers to buy more strawberries rather than to promote any particular grower's brand.

OBJECTIVES OF ADVERTISING

Marketers use advertising messages to accomplish three primary objectives: to inform, to persuade, and to remind. These objectives may be used individually or, more typically, in conjunction with each other. For example, an ad for a not-for-profit agency may inform the public of the existence of the organization and at the same time persuade the audience to make a donation, join the organization, or attend a function.

1 Identify the three major advertising objectives and the two basic categories of advertising.

figure 16.2

Advertising Objectives in Relation to Stage in the Product Life Cycle

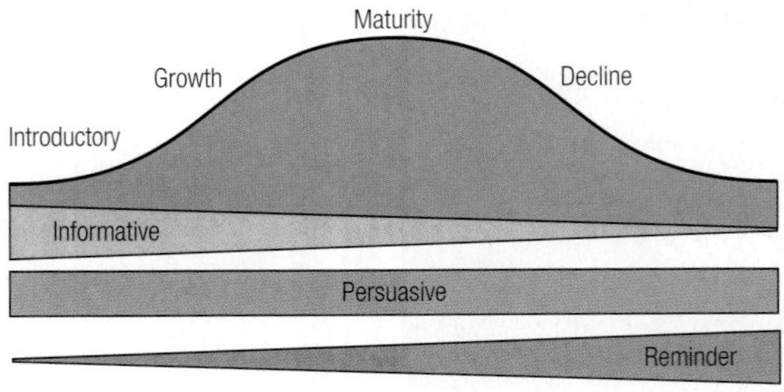

Informative advertising seeks to develop initial demand for a good, service, organization, person, place, idea, or cause. The promotion of any new market entry tends to pursue this objective because marketing success at this stage often depends simply on announcing availability. Therefore, informative advertising is common in the introductory stage of the product life cycle.

Persuasive advertising attempts to increase demand for an existing good, service, organization, person, place, idea, or cause. Persuasive advertising is a competitive type of promotion suited to the growth stage and the early part of the maturity stage of the product life cycle.

Reminder advertising strives to reinforce previous promotional activity by keeping the name of a good, service, organization, person, place, idea, or cause before the public. It is common in the latter part of the maturity stage and throughout the decline stage of the product life cycle.

informative advertising Promotion that seeks to develop initial demand for a good, service, organization, person, place, idea, or cause.

persuasive advertising Promotion that attempts to increase demand for an existing good, service, organization, person, place, idea, or cause.

reminder advertising Advertising that reinforces previous promotional activity by keeping the name of a good, service, organization, person, place, idea, or cause before the public.

Figure 16.2 illustrates the relationship between advertising objectives and the stages of the product life cycle. Informative advertising tends to work best during the early stages, while reminder advertising is effective later on. Persuasive advertising, if done well, can be effective through the entire life cycle.

Traditionally, marketers stated their advertising objectives as direct sales goals. A more current and realistic standard, however, views advertising as a way to achieve communications objectives, including informing, persuading, and reminding potential customers of the product. Advertising attempts to condition consumers to adopt favorable viewpoints toward a promotional message. The goal of an ad is to improve the likelihood that a customer will buy a particular good or service. In this sense, advertising illustrates the close relationship between marketing communications and promotional strategy.

To get the best value for a firm's advertising investment, marketers must first determine what that firm's advertising objectives are. Effective advertising can enhance consumer perceptions of quality in a good or service, leading to increased customer loyalty, repeat purchases, and protection against price wars. In addition, perceptions of superiority pay off in the firm's ability to raise prices without losing market share.

1. What are the goals of institutional advertising?
2. At what stage in the product life cycle are informative ads used? Why?
3. What is reminder advertising?

(2) List the major advertising strategies.

ADVERTISING STRATEGIES

If the primary function of marketing is to bring buyers and sellers together, then advertising is the means to an end. Effective advertising strategies accomplish at least one of three tasks: informing, persuading, or reminding consumers. The secret to success in choosing the best strategy is developing a message that best positions a firm's product in the audience's mind. Among the advertising strategies available for use by 21st century marketers are comparative advertising and celebrity advertising as well as decisions about global and interactive ads. Channel-oriented decisions such as retail and cooperative advertising can also be devised.

Marketers often combine several of these advertising strategies to ensure that the advertisement accomplishes set objectives. As markets become more segmented, the need for personalized advertising increases. The next sections describe strategies that contemporary marketers develop to reach their target markets.

comparative advertising Advertising strategy that emphasizes messages with direct or indirect promotional comparisons between competing brands.

COMPARATIVE ADVERTISING

Firms whose goods and services are not the leaders in their markets often favor **comparative advertising**, a promotional strategy that emphasizes advertising messages with direct or indirect comparisons to dominant brands in the industry. By contrast, market leaders seldom acknowledge in their advertising that competing products even exist, and when they do, they usually do not point out any benefits of the competing brand.

Brewing giants Miller and Anheuser-Busch have recently been slugging it out on network TV. Miller began a series of "President of Beers" commercials spoofing presidential debates and pointing out differences in the companies' products, with a Clydesdale at the opposing podium. Budweiser fired back with ads featuring the quirky Budweiser donkey discussing Miller's South African ownership with a Budweiser Clydesdale. These squabbles escalated to the point of lawsuits over false advertising.[6]

A generation ago, comparative advertising was not the norm; in fact, it was frowned on. But the Federal Trade Commission now encourages comparative advertising. Regulators believe such ads keep marketers competitive and consumers better informed about their choices. Generally speaking, where there is competition through advertising, prices tend to go down because people can shop around. This benefit has proved increasingly true for online consumers, who now use shopping bots to help find the best prices on goods and services.

CELEBRITY TESTIMONIALS

I was the only one there I never heard of.

Barry J. Farber (b. 1959)

American entrepreneur and author

A popular technique for increasing advertising readership in a cluttered promotional environment and improving overall effectiveness of a marketing message involves the use of celebrity spokespeople. About one of every five U.S. ads currently includes celebrities. This type of advertising is also popular in foreign countries. In Japan, 80 percent of all ads use celebrities, both local and international stars. U.S. celebrities featured in Japanese ads include actors Harrison Ford for Kirin Beer, Jodie Foster for Keri Cosmetics and Latte Coffee, and Paul Newman for Evance watch stores. Japanese consumers view foreign stars as images more than actual people, which helps marketers to sell products. They also associate American stars with quality.

Both the number of celebrity ads and the dollars spent on those ads have increased in recent years. Professional athletes are among the highest paid product endorsers, raking in millions each year. They appear in advertisements for a wide variety of products, many having little or nothing to do with sports. Retired basketball great Michael Jordan continues to earn more than $30 million annually as a spokesperson for underwear maker Hanes and for his MJ clothing line. Practically everyone has seen former boxer George Foreman in ads for Salton's Lean Mean Fat-Reducing Grilling Machine. And golfing great Tiger Woods has lucrative deals with dozens of products, ranging from telecommunications and credit-card giants to Buick automobiles, in addition to his $40 million agreement with Nike Golf.

One advantage of associations with big-name personalities is improved product recognition in a promotional environment filled with hundreds of competing 15- and 30-second commercials. Advertisers use the term *clutter* to describe this situation. As e-commerce continues to soar, one inevitable result has been the increase in advertising clutter as companies rush to market their goods and services online. But marketers need to remember that an effective online site must have meaningful content and helpful service.

Another advantage to using celebrities occurs when marketers are trying to reach consumers of another culture. Blockbuster Video and McDonald's have hired Hispanic stars to attract Hispanic consumers to their stores. Actress Daisy Fuentes appears in ads for McDonald's, while John Leguizamo and Hector Elizondo advertise for Blockbuster. "We see lots of new companies going into the Hispanic market who have never advertised before, and one way is hiring celebrities," explains Raul Mateu, a vice president at the William Morris talent agency. "It seems like an easy way of getting instant credibility in the marketplace is using [the celebrity's] equity."[7]

In addition to high-profile endorsement deals with Nike Golf, golfing sensation Tiger Woods's widespread appeal and instant recognition place him in demand as a celebrity endorser for firms like consulting giant Accenture.

A celebrity testimonial generally succeeds when the celebrity is a credible source of information for the product being promoted. The most effective ads of this type establish relevant links between the celebrities and the advertised goods or services, such as the models and actresses who endorse Revlon cosmetics. Note that in the examples mentioned earlier, even though many of the products are not sports related, they do make a link to the celebrity—likable boxing champion George Foreman seems like a person who enjoys eating. Several studies of consumer responses show that celebrities improve the product's believability, recall of the product, and brand recognition. Celebrity endorsements also create positive attitudes, leading to greater brand equity.

However, a celebrity who endorses too many products may create marketplace confusion. Customers may remember the celebrity but not the product or brand; worse, they might connect the celebrity to a competing brand. Another problem can arise if a celebrity is involved in a scandal or has legal problems, as marketers do not want their products associated with a negative image.

Some advertisers try to avoid such problems by using cartoon characters as endorsers. Snoopy, a character in the popular *Peanuts* comic strip and long-running TV animated programs, has appeared in MetLife ads for years. Some advertisers may actually prefer cartoon characters because the characters can never say anything negative about the product, they do exactly what the marketers want them to do, and they cannot get involved in scandals. The only drawback is high licensing fees; popular animated characters often cost more than live celebrities. Companies may create their own cartoon characters or "talking" animals, which eventually become celebrities in their own right as a result of many appearances in advertisements, as is the case with the Keebler elves and the Geico gecko.

In recent years, marketers have begun to consider celebrities as marketing partners rather than pretty or famous faces who can sell goods and services. Tiger Woods has been active in developing Nike's golf gear and apparel. Former supermodel Claudia Schiffer not only agreed to endorse a signature line of PalmPilots, but she also assisted in positioning the handheld computers in the electronics market by selecting fashionable colors and her own favorite software programs. Of course, George Foreman actually uses the grills he advertises. "George has been very active in the marketing of his grills and genuinely believes in them," says Jake Fuller, an equity research analyst at Credit Suisse First Boston in New York. The grills have served up $2 billion in sales for Salton to date.[8]

RETAIL ADVERTISING

Most consumers are confronted daily with **retail advertising,** which includes all advertising by retail stores that sell goods or services directly to the consuming public. While this activity accounts for a sizable portion of total annual advertising expenditures, retail advertising varies widely in its effectiveness. One study showed that consumers often respond with suspicion to retail price advertisements. Source, message, and shopping experience seem to affect consumer attitudes toward these advertisements.

An advertiser once quipped that the two most powerful words to use in an ad are "New" and "Free"—and these terms are often capitalized on in retail ads. Although "Free" may be featured only in discussions of customer services, the next best term—"Sale"—is often the centerpiece of retail promotions. And "New" typically describes new lines of products being offered. However, many retail stores continue to view advertising as a secondary activity, although that is changing. Local retailers rarely use independent advertising agencies, perhaps because of the expense associated with agencies. Instead, store managers may accept responsibility for advertising in addition to their other duties. Management can begin to correct this problem by assigning one individual the sole responsibility and authority for developing an effective retail advertising program.

cooperative advertising Strategy in which a retailer shares advertising costs with a manufacturer or wholesaler.

A retailer often shares advertising costs with a manufacturer or wholesaler in a technique called **cooperative advertising.** For example, an apparel marketer may pay a percentage of the cost of a retail store's newspaper advertisement featuring its product lines. Foot Locker highlights its special line of Skechers Sport shoes in the promotional message in Figure 16.3. Cooperative advertising campaigns originated to take advantage of the media's practice of offering lower rates to local advertisers than to national ones. Later, cooperative advertising became part of programs to improve dealer relations. The retailer likes the chance to secure advertising that it might not be able to afford otherwise. Cooperative advertising can strengthen vertical links in the marketing channel, as when a manufacturer and retailer coordinate their resources. It can also involve firms at the same level of the supply chain. In a horizontal arrangement, a group of retailers—for example, all the Ford dealers in the northeastern U.S.—might pool their resources.

INTERACTIVE ADVERTISING

Millions of advertising messages float across idle—and active—computer screens in homes and offices around the country every day. Net surfers play games that are embedded with ads from the site sponsors. Companies offer free e-mail service to people willing to receive ads with their personal messages. Video screens on grocery carts display ads for shoppers to see as they wheel down the aisles of grocery stores.

Since marketers realize that two-way communications provide more effective methods for achieving promotional objectives, they are interested in interactive media. **Interactive advertising** involves two-way promotional messages transmitted through communication channels that induce message recipients to participate actively in the promotional effort. Achieving this involvement is the difficult task facing contemporary marketers. Although interactive advertising has become nearly synonymous with e-commerce and the Web, it also includes other formats such as kiosks in shopping malls or text messages on cell phones, as the "Marketing Hit" feature discusses. Multimedia technology, the Internet, and commercial online services are changing the nature of advertising from a one-way, passive communication technique to more effective, two-way marketing communications. Interactive advertising creates dialogue between marketers and individual shoppers, providing more materials at the user's request. The advertiser's challenge is to gain and hold consumer interest in an environment where these individuals control what they want to see.

Interactive advertising changes the balance between marketers and consumers. Unlike the traditional role of advertising—providing brief, entertaining, attention-catching messages—interactive media provide information to help consumers throughout the purchase and

figure 16.3

Cooperative Advertising by Foot Locker and Skechers Sport Shoes

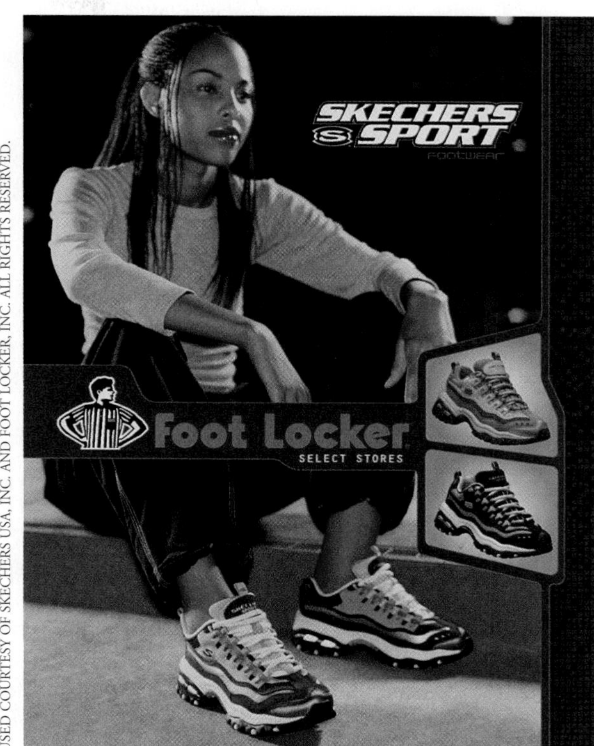

marketing hit — Cell Phone Messages Ring True

Background. Marketers want closer relationships with their customers, but advertising's typical anonymity—broadcasting messages to mass markets and hoping they hit their mark—has hindered that objective. Interactive advertising is beginning to open two-way communications, though. Marketers from local malls such as Cambridge, Massachusetts's Side Galleria Mall to national and global corporations such as Procter & Gamble and The Coca-Cola Co. are increasingly turning to cell phones to get their messages across. After all, an estimated 548 billion text messages were sent via cell phone last year.

The Challenge. Since no telephone directory for cell phone numbers exists, marketers need to entice customers to give them their numbers by getting them to respond to traditional advertising messages containing special five-digit cell phone numbers posted on TV or concert screens, posters, and print ads.

The Strategy. Marketers at the Cambridge mall collected 2,000 cell phone numbers from shoppers over a six-month period and then sent nearly 40 discount offers from the tenant stores directly to customers' cell phones. Respondents simply displayed their cell phone screens to the retailer to collect their discounts.

The Outcome. A whopping 80 percent of the text-message coupons were redeemed, resulting in a big uptick in sales for the mall stores. The key to the success of such offers is customers' willingness to participate. One marketer says that it is critical to knock and say "please" first; otherwise, the message could be viewed as just another form of spam.

Sources: Paul Davidson, "Cellphone Directory Gets Hoots, Hollers," *USA Today,* July 28, 2004, p. B3; Lora Kolodny, "112 Million Handsets Can't Be Wrong," *Inc.,* July 2004, p. 42; Stephen Baker, "A Marketer's Dream: Your Cell Phone," *TechNewsWorld,* June 22, 2004, http://www.technewsworld.com; Yuki Noguchi, "New Ad Frontier: Cell Phones," *The Washington Post,* November 7, 2003, accessed at *MSNBC,* http://msnbc.com.

1. What is comparative advertising?
2. What makes a successful celebrity testimonial?
3. What is cooperative advertising?

consumption processes. In a sense, it becomes closer to personal selling as consumers receive immediate responses to questions or requests for more information about goods and services. Interactive advertising provides consumers with more information in less time to help them make necessary comparisons between available products.

Successful interactive advertising adds value by offering the viewer more than just product-related information. An ad on the Web can do more than promote a brand; it can create a company store, provide customer service, and offer additional content.

(3) Describe the process of creating an advertisement.

Most firms deliver their interactive advertising messages through proprietary online services and through the Web. In fact, online ad spending will likely top $8 billion in 2006. Consumer advertisers typically spend the most dollars on online advertising, followed by the high-tech computing and media industries.[9]

figure 16.4

Elements of the Advertising Planning Process

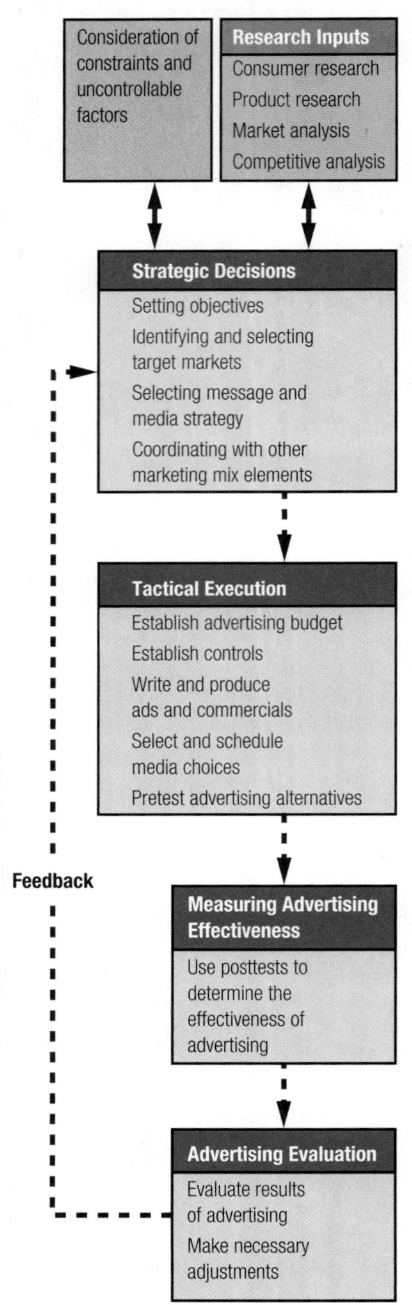

CREATING AN ADVERTISEMENT

Marketers spend about $300 billion a year on advertising campaigns in the U.S. alone.[10] With so much money at stake, they must create effective, memorable ads that increase sales and enhance their organizations' images. They cannot afford to waste resources on mediocre messages that fail to capture consumers' attention, communicate their sales message effectively, and lead to a purchase, donation, or other positive action for the organization.

Research helps marketers create better ads by pinpointing goals that an ad needs to accomplish, such as educating consumers about product features, enhancing brand loyalty, or improving consumer perception of the brand. These objectives should guide the design of the ad. Marketers can also discover what appeals to consumers and can test ads with potential buyers before committing funds for a campaign.

Marketers sometimes face specific challenges as they develop advertising objectives for services. They must find a creative way to fill out the intangible images of most services and successfully convey the benefits that consumers receive. The "You're in Good Hands" message of Allstate Insurance is a classic example of how creative advertising can make the intangible nature of services tangible.

TRANSLATING ADVERTISING OBJECTIVES INTO ADVERTISING PLANS

Once a company defines its objectives for an advertising campaign, it can develop its advertising plan. Marketing research assists managers in making strategic decisions that guide choices in technical areas such as budgeting, copywriting, scheduling, and media selection. Posttests, which are discussed in greater detail later in the chapter, measure the effectiveness of advertising and form the basis for feedback concerning possible adjustments. The elements of advertising planning are shown in Figure 16.4. Experienced marketers know the importance of following even the most basic steps in the process, such as market analysis.

As Chapter 9 explained, positioning involves developing a marketing strategy that aims to achieve a desired position in a prospective buyer's mind. Marketers use a positioning strategy that distinguishes their good or service from those of competitors. Effective advertising then communicates the desired position by emphasizing certain product characteristics, such as performance attributes, price/quality, competitors' shortcomings, applications, user needs, and product classes.

ADVERTISING MESSAGES

The strategy for creating a message starts with the benefits a product offers to potential customers and moves to the creative concept phase, in which marketers strive to bring an appropriate message to consumers using both visual and verbal components. Marketers work to create an ad with meaningful, believable, and distinctive appeals—one that stands out from the clutter and is more likely to escape "zapping" by the television remote control.

Usually, ads are created not individually but as part of specific campaigns. An **advertising campaign** is a series of different but related ads that use a single theme and appear in different media within a specified time period. The series of Sprint ads featuring a man in a black trench coat helping people obtain clear cell phone transmissions and McDonald's "I'm Lovin' It" ads represent just two of many recent advertising campaigns.

advertising campaign Series of different but related ads that use a single theme and appear in different media within a specified time period.

The City of Brotherly Love recently launched a campaign designed to attract gay tourists to Philadelphia. Ads featuring same-sex couples in colonial attire aired on cable networks such as Bravo, MTV, VH1, and Style and always ended with the tag line, "Come to Philadelphia. Get your history straight and your nightlife gay."[11]

In developing a creative strategy, advertisers must decide how to communicate their marketing message. They must balance message characteristics, such as the tone of the appeal, the extent of information provided and the conclusion to which it leads the consumer, the side of the story the ad tells, and its emphasis on verbal or visual primary elements.

ADVERTISING APPEALS

(4) Identify the major types of advertising appeals and discuss their uses.

Should the tone of the advertisement focus on a practical appeal such as price or gas mileage, or should it evoke an emotional response by appealing to, say, fear, humor, sex, guilt, or fantasy? This is another critical decision in the creation of memorable ads that possess the strengths needed to accomplish promotional objectives.

Fear Appeals

In recent years, marketers have relied increasingly on fear appeals. Ads for insurance, autos, health-care products, and even certain foods imply that incorrect buying decisions could lead to illness, injury, or other bad consequences. Even ads for business services imply that if a company doesn't purchase the advertised services, its competitors will move ahead or valuable information may be lost.

Pharmaceutical companies spend nearly $2 billion a year on advertising, much of which is directed toward consumer fears—whether fear of hair loss, fear of allergies, or fear of heart attacks. These drug advertisements have flourished in both print and broadcast media after the Food and Drug Administration lifted a ban on prescription drug advertising on television. Such ads have become a key component of marketers' pulling channel strategies. Typical ads encourage readers and viewers to ask their doctors whether the medication should be prescribed for their medical needs.

Fear appeals can backfire, however. Viewers are likely to practice selective perception and tune out statements they perceive as too strong or not credible. Some consumer researchers believe that viewer or reader backlash will eventually occur due to the amount of prescription drug advertising based on fear appeals.

Humor in Advertising Messages

A humorous ad seeks to create a positive mood related to a product. Humor can improve audience awareness and recall and enhance the consumer's favorable image of the brand. After all, if the ad makes the consumer feel good, then the product may do the same. But advertising professionals differ in their opinions of the effectiveness of humorous ads. Some believe that humor distracts attention from brand and product features; consumers remember the humor but not the product. Humorous ads, because they are so memorable, may lose their effectiveness sooner than ads with other kinds of appeals. In addition, humor can be tricky because what one group of consumers finds funny may not be funny at all to another group. Men and women sometimes have a different sense of humor, as do people of different ages. This distinction may become even greater across cultures.

Ads Based on Sex

Ads with sex-based appeals have what is called "stopping power" because they attract the reader's or viewer's attention. Research indicates, however, that sexual content in an ad boosts recall of the ad's content only if the appeal is appropriate to the type of product advertised.[12] Some advertisers have begun to tone down their appeals based on sex. CBS and Victoria's Secret canceled a recent season of *Victoria's Secret Fashion Show,* which had run for several years during the November sweeps, based partly on investigations into indecency in the media being conducted by the Federal Communications Commission following the Super Bowl halftime show that included singer Janet Jackson's bared breast. Marketers as diverse as Abercrombie & Fitch and Anheuser-Busch also announced plans to pull back from the unabashed sexuality of recent ad campaigns.[13]

DEVELOPING AND PREPARING ADS

The final step in the advertising process—the development and preparation of an advertisement—should flow logically from the promotional theme selected. This process should create an ad that becomes a complementary part of the marketing mix with a carefully determined role in the total marketing strategy. Preparation of an advertisement should emphasize features like its creativity, its continuity with past advertisements, and possibly its association with other company products.

What immediate tasks should an advertisement accomplish? Regardless of the chosen target, an advertisement should (1) gain attention and interest, (2) inform and/or persuade, and (3) eventually lead to a purchase or other desired action. It should gain attention in a productive way; that is, it should instill some recall of the good or service. Otherwise, it will not lead to buying action.

Gaining attention and generating interest—cutting through the clutter—can be formidable tasks. Recent studies revealed that ABC had the most clutter of any network, broadcasting 7.1 commercials and network promos per commercial break.[14] Stimulating buying action is often difficult because an advertisement cannot actually close a sale. Nevertheless, if an ad gains attention and informs or persuades, it probably represents a worthwhile investment of marketing resources. Too many advertisers fail to suggest how audience members can purchase their products if they desire to do so. Creative design should eliminate this shortcoming.

The headline is the most important element of an ad. It must offer a promise to the reader of a believable benefit. And it must be placed in a way to make it memorable.

Morris Hite (1910–1983)
American advertising pioneer

The eHarmony.com ad in Figure 16.5 shows the four major elements of this print advertisement: headline, illustration, body copy, and signature. *Headlines* and *illustrations* (photographs, drawings, or other artwork) should work together to generate interest and attention. *Body copy* serves to inform, persuade, and stimulate buying action. The *signature,* which may include the company name, address, phone number, Web address, slogan, trademark, or simply a product photo, names the sponsoring organization. An ad may also have one or more subheads—headings subordinate to the main headline that either link the main headline to the body copy or subdivide sections of the body copy.

After advertisers conceive an idea for an ad that gains attention, informs and persuades, and stimulates purchases, their next step involves refining the thought sketch into a rough layout. Continued refinements of the rough layout eventually produce the final version of the advertisement design that is ready to be executed, printed, or recorded.

The creation of each advertisement in a campaign requires an evolutionary process that begins with an idea and ultimately results in a finished ad that is ready for distribution through print or electronic media. The idea itself must first be converted into a thought sketch, which is a tangible summary of the intended message.

Advances in technology allow advertisers to create novel, eye-catching advertisements. Innovative computer software packages now allow artists to merge multiple images to create a single image with a natural, seamless appearance. Computer-generated images appeal to younger, computer-literate consumers.

CREATING INTERACTIVE ADS

Web surfers want engaging, lively content that takes advantage of the medium's capabilities and goes beyond what they find elsewhere. Increasingly, Web ads are competing with television ads by enhancing their content with video and audio clips. But this orientation overlooks the Web's major advantages: offering speed, providing information, exchanging input through two-way communications, offering self-directed entertainment, and allowing personal choice.

figure 16.5
Elements of a Typical Ad

The growing number of new ways to advertise on the Web attest to the rapidly changing environment marketers encounter on the Internet and in e-commerce in general. Web ads have grown from information-based home pages to innovative, interactive channels for transmitting messages to cyberaudiences, including banners, pop-ups, keyword ads, advertorials, and interstitials. In fact, many online ads now closely resemble television commercials.

Advertising banners were the trendsetters in online advertising, allowing customers to quickly access a company's goods and services through other Web site links. **Banners,** advertisements on a Web page that link to an advertiser's site, are the most common type of advertising on the Web. They can be free of charge or cost thousands of dollars per month depending on the amount of hits the site receives. Online advertisers often describe their Internet ads in terms of "richness," referring to the degree to which new technologies—such as streaming video, 3-D animation, JavaScript, and interactive capabilities—are implemented in the banners.

Banners have evolved into a more target-specific technique for Internet advertising with the advent of *missiles:* messages that appear on the screen at exactly the right moment. When a customer visits the site of Company A's competitor, a missile can be programmed to appear on the customer's monitor that allows the customer to click a direct link to Company A's site. However, many people feel the use of such missiles is a questionable practice.

Keyword ads are an outcropping of banner ads. Used in search engines, keyword ads appear on the results page of a search and are specific to the term being searched. Advertisers pay search engines to target their ads and only display the banners when users search for relevant keywords, allowing marketers to target specific audiences. For example, if a user searched the term "digital camera," keyword ads might appear for electronic boutiques or camera shops that sell digital cameras and film.

Banner designs that have also evolved into larger advertising squares that closely resemble advertisements in the telephone book's Yellow Pages are called *advertorials.* An advertorial on the *Forbes* Web site costs about $25,000 a month. Advertisers quickly expanded on these advertorials with *interstitials*—ads that appear between Web pages of related content. Interstitials appear in a separate browser window while the user waits for a Web page to download. Then there are pop-ups, which are little advertising windows that appear in front of the top window of a user's computer screen, and "pop-unders," which appear under the top window. All these ads are more aggressive than banners, forcing consumers to take action to eliminate them from their screens.[15] Many users complain that interstitials,

1. What is an advertising campaign?
2. What are an advertisement's three main goals?
3. What are the main types of interactive ads?

like pop-ups and missiles, are intrusive and unwanted. Interstitials are more likely to contain large graphics and streaming presentations than banner ads and therefore are more difficult to ignore than typical banner ads. But despite complaints, some studies show that users are more likely to click interstitials than banners.

Web site developers can now add 3-D effects to their sites, a capability that provides new opportunities for advertisers. For example, graphics can show products in lifelike representations.[16] Retailers can create 3-D stores where visitors can take a stroll through the virtual aisles viewing merchandise on display; Web sites need no longer provide their information in formats that resemble catalogs.

5 List and compare the major advertising media.

MEDIA SELECTION

One of the most important decisions in developing an advertising strategy is the selection of appropriate media to carry a firm's message to its audience. The media selected must be capable of accomplishing the communications objectives of informing, persuading, and reminding potential customers of the good, service, person, or idea being advertised.

Research identifies the ad's target market to determine its size and characteristics. Advertisers then match the target characteristics with the media best able to reach that particular audience. The objective of media selection is to achieve adequate media coverage without advertising beyond the identifiable limits of the potential market. Finally, cost comparisons between alternatives should determine the best possible media purchase.

Table 16.1 compares the major advertising media by noting their shares of overall advertising expenditures. It also compares the advantages and disadvantages of each media alternative. *Broadcast media* include television (network and cable) and radio. Newspapers, magazines, outdoor advertising, and direct mail represent the major types of print media. Electronic media include the Internet and kiosks.

TELEVISION

Television—network and cable combined—accounts for almost one of every four advertising dollars spent in the U.S. The attractiveness of television advertising is that marketers can reach local and national markets. Whereas most newspaper advertising revenues come from local advertisers, the greatest share of television advertising revenues comes from organizations that advertise nationally. The newest trend in television advertising is virtual ads—banner-type logos and brief messages that are superimposed onto television coverage of sporting events so that they seem to be a part of the arena's signage but cannot be seen by anyone attending the game. Then there are streaming headlines run by some news stations, which are paid for by corporate sponsors whose names and logos appear within the news stream. Another trend in television advertising is the abbreviated spot—a 15- or 30-second ad—that costs less to make and buy and is too quick for most viewers to zap with their remote controls. See the "Solving an Ethical Controversy" feature for more about ad-zapping.

In the past decade, cable television's share of ad spending and revenues has grown tremendously. Satellite television has contributed to increased cable penetration, which almost three-fourths of all Americans now have installed in their homes. In response to declining ratings and soaring costs, network television companies like NBC, CBS, ABC, Fox, and the WB (Warner Brothers) are refocusing their advertising strategies with a heavy emphasis on moving onto the Net to capture younger audiences.

As cable audiences grow, programming improves, and ratings rise, advertisers are compelled to earmark more of their advertising budgets to this medium. In fact, cable was the only advertising medium—other than direct mail—to actually grow in the advertising downturn that accompanied the recent recession.[17] Cable advertising offers marketers access to more narrowly defined target audiences than other broadcast media can provide—a characteristic referred to as *narrow-casting.* The top five cable networks, ranked in terms of ad revenues, are ESPN, Nickelodeon, MTV, Lifetime, and TBS.[18]

table 16.1 **Comparison of Advertising Media Alternatives**

MEDIA OUTLET	PERCENTAGE OF TOTAL*	ADVANTAGES	DISADVANTAGES
Broadcast			
Network television	18	Mass coverage; repetition; flexibility; prestige	High cost; temporary message; public distrust; lack of selectivity
Cable television	7	Same strengths as network TV; less market coverage since not every viewer is a cable subscriber	Same disadvantages as network TV, although cable TV ads are considerably more targeted to specific viewer segments
Radio	8	Immediacy; low cost; flexibility; targeted audience; mobility	Short life span; highly fragmented audience
Print			
Newspapers	19	Tailored to individual communities; ability to refer back to ads	Short life span
Direct mail	19	Selectivity; intense coverage; speed; flexibility; opportunity to convey complete information; personalization	High cost; consumer resistance; dependence on effective mailing list
Magazines	5	Selectivity; quality image reproduction; long life; prestige	Lack of flexibility
Outdoor	2	Quick, visual communication of simple ideas; link to local goods and services; repetition	Brief exposure; environmental concerns
Electronic			
Internet	2	Two-way communications; flexibility; link to self-directed entertainment	Poor image reproduction; limited scheduling options; difficult to measure effectiveness

*An estimated 21 percent is spent on a variety of miscellaneous media, including Yellow Pages, business papers, transit displays, point-of-purchase displays, cinema advertising, and regional farm papers.

SOURCE: Data from "U.S. Ad Spending Totals by Media," *FactPack 2004 Edition* (special supplement to *Advertising Age*), March 8, 2004, p. 15. Reprinted with permission from March 8, 2004 issue of *Advertising Age*. Copyright © 2004 Crain Communications Inc.

The great variety of special-interest channels devoted to subjects such as cooking, history, home and garden, health, and golf attract specialized audiences and permit niche marketing.

Television advertising offers the advantages of mass coverage, powerful impact on viewers, repetition of messages, flexibility, and prestige. Its disadvantages include loss of control of the promotional message to the telecaster (which can influence its impact), high costs, high mortality rates for commercials, and some public distrust. Compared with other media, television can suffer from lack of selectivity because specific TV programs may not reach consumers in a precisely defined target market without a significant degree of wasted coverage. However, the growing specialization of cable TV channels can help to resolve the problem.

Finally, it is important to note that some types of products are actually banned from television advertising. Tobacco goods, such as cigarettes, cigars, and smokeless tobacco, fall into this category.

RADIO

Radio advertising has always been a popular media choice for up-to-the-minute newscasts and for targeting advertising messages to local audiences. But in recent years, radio has become one of the fastest growing media alternatives. As more and more people find they have less and less time, radio provides immediate information and entertainment at work, at play, and in the car. In addition, as e-commerce

Solving an Ethical Controversy

WILL THE AD-ZAPPER MEAN THE DEATH OF TV COMMERCIALS?

NEW technology may soon free television audiences entirely from the need to sit through commercials. TiVo, the company that makes digital video recorders (DVRs), provides features that let viewers control the time at which they watch a program, pause, rewind, and skip commercials. With competitors like Time Warner and Comcast moving into the DVR market, and TiVo redoubling its R&D efforts, it's expected that the number of households with the ability to zap commercials cheaply and easily with on-demand TV will grow fivefold or more, to more than 25 million by 2007. One media analyst believes viewers will be able to ignore some 60 percent of commercials, or almost $7 billion worth of ads.

SHOULD TECHNOLOGY BE MADE AVAILABLE THAT ALLOWS VIEWERS TO ZAP COMMERCIALS?

PRO

1. Its effect will be minimal; some viewers will not learn to use the new technology and others won't bother to use it very much anyway.
2. Advertisers will just shift their efforts to other kinds of advertising.

CON

1. If TV advertising is no longer effective, the whole business model of television will have to change.
2. The advertising industry will lose so much revenue that the overall quality of programming on this free entertainment and news medium will be negatively affected.

SUMMARY

Satellite operators like EchoStar Communications Corp. and DirectTV and cable company Comcast all plan to begin providing new subscribers with DVRs either free or at very low cost. Top executives at TV networks say there is no immediate threat to the advertising that supports their broadcasts, but no one knows how many advertisers will begin looking elsewhere for their consumer audience.

Sources: E. Craig Stacey, "Abandon TV at Your Own Risk," *Advertising Age*, June 7, 2004, p. 32; Betsy Streisand, "Tuning Out TV," *U.S. News & World Report*, May 24, 2004, pp. 46–48; Brad Stone, "TiVo's Big Moment," *Newsweek*, February 16, 2004, p. 43; "Can Mad Ave. Make Zap-Proof Ads?" *BusinessWeek*, February 2, 2004, pp. 36–37; Stephen Baker, "My Son, the Ad-Zapper," *BusinessWeek*, November 10, 2003, p. 76; Michael Kraus, "Television Advertising in a Time of TiVo," *Marketing News*, January 6, 2003, p. 4.

continues to push the growth in global business, more people are traveling abroad to seek out new markets. For these travelers, radio, because many radio stations are airing over the Internet, is a means of staying in touch with home—wherever that may be. Marketers frequently use radio advertising to reach local audiences. But in recent years, it plays an increasingly important role as a national—and even global—listening favorite. Thousands of online listeners use the Internet to beam in on radio stations from almost every city—tuning in on an easy-listening station in London, a top-40 Hong Kong broadcaster, or a chat show from Toronto. Other listeners equip their vehicles with satellite radio to maintain contact with hometown or destination stations during long trips.

Radio ad revenues in the U.S. are slightly larger than those for cable television. Advertisers like the ability to reach people while they drive because they are a captive audience. With an increase in commuters, this market is growing. Stations can adapt to local preferences by changing format, such as going from country and western to an all-news or rock-and-talk station. The variety of stations allows advertisers to easily target audiences and tailor their messages to those listeners. Other benefits include low cost, flexibility, and mobility. Disadvantages include fragmentation (reaching most people in a market may require ads placed on 10 or more stations), the temporary nature of messages (unlike print ads, radio and TV ads are instantaneous and must be rebroadcast to reach consumers a second time), and a lack of research information as compared with television.

While most radio listening is done at home, in cars, or with headset-equipped portables, technology has given birth to Net radio. Web-cast radio allows customers to widen their listening times and choices through their computers. The potential for selling on this new channel is great. A listener

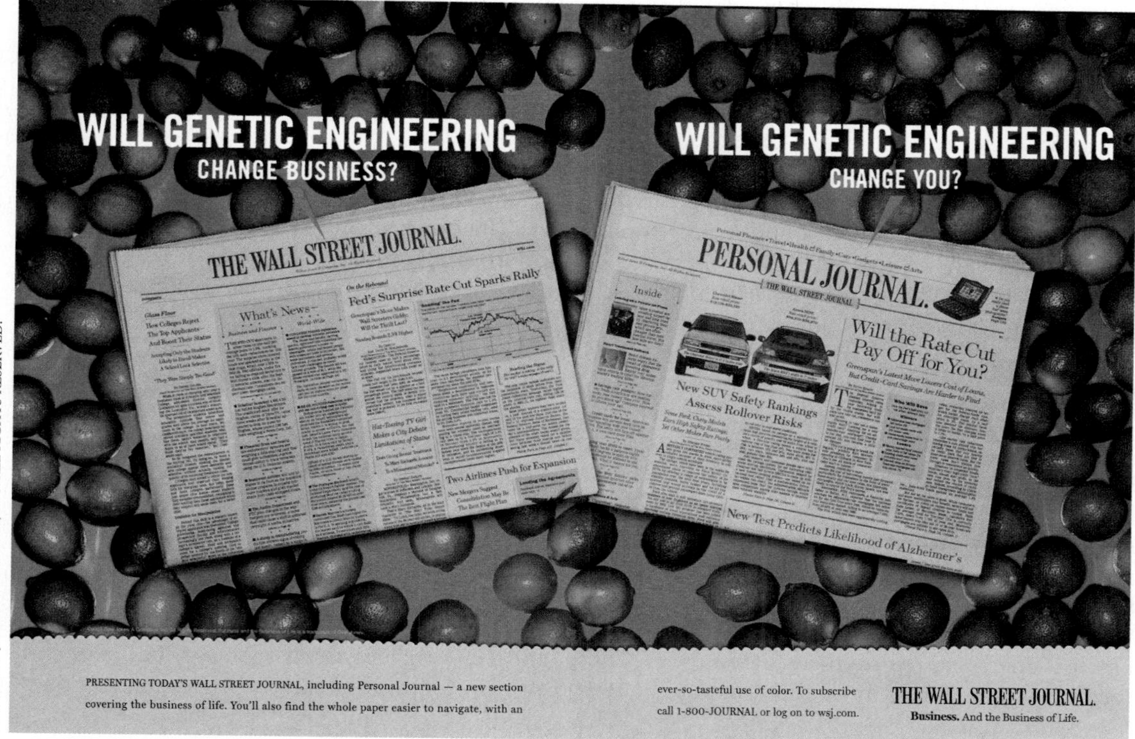

Newspapers offer intensive coverage in local markets, and a few, like* The Wall Street Journal *and* USA Today, *have national reach.

can simply "click here to purchase the song you're hearing." Other goods are easily adapted to click-and-sell possibilities.

NEWSPAPERS

Newspaper advertising continues to dominate local markets, accounting for $44 billion of annual advertising expenditures. In addition to retail advertisements, classified advertising is an important part of newspaper revenues.

Newspapers' primary advantages start with flexibility because advertising can vary from one locality to the next. Newspapers also offer community prestige since readers recognize they have deep impacts on their communities. And they allow intensive coverage for ads. In a typical location, a single newspaper may reach up to 90 percent of all homes and apartments. Readers control their exposure to the advertising message, unlike television or radio advertising messages, and can refer back to newspaper ads.

Newspaper advertising does have some disadvantages: a short life span, hasty reading (the typical reader spends about 40 minutes reading the newspaper), and relatively poor reproduction quality, although that is changing as technology improves. The high repro quality of ads in *USA Today* is an example of the recent strides in newspaper ad quality made possible by new technologies.

Newspapers have also begun to struggle to "get through the noise" of other advertisers. To retain big advertisers like trendy designers and national department stores, some have launched their own annual or semiannual fashion magazines, taking advantage of their finely tuned distribution capabilities.[19]

MAGAZINES

Advertisers divide magazines into two broad categories: consumer magazines and business magazines. These categories are also subdivided into monthly and weekly publications. The top five magazines in terms of circulation are *AARP The Magazine, Reader's Digest, TV Guide, Better Homes & Gardens,* and *National Geographic.*[20] The primary advantages of magazine advertising include the following: selectivity in reaching precise target markets, quality reproduction, long life, the prestige associated with some magazines, and the extra services that many publications offer. The primary disadvantage is that magazines lack the flexibility of newspapers, radio, and television.

Media buyers study circulation numbers and demographic information for various publications before choosing optimal placement opportunities and in negotiating rates. The same advertising categories have claimed the title for big spenders for several years running. Automotive, retail, and movies and media advertising have held their first, second, and third places, respectively, each year and have continued to show strong growth percentages. Advertisers seeking to promote their products to target markets can reach them by advertising in the appropriate magazines.

DIRECT MAIL

As discussed in Chapter 14, direct mail advertising consists of sales letters, postcards, leaflets, folders, booklets, catalogs, and house organs (periodicals published by organizations to cover internal issues). Its advantages come from direct mail's ability to segment large numbers of prospective customers into narrow market niches, speed, flexibility, detailed information, and personalization. Disadvantages of direct mail include high cost per reader, dependence on the quality of mailing lists, and some consumers' resistance to it.

The advantages of direct mail explain its widespread use. Data are available on previous purchase patterns and preferred payment methods, as well as household characteristics such as number of children or seniors. Direct mail accounts for about 19 percent of U.S. total advertising expenditures, or $46 billion annually.[21]

The downside to direct mail is clutter, otherwise known as *junk mail.* So much advertising material is stuffed into people's mailboxes every day that the task of grabbing consumers' attention and evoking some interest is daunting to direct mail advertisers. Three of every five respondents to a survey about "things most likely to get on consumers' nerves" rated junk mail at the top—above telemarketing, credit-card fees, and the fine print on billing statements.

OUTDOOR ADVERTISING

Outdoor advertising, perhaps the oldest and simplest media business around, represents just over 2 percent of total advertising spending. Traditional outdoor advertising takes the form of billboards, painted bulletins or displays (such as those that appear on the walls of buildings), and electronic spectaculars (large, illuminated, and sometimes animated signs and displays). But advertisers are finding new places to put their messages outdoors. You might find an advertising message stenciled guerilla-style on the base of a traffic light, drawn in colored chalk on the sidewalk, or drawn on the back of a park bench. In large, high foot-traffic cities, some brave souls agree—for a fee—to have company logos and brief slogans literally tattooed in visible locations on their bodies, shaved into their hair, or stenciled across their foreheads. A section of highway might be mowed and cleaned up by a local real estate company or restaurant, with a sign implanted where passersby can easily see it. All these are outgrowths of outdoor advertising.

This form of advertising has the advantages of immediate communication of quick and simple ideas, repeated exposure to a message, and strong promotion for locally available products. Outdoor advertising is particularly effective along metropolitan streets and in other high-traffic areas.

But outdoor advertising, just like every other type, is subject to clutter. It also suffers from the brevity of exposure to its messages by passing motorists. Driver concerns about rush-hour safety and limited time also combine to limit the length of exposure to outdoor messages. As a result, most of these ads use striking, simple illustrations, short selling points, and humor to attract people interested in products like beer, vacations, local entertainment, and lodging. As Figure 16.6 shows, United Colors of Benetton reminds people that humor is an important part of life, as well as new clothing.

A third problem involves public concern over aesthetics. The Highway Beautification Act of 1965, for example, regulates the placement of outdoor advertising near interstate highways. In addi-

figure 16.6

Outdoor Advertising: A Simple, Striking, and Humorous Image

tion, many cities have local ordinances that set regulations on the size and placement of outdoor advertising messages. Critics have even labeled billboard advertising as "pollution on a stick."

New technologies are helping to revive outdoor advertising, offsetting the huge drop that resulted from limitations on ads for tobacco and alcohol products. Technology livens up the billboards themselves with animation, large sculptures, and laser images. Digital message signboards can display winning lottery numbers or other timely messages like weather and traffic reports. The best-known digital signboard in the U.S. is in New York's Times Square. And very soon, certain billboards will be able to "beam" messages to consumers' cell phones as they drive past.

France spends the greatest amount on outdoor advertising—nearly 12 percent of total ad spending, compared with 6 percent for Europe as a whole and just over 2 percent for the U.S. But recent changes in advertising policy brought about by the European Union may disallow France's ban on TV advertising, which could shift revenues away from outdoor advertising. Retailers in France are eagerly awaiting the outcome.[22]

INTERACTIVE MEDIA

Interactive media—especially the Internet—are growing up. A recent survey conducted by the Online Publishers Association revealed that 57 percent of consumers prefer to find out about new products online, 43 percent report that the Internet contains advertising that is rich in information, and 42 percent feel that online advertising helps them decide what products to buy.[23] Not surprisingly, interactive advertising budgets are being beefed up at a growing number of companies.

OTHER ADVERTISING MEDIA

As consumers filter out appeals from traditional as well as Internet ads, marketers need new ways to catch their attention. In addition to the major media, firms use a vast number of other vehicles to communicate their messages. Transit advertising includes ads placed both inside and outside buses, subway trains and stations, and commuter trains. Some firms place ads on the roofs of taxicabs, on bus stop shelters and benches, on entertainment and sporting event turnstiles, in public restrooms, and even on parking meters. About half of the 23,000 U.S. movie theaters accept commercials.[24] The trend began as theater owners realized that a lag of 20 minutes between the time patrons enter the theater until the film actually starts could not be filled with upcoming previews, and they began to fill the time with ads. Each year, 1.6 billion tickets are sold, most to the teen to 35-year-old category, a prime target for many advertisers.

Autowraps are a new form of out-of-home advertising being used by many companies. Drivers can become ambassadors for the companies they advertise on their vehicles by handing out samples, coupons, and other information at stores, special events, and other places where traditional advertisers can't go.

Ads also appear on T-shirts, on text screens of cell phones, inlaid in store flooring, in printed programs of live theater productions, and as previews on movie DVDs. Directory advertising includes the familiar Yellow Pages in telephone books, along with thousands of business and industry directories. Some firms pay to have their advertising messages placed on hot-air balloons, blimps, banners behind airplanes, and on scoreboards at sporting events. Johnson & Johnson, Yahoo!, and Dreyers Ice Cream, among others, pay to have their logos and company messages placed on autos via the company Rush Hour Media, known by their drivers as http://www.autowrapped.com. Rush Hour Media uses regular people to literally drive the advertiser's message home. The drivers are chosen based on their driving habits, routes, occupations, and living and working locations and are paid a monthly fee for the use of the outside of their vehicles as advertising space.

MARKETING Concept Check

1. **What types of products are banned from advertising on television?**
2. **What are some advantages radio offers to advertisers? What about newspapers?**
3. **What types of ads would be classified as outdoor advertising?**

MEDIA SCHEDULING

Once advertisers have selected the media that best match their advertising objectives and promotional budget, attention shifts to **media scheduling**—setting the timing and sequence for a series of advertisements. A variety of factors influence this decision as well. Sales patterns, repurchase cycles, and competitors' activities are the most important variables.

Seasonal sales patterns are common in many industries. An airline might reduce advertising during peak travel periods and boost its media schedule during low travel months. Repurchase cycles may also play a role in media scheduling—products with shorter repurchase cycles will more likely require consistent media schedules throughout the year. Competitors' activities are still other influences on media scheduling. A small firm may avoid advertising during periods of heavy advertising by its rivals.

Briefly Speaking

In good times people want to advertise; in bad times they have to.

Bruce Barton (1886–1967)
American advertising executive

Advertisers use the concepts of reach, frequency, and gross rating points to measure the effectiveness of media scheduling plans. *Reach* refers to the number of different people or households exposed to an advertisement at least once during a certain time period, typically four weeks. *Frequency* refers to the number of times an individual is exposed to an advertisement during a certain time period. By multiplying reach times frequency, advertisers quantitatively describe the total weight of a media effort, which is called the campaign's *gross rating point (GRP).*

Recently, marketers have questioned the effectiveness of reach and frequency to measure ad success online. The theory behind frequency is that the average advertising viewer needs a minimum of three exposures to a message to understand it and connect it to a specific brand. For Web surfers, the "wear-out" is much quicker—hence, the greater importance of building customer relationships through advertisements.

A media schedule is typically created in the following way. Say an auto manufacturer wants to advertise a new model designed primarily to appeal to professional consumers in their 30s. The model would be introduced in November with a direct mail piece offering test drives. Outdoor, newspaper, and magazine advertising would support the direct mail campaign but also follow through the winter and into the spring and summer. The newspaper ads might actually be cooperative, for both the manufacturer and local dealers. Early television commercials might air during a holiday television special in mid-December, and then one or more expensively produced, highly creative spots would be first aired during the Super Bowl in late January. Another television commercial—along with new print ads—might be scheduled for fall clearance sales as the manufacturer gets ready to introduce next year's models. This example illustrates how marketers might plan their advertising year for just one product.

1. What is reach? Frequency?
2. How do advertisers calculate gross rating point?
3. Define *media scheduling* and identify the most important factors influencing the scheduling decision.

ORGANIZATION OF THE ADVERTISING FUNCTION

6 Outline the organization of the advertising function and the role of an advertising agency.

Although the ultimate responsibility for advertising decision making often rests with top marketing management, organizational arrangements for the advertising function vary among companies. A producer of a technical industrial product may operate with a one-person department within the company, who works primarily to write copy for submission to trade publications. A consumer goods company, on the other hand, may staff a large department with advertising specialists.

The advertising function is usually organized as a staff department reporting to the vice president (or director) of marketing. The director of advertising is an executive position with the responsibility for the functional activity of advertising. This position requires not only a skilled and experienced advertiser but also an individual who communicates effectively within the organization. The success of a firm's promotional strategy depends on the advertising director's willingness and ability to communicate both vertically and horizontally. The major tasks typically organized under advertising include advertising research, design, copywriting, media analysis, and in some cases, sales and trade promotion.

ADVERTISING AGENCIES

Most large companies in industries characterized by sizable advertising expenditures will hire an independent **advertising agency**, a firm whose marketing specialists assist businesses in planning and preparing advertisements. Advertising is a huge, global industry. Ranked by worldwide revenue, Japan's Dentsu is the world's largest advertising agency, followed by New York City–based McCann-Erickson Worldwide.[25]

advertising agency Firm whose marketing specialists assist advertisers in planning and preparing advertisements.

Most large advertisers cite several reasons for relying on agencies for at least some portion of their advertising. Agencies typically employ highly qualified specialists who provide a degree of creativity and objectivity that is difficult to sustain in a corporate advertising department. Some also manage to reduce the cost of advertising by allowing the advertiser to avoid many of the fixed expenses associated with maintaining an internal advertising department.

Figure 16.7 shows a hypothetical organization chart for a large advertising agency. Although job titles may vary among agencies, the major functions may be classified as creative services; account

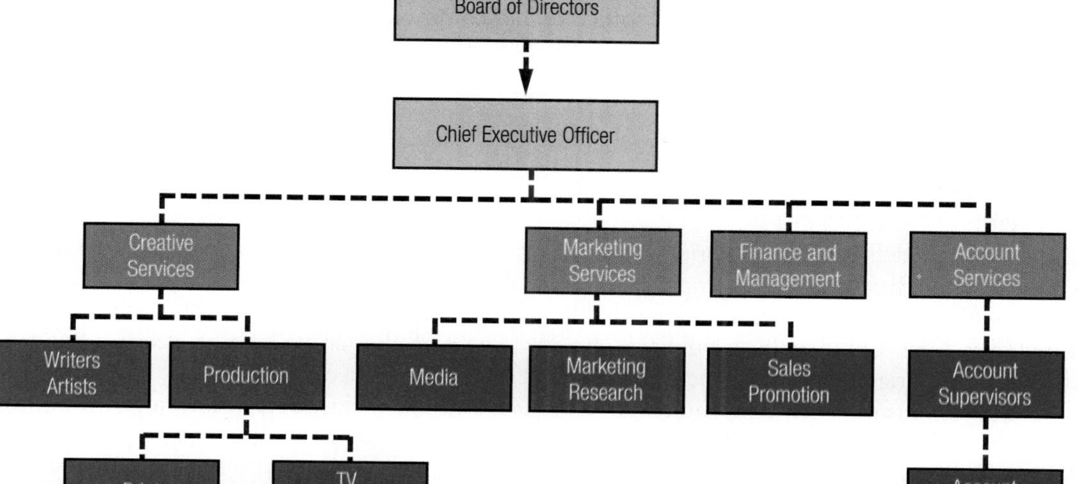

figure 16.7
Advertising Agency Organizational Chart

ETIQUETTE TIPS — FOR MARKETING PROFESSIONALS

Voice-Mail Etiquette

IT'S no secret that new communications technologies have changed the way we do business. New modes of communication require new skills if they are to be used effectively. How are your voice-mail manners? Check this list of tips and see what you might need to improve.

1. Whenever possible, answer your phone yourself, no later than the second or third ring. Identify yourself by name.
2. Avoid falling back on voice mail as a call-screening device. It is impolite, and it is better to deal with calls as they come than to let messages build up.
3. Set your voice mail to ring as few times as possible before playing your message.
4. Make your message professional but friendly—and short. Speak slowly and clearly and avoid slang.
5. Update your message often, especially if you travel a lot. Use the message to let callers know when you will return or when you will call back.
6. Provide directions for callers to reach someone else who can help them in person if they prefer.
7. Check your messages as often as possible, and return calls within one business day.
8. When you call back, thank the caller for his or her message.
9. If you leave a message for someone, begin with your full name, your company, and the day and time you called. Always include your own phone number to make it as easy as possible for the other person to return your call.
10. Leave a message that is concise. Make sure the person knows why you called and when he or she can reach you.

Remember that voice mail is not meant to replace you. It should be used only when you cannot answer your phone. As with many aspects of marketing, the personal touch is always best.

Sources: "Voice-Mail Etiquette," http://www.customerfocusinc.com, accessed April 23, 2004; "Voice Mail Etiquette FAQs," http://www.edu.gov.mb.ca, accessed April 23, 2004; "Telecommunications: Faculty/Staff," Rollins College, http://www.rollins.edu/telecom/etiquette.html, accessed April 23, 2004.

services; marketing services, including media services, marketing research, and sales promotion; and finance and management. Whatever organization structure is selected, an agency often stands or falls on its relationships with its clients. The fast pace and pressure of ad agencies are legendary, but good communication remains paramount to maintaining that relationship. A few important tips on the proper use of voice mail—an office tool as common as a PC—appear in the "Etiquette Tips for Marketing Professionals" feature.

1. What is the role of an advertising agency?
2. What are some advantages of using an agency?

(7) Explain the roles of cross promotions, public relations, publicity, and ethics in an organization's promotional strategy.

PUBLIC RELATIONS

In Chapter 15, we defined public relations as the firm's communications and relationships with its various publics, including customers, employees, stockholders, suppliers, government agencies, and the society in which it operates. Organizational public relations efforts date back to 1889, when George Westinghouse hired two people to publicize the advantages of alternating-current electricity and to refute arguments originally championed by Thomas Edison for direct-current systems.

Public relations is an efficient, indirect communications channel through which a firm can promote products, although it serves broader objectives than those of other components of promotional strategy. It is concerned with the prestige and image of all parts of the organization. Today, public relations plays a larger role than ever within the promotional mix, and it may emphasize more marketing-oriented information. In addition to its traditional activities, such as surveying public attitudes and creating a good corporate image, PR also supports advertising in promoting the organization's goods and services.[26]

Approximately 160,000 people work in public relations in both the not-for-profit and profit-oriented sectors. Some 1,800 public relations firms currently operate in the U.S. In addition, thousands of one-person operations compete to offer these services.

Public relations is in a period of major growth as a result of increased public pressure on industries regarding corporate ethical conduct and environmental and international issues. International expenditures on public relations are growing more rapidly than those for advertising and sales promotion. Many top executives are becoming more involved in public relations as well. The public expects top managers to take greater responsibility for company actions than they have accepted in the past. Those who refuse are widely criticized, censured, and even arrested.

Public relations can serve the community as well as the firm. ADT Security Systems recently installed security systems in the homes of battered women in five cities, working with the largest women's shelter in each area. The systems were installed and monitored at no charge, preventing assaults and even saving lives. At press conferences announcing the installations, ADT executives were joined by mayors, police chiefs, and the directors of the shelters. Coincidentally, the company saw increases in sales of its security systems in those cities, ranging from 15 to 33 percent.[27]

The PR department is the link between the firm and the media. It provides press releases and holds news conferences to announce new products, the formation of strategic alliances, management changes, financial results, or similar developments. The PR department may issue its own publications as well, including newsletters, brochures, and reports. Such innovations as the Segway personal transporter and Crest's WhiteStrips received tremendous boosts when their PR managers placed them on popular TV shows. The Segway transporter was demonstrated on *Good Morning America,* and WhiteStrips were launched on Rosie O'Donnell's former syndicated TV talk show.[28]

A PR plan begins much like an advertising plan, with research to define the role and scope of the firm's overall public relations and current challenges. Next come strategic decisions on short-term and long-term goals and markets, analysis of product features, and choices of messages and media channels—or other PR strategies such as speaking engagements or contests—for each market. Plan execution involves developing messages highlighting the benefits that the firm brings to each market. The final step is to measure results.

The Internet has actually changed some PR planning, as PR representatives now have more direct access to the public instead of having their messages filtered through journalists and the news media. This direct access gives them greater control over their messages.

MARKETING AND NONMARKETING PUBLIC RELATIONS

Nonmarketing public relations refers to a company's messages about general management issues. When a company makes a decision that affects any of its publics, input from public relations specialists can help smooth its dealings with those publics. A company that decides to close a plant would need advice on how to deal with the local community. Other examples include a company's attempts to gain favorable public opinion during a long strike or an open letter to Congress published in a newspaper during congressional debates on a bill that would affect a particular industry. Although some companies organize their public relations departments separately from their marketing divisions, PR activities invariably affect promotional strategies.

In contrast, **marketing public relations (MPR)** refers to narrowly focused public relations activities that directly support marketing goals. MPR involves an organization's relationships with consumers or other groups about marketing concerns and can be either proactive or reactive.

With proactive MPR, the marketer takes the initiative and seeks out opportunities for promoting the firm's products, often including distribution of press releases and feature articles. For example, companies send press releases about new products to newspapers, television stations, and relevant consumer, business, and trade publications. It is a powerful marketing tool since it adds news coverage that reinforces direct promotion activities.

Reactive MPR responds to an external situation that has potential negative consequences for the organization. Examples of reactive MPR are responses to product tamperings, such as the deaths caused by cyanide in Tylenol (1982) and Sudafed (1991) capsules. Prompt corrective action and strong

PR campaigns from Johnson & Johnson and GlaxoSmithKline, respectively, prevented these situations from becoming disasters. On the other hand, both Ford and Bridgestone/Firestone fumbled in their attempts to blame each other for injuries and deaths caused by defective tires. More recently, several major airlines have used MPR to try to attract more flying customers after the tragedies of September 11, 2001.

PUBLICITY

publicity Nonpersonal stimulation of demand for a good, service, place, idea, person, or organization by unpaid placement of significant news regarding the product in a print or broadcast medium.

The aspect of public relations that is most directly related to promoting a firm's products is **publicity:** nonpersonal stimulation of demand for a good, service, place, idea, person, or organization by unpaid placement of significant news regarding the product in a print or broadcast medium. It has been said that if advertising is the hammer, publicity is the nail. It creates credibility for the advertising to follow. Firms generate publicity by creating special events, holding press conferences, and preparing news releases and media kits. Many firms, such as Starbucks and Wal-Mart's Sam's Club, have built their brands with virtually no advertising. Pharmaceutical products including Viagra and Prozac became worldwide brands with relatively little advertising, although advertising—including a frequent-user awards program—is now used extensively in competing with a number of newly introduced competitors.

While publicity generates minimal costs compared with other forms of promotion, it does not deliver its message entirely for free. Publicity-related expenses include the costs of employing marketing personnel assigned to create and submit publicity releases, printing and mailing costs, and related expenses.

Firms often pursue publicity to promote their images or viewpoints. Other publicity efforts involve organizational activities such as plant expansions, mergers and acquisitions, management changes, and research breakthroughs. A significant amount of publicity, however, provides information about goods and services, particularly new products.

Because many consumers consider news stories to be more credible than advertisements as sources of information, publicity releases are often sent to media editors for possible inclusion in news stories. The media audiences perceive the news as coming from the communications media, not the sponsors. The information in a publicity release about a new good or service can provide valuable assistance for a television, newspaper, or magazine writer, leading to eventual broadcast or publication. Publicity releases sometimes fill voids in publications, and at other times, they become part of regular features. In either case, they offer firms valuable supplements to paid advertising messages.

1. **Distinguish between marketing public relations and nonmarketing public relations.**
2. **What is publicity?**

cross promotion Promotional technique in which marketing partners share the cost of a promotional campaign that meets their mutual needs.

CROSS PROMOTION

In recent years, marketers have begun to combine their promotional efforts for related products using a technique called **cross promotion,** in which marketing partners share the cost of a promotional campaign that meets their mutual needs—an important benefit in an environment of rising media costs. Relationship marketing strategies like comarketing and cobranding, discussed in Chapter 10, are forms of cross promotion. Marketers realize that these joint efforts between established brands provide greater benefits in return for both organizations; investments of time and money on such promotions will become increasingly important to many partners' growth prospects.

A recent advertisement for the Sony Liv CD clock radio promoted not only the clock but also its availability at Target. By signing an exclusive distribution deal with the retail giant, Sony marketers knew they would secure the cooperation of Target store managers in training their sales

1. **What is cross promotion?**
2. **What are the advantages of cross promotion?**

personnel to bring the new product to the attention of shoppers, secure effective display locations, and be included in Target promotions. Target marketers expected to gain as a result of their exclusive distribution of an exciting new product from one of the global leaders in consumer electronics.

MEASURING PROMOTIONAL EFFECTIVENESS

figure 16.8

Billboard Advertising: The Cheapest Way to Spend Ad Dollars

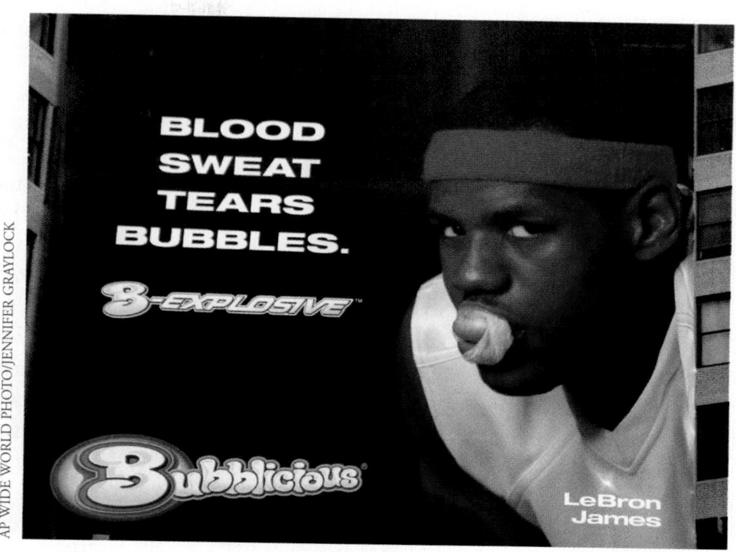

AP WIDE WORLD PHOTO/JENNIFER GRAYLOCK

Each element of the promotional mix represents a major expenditure for a firm. Although promotional prices vary widely, advertisers typically pay a fee based on cost to deliver the message to viewers, listeners, or readers—the so-called *cost per thousand (CPM).* Billboards are the cheapest way to spend advertising dollars, with television and some newspapers the most expensive. Despite the cost of paying LeBron James to appear in Figure 16.8, this billboard most likely cost much less than a television advertisement would have. So while price is an important factor in media selection, it is by no means the only one—or all ads would appear on billboards!

Because promotion represents such a major expenditure for many firms, they need to determine whether their campaigns accomplish appropriate promotional objectives. Companies want their advertising agencies and in-house marketing personnel to demonstrate how promotional programs contribute to increased sales and profits. Marketers are well aware of the number of advertising messages and sales promotions that consumers encounter daily, and they know that these people practice selective perception and simply screen out many messages.

8 **Explain how marketers assess promotional effectiveness.**

By measuring promotional effectiveness, organizations can evaluate different strategies, prevent mistakes before spending money on specific programs, and improve their promotional programs. As the earlier discussion of promotional planning explained, any evaluation program starts with objectives and goals; otherwise, marketers have no yardstick against which to measure effectiveness. However, determining whether an advertising message has achieved its intended objective is one of the most difficult undertakings in marketing. Sales promotions and direct marketing are somewhat easier to evaluate because they evoke measurable consumer responses. Like advertising, public relations is also difficult to assess on purely objective terms.

If you think advertising doesn't pay—we understand there are 25 mountains in Colorado higher than Pikes Peak. Can you name one?

Anonymous

MEASURING ADVERTISING EFFECTIVENESS

Measures to evaluate the effectiveness of advertising, while difficult and costly, are essential parts of any marketing plan. Without an assessment strategy, marketers will not know whether their advertising achieves the objectives of the marketing plan or whether the dollars in the advertising budget are well spent. To answer these questions, marketers can conduct two types of research. **Media research** assesses how well a particular medium delivers the advertiser's message, where and when to place the advertisement, and the size of the audience. Buyers of broadcast time base their purchases on estimated Nielsen rating points, and the networks have to make good if ratings do not reach promised levels. Buyers of print advertising space pay fees based on circulation. Circulation figures are independently certified by specialized research firms.

The other major category, **message research,** tests consumer reactions to an advertisement's creative message. Pretesting and posttesting, the two methods for performing message research, are discussed in the following sections.

Pretesting

To assess an advertisement's likely effectiveness before it actually appears in the chosen medium, marketers often conduct **pretesting.** The obvious advantage of this technique is the opportunity to

On-screen theater advertising is highly effective, especially for products targeted to younger audiences.

evaluate ads when they are being developed. Marketers can conduct a number of different pretests, beginning during the concept phase in the campaign's earliest stages, when they have only rough copy of the ad, and continuing until the ad layout and design are almost completed.

Pretesting employs a variety of evaluation methods. Focus groups can discuss their reactions to mock-ups of ads using different themes, headlines, or illustrations. To test magazine advertisements, the Batten, Barton, Durstine & Osborn ad agency cuts ads out of advance copies of magazines and then inserts the ads it wants to test. Interviewers later check the impact of the advertisements on readers who receive free copies of the revised magazines. Another ad agency, McCann-Erickson, uses a *sales conviction test* to evaluate magazine advertisements. Interviewers ask heavy users of a particular item to pick one of two alternative advertisements that would convince them to purchase it.

To screen potential radio and television advertisements, marketers often recruit consumers to sit in a studio and indicate their preferences by pressing two buttons, one for a positive reaction to the commercial and the other for a negative reaction. Sometimes proposed ad copy is printed on a postcard that also offers a free product; the number of cards returned represents an indication of the copy's effectiveness. *Blind product tests* are also frequently used. In these tests, people are asked to select unidentified products on the basis of available advertising copy.

Mechanical devices offer yet another method of assessing how people read advertising copy. One mechanical test uses a hidden camera to photograph eye movements of readers. The results help advertisers determine headline placement and copy length. Another mechanical approach measures the galvanic skin response—changes in the electrical resistance of the skin produced by emotional reactions.

The most important word in the vocabulary of advertising is TEST. If you pretest your product with consumers, and pretest your advertising, you will do well in the market place.

David Ogilvy (1911–1999)
founder, Ogilvy & Mather advertising agency

Posttesting

Posttesting assesses advertising copy after it has appeared in the appropriate medium. Pretesting generally is a more desirable measurement method than posttesting because it can save the cost of placing ineffective ads. However, posttesting can help in planning future advertisements and in adjusting current advertising programs.

In one of the most popular posttests, the *Starch Readership Report* interviews people who have read selected magazines to determine whether they observed various ads in them. A copy of the magazine is used as an interviewing aid, and each interviewer starts at a different point in the magazine. For larger ads, respondents are also asked about specifics, such as headlines and copy. Figure 16.9 shows a magazine advertisement with its Starch scores. All such *readership tests,* also called recognition tests, assume that future sales are related to advertising readership.

Unaided recall tests are another method of posttesting the effectiveness of advertisements. Respondents do not see copies of the magazine after their initial reading but are asked to recall the ads from memory. Burke Research Corp. conducts telephone interviews the day after a commercial has aired on television to test brand recognition and the advertisement's effectiveness. Another unaided recall test is adWatch, a joint project of *Advertising Age* magazine and the Gallup Organization. It measures ad awareness by telephone polling that asks each consumer to name the advertisement that first comes to mind of all the ads he or she has seen, heard, or read in the previous 30 days.

Inquiry tests are another popular form of posttest. Advertisements sometimes offer gifts—generally product samples—to people who respond to them. The number of inquiries relative to the advertisement's cost forms a measure of its effectiveness.

Split runs allow advertisers to test two or more ads at the same time. Although advertisers traditionally place different versions in newspapers and magazines, split runs on cable television systems frequently test the effectiveness of TV ads. With this method, advertisers divide the cable TV audience or a publication's subscribers in two: Half view advertisement A and the other half view advertisement

"AND YOU THOUGHT WE ONLY MADE CARS" ADVERTISEMENT IS COURTESY OF AMERICAN HONDA MOTORS CO., INC.

figure 16.9

Magazine Advertisement with Starch Scores

B. The relative effectiveness of the alternatives is then determined through inquiries or recall and recognition tests.

Regardless of the exact method they choose, marketers must realize that pretesting and posttesting are expensive efforts. As a result, they must plan to use these techniques as effectively as possible.

MEASURING PUBLIC RELATIONS EFFECTIVENESS

As with other forms of marketing communications, organizations must measure PR results based on their objectives both for the PR program as a whole and for specific activities. In the next step, marketers must decide what they want to measure. This choice includes determining whether the message was heard by the target audience and whether it had the desired influence on public opinion.

The simplest and least costly level of assessment involves outputs of the PR program: whether the target audience received, paid attention to, understood, and retained the messages directed to them. To make this judgment, the staff could count the number of media placements and gauge the extent of media coverage. They could count attendees at any press conference, evaluate the quality of brochures and other materials, and pursue similar activities. Formal techniques include tracking publicity placements, analyzing how favorably their contents portrayed the company, and conducting public opinion polls.

To analyze PR effectiveness more deeply, a firm could conduct focus groups, interviews with opinion leaders, and more detailed and extensive opinion polls. The highest level of effectiveness measurement looks at outcomes: Did the PR program change people's opinions, attitudes, and behavior? PR professionals measure these outcomes through before-and-after polls (similar to pretesting and posttesting) and more advanced techniques like psychographic analysis (discussed in Chapter 5) and marketing research tools such as cluster analysis and communicants audits.

EVALUATING INTERACTIVE MEDIA

Marketers employ several methods to measure how many users view Web advertisements: *hits* (user requests for a file), *impressions* (the number of times a viewer sees an ad), and *clickthroughs* (when the user clicks the ad to get more information). However, some of these measures can be misleading. Because each page, graphic, or multimedia file equals one hit, simple interactions can easily inflate the hit count, making it less accurate. To increase effectiveness, advertisers must give viewers who do click through their site something good to see. Successful Web campaigns use demonstrations, promotions, coupons, and interactive features.

Internet marketers price ad banners based on cost per thousand (CPM). Web sites that sell advertising typically guarantee a certain number of impressions—the number of times an ad banner is downloaded and presumably seen by visitors. Marketers then set a rate based on that guarantee times the CPM rate.

1. What is CPM and how is it measured?
2. Distinguish between media research and message research.
3. Describe several research techniques used in posttesting.

Although the Web does not yet have a standard measurement system, a number of companies like I/Pro, NetCount, and Interse offer different Web tracking and counting systems. At least two auditing services, Audit Bureau of Verification Services and BPA International, are available. Nielsen NetRatings rates Internet sites based on the number of different visitors they receive.

ETHICS IN NONPERSONAL SELLING

Chapter 3 introduced the topic of marketing ethics and noted that promotion is the element in the marketing mix that raises the most ethical questions. People actively debate the question of whether marketing communications contribute to better lives. The final section of this chapter takes a closer look at ethical concerns in advertising and public relations.

Briefly Speaking

We grew up founding our dreams on the infinite promise of American advertising. I still believe that one can learn to play the piano by mail and that mud will give you a perfect complexion.

Zelda Fitzgerald (1900–1948)

American artist, dancer, and writer

ADVERTISING ETHICS

Even though advertising to children and beer ads are legal, these types of promotions continue to be debated as important ethical issues. One area of controversy is advertising aimed at children. When it comes to influencing parents' purchase decisions, nothing beats influencing kids. By promoting goods and services directly to children, firms can sell not only to them but to the rest of the household, too. But many parents and consumer advocates question the ethics of promoting directly to children. Their argument: At a time when kids need to learn how to consume thoughtfully, they are being inundated with promotional messages teaching the opposite. To woo younger consumers, especially teens and those in their 20s, advertisers attempt to make these messages appear as different from advertisements as possible; they design ads that seem more like entertainment.

Alcoholic beverage advertising on television is another controversial area. Beer marketers advertise heavily on television and spend far more on advertising in print and outdoor media than do marketers of hard-liquor brands. Some members of Congress want much stricter regulation of all forms of such advertising on television and other media. This change would restrict ads in magazines with a 15 percent or more youth readership to black-and-white text only. Critics decry advertisements with messages implying that drinking the right beer will improve a person's personal life or help to win a sports contest. Many state and local authorities are considering more restrictive proposals on both alcohol and tobacco advertising.

In cyberspace ads, it is often difficult to separate advertising from editorial content since many sites resemble magazine and newspaper ads or television infomercials. Another ethical issue surrounding advertising online is the use of **cookies,** small text files that are automatically downloaded to a user's computer whenever a site is visited. Each time the user returns to that site, the site's server accesses the cookie and gathers information: What site was visited last? How long did the user stay? What was the next site visited? Marketers claim that this device helps them determine consumer preferences and argue that cookies are stored in the user's PC, not the company's Web site. The problem is that cookies can and do collect personal information without the user's knowledge.

Puffery and Deception

Puffery refers to exaggerated claims of a product's superiority or the use of subjective or vague statements that may not be literally true. A company might advertise the "most advanced system" or claim that its product is "most effective" in accomplishing its purpose.

Exaggeration in ads is not new. Consumers seem to accept advertisers' tendencies to stretch the truth in their efforts to distinguish their products and get consumers to buy. This inclination may provide one reason that advertising does not encourage purchase behavior as successfully as sales promotions do. A tendency toward puffery does raise some ethical questions, though: Where is the line between claims that attract attention and those that provide implied guarantees? To what degree do advertisers deliberately make misleading statements?

The *Uniform Commercial Code* standardizes sales and business practices throughout the U.S. It makes a distinction between puffery and any specific or quantifiable statement about product quality or performance that constitutes an "express warranty," which obligates the company to stand behind its claim. General boasts of product superiority and vague claims are puffery, not warranties. They are considered so self-praising or exaggerated that the average consumer would not rely on them to make a buying decision.

A quantifiable statement, on the other hand, implies a certain level of performance. For example, tests can establish the validity of a claim that a brand of long-life lightbulbs outlasts three regular lightbulbs.

ETHICS IN PUBLIC RELATIONS

Several public relations issues open organizations to criticism. Various PR firms perform services for the tobacco industry; publicity campaigns defend unsafe products. Also, marketers must weigh ethics before they respond to negative publicity. For example, do firms admit to problems or product deficiencies, or do they try to cover them up? It should be noted that PR practitioners violate the Public Relations Society of America's Code of Professional Standards if they promote products or causes widely known to be harmful to others.

1. **What is puffery?**
2. **What is the purpose of the Uniform Commercial Code?**

Strategic Implications of Marketing in the 21st Century

GREATER portions of corporate ad budgets will migrate to the Web in the near future. After experiencing huge growth since its beginnings, in just one recent year, Internet ad spending grew over 12 percent, and in Asia (excluding Japan), growth is expected to run in the triple digits over the next few years.[29] This trend means that marketers must be increasingly aware of the benefits and pitfalls of Internet advertising. But they should not forget the benefits of other types of advertising as well.

Promotion industry experts agree that e-commerce broadens marketers' job tasks, though many promotional objectives still remain the same. Today, advertisers need 75 different ways to market their products in 75 countries in the world and innumerable market segments. In years to come, advertisers also agree that channels will become more homogeneous while markets become more fragmented. ◆◆◆

REVIEW OF CHAPTER OBJECTIVES

(1) Identify the three major advertising objectives and the two basic categories of advertising.

The three major objectives of advertising are to inform, to persuade, and to remind. The two major categories of advertising are product advertising and institutional advertising. Product advertising involves the nonpersonal selling of a good or service. Institutional advertising is the nonpersonal promotion of a concept, idea, or philosophy of a company or organization.

1.1. Identify and define the two broad categories of advertising. Give an example of each.
1.2. What are the three primary objectives of advertising messages?
1.3. At what stage of the product life cycle is each type of advertising message most commonly used?

② List the major advertising strategies.

The major strategies are comparative advertising, which makes extensive use of messages with direct comparisons between competing brands; celebrity, which uses famous spokespeople to boost an advertising message; retail, which includes all advertising by retail stores selling products directly to consumers; and interactive, which encourages two-way communication either via the Internet or kiosks.

2.1. Describe each of the four major advertising strategies.

③ Describe the process of creating an advertisement.

An advertisement evolves from pinpointing goals, such as educating consumers, enhancing brand loyalty, or improving a product's image. From those goals, marketers move to the next stages: creating a plan, developing a message, developing and preparing the ad, and selecting the appropriate medium (or media). Advertisements often appeal to consumers' emotions with messages focusing on fear, humor, or sex.

3.1. What variables might marketers consider in creating an advertising message for a firm that offers financial services, including retirement accounts, credit cards, and other investments?

④ Identify the major types of advertising appeals and discuss their uses.

Advertisers often focus on making emotional appeals to the reader's or viewer's fear, humor, sex, guilt, or fantasy. While these can be effective, marketers need to recognize that fear appeals can backfire, people's sense of humor can differ according to sex, age, and other factors, and use of sexual imagery must not overstep the bounds of taste.

4.1. What are some common advertising appeals?
4.2. What are the advantages and disadvantages of these appeals?

⑤ List and compare the major advertising media.

The major media include broadcast (television and radio), newspapers and magazines, direct mail, outdoor, and interactive. Each medium has benefits and drawbacks. Newspapers are flexible and dominate local markets. Magazines can target niche markets. Interactive media encourage two-way communication. Outdoor advertising in a high-traffic location reaches many people every day; television and radio reach even more. Direct mail allows selective and intensive coverage.

5.1. Identify and describe the different advertising media. Give an example of one type of product that could best be advertised in each.
5.2. How is advertising through interactive media different from advertising in traditional media? Describe how you think a chain of golf resorts could use interactive advertising effectively.
5.3. When are celebrity spokespersons likely to be effective in advertising? Give recent examples of effective and ineffective spokespersons in advertisements.

⑥ Outline the organization of the advertising function and the role of an advertising agency.

Within a firm, the advertising department is usually a group that reports to a marketing executive. Advertising departments generally include research, art and design, copywriting, and media analysis. Outside advertising agencies assist and support firms that do not have their own advertising departments. These specialists are usually organized by creative services, account services, marketing services, and finance.

6.1. What is the role of an advertising agency?

⑦ Explain the roles of cross promotions, public relations, publicity, and ethics in an organization's promotional strategy.

Cross promotions, illustrated by tie-ins between popular movies and fast-food restaurants, permit the marketing partners to share the cost of a promotional campaign that meets their mutual needs. Public relations consists of the firm's communications and relationships with its various publics, including customers, employees, stockholders, suppliers, government, and the society in which it operates. Publicity is the dissemination of newsworthy information about a product or organization. This information activity is frequently used in new-product introductions. Although publicity is welcomed by firms, negative publicity is easily created when a company enters a gray ethical area with the use of its promotional efforts. Therefore, marketers should be careful to construct ethically sound promotional campaigns, avoiding such practices as puffery and deceit.

7.1. How can firms use marketing public relations (MPR) to their advantage?

7.2. Do you agree with the statement that publicity is free advertising?

⑧ Explain how marketers assess promotional effectiveness.

The effectiveness of advertising can be measured by both pretesting and posttesting. Pretesting is the assessment of an ad's effectiveness before it is actually used. It includes such methods as sales conviction tests and blind product tests. Posttesting is the assessment of the ad's effectiveness after it has been used. Commonly used posttests include readership tests, unaided recall tests, inquiry tests, and split runs.

8.1. Describe the ways in which marketers assess promotional effectiveness.

8.2. Identify the major ethical issues affecting advertising, sales promotion, and public relations.

MARKETING TERMS YOU NEED TO KNOW

advertising 520
product advertising 521
institutional advertising 521
informative advertising 522
persuasive advertising 522
reminder advertising 522
comparative advertising 522
cooperative advertising 524
advertising campaign 527
advertising agency 537
publicity 540
cross promotion 540

OTHER IMPORTANT MARKETING TERMS

retail advertising 524
interactive advertising 525
banners 529
media scheduling 536
nonmarketing public relations 539
marketing public relations (MPR) 539
media research 541
message research 541
pretesting 541
posttesting 542
split runs 542
cookies 544
puffery 544

PROJECTS AND TEAMWORK EXERCISES

1. With a classmate, review a number of advertising messages across several media and identify two effective messages and two you think are ineffective. Describe why you think each is effective or ineffective. Bring at least two of the ads to class to discuss with classmates.
2. Choose a magazine that interests you and analyze the advertisements in one issue. Describe whom you think the magazine's readers are by reviewing the ads.
3. With a classmate, find an example of cross promotion. If possible, bring it to class to discuss its effectiveness. Then create your own plan for cross promoting two products that you think would be good candidates for cross promotion.
4. Access the Internet and surf around to some sites that interest you. How many banner ads or pop-ups do you see? Do you like to view these ads, or do you find them intrusive? Which are most appealing? Which are least?
5. Select two different advertisers' television or print ads for the same product category (cars or soft drinks, for instance) and decide what emotion each appeals to. Which ad is more effective and why?
6. Which kind of appeal do you think would be most effective in advertising each of the following? Why?
   a. whitening toothpaste
   b. wireless Internet access
   c. diamond jewelry
   d. antilitter campaign
   e. anticavity toothpaste
   f. discount shoe store
7. Do outdoor ads and pop-up ads have any characteristics in common? What are they?
8. Research suggests that advertising appeals based on sex are successful only when they are appropriate to the type of product being advertised. With a classmate, discuss whether each of you agrees or disagrees with this observation. Prepare to present your reasoning to the class.
9. List as many advertisements as you can that you remember seeing, reading, or hearing in the last week. Narrow your list down to five or six ads you can recall with some detail and accuracy. What was memorable about each of these ads?
10. One media observer says that young audiences today may use television ads differently from the way their parents did. For example, they may copy an ad's editing style for a video of their own, or they may download the music because they like it. But unlike an earlier generation, they might not be focusing on the message of the ad at all. Do you agree or disagree with this suggestion? Why?

APPLYING CHAPTER CONCEPTS

1. Design a print ad, with rough-draft copy and an image (or a description of an image), for an electronics store you visit frequently. Be sure to include the elements of a typical ad and identify the appeal you chose.
2. One writer says that children exposed to puffery in ads grow into teens who are healthily skeptical of advertising claims. Find several print ads aimed at children, and identify what you think might be puffery in these ads. Select one ad that you think children would be influenced by, and rewrite the ad without the puffery.
3. Comparative advertising, in which marketers directly compare the advertised product with a competitor's, is controversial. The advertising industry is self-regulating on this issue, and disputes between companies regarding incorrect or misleading comparative ads are likely to result in lawsuits. Consequently, since the law provides few specific guidelines, advertisers who use comparative ads are responsible for monitoring the honesty and fairness of their messages. What do you think advertisers' criteria for fairness should be? Locate two or three comparative ads and compare the advertisers' criteria to your own. Which set of guidelines is stricter, yours or the advertisers'? Use the ads to illustrate a presentation to your class.
4. Some marketers believe that marketing in schools—through advertisements on book covers, product placement in lesson plans, and ads in educational videos and other programs—is acceptable only if the ads are designed to help schools financially by giving them supplies they cannot afford or helping them get money to buy these items. Others feel advertising has no place in schools at all. But the majority expect it to increase in the future. Find out about advertiser participation in the schools in your area. Do you agree that it has a benefit? Why or why not? Interview a few high school students you know and find out what they think. Prepare a brief report about your findings.

ETHICS EXERCISE

Major League Baseball recently canceled plans to plant a temporary Spider-Man logo on first, second, and third base to promote the film *Spider-Man 2* after sports fans voiced strong objections. Shocked by this sacrilege and convinced that, once advertising moved from signage to the field of play, the uniforms of players, coaches, and umpires would be covered with more brand images than a Nascar race car, tradition-oriented fans cried foul. They wrote letters; they called sports-talk radio programs. Their vocal media complaints proved successful, and baseball commissioner Bud Selig announced that the Spider-Man logo "proposal" had been rejected. But one sports marketing executive predicted that "marketers will always push the envelope, and I think somebody will try something like this again." New York Yankee pitching great Whitey Ford said of the proposed ads, "With the salaries they're paying now, they have to make money. . . . Today, television calls the shots."

1. Do you think marketing at sporting events and stadiums will become more aggressive if salaries for top players continue to climb? If the alternative is to charge higher ticket prices, which is preferable in the short term? In the long term? Why?
2. Some fans and sportswriters were outraged at the proposal to market a movie by using the bases, even though the plan was quickly canceled. Do you think advertisers should "test the waters" first for certain types of ads? Why or why not? If yes, what sort of feedback mechanism would you suggest marketers use?

'netWork EXERCISES

1. **Do not spam list.** The Federal Trade Commission, which manages the national Do Not Call list restricting telemarketing calls, recently refused to establish a Do Not Spam list. Visit the FTC's Web site (http://www.ftc.gov) and review the decision. What was the commission's rationale regarding its rejection of the Do Not Spam list? Do you feel such a list would be effective in reducing the amount of spam received by consumers? Why or why not? Then, visit the Web site listed below and read about a technology called Sender Policy Framework (SPF). How does this technology work? Would it be effective in reducing spam?

   http://spf.pobox.com
2. **Advertising.** Visit the *Advertising Age* Web site (http://www.adage.com/century) to access information on advertising during the last hundred years. Complete the following:
   a. What were the top five advertising campaigns?
   b. What were the top three advertising jingles?
   c. What were the top two advertising slogans?
   d. Who were the top five advertisers?
   e. Are any of the top campaigns, slogans, or jingles still in use today?
3. **Public relations.** Over the past five years, a number of retailers and manufacturers that outsource their production to foreign companies came under criticism from government, labor, and human rights organizations for selling clothing produced in factories where workers were poorly paid, often abused, and subjected to hazardous working conditions. In response, a number of these companies instituted new standards for vendors. Some retailers went even further. Visit the Web site of The Gap Stores (http://www.gap.com). Click "Company Info" and then "Social Responsibility." Read about the company's annual social audit and its other efforts to protect garment workers. Explain how these efforts are examples of the effective use of public relations and publicity as described in the chapter.

Note: Internet Web addresses change frequently. If you don't find the exact sites listed, you may need to access the organization's or company's home page and search from there or use a search engine such as Google.

INFOTRAC CITATIONS AND EXERCISES

Record: A116157929
Kentucky Derby Weekend Proves Anna's Back Once Again; Showing Up at the Most Posh Locations, Anna Impressed Everyone with Her Sexy New Look.
PR Newswire, May 3, 2004

Abstract: Hollywood's outrageous party girl is back and looking better than ever. Supermodel Anna Nicole Smith, best known for her candid reality TV show and ballooning weight issues following the death of nonagenarian millionaire husband J. Howard Marshall II, made the comeback of a lifetime in 2004 with help from the TRIMSPA diet program. After months of demonstrating incoherent behavior and baffling weight gain on E! Television's *The Anna Nicole Show,* Ms. Smith began taking the TRIMSPA X32 diet product and shed a remarkable 69 pounds in only eight months. Now, with voluptuous figure restored and showing a more sober face to the public, Anna Nicole has discovered a new career as TRIMSPA's premier spokeswoman. The Monroe-esque beauty queen has been seen touting the benefits of her ephedra-free weight-loss supplement in commercials, on *Larry King Live,* at sponsored NASCAR events, and during the Kentucky Derby.

1. Why do marketers spend enormous sums of money to get celebrities to endorse their products?
2. How does Anna Nicole Smith's celebrity testimonial help TRIMSPA break through the cluttered promotional environment and stand out from myriad weight-loss programs on the market today?
3. What risks to the advertiser are associated with using celebrity testimonials? Identify a celebrity endorsement that recently backfired on an advertiser. What was the situation, and what effect do you think it had on the brand?

CASE 16.1 Will Technology Kill the Advertising Star?

Unlike the annual fees charged in the UK to finance the BBC, most of the U.S. media's production and operating costs are covered by fees charged to advertisers. These fees still pay for many first-run programs, although at increasingly high prices. Per-viewer ad rates have more than doubled in the last 10 years even as the prime-time audience has declined by about a third. But marketers may not be so willing to foot the increased bill in the future.

Now they know that digital technology is putting viewers in the driver's seat for the first time, giving consumers the ability to bypass commercials. And although it got off to a slow start, the computer-based digital video recorder (DVR) technology that supports providers like TiVo is expected to move into U.S. homes at a much faster rate in the next couple of years, as prices go down and ease of use increases. Movies, sit-coms, dramas, and news will arrive on demand, either commercial-free or "zappable." Some programming executives see zapper technology as "a brutal attack on the underpinnings of our business," and others warn that "this is a tidal wave. It is happening, and it is profound. And we have got to figure out a way to deal with that." (See the "Solving an Ethical Controversy" box for a closer look at this issue.) Cable television and paid programming, aided by TiVo, offer even more commercial-free alternatives.

While marketers struggle to make up for the possibly vanishing audience for commercials, what will happen to the product spokesperson? It seems that U.S. consumers still love celebrities, no matter how and where they find them.

General Nutrition Centers has teamed up with Sylvester Stallone, of *Rocky* fame, to promote a new line of nutritional supplements. Increasing Stallone's visibility as product spokesperson is his new job as host of a reality series, *The Contender,* that pits amateur boxers against each other for a cash award and a chance to turn pro. Other reality shows use a new kind of product placement to get the word out. The savvy and sincere hosts of *Queer Eye for the Straight Guy,* for instance, recommend personal care products by name to their style-makeover subjects, in deals engineered between, say, Procter & Gamble and the network, turning the Fab Five into all-purpose product spokespersons. Contestants on *Survivor* wash Doritos down with Mountain Dew. Coca-Cola saturates the sets of *American Idol,* as the judges drink from logo-bearing cups. Penelope Cruz and Courtney Cox drink Coca-Cola in a new series of commercials, as have many celebrities before them, and Hugh Hefner, creator of the Playboy empire, promotes Carl's Jr. hamburgers. Jerry Seinfeld and Tiger Woods carry American Express cards, and Sarah Ferguson, Duchess of York, promotes Weight Watchers. Jessica Simpson stars in a series of breath mint commercials with her sister, promoting Ice Breakers Liquid Ice.

When the arrest of Michael Jackson on child molestation charges was shown 30 consecutive times on Fox News, it seemed to confirm the point made by author and advertising expert Jerry Della Femina: "We've become the world's largest fan club," he says. One researcher who has studied celebrity worship says, "We need celebrities as much as we need food, water and shelter. We need them to feel connected."

But a question that bothers marketers still remains. Do we need celebrities enough to want to watch their commercials?

Questions for Critical Thinking

1. Do you think celebrity spokespersons can help television advertising retain its effectiveness in spite of ad-zapping technology?
2. One television executive says of product placements and cameos, "These integrated packages are a fact of life, but they're not going to take over our schedule. The viewer can take only so much." What do you think is an appropriate mix of outright commercials and subtle product placements built into the show? How can marketers determine what balance will work best?

Sources: Sarah Hall, "Stallone Pumps Supplements," *E!Online,* May 21, 2004; "Jessica Simpson to Promote Breath Mints," Associated Press, May 18, 2004; Bruce Horovitz, "The Good, Bad and Ugly of America's Celeb Obsession," *USA Today,* December 19, 2003, pp.1B, 2B; Scott Woolley, "ZAP!" *Forbes,* September 29, 2003, pp. 76-84; Betsy McKay and Suzanne Vranica, "New Coke Ads with Celebrities Will Start Soon," *The Wall Street Journal,* January 9, 2003, pp. B1, B7.

VIDEO CASE 16.2 Ride the White Wave with Silk Soymilk

The written case on Silk Soymilk appears on page VC-19. The recently filmed Silk Soymilk video is designed to expand and highlight the concepts in this chapter and the concepts and questions covered in the written video case.

chapter 17

Personal Selling and Sales Promotion

chapter objectives

1. Outline the marketplace conditions that make personal selling a primary component of a firm's promotional mix.
2. Describe the four sales channels.
3. Describe the major trends in personal selling.
4. Identify and briefly describe the three basic sales tasks.
5. Outline the seven steps in the sales process.
6. Identify the seven basic functions of a sales manager.
7. Explain the role of ethical behavior in personal selling.
8. Describe the role of sales promotion in the promotional mix.
9. Identify the different types of consumer-oriented and trade-oriented sales promotions.

THE WILLIAMS SISTERS: SELLING TALENT AND TENNIS

They are the most successful sister duo in tennis history. When Venus and Serena Williams hit the court, people are glued to their television sets—even if they don't normally play or watch tennis. Perhaps it's because they are phenomenal tennis players—at age 17, Serena became the first African-American woman to win a Grand Slam title since Althea Gibson in 1958; at age 20, Venus won Wimbledon, the U.S. Open, a gold medal for singles, and another for doubles with her sister at the Sidney Olympics. (Since then, they have faced off against each other in the finals at Wimbledon, the French Open, and other tournaments.) Each has already won around $13 million in prize money during her career. In addition to powerful games and overall tennis skills, perhaps the reason for their unprecedented success lies in their personal charisma, their flamboyant fashion, or the confidence that accompanies the power of multimillion dollar endorsement deals with companies like Reebok and Nike. But

AP WIDE WORLD PHOTOS/JOHN D. MCHUGH

another major force in their lives was the most famous sports agent ever, a man named Mark McCormack, who acted as the sisters' agent until his death in June 2003.

Prior to McCormack and his International Management Group, few tennis players had agents. Professional tennis players negotiated their own contracts, managed their own finances, and typically were paid in merchandise as compensation for their endorsement of a product. McCormack, who got his start as Arnold Palmer's attorney, changed all that. As an agent, McCormack's job was to sell his athlete-clients to the public—and to companies interested in linking their products to the celebrity images of his clients. He once described his role this way: "I'm not an agent. I'm an engineer of careers." In turn, the athletes would be featured in advertising, make personal appearances, and take part in other sales promotions designed to sell the products of those companies. Eventually, they might even start their own businesses selling athletic apparel, equipment, golf course designs, cosmetics, or the like.

These deals have turned many athletes—including tennis players, golfers, and basketball stars—into celebrities that have little to do with their athletic abilities. Serena Williams recently signed a five-year endorsement deal with Nike worth about $40 million, making her one of the highest paid female athletes in the world, while Venus is a spokesperson for Reebok in a deal reported at about the same amount as her sister. Together, the pair has appeared in ads for toothpaste, chewing gum, McDonald's, and Avon. But in the past couple of years, both have branched out even farther. Venus is earning a degree in interior design and her design company, V Starr Interiors, has done several residential projects. Serena, the more extroverted sister, is interested in possibly pursuing an acting career, having made appearances on TV shows *Law & Order* and *The Division,* and is currently planning her feature-film debut. She has also launched her own line of designer clothes, called Aneres (Serena spelled backward).

All of these marketing efforts require careful management as well as personal selling to companies that might be interested in paying a lot of money to tie their products to the Williams sisters' celebrity. Meanwhile, their tournament schedules must be managed—after all, Serena and Venus are tennis players first. Still, Russian tennis player Anna Kournikova proved that winning titles is not a prerequisite to becoming a media star or a millionaire. The savvy Williams sisters understand the importance of marketing to their careers. When asked how she would describe herself professionally, Serena recently replied, "I am an entertainer." No one could argue with that.[1]

Chapter Overview

THE Williams sisters illustrate how it takes more than talent to become a sports celebrity. As in other types of marketing, building relationships—with fans, with companies, with other players and officials on the tennis tour—is a vital part of the sales process. In exploring personal selling strategies, this chapter gives special attention to the relationship-building opportunities that the selling situation presents.

(1) **Outline the marketplace conditions that make personal selling a primary component of a firm's promotional mix.**

personal selling Interpersonal influence process involving a seller's promotional presentation conducted on a person-to-person basis with the buyer.

Personal selling is the process of a seller's person-to-person promotional presentation to a buyer. The sales process is essentially interpersonal, and it is basic to any enterprise. Accounting, engineering, human resource management, production, and other organizational activities produce no benefits unless a seller matches the needs of a client or customer. The 15 million people employed in sales occupations in the U.S. testify to the importance of selling. While the average firm's advertising expenses may represent from 1 to 3 percent of total sales, personal selling expenses are likely to equal 10 to 15 percent. This makes personal selling the single largest marketing expense in many firms.

Personal selling is a primary component of a firm's promotional mix when one or more of several well-defined factors are present:

1. Customers are geographically concentrated.
2. Individual orders account for large amounts of revenue.
3. The firm markets goods and services that are expensive, are technically complex, or require special handling.
4. Trade-ins are involved.
5. Products move through short channels.
6. The firm markets to relatively few potential customers.

Briefly Speaking

People retire to do what I do every day—play golf with Arnold Palmer and tennis with Monica Seles. As long as I can contribute, I'll be around.

Mark McCormack (1931–2003)
founder and chairman, International Management Group

Table 17.1 summarizes the factors that influence the importance of personal selling in the overall promotional mix based on four variables: consumer, product, price, and marketing channels.

This chapter also explores *sales promotion,* which includes all those marketing activities other than personal selling, advertising, and publicity that enhance consumer purchasing and dealer effectiveness. The Williams sisters engage in sales promotions to market the sport of tennis as well as the products sold by companies with which they have endorsement agreements, such as Avon, Reebok, and Nike. ◆◆◆

THE EVOLUTION OF PERSONAL SELLING

Selling has been a standard business activity for thousands of years. As long ago as 2000 B.C., the Code of Hammurabi protected the rights of the Babylonian salesman, who was referred to as a "peddler." Throughout U.S. history, selling has been a major factor in economic growth. During the 1700s, Yankee peddlers pulled their carts full of goods from village to village and farm to farm, helping to expand trade among the colonies. In 1876, the invention of the telephone gave sellers a new way to communicate directly with their customers. Over the decades, stereotypes about salespeople as fast-talking, joke-telling, back-slapping hucksters began to develop.

table 17.1 *Factors Affecting the Importance of Personal Selling in the Promotional Mix*

VARIABLE	CONDITIONS THAT FAVOR PERSONAL SELLING	CONDITIONS THAT FAVOR ADVERTISING
Consumer	Geographically concentrated	Geographically dispersed
	Relatively low numbers	Relatively high numbers
Product	Expensive	Inexpensive
	Technically complex	Simple to understand
	Custom made	Standardized
	Special handling requirements	No special handling requirements
	Transactions frequently involve trade-ins	Transactions seldom involve trade-ins
Price	Relatively high	Relatively low
Channels	Relatively short	Relatively long

Personal selling is far different today. Today's salesperson is highly trained. Sales professionalism has been aptly defined as "a customer-oriented approach that employs truthful, nonmanipulative tactics to satisfy the long-term needs of both the customer and the selling firm."[2] Professional salespeople are problem solvers who focus on satisfying the needs of customers before, during, and after sales are made. Armed with knowledge about their firm's goods or services, those of competitors, and their customers' business needs, salespeople pursue a common goal of creating mutually beneficial long-term relationships with customers.

Personal selling is a vital, vibrant, dynamic process. As domestic and foreign competition increase emphasis on productivity, personal selling is taking on a more prominent role in the corporate marketing mix. Salespeople must communicate the subtle advantages of their firms' goods and services over those of competitors. The salesperson's role has changed from persuader to consultant and problem solver.[3] In addition, mergers and acquisitions, along with a host of new products and promotions, have expanded the scope and complexity of many selling jobs.

Relationship marketing affects all aspects of an organization's marketing function, including personal selling. This means that marketers in both internal and external relationships must develop different sales skills. Instead of working alone, many salespeople now unite their efforts in sales teams. The customer-focused firm wants its salespeople to form long-lasting relationships with buyers by providing high levels of customer service rather than going for quick sales. Even the way salespeople perform their jobs is constantly changing. Growing numbers of companies have integrated communications and computer technologies into the sales routine. These trends are covered in more detail later in the chapter.

Personal selling is an attractive career choice for today's college and university students. About three of every five marketing graduates choose a sales position as their first marketing job after graduation, in part because they see attractive salaries and career advancement potential. Bureau of Labor Statistics projections show that jobs in selling and marketing occupations requiring a college degree will grow faster than average rates of growth for all other occupations during the next 10 years. Company executives usually recognize a good salesperson as a

While advertising, public relations, and sales promotion are used by automakers and their retail outlets to create awareness and supply basic information about new auto models, the nature of this product purchase requires heavy emphasis on well-trained, professional salespeople in most purchase decisions.

1. What is personal selling?
2. What is the main difference between selling today and selling 100 years ago?

hard worker who can solve problems, communicate clearly, and be consistent.[4] In fact, many corporations are headed by executives who began their careers in sales.

over-the-counter selling Personal selling conducted in retail and some wholesale locations in which customers come to the seller's place of business.

THE FOUR SALES CHANNELS

(2) Describe the four sales channels.

Personal selling occurs through several types of communication channels: over-the-counter selling (including online selling), field selling, telemarketing, and inside selling. Each of these channels includes both business-to-business and direct-to-customer selling. Although telemarketing and online selling are lower cost alternatives, their lack of personal interaction with existing or prospective customers often makes them less effective than personalized, one-to-one field selling and over-the-counter channels. In fact, many organizations use a number of different channels. The promotional message in Figure 17.1 for the American Stock Exchange gives potential investors three ways to contact the exchange for more information on its product, MidCap Spiders: a toll-free number, a Web address, and recommendations for speaking to a financial adviser in person.

figure 17.1

Alternative Channels for Making Stock Purchases on the American Stock Exchange: Toll-Free Telephone, a Web Address, and Personal Contacts with a Financial Adviser

WWW.AMEX.COM

OVER-THE-COUNTER SELLING

The most frequently used sales channel, **over-the-counter selling**, typically describes selling in retail and some wholesale locations. Most over-the-counter sales are direct-to-customer, although business customers are frequently served by wholesalers with over-the-counter sales reps. Customers typically visit the seller's location on their own initiative to purchase desired items. Some visit their favorite stores because they enjoy shopping. Others respond to many kinds of invitations, including direct mail appeals, personal letters of invitation from store personnel, and advertisements for sales, special events, and new-product introductions. From the consumer electronics salesperson at Target to the diamond purveyor at Tiffany's, this type of selling typically involves providing product information and arranging for the completion of sales transactions.

Although Best Buy has put distance between itself and the likes of Circuit City, Ultimate Electronics, and Good Guys through skillful merchandising and marketing, the real secret of the retail chain's marketplace success is its unique sales culture. Each store's salesclerks—"blueshirts" as they call themselves—are trained, rewarded, motivated, monitored, and measured every hour the store is open. Their sales mantra is CARE Plus.

- *C is for Contact.* The initial approach is key. Salesclerks tell customers they're noncommissioned so they won't feel they're being hustled.
- *A is for Ask.* Questions are used to determine what customers are looking for and how eager they are to buy—and give salespeople a chance to show their expertise.
- *R is for Recommend.* Most customers aren't exactly sure what they want and respond to specific suggestions about which item is best for them.
- *E is for Encourage.* Praising the customer's purchase and showing how much fun the gadget will be strokes a customer's ego.

Does it work? Let's look at the numbers. On a square foot basis, the 640-plus Best Buy outlets sell almost twice as much electronic gizmos, services, music, and movies as Circuit City, some $25 billion a year.[5]

Before the advent of big chain retailers and discount stores, it was not unusual for local retailers to know their customers by name or to be familiar with their tastes and preferences. This is still the case in towns that have healthy downtown shopping areas with boutique stores offering everything from books to gifts to clothing to wine. Some astute marketers who work for larger firms are using the same tactics. Top direct marketers like Lands' End and L.L. Bean use sophisticated database technology to identify callers and any recent purchases made. This customer recognition helps build strong relationships in over-the-counter sales as well. Lands' End's use of its popular Virtual Model, which allows customers to "try on" clothes using a model they construct at the firm's Web site, as well as the publication of various specialty catalogs like the one for men in Figure 17.2 also help over-the-counter sales.

Web-driven sales are still elusive for certain types of industries. Most banks still rely heavily on face-to-face selling for insurance sales. Customer referral, followed by one-on-one meetings between insurance reps and potential customers, is the method most likely to result in a sale. Banks use their Web sites mainly to educate customers about insurance, not to close sales.[6]

field selling Sales presentations made at prospective customers' locations on a face-to-face basis.

figure 17.2

Lands' End: Building Strong Over-the-Counter Sales with the Aid of a High-Tech Web Site and Catalogs Targeting Specific Customer Segments

FIELD SELLING

Field selling involves making sales calls on prospective and existing customers at their businesses or homes. Some situations involve considerable creative effort, such as industrial sales of major computer installations. Often, the salesperson must convince customers first that they need the good or service and then that they need the particular brand the salesperson is selling. Field sales of large industrial installations like Boeing's new 7E7 Dreamliner also often require considerable technical expertise.[7]

Largely because it involves travel, field selling is considerably more expensive than other selling options. Figure 17.3 shows the average cost of sales calls across a range of industries. B2B sales calls, because of the sophistication or technical nature of products and the level of expertise needed to communicate to potential buyers, top the list.

In fairly routine field selling situations, such as calling on established customers in industries like food, textiles, or wholesaling, the salesperson basically acts as an order taker who processes regular customers' orders. Field selling may involve regular visits to local stores or businesses, or it may involve many days and nights of travel, by car or plane, every month. Salespeople who travel a great deal are frequently labeled *road warriors.* A recent study found that it costs an average of $215 per day to keep a salesperson on the road. However, communications technologies such as e-mail and videoconferencing have helped

figure 17.3

Cost of a Sales Call by Industry

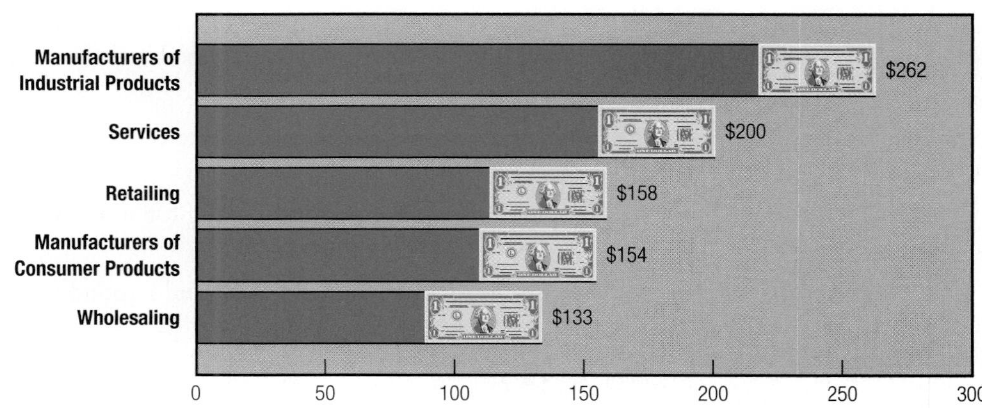

Source: Sales data reported in "Cost of a Call Survey," *Sales & Marketing Management,* September 2000, p. 82. © 2000 VNU Business Media. All rights reserved.

salespeople reduce their travel costs. In addition, more and more companies place routine orders online. Sunrider, a California-based seller of nutritional supplements and household products, reports that 20 percent of its $700 million in revenues comes from online orders made by its sales reps and its customers.[8]

Taking their cue from the successes of businesses like Avon, Mary Kay Cosmetics, and Tupperware, thousands of smaller businesses now rely on field selling in customers' homes. Often called **network marketing,** this type of personal selling relies on lists of family members and friends of the salesperson or "party host" who organizes a gathering of potential customers for an in-home demonstration of products. Rags Land, which sells children's clothing, is one such company. Rags Land customers enjoy sitting in a friend's living room and picking out clothes while their children play together; they don't have to find parking spaces or worry about losing a child at the mall. In addition, the costs of field selling are minimal compared to those of traditional firms. And according to the Direct Selling Association, $6.3 billion in sales were generated at these types of parties last year.[9]

Finally, industry experts have noted an increase in door-to-door selling attributable to the national Do Not Call Registry limiting telemarketing calls, as well as caller-ID and call-blocking devices like the TeleZapper. Cable companies, phone companies, and utilities are among the businesses now using door-to-door sales techniques. Cable giant Comcast reported that it registered 40,000 new customers during its most recent door-to-door campaign.[10]

TELEMARKETING

telemarketing Promotional presentation involving the use of the telephone on an outbound basis by salespeople or on an inbound basis by customers who initiate calls to obtain information and place orders.

Telemarketing, a channel in which the selling process is conducted by phone, serves two general purposes—sales and service—and two general markets—business-to-business and direct-to-customer. Both inbound and outbound telemarketing are forms of direct marketing.

Outbound telemarketing involves a sales force that relies on the telephone to contact customers, reducing the substantial costs of personal visits to customers' homes or businesses. Technologies such as predictive dialers, autodialing, and random-digit dialing increase chances that telemarketers will reach customers at home. *Predictive dialers* weed out busy signals and answering machines, nearly doubling the number of calls made per hour. *Autodialing* allows telemarketers to dial numbers continually; when a customer answers the phone, the call is automatically routed to a live sales agent. *Random-digit dialing* allows telemarketers to reach unlisted numbers and block caller-ID.

As demonstrated in the "Solving an Ethical Controversy" feature, a major drawback of telemarketing is that most consumers detest the practice, and 56 million have already signed up for the national Do Not Call Registry. If a telemarketer does call any of these numbers, the marketer is subject to an $11,000 fine.

Why, then, is outbound telemarketing such a popular sales technique? Companies still claim to like it because it is cost-effective and it works. An average telemarketing call costs $5, compared with hundreds of dollars for a field sales call. Millions of Americans continue to make purchases resulting from such calls each year. The industry employs roughly 6 million workers, many of whom represent

Solving an Ethical Controversy

WHO'S CALLING?

Did you sign up for the national Do Not Call Registry for telemarketers? If you did, are you glad? If not, do you wish you had? Since the list has gone into effect, the number of telemarketing calls received by the 56 million consumers who have already signed up for the registry has dropped dramatically. Charities, political candidates, and marketing researchers are still allowed to call, as are companies with whom a consumer has an existing relationship. Some telemarketers have complained, but others have accepted the regulation and are looking for other ways to expand their business. Still others are looking for loopholes.

DOES THE NATIONAL DO NOT CALL REGISTRY VIOLATE FREE SPEECH RIGHTS OF TELEMARKETERS?

PRO

1. This is the only way some businesses can reach out to potential customers. Being blocked this way may put them out of business.
2. Not all consumers reject unsolicited telemarketing calls. In fact, 66 million Americans made purchases resulting from such calls during a single 12-month period prior to the Do Not Call Registry.

CON

1. According to a federal appeals court, the registry "offers consumers a tool with which they can protect their homes against intrusions that Congress has determined to be particularly invasive."
2. Aggressive telemarketers are already finding loopholes in the law. Some are beginning to call people at the workplace if those phone numbers are not on the list. "We are rapidly trying to figure out ways to market over the telephone at places of work," says one telemarketer.

SUMMARY

Six months after the registry went into effect, a federal appeals court upheld its legality. "We hold that the do-not-call registry is a valid commercial speech regulation because it directly advances the government's important interests in safeguarding personal privacy and reducing the danger of telemarketing abuse without burdening an excessive amount of speech," wrote the court.

Sources: "Appeals Court Upholds Do-Not-Call List," *MSNBC*, February 17, 2004, http://www.msnbc.com; Catherine Arnold, "Law Gives Industry a Buzz," *Marketing News*, February 1, 2004, p. 11; Ellen Neuborne, "Telemarketing after 'Do Not Call,'" *Inc.* magazine, November 2003, pp. 32–34; Lorraine Woellart, "The Do-Not-Call Law Won't Stop the Calls," *BusinessWeek*, September 29, 2003, p. 89.

minorities or lower income groups. And the registry does not prohibit all telemarketing calls. Here is who may still call:

- Charities, political candidates, and marketing researchers
- Companies with whom you have an ongoing relationship
- Companies that have sold something to you, billed you, or made a delivery to you in the past 18 months
- Businesses you have contacted in the last 3 months
- Companies that have obtained your permission to call[11]

Inbound telemarketing typically involves a toll-free number that customers can call to obtain information, make reservations, and purchase goods and services. When a customer calls a toll-free number, the caller can be identified and routed to the sales agents with whom he or she has done business before, creating a human touch not possible before. This form of selling provides maximum convenience for customers who initiate the sales process. Many large catalog merchants, like Williams-Sonoma, Lillian Vernon, and Pottery Barn, keep their inbound telemarketing lines open 24 hours a day, 7 days a week.

Consumers want more control over their telephones. Today we give it to them.

Michael K. Powell (b. 1963)

chairman, Federal Communications Commission (announcing implementation of the national Do Not Call Registry)

INSIDE SELLING

The role of many of today's telemarketers is a combination of field selling techniques applied through inbound and outbound telemarketing channels with a strong customer orientation, called **inside selling.** Inside sales reps perform two primary jobs: They turn opportunities into actual sales, and they support technicians and purchasers with current solutions. Inside sales reps do far more than read a canned script to unwilling prospects. They perform a dynamic selling function that goes beyond taking orders to solving problems, providing customer service, and selling. eTapestry.com, an Indianapolis-based application service provider for nonprofit organizations, is one of many companies that successfully combines selling approaches. eTapestry's inside salespeople do far more than run down leads; they close major deals over the phone—some worth more than a quarter-million dollars. The team is made up of former outside sales pros. With revenues that exceed $3 million a year, eTapestry finds its inside reps more cost-effective and easier to manage than an outside sales force.[12] A successful inside sales force relies on close working relationships with field representatives to solidify customer relationships.

inside selling Selling by phone, mail, and electronic commerce.

INTEGRATING THE VARIOUS SELLING CHANNELS

Figure 17.4 illustrates how firms are likely to blend alternative sales channels—from over-the-counter selling and field selling to telemarketing and inside selling—to create a successful cost-effective sales organization. Existing customers whose business problems require complex solutions are likely to be best served by the traditional field sales force. Other current customers who need answers but not the same attention as the first group can be served by inside sales reps who call on them as needed. Over-the-counter sales reps serve existing customers by supplying information and advice and completing sales transactions. Telemarketers may be used to strengthen communication with customers or to reestablish relationships with customers that may have lapsed over a few months.

1. What is over-the-counter selling?
2. What is field selling?
3. Distinguish between inbound and outbound telemarketing.

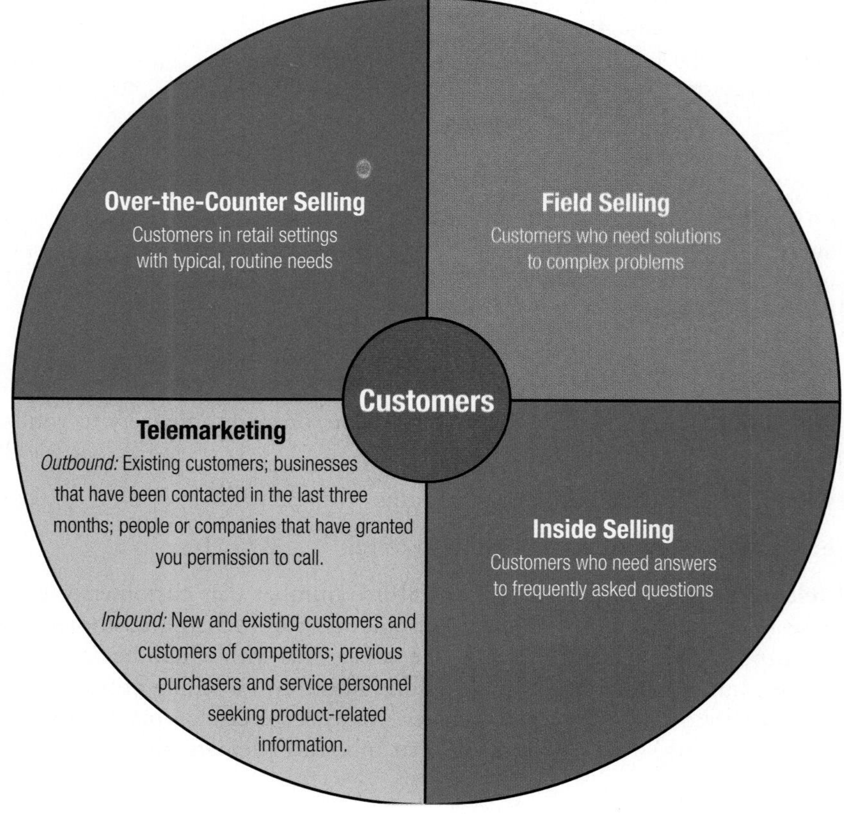

figure 17.4
Alternative Sales Channels for Serving Customers

TRENDS IN PERSONAL SELLING

(3) Describe the major trends in personal selling.

In today's complex marketing environment, effective personal selling requires different strategies from those used by salespeople in the past. As pointed out in the discussion of *buying centers* in Chapter 6, rather than selling one-on-one, in B2B settings it is now customary to sell to teams of corporate representatives who make up the client firm's decision-making units. In business-to-business sales situations involving technical products, customers expect salespeople to answer technical questions—or bring along someone who can. They also want representatives who understand technical jargon and can communicate using sophisticated technological tools. Patience is also a requirement because the B2B sales cycle, from initial contact to closing, may take months or even years.

To address all of these concerns, companies rely on four major personal selling approaches: relationship selling, consultative selling, team selling, and sales force automation. Regardless of the approach, however, experts agree on a few basic guidelines for conducting successful personal selling:

There are no problems we cannot solve together, and very few we can solve by ourselves.

Lyndon B. Johnson (1908-1973)

36th president of the United States

- *Listen instead of talk.* Instead of talking too much about what you have to offer, spend time listening to your customer. "[Listening] is so basic, it's overlooked," says Nick Elmer, a senior account executive for FedEx in Oklahoma City. "But it's the first step to respect."
- *Build trust and respect.* Take the time to build a relationship, even if it takes six months or a year to close the deal.
- *Find solutions for your customer.* "Right now, people want solutions," says Elmer. "Once you show them how to grow their businesses, you have an open door."[13]

RELATIONSHIP SELLING

Most firms now emphasize **relationship selling**, a technique for building a mutually beneficial partnership with a customer through regular contacts over an extended period. Such buyer–seller bonds become increasingly important as companies cut back on the number of suppliers and look for companies that provide high levels of customer service and satisfaction. Salespeople must also find ways to distinguish themselves and their products from competitors. To create strong, long-lasting relationships with customers, salespeople must meet buyers' expectations. Table 17.2 summarizes the results of several surveys that indicate what buyers expect of professional salespeople.

relationship selling Regular contacts between sales representatives and customers over an extended period to establish a sustained seller–buyer relationship.

The success of tomorrow's marketers depends on the relationships they build today in both the business-to-consumer and business-to-business markets. Merrill Lynch recently refocused its 10,000-plus U.S. brokers on a relationship selling approach. The company redirected its brokers to concentrate only on wealthy clients with $1 million or more to invest. Investors with more modest assets are now handled by call centers. The change not only has cut costs but it positions Merrill Lynch for faster growth, because brokers are able to offer more sophisticated advice to fewer but more profitable clients.

Relationship selling is equally important in business-to-business sales. ProSlide Technology sells water rides to amusement parks, but a closer look reveals that the company's success is centered on the

table 17.2 What Buyers Expect from Salespeople

Buyers prefer to do business with salespeople who:

- Orchestrate events and bring to bear whatever resources are necessary to satisfy the customer
- Provide counseling to the customer based on in-depth knowledge of the product, the market, and the customer's needs
- Solve problems proficiently to ensure satisfactory customer service over extended time periods
- Demonstrate high ethical standards and communicate honestly at all times
- Willingly advocate the customer's cause within the selling organization
- Create imaginative arrangements to meet buyers' needs
- Arrive well-prepared for sales calls

ETIQUETTE TIPS — FOR MARKETING PROFESSIONALS

Get in the Swing with Good Golf Manners

GOLF continues to be the sport of choice among many members of middle and top management. The fact is, many business discussions take place on the golf course and in the clubhouse. That's why so many managers with their eyes on the prize, whether it is an important deal or a top company position, take golf lessons. In addition to improving their swing and their knowledge of the rules, golfers must learn a fairly strict code of etiquette that not only affects the game but may also determine the business outcome of a golf outing. Here are a few tips:

1. Arrive well before your tee time in order to warm up properly.
2. When you receive your scorecard, check it to learn any local rules for the course.
3. Only one player should stand at the tee. Others should stand even with the ball, well outside of the tee area.
4. Play safely. Don't take practice swings near or toward another person.
5. Play at a reasonable speed so you keep pace with the group in front of you. Be at your ball and ready to hit when it is your turn. If your group is moving faster than the one in front, your host may ask them if you can "play through."
6. Replace any divots.
7. Be quiet on the course. When another player is getting ready to address (or hit) the ball, do not talk or move around.
8. Always exhibit good sportsmanship. Have a positive, pleasant attitude. Don't become outwardly frustrated if you play a poor game or blame the results on someone or something else. If you play a good game, accept the results modestly.

Following these tips can help you put your best foot forward with clients and coworkers. Respect, courtesy, and fair play are the watchwords of golf.

Sources: "The 10 Commandments of Golf Etiquette," *Legendinc.com,* http://www.legendinc.com, accessed May 22, 2004; Jim Corbett, "The General Concepts of Good Golf Etiquette," *Mr. Golf,* http://www.mrgolf.com, accessed May 22, 2004; "Golf Etiquette," *PGA.com,* February 26, 2003, http://www.pga.com.

ability of its sales force to customize each customer's order. New attractions like the CanonBOWL, an exhilarating water ride that allows parents to ride with children, are created by asking customers what they want and delivering both quality products and premium customer service. Rather than assume that established customers will remain loyal purchasers, ProSlide works to shape and reshape relationships with each new order it receives—from both established customers as well as new buyers. As a result, it has managed to retain an impressive number of loyal buyers—who comprise 70 percent of ProSlide's annual business—as well as continue to attract first-time customers.[14]

Sometimes B2B relationship selling takes place outside the workplace—in restaurants or on golf courses, as described in the "Etiquette Tips for Marketing Professionals" feature. Regardless of the venue, however, it is important for salespeople to maintain a professional attitude and demeanor.

CONSULTATIVE SELLING

consultative selling Meeting customer needs by listening to them, understanding their problems, paying attention to details, and following through after the sale.

Field representatives and inside sales reps require sales methods that satisfy today's cost-conscious, knowledgeable buyers. One such method, **consultative selling,** involves meeting customer needs by listening to customers, understanding—and caring about—their problems, paying attention to details, and following through after the sale. It works hand in hand with relationship selling in building customer loyalty. Kathy Williams, a top salesperson for North Carolina–based Chico's clothing store, greets every customer who comes in the door. She asks what the customer is looking for, listens, and determines the clothing or accessories that may be of interest to the customer. Since Chico's doesn't put mirrors in its dressing rooms, customers are more apt to turn to Williams for advice. "I don't consider myself a sales clerk. I'm a wardrobe consultant," says Williams. "I take the thinking out of it for [my customers]."[15] This type of consultative approach earns Williams many repeat customers.

As rapid technological changes drive business at an unprecedented pace, selling has become more complex, often changing the role of salespeople. At Zeks Compressed Air Solutions, for instance, every sales representative has a background in engineering. With the job title Application Engineer, they bring technical proficiency to the sales situation. The change in title has helped the company overcome resistance to sales calls, since the expertise offered brings extra value to the customer–seller relationship.

Online companies have instituted consultative selling models to create long-term customers. Particularly for complicated, high-priced products that require installation or specialized service, Web sellers must be able to quickly communicate the benefits and features of their products. They accomplish this through consultative selling.

Similar to consultative selling, **cross-selling**—offering multiple goods or services to the same customer—is another technique that capitalizes on a firm's strengths. It costs a bank five times more to acquire a new customer than to cross-sell to an existing one. Moreover, research shows that the more a customer buys from an institution, the less likely that person is to leave. So a customer who opens a checking account at a local bank may follow with a safety deposit box, retirement savings account, and a mortgage loan. In Figure 17.5, Pitney Bowes advertises a multitude of services for its business customers, ranging from postage meters to round-the-clock backup in case of disaster.

TEAM SELLING

One of the latest developments in the evolution of personal selling is **team selling**, in which the salesperson joins with specialists from other functional areas of the firm to complete the selling process. Teams can be formal and ongoing or created for a specific short-term selling situation. Although some salespeople have hesitated to embrace the idea of team selling, preferring to work alone, a growing number believe that team selling brings better results. Customers often prefer the team approach, which makes them feel well served. Another advantage of team selling is the formation of relationships between companies rather than between individuals.

team selling Selling situation in which several sales associates or other members of the organization are recruited to assist the lead sales representative in reaching all those who influence the purchase decision.

In sales situations that call for detailed knowledge of new, complex, and ever-changing technologies, team selling offers a distinct competitive edge in meeting customers' needs. In most computer software B2B departments, a third of the sales force is made up of technically trained, nonmarketing experts such as engineers or programmers. A salesperson continues to play the lead role in most sales

figure 17.5

Cross-Selling Efforts by Pitney Bowes

situations, but technical experts bring added value to the sales process. Some companies establish permanent sales-and-tech teams that conduct all sales presentations together; others have a pool of engineers or other professionals who are on call for different client visits.

sales force automation (SFA) Applications of computer and other technologies to make the sales function more efficient and competitive.

CDW Computer Centers, the largest direct seller of Hewlett-Packard, IBM, Microsoft, Toshiba, and other top-name computer industry brands, relies on team selling to serve its 600,000 consumer and business customers. Each customer is matched with a highly trained account manager who serves as the team leader of a group of specialists dedicated to finding solutions to this buyer's needs. In a typical day, more than 700 systems are custom configured for CDW customers. Customers can receive continuing lifetime technical support by visiting the CDW extranet or by calling a toll-free telephone number to speak with factory-trained technicians.[16]

figure 17.6

SAS: SFA Technology Supplier

Some resourceful entrepreneurs have begun building a **virtual sales team**—a network of strategic partners, trade associations, suppliers, and others who are qualified and willing to recommend a firm's goods or services. Clayton Banks, founder of Ember Media, a small firm that produces multimedia CD-ROMs, Web sites, and marketing materials for *Fortune* 500 companies, colleges, and nonprofit organizations, has built his own virtual sales team. Through these relationships, Ember Media has won five- and six-figure contracts with PepsiCo, Showtime, and VH-1 as well as other organizations.[17]

SALES FORCE AUTOMATION

A major component of the professional salesperson's 21st century arsenal of tools used in satisfying buyer needs is **sales force automation (SFA)**—the application of technologies to make the sales function more efficient and competitive, as described in the "Marketing Hit" feature. These technologies range from e-mail and voice mail to pagers, Web-browsing cell phones, laptop and notebook computers, and other devices.

With SFA tools, both large and small companies increase their efficiency and spend more time on client acquisition and retention. The benefits of SFA include improvements in the quality and effectiveness of sales calls due to improved access to information; lower selling, printing, and training costs; improved product launches; and attentive customer service. SAS, illustrated in Figure 17.6, provides businesses with customer intelligence software designed to help salespeople understand and meet the needs of their customers.

marketing hit — Salesforce.com Leases Software for Less

Background. The software industry has traditionally made its money by selling products to business customers at prices ranging from a few hundred dollars to several hundred thousand. When a software product is purchased, the customer owns it. But what if software could be rented via the Internet rather than purchased outright? And what if the software itself could help businesses enhance their own personal selling efforts?

The Challenge. Marc Benioff was looking for a better way to deliver software to business customers. His new company, Salesforce.com, couldn't compete with larger firms—Oracle and Siebel Systems—if it went about selling software in a conventional manner.

The Strategy. Benioff began thinking about software in a different way—as a utility. If large business customers could rent software accessed via the Web, they could save literally hundreds of thousands of dollars. So instead of offering multimillion-dollar software packages that might take months to install, Salesforce.com sells software as a service via the Internet, at about $65 per employee. Customers use the software to improve their own sales connections

SFA usage differs sharply by industry, although more and more marketers are recognizing its value. Food, beverage, and pharmaceutical industries are already using sophisticated third- or fourth-generation systems, whereas most apparel companies have not yet moved to SFA. The size of the firm does not matter—your local real estate agency is likely to be making use of SFA. Software for sales force automation also falls into several categories depending on its intended use. Most salespeople use basic productivity and general-purpose programs such as word processors, e-mail, and spreadsheets. Some programs help to organize prospect lists and remind salespeople to make follow-up calls. More expensive systems, such as those designed by SAS and similar firms, may integrate a wider range of information types.

1. Identify the four major personal selling approaches.
2. Distinguish between relationship selling and consultative selling.

SALES TASKS

(4) Identify and briefly describe the three basic sales tasks.

Today's salesperson is more concerned with establishing long-term buyer–seller relationships and helping customers select the correct products for meeting their needs than with simply selling whatever is available. Where repeat purchases are common, the salesperson must be certain that the buyer's purchases are in his or her best interest; otherwise, no future relationship will be possible. The seller's interests are tied to the buyer's in a symbiotic relationship.

While all sales activities assist the customer in some manner, they are not all alike. Three basic sales tasks can be identified: (1) order processing, (2) creative selling, and (3) missionary sales. Most of today's salespeople are not limited to performing tasks in a single category. Instead, they often perform all three tasks to some extent. A sales engineer for a computer firm may be doing 50 percent missionary sales, 45 percent creative selling, and 5 percent order processing. Most sales positions are classified on the basis of the primary selling task performed.

Then there's the philosophy that *everyone* in the organization, regardless of what his or her job description is, should be engaged in selling. When Norm Brodsky, a highly successful entrepreneur who currently owns six different businesses, got the bad news that customers weren't receiving the treatment they should when they phoned in to one of his companies, he and his wife (head of human resources) hired a trainer to correct the problem. The training sessions not only dealt with the employees' telephone-answering skills; they taught workers to think of themselves as salespeople—listening to customers, welcoming them, and offering help. Not only did the firm receive compliments about its improved service, but it also attracted new customers.[18]

by sharing data among members of a sales team. In addition, Benioff practices his own version of personal selling and sales promotion by inviting customers, potential customers, and the print and electronic media to high-profile events like movie openings.

The Outcome. Experts are watching Salesforce.com closely. Some believe the company's strategy will change the economics of the entire software industry. "Like Dell on the hardware side, they're a disruptive business model," says one global investment banker. Customers are enthusiastic about Salesforce.com's new way of delivering software. "We don't have an appetite to pay $18,000 [per employee] and spend years installing software," explains one customer. Another large group of believers consists of investors who snapped up shares when Salesforce.com recently went public and then bid the price up more than 50 percent the first day it traded. Benioff himself isn't modest about his company's prospects. "Microsoft is the present, but we have the potential to be the future," he predicts.

Sources: Company Web site, http://www.salesforce.com, accessed October 22, 2004; Matt Krantz, "IPO Investors Feel the Salesforce.com," *USA Today,* June 24, 2004, p. B1; Erick Schonfeld, "The Biggest Mouth in Silicon Valley," *Business 2.0,* September 2003, pp. 107–112; Steve Hamm, "Who Says CEOs Can't Find Inner Peace?" *BusinessWeek,* September 1, 2003, pp. 77–80.

ORDER PROCESSING

order processing Selling, mostly at the wholesale and retail levels, that involves identifying customer needs, pointing them out to customers, and completing orders.

Order processing, which can involve both field selling and telemarketing, is most often typified by selling at the wholesale and retail levels. For instance, a Pepsi-Cola route salesperson who performs this task must take the following steps:

1. *Identify customer needs.* The route salesperson determines that a store has only 7 cases left in stock when it normally carries an inventory of 40 cases.
2. *Point out the need to the customer.* The route salesperson informs the store manager of the inventory situation.
3. *Complete (write up) the order.* The store manager acknowledges the need for more of the product. The driver unloads 33 cases, and the manager signs the delivery slip.

Order processing is part of most selling positions. It becomes the primary task in situations where needs can be readily identified and are acknowledged by the customer. Even in such instances, however, salespeople whose primary responsibility involves order processing will devote some time convincing their wholesale or retail customers to carry more complete inventories of their firms' merchandise or to handle additional product lines. They also are likely to try to motivate purchasers to feature some of their firms' products, increase the amount of shelf space devoted to these items, and improve product location in the stores.

Sales force automation now streamlines order-processing tasks. In the past, salespeople would write up an order on the customer's premises but spend much time later, after the sales visit, completing the order and transmitting it to headquarters. Today, many companies have automated order processing. With portable computers and state-of-the-art software, the salesperson can place an order on the spot, directly to headquarters, and thus free up valuable time and energy. Computers have even eliminated the need for some of the traditional face-to-face contacts for routine reorders.

creative selling Personal selling that involves situations in which a considerable degree of analytical decision making on the buyer's part results in the need for skillful proposals of solutions for the customer's needs.

CREATIVE SELLING

When a considerable amount of decision making is involved in purchasing a good or service, an effective salesperson uses **creative selling** techniques to solicit an order. In contrast to the order-processing task, which deals mainly with maintaining existing business, creative selling generally is used to develop new business either by adding new customers or by introducing new goods and services. New products or upgrades to more expensive items often require creative selling. The salesperson must first identify the customer's problems and needs and then propose a solution in the form of the good or service being offered. Creative selling techniques are used in over-the-counter selling, field selling, inside selling, and telemarketing (when attempting to expand an existing business relationship).

Believing in your product 100 percent will make you a great salesperson, because you will be real. People can sense fakes, even if it's only 1 percent fake. You must be a solid 100 percent or you will not be successful for very long.

Donald J. Trump (b. 1946)
chairman and president, The Trump Organization

As competition among companies increases and the number of buyers for a product shrinks, creative selling is becoming more prominent. In the waiting room of one Texas Lexus dealership, customers can watch a big-screen TV, surf the Internet, or sip a latte. "We try to make it like a den would be in your home," explains dealer Jordan Case. He wants each customer to feel like a houseguest.[19] Imagine trying to sell something that is available elsewhere for free. Steve Gottlieb, CEO of TVT Records, an independent label, is doing exactly that. In an environment where consumers can simply burn their own CDs for free, TVT still manages to offer value. "It might be bonus tracks, access to online stuff, or special DVD footage," says Gottlieb. "[We] focus on making the appeal of the artist that much more personal, so the desire to have that personal token and connection to the artist holds sway."[20]

Sometimes creative selling can rejuvenate an old product. Newell Rubbermaid's Phoenix program is designed to train young salespeople to do whatever it takes to sell Rubbermaid products. They may be found stocking shelves, demonstrating new products, or organizing in-store scavenger hunts. Phoenix program trainees are energetic and enthusiastic—and they have helped turn the company around.[21]

missionary selling Indirect type of selling in which specialized salespeople promote the firm's goodwill among indirect customers, often by assisting customers in product use.

MISSIONARY SELLING

Missionary selling is an indirect approach to sales. Salespeople sell the firm's goodwill and provide their customers with information and technical or operational assistance. A cosmetics company salesperson may call on retailers to check on special promotions and overall product movement, even though a wholesaler takes orders and delivers merchandise. Large pharmaceutical companies are the most aggressive of missionary sales operations. Through extensive gift-giving, wining and dining, free seminars, and other incentives, teams of sales reps typically court doctors (the indirect customer) in the hope of persuading them to prescribe a particular brand to patients. They also provide physicians with glossy product literature. Here, the doctor is clearly the decision maker, even though the transaction is not complete until the patient hands the prescription over to a pharmacist.

Pharmaceutical firms are not the only ones who offer **sales incentives,** however. Banfe Products, a New Jersey–based firm that sells large loads of soil and mulch to businesses, has an extremely creative travel incentive program. Every January, a group of loyal customers and top-performing sales staff get to fly to the tropics for several days of fun in the sun—on Banfe's tab. Although it sounds extravagant, customers must purchase literally trailer loads of dirt, mulch, and manure to qualify—and they do. The program benefits everyone. "We get to know [our customers] so well and it's wonderful," says company founder Jerry Banfe. "Clients have told me, 'I hate talking to salespeople, but I love talking to you.'"[22]

WWW.BANFE.US/INDEX.HTML

Banfe Products, of New Jersey, sells soil and mulch. Banfe is well known in the northeastern United States for its creative travel incentive program for good customers.

Missionary sales may involve both field selling and telemarketing. Many aspects of team selling can also be seen as missionary sales, as when technical support salespeople help design, install, and maintain equipment; when they train customers' employees; and when they provide information or operational assistance.

1. What are the three major tasks performed by salespeople?
2. What type(s) of selling is/are associated with order processing?

THE SALES PROCESS

5 Outline the seven steps in the sales process.

If you have worked in a retail store, or if you've sold magazine subscriptions or candy to raise money for your school or sports team, you will recognize many of the activities involved in the following list of steps in the sales process. Personal selling encompasses the following sequence of activities: (1) prospecting and qualifying, (2) approach, (3) presentation, (4) demonstration, (5) handling objections, (6) closing, and (7) follow-up.

As Figure 17.7 indicates, these steps follow the attention-interest-desire-action concept (AIDA). Once a sales prospect has been qualified, an attempt is made to secure his or her attention. The presentation and demonstration steps are designed to generate interest and desire. Successful handling of buyer objections should arouse further desire. Action occurs at the close of the sale.

Salespeople modify the steps in this process to match their customers' buying processes. A neighbor who eagerly looks forward to the Girl Scout cookie sale each year needs no presentation—except for details about new types of cookie offerings. But the same neighbor would expect a demonstration from an auto dealer when looking for a new car or might appreciate a presentation of dinner specials by the waiter prior to ordering a meal at a restaurant.

PROSPECTING AND QUALIFYING

Prospecting, the process of identifying potential customers, may involve hours, days, or weeks of effort, but it is a necessary step. Leads about prospects come from many sources: the Internet, computerized databases, trade show exhibits, previous customers, friends and neighbors, other vendors, nonsales employees in the firm, suppliers, and social and professional contacts. Although a firm may emphasize personal selling as the primary component of its overall promotional strategy, direct mail and advertising campaigns are also effective in identifying prospective customers.

Before beginning a prospecting effort, a salesperson should be clear about what his or her firm is selling. But the salesperson's thoughts shouldn't be limited to a narrow definition of the product offerings. "People don't buy products or services," explains one sales trainer. "They buy the results (or

figure 17.7

The AIDA Concept and the Personal Selling Process

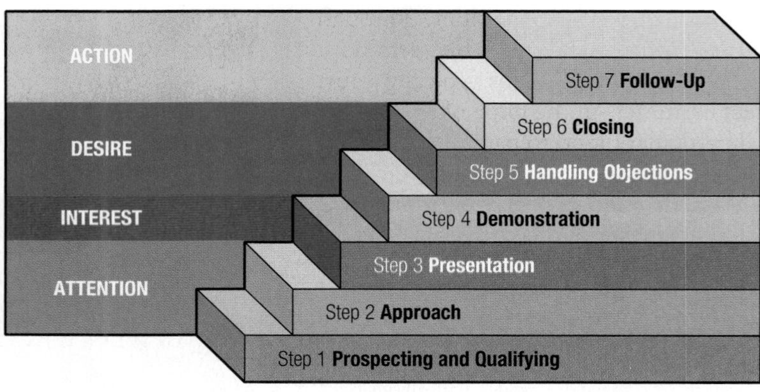

benefits) they expect to experience by using your product or services. You must therefore determine what your product or service really does for your customers."[23]

Qualifying—determining that the prospect really is a potential customer—is another important sales task. Not all prospects are qualified to make purchase decisions. A person with an annual income of $25,000 may wish to own a $200,000 house, but his or her ability to actually become a customer is questionable.

Qualifying can be a two-way street. The sales representative determines that the prospect has the authority and the resources to make the purchase decision. Likewise, prospects must agree that they are candidates for the goods or services being offered. If either of those conditions is not met, then further contact is not likely to lead to a sale and will be a waste of time for both salesperson and prospect.

APPROACH

Once the salesperson has identified a qualified prospect, he or she collects all available, relevant information and plans an **approach**—the salesperson's initial contact with the prospective customer. Information about the prospect can provide invaluable help to ease the initial contact for inside sales reps and field salespeople. If a firm already has a relationship with a customer or has permission to contact the person, telemarketing may be used as an approach. Salespeople can gather information from secondary sources—magazine or newspaper articles—or from the prospect's own published literature—annual reports, media releases, and even Internet sites. In collecting information, the salesperson must be sensitive to the issue of invading the prospect's privacy. A sales professional does not use unethical tactics to obtain personal information about a prospect.

Pretend that every single person you meet has a sign around his or her neck that says, "Make me feel important." Not only will you succeed in sales, you will succeed in life.

Mary Kay Ash (1915–2001)
founder, Mary Kay Cosmetics

Information gathering makes **precall planning** possible. A salesperson who has gathered relevant information about a prospect—essentially, done the homework—can make an initial contact armed with knowledge about the prospect's purchasing habits; his or her attitudes, activities, and opinions; and common interests between the salesperson and the prospect. It's also necessary to understand the industry as a whole by going to conferences, reading trade magazines, and the like. Finally, a salesperson needs to make a firm connection between his or her product and the customer's needs.[24] This preparation often provides key help for making the sale.

Retail salespeople usually cannot conduct precall planning, but they can compensate by asking leading questions to learn more about the purchase preferences of buyers. Business marketers have access to far more data than retail sellers, and they should review it before scheduling the first sales contact. Marketing research studies often provide invaluable information that serves as the basis of a sales approach. Answering the following questions can help salespeople complete effective precall planning:

- Who are the audience members and what jobs do they perform each day?
- What is their level of knowledge? Are they already informed about the idea you are going to present?
- What do they want to hear? Do they want detailed, technical jargon or general information?
- What do they need to hear? Do they need to know more about your company or more about the merchandise your company provides? Do they need to know more about the availability and cost of your product or more about how it actually works?

PRESENTATION

The salesperson gives the sales message to a prospective customer in a **presentation.** The seller describes the product's major features, points out its strengths, and concludes by citing illustrative successes. One popular form of presentation is a "features-benefits" framework wherein the seller's objective is to talk about the good or service in terms that are meaningful to the buyer. The salesperson relates product features to customer needs and explains benefits of those features rather than relating technical specifications.

The presentation should be well organized, clear, and concise, and it should emphasize the positive. Printed sales support materials (charts, product literature, marketing research, product reviews), charts designed on a laptop computer, and audiovisual aids such as CDs, videotapes, or streaming video enhance the clarity and effectiveness of presentations. The level of preparation depends on the type of call. For a routine sales call, up-to-date product knowledge and information about the prospect may be sufficient. When the salesperson is competing with several other companies for an account, a major presentation requires in-depth preparation and rehearsals to ensure that everything goes perfectly. Flexible presentations are nearly always needed to match the unique circumstances of each purchase decision. Proper planning and sensitivity to the customer's reactions are an important part of tailoring a presentation to each prospective customer.

Increasingly, presentations are going high-tech. Computer-based multimedia presentations are considered the next wave in sales force automation. With a multimedia-ready laptop or a larger PC or LCD projection computer, salespeople can bring color, animation, video, audio, and interactivity—as well as the latest product and pricing information—to their presentations. CNN Headline News salespeople previously used ordinary PowerPoint presentations to sell ads to cable operators. But when the company recently decided to change the look and feel of the Atlanta-based 24-hour cable news network, executives knew their sales force would need multimedia presentation materials that matched the network's more modern cutting-edge look. Presentations now include audio and video clips and high-tech graphics.[25]

DEMONSTRATION

One important advantage of personal selling over most advertising is the ability of salespeople to provide a **demonstration** of the good or service to the potential buyer. While you may typically think of a demonstration in terms of a software salesperson showing how a new anti-spam program works or being able to test-drive a car, cleverly designed advertising can simulate a demonstration as well, as illustrated by the ad for the Nissan XTerra in Figure 17.8. The intent of the ad is to show readers the off-road capabilities of the XTerra, even if they never actually drive the car up a snow-covered mountain. Instead, Nissan dealers hope the ad is sufficiently clever that it will prompt consumers to visit a dealership to try the car.

More firms use new technologies to make their demonstrations more effective. Multimedia interactive demonstrations are now common. Sales representatives for magazines such as *Forbes* and *Newsweek,* for instance, use data stored on CD-ROM or interactive laser discs to demonstrate the magazine's demographics and circulation patterns. These presentations use full-color video and sound, along with animation, statistics, and text, to demonstrate how a prospective client's ad will appear.

The key to an outstanding demonstration—one that gains the customer's attention, keeps his or her interest, is convincing, and stays in the customer's memory—is planning. But planning should also include time and space for improvisation. In other words, a salesperson should be prepared to take questions and give answers, interacting with customers.[26]

HANDLING OBJECTIONS

What if, after all the salesperson's effort, a potential customer says no? Handling the word "no" is part of the selling job. **Objections** are expressions of sales resistance by the prospect, and it is reasonable to expect them. Objections often appear in the form of stalling, such as, "I need to think about it" or "Let me call you back." They may focus on a product's features or price, such as, "I just don't like the color" or "I didn't want to spend that much."

A skilled salesperson knows how to answer objections without being aggressive or obtrusive. He or she can use an objection as a cue for providing additional information about the product. If the

figure 17.8

Nissan: How an Ad Can Simulate a Demonstration

customer says, "I just didn't want to spend that much," the salesperson may reinforce the benefits of the product, discuss a payment plan, or even offer a cheaper model. Testimonials from satisfied customers or providing a copy of the warranty may also help overcome this objection.

If a customer objects by comparing the salesperson's products to those of a competitor, it is possible to handle this as well. A good salesperson avoids criticizing the competition, focusing instead on the features and benefits of his or her offerings. Finally, handling objections may require some quick behind-the-scenes research, but sales force automation can help a sales representative handle certain objections by making needed information immediately available. For example, in just a few moments, the salesperson can confirm for the customer that the amount and type of a certain product are in stock and can be quickly shipped.

CLOSING

The moment of truth in selling is the **closing**—the point at which the salesperson asks the prospect for an order. If the sales representative has made an effective presentation based on applying the product to the customer's needs, the closing should be the natural conclusion. However, a surprising number of sales personnel find it difficult to actually ask for an order and thus risk losing the sale.

Closing does not have to be thought of in terms of a "hard sell." Instead, a salesperson can ask low-pressure questions such as, "Would you like to give this a try?" "Can I answer any more questions for you?" or "May I have your approval to proceed?" If a potential customer still seems unsure, reassurance such as, "I really think this would be an excellent solution to your problem," can work wonders.[27] Kathy Williams, the salesperson for Chico's clothing described earlier, closes many sales by reassuring customers about which clothing and accessories look attractive on them.

To be effective, salespeople must learn when and how to close a sale. In addition to those described previously, other methods of closing include the following:

1. Addressing the prospect's major concern about a purchase and then offering a convincing argument. ("If I can show you how the new heating system will reduce your energy costs by 25 percent, would you be willing to let us install it?")
2. Posing choices for the prospect in which either alternative is favorable to the salesperson. ("Will you take this sweater or that one?")

3. Warning the prospect that a sales agreement should be concluded now because the product may not be available later or an important feature, such as price, will soon change.
4. Remaining silent, since a discontinuance of a sales presentation forces the prospect to take some type of action (either positive or negative).
5. Offering an extra inducement designed to motivate a favorable buyer response. Extra inducements may include quantity discounts, special servicing arrangements, or layaway options.

FOLLOW-UP

The word *close* can be misleading because the point at which the prospect accepts the seller's offer is where much of the real work of selling begins. In today's increasingly competitive environment, the successful salesperson seeks to ensure that today's customers will be future purchasers. It is not enough to close the sale and move on. Relationship selling requires the salesperson to reinforce the customer's purchase decision and make sure that the company delivers high-quality goods or services on schedule. Salespeople must also ensure that customer service needs are met and that satisfaction results from all of a customer's dealings with the company. Otherwise, some other company may get the next order.

These postsale activities, which often determine whether a person will become a repeat customer, constitute the sales **follow-up.** Whenever possible, the sales representative should contact customers to find out whether they are satisfied with their purchases. This step allows the salesperson to psychologically reinforce the customer's original decision to buy. It also gives the seller an opportunity to correct any sources of discontent with the purchase and to secure important market information and make additional sales as well.

Follow-up helps to strengthen the bond salespeople try to build with customers in relationship selling. Automobile dealers, for example, often keep detailed records of their previous customers so that they can promote new models to individuals who already have shown a willingness to buy from them.[28] Many auto service departments will call several days after a customer's appointment to make sure the person is satisfied with the work and sometimes to schedule the next appointment. Verizon calls its local customers within a day or two to determine if a repair was successful and the customer is satisfied. Many doctors and dentists call patients after treatment to make sure they are doing well.

1. **Identify the seven steps of the sales process.**
2. **Are all the steps necessary for every sales effort? Why or why not?**
3. **Why is follow-up important to the sales effort?**

MANAGING THE SALES EFFORT

The overall direction and control of the personal selling effort are in the hands of sales managers, who are organized on a hierarchical basis. In a typical geographic sales structure, a district or divisional sales manager might report to a regional or zone manager. This manager in turn reports to a national sales manager or vice president of sales.

The sales manager's job requires a unique blend of administrative and sales skills depending on the specific level in the sales hierarchy. Sales skills are particularly important for first-level sales managers because they are involved daily in the continuing process of training and directly leading the sales force. But as people rise in the sales management hierarchy, they require more managerial skills and fewer sales skills to perform well. More than 60 percent of a typical salesperson's time is devoted to prospecting, face-to-face selling, and travel. Figure 17.9 shows the typical time allocations for a salesperson.

As with other promotional activities, personal selling requires effective planning and strategic objectives, including such strategies as selling existing products to new customers, selling new products, servicing customer accounts to enhance retention and satisfaction, and expanding customer relationships by selling more products to existing customers.

Sales force management is the administrative channel for sales personnel; it links individual salespeople to general management. The sales manager performs seven basic managerial functions:

figure 17.9

How Salespeople and Sales Managers Spend Their Time

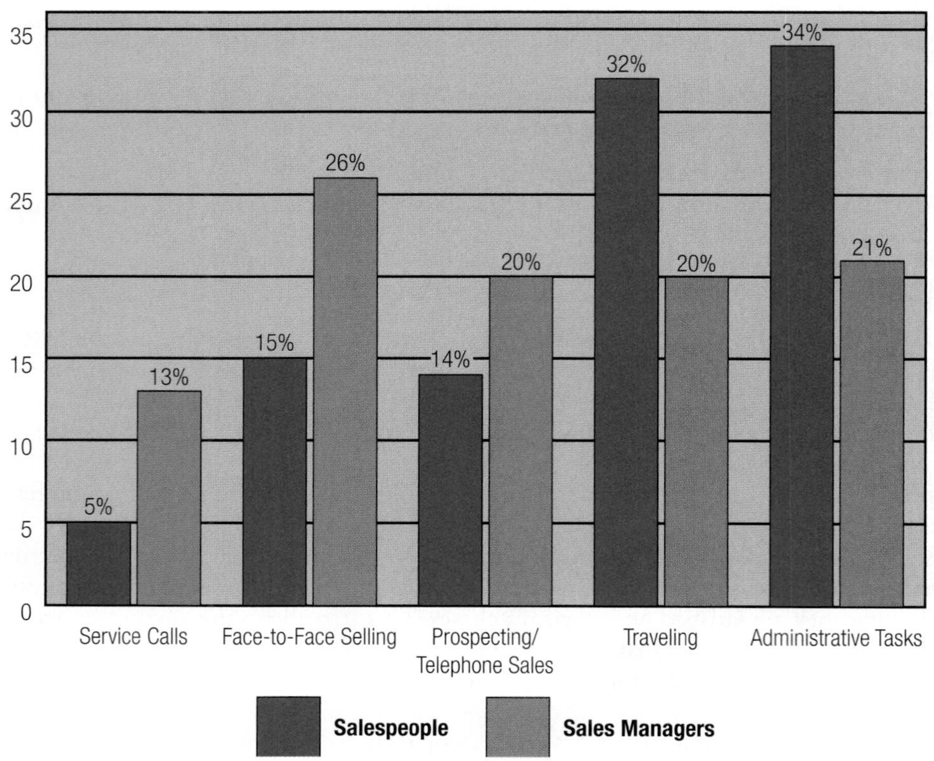

Source: Salesperson time allocation reported in "How Salespeople Spend Their Time," *Sales & Marketing Management,* March 1998, p. 96.

6 Identify the seven basic functions of a sales manager.

(1) recruitment and selection, (2) training, (3) organization, (4) supervision, (5) motivation, (6) compensation, and (7) evaluation and control. Sales managers perform these tasks in a demanding and complex environment. They must manage an increasingly diverse sales force that includes more women and minorities. Women account for almost half of U.S. professional salespeople, and their numbers are growing at a faster rate than that for men. The fastest growth rate is among salespeople of Hispanic and Asian descent, not a surprising development given the rapid growth of these two segments of the U.S. population.[29] However, women account for only one of every four business-to-business salespeople. As the workforce composition continues to change, an even more diverse blend of people will be needed to fill a growing number of sales positions.

RECRUITMENT AND SELECTION

Recruiting and selecting successful salespeople are among the sales manager's greatest challenges. After all, the people he or she hires will collectively determine just how successful the sales manager is. But there are still plenty of sources of new salespeople, including colleges and universities, trade and business schools, sales and nonsales personnel in other firms, and the firm's current nonsales employees. Some companies offer rewards or cash bonuses as incentives for existing employees who help find new salespeople. A successful sales career offers satisfaction in all of the following five areas that a person generally considers when deciding on a profession:

1. *Opportunity for advancement.* Studies have shown that successful sales representatives advance rapidly in most companies.
2. *Potential for high earnings.* Salespeople have the opportunity to earn a very comfortable living.
3. *Personal satisfaction.* A salesperson derives satisfaction from achieving success in a competitive environment and from helping customers satisfy their wants and needs.

4. *Job security.* Selling provides a high degree of job security because there is always a need for good salespeople.

5. *Independence and variety.* Salespeople often work independently, calling on customers in their territory. They have the freedom to make important decisions about meeting their customers' needs and frequently report that no two workdays are the same.

Careful selection of salespeople is important for two reasons. First, the selection process involves substantial amounts of money and management time. Second, selection mistakes are detrimental to customer relations and sales force performance and are costly to correct. Most larger firms use a seven-step process in selecting sales personnel: application screening, initial interview, in-depth interview, testing, reference checks, physical examination, and analysis and hiring decision. An application screening is typically followed by an initial interview. If the applicant looks promising, an in-depth interview is conducted. During the interview, a sales manager looks for personal characteristics like enthusiasm, good organizational skills, ambition, persuasiveness, the ability to follow instructions, and sociability.

Next, the company may use testing in its selection procedure, including aptitude, interest, and knowledge tests. One testing approach gaining in popularity is the assessment center. This technique, which uses situational exercises, group discussions, and various job simulations, allows the sales manager to measure a candidate's skills, knowledge, and ability. Assessment centers enable managers to see what potential salespeople can do rather than what they say they can do. Before hiring a candidate, specialists from the human resources department will check references, review company policies, and may request a physical examination for the candidate.

TRAINING

To shape new sales recruits into an efficient sales organization, managers must conduct an effective training program. The principal methods used in sales training are on-the-job training, individual instruction, in-house classes, and external seminars.

Popular training techniques include instructional videos or DVDs, lectures, role-playing exercises, and interactive computer programs. Simulations can help salespeople improve their selling techniques. Another area for training is sales force automation (SFA), described earlier in the chapter. Many firms supplement their training by enrolling salespeople in executive development programs at local colleges and universities and by hiring specialists to teach customized training programs. In other instances, sales reps attend courses and workshops developed by outside companies.

As mentioned earlier, Newell Rubbermaid has spent more than $100 million to recruit, hire, and train a young sales force through its Phoenix program. Phoenix trainees usually arrive with little or no sales experience but a lot of energy and enthusiasm. They take a training course, stock shelves, and brainstorm for ideas on how to help their customers. CEO Joe Galli prefers training a group with no experience rather than attempting to retrain or remotivate salespeople who have lost their edge. "This is the single most important thing we're doing," he says about the Phoenix program.[30]

Still, ongoing sales training is also important for veteran salespeople. Sales managers often conduct this type of training informally, traveling with field reps and then offering constructive criticism or suggestions. Sales meetings, classes, and workshops are other ways to reinforce training.

Mentoring is a key training tool at many organizations. Sealed Air Corporation, a New Jersey company, offers a sales mentoring program that cuts training costs, fosters loyalty, and helps groom future managers. Top sales performers spend three years coaching new or underperforming salespeople in their territories. While the trainee sets up calls and takes the lead in sales presentations, the mentor provides help and encouragement along the way.[31]

ORGANIZATION

Sales managers are responsible for the organization of the field sales force. General organizational alignments, which are usually made by top marketing management, may be based on geography, products, types of customers, or some combination of these factors. Figure 17.10 presents a streamlined organizational chart illustrating each of these alignments.

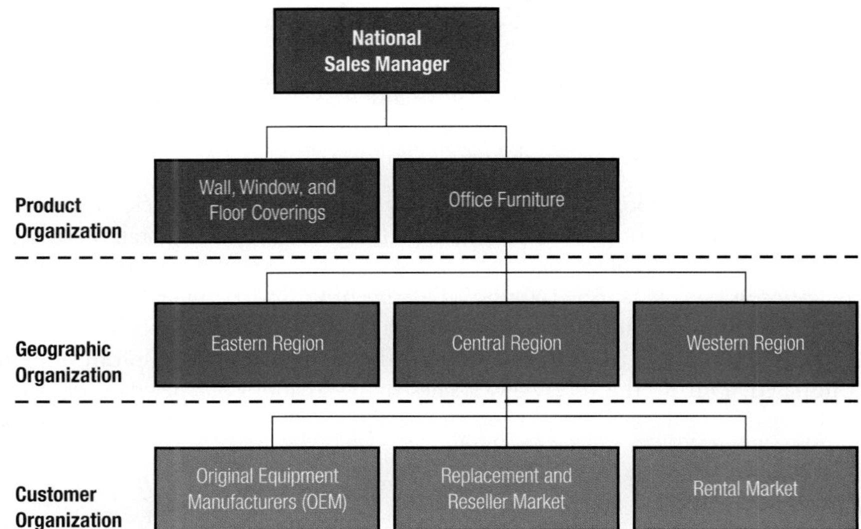

figure 17.10

Basic Approaches to Organizing the Sales Force

A product sales organization is likely to have a specialized sales force for each major category of the firm's products. This approach is common among industrial product companies that market large numbers of highly technical, complex products that are sold through different marketing channels.

Firms that market similar products throughout large territories often use geographic specialization. Multinational corporations may have different sales divisions on different continents. A geographic organization may also be combined with one of the other organizational methods. However, many companies are moving away from using territorial sales reps as they adopt customer-focused sales forces. For example, a single territory that contains two major customers might be redefined so the same sales rep covers both customers. Customer-oriented organizations use different sales force strategies for each major type of customer served. Some firms assign separate sales forces for their consumer and organizational customers. Others have sales forces for specific industries, such as financial services, educational, and automotive. Sales forces can also be organized by customer size, with a separate sales force assigned to large, medium, and small accounts.

A growing trend among firms using a customer-oriented organizational structure is the **national accounts organization.** This structure, designed to strengthen a firm's relationship with large and important customers, assigns senior sales managers or sales teams to major accounts in each market. Organizing by national accounts helps sales representatives develop cooperation between departments to meet special needs of the firm's most important customers. The classic example of a national account selling situation is the relationship between Wal-Mart and its major vendors. Clorox, Colgate, H.J. Heinz, Johnson & Johnson, Kraft, Nestlé, and PepsiCo are just some of the 500 or so companies that have set up sales offices near Wal-Mart's Bentonville, Arkansas, headquarters. Doing so places dedicated sales resources within an arm's length of this key account.

As companies expand their market coverage across national borders, they may use a variant of national account sales teams. These global account teams may be staffed by local sales representatives in the countries in which a company is operating. In other instances, the firm selects highly trained sales executives from its domestic operations. In either case, specialized training is critical to the success of a company's global sales force.

The individual sales manager also has the task of organizing the sales territories within his or her area of responsibility. Factors such as sales potential, strengths and weaknesses of available personnel, and workloads are considered in territory allocation decisions.

SUPERVISION

A source of constant debate among sales managers concerns the supervision of the sales force. It is impossible to pinpoint the exact amount of supervision that is correct in each situation since the individuals involved and the environments in which they operate vary. However, a concept known as **span of control** helps provide some general guidelines. Span of control refers to the number of sales representatives who report to first-level sales managers. The optimal span of control is affected by such factors as complexity of work activities being performed, ability of the individual sales manager, degree of interdependence among individual salespeople, and the extent of training each salesperson receives. A 6-to-1 ratio has been suggested as the optimal span of control for first-level sales managers supervising technical or industrial salespeople. In contrast, a 10-to-1 ratio is recommended if sales representatives are calling on wholesale and retail accounts.

MOTIVATION

What motivates salespeople to perform their best? The answer to this question is the sales manager's responsibility. Because the sales process involves problem solving, it often leads to considerable mental pressures and frustrations. Sales often result only after repeated calls on customers and may involve a long completion period, especially with new customers and complex technical products. Efforts to motivate salespeople usually take the form of debriefings, information sharing, and both psychological and financial encouragement. Appeals to emotional needs, such as ego needs, recognition, and peer acceptance, are examples of psychological encouragement. Monetary rewards and special benefits, such as club memberships and paid vacation awards, are types of financial incentives. Well-managed incentive programs can motivate salespeople and improve customer service. They typically include leisure trips or travel, gifts, recognition dinners, plaques and awards, and cash. Retailers such as Lowe's, L.L. Bean, and Blockbuster offer incentive awards that can be purchased by other firms that are looking for ways to motivate their sales staff. Blockbuster offers three incentive products that sales managers may offer their employees: a gift card, a movie card, and an entertainment card.[32] L.L. Bean offers gift certificates without expiration dates through its corporate sales department.[33] And Lowe's offers incentive gift cards in amounts ranging from $5 to $5,000 redeemable by a firm's sales reps. Lowe's offers a volume discount on the cards, which may be stockpiled by managers and handed out at appropriate times.[34]

Which types of incentives are the most effective? Some firms go all out, dangling luxury items such as computers, digital cameras, or trips in front of the sales force as rewards. "What really appeals to people today is an experience rather than a particular item," says Rodger Stotz, vice president of Maritz Performance Improvement, a firm that develops incentive programs for companies. He suggests that managers, rather than rewarding someone with a gas grill, offer classes in outdoor cooking. Stotz explains his recommendation this way. "When they choose these kinds of experiential rewards, you learn what motivates program participants as well as support their particular interests." In other words, sales managers can gain valuable insight into what motivates their staff by offering these types of incentives.[35]

Not all incentive programs are effective at motivating employees. A program with targets that are set too high, that isn't publicized, or that allows only certain sales personnel to participate can actually backfire. So it is important for sales management to plan carefully for an incentive program to succeed.

Sales managers can improve sales force productivity by understanding what motivates individual salespeople. They can gain insight into the subject of motivation by studying the various theories of motivation developed over the years. One theory that has been applied effectively to sales force motivation is **expectancy theory,** which states that motivation depends on the expectations an individual has of his or her ability to perform the job and on how performance relates to attaining rewards that the individual values.

Sales managers can apply the expectancy theory of motivation by following a five-step process:

1. Let each salesperson know in detail what is expected in terms of selling goals, service standards, and other areas of performance. Rather than setting goals just once a year, many firms do so on a semiannual, quarterly, or even monthly basis.
2. Make the work valuable by assessing the needs, values, and abilities of each salesperson and then assigning appropriate tasks.
3. Make the work achievable. As leaders, sales managers must inspire self-confidence in their salespeople and offer training and coaching to reassure them.
4. Provide immediate and specific feedback, guiding those who need improvement and giving positive feedback to those who do well.
5. Offer rewards that each salesperson values, whether it is an incentive as described above, opportunity for advancement, or a bonus.

COMPENSATION

Because monetary rewards are an important factor in motivating subordinates, compensating sales personnel is a critical matter for managers. Sales compensation can be based on a commission plan, a straight salary plan, or some combination of these options. Bonuses based on end-of-year results are another popular form of compensation. The increasing popularity of team selling has also forced companies to set up reward programs to recognize performance of business units and teams. Today, about one in four firms rewards business-unit performance.

A **commission** is a payment tied directly to the sales or profits that a salesperson achieves. A salesperson might receive a 5 percent commission on all sales up to a specified quota and a 7 percent commission on sales beyond that point. This approach to sales compensation is increasingly popular. But while commissions reinforce selling incentives, they may cause some sales force members to shortchange nonselling activities, such as completing sales reports, delivering sales promotion materials, and performing normal account servicing. Commission programs can also backfire. Sears recently modified its compensation system after discovering that salespeople were being too aggressive or recommending unnecessary services.[36] Another problem with commissions is that salespeople may focus on selling the most profitable products, ignoring those that do not result in the highest commissions. This happened at FedEx until the compensation program was revamped. "We needed to create a pay program that would encourage sales of all the products without displacing the sales of one product for the others," explains David Chichelli, whose consulting firm helped FedEx redesign its compensation structure.[37]

A **salary** is a fixed payment made periodically to an employee. A firm that bases compensation on salaries rather than commissions might pay a salesperson a set amount every week, twice a month, or once a month. A company must balance benefits and disadvantages in paying predetermined salaries to compensate managers and sales personnel. A straight salary plan gives management more control over how sales personnel allocate their efforts, but it reduces the incentive to expand sales. As a result, many firms develop compensation programs that combine features of both salary and commission plans. It is common for new salespeople to receive a base salary while they are in training, even if they move to full commission later on. A car, or an allowance toward a vehicle, is also usually part of an outside salesperson's compensation package because travel is an integral part of the job.[38]

Incomes for sales representatives vary widely. A Longaberger Baskets salesperson may earn $30,000 a year in commissions only, while a full-time, top-performing rep for a large pharmaceutical firm may earn $150,000 or more a year in salary, commissions, and bonus. Total compensation packages vary according to industry, with the finance, insurance, and real estate industries coming out on top, followed closely by general services. They also vary according to years of experience in sales. Figure 17.11 shows the average annual pay for sales representatives during one recent year.

EVALUATION AND CONTROL

Perhaps the most difficult tasks required of sales managers are evaluation and control. Sales managers are responsible for setting standards and choosing the best methods for measuring sales performance. Sales volume, profitability, and changes in market share are the usual means of evaluating sales effectiveness. They typically involve the use of **sales quotas**—specified sales or profit targets that the firm expects salespeople to achieve. A particular sales representative might be expected to generate sales of $720,000 in his or her territory during a given year. In many cases, the quota is tied to the compensation system. SFA has greatly improved the ability of sales managers to monitor the effectiveness of their sales staffs. Databases enable sales managers to quickly divide revenues by salesperson, by account, and by geographic area.

In addition to sales quotas, other measures such as customer satisfaction, profit contribution, share of product-category sales, and customer retention are also coming into play. The changes are the result of three factors:

1. An increasingly long-term orientation that results from greater use of customer relationship building efforts.
2. The realization that evaluations based on sales volume alone can lead to overselling and excessive inventory problems that work against customer relationship building.

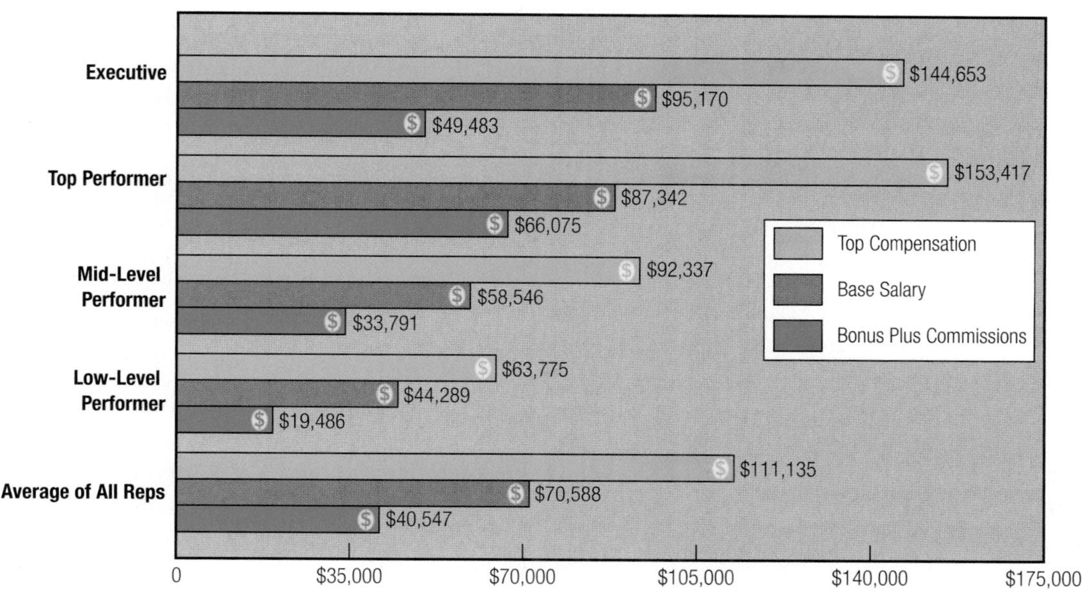

Source: Data from Christine Galea, "The 2004 Compensation Survey," *Sales & Marketing Management,* May 2004, pp. 28–34.

figure 17.11

Average Annual Pay for Sales Representatives

3. The need to encourage sales representatives to develop new accounts, provide customer service, and emphasize new products. A concentration on sales quotas tends to focus salespeople's attention on short-term selling from which they can generate the most sales today.

Regardless of the key elements in the evaluation program, the sales manager must follow a formal system that includes a series of decision rules. Such a system supplies information to the sales manager for action. This input helps the sales manager to answer three general questions.

First, where does each salesperson's performance rank relative to the predetermined standards? This comparison should fully consider the effect of uncontrollable variables on sales performance. Preferably, each adjusted rank should be stated as a percentage of the standard. This system simplifies evaluation and facilitates converting various ranks into a single composite index of performance.

The second evaluation question asks about the salesperson's strong points. One way to answer this question is to list areas of the salesperson's performance in which he or she has surpassed the respective standard. Another way is to categorize a salesperson's strong points in each of these areas of the work environment:

- *Task, or technical ability.* This strength appears in knowledge of the products (end uses), customers, and company, as well as selling skills.
- *Process, or sequence of work flow.* This strength pertains to actual sales transactions—the salesperson's application of technical ability and interaction with customers. Managers frequently measure process performance based on personal observation. Other measures are sales calls and expense reports.
- *Goal, or end results (output) of sales performance.* Sales managers usually state this aspect of the salesperson's work environment in terms of sales volume and profits.

The third evaluation question asks about the weak points, or negatives, in the salesperson's performance. The manager should categorize these faults as carefully as the salesperson's strong points. The sales manager should explain candidly, but kindly, the employee's weak areas. Because few people like to hear this part of an evaluation and consequently tend to "listen with only one ear," the manager should make sure the employee understands any performance problems that he or she needs to correct and ways the manager will measure progress. The manager and employee should then establish specific objectives for improvement and set a timetable for judging the employee's improvement.

In completing the evaluation summary, the sales manager should follow a set procedure:

- Each aspect of sales performance for which a standard exists should be measured separately. This helps prevent the so-called *halo effect,* in which the rating given on one factor influences those on other performance variables.
- Each salesperson should be judged on the basis of actual sales performance rather than potential ability. This emphasizes the importance of rankings in the evaluation.
- Sales managers should judge each salesperson on the basis of sales performance for the entire period under consideration rather than for a few particular incidents. As an evaluator, the sales manager should avoid reliance on isolated examples of the salesperson's success or failure.
- Each salesperson's evaluation should be reviewed for completeness and evidence of possible bias. Ideally, this review would be made by the sales manager's immediate superior.

1. **What are the seven basic functions performed by a sales manager?**
2. **Define *span of control.***
3. **Distinguish between a commission and a salary.**

Although evaluation includes both revision and correction, the sales manager must focus attention on correction. This priority translates into a drive to adjust actual performance to conform with predetermined standards. Corrective action, with its obviously negative connotations, typically poses a substantial challenge for the sales manager.

7 Explain the role of ethical behavior in personal selling.

ETHICAL ISSUES IN SALES

Promotional activities can raise ethical questions, and personal selling is no exception. A difficult economy or highly competitive environment may tempt some salespeople—particularly those new to the business—to behave in ways that they might later regret. They might use the company car for personal errands or pad an expense report. They might give or accept inappropriate or expensive gifts when negotiating a major business deal. But today's experienced, highly professional salespeople know that long-term success is based on building and maintaining mutually satisfying, ethical relationships with clients. They are also aware that the negative impact of any ethically questionable act is likely to affect the client's attitude toward the individual, his or her company, and any future relationships.

More and more companies are building ethics training into their overall sales training programs. One good example from the electronics industry is Texas Instruments. All new salespeople receive training in TI's code of ethics, including instruction in legal subjects such as proper disclosure of information and how to prepare sales contracts, along with human resources topics like sexual harassment and diversity. Trainers at Texas Instruments use role-playing exercises, case studies, video analysis, and even professional actors to convey their message. "We tell our salespeople that if you have to do something unethical to win business, don't do it," says Zoe Chapman, TI's director of human resources. "A reputation as an ethical vendor certainly makes customers want to do business with you."[39]

Some critics believe that ethical problems are inevitable because of the very nature of the sales function. And in the wake of corporate scandals in which top executives have benefited at the expense of customers, employees, and shareholders, ethical managers are working harder than ever to dispel the notion that many salespersons cannot be trusted. In fact, a growing number of firms have begun to realize that their greatest asset is an honest, reputable sales force. So they reinforce ethics codes that may already be in place and strengthen ethics training, as Texas Instruments has done. Today's savvy sales managers take the concept a step farther, using the sales force as emissaries of goodwill for the company. According to John Boatright, professor of business ethics at Loyola University and executive director of the Society of Business Ethics in Chicago, one of the best uses of a company's ethics code is "to make customers aware of it and to transmit it through the sales force. If companies are failing to do this, they are missing a good opportunity, because it increases the credibility of the company."[40]

Sales managers and top executives can do a lot to foster a corporate culture that encourages ethical behavior. Here are some characteristics of such a culture:

- *Employees understand what is expected of them.* "The ideal approach is for an organization to have a written code of conduct that everyone receives and reads," recommends Jim Eskin, a Texas-based public affairs consultant.
- *Open communication exists between employees and managers.* Employees who feel comfortable talking with their supervisors are more apt to report ethics violations.
- *Management leads by example.* Workers will naturally emulate the ethical behavior of management.
- *Employees are proud of and loyal to their organization.* Workers who feel good about their company are far more likely to behave ethically.[41]

1. Why is it important for salespeople to maintain ethical behavior?
2. What are the characteristics of companies that foster corporate cultures that encourage ethical behavior?

SALES PROMOTION

8 Describe the role of sales promotion in the promotional mix.

sales promotion Marketing activities other than personal selling, advertising, and publicity that enhance consumer purchasing and dealer effectiveness.

Sales promotion includes those marketing activities other than personal selling, advertising, and publicity designed to enhance consumer purchasing and dealer effectiveness. This component of the promotional mix traces its roots to the far reaches of antiquity, as examples have been found among the ruins of Pompeii and Ephesus. In the U.S., Adolphus Busch helped establish his brand by giving away samples of his beer and a pocket knife as a premium back in 1880. Ten years later, Procter & Gamble marketers built their market by exchanging watch-chain charms for Ivory soap wrappers. Today, over $250 billion is spent annually on consumer and trade sales promotion activities, including coupons, sampling, displays, trade shows and exhibitions, demonstrations, and the like.

Sales promotion techniques were originally intended as short-term incentives aimed at producing immediate consumer buying responses. Traditionally, these techniques were viewed as supplements to other elements of the firm's promotional mix. Today, however, marketers recognize them as integral parts of many marketing plans, and the focus of sales promotion has shifted from short-term goals to long-term aims of building brand equity and maintaining continuing purchases. A frequent-flyer program enables a new airline like JetBlue or Independence Air to build a base of loyal customers. A frequent-stay program allows a chain of hotels to attract regular guests.

Both retailers and manufacturers use sales promotions to offer consumers extra incentives to buy. Rather than emphasizing product features to make consumers feel good about their purchases, these promotions are likely to stress price advantages. The general objectives of sales promotion are to speed up the sales process and increase sales volume. Through a consumer promotion, a marketer encourages consumers to try the product, use more of it, and buy it again. The firm also hopes to foster sales of complementary items and increase impulse purchases.

Because sales promotion is so important to a marketing effort, an entire promotion industry exists to offer expert assistance in its use and to design unique promotions, just as an entire advertising industry offers similar services for advertisers. These companies, like advertising agencies, provide other firms with assistance in promoting their goods and services. Figure 17.12 shows current spending by companies for different types of sales promotions, many of which are conducted by these firms.

Sales promotions complement other types of promotion and often produce their best results when combined with other marketing activities. Ads create awareness, while sales promotions lead to trial or purchase. After a presentation, a salesperson may offer a potential customer a discount coupon for the good or service. Promotions encourage immediate action because they impose limited time frames. Discount coupons and rebates usually have expiration dates. In addition, sales promotions produce measurable results, making it relatively easy for marketers to evaluate their effectiveness. If an increased number of customers buy Honda Pilots from a certain dealer during its cash-back promotion, the dealership knows that the promotion was successful.

figure 17.12
Current Spending by Companies for Different Sales Promotions

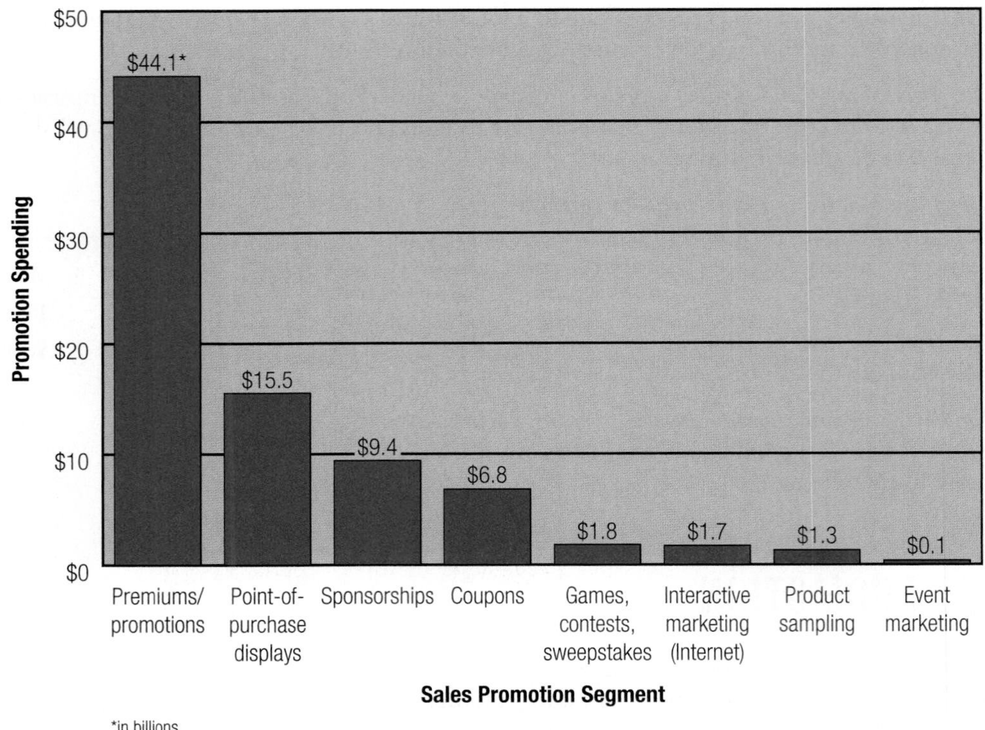

Source: Data from *PROMO* magazine and Promotion Marketing Association, as cited in "Promoting Promotions," *Marketing News,* July 7, 2003, p. 3. Used with permission from The American Marketing Association.

It is important to understand what sales promotions can and cannot do. They can encourage interest from salespeople and consumers for both new and mature products, help introduce new products, encourage trial and repeat purchases, increase usage rates, neutralize competition, and reinforce advertising and personal selling efforts. On the other hand, sales promotions cannot overcome poor brand images, product deficiencies, or poor training for salespeople. While sales promotions increase volume in the short term, they may not lead to sales and profit growth in the long run.

Sales promotion techniques may serve all members of a marketing channel. In addition, manufacturers may use trade promotion methods to promote their products to resellers. A single promotional strategy may combine more than one option, but probably no promotional strategy has ever used all of them in a single program. While the different types are not mutually exclusive, promotions generally are employed selectively. Sales promotion techniques include the following consumer-oriented promotions: samples, bonus packs, premiums, coupons, refunds, contests, sweepstakes, and specialty advertising. Trade-oriented promotions include trade allowances, point-of-purchase advertising, trade shows, dealer incentives, contests, and training programs.

9 Identify the different types of consumer-oriented and trade-oriented sales promotions.

CONSUMER-ORIENTED SALES PROMOTIONS

In the $85 billion promotion industry, marketers use all types of sales promotions, including games, contests, sweepstakes, and coupons to persuade new and existing customers to try their products. Consumer-oriented sales promotions encourage repurchases by rewarding current users, boosting sales of complementary products, and increasing impulse purchases. These promotions also attract consumer attention in the midst of advertising clutter. Table 17.3 lists the most popular consumer promotion techniques for firms using this element of the promotional mix.

It's important for marketers to use sales promotions selectively because, if they are overused, consumers begin to expect price discounts, which ultimately diminishes brand equity. The following sections briefly describe the various forms of consumer-oriented sales promotions.

Coupons and Refunds

Coupons, the most widely used form of sales promotion, offer discounts on the purchase price of goods and services. Consumers can redeem the coupons at retail outlets, which receive the face value of the coupon plus a handling fee from the manufacturer. The $5 billion coupon industry has been somewhat clipped in recent years due to more complex accounting rules that make couponing less attractive to some marketers, as well as the growing clout of retailers. In addition, consumers receive so many coupons that they can't possibly redeem them all. According to a recent survey sponsored by the Promotion Marketing Association, the average U.S. household received 3,000 coupons during a single 12-month period but only redeemed 40. Marketers spent nearly as much money distributing the coupons as consumers saved. Still, coupons continue to be a popular form of sales promotion.

table 17.3 **Seven Most Frequently Used Consumer Promotion Techniques**

TECHNIQUE	PERCENTAGE OF MARKETERS WHO USE IT
Coupons in retail ads	90
In-store coupons	88
Refunds	85
Electronic in-store displays	83
Samples of established products	78
Premiums	75
Sweepstakes	70

Mail, magazines, newspapers, package inserts, and, increasingly, the Internet are the standard methods of distributing coupons. A highly popular distribution method is printing them directly on receipts at supermarkets and other retail outlets. Free-standing inserts (FSIs) in certain magazines and Sunday newspapers account for nearly 75 percent of all coupons distributed.

Refunds, or rebates, offer cash back to consumers who send in proof of purchasing one or more products. Refunds help packaged goods companies to increase purchase rates, promote multiple purchases, and reward product users. Although many consumers find the refund forms too bothersome to complete, plenty still take the time and energy to do so.

Samples, Bonus Packs, and Premiums

Marketers are increasingly adopting the "try it, you'll like it" approach as an effective means of getting consumers to try and then purchase their goods and services. **Sampling** refers to the free distribution of a product in an attempt to obtain future sales. Samples may be distributed door-to-door, by mail, via demonstrations in stores or at events, or by including them in packages with other products.

Sampling produces a higher response rate than most other promotions. About three-quarters of the consumers who receive samples try them, particularly if they have requested the samples, and total annual spending on this sales promotion technique has topped $1 billion. A recent survey showed that 92 percent of consumers preferred receiving free samples rather than coupons. With sampling, marketers can target potential customers and be certain that the product reaches them. Sampling provides an especially useful way to promote new or unusual products because it gives the consumer a direct product experience.

A major disadvantage of sampling is the high cost involved. Not only must the marketer give away small quantities of a product that might otherwise have generated revenues through regular sales, but the market is also in effect closed for the time it takes consumers to use up the samples. In addition, the marketer may encounter problems in distributing the samples. Hellman's marketers annoyed consumers instead of pleasing them when the firm distributed sample packets of Italian and French salad dressing in home-delivered copies of *The New York Times.* Many of the packets burst when the papers hit the driveways.

Olay offers free samples of its products to consumers who visit the company's Web site.

A **bonus pack** is a specially packaged item that gives the purchaser a larger quantity at the regular price. For instance, Camay soap recently offered three bars for the price of two, and Salon Selectives often increases the size of its shampoos and conditioners for the same price as regular sizes.

Premiums are items given free or at reduced cost with purchases of other products. For example, Pantene frequently attaches a purse-size bottle of hairspray to the sides of its other hair-care products. Premiums have proven effective in motivating consumers to try new products or different brands. A premium should have some relationship with the product or brand it accompanies, though. A home improvement center might offer free nail aprons to its customers, for example.

Contests and Sweepstakes

Firms often sponsor contests and sweepstakes to introduce new goods and services and to attract additional customers. **Contests** require entrants to complete a task such as solving a puzzle or answering questions in a trivia quiz, and they may also require proofs of purchase. **Sweepstakes,** on the other hand, choose winners by chance, so no product purchase is necessary. They are more popular with consumers than contests because they do not take as much effort for consumers to enter. Marketers like them, too, because they are inexpensive to run and the number of winners is predetermined. With some contests, the sponsors cannot predict the number of people who will correctly complete the puzzles or gather the right number of symbols from scratch-off cards.

Not surprisingly, contests and sweepstakes have become more sophisticated and creative with the advent of the Internet. Saab recently ran a sweepstakes called "The Ultimate Drive of a Lifetime," in which consumers had a chance to win a new Saab 9-3 luxury sedan by visiting the company's Web site, as shown in Figure 17.13. Ads and e-mails were used to direct consumers to the site. Other prizes

figure 17.13

Saab's Online Sweepstakes

included flying winners to San Francisco for three days to test drive the car and go on a related outdoor adventure.[42]

With the recent rash of court rulings and legal restrictions, the use of contests requires careful administration. Any firm contemplating this promotional technique should engage the services of online promotion specialists such as WebStakes or NetStakes.

Specialty Advertising

The origin of specialty advertising has been traced to the Middle Ages, when artisans gave wooden pegs bearing their names to prospects, who drove them into the walls at home to serve as convenient hangers for armor. In more modern times, corporations began putting their names on a variety of products in the late 1800s, as newspapers and print shops explored new methods to earn additional revenues from their expensive printing presses.

Specialty advertising is a sales promotion technique that places the advertiser's name, address, and advertising message on useful articles that are then distributed to target consumers. Marketers give out more than $8 billion worth of specialty advertising items each year. Wearable products, including T-shirts and baseball caps, are the most popular products, accounting for nearly a third of specialty advertising sales. Writing instruments, glassware, and calendars are other popular forms.

specialty advertising Sales promotion technique that places the advertiser's name, address, and advertising message on useful articles that are then distributed to target consumers.

Advertising specialties help to reinforce previous or future advertising and sales messages. Consumers like these giveaways, which generate stronger responses to direct mail, resulting in three times the dollar volume of sales compared with direct mail alone. Companies use this form of promotion to highlight store openings and new products, motivate salespeople, increase visits to trade show booths, and improve customer relationships.

TRADE-ORIENTED PROMOTIONS

Sales promotion techniques can also contribute effectively to campaigns aimed at retailers and wholesalers. **Trade promotion** is sales promotion that appeals to marketing intermediaries rather than to final consumers. Marketers use trade promotions in push strategies by encouraging resellers to stock new products, continue to carry existing ones, and promote both effectively to consumers. The typical firm actually spends half of its promotional budget on trade promotion—as much money as it spends on advertising and consumer-oriented sales promotions combined. Successful trade promotions offer financial incentives. They require careful timing and attention to costs and are easy to implement by retailers. These promotions should bring quick results and improve retail sales.

trade promotion Sales promotion that appeals to marketing intermediaries rather than to consumers.

Trade Allowances

Among the most common trade promotion methods are **trade allowances**—special financial incentives offered to wholesalers and retailers that purchase or promote specific products. These offers take various forms. A buying allowance gives retailers a discount on goods. They include off-invoice allowances through which retailers deduct specified amounts from their invoices or receive free goods, such as one free case for every ten ordered, when they order certain quantities. When a manufacturer offers a promotional allowance, it agrees to pay the reseller a certain amount to cover the costs of special promotional displays or extensive advertising that features the manufacturer's product. The goal is to increase sales to consumers by encouraging resellers to promote their products effectively.

As mentioned in previous chapters, some retailers require vendors to pay a special slotting allowance before they agree to take on new products. These fees guarantee slots, or shelf space, for newly introduced items in the stores. This practice is common in large supermarket chains. Retailers defend these fees as essential to cover the added costs of carrying the products, such as redesigning display space and shelves, setting up and administering control systems, managing inventory, and taking the risks inherent in stocking new products. The fees can be sizable, from several hundred dollars per store to many thousands of dollars for a retail chain and millions of dollars for nationally distributed products.

Point-of-Purchase Advertising

point-of-purchase (POP) advertising Display or other promotion placed near the site of the actual buying decision.

A display or other promotion located near the site of the actual buying decision is known as **point-of-purchase (POP) advertising.** This method of sales promotion capitalizes on the fact that buyers make many purchase decisions within the store, so it encourages retailers to improve on-site merchandising. Product suppliers assist the retailer by creating special displays designed to stimulate sales of the item being promoted.

Free-standing POP promotions often appear at the ends of shopping aisles. On a typical trip to the supermarket, you might see a POP display for Disney videos, Coppertone sunscreen, or Pepsi's new reduced-calorie drink. Warehouse-style retailers such as Home Depot and Sam's Club, along with Staples and Kmart, all use POP advertising displays frequently. Electronic kiosks, which allow consumers to place orders for items not available in the store, have begun to transform the POP display industry, as creators of these displays look for ways to involve consumers more actively as well as entertain them.

Until recently, there have been few concrete measures of the success of POP promotions. However, several organizations have begun to develop research designed to help marketers evaluate the performance of POP promotions. "People have gone a lot on gut instinct in this business, but this research gives us a benchmark that confirms a lot of that instinct," says Dick Blatt, president and CEO of Point-of-Purchase Advertising International (POPAI), one of the groups conducting the research.[43]

Trade Shows

To influence resellers and other members of the distribution channel, many marketers participate in **trade shows.** These shows are often organized by industry trade associations; frequently, they are part of these associations' annual meetings or conventions. Vendors who serve the industries display and demonstrate their products for members.[44] Every year, over 4,300 different shows in the U.S. and Canada draw more than 1.3 million exhibitors and 85 million attendees. Industries that hold trade shows range from sporting goods to electronics, from toys to book publishing.

Because of the expense involved in trade shows, a company must assess the value of these shows on several criteria, such as direct sales, any increase in product awareness, image building, and any contribution to the firm's marketing communications efforts. Trade shows give especially effective opportunities to introduce new products and to generate sales leads. Some types of shows reach ultimate consumers as well as channel members. Home, recreation, and automobile shows, for instance, allow businesses to display and demonstrate home improvement, recreation, and other consumer products to entire communities.

Dealer Incentives, Contests, and Training Programs

Manufacturers run dealer incentive programs and contests to reward retailers and their salespeople who increase sales and, more generally, to promote specific products. These channel members receive incentives for performing promotion-related tasks and can win contests by reaching sales goals. Manufacturers may offer major prizes to resellers such as trips to exotic places. **Push money** (which retailers commonly refer to as *spiffs)* is another incentive that gives retail salespeople cash rewards for every unit of a product they sell. This benefit increases the likelihood that the salesperson will try to convince a customer to buy the product rather than a competing brand.

For more expensive and highly complex products, manufacturers often provide specialized training for retail salespeople. This background helps sales personnel explain features, competitive advantages, and other information to consumers. Training can be provided in several ways: A manufacturer's sales representative can conduct training sessions during regular sales calls, or the firm can distribute sales literature and DVDs.

MARKETING Concept Check

1. Define *sales promotion.*
2. Identify at least four types of consumer-oriented sales promotions.
3. Identify at least three types of trade-oriented sales promotions.

Strategic Implications of Marketing in the 21st Century

TODAY'S salespeople are a new breed. Richly nourished in a tradition of sales, their roles are strengthened even further through technology. However, as many companies are discovering, nothing can replace the power of personal selling in generating sales and in building strong, loyal customer relationships.

Salespeople today are a critical link in developing relationships between the customer and the company. They communicate customer needs and wants to coworkers in various units within an organization, enabling a cooperative, companywide effort in improving product offerings and in better satisfying individuals within the target market. For salespeople, the greatest benefit of electronic technologies is the ability to share knowledge when it is needed with those who need to know, including customers, suppliers, and employees.

Because buyers are now more sophisticated, demanding more rapid and lower cost transactions, salespeople must be quick and creative as they find solutions to their customers' problems. Product life cycles are accelerating, and customers who demand more are apt to switch from one product to another. Recognizing the long-term impact of keeping satisfied buyers—those who make repeat and cross-purchases and provide referrals—versus dissatisfied buyers, organizations are increasingly training their sales forces to provide superior customer service and rewarding them for increasing satisfaction levels.

The traditional skills of a salesperson included persuasion, selling ability, and product knowledge. But today's sales professional is more likely to possess communication skills, problem-solving skills, and knowledge of products, customers, industries, and applications. Earlier generations of salesperson tended to be self-driven; today's sales professional is more likely to be a team player as well as a customer advocate who serves his or her buyers by solving problems.

The modern professional salesperson is greatly assisted by the judicious use of both consumer- and trade-oriented sales promotions. Often overlooked in promotional discussions of high-profile advertising, the typical firm allocates more promotional dollars for sales promotion than for advertising. The proven effectiveness of sales promotion makes it a widely used promotional mix component for most B2C and B2B marketers.

REVIEW OF CHAPTER OBJECTIVES

① Outline the marketplace conditions that make personal selling a primary component of a firm's promotional mix.

Personal selling is likely to be a primary component when (1) customers are concentrated geographically; (2) individual orders account for large amounts of revenue; (3) the firm markets goods and services that are expensive, complex, or require special handling; (4) trade-ins are involved; (5) products move through short channels; and (6) the firm markets to relatively few customers.

1.1. Using the above criteria, give an example of a product that would require personal selling.

② Describe the four sales channels.

Over-the-counter (retail) selling involves providing product information and arranging for completion of the sales transaction when customers come to the retail location. Field selling involves sales calls to customers at their homes or businesses for the purpose of providing demonstrations or information about the good or service. Although its use has been severely limited by the recent do not call rules, telemarketing is used to provide product information and answer questions from customers who call. It also reduces the substantial cost involved in maintaining a sales force that makes personal calls at the homes of customers or businesses that are current customers or grant permission for such calls. Inside selling relies on phone, mail, and e-commerce to provide sales and product services for customers on a continuing basis.

2.1. Which sales channel is the most expensive to operate? Why?

2.2. If your telephone number is registered on the national do not call list, what types of organizations are still permitted to call you?

③ Describe the major trends in personal selling.

To address new challenges, companies are turning to relationship selling, consultative selling, team selling, and sales force automation. Relationship selling occurs when a salesperson builds a mutually beneficial relationship with a customer on a regular basis over an extended period. Consultative selling involves meeting customer needs by listening to customers, understanding and caring about their problems, paying attention to the details, and following through after the sale. Team selling occurs when the salesperson joins with specialists from other functional areas of the firm to complete the selling process. Sales force automation (SFA) is the use of various technologies to make the sales function more efficient and competitive.

3.1. Describe three basic guidelines for conducting successful personal selling.
3.2. What is cross-selling? Give an example.
3.3. How does SFA help make the sales function more efficient and competitive?

④ Identify and briefly describe the three basic sales tasks.

Order processing is the routine handling of an order. It characterizes a sales setting in which the need is made known to and is acknowledged by the customer. Creative selling is persuasion aimed at making the prospect see the value of the good or service being presented. Missionary selling is indirect selling, such as making goodwill calls and providing technical or operational assistance.

4.1. What are the three steps of order processing?
4.2. When might a salesperson engage in creative selling?

⑤ Outline the seven steps in the sales process.

The basic steps in the sales process are prospecting and qualifying, approach, presentation, demonstration, handling objections, closing, and follow-up.

5.1. Describe prospecting and qualifying.
5.2. How does precall planning help the approach?
5.3. How are presentation and demonstration related?
5.4. Which step do salespeople often have the most difficulty completing?

⑥ Identify the seven basic functions of a sales manager.

A sales manager links the sales force to other aspects of the internal and external environments. The manager's functions are recruitment and selection, training, organization, supervision, motivation, compensation, and evaluation and control.

6.1. Name two reasons the recruitment and selection process is so important to a firm.
6.2. Define *expectancy theory of motivation* and explain how sales managers can apply it to their sales force.

⑦ Explain the role of ethical behavior in personal selling.

Ethical behavior is vital to building good, long-term relationships with customers. More and more companies are building ethics training into their overall sales training programs. Today's savvy sales managers recognize that an ethical sales force can be a powerful emissary of goodwill for their company.

7.1. Give two examples of characteristics of a corporate culture that fosters ethical behavior among its workers.

8 Describe the role of sales promotion in the promotional mix.

Sales promotion methods were traditionally intended as short-term incentives aimed at producing immediate results; however, today's marketers recognize them as integral parts of their marketing plans. Sales promotion may now be part of a long-term goal to build brand equity and maintain continuing purchases.

8.1. How might a sales promotion be used in conjunction with personal selling?

9 Identify the different types of consumer-oriented and trade-oriented sales promotions.

Consumer-oriented sales promotions include coupons, refunds, samples, bonus packs, premiums, contests, sweepstakes, and specialty advertising. Trade-oriented promotions include trade allowances, point-of-purchase (POP) advertising, trade shows, and dealer incentives, contests, and training programs.

9.1. What is the most popular type of consumer-oriented sales promotion with marketers? Which type do consumers prefer?
9.2. Who is the intended audience for a trade promotion?

MARKETING TERMS YOU NEED TO KNOW

personal selling 554
over-the-counter selling 556
field selling 557
telemarketing 558
inside selling 560
relationship selling 561
consultative selling 562
team selling 563
sales force automation (SFA) 564
order processing 566
creative selling 566
missionary selling 566
sales promotion 579
specialty advertising 583
trade promotion 583
point-of-purchase (POP) advertising 584

OTHER IMPORTANT MARKETING TERMS

network marketing 558
outbound telemarketing 558
inbound telemarketing 559
cross-selling 563
virtual sales team 564
sales incentives 567
prospecting 567
qualifying 568
approach 568
precall planning 568
presentation 569
demonstration 569
objection 569
closing 570
follow-up 571
national accounts organization 574
span of control 574
expectancy theory 575
commission 576
salary 576
sales quota 576
coupon 581
refund 581
sampling 581
bonus pack 582
premium 582
contest 582
sweepstakes 582
trade allowance 583
trade show 584
push money 584

PROJECTS AND TEAMWORK EXERCISES

1. In pairs or small groups, explain and offer examples of how the following factors affect the decision to emphasize personal selling or nonpersonal advertising and/or sales promotion.
   a. geographic market concentration
   b. length of marketing channels
   c. degree of product technical complexity
   d. price
   e. number of customers
   f. prevalence of trade-ins
2. What sales tasks are involved in selling the following products? Have each team prepare a summary of one or more situations.
   a. Lexmark laser printers
   b. American Heart Association (to an employee group)
   c. used Honda Accord
   d. six blueberry bagels from Broadway Bagels
   e. janitorial supplies for use in plant maintenance
3. Describe the job of each of the following salespeople. In a group, discuss the differences and similarities.
   a. counterperson in a Blockbuster Video store
   b. Coldwell Banker real estate sales agent
   c. route driver for Keebler snack foods (sells and delivers to local food retailers)
   d. sales engineer for Dell
4. As sales representatives at a large paper company, your team is invited to make a sales presentation to a national warehouse and shipping company. List the five most important messages you wish to relate and then role-play the sales presentation.
5. Suppose you are the local sales manager for the telephone company's Yellow Pages and you employ six representatives who call on local firms to solicit advertising space sales. What type of compensation system would you use? What types of sales force automation would be effective in presenting the benefits of advertising in the Yellow Pages? How would you suggest that your sales personnel be evaluated?
6. Cross-selling can be an effective way for a firm to expand. On your own or with a classmate, locate an advertisement for a firm that you believe could benefit from cross-selling. List ways it could offer multiple products or services to the same customer. Then create a new ad illustrating the multiple offerings.
7. With a partner, choose one of the following sales situations. Then take turns coming up with creative ways to close the deal—one of you plays the customer and the other plays the salesperson. Present your closing scenarios to the class.
   a. You are a Toyota dealer, and a potential customer has just test-driven the hybrid Prius. You have handled all the customer's objections and settled on a price. You don't want the customer to leave without agreeing to purchase the car.
   b. You operate a lawn-care business and have visited several homeowners in a new development. Three of them have already agreed to give your service a try. You are meeting with the fourth and want to close that sale, too.
8. Design a coupon for one of the following or choose your own:
   a. ski resort
   b. Kellogg's cornflakes
   c. casual dining restaurant
   d. Wherehouse music store
9. Choose a product or firm that you think would benefit from a contest and write a brief proposal outlining your idea for the contest.
10. Go online and research a firm such as Kraft, General Mills, Ford, or Burger King to find out what kinds of consumer-oriented promotions the company is conducting for its various brands or individual products. Which promotions seem the most appealing to you as a consumer? Why? Present your findings to the class.

APPLYING CHAPTER CONCEPTS

1. Since the implementation of the national Do Not Call Registry, Americans have witnessed an increase in door-to-door selling. As a marketer, do you think this type of selling is effective? Why or why not?
2. Atlanta-based HomeBanc Mortgage Corp. often partners with construction companies that build housing developments and offices. As part of a deal, HomeBanc becomes a builder's preferred lender, allowing it to place marketing materials in completed homes offered for sale by the builder, as well as in the builder's offices. Potential homebuyers are not only exposed to the quality of the builder's product offerings but also receive printed materials on a recommended source of financing—whether they purchase from this builder or another firm. The builder also agrees to recommend HomeBanc to persons who actually make a home purchase. How might sales force automation (SFA) assist HomeBanc sales reps in their jobs? How important is relationship selling in a situation like this and why?
3. Imagine that you want to sell your parents on the idea of you taking a trip, buying a car, attending graduate school—something that is important to you. Outline your approach and presentation as a salesperson would.
4. Why is the recruitment and selection stage of the hiring process one of a sales manager's greatest challenges?
5. Describe a product that you think would benefit from the use of sampling.

ETHICS EXERCISE

Several years ago, the telecommunications firm WorldCom declared bankruptcy after admitting to multimillion-dollar accounting fraud. After changing its name to a less controversial MCI, WorldCom is now trying to rebuild itself and its reputation. As part of their training, all MCI salespeople are asked to read, sign, and adhere to the company's new ethics policy or risk being fired. Salespeople are also trained to tell customers about the new ethics program, the firm's independent ethics office, the new structure of the board of directors, and other steps the telecom giant has taken to ensure accurate and honest accounting. "We tell people exactly what we're doing," says Jonathan Crane, president of U.S. sales, marketing, and services.[45]

1. Do you think MCI's sales force can make a real difference in rebuilding the firm's reputation? Why or why not?
2. How might a sales manager's approach to recruiting, selecting, and hiring a salesperson now differ from the way these tasks were previously carried out at WorldCom?

'netWork EXERCISES

1. **Online product demonstrations.** As noted in the chapter, many companies now use the Internet to demonstrate their products. Visit the Web site listed below and view the product presentations. Make a list of your observations and bring your list to class to participate in a discussion on the subject.

   http://www.rebis.com/swf
2. **Job opportunities in sales.** Go to one of the major online employment sites, such as Monster (http://www.monster.com) and search for job opportunities in sales. Print the job description for a sales position in the location, and at a company, that would appeal to you if you were in the job market. Next, go the Bureau of Labor Statistics Web site (http://www.bls.gov) and click "Occupational Outlook Handbook." Here you will find detailed data on employment by occupation as well as employment trends and projections. How many people are currently employed in sales positions? What is the projected growth in employment for sales over the next few years?
3. **Online coupons.** Visit the Web site listed below and click "Couponing." Read the article entitled "The Power of Online Coupons." Next, visit several of the online coupon sites listed. Write a brief report summarizing what you learned and your impressions of online coupons.

   http://www.mommysavers.com

Note: Internet Web addresses change frequently. If you don't find the exact sites listed, you may need to access the organization's or company's home page and search from there or use a search engine such as Google.

INFOTRAC CITATIONS AND EXERCISES

Record: CJ118159552
Do Not Call Registry Forces Industry to Cut Jobs, Telemarketers Say. *William Glanz.*
The Washington Times, June 15, 2004

Abstract: The Federal Trade Commission's national Do Not Call Registry is a popular governmental regulation that enables consumers to block most telemarketers from calling them at home. Since its launch in 2003, the registry has garnered well over 56 million registrants who have expressed their desire not to be bothered by telemarketers. Direct marketing groups have challenged the new legislation in court, claiming that the law violates free speech rights and will result in huge job losses.

1. Given telemarketing's unpopularity with consumers, why is it still a popular sales technique for many businesses?
2. What effect is the Do Not Call legislation having on business, according to the article? Give examples.
3. Do you think the Do Not Call Registry is a violation of the right to free speech? Why or why not?

CASE 17.1 The Independent Sales Force

The sales rep used to be a company man. He lived, breathed, and retired a loyal employee. Then came the company woman, the sales rep who often outsold her male colleagues. Today, there is a whole new type of sales force taking shape: independent contractors. These salespeople are professional reps who sell goods and services for a variety of companies that are customers, rather than working for just one company as an employee.

Some companies have hired independent salespeople for decades. Avon, Tupperware, and Mary Kay are just three of the many firms that have always relied on independent contractors who sell their products directly to consumers. Hiring independent contractors, who develop one-to-one relationships with consumers, has been a successful strategy for all of these companies. But this type of direct selling is beginning to expand in new directions as well. Large corporations are attracted to its success—direct selling brings in almost $30 billion a year in U.S. sales alone—and are looking at new ways to use it to their advantage. Unilever has unveiled plans to start a direct-sales firm marketing cosmetics in South Africa. Hallmark's Binney and Smith unit is launching a direct-sales firm called Big Yellow Box by Crayola.

Some small firms are now experimenting with the use of independent sales contractors. Sven Harms, co-owner of Pioneer Research, a small firm that designs and markets binoculars and underwater cameras, would need to hire about 30 full-time salespeople at an annual cost of $160,000 each (including salaries and benefits) to serve his customers. Right now, though, he wants all of his current 45 employees to focus on designing and marketing Pioneer products. His firm doesn't have enough money to hire a full-time sales force. So Harms contracts with about 20 independent sales firms that provide about 60 salespeople who assist in bringing in the company's annual sales of $15 million. Hiring independent salespeople "was the only thing we could do," explains Harms. "Revenues were small. Cash flows were small. Credit lines were small. We couldn't hire a lot of people."

There are some downsides to hiring an independent sales force. Management of the sales force becomes one step removed. Firms have less control over impressions created by salespeople as they meet new customers for the first time. But professional reps often have worked their territories and industries for years and can provide access to customers based on relationships they have already built. In an age when marketing relationships are paramount, the independent sales force is finding new ways to create value for firms and their customers. Neil Offen, president of the Direct Selling Association (DSA), predicts, "The [direct-selling] industry has come of age."

Questions for Critical Thinking

1. Discuss how independent sales contractors can build relationships with the firms they represent as well as the customers to whom they sell products.
2. What steps might the owner of a firm that supplies other companies with sales reps take to motivate its sales force?

Sources: "Corporate America's New Sales Force," *Fortune,* August 11, 2003, pp. S2–S20; Kimberly Weisul, "Do You Dare Outsource Sales?" *BusinessWeek Online,* June 18, 2001, **http://www.businessweek.com**.

VIDEO CASE 17.2 Chicago Show, Inc. Puts On a Show

The written case on Chicago Show, Inc. appears on page VC-20. The recently filmed Chicago Show, Inc. video is designed to expand and highlight the concepts in this chapter and the concepts and questions covered in the written video case.

Talking about Marketing Careers with Suzy Christopher, Senior Director of Marketing for the Columbus Crew

Soccer is one of the most popular sports in the world, but it wasn't until the formation of the Major League Soccer organization in 1996 that American fans found a professional outlet for their appreciation of the sport. The Columbus Crew calls itself "America's Hardest Working Team," and the Black and Gold have a lot to be proud of. Although fans had to wait until 2002 to see the Crew win a championship, they were loyal from day one. In its first year, the team's fans were voted "Best Fans in the League" by *USA Today*. And they were rewarded in 1999 when Columbus became the site of the first soccer-only stadium in the United States.

BOONE & KURTZ: Suzy, you've got a job that thousands of our readers would give their eyeteeth for: applying your marketing knowledge and experience in the world of sport. Tell us a little about your background.

I certainly do not have your typical sports marketing educational background. I majored in political science at DePauw University in Greencastle, Indiana, and double minored in economics and religion. What is important to note from my education is that DePauw stresses writing, speech, and quantitative analysis across all disciplines, so I was very well prepared to think and present myself, regardless of my course of study. Those skills have served me better than any academic specifics would have. My first job in sports was as an operations intern for the Indianapolis Indians (AAA baseball). At the conclusion of that internship, I was fortunate enough to be the only intern, of about 15, to be offered a full-time position. After three years at the Indians, I was contacted by a headhunter to discuss a position with the Pittsburgh Pirates, and a few months later I was the manager of ticket sales and service there. The world of professional sports is very small, and I obtained my current job with the Columbus Crew through networking when, due to marriage, I needed to move to Columbus, Ohio. I was very fortunate to be able to continue my career in sports marketing with one of the few professional teams in Columbus.

SUZY CHRISTOPHER, SENIOR DIRECTOR OF MARKETING FOR THE COLUMBUS CREW

PHOTO: COURTESY OF SUZY CHRISTOPHER

BOONE & KURTZ: Major League Soccer is a relative newcomer to the field of professional sports. How do the Crew and other teams work to make themselves household names?

The league works very hard to brand itself nationally. They do that through nationally televised games, such as Soccer Saturday on ESPN2, and by building our marquee events (draft, all-star game, MLS Cup) in a manner to attract national media. In Columbus, we try to increase awareness of our team by participating in established community events and maintaining as much media presence as we can through ad buys, promos, and public relations.

BOONE & KURTZ: Between the stadium and the award-winning fans, the Crew seems to have quite a home in Columbus. Is the team better off here without the competition of several other major league sports teams? Do other MLS teams have less hometown support because of this?

Columbus is an interesting town because all professional sports take a backseat to Ohio State athletics, especially football. The competition we face when the Columbus Blue Jackets (NHL) are playing is minor compared to when there is an Ohio State football game, home or away. Obviously it helps to not have an MLB team in town because our schedules are so similar, but we do have a AAA baseball team that plays at the same time. In any market you are better off with fewer sports options, but we also view our competition as other entertainment options. We're competing for the same dollars that people spend on movies, miniature golf, amusement parks, and dining. I think, in that respect, all markets are oversaturated.

BOONE & KURTZ: The Crew is called "America's Hardest Working Team," and we bet that phrase doesn't just refer to the players. Tell us a little about how the Crew's front office operates.

There are between 29 and 32 full-time employees at any given time, and we operate the team and the stadium so that number includes everyone from the GM to the receptionist to the groundskeepers. Because of our small numbers, we work a lot. For example, on a weekend that the Crew is playing on the road, we may also be hosting a college soccer match on Friday night and a pair of high-school football games on Saturday. My experience is that a schedule like that is not uncommon anywhere in sports, especially when one office operates the venue and the team. This is definitely not an industry for people who need their weekends or evenings to themselves or have illusions of a 40-hour work week.

BOONE & KURTZ: Soccer is popular worldwide, both with athletes and fans. What does the Crew do to build its fan base, and how important are young people in the fan equation?

More youth play soccer than any other sport in the United States. Not only do they play, but they're well organized in state and local associations. A great deal of our sales and marketing efforts are focused on these associations and building relationships with their coaches and administrators.

BOONE & KURTZ: Tell us a bit about promotion for the Crew. Sports organizations have a special advantage in that newspapers devote an entire section to covering sports, and local TV news coverage does, too. How does your marketing group go about increasing the likelihood that this public relations–like coverage is positive?

Unfortunately we cannot control the tone of our sports coverage. We do try to anticipate negative articles and prepare talking points for the staff. We are very lucky in Columbus in the sense that although all of the articles about us are not positive, they are fair and frequent.

BOONE & KURTZ: How would you describe the objectives of your promotion? How do you attempt to measure the effectiveness of your promotional efforts?

Every single aspect of my job is geared toward increasing attendance. We measure everything through ticket sales; it is a very visible barometer.

BOONE & KURTZ: Promotional specialists talk about their promotional mix—the relative importance of personal selling, advertising, and sales promotion in accomplishing their promotional goals. How would you rank the relative importance of the three for the Columbus Crew?

It depends on what the product is. When we are selling three-year, six-figure corporate sponsorships, personal selling is key. When we are trying to attract suburban families, advertising and sales promotion are equal partners in the promotional mix.

BOONE & KURTZ: What types of grassroots marketing activities are used by your department in attracting fans, working with youth soccer, and securing corporate support from area organizations?

Our Mobile Marketing Unit is regularly at youth soccer fields and community events; we employ a street team to reach the sizeable Ohio State community; and on nice days you may spot members of the front office with our mascot passing out fliers and pocket schedules downtown.

BOONE & KURTZ: D.C. United reportedly signed Freddy Adu to a $500,000 annual contract—making him the highest-paid player in Major League Soccer. Has he achieved celebrity status to the point that his appearance in Columbus on the visiting team would increase attendance?

Absolutely—that was our first sellout of the year. It was amazing to talk to the guests that knew nothing of soccer, nothing specific of Freddy Adu but, regardless, attended the game. He received so much publicity that people came to see him anyway. It was a wonderful opportunity for guests to sample our product. Hopefully they enjoyed themselves and will attend another game in the future—this time for the Crew!

BOONE & KURTZ: By now, our readers have probably recognized that a great way of getting their foot in the door career-wise would be to complete an internship with an organization like the Crew. But they also realize that you must receive hundreds of internship applications every year. What advice would you give our readers about how to increase the chances that their application will receive serious consideration?

It always surprises me how few of the letters and résumés I receive are free of typographical errors. A well-written letter will always receive extra consideration because I receive so few (and a poorly written letter will not receive any). Probably because I did not have a background in sports when I began looking for a job I do not necessarily look for that in other people. I do want to see that an applicant has progressed at something, whether rising to lifeguard manager at their city pool or leading their church youth group.

MLS Promotes Soccer, and Reading, and Jobs

On a July night, thousands of soccer fans gathered at Washington D.C.'s RFK Stadium for the annual Sierra Mist MLS All-Star Game and "Soccer Celebration." The celebration consisted of dozens of fun soccer challenges for kids and families, informal competitions, and opportunities to meet stars like Cobi Jones and Tony Meola and get their autographs. "I think it's great for the youth to have something to do to come out before the game," said Jones.

Events such as Soccer Celebration are among the many public relations tools that MLS has honed throughout its first 10 years. The All-Star Game celebrated the first league game (played in 1996), and the RKF Stadium event also featured performances by the U.S. Army band and the Army drill team in a salute to the American armed forces. Fireworks and a fly-by of Black Hawk helicopters marked the moment of the kickoff. Other lucky fans, young and old, enjoyed opportunities to meet MLS players at a pregame party.

Public relations is just one of the promotional elements that MLS and the league's individual teams use in their integrated marketing communication programs. They also rely on advertising, personal selling, and publicity. And like all other sports, Major League Soccer commands a huge share of free public relations promotion in the form of sports sections printed in most daily newspapers, sports news reports on television and radio, magazines that include sports, and magazines devoted entirely to sports. All of these media keep the name of the local team and its successes and failures in front of fans on a daily basis. Personal selling is a big component in corporate ticket sales, revenue-producing advertising at the games, and sale of season tickets and luxury suites. It also factors into building relationships with coaches and administrators of youth leagues in each team's local area.

Reaching out to young players and their families is a big part of MLS's public relations effort. The league is opening youth soccer complexes at some of its fields and stadiums, including the Frisco, Texas, home of the Dallas Burn and has also signed a partnership deal with the Kroenke Sports Group to create as many as 20 youth soccer fields at the Colorado Rapids' new home in a Denver suburb. The league is pursuing a partnership with U.S. Soccer (a national youth soccer organization) to create a Youth Development League and to convert all the MLS teams into local or regional soccer clubs with individual youth development programs. Says commissioner Don Garber of this effort, "Our players and teams are deeply engaged in the communities we serve, and work tirelessly with local youth coaches and administrators to make a difference in the lives of young kids of all ethnicities in our country." Soccer camps and other training programs staffed by MLS players and coaches round out the league's current interactions with young players.

One promotional effort was a Kraft Foods venture that featured the images of MLS teams and players on Post cereal boxes. Past programs have included "Get a Kick Out of Reading," which teamed MLS, the National Education Association, and Honda in a bilingual, multicultural push to send kids positive messages about the fun and value of reading. MLS players from every team participated in a related broadcast public service campaign.

Internships with MLS teams are also offered to college students from time to time. These positions, in community relations, ticketing, technology, and other support areas, offer students valuable job experience and responsibility, often with college credit.

Questions for Critical Thinking

1. How do sports organizations like the member teams of the MLS gauge the effectiveness of their promotional efforts?
2. Which of the advertising strategies do you think is most effective in sports promotion? Why?
3. Do you think MLS is doing all it can to promote soccer to kids? What else might it do?
4. Why do you think personal selling is so important in selling corporate and season-ticket packages?

Sources: "Current Available Jobs in Internships," Major League Soccer Web site, http://mls.teamworkonline.com, accessed August 27, 2004; "On All-Star Weekend, MLS Partyers Kick It Up a Notch," *The Washington Post,* August 2, 2004, http://www.washingtonpost.com; Samantha Quigley, "Major League Soccer Salutes U.S. Troops at All-Star Game," American Forces Information Service, August 1, 2004, http://www.defenselink.mil/afis; Jonathan Nierman, "Celebration the Theme for All-Star," July 31, 2004, Major League Soccer Web site, http://www.mlsnet.com; Don Garber, "The State of the League Address," July 30, 2004, Major League Soccer Web site, http://metrostars.mlsnet.com; "Kids Got the Summer Blahs? Here's Something to Give Them a Kick," National Education Association news release, July 30, 2003, http://www.nea.org.

PHOTO: COURTESY OF WIREIMAGES.COM

part 7

PRICING DECISIONS

Chapter 18 Price Concepts and Approaches

Chapter 19 Pricing Strategies

PHOTO: COURTESY OF WIREIMAGES.COM

chapter 18

Price Concepts and Approaches

chapter objectives

1. Outline the legal constraints on pricing.
2. Identify the major categories of pricing objectives.
3. Explain price elasticity and its determinants.
4. List the practical problems involved in applying price theory concepts to actual pricing decisions.
5. Explain the major cost-plus approaches to price setting.
6. List the chief advantages and shortcomings of using breakeven analysis in pricing decisions.
7. Explain the superiority of modified breakeven analysis over the basic breakeven model and the role of yield management in pricing decisions.
8. Identify the major pricing challenges facing online and international marketers.

OUTFITTING A CHEERLEADING SQUAD: HOW MARKETERS TURN TEAM SPIRIT INTO BOOMING SALES

From the high school ranks to college and university athletic departments all over the country, the question is debated. Is cheerleading a sport or an activity? But whatever the answer, most agree on two points: The athletic prowess of today's cheerleaders is a far cry from earlier generations of so-called *yell leaders,* and cheerleading is definitely big business.

About 50 U.S. firms cater to the growing market for cheerleaders' uniforms and accessories, and the two biggest also run summer cheerleading camps and cheer competitions. With about 50 percent of the U.S. market, Varsity Spirit Corp., founded by

former cheerleader Jeffrey Webb, is riding a growing trend. Title IX has succeeded in its objective of increasing female participation in more high school and college sports, and cheerleading has turned out to be one of them. About 3 million students participate in cheerleading teams in the U.S., and another 1.5 million are on dance teams. Circulation of cheerleading and dance magazines is rising even as the number of publications increases. And kids can compete on "all-star teams" from the age of six. It's no wonder that Varsity Spirit recently sold its football headgear division because "football is not growing" while cheerleading, despite its high injury rate, clearly is.

© TAXI/GETTY IMAGES

Camps and competitions for cheer teams are both profitable and well attended. But the sale of cheerleading apparel accounts for about $3 of every $5 of Varsity Spirit's annual revenue. Outfitting a male cheerleader can cost about $180 for a top, pants, socks, and shoes, and a female cheerleader invests about $225 in skirt, briefs, top, bodysuit, pom-poms, and shoes. A megaphone can run another $26. Adding together the clothing, camps, and gym time, most cheerleaders spend about $1,000 a year or more to keep themselves on the squad.

Pricing its products right is an important part of Varsity Spirit's success. It has to consider not only what its competitors charge for cheerleading apparel but also what cheerleaders' families can afford to spend and what else they are buying in order to participate. One cheerleader's mother said of her daughter's cheer expenses, "You learn to eat one less meal a day, and it works out." In addition, Varsity Spirit must weigh the style and quality of apparel its market demands. It's doing something right. Though the privately owned cheerleading apparel supplier does not disclose its exact sales, independent estimates place Varsity Spirit's current annual sales at more than $150 million, and profits growing at an annual rate of 12 percent.[1]

Chapter Overview

AS parents of cheerleaders and other student athletes know, price has a powerful impact on consumer spending behavior. One of the first questions shoppers ask is, "How much does it cost?" Marketers understand the critical role that price plays in the consumer's decision-making process. From lipstick and perfume to automobiles and gasoline to doughnuts and coffee, marketers must develop strategies that price products to achieve their firms' objectives.

As a starting point for examining pricing strategies, consider the meaning of the term *price.* A **price** is the exchange value of a good or service—in other words, it represents whatever that product can be exchanged for in the marketplace. Price does not necessarily denote money. In earlier times, the price of an acre of land might have been 20 bushels of wheat, three head of cattle, or one boat. Even though the barter process continues to be used in some transactions, in the 21st century price typically refers to the amount of funds required to purchase a product.

Prices are both difficult to set and dynamic; they shift in response to a number of variables. A higher than average price can convey an image of prestige, while a lower than average price may connote good value. In other instances, though, a price that is much lower than average may be interpreted as an indicator of inferior quality. And price certainly affects a company's overall profitability and market share.

This chapter discusses the process of determining a profitable but justifiable (fair) price. The focus is on management of the pricing function, including pricing strategies, price-quality relationships, and pricing in various sectors of the economy. The chapter also looks at the effects of environmental conditions on price determination, including legal constraints, competitive pressures, and changes in global and online markets.

Briefly Speaking

The best way to cheer yourself up is to try to cheer somebody else up.

Mark Twain (1835–1910)
American writer and humorist

price Exchange value of a good or service.

① **Outline the legal constraints on pricing.**

PRICING AND THE LAW

Pricing decisions are influenced by a variety of legal constraints imposed by federal, state, and local governments. The next time you pull up to a gas station, consider where each dollar goes. Almost 50 percent of the price you pay goes to federal, state, local, and excise taxes.

In the global marketplace, prices are directly impacted by special types of taxes called *tariffs.* These taxes—levied on the sale of imported goods and services—often make it possible for firms to protect their local markets and still set prices on domestically produced goods well above world market levels. In other instances, tariffs are levied to prevent foreign producers from engaging in a practice described in Chapter 7: *dumping* foreign-produced products in international markets at prices lower than those set in their domestic market. Foreign industries that were recently accused of using below-market sales prices to gain shares of the U.S. market and threatened with retaliatory tariffs include industries as diverse as Chinese furniture manufacturers and shrimp suppliers.[2]

The U.S. is not the only country to use tariffs to protect domestic suppliers and produce a more level competitive playing field. To shield its sugar industry, the government of Mexico has levied a 20 percent tax on soft drinks made with high-fructose corn syrup imported from the U.S. The tax has succeeded in halting corn syrup imports and has helped shore up the Mexican sugar industry, which employs 3 million workers. The two countries are currently looking for a compromise that would allow some corn syrup into Mexico and some of Mexico's surplus sugar back into the U.S. at guaranteed high prices.[3] Tariffs on produce have a similar effect on price, resulting, for example, in higher prices for bananas in Europe than in the U.S.

Not every "regulatory" price increase is a tax, however. Rate increases to cover costly government regulations imposed on the telecommunications industry have been appearing on Internet and cell phone bills as "regulatory cost recovery fees" or similarly named costs. But these charges are not taxes, since the companies keep all the income from the fees and apply only some of it to complying with the regulations. In essence, such "fees" are a source of additional revenues in an industry so price-sensitive that any announced price increase is likely to send some customers fleeing to competitors.[4]

Almost every person looking for a ticket to a high-demand sporting or concert event has encountered an expensive—and often illegal—form of pricing called *ticket scalping*. Scalpers camp out in ticket lines (or hire someone else to stand in line) to purchase tickets they expect to resell at a higher price. Although some cities have enacted laws prohibiting the practice, it continues to occur almost everywhere.

But the ticket reselling market is both highly fragmented and susceptible to fraud and distorted pricing. In response, buyers and sellers are finding that the Internet is helping to create a market where both buyers and sellers can compare prices and seat locations. One Web firm called StubHub.com acts as a ticket clearinghouse for this secondary market and has signed deals with several professional sports teams that allow season ticket holders to sell unwanted tickets and for buyers to purchase them with a guarantee. Ticketmaster has quickly signed 20 similar deals. In addition, the nation's largest ticket seller has moved to capture some of the higher prices previously received by ticket scalpers by selling highly desirable seats to the highest bidder. The firm justifies the practice by pointing out that these sales are not resales and therefore not subject to legal prohibitions against scalping.[5]

Pricing is also regulated by the general constraints of U.S. antitrust legislation, as outlined in Chapter 3. The following sections review some of the most important pricing laws for contemporary marketers.

ROBINSON-PATMAN ACT

The **Robinson-Patman Act** (1936) typifies Depression-era legislation. Known as the Anti-A&P Act, it was inspired by price competition triggered by the rise of grocery store chains—in fact, the original draft was prepared by the U.S. Wholesale Grocers Association. Enacted in the midst of the Great Depression, when legislators viewed chain stores as a threat to employment in the traditional retail sector, the act was intended primarily to save jobs.

Robinson-Patman Act Federal legislation prohibiting price discrimination that is not based on a cost differential; also prohibits selling at an unreasonably low price to eliminate competition.

The Robinson-Patman Act was technically an amendment to the Clayton Act, enacted 22 years earlier, that had applied only to price discrimination between geographic areas, which injured local sellers. Broader in scope, Robinson-Patman prohibits price discrimination in sales to wholesalers, retailers, and other producers. It rules that differences in price must reflect cost differentials and prohibits selling at unreasonably low prices to drive competitors out of business. Supporters justified the amendment by arguing that the rapidly expanding chain stores of that era might be able to attract substantial discounts from suppliers anxious to secure their business, while small, independent stores would continue to pay regular prices.

Price discrimination, where some customers pay more than others for the same product, dates back to the very beginnings of trade and commerce. Today, however, technology has added to the frequency and complexity of price discrimination, as well as the strategies marketers adopt to get around it. For example, marketers may encourage repeat business by inviting purchasers to become "preferred customers," entitling them to average discounts of 10 percent. As long as companies can demonstrate that their price discounts and promotional allowances do not restrict competition, they avoid penalties under the Robinson-Patman Act. Direct mail marketers frequently send out catalogs of identical goods but with differing prices for different catalogs. Zip-code areas that traditionally consist of high spenders get the higher price catalogs, while price-sensitive zip-code customers receive a low-price catalog with lower prices. Victoria's Secret, Staples, and Simon & Schuster are among the hundreds of companies that employ legal price discrimination strategies.

Firms accused of price discrimination often argue that they set price differentials to meet competitors' prices and that cost differences justify variations in prices. When a firm asserts that it maintains price differentials as good-faith methods of competing with rivals, a logical question arises: What constitutes good-faith pricing behavior? The answer depends on the particular situation.

A defense based on cost differentials works only if the price differences do not exceed the cost differences resulting from selling to various classes of buyers. Marketers must then be prepared to justify the cost differences. Many authorities consider this provision one of the most confusing areas in the Robinson-Patman Act. Courts handle most charges brought under the act as individual cases.

Therefore, domestic marketers must continually evaluate their pricing actions to avoid potential Robinson-Patman violations.

UNFAIR-TRADE LAWS

unfair-trade laws State laws requiring sellers to maintain minimum prices for comparable merchandise.

More than 20 states supplement federal legislation with their own **unfair-trade laws,** which require sellers to maintain minimum prices for comparable merchandise. Enacted in the 1930s, these laws were intended to protect small specialty shops, such as dairy stores, from so-called *loss-leader* pricing tactics, in which chain stores might sell certain products below cost to attract customers. Typical state laws set retail price floors at cost plus some modest markup.

Although most unfair-trade laws have remained on the books for the past 70 years, marketers had all but forgotten them until recently. Then in 1993, Wal-Mart, the nation's largest retailer, was found guilty of violating Arkansas's unfair-trade law for selling drugs and health-and-beauty aids below cost. The lawsuit filed by three independent drugstore owners accused the mass merchandiser of attempting to drive them out of business through predatory pricing practices. Wal-Mart appealed and the decision was overturned, but similar lawsuits were filed in several other states.

fair-trade laws Statutes enacted in most states that once permitted manufacturers to stipulate a minimum retail price for their product.

FAIR-TRADE LAWS

The concept of fair trade has affected pricing decisions for decades. **Fair-trade laws** allow manufacturers to stipulate minimum retail prices for their products and to require dealers to sign contracts agreeing to abide by these prices.

figure 18.1

Designer Clothing: Protecting Brand Image by Avoiding Price Discounting

AP PHOTO/JENNIFER GRAYLOCK

Fair-trade laws assert that a product's image, determined in part by its price, is a property right of the manufacturer. Therefore, the manufacturer should have the authority to protect its asset by requiring retailers to maintain a minimum price. Exclusivity is one method manufacturers use to achieve this. By severely restricting the number of retail outlets that carry their upscale clothing, designers can exert more control over their prices and avoid discounting, which might adversely affect their image. The Christian Lacroix turquoise blue silk gown shown in Figure 18.1, which sells anywhere from $16,000 to $20,000, is not likely to be discounted.

Like the Robinson-Patman Act, fair-trade legislation has its roots in the Depression era. In 1931, California became the first state to enact fair-trade legislation. Most other states soon followed; only Missouri, the District of Columbia, Vermont, and Texas failed to adopt such laws.

A U.S. Supreme Court decision invalidated fair-trade contracts in interstate commerce, and Congress responded by passing the Miller Tydings Resale Maintenance Act (1937). This law exempted interstate fair-trade contracts from compliance with antitrust requirements, thus freeing states to keep these laws on their books if they so desired.

Over the years, fair-trade laws declined in importance as discounters emerged and price competition gained strength as a marketing strategy component. These laws became invalid with the passage of the Consumer Goods Pricing Act (1975), which halted all interstate enforcement of resale price maintenance provisions, an objective long sought by consumer groups.

In a new use of the term *fair trade,* some retailers are charging higher than market prices for commodities like coffee, bananas, and chocolate as part of an international campaign to help farmers earn a living wage in poor countries where such products are grown. Although thousands of farmers have already benefited from the funds, which pay for education, health care, and training projects, it remains to be seen whether experience with the practice in U.S. stores will be similar to that in Europe, where some retailers have simply used higher markups so they can benefit as well. It's often difficult for consumers to know how much of the added price is going to help those in need. One official of a Germany-based federation of fair-trade groups said of the situation in Europe, "Supermarkets are taking advantage of the label to make more profit because they know that consumers are willing to pay a bit more because it's fair trade."[6]

1. What was the purpose of the Robinson-Patman Act?
2. What laws require sellers to maintain minimum prices for comparable merchandise?
3. What laws allow manufacturers to set minimum retail prices for their products?

PRICING OBJECTIVES AND THE MARKETING MIX

(2) Identify the major categories of pricing objectives.

The extent to which any or all of the factors of production—natural resources, capital, human resources, and entrepreneurship—are employed depends on the prices those factors command. A firm's prices and the resulting purchases by its customers determine the company's revenue, influencing the profits it earns. Overall organizational objectives and more specific marketing objectives guide the development of pricing objectives, which in turn lead to the development and implementation of more specific pricing policies and procedures.

A firm might, for instance, set a major overall goal of becoming the dominant producer in its domestic market. It might then develop a marketing objective of achieving maximum sales penetration in each region, followed by a related pricing objective of setting prices at levels that maximize sales. These objectives might lead to the adoption of a low-price policy implemented by offering substantial price discounts to channel members.

Price affects and is affected by the other elements of the marketing mix. Product decisions, promotional plans, and distribution choices all impact the price of a good or service. For example, products distributed through complex channels involving several intermediaries must be priced high enough to cover the markups needed to compensate wholesalers and retailers for services they provide. Basic so-called "fighting brands" are intended to capture market share from higher priced, options-laden competitors by offering relatively low prices to entice customers to give up some options in return for a cost savings.

Pricing objectives vary from firm to firm, and they can be classified into four major groups: (1) profitability objectives, (2) volume objectives, (3) meeting competition objectives, and (4) prestige objectives. Not-for-profit organizations as well as for-profit companies must consider objectives of one kind or another when developing pricing strategies. Table 18.1 outlines the pricing objectives marketers rely on to meet their overall goals.

table 18.1 ***Pricing Objectives***

OBJECTIVE	PURPOSE	EXAMPLE
Profitability objectives	Profit maximization Target return	Low introductory interest rates on credit cards with higher standard rates after 6 months
Volume objectives	Sales maximization Market share	Dell's low-priced PCs increase market share and sales of services
Meeting competition objectives	Value pricing	Per-song charges for music downloads
Prestige objectives	Lifestyle Image	High-priced luxury autos such as BMW and watches by Piaget
Not-for-profit objectives	Profit maximization Cost recovery Market incentives Market suppression	High prices for tobacco and alcohol to reduce consumption

PROFITABILITY OBJECTIVES

Marketers at for-profit firms must set prices with profits in mind. Even not-for-profit organizations realize the importance of setting prices high enough to cover expenses and provide a financial cushion to cover unforeseen needs and expenses. As the Russian proverb says, "There are two fools in every market: One asks too little, one asks too much." For consumers to pay prices that are either above or below what they consider to be the going rate, they must be convinced they are receiving fair value for their money.

Economic theory is based on two major assumptions. It assumes, first, that firms will behave rationally and, second, that this rational behavior will result in an effort to maximize gains and minimize losses. Some marketers estimate profits by looking at historical sales data; others use elaborate calculations based on predicted future sales. It has been said that setting prices is an art, not a science. The talent lies in a marketer's ability to strike a balance between desired profits and the customer's perception of a product's value.

Marketers should evaluate and adjust prices continually to accommodate changes in the environment. The technological environment, for example, forces Internet marketers to respond quickly to competitors' pricing strategies. New search capabilities performed by shopping bots (described in Chapter 4) allow customers to compare prices locally, nationally, and globally in a matter of seconds.

Intense price competition—sometimes conducted even when it means forgoing profits altogether—often results when rival manufacturers battle for leadership positions in new-product categories. Recently, Microsoft—which has yet to turn a profit on its Xbox video game system—planned to slash prices to revive flagging sales. Sony stole its thunder by announcing that the retail price of its PlayStation 2 would drop by a third, a move that Microsoft decided to match. Meanwhile, Nintendo announced that it would undercut both products by pricing its Game Cube at $50 less than the two rival technologies.[7]

Profits are a function of revenue and expenses:

$$\text{Profits} = \text{Revenue} - \text{Expenses}$$

Revenue is determined by the product's selling price and number of units sold:

$$\text{Total Revenue} = \text{Price} \times \text{Quantity Sold}$$

Therefore, a profit-maximizing price rises to the point at which further increases will cause disproportionate decreases in the number of units sold. A 10 percent price increase that results in only an 8 percent cut in volume will add to the firm's revenue. However, a 10 percent price hike that results in an 11 percent sales decline will reduce revenue.

profit maximization Point at which the additional revenue gained by increasing the price of a product equals the increase in total costs.

target-return objective Short-run or long-run pricing objectives of achieving a specified return on either sales or investment.

Economists refer to this approach as **marginal analysis.** They identify **profit maximization** as the point at which the addition to total revenue is just balanced by the increase in total cost. Marketers must resolve a basic problem of how to achieve this delicate balance when they set prices. Relatively few firms actually hit this elusive target. A significantly larger number prefer to direct their effort toward more realistic goals.

Consequently, marketers commonly set **target-return objectives**—short-run or long-run goals usually stated as percentages of sales or investment. The practice has become particularly popular among large firms in which other pressures interfere with profit-maximization objectives. Target-return objectives offer several benefits for marketers in addition to resolving pricing questions. For example, these objectives serve as tools for evaluating performance. They also satisfy desires to generate "fair" profits as judged by management, stockholders, and the public.

VOLUME OBJECTIVES

Some economists and business executives argue that pricing behavior actually seeks to maximize sales within a given profit constraint. In other words, they set a minimum acceptable profit level and then seek to maximize sales (subject to this profit constraint) in the belief that the increased sales are more important in the long-run competitive picture than immediate high profits. As a result, companies should continue to expand sales as long as their total profits do not drop below the minimum return acceptable to management.

Sales maximization can also result from nonprice factors such as service and quality. Marketers succeeded in increasing sales for Dr. Scholl's new shoe insert, Dynastep, by advertising heavily in magazines. The ads explained how the Dynastep insert would help relieve leg and back pain. Priced around $14 for two inserts—twice as much as comparable offerings—Dynastep ran over its competitors to become number one in its category.

Another volume-related pricing objective is the **market-share objective**—the goal of controlling a specified minimum share of the market for a firm's good or service. Dr. Scholl's increased its market share to 29 percent by focusing on the benefits of Dynastep. A company's specific goal may be to maintain its present share of a particular market or to increase its share, for instance, from 10 to 20 percent. Volume-related objectives such as sales maximization and market share play an important role in most firms' pricing decisions.

The PIMS Studies

Market-share objectives may prove critical to the achievement of other organizational objectives. High sales, for example, often mean more profits. The **Profit Impact of Market Strategies (PIMS)** project, an extensive study conducted by the Marketing Science Institute, analyzed more than 2,000 firms and revealed that two of the most important factors influencing profitability were product quality and market share. Marketing campaigns with promotions like the one shown in Figure 18.2 help to enhance profitability for Southwest Airlines. By not restricting the number of seats available for its award travel on flights, Southwest's Rapid Rewards program focuses on customer satisfaction in the highly competitive airline industry. Numerous studies confirm the link between market share and profitability.

Profit Impact of Market Strategies (PIMS) project Research that discovered a strong positive relationship between a firm's market share and product quality and its return on investment.

The relationship between market share and profitability is evident in PIMS data that reveal an average 32 percent return on investment (ROI) for firms with market shares above 40 percent. In contrast, average ROI decreases to 24 percent for firms whose market shares are between 20 and 40 percent. Firms with a minor market share (less than 10 percent) generate average pretax investment returns of approximately 13 percent.[8]

The relationship also applies to a firm's individual brands. PIMS researchers compared the top four brands in each market segment they studied. Their data revealed that the leading brand typically generates after-tax ROI of 18 percent, considerably higher than the second-ranked brand. Weaker brands, on average, fail to earn adequate returns.

Marketers have developed an underlying explanation of the positive relationship between profitability and market share. Firms with large shares accumulate greater operating experience and lower overall costs relative to competitors with smaller market shares. Accordingly, effective segmentation strategies might focus on obtaining larger shares of smaller markets and on avoiding smaller shares of larger ones. A firm might achieve higher financial returns by becoming a major competitor in several smaller market segments than by remaining a relatively minor player in a larger market.

Meeting Competition Objectives

A third set of pricing objectives seeks simply to meet competitors' prices. In many lines of business, firms set their own prices to match those of established industry price leaders.

Price is a pivotal factor in the ongoing competition between long-distance telephone services and wireless carriers. When cellular companies began offering huge bundles of "use-anytime" minutes with free long-distance service, MCI rolled out its Select 200 program—offering customers 200 minutes of long-distance calling time, with no monthly fees, taxes, or surcharges attached. In its efforts to stem defections of customers to wireless services, AT&T recently offered unlimited long-distance calling at a flat rate of $19.95 a month—but only between households served by AT&T. Since, from the customer's perspective,

figure 18.2

Southwest Airlines: Focusing on Product Quality and Market Share

COURTESY SOUTHWEST AIRLINES

long-distance companies and cellular companies offer a service that is in many respects interchangeable, neither class of carrier could continue operations unless they came close to matching each other's prices.[9]

Pricing objectives tied directly to meeting prices charged by major competitors deemphasize the price element of the marketing mix and focus more strongly on nonprice variables. Pricing is a highly visible component of a firm's marketing mix and an easy and effective tool for obtaining a differential advantage over competitors. It is, however, a tool that other firms can easily duplicate through price reductions of their own. Airline price competition of recent years exemplifies the actions and reactions of competitors in this marketplace.[10] Rather than emphasizing the lowest fares of any carrier, most airlines choose to compete by offering convenient arrival and departure times, enhanced passenger comfort with more room between each row, an attractive frequent-flyer program, and customer-focused alliances with automobile rental, lodging, and other partners.[11] Some airlines even returned to providing passenger meals on long flights, a practice that had been discontinued in a cost-cutting effort. Even when price increases are needed to remain profitable, an announced price hike by one airline will be implemented only if its major competitors match the new price. Because price changes directly affect overall profitability in an industry, many firms attempt to promote stable prices by meeting competitors' prices and competing for market share by focusing on product strategies, promotional decisions, and distribution—the nonprice elements of the marketing mix.

Briefly Speaking

Price is what you pay. Value is what you get.

Warren Buffett (b. 1930)
American investor

value pricing Pricing strategy emphasizing benefits derived from a product in comparison to the price and quality levels of competing offerings.

Value Pricing

When discounts become normal elements of a competitive marketplace, other marketing mix elements gain importance in purchase decisions. In such instances, overall product value, not just price, determines product choice. In recent years, a new strategy—**value pricing**—has emerged that emphasizes the benefits a product provides in comparison to the price and quality levels of competing offerings. This strategy typically works best for relatively low-priced goods and services.

Laundry detergents are a good example of value pricing. The label on Dash detergent proclaims "Value Price," while Arm & Hammer's label assures customers that it "Cleans Great—Value Price, Too!" Yes detergent announces "Great Value!," while Ultra Rinso claims "Super Value," and the back label on Ultra Trend boasts that it offers "hard-working performance at a reasonable price." The label on another detergent, All, advises customers to "Compare & Save."

Value-priced products generally cost less than premium brands, but marketers point out that value does not necessarily mean *inexpensive.* The challenge for those who compete on value is to convince customers that low-priced brands offer quality comparable to that of a higher priced product. An increasing number of alternative products and private-label brands has resulted in a more competitive marketplace in recent years. Trader Joe's, a rapidly growing grocery chain that began in the Los Angeles area and has since expanded throughout the West, Midwest, and mid-Atlantic states, stands out from other specialty food stores with its cedar plank walls, nautical décor, and a captain (the store manager), first mate (the assistant manager), and the other employees (known as crew members) all attired in colorful Hawaiian shirts. The chain uses value pricing for the more than 2,000 upscale food products it develops or imports and generates annual sales of about $2.1 billion by selling wines, cheeses, meats, fish, and other unique gourmet items at closeout prices, mostly under its own brand names. If the high quality doesn't convince customers at its 210 stores, they can take comfort from the fact that Trader Joe's tuna are caught without environmentally dangerous nets, its dried apricots contain no sulfur preservatives, and its peanut butter is organic.[12]

© DAVID YOUNG WOLFF/PHOTOEDIT

Trader Joe's, a rapidly growing grocery store chain, makes a competitive play for customers by value-pricing upscale food products, imported wines, cheeses, and many organic foods.

Value pricing is perhaps best seen in the personal computer industry. In the past few years, PC prices have collapsed, reducing the effectiveness of traditional pricing strategies intended to meet competition. In fact, PCs priced at under $600 are now the fastest growing segment of the market. This category now accounts for almost 20 percent of PCs sold in stores. Industry leaders like Dell, Hewlett-Packard, and Gateway cannot continue to cut prices, so they are adding features such as increased memory and 3-D graphic accelerator cards that increase speed. Dell has even launched a home installation plan to offset tumbling prices in the PC market.[13]

figure 18.3

The "Diamond Is Forever" Campaign: Prestige Pricing

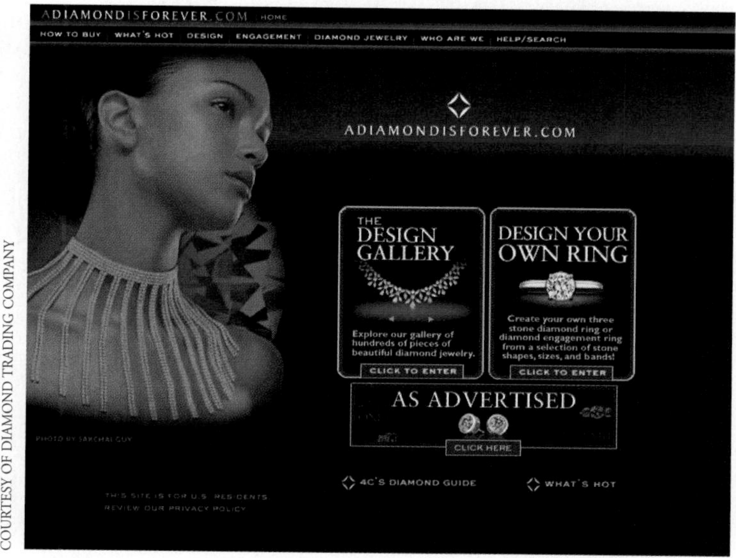

COURTESY OF DIAMOND TRADING COMPANY

PRESTIGE OBJECTIVES

The final category of pricing objectives, unrelated to either profitability or sales volume, is prestige objectives. Prestige pricing establishes a relatively high price to develop and maintain an image of quality and exclusiveness that appeals to status-conscious consumers. Such objectives reflect marketers' recognition of the role of price in creating an overall image of the firm and its product offerings.

Prestige objectives affect the price tags of such products as Waterford crystal, Alfa Romeo sports cars, Omega watches, and Tiffany jewelry. When a perfume marketer sets a price of $135 or more per ounce, this choice reflects an emphasis on image far more than the cost of ingredients. Analyses have shown that ingredients account for less than 5 percent of a perfume's cost. Thus, advertisements for Joy that promote the fragrance as the "costliest perfume in the world" use price to promote product prestige. As shown in the promotional message in Figure 18.3, diamond jewelry also uses prestige pricing to convey an image of quality and timelessness.

In the business world, private jet ownership imparts an image of prestige, power, and high price tags—too high for most business travelers to consider. Recognizing that cost is the primary factor that makes jet ownership prohibitive, companies like Flight Options and NetJets have created an alternative—fractional ownership. The companies target firms whose executives travel periodically rather than year round. Instead of buying a preowned plane, they join executives from other firms in purchasing shares in a new jet. Fractional ownership companies account for almost half the backlog of orders at the five major manufacturers of business jets.[14]

1. What are target-return objectives?
2. What is value pricing?
3. How do prestige objectives affect a seller's pricing strategy?

PRICING OBJECTIVES OF NOT-FOR-PROFIT ORGANIZATIONS

Pricing is also a key element of the marketing mix for not-for-profit organizations. Pricing strategy can help these groups achieve a variety of organizational goals:

1. *Profit maximization.* While not-for-profit organizations by definition do not cite profitability as a primary goal, there are numerous instances in which they do try to maximize their returns on single events or a series of events. A $1,000-a-plate political fund-raiser is a classic example.

2. *Cost recovery.* Some not-for-profit organizations attempt to recover only the actual cost of operating the unit. Mass transit, toll roads and bridges, and most private colleges and universities are common examples. The amount of recovered costs is often dictated by tradition, competition, or public opinion.

3. *Market incentives.* Other not-for-profit groups follow a lower than average pricing policy or offer a free service to encourage increased usage of the good or service. Seattle's bus system offers free service in the downtown area in an attempt to reduce traffic congestion, encourage retail sales, and minimize the effort required to access downtown public services.

Price is an essential factor in the ability of World Vision to assist millions of children and families affected by the HIV/AIDS crisis around the world. Funds secured by individuals, philanthropic organizations, corporations, and government agencies for World Vision's HIV/AIDS Hope Initiative are used to assist affected families with food, clean water, health care, education, and prevention in the fight against AIDS.

4. *Market suppression.* Price can also discourage consumption. High prices help to accomplish social objectives independent of the costs of providing goods or services. Illustrations include tobacco and alcohol taxes (the so-called "sin taxes"), parking fines, tolls, and gasoline excise taxes.

1. **What goals does pricing strategy help a not-for-profit organization achieve?**
2. **How does profit maximization apply to a not-for-profit organization or firm?**

METHODS FOR DETERMINING PRICES

Marketers determine prices in two basic ways—by applying the theoretical concepts of supply and demand and by completing cost-oriented analyses. During the first part of the 20th century, most discussions for price determination emphasized the classical concepts of supply and demand. During the last half of the century, however, the emphasis began to shift to a cost-oriented approach. Hindsight reveals certain flaws in both concepts.

Treatments of this subject often overlook another concept of price determination—one based on the impact of custom and tradition. **Customary prices** are retail prices that consumers expect as a result of tradition and social habit. Candy makers have attempted to maintain traditional price levels by greatly reducing overall product size. Similar practices have prevailed in the marketing of soft drinks as bottlers attempt to balance consumer expectations of customary prices with the realities of rising costs.

A thing is worth whatever the buyer will pay for it.

Publilius Syrus (first century B.C.E.)

Latin writer of mimes

customary prices Traditional prices that customers expect to pay for certain goods and services.

Wm. Wrigley Jr. Co., manufacturer of chewing gum standards Juicy Fruit, Doublemint, and Big Red, took advantage of the weakness in the industry's customary pricing strategy by introducing a smaller quantity pack at a lower price. While competitors continued to offer only seven-piece packs for 35 cents, Wrigley priced its five-piece packs at 25 cents. To spur impulse buying, the company prominently displayed the price on the package. The strategy was so successful that within two years of its inception, Wrigley discontinued selling seven-stick gum packs.

The soaring price of U.S. gasoline presents another example of supply and demand. As average prices for a gallon of gas rose above the $2-a-gallon mark and crude oil soared temporarily to $50 a barrel, frustrated drivers began demanding to know who, if anyone, was cashing in on the price spike. Democrats blamed Big Oil and the Bush administration. The oil industry and its backers blamed OPEC, and many consumers blamed their local gas station owners. Even though the U.S. is the world's largest refiner of gasoline, strong demand has led to an increase in oil imports. During the peak summer driving season, imports reach levels of 1 million barrels a day, more than twice the average imports of 20 years ago.

Although profits at U.S. refineries are at near-record levels, they continue to struggle to produce enough gasoline to meet demand. Adding to the supply problem is the fact that more than half the nation's refineries have shut down since 1981, no new ones have been built, and none is planned. Bill Greehey, chairman and CEO of refiner Valero Energy, explains the capacity problem this way: "Refiners are spending all of their money just meeting all the new [environmental] regulations. They don't have the money for strategic projects to add to their capacity." The largest single factor in today's record

ETIQUETTE TIPS — FOR MARKETING PROFESSIONALS

Learning the Rules about Tipping

TIPS become part of the price of dining out or using the services of door attendants, taxi drivers, bellhops, porters, valets, maître d's, and others with whom businesspeople come into contact. But many people are confused by tipping. How much is appropriate? Who gets a tip and who doesn't? What if the service isn't deserving of a tip? Here are a few guidelines to remember about tipping.

1. If the service is poor, give your server the benefit of the doubt and leave the standard 15 percent tip. But talk to the manager about improving the service.
2. Tip hairdressers 10 to 20 percent of the total price of the service. If the addition of a tip makes a salon cut a stretch for your budget, consider going less often or finding a cheaper place. Don't make up for an elevated price by cutting back on the tip.
3. Tip porters and skycaps $1 per bag; more if the bags are heavy.
4. Tip your taxi, limo, or van driver 15 percent of the total fare, but never less than $1, and more if the driver helps with your bags.
5. You need not tip a valet or parking attendant for parking your car, but always tip $2 to $5 for returning it.
6. Tip a door attendant or bellhop $1 to $2 per bag for bringing your luggage to your room and the same for hailing you a cab.
7. Tip the hotel maid daily because different maids are on duty each day. Leave $1 to $3 on your pillow each time, and remember to tip on the day you check out.
8. Tip the concierge $5 to $10 at the end of your stay if he or she has been helpful with dinner or theater reservations, particularly hard-to-get ones.
9. Tip for room service as you would in a restaurant—15 to 20 percent of the total charge.
10. If the maître d' in a restaurant merely seats you, no tip is required. If he gets you a special table or seats you without a reservation when the restaurant is busy, tip $5 to $10 or more depending on the average price of a meal.

In general, tips are used to thank any person who performs a special service for you—and makes your travel more convenient or meal more enjoyable. So thank the person who goes out of his or her way to make your day more pleasant. As you become more familiar with the business world, tipping will become second nature to you.

Sources: James G. Lewis, "Tipping Etiquette," http://www.findalink.net, accessed October 4, 2004; "Tipping Etiquette," http://www.etiquetteandimage.com, accessed October 4, 2004; Kristen Sullivan, "Proper Tipping Etiquette," http://msms.essortment.com, accessed October 4, 2004.

gasoline prices is the high cost of oil, which accounts for approximately $1 of every $2 motorists spend at the pump.[15]

Higher gas prices have effects on other consumer costs as well. With gas at record highs, hybrid cars like the Toyota Prius are in greater demand than ever before. Some dealers have months-long waiting lists and are beginning to demand above-sticker price tags for the vehicles, adding as much as $5,000 to the price of the car.[16]

At some point, someone has to set initial prices for products. In addition, competitive moves and cost changes necessitate periodic reviews of price structures. The remaining sections delve into the issue of price determination. They also consider how marketers can most effectively integrate the concepts to develop realistic pricing systems.

One price that's often difficult for businesspeople to set is the size of a tip. The "Etiquette Tips for Marketing Professionals" feature offers some guidelines for acknowledging the services of waiters, bellhops, taxi drivers, and others.

1. What are the two basic ways in which marketers determine prices?
2. What are customary prices?

PRICE DETERMINATION IN ECONOMIC THEORY

Microeconomics suggests a way of determining prices that assumes a profit-maximization objective. This technique attempts to derive correct equilibrium prices in the marketplace by comparing supply and demand. It also requires more complete analysis than actual business firms typically conduct.

Demand refers to a schedule of the amounts of a firm's product that consumers will purchase at different prices during a specified time period. **Supply** refers to a schedule of the amounts of a good or service that will be offered for sale at different prices during a specified period. These schedules may vary for different types of market structures. Businesses operate and set prices in four types of market structures: pure competition, monopolistic competition, oligopoly, and monopoly.

Pure competition is a market structure with so many buyers and sellers that no single participant can significantly influence price. Pure competition presupposes other market conditions as well: homogeneous products and ease of entry for sellers due to low start-up costs. The agricultural sector exhibits many characteristics of a purely competitive market, making it the closest actual example.

Monopolistic competition typifies most retailing and features large numbers of buyers and sellers. These diverse parties exchange heterogeneous, relatively well-differentiated products, giving marketers some control over prices.

Relatively few sellers compete in an **oligopoly.** Pricing decisions by each seller are likely to affect the market, but no single seller controls it. High start-up costs form significant barriers to entry for new competitors. Each firm's demand curve in an oligopolistic market displays a unique kink at the current market price. Because of the impact of a single competitor on total industry sales, competitors usually quickly match any attempt by one firm to generate additional sales by reducing prices. Price cutting in such industry structures is likely to reduce total industry revenues. Oligopolies operate in the petroleum refining, automobile, and tobacco industries.

The availability of alternative air transportation in the form of such discount carriers as Southwest Airlines, JetBlue, Ted, and Frontier Airlines forces established air carriers to maintain competitive airfares—or risk losing business to the upstarts. For example, before JetBlue and Southwest launched their first coast-to-coast flights from Washington to Los Angeles, transcontinental flights were the domain of bigger, higher fare airlines. If the discount carrier alternatives disappear, prices will probably rise.[17]

A **monopoly** is a market structure where only one seller of a product exists and for which there are no close substitutes. Antitrust legislation has nearly eliminated all but temporary monopolies, such as those created through patent protection. The "Solving an Ethical Controversy" feature explores how pharmaceutical companies protect their pricing policies through the exercise of patents. Regulated industries, such as utility companies, constitute another form of monopoly. The government allows regulated monopolies in markets in which competition would lead to an uneconomical duplication of services. In return for such a license, government reserves the right to regulate the monopoly's rate of return.

The four types of market structures are compared in Table 18.2 on the following bases: number of competitors, ease of entry into the industry by new firms, similarity of competing products, degree of control over price by individual firms, and the elasticity or inelasticity of the demand curve facing the individual firm. Elasticity—the degree of consumer responsiveness to changes in price—is discussed in more detail in a later section.

COST AND REVENUE CURVES

Marketers must set a price for a product that generates sufficient revenue to cover the costs of producing and marketing it. A product's total cost is composed of total variable costs and total fixed costs. **Variable costs** change with the level of production (such as raw materials and labor costs), and **fixed costs** remain stable at any production level within a certain range (such as lease payments or insurance costs). **Average total costs** are calculated by dividing the sum of the variable and fixed costs by the number of units produced. Finally, **marginal cost** is the change in total cost that results from producing an additional unit of output.

The demand side of the pricing equation focuses on revenue curves. Average revenue is calculated by dividing total revenue by the quantity associated with these revenues. Average revenue is actually the demand curve facing the firm. Marginal revenue is the change in total revenue that results from selling an additional unit of output. Figure 18.4 shows the relationships of various cost and revenue measures; the firm maximizes its profits when marginal costs equal marginal revenues.

Solving an Ethical Controversy

WHY DO PRESCRIPTION DRUGS COST SO MUCH?

U.S. consumers spent over $162 billion on prescription drugs last year, more than one and a half times as much as a decade ago. Not only are people consuming more prescription drugs, but they must also pay rising prices. Drug companies say they need to charge what the market will bear, both to make up for the high cost of developing and testing new drugs and to take advantage of the temporary monopoly on new medicines that patent protection provides. When imitators are allowed to produce a generic version of the new drug following the patent expiration, its price drops. But consumers are balking at drug prices across the board. Some are buying their medications in Mexico and Canada, where the government regulates the price of drugs. Even more worrisome, some patients, especially the uninsured and the elderly, are cutting back on prescribed doses of needed medication or going without.

SHOULD PRESCRIPTION DRUGS COST LESS?

PRO

1. Those who can't afford them should not be denied the health benefits of needed drugs.
2. The giant drug companies (often referred to as *Big Pharma*) already make too much money on their patented drugs and charge much higher prices to U.S. purchasers than to buyers in Europe, Canada, and Mexico.

CON

1. The price of drugs doesn't begin to cover the cost of developing treatments for such common diseases as cancer, AIDS, and Alzheimer's disease. In addition, many other countries have regulations that effectively limit the maximum prices that can be charged, forcing the drug companies to look to U.S. purchasers for additional revenue.
2. Drug companies that develop important—and widely needed—medical breakthroughs are entitled to rewards in the form of profits just as any other successful business.

SUMMARY

More and more consumers are taking prescription drugs on a regular basis. Medical practice is emphasizing the use of medications to control such chronic problems as high blood pressure and high cholesterol, and both children and the elderly consume more drugs than ever before. Some drug companies are beginning to donate free medicines to sick, uninsured patients in developing countries, but the demand for "cures" for the diseases of developed nations continues. As long as the demand is there and consumers (and insurance companies) are willing to pay, it is unlikely that anything short of government intervention will reduce drug prices.

Sources: Daren Fonda and Barbara Kiviat, "Curbing the Drug Marketers," *Time,* July 5, 2004, pp. 40–41; Jennifer Corbett Dooren, "AARP Endorses Senate Bill Allowing Drug Imports," *The Wall Street Journal,* June 17, 2004, p. D2; Julie Appleby, "U.S. Drug Needs Would Overwhelm Canada," *USA Today,* May 17, 2004, p. B1; Roger Parloff, "The New Drug War," *Fortune,* March 8, 2004, pp. 144–156; Lisa Gibbs, "Why Do Drugs Cost So Much?" *Money,* Fall 2003, pp. 95–99.

Table 18.3 illustrates why the intersection of the marginal cost and marginal revenue curves is the logical point at which to maximize revenue for the organization. Although the firm can earn a profit at several different prices, the price at which it earns maximum profits is $22. At a price of $24, $66 in profits are earned—$4 less than the $70 profit at the $22 price. If a price of $20 is set to attract additional sales, the marginal costs of the extra sales ($7) are greater than the marginal revenues received ($6), and total profits decline.

THE CONCEPT OF ELASTICITY IN PRICING STRATEGY

3 Explain price elasticity and its determinants.

Although the intersection of the marginal cost and marginal revenue curves determines the level of output, the impact of changes in price on sales varies greatly. To understand why it fluctuates, it is necessary to understand the concept of elasticity.

table 18.2 **Distinguishing Features of the Four Market Structures**

	Type of Market Structure			
CHARACTERISTICS	PURE COMPETITION	MONOPOLISTIC COMPETITION	OLIGOPOLY	MONOPOLY
Number of competitors	Many	Few to many	Few	No direct competitors
Ease of entry into industry by new firms	Easy	Somewhat difficult	Difficult	Regulated by government
Similarity of goods or services offered by competing firms	Similar	Different	Can be either similar or different	No directly competing goods or services
Control over prices by individual firms	None	Some	Some	Considerable
Demand curves facing individual firms	Totally elastic	Can be either elastic or inelastic	Kinked; inelastic below kink; more elastic above	Can be either elastic or inelastic
Examples	2,000-acre ranch	Banana Republic stores	BP	Commonwealth Edison

elasticity Measure of responsiveness of purchasers and suppliers to a change in price.

Elasticity is the measure of the responsiveness of purchasers and suppliers to price changes. The price elasticity of demand (or elasticity of demand) is the percentage change in the quantity of a good or service demanded divided by the percentage change in its price. A 10 percent increase in the price of eggs that results in a 5 percent decrease in the quantity of eggs demanded yields a price elasticity of demand for eggs of 0.5. The price elasticity of supply of a product is the percentage change in the quantity of a good or service supplied divided by the percentage change in its price. A 10 percent increase in the price of shampoo that results in a 25 percent increase in the quantity supplied yields a price elasticity of supply for shampoo of 2.5.

Consider a case in which a 1 percent change in price causes more than a 1 percent change in the quantity supplied or demanded. Numerically, that means an elasticity measurement greater than 1.0. When the elasticity of demand or supply is greater than 1.0, that demand or supply is said to be elastic. If a 1 percent change in price results in less than a 1 percent change in quantity, a product's elasticity of demand or supply will be less than 1.0. In that case, the demand or supply is called inelastic. For example, the demand for cigarettes is relatively inelastic; research studies have shown that a 10 percent increase in cigarette prices results in only a 4 percent sales decline.

figure 18.4

Determining Price by Relating Marginal Revenue to Marginal Cost

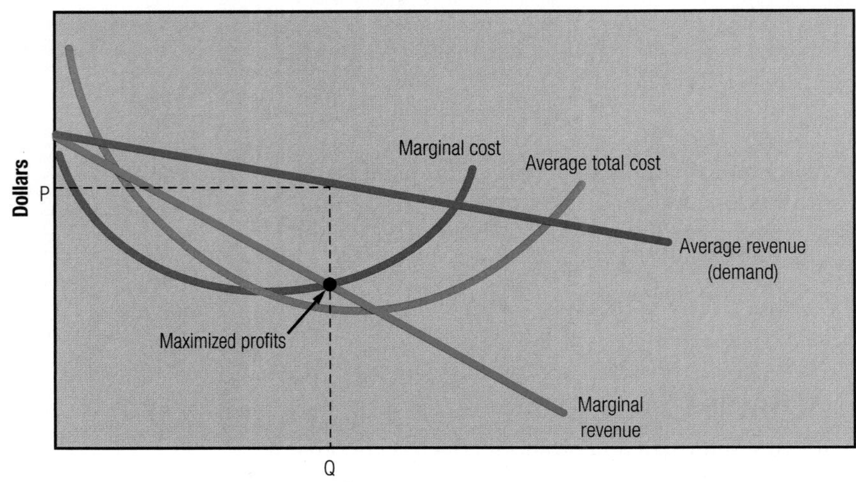

In countries such as Argentina or Brazil, where the annual inflation rate actually topped 100 percent a few decades ago, prices on almost all products rose accordingly. These higher prices led to elastic demand for some items, such as houses and cars; many of the cars on Argentina's roads were over 10 years old, and the nation's housing market was severely depressed. For other products, demand was inelastic; families continued to buy food because, after all, they needed to eat. However, even if they did not affect demand, inflationary prices did alter some consumer buying patterns. Lower income Brazilians, remembering the days when food prices

table 18.3 **Price Determination Using Marginal Analysis**

PRICE	NUMBER SOLD	TOTAL REVENUE	MARGINAL REVENUE	TOTAL COSTS	MARGINAL COSTS	PROFITS (TOTAL REVENUE MINUS TOTAL COSTS)
—	—	—	—	—	—	($50)
$34	1	$34	$34	57	$7	(23)
32	2	64	30	62	5	2
30	3	90	26	66	4	24
28	4	112	22	69	3	43
26	5	130	18	73	4	57
24	6	144	14	78	5	66
22	7	154	10	84	6	70
20	8	160	6	91	7	69
18	9	162	2	100	9	62
16	10	160	(2)	110	11	50

would increase dramatically from paycheck to paycheck, still buy much of the food items they will need for the next few weeks as soon as they get paid.

Determinants of Elasticity

Why is the elasticity of supply or demand high for some products and low for others? What determines demand elasticity? One major factor influencing the elasticity of demand is the availability of substitutes or complements. If consumers can easily find close substitutes for a good or service, the product's demand tends to be elastic. A product's role as a complement to the use of another product also affects its degree of price elasticity. For example, the relatively inelastic demand for motor oil reflects its role as a complement to a more important product, gasoline.

As increasing numbers of buyers and sellers complete their business transactions online, the elasticity of a product's demand is drastically affected. Take major discounters and other price-competitive box stores, for example. Small businesses and individual do-it-yourselfers shop Home Depot for tools, such as wheelbarrows; parents look for birthday gifts at Toys "R" Us; and homeowners go to Circuit City for new refrigerators or stoves. Today, however, the Internet lets consumers contact product manufacturers and service providers directly, often giving them better selections and prices for their efforts. Wheelbarrows, for instance, were once sold at almost identical prices at a relatively small number of retail outlets (inelastic demand). Today's shoppers can pick up a wheelbarrow at dozens of different locations—traditional hardware stores, plant nurseries, home improvement centers, discount stores, and even a few department stores (such as Sears). No longer does one wheelbarrow fit all—the product comes in different sizes, colors, and materials to match the specific needs of different users. The availability of different models and different prices for each combine to create a market characterized by demand elasticity.

Elasticity of demand also depends on whether a product is perceived as a necessity or a luxury. The Four Seasons chain of luxury hotels and resorts enjoys such a strong reputation for service, comfort, and exclusiveness that it has become a favorite among affluent individual travelers and business professionals. The combination of personal service and exclusiveness attracts a select group of upscale travelers who consider reservations at Four Seasons hotels essential components of their trips to Atlanta or Tokyo. Because its accommodations are viewed as a necessity, not a luxury, sales remain strong despite rising room rates.

© DAVE G. HAUSER/CORBIS

The world-renowned Four Seasons hotels and resorts continue to attract guests seeking unparalleled personal service and memorable stays in 22 countries around the world. Demand for rooms and suites at Four Seasons hotels and resorts by upscale travelers is likely to be inelastic.

Most people regard high-fashion clothes, such as a $2,000 Armani suit, as luxuries. If prices for designer outfits increase dramatically, people can respond by purchasing lower priced substitutes instead. In contrast, medical and dental care are considered necessities, so price changes have little effect on the frequency of visits to the doctor or dentist.

However, under the continuing influence of higher prices, some products once regarded as necessities may be dismissed as luxuries, leading to decreasing demand. Formerly booming personal computer sales have shown little or no growth in recent years.

Elasticity also depends on the portion of a person's budget that he or she spends on a good or service. People no longer really need matches. They can easily find good substitutes. Nonetheless, the demand for matches remains very inelastic because people spend so little on them that they hardly notice a price change. In contrast, the demand for housing or transportation is not totally inelastic, even though they are necessities, because both consume large parts of a consumer's budget. The "Marketing Miss" feature discusses how hidden fees can add to the price of some common services like banking, returning unwanted goods, and attending a football game.

Elasticity of demand also responds to consumers' time perspectives. Demand often shows less elasticity in the short run than in the long run. Consider the demand for home air conditioning. In the short run, people pay rising energy prices because they find it difficult to cut back on the quantities they use. Accustomed to living with specific temperature settings and dressing in certain ways, they prefer to pay more during a few months of the year than to explore other possibilities. Over time, though, with global warming becoming a real and present danger, they may find ways to economize. They can better insulate their homes, experiment with alternative cooling systems, or plant shade trees.

Sometimes the usual patterns do not hold true, though. Alcohol and tobacco, which are not necessities but do occupy large shares of some personal budgets, are also subject to inelastic demand.

Elasticity and Revenue

The elasticity of demand exerts an important influence on variations in total revenue as a result of changes in the price of a good or service. Assume, for example, that San Francisco's Bay Area Rapid Transit (BART) officials are considering alternative methods of raising more money for their budget. One possible method for increasing revenues would be to change rail pass fares for commuters. But should BART raise or lower the price of a pass? The correct answer depends on the elasticity of demand

marketing miss Oh, Those Fees and Hidden Charges

Background. Companies know that consumers are resistant to price increases, but they are still hoping to increase their bottom lines. So many of them, from banks to hotels to sports teams to retail stores, are charging hidden fees that have the same effect as a price increase. Brokerages may charge $2 to send you a copy of your monthly statement. One hotel in Florida charges $2.50 a day to clean your room. Best Buy is one of the retailers that charges a 15 percent restocking fee on returned items, and the New York Jets require $50 for placing your name on their season-ticket waiting list. Even local governments are raising penalties for traffic violations and court fees, and Alaskans who buy new tires pay the state $2.50 per tire as a recycling fee.

The Marketing Problem. These extra charges can add millions to a company's coffers. AT&T makes about $475 million on its "regulatory assessment fee" of 99 cents per long-distance customer. Banks and

for subway rides. A 10 percent decrease in fares should attract more riders, but unless it stimulates more than a 10 percent increase in riders, total revenue will fall. A 10 percent increase in fares will bring in more money per rider, but if more than 10 percent of the riders stop using the subway, total revenue will fall. A price cut will increase revenue only for a product with elastic demand, and a price increase will raise revenue only for a product with inelastic demand. BART officials seem to believe that the demand for rapid rail transit is inelastic; they raise fares when they need more money.

PRACTICAL PROBLEMS OF PRICE THEORY

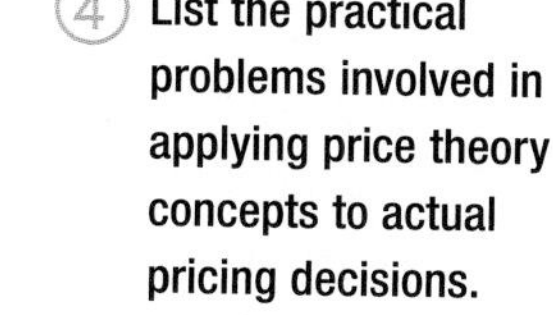

4 **List the practical problems involved in applying price theory concepts to actual pricing decisions.**

Marketers may thoroughly understand price theory concepts but still encounter difficulty applying them in practice. What practical limitations interfere with setting prices?

First, many firms do not attempt to maximize profits. Economic analysis is subject to the same limitations as the assumptions on which it is based—for example, the proposition that all firms attempt to maximize profits. Second, it is difficult to estimate demand curves. Modern accounting procedures provide managers with a clear understanding of cost structures, so managers can readily comprehend the supply side of the pricing equation. But they find it difficult to estimate demand at various price levels. Demand curves must be based on marketing research estimates that may be less exact than cost figures. Although the demand element can be identified, it is often difficult to measure in real-world settings.

1. **What are the determinants of elasticity?**
2. **What is the usual relationship between elasticity and revenue?**

PRICE DETERMINATION IN PRACTICE

5 **Explain the major cost-plus approaches to price setting.**

The practical limitations inherent in price theory have forced practitioners to turn to other techniques. **Cost-plus pricing,** the most popular method, uses a base-cost figure per unit and adds a markup to cover unassigned costs and to provide a profit. The only real difference among the multitude of cost-plus techniques is the relative sophistication of the costing procedures employed. For example, a local apparel shop may set prices by adding a 45 percent markup to the invoice price charged by the supplier. The markup is expected to cover all other expenses and permit the owner to earn a reasonable return on the sale of clothes.

In contrast to this rather simple pricing mechanism, a large manufacturer may employ a complex pricing formula requiring computer calculations. However, this method merely adds a more complicated procedure to the simpler, traditional method for calculating costs. In the end, someone still must make a decision about the markup. The apparel shop and the large manufacturer may figure costs differently, but they are remarkably similar in completing the markup side of the equation.

Cost-plus pricing often works well for a business that keeps its costs low, allowing it to set its prices lower than those of competitors and still make a profit. Wal-Mart keeps costs low by buying

credit-card companies collectively make billions on such "fees." "It's much easier to raise a price through obscure fees and surcharges than it is to raise a sales price," says a director of the Consumer Federation of America. But consumers are becoming more aware of such hidden costs and are beginning to rebel.

The Outcome. Consumers may soon be wise enough to avoid some fees by contacting the company to complain to a supervisor or switching companies if the fees are not waived. Some bank fees can be avoided by choosing services carefully. And if large numbers of customers complain, consumer groups or even the state attorney general may take notice.

Lessons Learned. Companies will need to look carefully at any added fees. With the Internet making it easier than ever to seek out information and find alternatives, and with competitors ready and waiting to acquire disgruntled customers, marketers need to identify the maximum "hidden" fees they can charge.

Sources: "Financial Services: Don't Get Taken by Hidden Fees," *ConsumerReports.org,* http://www.consumerreports.org, May 2004; Emily Thornton, "Readers Cry Foul over the Fee Frenzy," *BusinessWeek,* October 20, 2003, p. 14; Emily Thornton, "Fees! Fees! Fees!" *BusinessWeek,* September 29, 2003, pp. 99–104.

most of its inventory directly from manufacturers, using a supply chain that slashes inventory costs by quickly replenishing inventory as items are sold, and relying on wholesalers and other intermediaries only in special instances like localized items. This strategy has played a major role in the discounter becoming the world's largest retailer.

ALTERNATIVE PRICING PROCEDURES

The two most common cost-oriented pricing procedures are the full-cost method and the incremental-cost method. **Full-cost pricing** uses all relevant variable costs in setting a product's price. In addition, it allocates those fixed costs that cannot be directly attributed to the production of the specific item being priced. Under the full-cost method, if job order 515 in a printing plant amounts to 0.000127 percent of the plant's total output, then 0.000127 percent of the firm's overhead expenses are charged to that job. This approach allows the marketer to recover all costs plus the amount added as a profit margin.

The full-cost approach has two basic deficiencies. First, there is no consideration of competition or demand for the item. Perhaps no one wants to pay the price the firm has calculated. Second, any method for allocating overhead (fixed expenses) is arbitrary and may be unrealistic. In manufacturing, overhead allocations often are tied to direct labor hours. In retailing, the square footage of each profit center is sometimes the factor used in computations. Regardless of the technique employed, it is difficult to show a cause–effect relationship between the allocated cost and most products.

One way to overcome the arbitrary allocation of fixed expenses is with **incremental-cost pricing,** which attempts to use only those costs directly attributable to a specific output in setting prices. Consider a very small-scale manufacturer with the following income statement:

Sales (10,000 units at $10)		$100,000
Expenses:		
Variable	$50,000	
Fixed	40,000	90,000
Net Profit		$ 10,000

Suppose the firm is offered a contract for an additional 5,000 units. Since the peak season is over, these items can be produced at the same average variable cost. Assume that the labor force would otherwise be working on maintenance projects. How low should the firm price its product to get the contract?

Under the full-cost approach, the lowest price would be $9 per unit. This figure is obtained by dividing the $90,000 in expenses by an output of 10,000 units. The incremental approach, on the other hand, could permit any price above $5, which would significantly increase the possibility of securing the additional contract. This price would be composed of the $5 variable cost associated with each unit of production plus a $.10-per-unit contribution to fixed expenses and overhead. With a $5.10 proposed price, the income statement now looks like this:

Sales (10,000 at $10; 5,000 at $5.10)		$125,500
Expenses:		
Variable	$75,000	
Fixed	40,000	115,000
Net Profit	$ 10,500	

Profits thus increase under the incremental approach.

Admittedly, the illustration is based on two assumptions: (1) the ability to isolate markets such that selling at the lower price will not affect the price received in other markets and (2) the absence of legal restrictions on the firm. The example, however, does illustrate that profits can sometimes be enhanced by using the incremental approach.

breakeven analysis Pricing technique used to determine the number of products that must be sold at a specified price to generate enough revenue to cover total cost.

BREAKEVEN ANALYSIS

Breakeven analysis is a means of determining the number of goods or services that must be sold at a given price to generate sufficient revenue to cover total costs. Figure 18.5 graphically depicts this process. The total cost curve includes both fixed and variable segments, and total fixed cost is represented by a horizontal line. Average variable cost is assumed to be constant per unit as it was in the example for incremental pricing.

The breakeven point is the point at which total revenue equals total cost. In the example in Figure 18.5, a selling price of $10 and an average variable cost of $5 result in a per-unit contribution to fixed cost of $5. The breakeven point in terms of units is found by using the following formula, where the per-unit contribution equals the product's price less the variable cost per unit:

$$\text{Breakeven Point (in units)} = \frac{\text{Total Fixed Cost}}{\text{Per-Unit Contribution to Fixed Cost}}$$

$$\text{Breakeven Point (in units)} = \frac{\$40{,}000}{\$5} = 8{,}000 \text{ units}$$

The breakeven point in dollars is found with the following formula:

$$\text{Breakeven Point (in dollars)} = \frac{\text{Total Fixed Cost}}{1 - \text{Variable Cost per Unit Price}}$$

$$\text{Breakeven Point (in dollars)} = \frac{\$40{,}000}{1 - (\$5/\$10)} = \frac{\$40{,}000}{0.5} = \$80{,}000$$

Sometimes breakeven is reached by reducing costs. Isuzu Motors Ltd. plans to bring its unprofitable SUV business back to the breakeven point by canceling production of two of its vehicles, the Rodeo and Axiom, leaving only the Ascender in the North American market. The firm plans to import a Thai-made SUV it developed jointly with GM and may or may not contract with GM for the next generation of redesigned sport utility vehicles. The company's president said, "We'll decide what to do for SUVs after getting them back to a break-even."[18]

Once the breakeven point has been reached, sufficient revenues will have been obtained from sales to cover all fixed costs. Any additional sales will generate per-unit profits equal to the difference between the product's selling price and the variable cost of each unit. As Figure 18.5 reveals, sales of 8,001 units (1 unit above the breakeven point) will produce net profits of $5 ($10 sales price less per-unit variable cost of $5). Once all fixed costs have been covered, the per-unit contribution will become the per-unit profit.

figure 18.5

Breakeven Chart

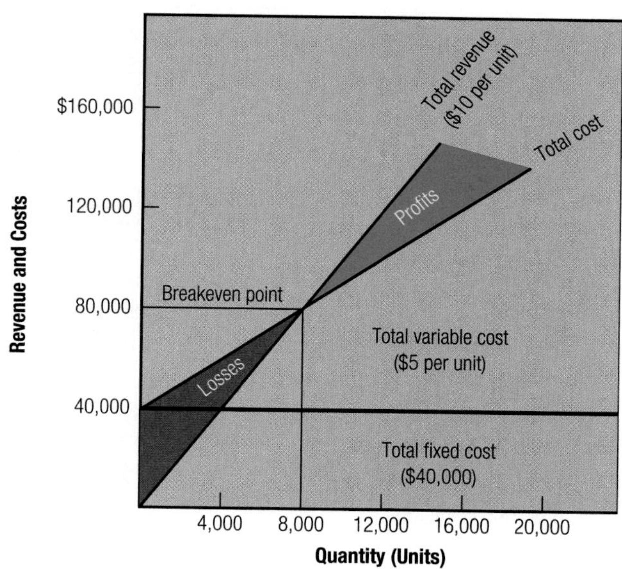

Target Returns

Although breakeven analysis indicates the sales level at which the firm will incur neither profits nor losses, most firms' managers include a targeted profit in their analyses. In some instances, management sets a desired dollar return when considering a proposed new product or other marketing action. A retailer may set a desired profit of $250,000 in considering whether to expand to a second location. In other instances, the target return may be expressed in percentages, such as a 15 percent return on sales. These target returns can be calculated as follows:

$$\text{Breakeven Point (including specific dollar target return)} = \frac{\text{Total Fixed Cost} + \text{Profit Objective}}{\text{Per-Unit Contribution}}$$

$$\text{Breakeven Point (in units)} = \frac{\$40{,}000 + \$15{,}000}{\$5} = 11{,}000 \text{ units}$$

If the target return is expressed as a percentage of sales, it can be included in the breakeven formula as a variable cost. Suppose the marketer in the preceding example seeks a 10 percent return on sales. The desired return is $1 for each product sold (the $10 per-unit selling price multiplied by the 10 percent return on sales). In this case, the basic breakeven formula will remain unchanged, although the variable cost per unit will be increased to reflect the target return, and the per-unit contribution to fixed cost will be reduced to $4. As a result, the breakeven point will increase from 8,000 to 10,000 units:

$$\text{Breakeven Point} = \frac{\$40,000}{\$4} = 10,000 \text{ units}$$

⑥ **List the chief advantages and shortcomings of using breakeven analysis in pricing decisions.**

Evaluation of Breakeven Analysis

Breakeven analysis is an effective tool for marketers in assessing the sales required for covering costs and achieving specified profit levels. It is easily understood by both marketing and nonmarketing executives and may help them decide whether required sales levels for a certain price are in fact realistic goals. However, it has its shortcomings.

First, the model assumes that costs can be divided into fixed and variable categories. Some costs, such as salaries and advertising outlays, may be either fixed or variable depending on the particular situation. In addition, the model assumes that per-unit variable costs do not change at different levels of operation. However, these may vary because of quantity discounts, more efficient utilization of the workforce, or other economies resulting from increased levels of production and sales. Finally, the basic breakeven model does not consider demand. It is a cost-based model and does not directly address the crucial question of whether consumers will purchase the product at the specified price and in the quantities required for breaking even or generating profits. The marketer's challenge is to modify the breakeven analysis and the other cost-oriented pricing approaches to incorporate demand analysis. Pricing must be examined from the buyer's perspective. Such decisions cannot be made by considering only cost factors.

1. **What is full-cost pricing?**
2. **Give the formula for finding the breakeven point, in units and in dollars.**
3. **What adjustments to the basic breakeven calculation must be made to include target returns?**

TOWARD REALISTIC PRICING

⑦ **Explain the superiority of modified breakeven analysis over the basic breakeven model and the role of yield management in pricing decisions.**

Traditional economic theory considers both costs and demand in determining an equilibrium price. The dual elements of supply and demand are balanced at the point of equilibrium. In actual practice, however, most pricing approaches are largely cost oriented. Since purely cost-oriented approaches to pricing violate the marketing concept, modifications that will add demand analysis to the pricing decision are required.

Consumer research on such issues as degree of price elasticity, consumer price expectations, existence and size of specific market segments, and buyer perceptions of strengths and weaknesses of substitute products is necessary for developing sales estimates at different prices. Because much of the resulting data involves perceptions, attitudes, and future expectations of present and potential customers, such estimates are likely to be less precise than cost estimates.

modified breakeven analysis Pricing technique used to evaluate consumer demand by comparing the number of products that must be sold at a variety of prices to cover total cost with estimates of expected sales at the various prices.

THE MODIFIED BREAKEVEN CONCEPT

The breakeven analysis method illustrated in Figure 18.5 assumes a constant $10 retail price regardless of quantity. But what happens at different retail prices? As Figure 18.6 shows, a more sophisticated approach called **modified breakeven analysis** combines the traditional breakeven analysis model with an evaluation of consumer demand.

Table 18.4 summarizes both the cost and revenue aspects of a number of alternative retail prices. The $5 per unit variable cost and the $40,000 total fixed cost are based on the costs utilized in the

figure 18.6

Modified Breakeven Chart: Parts A and B

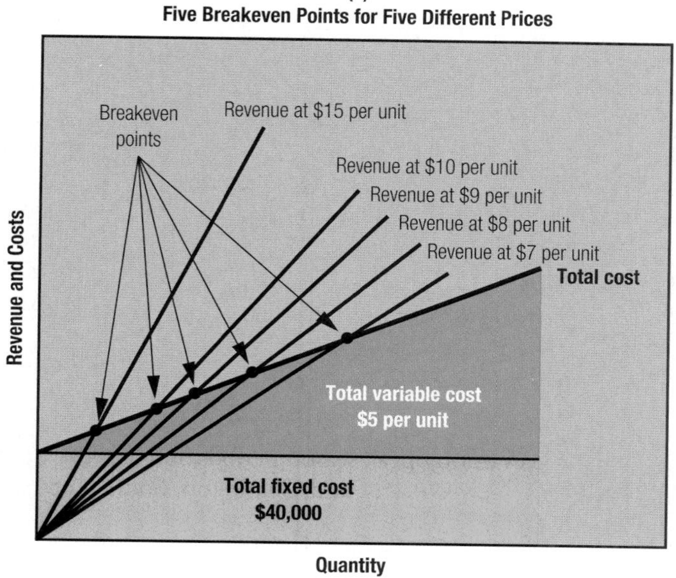

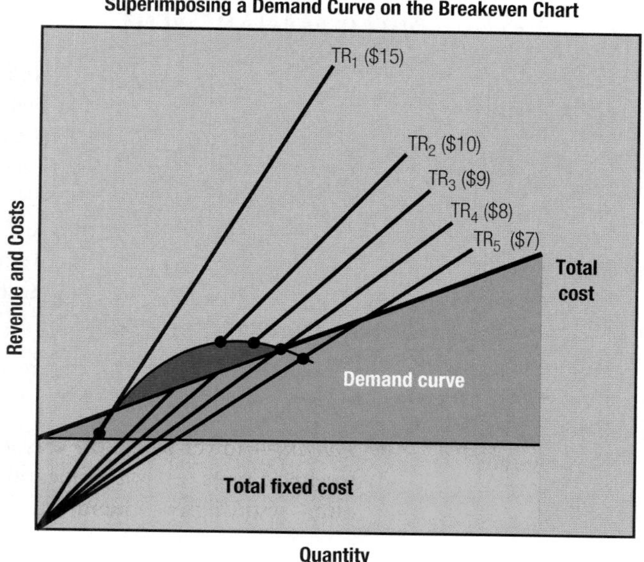

basic breakeven model. The expected unit sales for each specified retail price are obtained from marketing research. The table contains the information necessary for calculating the breakeven point for each of the five retail price alternatives. These points are shown in Figure 18.6(a).

The data shown in the first two columns of Table 18.4 represent a demand schedule that indicates the number of units consumers are expected to purchase at each of a series of retail prices. As Figure 18.6(b) shows, these data can be superimposed onto a breakeven chart to identify the range of feasible prices for the marketer to charge.

Figure 18.6 reveals that the range of profitable prices exists from a low of approximately $8 ($TR_4$) to a high of $10 ($TR_2$), with a price of $9 ($TR_3$) generating the greatest projected profits. Changing the retail price produces a new breakeven point. At a relatively high $15 ($TR_1$) retail price, the breakeven point is 4,000 units; at a $10 retail price, it is 8,000 units; and at the lowest price considered, $7 ($TR_5$), it is 20,000 units.

The contribution of modified breakeven analysis is that it forces the marketer to consider whether the consumer is likely to purchase the number of units required for achieving breakeven at a given

table 18.4 ***Revenue and Cost Data for Modified Breakeven Analysis***

	Revenues		Costs				
PRICE	QUANTITY DEMANDED	TOTAL REVENUE	TOTAL FIXED COST	TOTAL VARIABLE COST	TOTAL COST	BREAKEVEN POINT (NUMBER OF SALES REQUIRED TO BREAK EVEN)	TOTAL PROFIT (OR LOSS)
$15	2,500	$37,500	$40,000	$12,500	$52,500	4,000	$(15,000)
10	10,000	100,000	40,000	50,000	90,000	8,000	10,000
9	13,000	117,000	40,000	65,000	105,000	10,000	12,000
8	14,000	112,000	40,000	70,000	110,000	13,334	2,000
7	15,000	105,000	40,000	75,000	115,000	20,000	(10,000)

price. It demonstrates that a large number of units sold does not necessarily produce added profits, since—other things equal—lower prices are necessary for stimulating additional sales. Consequently, it is important to consider both costs and consumer demand in determining the most appropriate price.

YIELD MANAGEMENT

yield management Pricing strategy that allows marketers to vary prices based on such factors as demand, even though the cost of providing those goods or services remains the same; designed to maximize revenues in situations such as airfares, lodging, auto rentals, and theater tickets, where costs are fixed.

When most of a firm's costs are fixed over a wide range of outputs, the primary determinant of profitability will be the amount of revenue generated by sales. **Yield management** strategies allow marketers to vary prices based on such factors as demand, even though the cost of providing those goods or services remains the same. For example, sports teams like the San Francisco Giants charge more for weekend games, and the Colorado Rockies raise ticket prices based on the crowd-pleasing power of visiting teams. In the public sector, the Port Authority of New York and New Jersey recently experimented with variable pricing, charging more to cross the George Washington Bridge during peak rush hours.[19]

Similar yield management strategies typify the marketing of such goods and services as the following:

- *Theater tickets*—lower prices in the afternoons to offset low demand and higher prices in the evening when demand rises
- *Lodging*—lower prices off season and higher prices during peak season periods; low-priced weekend rates (except in locations like Las Vegas, New Orleans, and Charleston, South Carolina, with high weekend tourist visits)
- *Auto rental*—lower prices on weekends when business demand is low and higher prices during the week when business demand is higher
- *Airfares*—lower prices on nonrefundable tickets with travel restrictions such as advance-purchase and Saturday-night stay requirements and penalties for flight changes and higher prices on refundable tickets that can be changed without penalty

The following example from the airline industry demonstrates how yield management maximizes revenues in situations where costs are fixed.[20]

Airlines constantly monitor reservations on every flight. Beginning approximately 330 days before the flight, space is allocated between full-fare, discount-fare, and free tickets for frequent flyers who qualify for complimentary tickets. This allocation is monitored and adjusted at regular intervals until the flight departs.

Assume, for example, that Northwest Airlines has scheduled a 180-seat plane as Flight 1480 with an 8 A.M. departure from Memphis to Minneapolis on October 23. When Flight 1480 leaves its gate, all costs associated with the flight (fuel, crew, and other operating expenses) are fixed. The pricing that maximizes revenues on this flight will also maximize profits. An examination of past sales indicates that Northwest could sell 40 to 60 round-trip, full-fare tickets at $600 per passenger and 100 to 150 round-trip restricted-fare tickets at $200 per passenger. Demand for frequent-flyer space should be at least 10 seats.

If Northwest reserves 60 seats for full-fare passengers and accepts reservations for 110 restricted-fare tickets but sells only 40 full-fare tickets (leaving 20 vacant seats), total revenues will be:

$$\text{Revenues} = (40 \times \$600) + (110 \times \$200) = \$46{,}000$$

On the other hand, if Northwest's pricing decision makers want to reduce vacancies, they might decide to reduce the number of full-fare tickets to 20 and increase the restricted-fare tickets to 150. If the plane leaves the gate at full capacity, the flight will generate the following total revenues:

$$\text{Revenues} = (20 \times \$600) + (150 \times \$200) = \$42{,}000$$

Instead of rigidly maintaining the allocations established nearly a year before the flight, Northwest will use yield management to maximize the revenue per flight. In this example, the airline initially holds 60 full-fare seats and accepts reservations for up to 110 restricted-fare seats. Thirty days before the October 23 departure, updated computer projections indicate that 40 full-fare seats are likely to be sold. The allocation is now revised to 40 full-fare and 130 restricted-fare tickets. A full flight leaves the gate and revenues are:

$$\text{Revenues} = (40 \times \$600) + (130 \times \$200) = \$50{,}000$$

Applying yield management for the Memphis–Minneapolis flight increases revenues by at least $4,000 over the inflexible approach of making advance allocations and failing to adjust them based on passenger reservations and other data.

1. What is modified breakeven analysis?
2. Explain the goal of yield management.

GLOBAL ISSUES IN PRICE DETERMINATION

8 Identify the major pricing challenges facing online and international marketers.

It is equally important for a firm engaging in global marketing to use a pricing strategy that reflects its overall marketing strategy. Prices must support the company's broader goals, including product development, advertising and sales, customer support, competitive plans, and financial objectives.

In general, there are five pricing objectives that firms can use to set prices in global marketing. Four of these are the same pricing objectives that we discussed earlier in the chapter: profitability, volume, meeting competition, and prestige. In addition, international marketers work to achieve a fifth objective: price stability.

In the global arena, marketers may choose profitability objectives if their company is a price leader that tends to establish international prices. Profitability objectives also make sense if a firm is a low-cost supplier that can make a good profit on sales.

Volume objectives become especially important in situations where nations lower their trade barriers to expose domestic markets to foreign competition. As the European Union lowered economic barriers between countries, for instance, competition for customers soared. A recent trend has been mergers of European firms to form larger companies that can achieve volume objectives. For instance, Carrefour, France's largest discounter, recently acquired a former European competitor to become the world's second-largest retailer behind Wal-Mart.

Increased competition in Europe has also spurred firms to work toward the third pricing objective of meeting competitors' prices. Dutch corporation Philips Electronics offers U.S.-style coupons that give buyers 10 to 15 percent discounts off kitchen appliances. Aldi and Lidl, two German-owned food retailers, have opened discount outlets in France, forcing native French stores such as Carrefour to reduce prices. Automaker Fiat once boasted a 54 percent share of the Italian car market; its share has since dropped significantly due to inroads from competitively priced Ford of Europe. Fiat has fought back by offering $1,600 rebates and zero-interest financing on certain models.

Prestige is a valid pricing objective in international marketing when products are associated with intangible benefits, such as high quality, exclusiveness, or attractive design. The greater a product's perceived benefits, the higher its price can be. Marketers must be aware, however, that cultural perceptions of quality can differ from one country to the next. Sometimes items that command prestige prices in the U.S. are considered run-of-the-mill in other nations; sometimes products that are anything but prestigious in America seem exotic to overseas consumers. American patrons, for instance, view McDonald's restaurants as affordable fast-food eateries, but in China, they are seen as fashionable and relatively expensive.

AP WIDE WORLD PHOTOS/GREG BAKER

China's huge consumer base is attractive for companies hoping to expand globally. Companies must first gain a foothold in this new market—a factor to consider when setting prices.

The fifth pricing objective, price stability, is desirable in international markets, although it is difficult to achieve. Wars, terrorism, economic downturns, changing governments and political parties, and shifting trade policies can alter prices. An example is the computer industry. A few years ago, U.S. computer manufacturers sold their products in Europe for 30 to 50 percent more than U.S. prices. Today, greater competition within the European Union has forced computer prices down until they average only 10 percent higher than U.S. prices, barely enough to cover manufacturers' costs in retooling machines for the local market. Falling prices have slashed profits for both American and European manufacturers, including IBM, Hewlett-Packard, and Olivetti.

Price stability can be especially important for producers of commodities—goods and services that have easily accessible substitutes that other nations can supply quickly. Countries that export international commodities, such as wood, chemicals, and agricultural crops, suffer economically when their prices fluctuate. A nation such as Nicaragua, which exports sugarcane, can find that its balance of payments changes drastically when the international price for sugar shifts. This makes it vulnerable to stiff price competition from other sugarcane producers.

In contrast, countries that export value-oriented products, rather than commodities, tend to enjoy more stable prices. Prices of electronic equipment and automobiles tend to fluctuate far less than prices of crops like sugarcane and bananas.

Strategic Implications of Marketing in the 21st Century

THIS chapter has focused on traditional pricing concepts and methods—principles that are critical to all marketing strategies, especially in e-commerce. Consumers can now compare prices quickly, heightening the already intense competitive pricing environment. The Web allows for prices to be negotiated on the spot, and anything can be auctioned. From airline tickets to automobiles, the Web allows consumers to name their price.

While Internet shopping has not resulted in massive price cutting, it has increased the options available for consumers. Online price comparison engines, known as shopping bots, promise to help consumers find the lowest price for any good or service. Reverse auctions offered by sites like priceline.com, which allow customers to submit the highest price they are willing to pay for airline tickets, could conceivably be extended to other types of goods and are already gaining in popularity in business-to-business purchasing.[21]

Electronic delivery of music, books, and other goods and services will only lead to further price reductions. E-commerce has smoothed out the friction of time, which kept pricing relatively static. Microsoft cofounder Bill Gates recently gave a futuristic view of what he sees as a "friction-free economy." The current obsession with time and the ability to measure it will change perceptions and pricing of tangible goods. A growing number of products are not made until they are ordered, and increasingly, their prices are no longer fixed; instead, prices can shift up and down in response to changing market conditions.

While at least in the short term consumers are enjoying the benefits of competitive online pricing, retailers worry as they watch their profit margins shrink. The giant discount warehouse Costco, for example, offers housewares, furniture, and even office supplies delivered to your door through its Web site. Meanwhile, Buy.com goes a step further. The online superstore recently announced plans to price goods at wholesale—wiping out any profit margin and depending entirely on on-site advertising for revenues. The company offers a lowest price guarantee.[22] While there is no obvious blueprint for success, pricing strategies at Costco and Buy.com result from a similar way of thinking: Spend generously to win new customers, offer the lowest prices possible, and then give superior customer services to keep them loyal. ◆◆◆

REVIEW OF CHAPTER OBJECTIVES

1 Outline the legal constraints on pricing.

A variety of laws affect pricing decisions. Antitrust legislation provides a general set of constraints. The Robinson-Patman Act amended the Clayton Act to prohibit price discrimination in sales to other producers, wholesalers, or retailers that are not based on a cost differential. This law does not cover export markets or sales to the ultimate consumer. At the state level, unfair-trade laws require sellers to maintain minimum prices for comparable merchandise. These laws have become less frequently enforced in recent years. Fair-trade laws represented one legal barrier to competition that was removed in the face of growing price competition. These laws permitted manufacturers to set minimum retail prices for products and to require their dealers to sign contracts agreeing to abide by such prices. The Consumer Goods Pricing Act banned interstate use of fair-trade laws.

1.1. Distinguish between fair-trade and unfair-trade laws.
1.2. As a consumer, would you support either fair-trade or unfair-trade laws?
1.3. As the owner of a small retail store, would you support such laws?

2 Identify the major categories of pricing objectives.

Pricing objectives should be the natural consequence of overall organizational goals and more specific marketing goals. They can be classified into four major groups: (1) profitability objectives, including profit maximization and target returns; (2) volume objectives, including sales maximization and market share; (3) meeting competition objectives; and (4) prestige objectives.

2.1. Give an example of each of the major categories of pricing objectives.
2.2. What are the major price implications of the PIMS studies?
2.3. Suggest possible explanations for the relationships the PIMS studies reveal.

3 Explain price elasticity and its determinants.

Elasticity is an important element in price determination. The degree of consumer responsiveness to price changes is affected by such factors as (1) availability of substitute or complementary goods, (2) the classification of a good or service as a luxury or a necessity, (3) the portion of a person's budget spent on an item, and (4) the time perspective.

3.1. Explain the concept of elasticity.
3.2. Identify each factor influencing elasticity and give a specific example of how it affects the degree of elasticity in a good or service.

4 List the practical problems involved in applying price theory concepts to actual pricing decisions.

Three problems are present in using price theory in actual practice. First, many firms do not attempt to maximize profits, a basic assumption of price theory. Second, it is difficult to accurately estimate demand curves. Finally, inadequate training of managers and poor communication between economists and managers make it difficult to apply price theory in the real world.

4.1. What are the practical problems in applying price theory concepts to actual pricing decisions?

5 Explain the major cost-plus approaches to price setting.

Cost-plus pricing uses a base-cost figure per unit and adds a markup to cover unassigned costs and to provide a profit. It is the most commonly used method of setting prices today. There are two primary cost-oriented pricing procedures. Full-cost pricing uses all relevant variable costs in setting a product's price and allocates those fixed costs that cannot be directly attributed to the production of the specific item being priced. Incremental-cost pricing attempts to use only those costs directly attributable to a specific output in setting prices to overcome the arbitrary allocation of fixed expenses. The basic limitation of cost-oriented pricing is that it does not adequately account for product demand.

5.1. Explain the advantages of using incremental-cost pricing rather than full-cost pricing.
5.2. What are the potential drawbacks to incremental-cost pricing?
5.3. Why do many firms choose to deemphasize pricing as a marketing tool in favor of other marketing mix variables?

6 List the chief advantages and shortcomings of using breakeven analysis in pricing decisions.

Breakeven analysis is a means of determining the number of goods or services that must be sold at a given price to generate revenue sufficient for covering total costs. It is easily understood by managers and may help them decide whether required sales levels for a certain price are realistic goals. Its shortcomings are as follows. First, the model assumes that cost can be divided into fixed and variable categories and ignores the problems of arbitrarily making some allocations. Second, it assumes that per-unit variable costs do not change at different levels of operation, ignoring the possibility of quantity discounts, more efficient utilization of the workforce, and other possible economies. Third, the basic breakeven model does not consider demand. It is a cost-based model and fails to directly address the crucial question of whether consumers will actually purchase the product at the specified price and in the quantities required for breaking even or generating profits.

6.1. How can locating the breakeven point assist in price determination?
6.2. What are the primary dangers in relying solely on breakeven analysis in pricing decisions?
6.3. What is the breakeven point for a product with a selling price of $40, average variable costs of $24, and related fixed costs of $37,500? What impact would a $4-per-unit profit requirement have on the breakeven point?

7 Explain the superiority of modified breakeven analysis over the basic breakeven model and the role of yield management in pricing decisions.

Breakeven analysis is a means of determining the number of products that must be sold at a given price to generate sufficient revenue to cover total costs. The modified breakeven concept combines traditional breakeven analysis with an evaluation of consumer demand. It directly addresses the key question of whether consumers will actually purchase the product at different prices and in what quantities. Yield management pricing strategies are designed to maximize revenues in situations where costs are fixed, such as airfares, auto rentals, and theater tickets.

7.1. Explain the advantage of modified breakeven analysis over the basic breakeven formula.
7.2. Explain how the use of yield management can result in greater revenue than other pricing strategies.

8 Identify the major pricing challenges facing online and international marketers.

In general, firms can choose from among five pricing objectives to set prices in global marketing. Four of these objectives are the same pricing objectives discussed earlier: profitability, volume, meeting competition, and prestige. The fifth objective is price stability, which is difficult to achieve since wars, border conflicts, terrorism, economic trends, changing governments and political parties, and shifting trade policies can alter prices. The same types of changes can alter pricing in online marketing.

8.1. Identify the factors that can affect prices in international and online marketing.

MARKETING TERMS YOU NEED TO KNOW

price 598
Robinson-Patman Act 599
unfair-trade laws 600
fair-trade laws 600
profit maximization 602
target-return objective 602
Profit Impact of Market Strategies (PIMS) project 603
value pricing 604
customary prices 606
elasticity 610
breakeven analysis 614
modified breakeven analysis 616
yield management 618

OTHER IMPORTANT MARKETING TERMS

marginal analysis 602
market-share objective 603
demand 608
supply 608
pure competition 608
monopolistic competition 608
oligopoly 608
monopoly 608
variable costs 608
fixed costs 608
average total costs 608
marginal cost 608
cost-plus pricing 613
full-cost pricing 614
incremental-cost pricing 614

PROJECTS AND TEAMWORK EXERCISES

1. In small teams, categorize each of the following as a specific type of pricing objective. Suggest a company or product likely to utilize each pricing objective. Compare your findings.
   a. 5 percent increase in profits over the previous year
   b. prices no more than 6 percent higher than prices quoted by independent dealers
   c. 5 percent increase in market share
   d. 25 percent return on investment (before taxes)
   e. following the price set by the most important competitor in each market segment
   f. setting the highest prices in the product category to maintain favorable brand image
2. In pairs, discuss the market situations that exist for the following products. Defend your answers and present them to the class.
   a. desktop computer repair service
   b. DVD players
   c. golf clubs
   d. platinum
   e. soybeans
   f. remote control car alarms
   g. razors
   h. personal watercraft
3. How are the following prices determined and what do they have in common?
   a. ticket to a local museum
   b. your college tuition
   c. local sales tax rate
   d. printing of business cards
4. WebTech Development of Nashville, Tennessee, is considering the possible introduction of a new product proposed by its research and development staff. The firm's marketing director estimates that the product can be marketed at a price of $70. Total fixed cost is $278,000, and average variable cost is calculated at $48.
   a. What is the breakeven point in units for the proposed product?
   b. The firm's president has suggested a target profit return of $214,000 for the proposed product. How many units must be sold to both break even and achieve this target return?
5. The marketing research staff at Cleveland-based Cyber Novelties has developed the following sales estimates for a proposed new item the firm plans to market through direct mail sales:

Proposed Selling Price	Sales Estimate (units)
$8	55,000
10	22,000
15	14,000
20	5,000
24	2,800

The new product has a total fixed cost of $60,000 and a $7 variable cost per unit.
   a. Which of the proposed selling prices would generate a profit for Cyber Novelties?
   b. Cyber Novelties' director of marketing also estimates that an additional $0.50 per-unit allocation for extra promotion will produce the following increases in sales estimates: 60,000 units at an $8 unit selling price, 28,000 units at $10, 17,000 units at $15, 6,000 units at $20, and 3,500 units at $24. Indicate the feasible range of prices if this proposal is implemented and results in the predicted sales increases.
   c. Indicate the feasible price or prices if the $0.50 per-unit additional promotion proposal is not implemented but management insists on a $25,000 target return.
6. Research the price schedule at your local movie theater multiplex. What price strategy accounts for any price differentials you discover? Why don't matinee prices constitute price discrimination against those who don't qualify for the discounts?
7. Why is it more expensive to buy beer and a hot dog at a major league baseball game than it is to buy them at local retail stores?
8. Public funding of national parks has been declining for many years. What would you expect to happen to entry and use fees in this case? Research fees at parks in your state or region to verify your answer and report to the class.
9. How do cell phone companies make money by charging a flat rate per month for a set number of minutes, such as $35 for 300 minutes? Can you think of another plan that would be more profitable? Would it appeal to consumers?
10. Some airline industry executives believe that lower, simpler fares for the major carriers will earn goodwill from customers and send a clear marketing message that they are ready to compete with low-cost rivals. But few big airlines are embracing a new pricing system, frequently opting to launch new no-frills discount airlines to compete with AirTrans, JetBlue, Southwest, and the other low-cost carriers. Why do you think they are hesitating?

APPLYING CHAPTER CONCEPTS

1. Prices at amusement parks are expected to rise because operators like Disney and Universal Studios are adding new rides and coping with the rising cost of fuel; they are also copying each other's prices.[23] List as many things as you can think of that parks like these offer patrons in return for their money. Which of these do you think are directly reflected in the price of admission?
2. Musical artists earn only about 9 percent in royalties per CD, using a royalty base of retail price less 25 percent for packaging costs. The rest goes to the producer and to cover recording costs, promotion, copies given away to radio stations and reviewers, and other costs such as videos. What do you think happens to the artist's royalties when a CD is marked down to sell faster? Consider two cases: (1) the

marked-down CD sells more copies, and (2) it sells the same number of copies as before.

3. One writer advises consumers to worry not about rising gasoline prices, the cost of which can easily be covered by forgoing one takeout meal a month, but about how high energy prices will affect the rest of the economy. For example, each dollar-a-barrel price increase is equivalent to a $20 million-a-day "tax" on the economy. Explain what this means.
4. Ford Motor Co. recently announced that it will rely less on high-volume strategies like discounts and rebates to improve its profitability. Another strategy it will employ is to sell fewer cars to rental fleets, which eventually return the cars to Ford for sale at low auction prices. How do these types of sales affect Ford's profitability?

ETHICS EXERCISE

Real estate agents usually charge a 6 or 7 percent commission to list and sell a home, which earns them a fee of more than $10,000 on the sale of a median-priced home. But with homes in most of the U.S. selling at record rates, and at record prices, sellers are balking at those fees. "People are tired of paying higher and higher commissions just because houses are going up and up in value," says one realtor. Alternatives are springing up that include listing homes on the Internet, negotiating agents' fees down to the 4 percent range, and agreeing to flat fees for each separate task in the process such as setting the price of the home, holding an open house, or writing a sales contract with the buyer.

1. Since alternatives to costly commissions are now available to home sellers, should realtors still be setting the prices for their services the traditional way in the form of a set percentage of the sales price? Why do you think many of them are?
2. Do you think that negotiating a flat fee or lower commission helps or hurts the sense of trust that must be established between the seller and the agent? Why?

'netWork EXERCISES

1. **Breakeven analysis.** Visit the Web site listed below to learn more about breakeven analysis and how it can help in pricing decisions. Read the material and prepare a summary you can bring to class to participate in a discussion on the subject.

   http://www.businessknowhow.com/startup/break-even.htm
2. **Price discrimination.** As you know, most prescription drugs cost less in Canada than they do in the United States. Although not a violation of the Robinson-Patman Act, most purchasers would list this as an example of price discrimination—a seller charging different prices to different buyers. Use a major search engine, such as Google (http://www.google.com), to get current articles on the pricing of prescription drugs. Why do drug manufacturers charge Canadian customers less? Is there any justification, in your opinion, for these pricing practices?
3. **Yield management.** Yield management is an important component in the pricing of air travel. Visit the Web site of Southwest Airlines (http://www.southwest.com) and choose a round trip (say, from Chicago to Phoenix and back to Chicago). Review the different fares for your round trip. Why are some fares higher than others? Relate your explanation to the discussion of yield management found in the chapter.

Note: Internet Web addresses change frequently. If you don't find the exact sites listed, you may need to access the organization's or company's home page and search from there or use a search engine such as Google.

INFOTRAC CITATIONS AND EXERCISES

Record: A116588184
Variable Rate Pricing Coming to Online Music Services, Finally. *Charles Hall.*
The Online Reporter, May 15, 2004

Abstract: Online music services such as iTunes and Napster are successfully leading the way into the brave new world of legal online digital music, using fixed low-price strategies to woo music listeners to an Internet-based music distribution system. Apple launched its iTunes service by making a simple 99-cents-per-song appeal to consumers, and the pricing strategy has already proved profitable for the maker of iPod digital music players. However, big music companies that grant iTunes and Napster the right to sell music online are now planning to implement a new variable-pricing scheme for digital music downloads, seeking to jack up prices on some songs while lowering prices on others.

1. How will record companies determine which songs to offer at higher or lower prices, according to the article? Why is variable pricing an attractive option to businesses?
2. Why do some analysts believe the new digital music pricing strategy is a bad idea, both for record companies and online music services? Do you agree or disagree with the proposed pricing strategy? Explain.
3. According to the article, how has the Internet made variable pricing a viable and ultra-efficient pricing option for record companies?

CASE 18.1 Universal Slashes Prices of CDs by 30 Percent

Universal Music Group, with such labels as Island Def Jam, Interscope, and A&M, recently hit upon what looked like a surefire method of increasing sales and slowing the impact of music piracy. It cut the prices of its CDs by up to 30 percent.

Wholesalers received the price break in return for giving Universal 25 percent of their shelf space, and they were given a correspondingly lower suggested retail price to charge their customers. At the same time, to make sure consumers knew about the new lower prices, Universal switched from in-store and local marketing to a national TV and print ad campaign that included the broadcast networks and magazines like *Rolling Stone, People,* and *Entertainment Weekly.*

One record label executive said the move was a step in the right direction. "If you recognize competition includes illegal downloads and blank CDs," the industry needs "a more creative solution than suing college students." And Universal itself, which has the biggest share of the U.S. recorded music market, was optimistic. "Music fans will benefit from the price reductions we are announcing today," said the company's president. "Our new pricing model will enable U.S. retailers to offer music at a much more appealing price point in comparison to other entertainment products. We are confident this pricing approach will drive music fans back into retail stores."

But the price cut, called Jump Start, was a failure, partly because music buyers never saw the savings. Even though competitors were slow to copy the strategy, retail prices of Universal's CDs actually dropped only 5 percent during the first six months following the announcement of the price cut. Some stores never adopted the lower retail prices, charging the old higher prices while keeping the savings from the lower wholesale price for themselves, and others were slow to put the new prices into effect, first selling off old inventory that they had paid higher wholesale prices for. Many specialty music retailers were reluctant to cut the selling price of CDs because they thought they couldn't afford to discount CDs that much. Unlike big chain-store competitors like Wal-Mart, music stores don't have other merchandise on which to make up the price difference. "They [Universal] were trying to force a new pricing strategy upon us," said one record-store consultant. Other retailers disliked the pressure Universal applied to them to make a quick decision about signing up for the program. And many were upset that the firm cut its incentive payments and co-op advertising support.

The goal for Jump Start was to achieve a 21 percent sales increase to offset the lower wholesale price, but the actual increases were in the range of 8 to 13 percent for most weeks during the price break. A modified version of the program was soon put into place, with slightly higher wholesale prices and a goal of 17 percent increased volume. Within a few weeks of the new plan, Universal had racked up an increase of just over 16 percent. And its competitors are beginning to follow its lead, with some dropping their prices by moderate amounts. But none cut back on co-op advertising incentives to their retail partners, as Universal did.

Questions for Critical Thinking

1. Why are the music retailers important to the success of Universal's price-cutting plan? How could the company have avoided problems with the first version of Jump Start?
2. Do you think reduced retail prices for CDs are a good way to combat music piracy (downloading songs from the Internet)? Why or why not?

Sources: Don Clark, "New Rivals Lurk in Music-Recording Industry," *The Wall Street Journal,* June 30, 2004, pp. B1–B2; Ethan Smith, "Why a Plan to Cut CD Prices Went Off the Track," *Associated Press,* June 4, 2004, accessed at http://www.mlive.com; Ethan Smith, "Universal's CD Price Cuts Will Squeeze Music Retailers," *The Wall Street Journal,* September 18, 2003, p. B1; Jon Fine, "Universal Move Upends Music Biz," *Advertising Age,* September 8, 2003, pp. 3, 91.

VIDEO CASE 18.2 Wrigley's Gives Everyone Something to Chew On

The written case on The Wrigley Company appears on page VC-22. The recently filmed The Wrigley Company video is designed to expand and highlight the concepts in this chapter and the concepts and questions covered in the written video case.

chapter 19

Pricing Strategies

chapter objectives

1. Compare the alternative pricing strategies and explain when each strategy is most appropriate.
2. Describe how prices are quoted.
3. Identify the various pricing policy decisions that marketers must make.
4. Relate price to consumer perceptions of quality.
5. Contrast competitive bidding and negotiated prices.
6. Explain the importance of transfer pricing.
7. Compare the three alternative global pricing strategies.
8. Relate the concepts of cannibalization, bundle pricing, and bots to online pricing strategies.

HOW HOCKEY TEAMS SET TICKET PRICES

How much is a hockey game worth to you? Your answer to such a question is likely to be based on a number of factors, including the teams playing, where you were sitting, what night—or day—of the week the game was being played, the person accompanying you to the game, and how much you want to impress him or her. If you're a diehard fan with deep enough pockets to support your love for the sport, maybe you would purchase season tickets for your favorite team, which usually breaks down to a lower per-game price. If you just take in a game once in a while, maybe you'd splurge on the expensive seats—or perhaps you would decide the cheap seats are fine. But the ticket price alone isn't the only way National Hockey League (NHL) teams generate their total revenues. When you go to a game, you usually pay for parking, buy a hot dog and drink, pick up a game program, and perhaps spring for a souvenir cap or pennant. Setting prices is a complex process for team executives. Here are some of the strategies they use.

Like most NHL teams, the Pittsburgh Penguins offer a variety of plans ranging

AP WIDE WORLD PHOTO

from single-ticket sales to 10- and 20-game plans and up to full-season tickets. In addition, they calculate ticket prices based on the arena seating chart—the best seats cost more. And if fans want to attend a game on a weekday, they pay less than they would for a weekend game. So the cheapest ticket would be a full-season upper balcony seat at $17 per game, while the most expensive ticket would be a weekend A/B level seat at $90. Ticket buyers have a wide range of choices, including a new one for the Penguins: They can pay more or less depending on who the team's opponent is.

Recently, three NHL teams—the Penguins, the Ottawa Senators, and the Vancouver Canucks—began experimenting with a new pricing program: charging 10 to 20 percent more for single-game tickets for games featuring high-profile opponents. They don't charge less for games against the Atlanta Thrashers or Minnesota Wild; those prices remain at the original level. But if fans want to see the New York Rangers or Colorado Avalanche, they'll pay a few dollars more because there is greater demand for these tickets. "Rather than do an across-the-board, four-or-five percent increase, we thought we'd get a little bit more selective and try and keep the prices frozen for as many games as we can," explains Dave Cobb, chief operating officer for the Canucks. "We think it's a more effective way of getting the same amount of money because it allows us to maintain all our discount ticket programs that are in place now and also freezes prices on a majority of our games."

Other than the lower per-game price, what are the benefits of purchasing a full-season ticket from an NHL team? If you are a Dallas Stars fan, you get a host of benefits, including:

- invitations to special events
- a complimentary subscription to *Rinkside* magazine
- access to the unused ticket exchange program
- an additional discount on preseason games
- exclusive merchandise discounts
- complimentary ticket vouchers for other local professional sporting events, including Texas Rangers baseball games and the Mesquite Championship Rodeo

If you want to host a group of 20 or more friends or coworkers at a Dallas Stars game, the organization will give you a significant discount. Once your tickets are purchased, you may create your own "hospitality package" by adding food and beverages for $25 to $40 per guest. In addition, the Stars offer other packages—such as the combination package with discounted tickets to five hockey games and five Texas Rangers baseball games or the family package that includes four tickets, four pizzas, and four sodas at a discount price.

In recent years, fewer people are watching hockey on television, and players are commanding higher pay—three-fourths of the league's $1.93 billion in total annual revenues is spent on player salaries and benefits. "This is a level at which no business can survive," says Bill Daly, the NHL's chief legal officer. Critics disagree, saying that some teams are simply overspending. Either way, NHL team owners must be creative in implementing pricing strategies to attract more fans to the arena. It all depends on how much consumers are willing to pay for a ticket.[1]

Chapter Overview

SETTING prices is not a one-time decision, nor is it a standard routine. Instead, pricing is a dynamic function of the marketing mix. While about half of all companies change prices once a year or less frequently, one in ten does so every month. Online companies, which face enormous price pressures, often adjust prices daily. Some even negotiate prices on the spot. As described in the vignette on ticket pricing, NHL teams may change prices from season to season—or they may institute a new pricing program midseason as part of a promotional effort.

Companies translate pricing objectives into pricing decisions in two major steps. First, someone takes responsibility for making pricing decisions and administering the resulting pricing structure. Second, someone sets the overall pricing structure—that is, basic prices and appropriate discounts for channel members, quantity purchases, and geographic and promotional considerations.

The decision to make price adjustments is directly related to demand. Most businesses slowly change the amounts they charge customers, even when they clearly recognize strong demand. Instead of raising prices, they may choose to scale down customer service or add fees to cover added costs. They may also wait to raise prices until they see what their competitors will do.

Significant price changes in the retail gasoline and airline industries occur in the form of a *step out,* in which one firm will raise prices and then wait to see if others follow suit. If competitors fail to respond by increasing their prices, the company making the step out will usually reduce prices to the original level.

Few businesses want the distinction of being the first to charge higher prices. Since many firms base their prices on manufacturing costs rather than consumer demand, they may wait for increases in their own costs before responding with price changes. These increases generally emerge more slowly than changes in consumer demand. Finally, since many business executives believe that steady prices help preserve long-term relationships with customers, they are reluctant to raise prices even when strong demand probably justifies the change. Until recently, milk prices have remained fairly steady (see the "Marketing Miss" feature).

Chapter 18 introduced the concept of price and its role in the economic system and marketing strategy. This chapter examines various pricing strategies and price structures, such as reductions from list prices, and geographic considerations. It then looks at the primary pricing policies, including psychological pricing, price flexibility, product-line pricing, and promotional pricing, as well as price-quality relationships. Competitive and negotiated prices are discussed, and one section focuses entirely on transfer pricing. Finally, the chapter concludes by describing important factors in pricing goods and services for online and global markets. ◆◆◆

Briefly Speaking

How would you like a job where, if you made a mistake, a big red light goes on and 18,000 people boo?

Jacques Plante (1929–1986)

National Hockey League goalie

1 **Compare the alternative pricing strategies and explain when each strategy is most appropriate.**

skimming pricing strategy Pricing strategy involving the use of a high price relative to competitive offerings.

PRICING STRATEGIES

The specific strategies that firms use to price goods and services grow out of the marketing strategies they formulate to accomplish overall organizational objectives. One firm's marketers may price their products to attract customers across a wide range; another group of marketers may set prices to appeal to a small segment of a larger market; still another group may simply try to match competitors' price tags. In general, firms can choose from three pricing strategies: skimming, penetration, and competitive pricing. The following sections look at these choices in more detail.

SKIMMING PRICING STRATEGY

Derived from the expression "skimming the cream," **skimming pricing strategies** are also known as **market-plus pricing.** They involve the intentional setting of a relatively high price compared with the prices of competing products. Although some firms continue to utilize a skimming strategy throughout most stages of the product life cycle, it is more commonly used as a market entry price for distinctive goods or services with little or no initial competition. When the supply begins to exceed demand, or when competition catches up, the initial high price is dropped.

Such was the case with high-definition, flat-panel TVs, whose average price was $19,000, including installation, when they were introduced in 1999. The resulting sticker shock kept them out of the range of most household budgets. But a recent Consumer Electronics Association survey revealed that 40 to 50 percent of TV buyers are "interested" in purchasing a plasma or LCD set. As supply began to catch up with demand and prices on a 42-inch plasma TV dropped to around $1,000 by 2005, approximately 6 million units were purchased from such electronics firms as Sony, Sharp, Panasonic, Pioneer, and Samsung, whose large-screen plasma model is shown in Figure 19.1. Although flat panels are likely to stay more expensive than traditional TVs, prices should continue to fall through the decade as the technology matures.[2]

A company may practice a skimming strategy in setting a market-entry price when it introduces a distinctive good or service with little or no competition. Canon released its new S600 bubble-jet printer with a clever "Out of the Blue" ad campaign focusing on an innovative

figure 19.1

Distinctive Flat-Screen TVs Marketed with a Skimming Pricing Strategy

marketing miss — Milk Is in Demand

Background. Prices on agricultural products like fruit and grains often fluctuate depending on growing conditions, the weather, and acts of nature. But what about milk? Milk prices have traveled like yo-yos, going up and down in the past couple of years. But consumers haven't seen any of the decreases.

The Marketing Problem. As recently as 2003, the prices that farmers got for their milk were the lowest they had been in 25 years. Processors of ice cream, butter, and bottled milk were able to purchase milk for 30 percent less than the previous year. But in most regions of the U.S., consumers didn't see the savings. The average price of a gallon of milk at the supermarket dipped less than 10 percent or not at all. The New York State attorney general even investigated possible violations of the state law capping retail milk prices. Too much milk on the market should have resulted in a price-drop windfall for shoppers, but something seemed amiss in the supply–demand equation.

The Outcome. A year later, milk prices soared for dairy farmers, as much as 70 percent in a single four-month period. Suddenly, there wasn't enough milk to meet demand. Farmers who couldn't survive the low prices of the previous year had gone out of business or sold off part of their herds. Processors, including ice cream makers, worried that they would have to raise their prices to cover these increases—or go out of business themselves. Again, consumers paid more for milk products.

Lessons Learned. When prices—and demand—of raw ingredients like milk experience a dramatic rise or fall, every member of the channel is affected. Even if a large retailer declines to pass along savings to consumers, the decision may backfire, causing the retailer to lose the goodwill of its customers.

Sources: Marion Asnes, "Inflation: It's What's for Breakfast," *Money,* August 2004, pp. 29–30; Rhasheema A. Sweeting, "Ice Cream Parlors Sweating Over Surge in Milk Prices," *Chicago Tribune,* June 8, 2004, section 1, pp. 1, 24; Dawn Marks, "Farmers Say They're Happy Prices Are Mooving Up," *MyCattle.com,* May 26, 2004, http://www.mycattle.com; "Once Again, Milk Is a Cash Cow," *CBSNews.com,* April 16, 2004, http://www.litecarbs.com; Scott Kilman, "Secret in the Dairy Aisle: Milk Is a Cash Cow," *The Wall Street Journal,* July 28, 2003, pp. B1, B6.

figure 19.2

Skimming Pricing Strategy for Luxury Residences: Products for Which Price May Not Be a Key Consideration

WWW.CINNAMONBEACH.COM

product feature—individual ink tanks that let users replenish a single color without having to throw away an entire cartridge. This money-saving feature alone allowed Canon to price the printer at the top of the market.[3]

Skimming strategies are often used by marketers of high-end goods and services, such as the flat-screen TVs just described. The promotional message in Figure 19.2 for Cinnamon Beach, a private golf community along Florida's northeast coastline between St. Augustine and Daytona Beach, makes no mention of price. The club's marketers emphasize luxury, lifestyle, and the 2.5 miles of Atlantic beach adjacent to the community and the association of Cinnamon Beach with the Ocean Hammock Golf Course, which carries the name of legendary golfer Jack Nicklaus. They assume that consumers who are interested can afford the relatively high price for a new home or condominium at Cinnamon Beach and are willing to pay it.

In some cases, a firm may maintain a skimming strategy throughout most stages of a product's life cycle. The jewelry category is a good example. Even though relatively stable prices of gold bullion allow discounters such as Costco to offer heavier pieces for just a couple of hundred dollars, firms like Tiffany or Cartier are able to command prices 10 times that amount just for the brand name. Exclusivity justifies the pricing—and the price, once set, rarely falls.

Sometimes maintaining a high price through the product's life cycle works, but sometimes it does not. Consider the entertainment industry. From Disney World to Six Flags and from Cirque du Soleil to movie theaters, admission prices for popular entertainment have soared in recent years. The cost of tickets to concerts and sporting events has jumped as well. Broadway musicals top $100 a seat, and even a family outing to a nearby museum can cost $20 or more per person—not including parking or refreshments. In fact, prices have gone so high that many people have decided to stay home. Even a casual family restaurant chain can suffer from resistance to price increases. At the Red Lobster chain of seafood restaurants, continual price increases backfired. "Several years of aggressive menu price increases and higher-price menu introductions . . . has gotten the chain out of sync with its middle-class customers," noted restaurant industry expert David Palmer.[4]

But amusement park visitors, anxious to avoid long lines, have displayed a willingness to pay top prices for first-class treatment. During the past two years, Universal Studios Hollywood and Legoland California in Carlsbad have begun selling day passes that include line-cutting privileges for about twice the price of regular admission. Fearful of negative reactions by regular ticket holders, some major parks permit visitors to make "appointments" for popular rides, and Six Flags distributes pagers that buzz visitors for low-demand times on popular rides.[5]

Despite the risk of backlash, a skimming strategy does offer benefits. It allows a manufacturer to quickly recover its research and development (R&D) costs. Pharmaceutical companies, which fiercely protect their patents on new drugs, justify high prices because of astronomical R&D costs—an average of 16 cents of every sales dollar, compared with 8 cents for computer makers and 4 cents in the aerospace industry. To protect their brand names from competition from lower cost generics, drug makers frequently make small changes to their products—such as combining the original product with a complimentary prescription drug that treats different aspects of the ailment. The new combination often enables them to extend their patents. Just before the allergy medicine Claritin was scheduled to shift to over-the-counter sales, Schering-Plough introduced prescription Clarinex—a similar drug with minor alterations.

A skimming strategy also permits marketers to control demand in the introductory stages of a product's life cycle and then adjust productive capacity to match changing demand. A low initial price for a new product could lead to fulfillment problems and loss of shopper goodwill if demand outstrips the firm's production capacity. The result is likely to be consumer and retailer complaints and possibly permanent damage to the product's image. Excess demand occasionally leads to quality issues, as the firm strives to satisfy consumer desires for the product with inadequate production facilities.

During the late growth and early maturity stages of its life cycle, a product's price typically falls for two reasons: (1) the pressure of competition and (2) the desire to expand its market. Figure 19.3 shows that 10 percent of the market may buy Product X at $10.00, and another 20 percent could be added to its customer base at a price of $8.75. Successive price declines may expand the firm's market size and meet challenges posed by new competitors.

figure 19.3

Price Reductions to Increase Market Share

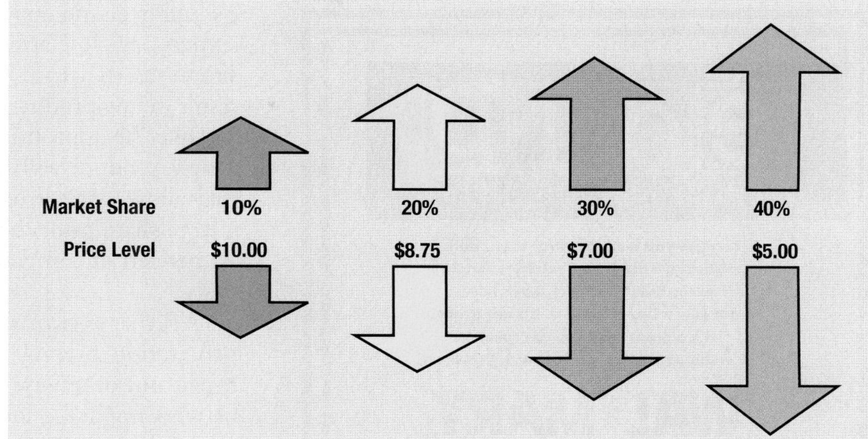

A skimming strategy has one inherent chief disadvantage: It attracts competition. Potential competitors see innovative firms reaping large financial returns and decide to enter the market. This new supply may force the price of the original product even lower than its eventual level under a sequential skimming procedure. However, if patent protection or some other unique proprietary ability allows a firm to exclude competitors from its market, it may extend a skimming strategy the way Schering-Plough did with Clarinex.

penetration pricing strategy Pricing strategy involving the use of a relatively low entry price compared with competitive offerings, based on the theory that this initial low price will help secure market acceptance.

PENETRATION PRICING STRATEGY

A **penetration pricing strategy** sets a low price as a major marketing weapon. Marketers often price products noticeably lower than competing offerings when they enter new industries characterized by dozens of competing brands. Once the product achieves some market recognition through consumer trial purchases stimulated by its low price, marketers may increase the price to the level of competing products. Marketers of consumer products such as detergents often use this strategy. A penetration pricing strategy may also extend over several stages of the product life cycle as the firm seeks to maintain a reputation as a low-price competitor.

A penetration pricing strategy is sometimes called *market-minus pricing* when it implements the premise that a lower than market price will attract buyers and move a brand from an unknown newcomer to at least the brand-recognition stage or even to the brand-preference stage. Since many firms begin penetration pricing with the intention of increasing prices in the future, success depends on generating many trial purchases. In its promotional message in Figure 19.4, Citibank states up front that it will increase its interest rate—its price—after a specific date. But the bank hopes to attract new customers with its zero-percent rate for the given time period.

figure 19.4

Credit-Card Offers: Penetration Pricing

If competitors view the new product as a threat, marketers attempting to use a penetration strategy often discover that rivals will simply match their prices. Discount air carriers like AirTran, America West, JetBlue, and Southwest continually face the problem of having their prices matched by larger competitors. As a result, they often compete with major carriers by offering not only low prices but a combination of attractive airfares, high customer-service levels, and routes that are often underserved by the majors. Aided by flight purchase guarantees from local businesses seeking improved air service, AirTran has established routes to smaller markets such as Myrtle Beach, South Carolina, and Biloxi, Mississippi.[6]

Retailers may use penetration pricing to lure shoppers to new stores. Strategies might take such forms as zero interest charges for credit purchases at a new furniture store, two-for-one offers for dinner

figure 19.5

Everyday Low Pricing (EDLP) at Wal-Mart

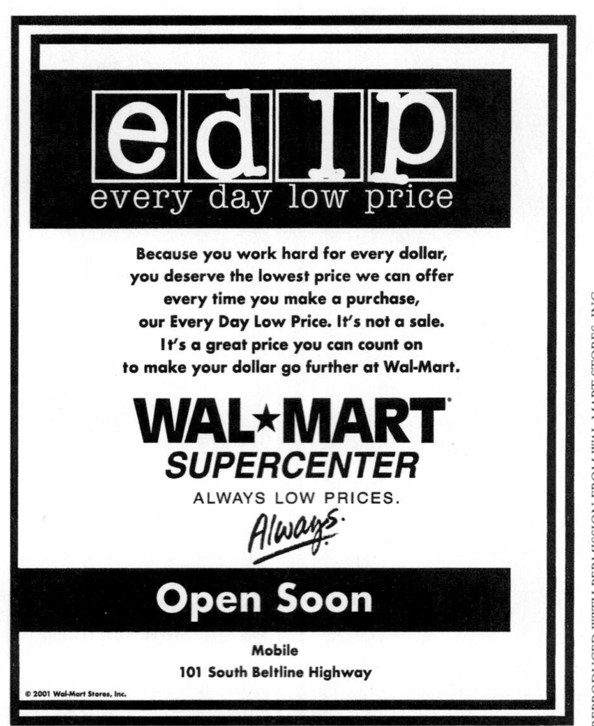

at a new restaurant, or an extremely low price on a single product purchase for first-time customers to get them to come in and shop.

Penetration pricing works best for goods or services characterized by highly elastic demand. Large numbers of highly price-sensitive consumers pay close attention to this type of appeal. The strategy also suits situations in which large-scale operations and long production runs result in low production and marketing costs. Finally, penetration pricing may be appropriate in market situations in which introduction of a new product will likely attract strong competitors. Such a strategy may allow a new product to reach the mass market quickly and capture a large share prior to entry by competitors. Research shows that about 25 percent of companies use penetration pricing strategies on a regular basis.

Perhaps surprisingly, some auto manufacturers have been using penetration pricing for some new models to attract customers who might not otherwise consider purchasing a vehicle during a given year or who might be looking at a more expensive competitor. Ford discounted its Freestar minivan by 13 percent almost as soon as it rolled off the assembly line to compete with the pricier Toyota Sienna and Nissan Quest. Chrysler immediately discounted its new Pacifica wagon by 16 percent.[7]

Everyday Low Pricing

Closely related to penetration pricing is **everyday low pricing (EDLP),** a strategy devoted to continuous low prices as opposed to relying on short-term, price-cutting tactics such as cents-off coupons, rebates, and special sales. EDLP can take two forms. In the first, retailers like Wal-Mart and Lowe's compete by consistently offering consumers low prices on a broad range of items. Through its EDLP policy, Lowe's offers not only to match any price the consumer sees elsewhere but also to take off an additional 10 percent. The promotional message in Figure 19.5 for a new Wal-Mart Supercenter emphasizes the retailer's EDLP policy.

The second form of the EDLP pricing strategy involves its use by the manufacturer in dealing with channel members. Manufacturers may seek to set stable wholesale prices that undercut offers that competitors make to retailers, offers that typically rise and fall with the latest trade promotion deals. Many marketers reduce the list prices on a number of products while simultaneously reducing promotion allowances to retailers. While reductions in allowances mean that retailers may not fund such in-store promotions as shelf merchandising and end-aisle displays, the manufacturers hope that stable low prices will stimulate sales instead.

Some retailers oppose EDLP strategies. Grocery stores, for instance, operate on "high–low" strategies that set profitable regular prices to offset losses of frequent specials and promotions. Other retailers believe that EDLP will ultimately benefit both sellers and buyers. Supporters of EDLP in the grocery industry point out that it already succeeds at two of the biggest competitors, Wal-Mart and warehouse clubs such as Costco.

One popular pricing myth is that a low price is a sure sell. Low prices are an easy means of distinguishing the offerings of one marketer from other sellers, but such moves are easy to counter by competitors. Unless overall demand is price elastic, overall price cuts will mean less revenue for all firms in the industry. In addition, low prices may generate an image of questionable quality. As 19th century art critic John Ruskin put it, "There is hardly anything in the world that some men can't make a little worse and sell a little cheaper, and the people who consider price only are this man's lawful prey." The astute marketer should evaluate both the benefits derived from low-price strategies and the costs involved before launching an EDLP strategy.

competitive pricing strategy Pricing strategy designed to deemphasize price as a competitive variable by pricing a good or service at the general level of comparable offerings.

COMPETITIVE PRICING STRATEGY

Although many organizations rely heavily on price as a competitive weapon, even more implement **competitive pricing strategies.** These organizations try to reduce the emphasis on price competition by matching other firms' prices and concentrating their own marketing efforts on the product, distribution, and promotion elements of the marketing mix. As pointed out earlier, while price offers a dramatic means of achieving competitive advantage, it is also the easiest marketing variable for competitors to match. In fact, in industries with relatively homogeneous products, competitors must match each other's price reductions to maintain market share and remain competitive.

Cutting prices is usually insanity if the competition can go as low as you can.

Michael E. Porter (b. 1947)
American educator

Retailers like Home Depot and Lowe's both use price-matching strategies, assuring consumers they will meet—and beat—competitors' prices. Grocery chains such as Safeway, Winn-Dixie, and Raley's often compete with seasonal items: watermelon, soft drinks, and hot dogs in the summer; apples, hot chocolate, and turkeys in the winter. As soon as one store lowers the price of an item like turkey, the rest follow suit.

When companies continually match each other's prices, prices can really drop. Dell and Hewlett-Packard are two computer makers that have been fighting it out in the laptop arena. Both companies say that laptops are big moneymakers, even if price reductions cut into profits. They both recently offered an entry-level laptop with Windows XP and a DVD player for about $700—several hundred dollars below the average price of $1,300. Shoppers who want even better deals can try discount retailers like Best Buy, which has been selling its Toshiba laptop (with Windows XP and DVD) for $499.[8]

Competitive pricing can be tricky because a price reduction results in financial effects not only through the first company that drops its prices but also throughout the entire industry as other firms match the price reduction. Unless the lower prices can attract new customers and expand the overall market enough to offset the loss of per-unit revenue, the price cut will leave all competitors with less revenue. Research shows that nearly two-thirds of all firms set prices using competitive pricing as their primary pricing strategy.

What happens when one discounter undercuts another? Although many retailers fear competition from Wal-Mart, one type of store seems well positioned against the powerful chain: the so-called dollar store. Dollar General, Family Dollar, and Dollar Tree are three examples of this sector, which has added more than 4,000 new stores across the U.S. in the past few years—an increase of more than one-third. Today's equivalent of the five-and-dime variety stores of the 20th century, dollar stores sell inexpensive items ranging from cleaning supplies, paper plates, toothpaste, greeting cards, and other household products—and compete on price and convenience, especially parking and easy access to the goods. Although these stores have yet to threaten Wal-Mart's position—their combined annual sales total just over $16 billion while Wal-Mart total sales exceeded $265 billion in 2004—the retail giant is paying attention. As these dollar store chains expand, adding more brand-name products and attracting more price-conscious customers, Wal-Mart is likely to take some competitive action. "[The dollar stores] are a major threat, so much so that Wal-Mart will eventually have to buy one of these chains or start one," predicts Harvard University professor John Stilgoe.[9]

Once competitors are routinely matching each other on price, marketers must turn away from price as a marketing strategy, emphasizing other variables to develop areas of distinctive competence and attract customers. Airlines, which are famous for competition based on price, must constantly look for other ways to get people to fly with them. The promotional message for American Airlines in Figure 19.6 emphasizes its new, roomier seating.

figure 19.6

American Airlines: Reducing the Emphasis on Price Competition

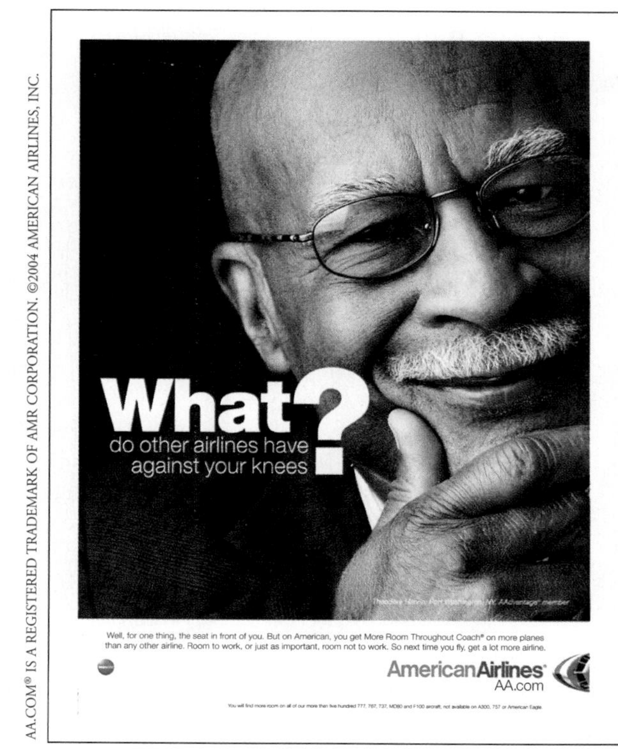

MARKETING Concept Check

1. **What is the difference between a penetration pricing strategy and EDLP?**
2. **Identify ways marketers use competitive pricing strategies.**

② Describe how prices are quoted.

PRICE QUOTATIONS

The choice of the best method for quoting prices depends on many industry conditions, including competitive trends, cost structures, and traditional practices, along with the policies of individual firms. This section examines the reasoning and methodology behind price quotation practices.

Most price structures are built around **list prices**—the rates normally quoted to potential buyers. Marketers usually determine list prices by one or a combination of the methods discussed in Chapter 18. The sticker price on a new automobile is a good example: It shows the list price for the basic model and then adds the prices of options. The window price information on a new Chrysler Crossfire states that the list price for the car is $34,960. But when the options included on the vehicle are added, the list price can grow to $39,000 or more—and not include taxes that will be added to the price at the time of purchase.

The price of oil is equally important to consumers—particularly those who drive cars—because it directly affects the list price of gasoline. Figure 19.7 shows where the money from a $1.99 gallon of gasoline goes on its journey from the oil field to your gas tank. Despite high prices, a strong demand for gasoline continues across the U.S.[10]

REDUCTIONS FROM LIST PRICE

The amount that a consumer pays for a product—its **market price**—may or may not equal the list price. Discounts and allowances sometimes reduce list prices. A list price often defines a starting point from which discounts set a lower market price. Marketers offer discounts in several classifications: cash, trade, and quantity discounts.

Cash Discounts

Consumers, industrial purchasers, or channel members sometimes receive reductions in price in exchange for prompt payment of bills; these price cuts are known as **cash discounts.** Discount terms usually specify exact time periods, such as 2/10, net 30. This notation means that the customer must pay within 30 days, but payment within 10 days entitles the customer to subtract 2 percent from the amount due. Consumers may receive a cash discount for immediate payment—say, paying with cash instead of a credit card at the gas pump or paying the full cash amount up front for elective healthcare services such as braces for teeth. Cash discounts represent a traditional pricing practice in

figure 19.7

Gasoline Prices: Where the Money Goes

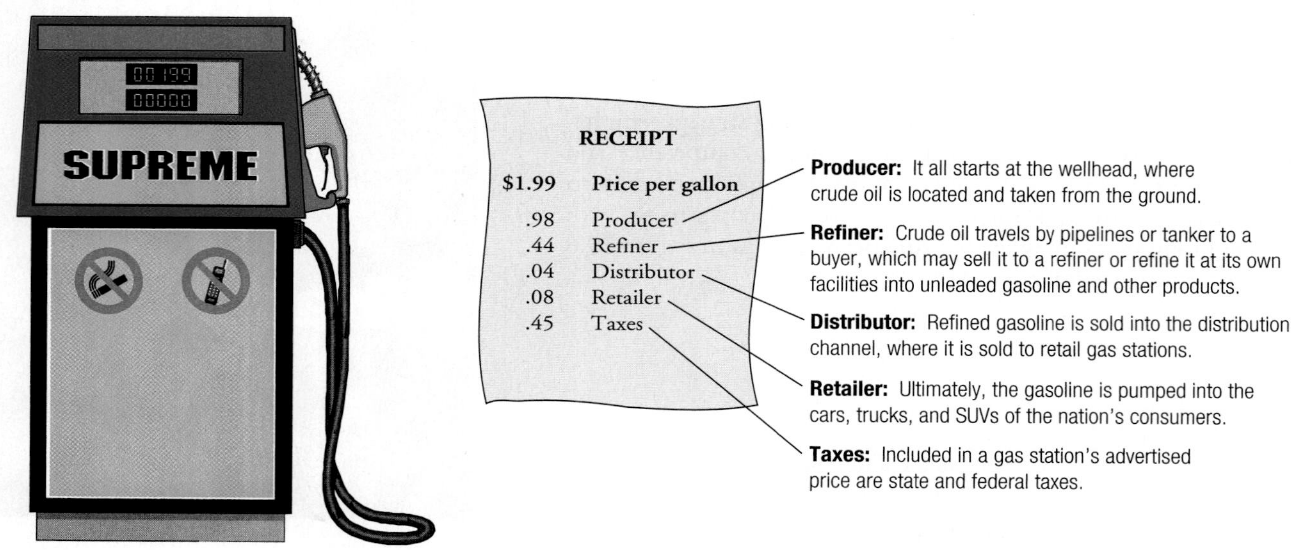

Source: Data from Lisa Sanders, "Look Who Gets Rich on $40-a-Barrel Oil," *CBS Marketwatch,* May 21, 2004, http://www.cbsmarketwatch.com. © 2004 MarketWatch, Inc.

many industries. They fulfill legal requirements provided that all customers can take the same reductions on the same terms.

In recent years, sellers have increasingly attempted to improve their own liquidity positions, reduce their bad-debt losses, and cut collection expenses by moving to a form of *negative cash discount.* Confronted with purchasers who may defer paying their bills as long as possible, a new notice has begun to appear on customer statements:

> **Due on Receipt.** A FINANCE CHARGE of 1.5% per month (18% A.P.R.) is computed on and added to the unpaid balance as of the statement date.

Past-due accounts may be turned over to collection agencies.

Trade Discounts

Payments to channel members for performing marketing functions are known as **trade discounts,** or functional discounts. Services performed by various channel members and the related costs were discussed in Chapters 13 and 14. A manufacturer's list price must incorporate the costs incurred by channel members in performing required marketing functions and expected profit margins for each member.

Trade discounts initially reflected the operating expenses of each category, but they have become more or less customary practices in some industries. The Robinson-Patman Act allows trade discounts as long as all buyers in the same category, such as all wholesalers or all retailers, receive the same discount privileges.

Figure 19.8 shows how a chain of trade discounts works. In the first instance, the trade discount is "40 percent, 10 percent off list price" for wholesalers. In other words, the 40 percent discount on the $40 product is the trade discount the retailer receives to cover operating expenses and earn a profit. The wholesaler receives 10 percent of the $24 price to retailers to cover expenses and earn a profit. The manufacturer receives $21.60 from the wholesaler for each order.

In the second example, the manufacturer and retailer decide to bypass the wholesaler. The producer offers a trade discount of 45 percent to the retailer. In this instance, the retailer receives $18 for each product sold at its list price, and the manufacturer receives the remaining $22. Either the retailer or the manufacturer must assume responsibility for the services previously performed by the wholesaler, or they can share these duties between them.

Quantity Discounts

Price reductions granted for large-volume purchases are known as **quantity discounts.** Sellers justify these discounts on the grounds that large orders reduce selling expenses and may shift some costs for storage, transportation, and financing to buyers. The law allows quantity discounts provided they are applied on the same basis to all customers.

Quantity discounts may specify either cumulative or noncumulative terms. **Cumulative quantity discounts** reduce prices in amounts determined by purchases over stated time periods. Annual purchases of at least $25,000 might entitle a buyer to a 3 percent rebate, and purchases exceeding $50,000 would increase the refund to 5 percent. These reductions are really patronage discounts because they tend to bind customers to a single supply source.

Noncumulative quantity discounts provide one-time reductions in the list price. For example, a firm might offer the following discount schedule for a product priced at $1,000 per unit:

1 unit	List: $1,000
2–5 units	List less 10 percent
6–10 units	List less 20 percent
Over 10 units	List less 25 percent

figure 19.8

Chain of Trade Discounts

"40 PERCENT, 10 PERCENT OFF" TRADE DISCOUNT

List Price	–	Retail Trade Discount	–	Wholesale Trade Discount	=	Manufacturer Proceeds
$40	–	$16 ($40 x 40%)	–	$2.40 ($24 x 10%)	=	$21.60 ($40 – $16 – $2.40)

"45 PERCENT" TRADE DISCOUNT

List Price	–	Retail Trade Discount	=	Manufacturer Proceeds
$40	–	$18 ($40 x 45%)	=	$22 ($40 – $18)

Many businesses have come to expect quantity discounts from suppliers. Ignoring these expectations can create competitive trouble for a firm. When United Parcel Service (UPS) balked at providing quantity discounts for large clients such as DuPont, it created an opportunity for competitors. One rival, Roadway Package System, lured several UPS customers by offering discounts to a wide range of organizational clients.

Marketers typically favor combinations of cash, trade, and quantity discounts. For example, catalogers like Oriental Trading Co., specializing in novelty products, and Current, Inc., specializing in stationery supplies, offer customers discounts according to how much they purchase. They typically place time limits on when such discounts are applicable for each catalog. In addition, Current includes free samples of seasonally timed greeting cards for customers on their mailing list.

Allowances

allowance Specified deduction from list price, including a trade-in or promotional allowance.

Allowances resemble discounts by specifying deductions from list price. The major categories of allowances are trade-ins and promotional allowances. **Trade-ins** are often used in sales of durable goods such as automobiles. The new product's basic list price remains unchanged, but the seller accepts less money from the customer along with a used product—usually the same kind of product as the buyer purchases.

Promotional allowances reduce prices as part of attempts to integrate promotional strategies within distribution channels. Manufacturers often return part of the prices that buyers pay in the form of advertising and sales-support allowances for channel members. Automobile manufacturers frequently offer allowances to retail dealers to induce them to lower prices and stimulate sales. In an effort to alert consumers to the difference between a car's sticker price and the price the dealer actually pays to the manufacturer, *Consumer Reports* recently began selling car and truck buyers a breakdown on dealers' wholesale costs. The information reveals undisclosed dealer profits such as manufacturers' "holdbacks"—amounts as high as 3 percent of the full sticker price, or \$750 on a \$25,000 car—that are refunded to dealers after sales are completed. The breakdown also reveals allowances for the dealers' advertising and other promotional costs. Once they are aware of the dealer's actual cost, car buyers are better able to negotiate a fair purchase price. Dealers dislike the move to reveal their markups, arguing that no other retail sector is forced to give consumers details of their promotional allowances.[11] Subsequently, *Consumer Reports* followed up with a list of seven other ways that car dealers profit from auto sales, some related to trade-ins and others to promotional allowances:

1. combining negotiations for the sales price of the automobile and the trade-in allowance granted to buyers who trade in their old automobile
2. zero-percent financing for a specified time period, after which all delayed payments are due
3. leasing
4. financing
5. adding options
6. offering services such as rust-proofing, fabric protection, or paint sealant
7. offering costly extended warranties[12]

For years, the price of music CDs has been artificially high, partly as a result of promotional allowances. Major record companies paid fees to stores that agreed not to advertise their CDs below set prices. Known as **minimum advertised pricing (MAP),** the policy in effect raised prices per CD by \$1 to \$2 across the board, eliminating most price competition. Under pressure from the Federal Trade Commission, major companies such as Bertelsmann, Sony, and EMI recently agreed to discontinue MAP allowances.[13] However, when Universal Music Group tried to cut its wholesale and suggested retail prices for CDs in an effort to boost business and satisfy consumers, the move backfired. Retailers thought they were being forced to make cuts they couldn't afford, and consumers didn't think a price cut to \$12.98 for a CD was a bargain.[14]

Rebates

In still another way to reduce the price paid by customers, marketers may offer a **rebate**—a refund of a portion of the purchase price. Rebates appear everywhere—on cosmetics packages, appliances, over-the-counter medications, and in automobile promotions—by manufacturers eager to get consumers to try their products or to move products during periods of slow sales. Mattress manufacturer Sealy has successfully used rebates to move consumers up to more expensive models in its product line, offering the biggest rebates for its top-priced mattresses.

Upromise.com offers rebates in the form of a point system related to the dollar amount of purchases that can be funneled into savings plans to pay for future college tuition. By purchasing products at participating retailers—including 15,000 grocery stores across the U.S., as well as major companies like ExxonMobil and AT&T—consumers can earn from 3 to 5 percent in rebates for college expenses when they buy any of the thousands of participating items, from Coca-Cola to Pop Tarts. If shoppers make purchases through the Upromise Web site from participating retailers such as Old Navy or L.L. Bean—using their Upromise MasterCard—they receive additional rebate points. Finally, every time they use their Upromise MasterCard for any purchase, consumers receive rebate points.[15]

With the exception of rebate programs like Upromise, which consumers make a conscious decision to join, rebates can have their problems. A major problem is that consumers come to expect them. Giant rebates, of several thousand dollars or more per vehicle, make a significant cut in the profits of the auto industry—but consumers now expect to receive a sizable rebate when they purchase a new vehicle. So, auto manufacturers believe they need to make this concession. "If we don't get off to a fast start, it makes it hard to reach our [sales] objectives," explains GM chief executive Rick Wagoner.[16] Another problem is that consumers tend to get fed up with rebates and begin to drift away from goods that require filling out a form, mailing it in, and then waiting weeks for a check in favor of goods that seem simpler to buy.[17] As Figure 19.9 reveals, computers and other electronic equipment commonly come with rebates. The "Solving an Ethical Controversy" feature illustrates the debate surrounding rebates tied to volume discounts in the healthcare industry.

GEOGRAPHIC CONSIDERATIONS

FOB (free on board) plant (FOB origin) Price quotation that does not include shipping charges.

In industries dominated by catalog and online marketers, geographic considerations weigh heavily on the firm's ability to deliver orders in a cost-effective manner at the right time and place. In other instances, geographic factors affect the marketer's ability to receive additional inventory quickly in response to demand fluctuations. And although geographic considerations strongly influence prices when costs include shipping heavy, bulky, low-unit-value products, they can also affect lightweight, lower cost products.

Buyers and sellers can handle transportation expenses in several ways: (1) The buyer pays all transportation charges, (2) the seller pays all transportation charges, or (3) the buyer and the seller share the charges. This decision has major effects on a firm's efforts to expand its geographic coverage to distant markets. How can marketers compete with local suppliers in distant markets who are able to avoid the considerable shipping costs that their firms must pay? Sellers can implement several alternatives for handling transportation costs in their pricing policies.

FOB Pricing

FOB (free on board) plant, or **FOB origin,** prices include no shipping charges. The buyer must pay all freight charges to transport the product from the manufacturer's loading dock. The seller pays only to load the merchandise aboard the carrier selected by the buyer. Legal

figure 19.9

Rebates for Computer-Related Goods

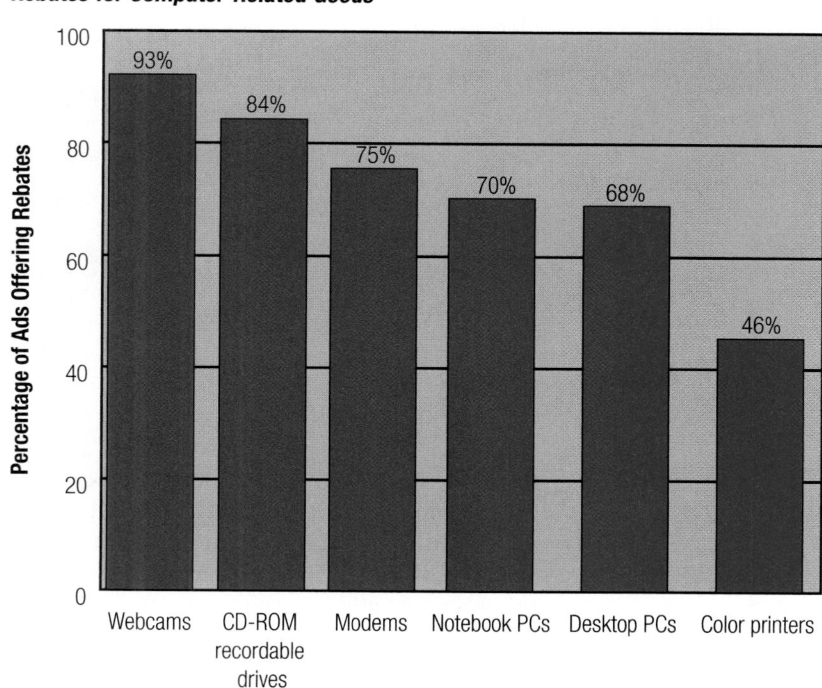

Source: Data from Daniel McGinn, "Let's Make a (Tough) Deal," *Newsweek,* June 23, 2003, p. 48.

Solving an Ethical Controversy

WHEN IS A REBATE NOT A REBATE?

IT seemed like a good idea a few years ago: U.S. health insurance companies could receive price breaks based on volume discounts for drugs through a newly created layer of marketing intermediaries. They hired companies—called *pharmacy benefit managers (PBMs)*—to negotiate prices with drug companies. Then they pressured doctors to prescribe the discounted drugs. These middlemen were responsible for cutting drug costs up to 30 percent. But gradually, the savings began to disappear—for everyone except the PBMs. Before long, by making deals, the PBMs gained enormous power, controlling which drugs doctors prescribed and which drugs were covered by health insurance plans for 200 million Americans. But the PBMs' revenue gradually shifted over the years from fees from the health insurance plans to rebates certain drug companies offered PBMs for prescribing their medications. The manufacturers' rebates they received went no farther than their own pockets. "We have to make some money," argued David Machlowitz, senior vice president and general counsel for Medco—a spinoff of the giant drug manufacturer Merck.

ARE PHARMACY BENEFIT MANAGERS DRIVING UP THE COST OF HEALTHCARE?

PRO

1. Rebates pocketed by PBMs add up to $12.2 billion per year according to some estimates. "The PBMs are driven by collecting rebates, not containing costs," says one benefits consultant.
2. A drug's price is often determined by the fee a pharmaceutical manufacturer is paying a PBM to recommend it rather than by how much it costs to produce the drug.

CON

1. "We generate competition," argues David Halbert, chief executive of AdvancePCS, the largest PBM in the U.S. "We are in the business of lowering drug costs."
2. PBMs usually recommend drugs that are not only as effective as their competitors' but also less expensive.

SUMMARY

Private lawsuits are seeking to reveal the size of the rebates received by PBMs—often hidden by both pharmaceutical manufacturers and PBMs—and ultimately stopping them. Drug manufacturers often label the fees they pay to PBMs as "educational grants," "data sales fees," or "health management fees" rather than rebates in order to circumvent the rebate law that ties the price of a drug to the amount of rebates offered. Prices continue to skyrocket. "This is a market structure based on reverse and perverse economics," criticizes Stephen Schondelmeyer, a professor of pharmaceutical economics at the University of Minnesota. "PBMs get paid more for doing what increases drug spending." Some PBMs have begun to share a portion of the rebates with their clients—the health insurance plans—although their contracts do not cover rebates. But with changes to Medicare prescription plans, PBMs may gain yet another slice of the market.

Sources: Tony Pugh, "The Prescription Cost Dilemma: Medicine Middlemen Limit HMOs' Drug Lists," *The Detroit Free Press,* February 8, 2003, http://www.freep.com; Julian E. Barnes, "When Is a Rebate a Kickback?" *U.S. News & World Report,* August 12, 2002, pp. 31–33.

title and responsibility pass to the buyer after the seller's employees load the purchase and get a receipt from the representative of the common carrier.

Many marketing intermediaries sell only on FOB plant terms to downstream channel members. These distributors believe that their customers have more clout than they do in negotiating with carriers. They prefer to assign transportation costs to the channel members in the best positions to secure the most cost-effective shipping terms.

FOB origin-freight allowed (freight absorbed) Price quotation system that allows the buyer to deduct shipping expenses from the cost of purchases.

Sellers may also quote prices as **FOB origin-freight allowed,** or **freight absorbed.** These terms permit buyers to subtract transportation expenses from their bills. The amount such a seller receives for its product varies with the freight charged against the invoice. This alternative is popular among firms with high fixed costs because it helps them to expand their markets considerably by quoting the same prices regardless of shipping expenses.

Uniform-Delivered Pricing

When a firm quotes the same price, including transportation expenses, to all buyers, it adopts a **uniform-delivered price** policy. This method of handling transportation expenses is the exact opposite of FOB origin pricing. The uniform-delivered system resembles the pricing structure for mail service, so it is sometimes called **postage-stamp pricing.** The price quote includes a transportation charge averaged over all of the firm's customers, meaning that distant customers actually pay a smaller share of shipping costs while nearby customers pay what is known as *phantom freight* (the amount by which the average transportation charge exceeds the actual cost of shipping).

uniform-delivered price Pricing system for handling transportation costs under which all buyers are quoted the same price, including transportation expenses. Sometimes known as *postage-stamp pricing.*

Zone Pricing

Zone pricing modifies a uniform-delivered pricing system by dividing the overall market into different zones and establishing a single price within each zone. This pricing structure incorporates average transportation costs for shipments within each zone as part of the delivered price of goods sold there; by narrowing distances, it greatly reduces but does not completely eliminate phantom freight. The primary advantage of zone pricing comes from easy administration methods that help a seller to compete in distant markets. The U.S. Postal Service's parcel rates depend on zone pricing.

zone pricing Pricing system for handling transportation costs under which the market is divided into geographic regions and a different price is set in each region.

Zone pricing helps explain why gasoline can cost more in one suburb than it costs in a neighborhood just two or three miles down the road. One way in which gasoline marketers boost profits is by mapping out areas based on formulas that factor in location, affluence, or simply what the local market will bear. Dealers are then charged different wholesale prices, which are reflected in the prices paid at the pump by customers. Some dealers argue that zone pricing should be prohibited. When drivers shop around for cheaper gas in other zones, stations in high-price zones are unable to compete. Ironically, it is the local dealer, not just the major oil company, which many consumers suspect of price gouging.

Basing-Point Pricing

In **basing-point pricing,** the price of a product includes the list price at the factory plus freight charges from the basing-point city nearest the buyer. The basing point specifies a location from which freight charges are calculated—not necessarily the point from which the goods are actually shipped. In either case, the actual shipping point does not affect the price quotation. Such a system seeks to equalize competition between distant marketers since all competitors quote identical transportation rates. Few buyers would accept a basing-point system today, however.

For many years, the best-known basing-point system was the Pittsburgh-plus pricing structure common in the steel industry. Steel buyers paid freight charges from Pittsburgh regardless of where the steel was produced. As the industry matured, manufacturing centers emerged in Chicago; Gary, Indiana; Cleveland; and Birmingham. Still, Pittsburgh remained the basing point for steel pricing, forcing a buyer in Atlanta who purchased steel from a Birmingham mill to pay phantom freight from Pittsburgh.

1. What are the three major types of discounts?
2. Identify two problems with rebates.
3. What are the three ways buyers and sellers can handle transportation expenses?

PRICING POLICIES

(3) Identify the various pricing policy decisions that marketers must make.

Pricing policies contribute important information to buyers as they assess the firm's total image. A coherent policy provides an overall framework and consistency that guide day-to-day pricing decisions. Formally, a **pricing policy** is a general guideline that reflects marketing objectives and influences specific pricing decisions.

Decisions concerning price structure generally tend to focus on technical, detailed questions, but decisions concerning pricing policies cover broader issues. Price-structure decisions take the firm's pricing policy as a given, from which they specify applicable discounts. Pricing policies have important strategic effects, particularly in guiding competitive efforts. They form the basis for more practical price-structure decisions.

Firms implement variations of four basic types of pricing policies: psychological pricing, price flexibility, product-line pricing, and promotional pricing. Specific policies deal effectively with various competitive situations; the final choice depends on the environment within which marketers must make their pricing decisions.

PSYCHOLOGICAL PRICING

psychological pricing Pricing policy based on the belief that certain prices or price ranges make a good or service more appealing than others to buyers.

Psychological pricing applies the belief that certain prices or price ranges make products more appealing than others to buyers. No research offers a consistent foundation for such thinking, however, and studies often report mixed findings. Nevertheless, marketers practice several forms of psychological pricing. Prestige pricing, discussed in Chapter 18, sets a relatively high price to convey an image of quality and exclusiveness. Two more psychological pricing techniques include odd pricing and unit pricing.

In **odd pricing,** marketers set prices at odd numbers just under round numbers. Many people assume that a price of $4.95 appeals more strongly to consumers than $5.00, supposedly because buyers interpret it as $4.00 plus change. Odd pricing originated as a way to force clerks to make change, thus serving as a cash-control device, and it remains a common feature of contemporary price quotations. Perhaps the most frequently seen example is at the local gas pump, where gas stations almost always price their fuels in tenths of a cent, believing that a posted price of $1.999 will be viewed as considerably less than $2 a gallon. In fact, a recent study reported in the *Harvard Business Review* concluded that consumers are more likely to make a purchase if a price ends in 9.[18]

However, some producers and retailers practice odd pricing but avoid prices ending in 5, 9, or 0. These marketers believe that customers view price tags of $5.95, $5.99, or $6.00 as regular retail prices, but they think of an amount like $5.97 as a discount price. Others, like Wal-Mart, avoid using 9s as ending prices for their items.

Unit pricing states prices in terms of some recognized unit of measurement (such as grams and liters) or a standard numerical count. Unit pricing began to be widely used during the late 1960s to make price comparisons more convenient following complaints by consumer advocates about the difficulty of comparing the true prices of products packaged in different sizes. These advocates thought that posting prices in terms of standard units would help shoppers make better informed purchases. However, unit pricing has not improved consumers' shopping habits as much as supporters originally envisioned. Instead, research shows that standard price quotes most often affect purchases only by relatively well-educated consumers with high earnings.

Wendy's uses odd pricing for its entire Super Value Menu, which is priced at 99 cents per item.

PRICE FLEXIBILITY

Marketing executives must also set company policies that determine whether their firm will permit **price flexibility**—that is, the decision of whether to set one price that applies to every buyer or to permit variable prices for different customers. Generally, one-price policies suit mass-selling marketing programs, whereas variable pricing is more likely to be applied in marketing programs based on individual bargaining. In a large department store, customers do not expect to haggle over prices with retail salespeople. Instead, they expect to pay the amounts shown on the price tags. Generally, customers pay less only when the retailer replaces regular prices with sale prices or offers discounts on damaged merchandise. Variable pricing usually applies to larger purchases such as automobiles, real estate, and hotel room rates. The fees associated with purchasing fractional ownership of a Bombardier Flexjet, described in Figure 19.10, could be open to variable pricing.

While variable pricing adds some flexibility to selling situations, it may conflict with provisions of the Robinson-Patman Act. It may also lead to retaliatory pricing by competitors, and it may stir complaints among customers who find that they paid higher prices than necessary. In an effort to reach Malaysian consumers—in conjunction with an initiative backed by the Malaysian government for PC ownership—Microsoft recently sold new PCs loaded with Microsoft software for around $300 in some Malaysian towns—while U.S. consumers were paying easily twice or three times that amount even at discount retailers like OfficeMax and Best Buy. The new policy was a radical departure from the firm's previous practice of global pricing, or charging the same amount for most of its products worldwide. Part of Microsoft's Malaysian pricing decision was in large part to fight its chief software competitor there, Linux, which provides free software via the Internet. Critics claim that the program will force a reduction of prices for Microsoft products worldwide, but supporters argue that the move was unavoidable if Microsoft planned to make headway in developing nations.[19]

figure 19.10

Fractional Ownership of a Personal Jet: Example of Variable Pricing

PRODUCT-LINE PRICING

Since most firms market multiple product lines, an effective pricing strategy must consider the relationships among all of these items instead of viewing each in isolation. **Product-line pricing** is the practice of setting a limited number of prices for a selection of merchandise. For example, a clothier might offer three lines of men's suits—one priced at $475, a second at $625, and the most expensive at $795. These price points help the retailer to define important product characteristics that differentiate the three product lines and assist the customer in deciding on whether to trade up or trade down.

Retailers practice extensive product-line pricing. In earlier days, five-and-dime variety stores exemplified this technique. It remains popular, however, because it offers advantages to both retailers and customers. Shoppers can choose desired price ranges and then concentrate on other product variables such as colors, styles, and materials. Retailers can purchase and offer specific lines in limited price categories instead of more general assortments with dozens of different prices.

Most airlines divide their seating areas on international flights according to product-line pricing. These flights offer a certain percentage of discount, business-class, first-class, and full-fare coach seats on each flight. On an overseas flight, for instance, the industry averages about 18 percent business-class seats. A round-trip business-class ticket from Houston to Paris on Continental Airlines costs almost twice the regular coach fare and several times more than the discount fare.

A potential problem with product-line pricing is that once marketers decide on a limited number of prices to use as their price lines, they may have difficulty making price changes on individual items. Rising costs, therefore, force sellers to either change the entire price-line structure, which results in confusion, or cut costs through production adjustments. The second option opens the firm to customer complaints that its merchandise is not what it used to be.

PROMOTIONAL PRICING

In **promotional pricing,** a lower than normal price is used as a temporary ingredient in a firm's marketing strategy. Some promotional pricing arrangements form part of recurrent marketing initiatives, such as a shoe store's annual "buy one pair, get the second pair for one cent" sale. Another example would be "7 CDs for 1 cent." This artificially low price attracts customers who must then agree to purchase a set number of CDs at regular prices within a specified time limit. Another firm may introduce a promotional model or brand with a special price to begin competing in a new market.

promotional pricing Pricing policy in which a lower than normal price is used as a temporary ingredient in a firm's marketing strategy.

Managing promotional pricing efforts requires marketing skill. As described earlier, customers may get hooked on sales and other promotional pricing events. If they know their favorite department store has a one-day sale every month, they are likely to wait to make their purchases on that day. Car shoppers have been offered so many price incentives that it is becoming harder and harder for manufacturers and dealers to take them away.[20] Women's clothing retailer Talbot's used to have just two sales a year; now it has four. Although the retailer is well known for being able to sell more items at full price than other apparel retailers, Talbot's is not immune to problems with promotional pricing. During a recent September, regular sales were doing so well that the firm decided to postpone its midseason sale by two weeks. But by the time the markdowns were taken, consumers weren't interested in past-season T-shirts and shorts—they were already looking for winter clothing. The firm was then left with unwanted inventory.[21]

Loss Leaders and Leader Pricing

loss leader Product offered to consumers at less than cost to attract them to stores in the hope that they will buy other merchandise at regular prices.

Retailers rely most heavily on promotional pricing. In one type of technique, stores offer **loss leaders**—goods priced below cost to attract customers who, the retailer hopes, will also buy other, regularly priced merchandise. Loss leaders can form part of an effective marketing program, but as pointed out in the previous chapter, states with unfair-trade laws prohibit the practice.

Retailers frequently use a variant of loss-leader pricing called **leader pricing.** To avoid violating minimum-markup regulations and to earn some return on promotional sales, they offer so-called leader merchandise at prices slightly above cost. Among the most frequent practitioners of this combination pricing/promotion strategy are supermarkets and mass merchandisers such as Wal-Mart, Target, and Kmart. Retailers sometimes treat private-label products (like Sam's Choice colas at Wal-Mart stores) as leader merchandise since prices of the store brands average 5 to 60 percent less than those of comparable national brands. While store brand items generate lower per-unit revenues than national brands would produce, higher sales volume will probably offset some of the difference, as will related sales of high-margin products like toiletries and cosmetics.

The personal computer industry provides an excellent example of this trend in pricing. Little more than a decade ago, PCs cost up to $5,000. Then prices tumbled as demand accelerated and production economies associated with large production runs drove down costs. But the industry became embroiled in a brutal price war that saw Dell not only slash PC prices to under $400 but also throw in free printers, free Internet access, and free delivery. Working on razor-thin profit margins, competitors struggled to match Dell's plunging prices. Apple focused on product image and caught buyers' eyes with the attractive iMac design. Both Apple and IBM realigned their operations to provide services they could bundle along with the basic PC offerings. Compaq and Hewlett-Packard (HP) consolidated in order to compete. An economic slowdown, combined with a saturated U.S. market and consumer expectations of low prices, set the stage for long-term problems ahead. Today, an Apple iMac with a 17-inch monitor is priced at around $1,799 on the Apple Web site, while Dell continues to offer lower prices. A visitor to the Dell Web site may find free shipping for a limited time, along with a 10 percent instant rebate, so that desktop prices range between $800 and $1,100.[22] Hewlett-Packard CEO Carly Fiorina describes her company as "high-tech, low-cost" in comparison with her competitors. "I would describe IBM as high-tech, high-cost," while she dubs Dell as "low-tech, low-cost."[23]

4 Relate price to consumer perceptions of quality.

Marketers should anticipate two potential pitfalls when making a promotional pricing decision:

1. Some buyers are not attracted by promotional pricing.
2. By maintaining an artificially low price for a period of time, marketers may lead customers to expect it as a customary feature of the product. In the airline industry, for example, pervasive ticket discounting has taught consumers to expect to pay prices below full fare. One of the reasons many airlines are losing money is many travelers will fly only if they can get discounted fares.

I have discovered in 20 years of moving around a ballpark that the knowledge of the game is usually in inverse proportion to the price of the seats.

Bill Veeck (1914–1986)
American baseball team owner

PRICE-QUALITY RELATIONSHIPS

One of the most thoroughly researched aspects of pricing is its relationship to consumer perceptions of product quality. In the absence of other cues, price serves as an important indicator of a product's quality to prospective purchasers. Many buyers interpret high prices as signals of high-quality products. Prestige is also often associated with high prices. Fashion trend watchers report that each season a popular, expensive handbag emerges as the "It Bag." The bag always appears on the arms of celebrities and is so expensive that average consumers cannot afford it. One such Louis Vuitton bag sells for $3,550—and has been carried by Sarah Jessica Parker and rapper Eve. Adding to the mystique is a one-month waiting list, which means that by the time the bag arrives, the next "It Bag" will soon appear.[24]

The relationship between price and perceived quality provides a widely used tool for contemporary marketers. Figure 19.11 shows that the Rolex Cellini Cellissima in an 18-karat white gold case bedecked with more than 100 diamonds and a crocodile strap is priced at around $15,000. But Rolex, recognized as one of the premier watchmakers in the world, has been in business for nearly a century. Its cutting-edge designers made international headlines in 1926 with the famed Oyster watch, the first water-resistant watch. Chuck Yeager wore a Rolex when he broke the sound barrier in 1947, and Sir Edmund Hillary wore one when he climbed Mt. Everest.

Probably the best statement of the price-quality connection is the idea of price limits. Consumers define certain limits within which their product-quality perceptions vary directly with price. A potential buyer regards a price below the lower limit as too cheap, and a price above the higher limit seems too expensive. This perception holds true for both national brands and private-label products.

In some South American and Asian countries, hyperinflation during the past decade has left consumers little evidence of the relationship between price and quality. In Brazil during the mid-1990s, for example, a consumer could buy a deluxe ice cream sundae or two kitchen blenders for 950 cruzados ($15). Moreover, prices for a single product also varied tremendously from store to store. As a result, a consumer could end up paying anywhere from 2 cruzados ($0.03) to 22 cruzados ($0.33) for a pencil eraser.

figure 19.11

Rolex Cellini Cellissima Watch: Example of the Price-Quality Relationship

1. **Define *pricing policy.***
2. **Distinguish between price flexibility and product-line pricing.**
3. **What are loss leaders?**

COMPETITIVE BIDDING AND NEGOTIATED PRICES

5 Contrast competitive bidding and negotiated prices.

Many government and organizational procurement departments do not pay set prices for their purchases, particularly for large purchases such as U.S. Department of Defense orders for MREs (Meals Ready to Eat) to replace those used by troops assigned to Afghanistan, Iraq, and other overseas deployments. Instead, they determine the lowest prices available for items that meet specifications through **competitive bidding.** This process consists of inviting potential suppliers to quote prices on proposed purchases or contracts. Detailed specifications describe the good or service that the government agency or business organization wishes to acquire. One of the most important procurement tasks is to develop accurate descriptions of products that the organization seeks to buy. This process generally requires the assistance of the firm's technical personnel, such as engineers, designers, and chemists.

Ford has been particularly successful in supplying state and federal agencies with auto models that meet their price and performance specifications. At present, 85 of every 100 U.S. police cars are Crown Victorias. Many police units also use Ford Explorers, and some even drive Lincoln Navigators.

In some cases, business and government purchasers negotiate contracts with favored suppliers instead of inviting competitive bids from all interested parties. The terms of such a contract emerge through offers and counteroffers between the buyer and the seller. Successful negotiating is a skill requiring some practice, as described in the "Etiquette Tips for Marketing Professionals" feature.

When only one supplier offers a desired product or when projects require extensive research and development, buyers and sellers often set purchase terms through negotiated contracts. In addition, some state and local governments permit their agencies to skip the formal bid process and negotiate

ETIQUETTE TIPS — FOR MARKETING PROFESSIONALS

How to Ask for a Price Break

WE'VE all been there as consumers—wanting to purchase something, but the price is just too high for our budget. Or we intend to buy several similar items and we feel that a discount for the whole bundle would be appropriate. As a marketer, you may have opportunities to negotiate prices as part of your job; you may bargain for advertising, bargain for an event location, ask for a better rate on a hotel room, or negotiate fees for shelf space in a supermarket. How you approach the situation may determine whether or not you succeed. Here are a few tips from the experts on negotiating prices:

1. Be polite and cooperative, not confrontational. You are not trying to conquer the seller; you are trying to work with him or her.
2. Do not question the value of the product you are considering, only the price. You might say, "I'm sorry, but that's just beyond our budget right now." Or you can ask, "Can you do a bit better on the price?"
3. Show respectful interest in the product. Make the seller believe you are more apt to purchase the product if the price is lowered.
4. Don't act embarrassed about bargaining. Project a positive attitude about the exchange—you really want to make the deal and you just need a lower price.
5. Although it is often worthwhile to research prices for certain products in advance, don't try to use your own formula to figure out how much profit the seller is making on the sale. Instead, focus on how much the product is worth to you and your company.
6. Let the seller know that you would like to develop a long-term relationship between the two businesses, giving the seller incentive to negotiate a more favorable price.

Using these simple tips can help you succeed in negotiating prices. Remember, though: If you don't ask for a price reduction, the seller probably won't offer one.

Sources: Christina Binkley, "Hotels Raise Prices as Travel Picks Up," *The Wall Street Journal,* July 6, 2004, pp. D1, D8; Lawrence Lustig, "Bargaining Tips for Travellers," *Travel Library,* http://www.travel-library.com, accessed June 5, 2004; "Hotels: Tips on How to Get a Hotel Discount," *Savvy,* http://www.savvy-discounts.com, accessed June 5, 2004; Willie Crawford, "Ask for a Better Price," *Small Business News,* July 25, 2003, http://www.smallbusinessnewz.com; Kit Davey, "Bargaining 101," *Palo Alto Weekly Online,* May 9, 2003, http://www.paloaltoonline.com.

purchases under certain dollar limits—say $500 or $1,000. This policy seeks to eliminate economic waste that would result from obtaining and processing bids for relatively minor purchases.

NEGOTIATING PRICES ONLINE

Many people see the Internet as one big auction site. Whether it's toys, art, or automobiles, there seems to be an online auction site to serve every person's needs—buyer and seller alike. Auctions are the purest form of negotiated pricing. As Figure 19.12 shows, buyers and sellers electronically communicate ask and bid prices until a mutually agreed-upon price is set.

Ticket sales are an online auction favorite. Whether it is a Broadway show, a NASCAR Nextel Cup race, a trip to the zoo, or an OzzFest concert, you can find tickets online. Tickets.com catalogs the dates, times, and locations of everything from concerts to museum exhibits. It recently partnered with the Advantix ticketing system to open a sales site for sports venues. In addition, Tickets.com also functions as a reseller through its own online auctions.

However, some businesses are beginning to back away from auctions. "If you have rare and collectible items, auctions seem to be the way to go," says Brian Schell, president and owner of Replay Media, which employs just three people to sell secondhand books and music recordings. "But for things we sell that aren't rare but may not be available locally, fixed pricing seems to be the way to go."[25] Other sellers agree. Although eBay rose to prominence as an online auction site, today 40 percent of eBay's transactions take place at fixed prices. Shoppers may use the site's "Buy It Now" option to purchase an item at a set price without bidding, or they may visit the company's fixed-price subsidiary Half.com.[26]

1. What is competitive bidding?
2. What are some products typically found at an online auction?

figure 19.12

Online Auctions: Purest Form of Negotiated Pricing

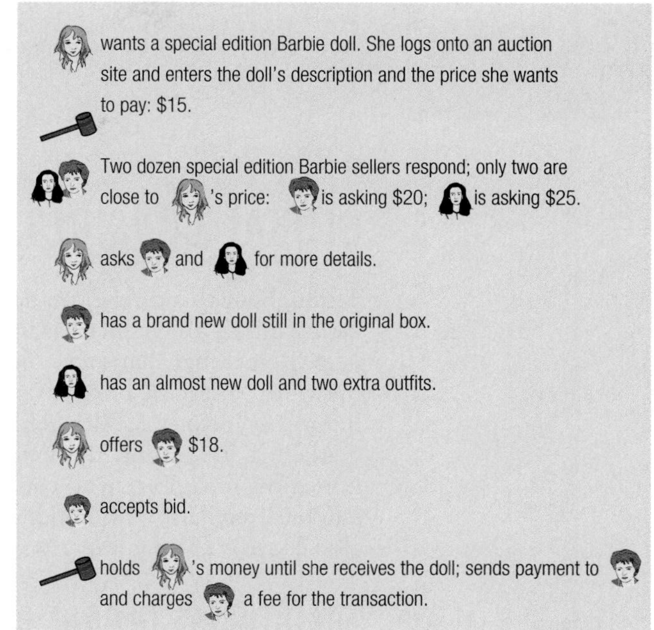

THE TRANSFER PRICING DILEMMA

A pricing problem peculiar to large-scale enterprises is the determination of an internal **transfer price**—the price for moving goods between **profit centers,** which are any part of the organization to which revenue and controllable costs can be assigned, such as a department. As companies expand, they tend to decentralize management and set up profit centers as a control device in the newly decentralized operation.

In a large company, profit centers might secure many needed resources from sellers within their own organization. The pricing problem thus poses several questions: What rate should profit center A (maintenance department) charge profit center B (production department) for the cleaning compound used on B's floors? Should the price be the same as it would be if A did the work for an outside party? Should B receive a discount? The answers to these questions depend on the philosophy of the firm involved.

(6) **Explain the importance of transfer pricing.**

Transfer pricing can be complicated, especially for multinational organizations. The government closely monitors transfer pricing practices because these exchanges offer easy ways for companies to avoid paying taxes on profits. Recent congressional investigations of the trend for U.S. firms to incorporate in Bermuda have focused on U.S. tax savings made possible by transfer pricing rates used between the firm's production location (U.S.) and its home country (Bermuda), even though no production takes place in Bermuda.

Figure 19.13 shows how this type of pricing manipulation might work. Suppose a South Korean manufacturer of DVD players sells its machines to its U.S. subsidiary for distribution to dealers. Although each unit costs $25 to build, the manufacturer charges the distributor $75. In

figure 19.13

Transfer Pricing to Escape Taxation

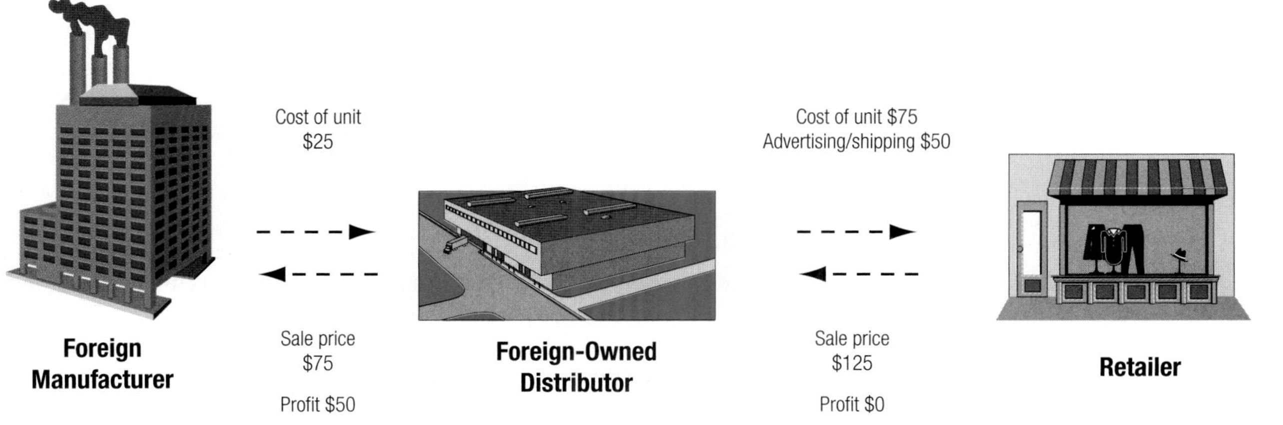

1. Define *transfer price.*
2. What is a profit center?

turn, the distributor sells the DVD players to retailers for $125 each. This arrangement gives the South Korean manufacturer a $50 profit on each machine, on which it pays taxes only in South Korea. Meanwhile, the American distributor writes off $50 for advertising and shipping costs, leaving it with no profits—and no tax liability.

GLOBAL CONSIDERATIONS AND ONLINE PRICING

Throughout this course, we have seen the impact of the Internet on every component of the marketing mix. This chapter has touched on the outer edges of the Internet's influence on pricing practices. Remember that every online marketer is inherently a global marketer who must understand the wide variety of internal and external conditions that affect global pricing strategies. Internal influences include the firm's goals and marketing strategies; the costs of developing, producing, and marketing its output; the nature of the products; and the firm's competitive strengths. External influences include general conditions in international markets, especially those in the firm's target markets, regulatory limitations, trade restrictions, competitors' actions, economic events, and the global status of the industry.

TRADITIONAL GLOBAL PRICING STRATEGIES

7 **Compare the three alternative global pricing strategies.**

In general, a company can implement one of three export pricing strategies: a standard worldwide price, dual pricing, or market-differentiated pricing. Exporters often set standard worldwide prices, regardless of their target markets. This strategy can succeed if foreign marketing costs remain low enough that they do not affect overall costs or if their prices reflect average unit costs. A company that implements a standard pricing program must monitor the international marketplace carefully, however, to make sure that domestic competitors do not undercut its prices.

The dual pricing strategy distinguishes prices for domestic and export sales. Some exporters practice cost-plus pricing to establish dual prices that fully allocate their true domestic and foreign costs to product sales in those markets. These prices ensure that an exporter makes a profit on any product it sells, but final prices may exceed those of competitors. Other companies opt for flexible cost-plus pricing schemes that allow marketers to grant discounts or change prices according to shifts in the competitive environment or fluctuations in the international exchange rate.

The third strategy, market-differentiated pricing, makes even more flexible arrangements to set prices according to local marketplace conditions. The dynamic global marketplace often requires frequent price changes by exporters who choose this approach. Effective market-differentiated pricing depends on access to quick, accurate market information.

Pharmaceutical marketers practice market-differentiated pricing in their global marketing strategies. While they cannot openly admit that they are levying a U.S. surcharge on the drug, marketers can set a high price on the treatment for wealthier patients in America while charging pennies for the same drug in needy areas of Africa.[27] However, it is more difficult to understand why some drugs are priced as much as 60 percent less in Europe or Canada than in the U.S. A month's supply of Claritin, for example, costs $17 in Canada and $13 in Australia, where it is available over the counter. American consumers—who until recently needed a prescription to get it—typically paid $62.[28]

CHARACTERISTICS OF ONLINE PRICING

To deal with the influences of the Internet on pricing policies and practices, marketers are applying old strategies in new ways and companies are updating operations to compete with new electronic technologies. Some firms offer online specials that do not appear in their stores or mail-order catalogs. These may take such forms as limited-time discounts, free shipping offers, or coupons that are good only online.

The Cannibalization Dilemma

By pricing the same products differently online, companies run the risk of **cannibalization.** The new twist to an old tactic is that companies are self-inflicting price cuts by creating competition among their own products. By building new e-businesses designed to compete head-on with the parent company, marketers are hoping to survive the transition from brick-and-mortar to electronic storefronts on the Web. Online securities trading company e.Schwab cannibalized its parent Charles Schwab when it offered online investors a flat $29.95 transaction fee. Traditional clients, who were still being charged $65 per trade, demanded and received the same flat fee.[29]

8 Relate the concepts of cannibalization, bundle pricing, and bots to online pricing strategies.

cannibalization
Loss of sales of an existing product due to competition from a new product in the same line.

Books-A-Million, the nation's third-largest bookstore chain, sells its top 20 bestsellers at 40 percent below list price. But click on the company's Web site, and you can buy the same books at discounts of 46 percent or more. Why sell books online at a lower price than you charge at the store? Books-A-Million's head of online marketing offers two reasons:

- It provides an additional channel to reach book buyers who do not regularly patronize their local Books-A-Million as well as those purchasers who live in areas with no BAM retail stores.
- It also represents a defensive move, since the company would rather have the business—even at extremely low margins—than lose it to Amazon.com.

Use of Shopping Bots

A second characteristic of online pricing is the use of search programs called **bots** or **shopbots**—derived from the word *robots*—that act as comparison shopping agents. Bots search the Web for a specific product and print a list of sites that offer the best prices. In online selling, bots force marketers to keep prices low. However, marketing researchers report that almost four of every five online shoppers will check out several sites before buying, and price is not the only variable they consider when making a purchase decision. Service quality and support information are powerful motivators in the decision process. Also, while price is an important factor with products such as books and CDs, it is not as important with complex or highly differentiated products, such as real estate or investment banking. Brand image and customer service may outweigh price in these purchase decisions.

BUNDLE PRICING

As marketers have watched e-commerce weaken their control over prices, they have modified their use of the price variable in the marketing mix. Whenever possible, they have moved to an approach called **bundle pricing,** where customers acquire a host of goods and services in addition to the tangible products they purchase.

bundle pricing
Offering two or more complementary products and selling them for a single price.

Concertgoers attending the recent Prince tour received more entertainment than they anticipated when they bought a ticket: a free copy of the artist's *Musicology,* a top 10 CD with total U.S. sales exceeding 2 million copies. Always more independent than most artists who often depend heavily on record companies to supply producers, songwriters, marketing, and money, Prince tabbed the typical industry model as "prehistoric and antiquated." As he put it, "All I ever said was, 'Let me drive.'" And drive he did, supplying the typical services of an independent record company, even owning the master recording—and with the assistance of his business partner, setting up the popular concert tour with the novel bundled price. A separate contract was signed with Columbia to handle U.S. distribution and license sales overseas—but the record company takes no cut of separate transactions, including the on-tour distribution. Columbia, with a proven marketplace name and no up-front guarantees, was happy with the partnership. As Prince's lawyer and business partner L. Londell McMillan points out, "Columbia is profitable from the first record sold because it didn't have to recoup unsold sums. We made a smart deal."[30]

Another typical example of bundled pricing is the selection of television stations you get through your cable or satellite TV service, as illustrated in Figure 19.14. At the lowest price level, you might receive the major networks, *Headline News,* your local public broadcast station, a home shopping channel, and one or two channels devoted to religious programming. As you move up to the next rung on the pricing ladder, you might get several sports channels, shopping channels, home and garden, cable news, and the like. As you climb, more channels are added to the package—MTV, Nickelodeon, Disney, HBO, and pay per view. But it seems that no matter which package you choose, you wind up with more channels than you need. "The average household watches no more than a dozen to 17 channels," notes Gene Kimmelman, head of Consumers Union, from a report compiled by the FCC. And because cable rates have been rising faster than the rate of inflation, critics of the bundle pricing practice are calling for reform. Cable subscribers "are being force-fed channels and features they don't want," argues Oregon's U.S. Senator Ron Wyden. Wyden and others in Congress are now calling for an "à la carte" pricing structure, which allows consumers to pick and choose the channels they want, paying only for those channels.[31]

figure 19.14

Cable TV Companies and Bundle Pricing

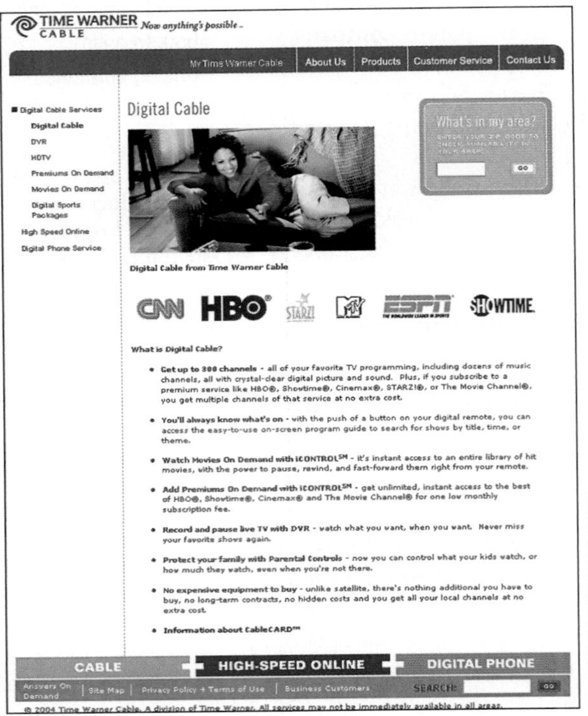

WWW.TIMEWARNERCABLE.COM

1. Identify some of the internal influences on global online prices.
2. Identify some of the external influences on global online prices.

Strategic Implications of Marketing in the 21st Century

PRICE has historically been the marketing variable least likely to be used as a source of competitive advantage. However, using price as part of a marketing program designed to meet a firm's overall organizational objectives can be a powerful strategy.

Technology has forever changed the marketplace, which affects the pricing function. Traditional geographic boundaries that allowed some businesses to operate have been broken by the Internet as well as mass merchandisers who offer a larger selection and lower prices. A customer in Wyoming might want to purchase an individually carved and painted walking cane from Kenya or an ornamental fan from Kyoto. Not a problem—the Web connects buyers and sellers around the globe. Similarly, the cost of shipping an overnight FedEx package from New York to California is no more than shipping it to a nearby city.

Not only is it possible to escape the boundaries of time and space on the Internet, but price is no longer a constant in the marketing process. With the increasing number of auction sites and search technologies like bots, customers now have more power to control the prices of goods and services. Consumers can find the lowest prices on the market, and they can also negotiate prices for many of the products they buy.

> ***Briefly Speaking***
>
> **What is a cynic? A man who knows the price of everything and the value of nothing.**
>
> *Oscar Wilde (1854–1900)*
> **Irish poet, playwright, and novelist**

To succeed, marketers must continue to offer value—fair prices for quality goods and services—and superior customer service. These are the critical success factors in marketing in the new millennium.

REVIEW OF CHAPTER OBJECTIVES

1 Compare the alternative pricing strategies and explain when each is most appropriate.

The alternative pricing strategies are skimming pricing strategy, penetration pricing strategy, and competitive pricing strategy. Skimming pricing is commonly used as a market-entry price for distinctive products with little or no initial competition. Penetration pricing is used when there is a wide array of competing brands. Everyday low pricing (EDLP), a variant of penetration pricing, is used by discounters that attempt to hold the line on prices without having to rely heavily on short-term coupons, rebates, and other price concessions. Competitive pricing is employed when marketers wish to concentrate their competitive efforts on marketing variables other than price.

1.1. Distinguish between a skimming pricing strategy and penetration pricing.
1.2. Why does EDLP stir debate among marketers and retailers?

2 Describe how prices are quoted.

Methods for quoting prices depend on such factors as cost structures, traditional practices in the particular industry, and policies of individual firms. Price quotes can involve list prices, market prices, cash discounts, trade discounts, quantity discounts, and allowances such as trade-ins, promotional allowances, and rebates. Shipping costs often figure heavily into the pricing of goods. A number of alternatives for dealing with these costs exist: FOB plant pricing, in which the price includes no shipping charges; FOB origin-freight allowed, or freight absorbed, which allows the buyer to deduct transportation expenses from the bill; uniform-delivered price, in which the same price, including shipping expenses, is charged to all buyers; and zone pricing, in which a set price exists within each region.

2.1. What is the difference between list price and market price?
2.2. Describe the three different types of allowances.
2.3. How does a basing-point system incorporate transportation costs?

3 Identify the various pricing policy decisions that marketers must make.

A pricing policy is a general guideline based on pricing objectives and is intended for use in specific pricing decisions. Pricing policies include psychological pricing, unit pricing, price flexibility, product-line pricing, and promotional pricing.

3.1. Describe the two different types of psychological pricing.
3.2. What are the benefits and potential pitfalls of price flexibility?
3.3. When does a price become a promotional price? What are the benefits and drawbacks of promotional pricing?

4 Relate price to consumer perceptions of quality.

The relationship between price and consumer perceptions of quality has been the subject of considerable research. In the absence of other cues, price is an important influence on how the consumer perceives the product's quality. A well-known and accepted concept is that of price limits—limits within which the perception of product quality varies directly with price. The concept of price limits suggests that extremely low prices may be considered too cheap, thus indicating inferior quality.

4.1. How does price relate to consumer perceptions of quality?
4.2. Give examples of your perception of an acceptable price range for a haircut, a deli sandwich, and toothpaste.

5 Contrast competitive bidding and negotiated prices.

Competitive bidding and negotiated prices are pricing techniques used primarily in the B2B sector and in government and organizational markets. Sometimes prices are negotiated through competitive bidding, in which several buyers quote prices on the same service or good. Buyer specifications describe the item that the government or B2B firm wishes to acquire. Negotiated contracts are another possibility in many procurement situations. The terms of the contract are set through negotiations between buyer and seller.

5.1. What is the difference between competitive bidding and negotiated price?
5.2. How has the Internet affected price negotiations?

6 Explain the importance of transfer pricing.

A phenomenon in large corporations is transfer pricing, in which a company sets prices for transferring goods or services from one company profit center to another. The term *profit center* refers to any part of the organization to which revenue and controllable costs can be assigned. In large companies whose profit centers acquire resources from other parts of the firm, the prices charged by one profit center to another will directly impact both the cost and profitability of the output of both profit centers.

6.1. In what ways does transfer pricing become complicated for a large organization?

7 Compare the three alternative global pricing strategies.

Companies can choose from three export pricing strategies: a standard worldwide price, dual pricing, or market-differentiated pricing. A standard worldwide price may be possible if foreign marketing costs are so low that they do not affect overall costs or if the price is based on an average unit cost. The dual pricing approach establishes separate domestic and export price strategies. Some exporters use cost-plus pricing methods to establish dual prices that fully allocate their true domestic and foreign costs to their product; others choose flexible cost-plus pricing. Market-differentiated pricing is the most flexible export pricing strategy, since it allows firms to price their products according to marketplace conditions. It requires easy access to quick, accurate market information.

7.1. What are the benefits and drawbacks of standard worldwide pricing?
7.2. What type of pricing strategy are pharmaceutical marketers likely to employ? Why?

8 Relate the concepts of cannibalization, bundle pricing, and bots to online pricing strategies.

To deal with the influences of the Internet on pricing policies and practices, marketers are applying old strategies in new ways, and companies are updating operations to compete with new electronic technologies. Cannibalization secures additional sales through lower prices that take sales away from the marketer's other products. Bots, also known as shopbots, act as comparison-shopping agents. Bundle pricing is offering two or more complementary products and selling them for a single price.

8.1. Give an example of bundle pricing.

MARKETING TERMS YOU NEED TO KNOW

skimming pricing strategy 629
penetration pricing strategy 631
competitive pricing strategy 632
allowance 636
FOB (free on board) plant (FOB origin) 637
FOB origin-freight allowed (freight absorbed) 638
uniform-delivered pricing 639
zone pricing 639
psychological pricing 640
promotional pricing 641
loss leader 642
cannibalization 647
bundle pricing 647

OTHER IMPORTANT MARKETING TERMS

market-plus pricing 629
everyday low pricing (EDLP) 632
list price 634
market price 634
cash discount 634
trade discount 635
quantity discount 635
cumulative quantity discount 635
noncumulative quantity discount 635
trade-in 636
promotional allowance 636
minimum advertised pricing (MAP) 636
rebate 636
postage-stamp pricing 639
basing-point pricing 639
pricing policy 639
odd pricing 640
unit pricing 640
price flexibility 640
product-line pricing 641
leader pricing 642
competitive bidding 643
transfer price 645
profit center 645
bots (shopbots) 647

PROJECTS AND TEAMWORK EXERCISES

1. Skimming pricing, penetration pricing, and competitive pricing are the three alternative pricing strategies. Divide your class into three teams. Then assign each team one of the three strategies and ask them to prepare a brief argument discussing the merits of their assigned pricing strategy for the following five products. Ask them to share their findings with the rest of the class. Once all three presentations have been completed, ask the class to vote on the most appropriate strategy for the products.
   a. video game
   b. digital television
   c. fuel additive that boosts automobile mileage
   d. monitored burglar, smoke, and fire alarm
   e. new brand of women's perfume or men's cologne
2. On your own or with a classmate, figure out how much it will cost to buy and own one of the following cars (or select another model):
   a. Toyota Prius
   b. Hummer
   c. Honda Accord
   d. Chrysler Crossfire
   e. Ford Explorer
3. Frequent-flyer programs are discount offers designed by airlines to secure and reward consumer loyalty. In what category of discount plans would you place these programs? Why? What potential dangers may limit the effectiveness of such programs?
4. How do sellers quote prices for each of the following products? In four teams, select one item per team. Research pricing practices within the industry and come up with a draft price quote.
   a. American Airlines ticket to Buenos Aires
   b. removing a 30-foot-high dead tree
   c. snowboard from a local dealer or an online dealer
   d. 23-foot Malibu motor boat (or something similar)
5. Assume that a product sells for $100 per ton and that Pittsburgh is the basing-point city for calculating transportation charges. Shipping from Pittsburgh to a potential customer in Cincinnati costs $10 per ton. The actual shipping costs of suppliers in three other cities are $8 per ton for Supplier A, $11 per ton for Supplier B, and $10 per ton for Supplier C. Using this information, answer the following questions:
   a. What delivered price would a salesperson for Supplier A quote to the Cincinnati customer?
   b. What delivered price would a salesperson for Supplier B quote to the Cincinnati customer?
   c. What delivered price would a salesperson for Supplier C quote to the Cincinnati customer?
   d. How much would each supplier net (after subtracting actual shipping costs) per ton on the sale?
6. On your own or with a classmate, visit a nearby supermarket. Choose one of the following types of products and chart the unit pricing for several different brands. Include in your chart the unit pricing for several sizes (if applicable) as well.
   a. bran flakes (or corn flakes) cereal
   b. laundry detergent
   c. dishwashing liquid
   d. salad dressing
   e. ice cream
7. Once you have the figures for the project described in Question 6, visit one or two more supermarkets and chart the unit pricing for the same product. Which supermarket is most expensive? Which is the least?
8. As an experiment in the relationship between price and quality, create a survey starting with the following products and adding four more of your own. Interview several consumers—members of your family, residents of your dorm or apartment, or other classmates and friends. Ask them the most they would pay for a quality item. Then ask them the lowest price they would pay before their perception of the item's quality would drop. Share your findings with the class.
   a. DVD player
   b. laptop computer
   c. cell phone
   d. leather jacket
   e. pair of jeans
   f. concert
9. Go online to eBay and browse through several auctions. In the auctions you browse, what is the percentage of items that are also listed as "Buy It Now"? Do you see a trend toward more fixed prices in certain product categories? Discuss your findings with the class.

APPLYING CHAPTER CONCEPTS

1. As a consumer, would you rather shop at a store that features a sale once a month or a store that practices everyday low pricing (EDLP)? Why?
2. Retailers of items like large appliances and furniture, as well as service providers like credit-card companies, have been offering zero percent financing to attract new customers. Is this a good deal for consumers? Why or why not? Do you think the practice will build long-term customer relationships? Why or why not?
3. Go online and search for some items that offer rebates. What types of products did you find? Do you think rebates are an effective enticement to purchase? Why or why not?

4. Flip through your local newspaper and note the prices for different types of products. Which firms seem to use psychological pricing? Do competing firms seem to use the same pricing policies?
5. Are you a bargain hunter, or do you routinely pay full price when you shop? Make a list of the items for which price is a major consideration in your purchase decision. Then make a second list of the products for which price is either secondary or hardly a consideration at all.

ETHICS EXERCISE

Recently, commission members from the European Union voted to fine Microsoft $618 million for doing business in such a manner that it blocked competition from other desktop PC software companies in Europe—in other words, creating a near monopoly. Microsoft uses bundle pricing to sell software packages that come with new PCs sold in Europe—a practice it also uses widely throughout the U.S., where it has been allowed. But European Competition Commissioner Mario Monti has been seeking to restrict bundling and wants the firm to release technical information that will make it easier for competitors to design server software that links together Windows PCs without Microsoft products. Microsoft plans to appeal the judgment, saying that the fine is "unprecedented and inappropriate" because it takes into account the firm's worldwide sales, not just its European sales.[32]

1. Do you agree with the position of the European Union or that of Microsoft? Why?
2. When can bundle pricing benefit consumers? When does it fail to create value?

'netWork EXERCISES

1. **Pricing strategies.** Visit several retailers who sell home audio and video equipment online. Examples include Best Buy (http://www.bestbuy.com), Circuit City (http://www.circuitcity.com), and Crutchfield (http://www.crutchfield.com). Check out several different products and brands, such as Bose and Sony. Do the prices of these products and brands vary from retailer to retailer? Do some brands cost the same regardless of where purchased? Why do prices vary for some product categories or brands but not for others?
2. **Price markups.** Assume you're in the market for a new car or truck. Visit Edmunds.com (http://www.edmunds.com). Pick two or three makes and models that interest you. Research the relationship between the invoice price and suggested retail price for each vehicle. Edmunds also includes something it calls the TVM® price for each vehicle. Is the TVM price closer to the invoice price or the suggested retail price? Summarize your findings and bring your report to class so you can participate in a discussion on pricing.
3. **Online auctions.** eBay is the largest and most successful of all the online auction sites. Visit the firm's Web site (http://www.ebay.com) and read about how auctions are conducted, how bids are entered, and how sellers are paid. Assume you have several items you would like to sell on eBay. How should you go about pricing your item to improve the chances of it selling for a good and fair price? Prepare a brief report on what you learned.

Note: Internet Web addresses change frequently. If you don't find the exact sites listed, you may need to access the organization's or company's home page and search from there or use a search engine such as Google.

INFOTRAC CITATIONS AND EXERCISES

Record: A114328603
What is music worth? If you think you're already paying too much for music, you should think again. *Andy Langer.*
Esquire, April 2004 v141 i4 p40 (2)

Abstract: Is it unreasonable for Lauryn Hill to expect fans to pay $15 for a single-song video that can be viewed only three times online? To music listeners accustomed to paying the same amount for an entire album of songs, Hill's pricey video play may seem absurd. Yet it is possible that Lauryn Hill has accidentally hit on an important truth: The biggest threat to the future of music is not piracy, it's pricing. In the minds of some analysts, consumers are not paying nearly enough for music. Such contrarian thinkers believe that music fans will get better quality music once they show they are willing to pay more.

1. How is price related to consumer perceptions of quality?
2. Why does the author think low prices are hurting the music industry?
3. According to the article, what would be the outcome of raising prices on music? Do you agree with this opinion? Why or why not?

CASE 19.1 Solving the Pricing Puzzle

It's hard to figure out why prices on some products soar while others crash. Demand, the economy, and pricing strategies all play a major part in determining how companies manage their pricing, but sometimes shoppers stand in the aisles of the supermarket or browse their favorite online sites and say, "Huh?" In general, prices for many durable goods such as automobiles, televisions, toys, sporting goods, and furniture have been declining, while prices for services such as insurance, healthcare, and a college education have been skyrocketing. In addition, some companies have adopted the strategy of charging the same price for less product. And some products are cheap to buy but expensive to maintain. All of these factors make it tough for consumers to figure out what's the best deal on the products they want to buy.

What about that new car or computer you've been putting off purchasing? Prices on many models have fallen. A Dodge minivan lists for $5,000 less than it did several years ago. Computer prices are down an overall 17 percent. But here's the catch: Car insurance is up 9 percent, while gas prices have topped off at an average of $2.00 per gallon.[33] And depending on what type of Internet service you decide to purchase for your new computer, your monthly bill could run anywhere from $10 to $50. Although manufacturers and service providers both have to cover rising labor costs, manufacturers have experienced record gains in productivity, offsetting the labor increases—whereas service providers have not. So the price of services will probably continue to rise.

If you're a Dannon yogurt fan, it's not your imagination: The containers are smaller. The standard 8-ounce containers have been replaced by 6-ounce containers. Although the price of the smaller container is lower—72 cents compared to 88 cents—the price per ounce is one cent more. Half-gallons of ice cream are disappearing as well. Edy's Grand has replaced its old 2 quart container with a 1.75 container, charging the same price for the new one. And if you pick up a container of Wisk liquid laundry detergent, it is lighter. The old container held 100 ounces, while the new one holds 80 ounces. Like the yogurt, the new Wisk size costs less—but more per quart.

Manufacturers insist that these adjustments are necessary to allow for increases in the cost of ingredients. "It's not just less yogurt," says Dannon spokesperson Anna Moses. "There are other things that go into the cost of a product." And Dannon claims that its customers like the new, smaller package. But in a survey of 2,000 consumers conducted by Supermarket Guru, 69 percent said they would rather have a price increase than receive less product. "From all the consumer surveys we do, people say, 'Raise the price and be honest with us,'" notes Phil Lempert, president of Supermarket Guru.

Sometimes consumers simply say no to price increases or volume reductions. They don't have to say a word to a store owner and they don't have to write a letter to a manufacturer. They just select lower priced items or don't buy the product at all. For several years, consumers have resisted paying $4 to $5 a box for branded cereal, selecting instead private-label brands at half the price. In one recent year, three of the four major food manufacturers—General Mills, Kraft Foods, and Quaker Oats—experienced a decline in sales of their cereals. In the end, firms must manage their prices so consumers continue to feel that they are getting the best value for their dollar—once they figure out the price.

Questions for Critical Thinking

1. As a consumer, how would you respond to the issue of reducing package size for a product but maintaining the price?
2. Do you think promotional pricing helps marketers gain customers in the case of durable goods like autos, computers, furniture, and the like? Why or why not? Why is it important for consumers to factor in the cost of maintaining these products?

Sources: Kathleen Madigan, "It Sure Doesn't Feel Like Low Inflation," *BusinessWeek,* May 19, 2003, p. 39; John E. Hilsenrath, "America's Pricing Paradox," *The Wall Street Journal,* May 16, 2003, p. B1; Stephanie Thompson, "Retailers Thwart Food-Price Hikes," *Advertising Age,* May 5, 2003, pp. 3, 35; Theresa Howard, "Pay the Same, Get Less as Package Volume Falls," *USA Today,* March 17, 2003, p. 3B.

VIDEO CASE 19.2 Jiffy Lube: The Well-Oiled Machine

The written case on Jiffy Lube appears on page VC-23. The recently filmed Jiffy Lube video is designed to expand and highlight the concepts in this chapter and the concepts and questions covered in the written video case.

Talking about Marketing Careers with Pat Gavin, Director of the Professional Golf Management (PGM) Program at New Mexico State University

A number of colleges and universities have introduced specialties within their marketing programs in which students apply their marketing and business backgrounds to nontraditional areas like sports. In a cooperative venture with the PGA, about 15 academic programs currently offer professional golf management (PGM) as an academic specialty for qualified students interested in a career in the golfing industry. To learn more about these programs, we visited with Professor Pat Gavin, director of one of the nation's first programs at New Mexico State University.

Boone & Kurtz: Tell us a little bit about yourself. What school and work experience led you to this position at NMSU?

While working on an MBA at New Mexico State University, I was fortunate enough to receive a graduate assistantship in the PGM program. Upon graduation, I moved to Phoenix to help develop and oversee a privately owned golf course management program. I was there for about three years when I learned of an opening at NMSU. I applied and was offered a position in 1993. I'm currently in my second decade of directing the program.

Boone & Kurtz: According to your Web site (http://cbae.nmsu.edu/~mktg www/pgm/pgm.htm), the professional golf management program's main goal is "to turn out the best educated and well-rounded future PGA Golf Professionals." How does the curriculum balance the golf instruction with traditional business classes?

The PGM curriculum requirements here at NMSU are that of a marketing degree. The difference that sets it apart is that we have added a series of golfing-related classes as electives. Classes such as Retailing, Merchandising, Turf Grass, Golf Course Landscape & Design, Food & Beverages of Country Clubs, and several PGA Education classes make up the core of the PGM electives. A student who successfully completes our PGM program earns a BBA with a major in marketing and a concentration in professional golf management. In addition to the 128-credit curriculum, students are also required to complete the PGA's Educational Program (which consists of three levels of testing), pass the PGA's Playing Ability Test, and work a minimum of 16 months of co-op (internship) at golf facilities all over the country. This is a very intense degree. Students find out quickly if this is the future for them.

PAT GAVIN, DIRECTOR OF THE PROFESSIONAL GOLF MANAGEMENT (PGM) PROGRAM AT NEW MEXICO STATE UNIVERSITY

PHOTO: COURTESY OF PAT GAVIN

Boone & Kurtz: Tell us more about your program, its size, and whether programs like yours are the typical approach for an individual to be trained as a golf professional.

NMSU's PGM program was launched in 1987 as the third university in the U.S. to offer a specialty in professional golf management. The first two schools were Ferris State University in Michigan and Mississippi State University; Pennsylvania State University's program began shortly after NMSU's as the fourth program. For several years, students had only four programs from which to choose. But during the past four years, 11 new schools have been added to the PGM network, increasing the total to 15 accredited PGA/PGM universities.

The traditional path to PGA membership involves working at an approved golf facility and completing the PGA's Educational Program. The PGM university offers qualified students the opportunity to become a PGA member while also earning a college degree in 4-1/2 years. Since 1987, we have graduated more than 450 PGM students. In recent years, about 20 students earn a degree in professional golf management each year.

Boone & Kurtz: What type of assistance do your graduates receive in finding employment?

Graduates receive assistance in finding co-op assignments as well as permanent jobs. As a matter of fact, we have a password-protected spot on our Web site, which allows our graduates to continue to receive information about job opportunities throughout the nation. We take pride in our alumni, and we try to help them continue to grow inside the golf industry.

Boone & Kurtz: Enrollment in the PGM program at New Mexico State University is limited to 300 students. The criteria spelled out for admission into the program are rigorous, both

academically and athletically. What is your advice for marketing students interested in gaining admission to the program?

Even though enrollment is capped at 300 students, we currently limit enrollment to about 200 students. With the addition of new PGM universities, students have more options regarding their choice of universities to attend. We pride ourselves in having the toughest admission requirements. True, it is a very rigorous degree, but our students learn early on the importance of time management. They are able to fit everything into a schedule that allows for class and study time as well as other PGM requirements and golf. My advice for an individual wanting to pursue this type of degree is to realize that it is a rigorous degree and not just playing golf every day. If a student wants to earn a college degree and pursue a job in the golf industry, then this is a perfect degree for them.

Boone & Kurtz: What kind of student does your program seek? Are most entrants typical college-age students, or do you prefer older students? What characteristics do you think a successful golf professional should possess?

Because of the rigorous degree, our program takes 4-1/2 years to complete. So it really attracts true incoming freshmen, but at the same time we do accept transfer students. To be a successful golf professional, you must have knowledge and experience in more than one area of the golf business. Merchandising, tournament operations, teaching, knowledge of the rules of golf, club repair, turf grass, food and beverage, and business planning are all very important areas in the golf business. Not only do we cover these areas in our curriculum, but students also gain hands-on experience from their co-op assignments.

Our goal at NMSU is to be viewed internally at the university as well as inside the golf industry as "the premier PGM university." With what we offer, I feel that we are meeting this goal.

Upon graduation, our students are expected to become golf professionals. The typical starting salary for someone coming out of a PGM program is between $24,000 and $27,000 a year. Those individuals can increase that with their golf lesson income. Within two to four years, they can move up to the position of head golf professional and from there continue to advance into a director of golf position. The ultimate goal would perhaps be to become the general manager of a facility.

Major League Soccer: The Price of Admission

Major League Soccer wants to continue showcasing the country's best soccer players in matches that draw fans to the stadiums in rising numbers. That means finding just the right price to make the ticket attractive.

The price of admission to an MLS game is a function of many factors. For MLS, a big one is player salaries. Like the National Football League, MLS has a cap on player contracts, which operates as a per-team limit of $1.73 million. Most players' earnings fall between a low of $24,000 to a high of $280,000, with an exceptional $500,000 a year being paid to teenage star Freddy Adu. Some U.S. players from the MLS have moved to European teams (most of which don't have caps) in pursuit of higher salaries, while others who stayed at home recently took pay cuts to newly lowered salaries.

With prices for hockey, basketball, baseball, and football tickets on a decade-long rise, many observers fear that average sports fans are being squeezed out of the game. A few college and professional teams have held or lowered their prices or introduced variable pricing, opponent pricing, and partial season plans, as well as enhancing season tickets with discounts, price breaks, complementary tickets, and preferred parking (for a fee). Others are increasing the number of inexpensive seats offered per game. "Instead of looking at making more money," says the senior associate athletics director of Arizona State University, "we are trying to fill all our seats at a lesser cost. If we get everybody in there and our team performs, they'll buy a Coke, a T-shirt, a program, and they'll come back." For ASU's football team, the strategy seems to be working; attendance rose 27 percent during a recent losing season. But the general price trend in these sports is still upward, and some team managers fear that cutting prices will cut revenue as well.

Prices for exhibition soccer matches, such as for Manchester United's annual tour, range from $30 to $125, partly due to travel expenses and the high costs of lavish accommodations. "Runaway salaries" dog the budgets of many European teams, and some are tying pay to performance (Man U limits salaries to 50 percent of its revenue), recruiting up-and-coming players at lower salaries, and turning over concessions and team shops for a fee to companies like Nike, adidas, and Puma. MLS counts Aquafina, Budweiser, Frito-Lay, Gatorade, Honda, Kraft, RadioShack, and Yahoo among its official sponsors. The league also earns money from its Chivas USA expansion team, which paid $15 million to share Home Depot Center's field with the L.A. Galaxy.

Regular single-game tickets for Chicago Fire home games range between $15 and $80. Executive suites offer entry to all home games for 12 to 30 people and include a host of amenities; they go for $15,000 to $30,000 a year. Columbus Crew offers six-game plans between $72 and $132 and also features less expensive youth tickets for those 18 and younger. Both teams offer various price packages. Dan Checketts, president of Utah Soccer LLC, offers a price range for the league's second expansion team, starting with a low of $8 per game, a high in the $20 range, and an average price between $14 and $15. With a special family package, said Checketts, "I have this dream that we're all going to be sitting in this great stadium with terrific views of the mountains and we won't have broken the bank to be there."

Questions for Critical Thinking

1. Do you think capping salary budgets for each team will help MLS avoid the high costs faced by European soccer teams? Why or why not? Is there any disadvantage to holding salaries down?
2. If you've attended a recent professional sports event, did you think you received good value for your ticket? Why or why not?
3. What are some of the costs MLS teams face besides player salaries and maintenance of their facilities?
4. What are some different price structures and strategies MLS could use to keep games affordable for fans?

Sources: Greg Boeck, "Teams Woo Fans with Cheaper Seats," *USA Today,* August 31, 2004, p. 3C; "Tickets," Chicago Fire Web site, http://chicago.fire.mlsnet.com, accessed September 27, 2004; "Tickets," Columbus Crew Web site, http://Columbus.crew.mlsnet.com, accessed September 27, 2004; "About MLS," Major League Soccer Web site, http://www.mlsnet.com, accessed August 2, 2004; Don Garber, "State of the League Address," Major League Soccer Web site, http://www.metrostars.mlsnet.com, accessed August 2, 2004; "MLS Exports Demonstrate League's Improvement While Diluting Talent Pool," *Sports Illustrated,* July 30, 2004, http://sportsillustrated.cnn.com; Jack Ewing with Laura Cohn, "Can Soccer Be Saved?" *BusinessWeek,* July 19, 2004, pp. 46–48; "MLS Quotesheet: Expansion Press Conference," *Sports Illustrated,* July 14, 2004, http://sportsillustrated.cnn.com; Grant Wahl, "Football vs. Fútbol," *Sports Illustrated,* July 4, 2004, pp. 68–72; Ridge Mahoney, "MLS Hits Road for Preseason," *USA Today,* February 18, 2004, p. C6; Amy Rosewater, "Manchester United Leads Soccer Invasion," *USA Today,* July 22, 2003, p. 3C.

appendix

Financial Analysis in Marketing

Without a yardstick, there is no measurement. And without measurement, there is no control.

—Pravin M. Shah (b. 1932)
Indian management consultant

A number of basic concepts from accounting and finance offer invaluable tools to marketers. Understanding the contributions made by these analytic tools can improve the quality of marketing decisions. In addition, marketers are frequently called on to explain and defend their decisions in financial terms. These accounting and financial tools can be used to supply quantitative data to justify decisions made by marketing managers. In this appendix, we describe the major accounting and finance concepts that have marketing implications and explain how they assist in making informed marketing decisions.

FINANCIAL STATEMENTS

All companies prepare a set of financial statements on a regular basis. Two of the most important financial statements are the income statement and balance sheet. The analogy of a motion picture is often used to describe an *income statement,* since it presents a financial record of a company's revenues, expenses, and profits over a period of time, such as a month, quarter, or year. By contrast, the *balance sheet* is a snapshot of what a company owns—called *assets*—and what it owes—called *liabilities*—at a point in time, such as at the end of the month, quarter, or year. The difference between assets and liabilities is referred to as *owner's, partners',* or *shareholders' equity*—the amount of funds the firm's owners have invested in its formation and continued operations. Of the two financial statements, the income statement contains more marketing-related information.

A sample income statement for Composite Technology is shown in Figure 1. Headquartered in a Boston suburb, Composite Technology is a B2B producer and marketer. The firm designs and manufactures a variety of composite components for manufacturers of consumer, industrial, and government products. Total sales revenues for 2006 amounted to $675 million. Total expenses, including taxes, for the year were $583.1 million. The year 2006 proved to be profitable for Composite Technology—the firm reported a profit, referred to as net income, of $91.9 million. While total revenue is a fairly straightforward number, several of the expenses shown on the income statement require additional explanation.

For any company that makes its own products (a manufacturer) or simply markets one or more items produced by others (an importer, retailer, or wholesaler), the largest single expense is usually a category called *cost of goods sold.* This reflects the cost, to the firm, of the goods that it markets to its customers. In the case of Composite Technology, the cost of goods sold represents the cost of components and raw materials as well as the cost of designing and manufacturing the composite panels the firm produces and markets to its business customers.

The income statement illustrates how cost of goods sold is calculated. The calculation begins with the value of the firm's inventory at the beginning of 2006. Inventory is the value of raw materials, partially completed products, and finished products held by the firm at the end of a specified time period, say, the end of the year. The cost of materials purchased by Composite Technology buyers during the year and the direct cost of manufacturing the finished products are then added to the beginning inventory figure. The result is cost of goods the firm has available for sale during the year. Once the firm's accountants subtract the value of inventory held by the firm at the end of 2006, they know the cost of

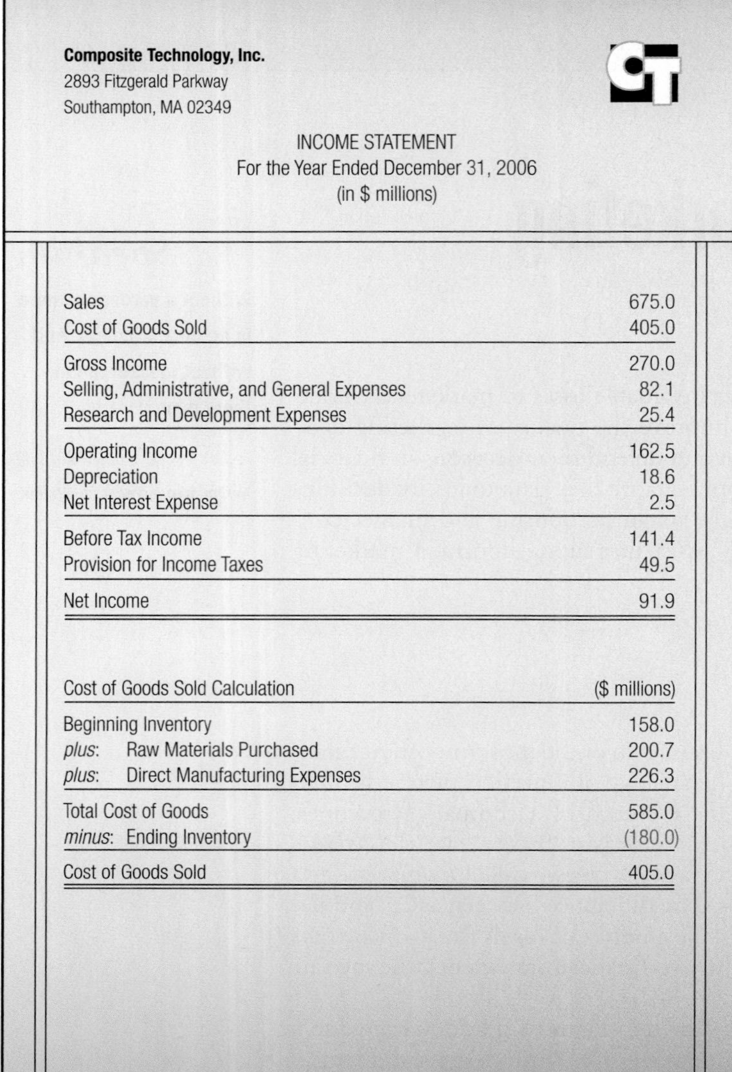

Composite Technology, Inc.
2893 Fitzgerald Parkway
Southampton, MA 02349

INCOME STATEMENT
For the Year Ended December 31, 2006
(in $ millions)

Sales	675.0
Cost of Goods Sold	405.0
Gross Income	270.0
Selling, Administrative, and General Expenses	82.1
Research and Development Expenses	25.4
Operating Income	162.5
Depreciation	18.6
Net Interest Expense	2.5
Before Tax Income	141.4
Provision for Income Taxes	49.5
Net Income	91.9

Cost of Goods Sold Calculation	($ millions)
Beginning Inventory	158.0
plus: Raw Materials Purchased	200.7
plus: Direct Manufacturing Expenses	226.3
Total Cost of Goods	585.0
minus: Ending Inventory	(180.0)
Cost of Goods Sold	405.0

figure 1

2006 Income Statement for Composite Technology, Inc.

goods sold. By simply subtracting cost of goods sold from total sales revenues generated during the year, they determine that Composite achieved gross profits of $270 million in 2006.

Operating expenses are another significant cost for most firms. This broad category includes such marketing outlays as sales compensation and expenses, advertising and other promotions, and other expenses incurred in implementing marketing plans. Accountants typically combine these financial outlays into a single category with the label *Selling, Administrative, and General Expenses.* Other expense items included in the operating expenses section of the income statement are administrative salaries, utilities, and insurance.

Another significant expense for Composite Technology is research and development (R&D). This includes the cost of developing new products and modifying existing ones. Firms such as pharmaceutical, biotechnology, and computer companies spend significant amounts of money each year on R&D. Subtracting selling, administrative, and general expenses and R&D expenses from the gross profit equals the firm's operating income. For 2006, Composite had operating income of $162.5 million.

Depreciation represents the systematic reduction over time in the value of certain company assets, such as production machinery, office furniture, or laptops provided for the firm's sales representatives. Depreciation is an unusual expense in that it does not involve an actual cash expenditure. However, it does reflect the reality that equipment owned by the company is physically wearing out over time from use and/or from technological obsolescence. Also, charging a portion of the total cost of these long-lived items to each of the years in which they are used results in a more accurate determination of the total costs involved in the firm's operation each year.

Net interest expense is the difference between what a firm paid in interest on various loans and what it collected in interest on any investments made during the time period involved. Subtracting depreciation and net interest expense from the firm's operating profit reveals the firm's *before tax income.* Composite had depreciation of $18.6 million and a net interest expense of $2.5 million for the year, so its 2006 taxable income was $141.4 million.

Profit-seeking firms pay taxes calculated as a percentage of their taxable income to the federal government, as well as state income taxes in most states, and—in some instances—city income taxes. Composite paid $49.5 million in taxes in 2006. Subtracting taxes from taxable income gives us the firm's *net income* of $91.9 million.

PERFORMANCE RATIOS

Managers often compute a variety of financial ratios to assess the performance of their firm. These ratios are calculated using data found on both the income statement and the balance sheet. Ratios are then compared with industry standards and with data from previous years. Several ratios are of particular interest to marketers.

A number of commonly used financial ratios focus on *profitability measures.* They are used to assess the firm's ability to generate revenues in excess of expenses and earn an adequate rate of return. Profitability measures include gross profit margin, net profit margin, and return on assets.

Gross Profit Margin

The gross profit margin equals the firm's gross profit divided by its sales revenues. In 2006, Composite had a gross profit margin of:

$$\frac{\text{Gross Profit}}{\text{Sales}} = \frac{\$270 \text{ million}}{\$675 \text{ million}} = 40\%$$

The gross profit margin is the percentage of each sales dollar that can be used to pay other expenses and meet the firm's profit objectives. Ideally, businesses would like to see gross profit margins that are equal to or higher than those of other firms in their industry. A declining gross profit margin may indicate that the firm is under some competitive price pressures or that its prices have not been adjusted to account for increases in raw materials or other product costs.

Net Profit Margin

The net profit margin equals net income divided by sales. For 2006, Composite had a net profit margin of:

$$\frac{\text{Net Income}}{\text{Sales}} = \frac{\$91.9 \text{ million}}{\$675 \text{ million}} = 13.6\%$$

The net profit margin is the percentage of each sales dollar that the firm earns in profit or retains after all expenses have been paid. Companies—and their shareholders—generally want to see rising, or at least stable, net profit margins.

The facts, all we want are the facts.

—Jack Webb (1920-1982)

***American actor* (as Sergeant Joe Friday in the 1950s television series *Dragnet*)**

Return on Assets (ROA)

A third profitability ratio, return on assets, measures the firm's efficiency in generating sales and profits from the total amount invested in the company. For 2006, Composite's ROA is calculated as follows:

$$\frac{\text{Net Income}}{\text{Average Assets}} = \frac{\text{Sales}}{\text{Average Assets}} \times \frac{\text{Net Income}}{\text{Sales}}$$

$$\frac{\$675 \text{ million}}{\$595 \text{ million}} \times \frac{91.9 \text{ million}}{\$675 \text{ million}} = 1.13 \times 13.6\% = 15.4\%$$

The ROA ratio actually consists of two components. The first component, called *asset turnover,* is the amount of sales generated for each dollar invested. The second component is *net profit margin.* Data for total assets are found on the firm's balance sheet.

Assume that Composite began 2006 with $560 million in assets and ended the year with $630 million in assets. Its average assets for the year would be $595 million. As was the case for the other profitability ratios, Composite's ROA should be compared with that of other firms in the industry and with its own previous performance to be meaningful.

Inventory Turnover

Inventory turnover is typically categorized as an *activity ratio* because it evaluates the effectiveness of the firm's resource use. Specifically, it measures the number of times a firm "turns" its inventory each year. The ratio can help answer the question of whether the firm has the appropriate level of inventory. Inventory turnover equals sales divided by average inventory. From the income statement, we see that Composite Technology began 2006 with $158 million in inventory and ended the year with $180 million in inventory. Therefore, the firm's average inventory was $169 million. The firm's inventory turnover ratio equals:

$$\frac{\text{Sales}}{\text{Average Inventory}} = \frac{\$675 \text{ million}}{\$169 \text{ million}} = 3.99$$

For 2006, Composite Technology turned its inventory almost four times a year. While a faster inventory turn is usually a sign of greater efficiency, to be really meaningful the inventory turnover ratio must be compared with historical data and appropriate peer firm averages. Different organizations can have very different inventory turnover ratios depending on the types of products they sell. For instance, a supermarket such as Safeway might turn its inventory every two weeks for an annual rate of 26 times per year. By contrast, a large furniture retailer is likely to average only about 2 turns per year. Again, the determination of a "good" or "inadequate" inventory turnover rate depends on typical rates in the industry and the firm's performance in previous years.

Accounts Receivable Turnover

Another activity ratio that may be of interest to marketers is accounts receivable turnover. This ratio measures the number of times per year a company "turns" its receivables. Dividing accounts receivable turnover into 365 gives us the average age of the company's receivables.

Companies make sales on either a cash or credit basis. Credit sales allow the buyer to obtain a product now and pay for it at a specified later date. In essence, the seller is providing credit to the buyer. Credit sales are common in B2B transactions. It should be noted that sales to buyers using credit cards such as MasterCard and Visa are included as cash sales since the issuer of the credit card, rather than the seller, is providing credit to the buyer. Consequently, most B2C sales are cash sales.

Receivables are uncollected credit sales. Measuring accounts receivable turnover and the average age of receivables are important for firms where credit sales make up a high proportion of total sales. Accounts receivable turnover is defined as:

$$\text{Accounts Receivable Turnover} = \frac{\text{Credit Sales}}{\text{Average Accounts Receivable}}$$

Assume that all of Composite Technology's sales are credit sales. Also assume that the firm began 2006 with $50 million in receivables and ended the year with $60 million in receivables (both numbers can be found on the balance sheet). Therefore, it had an average of $55 million in receivables. The firm's receivables turnover and average age equal:

$$\frac{\$675 \text{ million}}{\$55 \text{ million}} = 12.3 \text{ times}$$

$$\frac{365}{12.3} = 29.7 \text{ days}$$

Composite turned its receivables slightly more than 12 times per year. The average age of its receivables was slightly less than 30 days. Since Composite expects its customers to pay outstanding invoices within 30 days, these numbers appear appropriate. As with other ratios, however, receivables turnover and average age of receivables should also be compared with peer firms and historical data.

MARKUPS AND MARKDOWNS

In Chapters 14, 18, and 19, we discussed the importance of pricing decisions for firms. This section expands on our earlier discussion in Chapter 14 by introducing two important pricing concepts: markups and markdowns. They can help to establish selling prices and evaluate various pricing strategies and are closely tied to a firm's income statement.

Markups

The amount that a marketer adds to a product's cost to set the final selling price is the markup. The amount of the markup typically results from two marketing decisions:

1. The services performed by the marketer. Other things being equal, retailers who offer more services charge larger markups to cover their costs.

2. The inventory turnover rate. Other things being equal, retailers with a higher turnover rate can cover their costs and earn a profit while charging a smaller markup.

The markup included as part of a product's total price exerts an important influence on its image among present and potential customers. In addition, it affects the retailer's ability to attract shoppers. An excessive markup may drive away customers; an inadequate markup may fail to generate sufficient revenues needed by the retailer to cover costs and earn a profit.

Markups are typically stated as percentages of either the selling prices or the costs of the products. The formulas for calculating markups are as follows:

$$\text{Markup Percentage on Selling Price} = \frac{\text{Amount Added to Cost (Markup)}}{\text{Selling Price}}$$

$$\text{Markup Percentage on Cost} = \frac{\text{Amount Added to Cost (Markup)}}{\text{Cost}}$$

Consider a product with an invoice of 60 cents and a selling price of $1. The total markup (selling price less cost) is 40 cents. The two markup percentages are calculated as follows:

$$\text{Markup Percentage on Selling Price} = \frac{\$0.40}{\$1.00} = 40\%$$

$$\text{Markup Percentage on Cost} = \frac{\$0.40}{\$0.60} = 66.7\%$$

To determine the selling price knowing only the cost and markup percentage on selling price, a marketer applies the following formula:

$$\text{Price} = \frac{\text{Cost in Dollars}}{(100\% - \text{Markup Percentage on Selling Price})}$$

In the previous example, to determine the correct selling price of $1, the marketer would make the following calculation:

$$\text{Price} = \frac{\$0.60}{(100\% - 40\%)} = \$1.00$$

Similarly, you can convert the markup percentage for a specific item based on the selling price to one based on cost and the reverse using these formulas:

$$\text{Markup Percentage on Selling Price} = \frac{\text{Markup Percentage on Cost}}{(100\% + \text{Markup Percentage on Cost})}$$

$$\text{Markup Percentage on Cost} = \frac{\text{Markup Percentage on Selling Price}}{(100\% - \text{Markup Percentage on Selling Price})}$$

Again, data from the previous example give the following conversions:

$$\text{Markup Percentage on Selling Price} = \frac{66.7\%}{(100\% + 66.7\%)} = 40\%$$

$$\text{Markup Percentage on Cost} = \frac{40\%}{(100\% - 40\%)} = 66.7\%$$

Marketers decide on what they consider appropriate markups based on a number of factors:

- Typical markups on similar products offered by competitors

- Brand image of their product—which is influenced by price among other variables
- Number of marketing intermediaries in the channel and services performed by each
- Subjective judgments of the amounts that consumers will pay for a given product

When buyers refuse to pay a product's stated price, however, or when improvements in other products or fashion changes reduce the appeal of the current merchandise, a producer or retailer must take a markdown.

Markdowns

A markdown is a price reduction a firm makes on an item. Reasons for markdowns include sales promotions featuring price reductions or a decision that the initial price was too high. Unlike markups, markdowns cannot be determined from the income statement since the price reduction takes place before the sale occurs. The markdown percentage equals dollar markdowns divided by sales. For example, a retailer may decide to reduce the price of an item by $10, from $50 to $40, and sells 1,000 units. The markdown percentage equals:

$$\frac{(1{,}000 \times \$10)}{(1{,}000 \times \$40)} = \frac{\$10{,}000}{\$40{,}000} = 25\%$$

ASSIGNMENTS

1. Assume that a product has an invoice price of $45 and a selling price of $60. Calculate the markup as a percentage of both the selling price and the cost.
2. A product has an invoice price of $92.50. The seller wants to include a markup on the selling price of 25 percent. Calculate the selling price.
3. Assume a retailer decides to reduce the price of an item by $5, from $15 to $10, and sells 5,000 units. Calculate the markdown percentage.
4. Obtain a recent income statement and balance sheet for a business of your choosing whose stock is publicly traded. (A good source of recent financial statements is the MSN Investor Web site, http://investor.msn.com.) Use the relevant data included on the income statement to calculate each of the following ratios:
   a. gross profit margin
   b. net profit margin
   c. inventory turnover
   d. return on assets
   e. price markup
5. This appendix has described how the industry in which a firm operates affects its financial ratios. Solve this critical thinking exercise by matching the following set of financial ratios to each of the following firms: 3M, Gap, Pfizer, and Wal-Mart. Consider the industry in which each company operates and the way it is likely to affect profits, return on assets, and inventory turnover rates. For example, which of the four would you expect to have the lowest profit margin and which should have the highest profit margin?

FINANCIAL RATIO	FIRM A	FIRM B	FIRM C	FIRM D
Net profit margin	28.4%	3.5%	13.9%	6.5%
Return on assets	20.6%	8.6%	14.6%	10.0%
Inventory turnover	2.1	7.6	3.4	4.9

Video Case Contents

VIDEO CASE 1.2 TOYOTA'S HYBRID IS HIP WITH CUSTOMERS VC-2

VIDEO CASE 2.2 HEWLETT-PACKARD'S STRATEGIC PLANS SHINE IN B2B MARKETS VC-3

VIDEO CASE 3.2 GREEN MOUNTAIN COFFEE ROASTERS VC-4

VIDEO CASE 4.2 JOB-HUNTING IN THE DIGITAL AGE: MONSTER.COM VC-5

VIDEO CASE 5.2 VIDA WELLNESS SPA WISHES YOU WELL VC-6

VIDEO CASE 6.2 TECHNOMIC HELPS BUSINESSES SERVE GOOD FOOD VC-7

VIDEO CASE 7.2 DOC MARTENS MAKES STRIDES AROUND THE WORLD VC-9

VIDEO CASE 8.2 TEENAGE RESEARCH UNLIMITED HAS THE TRUE STORY ON TEENS VC-10

VIDEO CASE 9.2 ORANGE GLO CLEANS UP THE MARKETPLACE VC-11

VIDEO CASE 10.2 INTERNATIONAL FLAVORS & FRAGRANCES MAKES MARKETING PERSONAL VC-12

VIDEO CASE 11.2 CURVES: A NEW ANGLE ON FITNESS VC-13

VIDEO CASE 12.2 EVERYTHING IS BEAUTIFUL AT L'ORÉAL VC-15

VIDEO CASE 13.2 1-800-FLOWERS.COM: GREAT GIFTS BY PHONE OR ONLINE VC-16

VIDEO CASE 14.2 WESTFIELD GROUP CREATES A SHOPPER'S PARADISE VC-17

VIDEO CASE 15.2 JIMMY JOHN'S SANDWICH SHOPS GIVE CUSTOMERS SOMETHING TO CHEW ON VC-18

VIDEO CASE 16.2 RIDE THE WHITE WAVE WITH SILK SOYMILK VC-19

VIDEO CASE 17.2 CHICAGO SHOW, INC. PUTS ON A SHOW VC-20

VIDEO CASE 18.2 WRIGLEY'S GIVES EVERYONE SOMETHING TO CHEW ON VC-22

VIDEO CASE 19.2 JIFFY LUBE: THE WELL-OILED MACHINE VC-23

VIDEO CASE 1.2 Toyota's Hybrid Is Hip with Customers

Although younger auto buyers in Japan and the U.S. sometimes criticize Toyota styling as too "vanilla," the company's marketplace success indicates that its cars and trucks are on target with millions of purchasers. Toyota's well-known reputation for producing and marketing cars and trucks that people love has allowed it to leap over Ford into second place in global market share and even challenge General Motors for global dominance. Its vehicles are reliable, great on gas mileage, priced reasonably, and easy to drive. Toyota buyers are often loyal customers for all these reasons. So, when Toyota does something new, the auto world—and consumers—pay attention. It's true that hybrid vehicles—those that combine gasoline with electric power—have been around for a while. But not until the arrival of the Toyota Prius has there been a model that mainstream consumers would actually purchase and drive regularly. That success is due to Toyota's reputation for developing advanced technology that people can use and because of some skilled marketing.

Maybe you've seen the Toyota Prius around town. It has a distinctive body designed to accentuate the new generation of hybrid motor technology. Instead of simply putting a new engine in a Camry or Corolla body, Toyota's engineers designed a whole new look that people would notice and recognize immediately as a Prius. Built sleek and low to the ground like a sports car, the Prius has a spacious interior, delivers plenty of power, and lists for around $26,000. It also has features found on many conventional vehicles, such as keyless entry and startup. Toyota claims that the car can get up to 55 miles per gallon both on the highway and around town. An environmentally friendly vehicle appeals to conservation-minded consumers who are concerned about the consumption of fossil fuels and the preservation of the natural environment. But the technology of the Prius, which can operate either on gas or on electricity—or both at the same time—also appeals to mainstream consumers who want to preserve the environment, drive a convenient car, and cut their staggering gasoline expenditures. Toyota's marketers have their bases covered because the Prius appeals to both types of consumers.

The Prius has been an almost instant hit. When it made an appearance at the Academy Awards, celebrities immediately dubbed it the new trend. Because of this sudden and unexpected increase in demand, customers—including those Hollywood stars—had to wait up to six months after placing an order for the new car. *Motor Trend* awarded the Prius its coveted Car of the Year distinction over such entries as the Chrysler Crossfire, Cadillac XLR, and two series of new BMW models. Acknowledging that the selection of a hybrid vehicle was a first for *Motor Trend,* editor in chief Kevin Smith explained, "The Prius is a capable, comfortable, fun-to-drive car that just happens to get spectacular fuel economy. It also provides a promising look at a future where extreme fuel-efficiency, ultra-low emissions, and exceptional performance will happily coexist. That makes it meaningful to a wide range of buyers."

This type of success could not take place without building relationships throughout the marketing environment—among workers and the communities in which they live, with suppliers and dealers, industry experts, environmental groups, and the men and women who buy the vehicles. When demand for the Prius suddenly increased, dealers didn't have enough cars to satisfy their customers. One Toyota Motor Sales USA executive, Jim Press, pushed Toyota executives in Japan to increase production so that the company would not lose customers and damage relationships with its dealers. The company agreed and was able to boost production by 50 percent over a single 12-month period.

Toyota maintains a strong commitment to safe and environmentally friendly manufacturing methods as well as producing fuel-efficient vehicles. The firm welcomes input from workers and has developed strong relationships with environmental groups. "Toyota has placed great importance on protecting the environment," states its Web site. Nearly 99 percent of all scrap metal generated by Toyota plants is recycled, and the vehicles themselves are 85 percent recyclable. In addition, the firm seeks ways to reduce waste, such as applying paint with a roller rather than a sprayer, a process that reduces paint consumption by 40 percent. Consumers and environmental groups alike gravitate toward Toyota because of these practices. Toyota—and the Prius—have also won awards from groups like the National Wildlife Federation, the Sierra Club, and even the EPA. This commitment to the environment extends to the firm's relationship with its suppliers. "Toyota has a unique relationship with its suppliers," says Teruyuki Minoura, president and CEO of Toyota Manufacturing North America Inc. "We are known for expecting them to share our high-quality standards. Now we are asking them to join us in becoming environmental leaders." The Green Supplier guidelines developed by Toyota require suppliers to comply with a chemical ban list and ensure that hazardous materials are transported safely, according to Toyota's standards.

Instead of simply reacting to changes in the marketing environment, Toyota has taken a proactive role in improving its manufacturing processes, developing better cars, and building strong relationships. The Prius isn't a novelty—it's just the beginning of a whole new breed of cars.

Questions for Critical Thinking

1. How does Toyota create utility for consumers?
2. In what ways does Toyota practice relationship marketing?
3. How would you describe the role of critical and creative thinking in developing the Prius?
4. As a consumer, would you purchase a Prius? Why or why not?

Sources: Company Web site, http://www.toyota.com, accessed November 4, 2004; Kathleen Kerwin, "How to Market a Groundbreaker," *BusinessWeek,* October 18, 2004, pp. 104, 106; Alex Taylor III, "Toyota's Secret Weapon," *Fortune,* August 23, 2004, pp. 60–66; "*Motor Trend* Announces 2004 Car of the Year," *Motor Trend,* November 20, 2003, http://www.motortrend.com; Brian Bremner and Chester Dawson, "Can Anything Stop Toyota?" *BusinessWeek,* November 17, 2003, pp. 114–122.

VIDEO CASE 2.2

Hewlett-Packard's Strategic Plans Shine in B2B Markets

It takes creative minds to map out strategic plans in the computer industry. Technology and consumer preferences change so rapidly that marketers must remain nimble on their feet at all times to gain—and maintain—an advantage over competitors. Even in the business-to-business market, where purchase decisions are usually more deliberate and involve a number of decision makers, computer firms must be prepared to identify the problems and opportunities of their customers and design solutions for them.

At Hewlett-Packard, a technology giant founded in 1939 by Stanford University classmates Bill Hewlett and Dave Packard, marketers understand the importance of strategic planning for the business market. One of the company's early customers was Walt Disney Studios, which purchased eight units of HP's first product—an audio oscillator used by sound engineers—to test a new sound system for its movie *Fantasia.* Jump to 1966, when HP introduced its first computer, which gave its customers the ability to computerize instrument systems for science, manufacturing, and other fields. Woods Hole Oceanographic Institute purchased one to use aboard its research vessel. In 2002, HP merged with Compaq and is now able to serve more than 1 billion customers—consumer and business—in 162 countries.

HP is still guided by the original mission and corporate objectives that were formulated by founders Bill Hewlett and Dave Packard, even though CEO Carly Fiorina is now at the helm of the company. "It is necessary that people work together in unison toward common objectives," Hewlett and Packard wrote. Regarding customer loyalty, the firm strives to "provide products, services, and solutions of the highest quality and deliver more value to our customers that earns their respect and loyalty." In the realm of market leadership, HP intends to "grow by continually providing useful and significant products, services, and solutions to markets we already serve—and to expand into new areas that build on our technologies, competencies, and customer interests." Other objectives involve profitability, employee commitment, company leadership, and global citizenship. Each objective is supported by specific beliefs and strategies as outlined by the firm's founders.

One of HP's major strategies has been to target and serve small and medium-sized businesses—those with fewer than 1,000 employees—while maintaining a presence in the large business and consumer markets. "SMB [small and midsize business] customers around the world tell us that productivity, reliability, and affordability are the three issues that matter most to them when it comes to their IT [information technology]," notes Carly Fiorina. To fulfill those needs, HP recently launched an array of products, including PCs, data storage equipment, printers, support services, and financing services for small businesses. Tom Kucharvy, an analyst with *Summit Strategies,* praises the move because these companies are rapidly increasing their spending on technology. "It's the fastest-growing segment of the market," he observes.

HP isn't the only firm targeting this market. Competitors IBM, Dell, and Gateway have launched similar efforts. But HP now has Compaq in its stable, and Compaq has a strong history with customers in this market. One of the products HP has introduced is the HP Compaq Business Notebook nx5000, a laptop with Intel Centrino mobile technology and—perhaps most important—a battery life of up to nine hours, or one full workday. There's also a new desktop computer, the HP Compaq Business Desktop dx2000 microtower, along with low-cost switches for storage area networks (SANs), and an "affordable entry-level server" called the HP ProLiant ML110. The whole idea is to give small and midsize firms the capability to perform like their larger counterparts—at a reasonable price.

In a move that takes HP back to its entertainment roots, the firm has also announced partnerships with Warner Brothers and DreamWorks, in which it will design software and special services for the creators of content at these two Hollywood companies. HP hopes that Warner and DreamWorks will select its products for every stage of the production process, from creating animated characters to restoring film classics. Rob Enderle, principal analyst at the Enderle Group, compliments this strategic move. "[HP is] the only large-scale vendor that is still interested in [Hollywood] and capable of providing this kind of solution," he says.

Finally, in another component of HP's overall strategy, the firm has acquired the British computing services company Synstar, whose business customers include Audi, DuPont, Vodafone, Volkswagen, Grolsch, and London Taxis International. In addition, HP has acquired a similar German firm called Triaton. These moves should help Hewlett-Packard enhance its capabilities to serve customers throughout Europe. "Our strategy is to offer products, services, and solutions that are high tech, low cost and deliver the best customer service," claims the Web site. HP is doing its best to deliver on all three fronts.

Questions for Critical Thinking

1. Describe one or two tactics that HP might use as part of its strategy for expanding its presence in the entertainment market.
2. HP still abides by the mission objectives outlined by its founders almost 70 years ago. Do you think these should be revised? Why or why not?
3. What do you think are HP's core competencies?
4. This case identifies a large target market: small to midsize businesses. Within that market, describe an industry that you think could benefit from HP's products. How might HP help these businesses serve their customers?

Sources: Company Web site, http://www.hp.com, accessed November 4, 2004; "Continuing Its Effort to Reach Smaller Business, Hewlett-Packard Plans to Announce on Monday a Slew of New Offerings," *ZDNet,* http://news.zdnet.com, accessed November 4, 2004; "HP Buys British Services Company Synstar," *CNET News.com,* October 1, 2004, http://news.com.com; "Hewlett-Packard Goes Hollywood," *Wired News,* April 19, 2004, http://www.wired.com.

VIDEO CASE 3.2 Green Mountain Coffee Roasters

More than two decades ago, Robert Stiller visited a coffee shop in Waitsfield, Vermont, where he drank a cup that was so good he bought the coffee shop. Stiller, an entrepreneur, had recently sold another business and settled in Vermont because he was an avid skier. When he walked into the coffee shop—where the coffee was roasted on site—he smelled the sweet aroma of success. "I liked the idea that the product would be consumed, because if you do a great job, people will keep coming back," Stiller recalls. "I felt if you provide the best quality and service in whatever you pursue, you're going to do well." Within a few years, he'd bought a second coffee shop and founded Green Mountain Coffee Roasters, which—in addition to operating as retail shops—began wholesaling fresh-roasted coffee to restaurants and other outlets. When consumers complained of difficulty in going directly to the two Green Mountain Coffee shops and began to clamor for their favorite joe at home, the firm's mail-order business was born. Today, consumers can find all the flavors of Green Mountain Coffee in a variety of places—from restaurants and inns to doctors' offices and the Internet.

But just selling coffee isn't enough. Within two decades, the marketing environment had become amazingly complex. Competition from other firms like Starbucks is fierce, regulations govern international trade with coffee growers, economic factors affect how much consumers are willing to pay for premium coffee, and cultural factors may determine consumer preferences. Stiller and his executives must continually collect information about the marketing environment to provide the high-quality products that consumers want.

In addition, Green Mountain is well known for its ethical business practices and its commitment to social responsibility. Not long after Green Mountain was founded, a group of employees formed an environmental committee that became the foundation for the firm's social responsibility projects. The committee began with initiatives to turn off lights and turn down the heat in the company's offices to save energy. Then they redesigned some of the firm's shipping boxes to reduce weight—which also reduced costs. Next they came up with the idea for Rain Forest Nut coffee, the sale of which helped develop public awareness of the depletion of rain forests in South America *and* raised money for the Rainforest Alliance and Conservation International. (Historically, rain forests have been cleared by coffee farmers to produce additional spaces for growing more coffee.) Consumers loved the taste of Rain Forest Nut coffee, as well as the philosophy behind it, and sales took off.

As Green Mountain got more and more involved with rain-forest conservation, the firm developed alliances with coffee farmers, who agreed to specific conservation and quality criteria in return for guaranteed business. For example, to preserve the environment, the coffee is grown in the shade—which preserves habitats for certain birds and helps reduce global warming. Currently, Green Mountain is the world's largest supplier of double-certified coffee—products that meet qualifications for being organic as well as those of the Fair Trade initiative. Fair Trade certification signifies that coffee growers have been paid a fair price for their product, which means they can feed and clothe their families, send their children to school instead of requiring them to work in the fields, and use more environmentally sound farming practices.

Green Mountain donates 5 percent of its pretax earnings to nonprofit organizations and causes. The firm also creates alliances with these organizations or other companies for certain community projects. With the National Wildlife Federation, Green Mountain recently introduced two new shade-grown, Fair Trade coffees called National Wildlife Blend and National Wildlife Blend Decaf. Together, the two organizations are promoting the coffees as well as the link between the shaded coffee environments and the health of migratory birds that live there. Green Mountain is also an active supporter of Coffee Kids, an organization that works to improve the quality of life for children and families in the coffee-growing communities. Some of the Coffee Kids programs have included education, healthcare, hurricane relief, and funding for small businesses.

All the good business ethics and social responsibility projects in the world wouldn't amount to a hill of coffee beans if Green Mountain weren't a great place to work. Green Mountain has been ranked by *Forbes* magazine as one of the "200 Best Small Companies in America" four years in a row, and *Business Ethics* recently ranked Green Mountain fifth overall in its list of "100 Best Corporate Citizens." Company culture embraces teamwork, personal growth, and fun. And Green Mountain pays its employees for time they spend volunteering for various social responsibility programs.

Ethics and social responsibility are an integral part of Green Mountain's overall marketing strategy, which seeks to promote the highest quality products in a way that preserves the natural environment and enhances the well-being of people in need around the world. "We have distinguished ourselves with our focus both on superior execution and being a responsible corporate citizen," says Robert Stiller, "and now we can leverage these positions to competitive advantage."

Questions for Critical Thinking

1. Give two examples of the following types of competition faced by Green Mountain: direct competition and competition among substitute goods.
2. Describe how at least two major economic factors might affect Green Mountain's marketing decisions.
3. Design a label for one of Green Mountain's coffees: Autumn Harvest, Joyful Season, or Breakfast Blend. Include references to the firm's social responsibility projects and its ethical practices.
4. Give an example of each of the four levels of the social responsibility pyramid that you think is fulfilled by Green Mountain.

Sources: Company Web site, http://www.gmcr.com, accessed October 20, 2004; Adrienne Fox, "Green Mountain Coffee Roasters," in "50 Best Small & Medium Places to Work," *HR Magazine,* July 2004, http://www.shrm.org/hrmagazine; "Green Mountain Coffee Roasters Ranked #9 on List of Best Medium Companies to Work for in America," *Business Wire,* June 29, 2004, http://www.businesswire.com; "Green Mountain Coffee Roasters Now #5 on *Business Ethics* Magazine's List of Best 100 Corporate Citizens," *Business Wire,* May 4, 2004, http://www.businesswire.com; Virginia Lindaur Simmon, "Java Man," *Business People Vermont,* February 2, 2003, http://www.vermontguides.com.

VIDEO CASE 4.2 Job-Hunting in the Digital Age: Monster.com

"Life is too short not to enjoy what you do every day." This is an old adage with a contemporary twist: It has appeared on the home page of Monster.com, the Web site where employers and job-seekers meet each other online. Founded a decade ago in Massachusetts by Jeff Taylor, Monster.com initially had plenty of skeptics. How could anyone possibly find a job on the Internet? Who would hire someone they found on the Internet? To many people—including marketers, managers, and human resource professionals—the idea looked like just another of the hundreds of poorly planned business launches destined to become dot-com bombs. But it wasn't. Despite the initial dot-com boom and bust, Monster.com stayed tough. Now that e-commerce and other Internet activities are everyday occurrences, Monster has become one of the leading global career Web sites, receiving more than 41 million visits last year. Monster's goal is to link the "most progressive companies with the most qualified, career-minded individuals." To do so, the firm's global network operates local content and language sites in 15 countries, from the U.S. to India to Finland.

Since its inception, the services that Monster offers have grown tremendously. Job-seekers can log on to the site to search job postings and submit their résumés—Monster typically has more than 800,000 jobs posted at any one time—but they can accomplish much more as well. They can find detailed information on creating a résumé, network with other professionals, learn about different fields, and get career advice. On the other side of the job-hunting coin, employers who use Monster.com have instant access to thousands of qualified potential candidates who have been screened by the Web site.

Businesses and job-seekers didn't automatically flock to Monster.com, especially in the beginning. Marketers had to convince them that the whole idea was valid and then convince them that the Monster.com site could provide the best available services. So the firm came up with a marketing program that combined online efforts with traditional marketing channels such as direct marketing and advertising. Several years ago, Monster.com marketers took a huge risk and spent millions to purchase commercial time during the Super Bowl. Other dot-com ads on this most expensive of all advertising media failed, but Monster's "When I grow up" ad was a success. Within 24 hours following its airing on the Super Bowl, Monster experienced a 450 percent increase in job searches. So, the firm tackled the time slot again, purchasing four spots for $3 million. In addition, a Monster.com "ground crew" visited college football games and tailgating parties to get the word out to graduating seniors that the site was a good place to start their job search.

Monster.com is a bigger brand now, with considerably more clout. Its budget for global television, print, and online advertising, as well as direct marketing and other promotions, runs about $125 million per year. Its most recent campaign, called "Today's the Day," is designed to "encourage job seekers and employers to seize the day and not put off looking for a new job," says Carole Johnson, the firm's senior vice president for marketing. "It's also a very memorable line that can extend across advertising, promotions and sponsorships, both offline and online," she continues. On the site itself, job candidates can click a box that begins with the statement, "Today's the day I . . . " and select options that finish the sentence, such as "plan my relocation," "network with new people," or "find a new job." Each of those options provides tips on how to accomplish the task, as well as information about specific companies and other resources. If the person wants to find a job in a company that values diversity, the "diversity & inclusion" page offers listings by location and job category, as well as providing information on lucrative or popular fields. The "résumé center" page offers tips on how to create the best résumé—complete with sample résumés, examples of cover letters, expert advice, and tips for mastering tough résumé issues.

In addition to expanding its marketing programs, Monster.com has acquired other firms that complement its core business. The company recently purchased Tickle, a career assessment Web site with 18 million members. Monster.com also acquired India's JobsAhead.com, bolstering its presence in this huge Asian market.

In the last decade, Monster.com has helped launch an entirely new way for job-seekers and employers to connect. "Think Big. Be Happy," advises the company's site. It sounds as though Monster.com has been following a bit of its own advice.

Questions for Critical Thinking

1. Why is interactive marketing so important to Monster .com's business? Does Monster.com practice interactive marketing effectively?
2. In what ways does Monster.com practice B2B e-commerce?
3. What challenges might Monster.com face as it attempts to match employers and employees on a global basis?
4. Would you apply for a job through Monster.com? Why or why not?

Sources: Company Web site, http://www.monster.com, accessed October 22, 2004; "Monster.com Buys Tickle, Said to Be Near Another Buy," *Boston Business Journal,* May 25, 2004, http://boston.bizjournals.com; Kate Maddox, "Monster Boosts Ad Budget to $125 Million," *BtoB,* January 19, 2004, http://www.btobonline.com.

VIDEO CASE 5.2 Vida Wellness Spa Wishes You Well

Maybe you've never been to a spa. Maybe the juice bar attached to your gym is the closest you've come to the experience. Or perhaps you've ventured out for a facial or a pedicure. But even if you've never heard of Ayurvedic treatments or thought about having an exotic kona coffee exfoliation, Vida Wellness Spa wants you to consider the benefits of the spa experience.

As a consumer, you are subject to many influences that shape your attitudes toward the idea of a spa experience. Whether you consider it a luxury or a necessity, whether you continue to be an outside observer or become a loyal customer has much to do with the various influences on your behavior—including social influences like reference groups, personal friends, and family influences such as the household member who is most likely to make the purchasing decisions. Since British Columbia–based Vida Wellness is considered a first-class luxury spa, your decision about whether you become a customer will be influenced by cost as well. If you are a college student, the decision to take a spa-based vacation is likely to be a high-involvement purchase decision. By contrast, if you have a comfortable income, the involvement might not be quite as high.

The Vida Wellness Spa isn't your average spa where you can duck in for a quick manicure or massage. Instead, it offers a unique array of holistic treatments based on 5,000-year-old Indian health management principles called Ayurveda. According to the Ayurvedic philosophy, every human being inherits a unique combination of three elements that must remain in balance for optimal health. When those elements are tipped out of balance, ill health—or at least, less than optimal health—results. Ayurvedic treatments are designed to help restore this overall balance.

The first task Vida Wellness faces in attracting clients is education-based. The firm's marketers must inform them about the difference in Ayurveda and traditional spa methods and the benefits they will gain from these treatments. The objective of these efforts to educate potential clients is to change their behavior through trial visits.

For example, a massage at Vida Wellness isn't just a massage. Customers select from among a variety of choices ranging from a Swedish sports massage or a water massage to an ancient lava rock massage. And exfoliation isn't just a matter of peeling off old skin cells. Instead, exfoliation comes in flavors—kona coffee, warm ginger, orange, and wild rose, to name a few. Clients who choose the body sugar exfoliation get the full treatment—a full-body massage with a solution that combines cinnamon, lemon, and maple sugar. This is followed by a massage with essential oils of almond, peppermint, and sunflower. The treatment concludes with a maple body lotion and a spritz of glacier water—all designed to make even the most stressed and weary spa visitor feel energized but relaxed.

Who are Vida Wellness' customers? Generally, they are affluent, with a few celebrities appearing from time to time. And Vida claims that 40 percent of its clientele are men. Companies and not-for-profit organizations that want to treat their employees or members to a special day may sign them up for various treatments. These guests love the pampering. "It's so relaxing and enticing to the senses," says one businesswoman who was treated to the spa by the Vancouver Board of Trade. To serve its clients, Vida Wellness has spas in prime locations, such as the hotel Fairmont Chateau Whistler, where well-heeled travelers might enjoy an evening of pampering after a day on the ski slopes. Another Vida spa is located in Wall Centre One, a tony hotel and condominium complex in downtown Vancouver's tallest tower. Spa staff are well paid and are expected to appear radiant and impeccably groomed themselves, reflecting the well-being that Vida Wellness encourages.

A trip to the Vida Wellness Spa is a luxury, but one that its owners hope will be viewed by its customers as an integral part of their lives. "We are dedicated to helping our customers achieve and maintain balance," explains Kristina Hewlett, manager of Vida's Spa Services. "We go beyond the traditional spa experience by blending a holistic approach of Ayurveda with modern education and treatments."

Questions for Critical Thinking

1. Have you ever been to a spa? Why or why not? As a consumer, what is your perception of spas in general? What is your perception of Vida Wellness?
2. How might cultural influences affect a consumer's decision to go to a Vida Wellness Spa?
3. How would Vida Wellness be categorized on Maslow's hierarchy of needs? How might this categorization influence a consumer's attitude toward Vida Wellness?
4. Using the six steps in the consumer decision process, describe how a consumer might make the decision to try a spa treatment at Vida Wellness.

Sources: Company Web site, http://www.vidawellness.com, accessed July 30, 2004; Stephanie Morgan-Black, "Members' Reception at Vida Wellness Spa," The Vancouver Board of Trade, January 27, 2004, http://www.boardoftrade.com; Alexandra Gill, "Vida Wellness Spas, B.C.," *The Globe and Mail,* January 11, 2003, http://www.theglobeandmail.com.

VIDEO CASE 6.2 Technomic Helps Businesses Serve Good Food

When you sit down in a booth at your favorite chain restaurant to order dinner, you know what to expect: good food, attentive service, fair prices. As you cruise the aisles of your local supermarket, you select your favorite brand and variety of salad dressing and then grab a box of that breakfast cereal you've been eating since you were a kid. Many marketing decisions have gone into the selection of products to include on restaurant menus and retail store shelves, the way they are presented and promoted, and the way they are priced before you take a bite. While some firms conduct their own marketing research to determine who their customers are and how to reach and serve them, others hire outside specialists to do the job. Technomic is one such specialist. Founded in 1966, the Chicago-based firm supplies its business clients with services such as customer satisfaction studies, surveys of customers' needs and wants, and assistance with new product development. As a good stage manager would, Technomic works behind the scenes, helping companies in the food production and food service industry understand their customers, learn more about them, and ultimately serve them the food they want and need.

Technomic associates come from all corners of the food industry, including marketing, distribution, sales, research and development, and operations. So when Technomic assembles a team for a specific client, each individual contributes different types of expertise that can be used to assist the client. Say a restaurant chain wants to find out more about its level of customer satisfaction compared with that of competitors. Technomic will design a study, obtaining feedback from consumers, sales reps, distributors—everyone in the marketing channel who can provide valuable data to the restaurant. Perhaps a supermarket wants to know how its shelves compare with the competition's. Technomic will help the store identify its direct competitors and then create a specific benchmarking program that evaluates everything from business and financial performance to distribution efficiency to selection of products for consumers to see how it stacks up against the competition. The development and launch of a new product on a large scale can cost millions, so if a company like Campbell Soup is considering a new line of soups, Technomic might help the firm come up with strategies for effective test marketing and a successful product launch.

In addition to creating customized studies for its customers, Technomic publishes "shared research" programs that clients can use to learn more about their own customers and markets. These studies cover a wide range of topics, from the impact of obesity on the food service industry to evolving trends in adult beverages. The firm also offers broader programs, such as the Technomic Foodservice Planning Program, a compilation of six annual studies shared by more than 130 food service suppliers.

If all this sounds a bit dry, consider the nuts and bolts of the job of Technomic executive vice president Dennis Lombardi. Lombardi serves some of his customers by driving around the Chicago area visiting chain restaurants. As part of one ongoing study, he wants to see which full-service and fast-casual restaurants have chosen locations that best show off their brands. One particular area of Chicago reflects higher consumer incomes, so he spots trendy eateries like California Pizza Kitchen, the local South City Tavern, and Starbucks. He ponders the choice of location for California Pizza Kitchen, which is on the second floor of a building. The restaurant isn't really visible from the street, and he thinks it might do better on the first floor. On a trip through the western section of downtown Chicago, he spies a Spago, Rock Bottom Brewery, Roy's and Fogo de Chao, then a Red Lobster. Again, he ponders location. Competitors are everywhere. "If you're a conventioneer and you see a Spago, you'll go there because you don't have one in your town, even though [owner Wolfgang Puck] won't be there," he says. "But Red Lobster? They're going to say, 'I got a lot of them in my hometown.'"

Lombardi takes all of the notes he obtains during his drive-bys back to the office, where his written comments are analyzed and discussions take place. Other Technomic experts contribute their data, and useful information is produced. This is how Technomic serves its clients—by doing the legwork, crunching the numbers, and evaluating and interpreting the data so that valuable information emerges. Because business customers are paying a premium for the service, they expect results—and Technomic delivers the full-course meal.

Questions for Critical Thinking

1. How might Technomic segment its market?
2. Identify reasons why the buyer–seller relationship between Technomic and its food industry customers is an important part of Technomic's overall marketing strategy.
3. What are some of the environmental factors that might affect a restaurant chain's decision to purchase services from Technomic?
4. Imagine you are a marketer for Technomic, and you want to sell the firm's services to a regional supermarket chain. You have already done your homework, and you believe that Technomic can help the firm grow and establish a competitive advantage over other supermarkets in the area. Who in the buying center would you want to meet with and why?

Sources: Company Web site, http://www.technomic.com, accessed October 21, 2004; David Farkas, "Blowing through the Windy City," *Chain Leader,* July 2004, http://www.chainleader.com.

VIDEO CASE 7.2 Doc Martens Makes Strides around the World

Got a pair of Doc Martens in your closet? Maybe you're wearing them now. Perhaps you're wearing a pair of classic 1460 boots or a twin-strap sandal. Maybe your best friend is wearing a pair of guys' Grip Trax boots or even some wingtips. You're probably familiar with the distinctive yellow stitching, heel loop, and two-tone soles of Docs. The color names are pretty amazing, too—Bark Grizzly, Tan Analine, Aztec Crazy, Black Greasy. Even if you can't tell what colors these really are, you get curious. You scroll through the offerings online; you try on a pair in a shoe store. They look pretty clunky, but the Docs fit. When you walk around in them, your feet are really comfortable.

Doc Martens, or Docs or DMs, as they are often known, are officially called Dr. Martens, after their German inventor Dr. Klaus Maertens. Maertens, a physician in the German Army during World War II, injured his ankle on a ski trip to the Bavarian Alps in 1945. He'd been skiing in his uncomfortable army boots, and as he was recovering from his ankle injury, he spent a lot of time thinking about how to improve the boots. He came up with a design for a boot made of soft leather with air-padded soles.

Half a century later, consumers everywhere swear by their Docs. Now available in more than 250 styles of boots, sandals, and shoes, Doc Martens are worn by men, women, and children around the world. Madonna wears them. So does Pope John Paul II and his staff, who have their own exclusive line in pure white. Police officers and postal carriers, construction and factory workers, students and supermodels all wear them. Docs are sold in 78 countries, with two-thirds of them bought by American consumers. The firm has offices in such diverse places as Australia, Poland, the Philippines, Singapore, Turkey, the U.S., and the Ukraine. Even the United Arab Emirates boasts an office for Docs. People can buy them at retail stores or online from just about anywhere in the world. Unless you are stationed in Antarctica or climbing Mt. Everest, you can probably get a pair of Docs.

Since 1960, Doc Martens have been manufactured by R. Griggs, one of the two largest shoemakers in the United Kingdom (the other one is C&J Clark, maker of the Clarks brand). Despite its size, however, Griggs faces serious competition from other designer shoe manufacturers, as well as sports shoemakers such as Nike and Reebok. Because of fierce competition and uncertain economic times that have affected sales in the shoe industry in general, Griggs made the painful decision to move all of its manufacturing to China several years ago. Many companies in Europe have experienced similar pressures. Chinese manufacturers can produce goods cheaper than can European facilities. Since China is now considered a global trade power, having surpassed Taiwan and South Korea as the largest exporter of sport shoes to the U.S., footwear companies everywhere are feeling the pinch. But Griggs marketers believe that the move was critical to the survival of its Dr. Martens brand.

In addition, the marketers behind the Doc Martens brand have changed their entire global strategy, rescinding foreign licenses and focusing more on marketing the brand than on manufacturing the boots. Now, all marketing and sales efforts are overseen from the firm's UK headquarters. When Docs were allowed to return to South Africa, for example, it was under a stricter agreement than the one that was previously in force. "We are importing the Doc Martens—we don't manufacture them," explains Stewart Franks, international brand director for South Africa's Jordan Footwear. "That will ensure that there is standard uniformity in the quality of the shoes themselves."

Perhaps the most innovative effort by Docs marketers is the firm's current Web site. The site not only provides all the usual information and access to styles, but it also introduces "VEER: A Series of Documentaries," a program in conjunction with *Sports Illustrated* that is currently touring college campuses. Described as "6 films about people taking a different direction," the project focuses on six individuals who form the cutting edge of art, music, and other fields. Visitors to the site can click each one of the films, download it, and watch it. They can follow Janette as she struggles to make it as a DJ or John, Adam, Mark, Whylee, or Ndidi as they make their way in their various pursuits. The films have an edgy quality, as does the site itself, which features black-and-white photography. After 50 years, Doc Martens are cool again, on the feet of a new generation. You could say they are walking tall, around the world and back again.

Questions for Critical Thinking

1. China has become a global trade power, and Dr. Martens are now manufactured there. Assume the company also decides to market its shoes directly to Chinese shoppers. According to what you have read in the chapter, what considerations of the social-cultural environment might Doc Martens keep in mind when marketing to Chinese consumers?
2. Marketers for Doc Martens are using Internet technology to reach consumers via the documentaries presented on the Web site. Describe other creative ways they could use Internet technology to attract consumers.

3. How does the European Union affect the way Dr. Martens are marketed in Europe?
4. Do you think it was a good idea for Dr. Martens to rescind foreign licenses for its products at this time? Why or why not?

Sources: Company Web site, http://www.drmartens.com, accessed October 30, 2004; "R. Griggs, Limited, Company Profile," *Hoover's Online,* http://biz.yahoo.com, accessed October 21, 2004; "Dr. Martens Shoes," *Onlineshoes.com,* http://www.onlineshoes.com, accessed October 21, 2004; "Doc Martens," *TheFreeDictionary.com,* http://encyclopedia.thefreedictionary.com, accessed October 21, 2004; Karin Schimke and Mzolisi Witbooi, "Cool Doc Martens Is Back with a Thump," *Cape Argus,* September 7, 2004, http://www.capeargus.co.za; Matt Forney, "Tug-of-War over Trade," *Time Europe,* February 23, 2004, http://www.time.com/time/Europe; "Dr. Martens Moves to China," *BBC News,* October 24, 2002, http://news.bbc.co.uk.

VIDEO CASE 8.2 Teenage Research Unlimited Has the True Story on Teens

Teens are tricky. Trying to predict the next big trend—what they'll wear, what they'll eat and drink, which movies they'll watch, whose music they'll listen to—is like trying to run through a maze in record time. The buying power of teens—this year they'll spend a total of $175 billion—is mind-boggling. But Teenage Research Unlimited (TRU) isn't afraid of the challenge. Constantly developing new ways to research this ever-changing market, TRU employees consider themselves pioneers in the field of teen research. TRU's clients take this independent marketing research firm's work seriously. Their business clients make up an impressive list of the hottest retailers, including Aeropostale, Abercrombie & Fitch, Candies, Gap, Nike, and Perry Ellis International; the largest food and beverage firms, including Campbell Soup, The Coca-Cola Company, General Mills, Heinz, Kraft Foods, and PepsiCo; and media companies such as Time Warner, Cablevision, Sony Music Entertainment, and Walt Disney. Each of these firms, along with many others, listens closely to what TRU has to say about teens.

Founded more than two decades ago to specialize in researching and understanding the lifestyles and preferences of teenagers, TRU's original vision remains the same today: "To develop an unparalleled expertise in the teenage market and to offer our clients virtually unlimited methods for researching teens."

TRU uses a variety of methods to collect primary data. Not surprisingly, the most important sources of information are teens themselves. TRU conducts more than 1,000 focus groups and ethnographic interviews each year, in addition to several major quantitative studies. TRU's Trendwatch panel is composed if 300 "diverse, trendsetting, savvy teens." These teenage consumers—both boys and girls—are identified as some of the first to try, adopt, and spread the news about upcoming trends. TRU conducts focus groups, in-depth interviews, in-home studies including "closet checks," and field trips such as "shop-alongs" with some of Trendwatch's teen employees to gain firsthand, valuable data about teens as consumers. TRU also offers custom-designed Trendwatch programs for clients who want to integrate qualitative research into their teen marketing programs. In addition, TRU offers a biweekly teen trend report called TRU View to clients who want regular updates on teen consumer trends. Each multimedia issue, which is e-mailed to clients, contains an in-depth feature, trend alerts and forecasts, and relevant marketing news and analysis. TRU View also contains video clips from the Trendwatch panelists, who provide unscripted opinions on various topics.

It's one thing to capture the next big trend with teens, but it's another to grab it at just the right time. Because teens' preferences change rapidly, so do trends in general—which means marketers can be caught one step behind the beat. "Young people are particularly receptive to messages that promise either a new experience or one that satisfies a need-state unique to this age group," acknowledges TRU president Peter Zollo. "But they're also adept at blocking out messages that they deem false or misdirected." If a trend has passed, or if marketers misuse a message, teens are likely to tune out. Several years ago, the word *extreme* became popular among teens, so marketers dubbed everything from athletic clothing to high-energy snacks "extreme." Then they stepped over the line and began using it for shampoo and toothpaste—and teen consumers fled those brands. Teenage Research helps its clients avoid those missteps. "Rather than simply chasing after the latest and greatest," writes Zollo, "we advocate a more holistic approach. We prefer to help clients discover the nuances of how teens regard their brand: what young consumers expect of it and where else the brand can take them, including how to leverage trends that fit with and appropriately add to their brands."

Meanwhile, teens continue to wield their considerable purchasing power in markets ranging from clothing to automobiles. According to one study, more and more parents are buying their young teen drivers new cars—for around $20,000—rather than opting for used models. "You would be amazed by what high school students are driving these days. New. New!!" exclaims one 50-year-old mom. "Parents and teens obviously have vastly different priorities," says Rob Callender, senior trends manager at TRU. "Teens want something that will help their image and increase their esteem in the social world, and that is something new. Parents want something they can afford, and they want something that is reliable and safe."

Similar buying behavior occurs in clothing stores all around the nation. During a recent back-to-school season, the must-have clothing item for teens was a denim jacket. T-shirts with messages—particularly about self-esteem or religion—were in. And ponchos, cargo pants, and short, pleated skirts reappeared after decades of being banished to consignment shops. Teens routinely reported spending $400 to $800 on their new fall wardrobes. Fashion is "an independence thing," explained one clothing shop owner. That kind of spending may sound extreme—but marketers want to cash in on it.

Questions for Critical Thinking

1. Formulate a hypothesis for why teens are so quick to adopt new trends.
2. What kind of secondary data about teens is likely to be helpful to marketers?
3. TRU selects 300 "trendsetting" teens to participate in its Trendwatch program. Do you think this is an effective sampling technique? Why or why not?
4. TRU conducts interpretive research. Why is it so important in gathering data for TRU's clients?

Sources: Elizabeth Kenny, "What to Wear," *Seacoast Newspapers,* August 17, 2004, p. 1; "Hot on the Trends," *Knight Ridder Tribune Information Services, Seacoast Newspapers,* August 17, 2004, p. 1; TRU Web site, http://www.teenresearch.com, accessed July 23, 2004; Peter Zollo, "When Marketing to Teens, Trends Live Fast, Die Young," *Teenage Research Unlimited,* February 16, 2004, http://www.teenresearch.com; "Used Wheels Way to Go if Parents Are Paying," *Associated Press,* September 14, 2003, http://www.teenresearch.com.

VIDEO CASE 9.2 Orange Glo Cleans Up the Marketplace

Orange Glo is focused on getting things clean—your kitchen counters, your bathroom floor, your outdoor deck, your mirrors and windows. A visit to the company's Web site makes it perfectly clear: "At Orange Glo International, our mission is to delight people with magnificent new ways to clean that are innovative and healthy." Orange Glo offers three lines of branded products, all designed to scrub, scour, polish, and buff just about every surface in your home, garage, or yard: the Orange line, the OxiClean line, and the Kaboom! line. All of Orange Glo International's products are environmentally friendly as well. "We use only the best ingredients for your family and home," says the Web site. "That's why we take the time to use the most fragrant and powerful oil from fresh squeezed Valencia oranges, rather than using processed chemical extracts found in most other citrus products today."

What does all this mean in terms of segmenting and targeting markets and positioning products? First, Orange Glo's products are designed for consumers. That doesn't mean businesses can't use them to clean their offices, stores, or restaurants, but the products are categorized as consumer household products. Second, all of Orange Glo's products are designed for one purpose: cleaning. Third, everyone needs cleaning products—a fact that helps Orange Glo marketers select a marketing strategy to attract consumers from a broad population and turn them into loyal customers.

But marketing to a vast group of consumers who need cleaning products isn't specific enough; marketing segmentation requires that the overall marketplace be subdivided into more homogeneous groupings. Max and Elaine Appel, who founded Orange Glo in 1992—and whose family still owns and controls the company—understand this. So the firm's marketers practice segmentation and positioning strategies, relying a great deal on feedback from consumers themselves. "We actively seek input from consumers and customers about our products and services," say the Appels via their Web site. "Each of our products reflects input from people like you."

Segmentation for Orange Glo products is partially demographic, although consumers in certain geographic areas of the country might prefer one brand of cleaner to another. Orange Glo's consumers want the highest quality and are willing to pay a little more for it; they prefer to use products made with organic or natural ingredients; and they are adults (not children or teens). But because the market is so vast, Orange Glo's products lend themselves best to product-related segmentation. Orange Glo makes it very easy for consumers to identify the benefits of its products. Orange Eliminator Instant Spot Remover gets rid of spots on carpets or upholstered furniture—and it accomplishes this with natural ingredients and a pleasant scent. OxiClean Laundry Detergent cleans clothes—without chemical bleaches. Kaboom! Shower, Tub & Tile Cleaner wipes all bathroom surfaces clean without scrubbing.

As a direct seller, Orange Glo targets heavy, moderate, and light users of its products through infomercials and the Internet. "We constantly make our products fresh with extreme marketing," says Joel Appel, president and CEO. "If necessary I'll stand on my head to let my customers know about our features. Subtlety doesn't work for us." And because Orange Glo offers three distinct brands, the firm can concentrate on developing and strengthening brand loyalty among its customers. The company Web site makes use of a simple marketing tool to reinforce brand loyalty: testimonials. Visitors to the site can find comments from consumers praising all of Orange Glo's brands and many of the firm's individual products. One homeowner compliments the strength of OxiClean in removing the dirt and mildew covering her outside deck. A fisherman praises the ability of Orange for Hands to remove the fish smell from his hands. A bride tells the story of soaking her grandmother's discolored wedding dress in OxiClean Laundry Detergent—and being able to wear it to her own wedding.

Orange Glo can successfully position its products according to attributes, price/quality (they cost more, but deliver value), application, and product user. CEO Joel Appel says he doesn't worry about what his competitors are doing. "If we did market research and paid attention to the fact that our competitors were charging $3.50 for a can of furniture polish, we would never be charging $17 for ours," he insists. The Appel family, who are pictured on the Web site, look like a pretty clean-cut bunch. They're also pretty smart marketers. They know that consumers will always need cleaning products, and theirs are top-notch.

Questions for Critical Thinking

1. How might Orange Glo solicit feedback from consumers about the benefits they seek when purchasing the firm's products?
2. What do you think is the best strategy for reaching Orange Glo's target market?
3. Create a slogan that illustrates one of the positioning categories for Orange Glo products.
4. Suppose competition does begin to eat into Orange Glo's sales. What steps might the Appels take to reposition some of their products?

Sources: Company Web site, http://www.greatcleaners.com, accessed October 23, 2004; "Why Is Orange Glo So Appealing?" Happi.com, December 2002, http://www.happi.com; Monique Reece, "Entrepreneurs Share Their Secrets of Success," *Denver Business Journal,* December 15, 2000, http://www.bizjournals.com/denver.

VIDEO CASE 10.2 International Flavors & Fragrances Makes Marketing Personal

Take a deep breath. What do you smell? Maybe you've got a steaming cup of coffee beside you, or the window is open and you can sense a change of seasons. Perhaps you've been thinking about your favorite meal, or you're longing to take a walk in the park. Maybe you're absolutely certain your roommate's got a pair of dirty socks hidden somewhere in the room, or someone just let a wet dog into the dorm lounge.

International Flavors & Fragrances wants you to focus on the flavors and scents that recall or create the best memories—scents like freesia, rose, and dew or the crispness of linen and organza. In fact, International Flavors & Fragrances is behind some of the most famous flavors and fragrances on the market today. You've probably heard of some of them: Calvin Klein's Eternity, Lancôme's Trésor, Estée Lauder's Intuition for Men, Elizabeth Arden's Elizabeth Taylor White Diamonds, and Ralph Lauren's Polo. But chances are, you've never heard of International Flavors & Fragrances. That's because the firm's marketers, researchers, chemists, and technicians work behind the scenes to develop innovative flavors and scents, create them in the laboratory, and manufacture them for business customers. With more than 5,400 employees working in 66 facilities in 34 countries, IFF focuses on consumer preferences, cutting-edge technologies, customer relationships, and top-quality products.

IFF offers beginning-to-end services to its clients. "We have the expertise to take your product from idea to marketplace launch," explains the IFF Web site. "We work hand in glove with you every step of the way—and then we go the extra mile." Perhaps a firm such as Calvin Klein or Ralph Lauren wants to develop a new fragrance. IFF may consult independent research about consumer preferences for, say, vanilla or citrus scents or may decide to conduct its own research. IFF will create a program for the development of the product using a combination of proprietary technologies such as Vanilla Technology. IFF has its own vanilla plantation, which provides pesticide-free beans with a high vanillin content, resulting in the highest quality vanilla. If the project involves mint flavor, IFF scientists might turn to the firm's FlexiMint Technology, which is responsible for the creation of specific mint flavors for such products as candy, chewing gum, and toothpaste. Then IFF works with the client throughout the entire development process, from manufacturing to launch.

If a client wants to enter an international market, IFF can assist with its various facilities located around the world, from Bangkok to Barcelona. Recently, IFF opened its China Creative Center in Shanghai in order "to be wherever our customers need and want us to be," explains Richard A. Goldstein, chairman and CEO. "Our customers' businesses are growing in the Greater China region. They want us to leverage our global resources and insights and apply them in a way that makes sense in this part of the world." IFF is so committed to its relationships with its customers that it will build local facilities to be closer to them—and to the consumers served by those customers. "This new center [in Shanghai] will give our employees and customers unprecedented access to world-class equipment, applications, and technology," Goldstein continues. "That's good for our coworkers, good for our company as a whole, and good for the rapidly developing business community in Shanghai and throughout the Greater China region." The center in Shanghai is also a step toward the firm's goal of "One IFF," bringing together many of the components of flavor and fragrance development in one location to serve a regional market. "The new center allows us to bring management, commercial, creative, and application resources together for the first time in China," says Matt Rouse, general manager for IFF Greater China. "Previously, we had production in Hong Kong and Guangzhou, fragrance labs in Shanghai, flavor labs in Guangzhou, and management in Hong Kong."

In addition, the center is set up to enable IFF staff to work more closely with customers, meeting their needs and building stronger long-term relationships. "The center allows us to be that much closer to the customer, respond more quickly to new opportunities, and allocate the right resources in a much more efficient way," explains Matt Rouse. "Another great aspect of the center is that it gives us the ability to bring customers in to work with us in the flavor and fragrance labs. They can participate in evaluations and generally join in the selection process." Which means that, if a customer can imagine a scent or a flavor, IFF can create it.

Questions for Critical Thinking

1. How does the establishment of creative centers like the one in China help IFF monitor its interactions with customers?
2. IFF has many internal customers, ranging from scientists to marketers, in different locations around the world. What steps can the firm take to ensure these customers are satisfied—so that, in turn, they can satisfy external customers?
3. At what level on the relationship marketing continuum would you place IFF and its customers? Why?
4. Identify several ways in which IFF practices customer relationship management.

Source: Company Web site, http://www.iff.com, accessed November 23, 2004.

VIDEO CASE 11.2 Curves: A New Angle on Fitness

Gyms have been around for years, catering to the latest trends in fitness. From isometrics to aerobics, from step to spinning, over the decades gyms have offered a range of ways for consumers to get fit. But in recent years, the full-service gyms that were once so popular—with personal trainers, exotic classes and equipment, saunas, and juice bars—have created a significant problem for many would-be customers. They're expensive, sometimes costing many hundreds or even thousands of dollars per year, and they take up an awful lot of time. This might be fine for single professionals who have both time and money to spend on their fitness efforts—gyms are always crowded in the evenings and on weekends. But what about women—and particularly those who may be juggling family, job, and household duties? These consumers are also likely to be budgeting funds for children's clothing, sports, and braces; mortgage and car payments—while trying to plan ahead for college and retirement. They may join a gym as part of their New Year's resolution to get fit, only to discover by March that they can afford neither the time nor the money to maintain the membership.

Diane and Gary Heavin came up with a solution to this problem, which is a major part of their marketing strategy. Cofounders of Curves, they understood that the most valuable commodities to today's busy women are time and money. So they launched a chain offering a service that delivers value in both areas. Each Curves fitness center—there are now more than 8,000 in the U.S., Canada, and six other countries—specializes in a 30-minute, no-nonsense, no-frills workouts on 8 to 12 exercise machines. There are no pools, no classes, no juice bars. But women get what they want—a fast, effective workout at a low cost. The registration fee runs between $40 and $70, depending on location, with a monthly fee of $29 to $49. While other centers cater to consumers who want the latest in exercise equipment, clothing, and classes, Curves focuses on its 1 million customers who want to shed a few pounds, get fit, and feel better—on time and on budget. The friendly, encouraging atmosphere attracts women and keeps them coming back. "It's not a competitive environment, [it] is a supportive atmosphere," says one customer. "[It] provides an adequate level workout but doesn't kill you, so you can function the next day."

Now the largest fitness franchise in the world, Curves relies on real women for its marketing strategy. With their permission, Curves tells the stories of women customers who have lost weight and improved their physical fitness at Curves centers. The Curves International Web site contains at least a dozen testimonials from women around the country. There are stories from women who wanted to lose weight in time for their weddings, those who wanted to regain fitness after having children, and those who needed to gain strength after a serious illness.

But in an even more creative move, Curves looks to its customers as franchise ownership prospects. It's not unusual for a Curves customer to become a Curves franchise owner. This is possible because Curves franchises generally cost less to purchase and operate than other franchises, making them more accessible to women or couples looking for a new business opportunity within a limited budget. With its typical 1,200 square-foot size, a Curves franchise can be slipped into an existing storefront in a local strip mall, which costs less than building a new location and provides easy access to women customers who are already doing other errands. Don't expect to find showers or relaxing saunas there either. Curves customers expect an invigorating workout in a short time period and then move on to other items on their daily agenda.

Suzy Boerboom of Minnesota is an enthusiastic Curves franchise owner. A former nurse who also worked in customer service for Volunteers of America, Boerboom wanted to start her own business with husband, Tom. So the couple bought their first Curves franchise and have since added four more centers. "My mission is to enhance women's happiness through fitness," says Suzy. "For me as a nurse and customer-service person, that's been the most rewarding."

With about 18 million women in the U.S. belonging to health clubs and fitness centers, fitness marketers continue to look for ways to attract those customers. But it appears that Curves already has the answer to what women want. Still, the firm continues to add products to its line. Customers can order cofounder Gary Heavin's new book, read health and fitness articles on the Curves Web site, and download meal planner pages, progress reports, and a free foods list. "Only one place can give you the strength of a million women," promises the Web site. But Curves marketers know that their firm's real power lies in gaining one customer at a time.

Questions for Critical Thinking

1. Where would you place Curves on the goods–services continuum? Why?
2. What is the nature of Curves's service? Would you describe it as equipment based or people based? Why?
3. What types of business products might a Curves franchise owner have to purchase? Give an example of each category you cite.
4. Curves's product line is still rather limited. Imagine that Curves has asked you to come up with ideas for two or three more related products that you think Curves's customers would want to purchase. What would they be and why?

Sources: Company Web site, http://www.curvesinternational.com, accessed August 9, 2004; Chris Pentilla, "Hot Biz: Women's Fitness Centers," *Entrepreneur,* December 2003, http://www.findarticles.com; Bree Berss, "Curves for Women: A New Approach to Fitness," *Daily Sundial,* March 2002, http://sundial.csun.edu/sun/; Beth Ewen, "Workshop: Curves for Women," *The Business Journal,* March 1, 2002, http://www.bizjournals.com/twincities/stories/2002/03/04/smallb3.html.

VIDEO CASE 12.2 Everything Is Beautiful at L'Oréal

"I hope to share our passions with you: our passion for what we do, for our products, for innovation. . . . We are proud to be the world leader in cosmetics. Even more, we are filled with enthusiasm for the future, for the progress and discoveries of our research laboratories and for the wealth of opportunities to win new markets." These remarks by chairman and CEO Lindsay Owen-Jones welcome visitors to L'Oréal's Web site.

L'Oréal products have long been staples in many women's cosmetics drawers, medicine cabinets, and shower caddies. The firm's shampoo, skin-care products, and makeup have been represented by such stars as Cybill Shepherd, Heather Locklear, Dayle Haddon, and Andie MacDowell over the years. "Because I'm worth it" has been the L'Oréal Paris advertising slogan for almost 30 years, becoming a mantra for millions of women. Positioned as a mass-market premium brand, L'Oréal products have been the preference of consumers who want value—high quality without paying department-store prices—for nearly two generations.

The L'Oréal Paris line of lipsticks, eye colors, shampoos, conditioners, hair colorings, facial cleansers, moisturizers, and antiaging products—to name a few—is only one facet of the L'Oréal Group's business. The L'Oréal Group is now the parent company for several other highly recognizable brands, including Lancôme, Ralph Lauren Fragrances, Matrix, Redken, Maybelline, Garnier, and Dermablend. Maintaining the brand equity that each of these names represents—and using it to help the company as a whole continue to innovate and grow—is a challenge for the marketers of L'Oréal's various divisions.

Global branding is a large part of L'Oréal's overall marketing strategy. By acquiring existing international brands as well as developing new products—and introducing them to overseas markets—L'Oréal has developed a global portfolio of products that sell even while cosmetics sales in general may be faltering. That's because L'Oréal marketers have adopted CEO Lindsay Owen-Jones's approach: create marketing messages that transmit the allure of stylish foreign cultures. Marketers of Maybelline in Shanghai may emphasize its American popularity. Lancôme is conveyed to Americans as the epitome of French elegance. Consumers may not know or care that both Maybelline and Lancôme are L'Oréal brands, but they want to own a bit of American or European style—so they gladly purchase the products. Behind the image, though, are high-quality name-brand products that satisfy customers and ensure repeat purchases.

Recently, L'Oréal opened a multimillion-dollar facility devoted to researching and developing products for African American consumers. The L'Oréal Institute for Ethnic Hair & Skin Research is located outside Chicago and is focused specifically on reaching an ethnic market. Since ethnic consumers represent about 51 percent of all hair-care sales, new products coming from the institute will be important to L'Oréal. Eventually, the institute will expand the focus of its research to include Hispanic and Asian populations.

Sometimes maintaining brand equity requires defending a name. Although imitations are common in the fragrance industry, until recently courts have ruled that scents cannot be copyrighted because they belong to nature and not to a person or company. But when a Dutch manufacturer started selling a knock-off of Lancôme's Trésor, L'Oréal took the issue to court once again and won its case. The court decided that Trésor was a unique combination of ingredients "not only measurable by the senses but also, in the court's judgment, concrete and stable enough to be considered an authored work as intended in copyright law." In legal terms, Trésor is considered a work of art, not a conventional product, and is now protected by copyright.

What does Lindsay Owen-Jones see in his company's future? He believes strongly in making acquisitions that will add to the L'Oréal portfolio of products. And always, there's the message about the brand and the consumer who buys the brand—because she's worth it.

Questions for Critical Thinking

1. How can L'Oréal use its existing brand equity to create brand recognition and—it hopes—brand loyalty for new products or existing products in new markets?
2. Why would it be important for category managers for the different L'Oréal brands to communicate with each other?
3. Packaging has always been a major factor in marketing cosmetics, hair-care, and skin-care products. In what ways do you think packaging helps the success of L'Oréal's brands?
4. L'Oréal has already spent millions of dollars to build a research and development facility for products aimed at consumers with different ethnic backgrounds. How would you expect marketers to position the first of these product offerings?

Sources: Company Web site, http://www.loreal.com, accessed September 26, 2004; "Ruling Protects Lancôme Trésor," *Sun Journal,* July 25, 2004, http://www.sunjournal.com; "Lancôme Eyes $300M Global Effort," *Brandweek.com,* July 20, 2004, http://brandweek.com; Molly Prior, "L'Oréal Opens Ethnic Beauty Research Center," *Drug Store News,* July 21, 2003, http://www.findarticles.com.

VIDEO CASE 13.2 1-800-Flowers.com: Great Gifts by Phone or Online

When Jim McCann opened his first retail flower shop in 1976, he already knew something about consumers: They're busy, they need last-minute gifts, and they want the best. There was nothing new about the flower business, and merchants devoted most of their marketing focus to attractive, creative packaging and attempts to increase the frequency with which people bought flowers. McCann quickly built up his retail business, eventually opening 14 stores in the New York City area. But he was looking for new channels that would permit him to serve customers outside the immediate vicinity of his retail outlets. So in 1986, he purchased the 1-800-FLOWERS brand name. At the time, consumers were ordering more and more products by phone from all kinds of retailers. They liked the convenience and the freedom of selecting the products they wanted from a stack of catalog offerings. They loved the idea of dialing a single, toll-free number to order flowers for friends and loved ones far away—and knowing the flowers would arrive fresh and on time.

McCann focused on learning as much about his customers as he could. Then, when the timing was right, he expanded into the newest channel: the Internet. 1-800-Flowers.com went online in 1992, with a full Web site up and running in 1995. The firm survived the dot-com collapse and today offers a virtual bouquet of products online, including flowers, live plants, gourmet foods, candy, food baskets, and gifts. In addition, the firm now owns several other recognizable, complementary brands—Plow & Hearth, which offers gifts for the home and garden; HearthSong and Magic Cabin Dolls, which offer children's gifts and toys; The Popcorn Factory, which makes premium popcorn and other gourmet food gifts; and GreatFood.com, which provides gourmet foods.

1-800-Flowers.com has just about every channel covered. Consumers can choose from among 15,000 products by telephone, over the Internet, or at one of the firm's 111 retail stores. Say you want to purchase a birthday gift for your best friend, who lives in another state. You can call 1-800-FLOWERS 24/7 (which helps if you forgot your friend's birthday and need to place an order quickly). Order operators will help you select what you need. Or you can log online to http://www.1800flowers.com and browse through hundreds of choices. If you're in a hurry, you can click one of the featured gifts on the home page. Or if you're on a budget, you can click "By Price under $30." If you're feeling generous, you move to the $150+ price range. Or you can click the "Everyday Celebrations" button, which helps you select gifts for specific occasions—birthdays, anniversaries, weddings, new babies. Finally, if you're partial to certain gift brands, you can choose among favorites such as Gund, Godiva, and Waterford. If you've decided to send flowers and you need them to arrive the same day, you can do that, too—as long as you order before 2:00 P.M. on a weekday, before 12:30 P.M. on Saturday, and before 11:30 A.M. on Sunday. Essentially, if you have a credit card and a phone or a computer, you can send a quality gift anytime, anywhere, from 1-800-Flowers.com.

Achieving this type of fulfillment—and customer satisfaction—requires successful management of logistics and the supply chain as well as strong relationships with partners, suppliers, and affiliates. To make it even easier for consumers to make purchases online, 1-800-Flowers.com maintains strategic alliances with America Online, Microsoft Network, and Yahoo! as well as other Internet service providers. This means that customers can access 1-800-Flowers.com directly from their Internet service provider's site. In addition, the 1-800-Flowers.com account staff manages more than 40,000 affiliate relationships, through which business participants place banner ads with links for 1-800-Flowers.com on their Web sites. Affiliates earn commissions on items purchased by consumers who click the banner ads to reach 1-800-Flowers.com.

Of course, 1-800-Flowers.com couldn't fulfill its floral orders without florists. To accomplish this, the firm operates BloomNet, a network of 1,500 florists around the country, in addition to its own distribution and warehouse facilities. Nonfloral gift orders are fulfilled by local vendors who work in partnership with the company. Fulfilling orders this way means that products such as bakery goods arrive fresh at the recipient's door. It also means that 1-800-Flowers.com chooses not to carry most perishable foods in its brick-and-mortar stores. Instead, the stores carry gift baskets, small toys, candies, candles—and of course, flowers. 1-800-Flowers.com does everything possible to make sure your gift arrives as scheduled and exceeds the recipient's expectations. All you have to do is place the order.

Questions for Critical Thinking

1. Describe the components of 1-800-Flowers.com's dual distribution system. Do you think this system is effective? Why or why not?
2. What types of product factors might affect 1-800-Flowers .com's choice of marketing channel strategy?
3. Based on what you have learned about the company, would you consider 1-800-Flowers.com to be a channel captain? Why or why not?
4. Explain why combined transportation modes might be the best choice for 1-800-Flowers.com.

Sources: Company Web site, http://www.1800flowers.com, accessed November 30, 2004; Jack Hough, "The Data Mine: Flower Power," *Smartmoney.com,* July 28, 2003, http://www.smartmoney.com; "Business Intelligence," *Fortune,* June 2003, http://www.fortune.com; Paul Miller, "Merchandise by Medium," *Catalog Age,* June 1, 2003, http://www.findarticles.com.

VIDEO CASE 14.2 Westfield Group Creates a Shopper's Paradise

Americans love to shop. So do consumers in other countries, ranging from the United Kingdom to Australia and New Zealand. No one knows this better than the Westfield Group, which happens to own more shopping centers than any other company on Earth. Shoppers who dart in and out of their favorite stores at their favorite shopping malls may not be aware of the Westfield name yet—but Westfield is focused on bringing consumers the best merchandise and services under one roof. And the Westfield name is already well known among some of the best retailers in the world. Based in Australia, Westfield owns, operates, manages, and markets shopping malls in Australia, the U.S., the U.K., and New Zealand. Altogether, nearly 20,000 stores, covering about 27 million square feet, open their doors every morning in a Westfield-owned mall. That's enough to make even the most dedicated shopper pause—for a moment.

For Westfield to be successful, its shopping malls—known as Westfield Shoppingtowns—and the stores, restaurants, and movie theaters that operate in them must be successful. So, the development of strong, long-term relationships with retailers is vital. U.S. retailers likely to be found in a Westfield property range from Dillard's and Saks Fifth Avenue to Banana Republic and Gap. Lifestyle and entertainment businesses include Borders Books Music Café, AMC theaters, Dave & Buster's, and Sbarro's. Sometimes these and other retailers need one-to-one advice tailored to their needs. Westfield supplies consulting services that can evaluate various factors in a retailer's business and make recommendations designed to help boost business through merchandise planning, changes in shop design, financial management, improved customer service, and building a brand. In addition, Westfield offers training programs for retailers covering such topics as shop presentation, personal selling skills, customer service, financial management and planning, buying products, and marketing. Westfield also offers a series of meetings that focus on specific merchandise categories, in which retailers can gather to discuss issues surrounding their particular type of merchandise, whether it is fashion items or restaurant food. Those who are really ambitious can take a study tour of the world's best retail businesses to learn more about what makes them so successful. Finally, in partnership with the U.S.'s National Retail Federation (NRF), Westfield has been creating Retail Skills Centers to help qualified job candidates who are interested in retail careers develop the skills they need. "Retail Skills Centers are a win-win situation for retailers and the retail workforce," says Katherine Mance, vice president of NRF. "These Centers enable hard-working Americans to learn the skills necessary to begin good careers in retail. In turn, retailers gain access to a pool of qualified, prescreened potential employees."

There's an old saying that the three most important features of a piece of real estate are "location, location, location." Marketers for Westfield Shoppingtown centers understand the importance of locating their shopping malls in the right spot. Westfield is also working hard at creating a brand image for its shopping malls, so people recognize them wherever they go. Ideally, the mere mention of Westfield Shoppingtown will produce a mental image of the types of stores shoppers will encounter and the shopping experience they will enjoy if they decide to shop there. Whether Westfield purchases an existing mall or is involved in the construction of an entirely new one, the shopping center must be in an area where people want to shop and where at least one major "anchor" retailer is willing to commit to a long-term lease. When Westfield bought 50 percent of the Fashion Square mall in Sherman Oaks, California, it immediately began a transformation of the 848,000-square-foot shopping center. "Westfield is aggressively expanding in America," notes Michael Beyard, a senior research fellow for the Urban Land Institute. "They're looking for well-located shopping centers, which they then take to the next level." The Fashion Square mall already attracted customers from some of the area's wealthiest neighborhoods and included such stores as Bloomingdale's and Macy's. But Westfield wanted something more: a retail atmosphere and image that people would instantly recognize as the Westfield Shoppingtown's brand. "They brand their malls, which is the same strategy [individual] stores use," explains Beyard. "People have a very strong image of what that is."

Not far from Sherman Oaks, Westfield has also been renovating one of its latest acquisitions, Westfield Shoppingtown Santa Anita. When Westfield purchased the mall, it already had 151 specialty stores, 4 major department stores, and 11 food court restaurants. Westfield's $113 million renovation added a 16-screen AMC theater complex, 30 new stores, and an expanded food court. "At Santa Anita, we have taken an incredible shopping center and added new elements and energy to create a fun family experience," says David Doll, senior vice president of development. "This truly will be San Gabriel Valley's destination for shopping, dining, and entertainment." Westfield Shoppingtown Santa Anita is the perfect example of a planned shopping center that could be termed a lifestyle center. The next time you visit your local mall, double-check its name. If it isn't a Westfield Shoppingtown mall, it may become one very soon; and your perception of what a shopping mall should be could change.

Questions for Critical Thinking

1. Describe Westfield's target market.
2. Do you predict nationwide success of planned shopping centers that are considered lifestyle centers? Why or why not?
3. How might Westfield's training and support programs for participating retailers as well as job candidates help strengthen the Westfield Shoppingtown brand?
4. Select a retailer with whom you are familiar and explain why you think it would be a good candidate to include in a Westfield Shoppingtown center.

Sources: Company Web site, http://www.westfield.com, accessed November 23, 2004; "Westfield Shoppingtown Santa Anita: $113 Million Renovation Offers San Gabriel Valley Shoppers More Shopping, Dining, and Entertainment," press release, *Business Wire,* September 1, 2004, http://biz.yahoo.com; "Retail Skills Centers Offer Opportunities for Retailers, Employees," *National Retail Federation,* June 4, 2004, http://www.nrf.com; Brent Hopkins, "Westfield Buys into Fashion," *Los Angeles Daily News,* October 4, 2002, http://experts.uli.org/content/resfellows/Beyard/Beyard_c13.htm.

VIDEO CASE 15.2 Jimmy John's Sandwich Shops Give Customers Something to Chew On

What's your favorite sandwich? A steaming steak-and-cheese sub? Or perhaps you're longing to sink your teeth into a turkey club. Maybe you prefer the lighter side of the menu with a fresh veggie wrap. Whatever it is, Jimmy John's Sandwich Shops would love to have you try one of their gourmet sandwiches. Founded in 1983 by 19-year-old Jimmy John Liautaud with a loan from his dad and a bread recipe from his mom, the first Jimmy John's Gourmet Sandwich Shop opened its doors in a converted garage near the campus of Eastern Illinois University. Jimmy John targeted his market perfectly: hungry college students looking for quick, convenient, affordable, tasty food. Within two years, Jimmy John had paid back his dad—and thanked his mom for the bread recipe that proved such a crowd pleaser. Jimmy John is still CEO of his company, which today has expanded to more than 200 outlets—many of which are operated by franchisees—around the country, with another 200 scheduled to open soon.

The concept of integrated marketing communications may seem a little highbrow for a shop that started in a garage, but Jimmy John's wouldn't have grown to the business it is today, with the number of loyal customers it has, without some very astute marketing decisions that have resulted in the optimal promotional mix for the firm. It starts with the food itself—hearty, made-to-order sandwiches with names like Big John, Turkey Tom, Billy Club, Beach Club, Gourmet Veggie Club, and The J.J. Gargantuan. The French bread is fresh—never more than four hours old—and the sandwiches are bigger than those offered by other shops. Then there's the service. Hungry college students can call anytime before 3:00 A.M. (when the store closes), order a $3 sandwich, and have it delivered. That in itself is a very effective marketing message. Consumers who visit a Jimmy John's shop are greeted with the firm's and the founder's irreverent sense of humor in the form of signs and advertising posters. "Give us a call and we can start delivering these bad boys straight to your Barcalounger," says one. Next to a yardstick measure, which tells kids under 4 feet tall that they can get a half-priced sandwich, another sign whispers, "Do your folks a favor and slouch." To place an order, customers line up under a sign that says, "If you're a really good customer you'd order more." You can't help laughing. But some of the ads take a serious turn, encouraging consumers to make charitable donations. "Don't Buy My Sandwich Today," orders a Jimmy John's ad run in newspapers during the holidays. "Skip lunch. Take your . . . bucks to the Salvation Army."

It's no surprise that Jimmy John Liautaud is a firm believer in guerilla marketing, getting the message to consumers in innovative and unconventional ways. Liautaud speaks of the ideal marketing manager as someone who "really understands rolling up your sleeves and getting dirty and the guerilla tactics of making yourself known in the market." This type of marketing is particularly popular around college campuses, where many of Jimmy John's most loyal customers live. One such promotion is the "hot buns" team of three students hired on each college campus near a Jimmy John's shop to give away sandwiches and other free stuff. Locating stores near colleges and marketing to students are part of the firm's overall marketing strategy as well. Students who become loyal customers while in college often remain so after they graduate and move away. And new students are always arriving, beginning the cycle all over again. "It's like a brand-new opening every four years," says one franchise owner. "It keeps it kind of fresh."

Maintaining strong relationships with franchise owners is a vital part of marketing communications at Jimmy John's. For those interested in investigating the opportunity, the company Web site offers comprehensive information on where and how to get started, outlining the company's overall mission and approach, sales information, frequently asked questions, news stories and press releases, and testimonials from current franchise owners. All new franchisees participate in an 18-day training program and receive regularly scheduled deliveries of food products from a national distributor. The firm also encourages special promotional events, such as Customer Appreciation Days and grand-opening celebrations that include local media coverage, special pricing, and giveaways.

Despite a very effective promotional mix, Jimmy John Liautaud emphasizes that the success is not the result of complex planning; it is the result of his commitment to making a great sandwich. "I really believed that if people would taste them, they would eat them," he says, "and I got lucky—it happened."

Questions for Critical Thinking

1. How does the combination of marketing efforts create a unified personality for Jimmy John's Sandwich Shops?
2. Choose one of the marketing messages from the signs or the advertisement described in the case and analyze the effectiveness of its message using the criteria discussed in the chapter.
3. Create the copy of your own sign for a Jimmy John's shop. Your message should follow at least one of the objectives for promotion listed in the chapter.
4. Describe an event that you think would be appropriate for Jimmy John's to sponsor. Explain your answer.

Sources: Company Web site, http://www.jimmyjohns.com, accessed November 14, 2004; "Chicago's Rising Stars," *Crain's Chicago Business,* October 1, 2004, http://chicagobusiness.com; "Jimmy John's," *Tesg's Guide to Big Chain Road Food Consumption,* http://www.99w.com/evilsam/ff/jimmyjohns.htm, accessed October 1, 2004; Rachel Krier, "Jimmy John's Keeps It Simple, Yet So Good," *Kansas State Collegian,* October 1, 2004, http://www.kstate collegian.com; Kris Maher, "Help Wanted: Marketing Hero," *The Wall Street Journal Online,* http://www.careerjournal.com, accessed October 1, 2004.

VIDEO CASE 16.2 Ride the White Wave with Silk Soymilk

Soy milk doesn't sell itself, at least not in the U.S. Consumers who have grown up on cow's milk, whether it is whole milk, reduced fat, or skim milk, expect milk to taste a certain way. They pour it in their coffee, on their cereal, make hot chocolate and frappes with it, and drink it straight from the glass. Milk is creamy and tastes great to the millions of people who love it. But it does not taste anything like soy. So, when Steve Demos—a convert to soy—came home from a trip to India in the late 1970s determined to introduce the product to the U.S. public, he faced an uphill marketing battle. True, soy contains lots of beneficial nutrients, but Demos had to change the minds of consumers. To succeed, he knew he had to develop the best, most creative marketing strategy, including advertising and public relations, he possibly could.

Demos founded the firm White Wave and began selling tofu, a soy product. Then he turned his attention to developing a soy milk product that would actually taste good to Western palates. Ten years ago, Silk Soymilk was introduced to the market. Silk is now the best selling soy milk in the U.S. How did White Wave achieve this dominance in the marketplace? Answer: through advertising.

To start, White Wave had to create demand for soy products in general. Marketers needed to convince consumers that soy was not only good for them but tasted good—maybe even better than dairy products. So advertising focused first on providing information about the benefits of soy. White Wave began educating the public about soy, which people in Asia have made an important part of their diets for thousands of years. Information on the company Web site tells visitors that the FDA and American Heart Association recommend 25 grams of soy protein per day, that soy is thought to reduce the risks of certain types of cancers, and that it can contribute to stronger bones and also help manage diabetes. Consumers who want to try soy also need to know how to use it, so White Wave provides recipes.

But information alone isn't enough. People want to know why they should buy Silk Soymilk, or any other White Wave product, including tofu. They want to know if it tastes good. They want to know why they should change their milk-drinking habits. In short, they need to be persuaded. Understanding the importance of appealing to consumers' taste buds, the choice of the product name, Silk, is an important part of the marketing message that White Wave wants to convey. In addition, the firm has introduced flavored Silk products, including French vanilla, plain vanilla, and chocolate—all designed to appeal to mainstream preferences. Reviews, which generate effective publicity for the company, have been positive, encouraging people to try Silk. Stacy Porter, editor of the *Thrifty Planet Resource Guide,* writes that the flavored Silk is "the best tasting soy milk on the planet. . . . Silk Brand Soy Milk has not paid for any endorsement; I just really like it." Recently, Starbucks entered into an agreement to sell Silk at its shops, a powerful—and persuasive—endorsement from a popular consumer firm.

White Wave approaches its product advertising with humor. "Put a Smile on Your Prostate," says one Silk ad, which cleverly informs and persuades consumers. The ad shows a happy smile made of cereal bits laid out in a white bowl. "Milking soybeans. Dangerous but important work," reads another tag line. "Your body is a temple. Even if you do let cupcakes in once in awhile," jokes another. Other ads appeal to social values. One shows a mother patiently kissing her scowling son on the head and includes copy reading, "May today bring more connecting and less computer games; more exuberance and less grown-up-ness; more family and less saturated fat."

Not surprisingly, White Wave partners in event promotion and cooperative advertising with nonprofit organizations that share the firm's values. Silk Soymilk sponsors the Race for the Cure, presented by the Susan G. Komen Breast Cancer Foundation. In addition, White Wave supports Farm Aid, an annual music event that raises money for American farmers. Behind the scenes, White Wave purchases its soybeans from U.S. farms that practice sustainable, environmentally safe agriculture. White Wave also partners with Stonyfield Farm, which makes organic yogurt, to produce the Strong Women Summit and has joined the Undo It campaign, whose goal is to reduce global warming. All of these efforts are consistent with the firm's mission to "creatively lead the full integration of natural soyfoods into the average American diet through socially responsible and environmentally sustainable business practices." They also generate good public relations for the company.

Steve Demos says, "We're interested in promoting foods the world is better off with, rather than without." His firm has managed to take an unfamiliar product and turn it into a desired product with a recognizable brand. Consumers are catching the soymilk wave.

Questions for Critical Thinking

1. Imagine that you are a marketer for White Wave 10 years in the future, and Silk is facing major new competitors. Using reminder advertising, create an ad designed to reinforce the product in consumers' minds.
2. Would celebrity testimonials be an effective advertising tool for Silk? If so, which current high-profile celebrities might be effective in giving an effective and credible testimonial? What are some potential dangers of celebrity testimonials?
3. Do you think humor works well in the Silk ads described? Why or why not?
4. How does White Wave's public relations activities affect its other promotional strategies?

Sources: Company Web site, http://www.silkissoy.com, accessed November 6, 2004; "Naming Consumer Products: Silk, A Category Killer," *Igor International,* http://www.igorinternational.com, accessed November 6, 2004; Stacy Porter, "What's Hot This Month?" *Thrifty Planet Resource Guide,* June 10, 2004, http://www.thriftyplanet.com; "Starbucks to Sell Soy Milk from White Wave," *Denver Business Journal,* February 13, 2003, http://www.bizjournals.com.

VIDEO CASE 17.2 Chicago Show, Inc. Puts on a Show

Imagine being able to claim Ringling Brothers, Barnum & Bailey Circus *and* Harry Houdini as two of your first clients. Where do you go from there? These two customers are widely known as entertainers—the circus as "The Greatest Show on Earth" and the late Houdini as one of the greatest illusionists and escape artists of all time. But Chicago Show, Inc. isn't hiding behind the curtain—in fact, during its early years, the firm was responsible for some of the most creative sales promotions in the entertainment industry. Founded in 1902, Chicago Show began by producing high-quality printed handbills, theater posters, and outdoor billboard posters that were often plastered onto the sides of barns. A case in point was the 1910 poster for the Ringling Brothers, Barnum & Bailey Circus featuring a stampeding rhinoceros, claiming the circus to be "The World's Biggest Menagerie." Then the company began producing the playbills advertising Harry Houdini's escapades. More than 120 years later, the fourth generation of the firm's founders continue to be guided by the principles of client service, satisfaction, and long-term marketing relationships.

Today, Chicago Show develops entire sales display programs for its customers in a wide range of industries. The firm designs, engineers, produces, distributes, warehouses, and fulfills custom orders for its customers' display and merchandising programs. Displays incorporate a variety of materials, including electronics, illumination, wood, metal, and plastic. When Kellogg's wanted to improve the dispensers for bulk cereals at institutions—schools, hotels, and hospitals—the cereal giant turned to Chicago Show. The old dispensers got clogged, shot out crushed cereal, or didn't dispense at all. So Chicago Show designers came up with a new dispenser, which is now used for all of Kellogg's branded cereals that are sold in bulk.

The next time you cruise through the drive-thru at a Wendy's Restaurant, take another look at the menu sign. After producing these signs for more than a decade, Chicago Show designers recently introduced an improved sign for the fast-food chain. The new sign is both larger and easier to read than its predecessor. This molded polyethylene stand comes with an all-weather light fixture that can withstand the worst weather, meaning that Wendy's franchise owners don't need to continually replace their signs—they are durable and long-lasting. When GE came out with a newly designed, under-the-counter AM/FM/CD player for consumers, the company needed a new merchandising display for retailers that would attract consumers and show them the unique features of the product. So, Chicago Show's design team came up with the perfect display unit—with large, readable graphics and copy pointing out the features of the working player.

Valspar has been producing decorative paints and finishes for more than 100 years, but recently, the firm decided to update its retail displays. Chicago Show developed new merchandising centers that contain paint chips, "how-to" tips, graphics, literature, and products such as paintbrushes—all in one display stand. Each retailer can customize the center to include information and products relevant to local customers. Because the stand can be updated as new products arrive and as trends in color or techniques emerge, it provides long-lasting value to Valspar and its retailers.

It's one thing to create a single stand or merchandising center for a manufacturer. But what about an entire department? Even more challenging, what about one of the largest home improvement chains in the nation? Lowe's Home Centers marketers decided the time had come to evaluate their stores' wood flooring department, examining the mix of products and where they were placed in the stores. Chicago Show designers and engineers were able to present a comprehensive new plan to Lowe's executives. Their first moves added store-size flexibility by segmenting the product assortment to accommodate Lowe's smaller and larger stores. Next they placed certain products bought on impulse in a "see and reach" area so that customers would readily find them and drop them in their carts. Then they created their own display fixtures and graphics so each Lowe's store could select precisely what it needed—and the marketing message would remain constant from store to store.

Chicago Show has come a long way from the traditional advertising of circus posters and leaflets for escape artists. Trade show displays, retail store designs, and point-of-purchase items are now standard fare for the firm. In addition to the clients just described, the firm counts The Coca-Cola Co., Caterpillar, John Deere, and Wal-Mart among its best customers. Teamwork as well as attention to quality, service, and value begin at the top, with CEO James M. Snediker. Chicago Show's merchandising solutions are a bit like the stampeding rhinoceros—they get your attention, and they keep it.

Questions for Critical Thinking

1. Choose one of the companies whose displays are described in the case. In what ways does Chicago Show help this firm make sales promotion an integral part of its promotional mix? For the company you selected, outline a consumer-oriented sales promotion that could be integrated into a Chicago Show display or merchandising center.
2. Which of the four sales channels would be most effective for Chicago Show marketers to use when approaching a business customer to encourage him or her to purchase a new merchandising display?
3. The Valspar merchandising center functions as a point-of-purchase display. Describe another POP display you have seen recently. Did it attract your attention enough to stop and look at it? Did you purchase any of the products? Why or why not?
4. How might Lowe's use personal selling in conjunction with the new layout in its wood flooring department?

Source: Company Web site, http://www.chicagoshowinc.com, accessed September 8, 2004.

VIDEO CASE 18.2 Wrigley's Gives Everyone Something to Chew On

When his father passed away suddenly at age 66, William Wrigley Jr. became the fourth generation to head his family's company. He was only 35, but he became the leader of a sweet kingdom, presiding over such household name brands as Juicy Fruit, Freedent, Big Red, and Wrigley's Spearmint. Wrigley had been working at the company for 15 years, involved mostly in international operations and strategic planning, but the jolt of becoming CEO was a bit like chewing the first stick of cinnamon Big Red. Only a few years on the job, William Wrigley Jr. has continued his focus on strategic planning, and he recently outlined a six-point global strategy. "While we do not take this challenge lightly, we feel confident that we have the infrastructure and the strategic plan required to grow our leadership position in the chewing gum segment, while successfully expanding our business into other confectionery areas," notes Wrigley.

Part of the plan involves pricing. Chewing gum delivers value if it offers long-lasting flavor at a good price. Consumers can still pick up a pack of Wrigley's Spearmint, Juicy Fruit, Doublemint, or Big Red for a few cents. For many consumers, buying a pack of chewing gum is an impulse purchase. It's easy to throw a pack or two in the grocery cart while you're waiting in line or pick up a pack at the drug store while waiting for a prescription. However, Wrigley's premium sugar-free brands such as Eclipse and Orbit—whose promotion focuses on fresh breath and oral health—sell for more than a dollar a pack.

In a bold move, the firm recently announced a change in its pricing structure. The suggested retail price for five-stick packages of Wrigley's Spearmint, Doublemint, Juicy Fruit, Big Red, and Winterfresh is increasing from 25 cents to 30 cents. (The 25-cent price hasn't changed in 16 years.) But the suggested retail price for the same size package of sugar-free Extra is actually being reduced to 30 cents, aligning the five sugar brands and one sugar-free brand at the same price. What is the strategy behind such a move? "Our pricing strategy for Extra and our five sugar brands will create a powerhouse of Wrigley brands at the opening price point of the chewing gum category in both sugar-free and sugar segments," explains Ronald V. Waters, senior vice president and CFO of Wrigley.

New prices are not the only focus of the Wrigley marketing plan. Despite the fact that the company rakes in $2.2 billion annually from its chewing gum brands, competition in the industry is intense. The marketplace is flooded with products competing for consumers' attention, including Warner-Lambert's Trident and Dentyne and Nabisco's Bubble Yum and Care*Free. So, part of Wrigley's marketing program involves value pricing—emphasizing the combination of a low price with outstanding benefits. Visitors to the Wrigley Web site are informed that chewing gum improves concentration, eases tension, freshens breath, helps fight tooth decay, and substitutes as a low-calorie snack. "At work, chewing gum helps us concentrate on the task at hand," and chewing gum "moistens and refreshes the mouth and throat and sweetens the breath," states the Web site. The average stick of chewing gum contains no more than 10 calories, and chewing it promotes the production of saliva, which can help neutralize decay-causing acids. So, for an average price of 6 cents per stick, chewing gum creates a lot of value.

While Wrigley continues to promote its existing brands, the firm is moving into new markets with new products. Wrigley breath strips have reportedly sold well in the U.S., and Orbit Drops—a sugar-free candy—have been received positively by consumers in Europe. Eclipse Mints were launched recently in the U.S., while Extra Mints made a successful debut in the United Kingdom. All of this activity is part of an overall strategy that includes pricing. "Wrigley has traditionally been a very strong investor in its brands—enabling us to introduce successful new brands, while maintaining the vitality of brands that span a century," remarks CFO Waters. "That is no small feat in a consumer market where brands seem to churn with regularity. And it is our intention to continue investing to ensure that our brands remain relevant with consumers for the next 100 years." That gives everyone something to chew on.

Questions for Critical Thinking

1. Relate the recent pricing changes for Wrigley's Extra and the five sugar brands to Chapter 18's discussion of pricing objectives.
2. Why is value pricing an important strategy for a product like chewing gum?
3. How might Wrigley use prestige pricing to promote one of its premium brands?
4. As a consumer, is price part of your consideration when buying a product such as chewing gum? Why or why not?

Sources: Company Web site, http://www.wrigley.com, accessed September 8, 2004; J. Alex Tarquinio, "Chew on This," *Kiplinger's Personal Finance Magazine,* July 2004, http://www.kiplinger.com; "Wrigley Gives Update on Strategy and Business Results," company press release, October 22, 2003, http://www.corporate-ir.net; David Shook, "Online Extra: Wrigley: Solid Growth, by Gum," *BusinessWeek Online,* Spring 2003, http://www.businessweek.com.

VIDEO CASE 19.2 Jiffy Lube: The Well-Oiled Machine

If you're like most drivers, you want your car to run reliably, but you don't want to pay a lot for maintenance. Also, you're too busy to leave your car in the shop for hours or days. If someone asked you where you take your vehicle for service, you might answer with a blank stare because you can't remember the name of the place. And you think about regular oil changes about as often as you think about cleaning out your closets. All of these factors make Jiffy Lube's job a tough one.

Jiffy Lube, a subsidiary of Shell Oil, has 2,200 franchised and company-operated service centers around the U.S. offering a variety of auto maintenance services ranging from a simple oil change and lube to windshield repair. One of the first hurdles the firm faced was how best to distinguish itself from competitors, including dealers, independent mechanics, and other service chains like Valvoline and Pennzoil. "We compete ferociously with auto dealerships and auto mechanics," notes marketing executive Garry Lillian. Jiffy Lube had to establish itself in drivers' minds as the place to go for routine service. One effective marketing tool for accomplishing this is price—offering convenient, reliable service at prices lower than those of most competitors. Even so, some auto dealerships now throw in free oil changes with vehicle purchases, and of course, many drivers do their own oil changes—free, except for the cost of the oil and disposal costs for the old lubricants.

So a low price may not mean much unless customers are able to see some real value. In its marketing communications, Jiffy Lube strives to offer this value. If you pull in for an oil change, here's what you get for about $30: five quarts of clean oil; a new oil filter; visual inspection of brake fluid and antifreeze/coolant; inspection of air filtration, wiper blades, lights, belts, and tire pressure; vacuumed interior floors and cleaned exterior windows; lubricated chassis; and all essential fluids topped off. Through its diagnostic services, the Jiffy Lube staff will review and recommend any other necessary repairs.

Here's the best part: You don't have to leave your car all day or even overnight. Jiffy Lube's staff will handle the entire job within 15 to 20 minutes, while you wait. In fact, you don't even need an appointment—just show up during business hours. You don't get your driveway or your clothes dirty from changing the oil yourself, and you don't have to worry about legal disposal of the dirty oil. And Jiffy Lube isn't trying to sell you a new car or encouraging you to purchase more expensive parts and services on the spot. "Since we will not be performing any of the needed repair work that our services may uncover, our Jiffy Lube certified technicians can provide a completely unbiased evaluation of your car's critical operation systems," explains Anne Tawney, senior vice president of marketing. Consumers may purchase the diagnostic services as part of an oil change or separately, depending on what they think they may need. When they get the results, consumers can shop around for the best repair prices.

To strengthen its relationship with existing customers and possibly lure some of those do-it-yourselfers out of their driveways, Jiffy Lube offers other price incentives. Through its DriveAmerica program, regular customers can save up to $1,000 with a loyalty card. The company has also negotiated a special arrangement with AAA Motor Club, which offers a 15 percent discount on Jiffy Lube services at participating shops. Military personnel can get a 10 percent discount on oil changes and other services by showing a United Armed Forces Association membership card. People over the age of 55 also receive a 10 percent discount on Jiffy Lube services. And anyone who plans a trip through Jiffy Lube's Trip Tools program is entitled to a $5-off coupon on the next oil change. Other incentives include a 5 percent rebate on Shell gas and short-term promotions like movie ticket giveaways. Some of the larger franchise groups, such as California-based Broadbase Inc., offer coupons through their own Web sites that are good only at specific franchise locations. Broadbase uses these coupons to turn new customers into loyal customers. Each month, the franchise offers new coupons, such as $5 off an air filter change, $8 off a Jiffy Lube Signature oil change, and $20 off the fuel injection cleaning service. So customers can select savings on different services each time they visit.

The quick oil change industry is still growing, and although Jiffy Lube is the largest of these service providers—its annual customer base consists of 30 million drivers nationwide—the firm has plenty of room to expand. If a simple oil change saves on gasoline consumption, the high price of gas alone is likely to drive consumers into Jiffy Lube bays. Jiffy Lube likes to call itself The Well-Oiled Machine—meaning yours as well as theirs.

Questions for Critical Thinking

1. Since Jiffy Lube cannot match the price of do-it-yourselfers or auto dealers who offer free oil changes, what other factors does it emphasize to achieve a competitive advantage?
2. Jiffy Lube offers a lot of service for one low price. Do you think this affects consumers' perceptions of quality? Why or why not?
3. Jiffy Lube practices some product-line pricing, setting different price levels for different service packages. Do you think this is a good idea? Why or why not?
4. Do you think promotional pricing for certain Jiffy Lube services is a good strategy? Why or why not?

Sources: Broadbase Inc. Web site, http://www.broadbase.com, accessed November 13, 2004; Jiffy Lube Web site, http://www.jiffylube.com, accessed November 6, 2004; United Armed Forces Association Web site, http://www.uafa.org, accessed November 6, 2004; AAA Web site, http://www.autoclubgroup.com, accessed November 6, 2004; "Wheels: Best of 2002," *Valley Advocate,* 2002, http://old.valleyadvocate.com; "Jiffy Lube Expands Service Offering," *Houston Business Journal,* December 18, 2001, http://www.bizjournals.com.

notes

PROLOGUE

1. "Professional Golf Management," Florida State University, http://www.cob.fsu.edu/dsh/pgm, accessed October 30, 2004; "Bachelor of Science with a Major in Sport Management," Georgia Southern University, http://chhs.georgiasouthern.edu, accessed October 30, 2004; "Penn State University Professional Golf Management," Penn State University, http://www.hrrm.psu.edu/pgm/, accessed October 30, 2004.
2. Kris Maher, "Surprise Gifts for This Year's College Graduates: Job Offers," *The Wall Street Journal,* May 11, 2004; Eilene Zimmerman, Betsy Cummings, and Megan Sweas, "Job Market Thaw," *Sales & Marketing Management,* February 2004, pp. 24–30.
3. Sue Kirchoff, "Better Educated Find Jobs Faster," *USA Today,* June 16, 2003, www.usatoday.com.
4. Barbara Hagenbaugh, "Grads See Brighter Job Prospects," *USA Today,* April 14, 2004, p. 3B; Hilary Cassidy, "How's This for a Head Hunter?" *Brandweek,* March 8, 2004, pp. 20–23.
5. Jill Rachlin Marbaix, "Job Search 2.OH!" *U.S. News & World Report,* March 8, 2004, p. 60.
6. Joanne Gordon, "Battle of the Boards," *Forbes,* August 12, 2002, p. 50.
7. Peter Coy, "The Future of Work," *BusinessWeek,* March 22, 2004, pp. 50–52.
8. Hagenbaugh, "Grads See Brighter Job Prospects"; Diya Gullapalli, "Who Says Interns No Longer Get Any Perks?" *The Wall Street Journal,* July 30, 2002, pp. B1, B8.
9. Matthew D. Shank, *Sports Marketing: A Strategic Perspective,* 3rd ed. (Upper Saddle River, N.J.: Prentice Hall, 2005).
10. John Kador and Brian Caulfield, "A Résumé That Shows Them the Super-You," *Business 2.0,* April 2004, p. 134; Michelle Conlin, "The Resume Doctor Is In," *BusinessWeek,* July 14, 2003, pp. 115–117; Joann S. Lublin, "College Students Make Job-Hunting Tougher with Weak Resumes," *The Wall Street Journal,* April 29, 2003, p. B1.
11. Dale Dauten, "Cover Letters from Hell," *The Birmingham News,* December 7, 2003, p. G1.
12. "Job Tips for College Grads" in Steve Giegerich, "Some College Grads Opt to Delay Entry into Crowded Job Market," *Mobile Register,* May 16, 2003, p. A10.
13. Reported in Louis E. Boone, *Quotable Business,* 2nd ed. (New York: Random House, 1999), p. 103.

CHAPTER 1

1. Sonia Alleyne and T. R. Witcher, "The New Face of NASCAR," *Black Enterprise,* April 2004, pp. 108–118; Tom Lowry, "The Prince of NASCAR," *BusinessWeek,* February 23, 2004, pp. 91–98; Scott Lindlaw, "A Presidential Race," *Mobile Register,* February 16, 2004, p. C3; Lars Anderson, "The New NASCAR Nation," *Sports Illustrated,* February 16, 2004, pp. 83–88; Amy Rosewater, "Program Targets Minority Inclusion," *USA Today,* February 13, 2004, p. F15; Bruce Horovitz, "Dale Jr. Zooms to Front of Pack in Endorsements," *USA Today,* February 13, 2004, pp. B1–B2; "NASCAR Tracks Getting Soft Walls," *The Seattle Times,* January 23, 2004, http://www.seattletimes.com; Chris Jenkins, "The Changing Face of NASCAR," *USA Today,* August 29, 2003, pp. 1–2; "Politics Courting NASCAR Nation," *Sports Illustrated,* August 25, 2003, p. 18; Theresa Howard, "Auto Racing Drives into Mainstream Ads," *USA Today,* July 14, 2003, p. B4.
2. Steve Hamm, "Why High Tech Has to Stay Humble," *BusinessWeek,* January 19, 2004, pp. 76–77.
3. Larry Selden and Geoffrey Colvin, "What Customers Want," *Fortune,* July 7, 2003, pp. 122–128.
4. Shirley Leung, "Fast-Food Firms' Big Budgets Don't Buy Customer Loyalty," *The Wall Street Journal,* July 24, 2003, p. B4.
5. David M. Szymanski and David H. Henard, "Customer Satisfaction: A Meta-Analysis of the Empirical Evidence," *Journal of the Academy of Marketing Science,* Winter 2001, vol. 29, no. 1, pp. 16–35.
6. Barry Janoff, "Sirius Serious about NFL Ties; Phillies Share Joy of New Park," *Brandweek,* April 12, 2004, p. 10; Robert Barker, "Satellite Radio: Clear Growth, Far-Off Profits," *BusinessWeek,* February 2, 2004, p. 91.
7. Joseph P. Guiltinan and Gordon W. Paul, *Marketing Management,* 6th ed. (New York: McGraw-Hill), 1996, pp. 3–4.
8. Arlene Weintraub, "A High-Tech Race to Corral Mad Cow," *BusinessWeek,* March 1, 2004, pp. 107–108; Chris Woodward, "Beef Industry Looks to Reopen Markets," *USA Today,* December 29, 2003, p. 4B.
9. Rebecca Buckman, "Computer Giant in China Sets Sights on U.S.," *The Wall Street Journal,* June 19, 2003, pp. B1, B4.
10. Stephen Baker and Manjeet Kripalani, "Software: Will Outsourcing Hurt America's Supremacy?" *BusinessWeek,* March 1, 2004, pp. 84–94.
11. Laura Hillenbrand, *Seabiscuit: An American Legend* (New York: Random House, 2001), pp. 3–6.
12. Steven Rosenbush, "Armstrong's Last Stand," *BusinessWeek,* February 25, 2001, pp. 88–96.
13. David Court, Tom French, and Gary Singer, "How the CEO Sees Marketing," *Advertising Age,* March 3, 2003, p. 2B.
14. Elizabeth Goodgold, "Talking Shop," *Entrepreneur,* September 2003, pp. 62–67.
15. Goodgold, "Talking Shop."
16. Nonprofit Enterprise Institute, http://www.vcu.edu, accessed February 9, 2004.
17. John Bissell, "Opening the Doors to Cause Branding," *Brandweek,* October 27, 2003, p. 30.
18. Bill Hoffmann, "A-Rod Stock A-Ri$ing," *New York Post,* February 23, 2004, http://story.news.yahoo.com; Theresa Howard, "To Market, To Market: Advertisers Ponder A-Rod's Potential," *USA Today,* February 19, 2004, http://story.news.yahoo.com.
19. Terry Lefton, "Made in New York," *Brandweek,* December 8, 2003, pp. 29–32.
20. "Cause Marketing: After Two Decades of Growth, the $1 Billion Spending Mark Is in Sight," *Halo Awards: Cause Marketing Forum,* July 29, 2003, p. 4.
21. Sean Marcinek, "Uncle Sam Makes an Appeal to Mom," *The Wall Street Journal,* June 26, 2003, p. B6.
22. April Pennington, "Food for Thought," *Entrepreneur,* July 2003, p. 160.
23. Arundhati Parmar, "Marines, Air Force Scour Databases for Recruits," *Marketing News,* July 21, 2003, p. 17.
24. Christopher Helman, "Now Hear This," *Forbes,* September 15, 2003, pp. 122–124.
25. Catherine Arnold, "Technology Reels 'Em In," *Marketing News,* October 14, 2002, p. 13.
26. Stephen H. Wildstrom, "Net Phoning Is Starting to Make Sense," *BusinessWeek,* May 24, 2004, p. 28; Stephen H. Wildstrom, "At Last, You Can Ditch the Phone Company," *BusinessWeek,* May 17, 2004, p. 26; Xeni Jardin, "Why Your Next Phone Call May Be Online," *Wired,* January 2004, p. 32.
27. Charles Haddad, "Delta's Flight to Self-Service," *BusinessWeek,* July 7, 2003, pp. 92–93.
28. Benjamin Fulford, "Korea's Weird Wired World," *Forbes,* July 21, 2003, pp. 92–94.
29. Steve Jarvis, "A Whirlwind of Technologies May Sweep Up Marketers," *Outlook 2002,* January 7, 2002, p. 8.
30. Jarvis, "A Whirlwind of Technologies May Sweep Up Marketers," p. 8.
31. http://www.firstgov.gov, accessed February 12, 2004.
32. Mike Beirne, "The Mother of Incentives," *Brandweek,* January 26, 2004, p. 4.
33. Monte Burke, "Pop Music," *Forbes,* January 12, 2004, pp. 192–194.
34. Allison Fass, "Spot On," *Forbes,* June 23, 2003, p. 140.
35. Lisa Takeuchi Cullen, "Have It Your Way," *Time,* December 23, 2002, pp. 40–42.
36. Goodgold, "Talking Shop," pp. 62–67.
37. Tahl Raz, "A Recipe for Perfection," *Inc.,* July 2003, pp. 36–38.
38. Goodgold, "Talking Shop."
39. Company Web site, http://www.timberland.com, accessed February 13, 2004.
40. Del Jones, "Hasbro, Pfizer Get Award for Charity Efforts," *USA Today,* February 23, 2004, p. B9.

CHAPTER 2

1. Joe Flint, "Why Comcast Covets ESPN," *The Wall Street Journal,* February 13, 2004, p. B1; Monte Burke, "X-treme Economics," *Forbes,* February 2, 2004, pp. 42–44; Jon Friedman, "TV Sports: New Rules, New Games," *CBS MarketWatch,* January 30, 2004, http://www.cbs.marketwatch.com; Austin Murphy, "X Games Mark the Spot," *Sports Illustrated,* January 19, 2004, p. A16.
2. NBC News, April 5, 2004.
3. Nichole L. Torres, "Cloud Star Corp.," in Amanda Kooser et al., "Beyond Their Years," *Entrepreneur,* November 2003, pp. 74–85.
4. Sarah Ellison, "In Lean Times, Big Companies Make a Grab for Market Share," *The Wall Street Journal,* September 5, 2003, p. A1.
5. John Batelle, "The Net of Influence," *Business 2.0,* March 2004, p. 70.
6. Diane Brady, "Will Jeff Immelt's New Push Pay Off for GE?" *BusinessWeek,* October 13, 2003, pp. 94–98.
7. Bass Pro Shops promotional brochure, Bass Pro Shops, Springfield, MO.
8. Duff McDonald, "Roll Out the Blue Carpet," *Business 2.0,* May 2004, pp. 53–54.
9. NCAA Web site, http://www.ncaa.org, accessed April 5, 2004.
10. Kellogg's Web site, http://www.kelloggs.com, accessed April 5, 2004.
11. Dave Carpenter, "McDonald's to Dump Supersize Portions," *Associated Press,* March 3, 2004, http://story.news.yahoo.com.
12. Roger Parloff, "The New Drug War," *Fortune,* March 15, 2004, pp. 144–156.
13. Susan Horsburgh, Ron Arias, and Steve Helling, "eBay's eBoss," *People,* August 4, 2003, pp. 97–98.
14. Nick Wingfield, "Amazon Goes for Gold with Discount Jewelry," *The Wall Street Journal,* April 22, 2004, pp. B1, B2.
15. Company Web site, www.maldenmills.com, accessed April 5, 2004.

16. Derek F. Abell, "Strategic Window," *Journal of Marketing,* July 1978, pp. 21–26; John K. Ryans and William L. Shankin, *Strategic Planning: Concepts and Implementation* (New York: Random House, 1985), p. 11.
17. April Y. Pennington, in Kooser et al. "Beyond Their Years," p. 77.
18. Kerry A. Dolan, "It's Nice to Be Big," *Forbes,* September 1, 2003, p. 84.
19. Sandra O'Loughlin, "Brand Builders," *Brandweek,* March 31, 2003, pp. 16–17.
20. "Women on Their Way," Wyndham Hotels Web site, http://www.wyndham.com, accessed January 3, 2003; Katherine Conrad, "Hoteliers Cashing in with Women Business Travelers," *East Bay Business Times,* March 8, 2002, http://eastbay.bizjournals.com.
21. Horsburgh, Arias, and Helling, "eBay's eBoss."
22. Matthew Boyle, "Wal-Mart Keeps the Change," *Fortune,* November 10, 2003, p. 46.
23. Amy Cortese, "An Ancient Drink, Newly Exalted," *BusinessWeek,* March 1, 2004, pp. 122–123.
24. Keith Naughton, "Kicking Hyundai into High Gear," *Newsweek,* December 30, 2002, p. 73.
25. Shawn Young, "Night Rates to Start Two Hours Earlier on AT&T Cell Plan," *The Wall Street Journal,* March 9, 2004, pp. D1, D4.
26. "All Fired Up over Clean Coal," *BusinessWeek,* February 16, 2004, p. 76.
27. Andrew Gillies, "General Mills," in "Forbes Magnetic 40," *Forbes,* May 21, 2003, p. 86.
28. As mentioned in Jagdish Sheth and Rajendra Sisodia, *Surviving and Thriving in Competitive Markets* (New York: Free Press, 2002).
29. Wendy Zellner, "Is JetBlue's Flight Plan Flawed?" *BusinessWeek,* February 16, 2004, pp. 72–75.
30. Leigh Buchanan, "Death to Cool," *Inc.,* July 2003, pp. 82–87.
31. Peter Burrows, "Show Time!" *BusinessWeek,* February 2, 2004, pp. 58–64.
32. Burrows, "Show Time!"

APPENDIX

1. NCAA Web site, "NCAA Strategic Planning Process," http://www.ncaa.org, accessed April 5, 2004.
2. Keith Naughton, "Out of the Box," *Newsweek,* May 12, 2003, pp. 40–41.
3. April Y. Pennington, "Jenzabar Inc.," in "Beyond Their Years," *Entrepreneur,* November 2003, pp. 80–81.
4. Amanda C. Kooser, "Handango," in "Beyond Their Years," *Entrepreneur,* November 2003, p. 82.
5. Naughton, "Out of the Box."
6. Nichole L. Torres, "Raising Cane," in "Beyond Their Years," *Entrepreneur,* November 2003, p. 83.
7. Mike Steere, "A Timeless Recipe for Success," *Business 2.0,* September 2003, pp. 47–49.
8. Steere, "A Timeless Recipe for Success."
9. Susan Adams, "You, the Record Mogul," *Forbes,* October 27, 2003, p. 257.
10. Karen E. Spaeder, "Under Armour Performance Apparel," in "Beyond Their Years," *Entrepreneur,* November 2003, p. 76.
11. Andy Reinhardt, "Nokia's Big Leap," *BusinessWeek,* October 13, 2003, pp. 50–52.
12. Pui-Wing Tam, "Sony Puts Its Hand-Helds on Hold," *The Wall Street Journal,* June 2, 2004, p. B8.
13. "Levi Strauss Explores Sale of Dockers Brand," *USA Today,* May 11, 2004, http://www.usatoday.com.

CHAPTER 3

1. Greg Boeck, "At 14, Wie's Hour May Be at Hand," *USA Today,* March 24, 2004, pp. C1, C2; Geets Vincent, "A One-of-a-Kind Book: *The Unplayable Lie* by Marcia Chambers," http://www.womenonthegreen.com/clubhouse/getting.htm, accessed January 27, 2004; Steve Wilstein, "Some Sports Draw Jeers," *Mobile Register,* September 28, 2003, p. C2; Michael Bamberger, "Her Best Shot," *Sports Illustrated,* June 2, 2003, pp. 52–54; "Augusta's Money Matters," *Golf for Women,* May–June 2003, pp. 109–111; Jonathan R. Laing, "A Rough Round," *Barron's,* July 28, 2003, pp. 17–20; Marcia Chambers and Kim Gandy, "It's Not about Golf: Feminists Blast Discrimination at Home of Masters Tournament," National Organization for Women press release, April 10, 2003.
2. Sue Kirchoff, "Natural Beef Industry Might See Boost from Mad Cow Fears," *USA Today,* January 12, 2004, p. B1; Mark Sherman, "Organic Beef Growers Determined to Cash In on the Mad Cow Case," *Mobile Register,* January 12, 2003, p. A3.
3. Vanessa O'Connell, "Why Philip Morris Decided to Make Friends with FDA," *The Wall Street Journal,* November 25, 2003, p. 11.
4. Tim Weiner, "Low-Wage Costa Ricans Make Baseballs for Millionaires," *The New York Times,* January 25, 2004, http://www.nytimes.com.
5. Carrie Kirby, "RealNetworks Sues Microsoft on Antitrust," *San Francisco Chronicle,* December 19, 2003, http://www.sfgate.com.
6. Barbara Kiviat, "Buy Just the Broadband," *Time,* March 8, 2004, p. 84.
7. David Pringle, "Motorola Hopes Early Push in 3G Market Yields Gains," *The Wall Street Journal,* March 28, 2002, p. B4; Jennifer Tanaka, "Design: The Coolest Cell Phone Wins," *Newsweek,* February 25, 2002, p. 9; Maureen Tkacik, "Hey Dude, This Sure Isn't The Gap—Pink Fur Pants, Tongue Rings Draw 'Alternative' Teens to Hot Topic's Mall Stores," *The Wall Street Journal,* February 12, 2002, p. B1.
8. Jim Carlton, "People Favor Solar Power—But Not in Their Neighborhood," *The Wall Street Journal,* February 25, 2004, pp. B1, B4.
9. Yuki Noguchi, "Working WiFi," *Mobile Register,* February 29, 2004, p. F3; Michelle Kessler, "Wi-Fi Changes Virtually Everything," *USA Today,* February 19, 2004, pp. B1, B2; Karen Lowry Miller, "Is Wi-Fi Just a Bubble?" *Newsweek,* September 29, 2003, pp. E22–E24.
10. Gardiner Harris, "Back to the Lab," *The Wall Street Journal,* January 29, 2002, p. A1.
11. Dan Richman, "A Cingular Victory: AT&T Sale a Boon for Shareholders," *Seattle Post-Intelligencer,* February 18, 2004, http://seattlepi.nwsource.com.
12. Leigh Gallagher, "Pix Populi," *Forbes,* March 15, 2004, pp. 156–157.
13. David Lawsky, "EU Fighting Yesterday's War against Microsoft?" *Reuters Limited,* February 4, 2004, http://news.yahoo.com.
14. http://www.ftc.gov/bcp/conline/pubs/online/dotcons.htm, accessed February 4, 2004.
15. Jodie Kirshner, "Ta-ta, Telemarketers!" *U.S. News & World Report,* July 14, 2003, p. 34; Lorraine Woellert, "The Do-Not-Call Law Won't Stop the Calls," *BusinessWeek,* September 29, 2003, p. 89.
16. "Herbal Danger," *The Chicago Tribune,* January 3, 2004, Section 1, p. 26.
17. Jane Spencer, "Why You Have the Wrong Local Phone Service," *The Wall Street Journal,* January 8, 2003; Greg Farrell, "After 2 Years, Enron Task Force Finally Makes Progress," *USA Today,* January 26, 2004, p. B7; Bryan Gruly and Rebecca Smith, "Anatomy of a Fall: Keys to Success Left Kenneth Lay Open to Disaster," *The Wall Street Journal,* April 26, 2002, pp. A1, A5.
18. William Glanz, "Bankruptcies Climb to Record Levels in 2001," *The Washington Times,* February 20, 2002.
19. Jyoti Thottam, "Is Your Job Going Abroad?" *Time,* March 1, 2004, pp. 26–33; Emily Thornton, "The Small-Biz Job Machine Sputters," *BusinessWeek,* March 1, 2004, pp. 100–102; Anne Fisher, "Think Globally, Save Your Job Locally," *Fortune,* February 23, 2004, p. 60.
20. Michael Oneal, "Few Jobs Made in USA," *Chicago Tribune,* January 10, 2004, Section 1, pp. 1, 17.
21. www.hotjobs.com, accessed February 4, 2004; Joan Raymond, "The Jaws of Victory," *Newsweek,* March 18, 2002, p. 38P.
22. Betsy Shiffman, "Still Want to Teach the World to Sing?" *Forbes,* January 16, 2003.
23. "Boom or Gloom?" *The Economist,* November 20, 2003, http://www.economist.com.
24. Marc L. Songini, "Phillips Gives Petroleum Blending Software the Gas," *Computerworld,* March 18, 2002, p. 19.
25. David Welch, "Gentlemen, Start Your Hybrids," *BusinessWeek,* April 26, 2004, pp. 45–46; Richard J. Newman, "Red-Hot and Green," *U.S. News & World Report,* February 23/March 1, 2004, p. D6.
26. Ira Sager, ed., "The Price of Safety," *BusinessWeek,* September 15, 2003, p. 12.
27. Kerry A. Dolan and Quentin Hardy, "The Challenge from China," *Forbes,* May 13, 2002, pp. 73–76.
28. Fred Guterl, "Bright Light, Big Industry," *Newsweek,* September 23, 2002, p. 49.
29. Mary Kathleen Flynn, "Courting Calls," *U.S. News & World Report,* February 2, 2004, pp. 40–41.
30. Damien Cave, "Music's Top Cop," *Rolling Stone,* April 29, 2004, p. 18; Steve Knopper, "261 Music Fans Sued," *Rolling Stone,* October 16, 2003, pp. 25–26; Mike France and Ronald Grover, "Striking Back," *BusinessWeek,* September 29, 2003, pp. 94–96.
31. Brian Grow, "Hispanic Nation," *BusinessWeek,* March 15, 2004, pp. 58–70; Deborah L. Vence, "You Talkin' to Me?" *Marketing News,* March 1, 2004, pp. 1, 9–11; "Dieste Multicultural Shop of Year," *Advertising Age,* January 14, 2002, p. S-8.
32. Stephen Power and Karen Lundegaard, "One in Twelve Cars Recalled Last Year," *The Wall Street Journal,* March 4, 2004, pp. D1, D5.
33. Jonathan D. Salant, "FCC OKs Home-to-Cell Phone Number Rule," *Yahoo! News,* November 12, 2003, http://news.yahoo.com/.
34. "Corporate Crime: The Reckoning," *BusinessWeek,* March 15, 2004, p. 128.
35. Andrew Kramer, "Jury Finds Wal-Mart Owes Unpaid Overtime," *Associated Press,* February 18, 2004, http://story.news.yahoo.com.
36. William Spain, "Court Throws Out Tobacco Lawsuit," *CBS MarketWatch.com,* December 31, 2003; Barry Meier, "Huge Award for Smokers Is Voided by Appeals Court," *The New York Times,* May 22, 2003, http://www.nytimes.com.
37. "DoubleClick Settles Online-Privacy Suits, Plans to Ensure Protections, Pay Legal Fees," *The Wall Street Journal,* April 1, 2002, p. B8.
38. Cathy Booth-Thomas, "The See-It-All Chip," *Time,* October 2003, pp. A8–A16.
39. Nanci Hellmich, "School Vending Rated as Junk," *USA Today,* May 12, 2004, p. D12; Monica Roman, "Super Size Downsized," *BusinessWeek,* March 15, 2004, p. 44; "In Anti-Obesity Effort, Texas Schools Deep-Six Deep Fry," *AP Wire Story,* March 4, 2004; "McDonald's Phasing Out Super-Size Fries, Drinks," *USA Today,* March 4, 2004, p. B1; Mercedes M. Cardona, "Marketers Bite Back As Fat Fight Flares Up," *Advertising Age,* March 1, 2004, pp. 3, 35.
40. "Old Growth Campaign: Boise Victory!" *Rainforest Action Network,* http://www.ran.org, accessed February 19, 2004; Jim Carlton, "Boise Cascade Turns Green," *The Wall Street Journal,* September 3, 2002, p. B6.
41. Gregory Zuckerman, "Biovail Tactics on Marketing Focus of Probe," *The Wall Street Journal,* August 25, 2003, p. C1.
42. Cindy Starr, "Pharmaceutical Advertising Barrage Lures Consumers, Worries Doctors," *Scripps Howard News Service,* February 2, 2002; Devika Sennik, "Influence of Direct to Consumer Pharmaceutical Advertising and Patients' Requests on Prescribing Decision," *British Medical Journal,* February 2, 2002.

43. "Schering-Plough Corp.: U.S. Attorney Begins Issuing Subpoenas in Pricing Prove," *The Wall Street Journal,* April 1, 2002, p. C5.
44. Timothy J. Mullaney, with Brian Hindo, "Overstock: The Price Isn't Always Right," *BusinessWeek,* March 15, 2004, p. 11.
45. Marc Gunther, "Tree Huggers, Soy Lovers, and Profits," *Fortune,* June 23, 2003, pp. 89–104.
46. "Dell Recycling," Dell Web site, http://www.us.dell.com, accessed February 19, 2004; Jonathan Skillings, "Dell Partners for PC Recycling," *CNet News.com,* May 17, 2002, http://news.com.com.
47. Michelle Kessler, "PC Makers Soon May Be Forced to Recycle," *USA Today,* February 26, 2002, p. B1.
48. Bob Garfield, "Inspiration and Urge-to-Serve Mark the Best of Ad Council," *Advertising Age,* April 29, 2002, p. C2.
49. Christopher Tkaczyk, "Recycling," *Fortune,* April 1, 2002, p. 36.
50. Arlene Weintraub and Laura Cohn, "A Thousand-Year Plan for Nuclear Waste," *BusinessWeek,* May 6, 2002, pp. 94–96.
51. Nichole L. Torres, "Natural Instinct," *Entrepreneur,* August 2003, pp. 90–91.

CHAPTER 4

1. "In Quotes," *U.S. News & World Report,* April 12, 2004, p. 4; eBay Web site, http://www.ebay.com, accessed December 23, 2004; FansEdge Web site, http://www.fansedge.com, accessed December 23, 2004; Pro Sports Memorabilia Web site, http://www.prosportsmemorabilia.com, accessed December 23, 2004; Grandstand Sports & Memorabilia Web site, http://www.grandstandsports.com, accessed December 23, 2004; "No Long Lines, No Pushy Salespeople, No Problem Finding Parking," http://www.about.sportsline.com, accessed December 23, 2004; The National 25th Annual Sports Collectors Convention Web site, http://www.natlconv.com, accessed December 23, 2004; "The Sports Collectibles Industry," http://www.tristarproductions.com, accessed December 23, 2004.
2. Arundhati Parmar, "Student e-Union: Colleges Write Textbook on Internet Marketing," *Marketing News,* April 1, 2004, pp. 13–14.
3. Robyn Greenspan, "E-Tailers Will See Green," *ClickZ Network,* http://www.clickz.com, accessed February 2, 2004.
4. "Wireless Gets More Personal," http://www.apple.com/bluetooth/, accessed January 3, 2005.
5. Betsey Streisand, "Make New Sales," *U.S. News & World Report,* February 16, 2004, p. 41.
6. Ron Insana, "Dell Knows His Niche and He'll Stick with It," *USA Today,* April 5, 2004, p. B3.
7. Robert Hof, "Don't Cut Back Now," *BusinessWeek,* http://www.businessweek.com, February 24, 2004.
8. "Active Internet Users by Country," *ClickZ Network,* http://www.clickz.com/stats, accessed December 27, 2004.
9. Mark Dolliver, "Takes," *Adweek,* February 2, 2004, p. 30.
10. "iTunes Hits 50 Million Milestone," *BBC News,* http://newsvote.bbc.co.uk, accessed April 5, 2004.
11. Dan Reed, "Southwest Counters Cost Pressures with Longer Routes, Revved Growth," *USA Today,* March 2, 2004, p. 7B.
12. "B2B E-Commerce Headed for the Trillions," *ClickZ Network,* http://www.clickz.com/stats, accessed March 1, 2004.
13. "The Net's Good Fortune," *Wired,* March 2004, p. 967.
14. Robyn Greenspan, "Wireless Surfers Grow," *ClickZ Network,* http://www.clickz.com, accessed March 3, 2004.
15. Michelle Kessler, "Sales of Smart Phones Leave PDAs in the Dust," *USA Today,* January 29, 2004, p. B1.
16. Edward C. Baig, "It's Here, It's There, and Soon Everywhere," *USA Today,* March 29, 2004, p. B4; Scott Thurm, David Pringle, and Evan Ramstad, "Chill Hits Wi-Fi 'Hot Spots,'" *The Wall Street Journal,* March 18, 2004, pp. B1–B2.
17. Walter S. Mossberg, "Verizon Is Crossing the U.S. with Speedy, True Wireless Access," *The Wall Street Journal,* April 8, 2004, p. B1.
18. Laura Rush, "E-Commerce Growth Spurred by Maturation," *ClickZ Network,* http://www.clickz.com, accessed March 1, 2004.
19. Timothy Mullaney, "The E Biz Surprise," *BusinessWeek,* http://www.businessweek.com, accessed March 4, 2004.
20. "About," University of Phoenix, http://degrees.uofphx.info, accessed January 3, 2005.
21. Erick Schonfeld, "The Big Cheese of Online Grocers," *Business 2.0,* January/February 2004, pp. 60–61.
22. Deborah Vence, "Boston Orchestra Tunes Up Net Campaign," *Marketing News,* June 23, 2003, p. 5.
23. Robyn Greenspan, "Internet High on Travel Destinations," *ClickZ Network,* http://www.clickz.com, accessed March 1, 2004.
24. Mullaney, "The E Biz Surprise."
25. "Royal Mail Drive Major Cost Savings through FreeMarkets," press release, FreeMarkets, http://www.freemarkets.com, accessed March 5, 2004.
26. Erick Schonfeld, "Corporate America's New Outlet Mall," *Business 2.0,* April 2004, pp. 43–45.
27. "B2B E-Commerce Headed for the Trillions," *ClickZ Network,* http://www.clickz.com, accessed March 4, 2004.
28. IBM company profile, *MSN Investor,* http://moneycentral.msn.com, accessed January 4, 2005.
29. Robert Hof, "Reprogramming Amazon," *BusinessWeek,* http://www.businessweek.com, accessed March 4, 2004.
30. Steven Levy, "All Eyes on Google," *Newsweek,* March 29, 2004, pp. 49–59; Anick Jesdanun, "Google: The Trusted Name in Web Trolling," *Mobile Register,* March 28, 2004, p. F3.
31. "General Information" and "Benefits," State of North Carolina E-Procurement Program, http://www.ncgov.com/eprocurement/asp/section/ep_index.asp, accessed January 5, 2005.
32. Greenspan, "E-Tailers Will See Green."
33. Chris Woodyard and Barbara De Lollis, "Small-Car-Rental Firms Take Jab at Big Guys," *USA Today,* April 5, 2004, p. B1.
34. *Historybuff.com,* http://www.historybuff.com, accessed January 5, 2005.
35. Robyn Greenspan, "Merchants Need Some Timely Improvements," *ClickZ Network,* http://www.clickz.com, accessed March 15, 2004.
36. Amy Tsao, "Where Retailers Shop for Savings," *BusinessWeek,* http://www.businessweek.com, accessed March 8, 2004.
37. *AutoNetwork.com,* http://www.autonetwork.com, accessed December 8, 2004.
38. "Active Internet Users by Country," *ClickZ Network,* http://www.clickz.com, accessed March 6, 2004.
39. Pamela Parker, "Blame It on Surprises," *ClickZ Network,* http://www.clickz.com, accessed March 8, 2004.
40. Brian Krebs, "Senators Try to Smoke Out Spyware," *The Washington Post,* http://www.washingtonpost.com, accessed March 8, 2004.
41. Amazon.com Privacy Notice, http://www.amazon.com, accessed January 7, 2005.
42. "FTC Announces Settlement with Bankrupt Website, Toysmart.com, Regarding Alleged Privacy Policy Violations," press release, Federal Trade Commission, http://www.ftc.gov, accessed March 8, 2004.
43. Krebs, "Senators Try to Smoke Out Spyware."
44. Laura Rush, "E-Commerce Growth Spurred by Maturation," *ClickZ Network,* http://www.clickz.com, accessed March 8, 2004.
45. *America's Online Pursuits,* Pew Internet and American Life Project, http://www.pewinternet.org, accessed March 8, 2004.
46. Laura Rush, "Women, Comparison Shopping Help Boost Holiday Revenues," *ClickZ Network,* http://www.clickz.com, accessed March 10, 2004.
47. "Irrelevance through Constant Consumer Analysis," *Jupiter Media Metrix,* http://www.jmm.com, accessed March 6, 2004.
48. Nicole Maestri, "Target Phasing Out 'Smart' Visa Cards," *Yahoo! News,* http://news.yahoo.com, accessed March 5, 2004.
49. Jena McGregor, "It's a Blog World After All," *Fast Company,* April 2004, pp. 84–85; Catherine Arnold, "Vox Venditori: Marketers Discover Weblogs' Power To Sell—Minus the Pitch," *Marketing News,* March 15, 2004, pp. 1, 11–12.
50. Robyn Greenspan, "Online Ads, E-Marketing on Upswing," *ClickZ Network,* http://www.clickz.com, accessed March 10, 2004.
51. "Learning How Shoppers Shop, Sharper Image Considers Site Modification," *Internet Retailer,* http://internetretailer.com, accessed March 10, 2004.

CHAPTER 5

1. Tom Lowry, "Take Me Out to the Webcast?" *BusinessWeek,* April 12, 2004, p. 42; "Paul Tagliabue, National Football League," in "Best Managers," *BusinessWeek,* January 12, 2004, p. 66; Stefan Fatsis, "Can New $220 Million NFL Deal Appease Restive Owners?" *The Wall Street Journal,* December 16, 2003, p. B1; Peter Meyers, "Take Me Out . . . to the Webcast," *The Wall Street Journal,* October 7, 2003, p. D1; Michael Hiestand, "Sports on Cable TV: Will You Have to Pay More?" *USA Today,* October 9, 2003, p. 3C; Sam Walker, "The Long-Distance Fan," *The Wall Street Journal,* July 18, 2003, pp. W1, W4; Bill Syken, "A Big Web Catch," *Sports Illustrated,* June 9, 2003; Byron Acohido, "Golf Fever Proves Fans Will Pay to Log On," *USA Today,* May 23, 2003, p. B1.
2. Lynn Cook, "How Sweet It Is," *Forbes,* March 1, 2004, pp. 90–92; Laurel Wentz, "Nissan Boosts Hispanic Efforts," *Advertising Age,* December 1, 2003, p. 26.
3. Tobi Elkin, "Sony Marketing Aims at Lifestyle Segments," *Advertising Age,* March 18, 2002, p. 72.
4. Normandy Madden, "Study: Chinese Youth Aren't Patriotic Purchasers," *Advertising Age,* January 5, 2004, p. 6.
5. Haya El Nasser, "Census Projects Growing Diversity," *USA Today,* March 18, 2004, p. A1.
6. El Nasser, "Census Projects Growing Diversity."
7. Haya El Nasser, "39 Million Make Hispanics Largest Minority Group," *USA Today,* June 19, 2003, p. 1A.
8. El Nasser, "39 Million Make Hispanics Largest Minority Group."
9. Brian Grow, "Hispanic Nation," *BusinessWeek,* March 15, 2004, pp. 58–70.
10. Charles Schwab & Co., http://www.schwab.com, accessed March 8, 2004.
11. Patricia Sellers, "The Business of Being Oprah," *Fortune,* April 1, 2002, pp. 52–53.

12. "Asians Are an Unseen Minority," *MMR,* June 16, 2003, p. 117.
13. "NBA Uses Chinese Talent in Asian Marketing," *PR Week,* November 3, 2003, p. 3.
14. U.S. Census Bureau, http://www.census.gov, accessed March 9, 2004.
15. Stephanie Thompson, "Hip-Hop Bounces into Toddler Fashions," *Advertising Age,* March 15, 2004, pp. 3, 81; Barbara Lippert, "Her Favorite Things," *Adweek,* March 8, 2004, p. 30.
16. Melanie Wells, "Kid Nabbing," *Forbes,* February 2, 2004, pp. 84–88.
17. James D. Speros, "Why the Harley Brand's So Hot," *Advertising Age,* March 15, 2004, p. 26.
18. Arundhati Parmar, "Marketers Ask: Hues on First?" *Marketing News,* February 15, 2004, pp. 8, 10.
19. David Welch, "A Bummer for the Hummer," *BusinessWeek,* February 23, 2004, p. 49.
20. These categories were originally suggested in John A. Howard, *Marketing Management: Analysis and Planning* (Homewood, IL: Richard D. Irwin, 1963).

CHAPTER 6

1. Company Web site, http://www.rawlings.com, accessed February 6, 2004; "K2 Inc.'s Rawlings Sporting Goods Division Signs New Five Year Contract for Minor League Baseball," *Business Wire,* September 3, 2003, http://www.businesswire.com; "K2 and Rawlings Sign Agreement to Merge," Business Wire, December 16, 2002, http://www.businesswire.com; Stan McNeal, "Nothing Unseemly . . . or Unseamly," *The Sporting News,* June 5, 2000, http://www.findarticles.com; Terry Lefton, "MLB Sends Balls to the Mall," *Brandweek,* February 7, 2000, http://www.brandweek.com.
2. Robert A. Hamilton, "Budget Plan Has Billions for the State," *The New York Times,* February 10, 2002, p. 4.
3. "B2B E-Commerce Headed for Trillions," *ClickZ Network,* March 6, 2002, http://www.clickz.com.
4. Company Web site, http://www.kellyservices.com, accessed February 19, 2004.
5. Riza Cruz, "Things I Can't Live Without," *Inc.,* January 2004, p. 58.
6. Haya El Nasser, "Governments Use eBay to Sell High," *USA Today,* December 8, 2003, p. A1.
7. http://www.firstgov.gov, accessed February 12, 2004.
8. "Where B2B Exchanges Went Wrong," *Cnet News.com,* December 14, 2002, http://www.cnetnews.com.
9. Rene Pastor, "Online Cotton Exchange Eyes China and Brazil," *Reuters,* January 7, 2004, http://www.reuters.com.
10. Pastor, "Online Cotton Exchange Eyes China and Brazil."
11. Marketing materials supplied by Tetra Tech FW, Inc., February 2004.
12. "North American Industry Classification System (NAICS)," *U.S. Census Bureau,* January 7, 2004, http://www.census.gov.
13. Mike Troy, "PL Push and Power Users Put Profit Back in the Picture," *DSN Retailing Today,* September 8, 2003, http://www.findarticles.com.
14. "Ford Announces More Jobs and Another New Mercury Vehicle for Chicago Operations," company press release, *PRNewswire,* February 4, 2004; Jim Mateja, "Ford Suppliers Coming to First-of-Kind Campus," *Chicago Tribune,* May 16, 2002, S3, p. 1.
15. Ricky Anderson, "Tracking Your Deliveries in Your Hospital," *Healthcare Purchasing News,* June 2003, http://www.findarticles.com.
16. Marketing materials supplied by Tetra Tech FW, Inc., February 2004.
17. Sean Callahan, "China Calling," *BtoBonline,* March 11, 2002, http://www.btobonline.com.
18. Jon E. Hilsenrath, "Globalization Persists in Precarious New Age," *The Wall Street Journal,* December 31, 2001, p. A1.
19. Tom Krazit, "Intel's 90-Nanometer Prescott Chips Unveiled in Four Speeds," *ComputerWorld,* February 2, 2004, http://www.computerworld.com; Tom Smith, "Chipmakers' Circuits Are Humming," *BusinessWeek,* January 16, 2004, http://www.businessweek.com; Cliff Edwards, "Intel: Powered Up for Another Hot Year," *BusinessWeek,* January 15, 2004, http://www.businessweek.com.
20. Jack Neff, "Wal-Marketing: How to Benefit in Bentonville," *Advertising Age,* October 6, 2003, pp. 1, 24–28.
21. Stephanie Moore, "IT Trends 2004: Offshore Outsourcing," *Giga Research,* December 17, 2003, http://www.gigaweb.com.
22. Robyn Greenspan, "Companies Look Outside Themselves," *ClickZ Network,* May 3, 2002, http://www.clickz.com.
23. Company Web site, http://www.paychex.com, accessed February 5, 2004.
24. Stephen Baker and Manjeet Kripalani, "Software: Will Outsourcing Hurt America's Supremacy?" *BusinessWeek,* March 1, 2004, pp. 84–95; Stephanie Moore, "IT Trends 2004: High-Tech Battle Heats Up," *International Herald Tribune,* November 20, 2003, http://www.iht.com.
25. Andy Reinhardt, "Forget India, Let's Go to Bulgaria," *BusinessWeek,* March 1, 2004, p. 93.
26. Baker and Kripalani, "Software: Will Outsourcing Hurt America's Supremacy?"
27. David Clarke, "The Dangers of Outsourcing (and What to Do about Them)," *CIO,* February 1, 2004, http://www.cio.com.
28. Desiree De Myer, "Combat the Downside of Outsourcing Sprint," *Ziff Davis Smart Business,* May 1, 2002, p. 47.
29. Edward Prewitt, "Filing for Divorce," *CIO Magazine,* February 1, 2004, http://www.cio.com.
30. Bob Frances, "Gold Winner: Color My World Boise," *Brandweek,* March 18, 2002, p. R17.
31. Michelle Leder, "Taking a Niche Player Big-Time," *Inc.,* January 2004, pp. 34, 37.
32. Leder, "Taking a Niche Player Big-Time."
33. Leder, "Taking a Niche Player Big-Time."
34. Betsy McKay, "Pepsi Is Set to Become the Cola of Choice for United Airlines," *The Wall Street Journal,* March 25, 2002, p. A3.
35. Leder, "Taking a Niche Player Big-Time."
36. Ian Mount, "Be Fast, Be Frugal, Be Right," *Inc.,* January 2004, pp. 64–70.
37. "Setting New Standards for Innovation," *DSN Retailing Today,* May 20, 2002, http://www.findarticles.com.
38. Mount, "Be Fast, Be Frugal, Be Right."
39. Fibre Containers Web site, http://www.fibrecontainers.com, accessed March 12, 2004; Don Green, "Count on Strong Relationships," *Paperboard Packaging,* November 2001, p. 8.
40. Spencer S. Hsu, "Federal Spending in Region Surged," *The Washington Post,* April 21, 2001, p. E1.
41. Allan V. Burman, "Buying Better All the Time," *Government Executive,* December 2001, p. 72.
42. Shane Harris, "The Only Game in Town," *Government Executive,* December 2001, pp. 16–26.
43. Company Web site, http://www.baxter.com, accessed February 28, 2004.

CHAPTER 7

1. Bruce Horovitz, "Gillette Signs Soccer Star Even as Rumors Buzz," *USA Today,* May 28, 2004, p. B3; Michael Freedman, "Madness of Crowds," *Forbes 2000,* April 12, 2004, pp. 120–125; Cecily Fluke and Michael K. Ozanian, "Goal, Man U!" *Forbes 2000,* April 12, 2004, pp. 126–127; Grant Wahl, "Ready for Freddy?" *Sports Illustrated,* March 29, 2004, pp. 59–61; Barry Janoff, "U.S. Beckons Beckham, Réal," *Brandweek,* March 22, 2004, p. 12.
2. Steven B. Kamin, "U.S. International Transactions in 2002," *Federal Reserve,* May 3, 2003, http://www.federalreserve.gov.
3. Nuchhi R. Currier, "World Investment Report 2002: Transnational Corporations and Export Competitiveness," *United Nations Chronicle Online Edition,* March 2003, http://www.un.org.
4. Jeffrey E. Garten, "Wal-Mart Gives Globalism a Bad Name," *BusinessWeek,* March 8, 2004, p. 24; Ann Zimmerman and Martin Fackler, "Wal-Mart's Foray into Japan Spurs a Retail Upheaval," *The Wall Street Journal,* September 19, 2003, pp. A1, A6.
5. "About New York Metro Weddings," company Web site, http://www.newyorkmetroweddings.com, accessed February 18, 2004.
6. Ad for Hilton HHonors Worldwide, copyright 2002, Hilton HHonors Worldwide.
7. News Release, "U.S. International Trade in Goods and Services," Bureau of Economic Analysis, February 13, 2004, http://www.bea.gov.; Mitchell Pacelle, "Citigroup Looks Ahead for Its Future Growth," *The Wall Street Journal,* March 15, 2004, pp. C1, C3.
8. "Finance Site the Stickiest Online," *ClickZ Network,* http://www.clickz.com, February 28, 2002; Michael Pastore, "Branches Still Rule Banking in Europe," *ClickZ Network,* http://www.clickz.com, November 19, 2002.
9. Ira Sager, ed., "Over There: Starbucks—An American in Paris," *BusinessWeek,* December 8, 2003, p. 11; Ellen Hale, "Krispy Kreme's Sweet on Britain," *USA Today,* August 12, 2003, p. 1; Martin Fackler, "Will Ratatouille Bring Japanese to McDonald's?" *The Wall Street Journal,* August 14, 2003, p. B1; Leslie Chang, "Amway in China: Once Barred, Now Booming," *The Wall Street Journal,* March 12, 2003, pp. B1, B5.
10. Geoffrey A. Fowler, "China's Cultural Fabric Is a Challenge to Marketers," *The Wall Street Journal,* January 21, 2004, p. B7A.
11. "World Population Profile: 1998 Highlights," U.S. Census Bureau, http://www.census.gov, accessed February 18, 2004.
12. Chad Terhune and Gabriel Kahn, "Coke Lures Japanese Customers with Cellphone Come-Ons," *The Wall Street Journal,* September 8, 2003, p. B1.
13. Betsy McKay, "Pepsi and Coke Roll Out Flavors to Boost Sales," *The Wall Street Journal,* May 7, 2002, pp. B1, B4; "The Coca-Cola Co.," Hoover's Online company capsule, http://www.hoovers.com, accessed February 19, 2004.
14. Shusaku Hattori, "Blockbuster Shuts Down in Hong Kong," *CBS Market Watch,* January 30, 2004, http://cbs.marketwatch.com.
15. Bruce Einhorn, "The Net's Second Superpower," *BusinessWeek,* March 15, 2004, pp. 54–56; Jeffrey D. Sachs, "Welcome to the Asian Century," *Fortune,* January 12, 2004, pp. 53–54.
16. Evan Ramstad and Ken Brown, "China Expands Phone Service Via Internet," *The Wall Street Journal,* April 22, 2004, p. B4; *Reuters Limited,* "Nokia Looks to Dominate Sales in China," *Cnet Asia,* February 26, 2002, http://www.asia.cnet.com.
17. Colleen Barry, "Euro Currency Begins in Europe," *Mobile Register,* January 1, 2002, p. A11.
18. "Doing Business Abroad," http://www.getcustoms.com, accessed February 19, 2004.
19. Anton Piëch, "Speaking in Tongues," *Inc.,* June 2003, p. 50.
20. James Cox, "U.S. Challenges Europe's Biotech Crop Ban in Court," *USA Today,* May 14, 2003, p. 3B; "Europe to Demand Strict Molecular Characterization for GMOs?" Institute of Science in Society press release, May 21, 2002, http://www.i-sis.org.uk/biotech-info-net.
21. Dexter Roberts et al., "Days of Rage," *BusinessWeek,* April 8, 2002, pp. 50–51.
22. Antoaneta Bezlova, "McDonald's Arches Outlawed in Beijing," *USA Today,* March 5, 2002, p. 7B.
23. "U.S. Reaches Free Trade Deal with Four Central American Countries," *USA Today,* December 17, 2003, http://usatoday.com.

24. Michael Erman, "Steelmakers Displeased in End to Tariffs," *Reuters Limited,* December 4, 2003; James Cox, "Bush Scraps Tariffs on Steel," *USA Today,* December 5, 2003.
25. Office of Foreign Assets Control, "Cuba: What You Need to Know about the U.S. Embargo," U.S. Department of the Treasury, March 24, 2003, http://www.ustreas.gov.
26. Andy Mukherjee, "First, Brassieres. Now, Shrimp. Who Gains?" *Bloomberg News,* January 7, 2004, http://www.bloomberg.com.
27. Eric Wahlgren, "The Outsourcing Dilemma," *Inc.,* April 2004, pp. 41–42; Bruce Nussbaum, "Where Are the Jobs?" *BusinessWeek,* March 22, 2004, pp. 36–48; Stephanie Armour, "Companies Crow about Keeping Jobs in the USA," *USA Today,* March 12, 2004, p. B1; Jesse Drucker, "Global Talk Gets Cheaper," *The Wall Street Journal,* March 11, 2004, pp. B1–B2; Scott Thurm, "Lesson in India: Not Every Job Translates Overseas," *The Wall Street Journal,* March 3, 2004, pp. A1, A10; Peronet Despeignes, "Poll: Enthusiasm for Free Trade Fades," *USA Today,* February 24, 2004, p. B1.
28. Jay Greene and Andy Reinhardt, "Microsoft: First Europe, Then . . . ?" *BusinessWeek,* March 22, 2004, pp. 86–87; Paul Geitner, "World Trade Organization Hands Major Loss to U.S.," *Mobile Register,* January 15, 2002, p. B5.
29. Kris Axtman, "NAFTA's Shop-Floor Impact," *Christian Science Monitor,* November 4, 2003, http://www.csmonitor.com.
30. Robert A. Pastor, "Wanted: A Real NAFTA Partnership," *Worth,* March 2004, p. 34.
31. Geri Smith and Cristina Lindblad, "Mexico: Was NAFTA Worth It?" *BusinessWeek,* December 22, 2003, p. 66–72; Geri Smith, "Wasting Away," *BusinessWeek,* June 2, 2003, p. 42–44; Jim Rogers, "Running on Empty," *Worth,* January/February 2002, pp. 55–56.
32. Noelle Knox, "EU Expansion Brings USA Opportunities," *USA Today,* April 27, 2004, pp. B1, B2; Joshua Kurlantzick, "New World Order," *Entrepreneur,* April 2004, pp. 19–20.
33. Brian Caulfield and Ting Shi, "An American Icon in China," *Business 2.0,* March 2004, p. 58; Russell Flannery, "China Is a Big Prize," *Forbes,* May 10, 2004, pp. 163–166.
34. "Foreign Direct Investment Is on the Rise around the World," *The New Economy Index,* http://www.neweconomyindex.org, accessed April 26, 2004.
35. Normandy Madden and Jack Neff, "P&G Adapts Attitude Toward Local Markets," *Advertising Age,* February 23, 2004, pp. 28–29.
36. Lisa Bannon and Carlta Vitzthum, "One-Toy-Fits-All: How Industry Learned to Love the Global Kid," *The Wall Street Journal,* April 29, 2003, p. A1.
37. The Coca-Cola Co. Web site, http://www.coca-cola.com, accessed February 20, 2004.
38. "The World's 10 Most Valuable Brands," *BusinessWeek,* August 4, 2003, http://www.businessweek.com.
39. Robert J. Samuelson, "The Cartel We Love to Hate," *Newsweek,* February 23, 2004, p. 47.
40. Venture Safenet Web site, http://www.venturesafenet.com, accessed February 20, 2004.
41. "Table 1: Foreign Direct Investment in the United States," International Accounts, Bureau of Economic Analysis, http://www.bea.gov, accessed February 20, 2004; "Who Owns What," *Columbia Journalism Review,* http://www.cjr.org, accessed February 20, 2004; "L'Oréal," http://www.hoovers.com, accessed February 21, 2004; L'Oréal Web site, http://www.loreal.com, accessed February 20, 2004; "Grand Metropolitan," *Business.com,* http://www.business.com, accessed February 20, 2004.

CHAPTER 8

1. Hillary Cassidy, "Out with the Old . . . In with the New," *Brandweek,* May 10, 2004, pp. 44–54; Darren Rovell, "The Making of a Name (and Logo)," *ESPN.com,* March 10, 2004, http://sports.espn.go.com; "Charlotte Welcomes the Bobcats," *Jet,* June 30, 2003, infotrac-college.thomsonlearning.com; "NBA Expansion Franchise to Be Named Charlotte Bobcats," Charlotte Bobcats Web site, June 11, 2003, http://www.nba.com/bobcats; "Ad Pros Weigh In on Charlotte Bobcats' Design," The Society for Sports Uniforms Research, June 12, 2003, http://www.ssur.org; "Johnson Will Be NBA's First Black Majority Owner," *ESPN.com,* December 17, 2002, http://espn.go.com/nba.
2. Daniel Kruger, "You Want Data with That?" *Forbes,* March 29, 2004, pp. 58–60.
3. Kevin Kelleher, "66,207,896 Bottles of Beer on the Wall," *Business 2.0,* January/February 2004, pp. 47–49.
4. Stephanie Thompson, "Wal-Mart Tops List for New Food Lines," *Advertising Age,* April 29, 2002, pp. 4, 61.
5. Jerry W. Thomas, "Skipping MR a Major Error," *Marketing News,* March 4, 2002, p. 50.
6. http://www.census.gov/mp/www/rom/geoprod.html, accessed March 29, 2004.
7. Matt Michell, "The Internet as a Market Research Tool," *Public Relations Tactics,* March 2002, p. 6; Theano Nikitas, "Your Customers Are Talking. Are You Listening?" *Ziff Davis Smart Business,* February 2002, p. 50.
8. Deborah Szynal, "Big Bytes," *Marketing News,* March 18, 2002, p. 3.
9. Steve Jarvis, "Sum of the Parts," *Marketing News,* January 21, 2002, p. 1.
10. Claire Atkinson, "Nielsen Local Ratings Under Gov't Scrutiny," *Advertising Age,* May 17, 2004, p. 6; Linda Moss, "A Constant Companion," *Broadcasting & Cable,* February 11, 2002.
11. Suzanne Vranica and Charles Goldsmith, "Nielsen Adapts Its Methods as TV Evolves," *The Wall Street Journal,* September 29, 2003, pp. B1, B10; Lee Hall, "People Meters Push Right Button," *Advertising Age,* May 12, 2003, p. S–22.
12. Nick Wingfield and Jennifer Saranow, "TiVo Tunes in to Its Users' Viewing Habits," *The Wall Street Journal,* February 9, 2004, pp. B1, B4.
13. Lev Grossman, "The Quest for Cool," *Time,* September 8, 2003, pp. 48–54.
14. Steve Jarvis, "CMOR Finds Survey Refusal Rate Still Rising," *Marketing News,* February 4, 2002, p. 4.
15. Ken Peterson, "Despite New Law, Phone Surveys Still Effective," *Marketing News,* September 15, 2003, pp. 22–23.
16. Kenneth Wade, "Focus Groups' Research Role Is Shifting," *Marketing News,* March 4, 2002, p. 47.
17. Henry Gomez, "Wyse Remakes Focus Groups with Laptop Program," *Crain's Cleveland Business,* November 17, 2003, p. 9.
18. Sylvia Marino, "Survey Says!" *Econtent,* April 2002, pp. 32–36.
19. Nina M. Ray and Sharon W. Tabor, "Several Issues Affect E-Research Validity," *Marketing News,* September 15, 2003, pp. 50–51; Dana James, "This Bulletin Just In," *Marketing News,* March 4, 2002, p. 45.
20. Kris Oser, "Speedway Effort Decodes Nascar Fans," *Advertising Age,* May 17, 2004, p. 150; Anni Layne Rodgers, "More Than a Game," *Fast Company,* May 2002, p. 46.
21. Jim Kirk, "Wait Nearly Over for U.S. Rollout of Low-Carb Beer," *Chicago Tribune,* May 2, 2002, S3, p. 3.
22. Carlos Denton, "Time Differentiates Latino Focus Groups," *Marketing News,* March 15, 2004, p. 52.
23. Jagdish N. Sheth and Banwari Mittal, *Customer Behavior: A Managerial Perspective,* second edition (Mason, OH: South-Western, 2004), p. 240.
24. Linda Tischler, "Every Move You Make," *Fast Company,* April 2004, pp. 73–75.
25. Todd Wasserman, "Sharpening the Focus," *Brandweek,* November 3, 2003, pp. 28–32.
26. Tischler, "Every Move You Make."
27. Wesley Sprinkle, "In Sync with Customers," *Bests Review,* April 2002.
28. Julia King, "One Version of the Truth," *Computerworld,* December 22, 2003, p. 38.
29. Gary H. Anthes, "The Search Is On," *Computerworld,* April 15, 2002, pp. 54–56.
30. Ron Miller, "Get Smart with Business Intelligence Software," *Econtent,* November 2003, p. 24.
31. Stefanie Olsen, "IBM Sets Out to Make Sense of the Web," *CNETnews.com,* February 5, 2004.
32. Thomas, "Skipping MR a Major Error."

CHAPTER 9

1. Phil Taylor, "Pennies from Heaven," *Sports Illustrated,* February 9, 2004, pp. 58–62; David Whitford, "The People's Owner," *Fortune,* October 13, 2003, pp. 181–188; Mark Hyman, "Sure, He's Latino. But Don't Expect Salsa at the Park," *BusinessWeek,* June 2, 2003, p. 85; Bob Nightengale, "First Hispanic MLB Owner Loves the Game," *USA Today Sports Weekly,* May 21–27, 2003, p. 13.
2. Edith M. Lederer, "U.N. Predicts 9 Billion People by 2300," *Associated Press,* http://story.news.yahoo.com.
3. May Wong, "Consumer Electronics Companies Woo Women," *Associated Press,* January 15, 2004, http://news.yahoo.com.
4. Company Web site, http://www.lowes.com, accessed March 31, 2004; Bruce Upbin, "Merchant Princes," *Forbes,* January 20, 2003, pp. 52–56; "Robert Tillman," *BusinessWeek,* January 13, 2003, p. 63.
5. Wong, "Consumer Electronics Companies Woo Women"; Samar Farah, "What Women Want," *Metro,* February 14, 2002, p. 11 [originally published in the *Christian Science Monitor*].
6. Wong, "Consumer Electronics Companies Woo Women."
7. Wong, "Consumer Electronics Companies Woo Women."
8. U.S. Census Bureau, http://www.firstgov.gov, accessed March 10, 2004.
9. U.S. Census Bureau, http://www.census.gov/population/projections/state/stpjrace.txt, May 2, 2002.
10. "The Twenty Most Populous Countries," *United Nations Population Division,* http://www.un.org/esa/population, accessed March 10, 2004.
11. Mark Dolliver, "Sure, We're Still a Mobile People, but Not as Mobile as We Used to Be," *Adweek,* March 29, 2004, p. 30.
12. U.S. Census Bureau, http://www.firstgov.gov, accessed March 10, 2004.
13. Genaro C. Armas, "Western Suburbs Lead U.S. in Growth," *Mobile Register,* July 10, 2003, p. A11.
14. U.S. Census Bureau, http://www.census.gov/population/www/pop-profile/stproj.html, May 2, 2002.
15. Haya el Nasser, "Moving West Is No Longer the Norm," *USA Today,* August 6, 2003, http://www.usatoday.com.
16. "Metropolitan Areas and Primary Metropolitan Statistical Areas," http://www.census.gov/population/www/estimates/aboutmetro.html.
17. Joan Voigt, "Don't Box Me In," *Brandweek,* September 1, 2003, pp. 14–16.
18. Laurel Scheffel, "Co-Masters of Their Domain," *Brandweek,* September 8, 2003, p. 20.
19. "Do Gender Specific Razors Differ?" *Fortune,* November 12, 2001, p. 48.
20. Steve Cooper, "It Figures," *Entrepreneur,* p. 36.
21. Susan Linn and Diane E. Levin, "Stop Marketing Yummy Food to Children," *Christian Science Monitor,* June 20, 2002, http://www.csmonitor.com.
22. Diane Scharper, "Study Shows Young Generation's Brand-Name Playgrounds," *USA Today,* April 21, 2003, p. B6; Becky Ebenkamp, "Youth Shall Be Served," *Brandweek,* June 24, 2002, p. 21.

23. Ebenkamp, "Youth Shall Be Served."
24. Ebenkamp, "Youth Shall Be Served."
25. Matthew Maier, "What Works: Hooking Up with Gen Y," *Business 2.0,* October 2003, pp. 49–52.
26. Dean Faust and Brian Grow, "Coke: Wooing the TiVo Generation," *BusinessWeek,* March 1, 2004, pp. 77, 80.
27. Overseas Adventure Travel catalog, 2003–2004.
28. Roger Simon and Angie Cannon, "An Amazing Journey," *U.S. News & World Report,* August 6, 2001, p. 13.
29. Simon and Cannon, "An Amazing Journey."
30. "Longer Life for 50-Plus Americans," *AARP Bulletin,* November 2001, p. 4.
31. Voigt, "Don't Box Me In."
32. Kelly Greene, "Marketing Surprise: Older Consumers Buy Stuff, Too," *The Wall Street Journal,* April 4, 2004, pp. A1, A12.
33. Haya El Nasser, "Census Projects Growing Diversity," *USA Today,* March 18, 2004, p. A1.
34. Brian Grow, "Hispanic Nation," *BusinessWeek,* March 15, 2004, p. 60; Haya el Nasser, "39 Million Make Hispanics Largest U.S. Minority Group," *USA Today,* June 18, 2003, http://www.usatoday.com.
35. El Nasser, "39 Million Make Hispanics Largest U.S. Minority Group"; Simon and Cannon, "An Amazing Journey."
36. Grow, "Hispanic Nation"; Jeffery D. Zbar, "Networks Give New Voice to Hispanic Households," *Advertising Age,* May 21, 2004, p. S10; Sandy Brown, "A New Portrait of Hispanic Consumers," *Adweek,* May 10, 2004, p. 10; Mercedes M. Cardona, "Home Chains Focus on Hispanic Market," *Advertising Age,* March 22, 2004, p. 6.
37. Catherine Arnold, "Change-up Pitch," *Marketing News,* October 13, 2003, pp. 5, 12.
38. Jeffrey D. Zbar, "Latinos Make Mark on U.S. Sports," *Advertising Age,* October 27, 2003, p. S–10.
39. Anne D'Innocenzio, "Retailers Try to Woo Hispanic Consumers," *Mobile Register,* May 11, 2003, p. B7.
40. Jane Weaver, "A Hot Hispanicized Consumer Market," *MSNBC,* May 12, 2003, http://www.msnbc.com.
41. "Marketing Fact Book," *Marketing News,* July 7, 2003, p. 24; *Hispanic Business Magazine,* Hispanic Business Inc., Santa Barbara, CA; Competitive Media Reporting, NY.
42. Voigt, "Don't Box Me In."
43. "Hispanics, Asians Continuing Explosive Population Growth," http://www.usatoday.com, June 14, 2004; Wilfred Masumara, "Money Income," U.S. Census Bureau, http://www.census.gov/population/www/pop-profile/minc.html, March 9, 2000.
44. Terrance Reeves and Claudette Bennett, "The Asian and Pacific Islander Population in the United States: March 2002," *U.S. Census Bureau Current Population Reports,* March 2003, http://www.census.gov.
45. Stella U. Ogunwole, "The American Indian and Alaska Native Population: 2000," *U.S. Census Bureau Current Population Reports,* February 2002, http://www.census.gov.
46. Catherine Arnold, "Native American Segment Is Ripe for New Research," *Marketing News,* July 21, 2003, p. 4.
47. Matt Krantz, "Indian Tribe Bets on Diversification for Longevity," *USA Today,* January 30, 2004, p. 5B; Arnold, "Native American Segment Is Ripe for New Research."
48. Krantz, "Indian Tribe Bets on Diversification for Longevity."
49. Daniel Yee, "U.S. Women Waiting until 25 to Have Kids," *Associated Press,* December 17, 2003, http://story.news.yahoo.com.
50. Eileen Daspin, "The End of Nesting," *The Wall Street Journal,* May 16, 2003, pp. W1, W9.
51. Michelle Conlin, "Unmarried America," *BusinessWeek,* October 20, 2003, pp. 106–116.
52. Genaro C. Armas, "More Older Couples Choose to Live Together," *The Morning News,* July 30, 2002, p. 3D.
53. Conlin, "Unmarried America."
54. Sue Shellenbarger, "Amid Gay Marriage Debate, Companies Offer More Benefits to Same-Sex Couples," *The Wall Street Journal,* March 18, 2004, p. D1.
55. Christine Dugas, "Middle Class Barely Treads Water," *USA Today,* September 15, 2003, pp. 1B, 2B.
56. Tony Case, "No Stopping Shopping," *Brandweek,* September 8, 2003, pp. 22–26.
57. Pamela Paul, "Sell It to the Psyche," *Time Inside Business,* October 2003.
58. Roper ASW, http://www.roperasw.com, accessed May 7, 2002.
59. Paul, "Sell It to the Psyche."
60. Michelle Andrews, "If It Feels Good, Buy It," *U.S. News & World Report,* February 23–March 1, 2004, pp. D2–D4.
61. "FedEx Completes Acquisition of Kinko's," company press release, February 12, 2004, http://www.kinkos.com; Alison Overholt, "New Leaders, New Agenda," *Fast Company,* May 2002, p. 52.
62. Kimberly L. Allers, "Retail's Rebel Yell," *Fortune,* November 10, 2003, pp. 137–141.
63. David Kiley and James R. Healey, "GM Plans to Boldly Go after Niche Markets," *USA Today,* February 19, 2004, p. B3.
64. Jennifer Barrett, "Travel/Flying High," *Newsweek,* January 12, 2004, p. 59.
65. Paul Frumkin, "Bertucci's Turns the Corner as Repositioning Drives Sales," *Nation's Restaurant News,* June 2, 2003, http://www.findarticles.com.
66. Shelly Branch and Nick Wingfield, "Chic at a Click: eBay Fashions a Deal with Designers," *The Wall Street Journal,* September 15, 2003, pp. B1, B10.

CHAPTER 10

1. WNBA Web site, http://www.wnba.com, accessed March 9, 2004; Mohegan Sun Web site, http://www.mohegansun.com, accessed March 9, 2004; Michael Hiestand, "Slots and Jump Shots," *USA Today,* June 19, 2003, pp. C1, C2; Karen Benezra, "WNBA Challenge: Boost Ratings, Sponsor Activity," *Brandweek,* July 28, 2003, p. 8; Hilary Cassidy, "The Game," *Brandweek,* May 26, 2003, p. 16.
2. Christine Dugas, "MBNA Adds AmEx to Visa, MasterCard Lineup," *USA Today,* January 30, 2004, p. B1.
3. Lawrence A. Crosby and Sheree L. Johnston, "CRM and Management," *Marketing Management,* January/February 2002, p. 10.
4. Veronica Agosta, "Nat City Takes Customer Focus to the Airwaves," *American Banker,* March 19, 2002, p. 1.
5. Andy Serwer, "The Hottest Thing in the Sky," *Fortune,* March 8, 2004, pp. 86–88, 101–102.
6. "Deals and Discounts," *The New York Times,* March 17, 2002, p. 3.
7. Sean Hargrave, "Making Waves," *New Media Age,* January 15, 2004, http://infotrac-college.thomsonlearning.com.
8. Bernard Stamler, "The Web Doesn't Sell Cars, but Lets Buyers Build Their Own," *The New York Times,* September 26, 2001, p. H10.
9. Jane M. Von Bergen, "FAO Schwarz, Zany Brainy's Parent Company Files for Bankruptcy," *Knight-Ridder/Tribune Business News,* January 14, 2003.
10. Hargrave, "Making Waves."
11. Andy Serwer, "Music Retailers Are Starting to Sing the Blues," *Fortune,* March 8, 2004, p. 73.
12. Marriott Web site, http://www.marriott.com, accessed March 21, 2004.
13. Mike Koller, "Harrah's Rewards Gamblers," *Internetweek,* October 8, 2001, pp. 10–11.
14. "On Demand Business Software," *Association Management,* November 2003, http://0-web3.infotrac.galegroup.com.lrc.cod.edu:80.
15. "Affinity Marketing Efforts Gain Momentum," *Bank Marketing International,* November 30, 2003, http://0-web3.infotrac.galegroup.com.lrc.cod.edu:80.
16. "Tip of the Iceberg," *Health Management Technology,* 2003, http://www.nelsonpublishingcompany.com.
17. Arundhati Parmar, "Marines, Air Force Scour Databases for Recruits," *Marketing News,* July 21, 2003, p. 17.
18. Jeff Howe, "Ready for Prime Time," *Adweek,* September 10, 2001, p. Q10.
19. Ian McKenna, "Touching Database," *Money Marketing,* 2003, http://www.moneymarketing.co.uk.
20. "Farm Aid Uses Convio to Cultivate Broader Base of Supporters," *PrimeZone Media Network,* February 9, 2004, http://media.primezone.com.
21. "Deliver a Punch to Your Gut Market," *On Wall Street,* February 1, 2004, http://www.thomsonmedia.com.
22. William M. Bulkeley, "IBM Highlights Service on Demand," *The Wall Street Journal,* April 21, 2003, p. B8.
23. Susan Greco, "1+1+1=The New Mass Market," *Inc.,* January 2003, p. 32.
24. "Custom CDs," *Sony Music Marketing Group,* company Web site, http://www.sonycustommarketing.com.
25. "Grassroots Marketing Defined," *Onpoint Marketing and Promotions,* company Web site, http://www.onpoint-marketing.com, accessed February 4, 2004.
26. "Grassroots Marketing," *ITMS Sports,* company Web site, http://www.itmssports.com, accessed February 4, 2004.
27. "Hanes Body Enhancers," *Alliance,* company Web site, http://www.alianco.com, accessed February 4, 2004.
28. Theresa Lindeman, "More Firms Use Unique Guerilla Marketing Techniques to Garner Attention," *Pittsburgh Post Gazette,* January 18, 2004, http://www.post-gazette.com.
29. "The Good Ad and the Ugly," *Internet Magazine,* January 15, 2004, http://infotrac-college.thomsonlearning.com.
30. Jean Halliday, "Mazda Goes Viral to Tout New Cars," *Automotive News,* November 24, 2003, http://infotrac-college.thomsonlearning.com.
31. Carleen Hawn, "The Man Who Sees Around Corners," *Forbes,* January 21, 2002, p. 72.
32. Hawn, "The Man Who Sees Around Corners"; Michael Krauss, "Siebel Leverages Hosted CRM Apps' Value," *Marketing News,* April 1, 2004, pp. 6, 7.
33. Daniel Tynan, "CRM: Buy or Rent?" *Sales & Marketing Management,* March 2004, pp. 41–45.
34. Kathleen Cholewka, "CRM: The Failures Are Your Fault," *emanager,* January 2002, pp. 23–24.
35. Colin Shearer, "Make Predictions to Improve CRM Results," *Marketing News,* July 21, 2003, p. 19.
36. Amanda C. Kooser, "Crowd Control," *Entrepreneur,* August 2003, pp. 33–41.
37. Geoff Ables, "Getting (Re)Started with Relationship Marketing," *CRM Today,* http://www.crm2day.com/relationship_marketing, accessed January 13, 2004.
38. Kooser, "Crowd Control."
39. Ellen Neuborne, "The Virtual Relationship," *Sales & Marketing Management,* http://www.salesandmarketing.com, accessed December 18, 2003.
40. Jacquelyn S. Thomas, Robert C. Blattberg, and Edward J. Fox, "Recapturing Lost Customers," *Journal of Marketing Research,* February 2004, pp. 31–45.
41. Ellen Neuborne, "Customer Rehab," *Sales & Marketing Management,* August 2003, p. 18.

42. Neuborne, "Customer Rehab."
43. David Finnegan, "The Biz," *Brandweek,* April 8, 2002.
44. Paul Kaihla, "The Matchmaker in the Machine," *Business 2.0,* January/February 2004, pp. 52–55.
45. Becky Ebenkamp, "BK, Kellogg Dish Out *SpongeBob* Support," *Brandweek,* February 9, 2004, p. 4.
46. Heather Harreld, "Supply Chain Collaboration," *InfoWorld,* December 24, 2001, pp. 22–25.
47. Mary Aichlmayr, "Is CPFR Worth the Effort?" *Transportation & Distribution,* 2003.
48. "Sky Team Gets on Board with $18 M Effort," *Brandweek,* April 11, 2002.

CHAPTER 11

1. Wal-Mart Fishing and Boating Web site, **http://www.walmart.com**, accessed May 27, 2004; Wal-Mart FLW Tour Web site, **http://flw.flwoutdoors.com**, accessed May 27, 2004; American Sport Fishing Association Web site, **http://www.asafishing.org**, accessed May 27, 2004; Bass Pro Shops Web site, **http://www.basspro-shops.com**, accessed April 30, 2004; Bassmaster, **http://espn.go.com/outdoors/Bassmaster**, accessed April 17, 2004; American Bass Anglers Web site, **http://www.americanbassangler.com**, accessed April 17, 2004; ProBass Web site, **http://www.probass.com**, accessed April 17, 2004.
2. Concept first introduced by G. Lynn Shostack, "Breaking Free from Product Marketing," *Journal of Marketing,* April 1977, p. 77; John M. Rathmell, "What Is Meant by Services?" *Journal of Marketing,* October 1980, pp. 32–36.
3. Bruce Horovitz, "You Want It Your Way," *USA Today,* March 5–7, 2004, pp. 1–2.
4. Ann Harrington, "America's Most Admired Companies," *Fortune,* March 8, 2004, pp. 80–81.
5. Sue Kirchoff, "Service Sector Outpaces Predictions, Hits Six-Year High," *USA Today,* August 6, 2003, p. B2.
6. Bureau of Labor Statistics, **http://www.firstgov.gov**, accessed May 3, 2004.
7. Jesse Drucker and Ken Brown, "Press 1 for Delhi, 2 for Dallas," *The Wall Street Journal,* March 9, 2004, p. B1.
8. Catharine P. Taylor, "The Buck Stops Here; Doctors and Their Rx Pads at the Forefront of DTC," *Advertising Age Special Report on Direct-to-Consumer Marketing,* May 27, 2002, pp. S-2, S-8.
9. John Simons, "Merck's Man in the Hot Seat," *Fortune,* February 23, 2004, pp. 111–114.
10. Company Web site, **http://www.giftbaskets.com**, accessed May 4, 2004.
11. Delroy Alexander, "High-Stakes Shelf Games," *Chicago Tribune,* December 14, 2003, pp. 5–1, 5–7.
12. Concept introduced by Christopher H. Lovelock, "Classifying Services to Gain Strategic Marketing Insights," *Journal of Marketing,* Summer 1983, p. 10.
13. Michael D. Hutt and Thomas W. Speh, *Business Marketing Management,* eighth edition (Mason, OH: South-Western, 2004).
14. "JetBlue Ranked No. 1 Airline, Report Says," *USA Today,* April 5, 2004, **http://www.usatoday.com**.
15. Alex Taylor III, "OnStar Is a Nonstarter for GM," *Fortune,* July 21, 2003, p. 28.
16. L.L. Bean catalog, summer 2004.
17. L.L. Bean catalog, summer 2004, pp. 66–67.
18. Anand Natarajan, "Interiors by Smith & Wesson," *BusinessWeek,* November 10, 2003, p. 16.
19. Diane Brady, "Teaching an Old Bag New Tricks," *BusinessWeek,* June 9, 2003, pp. 78–80.
20. Jefferson Graham, "Camera Phones Rival DVD Players as Fastest Growing," *USA Today,* November 18, 2003, p. B1.
21. Graham, "Camera Phones Rival DVD Players as Fastest Growing."
22. "Flat Is Beautiful," *Business 2.0,* April 2004, p. 36.
23. Benjamin Fulford, "Adventures in the Third Dimension," *Forbes,* May 24, 2004, pp. 166–170.
24. Zippo Web site, **http://www.zippo.com**, accessed May 28, 2004; Cara Beardi, "Zippo's Eternal Flame," *Advertising Age,* August 13, 2001, p. 4.
25. Stephen Manes, "Time to Trash Your VCR?" *Forbes,* April 19, 2004, pp. 90–92.
26. James Bandler, "Ending Era, Kodak Will Stop Selling Most Cameras," *The Wall Street Journal,* January 14, 2004, pp. B1, B4; James Bandler, "Kodak Shifts Focus from Film, Betting Future on Digital Lines," *The Wall Street Journal,* September 25, 2003, pp. A1, A12.
27. David Colker, "Video Games Are Going Gray to Keep Growing," *Los Angeles Times,* May 10, 2004, accessed at **http://story.news.yahoo.com**.
28. WD-40 Company Web site, **http://www.wd40.com**, accessed May 10, 2004; Gary Dymski, "WD-40 More Than Slick Packaging," *The Morning News,* December 11, 2001, pp. E1, E2.

CHAPTER 12

1. "The Collegiate Licensing Company Names Top Selling Universities, Manufacturers for July 1, 2003–March 31, 2004," The Collegiate Licensing Company press release, April 21, 2004, **http://www.clc.com**; CollegeGear.com Web site, **http://www.collegegear.com**, accessed April 17, 2004; Jeffrey Zaslow, "Taunting Products Aid Losing College Teams," *Mobile Register,* November 15, 2003, p. B7; Stedman Graham, Lisa Delpy Neirotti, and Joe Jeff Goldblatt, *The Ultimate Guide to Sports Marketing* (New York: McGraw-Hill, 2001); Bernard J. Mullin, Stephen Hardy, and William A. Sutton, *Sport Marketing,* second edition (Champaign, IL: Human Kinetics, 2000).
2. Mercedes M. Cardona, "Penney's Markets Way to Turnaround," *Advertising Age,* April 26, 2004, pp. 26, 95.
3. Interbrand, "Best Global Brands of 2003," *Biz-Community,* **http://www.biz-community.com**, July 28, 2003.
4. Gerry Khermouch, Diane Brady, and others, "Brands in an Age of Anti-Americanism," *BusinessWeek,* August 4, 2003, pp. 69–78.
5. "Young & Rubicam Inc. Launches the Media Edge," Young & Rubicam press release, September 25, 1998, **http://www.youngandrubicam.com/news**, accessed May 11, 2004.
6. Khermouch, "Brands in an Age of Anti-Americanism."
7. Jean Halliday, "GM Puts Final Nail in Coffin of Brand-Management Effort," *Advertising Age,* April 5, 2004, p. 8; David Welch, "GM Brand Managers Get the Boot," *BusinessWeek,* April 22, 2002, p. 14.
8. Brandon Copple, "Shelf-Determination," *Forbes,* April 15, 2002, pp. 131–142.
9. "Itch Doctor," *People,* October 20, 2003, p. 130.
10. The concept of trade dress is examined in Michael Harvey, James T. Rothe, and Laurie A. Lucas, "The 'Trade Dress' Controversy: A Base of Strategic Cross-Brand Cannibalization," *Journal of Marketing Theory and Practice,* 6, Spring 1998, pp. 1–15. The *Kendall-Jackson v. Gallo* case is discussed in "Jury Clears E&J Gallo-Winery in Lawsuit over Bottle Design," *The Wall Street Journal,* April 7, 1997.
11. Paxan company Web site, **http://www.iran-export.com/exporter/company/PAXAN**, accessed May 4, 2004.
12. Deborah Ball, "Osama Relative Fashions Apparel Bin Ladin Line," *The Wall Street Journal,* June 17, 2002, p. B1.
13. Dana Tims, "More Vintners Are Kicking the Cork," *Mobile Register,* December 31, 2003, p. 4D.
14. Deborah L. Vence, "The Lowdown on Trans Fats," *Marketing News,* March 15, 2004, p. 13.
15. "Brand Extension, with Jacuzzi, Luxury-Goods Companies, and Hotels," *The Economist,* February 28, 2004, accessed at **http://infotrac-college.thomsonlearning.com**.
16. Michael McCarthy, "Judge Pooh-Poohs Lawsuit over Disney Licensing Fees," *USA Today,* March 30, 2004, p. B1; Bruce Orwall, "Disney Wins Bear-Knuckled, 13-Year Fight over Royalties," *The Wall Street Journal,* March 30, 2004, p. B1.
17. Robert Berner, "P&G: New and Improved," *BusinessWeek,* July 7, 2003, pp. 52–63.
18. Chuck Stogel, "It's Easier Being Green," *Brandweek,* January 28, 2002, pp. 16, 18, 20.
19. Julie Naughton and Kristin Finn, "Flanker Scents Spark Controversy," *Women's Wear Daily,* April 2004, accessed at **http://infotrac-college.thomsonlearning.com**.
20. Kevin Maney, "Dell to Dive into Consumer Electronics Market," *USA Today,* November 22, 2003, p. B1.
21. Everett M. Rogers and F. Floyd Shoemaker, *Communication of Innovation* (New York: Free Press, 1971), pp. 135–157. Rogers later relabeled his model as an innovation-decision process. He called the five steps knowledge, persuasion, decision, implementation, and information. See Everett M. Rogers, *Diffusion of Innovations,* third edition (New York: Free Press, 1983), pp. 164–165.
22. Darren Fonda, "Make *Vroom* for the Hybrids," *Time,* May 25, 2004, pp. 52–54.
23. Wyeth Web site, **http://www.wyeth.com**, accessed May 4, 2004; Rob Wherry, "No Worries," *Forbes,* July 23, 2001, p. 168.
24. Chuck Stogel, "It's Easier Being Green."
25. Anne Fisher, "How to Encourage Bright Ideas," *Fortune,* May 3, 2004, p. 70; Lyne quotation from Allison Overholt, "New Leaders, New Agenda," *Fast Company,* May 2002, p. 54.
26. Theresa Howard, "Brawny Man, and His Towels, Get Makeovers," *USA Today,* October 23, 2003, **http://www.usatoday.com**.
27. E. Michael Johnson, "The Swoosh Swoops In," *Golf Digest,* January 25, 2002, **http://www.golfdigest.com**.

CHAPTER 13

1. Stephanie King, "Foot Locker Profit Jumps 25%, Boosted by Influx of Nike Shoes," *The Wall Street Journal,* March 3, 2004, p. B3; Rukmini Callimachi, "Nike to End Feud with Foot Locker," *Birmingham News,* December 6, 2003, p. C4; Brendan Coffey, "Stepping Out," *Forbes,* September 15, 2003, p. 214; Maureen Tkacik, "In a Clash of Sneaker Titans, Nike Gets Leg Up on Foot Locker," *The Wall Street Journal,* May 18, 2003, pp. A1, A10.
2. Jack Neff, "Wal-Mart Softens Stance on Price Increases," *Advertising Age,* April 12, 2004, p. 12.
3. Rich Thomaselli, "Nike Makes Web a Destination," *Advertising Age,* February 23, 2004, p. 38.
4. Scott McMurray, "Return of the Middleman," *Business 2.0,* March 2003, pp. 53–54.
5. Warren Brown, "Savvy Buyers Might Appreciate the Smart Approach," *The Washington Post,* May 2, 2004, p. 6E.
6. Alice Z. Cuneo and Elizabeth Boston, "Home Depot Tries Direct Response TV," *Advertising Age,* May 19, 2003, pp. 3, 143.
7. Joe Cappo, "How Retailer Power Changes Marketing," *Advertising Age,* July 21, 2003, p. 16.
8. Jack Neff, "Wal-Mart Weans Suppliers," *Advertising Age,* December 1, 2003, p. 1.
9. Christopher Null, "How Netflix Is Fixing Hollywood," *Business 2.0,* July 2003, pp. 41–43.
10. Paul Nowell, "Furniture Makers, Sellers Spar over Trade," *Mobile Register,* May 2, 2004, pp. 1F, 5F.
11. Julie Appleby, "U.S. Drug Needs Would Overwhelm Canada," *USA Today,* May 17, 2004, p. B1; Megan Barnett, "The New Pill Pushers," *U.S. News & World Report,* April 26, 2004, pp. 40–41.
12. Andy Cohen, "Winds of Change," *Sales & Marketing Management,* May 2004, pp. 44–51.

13. Victoria Murphy, "The Logistics of a Dinner Plate," *Forbes,* January 21, 2002, pp. 96–97.
14. Jeffrey A. Krames, *What the Best CEOs Know* (New York: McGraw-Hill, 2003).
15. Wendy Zellner, "Wal-Mart," *BusinessWeek,* November 24, 2003, p. 104.
16. David McHugh, "German Chain Has High-Tech Vision for Shoppers," *The Morning News,* April 30, 2003, p. 3D.
17. James Covert, "Down, but Far from Out," *The Wall Street Journal,* January 12, 2004, p. R5.
18. Brian Bergstein, "Radio Cards Could Mean No Swipes," *The Morning News,* December 14, 2003, p. 5D.
19. Rod Kurtz, "Safer Harbors, Higher Fees," *Inc.,* January 2004, p. 27.
20. John Gorsuch, "Examining the Links," *Overhaul and Maintenance,* April 20, 2002, p. 38.
21. Susan Declercq Brown and Phyllis Rhodes, "The Defense Logistics Agency Contributes to Operation Iraqi Freedom," *Navy Supply Corps Newsletter,* July–August 2003, accessed at http://www.findarticles.com.
22. "The Lifelong Lure of the Open Road," *U.S. News & World Report,* February 18, 2002, p. 48.
23. Warren S. Hersch, "Midrange Distributors' Role Broadens in E-Commerce World," *Computer Reseller News,* accessed at the CRN Web site, http://www.crn.com, August 4, 2002.
24. Imran Vittachi, "Container Squeeze Tightens Prices," *Chicago Tribune Online,* January 9, 2004, http://www.chicagotribune.com.
25. Andrew Tanzer, "Warehouses That Fly," *Forbes,* http://www.forbes.com, accessed August 4, 2002.
26. Mike Troy, "Logistics Still Cornerstone of Competitive Advantage," *DSN Retailing Today,* June 9, 2003, accessed at http://www.findarticles.com.
27. Richard Jerome and Vickie Bane, "Spam I Am," *People,* May 3, 2004, pp. 125–126.

CHAPTER 14

1. Company Web site, http://www.rei.com, accessed April 17, 2004; "Dennis Madsen," interview, *Chain Store Age,* February 2004, p. 24; "REI Store Opens in Downtown San Francisco," *PR Newswire,* October 3, 2003; Mike Gorrell, "New REI Store Opens in Salt Lake City Area," *Knight Ridder/Tribune Business News,* March 28, 2003, http://infotrac-college.thomsonlearning.com.
2. Jonathan Fahey, "The Lexus Nexus," *Forbes,* June 21, 2004, pp. 68–70.
3. Anne D'Innocenzio, "Designer Names Helping Target Offer Cheap Chic," *Mobile Register,* March 16, 2002, p. B7; Teri Agins, "Todd Does Target," *The Wall Street Journal,* April 11, 2002, p. B1.
4. Family Dollar Web site, http://www.familydollar.com, accessed July 2, 2004; "Family Dollar Reports Record Third Quarter and First Three Quarters Sales and Earnings and Announces Plans to Open 575 New Stores in Fiscal 2003," Family Dollar Stores press release, *PR Newswire,* June 25, 2002.
5. Lowe's Web site, http://www.lowes.com, accessed July 2, 2004; Aixa M. Pascual, "Lowe's Is Sprucing Up Its House," *BusinessWeek,* June 3, 2002, pp. 56–58.
6. SuperTarget Web site, http://www.target.com, accessed July 2, 2004; Calmetta Y. Coleman, "Target's Aim: 'Bring Fashion to Food' on a National Scale," *The Wall Street Journal,* March 1, 2001, p. 4.
7. Delroy Alexander, "High-Stakes Shelf Games," *Chicago Tribune,* December 14, 2003, pp. 5-1, 5-7.
8. Mercedes M. Cardona, "Home Depot Revamps Results," *Advertising Age,* November 24, 2003, pp. 1, 23.
9. Lorrie Grant and Teresa Howard, "Shopping Shifts to 'Off-Mall' Stores," *USA Today,* April 26, 2004, p. B4; Kortney Stringer, "Abandoning the Mall," *The Wall Street Journal,* March 24, 2004, p. B1.
10. "General Growth to Open Lifestyle Center in Ohio," *Chain Store Age,* March 24, 2004, p. 124; "National Tenants Bite Big Apple: Lifestyle Shopping Center under Development in Queens, N.Y.," *Chain Store Age,* February 2004, p. 127; C. R. Roberts, "Plans for Retail 'Lifestyle Center' Move Forward in Tacoma, Wash.," *The News Tribune,* November 13, 2003; Henry Gomez, "Legacy Village: More Main Street Than Mall," *Crain's Cleveland Business,* October 20, 2003, p. 1; Allison Kaplan, "That's Not a Mall, It's a Lifestyle Center!" *Knight Ridder/Tribune News Service,* September 23, 2003, http://infotrac-college.thomsonlearning.com.
11. Alice Z. Cuneo, "What's in Store?" *Advertising Age,* February 25, 2002, pp. 30–31.
12. Emma Hall and Normandy Madden, "IKEA Courts Buyers with Offbeat Ideas," *Advertising Age,* April 12, 2002, p. 10.
13. Monica Khemsurov, "Sexing Up Victoria's Secret," *Business 2.0,* April 2004, pp. 54–55.
14. Joanne Cleaver, "Diversity Training Ups Saks' Sales," *Marketing News,* November 1, 2003, pp. 24–25.
15. Mike Troy, "Sam's Rewrites Business Plan," *DSN Retailing Today,* June 9, 2003, http://infotrac-college.thomsonlearning.com.
16. Lorrie Grant, "Maytag Stores Let Shoppers Try before They Buy," *USA Today,* June 7, 2004, p. B7.
17. Erin White and Kimberly Palmer, "U.S. Retailing, 101," *The Wall Street Journal,* August 12, 2003, pp. B1, B9.
18. Erin White and Susanna Ray, "Bare-Bones Shopping," *The Wall Street Journal,* May 10, 2004, p. R6.
19. Mike Troy, "A Force Even Category Killers Can't Catch," *DSN Retailing Today,* June 9, 2003, p. 77.
20. Anne D'Innocenzo, "Back in Fashion," *Mobile Register,* May 2, 2004, p. F1.
21. Cuneo, "What's in Store?"
22. "Products & Services," 7-Eleven Web site, http://www.//7-Eleven.com/products, accessed May 15, 2004.
23. Russell Flannery, "Happy in the Middle," *Forbes,* April 1, 2002, p. 62.
24. United Stationers Web site, http://www.unitedstationers.com, accessed May 15, 2004; "United Stationers Opens New State-of-the-Art Distribution Center in Denver," United Stationers' press release, June 25, 2001.
25. Don Debelak, "Farmers' Market," *Entrepreneur,* February 2002, p. 104.
26. Yahoo Web site, http://www.yahoo.com, accessed July 2, 2004; Tobi Elkin, "Yahoo! Increases Direct Marketing," *Advertising Age,* April 22, 2002, p. 20; Ellen Neuborne, "Coaxing with Catalogs," *BusinessWeek e.biz,* August 6, 2001, p. EB6.
27. Deborah Szynal, "Anthrax and You," *Marketing News,* April 29, 2002, pp. 1, 4.
28. Office Depot Web site, http://www.officedepot.com, accessed May 15, 2004; Jon Swartz, "E-Tailers Turn Net Profits," *USA Today,* December 13, 2000, pp. 1B-2B.
29. Japan Scan Food Industry Bulletin, http://www.japanscan.com, accessed July 2, 2004; JapanScan Market Report, "Automatic Vending Machines in Japan," January 2002, http://www.foodindustryjapan.com/automatic_Vending.htm; Tim Sanford, "Vending and Beyond," *Vending Times,* March 25–April 24, 2001, http://www.vendingtimes.com.

CHAPTER 15

1. S. L. Price, "Lance in France (Part 6)," *Sports Illustrated,* June 28, 2004, pp. 46–53; David B. Wilkerson, "Discovery to Sponsor Armstrong," June 15, 2004, CBS.MarketWatch.com, accessed June 16, 2004; Sal Ruibal, "U.S. Postal Nears Final Delivery," *USA Today,* May 7, 2004, p. C13; Rick Reilly, "Tour de Romance," *Sports Illustrated,* February 16, 2004, p. 88; Bill Saporito, "10 Questions for Lance Armstrong," *Time,* September 29, 2003, p. 8; Kelli Anderson, "Tour de Lance," *Sports Illustrated,* August 4, 2003, pp. 51–53; Sal Ruibal, "Armstrong Flags Down No. 5," *USA Today,* July 28, 2003, pp. C1-C2; Jack Ewing and Christina Passariello, "Is Lance Just Too Good?" *BusinessWeek,* June 30, 2003, p. 44.
2. Dale Buss, "Art of Gaining Impressions," *Brandweek,* March 18, 2002, p. R14 ("Reggie Awards").
3. Laurel Wentaz, "Banks Tailor Efforts to Homesick Hispanics," *Advertising Age,* April 5, 2004, p. 30.
4. Betsy Cummings, "Making It Click," *Sales & Marketing Management,* April 2002, p. 21.
5. Cummings, "Making It Click," p. 22.
6. Jim Edwards, "Got Milk? (Got Mess)," *Adweek,* April 19, 2004, pp. 36–43.
7. Kenneth Hein, "Pepsi Pops New Formula," *Brandweek,* March 22, 2004, p. 4; Becky Ebenkamp and Todd Wasserman, "Have You Heard the Latest about Pepsi's Sierra Mist?" *Brandweek,* March 22, 2004, p. 10.
8. Jon Swartz, "EarthLink Joins Movement to Kill Pop-up Ads," *USA Today,* August 20, 2002, p. B1; "EarthLink Will Offer Subscribers Software to Block Pop-up Ads," *The Wall Street Journal,* August 20, 2002, p. B6.
9. Mike Beirne, "Hoteliers Take Different Roads to Travelers," *Brandweek,* June 10, 2002, p. 4.
10. Lisa Sanders, "Ford SUV Gets Starring Role in Film," *Advertising Age,* April 19, 2004, p. 8.
11. Ronald Grover and Gerry Khermouch, "The Trouble with Tie-ins," *BusinessWeek,* June 3, 2002, p. 63.
12. Katy Kelly, Kim Clark, and Linda Kulman, "Trash TV," *U.S. News & World Report,* February 16, 2004, pp. 48–52.
13. Kenneth Hein, "Cracking the Code for Pepsi," *Brandweek,* October 14, 2002, pp. M13–M16.
14. Jean Halliday, "Toyota Goes Guerilla to Roll Scion," *Advertising Age,* August 11, 2003, pp. 4, 41; Amy Moerke, "It's a Jungle Out There," *Sales of Marketing Management,* May 2004, p. 12.
15. Donna Fuscaldo, "Create a Buzz for Your Product," *The Wall Street Journal,* September 15, 2003, p. R8.
16. Sheri Qualters, "Advertisers Seek More Bang for Sports–Marketing Bucks," *Boston Business Journal,* June 9, 2003, http://www.bizjournals.com/boston.
17. Bartley Morrisroe, "Second-Tier Sponsorships Get Personal," *Marketing News,* June 23, 2003, p. 4.
18. David Dukcevich, "Whither College Hoops?" *Forbes,* March 31, 2003, http://www.forbes.com; Betsy McKay, "Coke Beats Pepsi for NCAA Rights in a Deal That Tops $500 Million," *The Wall Street Journal,* June 12, 2002, accessed at http://www.sportsbusinessdaily.com.
19. Gabriel Kahn, "Soccer's FIFA Cries Foul as Ambushers Crash World Cup," *The Wall Street Journal,* June 21, 2002, p. B1.
20. Direct Marketing Association, http://www.the-dma.org, accessed December 22, 2004.
21. Laird Harrison, "You've Got Ads!" *Time* Bonus Section—Inside Business, January 2002, p. Y7.
22. "Home Depot Announces First-Ever Holiday Catalog," *DSN Retailing Today,* November 11, 2003, http://www.dsnretailingtoday.com.
23. Direct Marketing Association, http://www.the-dma.org, accessed January 2, 2005.
24. "Pay Your Verizon Phone Bill When You Get a Cup of Coffee at 7-Eleven," *PR Newswire,* April 8, 2003, http://infotrac-college.thomsonlearning.com.
25. Kenneth Hein, "Memo from the Front," *Brandweek,* February 11, 2002, p. 38.

26. Gregory Solman, "Marketers, Music Sites Find It Takes Two to Tango," *Adweek,* April 5, 2004, p. 9.
27. Kenneth Hein, "Got a Thrilla in the Mist," *Brandweek,* January 10, 2004, pp. 16–17.
28. Bob Francis, "Pepsi Celebrates History and Bridges Digital Divide," *Brandweek,* March 22, 2004, p. R9.
29. John Densmore, "Should The Doors Sell Out?" *Rolling Stone,* December 2002–January 2003, pp. 44–45.
30. Theresa Howard, "Teens Actually Like Being Told Why Smoking's Dumb," *USA Today,* May 3, 2004, p. B7.

CHAPTER 16

1. Gabriel Kahn, "Tiger's New Threads," *The Wall Street Journal,* March 26, 2004, p. B1; "McDonald's Goes Supersize with Yao," *USA Today,* February 13, 2004, p. C23; Rich Thomaselli, "Nike Bets Big on Range of Endorsers," *Advertising Age,* January 5, 2004, p. 8; Stephanie Kang, "Postgame Strategy," *The Wall Street Journal,* November 11, 2003, pp. B1, B5; Harry R. Weber, "LeBron James Replaces Kobe in Sprite Ads," *Marketing News,* September 15, 2003, p. 28; Kenneth Hein, "A Broken Field of Marketing Dreams," *Brandweek,* July 14, 2003, p. 6; Richard O'Brien and Mark Bechtel, "James and the Giant Deal," *Sports Illustrated,* June 2, 2003, p. 23.
2. Dorothy Pomerants, "Coming Distractions," *Forbes,* June 10, 2002, p. 50.
3. "Beyoncé Knowles Headed for Superstardom," *ABS CBN Interactive,* February 15, 2004, http://www.abs-cbnnews.com.
4. "Top 25 U.S. Advertisers," *FactPack 2004 Edition* (special supplement to *Advertising Age*), March 8, 2004, p. 12.
5. "Top 25 U.S. Megabrands," *FactPack 2004 Edition* (special supplement to *Advertising Age*), March 8, 2004, p. 13.
6. James B. Amdorfer, "Miller Brewing Sues Anheuser-Busch over Ads," *Advertising Age,* May 27, 2004, http://www.adage.com; James. B. Amdorfer, "Budweiser Launches Major Ad Offensive against Miller," *Advertising Age,* May 20, 2004, http://www.adage.com.
7. Laurel Wentz, "Marketers Turn to Celebrities to Lure Hispanic Consumers," *Advertising Age,* May 13, 2002, p. 20.
8. Bruce Horovitz, "Foreman Puts Up His Dukes for Big, Tall," *USA Today,* March 4, 2004, p. B3.
9. Robyn Greenspan, "U.S. Online Ad Growth Under Way," *ClickZ Network,* July 15, 2003, http://www.clickz.com; Michael Krauss, "Google Changes the Context of Advertising," *Marketing News,* June 1, 2004, p. 6.
10. Theresa Howard, "Ad Sales Increase Shows Slump May Be Past," *USA Today,* June 4, 2004, p. B1.
11. "Philadelphia to Air Ads to Attract Gays," *The Morning News,* June 3, 2004, p. B5.
12. Terence A. Shimp, *Advertising, Promotion, and Supplemental Aspects of Integrated Marketing Communications,* sixth edition (Mason, OH: South-Western, 2003), pp. 306–309.
13. Betsy McKay and Chad Terhune, "Coke Pulls TV Ad after Some Call It the Pits," *The Wall Street Journal,* June 8, 2004, pp. B1, B8; Bruce Horovitz, "Risqué May Be Too Risky for Ads," *USA Today,* April 16, 2004, p. B1; Christine Bittar, "Victoria's Secret Special Shelved Amid FCC Probes," *Brandweek,* April 12, 2004, p. 5.
14. Claire Atkinson, "Which Nets Are Kings of Clutter?" *Advertising Age,* June 7, 2004, p. 53.
15. Jon Swartz, "EarthLink Joins Movement to Kill Pop-Up Ads," *USA Today,* August 20, 2002, p. B1; Tobi Elkin, "'Intrusive' Pop-Ups Get Closer Scrutiny after iVillage Block," *Advertising Age,* August 5, 2002, p. 6.
16. Karl Greenberg, "Sea-Doo Sees Alternative Ways to Craft 3D Strategy," *Brandweek,* June 2, 2004, p. 3.
17. Robert J. Coen, "Advertising Boom in U.S. Ended in '01," *Advertising Age,* May 13, 2002, p. 24.
18. "Top 25 Cable Networks," *Advertising Age,* May 31, 2004, p. S-17.
19. Chuck Bartels, "Newspaper Ads No Longer Best Fit for Dillard's," *Marketing News,* November 15, 2003, p. 5.
20. "Top 25 Magazines by Circulation," *FactPack 2004 Edition* (special supplement to *Advertising Age*), March 8, 2004, p. 36.
21. "U.S. Ad Spending Totals by Media," *FactPack 2004* (special supplement to *Advertising Age),* March 8, 2004. p. 15
22. Erin White, "Outdoor Ads May Get Indoor Rival," *The Wall Street Journal,* July 17, 2002, p. B10.
23. Kris Oser, "Internet Advertising Reaches $2.3 Bil High," *Advertising Age,* May 3, 2004, pp. 3, 65; Scott Hays, "Has Online Advertising Finally Grown Up?" *Advertising Age,* April 1, 2002, p. C1.
24. Russ Britt, "Theaters Reap More Revenues from Ads," http://www.CBS.MarketWatch.com, June 14, 2004.
25. "World's Top 10 Core Agencies," *FactPack 2004 Edition* (special supplement to *Advertising Age*), March 8, 2004, p. 51.
26. Jordana Mishory, "Loud and Clear," *Sales & Marketing Management,* June 2004, p. 14.
27. Janine Gordon, "When PR Makes More Sense Than Ads," *Brandweek,* April 21, 2003, p. 26.
28. Jack Neff, "Ries' Thesis: Ads Don't Build Brands, PR Does," *Advertising Age,* July 15, 2002, pp. 14–15.
29. Oser, "Internet Advertising Reaches $2.3 Bil High"; Normandy Madden, "Levi's Enjoys 'Rebirth' on the Web in Asia," *Advertising Age,* April 19, 2004, p. N-8.

CHAPTER 17

1. Diane Brady, "IMG: Show Me the Bottom Line," *BusinessWeek,* July 12, 2004, pp. 82–84; Alex Tresniowski and Lori Rozsa, "Second Serve," *People,* June 28, 2004, pp. 136–139; Douglas Robson, "Women's Tennis: Back on Serve," *BusinessWeek,* June 7, 2004, pp. 111–112; Howard Fendrich, "Afresh Start for Williams Sisters," *Mobile Register,* June 21, 2004, p. C2; Hamil R. Harris, "Serena Aces on Nike Deal," *Black Enterprise,* December 15, 2003, http://www.blackenterprise.com; Stephanie Kang, "Nike, Serena Williams Partner Up," *The Wall Street Journal,* December 12, 2003, p. B2; Nicole Gull, "Venus's Designs," *Inc.,* September 2003, p. 19.
2. "Corporate America's New Sales Force," *Fortune,* August 11, 2003, pp. S2–S20.
3. Stephanie B. Goldberg, "Sales: What Works Now," *Inc.,* June 2004, pp. 65–80.
4. Barry Farber, "Natural-Born Sellers?" *Entrepreneur,* May 2004, pp. 89–90; Kimberly McCall, "Leading the Pack," *Entrepreneur,* May 2004, p. 90.
5. Michael V. Copeland, "Best Buy's Selling Machine," *Business 2.0,* July 2004, pp. 93–103.
6. Trevor Thomas, "FIIA Study Finds Banks Favor One-on-One Selling for Insurance," *National Underwriter,* May 6, 2002, p. 41.
7. Matthew Maier, "Boeing's Dreamliner: 52 Sold, 3,448 to Go," *Business 2.0,* July 2004, pp. 27–28.
8. "Automating the Sales Force," *Fortune,* August 11, 2003, p. S10.
9. Becki Connally, "Marketing Comes to the Home," *Mobile Register,* March 11, 2004, p. S-1.
10. Jane Spencer, "Ignore That Knocking: Door-to-Door Sales Make a Comeback," *The Wall Street Journal,* April 30, 2004, p. D1.
11. Lorraine Woellart, "The Do Not Call Law Won't Stop the Calls," *BusinessWeek,* September 29, 2003, p. 89.
12. Kimberly L. McCall, "The Ins and Outs," *Sales & Marketing Management,* March 2002, pp. 87–88.
13. Chris Penttila, "The Art of the Sale," *Entrepreneur,* August 2003, pp. 58–61.
14. Tim O'Brien, "Kahuna Lagoon Makes a Splash at Camelbeach," *Amusement Business,* May 20, 2002, p. 6.
15. Penttila, "The Art of the Sale."
16. L. Biff, "Customers Still Want Expert Advice," *Bank Marketing,* May 2002, p. 41.
17. Joseph C. Panetteri, "Birth of a Salesman," *Priority,* July–August 2003, pp. 20–23.
18. Norm Brodsky, "Street Smarts," *Inc.,* June 2004, pp. 53–54.
19. Jean Halliday, "Car Dealers Court Existing Buyers," *Advertising Age,* March 1, 2004, p. 6.
20. Steve Gottlieb, "How to Sell a Product Everyone Is Getting for Free," *Business 2.0,* April 2004, p. 48.
21. Matthew Boyle, "Joe Galli's Army," *Fortune,* December 30, 2002, pp. 135–138.
22. Jess McCuan, "The Ultimate Sales Incentive," *Inc.,* May 2004, p. 32.
23. Brian Tracy, "Top Secrets," *Entrepreneur,* August 2003, pp. 62–63.
24. Brian Caulfield, "How to Land the Deal," *Business 2.0,* April 2004, p. 85.
25. "Multimedia Information Services," http://viswiz.gmd.de/MultimediaInfo/, accessed January 18, 2005.
26. Michael Schrage, "The Dynamic Duo," *Sales & Marketing Management,* May 2004, p. 26.
27. Tracy, "Top Secrets."
28. "Post-Sale Selling," *Sales & Marketing Management,* June 2004, p. 12.
29. Deborah L. Vence, "Top Niche," *Marketing News,* June 1, 2004, pp. 11–13; "Hispanics Wanted," *Brandweek,* April 12, 2004, pp. 22, 24.
30. Boyle, "Joe Galli's Army."
31. Michele Marchetti, "The Case for Mentors," *Sales & Marketing Management,* June 2004, p. 16.
32. David Lieberman, "Blockbuster Jabs Back at Its Rivals," *USA Today,* June 22, 2004, pp. B1–B2; "Blockbuster: The Ticket to Performance," special advertising section to *Sales & Marketing Management,* August 9, 2002, p. S-4.
33. *Sales & Marketing Management,* May 2004, p. 43.
34. "Lowe's Gift Cards," special advertising section to *Sales & Marketing Management,* August 9, 2002, p. S-6.
35. David Kaufman, "Perking up the Workforce," special advertising section to *Fortune,* September 29, 2003, pp. S1–S8.
36. Sandra Jones, "How Sears Came Down with Seasonal Disorder," *Business 2.0,* July 2004, pp. 66–67.
37. Andy Cohen, "A Push for Product Diversity," *Sales & Marketing Management,* May 2004, pp. 38–39.
38. Jennifer Gilbert, "Building in Loyalty," *Sales & Marketing Management,* May 2004, pp. 40–41.
39. Julia Chang, "Codes of Conduct," *Sales & Marketing Management,* November 2003, p. 22.
40. Jennifer Gilbert, "A Matter of Trust," *Sales & Marketing Management,* March 2003, pp. 30–35.
41. Gilbert, "A Matter of Trust."
42. Jean Halliday, "Saab's Sweepstakes," *Advertising Age,* September 9, 2002, p. 24.
43. "POP Sharpens Its Focus," *Brandweek,* June 16, 2003, pp. 31–36.
44. Bob Donath, "Maximize Trade Show Power to Support Your Field Sales Reps," *Marketing News,* June 1, 2004, p. 7.
45. Gilbert, "A Matter of Trust."

CHAPTER 18

1. Varsity Spirit Web site, http://varsity.com, accessed August 12, 2004; "Leonard Green Shows School Spirit," *Buyouts,* May 12, 2003, http://infotrac-college.thomsonlearning .com; Erik Brady, "From Megaphones to Mega-Profits," *USA Today,* April 26, 2002, p. 3C; Erik Brady, "Cheerleading in the USA: A Sport and an Industry," *USA Today,* April 26, 2002, pp. A1, A2.
2. Chuck Salter, "When Couches Fly," *Fast Company,* July 2004, pp. 80–81; Pete England, "Dumping: China Strikes Back," *BusinessWeek,* July 5, 2004, p. 58; David Lynch, "Chinese Shrimp Farmers Feel Pain of U.S. Trade War," *USA Today,* June 30, 2004, pp. B1–B2; Dan Morse, "In North Carolina, Furniture Makers Try to Stay Alive," *The Wall Street Journal,* February 20, 2004, pp. A1, A6.
3. Elisabeth Malkin, "In Mexico, Sugar vs. U.S. Corn Syrup," *The New York Times,* June 9, 2004, http://nytimes.com.
4. Jesse Drucker and Almar Latour, "The Spread of Hidden Fees," *The Wall Street Journal,* April 13, 2004, pp. D1, D5.
5. William Grimes, "That Invisible Hand Guides the Game of Ticket Hunting," *The New York Times,* June 18, 2004, pp. E1, E6.
6. Steve Stecklow and Erin White, "At Some Retailers, 'Fair Trade' Carries a Very High Cost," *The Wall Street Journal,* June 8, 2004, pp. A1, A10.
7. Byron Acohido, "Will Microsoft's Xbox Hit the Spot?" *USA Today,* June 4, 2004, pp. B1, B2.
8. Robert D. Buzzell and Frederick D. Wiersema, "Successful Share Building Strategies," *Harvard Business Review,* January–February 1981, pp. 135–144.
9. David Lieberman, "Comcast Forecasts Digital TV, PC, Phone Convergence," *USA Today,* July 1, 2004, p. B1; Almar LaTour, "After 20 Years, Baby Bells Face Some Grown-Up Competition," *The Wall Street Journal,* May 28, 2004, pp. A1, A5; Heather Green, "No Wires No Rules," *BusinessWeek,* April 26, 2004, pp. 95–102.
10. Marilyn Adams, "Price War Erupts as Start-Up Begins Selling Tickets," *USA Today,* May 20, 2004, p. A1.
11. Melanie Trottman, "Airlines Cut Fares, Add Routes to Fight with Low-Cost Carriers," *The Wall Street Journal,* February 6, 2004, p. A1.
12. "The Story of Trader Joe's," http://www.traderjoes.com/about/index.asp, accessed October 25, 2004; Larry Armstrong, "Trader Joe's: The Trendy American Cousin," *BusinessWeek,* April 25, 2004, p. 62.
13. Dell Web site, http://dell.com, accessed January 4, 2005.
14. Joe Sharkey, "Life Can Be Pretty Good Five Miles Up," *The New York Times,* May 14, 2002, p. C7.
15. Brad Foss, "America Relies More Heavily on Imported Gasoline," *Mobile Register,* May 22, 2004, p. B7.
16. Keith Naughton, "Fed Up with Filling Up," *Newsweek,* June 28, 2004, pp. 38–39; Karl Greenberg, "Pumping Up the Volume," *Adweek,* June 14, 2004, p. 6; Sholan Freeman, "Forget Rebates: The Hybrid-Car Markup," *The Wall Street Journal,* June 10, 2004, pp. D1, D6.
17. Barbara De Lollis, Chris Woodyard, and Marilyn Adams, "Savvy Travelers Fly for Less," *USA Today,* April 21, 2002.
18. Yuzo Yamaguchi, "Isuzu: Fewer U.S. Models Will Help Bottom Line," *Automotive News,* May 24, 2004, p. 49.
19. David Leonhardt, "Tiptoeing toward Variable Pricing," *The New York Times,* May 12, 2002, p. C7.
20. James L. McKenney, *Stouffer Yield Management System,* Harvard Business School Case 9-190-193 (Boston: Harvard Business School, 1994); Anirudh Dhebar and Adam Brandenburger, *American Airlines, Inc.: Revenue Management,* Harvard Business School Case 9-190-029 (Boston: Harvard Business School, 1992).
21. Michael Sasso, "Tampa, Fla.-Based Company Rides Wave of Internet Auctions," *Tampa Tribune,* February 19, 2004; Valerie L. Merahn, "Priced to Go: A Quick Search for Soda," *Brandweek,* February 2, 2004, pp. 22, 23.
22. Buy.com Web site, http://buy.com, accessed June 13, 2004; David P. Hamilton, "E-Commerce: The Price Isn't Right," *The Wall Street Journal,* February 12, 2001, p. B1.
23. Eleena de Lisser, "A New Twist in Theme-Park Pricing," *The Wall Street Journal,* June 24, 2004, pp. D1, D4.

CHAPTER 19

1. Dallas Stars Web site, http://www.dallasstars.com, accessed October 14, 2004; Jim Morris, "Charging More for Some Games Allows NHL Teams to Hold Line on Ticket Prices," *Canoe,* http://www.canoe.com, accessed June 5, 2004; "Pittsburgh Penguins," *Post-Gazette.com Sports,* http://www.post-gazette.com, accessed June 4, 2004; Stefan Fatsis, "NHL Says Players' Salaries Put League in Financial Peril," *The Wall Street Journal,* September 19, 2003, pp. B1, B3.
2. Heidi Brown and Justin Doebele, "Samsung's Next Act," *Forbes,* July 26, 2004, pp. 102–107; Michelle Kessler, "Prices of Flat-Panel TVs, Monitors Could Drop More," *USA Today,* June 30, 2004, p. B1; Beth Snyder Bulik, "Consumers Flock to Flat-Screen TVs as Prices Fall," *Advertising Age,* June 28, 2004, p. S-8; Peter Kafka, "Is the Price Right?" *Forbes,* March 1, 2004, p. 80.
3. "Canon News," http://www.canon.com, accessed January 22, 2003.
4. Richard Gibson, "Red Lobster Hopes to Lure Diners Back," *The Morning News,* December 21, 2003, p. 10D.
5. Ramin Setoodeh, "Step Right Up!" *The Wall Street Journal,* July 13, 2004, pp. B1, B6.
6. Chris Woodyard, "JetBlue Jumps on Board for Fall Fare Wars," *USA Today,* July 14, 2004, p. B1; Chris Woodyard, "Pitting Southwest vs. JetBlue," *USA Today,* July 6, 2004, p. B5.
7. Richard J. Newman, "The Lowdown on List Prices," *U.S. News & World Report,* January 5, 2004, pp. D12–D14.
8. Michelle Kessler, "Competition Helps Drop Laptop Prices," *USA Today,* December 8, 2003, p. B1.
9. Robert Berner and Brian Grow, "Out-Discounting the Discounter," *BusinessWeek,* May 10, 2004, p. 78.
10. Brad Foss, "America Relies More Heavily on Imported Gasoline," *Mobile Register,* May 22, 2004, p. B7.
11. "Dealer Holdbacks: What Are They and What Do They Do?" http://www.carbuytip.com/dealer-holdbacks.html, accessed January 23, 2003.
12. "7 Ways Dealers Make You Pay Extra," *Consumer Reports,* New Car Preview 2004, pp. 12-13.
13. "The Music Industry and the New Digital Economics," http:nfo.net/usa/digecon.html, accessed January 24, 2003.
14. Ethan Smith, "Why a Grand Plan to Cut CD Prices Went off the Track," *The Wall Street Journal,* June 4, 2004, pp. A1, A3.
15. Upromise Web site, http://www.upromise.com, accessed October 21, 2004.
16. Earle Eldridge, "Car Sales Go Down, Rebates Go Up," *USA Today,* July 8, 2004, p. B1; Wagoner quotation from David Kiley, "GM Tries to Cut Cord on Costly Rebates," *USA Today,* January 23, 2004, pp. B1, B2.
17. Daniel McGinn, "Let's Make a (Tough) Deal," *Newsweek,* June 23, 2003, pp. 48-49.
18. Barbara Kiviat, "Sneaky Pricing," *Time,* September 29, 2003.
19. Rebecca Buckman, "Microsoft's Malaysia Policy," *The Wall Street Journal,* May 20, 2004, p. B1.
20. Sharon Silke Carty, "Auto Makers Offer More Incentives," *The Wall Street Journal,* July 8, 2004, p D5; John Porretto, "GM, Ford Heat Up Incentives Battle," *Mobile Register,* July 8, 2004, p. B6; David Welch, "Those Price Breaks Are Habit Forming," *BusinessWeek,* February 16, 2004, p. 39.
21. Shelly Branch, "Long Used to Getting Full Price, a Retailer Faces New Pressures," *The Wall Street Journal,* February 4, 2004, pp. A1, A9.
22. Company Web sites, http://store.apple.com; and http://www.dell.com, accessed October 22, 2004.
23. David Kirkpatrick, "Inside Sam's $100 Billion Growth Machine," *Fortune,* June 14, 2004, pp. 80–98.
24. Kate Bonamici, "Tag! You're the It Bag," *Fortune,* June 14, 2004, p. 50.
25. Mark Henricks, "Get Your Fix," *Entrepreneur,* April 2003, pp. 75–76.
26. Henricks, "Get Your Fix."
27. Kerry Capell, "Vaccinating the World's Poor," *BusinessWeek,* April 26, 2004, pp. 65–69.
28. Kwame Kuadey, "The Politics of AIDS Drugs in Africa." *AIDS in Africa,* http://www.aidsandafrica.com/, accessed September 1, 2004.
29. "Product Preannouncement, Market Cannibalization, and Price Competition," http://netec.mcc.ac.uk/BibEc/data/Papers/fthecsucp98-136.html, accessed January 25, 2003.
30. Edna Gundersen, "Prince Reaches Out 2U with Marketing That's All His," *USA Today,* June 24, 2004, p. D1; Edna Gundersen, "For Prince, It's Good to Be King," *USA Today,* June 24, 2004, p. D3.
31. Anne Marie Squeo and Joe Flint, "Should Cable Be à la Carte, Not Flat Rate?" *The Wall Street Journal,* March 26, 2004, pp. B1, B4.
32. Noelle Knox and Byron Acohido, "Microsoft Faces Fine of $618 M in EU Case," *USA Today,* March 23, 2004, p. B1.
33. Jeffrey Ball, "For Many Low-Income Workers, High Gasoline Prices Take a Toll," *The Wall Street Journal,* July 12, 2004, pp. A1, A8.

glossary

A

accessory equipment Capital items like desktop computers and printers that typically cost less and last for shorter periods of time than installations.

acculturation Process of learning a new culture foreign to one's own.

administered marketing system VMS that achieves channel coordination when a dominant channel member exercises its power.

adoption process Stages that consumers go through in learning about a new product, trying it, and deciding whether to purchase it again.

advertising Any paid, nonpersonal communication through various media about a business firm, not-for-profit organization, product, or idea by a sponsor identified in a message that is intended to inform or persuade members of a particular audience.

advertising agency Firm whose marketing specialists assist advertisers in planning and preparing advertisements.

advertising campaign Series of different but related ads that use a single theme and appear in different media within a specified time period.

affinity marketing Marketing effort sponsored by an organization that solicits responses from individuals who share common interests and activities.

AIDA concept Steps through which an individual reaches a purchase decision: attention, interest, desire, and action.

AIO statements Items on lifestyle surveys that describe various activities, interests, and opinions of respondents.

allowance Specified deduction from list price, including a trade-in or promotional allowance.

ambush marketing Attempt by a firm that is not an official sponsor of an event or activity to link itself to the event or activity.

application service providers (ASPs) Outside companies that specialize in providing both the computers and the application support for managing information systems of business clients.

approach Salesperson's initial contact with a prospective customer.

Asch phenomenon Impact of groups and group norms on individual behavior, as described by S. E. Asch. People often conform to majority rule, even when majority rule goes against their beliefs.

atmospherics Combination of physical characteristics and amenities that contribute to a store's image.

attitudes Person's enduring favorable or unfavorable evaluations, emotions, or action tendencies toward some object or idea.

average total costs Costs calculated by dividing the sum of the variable and fixed costs by the number of units produced.

B

baby boomers People born between the years of 1946 and 1965.

backward integration Process through which a manufacturer attempts to gain greater control over inputs in its production process, such as raw materials.

banner ads Promotional messages on a Web page that link to an advertiser's site.

banners Advertisements on a Web page that link to an advertiser's site.

basing-point pricing System used in some industries during the early 20th century in which the buyer paid the factory price plus freight charges from the basing-point city nearest the buyer.

benchmarking Method of measuring quality by comparing performance against industry leaders.

blog (short for Web log) Web page that serves as a publicly accessible personal journal for individuals and, in more and more instances, for marketers.

bonus pack Specially packaged item that gives the purchaser a larger quantity at the regular price.

bot Search program that checks hundreds of sites, gathers and assembles information, and brings it back to the sender.

bots (shopbots) Online search programs that act as comparison shopping agents.

bottom line Business jargon referring to the overall profitability of an organization.

brand Name, term, sign, symbol, design, or some combination that identifies the products of one firm while differentiating them from the competition's.

brand equity Added value that a respected, well-known brand name gives to a product in the marketplace.

brand extension Strategy of attaching a popular brand name to a new product in an unrelated product category.

brand insistence Consumer refusals of alternatives and extensive search for desired merchandise.

brand licensing Firm's authorization of other companies to use its brand names.

brand manager Marketer within an organization who is responsible for a single brand.

brand mark Symbol or pictorial design that distinguishes a product.

brand name Part of a brand consisting of words or letters that form a name that identifies and distinguishes a firm's offerings from those of its competitors.

brand preference Consumer reliance on previous experiences with a product to choose that product again.

brand recognition Consumer awareness and identification of a brand.

breakeven analysis Pricing technique used to determine the number of products that must be sold at a specified price to generate enough revenue to cover total cost.

broadband technology Extremely high-speed, always-on Internet connection.

broker Agent wholesaling intermediary who does not take title to or possession of goods in the course of its primary function, which is to bring together buyers and sellers.

B2C products *See* consumer product.

bundle pricing Offering two or more complementary products and selling them for a single price.

business cycle Pattern of differing stages in the level of economic activity of a nation or region. Although the traditional cycle includes the four stages of prosperity, recession, depression, and recovery, most economists believe that future depressions can be prevented through effective economic policies.

business products Goods and services purchased for use either directly or indirectly in the production of other goods and services for resale.

business services Intangible products that firms buy to facilitate their production and operating processes.

business-to-business (B2B) marketing Organizational sales and purchases of goods and services to support production of other products, for daily company operations, or for resale.

business-to-business (B2B) product Product that contributes directly or indirectly to the output of other products for resale; also called industrial or organizational product.

buyer Person who has the formal authority to select a supplier and to implement the procedures for securing a good or service.

buyer partnership Relationship in which a firm purchases goods or services from one or more providers.

buyer's market Market in which there are more goods and services than people willing to buy them.

buying center Participants in an organizational buying action.

C

cannibalization Loss of sales of an existing product due to competition from a new product in the same line.

captive brand National brands that are sold exclusively by a retail chain.

cash discount Price reduction offered to a consumer, business user, or marketing intermediary in return for prompt payment of a bill.

category Key business unit within diversified firms; also called a *strategic business unit (SBU).*

category captain Vendor who is responsible for dealing with all of the suppliers for a project and then presenting the entire package to the buyer.

category killer Store that offers huge selections and low prices in single product lines.

category management Product management system in which a category manager—with profit and loss responsibility—oversees a product line.

cause marketing Identification and marketing of a social issue, cause, or idea to selected target markets.

channel Medium through which a message is delivered.

channel captain Dominant and controlling member of a marketing channel.

click-through rate The percentage of people presented with a Web banner ad who click it.

click-throughs *See* cost per response.

closed sales territory Exclusive geographic selling region of a distributor.

closing Stage of the personal selling process where the salesperson asks the customer to make a purchase decision.

cluster sample Probability sample in which researchers select a sample of subgroups (or clusters) from which they draw respondents; each cluster reflects the diversity of the whole population being sampled.

cobranding Cooperative arrangement in which two or more businesses team up to closely link their names on a single product.

cognitive dissonance Imbalance between beliefs and attitudes that occurs after an action or decision is taken, such as a purchase.

cohort effect Tendency of members of a generation to be influenced and bound together by events occurring during their key formative years—roughly 17 to 22 years of age.

collaborative planning, forecasting, and replenishment (CPFaR) Inventory management technique involving collaborative efforts by both purchasers and vendors.

comarketing Cooperative arrangement in which two businesses jointly market each other's products.

commercial market Individuals and firms that acquire products to support, directly or indirectly, production of other goods and services.

commission Incentive compensation directly related to the sales or profits achieved by a salesperson.

commission merchant Agent wholesaling intermediary who takes possession of goods shipped to a central market for sale, acts as the producer's agent, and collects an agreed-upon fee at the time of the sale.

common carriers Businesses that provide transportation services as for-hire carriers to the general public.

common market Extension of a customs union by seeking to reconcile all government regulations affecting trade.

comparative advertising Advertising strategy that emphasizes messages with direct or indirect promotional comparisons between competing brands.

competitive bidding Inviting potential suppliers to quote prices on proposed purchases or contracts.

competitive environment Interactive process that occurs in the marketplace among marketers of directly competitive products, marketers of products that can be substituted for one another, and marketers competing for the consumer's purchasing power.

competitive pricing strategy Pricing strategy designed to deemphasize price as a competitive variable by pricing a good or service at the general level of comparable offerings.

competitive strategy Methods through which a firm deals with its competitive environment.

component parts and materials Finished business products of one producer that become part of the final products of another producer.

concentrated marketing Focusing marketing efforts on satisfying a single market segment; also called *niche marketing.*

concept testing Method for subjecting a product idea to additional study before actual development by involving consumers through focus groups, surveys, in-store polling, and the like.

consolidated metropolitan statistical area (CMSA) Urban area that includes two or more PMSAs.

consultive selling Meeting customer needs by listening to them, understanding their problems, paying attention to details, and following through after the sale.

consumer behavior Mental and physical activities of individuals who actually use the purchased goods and services.

consumer innovators People who purchase new products almost as soon as the products reach the market.

consumer orientation Business philosophy incorporating the marketing concept that emphasizes first determining unmet consumer needs and then designing a system for satisfying them.

consumer products Products bought by ultimate consumers for personal use.

consumer rights In their most basic form, these rights include a person's right to choose goods and services freely, to be informed about these products and services, to be heard, and to be safe. These four basic rights form the conceptual framework for a more thorough and legislative explanation of consumer rights that has developed and changed since 1962 when President Kennedy outlined consumer rights.

consumerism Social force within the environment designed to aid and protect the consumer by exerting legal, moral, and economic pressures on business and government.

containerization Process of combining several unitized loads into a single, well-protected load for shipment.

contest Sales promotional technique that requires entrants to complete a task such as solving a puzzle or answering questions on a quiz for the chance to win a prize.

contract carriers For-hire transporters that do not offer their services to the general public.

contractual marketing system VMS that coordinates channel activities through formal agreements among participants.

controlled experiment Scientific investigation in which a researcher manipulates a test group (or groups) and compares the results with those of a control group that did not receive the experimental controls or manipulations.

convenience products Goods and services that consumers want to purchase frequently, immediately, and with minimal effort.

convenience retailer Store that appeals to customers on accessible location, long hours, rapid checkout, and adequate parking.

convenience sample Nonprobability sample selected from among readily available respondents.

conversion rate The percentage of visitors to a Web site who make a purchase.

cookies Controversial techniques for collecting information about online Web site visitors in which small text files are automatically downloaded to a user's computer to gather such data as length of visit and the site visited next.

cooperative advertising Agreement under which the manufacturer pays a percentage of the retailer's advertising expenditures and the retailer prominently displays the firm's products.

core based statistical area (CBSA) Collective term for metropolitan and micropolitan statistical areas.

core competencies Activities that a company performs well and that customers value and competitors find difficult to duplicate.

core region Region from which most major brands get 40 to 80 percent of their sales.

corporate marketing system VMS in which a single owner operates the entire marketing channel.

corporate Web sites Web sites that seek to build customer goodwill and supplement other sales channels rather than to sell goods and services.

cost per impression Measurement technique that relates the cost of an ad to every thousand people who view it.

cost per response (also called *click-throughs*) Direct marketing technique that relates the cost of an ad to the number of people who click it.

cost-plus pricing Practice of adding a percentage of specified dollar amount—or markup—to the base cost of a product to cover unassigned costs and to provide a profit.

countertrade Form of exporting whereby goods and services are bartered rather than sold for cash.

coupon Sales promotional technique that offers a discount on the purchase price of goods or services.

creative selling Personal selling that involves situations in which a considerable degree of analytical decision making on the buyer's part results in the need for skillful proposals of solutions for the customer's needs.

creativity Human activity that produces original ideas or knowledge, frequently by testing combinations of ideas or data to produce unique results.

critical thinking Process of determining the authenticity, accuracy, and worth of information, knowledge, claims, and arguments.

cross promotion Promotional technique in which marketing partners share the cost of a promotional campaign that meets their mutual needs.

cross-selling Selling of multiple, often unrelated goods and services to the same customer based on knowledge of that customer's needs.

cue Any object in the environment that determines the nature of a consumer's response to a drive.

culture Values, beliefs, preferences, and tastes handed down from one generation to the next in a society.

cumulative quantity discount Price discount determined by amounts of purchases over stated time periods.

customary prices Traditional prices that customers expect to pay for certain goods and services.

customer behavior Mental and physical activities that occur during selection and purchase of a product.

customer relationship management (CRM) Strategies and tools that drive relationship programs, reorienting an entire organization to a concentrated focus on satisfying customers.

customer satisfaction Extent to which customers are satisfied with their purchases.

customer winback Process of rejuvenating lost relationships with customers.

customer-based segmentation Dividing a business-to-business market into homogeneous groups based on buyers' product specifications.

customer-service standards Statement of goals and acceptable performance for the quality of service that a firm expects to deliver to its customers.

customs union Establishment of a free trade area plus a uniform tariff for trade with nonmember unions.

cybermall Group of virtual stores planned, coordinated, and operated as a unit for online shoppers.

D

data mining Process of searching through customer databases to detect patterns that guide marketing decision making.

database marketing Use of software to analyze marketing information, identifying and targeting messages toward specific groups of potential customers.

decider Person who chooses a good or service, although another person may have the formal authority to do so.

decline stage Final stage of the product life cycle, in which a decline in total industry sales occurs.

decoding Receiver's interpretation of a message.

Delphi technique Qualitative sales forecasting method that gathers and redistributes several rounds of anonymous forecasts until the participants reach a consensus.

demand Schedule of the amounts of a firm's product that consumers will purchase at different prices during a specified time period.

demarketing Process of reducing consumer demand for a good or service to a level that the firm can supply.

demographic segmentation Division of an overall market into homogeneous groups based on variables such as gender, age, income, occupation, education, sexual orientation, household size, and stage in the family life cycle; also called *socioeconomic segmentation.*

demonstration Stage in the personal selling process in which the customer has the opportunity to try out or otherwise see how a good or service works before purchase.

department store Large store that handles a variety of merchandise, including clothing, household goods, appliances, and furniture.

deregulation movement Opening of markets previously subject to government control.

derived demand Demand for a resource that results from demand for the goods and services that are produced by that resource.

differentiated marketing Market strategy that focuses on producing several products and pricing, promoting, and distributing them with different marketing mixes designed to satisfy smaller segments.

diffusion process Process by which new goods or services are accepted in the marketplace.

digital tools Electronic technologies used in e-commerce, including fax machines, personal digital assistants (PDAs) like Bluetooth, smart phones, and DVDs.

direct channel Marketing channel that moves goods directly from a producer to the business purchaser or ultimate user.

direct mail Communications in the form of sales letters, postcards, brochures, catalogs, and the like conveying messages directly from the marketer to the customer.

direct marketing Direct communications, other than personal sales contacts, between buyer and seller, designed to generate sales, information requests, or store or Web site visits.

direct sales results test Method for measuring promotional effectiveness based on the specific impact on sales revenues for each dollar of promotional spending.

direct selling Strategy designed to establish direct sales contact between producer and final user.

discount house Store that charges low prices but may not offer services such as credit.

discretionary income Money people have available to spend after buying necessities such as food, clothing, and housing.

distribution Movement of goods and services from producers to customers.

distribution strategy Planning that ensures that consumers find their products in the proper quantities at the right times and places.

downstream management Controlling part of the supply chain that involves finished product storage, outbound logistics, marketing and sales, and customer service.

drive Any strong stimulus that impels a person to act.

drop shipper Limited-function merchant wholesaler who accepts orders from customers and forwards these orders to producers, which then ship directly to the customers who place the orders.

dual distribution Network that moves products to a firm's target market through more than one marketing channel.

dumping Controversial practice of selling a product in a foreign market at a price lower than what it receives in the producer's domestic market.

E

economic environment Factors that influence consumer buying power and marketing strategies, including stage of the business cycle, inflation, unemployment, income, and resource availability.

80/20 principle Generally accepted rule that 80 percent of a product's revenues come from 20 percent of its total customers.

elasticity Measure of responsiveness of purchasers and suppliers to a change in price.

electronic bulletin board Specialized online service that provides information on a specific topic or area of interest.

electronic commerce (e-commerce) Targeting customers by collecting and analyzing business information, conducting customer transactions, and maintaining online relationships with customers by means of computer networks.

electronic data interchange (EDI) Computer-to-computer exchanges of invoices, orders, and other business documents.

electronic exchange Online marketplace that brings buyers and sellers together.

electronic marketing (e-marketing) Strategic process of creating, distributing, promoting, and pricing goods and services to a target market over the Internet or through digital tools.

electronic signature Electronic approval of a document that has the same legal status as a written signature.

electronic storefront Online store where customers can view and order merchandise much like window shopping at traditional retail establishments.

embargo Complete ban on the import of specified products.

emergency goods and services Products bought in response to unexpected and urgent needs.

employee satisfaction Employee's level of satisfaction for his or her company and the extent to which that loyalty or lack of loyalty is communicated to external customers.

encoding Translating a message into understandable terms.

end-use application segmentation Segmenting a business-to-business market based on how industrial purchasers will use the product.

Engel's laws Three general statements based on Engel's studies of the impact of household income changes on consumer spending behavior: As household income increases, a smaller percentage of expenditures go for food, the percentage spent on housing and household operations and clothing remains constant, and the percentage spent on other items (such as recreation and education) increases.

enterprise resource planning (ERP) system Software system that consolidates data from among a firm's various business units.

environmental management Attainment of organizational objectives by predicting and influencing the competitive, political-legal, economic, technological, and social-cultural environments.

environmental scanning Process of collecting information about the external marketing environment to identify and interpret potential trends.

ethics Moral standards of behavior expected by a society.

European Union (EU) Customs union that is moving in the direction of an economic union by adopting a common currency, removing trade restrictions, and permitting free flow of goods and workers throughout the member nations.

evaluative criteria Features that a consumer considers in choosing among alternatives.

event marketing Marketing of sporting, cultural, and charitable activities to selected target markets.

everyday low pricing (EDLP) Pricing strategy of continuously offering low prices rather than relying on such short-term price cuts as cents-off coupons, rebates, and special sales.

evoked set Number of alternatives that a consumer actually considers in making a purchase decision.

exchange control Method used to regulate the privilege of international trade among importing organizations by controlling access to foreign currencies.

exchange function Buying and selling functions of marketing.

exchange process Activity in which two or more parties give something of value to each other to satisfy perceived needs.

exchange rate Price of one nation's currency in terms of another country's currency.

exclusive dealing agreement Arrangement between a manufacturer and a marketing intermediary that prohibits the intermediary from handling competing product lines.

exclusive distribution Distribution of a product through a single wholesaler or retailer in a specific geographic region.

expectancy theory Theory stating that motivation depends on an individual's expectations of his or her ability to perform a job and how that performance relates to attaining a desired reward.

exploratory research Process of discussing a marketing problem with informed sources both within and outside the firm and examining information from secondary sources.

exponential smoothing Quantitative forecasting technique that assigns weights to historical sales data, giving the greatest weight to the most recent data.

exporting Marketing domestically produced goods and services in foreign countries.

extended problem solving Situation that involves lengthy external searches and long deliberation; results when brands are difficult to categorize or evaluate.

external customer People or organizations that buy or use another firm's goods or services.

extranet Secure network accessible through a Web site by external customers or organizations for electronic commerce. It provides more customer-specific information than a public site.

F

facilitating functions Functions that assist the marketer in performing the exchange and physical distribution functions.

fair-trade laws Statutes enacted in most states that once permitted manufacturers to stipulate a minimum retail price for their product.

family brand Single brand name that identifies several related products.

family life cycle Process of family formation and dissolution.

feedback Receiver's response to a message.

field selling Sales presentations made at prospective customers' locations on a face-to-face basis.

first mover strategy Theory advocating that the company that is first to offer a product in a marketplace will be the long-term market winner.

fixed costs Costs that remain stable at any production level within a certain range (such as lease payments or insurance costs).

fixed-sum-per-unit method Method of promotional budgeting in which a predetermined amount is allocated to each sales or production unit.

FOB (free on board) plant (FOB origin) Price quotation that does not include shipping charges.

FOB origin-freight allowed (freight absorbed) Price quotation system that allows the buyer to deduct shipping expenses from the cost of purchases.

focus group Simultaneous personal interview of a small group of individuals, which relies on group discussion about a certain topic.

follow-up Postsales activities that often determine whether an individual who has made a recent purchase will become a repeat customer.

foreign licensing Agreement that grants foreign marketers the right to distribute a firm's merchandise or to use its trademark, patent, or process in a specified geographic area.

forward integration Process through which a firm attempts to control downstream distribution.

franchise Vertical marketing system in which a wholesaler or dealer (the franchisee) agrees to meet the operating requirements of a manufacturer or other franchiser.

free trade area Region in which participating nations agree to the free trade of goods among themselves, abolishing tariffs and trade restrictions.

Free Trade Area of the Americas (FTAA) Proposed free trade area stretching the length of the entire Western hemisphere and designed to extend free trade benefits to additional nations in North, Central, and South America.

frequency marketing Frequent buyer or user marketing programs that reward customers with cash, rebates, merchandise, or other premiums.

friendship, commerce, and navigation (FCN) treaties International agreements that deal with many aspects of commercial relations among nations.

full-cost pricing Pricing method that uses all relevant variable costs in setting a product's price and also allocates those fixed costs that cannot be directly attributed to the production of the specific item being priced.

full-service research supplier Marketing research organization that offers all aspects of the marketing research process.

G

gatekeeper Person who controls the information that all buying center members will review.

General Agreement on Tariffs and Trade (GATT) International trade accord that has helped reduce world tariffs.

general merchandise retailer Store that carries a wide variety of product lines, stocking all of them in some depth.

generic products Products characterized by plain labels, no advertising, and the absence of brand names.

geographic information systems (GISs) Computer systems that assemble, store, manipulate, and display data by their location.

geographic segmentation Division of an overall market into homogeneous groups based on their locations.

global marketing strategy Standardized marketing mix with minimal modifications that a firm uses in all of its domestic and foreign markets.

global sourcing Purchasing goods and services from suppliers worldwide.

good Tangible product that customers can see, hear, smell, taste, or touch.

goods–services continuum Spectrum along which goods and services fall according to their attributes, from pure good to pure service.

grassroots marketing Efforts that connect directly with existing and potential customers through nonmainstream channels.

green marketing Production, promotion, and reclamation of environmentally sensitive products.

grey goods Products manufactured abroad under license from a U.S. firm and then sold in the U.S. market in competition with that firm's own domestic output.

growth stage Second stage of the product life cycle, which begins when a firm starts to realize substantial profits from its investment in the product.

guerilla marketing Unconventional, innovative, and low-cost marketing techniques designed to get consumers' attention in unusual ways.

H

high-involvement purchase decision Buying decision that evokes high levels of potential social or economic consequence.

home shopping channel Television direct marketing in which a variety of products are offered and consumers can order them directly by phone or online.

hypothesis Tentative explanation for some specific event.

I

import quotas Trade restrictions that limit the number of units of certain goods that can enter a country for resale.

importing Purchasing foreign goods, services, and raw materials.

impulse goods and services Products purchased on the spur of the moment.

inbound telemarketing Sales method in which prospects call a toll-free number to obtain information, make reservations, and purchase goods and services.

incremental-cost pricing Pricing method that attempts to use only those costs directly attributable to a specific output in setting prices.

indirect evaluation Method for measuring promotional effectiveness by concentrating on quantifiable indicators of effectiveness such as recall and readership.

individual brand Single brand that uniquely identifies a product itself.

industrial products *See* business-to-business (B2B) product.

inelastic demand Demand that, throughout an industry, will not change significantly due to a price change.

inflation Rising prices caused by some combination of excess consumer demand and increases in the costs of one or more factors of production.

influencer Typically, technical staff such as engineers who affect the buying decision by supplying information to guide evaluation of alternatives or by setting buying specifications.

infomercial Paid 30-minute product commercial that resembles a regular television program.

informative advertising Promotion that seeks to develop initial demand for a good, service, organization, person, place, idea, or cause.

infrastructure Nation's basic system of transportation networks, communications systems, and energy facilities.

inside selling Selling by phone, mail, and electronic commerce.

installations Business products like factories, assembly lines, and huge machinery that are major capital investments.

instant messaging E-mail service that allows for the immediate exchange of short messages between online users.

institutional advertising Promotion of a concept, idea, philosophy, or goodwill of an industry, company, organization, person, geographic location, or government agency.

integrated marketing communications (IMC) Coordination of all promotional activities to produce a unified, customer-focused promotional message.

intensive distribution Distribution of a product through all available channels.

interactive advertising Two-way promotional messages transmitted through communication channels that induce message recipients to participate actively in the promotional effort.

interactive marketing Buyer–seller communications in which the customer controls the amount and type of information received from a marketer through such channels as the Internet, CD-ROMs, interactive toll-free telephone numbers, and virtual reality kiosks.

interactive television (iTV) Television service package that includes a return path for viewers to interact with programs or commercials by clicking their remote controls.

intermodal operations Combination of transport modes such as rail and highway carriers (piggyback), air and highway carriers (birdyback), and water and air carriers (fishyback) to improve customer service and achieve cost advantages.

internal customer Employees or departments within an organization that depend on the work of another employee or department to perform tasks.

internal marketing Managerial actions that help all members of the organization understand and accept their respective roles in implementing a marketing strategy.

internal partnership Relationship involving customers within an organization.

Internet (or **Net)** Worldwide network of interconnected computers that lets anyone with access to a personal computer send and receive images and data anywhere.

Internet service provider (ISP) Organization that provides access to the Internet via a telephone, satellite TV service, or cable TV network.

interpretative research Observational research method developed by social anthropologists in which customers are observed in their natural setting and their behavior is interpreted based on an understanding of social and cultural characteristics; also known as *ethnography,* or "going native."

intranet Internal corporate network that allows employees within an organization to communicate with each other and gain access to corporate information.

introductory stage First stage of the product life cycle, in which a firm works to stimulate the new market entry.

ISO (International Organization for Standarization) certification Internationally recognized standards that ensure a company's goods and services meet established quality levels and that ensure its operations minimize harm to the environment.

ISO 9002 International quality standards developed by the International Organization for Standardization in Switzerland to ensure consistent quality among products manufactured and sold throughout the European Union (EU).

J

joint demand Demand for a product that depends on the demand for another product used in combination with it.

jury of executive opinion Qualitative sales forecasting method that assesses the sales expectations of various executives.

just-in-time (JIT)/just-in-time II (JIT II) Inventory practices that seek to boost efficiency by cutting inventories to absolute minimum levels. With JIT II, suppliers' representatives work at the customer's facility.

L

label Branding component that carries an item's brand name or symbol, the name and address of the manufacturer or distributor, information about the product, and recommended uses.

lateral partnerships Strategic relationships that extend to external entities but involve no direct buyer–seller interactions.

leader pricing Variant of loss-leader pricing in which marketers offer prices slightly above cost to avoid violating minimum-markup regulations and earn a minimal return on promotional sales.

learning Knowledge or skill that is acquired as a result of experience, which changes consumer behavior.

lifetime value of a customer Revenues and intangible benefits that a customer brings to an organization over an average lifetime, minus the investment the firm has made to the customer.

limited problem solving Situation in which the consumer invests some small amount of time and energy in searching for and evaluating alternatives.

limited-line store Retailer that offers a large assortment within a single product line or within a few related product lines.

limited-service research supplier Marketing research firm that specializes in a limited number of research activities, such as conducting field interviews or performing data processing.

line extension Development of individual offerings that appeal to different market segments while remaining closely related to the existing product line.

list price Established price normally quoted to potential buyers.

logistics Process of coordinating the flow of information, goods, and services among members of the distribution channel.

loss leader Product offered to consumers at less than cost to attract them to stores in the hope that they will buy other merchandise at regular prices.

low-involvement purchase decision Routine purchase that poses little risk to the consumer, either socially or economically.

M

mail-order wholesaler Limited-function merchant wholesaler who distributes catalogs instead of sending sales representatives to contact customers.

mall intercept Interviews conducted inside retail shopping centers.

manufacturer's brand Brand name owned by a manufacturer or other producer.

manufacturers' representative Agent wholesaling intermediary who represents a number of manufacturers of related but noncompeting products and who receives a commission on each sale.

marginal analysis Method of analyzing the relationship between costs, sales price, and increased sales volume.

marginal cost Change in total cost that results from producing an additional unit of output.

markdown Amount by which a retailer reduces the original selling price of a product.

market Group of people with sufficient purchasing power, authority, and willingness to buy.

market development strategy Strategy that concentrates on finding new markets for existing products.

market penetration strategy Strategy that seeks to increase sales of existing products in existing markets.

market price Price that a consumer or marketing intermediary actually pays for a product after subtracting any discounts, allowances, or rebates from the list price.

market segmentation Division of the total market into smaller, relatively homogeneous groups.

market share/market growth matrix Framework that places SBUs on a chart that plots market share against market growth potential.

marketing Process of planning and executing the conception, pricing, and distribution of ideas, goods, services, organizations, and events to create and maintain relationships that will satisfy individual and organizational objectives.

marketing (distribution) channel System of marketing institutions that enhances the physical flow of goods and services, along with ownership title, from producer to consumer or business user.

marketing communications Messages that deal with buyer–seller relationships.

marketing concept Companywide consumer orientation with the objective of achieving long-run success.

marketing decision support system (MDSS) Marketing information system component that links a decision maker with relevant databases and analysis tools.

marketing ethics Marketers' standards of conduct and moral values.

marketing information system (MIS) Planned, computer-based system designed to provide managers with a continuous flow of information relevant to their specific decisions and areas of responsibility.

marketing intermediary (middleman) Wholesaler or retailer that operates between producers and consumers or business users.

marketing mix Blending of the four strategy elements—product, distribution, promotion, and pricing—to fit the needs and preferences of a specific target market.

marketing myopia Management's failure to recognize the scope of its business.

marketing planning Implementing planning activities devoted to achieving marketing objectives.

marketing public relations (MPR) Narrowly focused public relations activities that directly support marketing goals.

marketing research Process of collecting and using information for marketing decision making.

marketing strategy Overall companywide program for selecting a particular target market and then satisfying consumers in that market through the marketing mix.

marketing Web sites Web sites whose primary objective is to increase purchases by online visitors.

market-plus pricing The intentional setting of a relatively high price compared with the prices of competing products; also known as *skimming pricing.*

market-share objective Volume-related pricing objective in which the goal is to achieve control of a portion of the market for a firm's good or service.

markup Amount that a retailer adds to the cost of a product to determine its selling price.

mass merchandiser Store that stocks a wider line of goods than a department store, usually without the same depth of assortment within each line.

materials handling system Set of activities that move production inputs and other goods within plants, warehouses, and transportation terminals.

maturity stage Third stage of the product life cycle, in which industry sales level out.

media research Advertising research that assesses how well a particular medium delivers an advertiser's message, where and when to place the advertisement, and the size of the audience.

media scheduling Setting the timing and sequence for a series of advertisements.

meeting competition method Method of promotional budgeting that simply matches competitors' outlays.

merchandisers Buyers who are responsible for securing needed business products at the best possible prices.

merchant wholesaler Independently owned wholesaling intermediary who takes title to the goods that it handles; also known as an industrial distributor in the business-goods market.

message Communication of information, advice, or a request by the sender to the receiver.

message research Advertising research that tests consumer reactions to an advertisement's creative message.

metropolitan statistical area (MSA) Freestanding urban area with a population in the urban center of at least 50,000 and a total MSA population of 100,000 or more.

micromarketing Targeting potential customers at very narrow, basic levels, such as by zip code, specific occupation, or lifestyle—possibly even individuals themselves.

micropolitan statistical area Area comprised of at least one town of 10,000 to 49,999 people with proportionally few of its residents commuting to outside the area.

middleman *See* marketing intermediary.

minimum advertised pricing (MAP) Fees paid to retailers that agree not to advertise products below set prices.

mission Essential purpose that differentiates one company from others.

missionary selling Indirect type of selling in which specialized salespeople promote the firm's goodwill among indirect customers, often by assisting customers in product use.

modified breakeven analysis Pricing technique used to evaluate consumer demand by comparing the number of products that must be sold at a variety of prices to cover total cost with estimates of expected sales at the various prices.

modified rebuy Situation in which a purchaser is willing to reevaluate available options for repurchasing a good or service.

monopolistic competition Market structure involving a heterogeneous product and product differentiation among competing suppliers, allowing the marketer some degree of control over prices.

monopoly Market structure in which a single seller dominates trade in a good or service for which buyers can find no close substitutes.

motive Inner state that directs a person toward the goal of satisfying a need.

MRO items Business supplies that include maintenance items, repair items, and operating supplies.

multidomestic marketing strategy Application of market segmentation to foreign markets by tailoring the firm's marketing mix to match specific target markets in each nation.

multinational corporation Firm with significant operations and marketing activities outside its home country.

multiple sourcing Purchasing from several vendors.

N

national account selling Promotional effort in which a dedicated sales team is assigned to a firm's major customers to provide sales and service needs.

national accounts organization Organizational arrangement that assigns sales teams to a firm's largest accounts.

need Imbalance between a consumer's actual and desired states.

network marketing Personal selling that relies on lists of family members and friends of the salesperson who organizes a gathering of potential customers for a demonstration of products.

new-task buying First-time or unique purchase situation that requires considerable effort by decision makers.

niche marketing Marketing strategy that focuses on profitably satisfying a single market segment; also called *concentrated marketing.*

9/11 Generation People in their formative years at the time of the September 11 terrorist attacks.

noise Any stimulus that distracts a receiver from receiving a message.

noncumulative quantity discount Price reduction granted on a one-time-only basis.

nonmarketing public relations Organizational messages about general management issues.

nonpersonal selling Promotion that includes advertising, sales promotion, direct marketing, guerilla marketing, and public relations—all conducted without being face to face with the buyer.

nonprobability sample Sample that involves personal judgment somewhere in the selection process.

norms Values, attitudes, and behaviors that a group deems appropriate for its members.

North American Free Trade Agreement (NAFTA) Accord removing trade barriers among Canada, Mexico, and the United States.

North American Industrial Classification System (NAICS) Classification used by NAFTA countries to categorize the business marketplace into detailed market segments.

O

objection Expression of sales resistance by the prospect.

objectives Goals that guide the development of supporting marketing strategy to fulfill a firm's mission.

odd pricing Pricing policy based on the belief that a price ending with an odd number just under a round number is more appealing—for instance, $9.97 rather than $10.

offshoring Movement of high-wage jobs from the U.S. to lower-cost overseas locations.

oligopoly Market structure, like those in the steel and telecommunications industries, in which relatively few sellers compete, and where high start-up costs form barriers to keep out new competitors.

one-to-one marketing Program that is customized to build long-term relationships with customers, one at a time.

online sample offerings Product offerings designed to encourage trial use that may lead to future purchases that can be ordered online directly from companies making such orders or indirectly from Web sites such as Freesite.com and All-free-samples.com.

opinion leaders Trendsetters who purchase new products before others in a group and then influence others in their purchases.

order processing Selling, mostly at the wholesale and retail levels, that involves identifying customer needs, pointing them out to customers, and completing orders.

organization marketing Marketing by mutual-benefit organizations, service organizations, and government organizations intended to influence others to accept their goals, receive their services, or contribute to them in some way.

organizational products *See* business-to-business (B2B) product.

outbound telemarketing Sales method in which sales representatives place phone calls to prospects and try to conclude the sale over the phone.

outsourcing Using outside vendors to produce goods and services formerly produced in-house.

over-the-counter selling Personal selling conducted in retail and some wholesale locations in which customers come to the seller's place of business.

P

partnership Affiliation of two or more companies that assist each other in the achievement of common goals.

penetration pricing strategy Pricing strategy involving the use of a relatively low entry price compared with competitive offerings, based on the theory that this initial low price will help secure market acceptance.

percentage-of-sales method Method of promotional budgeting in which a dollar amount is based on a percentage of past or projected sales.

perception Meaning that a person attributes to incoming stimuli gathered through the five senses.

perceptual screen Mental filter or block through which all inputs must pass to be noticed.

person marketing Marketing efforts designed to cultivate the attention, interest, and preference of a target market toward a person (typically a political candidate or celebrity).

personal selling Interpersonal influence process involving a seller's promotional presentation conducted on a person-to-person basis with the buyer.

persuasive advertising Promotion that attempts to increase demand for an existing good, service, organization, person, place, idea, or cause.

physical distribution Broad range of activities aimed at efficient movement of finished goods from the end of the production line to the consumer.

physical distribution function Transportation and distribution of goods and services.

place marketing Marketing efforts to attract people and organizations to a particular geographic area.

planned obsolescence Intentional design, manufacture, and marketing of products with limited durability.

planned shopping center Group of retail stores planned, coordinated, and marketed as a unit.

planning Process of anticipating future events and conditions and of determining the best way to achieve organizational goals.

point-of-purchase (POP) advertising Display or other promotion placed near the site of the actual buying decision.

political risk assessment (PRA) Units within a firm that evaluate the political risks of the marketplaces in which they operate as well as proposed new marketplaces.

political-legal environment Component of the marketing environment consisting of laws and interpretations of laws that require firms to operate under competitive conditions and to protect consumer rights.

population (universe) Total group that researchers want to study.

pop-up ads Promotional messages that appear unsolicited as windows on a computer screen.

Porter's Five Forces Model developed by strategy expert Michael Porter, which identifies five competitive forces that influence planning strategies: the threat of new entrants, the threat of substitute products, rivalry among competitors, the bargaining power of buyers, and the bargaining power of suppliers.

portfolio analysis Evaluation of a company's products and divisions to determine which are strongest and which are weakest.

positioning Placing a product at a certain point or location within a market in the minds of prospective buyers.

positioning map A valuable tool that helps marketers place products in a market by graphically illustrating consumers' perceptions of competing products within an industry.

postage-stamp pricing System for handling transportation costs under which all buyers are quoted the same price, including transportation expenses; also known as *uniform-delivered price.*

posttesting Research that assesses advertising effectiveness after it has appeared in a print or broadcast medium.

precall planning Use of information collected during the prospecting and qualifying stages of the sales process and during previous contacts with the prospect to tailor the approach and presentation to match the customer's needs.

premium Item given free or at reduced cost with purchases of other products.

presentation Personal selling function of describing a product's major features and relating them to a customer's problems or needs.

pretesting Research that evaluates an ad during its development stage.

price Exchange value of a good or service.

price flexibility Pricing policy permitting variable prices for goods and services.

pricing policy General guideline that reflects marketing objectives and influences specific pricing decisions.

pricing strategy Methods of setting profitable and justifiable prices.

primary data Information collected specifically for the investigation at hand.

primary demand Desire for a general product category.

primary metropolitan statistical area (PMSA) Urbanized county or set of counties with social and economic ties to nearby areas.

private brand Brand offered by a wholesaler or retailer.

private carriers Transporters that provide service solely for internally generated freight.

probability sample Sample that gives every member of the population a known chance of being selected.

product Bundle of physical, service, and symbolic attributes designed to satisfy a customer's wants and needs.

product advertising Nonpersonal selling of a particular good or service.

product development Introduction of new products into identifiable or established markets.

product differentiation When consumers regard a firm's products as different in some way from those of competitors.

product diversification strategy Developing entirely new products for new markets.

product liability Responsibility of manufacturers and marketers for injuries and damages caused by their products.

product life cycle Progression of a product through introduction, growth, maturity, and decline stages.

product line Series of related products offered by one company.

product manager Marketer within an organization who is responsible for an individual product or product line; also called a brand manager.

product mix Assortment of product lines and individual product offerings that a company sells.

product placement Form of promotion in which a marketer pays a motion picture or television program owner a fee to display a product prominently in the film or show.

product positioning Consumers' perceptions of a product's attributes, uses, quality, and advantages and disadvantages relative to competing brands.

product strategy Decisions about what goods or services a firm will offer its customers; also includes decisions about customer service, packaging, brand names, and the like.

production orientation Business philosophy stressing efficiency in producing a quality product, with the attitude toward marketing that "a good product will sell itself."

product-line pricing Practice of setting a limited number of prices for a selection of merchandise and marketing different product lines in each of these price levels.

product-related segmentation Division of a population into homogeneous groups based on their relationships to the product.

profit center Any part of an organization to which revenue and controllable costs can be assigned.

Profit Impact of Market Strategies (PIMS) project Research that discovered a strong positive relationship between a firm's market share and product quality and its return on investment.

profit maximization Point at which the additional revenue gained by increasing the price of a product equals the increase in total costs.

promotion Communications link between buyers and sellers. Function of informing, persuading, and influencing a consumer's purchase decision.

promotional allowance Promotional incentive in which the manufacturer agrees to pay the reseller a certain amount to cover the costs of special promotional displays or extensive advertising.

promotional mix Subset of the marketing mix in which marketers attempt to achieve the optimal blending of the elements of personal and nonpersonal selling to achieve promotional objectives.

promotional pricing Pricing policy in which a lower than normal price is used as a temporary ingredient in a firm's marketing strategy.

prospecting Personal selling function of identifying potential customers.

protective tariff Taxes designed to raise the retail price of an imported product to match or exceed that of a similar domestic tariff.

psychographic segmentation Division of a population into groups that have similar psychological characteristics, values, and lifestyles.

psychological pricing Pricing policy based on the belief that certain prices or price ranges make a good or service more appealing than others to buyers.

public relations Firm's communications and relationships with its various publics.

public service announcements (PSAs) Advertisements aimed at achieving socially oriented objectives by focusing on causes and charitable organizations that are included in print and electronic media without charge.

publicity Nonpersonal stimulation of demand for a good, service, place, idea, person, or organization by unpaid placement of significant news regarding the product in a print or broadcast medium.

puffery Exaggerated claims of a product's superiority, or the use of subjective or vague statements that may not be literally true.

pulling strategy Promotional effort by the seller to stimulate final-user demand, which then exerts pressure on the distribution channel.

pure competition Market structure characterized by homogeneous products in which there are so many buyers and sellers that none has a significant influence on price.

push money Financial incentive that gives retail salespeople cash rewards for every unit of a product they sell.

pushing strategy Promotional effort by the seller directed to members of the marketing channel rather than final users.

Q

qualifying Determining that a prospect has the needs, income, and purchase authority necessary for being a potential customer.

qualitative forecasting Use of subjective techniques to forecast sales, such as the jury of executive opinion, Delphi technique, sales force composite, and surveys of buyer intentions.

quantitative forecasting Use of statistical forecasting techniques such as trend analysis and exponential smoothing.

quantity discount Price reduction granted for a large-volume purchase.

quick-response merchandising Just-in-time strategy that reduces the time a retailer must hold merchandise in inventory, resulting in substantial cost savings.

quota sample Nonprobability sample divided to maintain the proportion of certain characteristics among different segments or groups as the population as a whole.

R

rack jobber Full-function merchant wholesaler who markets specialized lines of merchandise to retail stores.

radio frequency identification (RFID) Technology that uses a tiny chip with identification information that can be read from a distance by a scanner using radio waves.

raw materials Natural resources such as farm products, coal, copper, or lumber, which become part of a final product.

rebate Refund of a portion of the purchase price, usually granted by the product's manufacturer.

reciprocity Policy to extend purchasing preference to suppliers that are also customers.

reference groups People or institutions whose opinions are valued and to whom a person looks for guidance in his or her own behavior, values, and conduct, such as family, friends, or celebrities.

refund Cash given back to consumers who send in proof of purchasing one or more products.

reinforcement Reduction in drive that results from a proper response.

relationship marketing Development and maintenance of long-term, cost-effective relationships with individual customers, suppliers, employees, and other partners for mutual benefit.

relationship selling Regular contacts between sales representatives and customers over an extended period to establish a sustained seller–buyer relationship.

remanufacturing Production to restore worn-out products to like-new condition.

reminder advertising Advertising that reinforces previous promotional activity by keeping the name of a good, service, organization, person, place, idea, or cause before the public.

repositioning Changing the position of a product within the minds of prospective buyers relative to the positions of competing products.

research design Master plan for conducting marketing research.

reseller Marketing intermediaries that operate in the trade sector.

response Individual's reaction to a set of cues and drives.

retail advertising Advertising by stores that sell goods or services directly to the consuming public.

retail convergence A situation in which similar merchandise is available from multiple retail outlets, resulting in the blurring of distinctions between type of retailer and merchandise offered.

retail cooperative Group of retailers that establish a shared wholesaling operation to help them compete with chains.

retailing Activities involved in selling merchandise to ultimate consumers.

revenue tariff Taxes designed to raise funds for the importing government.

reverse channel Channel designed to return goods to their producers.

Robinson-Patman Act Federal legislation prohibiting price discrimination that is not based on a cost differential; also prohibits selling at an unreasonably low price to eliminate competition.

role Behavior that members of a group expect of individuals who hold specific positions within that group.

routinized response behavior Rapid consumer problem solving in which no new information is considered; the consumer has already set evaluative criteria and identified available options.

rule of three Three strongest, most efficient companies in an industry will dominate 70 to 90 percent of the market.

S

salary Fixed compensation payment made periodically to an employee.

sales analysis In-depth evaluation of a firm's sales.

sales force automation (SFA) Applications of computer and other technologies to make the sales function more efficient and competitive.

sales force composite Qualitative sales forecasting method based on the combined sales estimates of the firm's salespeople.

sales forecast Estimate of company revenue for a specified future period.

sales incentives Programs that reward salespeople for superior performance.

sales orientation Business assumption that consumers will resist purchasing nonessential goods and services with the attitude toward marketing that only creative advertising and personal selling can overcome consumers' resistance and convince them to buy.

sales promotion Marketing activities other than personal selling, advertising, guerilla marketing, and public relations that stimulate consumer purchasing and dealer effectiveness.

sales quota Level of expected sales for a territory, product, customer, or salesperson against which actual results are compared.

sampling In marketing research, the process of selecting survey respondents or research participants; in sales promotion, free distribution of a product in an attempt to obtain future sales.

scrambled merchandising Retailing practice of combining dissimilar product lines to boost sales volume.

search engine Tool to help online users find specific Web sites and pages.

search marketing Technique employed by online marketers who pay fees to search engines to have their Web sites or ads pop up after a computer user enters certain words into the search engine or to ensure that their firm's listing appears near the top of the search results.

second mover strategy Theory that advocates observing closely the innovations of first movers and then introducing new products that improve on the original offering to gain advantage in the marketplace.

secondary data Previously published information.

selective demand Desire for a specific brand within a product category.

selective distribution Distribution of a product through a limited number of channels.

self-concept Person's multifaceted picture of himself or herself.

seller partnership Relationship involving long-term exchanges of goods or services in return for cash or other valuable consideration.

seller's market Market in which there are more buyers for fewer goods and services.

selling agent Agent wholesaling intermediary responsible for the entire marketing program of a firm's product line.

sender Source of the message communicated to the receiver.

service Intangible task that satisfies the needs of consumer and business users.

service encounter Point at which the customer and service provider interact.

service quality Expected and perceived quality of a service offering.

shaping Process of applying a series of rewards and reinforcements to permit more complex behavior to evolve over time.

shopping products Products that consumers purchase after comparing competing offerings.

simple random sample Basic type of probability sample in which every individual in the relevant universe has an equal opportunity of being selected.

skimming pricing strategy Pricing strategy involving the use of a high price relative to competitive offerings.

slotting allowances Money paid by vendors to retailers to guarantee display of merchandise.

smart card Multipurpose card embedded with computer chips that store personal and financial information, such as credit-card data, health records, and driver's license numbers.

social responsibility Marketing philosophies, policies, procedures, and actions whose primary objective is the enhancement of society.

social-cultural environment Component of the marketing environment consisting of the relationship between the marketer and society and its culture.

sole sourcing Purchasing a firm's entire stock of an item from just one vendor.

span of control The number of representatives who report to first-level sales managers.

specialty advertising Sales promotion technique that places the advertiser's name, address, and advertising message on useful articles that are then distributed to target consumers.

specialty products Products that offer unique characteristics that cause buyers to prize those particular brands.

specialty retailer Store that combines carefully defined product lines, services, and reputation to convince shoppers to spend considerable shopping effort there.

split runs Methods of testing alternate ads by dividing a cable TV audience or a publication's subscribers in two, using two different ads, and then evaluating the relative effectiveness of each.

sponsorship Event/sponsor relationship in which an organization provides funds or in-kind resources to an event or activity in exchange for a direct association with that event or activity.

staples Convenience goods and services that consumers constantly replenish to maintain a ready inventory.

status Relative position of any individual member in a group.

stockkeeping unit (SKU) Offering within a product line such as a specific size of liquid detergent.

straight rebuy Recurring purchase decision in which a customer repurchases a good or service that has performed satisfactorily in the past.

strategic alliance Partnership in which two or more companies combine resources and capital to create competitive advantages in a new market.

strategic business unit (SBU) *See* category.

strategic business units (SBUs) Key business units within diversified firms.

strategic planning Process of determining an organization's primary objectives and adopting courses of action that will achieve these objectives.

strategic window Limited periods during which the key requirements of a market and the particular competencies of a firm best fit together.

stratified sample Probability sample constructed to represent randomly selected subsamples of different groups within the total sample; each subgroup is relatively homogeneous for a certain characteristic.

subcontracting Contractual agreements that assign the production of goods or services to local or smaller firms.

subcultures Smaller groups within a society that have their own distinct characteristics and modes of behavior, defined by ethnicity, race, region, age, religion, gender, social class, or profession.

subliminal perception Subconscious receipt of incoming information.

suboptimization Condition that results when individual operations achieve their objectives but interfere with progress toward broader organizational goals.

subsidy Government financial support of a private industry.

supercenter Large store, smaller than a hypermarket, that combines groceries with discount store merchandise.

supplies Regular expenses that a firm incurs in its daily operations.

supply Schedule of the amounts of a good or service that firms will offer for sale at different prices during a specified time period.

supply chain Complete sequence of suppliers and activities that contribute to the creation and delivery of merchandise.

supply-chain management Control of the activities of purchasing, processing, and delivery through which raw materials are transformed into products and made available to final consumers.

survey of buyer intentions Qualitative sales forecasting method that samples opinions among groups of present and potential customers concerning their purchase intentions.

sustainable competitive advantage Superior market position that a firm possesses and can maintain for an extended period of time.

sweepstakes Sales promotional technique in which prize winners are selected by chance.

switchless reseller Telecommunications company with no lines or equipment that buys blocks of long-distance time from major carriers and resells them by the minute at a discount.

SWOT analysis Analysis that helps planners compare internal organizational strengths and weaknesses with external opportunities and threats.

syndicated service Organization that provides standardized data on a periodic basis to its subscribers.

systems integration Centralization of the procurement function within an internal division or as a service of an external supplier.

T

tactical planning Planning that guides the implementation of activities specified in the strategic plan.

target market Group of people to whom a firm decides to direct its marketing efforts and ultimately its goods and services.

target-return objective Short-run or long-run pricing objectives of achieving a specified return on either sales or investment.

tariff Tax levied against imported goods.

task-objective method Development of a promotional budget based on evaluation of the firm's promotional objectives.

team selling Selling situation in which several sales associates or other members of the organization are recruited to assist the lead sales representative in reaching all those who influence the purchase decision.

technological environment Applications to marketing of knowledge based on discoveries in science, inventions, and innovations.

technology Business application of knowledge based on scientific discoveries, inventions, and innovations.

telemarketing Promotional presentation involving the use of the telephone on an outbound basis by salespeople or on an inbound basis by customers who initiate calls to obtain information and place orders.

test market Quantitative forecasting method that introduces a new product, price, promotional campaign, or other marketing variable in a test-market location to assess consumer reactions.

test marketing Marketing research technique that involves introducing a new product in a specific area and then measuring its degree of success.

third-party (contract) logistics firm Company that specializes in handling logistics activities for other firms.

time-based competition Strategy of developing and distributing goods and services more quickly than competitors.

total quality management (TQM) Continuous effort to improve products and work processes with the goal of achieving customer satisfaction and world-class performance.

trade allowance Special financial incentive offered to wholesalers and retailers that purchase or promote specific products.

trade discount Payment to a channel member or buyer for performing marketing functions; also known as a *functional discount.*

trade dress Visual components that contribute to the overall look of a brand.

trade industries Retailers or wholesalers that purchase products for resale to others.

trade promotion Sales promotion that appeals to marketing intermediaries rather than to consumers.

trade show Product exhibition organized by industry trade associations to showcase goods and services.

trade-in Credit allowance given for a used item when a customer purchases a new item.

trademark Brand for which the owner claims exclusive legal protection.

transaction-based marketing Buyer and seller exchanges characterized by limited communications and little or no ongoing relationships between the parties.

transfer price Cost assessed when a product is moved from one profit center in a firm to another.

trend analysis Quantitative sales forecasting method that estimates future sales through statistical analyses of historical sales patterns.

truck wholesaler Limited-function merchant wholesaler who markets perishable food items; also called a *truck jobber.*

tying agreement Arrangement that requires a marketing intermediary to carry items other than those they want to sell.

U

undifferentiated marketing Market strategy that focuses on producing a single product and marketing it to all customers; also called *mass marketing.*

unemployment Proportion of people in the economy who are actively seeking work but do not have jobs.

unfair-trade laws State laws requiring sellers to maintain minimum prices for comparable merchandise.

uniform-delivered price Pricing system for handling transportation costs under which all buyers are quoted the same price, including transportation expenses. Sometimes known as *postage-stamp pricing.*

unit pricing Pricing policy in which prices are stated in terms of a recognized unit of measurement or a standard numerical count.

Universal Product Code (UPC) Numerical bar code system used to record product and price information.

unsought products Products marketed to consumers who may not yet recognize a need for them.

upstream management Controlling part of the supply chain that involves raw materials, inbound logistics, and warehouse and storage facilities.

user Individual or group that actually uses a business good or service.

utility Want-satisfying power of a good or service.

V

VALS2 Segmentation system that divides consumers into eight psychographic categories: actualizers, fulfilleds, believers, achievers, strivers, experiencers, makers, and strugglers.

value analysis Systematic study of the components of a purchase to determine the most cost-effective approach.

value pricing Pricing strategy emphasizing benefits derived from a product in comparison to the price and quality levels of competing offerings.

variable costs Costs that change with the level of production (such as labor and raw materials costs).

vendor analysis Assessment of supplier performance in areas such as price, back orders, timely delivery, and attention to special requests.

vendor-managed inventory (VMI) System that provides inventory information, based on the assumption that suppliers are in the best position to spot understocks or surpluses.

venture team Associates from different areas of an organization who work together in developing new products.

vertical marketing system (VMS) Planned channel system designed to improve distribution efficiency and cost effectiveness by integrating various functions throughout the distribution chain.

viral marketing Efforts that allow satisfied customers to spread the word about products to other consumers.

virtual coupons Sales promotional price discount offers that are downloaded by request on a home computer or via e-mail.

virtual relationships Links between businesses and customers that are developed without person-to-person contact.

virtual sales team Network of strategic partners, trade associations, suppliers, and others who recommend a firm's goods or services.

W

Web kiosk Small, freestanding computer, often located in a store, that provides consumers with Internet connections to a firm and its goods and services.

wheel of retailing Hypothesis that each new type of retailer gains a competitive foothold by offering lower prices than current suppliers charge; the result of reducing or eliminating services.

wholesaler Channel intermediary that takes title to goods it handles and then distributes these goods to retailers, other distributors, or B2B customers.

wholesaling intermediary Comprehensive term that describes wholesalers as well as agents and brokers.

Wi-Fi (wireless fidelity) Wireless Internet access.

wireless technology Technology that allows communications connections without wires.

World Trade Organization (WTO) Organization that replaces GATT, overseeing GATT agreements, making binding decisions in mediating disputes, and reducing trade barriers.

World Wide Web (WWW or **Web)** Collection of resources on the Internet that offers easy access to text, graphics, sound, and other multimedia resources.

Y

yield management Pricing strategy that allows marketers to vary prices based on such factors as demand, even though the cost of providing those goods or services remains the same; designed to maximize revenues in situations such as airfares, lodging, auto rentals, and theater tickets, where costs are fixed.

Z

zone pricing Pricing system for handling transportation costs under which the market is divided into geographic regions and a different price is set in each region.

name and company index

A

Abell, Derek, 48
Ace Hardware, 133
Ackerman, Val, 317
ACNielsen, 145, 266
Ad Council, 107
Adobe, 141
ADT Security Systems, 538
Adu, Freddy, 220
Advertising Age, 542
adWatch, 542
A&E Network, 484
Aetna, 324
Akamai Technologies, 364
Alabama Power, 80
Alliance, 329
Allstate Insurance, 526
Altria, 79
Amazon.com, 46, 52, 468
  e-commerce and, 135, 144
  interactive marketing by, 119
  market segmentation and, 296
American Airlines, 174, 322, 633
American Express, 20, 29, 30, 192, 326
  quality program, 366
  supply chain, 432
American Family Insurance, 354, 355
American Legacy Foundation, 88, 511
American Marketing Association, 239
American National Standards Institute, 364
American Plastics Council, 394
American Red Cross, 21
American Stock Exchange, 556
American Technology Corporation, 22–23
American Tobacco Co., 115
Amgen, 330
Amos, Diane, 297
Amway Corp., 223
Anderson, Stuart, 201
Anecharico, Paul, 113
Angle, Colin, 55
Anheuser-Busch, 32, 262, 523
  Budweiser trademark, 391–392
  marketing research by, 273
Anthropologie, 15
Apple, 29, 46, 55
  e-commerce and, 118, 123
  pricing, 642
Applegate, Meredith Collura, 49
Applica, 197
Arad, Avi, 285
Arbitron, 268
Argyle Winery, 394
ARIBA, 338
Armstrong, Lance, 480–481, 519
Arthur Andersen, 31
Art Institute of Chicago, 16
Asch, S.E., 163
Atkins Nutritional Approach, 169
AT&T, 603–604, 612
AT&T Wireless, 82, 325
Augusta (Georgia) National Golf Club, 77
AutoNetwork.com, 133
Autowraps, 536
Avon, 20
Ayds, 391
Ayer, N.W., 258

B

Baldrige, Malcolm, 364
Ballmer, Stephen A., 200
Banfe, Jerry, 567
Banfe Products, 567
Bank of America, 484
Bank One, 11
Barnes & Noble, 52, 131
Barrow, Clyde, 259
BASS, 350–351
Bass Pro Shops, 42, 184, 351
Bateer, Mengke, 162
Batten, Barton, Durstine & Osborn, 542
BAX Global, 445
Baxter Healthcare, 212
Bazadona, Damian, 331
Beckham, David, 219–220
Behar, Yves, 370
Ben & Jerry's, 276
Benetton, 535
Benioff, Marc, 564–565
Bergquist, Rick, 53
Bertelsmann AG, 247
Bertucci's, 309
Best Buy, 454, 456, 556, 612
Best Western, 492
Bezos, Jeff, 52
Bin Laden, Osama, 392–393
Binladin, Yeslam, 392–393
Biovail Corp., 101–102
Birkenstock, 370–371
BJ's, 460
Blades, Herbert, 379
Blatt, Dick, 584
Blockbuster Video, 226, 297, 523, 575
Blog for America, 142
Blue Bell Creameries, 159
BMW, 97, 483
Boatright, John, 578
Boise Cascade, 101, 203
Books-A-Million, 647
Boost, 295
Boselli, Mario, 393
Boston Consulting Group, 55
Boston Symphony Orchestra, 126
Boudreaux, George, 390
Boys and Girls Clubs of America, 20
Bridgestone/Firestone, 387
Brinkley, Kevin, 191
British Petroleum (BP), 81
Broden, Dan, 175
Brodsky, Norm, 565
Brookings Institution, 126
Brooks, Rodney, 55
Brooks Brothers, 310
Brotman, Jeff, 475
Brown, George, 53
Brown, Rick, 133
Bryant, John, 162
Bryant, Kobe, 519
Build-a-Bear Workshop, 29
Burger King, 5, 263
Burke Research Corp., 542
Busch, Adolphus, 579
Busch Gardens, 19
Bush, George W., 3, 210

C

Cabela, Dick, 184
Cabela's, 184
Cadbury, 68
California Avocado Commission, 491
Campbell Soup Co., 258
Camps, Christopher, 294
Canon, 188, 629–630
Canopy Walk, 304
Cantalupo, James, 261
Captain Morgan Rum, 270–271
Carmax.com, 323
Carnahan, Sherry, 331
Carrefour, 619
carsdirect.com, 334
Case, Jordan, 566
Cause Marketing Forum, 20
CBS, 528
CDW Computer Centers, 418, 462, 564
Central DuPage Health, 327
Cereal Partners Worldwide, 52
Chambers, Marcia, 78
Chapman, Zoe, 578
Charles Schwab & Co., 162, 647
Charlotte Bobcats, 256–257
Chico's, 358, 562, 570
Cigna, 353
Cingular Wireless, 82, 330
Cinnamon Beach, 630
Citibank, 484

Citigroup, 14
Civic Entertainment Group, 484
Clark, Maxine, 29
Clinique, 397
Cloud Star Corporation, 41
CMG Information Services, 272
CNN, 569
Coach, 370
Coalition of Black Investors, 162
Coca-Cola Co., 92–93, 226, 244
  advertising by, 519
  brand equity of, 387, 393
  consumer behavior and, 167
  marketing research by, 263
  market segmentation and, 295
  promotional mix used by, 505
  trademark by, 391
Cody, Iron Eyes, 107
Commerce One, 501
CompUSA, 141
CompuServe, 265
ConocoPhillips, 93
Consumer Product Safety Commission (CPSC), 404
Consumer Reports, 636
Convio, 328
Cordis Corporation, 368
Coremetrics, 145
Costco, 65, 66, 439, 456, 460, 475
Council of Better Business Bureaus, 88
Crest, 20, 538
Cridland, James, 322
Cummings, John W., 4
Cunningham, 260
Curves International, 82, 83

D

DaimlerChrysler, 23, 40–41, 91, 323, 485
  marketing channels of, 422
  technological environment and, 113
Daly, Bill, 627
Daniel, Lynn, 331
Dannon, 653
Davids, Den, 206
Dean, Howard, 142
Decision Analyst, 272
Defense Logistics Agency, 433
Dell, Michael, 4, 231, 429–431
Dell Computer, 4, 5, 8, 429
  ecology and, 106
  e-commerce and, 116, 137, 143
  pricing by, 633, 642
  product diversification strategy of, 397
Delta Airlines, 23, 131
Dembek, Alexa, 379
Demos, Steve, 328
Dentsu, 537
De St. Croix, Lance, 370
DHL, 6
Dialog, 265
Diamond Trading Company, 605
Dieste Harmel, 95–96
Direct Marketing Association (DMA), 88, 100, 502
Disney World, 290
Dolce & Gabbana, 423
Domino's Pizza, 3, 498
DoubleClick.com, 99–100
Doubletree, 223
Dr. Pepper/Seven Up, 142
Dr. Scholl's, 603
Draper, Peter, 219
Drexler, Mickey, 489
Drucker, Beth, 222
Drucker, Lou, 222
Drucker, Peter, 42
Drugstore.com, 232
Dubai's Emaar Properties, 396
Duet, 50
DuPont, 106, 207, 379
Durasol, 293

E

Eames, Charles, 191
Eames, Ray, 191
Earnhardt, Dale, Jr., 4
Earnhardt, Dale, Sr., 4
Earth Bud-Eze, 466
EarthLink, 492
eBay, 24, 114, 116, 310, 466
  e-commerce and, 127
  pricing, 644–645
Edwardson, John, 418
Elaine's Tea Shoppe, 51
Elbow Beach, Bermuda, 90
Electronic Arts, 3, 374
Electron Stream Carbon Dioxide Reduction, 52
Elfers, Jane, 460
Elmer, Nick, 561
Enron, 31, 87
Environmental Inks, 331–332
Equal, 45–46
Ernest & Julio Gallo Winery, 392
Ernst, Caroline, 502
ESPN, 38–39
E.T., 493
eTapestry.com, 560
E*Trade, 116
Evans, Pamela, 217
Expedia.com, 116
ExxonMobil, 23
eZiba.com, 468

F

FAO Schwartz, 324
Federal Communications Commission (FCC), 85, 367
Federal Trade Commission (FTC), 14, 85, 87, 100, 135, 503
  on advertising, 523
  on consumer research practices, 99–100
  e-commerce and, 135
  on slotting allowances, 357
FedEx, 126, 192, 306, 354
Fernandez, Kirk, 49
Fiat, 619
Fibre Containers, 209
Fidelity Investments, 201
Find/SVP, 265
Fiorina, Carly, 642
Fischer, Susan, 145
Fishman, Neil, 331
FlexJet, 641
FocusVision, 271
Focus World International, 274
Food and Drug Administration (FDA)
  on advertising, 527
  on labeling, 395
  product development and, 404
Foot Locker, 414–415, 524, 525
Foot-Smart, 502
Foran-Owens, Betsy, 432
Ford, Henry, 9–10, 259, 289
Ford Motor Company, 3, 9–10, 25, 97, 194
  brand equity of, 387
  as multinational corporation, 242
  pricing by, 643
  product placement of, 493–494
  technological environment and, 93, 113
Foreman, George, 523, 524
Four Seasons, 611, 612
Foxwoods, 298
France, "Big Bill," 2–3
France, Bill, Jr., 3
France, Brian, 2, 3
France, Lesa, 2, 3
Frankfort, Lew, 370
Freeman, Laura, 133
FreeMarkets, 127
French's, 165
FreshDirect, 126
Frontier Airlines, 274
Fujitsu, 127
Fuller, Jake, 524
Furniture.com, 125
Furst Group, 89

G

Gale Publishing, 265
Galli, Joe, 573
Gallup Organization, 542
Gap, 489
Garcia, Luis, 297
General Electric, 11, 42, 194, 201
General Foods, 391, 492
General Mills, 52
General Motors, 113, 172–173, 197, 308, 366, 388
General Nutrition Centers, 551

General Services Administration (GSA), 209–211
George Weston Bakeries, 169
Georgia-Pacific, 402
Gerstein, Richard, 29
GiftBaskets.com, 356
Gillette, 219, 294
Giorgio Armani, 396
Gist, Roosevelt, 133
Givens, Beth, 14
Givens, Holly, 107
GlaxoSmithKline, 539–540
Glazier, Mitch, 137
Goliath Casket Co., 168
Goodyear, 195, 428
Gottlieb, Steve, 566
Grand Metropolitan, 247
Graves, Todd, 66
Great Harvest Bread Co., 169
Greehey, Bill, 606
Greiner, Helen, 55
GroupSpark, 271
Grupo Vips, 60
Gwynn, Tony, 116

H

Halbert, David, 638
Hallmark, 297
Handango, 66
Hanero, 25
Hanes, 329
Hanson, John, 113
Harley-Davidson, 168
Harms, Sven, 591
Harrah's Casino, 326
Harris Interactive, 269–270
Harry Potter, 170, 294
Harvey, Tim, 345
Hasbro, 32
Headley, Dean, 365
Hearst, 39
Heavin, Diane, 83
Heavin, Gary, 83
Heckman, Richard J., 187
Hershey, 432
Hewlett-Packard (HP), 8, 55, 199, 201
  new-task buying, 206
  pricing by, 633, 642
Hidden Valley, 309
Hilton, 222, 345
Hitachi, 106
H.J. Heinz, 394
H&M, 457
Hogan, Christopher, 388
Holiday Inn, 27
Home Depot, 16, 422, 451, 502
Honda, 113, 297, 386, 543
Hormel Foods Co., 390–391
HotJobs.com, 92
Hot Topic, 81
HSBC, 3
Hulk, The, 285
Hypersonic Sound (HSS) emitter, 22–23, 27
Hyundai, 51

I

IBM, 128, 189, 203, 329
  marketing research for, 276
  as multinational corporation, 242
  pricing, 642
  supply chain of, 431
iBot, 55
iHarvest.com, 125
IKEA, 454, 459
Immelt, Jeffrey, 42
Inamoto, Rei, 417
Inland Empire Components, 331
Inn at Little Washington, 29
In-N-Out, 66–67
Intel, 198
International Monetary Fund, 231
International Programs Center (IPC), 301
Internet Initiative, 134
Interstate Commerce Commission (ICC), 435
Isuzu Motors Ltd., 615
ITMS Sports, 329
iwon.com, 488

J

Jackson, Janet, 367, 528
Jackson, Michael, 551
Jackson, Peter, 285
Jagger, Mick, 37
James, LeBron, 541
Japan, 223
JCPenney, 385
J.D. Power and Associates, 206
Jenn-Air, 30
JetBlue, 52, 309, 365
Jiron, Dana, 331
Jiron, Ron, 331
Jofré, Christian, 251
Johnson, Brennan, 41
Johnson, Robert L., 256–257
Johnson Controls, 362, 364
Johnson & Johnson, 368, 369, 539–540
Jordan, Michael, 18, 519, 523
JRP Marketing Research Services, 259, 260
Junglee Corp., 144
Jupiter Media Metrix, 118
Just My Size, 49

K

Kabana, 359
Kamen, Dean, 12–13
Kazaa, 137
Keefer, Brian, 14
Keene, Howard, 187
Keller, Ed, 304
Kelley Blue Book, 322–323
Kellogg's, 43, 166, 170, 333
Kelly Services, 189
Kendall-Jackson Vineyards and Winery, 392
Keogh, Scott, 422
KETC-TV, 327
Keurig, 204–205
Kevlar, 379
KFC Corp., 102
Kimberly-Clark, 41
Kimmelman, Gene, 648
Kingsley, Al, 415
Kinko's, 101, 306
Kleenex, 391
Knight, Phil, 415
Knowles, Beyoncé, 18, 521
Kodak, 373
Kohl's, 48–49, 449
Korea Telecom, 25
Kozler, Amber, 329
Kozmo.com, 125
Kraft, 3
Kraft General Foods, 500
KraftMaid Cabinetry, 176
Krasny, Michael, 418
Krill, Jennifer, 101
Krispy Kreme, 223
Kusin, Gary, 306–307
Kwolek, Stephanie, 379
Kyocera Mita, 321

L

Lands' End, 29, 129–130
  brand of, 390
  consumer behavior and, 173
  e-commerce and, 140
  mail order, 370
  retailing classification of, 459
  sales, 557
Lanier, 206
Las Vegas, 7
Lazaris, Nick, 204–205
Lee, Ang, 285
Lee, Sharon, 268
Legend Group Ltd., 8
Lego, 266
Lending Tree, 116
Levi Strauss, 68, 426
Levitt, Theodore, 10, 13
Levy, Jerry, 445
Lewin, Kurt, 158
Lexus, 449
LidRock, 27–28
LifeMatrix, 302–303
Liftomatic Materials Handling, 196–197
Lillian Vernon, 468
Limited Too, 29
Lindsay, James, 21–22
Ling Chai, 66
Linksys, 208
L.L. Bean, 239, 333–334, 367–368, 575

Look-Look, 268
Lord of the Rings, 285
Lord & Taylor, 460
L'Oréal, 247
Lowe's, 16, 420, 450, 575
Lucent Technologies, 436
Luke, Tim, 67
Lynch, Reinhardt, 29
Lyne, Susan, 402

M

Machlowitz, David, 638
Madsen, Dennis, 447
Maersk Sealand, 436
Maharam, Michael, 190
Maharam, Stephen, 190
Major League Baseball, 123, 156, 157
  B2B marketing and, 187
  market segmentation, 286–287, 297
  relationship marketing by, 329
Major League Soccer, 153–154, 220, 253–254, 347–348, 411–412, 477–478, 593–594, 655–656
Make-a-Wish Foundation, 16
Malaga, Mark, 356
Malcolm Baldrige National Quality Award, 364
Malden Mills, 48
Mall of America, 454
Manchester United (Man U), 219
Maritz Performance, 575
Market Place Mall, 454
Markman, Catherine, 290
Marriott, 325–326
Marshall Associates, 466
Mars Inc., 20, 374, 493
Marstellar Inc., 107
Maslow, Abraham H., 167–168
MasterCard, 296, 432
Masters Tournament, 77
Mastro, Bill, 116
Match.com, 150–151
Mattel, 143, 244
Matusovich, Wendy, 328
Maytag, 456
Mazda, 41, 329
MBNA Corporation, 319
McAndrew, Terry, 77
McCann Erickson, 537, 542
McCormack, Mark, 553
McDonald's, 5, 15, 23, 44, 101
  advertising by, 519, 523
  atmospherics, 456
  in global markets, 223, 233, 241
  location strategy of, 453
  marketing research by, 261
  pricing, 619
  promotion by, 506
  relationship marketing by, 322
  Ronald McDonald House Charities, 16
MCI, 603
McKinsey & Co., 77
McKittrick, Jane, 466
McMahan, Don, 127
McMillan, L. Londell, 647
Meakem, Glen, 127
Meijer, 461
Melton, Jennifer, 41
Menlo Worldwide, 431
Merck, 82, 355
Merkle Direct Marketing, 327
Merrill Lynch, 561
MetalRoofing.com, 300
Metech International, 107
MetLife, 524
Metz & Associates, 329
Microsoft, 80, 84, 602, 641
Miller Brewing Co., 274, 523
Ming, Yao, 162
Minor League Baseball, 195
Missano, Anthony, 28
Moffatt, Robert, 431
Mohegan Sun, 317
Monsanto, 31
Monster.com, 92
Moreno, Arte, 286–287
Morrison, David, 295
Moseley, Keith, 425
Moses, Anna, 653
Motorola, 80–81, 242, 251
Moulin International Holdings Ltd., 227
Mountain Dew, 39
MTV, 251, 367
Munick, Paul, 317
Murray, Chris, 97
MySpace.com, 125

N

Namath, Joe, 115
Nance, Gary, 331–332
Napster, 95
NASCAR, 2–4, 499, 500
National Bread Leadership Council, 169
National City Corp., 320
National Collegiate Athletic Association (NCAA), 43, 187
National Crime Prevention Council, 19
National Fatherhood Initiative (NFI), 512
National Football League (NFL), 157
National Geographic Society, 16
National Golf Foundation, 77
National Hockey League, 156–157
National Wildlife Federation, 16
NCSoft, 25
NEC, 328
Neeleman, David G., 52
Nelson, David, 379
Nestlé, 52
Netflix, 451
Netscape, 84, 189, 190
Nevada, 107
New Balance, 498
Newell Rubbermaid, 566, 573
New Line Cinema, 285
Newspaper Collectors Society of America, 133
New York City, 19
newyorkmetroweddings.com, 222
New York Stock Exchange, 8
Nextel Communications, 3
Nham, Nguyen Van, 235
Nicholson, Cie, 505
Nickelodeon, 160, 334
Nielsen Media Research, 268
Nielsen National Research Group, 260
Nike, 132, 397
  advertising by, 518–519
  channel strategy of, 414–415, 417
  product development by, 402, 403
99¢ Only Stores, 455
Nintendo, 602
Nissan, 15, 159, 246, 289, 501–502, 569
Nokia, 67, 80–81, 142, 371
NonObvious Relationship Awareness (NORA), 276
Nordstrom, 420
Norris, Woody, 22–23
Nortel Networks, 41
North Carolina, 129
Northrup Grumman, 333

O

O, The Oprah Magazine, 162
O'Connell, Patrick, 29
Offen, Neil, 591
Office Depot, 207–208, 469
Ogilvy & Mather, 274
Olson, Millie, 296
Olympics, 20
Omnibus Trade and Competitiveness Act, 234
Operation Hope, 162
Optibrand Ltd., 8
Oracle, 53
Orbitz, 133
Oscar Meyer, 307
Ottawa Senators, 627
Outlaw, Joe, 331
Overstock.com, 102
Owens Corning, 392

P

Pacific Internet, 134
Palmer, David, 630
Palmisano, Samuel J., 328, 431
Pampered Chef, 419
Panasonic, 373
Panera Bread, 5, 169
Parker, George S., 336
Parker, Jim, 321
Parker, Sarah Jessica, 164
Parlin, Charles C., 258
Parloff, Roger, 232

Pawlenty, Tim, 232
Paxan Corp., 392
Paychex, 200
Peanuts, 524
Pearl Jam, 425
Pella, 492
PeopleSoft, 53
PepsiCo, 29, 246, 521
  demand for, 491
  guerilla marketing by, 496
  promotional mix used by, 505, 506
Perdue Farms, 229
Perello, Joe, 19
Petrucelli, Leonard, 433
Pfizer, 32, 93–94, 232
Philadelphia, 527
Philip Morris. *see* Altria
Philips Electronics, 362, 364, 500, 619
Phillips, 428
Pier 1 Imports, 429
Pinacor, 436
Pioneer Research, 591
Pitney Bowes, 195, 563
Pittsburgh Penguins, 626–627
Pizza Hut, 325
PlanetAll, 144
PlanetOut, 334
Polycom, 362
Porsche, 178
Porter, Michael E., 44–46
Potts, Wendy, 105
Powell, Michael, 367
Praxair, 193
Premier Cru, 67
Pressler, Paul, 489
Priceline.com, 143
PricewaterhouseCoopers, 204–205
Prince, 647
Princess Cruise Lines, 301
Procter & Gamble, 41, 199
  consumer behavior and, 166
  international marketing strategy of, 243–244
  product managers at, 400
  product positioning by, 397
  relationship marketing by, 317
  sales promotion by, 579
ProSlide Technology, 561–562
Public Relations Society of America (PRSA), 545
Purina, 422
Pyne, George, 3

Q

Quaker, 50

R

Radio Shack, 290
Rags Land, 558
Rainforest Action Network, 101
Raising Cane, 66
Ramada, 492
Random House, 142
RapSnacks, 21–22
Rawlings Sporting Goods, 80, 186–187
Reagan, Michael, 217
RealNetworks, 80, 84, 157
Rech, Millie, 77
Recording Industry Association of America (RIAA), 95, 137
Recreational Equipment Inc. (REI), 440, 446–447
Reebok International, 496
Reese's, 493
Reeves, Ernie, 79
Reflect.com, 28–29
Replay Media, 644
Revlon, 15
Revson, Charles, 13–15
Reynolds Metal Co., 92
R/GA, 417
Ritz-Carlton Hotels, 42
RJR Tobacco, 499
Rodriguez, Alex, 18
Rolex, 643
Rolling Stones, 37
Rollins, Kevin, 397
Rolls-Royce, 194
Romero, Sandra, 201
Roomba, 55
Roper, 266
Rorsted, Kasper, 201
Royal Mail, 127
Ruskin, John, 632
Ruth Cain, 456
RxNorth.com, 232
Ryder System, 11–12

S

Saab, 582–583
Saffo, Paul, 100
Saks Fifth Avenue, 456
Salesforce.com, 564–565
Sales & Marketing Management, 265
Sam's Club, 456, 460, 475
Samsung Electronics, 427, 500, 629
Sanabria, David, 329
San Francisco Giants, 157
Sanyo Electric, 372
SAP AG, 201
Sarnow, Greg, 422
SAS Insitute, 564
Saturn, 178, 323, 390
Save the Children, 29
Sazaby, 60
Sbarro, 27–28
Schell, Brian, 644
Schering-Plough Corp., 102, 630
Schick, 491
Schultz, Howard, 11, 60
Sealed Air Corporation, 573
Sealy, 637
Seam, 191
Sears, 173, 370
SecureWorks, 331
Segway, 12–13, 538
Sekiguchi, Fusao, 246
Selig, Bud, 187
Semiao, Ron, 39
Serra, Matt, 415
Share Our Strength, 29, 30
Sharp, 290
Sharper Image, 145
Shell, 492
Sherman, Cary, 95
Sherwood, Amy, 495
Shopping.com, 131
Siebel Systems, 217, 330
Sierra Mist, 505
Silk Soymilk, 328
Silvey, Greg, 66
Sinegal, Jim, 475
Singapore Airlines, 8
Sirius Satellite Radio, 7, 26, 157
SkyTeam, 339
Smart Technologies, 501
Smith, Scott, 133
Smith & Wesson, 369
Snapple Beverage Group, 19, 68
Snyder, Esther, 67
Snyder Communications, 486
Solucient, 330
Solutionz, 49
Song, 309
Sony, 50, 68, 139, 159, 361, 602
Sony Music, 328–329
Southern Co., 80
Southwest Airlines, 52, 321, 354, 603
SPAM, 390–391
Special Olympics, 20
Spencer, Mary Reiling, 317
Splenda, 45–46
SpongeBob Squarepants Movie, 334
SportsLine USA, 115
Sprint, 51, 201–202
St. Jude Children's Research Hospital, 195
Stallone, Sylvester, 551
Starbucks, 11, 60, 139, 223, 387
Steelcase, 168
steinersports.com, 115
Stephen Slesinger Inc., 396
Stilgoe, John, 633
Stotz, Rodger, 575
Stouffer's, 49
Stride Rite, 29
String Cheese Incident, 425
Subaru, 333–334, 334
Subway, 5
Sullivan, Tim, 150
Sumitomo, 134
Sun Microsystems, 217

Super Bowl (2004), 367, 528
Super Size Me, 101
SurveySite, 271
SwapIt.com, 125
Symantec, 12
Synnex Information Technologies, 462
Systems Research & Development (SRD), 276

T

Tacit Knowledge Systems, 333
Taco Bell, 495
Tagliabue, Paul, 157
Talbot's, 139, 641–642
Target, 46–47, 142, 449, 450, 459
Taste of the Nation, 29, 30
Taylor-Hines, Charles, 496
TCL International Holdings Ltd., 227
Tebo, Paul, 106
Tetra Tech FW, 192, 195, 210
Texas Agriculture Department, 101
Texas Instruments, 82, 578
T.G.I. Friday's, 27
theonering.net, 285
Thomson, Mark, 150
Ticketmaster, 425
Tickets.com, 644
Tide, 243
Timberlake, Justin, 367, 528
Timberland Company, 32, 49
Time Inc., 160
Time Warner, 398, 648
Timex, 52
TiVo, 268, 532, 551
T-Mobile, 372
Tommy Hilfiger, 383
Toronto Globe and Mail, 328
Tower Records, 325
Toyota Motor Corp., 224
  guerilla marketing by, 496
  market segmentation and, 295, 315
  pricing, 607
  relationship marketing by, 322
  technological environment and, 93, 94, 113
Toyota Tsusho America, 11–12, 52
Toysmart.com, 135
Trader Joe's, 604
Tri-City Electronics, 290
Tropicana, 421
TRUSTe, 135
TRW Aeronautical Systems, 432–433
Tsao, Victor, 208
TTR Logistics, 12
Tueffert, Curt, 332
TVT Records, 566
Tyco, 31
Tyson Foods, 16

U

Uhlich, Kevin, 287
Ulrich, 265
Under Armour Performance Apparel, 67
Unilever, 199, 337
Union Pacific, 435, 437
United States Potato Board, 97
United Stationers, 463
United Technologies, 194–195, 361
Universal Music Group, 50, 625
University of Michigan, 380–381
University of Phoenix, 126
Upromise.com, 637
UPS, 196, 435, 636
Urban Outfitters, 82, 83
U.S. Bureau of the Census, 264, 293, 301
U.S. Department of Agriculture (USDA), 172
U.S. Department of Commerce, 211, 239, 273, 300
U.S. Department of Defense, 20, 188, 210, 211, 643
U.S. Department of Homeland Security, 432
U.S. Department of Justice, 84, 85
U.S. Department of State, 239
U.S. Food and Drug Administration, 80, 232
U.S. General Accounting Office, 357
U.S. International Trade Commission (ITC), 235
U.S. Navy, 402
U.S. Postal Service, 224, 245, 480–481
U.S. Supreme Court, 424, 600
U.S. Treasury, 211
Usenet, 266

V

ValPak Direct Marketing Systems, 142
Vancouver Canucks, 627
Varsity Spirit Corp., 596–597
Venture Safenet, 246
Verizon Wireless, 96
Veterinary Pet Insurance, 356
Viacom, 251
Victoria's Secret, 455, 528
Virgin Mobile USA, 295
Virgin Radio, 322, 324–325
Visa, 14, 135
Visible World, 28
Volvo, 404
Vonage, 95

W

Wagner, Honus, 114–115
Wagoner, Rick, 637
Wall Street Journal (New York), 533
Wal-Mart, 49, 50, 98, 197, 462
  B2B marketing, 199
  channel strategy of, 426
  distribution network of, 439
  e-commerce and, 120, 137
  global marketing by, 221
  marketing channels of, 417
  marketing research by, 276
  market segmentation and, 297
  pricing by, 613–614, 633
  sales organization of, 574
  unfair-trade laws and, 600
Walt Disney Company, 39, 290, 374, 396
Walt Disney Records, 333
Wanamaker, John, 510
Warner, W. Lloyd, 164
Warner Brothers, 456
Water Country USA, 19
WD-40, 374
Webb, Jeffrey, 597
Wendy's, 90, 640
Western Union, 484
Westinghouse, George, 538
White, Constance, 310
Whole Latte Love, 123
Williams, Kathy, 562, 570
Williams, Serena, 552–553
Williams, Venus, 552–553
Winfrey, Oprah, 162
Winkler, Tyler, 331
Wipro, 354
Wm. Wrigley Jr. Co., 358, 606
Women's National Basketball Association (WNBA), 316–317
Woods, Tiger, 18, 76–78, 523
World Trade Organization (WTO), 233, 234
W.R. Grace, 362
Wyden, Ron, 136, 648
Wyeth, 402
Wyndham Hotels & Resorts, 50

X

Xerox, 325, 391
X Games, 39
XM Satellite Radio Holdings, 77

Y

Yahoo!, 125, 468
Yank, The, 285
YaYa LLC, 272
Yokohama Metals, 107
Young & Rubicam (Y&R), 387
Yucca Mountain, 107
Yum! Brands, 368

Z

Zehren, Anne, 295
Zeks Compressed Air Solutions, 563
Zetsche, Dieter, 323
Zhang Shangguang , 231
Zhizhi, Wang, 162
Zippo, 238, 372

subject index

Note: **Bold** entries refer to major discussions or definitions.

A

ABI/Inform (Dialog), 265
accessory equipment, 361, 363
accidental sample, 267
accounting data, 262
acculturation, 161
administered marketing system, 428
adoption process, 398–400
"advergames," 272
advertising, 454, **493,** 497, 518–520, **520–522,** 619. *see also* **integrated marketing communications (IMC)**
  on cell phones, 525
  creating campaigns for, 526
  cross promotion in, 540–541
  effectiveness of, 541–544
  ethics in nonpersonal selling, 544–545
  media scheduling, 536–537
  media selection, 530–536
  messages of, 527–530
  organization of, 537–538
  public relations and, 538–540, 545
  sponsorship *vs.,* 499–500
  strategies, 522–526
  technology and, 551
  tobacco, 3
advertising agencies, 486, **537–538**
advertising campaigns, 527
advertorials, 529
ad-zappers, 532
affinity marketing, 326
African Americans, 161–162, 296
age factors, 294–295
agents, 420, 465–466
AIDA concept (attention-interest-desire-action), **487,** 567, 568
AIO statements, 302
air freight, 437
airline industry, 52
  positioning by, 309
  pricing by, 603–604, 618–619, 631, 641
  strategic alliances of, 339
allowances, 636
"altruists," 304
ambush marketing, 500
antimonopoly period, 84
antitrust lawsuits, 80, 84
application service providers (ASPs), 328
approach, sales, **568**
Asch phenomenon, 163
Asian Americans
  consumer behavior of, 161, 162
  market segmentation and, 296–298
  in sales force, 572
assurances, 366
atmospherics, 456–457
attitudes, 171–173
auction houses, 466
autodialing, 558
auto industry
  channel strategy of, 425
  consumer adoption process and, 399
  consumerism and, 97
  market segmentation and, 289–290
  personal selling by, 571
  relationship marketing by, 334
  technological environment and, 93, 94, 113
automatic merchandising, 469
autonomic role, 165
average total costs, 608

B

baby boomers, 295–296
backward integration, 427
banner ads, 140, 141, **529**
basing-point pricing, 639
BCG (Boston Consulting Group), 55
beef industry, 79, 172, 198
benchmarking, 364
bicycle racing, 480–481
bidding, competitive, 643–646
billboards, 534–535, 541
birdyback service, 438
blind product tests, 542
block-numbering areas (BNAs), 264–265
blogs, 142
body art, 303
body copy, in advertisements, 528, 529
body language, 175
bonus packs, 582
bots, 131, 647
bottom line, 15
boundaries, of marketing, 15–17
Brand Asset Valuator (Young & Rubicam), 387
brand equity, 387, 391
brand extension, 395–396
brand insistence, 383
brand licensing, 396
brand managers, 388
brand marks, 388–390
brand names, 388–390, 392–393
brand preference, 383
brand recognition, 383
brands, 226–227, 245, 380–381, 382, **382–384,** 409. *see also* **category management**
  brand loyalty, 305
  counterfeit goods, 383
  managing for competitive advantage, 382–388
  new-product development, 401–403
  new-product planning, 396–401
  product identification, 388–396
  product safety and liability, 403–404
  types of, 384–387
bread industry, 168–169
breakeven analysis, 614–616, 616–618
broadband technology, 24–25, 124, 134
broadcast media, 503
  radio, 531–533
  television, 25, 327, 530–532, 629
brokers, 465, **466**
budgeting, 67–68, 74, 506–509. *see also* costs, of marketing
bulletin boards (Internet), 122–123
bundle pricing, 647–648
business analysis, 402–403, 512
business cycle, 89–91
business dinners, 196
business intelligence, 276
business invitations, 455
business meetings, 389
business plans, 62–63. *see also* **marketing plans**
business products, 288–289, 360–363
business services, 362–363
business-to-business (B2B) marketing, 26, 186–187, **188,** 217
  business buying process, 202–207
  business dinners, 196
  buyer-seller relationships in, 332–339
  buying center concept, 207–209
  characteristics of, 194–197
  components of, 190–191
  demand, 197–199
  effective strategies for, 209–213
  international market differences, 191, 196–197
  Internet and, 191
  make, buy, lease decisions, 199–202
  nature of market, 188–191
  online marketing, 126–129
  personal selling and, 561
  segmentation, 192–194
  stages in process, 204
business-to-business (B2B) products, 355
business-to-consumer (B2C) e-commerce, 129–133, 189
buyer behavior, 226–227
buyer partnerships, 333
buyers, 203–204, **208**. *see also* buying
buyer-seller relationships
  B2B marketing and, 195, 332–339
  relationship marketing for, 325–329

buyer's market, 11
buying, 30, 31
B2B process of, 202–207
business decisions about, 199–202
buyers, 203–204, 208
buying center concept, 207–209
classifying B2B situations, 206–207
offices, for retailing, 467
wholesaling and, 463
buying center concept, 207–209

C

call centers, 200
caller-ID systems, 269–270
"call to action," 492
cannibalization, 397, 647
captive advertising, 494
captive brands, 386
cartoon characters, 524
cash-and-carry wholesalers, 465
"cash cows," 55
cash discounts, 634–635
casinos, 298, 317, 326
catalogs, 370, 468, 502
categories, 55
category captains, 204
category killers, 459
category management, 380–381, **388–390,** 450. *see also* **brands**
category managers, 382
cause marketing, 17, **19–20**
CDs (compact disks), 625, 636
celebrity endorsements, 518–519, 523–524. *see also* **person marketing**
cell phone industry, 80–81, 82–83, 124
advertising and, 525
global markets and, 228
market segmentation and, 295
product life cycle and, 372
videophones, 105
Census of Manufacturers, 194
cereals, 409
chain stores, 458–459
channel captains, 426
channels, of communication, **487**
chat rooms, 122–123
cheerleading, 596–597
children
influence on consumer behavior by, 165–166
market segmentation and, 294–295
Children's Online Privacy Protection Act, 85, 86, 135
Clayton Act, 86, 424, 599
click-through rate, 144, 511, 543–544
climate, 292–293
closed sales territories, 424
closing, 570–571
closure, 170
cluster sample, 267
clutter, in advertising, 523, 534
cobranding, 333–335
cognitive dissonance, 178–179
cohort effect, 295
collaborative planning, forecasting, and replenishment (CPFaR), 337
color, 170
comarketing, 334–335
commercialization, of new products, 403
commercial market, 190
commission merchants, 466
commissions, 576
common carriers, 434
common market, 236
communication, 121–123, 486–490, 501–504
community shopping centers, 453
Community Trademark (CTM), 238
company description, 66, 68
comparative advertising, 522–523
compensation, of sales forces, 576, 577
competitive analysis, 62, 65–66, 71–72
competitive bidding, 643
competitive environment, 80–84
competitive factors
of channel strategy, 422, 423
pricing and, 619
competitive intelligence, 277
competitive pricing strategies, 632–633
competitive strategy, 82
component parts and materials, 362, 363
concentrated marketing, 308
concept testing, 402–403
consolidated metropolitan statistical areas (CMSA), 292
consultative selling, 562–563
consumer behavior, 156–157, **158,** 180, 184
decision process, 175–179
interpersonal determinants of, 158–166
personal determinants of, 166–175
consumer goods, 419
Consumer Goods Pricing Act (1975), 600
consumer innovators, 398–399
consumer interest organizations, 87–88
consumerism, 96–97
consumer orientation, 11
consumer products, 288–289, 355
consumer rights, 96–97
consumers, 419–420
adoption process, 398–400
buying patterns, 360, 512
classification of services and, 358
protection of, 84–85, 96–97
sales promotions aimed at, 580–583
contact carriers, 434–435
containerization, 440
contests, 582
contractual agreements, 240–242
contractual marketing system, 428
controlled experiments, 272–273
convenience products, 355–356, 359
convenience retailers, 458
convenience sample, 267
conversion rate, 144
cookies (data collection method), 135, **544**
cooperative advertising, 423, 524
copyrighted material, 137, 384
core based statistical areas (CBSAs), 292
core competencies, 66, 70
core regions, 292
core values, 159
corporate advertising, 521
corporate marketing system, 428
corporate Web sites, 139
cost per impression, 511
cost per response (click-throughs), 144, 511, 543–544
cost per thousand (CPM), 541, 544
cost-plus pricing, 613
cost recovery, 605
costs, of marketing, 30–31, 133. *see also* budgeting
counterfeit goods, 383
countertrade, 246
County and City Data Book, 265
coupons, 173, 579–580, **581**
"creatives," 304
creative selling, 566
creativity, 21–22
credit cards
pricing, 631
privacy issues, 135–136
relationship marketing and, 322, 326
supply chain, 432
critical path method (CPM), 402
critical thinking, 21–22
cross promotion, 540–541
cross-selling, 563
cues, 173
culture, 159. *see also* **social-cultural environment**
B2B and, 191
IMC programs and, 489
relationship marketing and, 336
subcultures, 160–162
supply chain and, 430
cumulative quantity discounts, 635
currency
countertrade and, 246
global markets and, 228
customary prices, 606
customer-based segmentation, 192–194
customer behavior, 158. *see also* **consumer behavior**
customer loyalty, 4–5, 37
customer-oriented marketing strategies. *see* **customer relationship management (CRM); e-commerce (electronic commerce); ethics;** marketing environment; **social responsibility; strategic planning**
customer relationship management (CRM), 173, **193–194,** 202, **329–332,** 339, 345

boundaries of marketing, 15–17
B2B marketing and, 217
creativity and critical thinking, 21–22
customer loyalty, 4–5
customer retention, 325–326, 331–332
customer satisfaction, 324–325
customer service, 25, 451
customer-specific marketing strategy, 486
globalization, 8
history of marketing and, 9–12
marketing, defined, 7
marketing myopia, 13–15
measurement programs, 260
nontraditional marketing, 17–21
transaction-based marketing, 26–30
utility, 6–7
customer satisfaction, 324–325
customer-service standards, 434
customer winback, 331
customs union, 236
cybermalls, 139
"cyberspace," 85

D

dairy industry, 374, 629
database marketing, 327–328
databases, 22
B2B, 335–336
for direct marketing, 501
used in IMC programs, 486
data collection, 135, 262–263
market segmentation and, 299
primary, 262–263, 267–273
secondary, 262–267
data mining, 275–276
deciders, 208
decline stage, of product life cycle, **372**
decoding, 487
deep-discount chains, 449
deflation, 91
Delphi technique, 277–278
demand, 491, **608**
demarketing, 92
demographics, 3
e-commerce and, 136
of golf fans/players, 76–78
of online sellers, 138
segmentation by, 192–194
demographic segmentation, 293–301
demonstration, 569
department stores, 460
depreciation, 198
depression, in business cycle, 89–91
depth, of a product, 369
deregulation movement, 80
derived demand, 197–198
"devouts," 303
differentiated marketing, 307
differentiation, brand, 387
diffusion process, 398
digital cameras, 373
Digital Millennium Copyright Act, 137
digital tools, 118
digital video recorders (DVR), 551
direct channel, 419
direct competition, 80–81
direct mail, 467–468, 501–502, 534
direct marketing, 467, 495, 497, **500–504**
direct sales results test, 510
direct sampling, 486
direct selling, 419, 591
discount houses, 460
discretionary buying power, 81–82
discretionary income, 92
discrimination, 133
dissonance, 178–179
distribution channels, 416
distribution intensity, 422–424
distribution strategy, 50, 73. *see also* **marketing channels; supply-chain management**
ethics and, 1
international, 245
diversity, 49, 53, 76–78. *see also* **culture**
"dogs," 56
Do Not Call Registry, 85, 100, 269, 503, 558, 559
downstream management, 429
drive, 173
drop shippers, 465
dual distribution, 420
dumping, 234–235, 598
DVD players, 373

E

ecology, 106–107
e-commerce (electronic commerce), 114–115, **117–119,** 145, 150–151. *see also* **business-to-business (B2B) marketing**
dot.com failures, 125
economy and, 126–138
effective web presence for, 143–145
e-mail and fax etiquette, 122
interactivity and, 119–124, 138–142
Internet access and, 124–125
Internet piracy, 137
online marketing, 127–130, 136–138, 510–511
products sold online, 138
economic environment, 89–93
global markets and, 227–228
IMC programs, 512
multinational economic integration, 235–238
economic theory, pricing and, 608–613
e-fraud scams, 85
80/20 principle, 305
elasticity, pricing and, 609–613
electronic bulletin boards, 141
electronic data interchanges (EDIs), 335–336
electronic direct marketing channels, 503–504
electronic exchanges, 127
electronic industry, 290
electronic signatures, 135
electronic storefronts, 139
e-mail
direct marketing and, 503–504
etiquette, 122
spam, 390–391
e-marketing (electronic marketing), 117–118
embargo, 234
emergency goods and services, 356–357
empathy, 366
employee satisfaction, 321
employment
in marketing, 555–556
in sales, 572–573, 576, 577
encoded messages, 487
Encyclopedia of Associations (Gale Publishing), 265
end-use application segmentation, 193
energy industry, 94–95
Engel's laws, 300–301
English language, 489–490
enterprise resource planning (ERP) system, 53, **432**
entertaining, for business, 455
entertainment industry
advertising venues of, 535
e-commerce and, 123
global marketing by, 223
marketing research by, 285
pricing, 630
product placement and, 494–495
environmental factors, 51–53, 202. *see also* situation analysis
environmental management, 79
environmental scanning, 79
Esomar (European Society of Opinion and Market Research), 239
esteem, brand equity and, 387
esteem needs, 167–168
ethics, 31–32, 97–102, 107–108. *see also* marketing environment; **social responsibility**
buyers and markets, 172, 210
buyers and sellers, 232
of data collection, 299
e-commerce and, 123, 137
in marketing research, 263
in nonpersonal selling, 544–545
in sales, 578–579
ten steps to improve standards, 99
workplace ethics quiz, 100
ethnic groups, 296–298. see also *individual names of ethnic groups*
ethnographic studies, 274
European Society of Opinion and Market Research, 239
evaluative criteria, 177
event marketing, 17, **20**
everyday low pricing (EDLP), 632

evoked set, 177
"e-waste," 106
exchange control, 234
exchange functions, 30
exchange process, 9
exchange rate, 228, 229
exclusive dealing agreements, 424
exclusive distribution, 423–424
executive summary, 62, 65–66, 69
exit strategy, 68
expectancy theory, 575
experimental research methods, 272–273
exploratory research, 261–262
exponential smoothing, 278, **279**
exporting, 220, 221, 240
  export brokers, 466
  export-management companies (EMC), 240
  export-trading companies (ETC), 240
  Export Trading Company Act of 1982, 231
  security issues and, 432
  of services and retail, 222–223
extended problem solving, 179
external customers, 320–321
extranets, 120

F

facilitating functions, 30
facilities plans, 63
Fair Packaging and Labeling Act in 1966, 395, 404
fair trade, 600–601
fair-trade laws, 600
families, consumer behavior and, 164–166
family brands, 386
family life cycle, 298–299
fashion industry, 373
fax etiquette, 122
fax surveys, 271
fear appeal, in advertising, 527
Federal Acquisition Regulation (FAR), 210
Federal Food and Drug Act, 84, 86
Federal Sentencing Guidelines for Organizations, 98
Federal Trade Commission Act, 86, 424
Federal Trademark Dilution Act of 1995, 392
feedback, 324–325, **487,** 488–489
fees, charged by sellers, 612–613
field selling, 557–558
financial services industry, 223
financing, wholesaling and, 463
financing plans, 63
FindEx (Find/SVP), 265
first mover strategy, 46
fishing, 350–351
fishyback service, 438
fixed costs, 608
fixed-sum-per-unit method, 509
Flammable Fabrics Act of 1953, 404
flanker brands, 397
FOB (free on board) plant/origin, 637–638
FOB origin-freight allowed (freight absorbed), 638
focus groups, 270–271
follow-up, 571
forecasting, of market potential, 306
Foreign Corrupt Practices Act, 231
Foreign Economic Trends (U.S. Department of Commerce), 273
foreign licensing, 241
form utility, 6–7
forward integration, 427
franchises, 241, 428–429
"frankenfoods," 230
free trade areas, 235–236
freight forwarders, 438
frequency, 536
frequency marketing, 326
friendships, commerce, and navigation (FCN) treaties, 231
FTC Act, 84
full-cost pricing, 614
full-function merchant wholesalers, 464
full-service research suppliers, 259
"fun seekers," 304

G

gatekeepers, 208
gay community, 334, 527
gender, 293–294. *see also* women
General Agreement on Tariffs and Trade (GATT), 233, **236**
general merchandise retailers, 459–461
Generations X/Y, 294–295, 315
generic products, 385
genetically modified organisms (GMOs), 230, 231
geographic consumer markets, 194, 637–639
geographic information systems (GISs), 293
geographic segmentation, 291–293. *see also* **market segmentation**
globalization, 5, 8, 238–239
  e-commerce and, 134
  international economic environment and, 92–93
global marketing strategy, 218–221, **243–246,** 251
  brand equity and, 387
  decision process to market globally, 239–242
  developing strategy for, 243–246
  globalization, 238–239
  importance of, 221–224
  international economic environment and, 92–93
  international marketing environment, 227–235
  international marketplace, 224–227
  multinational corporations, 242–243
  multinational economic integration, 235–238
  online pricing and, 646–648
  prescription drugs and, 232
  price determination and, 619–620
  psychographic segmentation of, 303–304
  U.S. as target for international marketers, 246–247
global reach, 118, 119
global sourcing, 197
goals, 66, 70
golf, 76–78, 397, 402
  advertising, 518–519
  etiquette, 562
goods-services continuum, 353–354
government data, 264–265
government markets, 209–211
government regulation. *see* legal issues; **political-legal environment**
grading, 30, 31
grassroots marketing, 329
Green Book, The (American Marketing Association), 239
green marketing, 107
grey goods, 427
gross rating point (GRP), 536
growth stage, of product life cycle, **372**
guerilla marketing, 496–497
Guide to International Periodicals (Ulrich), 265

H

halo effect, 578
headlines, in advertisements, 528, 529
Helms-Burton Act, 231
hierarchy of needs theory, 167–168
high-involvement purchase decisions, 175
Highway Beautification Act of 1965, 534–535
Hispanics, 523
  consumer behavior of, 159–161
  integrated marketing communications and, 484
  market segmentation and, 287, 289, 296–297
  in sales, 572
history, of marketing, 9–12
hits, 543–544
hockey, 626–627
home pages, 129
home shopping channels, 503
horizontal conflict, in channel strategy, 426
human resources plans, 63
humor, in advertising, 527
husband-dominant role, 165
hypermarkets, 461
hypermedia resources, 24
hypotheses, 262

I

ideal self, 174
ideas, generating, 402–403
identity theft, 14
illustrations, in advertisements, 528, 529
image, product, 389
importing, 220, 221, 232, 432
import quotas, 234

impressions, 543–544
impulse goods and services, 356
inbound telemarketing, 559
incentive programs, in sales, 575
income, 92, 300–301
incremental-cost pricing, 614
independent contractors, in sales, 591
independent retailers, 458
indirect competition, 81
indirect evaluation, 510
individual brands, 386
industrial distributors, 419, 464
industrial products, 355
industry deregulation, 84–85
industry regulation phase, 84–85
inelastic demand, 198, 199
inflation, 91
influencers, 208
infomercials, 469, **503**
information, 490–491
  e-commerce and, 123
  web sites for, 130
informational investigation, 261
informative advertising, 522
infrastructure, 225, 228
innovators, 398–399
inquiry tests, 542
inside selling, 560
installations, 360–361, 363
instant messaging, 122
institutional advertising, 521
institutional markets, 211–212
integrated marketing communications (IMC), 51, 480–481, **482, 483–486,** 513, 517. *see also* **advertising**
  budgeting for promotional strategy, 508–509
  communication process and, 486–490
  direct marketing, 500–504
  effectiveness of, 510–511
  elements of promotional mix and, 492–497
  Internet and, 118, 119
  objectives of promotion and, 490–492
  promotional mix, 504–507
  pulling and pushing promotional strategies, 507–508
  sponsorships, 497–500
  value of, 511–512
intensive distribution, 423
interactive advertising, 525–526, 528–530
interactive brochures, 25
interactive marketing, 23, 118, **119–124,** 138–142
interactive television (iTV), 25, 327
interdependent partnership, relationship marketing and, 322–323
intermodal operations, 436
internal customers, 320–321
internal marketing, 320–321
internal partnerships, 333
international direct investment, 242
international marketing, 134, 212–213
international marketing research, 273–274
Internet (Net), 23–26, 119–120. *see also* **e-commerce (electronic commerce);** online marketing
  accessing, 124–125
  advertising on, 503–504, 529–530, 531, 535, 543–544
  auction houses on, 466
  B2B marketing and, 191
  for competitive strategy, 84
  consumer behavior and, 163
  employment advertising on, 91–92
  frequency marketing and, 326
  functions of, 121–123
  global markets and, 230
  international marketing on, 222
  marketing environment and, 52
  marketing intermediaries and, 418
  for marketing research, 285
  piracy, 137
  retailing, 469
  for secondary data, 266
  spam, 390–391
  survey methods for, 271–272
  Wi-Fi, 81
Internet service providers (ISPs), 124
interpretative research, 268, 274–275
interstitial advertisements, 529
"intimates," 304
intranets, 120
introductory stage, of product life cycle, **371–372**
inventory
  adjustments to, 199
  control systems, 439–440
ISO (International Organization for Standardization) certification, 231
ISO 9002, 364

J

joint demand, 198
junk mail, 534
jury of executive opinion, 277, 278
just-in-time (JIT)/JIT II inventory, 199

K

keyword advertisements, 529
"killer app," 150
kiosks, 504
knowledge, 387
Knowledge Index (CompuServe), 265

L

labels, 395
laggards, 399
language, 229, 230, 489–490
Lanham Act of 1946, 389
lateral partnerships, 333
leader pricing, 642
learning, 173–174
leasing, 199–202
legal issues. *see also* **political-legal environment**
  e-commerce and, 123
  of exclusive distribution, 424
  laws maintaining competitive environment, 86
  of pricing, 598–601
length, of a product, 369
letter writing, 488
liability, 403–404
licensing, 396, 524
lifestyle, 302
lifestyle centers, 454
lifetime value of a customer, 26, 339
limited-line stores, 459
limited problem solving, 179
limited-service research suppliers, 260
line extension, 370, 395–396
listening skills, 269, 561
list prices, 634
location
  distribution strategy and, 453–454
  retail transactions by, 461–462
logistics, 416, 429–433, 439
looking-glass self, 174
loss leaders, 642
low-involvement purchase decisions, 175
loyalty cards, 326
luxury products, 475
  elasticity and, 611
  global marketing of, 243
  market segmentation and, 301, 304
  prestige objectives, pricing and, 605

M

magazine advertising, 533
mail-order wholesalers, 465
mail surveys, 271
mall intercepts, 270
management, planning by, 41–42
manufacturers, 30–31, 199–202, 430, 464
manufacturer's brands, 385
manufacturers' representatives, 420, 466
marginal analysis, 602
marginal cost, 608, 611
markdown, 453
market development strategy, 397
marketing, defined, **7**
marketing channels, 414–415, **416**
  channel management, 426–427
  logistics and supply-chain management, 429–433, 445
  physical distribution, 433–440
  role of, in marketing strategy, 416–417
  strategic decisions about, 421–425
  types of, 417–421
  vertical marketing systems, 427–429
marketing communications, 482
marketing concept, 11
marketing cost analysis, 262

marketing decision support systems (MDSSs), 259, **275**
marketing environment, 76–78, 107–108. *see also* **ethics; social responsibility**
competitive environment, 80–84
economic environment, 89–93
environmental management, 79
environmental scanning, 79
political-legal environment, 84–89
social-cultural environment, 95–97
technological environment, 93–95
marketing ethics, 98. *see also* **ethics**
marketing information, wholesaling and, 463
marketing information systems (MISs), 275
marketing intermediaries, 417, 419–420
marketing mix, 49–51, 65, 67, 72–74, **352,** 601–605. *see also* **distribution strategy; pricing strategy; product strategy;** promotional strategy
marketing myopia, 13–15
marketing planning, 41
marketing plans, 62
business plan components, 62–63
creation of, 63–68
sample, 68–75
marketing public relations (MPR), 539
marketing research, 256–257, **258,** 285
computer technology in, 275–277
ethics and, 99–100
function of, 258–260
interpretative research, 274–275
listening skills for, 269
manipulation of test results, 263
methods, 264–274
personal selling and, 568
process of, 260–264
sales forecasting and, 277–279
marketing strategy, 44
elements of, 48–54
formulation of, 63–65
marketing channels and, 416–417
for market segmentation, 308–310
marketing Web sites, 139
market-minus pricing, 631
market penetration strategy, 397
market-plus pricing, 629
market price, 634
markets, 288
market segmentation, 192–194, 286–287, **289–290,** 397, 498
demographic, 293–301
ethical data collection and, 299
geographic, 291–293
process of, 306–307
product-related, 305–306
psychographic, 301–305
segmenting consumer markets, 290
strategies for, 307–310
types of markets, 288–289
market share/market growth matrix, 55–56
market-share objective, 603
markup, 452
mass merchandisers, 460
materials handling system, 440
measurement
of advertising, 541–544
of customer relationship programs, 339
of customer satisfaction, 260
of online marketing effectiveness, 144–145
of promotion decisions, 510–511
of public relations, 543
of sales, 576–578
of sponsorship results, 500
media buying, 500–501
media research, 541–543
media scheduling, 536–537
media selection, 530–536. see also *individual names of media*
meeting competition, 509
memorabilia, 114–116
merchandise marts, 464
merchandisers, 203–204
merchandising strategy, 450–451
merchant wholesalers, 464
message research, 541
messages, 486
metropolitan statistical areas, 292
micromarketing, 308
micropolitan statistical areas, 292
milk, 629. *see also* dairy industry
Miller Tydings Resale Maintenance Act, 600
minimum advertised pricing (MAP), 636
missiles, in advertisements, 529
mission, 42–43, 70
mission statements, 62, 65–66
for web sites, 143
missionary selling, 566–567
mixed-race U.S. residents, 298
modified breakeven analysis, 616–618
modified rebuying, 206
monitoring, of marketing plans, 67–68, 74–75
monopolistic competition, 608, 610
monopoly, 80, 608, 610
Monthly Catalog of the United States Government Publications, 265
motives, 167–168, 575
motor carriers, 436–438
movie theater advertising, 535
MRO items, 362, 363
multidomestic marketing strategy, 243
multinational corporations, 242–243
multiple sourcing, 203

N

name recall, 28
narrow-casting, 530–531
"NASCAR dads," 3
national account selling, 335
national accounts organization, 574
national brands, 385
Native Americans, 298
needs, 12, **167–168**
negotiation, of prices, 643–646
neighborhood shopping centers, 453
networking, 54
network marketing, 558
newsgroups, 141
newspaper advertising, 533
new-task rebuying, 206–207
niche marketing, 308
9/11 Generation, 295
1988 Trade Act, 231
noise, 487, 489
noncumulative quantity discounts, 635–636
nonmarketing public relations (MPR), 539–540
nonpersonal selling, 493, 497. *see also* **advertising**
nonprobability sample, 267
nontraditional marketing, 17–21
norms, 163
North American Free Trade Agreement (NAFTA), 237
North American Industrial Classification System (NAICS), 192–193, 195
not-for-profit organizations, 15–16, 605–606
nuclear waste, 107
Nutrition Labeling and Education Act of 1990, 395

O

objections, 569–570
objectives, 43
observational studies, 268
odd pricing, 640
off-price retailers, 460–461
offshoring, 201–202, 354
oil industry, 606–607, 634
oil pipelines, as transportation, 436–437
oligopoly, 80, 608, 610
one-to-one marketing, 27–29, 118, 119, **328–329**
online marketing, 118. *see also* **e-commerce (electronic commerce); Internet (Net)**
business-to-business e-commerce, 26, 126–129
business-to-consumer e-commerce, 129–133
buyers and sellers, 136–138
effectiveness, 143–145
interactive channels, 138–142
international, 134
measuring promotions, 510–511
online communities, 140–141
online dating, 150–151
pricing, 644–648
problems of, 128–129
security and privacy issues of, 135–136
by U.S. federal government, 211, 212
online samples, 142
online surveys, 271–272
opinion leaders, 164

opportunity recognition, 176–177
order processing, 439–440, **566**
organic farming, 79
organizational factors
of business buying, 203
of channel strategy, 422, 423
organizational products, 355
organization marketing, 17, **20–21**
outdoor advertising, 534–535
outlet malls, 461
outsourcing, 199, **200–202,** 236
Overseas Business Reports (U.S. Department of Commerce), 273
over-the-counter selling, 556–557

P

packaging, 170, 374, 393–395, 409
cost-effectiveness of, 395
pricing and, 653
partnerships, 332. *see also* **strategic alliances**
party plans, 419
penetration pricing strategy, 631–632
percentage-of-sales method, 508–509
perception, 169–171
perceptual screens, 169
personal computer industry, 12, 604–605, 642, 653
personal interviews, 270
personalization, 118, 119, 132
personal selling, 493, 497, 552–553, 585
ethics of, 578–579
evolution of, 554–556
independent sales forces, 591
management of, 571–578
process of, 567–571
sales channels, 556–560
sales promotion and, 579–584
sales tasks of, 565–567
trends in, 561–565
person marketing, 17–18
persuasive advertising, 522
phantom freight, 639
pharmaceutical industry, 80, 82, 232, 457
advertising by, 527, 540
ethics and, 101–102
importing prescription drugs, 232
marketing channels of, 427
pricing and, 609, 630
product strategies of, 355
pharmacy benefit managers (PBMs), 638
physical distribution functions, 30, 416, 433–440
physiological needs, 167
piggyback service, 436, 438
place marketing, 17, **18–19**
planned obsolescence, 106
planned shopping centers, 453
planning, 40–44
for advertising, 526
at different organizational levels, 41–42
methods for, 54–55
process of, 42–44
planograms, 450
point-of-purchase (POP) advertising, 584
Poison Prevention Packaging Act, 404
political-legal environment, 84–89. *see also* legal issues
control of, 88–89
international, 230–233
political risk assessment (PRA), 230
population, 266–267. see also *individual names of ethnic groups*
geographic segmentation and, 291–293
global markets and, 224–225
minority groups, 296–298
pop-up ads, 140
portable people meters (PPMs), 268
Porter's Five Forces Model, 44–46
portfolio analysis, 54–55
positioning, 309
positioning map, 309, 310
postage-stamp pricing, 639
posttesting, 542–543
power centers, 453
Praedo's Law, 305
precall planning, 568
predictive dialer devices, 502–503, 558
premiums, 582
prescription drugs. *see* pharmaceutical industry
presentation, 569
prestige objectives, pricing and, 605, 619
preteens, 294–295
pretesting, 541–542
price, 598. *see also* **pricing strategy**
discrimination, 599
price-quality relationships, 642–643
purchase decisions and, 361, 363
quotations, 634–639
relationship marketing and, 322
stability, 620
price flexibility, 640
pricing policy, 639–640
pricing strategy, 51, 73–74, 596–597, 625, 626–627, 653. *see also* **price**
competitive bidding and negotiated prices, 643–646
determining, 606–607
economic theory and, 608–613
ethics and, 102
global issue in, 619–620
international, 245–246
legal issues of, 598–601
marketing mix and, 601–605
objectives of not-for-profit organizations, 605–606
policies, 639–640
practice of, 613–616
in promotional mix, 506
psychological, 640–643
quotations, 634–639
realistic, 616–619
rebates, 638
for retailing, 452–453
strategies, 628–633
tipping and, 607
primary data, 262–263, 267–273
primary demand, 491
primary statistical areas (PMSA), 292
print media
advertising in, 528, 529, 531, 533–534
direct marketing and, 504
privacy, 12–14, 86
child protection and, 85
ethics and, 99–100
security and, 135–136
telephone interviews and, 269–270
videophones and, 105
private brands, 385
private carriers, 434–435
private data, 265–266
probability sample, 267
probable market share, 306–307
problem recognition, 176–177
classification of problem-solving, 179
marketing research and, 260–261
producers, 419–420
product advertising, 521
product and service strategies, 350–351, 379
business products, 360–363
consumer products, 355–358
consumer services, 358–360
goods and services, defined, 352–354
product deletion, 375
product life cycle, 370–375, 396–401, 505–506
product line development, 366–368
product mix, 368–370
products, defined, 352
quality as product strategy, 364–366
service sector importance, 354–355
product development, 397. *see also* **product life cycle**
new-product process, 401–403
organizing for, 400–401
product lines, 366–368
product differentiation, 491–492
product diversification strategy, 397
product factors, channel strategy and, 421–422, 423
product identification, 388–396
brand extensions and, 395–396
brand licensing and, 396
brand names and brand marks, 388–390
packaging and, 393–395
trademarks, 391–393
production era, of marketing, 9–10
production orientation, 9
production plans, 63
product liability, 403–404

product life cycle, 370, 505–506. *see also* product and service strategies; **product development**
extending, 373–375
new-product planning and, 396–401
product deletion decisions, 375
stages of, 371–373
product-line pricing, 641
product lines, 366–368
product managers, 400
product mix, 368–370
product placement, 493–494, 495
product planning, 396–401
product positioning, 397
product-related segmentation, 305–306
products, 352
product strategy, 49–50, 72. *see also* product and service strategies
development, 396–397
ethics and, 100–101
international, 244–245
quality as, 364–366
profitability, 602, 619
profit centers, 645
Profit Impact of Market Strategies (PIMS), 603
profit maximization, 602, 605
program evaluation and review technique (PERT), 402
promotion, 51, 482
objectives of, 490–492
sales promotion, 579–584
promotional allowances, 636
promotional mix, 492–497. *see also* **marketing mix**
comparison of elements, 497
developing, 504–507
personal selling in, 555
promotional pricing, 641
promotional strategy, 73
budgeting for, 508–509
effectiveness of, 510–511
ethics and, 101–102
international, 244–245
of retailing, 454–456
prospecting, 567–568
prosperity, 89
protecting competitors phase, of government regulation, 84
protective tariffs, 233–234
psychographic segmentation, 301–306
psychological pricing, 640
publicity, 495, 540
public relations, 495, 497, 538–540, 543, 545
public service announcements (PSAs), 512
puffery, 544–545
pulling strategy, 507–508
purchase decision process, 175–179, 195, 202–204
purchasing functions, segmentation and, 193–194
pure competition, 608, 610
pushing strategy, 507–508
push money, 584

Q

qualifying, 568
qualitative forecasing, 277–278
quality
price-quality relationships, 642–643
as product strategy, 364–366
quantitative forecasting, 277, 278–280
quantity discounts, 635
"question marks," 55
quick-response merchandising, 336
quota sample, 267

R

rack jobbers, 464
radio advertising, 531–533
radio frequency identification (RFID), 50, 100, **431–432,** 439
railroads, 435–438
random-digit dialing, 558
raw materials, 362, 363
reach, 536
readership tests, 542
reality show, 551
real self, 174
rebates, 636–637, 638
recession, 89–90
reciprocity, 207
recovery, in business cycle, 89, 91
reference groups, 163–164
refunds, 579–580, **581**
regional shopping centers, 453
reinforcement, 173
relationship marketing, 11–12, 26–30, 316–317, **318,** 340
in B2B marketing, 332–339
buyer-seller relationships, 325–329
and culture, 336
customer relationship management and, 329–332
customer satisfaction and, 324–325
effectiveness of, 339
ethical management of, 323
levels of, 321–323
one-to-one marketing, 328–329
online marketing and, 132
from transaction-based marketing to, 318–321
relationship selling, 561
relevance, 387
reliability, 366
remanufacturing, 212–213
reminder advertising, 522
repositioning, 309
research aggregators, 266
research design, 262
resellers, 190
resources, 44, 92, 338
response, 173
responsiveness, 366
retail advertising, 524
retail convergence, 461
retail cooperatives, 428
retailing, 222–223, 419–420, **448–449,** 469–470, 475. *see also* **pricing strategy**
classification of ownership, 458–459
direct marketing and, 467–469
strategy, 449–457
types of, 457–462
wholesaling intermediaries and, 462–467
revenue curves, pricing, 608–609, 612–613
revenue tariffs, 233
reverse channels, 420–421
right-time marketing, 118, 119
risk taking, 30, 31, 240, 463
rivalry merchandise, 381
Robinson-Patman Act (1936), 84, 86, **599–600**
roles, 163
Roper Starch Worldwide (Roper), 266
routinized response behavior, 179
rule of three, 52

S

safety, 403–404
safety needs, 167
salaries, 576
sales analysis, 261
sales branches, 464
sales channels, 556–560
sales conviction test, 542
sales era, of marketing, 10
sales force automation (SFA), 564–565, 573
sales force composite, 278
sales forecasting, 277–278
sales incentives, 567
sales offices, 464
sales orientation, 10
sales promotion, 494–495, 497, **579–584**
sales quotas, 576
sampling, as research technique, **266–267**
sampling, of products, **581–582**
scheduling, for marketing plans, 67–68, 74–75
scrambled merchandising, 461–462
screening, 402
search engines, 123, **125,** 128, 140
search marketing, 128, 129
secondary data, 262–263, 262–267
second mover strategy, 46, 47
securing market information, 30, 31
selective demand, 491
selective distribution, 423
self-actualization needs, 167–168
self-concept, 174–175
self-image, 174
self-regulatory organizations, 87–88, 88
seller partnerships, 333
seller's market, 11
selling agents, 466
selling up, 455

senders, 486
senior citizens, 296
service encounter, 365
service quality, 365
services, 352–354. *see also* product and service strategies
provided by retailers, 458–459
provided by wholesaling intermediaries, 462, 463, 466
quality of, 365–366
retail exports and, 222–223
service sector importance, 354–355
sex appeal, in advertising, 528
shaping, 173
Sherman Act, 84, 86, 424
shopbots, 647
shopping products, 357, 359
shopping web sites, 130
showroom retailers, 461
shrimping industry, 235
signature, in advertisements, 528, 529
simple random sample, 267
situation analysis, 66–67, 70. *see also* marketing environment
skimming pricing strategy, 628–631
slotting allowances, 449–450
slotting fees, 262, 426
smart cards, 142
smart phones, 124–125
smoking etiquette, 104. *see also* tobacco industry
social/belongingness needs, 167–168
social classes, 164
social-cultural environment, 53, **95–97**. *see also* **culture**
IMC programs and, 511–512
influence on consumer behavior, 163–166
international, 228–230
social interactions, relationship marketing and, 322
social responsibility, 32, 102–107, 107–108. *see also* **ethics;** marketing environment
four-step pyramid and, 103
smoking etiquette and, 104
videophones and privacy, 105
socioeconomic segmentation, 293. *see also* **demographic segmentation**
soft currencies, 228
software industry, 200
solar power, 81
sorting, 417
spam, 85, 390–391
span of control, 574–575
specialty advertising, 583
specialty products, 357–358, 359
specialty retailers, 458
specialty stores, 459
spiffs, 584
split runs, 542
sponsorship, 497–500
spreadsheet analysis, 64–65
spyware, 135
Standard Industrial Classification (SIC) system, 192–193
standardization, 30, 31, 417
staples, 356
Starch Readership Report, 542
"stars," 55
status, 163
stealth marketing, 142
stockkeeping units (SKUs), 450
"stopping power," 528
storing, 30, 31, 438–439, 463
straight rebuying, 206
strategic alliances, 29, 60, **79, 337–339**. *see also* **partnerships**
strategic business units (SBUs), 55
strategic planning, 38–39, **40–42,** 56, 60, 62
elements of, 48–54
methods for, 54–55
methods of, 54–55
process of, 42–44
techniques of, 44–48
tools and techniques for, 44–48
strategic window, 48
stratified sample, 267
"strivers," 303
subcontracting, 241
subcultures, 160–162
subliminal perception, 170–171
suboptimization, 433–434
subsidies, 234
sugar industry, 45–46
suggestion selling, 455–456
supercenters, 461
supermarkets, 169
Super Size Me, 44
supplies, 362, 363
supply, 608
supply chain, 337, 429–433
supply-chain management, 416
survey methods, 268–272
survey of buyer intentions, 278
Survey of Current Business, 265
Survey of Media Markets (Sales & Marketing Management), 265
sustainable competitive advantage, 44
sweepstakes, 582
switchless resellers, 89
SWOT (strengths, weaknesses, opportunities, threats) analysis, 46–48, 67, 70–71
sydicated service, 259
syncratic role, 165
systems integration, 204

T

tactical planning, 41
tangibles, 366
target markets, 48–49, 67, 72, 288. *see also* **customer relationship management (CRM); marketing research; market segmentation; one-to-one marketing; relationship marketing**
promotion methods and, 504–505
for retailing, 449–450
strategies for reaching, 307–310
target-return objectives, 602, 615–616
tariffs, 233, 598
task-objective method, 509
taxation, transfer pricing and, 645–646
team selling, 209, **563**
teamwork, 485–486
technological environment, 93–95. see also *individual names of technological innovations*
auto industry and, 113
distribution and, 50
international, 230
marketing environment and, 52
marketing research and, 275–277
technology, 5, **22–26**
teenagers, 294–295
Telecommunications Act of 1996, 86, 87
telecommunications industry, 88–89
advertising by, 520
consumerism and, 97
e-commerce and, 134
regulation of, 85–86
technological environment and, 95
telemarketing, 469, **502–503, 558–560**
Telemarketing Sales Rule (1996), 86, 503
telephone etiquette, 365
telephone interviews, 268–270
television
advertising, 530–531, 532
equipment, 629
interactive television (iTV), 25, 327
tennis, 552
terrorism
effect on direct mail, 501
effect on relationship marketing, 321
importing and exporting concerns, 432
marketing logistics and, 445
9/11 Generation and, 295
test-marketing method, 272–273, 403
test markets, 278, 279
third-party (contract) logistics firms, 432–433
ticket scalping, 599
TIGER (Topographically Integrated Geographic Encoding and Referencing) system, 265
time-based competition, 81–82
tipping, 607
tobacco industry, 511
advertising, 3, 531
ethics and, 99
ton-miles, 435
total quality management (TQM), 364
trade, 8. *see also* **global marketing strategy**
barriers, 233–234
international law and, 230–233
Trade Act (1988), 231
trade allowances, 583

trade discounts, 635
trade dress, 392
trade fairs, 464
trade industries, 190
trade-ins, 636
trademarks, 391–393
trade promotion, 495, 583
trade shows, 584
training, of sales forces, 573
transaction-based marketing, 26–30, 318–321
transfer price, 645
transfer pricing, 645–646
transportation, 30, 31, 434–438, 463, 637
travel industry
  e-commerce and, 116, 126
  global markets and, 222, 228
  market segmentation and, 295
trend analysis, 278, **279**
truck jobbers, 465
trucks, 436–438
truck wholesalers, 465
"tweens," 294–295
tying agreements, 424

U

unaided recall tests, 542
undifferentiated marketing, 307
unemployment, 91–92
unfair-trade laws, 600
Uniform Commercial Code, 545
uniform-delivered price, 639
unitizing, 440
unit pricing, 640
Universal Product Code (UPC), 395
universe, 266–267
Unplayable Lie, The (Chambers), 78
unsought products, 355
UPC bar codes, 266
upstream management, 429
Uruguay Round, 236
users, 207
utilities, 80, 85–86
utility, 6–7, 462

V

VALS2 (values and lifestyles), **302–303**
value-added service, 431
value analysis, 207
value chain, 337, 429
value pricing, 604–605
variable costs, 608
variety stores, 460
VCRs, 373
vending machines, 422
vendor analysis, 207
vendor-managed inventory (VMI), 336–337, 439
venture teams, 401
vertical conflict, in channel strategy, 426–427
vertical marketing system (VMS), 427–429
videophones, 105
viral marketing, 329
virtual coupons, 142
virtual sales teams, 564
virtual storefronts, 25
voice mail etiquette, 538
volatile demand, 198
volume objectives, pricing and, 602–603, 619

W

warehouse clubs, 460, 461, 475
warehousing, 30, 31, 438–439, 463
water carriers, 436–438
wealth effect, 89, 90
Web Commerce Today, 25
web kiosks, 141
web sites, effectiveness of, 143–145. *see also* **Internet (Net)**
wheel of retailing, 448–449
wholesalers, 30, 417–418, 419–420
wholesaling intermediaries, 462–467
wife-dominant role, 165
Wi-Fi (wireless fidelity), 81, **125**
wireless, 25
women
  discrimination against, 77–78
  e-commerce and, 138
  market segmentation and, 289–290
  in sales, 572
  as target market, 49, 50
workplace rights, 303
World Cup, 219
World Trade Organization (WTO), 236
World Wide Web (WWW, Web), 24, 120–121. *see also* **Internet (Net)**

Y

yield management, 618–619

Z

zone pricing, 639

international index

Bold entries refer to major discussions or definitions.

A

Africa, 224, 646
Argentina, 610–611
Asia, 643. see also *individual names of countries*
  B2B marketing in, 198, 200, 212
  e-commerce and, 128, 134
  global marketing, 221–224, 224
  international product, promotional strategy and, 244
  trade agreements and, 236
Australia, 134

B

Bermuda, 645
Brazil, 229, 610–611, 643

C

Canada
  B2B marketing in, 207
  labeling in, 395
  market segmentation, 301
  NAFTA and, 237
  prescription drugs, 427
Central America, 200. see also *individual names of countries*
Chile, 237
China, 79
  B2B marketing in, 196–197, 200–201
  consumer behavior and, 160
  e-commerce and, 134
  exports by, 8
  global marketing, 222–229, 238–239
  international trade law, 233
  political environment in, 230–231
  pricing, 619
  product positioning in, 397
  promotional strategy in, 454
  relationship marketing in, 336
  supply chain in, 430
  technological environment and, 94
  trade agreements and, 236
Cuba, 231, 234

E

England, 219, 295, 327
Europe. *see also* **European Union (EU)**; *individual names of countries*
  B2B marketing in, 200, 201
  e-commerce and, 128, 134
  fair trade in, 600–601
  relationship marketing in, 327
European Union (EU), 237–238. see also *individual names of countries*
  B2B marketing in, 208
  global markets and, 228
  government regulation by, 84
  ISO 9002, 364
  pricing, 620

F

France, 60
  B2B marketing in, 210
  e-commerce in, 133
  global marketing, 223
  market segmentation, 301
  marketing channel strategy in, 422
  outdoor advertising in, 535
  pricing in, 619
Free Trade Area of the Americas (FTAA), 237

G

General Agreement on Tariffs and Trade (GATT), 236
Germany, 244, 301
  B2B marketing in, 210
  fair trade in, 600–601
  relationship marketing in, 329
global marketing strategy, 218–221, **243–246,** 251
  brand equity and, 387
  decision process to market globally, 239–242
  developing strategy for, 243–246
  globalization, 238–239
  importance of, 221–224
  international economic environment and, 92–93
  international marketing environment, 227–235
  international marketplace, 224–227
  multinational corporations, 242–243
  multinational economic integration, 235–238
  online pricing and, 646–648
  prescription drugs and, 232
  price determination and, 619–620
  psychographic segmentation of, 303–304
  U.S. as target for international marketers, 246–247
globalization, 5, 8, 238–239
  e-commerce and, 134
  international economic environment and, 92–93
government markets, 209–211

H

Hong Kong, 226, 227
Hungary, 491

I

India
  B2B marketing in, 200
  global markets, 227–228, 251
  product/service strategies and, 354
  relationship marketing in, 336
international direct investment, 242
international marketing, 134, 212–213
international marketing research, 273–274
Iran, 392
Iraq, 210
Israel, 60, 242
Italy, 489

J

Japan, 60, 225
  advertising and, 537
  B2B marketing in, 207
  global markets, 239, 246–247
  market segmentation, 301
  relationship marketing in, 336
  technological environment and, 93

L

Latin America. see also *individual names of countries*
  global marketing, 224
  marketing research in, 273–274
Lebanon, 60

M

Malaysia, 641
Mexico, 79, 221
  global marketing, 225
  NAFTA and, 237
  pricing in, 598
  trade agreements of, 238
Middle Eastern, 336
multinational corporations, 242–243

N

North American Free Trade Agreement (NAFTA), 237
North American Industrial Classification System (NAICS), 192–193, 195

S

South Africa, 229
South America, 643
South Korea, 25

Soviet Union, 246
Spain, 212, 295

T

Thailand, 228
The Netherlands, 208, 301
trademarks, global, 392–393
Turkey, 244

U

United States
  B2B marketing in, 207
  core cultural values in, 159
  exports of, 221
  globalization and, 8
  international trade by, 220
  international trade law of, 231
  marketing research, 273
  NAFTA and, 237
  purchasing procedures of, 209–211
  relationship marketing by government agencies, 327
  technological environment and, 94
  tourism, 222
  trade partners of, 221